Natural Resource Conservation

Natural Resource Conservation

AN ECOLOGICAL APPROACH

4th edition

Oliver S. Owen

Department of Biology, University of Wisconsin–Eau Claire

Macmillan Publishing Company
New York

Collier Macmillan Publishers
London

Macmillan Publishing Company
866 Third Avenue, New York, New York 10022

Collier Macmillan Canada, Inc.

Library of Congress Cataloging in Publication Data

Owen, Oliver S.,
  Natural resource conservation.

  Includes bibliographies and index.
  1. Conservation of natural resources.   2. Ecology.
3. Environmental protection.   4. Conservation of natural
resources — United States.   5. Ecology — United States.
6. Environmental protection — United States.   I. Title.
S938.087 1985   333.7′2′0973   83-11292
ISBN 0-02-390100-4

Printing: 1 2 3 4 5 6 7 8   Year: 5 6 7 8 9 0 1 2

ISBN 0-02-390100-4

**To my loving wife,
Carol
and our children
Tom, Tim, and Stephanie**

May they never be denied the privilege of hiking through a forest wilderness, stalking a deer, or listening to the dusk-chant of a whippoorwill.

PREFACE

The wide and enthusiastic acceptance of the third edition of this text by teachers and students throughout the United States has been very gratifying. However, during the writing of this fourth edition, strenuous efforts have been made to make the book an even more effective educational medium. To this end the following structural and organizational changes have been made:

1. An entirely new chapter entitled "Minerals, Mining, and Society's Needs" has been added.
2. A number of guest articles have been included. All are written by leading national authorities, among them researchers at major universities as well as members of private research groups and officials of environmental organizations.
3. Each chapter ends with (a) a concisely written rapid review, (b) a list of key words and phrases, (c) questions and topics for discussion, and (d) a list of suggested readings for interested students.
4. A number of special topics have been enclosed in boxes. This arrangement gives the instructor an effective means of including or excluding this material from the students' reading assignment.
5. An appendix is included, listing information sources for environmental research.
6. This fourth edition has many more line drawings, graphs, charts, and tables than earlier editions, to enhance and clarify the text.

This Edition also embraces a number of topics that have not been treated previously in the book:

1. The Reagan administration and the environment.
2. The phosphorus cycle.
3. Growing, aging, and steady-state ecosystems.
4. Soil-water budgets.
5. Desertification.
6. Harvesting icebergs.
7. Lake renewal projects.
8. The destruction of tropical forests.
9. The Forest Management Act.
10. Chesapeake Bay: Case study of an estuary.
11. Indoor air pollution.
12. Hybrid cars.
13. The California Medfly controversy.
14. The chemical "time bomb" at Love Canal.
15. The PCB problem.
16. The Superfund controversy and the EPA.
17. Minerals, mining, and society's needs.

Several topics have received more intensive treatment than in earlier editions:

1. Stability of ecosystems.
2. Laws of matter and energy.
3. "Buckshot" urbanization.
4. Conservation tillage.
5. Groundwater shortages.
6. Population dynamics.
7. Environmental stress caused by food production.
8. Water pollution caused by detergents.
9. The dioxin problem.
10. Wildlife extinction.
11. Predator control.

12. Whale survival.
13. 200-mile fishing zone.
14. Fish farming.
15. The carbon dioxide buildup and the greenhouse effect.
16. Acid rain.
17. An energy policy for the United States.
18. Hydropower.
19. Tidal power.
20. Energy conservation.
21. Ocean thermal-energy conversion.
22. Pros and cons of alternative energy sources.
23. The energy demands of American agriculture.

All the guest authors are experts in their respective research or administrative areas and a number of them have an international reputation. A list of the guest authors, listed alphabetically, follows:

Dean Abrahamson, Director, Hubert H. Humphrey Institute of Public Affairs, University of Minnesota at Minneapolis St. Paul.

John E. Bardach, East-West Resource Systems Institute, Honolulu, Hawaii.

John E. Benneth, Western Regional Manager, The American Forest Institute.

Georg Borgstrom, Emeritus Professor of Food Science, Michigan State University, East Lansing, Michigan.

Reid Bryson, Director, Institute of Environmental Studies, University of Wisconsin–Madison.

Robert A. Canham, Executive Director, Water Pollution Control Federation, Washington, D.C.

Earl Cook. Distinguished Professor of Geology, Texas A&M University, College Station, Texas.

Robert B. Delano, President, American Farm Bureau Federation.

Howard Eastin, Director, California Department of Water Resources, Sacramento, California.

W. T. Edmondson, Professor of Zoology, University of Washington, Seattle, Washington.

David A. Etnier, Professor of Zoology, University of Tennessee at Knoxville.

Thomas M. Gerusky, Director, Pennsylvania Bureau of Radiation Protection, Harrisburg, Pennsylvania.

Milton Hakel, Presidential Assistant, National Farmers Union.

Edward J. Kormondy, Vice-President of Academic Affairs, California State University at Los Angeles.

Robert A. McCabe, Professor of Wildlife Ecology, University of Wisconsin–Madison.

E. Willard Miller, Professor of Geography. The Pennsylvania State University, University Park, Pennsylvania.

B. Thomas Parry, Forest Policy Analyst, Center for Natural Resource Studies, Berkeley, California.

Russell W. Peterson, President, National Audubon Society.

David Pimentel, Professor of Entomology, Cornell University, Ithaca, New York.

Fred O. Pinkham, President, Population Crisis Committee, Washington, D.C.

Robert Leo Smith, Professor of Wildlife Biology. Division of Forestry, West Virginia University, Morgantown, West Virginia.

Paul Springer, Chief Biologist, Wildlife Research Field Station, U.S. Fish and Wildlife Service, Humboldt State University, Arcata, California.

T. B. Thompson, Professor of Geology, Colorado State University, Fort Collins, Colorado.

Charles E. Warren, Professor of Fisheries and Wildlife, Oregon State University, Corvallis, Oregon.

Charles F. Wurster, Marine Sciences Research Center, State University of New York at Stony Brook.

The author is greatly indebted to several college professors who have critically reviewed the manuscript and have given extremely helpful suggestions. They include Richard Alexander, Rider College; Edmund Bedecarrax, San Francisco City College; Robert Frey, Plymouth State College; G. Patterson, Glassboro State College; Gary San Julian, North Carolina State University; Alan Teramura and George Bean, University of Maryland; Robert VanKirk, Humbolt State University; and Erik Fritzell, University of Missouri.

The author wishes to thank also Mr. Gregory Payne and Ms. Dora Rizzuto of the Macmillan staff, for their cooperation and assistance. Thanks are also due to Linda Glenna for typing the manuscript. I am very grateful to my brother, Earl Owen, for his inspiration and encouragement. Most importantly, I affectionately acknowledge the patience, understanding, and cooperation of my loving wife Carol, without whose help this book would not have materialized.

Oliver S. Owen

CONTENTS

Contents

Contents

List of Guest Articles

Natural Resource Conservation

1 Introduction: Conservation, Ecology, and Spaceship Earth

The Crisis on Planet Earth

Human beings are degrading their natural environment. We pride ourselves on conquering outer space, yet after two centuries of technological "progress" we still do not know how to manage the space right around us here on planet Earth. This global environmental crisis is the result of three major factors: (1) rapid population increase, (2) excessive consumption of resources, and (3) pollution.

Population Increase

Experts inform us that the global population will surge upward from the 4.6 billion of 1982 to roughly six billion by 2000. This "cancerous" growth of the human population clouds the future of planet Earth and is the underlying cause of our environmental crisis. Unless this population surge is restrained within the very near future, even the most soundly conceived and effectively implemented conservation and environmental practices will be to no avail. An increase in people means an increase in all types of environmental pollution. It means an accelerated depletion of natural resources, most of which are already in short supply or of deteriorating quality. It means that greater numbers of people, living in overcrowded conditions, will suffer from increasing emotional stress and will make increasing demands on wilderness and recreation areas to "get away from it all." With each upward surge of the number of human beings on earth, there will be a corresponding surge in the urgency and complexity of our conservation and environmental task.

After two million years of gradual population growth, our global population has moved around the bend of a J-curve and is now moving almost straight up. By this time tomorrow there will be 205,000 more people on the planet; by next week 1.4 million more, and by next year an additional 75 million. On Memorial Day our nation honors the memory of those Americans who have given their lives for their country on the world's battlefields. The fatalities have indeed been numerous — 57,000 in the Vietnam War alone. Yet the rate of population growth is so high that all the battlefield deaths of soldiers the world over, since the discovery of America by Columbus, *will have been replaced in only six months* (7).

And these additional people must be fed. For a number of political, economic, and ecological reasons, however, the food is not available. During the time it takes the average American family to polish off its Thanksgiving turkey (and cranberry sauce, and apple pie, and . . .) 1,400 people took their last breath — dead either directly or indirectly from a lack of food. One year from now an estimated 15 million people will have starved — a population equal to that of Pennsylvania and Kentucky combined!

1

1 – 1 *America prides herself on conquering outer space, yet after two centuries she still does not know how to manage her "inner space" here on earth.*

Excessive Resource Consumption

The world's industrialized nations are consuming nonrenewable resources (coal, oil, gas, copper, zinc, and cobalt, for example) at an accelerating pace, with the United States ranking first on a per capita basis. Although our nation has only 5 percent of the global population, it is consuming 30 percent of our world's resources. Furthermore, during the brief period since World War I (1918), Americans have consumed more of most resources than were consumed by human beings in the earth's previous entire history.

Many demands made by Americans on natural resources are excessive and do not contribute to human happiness in any substantial way. Americans are the most overfed, overhoused, overclothed, overmobilized, and overentertained people in the world. Our enormous consumption of cars, color television sets, dishwashers, air conditioners, golf carts, home computers, swimming pools, speed boats, and video games certainly does not stem from need. For the sake of a quick pickup we use high-octane gasoline and spew thousands of tons of irreplaceable lead into the atmosphere.

It is highly questionable whether our Gross National Product (GNP) or the sales of motor cars, home computers, and video games is a valid measure of real human happiness in America. And in this excessive production and consumption, called *throughput* by economists, the United States and other highly industrialized nations (Japan, West Germany, Great Britain, and Russia) are accelerating the depletion of our planet's stock of resources.

Pollution

The United States, the world's most *affluent* nation, has also become the most *effluent*. Together with other industrialized segments of the global community we have degraded our environment with an ever-increasing variety and volume of contaminants. We are polluting lakes and streams with raw sewage, industrial wastes, radioactive materials, heat, detergents, agricultural fertilizers, pesticides, and a complex mixture of synthetic chemicals whose harmful effects on human health are just beginning to be recognized. We are releasing so many toxic materials into the air, water, and land around us that this period in human history has been called the Age of Poisons. Our uncontrolled and indiscriminate use of pesticides has contaminated global

1–2 *Greater numbers of people, living in overcrowded conditions, will make increasing demands on wilderness and recreation areas to get away from it all. This family tried to escape from the city's crowds to the "serenity" of Shenandoah National Park in Virginia. Unfortunately, the escape is no escape after all, for the park itself appears to be crowded with cars and people.*

1–3 *As a result of our expanding population, even our national parks are being defiled. Note the debris being removed from Blue Star Spring, Yellowstone National Park.*

1–4 *America is polluting her lakes and streams with raw sewage, industrial wastes, radioactive materials, heat, detergents, agricultural fertilizers, and pesticides. Massive fish kills may result.*

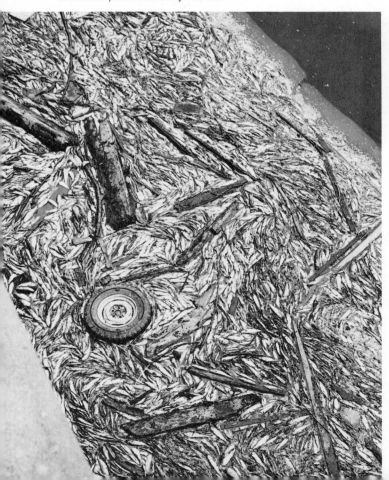

food chains to such an extent that virtually all animals, including humans, have been affected. For example, you the reader have perhaps about six parts per million of DDT in your tissues at this very moment. The long-term effects of such concentrations are unknown. However, laboratory studies on experimental animals like rats and mice have shown that a concentration of seven parts per million of DDT may have deleterious effects on heart and liver functions, and higher concentrations may interfere with reproductive processes, generate harmful mutations, and induce cancers. Millions of tons of gases, such as carbon monoxide, sulfur dioxide, and

3

nitrous oxide, which can contribute to serious respiratory ailments, are being spewed into the atmosphere. Our increasing dependence on nuclear power, as well as on nuclear armaments, has led to the accumulation of disturbingly large amounts of radioactive waste, some of which will pose a threat to genetic material and to human health and life for thousands of years.

To summarize, then, the three most important causes of our global environmental problems today are rapid population growth, excessive resource consumption, and high levels of pollution. The major thrust of this book is (1) the identification of these problems as they occur in the United States, and to a lesser degree also in the rest of the world, (2) the methods by which the conservationist and environmentalist may control, reduce, or actually solve a specific problem, and (3) the nature of our ongoing task to ensure that all people on earth some day have a life worth living. (See Charles E. Warren's guest article, on page 14, concerning our nation's need for a proper perspective regarding protection of the environment.)

Limits to Industrial and Economic Growth

Will the planet Earth still be capable of supporting a reasonably high quality of life for the human species by the time your children are in college? Or by the year 2050? Or by the year 2100? This is an exceedingly important and challenging question. It is almost impossible to answer with any degree of certainty. The problem is that there are so many interacting variables: population levels, resource availability, degree of environmental pollution, climatic patterns, industrial production, national and international politics, social attitudes, changing patterns of war and peace, and so on. In fact, the task we face in maintaining a reasonably high standard of living is much more formidable than developing the atom bomb or putting a man on the moon.

An extremely important book entitled *Limits to Growth* was published in 1972 by a group of researchers at the Massachusetts Institute of Technology (MIT). The book summarizes their computer studies of the projected future of humans on earth. The scientists fed statistical data for the current

1–5 *America is spewing large quantities of solid and gaseous contaminants into the atmosphere. This smoke is from burning auto batteries.*

global rates of population growth, resource depletion, environmental pollution, food production, and consumption into a computer. It was an attempt to determine the gradual changes in environmental quality that might take place through the year 2100, assuming that population growth, resource depletion, pollution, industrial production, and so on, continue at exponential (extremely high) rates — in other words moving almost straight up on a J-curve. The graphed projections that appeared on their computer printout sheets are not only of extreme interest, they are highly disturbing as well (6).

Notice in Figure 1-6 that, even though the global population zooms sharply upward until about 2030, increased amounts of food will be available per capita because of the simultaneous expansion of industrial and agricultural output. These industrial and food-production gains, however, will only be made at the expense of severe resource depletion and massive pollution. Thus, by the year 2030, perhaps a few more of the world's stomachs and wallets will be filled, but the quality of human life in most other respects will have deteriorated. Several decades later, many natural resources will either be so severely depleted (fertile soil, oil, and metals) or so seriously polluted (air, water, and land) that both food and industrial production will drop off sharply. Aggravating the problem then will be the continuing upsurge of global population. Eventually, by the year 2070, well within the lifetime of your children, there will be a massive die-off of the human species, primarily as the result of starvation. The prospects for human survival beyond 2100 appear not to be very good, simply because the global stock of natural resources, upon which humans have depended during our entire two-million-year tenure on this planet, will have reached the point of exhaustion, and life will have become incompatible with pollution levels (6).

Can Technology Save Us?

These somber projections have been ridiculed by those who believe that somehow technology will solve all of our resource and environmental problems. History is full of examples showing that "necessity is the mother of invention." The optimists suggest that the Western world is on the brink of another technological revolution. After all, isn't the current crisis the greatest in human history? If small crises result in small innovations, then certainly

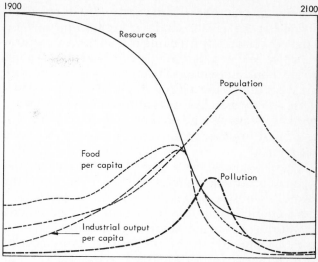

Today's spend-thrift society (cowboy economy)

1–6 *Computer predictions of different variables (food, population, industrial output, pollution, resources) if current-trends continue.*

today's composite population-resources-pollution dilemma may just be the necessary stimulus for the greatest technological breakthroughs of all time. These optimists confidently claim that "a breakthrough a day will keep the crises at bay." Wherever something has gone awry, technology will provide a "fix." Athelstan Spilhaus of the University of Minnesota is a leading spokesman for this school of thought. He has suggested, for example, that "energy is the ultimate currency of civilization"— in other words, if enough cheap energy is available, all things can be accomplished, pollution will be controlled, the world's stomachs will be filled, and clothing and shelter for the needy millions will be provided. Indeed, the nuclear power enthusiasts are predicting unlimited energy supplies once the breeder reactor has been perfected. (See Chapter 19.) As the editor of *Skeptic* magazine has remarked: "With limitless energy we can plumb the depths of the earth and the ocean or colonize the moon in our search for resources. We can sink mines to far greater depth economically, refine ores that do not now yield enough to interest us, transform old resources into new, reclaim resources already used. We can farm the seas, melt the icecaps, level the mountains to make arable land . . ." (10). To increase food production the optimists suggest a variety of schemes from fish farming to synthesiz-

5

ing food in test tubes; from yeast and algal culture to irrigating the Sahara sands; from draining swamplands to selectively breeding miracle wheats and supercorn. We can derive oil from worn-out rubber tires, refine methane gas from cow and pig manure, and obtain construction materials from broken glass and fly ash. Yes, according to these optimists, we can always depend on human ingenuity and skill to "bring another rabbit out of our technological hat."

Unfortunately, there is one big fly in this technological ointment that is supposed to heal this planet's wounds — the matter of *time*. There simply isn't enough time left for a technology-mediated salvation. (At the present moment energy also poses a big problem. If the breeder reactor or nuclear fusion is never fully developed, the possibility for technology ever to bring about the "good life" is very small indeed.) Why is time so crucial? The key to the answer is the word *exponential*. Remember the J-curves? They represent exponential growth — of populations, of resource depletion rates, of pollution. Such growth increases *geometrically*, as symbolized by the numerical sequence 1, 2, 4, 8, 16, and so on. This is in contrast to *arithmetic* growth, which is symbolized as 1, 2, 3, 4, 5, 6, and so on. The sheer rapidity of exponential growth is difficult to grasp. Let us use an analogy.

Suppose that there is a cancerous tumor in the windpipe that carries oxygen to your lungs — a tumor that doubles its size each day. Suppose now that it will take only thirty days for this cancer to close off your windpipe completely and cause your death from suffocation. Suppose now that on Day 29 you are rushed to the hospital for emergency surgery. The surgeon examines the tumor and discovers that it has blocked off half of your windpipe. Now, if he were unfamiliar with the dynamics of exponential growth, he would probably suppose that he has plenty of time to remove the tumor and save your life. Wrong. He would have just one day left. In this metaphor the windpipe represents the fragile and highly vulnerable life-support systems for humans. The cancerous tumor represents the exponentially growing levels of global population, resource consumption, and pollution. Even though the world's best scientists, technologists, ecologists, sociologists, and economists struggle valiantly to remove this rapidly growing environmental cancer, it will be too late. For this is Day 29. There is only one day left (6).

The Simple Life in Our Future

Many authorities in the areas of political science, sociology, economics, and ecology are convinced that eventually some kind of simple life will be our fate, one way or another. It could be simple life Type A, the *steady-state society* shown in Figure 1–7, with an emphasis on cultural, moral, and spiritual values rather than on material wealth. Life-styles in this steady-state society, which could be attainable by 2025, would be much simpler than today. The average American, for example, would have to get along without some of the traditional status symbols such as membership in the country club, the second or third family car, the home computer, and the speedboat. That life-style, however, would be *ecologically sound* rather than *ecologically suicidal* and probably would offer a better chance of finding real happiness. In today's resource-spending society happiness may be a jet flight to Vegas, a holiday in Spain, or watching Pac-Man feeding on blue monsters. However, in the resource-conserving, steady-state, ecologically sound and sustainable society of the year 2025, human happiness might well be served by canoeing down the Apple River, growing pumpkins in a backyard garden, learning the stars in the Big Dipper on a warm summer's night, or getting acquainted with Mozart, Rembrandt, or Thoreau. The attainment of simple life Type A, our steady-state society, may ultimately depend on a

1–7 *Note that if strenuous attempts are made now (1980–1985), the steady-state society might be achieved by 2025.*

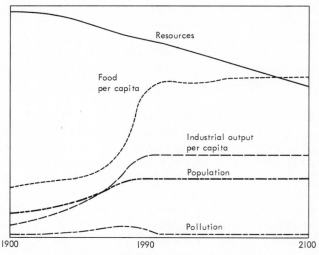

The steady-state society (space ship economy)

1-8 *Flowchart for events on planet Earth leading to a desired or imposed type of "simple life."*

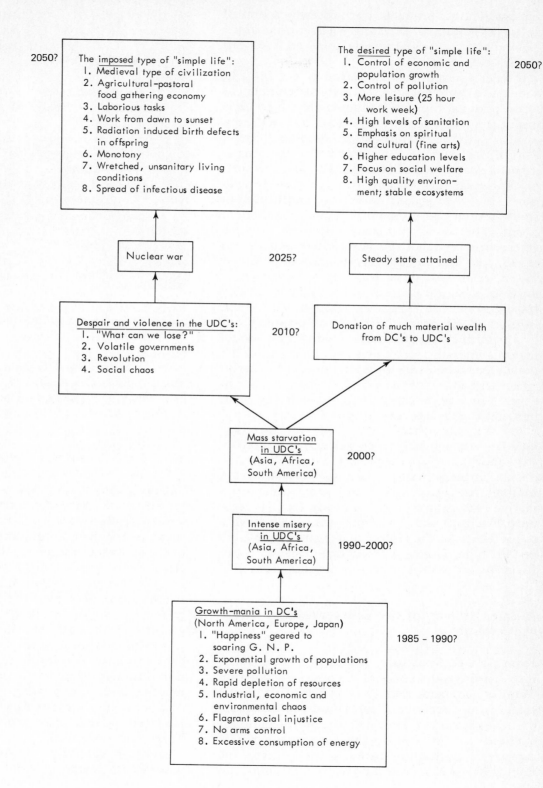

2050? The imposed type of "simple life":
1. Medieval type of civilization
2. Agricultural-pastoral food gathering economy
3. Laborious tasks
4. Work from dawn to sunset
5. Radiation induced birth defects in offspring
6. Monotony
7. Wretched, unsanitary living conditions
8. Spread of infectious disease

The desired type of "simple life":
1. Control of economic and population growth
2. Control of pollution
3. More leisure (25 hour work week)
4. High levels of sanitation
5. Emphasis on spiritual and cultural (fine arts)
6. Higher education levels
7. Focus on social welfare
8. High quality environment; stable ecosystems
2050?

Nuclear war   2025?   Steady state attained

Despair and violence in the UDC's:
1. "What can we lose?"
2. Volatile governments
3. Revolution
4. Social chaos
2010?
Donation of much material wealth from DC's to UDC's

Mass starvation in UDC's (Asia, Africa, South America)   2000?

Intense misery in UDC's (Asia, Africa, South America)   1990-2000?

Growth-mania in DC's (North America, Europe, Japan)
1. "Happiness" geared to soaring G. N. P.
2. Exponential growth of populations
3. Severe pollution
4. Rapid depletion of resources
5. Industrial, economic and environmental chaos
6. Flagrant social injustice
7. No arms control
8. Excessive consumption of energy
1985 - 1990?

7

massive redistribution of our spaceship's limited resources so that all the Earth's passengers, white, black, brown, red, and yellow alike, get their fair share (13).

If such a resource distribution is not brought about, it is quite possible that the frustrated hopes of the poor nations will lead inevitably to political unrest, violence, food riots, revolution, and even nuclear war. The great British philosopher Bertrand Russell, for example, once noted that "nothing is more likely to lead to an H-bomb war than the threat of universal destitution through overpopulation. . . ." Newspaper columnist Smith Hempstone makes the following somber prediction: "Neither democracy nor peace will survive in areas where the roots of both are weak. Governments will fall like ten-pins and hungry nations will go to war in an effort to sieze what they cannot produce. . . ." A nuclear exchange could conceivably impose simple life Type B on mankind, as shown in Figure 1 – 8. It is characterized not by happiness, but by a primitive level of existence, with remnant populations literally scratching for survival in the moonscape rubble of what is left of spaceship Earth.

Our task, to achieve a true steady-state, spaceship type of society, is exceedingly difficult and challenging. It requires the dedicated, highly coordinated, and long-sustained efforts of many members on our space vehicle's passenger list, from factory workers to business executives, from college students to farmers, from scientists to politicians, from food specialists to geographers. It will require imaginative and inspirational leadership from government leaders at all levels, from small-town mayors to presidents of the United States and commissars of the Soviet Union, from village tribal chiefs in Africa to benevolent despots in South America.

A Brief History of the Conservation Movement

From time to time, early in our nation's history, men with vision such as George Washington, Thomas Jefferson, and Patrick Henry expressed their concern over our nation's unrestrained squandering of resources. However, the most significant advances in conservation have been made in this century. They have occurred in three waves: the first (1901 – 1909) was under the dynamic and

1 – 9 *President Theodore Roosevelt, outdoors man, big-game hunter, and conservationist, at Yosemite National Park.*

forceful leadership of Theodore Roosevelt and Gifford Pinchot; the second (1930s) was during the presidency of Franklin D. Roosevelt; and the third (1962 – 1980) was given impetus by John F. Kennedy.

The First Wave (1901 – 1909)

The White House conference called by President "Teddy" Roosevelt in 1908 was a high-water mark for the cause of conservation. Several developments influenced Roosevelt's decision to call the conference. Among them were (1) the deep concern among scientists over the severe depletion of timber in the Great Lakes states, (2) the study of arid western lands by Major J. W. Powell in the 1870s that had stimulated great interest in the possibilities of irrigation farming and converting deserts to vegetable gardens; (3) the 1907 report by the Inland Waterways Commission pointing out that the excessive use of water would inevitably have a negative impact on other resources, such as timber, soils, and wildlife; and (4) a growing apprehension in 1908 that our nation's resources were being grossly mismanaged and that severe economic hardship would be the inevitable result (1).

Invited to the White House Conference on Natural Resources were governors, congressional leaders, scientists, informed sportsmen, and resource experts from several foreign nations. As a result of the conference, a fifty-member National Conservation Commission was formed, composed of scientists, legislators and businessmen; inspirational leadership was provided by Gifford Pinchot, a professional forester. The commission completed our nation's first comprehensive *Natural Resources Inventory*. The White House conference also resulted indirectly in the formation of 41 state conservation departments, almost all of which are still operating vigorously today (1).

The Second Wave (1933–1941)

Franklin D. Roosevelt is a notable example of "the right man in the right place at the right time." When he assumed the presidency in 1933 there was an urgent need for an imaginative program in job creation. Not only did his administration create employment, but it solved many natural-resource problems plaguing our nation as well.

1. The Prairie States Forestry Project was begun in 1934. Its goal was the establishment of shelter belts of trees and shrubs along the one-hundredth meridian extending from the Canadian border of North Dakota south to Texas. This project did much to reduce soil erosion on both crop and range lands (1).

2. The National Resources Board appointed by Roosevelt completed our nation's second comprehensive *Natural Resources Inventory* in 1934. In its report the board not only identified serious resource problems plaguing our country, but described methods for solving them as well.

3. The Civilian Conservation Corps (CCC), which was organized in 1933 and functioned until 1949, was organized into 2,652 camps of two hundred men each. Many were located in our national parks and forests. The forest workers constructed fire lanes, removed fire hazards, fought forest fires, controlled pests, and planted millions of trees. The park workers constructed bridges, improved roads, and built nature trails. In addition, the CCC made lake and stream improvements and participated in flood-control projects (1, 4).

4. In 1935 the Soil Conservation Service (SCS) was established. The time was ripe for such a program. The frequent occurrence of severe dust storms over the Dust Bowl of the Great Plains bore eloquent testimony to the vulnerability of our nation's soils. The SCS conducted soil-conservation demonstrations to show farmers the techniques and importance of erosion control (4).

5. The establishment of the Tennessee Valley Authority (TVA) in 1933 was a bold experiment,

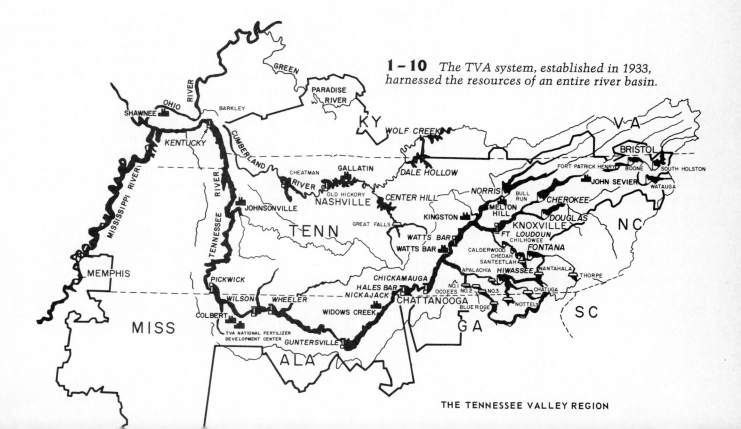

1–10 *The TVA system, established in 1933, harnessed the resources of an entire river basin.*

THE TENNESSEE VALLEY REGION

unique in conservation history, to integrate the use of the resources (water, soil, forests, and wildlife) of an entire river basin. Although highly controversial at the time, it has received international acclaim and has served as a model for similar projects in India and other nations (4).

6. The first North American Wildlife and Resources Conference was convened by President Roosevelt in 1936. Attended by wildlife management specialists, interested sportsmen, and concerned government officials, it had as its objectives (a) an inventory of our nation's wildlife resources, (b) a statement of wildlife and other related conservation problems, and (c) the formulation of techniques and policies by which those problems might be solved. This conference meets annually to this day.

The Third Wave (1962–1980)

John F. Kennedy, who assumed the presidency in 1961, spearheaded the third wave of our nation's conservation efforts. The main features of Kennedy's natural resource program included

1. Preserving wilderness areas.
2. Developing marine resources.
3. Reserving remaining shorelines for public use.
4. Expanding outdoor recreation opportunities.
5. Enhancing freshwater supplies by the process of desalinization.
6. Aiding metropolitan areas in solving land-use problems.
7. Developing the water resources of all river basins.
8. Vigorously opposing all forms of pollution.
9. Encouraging scientists and technologists to develop suitable substitutes for resources in short supply.
10. Organizing the Youth Conservation Corps to provide the muscle to implement much of his program.

The impetus to the conservation movement provided by Kennedy (1) was sustained after his assassination by his successor, President Lyndon B. Johnson. Many of the bills signed by Johnson were concerned with (1) upgrading human resources, (2) controlling air and water pollution, (3) preserving wilderness areas, and (4) beautifying the environment.

The twin functions of natural-resource conservation and the upgrading of environmental quality were served well during the decade of the 1970s under the Nixon, Ford, and Carter administrations. To this end outmoded federal agencies were dissolved and new, more effective ones were created. Certainly one of the major accomplishments of the Nixon administration was the organization of the Environmental Protection Agency (EPA). The EPA absorbed the environment-related responsibilities of at least six other agencies. Consolidation of many programs under the sole administration of the EPA eliminated much duplication of effort and promoted more effective use of available funds. Much petty feuding between agencies concerning areas of authority also was eliminated.

Ever since the Arab oil embargo of 1973–1974 our nation has become painfully aware that one of its major energy sources is in extremely precarious supply. The serious implications of this dilemma for the economic, political, and military well-being of the United States prompted the integration of all our energy programs under a newly established top-level Department of Energy (DOE). The importance of this new department is reflected in its 20,000-member staff and $12-billion annual budget.

The Reagan Administration

The encouraging progress that had been made in the areas of resource conservation and environmental quality during the past few decades was abruptly halted by the shocking policies of the Reagan Administration, which came into office in 1981. Conservationists, among them many staunch Republicans, have been dismayed by the statements and actions not only of the President, but also of such key Reagan appointees, as James Watt, Secretary of the Interior, and Anne Gorsuch, head of the Environmental Protection Agency (EPA). Gorsuch, under mounting pressure from environmentalists and some congressmen, eventually resigned in 1983.

The adverse effects of the Reagan Administration on our nation's resource and environmental posture may not be assessed for several years. Some may never be fully evaluated. For example, how does one assess the effects of the virtual wholesale dismantling of the Council on Environmental Quality — an organization whose major function is to advise the President on resource and environmental matters? Or how can one evaluate the effects of a massive cut in the research budgets of scientists who are trying to determine whether contaminants in ground-water may cause cancer in the human organism?

The Conservation Foundation, a nonprofit organization, is dedicated to promoting the quality of the human environment. Highly respected, its interdisciplinary staff is composed of economists, scientists, lawyers, political scientists, and specialists on federal programs. It described some of the negative impacts of the Reagan Administration on resource-environmental programs in its annual report. We have listed some of them:

1. The bipartisan consensus that supported federal protection of the environment for more than a decade has been broken by an Administration that has given priority to deregulation, defederalization, and defunding domestic programs.
2. Reagan Administration initiatives have polarized relations between the executive branch and conservationists in Congress and throughout the country. The polarization has disrupted the communication necessary to formulate and carry out environmental programs.
3. Without question the Reagan Administration has introduced a fundamental discontinuity into national resource and environmental policy. It has pursued its domestic goals with such single-mindedness, so aggressively, as to allow conservationists no alternative but to protest.
4. At the Environmental Protection Agency the 1983 budget calls for a 40 percent reduction from the 1981 level for research and development.
5. Cuts already made have done away with the noise-control program, sharply reduced efforts to deal with toxic substances, and cast doubt on the EPA's ability to fulfill its mandates under the Clean Air and Clean Water Acts.
6. At the Department of Energy, programs in energy conservation and renewable energy sources have given way to increased spending for nuclear reactor research.
7. At the Department of Interior, the emphasis has been on selling off federal land, encouraging accelerated mineral exploration and extraction; . . . the tendency has been either to neglect or exploit natural resources. (11)

Conservation Defined

The late Aldo Leopold, who was this writer's ecology professor at the University of Wisconsin – Madison, defined conservation as "a state of harmony between man and the land." Eugene P. Odum, the distinguished ecologist from the University of Georgia, has written: "*Conservation in the broadest sense is probably the most important application of ecology.* Unfortunately, the term *conservation* suggests *hoarding,* as if the idea were simply to ration static supplies to that there would be some left for the future. The aim of good conservation is to ensure a continuous yield of useful plants, animals, and materials by establishing a balanced cycle of harvest and renewal . . ." (9).

Recently, Spenser Havlick, an environmentalist at California State University – San Jose, defined modern conservation as "an operational collection of ecological knowledge and skill applied in a way to understand and manage as many consequences of an environmental activity as possible in keeping with the expectations of all participants — plants and animals including man" (3).

Basic Conservation Practices

For many years Stanley A. Cain taught a course at the University of Michigan – Ann Arbor called *Natural Resources Ecology.* In the course he identified some of the basic practices of the modern conservationist. They include the following:

1. *Preservation.* Our nation's conservation movement placed an early emphasis on preserving resources from human destruction. Good examples are the designation of millions of acres of magnificent redwood stands as National Forests, or the designation of sites of awesome scenic beauty, such as Yosemite Falls and the Grand Canyon, as National Parks. Also included under preservation practice is the establishment of wildlife refuges for such endangered species as the whooping crane (Aransas Wildlife Refuge) and timber wolf (Isle Royal).
2. *Restoration.* Despite our best intentions, we often make mistakes when making use of our natural resource heritage. Once those errors are identified, the professional conservationist has the responsibility of repairing the damage, so that the original value and productivity of the resource can be restored. A classic example is Lake Erie. In the early 1970s the lake was badly polluted with human and industrial sewage, barnyard runoff, airborne chemicals, and warm-water discharges from power plants located on its shores. As a result, the once multimillion-dollar lake-trout fishery was virtually destroyed. Shallow waters near shore became clogged with

Natural Resource Classification

Any portion of our natural environment — soil, water, rangeland, forest, wildlife, or minerals — that human beings can use to promote their welfare is a natural resource. Such resources vary greatly in *abundance, degree of use, exhaustibility,* and *renewability.* The best type of management employed depends on these characteristics. The following classification was modified from that of Richard J. Hartesveldt of San Jose State College, San Jose, California:

I. Inexhaustible

1. *Atomic energy.* Vast quantities of fissionable materials available in granitic rocks.
2. *Wind power.* The result of heating air masses by the sun.
3. *Precipitation.* An unlimited supply. However, we will very likely alter the distribution patterns in the future — accidentally from air pollution, and purposefully by means of cloud seeding to induce rainfall.
4. *Water power of tides.* Resulting from sun-moon-earth relationships.
5. *Solar power.* Total amount being received by forests, crops, and aquatic vegetation has been reduced because of air pollution.
6. *Atmosphere.* Quality has been impaired because of virtual worldwide pollution (smoke, fly ash, sulphur dioxide, radioactive dust, and pesticides).
7. *Waters of oceans, lakes, and streams.* All are currently being polluted with infectious organisms, heat, sediment, toxic chemicals, nutrients, radioactive wastes, and sewage.
8. *Water power of flowing streams.* Available extensively on a global basis. However, harnessing this power tends to destroy the scenic beauty of a once free-flowing stream.
9. *Natural scenic beauty. Mount Ranier, Blue Ridge Mountains, Grand Canyon, and the coastlines of California, Oregon, and Maine.*

II. Exhaustible

1. *Renewable.* Resources whose continued harvest or use depends on proper human planning and management. Improper use and/or management results in impairment or exhaustion, with resulting harmful social and economic effects.
   (a) *Fertile soil.* The fertility of soil can be renewed, but the process is expensive and takes time.
   (b) *Products of the land.* Resources grown in or dependent on the soil.
       (1) *Agricultural products.* Vegetables, grains, fruits, and fibers.
       (2) *Forests.* Source of timber and paper pulp. Valuable as source of scenic beauty, as an agent in erosion control, as recreational areas, and as wildlife habitat.
       (3) *Rangeland.* Sustains herds of cattle, sheep, and goats for the production of meat, leather, and wool.
       (4) *Wild animals.* Provide aesthetic values, hunting sport, and food. Examples are deer, wolves, eagles, bluebirds, and fireflies.
   (c) *Products of lakes, streams, and oceans.* Black bass, lake trout, salmon, cod, mackerel, lobsters, oysters, and seaweed.
   (d) *Human powers.* Physical and spiritual.
2. *Nonrenewable.* Mineral resources such as coal, oil, metals, phosphate rock, and salt. Amount of resource is finite. When destroyed or con-

12

sumptively used, such as the burning of coal, the resource cannot be replaced.

(a) *Fossil fuels.* Produced by processes that occurred millions of years ago. When consumed (burned), heat, water, and gases (carbon monoxide, carbon dioxide, and sulphur dioxide) are released. The gases may pose serious air-pollution problems.

(b) *Nonmetallic minerals.* Phosphate rock, glass sand, and salt. Phosphate rock is of crucial importance as a source of fertilizer.

(c) *Metals.* Gold, platinum, silver, cobalt, lead, iron, zinc, and copper. Without these, modern civilization would be impossible. Lead is used in high-octane gasoline and in paint; zinc is used in galvanized iron to protect it from rusting; tin is used in toothpaste tubes; and iron is used in cans, auto bodies, and bridges.

masses of rotting weeds. Recreational swimming and boating were severely disrupted. The lake's natural beauty was sullied. Some scientists even claimed, "Lake Erie is dead!" However, thanks to the establishment of strict pollution-control regulations, the lake is rapidly regaining its former status as one of our nation's most valuable aquatic resources.

3. *Beneficiation, or upgrading a resource.* Originally the term *beneficiation* was used in connection with the development of techniques that made it profitable for the mining industry to mine low-grade ores once considered worthless. The history of copper mining in the United States is a good example. At the beginning of this century only the very high-grade ore containing sixty pounds of copper per ton (3 percent copper) was mined. However, as new advances were made in ore processing, progressively leaner ores with fifty, forty, thirty, and then twenty pounds of copper per ton could be used. Today a very low-grade of ore containing only six pounds of copper per ton (.3 percent copper) can be mined at a profit (8). Beneficiation may be used in a much broader sense to include the upgrading of any natural resource — forest, farmland, or fishery.

4. *Substitution.* The replacement of a scarce resource with one that is more abundant, or the replacement of a nonrenewable resource with one that is renewable is known as substitution. Examples are the replacement of steel with aluminum in motor cars and airplanes, and the substitution of nonrenewable oil with inexhaustible solar power. In the area of fisheries management, the European brown trout, which was introduced from Europe and is highly resistant to pollution, has, in a sense, been substituted for our native brook trout — a species highly sensitive to the changing physical characteristics of the water.

5. *Maximization.* Maximization refers to the reduction of waste by the most efficient use of a resource that is possible. A classic example of waste reduction can be drawn from the lumber industry. During the "cut-out-and-get-out" logging days of the late nineteenth century, the loggers were interested only in *logs.* The rest of the tree — stump, limbs, foliage, and bark — was left in the forest as worthless debris. Today, however, thanks to researchers at the U.S. Forest Products Laboratory in Madison, Wisconsin, several ingenious methods have been developed for making extremely useful products from scrap boards, shavings, wood chips, sawdust and even bark. From the bark, for example, a variety of substances has been derived, ranging from oil-well-drilling compounds to chemicals used to check bleeding during surgery.

6. *Reusing and recycling.* Water has been intensively recycled and reused in the more densely populated regions of the United States. Environmentalist Paul Ehrlich of Stanford University describes it this way: "Don't be startled, but that last glass of water you drank *may already have passed through the bodies of eight people.*" This fact concerning the "toilet-to-mouth" pipeline has been the subject of some humor. Thus, scrawlings on the walls of public bathrooms along the Mississippi River say: "Flush the toilet, they need the water in St. Louis." These words appropriately describe the use and reuse of sew-

13

Environmental Protection: A Perspective

Charles E. Warren
OREGON STATE UNIVERSITY

After a generation of effort to understand and deal with problems of environmental pollution — a generation in which we have progressed in some areas only to find even greater problems in others — we are told by otherwise responsible persons that those concerned with the environment have gone too far. Proper resource utilization and waste management cost too much — more than their benefits. And too many of us nod in agreement. How can this be?

It comes from a narrowness of perspective that endangers our very society. It comes from failure to appreciate the systemic nature of society and its resources in all their interpenetrating dependencies. The cost of environmental protection is seen by too many as an unnecessary increase in the costs of utilities and products we need. But environmental degradation means only that we and others, often unknowingly or with little say, bear these costs in loss of pleasure, health, and even life's bare necessities. And these costs will continue to be borne by generations to come. Our legislatures have begun to articulate this truth into law. But we have allowed ourselves to be diverted from legitimate strengthening and enforcement of resource law.

The quality and even the persistence of a society depend upon its developing its capacities in concordance — in harmonious and rulelike relation — with the capacities of its natural resources. To this time in history our society has failed in this. Our great material and cultural wealth have been bought with the destruction of much of a continent's resources. Still the resources of this continent are vast, and a stable concordance of our society and environment could yet be reached. If only we are not diverted from the development of a truly good and persistent society by those having little perspective.

age-contaminated river water throughout urban America.

7. *Integration.* A given natural resource, such as a forest, does not stand in isolation. It is frequently associated with other resources such as soil, water, wildlife, and scenic beauty. The conservationist must decide, therefore, whether a given stand of mature pine is more valuable to society as timber or as part of the forest-soil-water-wildlife-scenic-beauty complex. Certainly, if the stand were logged off, the soil would erode, trout streams would become muddied, wildlife would be deprived of food and cover, and scenic beauty would be instantly destroyed. The determination of how the maximal value for society may be obtained from such a complex of interrelated and interacting resources is known as integration (3).

An Ecological Approach to Conservation

More than one hundred years ago the American diplomat-naturalist George Perkins Marsh observed how human beings had abused once-fertile agricultural lands in Europe and Asia. He further observed how this abuse resulted in massive waste, water pollution, dust storms, and the inevitable erosion of the nation's economy and well-being. After returning to the United States, Marsh advanced the concept that humans cannot degrade *one part of the environment without at the same time harming other parts as well* (11). In other words, our natural environment, although infinitely complex and varied, is a dynamic and organic whole. As a result, it cannot be properly studied only one part at a time. Today's conservationists know that Marsh was correct. The study of the interrelationships that exist between organisms and their environment is known as ecology. The fundamental practices of conservation described here operate in the context of ecology. Leopold, the highly respected ecologist and pioneer in wildlife management, was a leading exponent of the application of sound ecological principles to solve resource problems. The following passage from Leopold's book *Sand County Al-*

14

manac reveals his deep understanding of the interaction of plants, animals, climate, and fire in the development of a mature prairie soil such as we might find in Kansas or Iowa:

The black prairie (soil) was built by the prairie plants, a hundred distinctive species of grasses, herbs, and shrubs; by the prairie fungi, insects, and bacteria; by the prairie mammals and birds, all interlocked in one humming community of cooperations and competitions — one biota. This biota, through ten thousand years of living and dying, burning and growing, preying and fleeing, freezing and thawing, built that dark and bloody ground we call prairie. (5)

In the next chapter we will examine some basic ecological principles. They will provide us with a conceptual framework for a discussion of our nation's resource problems and the methods by which they may be solved, or at least brought under control. In the broader context, however, the study of ecological concepts will enable us to understand the functions of the conservationist in bringing about an ecologically sound, sustainable, steady-state type of life here on earth.

Rapid Review

1. The global environmental crisis is the result of three major factors: (a) rapid population increase, (b) depletion of natural resources, and (c) pollution.

2. The global population will surge upward from 4.6 billion in 1983 to almost six billion by 2000.

3. Each year 15 million people starve to death.

4. Although America has only 5 percent of the world's population, it consumes 30 percent of the world's resources.

5. Americans are degrading the environment more intensely than any other nation on earth.

6. The major thrust of this book is (a) to identify our nation's resource-environmental problems, (b) to consider the methods by which those problems might be brought under control, and (c) to consider the nature of the on-going task that will promote the quality of life for Americans, in particular, and, in a general way, for all humanity.

7. The *Limits to Growth* suggests that the world's population-resource-pollution problems place limits on the level of agricultural, industrial, and economic growth possible in human society.

8. Because population-resource-pollution problems are increasing at an exponential rate, the chance of technological breakthroughs solving them is rather remote.

9. The planet on which we live can be compared to a spaceship: a fairly closed system, except for incoming solar energy, with limited supplies of resources and living space.

10. The most significant conservation developments in the United States were made in this century in three waves: under the leadership of Teddy Roosevelt (1901–1909); during the presidency of Franklin D. Roosevelt in the 1930s; and under the impetus provided by John F. Kennedy (1962–1980).

11. The Reagan Administration's policies, for the most part, have been disastrous for the cause of conservation and environmental quality.

12. The National Environmental Policy Act (NEPA) of 1970 has proved to be one of the most important legal instruments for advancing the twin causes of resource conservation and environmental protection.

13. Resources can be placed in two broad categories: inexhaustible and exhaustible.

14. Inexhaustible resources are represented by wind, solar power, and atmosphere. Exhaustible resources may either be renewable or nonrenewable. Renewable resources are represented by soil, forests, and wildlife; nonrenewable resources include fossil fuels and metals.

15. In a broad sense, conservation can be defined as "the most important application of ecology."

16. Some of the major practices of the modern conservationist are (a) preservation, (b) restoration, (c) beneficiation, or resource upgrading, (d) substitution, (e) maximization, (f) reutilization and/or recycling, and (g) integration.

Key Words and Phrases

Beneficiation	Exponential growth
Civilian Conservation Corps (CCC)	Inexhaustible resources
	Integration
Conservation	Kennedy (John F.)
Ecology	Limits to growth
Environmental Protection Agency (EPA)	Maximization
	National Environmental Policy Act (NEPA)
Exhaustible resources	National Resource Board

15

Natural Resource
   Classification
Nonrenewable resource
Preservation
Renewable resource
Reutilization

Soil Conservation
   Service (SCS)
Tennessee Valley
   Authority (TVA)
White House
   Conference

Questions and Topics for Discussion

1. Name the three most important factors that have contributed to the world's current environmental crisis.
2. In what ways does population increase contribute to resource and other global environmental problems?
3. Discuss the statement: "America, the world's most *affluent* nation, has also become the most *effluent.*"
4. What is the major message of *limits to growth?*
5. Discuss the statement: "Technology will solve all our population-resource-pollution problems," from the standpoint of an optimist. From the standpoint of a pessimist.
6. List five examples of inexhaustible resources.
7. List five examples of exhaustible resources that are renewable.
8. List three examples of exhaustible resources that are nonrenewable.
9. Discuss and give an example of each of the following conservation practices: (a) preservation, (b) beneficiation, (c) substitution, and (d) integration.

Endnotes

1. Allen, Shirley W., and Justin W. Leonard. *Conserving Natural Resources.* New York: McGraw-Hill, 1966.
2. Boulding, Kenneth E. "The Economics of the Coming Spaceship Earth," in Henry Jarrett, ed., *Environmental Quality in a Growing Economy.* Baltimore: Johns Hopkins, 1966.
3. Havlick, Spenser W. *The Urban Organism.* New York: Macmillan, 1974.
4. Highsmith, Richard M., Jr., Granville Jensen, and Robert D. Rudd. *Conservation in the United States.* Chicago: Rand McNally, 1962.
5. Leopold, Aldo. *A Sand County Almanac.* New York: Oxford U.P., 1966.
6. Meadows, Donella H., et al. *The Limits to Growth.* New York: Universe, 1972.
7. Miller, G. Tyler. *Living in the Environment,* 2nd ed. Belmont, CA: Wadsworth, 1982.
8. Moriber, George. *Environmental Science.* Boston: Allyn and Bacon, 1974.
9. Odum, Eugene P. *Fundamentals of Ecology,* 3rd ed. Philadelphia: Saunders, 1971.
10. *Skeptic.* "Can Technology Come to Our Rescue?" (Editorial). Special Issue No. 2 (1974). The Forum for Contemporary History. Santa Barbara, CA.
11. The Conservation Foundation. *State of the Environment—1982.* Washington, DC: The Conservation Foundation, 1982.
12. Udall, Stewart L. *The Quiet Crisis.* New York: Holt, 1963.
13. Van Vleck, David B. *The Crucial Generation.* Charlotte, VT: Optimum Population, 1971.

Suggested Readings for the Interested Student

"Action for Survival" (Editorial). *Progressive* (April 1970), 3–6.

Allen, D. L. *The Life of Prairies and Plains.* New York: McGraw-Hill, 1967.

Carson, Rachel. *Silent Spring.* Boston: Houghton, 1962.

Bates, M. "Crowded People." *Natural History,* 77(8):20–25, 1968.

Ehrlich, Paul R., and A. H. Ehrlich. *The End of Affluence.* New York: Ballantine, 1974.

Leopold, Aldo. *Game Management* New York: Scribner, 1933.

———. *Sand County Almanac.* New York: Oxford U.P., 1949.

Malthus, T. R. *An Essay on the Principle of Population.* London: Johnson, 1798.

Meadows, D. H., D. L. Meadows, J. Randers, and W. W. Behrens III. *The Limits to Growth.* New York: Universe, 1972.

2 Lessons from Ecology

We have defined *ecology* as the study of the interrelationships that exist between organisms and their environment. An understanding of certain basic ecological concepts will aid in developing an appreciation not only of the problems facing the conservationist and environmentalist, but also of the policies, strategies, and regulations by which the problems might be resolved.

Levels of Organization Studied by Ecologists

As anyone who has ever taken a course in biology knows, one of the outstanding characteristics of any living organism is its organization. In ascending order of complexity, the organization levels of the human body are the following: atom, molecule, cell, tissue, organ, organ system, and organism. Although the ecologist is certainly concerned with

each of these levels, most of his or her attention is usually focused on levels above that of the organism: the *population*, *community*, and *ecological system*, or *ecosystem*, as seen in Figure 2–1.

Population

When the layperson uses the term population it invariably refers to the number of human beings in a given locality. For example the population of Pittsburgh, Pennsylvania, is 520,117. The ecologist, however, extends the term to include any organism, human or nonhuman. Thus, we may speak of populations of white pine, black bass, or deer.

Community

The layperson uses the word community to refer to a town or city. The ecologist, on the other hand, would define a *community* as the "sum of all living organisms occupying a given locality." We refer to the community of a woodlot, lake, prairie, marsh, or

2–1 *Levels of ecological organization.*

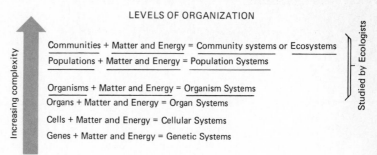

LEVELS OF ORGANIZATION

Increasing complexity

Communities + Matter and Energy = Community systems or Ecosystems
Populations + Matter and Energy = Population Systems

Organisms + Matter and Energy = Organism Systems
Organs + Matter and Energy = Organ Systems
Cells + Matter and Energy = Cellular Systems
Genes + Matter and Energy = Genetic Systems

Studied by Ecologists

17

even that of a rotting log or drop of pond water. The community of your backyard might embrace millions of individual organisms, which represent a great assemblage of species, from soil bacteria and earthworms to thrushes and oaks.

Ecosystem

A community of organisms does not operate in a vacuum. It operates in an environment. And this environment is composed of both living (biotic) and nonliving (abiotic) parts. The community of organisms can cause changes in the environment; the environment, in turn, may have effects on the community. The ecologist refers to the community plus the environment with which it interacts as an *ecological system*, or *ecosystem*. (See Figure 2–2.) As shown in Figure 2–3, ecosystems may be either balanced or unbalanced.

Eugene Odum of the University of Georgia has a definition for ecology: *The study of the structure and function of ecosystems (6).* Let us see now what is meant by structure and function, by examining a lake ecosystem.

1. By structure is meant
   a. The kinds, numbers, and distribution of plants (algae, water lilies, and cattails) and an-

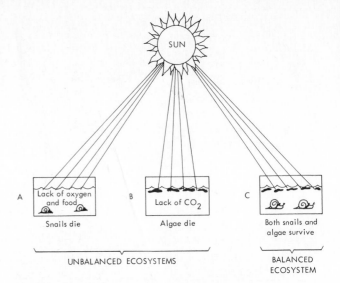

2–3 *Balanced and unbalanced ecosystems. In aquarium A, the snails die because of lack of food and oxygen. In B, the algae die from lack of the carbon dioxide necessary for photosynthesis. In C, the aquarium occupied by both snails and algae, all organisms survive. There is sufficient food and oxygen for the algae-consuming snails; the algae are able to photosynthesize because they have an adequate supply of carbon dioxide (released by the snails).*

imals (crustaceans, snails, insects, fish, turtles, and muskrats).
   b. The kinds, quantity, and distribution of nonliving components, such as oxygen, carbon dioxide, water, sand, nitrates, heat, and sunlight.
2. By function is meant
   a. The volume and rate at which various elements (carbon, nitrogen, and phosphorus) circulate through the ecosystem.
   b. The quantity and rate at which energy flows through the ecosystem.
   c. The processes by which living organisms change the abiotic environment. (For example, when feeding on the lake bottom, a carp may muddy the water. Similarly, in the process of decomposing a dead frog, bacteria will cause the release of nitrates into the surrounding water.)
   d. The processes by which the nonliving environment affects living organisms. (For example, as water temperature rises, so does the rate of breathing, heart action, feeding, locomotion, and excretion in fish, frogs, and tur-

2–2 *Concept of the ecological system, or ecosystem.*

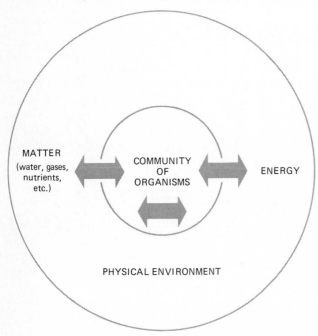

tles. Conversely, as water temperature decreases, so does the rate of all those activities.)

e. Events by which population levels of organisms are regulated. (For example, breeding activities in the spring result in a sudden increase of the black bass population. However, this increase is counteracted by mortality factors, such as cannibalism, predation, disease, oxygen starvation, and various forms of water pollution.)

As we will see in later chapters, most measures applied by the conservationist involve ecosystem manipulation. Thus, the removal of snow cover from an icebound lake might prevent the winter kill of fish from oxygen-depleted waters. This permits sunlight to penetrate the ice and become available to submerged aquatic plants for photosynthesis. The resultant increase in dissolved oxygen could prevent massive fish mortality. In this relatively simple example are interactions between such nonliving components as water, solar energy, and oxygen and the biotic components represented by aquatic plants, fish, and humans.

Although it is convenient to consider ecosystems as separate entities, they are isolated only on the pages of ecology textbooks. In the actual living world there is frequently some movement from one ecosystem to another, whether immediately adjacent or thousands of miles distant. The movement of energy and chemicals from one ecosystem to another is accomplished by biological (animal migration), meteorological (dust storms and hurricanes), and geological (flowing rivers and volcanic eruptions) processes. Thus, topsoil may be blown from an Oklahoma wheat field to the Atlantic Ocean, or it may be washed by spring rains into a nearby stream. Snow geese may migrate from the Canadian tundra to a Louisiana rice field. Phosphorus originating in deep marine sediments may eventually be transferred to terrestrial ecosystems as guano deposits (bird droppings) by means of the algae-crustacean-fish-cormorant food chain, as has occurred conspicuously on islands off the coast of Peru. In a sense,

Human Disruption of Ecosystems

Edward J. Kormondy
Vice-President of Academic Affairs CALIFORNIA STATE UNIVERSITY – LOS ANGELES

All organisms affect and are affected by their environment. There is a constant give and take of energy, minerals, liquids, and gases. When the give and take is more or less in balance, as in the case of oxygen production by plants and its consumption by animals and plants, an ecosystem functions smoothly. When the give and take is disproportionate, as in the case of carbon dioxide, ecosystems are in for trouble. The release of carbon dioxide to the atmosphere exceeds its uptake in photosynthesis. This is resulting in the buildup of carbon dioxide, causing the greenhouse effect — so named because carbon dioxide traps heat similar to the way glass does in a greenhouse. Eventually this increased heat can result in melting of the polar ice caps — which in turn will raise sea level and flood coastal areas.

Mercury, lead, and other metals are important to the human economy. But, released in an ecosystem, they can be incorporated into the human body and lead to neurological and other pathological conditions. Sulfuric acid has its proper place in various metallurgical processes. But, as the primary agent in acid rain, it wreaks havoc on unbuffered lakes, raising their acidity and destroying their aquatic life.

Though all organisms interact with their environment, no other organism is as wide-ranging or powerful in doing so as are we humans. Most often our actions are unintentional or derive from misplaced conceptions about unlimited resources or an environment resistant to assault. Sometimes there is purposive mismanagement as in the case of using pesticides and herbicides harmful to human health and the storage of toxic wastes proximal to water supplies. Planet Earth is our only habitat now and in the foreseeable future. We cannot treat it unthinkingly but instead must shepherd our resources and husband our environment. It's all we have.

therefore, all the ecosystems on earth are tied together to form one all-encompassing ecosystem known as the ecosphere. The ecosphere exists as a thin envelope around the surface of this planet.

Principles of Ecology

The Law of Conservation of Matter

One of the basic laws of physics (and ecology) is the law of conservation of matter. In a nutshell it states: *Although matter can be changed from one form to another, it can neither be created nor destroyed by ordinary physical and chemical changes.* This law relates directly to the massive pollution problems facing our nation. We are consuming natural resources at a record-breaking pace to support a life-style enjoyed by no other nation on earth. But in the process we are also generating wastes at a record-breaking pace. The wastes are difficult to remove. The law of conservation of matter informs us that we just can't throw those wastes away, or burn or flush them away. Everything must go somewhere. Take as an example the solid waste that accumulates in the average community. In order to prevent land pollution, we might collect the waste and bury it in a landfill. That sounds great, but if the landfill is not properly situated or designed, some of the waste may leach into a nearby stream, cause water pollution, and destroy aquatic life. You say, "Why not burn the waste?" That should do it. But wait a minute. The waste certainly would be reduced in volume — to a few ashes — but in the act of burning we would cause air pollution by generating large amounts of fly ash, smoke, and gases (carbon monoxide and sulfur dioxide, for example) that could be harmful to our health. So no matter what waste disposal method we try, pollution (matter) is still very much with us. Perhaps the best approach would be to consider solid waste as no waste at all but as a sort of natural resource in disguise, which, with a little creativity on our part, could be recycled and used over and over again.

Matter and Energy Laws: Their Ultimatum to Spaceship Earth

Consider some of your activities as a college student for a moment: (1) shutting off that horrible alarm clock so that you can rush to your 8 o'clock class, (2) taking lecture notes from that distinguished professor in Conservation class, (3) "whooping it up" at a basketball game, or (4) scuffling with your roommate in the dorm. All of these actions are under the control of the basic matter and energy laws we have just discussed. In a more serious vein, however, these laws also control the activities of all ecosystems on spaceship Earth. In a sense they shape and determine a whole series of resource and other environment problems from bark-beetle outbreaks in a pine forest in Colorado to the toxic contamination of well water on Long Island. These laws provide us with a key to understanding (1) the urgency of our nation's environmental problems, and (2) how those problems can be solved or brought under control.

The matter and energy laws, moreover, provide us with a stern ultimatum: "You must shift from a high-entropy, ecologically unsound, nonsustainable society to a low-entropy, ecologically sound, sustainable society. Unless you do this soon, it is inevitable that your system will collapse." We can no longer continue a system that is characterized by faster and faster rates of matter and energy flow. The ultimate result will be an increasing degree of *entropy*, or disorder. Industrialized societies have for centuries believed that progress could only be achieved by the intensive conversion of resources into the products (cars, bridges, computers) desired by human beings. Unfortunately, this long-cherished belief completely ignores the all-pervasive, unchanging matter and energy laws.

Indeed, those laws compel us to convert to a system that emphasizes resource conservation and reuse, pollution control, and low levels of entropy. We cannot continue to act as if we rule nature; we must act as though nature rules us. It is a curious paradox that while the world's industrialized nations have raised their standard of living, they have unavoidably lowered their standard of environment. We cannot look at nature and wonder what we can get out of it and how fast. Rather we must regard nature with the respect it deserves as the source of life and bounty for all humankind. We must learn to adapt ourselves to nature's basic ecological laws rather than to heavy-handedly disrupt its exquisitely intricate and delicate workings, and in the process eventually destroy ourselves.

The Elemental Cycles

Suppose that the following figure represents planet Earth:

Now suppose that we draw another figure to represent the total amount of living substance (protoplasm) that has ever existed since the first living organism evolved over two billion years ago. This sphere, of course, would include your own body, as well as those of Stone Age people, ancient tree ferns, and dinosaurs. Now, how big do you think this ball of protoplasm would be? You might be surprised to know that it would be considerably larger than the Earth. Thus:

Of the 103 elements known to science, only about 35 contribute to the formation of protoplasm. Carbon, hydrogen, oxygen, and nitrogen form about 96 percent of the human body, whereas such elements as sodium, calcium, potassium, magnesium, sulfur, cobalt, zinc, iron, iodine, and many others occur in smaller amounts. All the elements forming the bodies of living organisms were derived either from the top few inches of the earth's crust (soil), from the rivers, lakes, oceans, and aquifers on or near the surface of the earth, or from the thin atmospheric "blanket" of air that envelops the earth. If this is true, then the only way we can explain a cumulative ball of protoplasm larger than the planet Earth is to assume that the elements forming the protoplasm were used over and over again. In other words, a given atom of, say, nitrogen, which was once part of a dinosaur's jawbone, might eventually have formed part of a professor's brain and, at some time in the future, may form part of a cabbage some college student will have for dinner one evening. The circular flow of an element from the nonliving (abiotic) environment, such as rocks, air, and water, into the bodies of living organisms and then back into the nonliving environment once again is known as an *elemental cycle.*

For eons of time these elemental cycles have been in equilibrium. In other words, the *same* amount of

an element had been moving into the various elemental reservoirs as had been moving out. However, in the last 150 years or so, we have caused imbalances of some elemental cycles. The result has been the buildup of large concentrations of certain elements, such as carbon, nitrogen, and phosphorus, that have had a harmful effect on human welfare. In other words, these imbalances have caused pollution.

THE NITROGEN CYCLE. In pure form nitrogen is a colorless, tasteless, odorless gas that forms about 3 percent (by weight) of living protoplasm. It is an essential component of many important compounds, such as chlorophyll in plants, and hemoglobin, insulin, and DNA (the heredity-determining molecule) in animals. With the aid of Figure 2–5, let us follow nitrogen along its circular pathway through the environment.

Nitrogen is extremely abundant. It forms about 80 percent of the atmosphere. There are about 34,000 tons of nitrogen in the air column above each acre of the earth's surface. One would suppose, therefore, that securing adequate supplies of nitrogen would be relatively simple for living organisms. The problem is, however, that nitrogen is chemically inactive. It does not combine readily with other elements, and it cannot be used by most organisms in the pure elemental form. The 11,000 quarts of nitrogen you breathe into your lungs each day are exhaled right back into the atmosphere.

How, then, can we and the great majority of living organisms make use of gaseous nitrogen in the synthesis of life-sustaining proteins? We cannot. First the nitrogen has to be fixed — converted to a usable form. There are several mechanisms by which nitrogen is fixed in nature.

One type of nitrogen fixation is *atmospheric fixation.* In this process the energy of lightning or sunlight causes the nitrogen to combine with oxygen to form nitrate (NO_3). About 7.6×10^6 metric tons of nitrate are formed annually in this way. This nitrate is then washed to earth by rain and snow and is absorbed by the roots of growing plants(5).

A second type of nitrogen fixation is *biological fixation.* It is much more important than atmospheric fixation. About 54×10^6 metric tons of nitrogen are fixed annually by biological fixation. It is accomplished by microscopic organisms such as bacteria and blue-green algae, which occur abundantly in soil and water. In this process nitrogen is

The Laws of Energy

The leap of a tiger, the beat of your heart, the scream of an eagle, the turn of a wheel, the dip of a canoe paddle — all of these seeming diverse events have something in common: they require energy and they represent change, or work. Just what is energy? The physicists define it as ''the ability to do work or cause change.'' Unlike matter, such as nitrogen, carbon, and phosphorus, *energy cannot be recycled.* Instead energy flows through systems, whether the system is a single organism, like a college student, or the entire ecosphere.

Energy tends to move spontaneously from a highly concentrated or highly *organized* state (food or fuel) to a more *dispersed* or disorganized state (motion and heat). Energy in a concentrated state can perform a great deal of useful work and can be considered to be of high quality. Energy in the dispersed condition, on the other hand, cannot perform as much work and therefore is considered to be of relatively low quality. The measurement of the degree of disorder of a system is known as entropy. All systems, from tigers and oak trees to volcanoes and thunder storms, spontaneously move toward disorder. Living organisms can be considered to be islands of order living in an ocean of disorder. However, energy is continuously being lost from the bodies of organisms in the form of *heat.* Therefore, to retain organization, organisms must have access to a continuous inflow of high-quality energy. In the case of animals this inflow is achieved by the consumption of energy-rich foods. In the case of plants the energy inflow is represented by the solar energy captured by chlorophyll during photosynthesis (4, 5).

First Law of Energy

Pertinent to our study of food chains, food webs, and energy pyramids in the next few pages, are the laws of energy. The first law of energy states: *Although energy cannot be created or destroyed, it can be converted from one form to another.* We might ask: ''What are some of the forms in which energy exists?'' Let's see. When you opened this book a few minutes ago, the contraction of your arm and hand muscles represented the *energy of motion,* or *kinetic energy.* But this kinetic energy was derived from the *chemical energy* of the food you recently ate. And this energy, in turn, was derived directly or indirectly from *solar* or *radiant* energy, during the process of photosynthesis. In this brief description of energy flow we have identified kinetic, chemical, and radiant energy. But there are other forms such as *nuclear* and *heat* energy. Each of these energy forms can be converted into other forms. With each conversion, surprisingly, *energy is neither created nor destroyed.*

Let's consider another example of energy conversions. (See Figure 2 – 4.)

2 – 4 *Energy can be changed from one form to another. However, with each change a certain amount is lost as heat.*

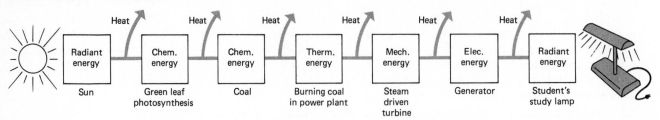

22

The fuel energy of the coal we burn today actually represents the energy of sunlight that shone on the earth about 300 million years ago. This solar energy was trapped by chlorophyll, converted into chemical energy, and locked in the organic molecules of the plant. Eventually, those plants were converted into coal. Today, when this coal is burned by the electrical power industry, the coal's chemical energy is converted into heat energy, which is used to generate steam. The steam in turn spins a turbine (kinetic energy) that then converts the kinetic energy into electrical energy. Eventually, when you turn on your study lamp in your dormitory room (to study ecology) the electrical energy is converted into radiant energy. In this example energy was progressively changed from radiant to chemical to heat to kinetic to electrical and back to radiant energy. And in all those conversions, energy was neither created nor destroyed (4, 5).

Second Law of Energy

As stated before, the quality of energy varies greatly. Thus, the energy in sunshine, food, or fuel (coal, wood, or oil) is highly concentrated and of high quality. On the other hand, the energy in heat is more dispersed and is of low quality. The second law of energy states: *Whenever energy is converted from one form to another, a certain amount is lost in the form of heat.* (In terms of quality, energy is constantly flowing downhill.) Note that "lost" does not mean the same as "destroyed." When we say that energy is lost, we simply mean that it no longer can perform useful work. Now let's examine once more the energy conversion series already described here. Only about 1 percent of the solar energy that bathes a plant leaf actually is converted to chemical energy during photosynthesis. Most of it is reflected or is converted into heat energy and simply warms up the surface of the leaf. That heat is low-quality energy — it cannot perform useful work and, therefore, in a sense is lost. Heat is lost in each successive conversion in the series. During the conversion of electrical energy to radiant (light) energy, again heat is lost — as everyone who has accidentally touched a hot light bulb well knows. (See Figure 2–4.)

Let's consider another example dealing with the internal combustion engine in your car. Only about 25 percent of the high-quality chemical energy consumed by the engine is converted into high-quality kinetic energy that propels you along the highway. On the other hand, about 75 percent of the energy in the gasoline is converted to low-quality heat energy — useless as power but nice to have for warming your car during a midwinter trip. Eventually this heat energy radiates from the car and cannot be used again. The second energy law also operates in living systems. For example, during photosynthesis high-quality solar energy is converted to high-quality chemical energy by green plants during photosynthesis. When you eat plants, whether beans or bananas, the chemical energy of the food is eventually converted by your body to the high-quality chemical energy stored in your body tissues. Sooner or later your body converts it into high-quality kinetic energy that powers such life-sustaining activities as breathing, the beating of the heart, and the muscle contractions of such organs as the stomach, intestine, and throat. However, here again, with each conversion, from solar energy to chemical energy, and from chemical energy to kinetic, a certain amount of energy was lost as heat. Of course, in the latter conversion, the heat serves to help keep your body temperature at about 98.6° F. Eventually, however, it radiates into the surrounding atmosphere and is lost (4, 5).

2 – 5 *The nitrogen cycle.*

combined with hydrogen to form ammonia (NH_3). Then other bacteria convert the ammonia to nitrate, which is usable by plants. Many types of nitrogen-fixing bacteria live inside the root systems of about 190 species of plants, including legumes (alfalfa, peas, beans, soybeans, and clover) and some pines and alders. (See Figure 2 – 6.) The nitrogen-fixing bacteria in the legume plants actually produce more fixed nitrogen than is needed by either the bacteria or the legumes. This surplus is then secreted. As a result, a farmer may increase the nitrogen content (and hence fertility) of a given acre by 80 pounds per year simply by growing legumes. Similarly, the fertility (and hence fish production) of certain mountain lakes may well depend on the nitrogen-fixing bacteria living in the roots of the alders fringing its shores.

A third type of nitrogen fixation is *industrial fixation;* it is a process in which nitrogen is initially combined with hydrogen to form ammonia. Later the ammonia is converted into ammonium salts that can be used as fertilizers. Such commercial production of fertilizer, which requires large amounts of energy, has increased enormously since World War II.

Let us now, with the aid of Figure 2 – 5, follow nitrogen through a hypothetical cycle:

1. Nitrogen diffuses from the atmosphere into the air spaces of soil.
2. It enters the root swellings (nodules) of an alfalfa plant, where the nitrogen-fixing bacteria are located.
3. Here the nitrogen-fixing bacteria combine the

2-6 *Nitrogen-fixing legume. Root system of black-eyed peas taken from a Texas farm. Note the nodules. Nitrogen-fixing bacteria are abundant in the black clay soil of this farm because peas have been grown in rotation for the past 40 years.*

nitrogen with hydrogen to form ammonia and eventually incorporate the nitrogen into amino acids, the building blocks of proteins.

4. The host alfalfa plant then builds up its own protein from the surplus amino acids not required by the bacteria.
5. After a cow (or other consumer) feeds on the alfalfa, the nitrogen in the alfalfa eventually is incorporated into cow protein.
6. The cow excretes nitrogen-containing wastes (manure and urine), or the cow may die, and its carcass may lie on the ground.
7. The large, complex, nitrogen-containing protein molecules in the wastes (or carcass) are then eventually broken down (decomposed) by successive groups of bacteria into nitrates. This process in which nitrate compounds usable to plants are produced by the action of bacteria on nitrogen-containing organic material is known as *nitrification.*
8. A plant, such as corn, wheat, or oak, can now absorb the soluble nitrate through its roots and use them to build up its own essential protein compounds.

We have suggested that ecosystems are not rigidly isolated from each other, but that there exists a limited flow of energy and materials from one to another. Nitrogen also flows from one ecosystem to another. For example, it may flow from a terrestrial ecosystem to an aquatic ecosystem and back to a terrestrial ecosystem again, as shown in Figure 2-5. Thus,

1. The soluble nitrate salts formed by the decay of a rabbit carcass may be washed into a stream and eventually carried to the ocean.
2. The nitrates may be absorbed by marine algae.
3. The algae may be consumed by crustaceans that, in turn, are eaten by fish that, in turn, are consumed by cormorants.
4. The cormorants then fly back to their nesting colony on the California coast and feed some of the partially digested fish to their young. Or the adult bird may excrete some waste as it flies over California farmland, thus to a slight degree contributing to its fertility.

So we have traced nitrogen through a part of its cycle. The perceptive student will realize, however, that one big question remains. If the flow of nitrogen is truly circular, then somehow it must eventually pass back into the atmospheric reservoir from which it originally came. How is this accomplished? *Denitrifying bacteria,* which live in the soil and water, are able to break down nitrates. They then use the energy released to sustain their own life processes. Gaseous nitrogen (N_2) is given off as a byproduct. The nitrogen gas then escapes into the atmosphere from which it originally came. This process, by means of which gaseous nitrogen is temporarily removed from circulation and made unavailable for plant and animal life, is known as *denitrification.* Note then that the role of the denitrifying bacteria is exactly the reverse of that of the nitrifying bacteria. The former remove nitrogen from soil and water and return it to the atmosphere; the latter remove nitrogen from the air and add it to the soil and water.

Imbalance of the Nitrogen Cycle Caused by Humans. Research in Florida has shown that some chlorinated hydrocarbon pesticides are detrimental to the bacteria responsible for nitrification. Pesticide use, therefore, should be restricted to a minimum; for if populations of soil bacteria are greatly diminished, the nutrient cycle on which plants, and eventually animals and humans, depend would be severely disrupted (15). Paul R. Ehrlich of Stanford University views the phenomenon with considerable gravity. In his opinion, "our general lack of attention to the possible long-range effects of these and similar subtle problems in our environment could ultimately prove to be fatal to mankind" (1).

By the year 2000 it is estimated that 100×10^6 metric tons of nitrogen fertilizers will be produced annually (3). One authority has suggested that at the present time as much nitrogen is being fixed by industry to produce fertilizers as was fixed by biological methods before the advent of modern agriculture (3). Another form of industrial fixation, which is completely accidental, is caused when gasoline is burned in the internal combustion engines of automobiles. In this case atmospheric nitrogen is combined with oxygen to form nitrogen dioxide, which is later converted to nitrates and becomes available as nutrients for plants.

For many thousands of years prior to commercial fertilizer production and the modern motor car, the nitrogen cycle was in *dynamic equilibrium.* In other words, the amount of nitrogen leaving the atmosphere by nitrogen fixation was precisely balanced by the amount of nitrogen entering the atmosphere as a result of denitrification. But the fixation of increasing amounts of nitrogen by industrial processes has caused an imbalance; the excess nitrate has been washed from terrestrial to aquatic ecosystems and has caused *eutrophication.* This form of pollution, which is discussed at length in Chapter 8, is characterized by explosive growths of aquatic plants that render lakes unsightly, decrease their recreational value, and cause the replacement of valuable game fish with trash species.

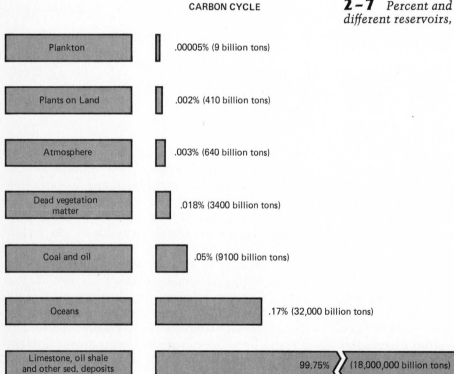

CARBON CYCLE

Plankton — .00005% (9 billion tons)

Plants on Land — .002% (410 billion tons)

Atmosphere — .003% (640 billion tons)

Dead vegetation matter — .018% (3400 billion tons)

Coal and oil — .05% (9100 billion tons)

Oceans — .17% (32,000 billion tons)

Limestone, oil shale and other sed. deposits — 99.75% (18,000,000 billion tons)

2–7 *Percent and actual tonnage of carbon present in different reservoirs, or "pools," of the carbon cycle.*

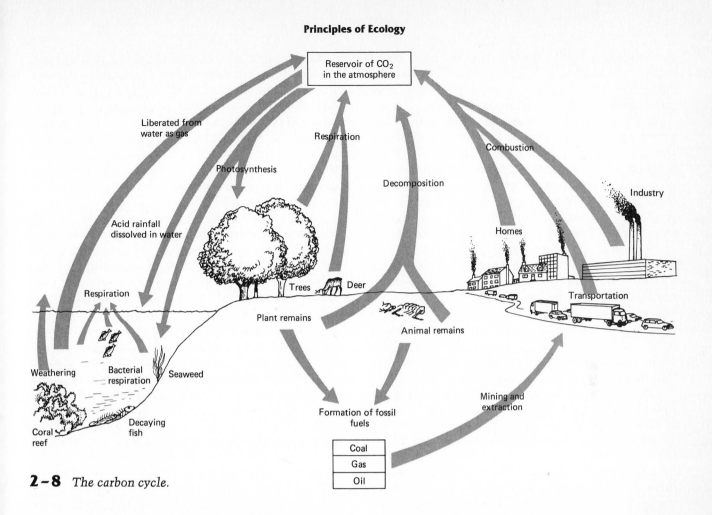

2-8 *The carbon cycle.*

The Carbon Cycle. Carbon is the key element in the molecular structure of all organisms, from bacteria to humans. It forms 49 percent of the dry weight of the body. It is an indispensable element in all the organic compounds characteristic of life, such as carbohydrates, fats, and proteins. Carbon exists in several different reservoirs, including the atmosphere, the bodies of organisms, the ocean, ocean sediments, and as calcium carbonate (rocks, shells, and skeletons). Although the actual *size* of the atmospheric and organism reservoirs is relatively *small*, the rate of flow of carbon into and out of those reservoirs is relatively *high*. As we discuss the carbon cycle, refer to Figure 2-8. Six tons of carbon occur in the air column above each acre of the earth's surface. One acre of lush vegetation will remove 20 tons of carbon from the atmosphere annually. After moving into the breathing pores of a plant, such as clover, it is combined with hydrogen to form sugar during photosynthesis. Later, when those clover leaves are consumed by an animal, such

as a deer, the carbon-containing organic compounds of the clover are digested and converted into deer protoplasm. When humans consume and digest venison, the digested meat is eventually transformed into human protoplasm. In all these organisms, clover, deer, and humans, some carbon is released during respiration — a process in which the organism burns the organic fuels (carbohydrates, protein, and fats) in its cells and extracts the energy in a usable form. Among plants the carbon is released (as carbon dioxide) to the atmosphere via breathing pores; in animals, such as deer and humans, the carbon dioxide is exhaled from the lungs. The carbon-containing remains of dead organisms (clover, deer, man, and so on) or the wastes (feces and urine) of animals are broken down by the bacteria and fungi that occur abundantly in soil, air, and water. Such decomposition releases carbon into soil and air. (Researchers at the University of Notre Dame are conducting experiments with bacteria-free animals kept in sterile chambers. Although

27

the animals — mice, rabbits, and so on — eventually grow old and die, their bodies do not decay. Hence, the carbon content of the carcasses is temporarily taken out of circulation.)

About 300 million years ago, during the Carboniferous period, giant tree ferns and other plants grew in areas now known as Pennsylvania, West Virginia, Ohio, Kentucky, Tennessee, Indiana, and Illinois. Many of those plants were buried by sediment and therefore escaped decomposition. Instead, they were eventually converted into lignite and coal. In a somewhat similar fashion, both plant and animal bodies were converted to crude oil and natural gas. The carbon in these so-called *fossil fuels* was removed from circulation for 300 million years, until in industrialization they were consumed for heat and power. As we will discuss in more detail in Chapter 16, our accelerated combustion of fossil fuels has resulted in a 10 percent increase in the amount of carbon in the atmosphere during the last century. This increase may result in climatic changes that will be harmful to human welfare. Each year forest fires consume about three million acres of timberland in the United States. Each such fire results in a temporary localized increase in atmospheric carbon.

The oceans, which cover 70 percent of the earth's surface, also serve as a reservoir. Carbon dioxide is continuously being exchanged between the atmosphere and the ocean. When atmospheric carbon dioxide increases, more is dissolved in the ocean. Conversely, when atmospheric carbon dioxide decreases, more carbon dioxide is liberated from the ocean as a gas. By this mechanism the carbon dioxide in the atmosphere has been maintained at a fairly constant level for thousands of years — at least until the last century. The carbon dioxide dissolved in the ocean may move through an alga-crustacean-fish food chain. The fish in turn may be eaten by such organisms as shark, tuna, waterfowl, whales, or humans. Some of this carbon is returned to the ocean by the respiration of marine organisms, and some is used by clams, oysters, scallops, and corals to build limestone shells and skeletons. Tremendous quantities of carbon are locked up in coral reefs off the coasts of California and Florida. The Great Barrier Reef off the Australian coast — a mass of limestone 180 feet thick and 1,260 miles long — is composed of countless billions of coral skeletons.

Eventually, as a result of weathering processes that operate for millennia, small amounts of the carbon from coral reefs and the shells of clams and oysters are returned to solution in the ocean waters.

The Phosphorus Cycle. Roughly 1 percent of the human body is composed of phosphorus. It is an essential component of such compounds as deoxyribonucleic acid (DNA) — the heredity-determining molecule — as well as adenosine triphosphate (ATP) — the energy-rich molecule that powers the life activities of virtually all organisms, from bacteria to the whale.

Let us now trace the circular flow of a given phosphorus atom with the aid of Figure 2–9. We begin with its reservoir in phosphate rock. Because of the process of weathering, some of the phosphate dissolves in raindrops and is washed into the soil. There it represents a potential plant nutrient just like nitrogen. However, the ratio of nitrogen to phosphorus in the soil is about 23:1. Because phosphorus is much less abundant than nitrogen, it plays a more important role as a limiting factor for plant growth. The phosphorus atom passes into the body of an animal when it consumes the plant. When the plant or animal dies, its body is decomposed by bacteria and fungi. Phosphate is released to the soil as a result. Some of this phosphate-containing soil may then be washed into a stream after a rain storm. The stream may transport it to a lake or to the ocean. In each of these aquatic ecosystems the phosphorus may be absorbed by algae and rooted plants. From these plants it may then flow through the aquatic food web to such organisms as crustaceans and eventually fish. When phosphorus-containing materials are transported to the ocean, when marine organisms die and are decomposed, or when the marine animals excrete wastes, the phosphorus may gravitate to the ocean floor and form part of the sediment. Over a period of millions of years these sediments may eventually form phosphate rock. Ultimately, by some geological process such as upheaval, the rock may become exposed to the atmosphere. Then, by the action of weathering and erosion, some of the phosphorus in the rock may become part of the soil once again.

Imbalance of the Phosphorus Cycle Caused by Humans. For eons the amount of phosphorus moving from its phosphate rock reservoir into the bodies of living organisms was in equilibrium with the amount moving from living organisms into the phosphate rock reservoir. The total amount of phosphorus in circulation was relatively small. However, in the last few decades the intensive fertiliza-

PHOSPHORUS CYCLE

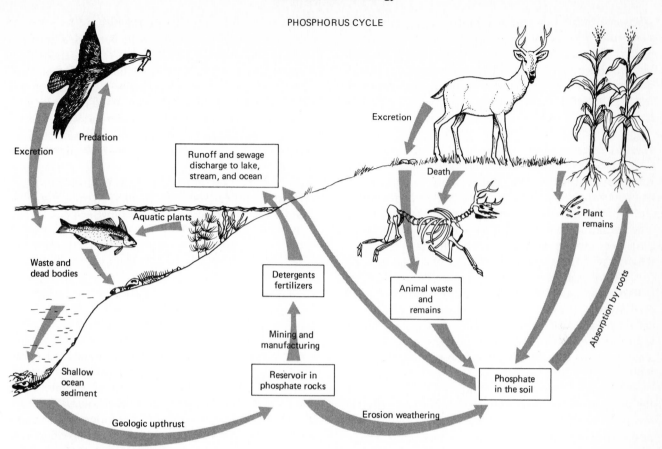

2-9 *The phosphorus cycle.*

tion of agricultural lands to feed a mushrooming human population, as well as the use of phosphorus-containing detergents, has caused an imbalance in the phosphorus cycle. The loss of phosphorus from agricultural lands as a result of erosion is estimated to be about 34 metric tons per square kilometer per year (6). The increased levels of phosphorus in our lakes and streams has been a significant factor in their eutrophication — the accelerated process of aging.

The Global Flow of Energy

The Electromagnetic Spectrum

Suppose that the bulb in your study lamp suddenly burned out while you were preparing for a final exam. It would be just cause for some unmentionable mutterings on your part. Further suppose

that the sun burned out. Far more than mere irritation on the part of one individual, it would bring an end to all life on earth, from the bean to the banana, from the bumblebee to the whale.

The sunshine that warms your nose on your way to class reached your skin only eight minutes after leaving the sun's surface, roughly 93 million miles away. The total range of radiant energy released from the sun is known as the *electromagnetic spectrum.* Note that the visible light (sunshine) we are familiar with forms only a small portion of the entire spectrum. The types of energy represented in the spectrum range from low-energy radio waves at one end, to high-energy gamma rays at the other. This energy may be thought of as coming to the earth in the form of waves. The distance between two successive wave peaks is known as the *wave length.* Both the level of energy and the wave frequency (number of waves per unit distance) increase

29

from the radio wave to the gamma-ray end of the spectrum. The potentially harmful effects of ultraviolet, X rays, and gamma rays will be discussed later in this book. In fact, human survival would not be possible were it not that 90 percent of ultraviolet rays are filtered out by a screen of ozone gas that is located high in the atmosphere.

Global Energy Flow

Let us now examine the fate of solar energy once it has been received by our planet. Only 66 percent of the incoming solar energy is actually absorbed by the earth's atmosphere, land, water, and vegetation. The remainder is reflected back into space by dust particles, clouds, and the earth's surface. This reflectivity of the earth is known as the *albedo*. Improper soil-management practices on the part of the farmer that cause soil erosion and the formation of dust storms will therefore have a cooling effect because of the increased albedo. A similar effect would be caused by a volcanic eruption or the release of soot and fly ash from the smokestacks of factories (4).

About 22 percent of the solar radiation actually absorbed by the earth serves to drive the water cycle — in other words to move the water, by evaporation, from the oceans into the atmosphere, from where it is released as rain, falls to earth, and eventually flows back to the oceans once again.

One important reason humans cannot live on the planet Neptune is its extremely low average temperature — about $-280°$ F $(-173°$ C$)$. However, on planet Earth, 42 percent of the incoming solar energy is used to keep the earth's average temperature at about $58°$ F — well within the range of human temperature tolerance. You may be surprised to learn that only .023 percent of the solar energy absorbed by earth is actually converted to chemical form (food) by photosynthesis (4).

Almost all of the solar energy absorbed by the earth is eventually degraded into low-quality infrared (heat) energy in accordance with the second energy law. This energy then leaves the earth's surface and radiates into space. The ability of the earth to release this energy is known as its *emissivity*. Certain chemicals in the atmosphere, such as carbon dioxide molecules, block the release of some of this energy. The result is a warming effect. The accelerated consumption of fossil fuels during the last fifty years in the United States has had such an influence.

The Flow of Energy in Ecosystems

All the energy that powers the activities of life — from the growth of a cabbage to the beating of the human heart — can be traced back to its original source, the sun. Photosynthesis is defined as the process by which solar energy is used in the conversion of carbon dioxide and water into sugar. With a few minor exceptions, this process can occur only in the presence of chlorophyll, a green pigment found in plants. (See Figure 2–10.) In a sense, the solar energy is trapped by the chlorophyll and channeled into sugar molecules in the form of chemical energy. The overall equation for photosynthesis is

$$\text{solar energy} + \underset{\substack{\text{(carbon} \\ \text{dioxide)}}}{6CO_2} + \underset{\text{(water)}}{6H_2O} \rightarrow$$
$$\underset{\text{(sugar)}}{C_6H_{12}O_6} + \underset{\text{(oxygen)}}{6O_2} + \text{chemical energy.}$$

Some of the released oxygen may be used directly by the plant or may pass from the leaf through microscopic "breathing" pores into the atmosphere. Here the oxygen may be used by other organisms from bacteria to humans. There is considerable concern among some ecologists that the progressive contamination of the oceans with pesticides and industrial wastes may sharply reduce the photosynthetic activity of marine algae and therefore greatly diminish the earth's supply of atmospheric oxygen. Another harmful result, of course, would be sharply limited food supplies for a rapidly expanding population of human consumers, which might reach six billion by the year 2000.

Primary production is the total amount of sugar produced by photosynthesis. In the world as a whole, it amounts to 270 billion tons yearly. Ecologists refer to the primary production of a lake, meadow, woodlot, or some other ecosystem. All living plants and animals carry on respiration, a process by means of which sugar (and other organic compounds) is burned up or oxidized. The function of respiration is to make energy available to the organism so that it can power its life-maintaining activities. The generalized equation for respiration is

$$\underset{\text{(sugar)}}{C_6H_{12}O_6} + \underset{\text{(oxygen)}}{6O_2} \rightarrow \underset{\substack{\text{(carbon} \\ \text{dioxide)}}}{6CO_2} + \underset{\text{(water)}}{6H_2O} + \text{energy.}$$

2-10 *A food "factory." A cross section of a green plant leaf showing some of the aspects of photo-synthesis, the food-manufacturing process that occurs in the chloroplasts of the palisade and spongy tissue cells.*

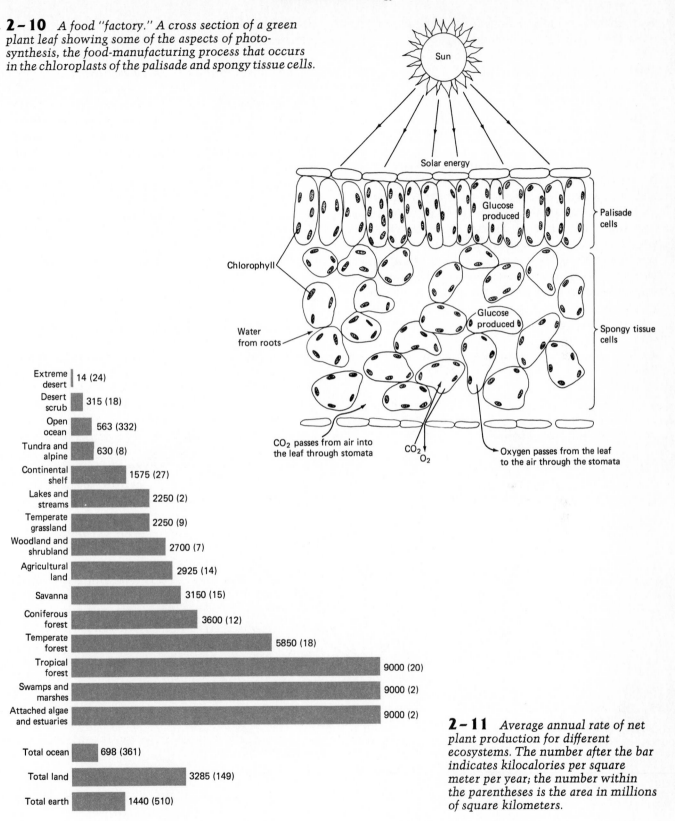

Sun

Solar energy

Glucose produced

Palisade cells

Chlorophyll

Spongy tissue cells

Water from roots

Glucose produced

CO_2 passes from air into the leaf through stomata

CO_2
O_2

Oxygen passes from the leaf to the air through the stomata

Ecosystem	Value
Extreme desert	14 (24)
Desert scrub	315 (18)
Open ocean	563 (332)
Tundra and alpine	630 (8)
Continental shelf	1575 (27)
Lakes and streams	2250 (2)
Temperate grassland	2250 (9)
Woodland and shrubland	2700 (7)
Agricultural land	2925 (14)
Savanna	3150 (15)
Coniferous forest	3600 (12)
Temperate forest	5850 (18)
Tropical forest	9000 (20)
Swamps and marshes	9000 (2)
Attached algae and estuaries	9000 (2)
Total ocean	698 (361)
Total land	3285 (149)
Total earth	1440 (510)

2-11 *Average annual rate of net plant production for different ecosystems. The number after the bar indicates kilocalories per square meter per year; the number within the parentheses is the area in millions of square kilometers.*

31

Note that this equation is exactly the opposite of the overall equation for photosynthesis:

solar energy $+ 6CO_2 + 6H_2O \rightarrow$
(carbon   (water)
dioxide)

$$C_6H_{12}O_6 + 6O_2.$$
(sugar)   (oxygen)

Thus, the *raw materials* of photosynthesis — carbon dioxide and water — are the *products* of respiration, whereas the *products* of photosynthesis — glucose and oxygen — are the *raw materials* of respiration. All plants, of course, must respire, and therefore they burn up glucose. For that reason ecologists distinguish between gross production, which is the *total* amount of energy captured by the plant during photosynthesis, and *net production*, which is the chemical energy that remains after respira-

tion. The net production may serve as food for plant-eating animals. (See Figure 2–11.) Unlike green plants, animals are able to capture energy only by the consumption of energy-bearing food.

Food Chains

A *food chain* is the sequence of organisms through which energy and nutrients move. A representative food chain that might operate in a wet meadow would be

grass   → grasshopper →
(producer)   (primary
             consumer)
             [herbivore]

frog   →   snake   →   hawk
(secondary   (tertiary   (quarternary
consumer)   consumer)   consumer)
─────────────────────────────
[carnivores]

2–12   *One possible food chain for a wet meadow is shown along with the web of which it is a part. The food web is highly simplified.*

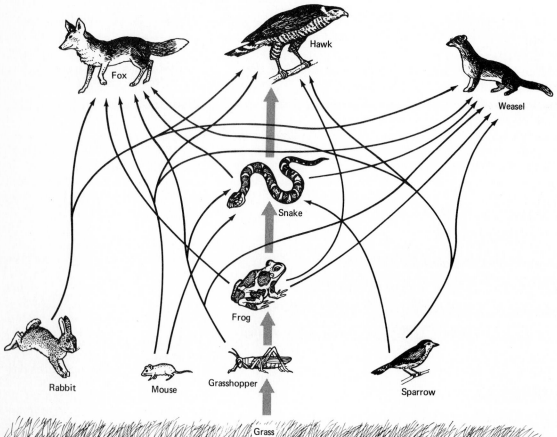

In this food chain the initial link (grass) is classified as a *producer* because it converts unusable solar energy into usable chemical energy by the process of photosynthesis. Any food chain that has a green plant as its first link is known as a *grazing food chain.* This chemical energy is available to later links in the food chain. This is indeed the energy that either directly or indirectly powers the activities of all organisms on earth. Over 270 billion tons of sugar are produced annually by marine, terrestrial, and freshwater vegetation. Link Number 2, the grasshopper, is classified as an *herbivore* because it is a plant eater. The flesh-eating links Number 3 (frog), Number 4 (snake), and Number 5 (hawk) are classified as *carnivores.* Actually this food chain is rather long; most terrestrial food chains have only two or three links.

Another type of consumer, not represented in our food chain diagram, is the *detritus feeder.* These organisms obtain their energy and nutrients from detritus—lifeless remains of plants and animals. Detritus feeders in a forest are represented by bacteria and fungi (mushrooms and molds), as well as by such animals as maggots and termites. As a result of their activities, the large, complex molecules in plant and animal remains are broken down (decomposed) into smaller molecules such as nitrates. Those compounds may then enrich the soil and be used as nutrients by future generations of plants (producers). In some shallow lakes, detritus is abundantly represented by decaying vegetation. This material in turn is fed on by crayfish and snails, which in turn are consumed by fish.

Any food chain that has its base in the dead remains of plants and animals is known as a *detritus food chain.* Roughly 90 percent of the biomass in an oak woods eventually dies and becomes the base of *detritus* food chains. In the open water of a lake, on the other hand, the situation is just reversed. There the floating algae represent the principal producers. Roughly 90 percent of the algal producers are consumed by small crustaceans and thus serve as the food base for *grazing* food chains (5).

Food Webs

A food web is an interconnected series of food chains. In actuality a food chain virtually never exists as an isolated entity. Consider the food chain corn–pig–human, for example. A pig eats other foods beside corn, such as rats, mice, insects, grubs, earthworms, baby chicks, grass, weeds, and garbage.

Similarly, in addition to pork, humans consume everything from artichokes to zweiback, from kippered herring to pheasant under glass. In nature, therefore, food chains exist primarily as separate strands of an interwoven *food web.*

Let us connect our original grass–grasshopper–frog–snake–hawk food chain of a wet meadow with a few other food chains, in order to form a food *web*, as shown in Figure 2–12. Actually, this food web is still a gross oversimplification. Probably hundreds of species of organisms are involved in the complete food web of a wet meadow.

As a general rule, the greater the number of alternative channels through which energy can flow, the greater the stability of the food web and ecosystem. Just why should a complex food web have stability? Let us see. In our wet meadow foxes obtain their nourishment by preying on rabbits, mice, grasshoppers, sparrows, frogs, and snakes. Now suppose that the rabbit population was reduced, possibly because of adverse weather during the breeding period. Under those conditions the fox population would shift the predatory pressure it had exerted on rabbits to some (or all) of its alternative prey (mouse, grasshopper, sparrow, frog, and snake) without suffering from nutritional hardship. Reduced predatory pressure on the resilient rabbit population, in turn, might permit it to rebound quickly when breeding conditions are favorable.

Many of the ecological problems we humans have unwittingly brought on ourselves have resulted from our attempt to simplify ecosystems and hence promote their instability. The Irish potato famine of the 1840s is a particularly illuminating example, as described by J. M. Moran, M. D. Morgan, and J. H. Wiersma of the University of Wisconsin at Green Bay(5):

Ireland's soil and climate are ill-suited for most crops. From the time of its introduction at the end of the sixteenth century, the potato was the main source of Ireland's food energy because it grew well and yielded a much higher number of calories per acre than other food crops. As potato production flourished, the population approximately doubled between 1780 and 1845 to a level of 8,500,000. In that year a fungus that caused a plant disease known as potato blight entered Ireland from Europe. The potatoes were susceptible to the fungus and large numbers of potato plants died during the five years that the blight lasted. Because the Irish had no substitute food source, roughly *one million* of them died from starvation or disease between 1845 and 1850 and another

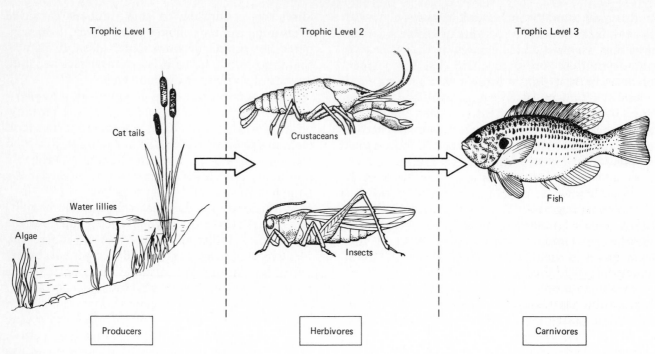

2 – 13 *Trophic levels of a lake ecosystem.*

million emigrated. In a period of five years the population declined 25 percent, and the country's economic and social structure was dealt a staggering blow — all largely the result of oversimplifying the food web. (5) *[Italics mine.]*

TROPHIC LEVELS. Suppose that we consider, for a moment, the food web of a lake ecosystem. Each nourishment, or food level in that community is known as a *trophic level*. (See Figure 2 – 13.) Thus, all the producers (algae, rooted plants, water lilies, cattails, and so on) form the first trophic level. All the plant eaters, known as primary consumers, or herbivores, such as crustaceans and insects, form the second trophic level. The secondary consumers (carnivores), such as fish, feed on the primary consumers and form the next trophic level, and so on.

PYRAMID OF ENERGY. Not all the energy in a given trophic level can be harvested by the next level. In fact, most consumers in a food web can harvest only about 10 percent of the energy in the trophic level from which they obtain their nourishment. Thus, the primary consumers (herbivores) harvest only 10 percent of the food energy in the producer (green plant) level. Similarly, the secondary consumers (carnivores) in turn harvest only 10

percent of the food energy present in the primary consumer level. As a result, the energy relationships between the various trophic levels of a food web may be represented in the form of an *energy pyramid*, as shown in Figure 2 – 14.

Our description of trophic levels has been greatly simplified for purposes of clarity. We must not get the idea that a given species of organism can belong to only one trophic level. For example, although some fish are either exclusively herbivorous or exclusively carnivorous, some species of fish, such as

2 – 14 *Pyramid of energy for a lake ecosystem.*

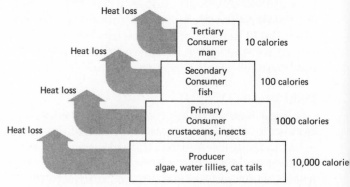

34

the carp, are *omnivorous*—they feed on plants and animals. Therefore, in terms of its food-energy relationships, we would have to consider that the carp occupies both the primary *and* secondary consumer level in the energy pyramid of the food web of a lake.

Reasons for Low Efficiencies. As a curious student you will now ask: "Why can these energy relationships be represented by a pyramid? Why is each consumer level only about 10 percent efficient in harvesting food energy?" Let's see if we can answer these questions. There are three main reasons for the low efficiencies. First, by means of evolutionary processes taking place over eons of time, most organisms have acquired adaptations to avoid being eaten by consumers. Plants can deter herbivores with spines, thorns, thick protective bark, irritating secretions, or foul odors. Animals such as insects, trout, and antelope can fly, swim, or run from the approaching predator at high speed. Some animals rely on protective coloration to escape detection by predators. This is well exemplified in certain species of moths whose colors make them almost invisible against the bark of a tree. Similarly, many ground-nesting birds like pheasants and grouse are extremely difficult to detect while they are incubating their eggs, even from a distance of a few feet. If an organism escapes predators, it will eventually die from some other cause, such as disease or starvation. Its carcass will then be decomposed by bacteria and/or fungi and will then serve as an energy base for detritus food webs (5).

Second, the low efficiency in energy transfer from one trophic level to another can be explained by the fact that not all the body of the food organism is digestible. For example, an owl that has eaten a mouse is unable to digest the bones and fur. This material is formed into a pellet and later ejected through the mouth. Similarly, many herbivores, such as porcupines, beaver, deer, and rabbits, cannot digest cellulose, a characteristic compound in plant tissue. Therefore, many cellulose fibers are voided from the body as waste. Humans do not eat celery because it is a rich source of energy; we eat it because the indigestible celery fibers serve as roughage and stimulate the digestive action of the gut. Such waste will eventually serve as an energy base for a detritus food web (5).

Third, the low efficiency in energy transfer can be partially explained by the need of every organism to respire. You will recall that respiration is the process

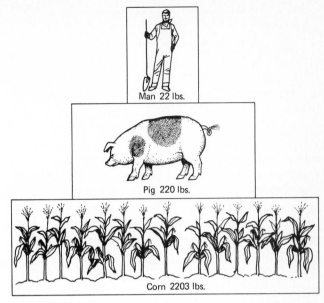

2–15 *Pyramid of biomass. It takes 2,203 pounds of corn to produce the 220 pounds of pork required to produce 22 pounds of human biomass.*

by which organisms oxidize, or burn, energy-rich organic compounds in order to release the energy they need to power their life activities. Respiration itself is a relatively inefficient process. For example, often less than 50 percent of the energy in a given sugar molecule may actually work for an organism. The remainder is largely converted to useless heat that escapes into the environment.

THE PYRAMID OF BIOMASS. Ecologists refer to the weight of living substance (protoplasm) in an organism, a population, or community as its biological mass, or *biomass*. In typical food webs based on small green plants and ending in predators like hawks, there is a *progressive reduction in the total biomass represented at each succeeding trophic level.* This, of course, is the result of the progressive reduction in food energy available for biomass synthesis at each succeeding trophic level.

A good example is the corn–pig–human biomass pyramid. For example, 1,000 kilograms (2,203 pounds) of corn are needed to produce 100 kilograms (220 pounds) of pork and ham, which in turn can be converted into 10 kilograms (22 pounds) of your flesh when you sit down at the dinner table. (See Figure 2–15.)

In some cases the biomass pyramid may be *upside*

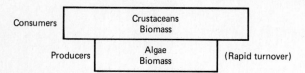

2–16 *Inverted biomass pyramid, such as might occur in a lake ecosystem.*

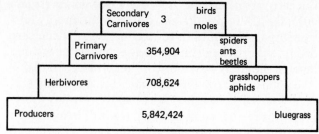

A. Pyramid of Numbers

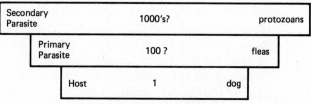

B. Inverted Pyramid of Numbers

2–17 *Two kinds of number pyramids. The upper pyramid (A) is for a weedy field; the lower (B) for a dog-parasite system.*

down. This may be the case in some aquatic ecosystems where the food webs are based on billions of microscopic algae. The algae reproduce very rapidly — doubling their numbers every few days. The consumers, however (crustaceans and fish), feed on the algae almost as rapidly as they are produced. As a result the algae (producer) trophic level has less biomass than the crustacean-fish (consumer) trophic level (4). (See Figure 2–16.)

The Pyramid of Numbers. In typical food webs based on small green plants like grasses or algae and ending in predators like hawks and fish, the numbers of individuals are frequently greatest at the producer level, less at the herbivore level, and least at the carnivore level. This concept is known as the *pyramid of numbers.* Figure 2–17A illustrates the pyramid of numbers in the food web of an acre of blue grass in Michigan. In food webs ending in parasites, the pyramid of numbers is upside down. This is evident in the dog–flea–protozoan food chain,

where the protozoans are parasites of the parasitic fleas (Figure 2–17B). Because, however, number pyramids do not provide accurate pictures of either biomass or energy relationships between trophic levels, they are of somewhat limited value.

2–18 *Hypothetical energy pyramids. Note that the efficiency of humans in obtaining energy increases as the food chains shorten. By feeding on algae humans can obtain 125 times more energy than by feeding on trout.*

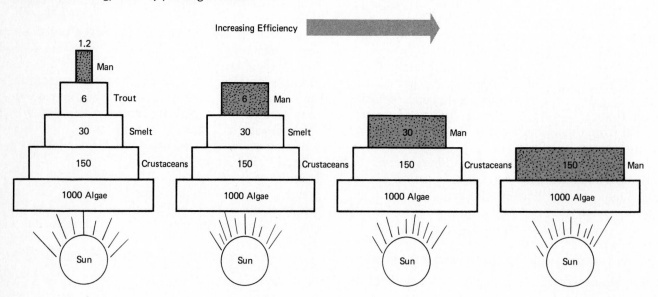

36

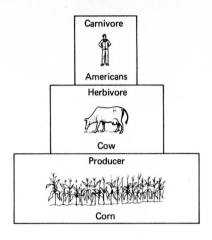

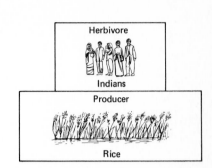

2–19

The Pyramid of Energy and Human Nutrition. It is apparent that the second law of energy imposes a limit on food-chain length. Most terrestrial food chains have only three or four links. In the unusually long food chain clover–grasshopper–frog–snake–hawk, which might operate in a wet meadow, the hawk uses only 0.0001 percent of the incoming solar energy. Some marine food chains leading from algae to tuna are so long that 100,000 pounds of algae would be required to produce a single pound of tuna usable by humans. Figure 2–18 shows similar relationships in a lake ecosystem using hypothetical energy pyramids.

Knowledge of these energy relationships enables us to understand the striking difference between Indian and American diets, for example. If, as an American, you live to be seventy, you probably will have consumed 10,000 pounds of meat, 28,000 pounds of milk and cream, and additional thousands of pounds of grain, sugar, and specialty foods. However, a seventy-year-old Indian probably would have eaten only 1 percent as much meat as you. In overpopulated nations like India and China, where one of every three people go to bed hungry, it is no accident that human food chains frequently have only two links, in which herbivorous *humans* have replaced the herbivorous *cow, sheep,* or *pig.* (See Figure 2–19.) More energy is available to the Asian (or to the New York slum dweller) by moving up the chain—closer to the producer base. Americans still live in a "land of milk and honey" (as well as pork chops and tuna). However, the time may well come, as a result of our mushrooming population (expected to reach 265 million by the year 2000), when we will be faced with the ecological ultimatum: "Shorten your food chains or tighten your belts." Of course, it is much more delightful to feast on chops and tuna, but the second energy law may yet make us shift to bean soup and cornmeal mush.

The Law of Tolerance

The survival of any organism depends on essential factors in its physical environment, such as water, temperature, oxygen, and nutrients. The concentrations or values of these factors may vary greatly. For each factor a given species has a range of tolerance that is determined by its genetic makeup. The organism will be adversely affected when the factor approaches values beyond its tolerance limits. Let us take your tolerance for air temperature as an example. If the air temperature gets too high, you sweat and feel uncomfortable. If it gets too low, you shiver and again are uncomfortable. However, if the air temperature is about 70° F., you operate most efficiently and feel comfortable. (Figure 2–20 shows the house fly's range of tolerance for air temperature.)

Let's give another example. You require four grams of iodine in your diet each year. The reason? It is needed in the synthesis of the hormone thyroxine, which plays an important role in regulating your body's metabolism and, therefore, your body temperature, heart rate, and physical and mental development. An absence of iodine in your diet would surely result in death. On the other hand if you mixed a few pounds of iodine in your breakfast cereal tomorrow morning, your early funeral would be virtually assured. The concept that either too *little* or too *much* of a given factor may have an ad-

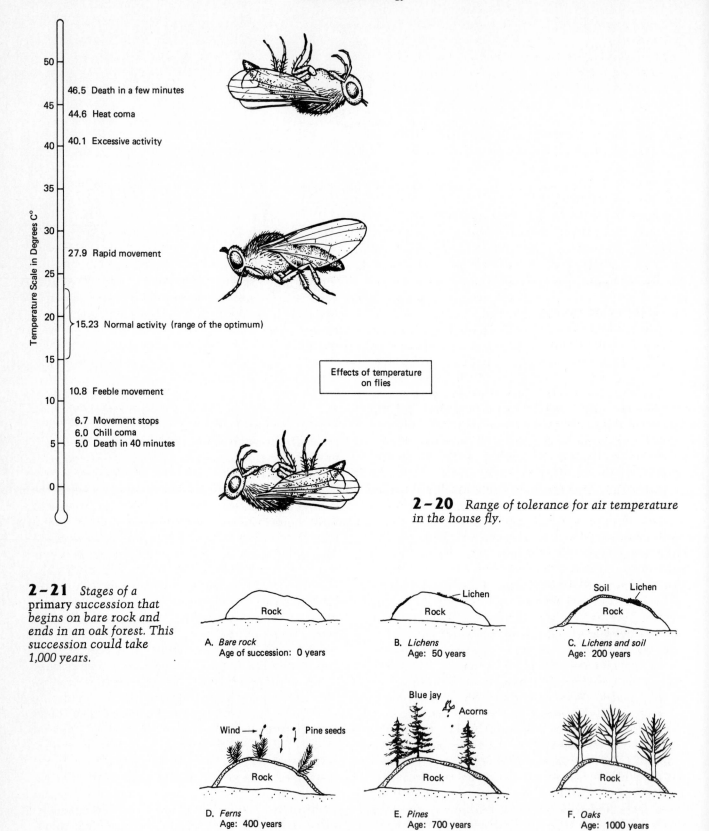

Temperature Scale in Degrees C°

46.5 Death in a few minutes

44.6 Heat coma

40.1 Excessive activity

27.9 Rapid movement

15.23 Normal activity (range of the optimum)

Effects of temperature on flies

10.8 Feeble movement

6.7 Movement stops
6.0 Chill coma
5.0 Death in 40 minutes

2–20 *Range of tolerance for air temperature in the house fly.*

2–21 *Stages of a primary succession that begins on bare rock and ends in an oak forest. This succession could take 1,000 years.*

Rock

A. *Bare rock*
Age of succession: 0 years

Lichen

Rock

B. *Lichens*
Age: 50 years

Soil   Lichen

Rock

C. *Lichens and soil*
Age: 200 years

Wind ⟶   Pine seeds

Rock

D. *Ferns*
Age: 400 years

Blue jay   Acorns

Rock

E. *Pines*
Age: 700 years

Rock

F. *Oaks*
Age: 1000 years

verse effect on an organism is known as the *law of tolerance.*

The tolerance of a given species for an environmental factor may vary with the age of the organism. Thus, newly hatched salmon are much more vulnerable to such water contaminants as heat, toxic metals, and pesticides than adults. Tolerance may also vary with the generation of the organism. For example, when DDT is first sprayed on a given population of house flies, almost all of them are destroyed. However, when DDT is applied to the second generation of flies (which has been produced from the few survivors of the initial spraying), the insecticide is not quite as effective. Eventually, after many generations of flies have been sprayed with DDT, a generation develops that is highly resistant to the chemical.

Biological Succession

Biological succession is the replacement of one community of organisms (plant or animal) by another in an orderly and predictable manner. In a plant succession the plants of each successional stage (grass, shrub, tree) cause changes in sunlight intensity, wind velocity, humidity, and temperature, as well as in the structure, depth, moisture, and fertility of the soil. These changes result in the replacement of the original stage by a later stage better adapted to the modified environment.

Primary Succession. A succession that develops in an area not previously occupied by organisms is known as a *primary succession.* It must start from scratch, so to speak. It may become established on a jagged outcrop of granite, on a lava-covered slope, on rubble left in the wake of a landslide, or even on the slag heaps of an open-pit mine. At the present time a primary succession is slowly getting started on the lava-covered slopes of Mount St. Helens, the volcanic mountain that erupted May 18, 1980 (see Box on page 41).

We will trace a primary succession that might occur on a rocky surface in the deciduous forest region of the eastern United States. (See Figure 2–21.) The first stage is the pioneer community. Plants of this stage are adapted to withstand great extremes of temperature and moisture. A typical pioneer plant that might become established on a bare, windswept rocky outcrop is the lichen, whose wind-dispersed reproductive bodies — spores — might be blown into the area. The lichens gradually form a grayish-green crust on the rocks. Even if the rock is completely dry, the lichen spores will develop if adequate atmospheric moisture is available. Once established, lichens begin to modify the immediate environment around them. Weak carbonic acid (H_2CO_3) produced by the lichen begins to dissolve the underlying rock. Lichens growing side by side form a trap in which particles of windblown sand, dust, and organic debris begin to accumulate. When an occasional lichen dies, bacteria and small fungi cause its decay. The resultant organic material and the excreta of minute lichen-eating insects that have invaded the microhabitat enrich the relatively sterile soil that has accumulated. This soil now acts as a sponge, rapidly absorbing water that falls as dew or rain. Once sufficient soil has accumulated, mosses and ferns may become established, also by means of wind-distributed spores. Ferns eventually shade out the lichens and replace them in the succession. The soil becomes further enriched each fall with the decay of the ferns. Eventually, as the decades pass, windblown pine seeds that may have originated in some hilltop pine forest may fall in the area. They may have been dropped by seed-eating birds, such as the pine siskin, as they flew overhead. The young sun-loving pine seedlings in turn compete successfully with the ferns. Eventually the pines shade out the ferns and replace them in the succession.

With the passage of time, gray squirrels may temporarily enter the area to bury acorns brought in from a neighboring oak woods. Acorns may also be accidentally dropped by a wandering raccoon or by a bluejay during a flight over the young pines. The acorns germinate readily in the relatively fertile soil, which by now has been developing for centuries since the succession began. The young oak seedlings grow well in the reduced light under the pine canopy. The oaks (and other species such as hickory, red maple, and red gum) have long roots and therefore can make use of soil moisture that is unavailable to the shallow-rooted pines. As an occasional pine dies, its position in the forest community will be filled by an oak. Ultimately an oak forest, with its characteristic complement of plants and animals, will become established, as the stable terminal community, or *climax*, of the succession. (See Fig. 2–21.) Thus, the bare windswept rock outcrop is eventually replaced after hundreds of years by a mature oak woods.

Secondary Succession. A succession that develops in an area that was previously occupied by

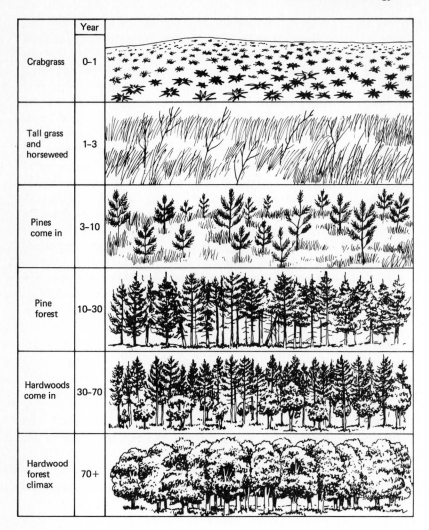

	Year	
Crabgrass	0–1	
Tall grass and horseweed	1–3	
Pines come in	3–10	
Pine forest	10–30	
Hardwoods come in	30–70	
Hardwood forest climax	70+	

2–22 *Stages of a secondary succession that begins on abandoned farmland and, after 70 years, ends in a hardwood forest.*

organisms is a *secondary succession.* It is much more common than the primary succession. It occurs when a given ecosystem is partially destroyed and is therefore moved back to an earlier stage of succession. For example, a secondary succession may get started in a burned-over forest or in a lake that had been accidentally poisoned with waste from a chemical plant. With the help of Figure 2–22, let us examine the secondary succession that develops in abandoned cotton fields in the Piedmont region of Georgia (2).

During the first year following abandonment, the land is populated by two pioneer species: crabgrass and horseweed. During the second year they are replaced by aster. Tall grass in turn replaces the aster

by the third year. Shrubs and young pines become established in about the fifth year and gradually shade out the tall grass. The pine forest dominates the succession until it is about 50 years old. At this point sun-loving pine seedlings can no longer survive in the dense shade on the forest floor. They are replaced by the shade-loving seedlings of oaks and hickories. With the passage of time, one by one, a mature pine dies and its place is taken by young oaks and hickories. About 100 years after the succession began, the pines are shaded out by the oaks and hickories. The latter species eventually form the climax stage of the succession. Note that this secondary succession required only 100 years to move from the pioneer stage to the climax. On the other hand, a primary succession that starts on bare rock or sand may require 500 to 1,000 years before the climax stage is reached (6).

Although we have stressed the succession of plant communities because vegetational changes are more basic and conspicuous, it should be emphasized that a succession of animal communities occurs as well. This is understandable, because the occurrence of a given species of animal in a particular stage of a succession depends on such factors as food, water, protective cover against predators and storms, breeding sites, temperature, and humidity, all of which change as the succession proceeds. In the Georgia study, marked changes in breeding bird populations were observed in the various stages. In this succession the field sparrow, towhee, and cardinal played important roles in seed dispersal. The seeds of some plants actually germinate better after passing through a bird's digestive tract, apparently because its digestive juices dissolve the seed coat.

Mammalian communities show a similar change in species composition and density with the prog-

Life Returns to Mount St. Helens: A Dramatic Example of Succession

Mount St. Helens erupted on May 18, 1980. It was one of the most spectacular volcanic eruptions witnessed on the planet Earth. Mortality to both plant and animal life was awesome. Some ecosystems were literally knocked back to ground zero and had to start from scratch. Roger del Moral described the dramatic comeback of life in an article entitled "Life Returns to Mount St. Helens." Excerpts from his article follow:

At 8:32 A.M. superheated groundwater close to the magma flashed into steam, resulting in a lateral explosion that pulverized rocks and trees and sent a hurricane-force . . . bolt of ash off the north face and across the Toutle River Valley to the north and west. Temperatures in this inferno were estimated to exceed 900° F. Comparable to a 400-megaton blast, the explosion blew down trees in a 160° arc up to 14 miles north of the crater. As the summit of the mountain collapsed, two vertical columns of gas and steam were injected more than 65,000 feet into the air. The ash was eventually deposited, in layers up to five inches thick, over 49 percent of Washington State and beyond.

The number of animals killed as a direct result of the explosion was high. Subterranean animals, such as pocket gophers, appear to have survived in many places even within the blast zone, but mammals and birds living above ground had no protection from the blast. The Washington Department of Game estimates that among the more important casualties were 5,200 elk, 6,000 black-tailed deer, 200 black bears, 11,000 hares, 15 mountain lions, 300 bobcats, 27,000 grouse, and 1,400 coyotes. . . . The eruption also severely damaged 26 lakes and killed some 11 million fish, including trout and young salmon.

Larger vertebrates may form a crucial link in the process of vegetation recolonization. Where heavy ash or mudflows dried to form a hard, uniform crust, there are few cracks to shelter germinating seeds. But large animals wandering in search of food or water make tracks that trap seeds.

Higher terrestrial life may be scarce in the blast zone but dead organic matter is abundant, and such a resource is never unexploited for long. Here, where many humans died, where entire ecosystems ceased to exist in a matter of seconds, Dave Hosford of Central Washington State College has found a mushroom growing from the ash, slowly decomposing organic matter found there and beginning a terrestrial succession.

Of all the regions on the mountain, the most severely affected was the blast zone immediately north of the crater, including Spirit Lake. Every type of volcanic behavior displayed by the mountain has assailed this terrain. All life was seemingly obliterated. Trees were pulverized and soil vaporized. Yet, even here life is returning.

41

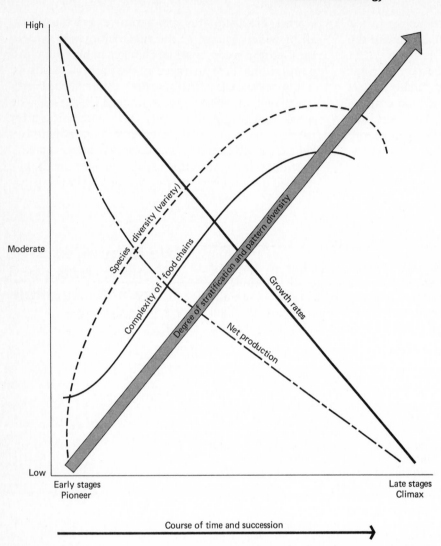

High

Moderate

Species diversity (variety)

Complexity of food chains

Degree of stratification and pattern diversity

Growth rates

Net production

Low

Early stages
Pioneer

Late stages
Climax

Course of time and succession

2–23 *Summary of some of the trends occurring during an ecological succession. Note that the number of species (species diversity), complexity of food chains, and degree of stratification (vegetational layers) increase. However, the growth and net production rates decrease.*

ress of the succession. Thus, in the secondary succession we have just described, cottontails and grass snakes of the grass stage were succeeded by such oak-hickory representatives as the opossum, raccoon, and squirrel. A summary of some of the major trends occurring in a succession is shown in Figure 2–23.

The Biomes

Anyone who has driven from New England to California is acutely aware of the marked changes in landscape that unfold as one speeds along the highway — from the evergreen forests of Maine to the beech-maple woodlands of Ohio, from the windswept Kansas prairie to the hot Arizona desert. Each of those distinctive areas represents a different

biome. The biomes of the world are shown in Figure 2–24. We may define a biome as the largest terrestrial community that can be easily recognized by a biologist. A biome is the biological expression of the interaction of climate, soil, water, and organisms (13). (See Figure 2–25.)

TUNDRA. The Siberian word tundra means "north of the timberline." The term is highly appropriate because it extends from the timberline in the south to the belt of perpetual ice and snow in the north. The surface rolls gently. The tundra embraces about twenty million square miles. It extends around the globe in the northern latitudes. Because of its relative simplicity, the ecology of the tundra is better understood than that of other biomes. The

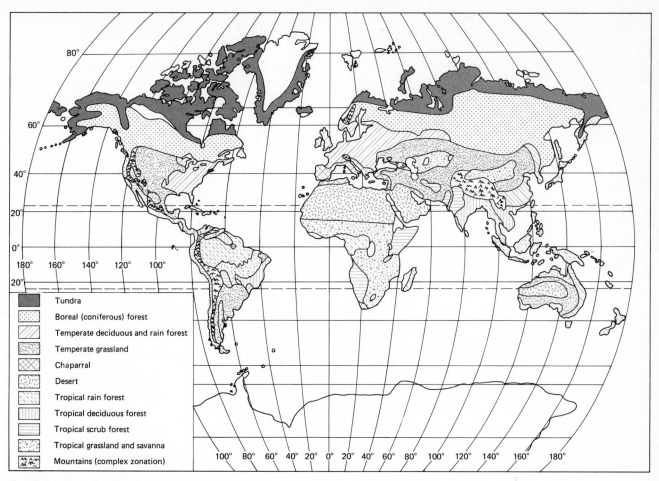

2–24 *Biomes of the world.*

Tundra

Boreal (coniferous) forest

Temperate deciduous and rain forest

Temperate grassland

Chaparral

Desert

Tropical rain forest

Tropical deciduous forest

Tropical scrub forest

Tropical grassland and savanna

Mountains (complex zonation)

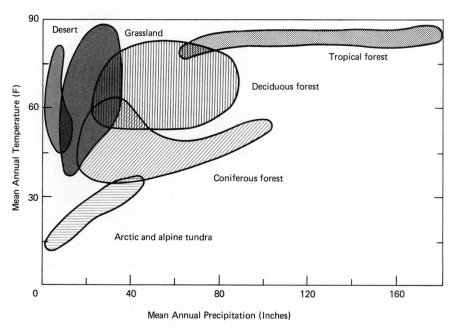

2–25 *Roles of temperature and precipitation in determining biome types.*

2–26 *The caribou, a characteristic herbivore of the tundra. Note the low-lying vegetation, composed primarily of lichens, grasses, and mosses.*

principal limiting factors are the small amount of solar energy and the bitter cold. During June and July the tundra on the edge of the Arctic Circle is a "land of the midnight sun." On the other hand, in January this same region is a "land of daytime darkness," for the sun never rises. Annual precipitation is fewer than ten inches, most of which falls in summer or autumn as rain. Snowfall is scant. Because of the cold weather and the short six-week growing season, the vegetation in the northern tundra is quite sparse. As a result, this region is sometimes referred as an Arctic desert. In fact, plant productivity in the tundra is just slightly higher than in the true desert biome. (See Figure 2–26.) The low temperature slows down the chemical and biological activities that are necessary for the formation of mature soils. The upper level of the permanently frozen soil (or permafrost) occurs at a depth of about 6 to 18 inches. In spring and summer the thawed-out ground is turned into a quagmire. The melt-waters of late spring form thousands of tiny lakes because of poor drainage and low rates of evaporation. Dwarf willows are characteristic producers. Although only a few feet high, some of these willows may be more than one hundred years old.

The tundra is a very fragile ecosystem. One reason is the very slow rate of recovery from human disturbance. Thus, wagon wheel tracks that were formed

2–27 *Aerial view of a migrating herd of caribou. Note the large number of small lakes dotting the tundra landscape.*

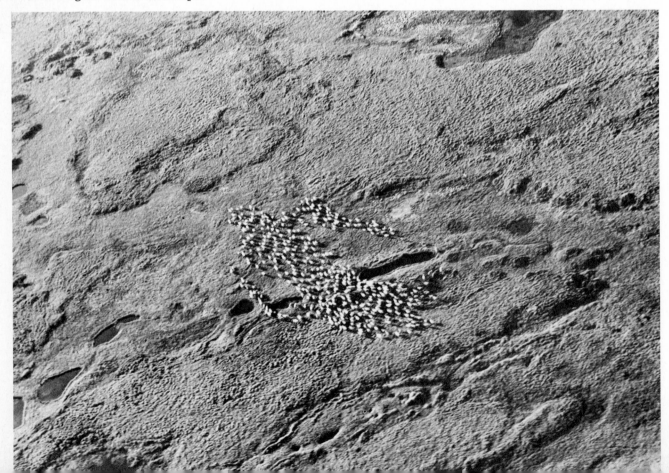

2–28 *The ptarmigan, another characteristic herbivore of the tundra. It is consumed by snowy owls, Arctic foxes, and other predators.*

more than one hundred years ago are still plainly visible. The tundra may be very seriously disturbed in the next few years as a result of our never-ending quest for energy. In 1968 the richest oil deposit in the Western Hemisphere was discovered on Alaska's North Slope. A 789-mile-long pipeline was constructed to transport this oil to the port of Valdez on Alaska's southern coast. This caused the destruction of much vegetation and valuable wildlife habitat and an excessive amount of soil erosion. In addition to oil the tundra contains two thirds of the North American continent's known reserves of coal, and substantial amounts of zinc, lead, and copper lie under the permafrost. These resources will almost certainly be exploited in the not-too-distant future. When that happens, additional stress on this biome can be expected.

Representative consumer species include herbivores such as the lemming, ptarmigan, caribou, and musk ox. The snowy owl and Arctic fox are characteristic carnivores in the area.

NORTHERN CONIFEROUS FOREST. As shown on the global biome map (Figure 2–24) the northern coniferous biome forms an extensive east-west belt just south of the Arctic tundra in North America, Sweden, Finland, Russia, and Siberia. Characteristic *physical features* include an annual rainfall of from

15 to 40 inches, average temperatures of from 20° F in the winter to more than 70° F in the summer, and a 150-day growing season. Dominant climax vegetation includes black spruce, white spruce, balsam fir, and tamarack. The evergreen trees are well adapted to survive — their branches are so flexible that they bend under the burden of a heavy snow fall without snapping. Lightning-triggered crown fires are fairly common because the dead, dry needles, which persist on the branches, are easily ignited. Over fifty species of insects are adapted to feed on the conifers. The populations of some species, such as spruce budworm, tussock moth, pine-bark beetle, and pine sawfly, may suddenly explode, thus causing considerable mortality of timber-valuable spruce, fir, and pine. White birch and quaking aspen are representative of the earlier successional stages. Typical animals include the moose, snowshoe hare, lynx, pine grosbeak, and red crossbill (10, 13, 14).

DECIDUOUS FOREST. The global biome map (Figure 2–24) also shows that the deciduous (broadleafed) forest originally covered eastern North America, all of Europe, and parts of China, Japan, and Australia. In the United States the deciduous forest biome attains its greatest development east of the Mississippi River and south of the northern coniferous forest. In precolonial times, of course, the deciduous forest was virtually continuous and unbroken. Today, however, as a result of settlement, agricultural development, logging, and mining activities, as well as highway construction, the biome has been reduced to only .1 percent of its original area. Fingers of deciduous forest extend westward into the prairie country along major river valleys, in response to increased levels of soil moisture. Because of abundant precipitation (at least thirty inches annually) and the fairly long growing season, plant productivity is the highest of any biome in North America, except the rain forest. Characteristic trees are oak, hickory, beech, maple, black walnut, black cherry, and yellow poplar. Representative consumers include the gray squirrel, skunk, black bear, and white-tailed deer.

TROPICAL RAIN FOREST. The tropical rain-forest biome is located in the equatorial regions wherever there is more than eighty inches of rainfall annually. As shown in Figure 2–24, rain forests are located primarily in Central America, in South America along the Amazon and Orinoco rivers, in the Congo

River basin of Africa, in Madagascar, and in southeast Asia. The day–night temperature variations are greater than those of summer–winter. Heavy rains may fall *daily* through much of the year, and so moisture drips almost continuously from the canopy. Because so much sunlight is screened out by the canopy, the forest floor is relatively dark and poorly vegetated. To the optimists, the rain forest is a "green cathedral" — to the pessimists, it's a "humid hell" (4).

Plant life is highly diverse in the rain forest. Two hundred species of trees may be found in one hectare (2.47 acres) compared to only ten species per hectare in the temperate deciduous forests of the United States. There may be more species of trees in a few acres of rain forest than in all of Europe (6). The number of species of organisms living in or on a *single tree* may be greater than occurs in the entire northern coniferous forest (4). The forests are highly layered, or stratified — with the tree crowns occurring at three or even four different levels.

The majority of animals occur in the canopy, in contrast to the situation in deciduous forests of the United States, where most species of animals live on the forest floor. In Guyana, for example, 31 of 59 (52.5 percent) species of mammals are canopy-dwellers. Animal life is abundant and highly diverse. At least 369 species of birds have been identified in just two hectares of Costa Rican rain forest — more than are found in Alaska. Whereas only a few hundred species of insects occur in all of France, more than 20,000 have been recorded in the tropical rain forest of a small island in the Panama Canal Zone (6). Some insects are extremely large. In the Amazon rain forest the wingspread of one species of moth is nearly a foot, and some spiders are large enough to feed on birds caught in their webs (4).

Unfortunately, human beings are cutting the rain forest up into small pieces. The reasons are multiple: (1) to develop settlements, (2) for logging purposes, and (3) to establish farms and rangelands. Agricultural ventures usually result in failure, not only because the soil is very infertile, but also because it frequently contains iron compounds that bake brick-hard under the tropic sun.

TROPICAL SAVANNAH. A savannah is a warm climate grassland characterized by scattered trees. As shown in the global biome map (Figure 2–24), savannahs are located primarily in South America,

Africa, India, and Australia. Rainfall averages forty to sixty inches per year. Wet seasons alternate with dry seasons, and fires are characteristic during the prolonged dry spells. Plants and animals must be both drought- and fire-resistant. As a result, the diversity of species is not great. The African savannah is characterized by the picturesque baobab and thorny acacia trees. This savannah supports the greatest variety and largest number of hoofed herbivores in the world. They include the zebra, giraffe, wildebeest, elephant, and many species of antelope. Many of the herbivores travel in migratory herds, whose pattern of movements is dictated by the availability of suitable watering holes. Because the newly born young are highly dependent on the protection provided by the herd, they must be able to walk within a few hours of birth or be left behind, vulnerable to predation by lions and cheetahs. The Australian savannahs are populated by kangaroos, whose survival depends partly on its ability to jump above the tall grasses and thus be able to keep an eye on nearby predators. In the struggle to produce more food, many people in Africa and India have converted extensive acreages of savannah into farms and livestock pasture. Those disturbances, along with illegal hunting, have caused a rapid decline in the herds of big game.

GRASSLAND. On a global basis, as shown in Figure 2–24, the principal grasslands include the *prairies* of Canada and the United States, the *pampas* of South America, the *steppes* of Eurasia, and the *veldts* of Africa. Major grasslands occur in two regions in the United States: the Great Plains, a vast area extending from the eastern slopes of the Rockies to the Mississippi River, and the more moist portions of the Great Basin lying between the Sierras to the west and the Rockies to the east. In north temperate latitudes, grasslands apparently represent the vegetational expression of an average annual precipitation that is excessive (over ten inches) for the development of desert vegetation and inadequate (under thirty inches) for the development of forest. Winter blizzards and summer drought can be severe. There is evidence that devastating fires periodically have burned the prairie. The dominant vegetation includes the big bluestem, little bluestem, buffalo grass, and grama grass. The horned lark, meadowlark, and burrowing owl are characteristic birds in that grassland. The dominant mammals include the pronghorned antelope,

Asia (Tibet and Gobi) and Australia. American deserts are located in the hotter, drier portions of the Great Basin and in parts of California, New Mexico, Arizona, Texas, Nevada, Idaho, Utah, and Oregon. Deserts occur primarily to the leeward of prominent mountain ranges, such as the Sierra Nevada and the Rocky Mountains. The prevailing warm, humid air masses from the Pacific Ocean gradually cool as they move up windward slopes and release their moisture as rain or snow. The region to leeward of the mountains lies in the "rain shadow," where precipitation is minimal. (See Figure 2–31.) A desert type of community generally receives fewer than ten inches of annual precipitation. Rainfall, moreover, may not be uniformly distributed, but may fall periodically in the form of cloudbursts that cause flash floods and soil-eroding runoff. An

2–30 *Pronghorn antelope, characteristic herbivore of the grassland biome.*

2–29 *Resident of the grassland biome. The black-tailed prairie dog at the edge of its craterlike burrow entrance. The levee not only serves as a lookout post, but prevents flash flooding of the burrow.*

badger, white-tailed jackrabbit, coyote, and pocket gopher. (See Figure 2–29.) It must be emphasized that only scattered remnants of the climax grassland biome remain. Humans have replaced the original wild grasses with cultivated "grasses" such as corn and wheat. In addition, humans have almost eradicated the bison and replaced it with domesticated herbivores such as cattle and sheep.

DESERT. As shown in the global biome map (Figure 2–24), the world's deserts are primarily located in the United States, Mexico, Chile, Africa (Sahara),

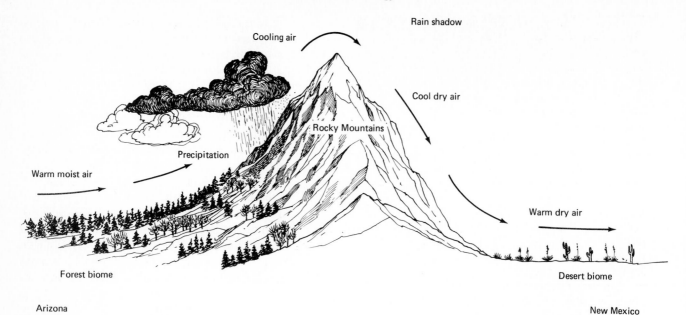

Cooling air

Rain shadow

Cool dry air

Rocky Mountains

Precipitation

Warm moist air

Warm dry air

Forest biome

Desert biome

Arizona

New Mexico

2–31 *The desert biome frequently lies in the rain shadow on the lee side of a mountain range.*

2–32 *Desert biome, Arizona. Note the gravel pavement and widely spaced plants. The tall plant in the right background is the saguaro cactus, many of which live to be 100 years old.*

2–33 *An antelope jackrabbit cools off in the shadows of a desert shrub. Its enormous ears serve as "radiators" in promoting heat loss from the body.*

Ecology and Resource Management

Robert Leo Smith
WEST VIRGINIA UNIVERSITY

The environmental movement of the early 1970s, a rapid accumulation of ecological knowledge in the past several decades, and better ecological training of resource managers have stimulated an ecological approach to resource management.

In forestry, for example, silviculturists once emphasized the cultural aspects of growing trees, stressing the physiological requirements of individual species. Now forestry is concerned with nutrient cycling in forest ecosystems, biomass accumulation, net productivity, mycorrhizal relationships, forest succession, and modeling forest growth.

Range management, once interested primarily in how many grazing animals could be supported per unit of grassland, is now investigating herbivore-vegetation interactions, role of grassland invertebrates in ecosystem functioning, and constraints on productivity.

Wildlife management in the past was equated with game species; now it embraces nongame and endangered species as well. Wildlife biologists are investigating ways of applying population theory such as optimal foraging, island biogeography, and the guild concept to management problems. They are also developing an interest in population genetics, particularly as it relates to the removal of trophy animals from game populations.

Agriculture, with its emphasis on monocultural cropping on the same ground year after year, is the antithesis of an ecological approach. Yet there is a developing interest in organic farming which includes crop rotation and the return of manures to fields. In the tropics and subtropics, where European-and American-style agriculture is a failure, attention is being given to more traditional agroforestry systems. This involves the growing of woody plants with agricultural crops and livestock on the same ground. Thus, agroforestry is an ecological approach to land management that involves diversification of plant life, conservation of nutrients and soil, and reduction in crop failures.

Although a start has been made in the application of ecological principles to resource management, we still have a long way to go. How quickly we achieve such a goal depends on how rapidly we can overcome the restraints imposed by political and economic self-interests.

---

extremely high evaporation rate aggravates the severe moisture problem. For example, the water that theoretically *could* evaporate from a given land acre in one year may be thirty times the actual amount received as precipitation. Summer temperatures range from about 50° F at night to about 120° F during the day. Desert-floor temperature reaches 145° F in summer.

Only organisms that have evolved specialized structural, physiological, and behavioral adaptations to extreme heat and dryness can survive in the desert. Characteristic producers are prickly-pear cactus, saguaro cactus, creosote bush, and mesquite. (See Figure 2–32.)

Conspicuous among desert consumers are the western diamondback rattlesnake, Gila monster, roadrunner, jackrabbit, kangaroo rat, and wild pig.

ALTITUDINAL BIOMES. Examine the biome map of North America once again. Note that by traveling several thousand miles from Texas northeastward to northern Canada you could pass through a series of different biomes — desert, grassland, deciduous forest, coniferous forest, and tundra. These biome changes, of course, reflect progressive changes in temperature and precipitation. Such a series of biomes also exists on the slopes of tall mountains, such as the 12,000-foot-high Colorado Rockies. Here again, the gradual changes in biome type are dictated by climatic factors, which in this case, change progressively with *altitude* rather than with latitude.

Rapid Review

1. Ecology is the study of the interrelationships that exist between organisms and their environment. Ecologists focus their studies primarily on three levels of organization: the *population*, the *community*, and the ecological system, or *ecosystem*. A population is the total number of individuals of *one species* occupying a given area. A community is the sum of all living organisms in a given area. The ecologist refers to the community plus the environment with which it interacts as an ecological system, or *ecosystem*.

2. The circular flow of an element from the nonliving environment into the bodies of living organisms and then back into the nonliving environment once again is known as an *elemental cycle*. For millions of years before the advent of human technology, the elemental cycles were delicately balanced. However, in recent years our technology has caused many elemental cycles to become unbalanced. In other words, we have accelerated the movement of a given element from one point to another in its cycle. The result is the *pollution* of the air, water, and land..

3. The first law of energy states: Although energy cannot be created or destroyed, it can be converted from one form to another. The second law of energy states: Whenever one form of energy is converted to another, a certain amount is lost as heat.

4. Photosynthesis is the process by which green plants convert the raw materials carbon dioxide and water to glucose in the presence of sunlight. The green pigment in plants, known as *chlorophyll*, serves as a catalyst in the process.

5. A food chain is a sequence of organisms through which nutrients and energy move. A network of food chains is known as a *food web*.

6. The *stability* of a food web increases in proportion to its complexity. Green plants convert energy from the sun to organic food energy that can be used by other organisms. Because of this green plants are called *producers*. Plant-eating animals, such as the rabbit, are called *herbivores* (primary consumers). Animals like the wolf, which feed on other animals, are known as *carnivores*, or *secondary consumers*.

7. The total weight of living substance (protoplasm) in a given organism, population, or community is known as biological mass, or *biomass*. There is a progressive reduction in biomass in each succeeding feeding level, or *trophic level*, of a given food web. This is known as the *pyramid of biomass*.

8. *Energy* is the capacity to do work. Unlike the elements, energy cannot be recycled. As we have learned from the second law of energy, whenever energy is converted into another form, a certain amount is lost as heat. Living organisms are only about 10 percent efficient in converting the energy of their food into the energy of their own biomass. As a result, there is a progressive reduction in the amount of food energy represented by the successive trophic levels (feeding levels) of a given food web. This is known as the *pyramid of energy*. In other words, more energy is available to plants than to herbivores, and more energy is available to herbivores than to carnivores. More food energy would be available to human beings if we would move up the food chain — closer to the producer base.

9. For each organism there exists a specific tolerance range for any essential environmental factor, below or above which the organism is adversely affected. This principle is known as the *range of tolerance*.

10. The replacement of one community by another under constant climatic conditions is known as an *ecological succession*. The initial stage of a succession is known as a *pioneer community*. This community usually can withstand considerable extremes in temperature and moisture. The final stage of a succession is known as the *climax community*. This stage is stable. In theory it will persist indefinitely unless the climate changes. A succession that becomes established in an area where living organisms were not previously present, such as bare rock or a lava flow, is known as a *primary succession*. However, a succession that becomes established in an area that once supported life, such as a burned-over forest or an abandoned corn field, is known as a *secondary succession*.

11. A *biome* is the largest terrestrial community that is easily recognized by a biologist. It is the biological expression of the interaction of climate, soil, water, and organisms. Representative biomes discussed in this chapter were the following: tundra, northern coniferous forest, deciduous forest, tropical rain forest, grassland, tropical savannah, and desert. Each biome is characterized by a unique assemblage of plants and animals. On the slopes of tall mountains, such as the Rockies, a series of *altitudinal biomes* can be recognized.

50

Key Words and Phrases

Altitudinal biomes	Legume
Atmospheric fixation	Limiting factor
Biological fixation	Mechanical energy
Biomass	Mount St. Helens
Biome	Net production
Carnivore	Nitrification
Chlorophyll	Nitrogen cycle
Climax community	Nitrogen fixation
Community	Permafrost
Coniferous forest biome	Phosphorus cycle
Decomposer	Photosynthesis
Denitrification	Pioneer community
Desert	Population
Detritus	Primary consumer
Ecological succession	Primary production
Ecology	Primary succession
Ecosphere	Producer
Ecosystem	Pyramid of biomass
Elemental cycle	Pyramid of energy
Energy	Pyramid of numbers
Eutrophication	Radiant energy
Food chain	Respiration
Food web	Savannah
Fossil fuel	Secondary succession
Herbivore	Stomata
Industrial fixation	Stratification
Kinetic energy	Trophic level
Law of conservation of	Tropical rain forest
matter	Tundra
Laws of energy	

Questions and Topics for Discussion

1. *Levels of organization.* Give an example of each of the following: community, ecosphere, population, ecosystem. List the levels in order of increasing complexity.

   (a) *Ecosystem.* Do large cities like Chicago or New York have the characteristics of a balanced ecosystem? In other words, could those cities continue to exist completely isolated from all other ecosystems? Why or why not?

   (b) *Ecosystem.* For many years a lake has been operating as a balanced ecosystem. Suppose now that a disease kills off all the plants. What effect would this have on the animals in that ecosystem? Suppose that instead of killing off all the plants, a disease destroyed all the bacteria in the lake. What effect would this have on the lake ecosystem? Discuss your answer.

   (c) *Ecosystem.* Suppose your professor made one of the following statements in class: "There is just one big ecosystem on planet Earth." "There are thousands of little ecosystems on planet Earth." Which of these statements do you think is correct? Or are they both, in a sense, correct? Discuss your answer.

   (d) *Ecosystems.* Describe and discuss the structure and function of the ecosystems represented by your college campus. Does your college campus represent a balanced ecosystem? Why or why not? What sort of disturbances would tend to promote imbalance?

2. *Elemental cycles.* Make labeled diagrams of the shortest nitrogen, carbon, and phosphorus cycles you can think of.

3. *Nitrogen cycle.* Trace a given nitrogen atom from the air over the state of Washington into some land-dwelling organisms. Then follow its path through additional organisms until it is excreted as guano by cormorants on the coast of Peru. Then trace it back to a corn field in Illinois. Finally, show how it might pass back into the air once again.

4. *Nitrogen cycle.* Describe three ways by which nitrogen can be fixed.

5. *Carbon cycle.* Trace a given carbon atom from the air that existed over Pennsylvania during the Carboniferous period 150 million years ago to the fried egg you had for breakfast this morning.

6. *Elemental cycles.* In one sense pollution can be defined as an imbalance of an elemental cycle. Explain. In this context can you give one example each of land, air, and water pollution?

7. *Elemental cycles.* Discuss the movement of elements (both nutrients and wastes) through your body. Trace those elements back to soil, rocks, air, and water. Does your body recycle some elements such as iron and sodium? Does it recycle water? By what processes do elements leave your body and pass back into the external environment?

8. *Range of tolerance.* Discuss the range of tolerance that you have for various physical conditions of the daily environment to which you are exposed. Bring to class some newspaper clippings describing recent human fatalities that

51

resulted because tolerance ranges were exceeded. Do some library research and discuss the extinction of dinosaurs, mammoths, the saber-toothed tiger, dodo, and passenger pigeon in terms of tolerance ranges.

9. *Second law of energy.* Trace the radiant energy from your study lamp backward in time to its ultimate source in solar energy.

10. *Photosynthesis.* Compare photosynthesis with respiration. Does a green plant give off oxygen both day and night? Does a green plant take in carbon dioxide both day and night?

11. *Food chains.* Distinguish between grazing food chains and detritus food chains. Give an example of each type. Which type is the most easily observed? Which type of food chain is the most important in a forest ecosystem? Which type is the most important in a marine ecosystem?

12. *Food web.* How many different species of organisms can you identify that are living either in your dormitory or in your home? Identify their trophic level. In other words, are they producers, herbivores, carnivores, detritus feeders, and so on? Compare your results with those of members of your class.

13. *Food web.* List all the food organisms you consumed in part or in entirety in your last three meals. Now construct a food web using this list and yourself as a starting point. You may include other organisms not actually represented in your meals. When completed, your food-web diagram should include at least 25 species of organisms. Identify the trophic level of each species in the web.

14. *Pyramid of biomass.* The total biomass of the animals living in the English Channel is five times greater than that of the plants. Consider this fact in relation to the pyramid of biomass concept. Can you offer any explanation for this seeming contradiction of the concept?

15. *Trophic levels.* Suppose that you are in charge of a unique wildlife refuge that is completely isolated from other ecosystems. This refuge is composed of one kind of producer (grass), one kind of herbivore (rabbits), and one kind of carnivore (hawks). Assume that one rabbit weighs as much as one hawk. Assume further that the rabbits consume only grass and that the hawks feed only on rabbits. Suppose that you originally stocked the refuge with three rabbits and six hawks, in other words a 2 : 1 ratio of hawks to rabbits. After about five years would you expect that this same ratio would exist? Why or why not? What ratio would you expect?

16. *Energy flow.* Discuss the flow of energy through your body. Trace the energy you are using to read this sentence back to the sun. In what form does your body store energy? In what form(s) does your body use energy? In what form does your body lose energy?

17. (a) *Energy flow.* As we have learned in this chapter, elements are recycled through ecosystems but energy is not. Suppose, however, that energy was recycled and elements were not. What would be the effects on ecosystems? Discuss your answer.

(b) *Energy flow.* Suppose that the sun stopped shining. What effect would this have on life on earth? Would life still be possible? Discuss your answer.

18. *Pyramid of energy.* Suppose that 20,000 calories of solar energy are available to grass for photosynthesis. Suppose that grass converts 1 percent of the solar energy available to it. Suppose that animals can store 10 percent of the food energy they consume in their own protoplasm. How many food calories would you get if you consumed the grass? If you lived on beef derived from grass-eating cattle? How much food energy would be available to a hawk at the end of a grass–grasshopper–frog–snake–hawk food chain? What percentage of the original 20,000 calories would be stored in the body of the hawk?

19. *Ecological succession.* Describe three sites at which a primary succession might get started. Describe three sites at which a secondary succession might become established.

20. *Ecological succession.* Construct a chart in which you list eight basic differences between the pioneer and climax stages of an ecological succession.

21. *Ecological succession.* Suppose that a square mile of oak woods in Ohio is removed and replaced with a huge slab of polished marble. One thousand years pass. Will the marble slab still be visible? Why or why not? Give a detailed explanation of the probable events that occurred.

22. *Biomass.* Suppose that in 5,000 years a glacier moved into northern New York. Consult the biome map (Figure 2–24). Do you suppose that

any changes in biome distribution in New York State would occur? If so, what would they be?

23. *Biomes.* Describe the physical features of the tundra biome. Why is it sometimes called an Arctic desert? Why is it considered a fragile ecosystem? Would it be a good place to study succession? Why or why not? Explain.

24. *Biomes.* Which of the biomes discussed in the text has the greatest diversity of animal life? Which features of the biome make this diversity possible?

25. *Biomes.* To which biome does each of the following organisms belong: beech, little blue stem, mesquite, dwarf willow, acacia, antelope, lemming, elephant, fruit bat, white-tailed deer?

Endnotes

1. Ehrlich, Paul R., and Anne H. Ehrlich. *Population, Resources, Environment.* San Francisco: Freeman, 1970.
2. Johnston, David W., and Eugene P. Odum. "Breeding Bird Populations in Relation to Plant Succession on the Piedmont of Georgia." *Ecology,* **37** (1956), 50–62.
3. Kormondy, Edward J. *Concepts of Ecology.* 2nd ed. Englewood Cliffs, NJ: Prentice-Hall, 1976.
4. Miller, G. Tyler, Jr. *Living in the Environment.* 3rd ed. New York: Wadsworth, 1982.
5. Moran, Joseph M., Michael D. Morgan, and James H. Wiersma. *An Introduction to Environmental Sciences.* San Francisco: Freeman, 1980.
6. Odum, Eugene P. *Fundamentals of Ecology.* 3rd ed. Philadelphia: Saunders, 1971.
7. Southwick, Charles H. *Ecology and the Quality of Our Environment.* New York: Van Nostrand, 1972.

Suggested Readings for the Interested Student

Billings, W. D. *Plants, Man, and the Ecosystem.* 2nd ed. New York: Wadsworth, 1970. The material on biomes is excellent.

Clapham, W. B., Jr. *Natural Ecosystems.* New York: Macmillan. 1973. This is a splendid treatment of basic ecological concepts.

Cooper, C. F. "The Ecology of Fire." *Scientific American,* **204** (April 1961), 150–160. This is a fascinating study of the influence of fire on ecological succession.

Darnell, Rezneat. *Ecology and Man.* Dubuque, Iowa: Brown, 1973. This is an excellent presentation of the principles of ecology.

Dasmann, Raymond F. *Environmental Conservation.* 4th ed. New York: Wiley, 1976. This is an authoritative study of the relation between resources, humans, and the environment.

del Moral, Roger. "Life Returns to Mount St. Helens." *Natural History* (May 1981), 36–46. The author gives a fascinating description of the ecological succession occurring shortly after the eruption of Mount St. Helens.

Ehrlich, Paul R., Anne H. Ehrlich, and John P. Holdren. *Ecoscience: Population, Resources and Environment.* San Francisco: Freeman, 1977. This is a scholarly treatment of basic environmental issues facing society.

Gosz, J. R., R. T. Holmes, G. E. Likens, and F. H. Bormann. "The Flow of Energy in a Forest Ecosystem." *Scientific American,* **238** (March 1978), 93–102. The authors provide an understanding of energy flow rates and patterns.

Levine, Norman D., ed. *Human Ecology.* North Scituate, MA: Duxbury, 1975. This is a superior introduction to the fundamentals of ecology.

Odum, Eugene P. *Fundamentals of Ecology.* 3rd ed. Philadelphia: Saunders, 1971. This is one of the finest texts available in the area of ecology.

———. *Ecology.* 2nd ed. New York: Holt, 1975. This shortened treatment of the science of ecology is highly authoritative.

Smith, Robert L. *Ecology and Field Biology.* 3rd ed. New York: Harper 1980. This is a highly readable, lavishly illustrated text.

Woodwell, George M. "The Energy Cycle of the Biosphere." *Scientific American,* **223** (September 1970), 64–74. This is an excellent discussion of energy flow in intact, degraded, and agricultural ecosystems.

3 The Ecology of Human Populations

Rapid Population Growth

Biologists place humans at the pinnacle of the animal kingdom because of our ability to assess a problem, to devise a solution, and to put that solution into operation. However, at this crucial period in human history, we have as yet not effectively applied our talents to solving the problem of exploding population. If unresolved, this population increase may bring calamity to the human species. Currently the global population is increasing at the rate of more than 225,000 people per day, equal to another Syracuse, New York, or a Richmond, Virginia. To give each person in this daily increase a glass of milk would require milk from 15,000 cows; it would take more than 300 acres of wheat to give each a loaf of bread. Each year the world has to provide the necessary food, water, shelter, and living space to sustain 80 million additional people. Every three years the global environment and its resources must somehow support another 240 million people — equal to another United States. At present the earth's population is increasing at the rate of 1.7 percent annually — a rate at which the global population will double in only 41.1 years. (See Figure 3–2.)

Examining world population doubling rates can be quite informative. For example, it took the first humans almost two million years to build up to a population of a mere 0.25-billion by the year 1 AD. However, in only 1,650 years human population doubled (to 0.50-billion), then doubled again (to one billion) in only 200 years, doubled again (to two billion) in only 90 years; the doubling to four billion was accomplished in only 35 years — from 1941 to 1976 (15). And by 1989, only 13 years later, the global population will have increased by another billion. Each year there is an increment of 80 million, equal to nine New York Cities or two Englands.

It is indeed sobering to note that our global population growth was greater in the 1970s than in any

3–1

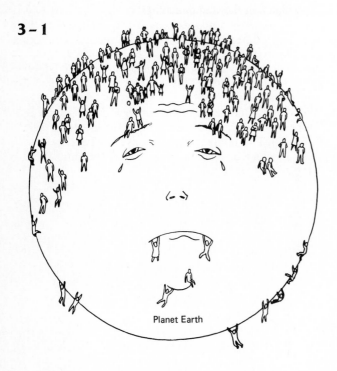

Planet Earth

54

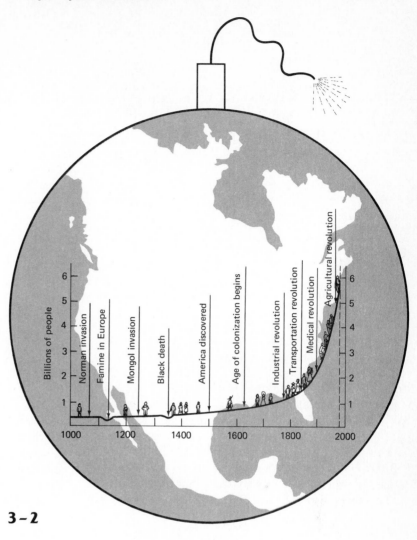

3-2

previous decade in history — it was more than 800 million. Almost 90 percent of that increase was contributed by the less developed nations of Asia, Africa, and South America. Living standards in those nations are already in a woeful state. Certainly the increased population pressure will severely strain their economic, social, political, and environmental structure. (See Fred O. Pinkham's guest article on page 63 for further discussion of this problem.)

Since 1970 the population growth *rate* has slowly decreased. Most of the slowdown apparently has occurred in the undeveloped nations of Asia and South America. Zero Population Growth has actually been attained in some eastern European countries. However, simply because the growth rate decreases does not mean that the global population will not continue to grow. (See Figure 3-3.) For example, according to Harvard University's Center for Population Studies, the global population will increase from the 4.6 billion of 1982 to about 5.7 billion by 2000. The Harvard experts predict that at some time in the next century the planet Earth will be crowded with at least ten billion people.

Birth and Death Rates

The *birth rate* is the number of persons born per 1,000 individuals in a given year. On the other hand, the *death rate* is the number of persons per 1,000 individuals that die in a given year. The *difference* between the birth and death rates is known as the *rate of natural increase* (or *decrease*). Of course, if

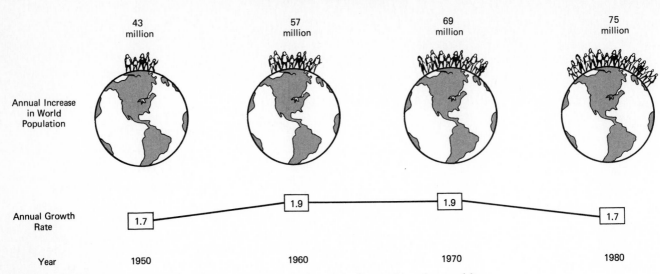

3-3 *Despite the fact that the world's annual growth rate is* decreasing, *the world's annual population continues to* increase.

the death rate is higher, then the population will drop. However, if the birth rate is higher, the population will rise. (See Figure 3-4 for data on the United States.) The global birth rate in 1981 was 28, while the death rate was 11. Therefore, the rate of natural increase was 17 per thousand (2). Figure 3-5 shows the rate of natural increase for the developed (rich) and undeveloped (poor) nations. Note that the population of the poor nations is increasing much more rapidly than that of the rich.

The population growth of a nation can be given in percentage. It is determined as follows (2):

percent annual growth rate
$$= \frac{\text{birth rate} - \text{death rate}}{10}.$$

3-4 *Components of change in the U.S. population.*

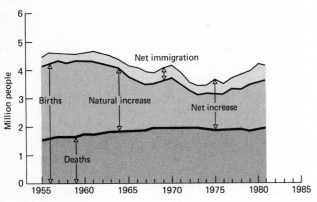

Therefore, the percent annual growth rate for the world in 1981 is determined as follows:

$$\frac{28 - 11}{10} = \frac{17}{10} = 1.7 \text{ percent.}$$

It is interesting to know how long it would take a given population to *double* in size. This can be determined simply by dividing 70 by the percent annual growth rate. Thus, the doubling time for the global population is

$$\frac{70}{1.7} = 41.1 \text{ years.}$$

REDUCTION IN DEATH RATES. We regard today's medical technology as a wonder, a boon for human life. However, this advanced medical technology is largely responsible for the present surge in human numbers. Before the advent of modern medicine, human mortality rates were much higher. Three centuries before Christ, Aristotle noted that "most babies die before the week is out." Man was at one time extremely vulnerable to the lethal attacks of infectious parasites such as viruses, bacteria, and protozoa. Medieval lands were scourged with the horror of plague. It killed over 25 million people in Asia and Europe. Smallpox spread like wildfire and killed one out of every four afflicted, until Jenner developed his vaccine at the close of the eighteenth

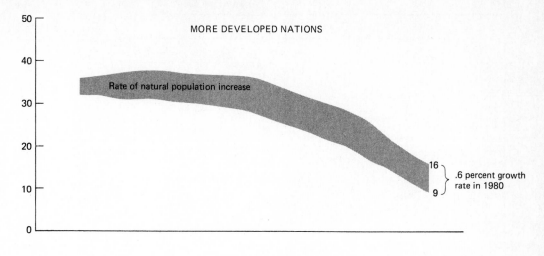

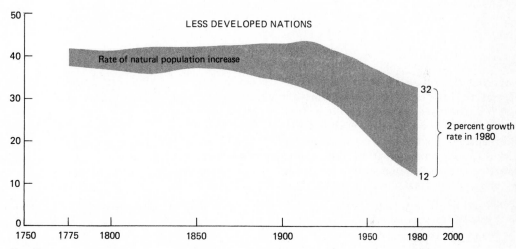

3 – 5 *Comparison of population growth rates in developed and less developed countries.*

century. A child born in 1550 had a life expectancy of only *eight and one-half* years. In 1900 the prime killer was tuberculosis, with pneumonia running a close second. As late as 1919 the influenza virus took a toll of 25 million people. The mortality picture has drastically changed. Tuberculosis and pneumonia are controlled with antibiotics, and effective vaccines have been developed against smallpox, tetanus, diptheria, whooping cough, and many other diseases. Largely because of modern medicine the world death rate of 25 per thousand in 1935 fell to about 12.7 per thousand by 1980.

Early in the twentieth century the mosquito-borne disease malaria was either directly or indirectly responsible for 50 percent of all human mortality. Today, thanks to mosquito-killing insecticides such as DDT, the malarial threat has greatly diminished. Consider Ceylon. Because of the intensive malaria-control campaign launched there in 1946, the Ceylonese mortality rate was reduced from 22 to 13 per thousand in only six years. Today, the primary fatal diseases are heart disease and cancer, in that order; both are primarily associated with the aging process. Advances in medical and paramedical technology, then, have largely contributed to our "golden" opportunity for growing old. As Harvard University's Roy Greep writes:

In a nutshell, the reason for the present unprecedented increase in population growth is the introduction of *death*

57

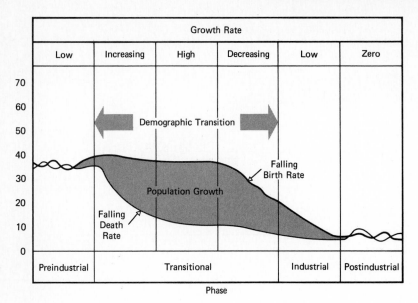

3-6 *Characteristic features of the demographic transition.*

control without birth control. In the emerging nations it is now possible to cut the death rate in half within a period of five to ten years but with no reduction or even an increase in the birth rate. The result of these changes is that the advanced countries, constituting one third of the world's population, are growing at a modest rate, whereas the less developed and heavily populated areas of the world are showing fantastic population increments. (1) [*Italics mine.*]

DEMOGRAPHIC TRANSITION. *Demographic transition* is the name given to a change in a population characterized by decreasing birth and death rates (2) (see Figure 3-6). The transition usually occurs when a nation becomes industrialized. Most of the industrialized European nations, as well as the United States, Canada, and Japan, have already experienced demographic transition. The decline in death rates is caused by the improvements in medical care and nutrition that are made possible by greater per capita income. The decline in birth rates may have a number of explanations:

1. An increasing percentage of families moves from rural areas to urban areas where a large number of children, especially boys, are not needed to perform household chores.
2. Increasing educational and employment opportunities for women causes them to delay marriage and, hence, have fewer children.
3. The high standard of living demanded by a mar-

ried couple makes it financially impossible for them to have many children.

As the undeveloped nations gradually develop, or become industrialized, it is expected that they too will enter the demographic transition. (See Figure 3-7.)

IMMIGRATION. The United States, of course, is a nation made up of immigrants or their descendants. America is indeed a melting pot of many ethnic groups, from Irish to Polish, Norwegian to Italian, and Bohemian to Welsh. These people have immigrated to the United States for a number of political, religious, and economic reasons. Consider the Irish: More than one million immigrated to the United States between 1845 and 1850 because of the potato famine. Today the United States has an influx of roughly 500,000 legal and 400,000 illegal immigrants each year (2). The illegal immigration of thousands of Mexican "wetbacks" across the Rio Grande River into the United States is only one of the immigration problems of continuing concern. (See Figure 3-8.)

AGE STRUCTURE OF A POPULATION. During the last few years the fertility rate of American women has been declining. If this is true, then we might well ask why experts predict that our nation's population will continue to increase by two million per year well into the twenty-first century. This seem-

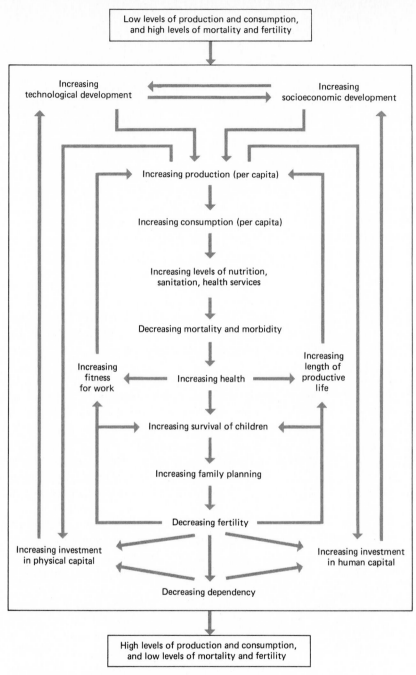

3-7 *A flowchart for demographic transition.*

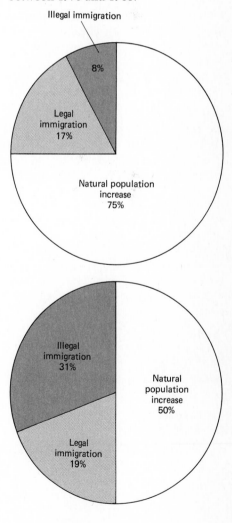

3-8 *Illegal immigration increased substantially in the United States between 1970 and 1980.*

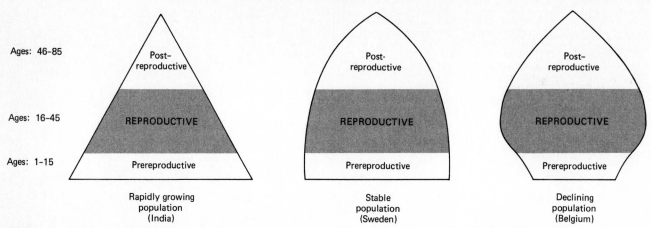

3–9 *Characteristic population age-structure profiles for (a) rapidly growing, (b) stable, and (c) declining populations.*

ing contradiction can be explained on the basis of the age structure of our population. The age structure is "the number of individuals occurring in each age class within the population" (2).

By examining the profile of an age-structure diagram it is possible to determine whether a given population is growing rapidly, growing slowly, or remaining stable. (See Figure 3–9.) An age-structure diagram for a typical underdeveloped nation has a very broad base and a narrow apex—a shape characteristic of a rapidly growing population. Indeed, the doubling time for these populations is about twenty to forty years. Typical age-structure

diagrams for a developed nation like the United States have a somewhat narrower base and steeper sides. They are characteristic of a slowly growing population where the doubling time is 40 to 120 years. The age-structure diagram for most European countries has a still narrower base and indicates an extremely slow growth rate, with a doubling time of 121 to 693 years (2).

When considering age structure it is useful to divide the population into three major age groups: *prereproductive* (ages one to fifteen), *reproductive* (sixteen to forty-five), and *postreproductive* (forty-six to eighty-five plus). (A comparison of age struc-

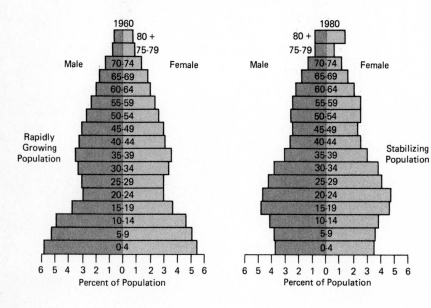

3–10 *A comparison of U.S. population profiles for 1960, when it was rapidly growing, and 1980, when it was stabilizing.*

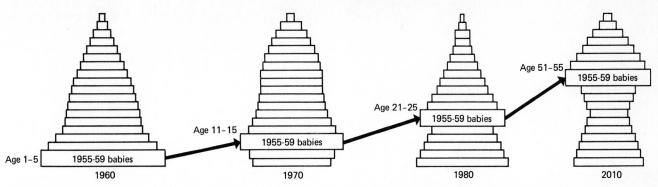

3 – 11 *Movement up the population profile of the U.S. "baby-boom" population bulge of 1955–1959.*

ture diagrams for the years 1960 and 1980 in the United States is shown in Figure 3–10.) *Current* population growth, of course, would depend on the number and fertility of the females in the age group fifteen to forty-five. *Future* population growth, on the other hand, would depend ultimately on the females who are now in the age group one to fifteen (2).

Let us use an example. The United States experienced a "baby boom" during the years 1955–1959, as indicated by the broad base in Figure 3–11. As the years passed this population bulge gradually moved upward in the age-structure pyramid. Eventually many of the females in the baby-boom population attained reproductive age. As G. Tyler Miller has stated, the passage of time had converted the original baby boom into a "mother boom."

At the present time roughly 35 percent of the world's population is under fifteen years of age. (In Madagascar the figure is 50 percent.) Thus, we have a built-in mechanism for explosive population growth in the near future. From the standpoint of population control, this is an extremely distressing situation. After all, there are already more women of childbearing age on this planet than there have ever been — about 800 million (2).

Two Kinds of Overpopulation

As Miller has pointed out, the adverse environmental impact of a nation depends on three factors: the size of the population, the amount of resources used by each individual, and the pollution released for each unit of resource (barrel of oil, ton of coal) consumed. As shown by Miller, these relationships can be expressed in the following formula:

$$\text{size of population} \times \begin{array}{c}\text{amount of}\\\text{resource used}\\\text{per person}\end{array} \times \begin{array}{c}\text{pollution from}\\\text{each resource}\\\text{unit}\end{array}$$

$$= \begin{array}{c}\text{harmful}\\\text{environmental}\\\text{impact or pollution.}\end{array}$$

The fragile life-support systems of planet Earth are being stressed by two types of overpopulation. *Malthusian overpopulation* is the kind occurring in the poor nations of the world (India, Pakistan, Bangladesh, Costa Rica, and Ethiopia, for example); it results in malnutrition and starvation (see Figure 3–12). It is named after Robert Malthus, a British economist, who stated in 1798 that populations tend to increase faster than food supplies. The only way population will come into balance with the available food supply, according to Malthus, is by a massive die-off caused by starvation, disease, war, or some other calamity. The most important factor in Malthusian overpopulation is population size. It is simply a matter of too many stomachs and not enough food.

The effects of Malthusian overpopulation are grimly described by an executive of an international relief organization. The following is merely one of many similar tragedies that he often observed while on an extended tour through several of the 100-odd less developed nations, where a majority of people live in appalling poverty and chronic malnutrition (see Figure 3–13).

Hunger is more than cold facts and awesome statistics. Hunger has a face. I know. I have looked into it. Hunger is a Bengali face — a little mother named Jobeda whom I

61

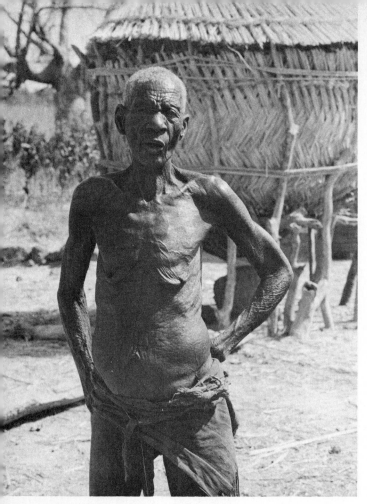

3-12 *An aged woman in a famine-plagued region of Africa. The World Food Programme (WFP) is currently assisting the government in its efforts to improve the living conditions of the population.*

found in the shade of a tattered lean-to in a refugee camp in Dacca. A small withered form lying close beside her whimpered and stirred. Instinctively she reached down to brush away the flies. Her hand carefully wiped the fevered face of her child. At six years acute malnutrition had crippled his legs, left him dumb, and robbed him of his hearing. All that was left was the shallow, labored breathing of life itself, and that, too, would soon be gone. But death is no stranger to Jobeda. She has seen starvation take away her husband and five of her seven children. . . . (3)

Today 40,000 people will die either directly or indirectly from starvation and malnutrition. Tomorrow 40,000 more. Although the causes of these deaths are multiple, certainly the basic cause is Malthusian overpopulation: too many human stomachs and not enough food.

The second type of overpopulation taxing the earth's life-support systems is *neo-Malthusian* or *technological overpopulation.* It is characteristic of the heavily industrialized nations (United States, Japan, West Germany, and Russia). Here the most important factors in our environmental-impact formula are the resources used and the pollution generated per unit of resource consumed. A relatively small population may therefore really be a neo-Malthusian *overpopulation* in terms of its harmful effects on the environment. As Miller states, "In this type of overpopulation, people do not get sick or die from a lack of food. Instead, they can sicken and die from contaminated air, water, and soil." In fact, the average American may have forty times as great a harmful environmental impact as the average Indian (2).

The effects of neo-Malthusian overpopulation are

3-13 *A six-month-old baby, suffering from malnutrition, is treated in a Chilean hospital.*

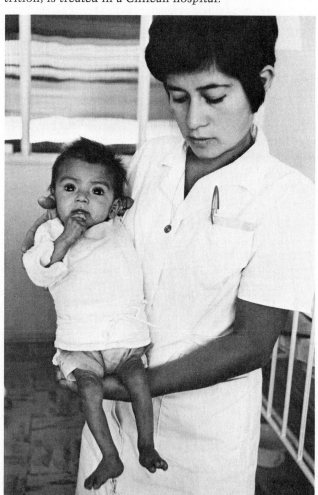

62

not hard to find. They are visible all around us — right here in the United States. Let's list a few examples:

1. Between 1965 and 2000 Americans will generate ten billion tons of solid waste — sufficient to fill a gigantic landfill the size of Delaware.

2. The release of thousands of tons of sulfur dioxide into the atmosphere from the stacks of power plants is triggering the formation of an acid rain that is destroying the fish populations of hundreds of lakes, leaching valuable nutrients from agricultural lands, and stunting the growth of forests and food crops.

The Population Crisis

Fred O. Pinkham
President
POPULATION CRISIS
COMMITTEE,
WASHINGTON, D.C.

The world faces an horrendous, historically unprecedented problem of excessive population growth. It is a silent explosion, insidious, exacerbating all other social and economic, even political, conditions, especially in the Third World. A veritable explosion of people is occurring, particularly in those countries least able to cope with the burgeoning numbers. No threat, not even the possibility of nuclear war, should be of greater concern to thinking people everywhere. And the situation worsens daily as the abnormally high proportion of young people in the populations of the less developed countries enter their fertile years.

In locust fashion they stream into cities, deplete forests and soils, pollute the environment, foment social and economic conditions as unsettling and threatening to political stability as to biological balances.

The consequences of this situation are everywhere evident. Hard won developing country production gains are dissipated by ever more people to feed, clothe, house, and employ. Almost one third of the Third World labor force is unemployed or underemployed at the present. The United Nations International Labor Organization (ILO) projects 900 million new jobs must be created in the next twenty years just to maintain the present level of employment (or unemployment). That's more jobs than now exist in the entire Western world. Grave environmental damage is done by overcropping, overgrazing, overcutting, and other desperate efforts to survive.

The rich-poor gap within and between nations widens, a further source of dissension and instability. All these conditions can only worsen as the flood of children from parents already born increases. Some of our most precious and critical natural resources are concentrated in the less developed countries most beset by overpopulation and consequent receding economies and diminishing resources. On this globe where we are all now so interdependent, no one and no land is beyond the reach of the effects of overpopulation.

It sounds hopeless. But much has been done, and much more can be done, to bring family planning information and services to every couple worldwide no matter how poor or remote. (In fifteen years over sixty countries, accounting for over 90 percent of the world's population, have instituted such programs.) This task is both urgent and long term. Every averted birth of a child who is unwanted and who cannot be properly supported is an immediate humanitarian gain. And it is also a contribution to what must be a decades-long struggle to achieve a leveling off in world population at double our present 4.6 billion some time in the twenty-first century. The implications of "overpopulation" for conservation of resources, although obvious, are seemingly as unseen by the minority of us who live in abundant lands as it is, in contrast, overwhelming to the hundreds of millions who suffer the consequences, even at this time.

3. Industrial plants along the Mahoning River in Ohio have discharged so much heated water into the stream that water temperatures have been known to reach 140°F. The result is massive fish kills.

4. Each year more than one billion pounds of phosphorus is washed from freshly fertilized American farmlands into lakes and streams. The result is wide-scale degradation characterized by the explosive growth of algae and weeds, lowered levels of dissolved oxygen, fish kills, foul smells, and the defilement of scenic beauty.

5. The operation of nuclear power plants as well as the development and testing of nuclear weapons (which have sufficient explosive force to destroy civilization) have resulted in a serious problem: How will the wastes, which may remain highly radioactive for thousands of years, be safely stored? No one as yet seems to know the answer.

6. In 1956 more than 1,000 people died in New York City because of high concentrations of atmospheric pollutants released from motor cars and industrial plants.

7. Each year Americans attempt to dispose of seven million junked cars, 20 million tons of waste paper, 50 billion cans, and 26 billion bottles.

8. "Buckshot" urbanization results in the loss of one million acres of top-quality farmland in the United States each year.

9. The aesthetics of many a lovely Appalachian mountainside has been destroyed by strip-mining to provide more coal to power the industrial activities (power plants, steel, chemical, pulp and paper, and automobile-manufacturing plants) that are responsible for even more environmental degradation.

10. In recent years 220 million Americans have consumed more energy just to power their air conditioners than 800 million Chinese have used for all purposes.

11. Massive bulldozers and other earth-moving

Letter to an Unborn Child

Is it morally right for any couple to bring children into the world at a time when ecological systems are being strained to the point of collapse? If truly significant population control is to be achieved over the long term, it is essential that the world's prospective parents demonstrate the same kind of sensitivity, concern, and thoughtfulness that was recently shown by Dave, a twenty-seven-year-old man from Rosslyn, Virginia (just across the Potomac River from crowded downtown Washington, D.C.). After his wife Cindy announced that they were going to have their first baby, Dave tried to express his feelings in a letter to his unborn child:

Your mother and I are looking forward to seeing you with a love that we have never had the opportunity to feel before. . . . But, every once in a while, when I look out the window or walk down the street, I sense an apology in the recesses of my mind when I think of you. When I stand at a bus stop in a cloud of exhaust that lingers around me so I smell the city when I go home or try to shield my eyes against the flying debris that litters the streets I wonder how your eyes and lungs will react to it. When I think of showing you this land of ours, I think of trash-lined highways, littered beaches, and no-fishing signs warning of polluted waters. When I think of your mother taking you for a stroll in the fresh air, I wonder how far she will have to go to find that fresh air. How long will you be able to sleep with jets overhead and the trucks below? And if you should survive the earth, sea, and sky, will you survive your fellow man? I must apologize for what the past generation has left and what some of the present generation is creating.

It is a selfish love that welcomes a newborn child into the world. We hope you don't suffer because of it.

From "Expectant Father Composes Letter to His Unborn Child," a newspaper article by UPI Senior Editor Louis Cassels.

equipment have laid bare the soil during highway and building construction projects. The result is accelerated erosion, which contributes to the two million tons of soil discharged each day by the Mississippi River into the Gulf of Mexico.

12. In the Love Canal region of Niagara Falls, New York, the ground and water were so badly polluted by toxic chemicals that the federal government designated it a disaster area. Many families were forced to move elsewhere because of the imminent hazard to their health.

Taken together, the events described here represent an environmental horror picture fully as serious as the starvation and malnutrition problem in the poor nations of the world. In a sense the problems occurring in the United States (and other industrialized nations) are also the result of *overpopulation* — an overpopulation of Americans who demand a life-style that cannot be supported without the intensive consumption of resources and considerable environmental contamination.

Throughout the remainder of this book we will emphasize the underlying importance of these two types of overpopulation. Whether we are discussing soil erosion, air and water pollution, wildlife extinction, the energy crisis, the toxic chemical problem, or global starvation, either Malthusian or neo-Malthusian overpopulation is importantly involved.

Rapid Review

1. The global population is increasing at the rate of 225,000 per *day* — equal to the daily increase of another Syracuse, New York.

2. Each *year* the world's population is increasing by 90 million — equal to nine New York Cities or two Englands.

3. The *birth rate* is the number of persons born per 1,000 individuals in a given year.

4. The *death rate* is the number of deaths per 1,000 individuals in a given year.

5. The *rate of natural increase* (or decrease) is the *difference* between the birth and death rates. The world's rate of natural increase at present is about 17 per thousand.

6. The percent annual growth rate for the world population at present is about 1.7.

7. The doubling time for the global population at present is about 41 years.

8. When nations become industrialized they frequently undergo a *demographic transition*. This is characterized by a reduction in both birth and death rates.

9. The United States has an influx of about 500,000 legal and 400,000 illegal immigrants yearly.

10. The *age structure* of a population is the number of individuals occurring in each age class.

11. The age-structure diagram of a rapidly growing population has a broad base, whereas the diagram of one that is growing very slowly has a narrow base.

12. At the present time roughly 35 percent of the world's population is under fifteen years of age.

13. By *Malthusian overpopulation* is meant too many people for the available food supply. It is characteristic of the less developed nations of Asia, Africa, and South America.

14. By *neo-Malthusian overpopulation* is meant an overpopulation of people, usually in industrialized countries, who, because of their use of advanced technology, have a harmful effect on the environment.

15. Environmental damage caused by neo-Malthusian overpopulations includes excessive consumption of resources; pollution of air, land, and water; defilement of scenic beauty; wildlife extinction; and the release of chemicals that may be hazardous to human health.

16. Advances in medicine (including modern surgical techniques and the development of vaccines and antibiotics) have, ironically, contributed to the present rapid buildup of people on this earth.

Key Words and Phrases

Acid rain	Malthusian
Age structure	overpopulation
Birth rate	Neo-Malthusian
Death rate	overpopulation
Demographic transition	Percent annual growth
Developed nation	rate
Immigration	Radioactive waste
Less developed nation	Rate of natural increase
Love Canal	Strip-mining
Mahoning River (Ohio)	

Questions and Topics for Discussion

1. Construct a simple graph that indicates (roughly) the buildup of the human population since humans appeared on earth.
2. Compare public health conditions that prevailed in medieval ages with today's. What were the major causes of mortality then? What are the major causes today?
3. What were the global birth, death, and natural increase rates for the early 1980s?
4. How is the percent annual growth rate determined?
5. How do we determine how long it would take for a population to double?
6. List three reasons why birth rates tend to decrease when the standard of living rises.
7. The United States receives an influx of almost one million immigrants yearly. Do you approve of such an influx? Why or why not? What benefits might result? What might be the disadvantages to the United States?
8. Does a decrease in the fertility rate of a nation necessarily indicate that that nation's population is decreasing as well? Why or why not?
9. Describe the shape of age-structure diagrams for (a) rapidly growing populations, (b) slowly growing populations, (c) stable populations, and (d) declining populations.
10. Would a study of age-structure diagrams of the American population be of benefit to automobile manufacturers? The agricultural industry? To school administrators?
11. Give the generalized formula that indicates the degree to which a neo-Malthusian overpopulation can harm its environment.
12. Give five examples of environmental stress caused by the neo-Malthusian overpopulation experienced by the United States today.

Endnotes

1. Greep, Roy O. "Prevalence of People." *Perspectives in Biology and Medicine,* **12** (Spring, 1969), 332–343.
2. Miller, G. Tyler. *Living in the Environment.* 3rd ed. New York: Wadsworth, 1982.
3. Ranck, Lee. "Much More than Relief." *Engage/Social Action,* (Feb. 1975), 18–29.

Suggested Readings for the Interested Student

Bachrach, C. A. "Old Age Isolation and Low Fertility." *Population Bulletin,* **7** (Jan. 1979). This is a superb examination of the social and economic changes resulting from population stabilization.

Bouvier, Leon F. "America's Baby Boom Generation." *Population Bulletin* (April), 1–35. This is an excellent analysis of the adverse effects of the baby explosion.

Chrispeels, Maarten J., and David Sadava. *Plants, Food and People.* San Francisco: Freeman, 1977. This is an excellent discussion of methods for boosting food production.

Day, L. H. "What Will a ZPG Society Be Like?" *Population Bulletin,* **33** (June 1978). This discussion explores the ways in which a stable population benefits society.

Population Reference Bureau. World Population Data Sheet. Washington, DC, 1983. This is an annual summary of global population statistics.

U.S. Bureau of the Census. *Current Population Reports.* Washington, DC: U.S. Government Printing Office. These are up-to-date statistics on population dynamics for the United States.

4 The Nature of Soils

Soils and Ecosystems

You recall that we have defined an ecosystem as a community of organisms plus the environment with which it interacts. If that definition is valid, then we must certainly consider soil to be an ecosystem. The living community of soil organisms includes bacteria, molds, protozoa, mites, insect larvae, millipedes, earthworms, burrowing mammals (moles), and so on. The environment with which this soil community interacts is composed of trillions of rock particles, detritus (decaying organic matter), water, gases (oxygen, carbon dioxide, etc.), chemical energy, heat energy, and so on. The activities of living organisms play an important role in soil development. The soil, in turn, is an important factor in the distribution of both plants and animals. In Wisconsin, Michigan, and Minnesota, for example, jack pine is usually confined to *sandy* soils, while black spruce is normally found in soils that are *acid*. In Missouri, the ring-necked pheasant is found primarily in regions where the soil is rich in *calcium*. Apparently this element is needed for the development of strong bones and thick eggshells.

It is from the soil that most of the nutrients which sustain our nation's renewable resources (such as farm crops, range lands, forests, wildlife, and fisheries) are derived. Range grasses, farm crops, and forests, of course, obtain their nutrients *directly* from the soil. Wildlife obtain their nutrients *indirectly* from the soil by feeding either on plants, or on plant-eating animals. And even though fish are con-

sidered members of aquatic rather than terrestrial ecosystems, they also depend, by way of their food chains, upon nutrients that are washed into lakes, streams, and oceans from the surface of the land.

Although soil ordinarily is indeed a most valuable resource, under certain conditions its effect on ecosystems can be exceedingly adverse. For example, when transported by the wind as a "dust storm," soil may cause serious respiratory problems for both wildlife and man. When washed into a lake in excessive amounts soil may destroy the spawning sites of fish, interfere with sunlight penetration, or cause an over-enrichment of the water characterized by dense growths of weeds. Moreover, a number of toxic substances like pesticides and heavy metals (lead, mercury, and so on) may become attached to soil particles and be transported for considerable distances. This mechanism was partly responsible for the dispersion of DDT to almost every part of the ecosphere — both land and sea.

"In the sweat of thy face shalt thou eat bread, till thou return unto the ground, for out of it wast thou taken: for dust thou art, and unto dust shalt thou return." This passage from the biblical story of creation (Genesis 3:19) was written over 3,000 years ago. It can well be appreciated by the soil scientist and ecologist today. As we have learned in our discussion of food chains and pyramids, it is in the soil that all higher terrestrial plants have their roots and from which they absorb life-sustaining moisture and nutrients. Humans, in turn, feed directly on plants, on plant-eating animals, or on the carnivores

67

that prey on herbivores. Thus, virtually all terrestrial life ultimately is derived from the "dust of the earth." And when we eventually die, the soil-derived elements in our body will be restored to the earth by the process of bacterial decay.

The Value of Soil to Humanity

The average city dweller equates soil with "dirt," but to the farmer soil is the essence of survival. The farmer's economic well-being is inextricably linked with the quality of the land. It may mean the difference between a squalid four-room shack and a comfortable ranch house, between an old "klunker" and a new car, or between an eighth-grade and a university education for the children. A few years ago there were *3.7 million individual farms in America, embracing somewhat over one billion acres of land.* The total value of both farmland and buildings was estimated at $200 billion.

Empires and nations, like individuals, are dependent on the soil. As a nation's soil resources are fertile and abundant, in like measure will that state have vigor and stability. When that resource is exhausted because of the mounting demands of a swelling population or long mismanagement, the nation's survival is in jeopardy. Some authorities believe that the decline and fall of the mighty Roman Empire may be attributed as much to the deterioration of the soils in the Roman granary of northern Africa as to political corruption and the invader's prowess. Throughout the annals of recorded human history, soil has been valued highly and has been as attractive a war prize as armaments, buildings, industries, or slaves. During the long search for fertile soil, hitherto peaceable, responsible empires have turned into militant aggressors.

Soil Formation

The development of a mature soil is a complex process. It involves the interaction of physical, chemical, and biological processes. The time required depends not only on the intensity of those processes, but on the nature of the parent material. Authorities estimate that the development of one inch of topsoil derived from hard, rocklike basalt or granite may require from 200 to 1,200 years. However, soft rocks, such as volcanic ash and shale, and such parent material as sand dunes and river sediments, may develop into mature vegetation-supporting soil within a few decades. Many soils do not develop directly from underlying bedrock but are derived from materials transported by glaciers, wind, or water. The major processes in soil formation are *physical, chemical,* and *biological.* Some of these processes are shown in Figure 4–1.

Physical Processes

Rapid heating and cooling may induce differential contraction and expansion, which eventually cause rocks to scale, split, and shatter. This process

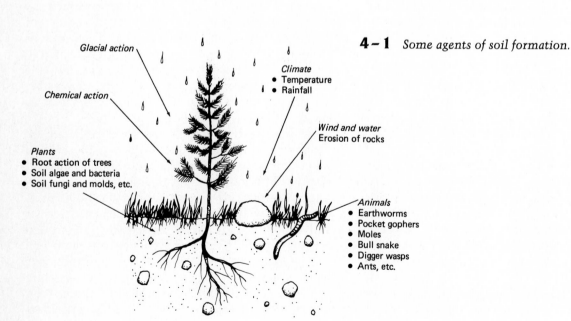

4–1 *Some agents of soil formation.*

Glacial action

Climate
• Temperature
• Rainfall

Chemical action

Wind and water
Erosion of rocks

Plants
• Root action of trees
• Soil algae and bacteria
• Soil fungi and molds, etc.

Animals
• Earthworms
• Pocket gophers
• Moles
• Bull snake
• Digger wasps
• Ants, etc.

assumes a particularly prominent role in the arid climates of the desert biome, where the day-night cycle, especially during summer, may be marked by major shifts in temperature. Thus, at noon the hot floor of the Arizona desert may register 145° F and by midnight may have dropped to 65° F.

Thawing and freezing are characteristic of temperature latitudes where there is relatively abundant rainfall. During a winter thaw, rivulets of water from melted snow and ice gradually infiltrate the pores and cracks of surface rock. During a subsequent freeze, the water expands with considerable force, causing rock to flake and fragment.

Chemical Processes

The chemical processes of soil formation frequently occur simultaneously with the physical processes. Both water and oxygen will react with rock and cause it to soften and break up. Some rocks, like limestone, are dissolved readily by water. The water, which is slightly acidic, gradually eats away the rock to form minute pores, channels, and crevices. The dissolved materials may be transported a considerable distance before precipitating out and eventually contributing to the formation of soil. The type of bedrock largely determines the texture and fertility of the soil. Thus, soils derived from sandstone are coarse, sandy, and infertile, and those derived from limestone are fine-grained and very fertile.

Biological Processes

The development of a mature soil also depends on the activity of a great number and diversity of organisms. The all-important bacteria influence soil structure, aeration, moisture content, and fertility in many ways that will be discussed later in this chapter. Lichens and mosses that have become established on rock may trap wind-blown organic debris, such as plant fibers, seeds, dead insects, excrement, and so on, to a depth sufficient to form a film over the rock's surface. They may also secrete a very dilute carbonic acid (H_2CO_3) that slowly dissolves the rock, thus accelerating its ultimate incorporation into a mature soil. Finally, upon their death, the lichens and mosses will decompose and eventually enrich the soil with their constituent elements. Rock may be splintered by the actively

4-2 *Common soil-dwelling animals that feed on decomposing plant material (detritus) and are important in contributing to soil fertility.*

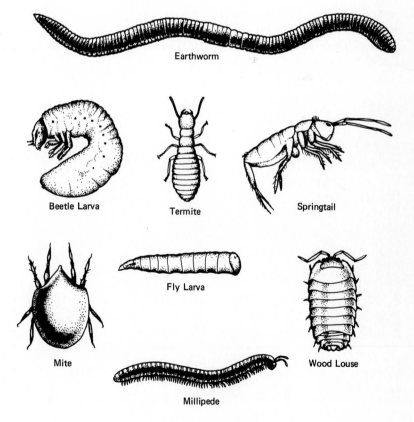

Earthworm

Beetle Larva

Termite

Springtail

Fly Larva

Mite

Wood Louse

Millipede

growing roots of trees. Rooted vegetation absorbs nutrient salts from lower levels and deposits them at the soil surface when it dies. Through the centuries, the hoofs of antelope, buffalo, mountain sheep, deer, and livestock have gradually fragmented and pulverized underlying rock. The burrowing activities of earthworms, beetle larvae, bull snakes, pocket gophers, and ground squirrels aid in the movement of air and water through the soil. (See Figure 4–2.) Soil fertility is improved by animal wastes, especially those of earthworms, insects, birds, and mammals.

Sources of Parent Materials

The *parent material* from which soils develop may be the underlying weathered bedrock. Most parent materials, however, are carried for considerable distances by the action of water, wind, and glaciers.

GLACIAL ACTIVITY. During the Pleistocene period (one million to 10,000 BC), four massive glacial advances moved southwestward from Canada into the northeastern states as far as Ohio, Indiana, Illinois, and Iowa. The massive dome-shaped glaciers sheared off hilltops and mountain peaks, gouged out depressions, and pulverized large boulders. Rocks, gravel, sand, silt, and clay accumulated underneath the moving glacier. (See Figure 4–3.) Con-

sequently, when the ice finally melted, a mantle of *glacial drift* remained, which served as fresh parent material for the development of future soils. Glaciation has generally enhanced the value of soils for agriculture by increasing soil fertility and by leveling the land.

OCEAN WAVES AND RIVER CURRENTS. Ocean waves are powerful rock grinders. Boulders may be dashed about in the raging surf like so many marbles, many of them being chipped and broken in the process. Rivers also play an important role in soil building. Pebbles of a streambed may be worn smooth by the scouring action of the current. Each stream carries in suspension a load of sand, silt, and clay. Much of that material may ultimately be transported to the ocean at the river's mouth to form a delta. (See Figure 4–4.) The Mississippi River alone discharges roughly 700 million tons of sediment into the Gulf of Mexico each year. When the major rivers of the world, such as the Mississippi, Nile, and Amazon, periodically overflow their banks, a nutrient-rich load of sediment is deposited along the river bottoms. This special type of soil, *alluvial soil*, is said to support almost one third of the world's agriculture.

WIND ACTION. Wind-blown parent material is *loess*. In the Corn Belt of the Midwest some loess

4–3 *Geological erosion. Note the glacial striations on this rock formation in Wyoming. The boulder in the foreground has been smoothed and rounded by moving glaciers, one of the physical processes involved in soil formation.*

4–4 *Infrared aerial view of the Missisquoi River watershed, Vermont. The delta of the river, formed by the water transport of thousands of tons of silt, is visible in the foreground.*

deposits are about 100 feet thick. Loess is of considerable importance to American agriculture. Corn grows tall in the fertile loess soils of Iowa and Illinois. Loess makes possible the thousands of wheat farms in Kansas and Nebraska which form much of our nation's "Breadbasket" (2).

The Role of Climate

All other things being equal, the warmer the climate, the faster the development of soil. Thus, in the relatively cold climate of northern Michigan it takes twice as long to form soil from limestone as it does in Indiana, which is somewhat warmer. Climate (temperature and precipitation) plays a role in controlling the development of major vegetational types (biomes). Vegetation (and therefore, indirectly, climate) also has a role in the development of major soil groups (5). The animal communities supported by the plant communities also play a role, although a lesser one, in the development of soil.

A major climatic change, such as the dawning of a new Ice Age (which some authorities believe we are experiencing at the present time), would result in the southward extension of the northern coniferous forest into such states as Illinois, Indiana, and Ohio. Ultimately, the replacement of deciduous forest (oak, elm, maple) by coniferous forest (spruce, fir, pine) would gradually be expressed in a change in the kind of soil. Of course, these changes would proceed very slowly over many thousands of years.

71

The Characteristics of Soil

The major characteristics of soils are texture, acidity, nutrient content, gaseous content, and moisture content. An understanding of the nature of these characteristics is an essential prerequisite to the study of soil profiles, soil types, soil productivity, and soil management.

Soil Texture

Texture is the size and shape of the individual soil particles as well as the proportions in which they occur. For convenience and efficiency in the study of mineral particles, the U.S. Department of Agriculture (USDA) has classified soil particles in categories of diminishing size as *gravel, sand, silt,* and *clay.* (See Figure 4–5.) It should be emphasized that these textural classes are relatively stable. Despite the dynamic nature of soil, despite the continuous physical, chemical, and biological activities that are continuously transforming it, and regardless of the soil-management activities of the farmer, gravel will not change to sand, nor silt to clay, within the average human life span.

CLAY. Clay particles are so small (less than 0.004 mm) that they are not even visible under an

4–5 *Soil-texture designations as a function of percentages of sand, silt, and clay.*

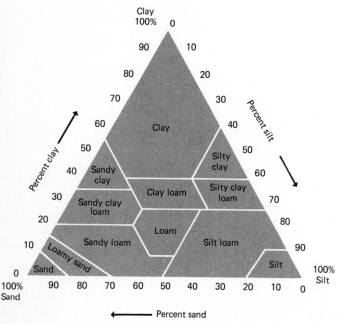

ordinary microscope. Each clay particle has the shape of a flat, many-sided wafer. The plasticity and cohesiveness of moistened clay permit it to be fashioned into pots, bowls, and vases. Because of its stickiness when wet, clay soils are worked only with difficulty and are therefore called *heavy* soils, in contrast to the easily worked *light* soils that are composed primarily of sand. When clay soils dry out, the individual particles contract and form hard clods. As science writer John Vosburgh observes: "Baked by the sun, clay soil will keep out water almost as effectively as tile, which is but clay baked by man" (6).

The total amount of air space in clay is somewhat greater than in sand; however, because much of the air space is represented by extremely minute pores, the actual rate of water and air movement through clay is much slower than through sand. Water is held so tenaciously that most plant root systems cannot absorb it. Moreover, because young plant rootlets do not readily penetrate poorly oxygenated clay, soil composed exclusively of clay is poor for raising crops.

Clay serves as an important *reservoir* of plant food, a function that largely depends on two characteristics of clay particles: (1) their *very large surface area* and (2) their *negative electrical charge.* It has been estimated that the aggregate surface area of the clay particles in the topsoil of only five acres of an Iowa cornfield is roughly equal to the *entire surface area of the North American continent.* The negatively charged surface of the clay particle attracts positively charged atoms (cations) of nutrient elements such as calcium, potassium, magnesium, phosphorus, zinc, and iron. (See Figure 4–6.) Those nutrient particles then form a loose chemical bond with the clay particles. This process is called *adsorption.* From the standpoint of soil fertility, it is of fundamental importance. As W. B. Clapham, Jr., states:

Because most rainfall is lost either through evaporation or percolation downward through the soil, it is not possible for nutrients to persist dissolved in water, as in aquatic ecosystems. If there were no mechanism for nutrient storage in the solid fraction of the soil, whatever nutrients were originally present would be quickly leached out. But adsorption of these nutrients onto soil particles provides a mechanism whereby they can be stored in the solid fraction of the soil in a form that is available to living organisms. (1)

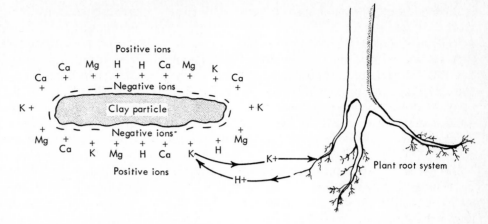

4–6 *The positive ions of various nutrient elements such as potassium (K), calcium (Ca), and magnesium (Mg) are attracted to the negatively charged surface of the clay particle. Note that these nutrient ions are replaced by hydrogen ions from the root systems of plants and then absorbed by the plants. It is this role of the clay particle that makes it an invaluable component of agricultural soil.*

On the other hand, clay particles have a relatively poor ability to retain *negatively charged* nitrate particles (anions). As a result, nitrates are leached from the soil by rainfall or washed away with runoff waters. The nitrates then fertilize lake and pond waters and eventually convert open-water, game-fish lakes to weed-grown, trash-fish lakes — a process called *eutrophication*, which will be discussed later. To prevent such excessive nitrate loss from farmlands, James Bonner of the California Institute of Technology has suggested adding a resin to the soil that has the ability to hold the negatively charged nitrate particles. Such a proposal, of course, would have to be studied very carefully, lest this new technological "fix" create a more serious problem than the one it was supposed to cure (3).

LOAM. Very few agricultural soils are composed exclusively of one textural class; usually they represent a mixture in which all four of the major classes (gravel, sand, silt, and clay) are represented in varying proportions. (See Figure 4–5.) The most desirable soil from an agricultural standpoint is *loam*, which represents a mixture of heavy and light soil materials in the following proportions: sand, 30 to 50 percent; silt, 30 to 50 percent; and clay 0 to 20 percent. In the best loams the most desirable qualities of sand and clay are combined and their undesirable traits are minimized.

Soil Acidity (pH)

Soil scientists employ the symbol *pH* as a quantitative measure of *hydrogen-ion concentration*. (The hydrogen ion is a positively charged hydrogen atom.) Soils may vary from a pH of 4.5 (strongly acid) to 9 (strongly alkaline). (See Figure 4–7.) Soils

having a pH of 7 are considered neutral. Most vegetables, grains, trees, and grass grow best in soil that is very mildly acid (about 6.8). A few species of plants, such as the valuable long-leaf pine of the South, prefer a more acidic soil. Hardwood-forest

4–7 *The pH scale, showing the pH of some commonly known substances (left) and the preferred soil pH of certain plants (right).*

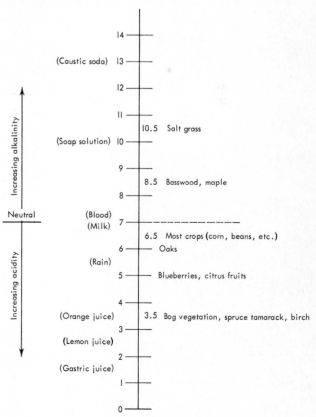

(oak-maple-beech) soils are usually more alkaline than coniferous-forest (pine-spruce) soils. With the help of a soil scientist from the local Soil Conservation Service district, the farmer or city dweller can determine the pH of his or her land. If it is too acid, the use of limestone may be advised. For example, to raise the pH of a seven-inch layer of acid soil over a 1,000-square-foot area from 5.5 to 6.5 would require the use of 30 pounds of finely ground limestone.

Soil pH is an important factor in determining the distribution of vegetation in natural ecosystems. Extreme acidity (low pH) or alkalinity (high pH) may exceed the tolerance range of all but a few highly specialized species. Some species of *Aster*, as well as an appropriately named plant called *salt-grass*, occur only in highly alkaline soils. In northern Minnesota, Wisconsin, and Michigan certain species of trees like sugar maple, red maple, and ash, which are highly intolerant of very acid soils, may occur abundantly right up to the margin of an acid bog. However, in the bog itself they are abruptly replaced by "acid-loving" species like tamarack and black spruce.

Acid Rain. One of the most serious environmental problems plaguing our nation is that of *acid rain* (see Chapter 16). It has had harmful effects on both terrestrial and aquatic organisms. The severity of the effects depends to a large degree on the soil pH. If the pH is high (alkaline soil) the acid rain will tend to be neutralized and the adverse effects will be minimized.

4–8 *How soil gains or loses soil nutrients.*

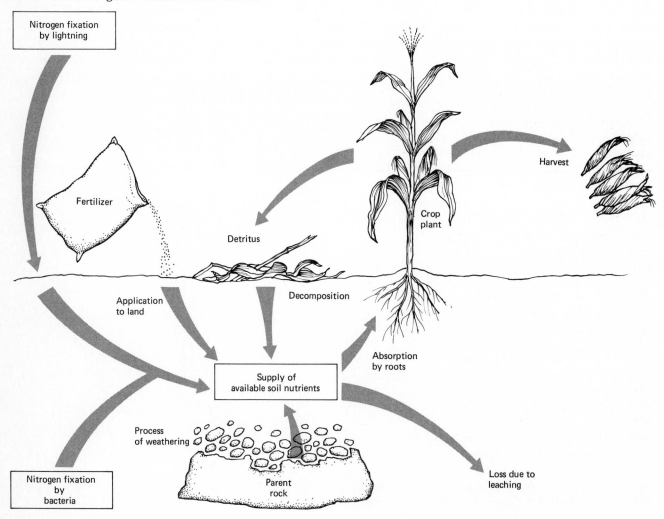

Nutrient Content

Of the 89 naturally occurring chemical elements, about 17 are required by plants and about 19 are required by animals, including humans, for health, growth, and reproduction. Mineral nutrients that are used by organisms in large quantities are classified as *macronutrients;* those that are needed in only extremely small amounts are called *micronutrients.* (See Figure 4–8.)

MACRONUTRIENTS. The macronutrients essential for plants include carbon, hydrogen, oxygen, nitrogen, phosphorus, potassium, magnesium, and sulfur. *Carbon, hydrogen,* and *oxygen* are usually abundantly present in air and water. As a result they do not ordinarily represent limiting factors for plant development. *Nitrogen* is required by plants for the synthesis of proteins, which are needed as enzymes and as structural components of cells. Nitrogen is also required for the synthesis of nucleoproteins — the chemicals of heredity. Nitrogen is necessary for growth, respiration, photosynthesis, and seed production. Although there are 34,500 tons of gaseous nitrogen in the air column above each acre of the earth's surface, this cannot be used by plants until it has been fixed by nitrogen-fixing bacteria and algae.

Phosphorus. Phosphorus is obtained by plants in the form of phosphate (PO_4) ion. Some phosphate is derived from the weathering of rock; however, the amount obtained from this source is small. Plants get most of their phosphorus from the decomposing remains of dead plants and animals — in other words, from organic compounds. (In agricultural ecosystems the farmer frequently adds much nitrogen and phosphorus to the soil by applying organic fertilizer, such as manure or sewage sludge, or by applying inorganic commercial fertilizers.)

Magnesium. Magnesium is essential for the synthesis of chlorophyll, the green pigment of photosynthesis. It is usually fairly abundant and does not ordinarily represent a limiting factor.

MICRONUTRIENTS. The micronutrients essential to plants include molybdenum, boron, zinc, manganese, iron, copper, and chlorine. The amounts of these trace elements required by crops are exceedingly small. A clover field, for example, requires only *one ounce of molybdenum per acre.* *Boron* requirements are met with a concentration of only one part boron per million parts water. Seven

tons of Maine potatoes may possess 143 pounds of nitrogen but only .2 pound of boron!

The range of tolerance that some plants have for trace elements may be extremely narrow. For example, for some plants a one part per million concentration of boron in the soil may be optimal. However, an increase to five parts per million may exceed the plant's tolerance and cause death.

NUTRIENT DEFICIENCY SYMPTOMS. Sometimes it is exceedingly difficult for the farmer, forester, or rancher to determine whether or not trees, vegetables, grains, range grasses, and so on, are in fact suffering from a nutrient deficiency. The problem is that such nutrient deficiency symptoms as unusual leaf color, stuntedness, abnormal leaf shape, and leaf and root deterioration, are virtually identical to symptoms caused by parasitic bacteria, fungi and insects.

NUTRIENT AVAILABILITY. Even though a given nutrient element may be present in the soil in adequate amounts, it may not occur in a form that makes it *available* to a given plant. This availability may be determined by the pH of the soil. (See Figure 4–9.) For example, if the soil is too alkaline, iron, manganese, magnesium, zinc, and sometimes phosphorus may remain unavailable to most plants. On the other hand, if the soil is too acid, an element like phosphorus may become unavailable because it has combined with iron or aluminum to form an insoluble phosphate salt. A major reason for adding lime to correct soil acidity is to make important nutrients available for absorption by plants.

Gaseous Content

Only about 50 percent of soil volume is actually represented by solid materials such as minerals, plant and animal bodies, and organic residues. The remaining 50 percent is represented by pore spaces, which occur between the individual soil particles. When soil is extremely dry because of a protracted drought, the spaces are filled with air. When soil is waterlogged after a violent thunderstorm, they may be filled with water.

In a sense, soil can be considered to "inhale and exhale" continuously. *Oxygen,* which is present in greater concentration in the atmosphere than in the soil, diffuses *into* the soil pores. *Carbon dioxide* continuously moves from soil into the atmosphere.

75

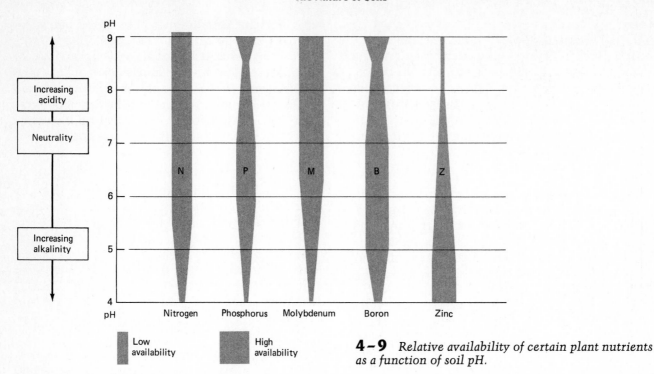

4–9 *Relative availability of certain plant nutrients as a function of soil pH.*

When soil is poorly aerated, the activity of nitrogen-fixing bacteria is slowed down. This results in reduced soil fertility. Moreover, an oxygen-deficient soil slows the development of crop roots and may hamper their ability to absorb water and nutrients.

Moisture Content

Water serves several important plant functions. It is an essential raw material for photosynthesis; it is the solvent medium by which minerals are transported upward to the leaves and sugar is transported downward to the roots; and it is an essential component protoplasm forming 90 percent of the weight of actively growing organs such as buds, roots, and flowers.

Soil is said to be *saturated* when the air in all the pores has become replaced with water (see Figure 4–6). This may occur after low-lying fields have been flooded following a severe thunderstorm or intensive irrigation.

Most upland crops such as corn and cotton cannot survive in soils that are water-saturated because of the greatly reduced oxygen content. Rice, however, grows well under these conditions. The amount of water that remains after the excess has drained away

from the saturated soil is known as the *field capacity*.

Crops continuously remove soil moisture. As the soil dries out a critical point is reached when the "pull" of the plant roots for water is not sufficient to prevent permanent wilting. This is known as the *permanent wilting point* — a condition experienced by many a farmer or suburban gardener who has seen his plot of beans and lettuce wilt and shrivel during a late summer drought.

The Soil Profile

When one looks at the exposed face of a road cut or the side of a stone quarry, it is apparent that some soil is organized into horizontally ranged layers, or *horizons*. Each of these horizons is distinct with regard to thickness, color, texture, structure, and chemical composition. Such a cross-sectional view of the various horizons is known as the *soil profile*. Each profile is the expression of a specific combination of soil formation factors, including parent rock, soil age, topography, climate, and organisms. (See Figure 4–10.)

The major layers from the ground surface down-

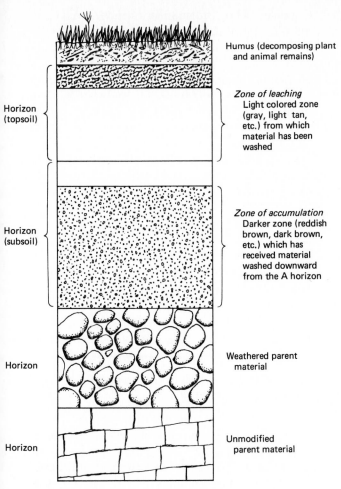

Humus (decomposing plant and animal remains)

Horizon (topsoil)

Zone of leaching
Light colored zone (gray, light tan, etc.) from which material has been washed

Horizon (subsoil)

Zone of accumulation
Darker zone (reddish brown, dark brown, etc.) which has received material washed downward from the A horizon

Horizon

Weathered parent material

Horizon

Unmodified parent material

4 – 10 *Highly simplified soil profile.*

cal standpoint the soil profile is of great economic importance, for it can tell the soil scientist immediately whether the soil is best suited for agricultural crops, for rangeland, for timber, or for wildlife habitat and recreation. The profile also reveals the suitability of the soil for various urban uses, such as home sites, highways, sewage-disposal plants, sanitary landfills, septic tanks, and the laying of power cables.

Let us examine the basic characteristics of a soil profile, beginning with the uppermost horizon and moving downward to bedrock (see Figure. 4 – 10).

A Horizon. Human survival depends on the thin layer of *topsoil* that covers much of the earth. In the United States its thickness ranges from one inch on the slopes of the Rockies to almost two feet in Iowa corn country. It is from the topsoil, or A horizon, that crop roots absorb vital water and nutrients. It is within this layer also that most soil organisms live. This A horizon is sometimes called the *zone of leaching* because many soluble salts are dissolved and carried downward to the B horizon by water.

B Horizon. The B horizon, commonly called the *subsoil* (see Figure 4 – 10), is an *accumulation zone* which receives and accumulates the soluble salts and organic matter that are carried by percolating waters from the A horizon. Sometimes strip-mining activities will rip away all of the topsoil and much of

4 – 11 *Some shapes of soil particles.*

SOME KINDS OF SOIL PARTICLES

Description		Location in Soil Profile
Spherical		Topsoil
Block-like		Subsoil (humid regions)
Columnar		Subsoil (dry regions)
Plate-like		All horizons

ward to bedrock are designated as horizons A (topsoil), B (subsoil), C (parent material), and D (bedrock). These horizons will not be equally distinct in all soil types. In fact, in immature soils, where weathering has not fully progressed, some horizons may be missing. In certain soils derived from water-borne sediment *(alluvial soils)*, or in soils that have been thoroughly mixed by the burrowing activity of mammals, the stratified pattern may be lacking completely.

The soil profile is the end product of the action of vegetation, temperature, rainfall, and soil organisms on parent-rock materials, operating for many thousands of years. The soil profile, therefore, tells us a great deal about soil *history.* It represents a kind of soil *autobiography* by which we can learn much about its origin and development. From the practi-

the B horizon or the subsoil. The exposed subsoil that remains becomes a barren wasteland in many cases. It is in the B horizon that a dense, impermeable *hardpan* might form. A flat, well-drained land favors hardpan formation. Minerals may be leached downward from the A horizon and be "cemented" by iron. Such hardpans cannot be penetrated by oxygen, water, plant root systems, or soil animals. The presence of a hardpan, of course, severely limits crop yields, whether the crop is corn, oats, or timber. For example, on the coast of northern California *giant* redwoods and *dwarf* conifers grow side by side *only a few feet apart*. Although dramatically different in size, both types of trees experience the same climate, and the soils in which they grow have developed from the same underlying sandstone. The crucial difference however, is that the dwarf trees are located above a dense hardpan that formed 18 inches below the forest floor (5).

C Horizon. The C horizon is composed of weathered parent material. It is the source of the mineral content (calcium, phosphorus, and so on) of A and B horizons. About 97 percent of the parent materials in the United States were transported to their present sites by ice, water, wind, and gravity. This parent material will in part determine soil texture and the rate of water absorption and release. It will also determine much of the future soil's nutrient content, such as nitrogen, phosphorus, calcium, and potassium. Moreover, it will influence the soil's acidity or alkalinity. Thus, if the parent material is granite, the soil will mature slowly and tend to be acid. On the other hand, if the parent material is limestone, the soil will develop rapidly and tend to be alkaline. Soils derived from granite are usually less productive than limestone soils.

D Horizon. The D horizon consists of the unweathered bedrock.

Kinds of Soils

The U.S. Department of Agriculture (USDA), with the assistance of the various state agricultural stations, has mapped more than 70,000 *soil types* over an area of 500 million acres. (See Figures 4–12 and 4–13.) Soil types are designated by locality (city, river, county, and so on) and by texture — for example, *Miami silt loam, Fargo clay,* and *Plainfield sand.* In a 1,100-square-mile region near Merced, California, at least 290 soil types have been distinguished. Soil types are assembled into ten major classification units called *orders.* Major soil orders of North America are shown in Figure 4–14. For our purposes it will be necessary only to identify and describe three representative soil orders, the spodosols, the mollisols, and the laterite soils of tropical rain forests.

The Spodosols

Spodosols develop in a cool, relatively humid climate under coniferous forest vegetation in the northern Lake states, in the uplands of New England, and at high elevations in the western mountains. (See Figure 4–15.) The litter of forest needles, cones, and branches decomposes, largely because of fungal activity, to produce a dark-brown, extremely acid humus. Percolating water and organic acids carry soluble carbonate and sulphate salts, as well as aluminum and iron compounds, downward from the A to the B horizon. This leaching causes the lower part of the A horizon to assume a gray, ashlike appearance. (The term spodosol is derived from the Greek word *spodos* meaning "wood ash" and the Latin *solum* meaning "ground.") The lower portion of the B horizon, on the other hand, because of the accumulation of iron compounds and organic materials, assumes a distinctive coffee-brown color.

Because these soils are infertile, they can best be used for timber production, wildlife habitat, and scenic wilderness. Many an enterprising farming venture based on tilling the spodosols of northern Michigan and Wisconsin in the early part of this century ultimately failed because of the relatively

4 – 12 *Taking aerial photographs of farmland. Such photos are used by the SCS specialist who aids the farmer in drawing up a farm plan. The soil capability map is superimposed on the aerial photo of the farm. The men in the plane are taking pictures. They are working in a converted World War II bomber. The camera is located in the bomb bay. The man on the left controls the intervals at which the photos are taken; the man on the right sees to it that the correct flight line is maintained.*

4 – 13 *Soil maps. The U.S. Soil Conservation Service has probed, examined, and mapped the 70,000 different soil types in the United States. Soil surveys hold the key to proper land management and are used primarily by private land owners— farmers and ranchers—to determine the proper cultivation and conservation measures for their land. But the soil surveys are also important to foresters, country agents, land developers, real estate offices, highway engineers, libraries, and sanitation boards.*

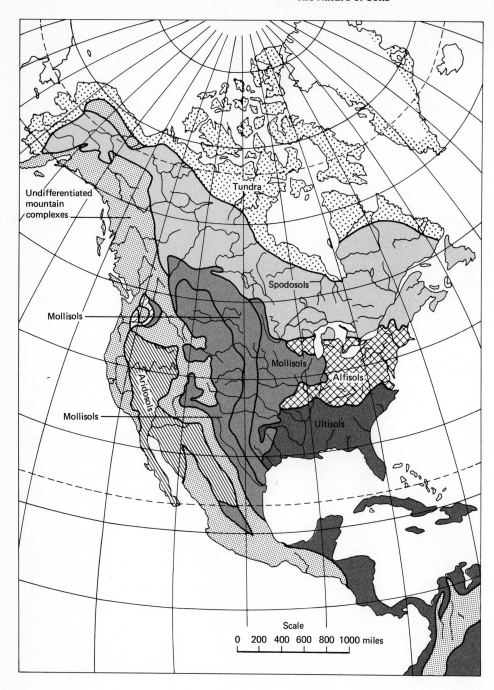

4–14 *Major soil orders of North America.*

short growing season and the extremely acid and infertile soil. Unless spodosol soil is heavily limed and fertilized, it depreciates rapidly. This is corroborated by many an abandoned farm home now being swallowed up by encroaching second-growth forest. An outstanding exception to the general failure of spodosols as agriculturally productive soils is the famous potato-growing area in Aroostook County, Maine, where intensive fertilization is practiced.

80

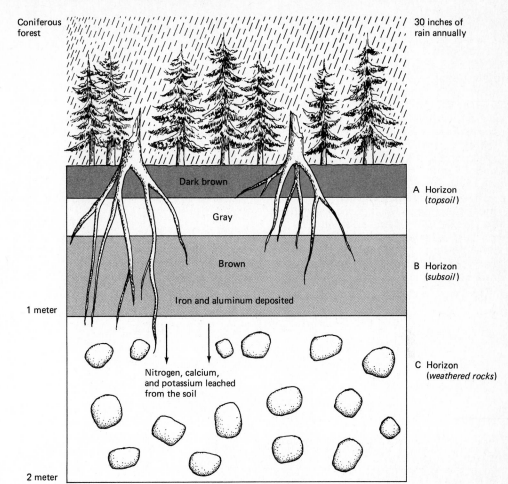

Coniferous forest

30 inches of rain annually

Dark brown — A Horizon (*topsoil*)

Gray

Brown — B Horizon (*subsoil*)

Iron and aluminum deposited

1 meter

C Horizon (*weathered rocks*)

Nitrogen, calcium, and potassium leached from the soil

2 meter

4 – 15 *A highly simplified profile of spodosol soil.*

The Mollisols (Prairie Soils)

The term mollisol means "soft soil" and refers to the soft, crumbly texture of prairie soils. The extremely fertile, blackish-brown topsoil may be up to four feet thick. The mollisols extend in a north-south belt in the Great Plains from the Dakotas south to Texas. (See Figure 4 – 16.) Calcification of the subsoil resulting from the leaching of soluble calcium carbonate from above is a dominant characteristic. However, because of an annual rainfall of only 15 to 25 inches, which is usually in the form of brief summer thundershowers, leaching does not carry the calcium through to the C horizon. It is deposited in the lower subsoil instead, where it precipitates out and forms a grayish or yellowish band. (See Figure 4 – 17.) The topsoil of the mollisols, characterized by a rich organic and nutrient content, is intrinsically *more fertile than any other soil in the United States.* This is in part because of the dense mesh of roots extending down through the A horizon. It has been estimated that a single rye plant (which is actually a cultivated grass), only 20 inches tall, may have more than 14 million branches in its root system. If laid end to end those branches would form a line over 300 miles long. When a grass plant dies, of course, its root system decomposes *in place* and releases nutrients that are immediately available to future plant generations.

4 – 16 *Profile of mollisol soil. The black color of the 2-foot thick A horizon contrasts with the light color of the 1-foot thick B horizon. Note that because of the light rainfall (10 to 30 inches annually) the soluble mineral salts (except for lime, which accumulates at the base of the B horizon) are not leached extensively from the A horizon but are available to plants. Observe the extensive mesh of root systems in the A horizon. Upon plant death, the in situ decomposition of the root systems releases nutrients that become immediately available for future plant generations. Loss of these nutrients by erosion is obviously minimal. The actual dimensions of the mollisol horizons illustrated are typical but may vary considerably, depending on regional differences in parental material and climate.*

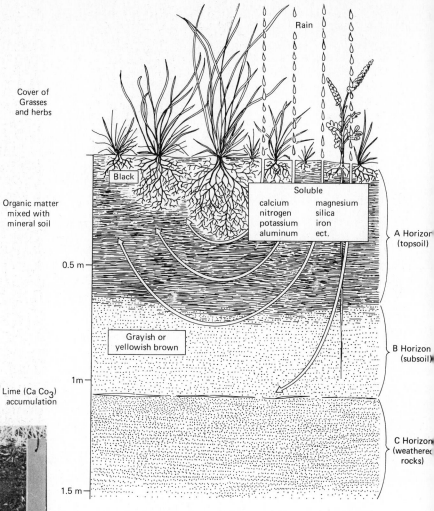

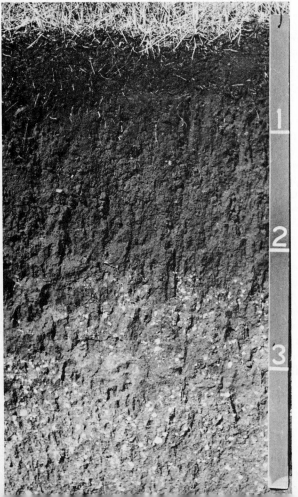

4 – 17 *Profile of mollisol soil formed from glacial till in South Dakota. Note thick, dark A horizon and the whitish flecks (calcium deposits) in the B horizon. Scale is calibrated in feet.*

Typical mollisol soils contain about 600 tons of *humus* (decaying organic material, such as roots) per acre, as compared with only 50 tons per acre for spodosol soils (15). The relatively undependable and low annual rainfall limits this soil's productivity, however. During wet years bumper crops are commonplace, but during years of excessive heat and drought, crop failures may be extensive. Major northern crops produced on these soils are high-quality corn, wheat, barley, oats, and rye. Sorghum is a prominent southern crop.

Laterite Soils of the Tropical Rain Forest

When you think of a tropical forest you picture lush jungles of vegetation. That thick vegetation in turn must be possible only because the soil is very fertile. Right? Wrong. In a sense, the nutrients are locked up in the vegetation. Actually, most tropical forest soils are *highly infertile.* The topsoil is extremely thin. Much of the dead plant and animal material on the forest floor is rapidly decomposed by fungi that live partly *inside* and partly *outside* the living plant roots. As a result, the nutrients that are released during decomposition are absorbed *directly* into the living plant roots. The heavy rainfall quickly washes away any nutrients that might be released to the soil (4).

Another problem with these soils is the high iron content in the B horizon. Suppose that hopeful farmers remove the trees and plant crops in infertile, iron-rich soil. What will be the result? After a few years this laterite soil will bake brick hard in the "kiln" of the hot equatorial sun. Such lateritic bricks were actually used by the ancient Khmer civilization of Cambodia to construct the magnificent temples at Angkor Wat. Modern buildings in Thailand are being built today of those bricks. Such hardness and durability may be good for buildings and temples but certainly are highly undesirable for growing crops.

Rapid Review

1. All terrestrial life is derived from "the dust of the earth"—the soil.

2. The development of a mature soil is complex. It involves the interaction of physical, biological, chemical, and climatic processes.

3. Physical processes in soil formation include rapid heating and cooling, and thawing and freezing.

4. The solution of rock by water is an important chemical process in soil formation.

5. Soil bacteria influence the aeration, moisture content, and fertility of the soil.

6. In addition to the action of soil bacteria, other biological processes involved in soil formation include (a) the splitting of rock by plant roots, (b) the fragmentation of rocks by hoofed animals, (c) the burrowing activities of earthworms, pocket gophers, and ground squirrels, and (d) the pumping of nutrients to the soil surface by rooted vegetation.

7. The parent material from which soil is derived may be the underlying bedrock. However, more than 95 percent of the parent materials in the United States have been transported by the action of wind, water, and glaciers.

8. *Alluvial* soils support almost one third of the world's agriculture.

9. *Loess* soils support the production of corn in Iowa and Illinois and of wheat in Kansas and Nebraska.

10. All factors being equal, the warmer the climate the more rapid the process of soil development.

11. Soil particles are classified as gravel, sand, silt, and clay on the basis of size.

12. Pure clay is not a good soil for growing crops because air and water move through it very slowly.

13. Clay serves as an important reservoir for plant nutrients. The negatively charged surface of the clay particle attracts positively charged atoms of such nutrients as calcium, potassium, and magnesium.

14. Clay particles do not retain negatively charged nitrate particles. As a result, nitrates are easily washed from clay soils by rainfall.

15. The most desirable agricultural soil is *loam* —a mixture of sand, silt, and clay.

16. The pH of soils varies from 4.5 (strongly acid) to 9 (strongly alkaline). Most plants grow best in soil with a pH of about 6.8 (mildly acid).

17. Alkaline soils tend to minimize the harmful effects of acid rain on ecosystems.

18. Roughly 50 percent of the soil volume is represented by pore space.

19. Oxygen continuously moves from the atmosphere into the soil, whereas carbon dioxide moves from the soil into the atmosphere.

20. The major soil layers from the ground surface downward are known as the A, B, C, and D horizons.

21. The soil profile is the end product of the action of temperature, rainfall, vegetation, and soil organisms on parent materials through time frequently measured in thousands of years.

22. The presence of a hardpan severely limits the growth of both food crops and timber.

23. The USDA has mapped more than 70,000 soil types.

24. Because of their infertility, spodosol soils are best suited for timber production, wildlife habitat, and scenic beauty.

25. Mollisol soils are characterized by an extremely fertile, blackish-brown topsoil that may be up to four feet thick.

26. The productivity of mollisols is limited by an unpredictable and low average rainfall.

27. Most of the nutrients in tropical forests are locked up in the vegetation; as a result, the soil itself is infertile.

28. The iron-rich laterite soils of tropical forest regions can be farmed for only a few years before they bake brick hard under the hot equatorial sun.

Key Words and Phrases

Acidity	B horizon
Acid rain	Calcification
Adsorption	C horizon
A horizon	Clay
Alluvial soil	D horizon
Anions	Eutrophication
Bedrock	Field capacity

Glacial drift	pH
Glaciers	Sand
Granite	Saturated soil
Gravel	Silt
Hardpan	Soil
Heavy soil	Soil order
Hydrogen ions	Soil profile
Laterite	Soil texture
Light soil	Soil type
Limestone	Spodosol
Loam	Subsoil
Loess	Topsoil
Mollisol	Zone of deposition
Parent material	Zone of leaching
Permanent wilting point	

Questions and Topics for Discussion

1. Discuss the ecological implications of the biblical statement: "In the sweat of thy face shalt thou eat bread, till thou return unto the ground, for out of it wast thou taken; for dust thou art, and unto dust shalt thou return."

2. Is there any correlation between soil fertility and the power and influence of nations like the United States and Russia? Discuss your answer.

3. Describe five biological processes involved in the development of soils. What is the importance of each?

4. List three agencies that play an important role in the transport of parent materials for soil development.

5. Discuss the role of glaciers in the development of the soils of Minnesota, Wisconsin, and Michigan.

6. How could a climatic change eventually cause a change in the type of soil occurring in a given region?

7. List five major properties of soils.

8. A farmer has a couple acres of land that is almost pure sand. If he fertilizes the soil well, carefully plants seeds, keeps the young plants well watered, and diligently removes weeds from his acreage, will he eventually be successful in growing a crop? Discuss your answer.

9. What characteristics of clay are undesirable for crop production? What characteristics are desirable?

10. What does pH mean? What pH is desirable for most trees and food crops?

11. Suppose a farmer has soil with a pH of 5.0 but wishes to raise a crop that requires a pH of 6.0. What can he do?

12. What is meant by the statement: "Soil inhales and exhales"?

13. Give three reasons why a plant cannot survive without water.

14. Discuss the statement: "A soil profile represents a kind of autobiography." Is this statement valid? Why or why not?

15. What is the basis for naming a soil type? Give an example.

16. Compare the profiles of spodosol and mollisol soils. What are the major differences?

17. A Brazilian farmer living in the Amazon River valley cleared his land of forest cover and started to farm it. Were his prospects of long-term success very good? Why or why not?

Endnotes

1. Clapham, W. B., Jr. *Natural Ecosystems.* New York: Macmillan, 1981.

2. Donahue, Roy L., Roy H. Follett, and Rodney W. Tulloch. *Our Soils and Their Management.* Danville, IL: Interstate, 1976.

3. Ehrlich, Paul R., and Anne H. Ehrlich. *Population, Resources, Environment.* San Francisco: Freeman, 1970.

4. Moran, Joseph M., Michael D. Morgan, and James H. Wiersma. *Introduction to Environmental Science.* San Francisco: Freeman, 1980.

5. Odum, Eugene P. *Fundamentals of Ecology.* 3rd ed. Philadelphia: Saunders, 1971.

6. Vosburgh, John. *Living with Your Land.* New York: Scribner, 1968.

Suggested Readings for the Interested Student

Brady, N. C. *The Nature and Property of Soils.* 8th ed. New York: Macmillan, 1974. This is a comprehensive treatment of soils by a top authority.

Clapham, W. B., Jr., *Human Ecosystems.* New York: Macmillan, 1981. This book offers excellent material on the composition, nutrient balance, and fertility of soils.

Donahue, Roy L., Roy L. Follett, and Rodney W. Tulloch. *Our Soils and Their Management.* Danville, IL: Interstate, 1976. The authors' treatment is comprehensive and easily understood by the general reader not majoring in soil science.

Eckholm, Eric. *Losing Ground.* New York: Norton, 1976. The author discusses the harmful effects of soil mismanagement.

Hunt, C. B. *Natural Regions of the United States and Canada.* San Francisco: Freeman, 1974. This is a well-written treatment of the interrelationships of soil, water, and vegetation.

Janick, J., R. W. Schery, F. W. Woods, and V. W. Ruttan. *Plant Science.* 2nd ed. San Francisco: Freeman, 1974. This is an excellent account of the relationship between soil chemistry and crop yields.

Odum, Eugene P., *Fundamentals of Ecology.* Philadelphia: Saunders, 1971. The author discusses soil development, soil profiles, kinds of soils, and the role played by soil organisms.

Smith, Robert Leo. *Ecology and Field Biology.* 3rd ed. New York: Harper, 1980. This is a superb treatment of soil development, soil horizons and profiles, nutrient cycling in soils, and the nature of soil as an environment. The illustrations are outstanding.

Walter, H. *Vegetation of the Earth.* New York: Springer-Verlag, 1973. The author discusses the characteristics of the soils in each major biome.

5 Soil Management

The modern farm is a special type of ecosystem consisting of both natural and human-made components. We shall call it an *agroecosystem*. The *structure* of this ecosystem consists of both biotic (farmer, crop, insect pests, and so on) and abiotic (soil minerals, climate, solar energy, and fossil fuels) components which interact. The *function* of the agroecosystem includes such processes as: plowing, fertilizer application, photosynthesis, irrigation, and soil erosion.

Farming in America

Need for Greater Food Production by American Farmers

The average farmer in the United States is producing enough food to satisfy the needs of 55 people. But he must do even better to meet the future food demands both at home and abroad.

First, he must produce more food, because by the year 2000 there will be about 50 million additional American stomachs to fill. In addition, each stomach's demand for food is increasing as well. Population and crop production trends in the United States are compared in Figure 5–1.

Second, the American farmer must increase food production because the export of food to foreign nations is vital to our nation's economic health. In 1978, for example, we exported 127 million tons of food for which we received $27.2 billion. Without those food sales our trade deficit for that year would have been almost twice as large as it was. Foreign demand for American-grown food is increasing. Spain, Italy, Russia, and China will be sharply boosting their purchases of American farm products — especially grain. So will countries that have become wealthy from multibillion-dollar oil sales, such as the OPEC nations of the Middle East and North Africa.

Third, greater food yields are needed to help prevent undernourishment and starvation in the have-not nations of Africa, Asia, and South America. Certainly, as a nation blessed with fertile soil, fairly abundant water, and long growing seasons, we have a moral commitment to serve as a breadbasket for countries not so well endowed.

Problems Facing the American Farmers

Although at first glance, at least to the "city slicker," farming might appear to involve not much more than throwing some seeds on the ground and watching them grow, as practiced in today's America it is anything but a simple occupation. As a result of a complex web of interacting factors, continued high levels of crop yields might be impossible to maintain were some of the supporting strands to weaken or unravel. Let us briefly examine a few of the problems which are currently hampering our nation's agricultural effort.

1. American agriculture is impaled on the horns of a dilemma. At the same time that it is under pressure to increase the acreage devoted to food

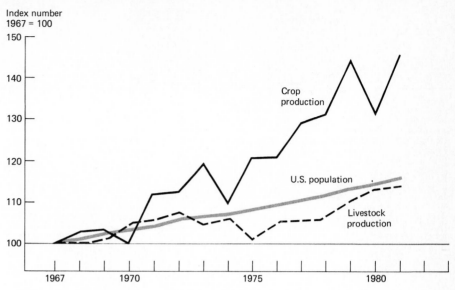

Index number
1967 = 100

5 – 1 *Crop production in the United States between 1967 and 1981 increased at a faster rate than population.*

5 – 2 *Land use in the United States. Note that 27 percent of our nonfederal land (413 million acres) is devoted to crop production. This represents an 8 percent reduction from the 448 million acres in cropland in 1958. Much of this reduction is due to "buckshot urbanization."*

LAND USE IN THE UNITED STATES

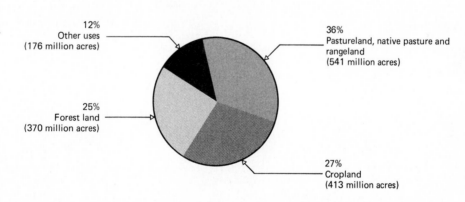

Use of Nonfederal Land

Includes United States,
Puerto Rico, and Virgin Islands.
Excludes Alaska.

12%
Other uses
(176 million acres)

36%
Pastureland, native pasture and rangeland
(541 million acres)

25%
Forest land
(370 million acres)

27%
Cropland
(413 million acres)

Trends in Land Use

Includes United States,
Puerto Rico, and Virgin Islands.
Excludes Alaska.

	1958	1977	Percent Changed
	(millions of acres)		
Cropland	448	413	− 8
Pastureland, native pasture, and rangeland	485	541	+12
Forest land	453	370	−18
Urban land (over 10 acres)	51	90	+76
Small areas of open water	7	9	+29
Other	60	77	+27
Total	1,504	1,500	

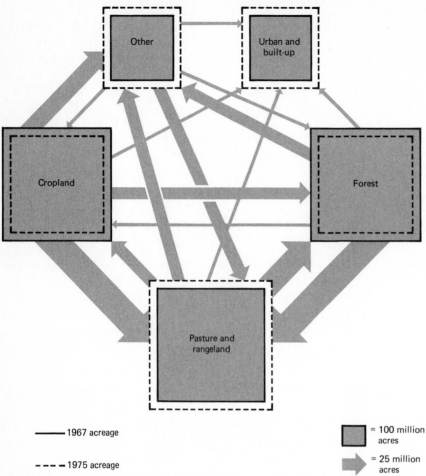

—— 1967 acreage

– – – 1975 acreage

Boxes represent the total amount of nonfederal land in each category for a given year. Arrows represent amount of land converted from one use to another between 1967 and 1975.

▨ = 100 million acres

➤ = 25 million acres

5-3 *Land-use conversions. Note that the amount of land devoted to crop production in the United States is decreasing. Much has been converted to pasture, rangeland, and forest or has been lost to "buckshot urbanization."*

production, much prime farmland is being covered over with suburban homes, shopping centers, factories, and highways: "buckshot" urbanization. Concrete is invading the cornfields. Highway "cloverleafs" are replacing the clover. Much of this urbanization is occurring in a hit-or-miss "buckshot" pattern. Thus for every acre that is actually destroyed for crop-growing purposes, another acre is rendered useless because of its isolation from adjoining farmlands. Because of this insidious process, our nation is losing 8,000 acres of agricultural land per day — and this loss is forever! (See Figure 5 – 3.) Buckshot urbanization has been particularly destructive in the industrial states east of the Mississippi River. Maryland, for example, is losing 30,000 acres per year. New England has lost about 50 percent of its best acreage. Florida might lose all of its high quality farm land by the year 2000.

2. Food production is being hindered because of slowly decreasing average temperatures. Climatologists inform us that the average temperature in the Northern Hemisphere has declined 0.4° C between 1940 and 1980. This represents a shortening of the growing season by roughly nine days. A two-week shortening of the corn-growing season would result in a 14-bushel-per-acre reduction in yield (26).

3. Soil erosion has either destroyed or seriously impaired about 150 million acres of once food-productive land in the United States. In an important address to the American Farm Bureau, Douglas M. Costle, then head of the Environ-

mental Protection Agency (EPA), emphasized how seriously accelerated erosion is affecting crop yields: "Soil scientists generally agree that even deep soils cannot sustain losses of more than five tons an acre per year without harming productivity. Yet erosion losses nationally, from all sources, are estimated at between 9 and 12 tons an acre per year. In some cases 60 tons or more are recorded" (8).

4. Modern American agriculture depends on huge inputs of energy derived from increasingly costly fossil fuels, such as oil and natural gas, which are already in short supply. Over 50 percent of the world's known reserves of oil and natural gas will be consumed by the year 2000.

5. Flood and sediment damage, caused in part by overgrazing, clear cutting forests, strip-mining, and construction projects, destroy $1.3 billion worth of crops and pastures annually (26).

6. The availability of water for irrigation will sharply diminish in the near future because of the competitive demands of expanding urban populations, industrial development, and newly established oil-shale and strip-mining operations.

7. Because of improper irrigation practices some farmland in California is now producing only one major crop: Imperial Valley "snow"—a whitish crust of aluminum sulfate. This salt is deposited when irrigation water evaporates from poorly-drained land.) Such snow has reduced crop yields on eight million acres in the West (21).

8. American agriculture has been increasingly dependent on costly synthetic fertilizers. Since 1950 the nation's farmers have boosted their annual use of fertilizer at least sixteenfold. However, this has caused extensive and severe water-pollution problems. Environmentalists strongly urge a restriction of the use of synthetic fertilizers.

9. The intensive application of persistent pesticides, such as DDT, to croplands has resulted in soil contamination with residues. Some of those pesticides have adversely affected the process of nitrification by which soil bacteria convert nitrogen to a form that is usable by crops.

10. Atmospheric pollution is inflicting about a $350 million annual loss on the agricultural industry. At least 36 commercial crops are affected. The flood of vehicles along our interstate highway network has seriously diminished yields on nearby farms.

11. Because of the continued intensive use of heavy machinery such as tractors and harvesters, agricultural soils in many areas are becoming increasingly compacted. The capability of such soils to hold water and air is markedly reduced. As a result crop yields decline.

Although this chapter deals primarily with soil problems in the United States, we should emphasize that one or more of those problems is being experienced by almost *all nations.* For example, two thirds of Indian farmland has been either partly or completely destroyed by erosion. Pakistan is losing many acres every day as a result of irrigation-induced salt deposition. Misguided farming ventures in the tropics of South America, Africa, and Asia have failed miserably because of the eventual hardening of the iron-rich soil into a bricklike "pavement" that is virtually impenetrable to crop root systems. Yet, paradoxically, never before in history have we been so dependent on the very soil we seemingly disdain. Two of every three people in the world are either malnourished or go to bed hungry. This very day about 15,000 unfortunates will quietly starve to death; tomorrow 15,000 more. And the situation will probably worsen, dramatically, for by the year 2000 the number of human stomachs in the world will have increased from about 4.8 billion to almost six billion. Certainly never in history has it been so urgent for us to develop a sense of stewardship toward our soil heritage.

Erosion

The Dust Bowl

Twenty inches of precipitation annually is considered marginal for crop production. The arid and semiarid Great Plains frequently have less. During periods of severe drought, rainfall may be considerably less than five inches annually. Throughout history, the Great Plains experienced alternating periods of drought and adequate rainfall. Although major drought appears to have recurred at roughly twenty-two year intervals, the precise time of its occurrence has not been predictable. (See Figure 5–4.) Drought visited the Great Plains in 1890 and

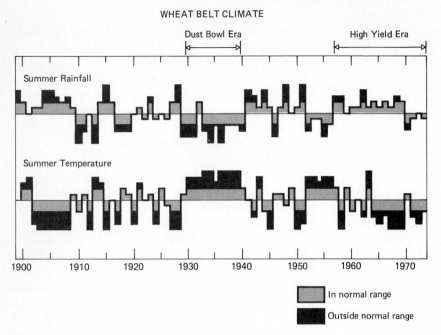

WHEAT BELT CLIMATE

5–4 *A 75-year record of rainfall and temperature in the wheat-growing states of Kansas, Nebraska, North Dakota, South Dakota, and Oklahoma. The graph indicates a drought cycle of about 22 years. The Dust Bowl era was characterized by extreme drought.*

again in 1910. During each dry spell, crops withered and died. Farms and ranches were abandoned only to be reoccupied during the ensuing years of adequate rainfall.

Then came the Big Drought. For five years, from 1927 to 1932, there was hardly enough rain to settle the dust. On the ranches the buffalo grass and the other prairie grasses lost their vigor and withered. Overstocked pastures were clipped to ground level by scrawny cattle. Much livestock was mercifully slaughtered. Droughts had visited the plains before. So had windstorms. But never before in the history of the North American prairie was the land more

5–5 *Dust storm approaching Springfield, Colorado, on May 21, 1937. This storm reached the city limits at exactly 4:47 P.M. Total darkness lasted about one-half hour.*

vulnerable to their combined assault. Gone were the profusely branching root systems of the buffalo grass, the grama grass, the big bluestem, and the little bluestem, which had originally kept the rich brown soil firmly in place. Gone was the decomposing organic material that had aided in building up stable soil aggregates and the soil cover of grass mat and sagebrush. On the ranches soil structure deteriorated under the concerted pounding given it by millions of cattle. On the wheat and cotton farms, soil structure broke down under the abuse inflicted by the huge machinery used in plowing, cultivating, and harvesting. The stage was set for the "black blizzards."

In the spring of 1934 and again in 1935, winds of gale velocity swept over the Great Plains. In western Kansas and Oklahoma, as well as in the neighboring parts of Texas, Colorado, and Nebraska, the wind whirled minute particles of clay and silt far upward into the prairie sky. (See Figure 5–5.) Brown dust clouds up to 7,000 feet thick filled the air with an upper edge almost two miles high (23). One storm on May 11, 1934, lifted 300 million tons of fertile soil into the air. (This roughly equals the total soil tonnage scooped from Central America to form the Panama Canal.) In many areas the wilted wheat was uprooted and blown into the air. In the Amarillo, Texas area during March and April 1935, 15 windstorms raged for 24 hours; four lasted more than 55 hours (17).

In his celebrated novel *The Grapes of Wrath*, John Steinbeck described this event:

The wind grew stronger, whisked under stones, carried up straws and old leaves, and even little clods, marking its course as it sailed across the fields. The air and the sky darkened and through them the sun shone redly, and there was a raw sting in the air . . . as that day advanced the dusk slipped back toward darkness, and the wind cried and whimpered over the fallen corn. . . . In the morning the dust hung like fog, and the sun was as red as ripe new blood. All day the dust sifted down from the sky, and the next day it sifted down. . . . It settled on the corn, piled up on the tops of the fence posts, piled up on the wires; it settled on roofs, blanketed the weeds and trees. And the women came out of the houses to stand beside their men—to feel whether this time the men would break. (27)

Dust from Oklahoma prairies came to rest on the deck of a steamer 200 miles out in the Atlantic. (See Figure 5–6.) Dust sifted into the plush offices of Wall Street and smudged the luxury apartments of Park Avenue. When it rained in the blow area, the drops would sometimes come down as diluted mud. In Washington, D.C., mud splattered buildings of the Department of Agriculture, a rude reminder of the problem facing it and the nation. A thousand miles westward, harried housewives stuffed water-soaked newspapers into window cracks to no avail. The dust sifted into kitchens, forming a thin film on pots and pans and freshly baked bread. Blinded by swirling dust clouds, ranchers got lost in their own backyards. Motorists pulled off to the side of highways. Hundreds of airplanes were grounded. Trains were stalled by huge drifts. Hospital nurses placed wet cloth on patients' faces to ease their breathing. In Colorado's Baca County (March 1935), forty-eight relief workers contracted "dust pneumonia," and four of them died. Five youngsters belonging to a New Mexico mother were smothered to death in their cribs (16).

When the winds finally subsided, ranchers and farmers wearily emerged to survey the desolation. Two to twelve inches of fertile clay and silt soils had

5–6 *The Dust Bowl region. Stippled areas on this map incurred severe wind erosion during the 1930s. Topsoil was blown as far as the Atlantic Ocean. Over one million farm-acres lost 2 to 12 inches of topsoil.*

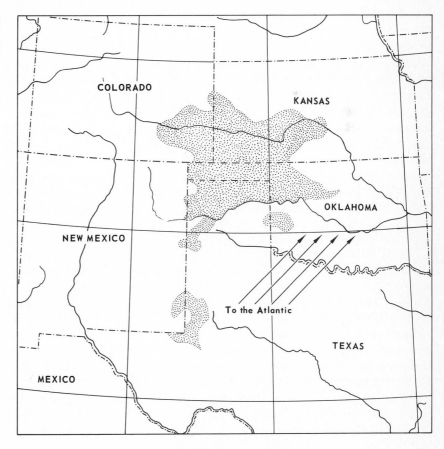

5–7 *Abandoned Oklahoma farmstead, showing the disastrous results of wind erosion.*

been carried to the Atlantic seaboard. The coarser sand, too heavy to be airborne, bounced across the land, sheared off young wheat, and finally accumulated as dunes to the leeward of homes and barns. Heavily mortgaged power machinery was shrouded in sand. (See Figure 5 – 7.)

The dust storms of the 1930s inflicted both social and economic suffering. Yet a few ranchers and farmers were philosophical about their misfortunes and could even crack jokes about the birds flying backward "to keep the sand out of their eyes" and about the prairie dogs "digging burrows 100 feet in the air." However, for most Dust Bowl victims, the dusters were not very funny. Many victims were virtually penniless. The 300 million tons of topsoil removed in a single storm on May 11, 1934, represented the equivalent of taking 3,000 farms of 100 acres each out of crop production. Dust Bowl relief up until 1940 alone cost American taxpayers over $1 billion. A single county in Colorado received $7 million, more than was paid to purchase all of Alaska. The only recourse for many of those ill-fated farmers was to find a new way of life. They piled their belongings into rickety cars and trucks and moved out — some to the Pacific coast, some to the big industrial cities of the Midwest and the East. However, our nation was still in the throes of a depression, and many an emigrating family found nothing but frustration, bitterness, and suffering at the end of the road.

Soil Erosion Today

The Dust Bowl period was devastating to our nation's soil resource, to our economy, and to the emotional well-being of millions of Americans. In the fifty years that have passed since that critical period in American agriculture, the federal government has spent more than $20 billion to control erosion. Scientists at many of our major universities have conducted erosion-control research with tax-money support. Hundreds of scientific publications have been written on the subject. The USDA has established more than 3,000 Soil Conservation Districts whose prime function is to assist the farmer with his erosion problems. So, after all this time, energy, and money devoted to soil erosion control, we are justified, as taxpayers, to ask the question: "Is the American farmer doing any better in controlling erosion today than during the Dust Bowl years?" Unfortunately, the highly disturbing answer is an emphatic "No." In fact, soil erosion today, almost incredibly, is even more severe than back in the 1930s. (See Figure 5 – 8.)

Soil erosion is sharply reducing the American farmer's capacity to produce food and fiber, at a time when both domestic and foreign demands for our crops are reaching an all-time high. Crop production in the United States grew at a rate of 2.1 percent per year from 1939 through 1965. Recently, however, the growth rate has been reduced to only 1.7 percent, largely the result of soil losses, which

92

recently have amounted to almost 4 billion tons annually, substantially more than was lost during the Dust Bowl era. At the present time one third of our cropland base is losing top soil at an excessive rate. To transport the soil lost annually in the United States would require a train of freight cars more than 633,000 miles long—sufficient to circle the earth 24 times (4)! To compensate for the nutrient losses caused by erosion would require an expenditure of $1 billion worth of fertilizer (4).

Top soil depth in the United States ranges from a few inches to several feet. The USDA has determined that soils with a thick layer of top soil can withstand erosion losses of five tons per acre per year without losing their ability to support crops. This amount of soil loss is normally regained by the natural processes of soil formation. However, in some areas of Washington, Oregon and Idaho, 50 to 100 tons per acre per year are lost due to a combination of steep slopes and highly erodible soil types. Under the Soil and Water Resources Conservation Act of 1977, the U.S. Dept. of Agriculture was charged to make a comprehensive appraisal of the quantity and quality of America's soil resources. It was found that our nation's soils differ greatly in their susceptibility to erosion. Some are 1000 times more erodible than others. Cropland planted to corn showed losses which ranged from about eight tons per acre per year on 17 million acres to more than 200 tons per acre per year on 49,000 acres. In many of the Midwestern states such as Iowa and Illinois, two bushels of soil are being lost for each bushel of corn harvested (4).

The Nature of Soil Erosion

During the three-century history of soil deterioration in the United States, erosion has played a dominant role. Let us now examine this insidious process.

The word *erosion* is derived from the Latin word *erodere*, meaning "to gnaw out." Erosion is, thus, the process by which rock fragments and soil are detached from their original site, transported, and then eventually deposited at some new locality. The principal agents of erosion are wind and water.

GEOLOGICAL EROSION, OR NATURAL EROSION. *Geological erosion* is a process that has occurred at

5–8 *Wind erosion in the Great Plains.*

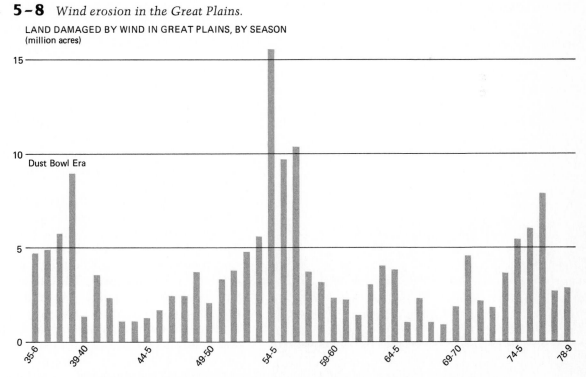

LAND DAMAGED BY WIND IN GREAT PLAINS, BY SEASON
(million acres)

Note: Data for period 1943-44 through 1952-53 were obtained from reports of the Great Plains Council.
All other data were obtained from SCS reports. (The number of counties reporting may vary from year to year.)

5–9 *Geological erosion. The Grand Canyon of the Colorado River, Arizona, as seen from the north rim, a colossal example of the effects of geological erosion operating for millennia.*

an extremely *slow* rate ever since the earth was formed four to five billion years ago. It has been estimated that water erodes a rocky surface at the rate of one-fourth to one-fiftieth of a millimeter per year — the rate depending, of course, on the force of

5–10 *Accelerated erosion. Water erosion caused the severe gullies on this North Carolina farm.*

the water and the nature of the rock. The mountains, valleys, canyons, coastlines, and deltas on the earth's surface have been sculptured by water and wind erosion working through vast periods of time. The Appalachian Mountains were at one time as tall and rugged as the Rocky Mountains, but since their formation 200 million years ago they have been gradually worn down by erosive forces. Were it not for geological erosion, New Orleans would be resting on the bottom of the Gulf of Mexico, for the delta on which it is built was formed by a deposit of soil transported by the Mississippi River from sites as far as 1,000 miles away. The Grand Canyon originated as a shallow channel 100 million years ago. It was ultimately scoured to its awesome one-mile depth by the churning waters of the Colorado River. (See Figure 5–9.)

ACCELERATED EROSION. Geological erosion, then, has continued to operate at a slow, deliberate

Erosion

1780's   1980's

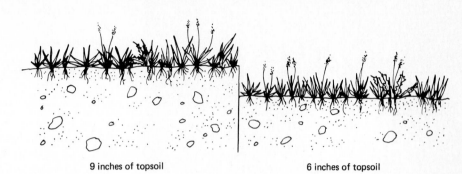

9 inches of topsoil   6 inches of topsoil

5–11 *When the United States was still largely a wilderness, the topsoil was about nine inches deep. Today, however, it is about six inches deep, one-third loss in only 200 years.*

pace for millions of years. However, with the appearance of humans on the world scene, a species of organisms intruded that could "reshape" the natural environment. As a result of human activities, an artificial type of erosion began that has operated at a much faster rate than natural erosion. (The severity of erosion in the United States is shown in Figures 5–11 and 5–12.) Surveys by the Soil Conservation Service have indicated that over a *billion* tons of soil are washed from land in the United States each year —an average soil loss of more than 300 tons for every square mile. This annual soil loss would fill

5–12 *Average annual sheet and rill erosion on cropland in tons per acre. The national average is 4.66 tons per acre.*

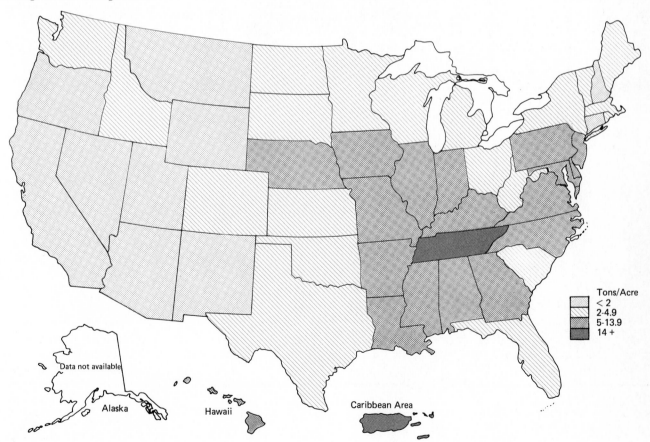

Data not available

Alaska

Hawaii

Caribbean Area

Tons/Acre
< 2
2-4.9
5-13.9
14 +

95

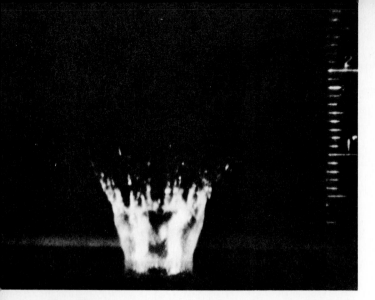

5-13 *A water explosion! This is a picture of a raindrop falling on farm soil. The duration of the splash from a raindrop is about 40 milliseconds. Nevertheless, the force generated by this tiny raindrop, together with millions of similar drops, triggers processes that lead to massive erosion of valuable topsoil.*

the boxcars of 18 freight trains, each long enough to circle the world at the equator (21). It is with this *accelerated erosion* that the conservationist is primarily concerned.

FACTORS DETERMINING THE RATE OF WATER EROSION

Volume and Intensity of Precipitation. Annual precipitation in the United States ranges from virtually nothing in some parts of Death Valley, California, to 140 inches in parts of Washington State. Such pronounced differences in rainfall will be expressed in part by differential erosion rates. However, even more important is the seasonal rainfall pattern.

A town in Florida once experienced a deluge of 24 inches of rain in only 24 hours. The soil loss resulting from runoff waters must have been severe. On

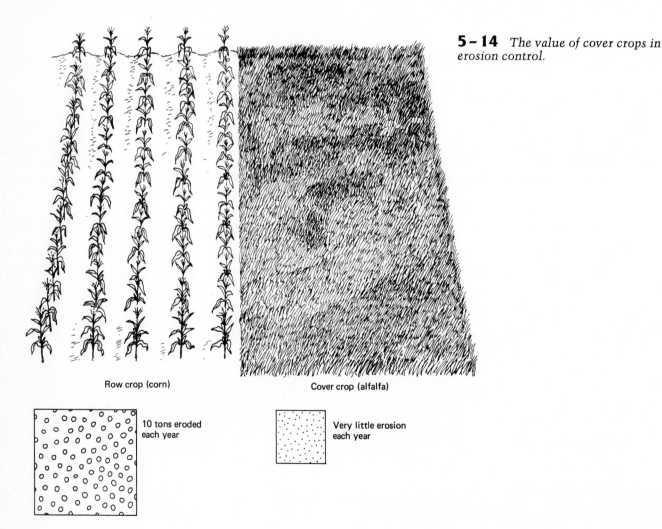

Row crop (corn)

Cover crop (alfalfa)

10 tons eroded each year

Very little erosion each year

5-14 *The value of cover crops in erosion control.*

96

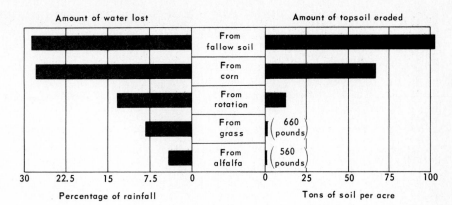

5 – 15 *Influence of vegetational cover on soil erosion and water runoff. Data from research conducted by the Soil Conservation Service at Bethany, Missouri, on Shelby loam on land with an 8 percent slope. Average annual rainfall in the area is 40 inches.*

the other hand, were this 24-inch rainfall the result of daily one-inch drizzles occurring over a period of 24 consecutive days, the erosion threat would have been negligible, simply because the soil would have had sufficient time in which to absorb the water. Surprisingly, even in the arid deserts of Nevada and Arizona, where annual rainfall averages five inches, excessive erosion occurs because the entire annual precipitation materializes in the form of a few torrential cloudbursts. As a result, the desert floor is dissected with canyons gouged out by runoff waters.

Topography of the Terrain. It would be expected that the intensity of water runoff and soil erosion would partially depend on the relative slope of the terrain. Steepness of slope is indicated in terms of percentages. Thus, a 10 percent slope would be one that drops ten feet over a horizontal distance of 100 feet. On farms planted with row crops like corn and cotton, a 100 percent increase in slope will result in an approximately 300 percent increase in soil loss caused by erosion.

Kind of Vegetational Cover. In the foothills of the southern Appalachians, where sandy clay loam is a representative erosible soil, pronounced differences in soil loss occur under varying types of vegetational cover. Bare soil erodes 2.5 times more rapidly than land planted to cotton, more than 4,000 times as rapidly as grass-covered land, and almost 32,000 times more quickly than land covered with virgin forests (4). (See Figures 5 – 14 and 5 – 15.)

Soil Condition. The structure of a soil can be improved by plowing under a crop of clover or alfalfa (green manuring) or simply by adding decaying organic material, such as leaves or barnyard manure. In Iowa, lands manured with 16, 8, and 0 tons

per acre incurred soil losses of roughly 4, 9, and 22 tons per acre, respectively (6). Soil loss from non-manured land was over five times that from heavily manured soil. The addition of organic material apparently improved the soil's water-absorbing ability. This trait, in turn, would be expressed in a more dense, vigorous growth of corn. The vegetative mantle thus established would further protect the soil. The developing corn root systems would also penetrate more vigorously between the individual soil particles and tend to bind them in place.

Control of Soil Erosion

We shall now discuss some of the major land management practices by which soil erosion may be controlled. These practices include: (1) contour farming, (2) strip-cropping, (3) conservation tillage, (4) terracing, (5) gully reclamation, and (6) establishment of shelterbelts.

CONTOUR FARMING. This erosion control practice may be defined as "plowing, seeding, cultivating, and harvesting *across* the slope, rather than *with* it. It was used by Thomas Jefferson, who wrote in 1813, "We now plow horizontally, following the curvature of the hills . . . scarcely an ounce of soil is now carried off." Jefferson, however, was an exception. In the early days of American agriculture, the farmer who could plow the straightest furrows (usually up and down slopes) was considered a master plowman and was praised by his neighbors.

An experiment conducted on a Texas cotton field with a 3 to 5 percent slope revealed that average annual water runoff from a noncontoured plot was 4.6 inches, whereas that for a contoured plot was 65.3 percent less, or 1.6 inches. (See Figure 5 – 16.)

97

5 – 16 *Bell County, Texas. The pattern of farm conservation is reflected in the fields of this Texas farmer, who uses contour farming to reduce rainwater runoff and its erosive effects on soil. The different shades are caused by different crops (strip-cropping); the pattern conforms to the contours of his fields, with the highest elevation where the smaller rings are. Besides slowing water so that it can soak into the soil better, such measures reduce siltation, the most common cause of water pollution in the United States, according to the U.S. Department of Agriculture.*

STRIP-CROPPING.   On land with a decided slope, planting crops on contour strips will be an effective erosion deterrent. For effective control the width of the contour strip should vary inversely with the length of the slope. When viewed from a distance, such farmland appears as a series of slender, curving belts of color. A row crop, such as corn, cotton, to-

5 – 17 *Contour strip-cropping on a Washara County, Wisconsin farm. The land is slightly sloping. Soil is silt loam.*

bacco, or potatoes, and a cover crop of hay or legumes are alternated along the contours. Strip-cropping is combined frequently with crop rotation, so that a strip planted to a soil-depleting, erosion-facilitating corn crop one year will be sown to a soil-enriching legume the next. (See Figure 5 – 17.)

CONSERVATION TILLAGE.   The highly effective erosion-control practice of conservation tillage is becoming more and more popular. Sometimes called minimum tillage, it involves reducing soil disturbance, associated with seeding, cultivating and harvesting, to an absolute minimum. The conventional moldboard plow, which cuts deep furrows, turns over the soil, and buries stubble, of course, cannot be used. It is replaced with heavy-duty seed drills, which plant the crops right through the stubble and dead weeds. This technique reduces soil disturbance to a minimum. It is used most effectively on cotton, corn, soybeans, and small grains.

An experiment conducted by the Soil Conservation Service in Georgia recently showed that conservation tillage reduced soil erosion from 26 tons to only .1 ton per acre annually (5). In addition to controlling erosion, conservation tillage reduces field preparation time by 20 percent and the

5–18 *Kit Carson County, Colorado. Conservation farming has brought about many new cultural methods. Conservation tillage, shown here, a method of cultivation that leaves the soil surface protected, was encouraged by the SCS in the Great Plains and has spread to many other areas through the nation.*

farmer's tractor expenses by 50 percent. It is estimated that in Texas alone conservation tillage saves farmers more than 2 million gallons in tractor fuel each year. Moreover, the decomposing plant residues serve as a source of soil nutrients. The practice of conservation tillage is growing rapidly on U.S. farmlands. (See Figures 5–18 and 5–19.)

One negative feature of this tillage technique, however, is that weeds, crop diseases, and insects tend to multiply in the stubble and other plant residue left on the ground. As a result, therefore, periodic applications of appropriate herbicides, fungicides, and pesticides must be made.

5–19 *Acreage under conservation tillage in the United States is increasing rapidly.*

GROWTH IN CONSERVATION TILLAGE
Includes mulch tillage, no-till, and other reduced tillage techniques

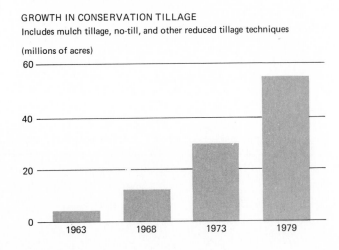

TERRACING. Terracing has been practiced by man for centuries. It was used by the Incas of Peru and by the ancient Chinese. Plagued with relatively dense populations and a scarcity of arable land, those civilizations were forced to till extremely steep slopes, even mountainsides, in order to prevent extensive hunger. The flat, steplike bench terraces that those ancient agriculturists constructed, however, are not amenable to today's farming methods. To be effective, terraces must check water flow before it attains sufficient velocity (three feet per second) to loosen and transport soil. (See Figure 5–20.) In the United States two major types of terraces are constructed to control erosion—the *ridge terrace* and the *channel terrace.*

1. *Ridge terrace.* This type of terrace is formed simply by constructing a ridge of earth at right angles to the slope—in other words across the path of water runoff. It is the characteristic terrace used on the Great Plains.
2. *Channel terrace.* This type of terrace is formed by digging a channel across the slope. It is frequently used in the Tennessee and Ohio Valleys, as well as the Southeast and the Mid-Atlantic States, where rainfall is high but the water-absorbing capacity of the soil is poor.

GULLY RECLAMATION. Gullies are especially frequent in the Southeast due to a long history of soil abuse and high-intensity rains which are common in this region. Gullies are danger signals that

99

5-20 *Terracing. A system of parallel level terraces has controlled sheet erosion on this farm near Templeton, Iowa. Slope is moderate to steep.*

indicate land is eroding rapidly and may become a wasteland unless erosion is promptly controlled. Some gullies work their way up a slope at the rate of fifteen feet a year. (See Figure 5-21A.) In North Carolina a 150-foot-deep gully was gouged out in only sixty years, "swallowing up" fence posts, farm implements, and buildings in the process. If relatively small, a gully can be plowed in and then seeded to a quick-growing "nurse" crop of barley, oats, or wheat. In this way, erosion will be checked until sod can become established. In cases of severe gullying, small check dams of manure and straw constructed at twenty-foot intervals may be effective, because silt will collect behind the dams and gradually fill in the channel. Dams may be constructed of brush or stakes held securely with a woven wire netting. Earthen, stone, and even concrete dams may be built at intervals along the gully. Once dams have been constructed and water runoff has been restrained, soil may be stabilized by planting rapidly growing shrubs, vines, and trees. Willows are effective. Not only does such pioneer vegetation discourage all future erosion, but it obliterates the ugliness of gaping gullies and provides food, cover, and breeding sites for wildlife. (See Figure 5-21B.)

SHELTER BELTS. In a strenuous attempt to prevent future dust bowls, the federal government

5-21 *(A) Gully erosion on a Minnesota farm. It was scalped and then planted with productive vegetation, primarily locust trees. (B) Five growing seasons later, the locust trees averaged 15 feet in height and not only served to control erosion, but provided wildlife cover and beautified the landscape.*

(B)

5–22 *This North Dakota farm is well protected from wind and snow by a 17-year-old windbreak of conifers, fruit trees, and shrubs.*

launched a massive shelter belt system in 1935. More than 218 million trees were planted on 30,000 farms across the Great Plains from North Dakota south to Texas. The green checkerboard patterns formed by the 20,000 miles of windbreaks have added color and variety to an otherwise monotonous prairie landscape. (See Figure 5–22.) In the Central Plains a typical shelter belt consists of one to five rows of trees planted on the western margin of a farm in a north-south line, to intercept winter's prevailing westerly winds. Conifers such as red cedar, spruce, and pine provide the best year-round protection. Soil blowing can be retarded even further by planting a few rows of grain between the rows of trees. A properly designed shelter belt of adequate height and thickness can reduce a wind

5–23 *Influence of a shelterbelt on wind velocity.*

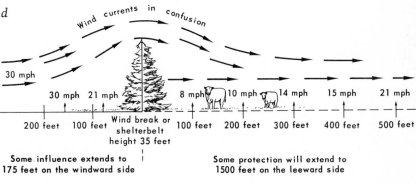

velocity of thirty miles per hour to only eight miles per hour to leeward of the trees (1). (See Figure 5–23.) Although windbreaks occupy valuable land that otherwise could be used for crop production, are relatively slow to grow, and must be fenced from livestock until the stands are well established, the accrued benefits far outweigh these minor disadvantages. In addition to controlling wind erosion, properly designed windbreaks provide aesthetic benefits, increase soil moisture by reducing evaporation and trapping snow, and provide habitat for wildlife. Moreover, the fuel requirements for heating and cooling nearby homes is reduced by about 28 percent (5). Unfortunately, a number of shelterbelts planted in the 1930s are now being removed — in some cases so that the farmer can use the wood as fuel, in other cases to make room for crops. Roughly 25 percent of the shelter belts in Oklahoma had been removed by the early 1980s.

The Price Support Program. Some government programs, such as those designed to stabilize farm income, may actually be more effective in controlling soil erosion than a number of the practices just described. For example, under some price support programs, the federal government pays the farmer to remove a specified acreage from production — in other words to let it stand idle. The primary objective, of course, is to reduce agricultural output and thus keep crop prices at a reasonably high level. Frequently the cropland taken out of production is that which is most vulnerable to erosion when cultivated. When those lands are idle, biological succession eventually covers the soil with an erosion-controlling mantle of vegetation.

The Soil Conservation Service and Its Program

The "black blizzards" of the 1930s may have had one redeeming feature: they alerted a hitherto apathetic nation to the plight of her soil resources more forcefully than a thousand urgent speeches could have done.

The federal government finally faced up to the soil erosion problem. It has spent about $20 billion on soil conservation programs in the last 45 years. In 1934 the newly organized Soil Erosion Service (SES) set up forty-one soil- and water-conservation demonstration projects. The labor force for these projects was supplied by Civilian Conservation Corps (CCC) workers drawn from about fifty camps (15). The projects impressed Congress so forcefully that it established the Soil Conservation Service (SCS) in 1935. The major function of the SCS has been to provide technical assistance to farmers and ranchers so that they can utilize each acre of land according to its capability, with methods that are as consistent with the needs of the soil as with those of the landowner.

The administrative and operative unit of the SCS program is the SCS district, which is organized and run by farmers and ranchers. Each district is staffed with a professional conservationist and several

5–24 *A conservationist and a soil scientist examine an alfalfa stand at Maple Lake, Minnesota, for insect damage and phosphate-potash deficiency. The land is class III with 7 percent slope. The corn will yield 80 to 85 bushels per acre.*

aides who work directly with the farmer on his land. (See Figure 5–24.) The technicians have had training in many related areas and include, ideally, a soil scientist, hydrologist, land appraiser, botanist, zoologist, agronomist, chemist, forester, game manager, and agricultural engineer all wrapped up in one superindividual. Any farmer located within the SCS district can request assistance in setting up and maintaining sound conservation practices in managing his farm. Participation in the SCS program is purely voluntary. As of today, more than 3,000 SCS districts have been organized (16), embracing roughly five million farms and 96 percent of the nation's farm and ranchlands.

One of the most significant accomplishments of the SCS early in its history was the development of a *land capability* classification. In this scheme land is classified into eight categories on the basis of its capability. Class I land is most suitable for crop production, being flat, fertile, and not vulnerable to erosion. Classes II and III may be used for growing crops, but proper erosion control measures must be practiced. Class IV land is suitable for grazing livestock. Classes V, VI, and VII may be used as rangeland or forest. Class VIII land, being stony, infertile, and/or hilly, is suitable only as wildlife habitat, wilderness, and/or recreation.

Each year more than one million acres of agricultural land, lying primarily on "the edge of town," are converted to urban use. Concrete has invaded the cornfield. "Jaguars" and "Mustangs" roar where cattle once roamed. As a result, the SCS has found a new challenge. As one SCS spokesman has

expressed it, "The country's 3,000 soil and water conservation districts have inherited the problems and opportunities of exploding suburbia. A common experience has been the replacement of two or three problems of individual farmers by the soil and water ailments of thousands of new homeowners." And the SCS has prepared soil-survey maps to meet not only the needs of prospective homeowners, but also those of highway engineers and layers of underground electric cables. Soils data are very useful to urban planners in helping them "to select and develop desirable spatial distribution patterns for industrial, commercial, residential . . . and recreational development" (30).

The Development of an SCS Farm Plan

In the event that a farmer requests technical assistance from his SCS district, four principal steps are followed in executing the conservation plan for his farm.

First, the technician and the farmer make an intensive acre-by-acre *survey* of the farm. On the basis of such criteria, including slope, fertility, stoniness, drainage, topsoil thickness, and susceptibility to erosion, the technician maps out each parcel of land on the basis of its capability. Each plot is ascribed a capability symbol in the form of a Roman numeral or color. This capability map is then superimposed on an aerial photograph.

Second, the farmer draws up a *farm plan* with

5–25 *Result of magnesium deficiency on potatoes. Healthy, normal plant is on left. Plants on right show progressive magnesium deficiency in the soil and fertilizer.*

assistance from the technician. This plan involves decisions on how each acre will be used and how it will be improved and protected. In other words, shall a given acre be used for crops, pasture, forests, or wilderness area? Usually alternative uses and treatments are considered. Some changes, of course, will not be made simply because they are impractical. The farmer would not move his barn, for example, just because the soil underneath is good for growing corn! In addition to the type of soil, such factors as farm size, amount of rainfall, potential market for crops, and the farmer's age and skills all enter into his ultimate choice concerning the use of his land.

Third, the treatment and uses called for in the plan are actually *applied* to the farm by the farmer, with assistance from one or more technicians. Although much of this application can be completed by the farmer himself, he may find it helpful to enlist the aid of the conservation technicians in connection with such techniques as terracing, contour plowing, strip cropping, establishment of farm ponds, gully control, shelter belting, proper use of cover crops in erosion control, use of legumes in fertility improvement, development of hedgerows as wildlife habitat, and selective cutting involved in the periodic harvest of his wood lot.

The final and most important phase of the program is its *maintenance* from year to year with the assistance of conservation technicians. As time passes, agricultural geneticists might develop a new strain of rust-resistant wheat or a tick-resistant breed of cattle; a plant may be introduced from the Orient or from South America which is more effective in fixing nitrogen than are native legumes; a new subspecies of bluegill may be discovered which thrives in farm ponds, or perhaps a new method of tilling wetlands will be available. These new developments then can gradually be incorporated into the over-all conservation program.

The SCS program has shown considerable stability despite minor variations from year to year. Each year roughly 3 per cent of our nation's farms are involved in about 100,000 basic conservation plans formulated by the SCS. Typically, contour farming practices under SCS technical aid are newly applied to about 3 to 5 million acres annually. Roughly 4 million acres of land are newly cover cropped. Each year, 50,000 to 75,000 new farm ponds are constructed, and 40,000 to 50,000 new terraces are built.

Loss of Soil Nutrients

Loss by Cropping

Before settlers came to North America, this vast continent was populated by ten million native Indians, considerably fewer people than inhabit the Chicago area today. Although those Indians raised a few crops (corn, pumpkins, beans, squash, and potatoes), for the most part they depended on hunting, fishing, and gathering berries, fruits, and nuts. The extensive biomes of prairies, deciduous forest, and coniferous forest were modified very little by human activity. Generation after generation of big bluestem grass, oak, hickory, beach, maple, spruce, fir, and pine lived and died. During their life span these plants absorbed large quantities of life-sustaining nutrients from the soil, channeling them into billions of tons of wood, bark, leaves, flowers, roots, and seeds. Eventually, however, when those organisms died, their body nutrients were restored to the soil from which they originated. Soil fertility was also replenished by the wastes and decaying bodies of animals.

Then came the settlers' agriculture, which replaced forest and prairie vegetation with corn, wheat, cabbage, beans, and potatoes. As a result, the normal circular flow of soil elements was greatly disrupted. Where once they were cycled, many soil nutrients now move down a one-way street — first being channeled into plant or animal crops, then into human digestive tracts and biomass, and then finally as human waste being flushed by sewage systems into rivers, lakes, and oceans. Livestock manure may have returned soil nutrients in some regions, especially before the farm tractor, but it was not sufficient to halt the trend toward soil impoverishment. As soil scientist Firman Bear so aptly states, "in many areas of the United States, the land has been turned into a nearly lifeless organic medium that must be nursed along like an invalid at the threshold of death" (2).

Loss by Erosion

Along with land cropping, erosion has also exacted a heavy toll on soil fertility. An example is the fertility-depleting effects of a dust storm that originated in Texas and moved northeastward into Iowa. The lighter soil, which was released on snow-covered land in Iowa, was compared with heavier soil released in Texas. Analyses revealed that the soil blown into Iowa contained ten times as much organic matter, nine times as much nitrogen, and nineteen times as much phosphoric acid as the heavier soil released in Texas (6). Theoretically it might be conceivable that Iowa farmers would benefit from this nutrient "windfall" by growing bumper corn crops on transplanted Texas soil. Unfortunately, however, much windblown topsoil accumulates on roof tops, city streets, parking lots, and factories. Some nutrient-rich soil may fall into lakes or even be blown out to sea and lost forever.

Water erosion has also taken its toll of productive soil. The Mississippi River is discharging 15 tons of valuable topsoil into the Gulf of Mexico every second. (Swish! Thirty tons were lost while you read that sentence!) Each year the combined agents of wind and water deprive America's future generations of crops, livestock, wildlife, and human beings of four billion tons of potentially valuable topsoil.

Loss Caused by Pesticides

Ironically, the very wonder chemicals — pesticides — that many farmers spray on their crops to increase yields may, in the final analysis, play an important role in *reducing* their ability to raise crops over the long run. Studies have shown that roughly *40 percent* of such persistent pesticides as chlordane, DDT, and toxaphene will remain in sandy loam soil intact at least fourteen years after they are applied (11). The use of such pesticides would seriously reduce soil fertility if they interfered with the activity of nitrogen-fixing bacteria. As Amos Turk of the City College of New York has written:

The effect on these organisms of an increasing concentration of poison in the soil is largely unknown. In many heavily sprayed areas of the world man is harvesting more food per acre than ever before. Yet some facts are coming to light which may presage future disaster. Studies in Florida have shown that *some chlorinated pesticides seriously inhibit nitrification by soil bacteria.* As is the case for many types of ecological disruptions, the long-term results are not known. Perhaps bacteria are immune, or will become immune, to pesticide spraying. But the stakes in the gamble are large, for if the microorganisms in the soil die, large plants . . . cannot live. . . . (29) [*Italics mine.*]

Temporary Restoration of Soil Fertility

USE OF LEGUMES. An acre of agricultural land probably loses 60 to 70 pounds of nitrogen yearly in the form of crops that have been harvested, as well as 20 to 25 pounds because of soil erosion. Thus, roughly 80 to 95 pounds of nitrogen per acre will be required annually to prevent a deficit. This can be met with *legumes.* Several species can be utilized, including alfalfa, clover, soybeans, and vetch. Some of the nitrogen fixed by the nodule bacteria is added to the soil and becomes available to the next crop in the rotation.

CROP ROTATION. Effective crop-rotation techniques may promote soil fertility as well as minimize erosion. A typical three-year rotation pattern might involve a wide-row, cultivated soil-depleting crop (corn, tobacco, or cotton) the first year; a narrow-row, noncultivated soil-depleting crop of wheat, barley, or oats the second year; and a dense, noncultivated cover crop (grasses or legumes) the third year. The grass-legume crop of the terminal rotation year would cover the soil with an almost continuous shield of leaves and stems; it would receive the full impact of rainfall and minimize erosion. Moreover, the nitrogen-fixing bacteria of the legume nodules would fix about 200 pounds of nitrogen per acre. When properly practiced, crop rotation would do much either to build up impoverished soils or to maintain the fertility of good soils.

Regrettably, in recent years the intensive use of commercial fertilizers has enabled farmers to shift from the soil-conserving practice of crop rotation to the soil-abusing practice of planting the same cash crop year after year on the same acreage. The eventual long-term results of such malpractice are always soil erosion and loss of fertility.

USE OF ORGANIC FERTILIZERS. When the American Indian put a fish head in each hill of corn, he was using a form of organic fertilizer. About 2 million tons of organic wastes are formed in the United States each year. Much of this could be used as fertilizer, including slaughterhouse and cannery waste, steam-treated garbage, and sludge from human sewage; ground-up horseshoe crabs are used along the Atlantic coast.

Soil Benefits. In addition to providing nutrients, the advantages of using organic fertilizers are multiple:

1. Erosion is reduced.
2. Soil moisture is more readily retained.
3. Soil is better aerated.

4. Soil bacteria grow and multiply.

5. Soil is buffered against sudden shifts in acidity and alkalinity.

Use of Animal Manure. Animal manure is the dung and urine of all farm animals such as horses, cattle, swine, sheep, goats, and poultry. Human beings have used animal excrement to fertilize crops for thousands of years. The ancient King Laertes was not too proud to put dung (animal manure) on his farmland with his bare hands.

A corn-fed dairy cow returns to the soil (in excrement) 75 percent of the nitrogen, 80 percent of the phosphoric acid, and 90 percent of the potash obtained from her feed. Even then, a rather large volume of manure is required for proper fertilization. For example, in order to provide a given acre with adequate supplies of nitrogen, phosphorus, and potassium would require all the manure produced by 3 cows, 22 hogs, or 207 chickens (26). The application of 5 tons of manure per acre in Michigan yielded 46 bushels of corn per acre, in contrast to the 35-bushel-per-acre yield of nonmanured land — a 31.4 percent increase.

An interesting source of organic fertilizer is the excrement, or *guano*, of wild birds and bats. For many years, four to five million fish-eating cormorants have maintained dense breeding colonies on the Chincha Islands off the coast of Peru. Over the centuries, the guano of those birds has hardened and accumulated to a depth of over 100 feet. Rich in both nitrogen and phosphorus, the deposits have been mined and shipped all over the world as a form of fertilizer.

5–26 *Use of treated sewage as fertilizer and soil builder on farmland. Spreading of sewage effluent on terraced land is shown near Monticello, Missouri. Crops will be planted after spreading operation has been completed.*

5–27 *Green manuring. Hairy vetch (a legume) being plowed under at a farm near Storey, Oklahoma, prior to planting of a cotton crop.*

Even though most countries utilize human waste to increase soil fertility, this practice has been largely shunned in the United States. However, a few sewage-disposal plants have prepared commercial fertilizer from sewage sludge. For many years the city of Milwaukee has marketed a sludge product called Milorganite, which has been used as a fertilizer and soil conditioner. Chicago is exporting its sewage sludge to fertilize sandy farmlands sixty miles away. It is expected that by the year 2015 that nitrogen- and phosphorus-rich sludge will have been piped or sprayed on 21,500 acres, and that bumper crops of field corn and pasture grasses will be raised on the previously infertile soil (20). (See Figure 5–26.)

Use of Plant Manure. The process of turning under green crops to improve soil productivity is known as green manuring. Its effect on soil is similar to that of animal manure. With the latter becoming more scarce in some areas as farms become more mechanized, green manure has assumed an especially significant role. (See Figure 5–27.)

USE OF INORGANIC FERTILIZERS

Nitrogen Fertilizers. Nitrogen forms up to 0.3 percent by weight of dark-brown prairie topsoil — a total of 4,000 pounds per acre (1). Once such soil is subjected to intensive cropping or severe erosion, however, the initially abundant nitrogen content may be rapidly depleted.

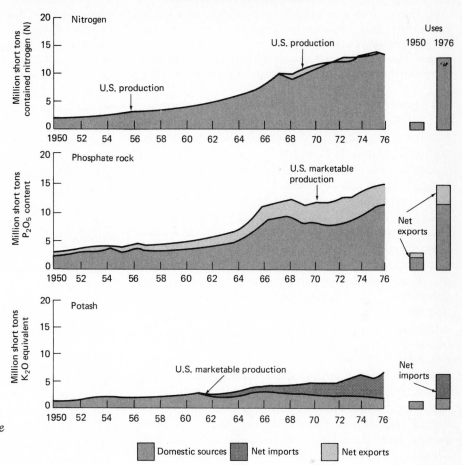

FERTILIZERS AND CHEMICALS

5-28 *Sources and uses of major fertilizers in the United States. Note that fertilizer use is increasing rapidly.*

The greatest single inorganic source of nitrogen currently used in American agriculture is the Haber process, in which nitrogen and hydrogen are combined under pressure in the presence of a catalyst to form ammonia. The nitrogen may be in the form of ammonia and ammonium salts or in the form of urea and nitrates derived from the ammonia.

Balanced Fertilizers. A balanced fertilizer is a mixture (in varying ratios) of nitrogen, phosphorus, and potassium. A bag of balanced fertilizer must carry a printed guarantee of the nutrients it contains. The guarantee is usually stated in percentages. Thus, a 5-10-5 mixture contains 5 percent total nitrogen, 10 percent available phosphoric acid, and 5 percent water-soluble potash. The tonnage of fertilizers used in the United States has increased greatly in recent years. (See Figure 5-28.) Unfortunately, the world's known reserves of phosphate rock, from which phosphorus is obtained for fertil-

izer manufacture, are rapidly dwindling. They will be gone in forty years. When this occurs, the high level of food production that characterizes America and a few other nations will come to an end.

Disadvantages of Inorganic Fertilizers. The inorganic fertilizers, however, are not an unmixed blessing, for their continued use may result in subtle adverse changes of soil structure, contribute to water-pollution problems, and be harmful to human health. Barry Commoner, the noted ecologist from Washington University, St. Louis, Missouri, has aptly described the pollution problem:

These fertilizers greatly increase immediate crop yields; but at the same time, the impoverishment of soil organic matter, by altering the physical character of the soil (especially its porosity to oxygen), sharply reduces the efficiency with which the added fertilizer is taken up by the crop. As a result, unused nitrogen fertilizer drains out of the soil into rivers and lakes, where it joins with the nitrate imposed on the water by the effluent of sewage treatment plants, causing overgrowths of green plants and the resultant organic pollution. The drainage of nitrogen from fertilizer has already destroyed the self-purifying capability of nearly every river in Illinois. (6)

The gravity of these problems can be better appreciated when we consider that the use of commercial fertilizers in the United States has increased sixteenfold in the last 25 years.

The exorbitant use of nitrate fertilizers in the United States has also been indirectly responsible for an increased rate of *methemoglobinemia*, a serious blood disease of infants that may be lethal. The excessive nitrate not absorbed by crop root systems may be leached downward to the water table by rainwater and eventually contaminate private or municipal wells. The nitrate in itself is not highly deleterious. However, when it enters an infant's intestines, the *nitrate* is converted into *nitrite.* The nitrite them combines with the hemoglobin (the red-blood pigment) to form methemoglobin. Unfortunately, the capacity of methemoglobin to carry oxygen is much less than that of hemoglobin. As a result, the infant attempts to compensate by breathing more rapidly and strenuously. In severe cases, mental impairment results, because the brain does not get enough oxygen. Occasionally this disorder causes an infant to suffocate. The streams of California's Central Valley have perhaps the highest nitrate level in the nation. Public health authorities in the area have therefore suggested that babies be given only bottled water (12). Illinois, Missouri, Minnesota, and Wisconsin have all had disturbing numbers of cases of methemoglobinemia.

Soil Nutrients and Human Health

Some authorities have been concerned that both agronomists and farmers are so preoccupied with crop yield that the crop's nutritional value is inadvertently being ignored. *Quantity* is being confused with *quality.* And to increase crop quantity, American farmers add inorganic nitrate fertilizers. As Commoner has so pungently stated, "farmers are hooked on nitrates like a junkie is hooked on heroin" (6). Soil scientist A. G. Norman, of the University of Michigan, writes, "High yields are not . . . synonymous with a high content of nu-

trient elements. . . . Crops from well-fertilized plots may have a *lower* content of some health-essential elements than those from poorly yielding plots; the *addition* of a fertilizer may cause a *reduction* in content of some of the other nutrient elements. . ." (14). [*Italics mine.*]

Despite remarkable accomplishments in nutritional research within the last few decades, frankly, we are not able to pinpoint all the nutrients in vegetables and grains that are essential to human health. An ear of corn, an orange, or a cabbage may appear attractive and wholesome and may even be delicious. However, if certain health-essential constituents are lacking, human beings may well incur serious nutritional inadequacies by subsisting extensively on food grown in soil "doctored up" with a few inorganic commercial fertilizers in the interests of *crop volume* rather than human health.

Why Don't American Farmers Do a Better Job of Soil Conservation?

It is extremely difficult for an American citizen who is not a member of the agricultural community to understand why our nation's farmers have permitted their soils to deteriorate. After all, the technical knowledge for insuring that almost *no* erosion could occur from a given farm acre is available. Moreover, professional assistance to apply that knowledge is also to be had at the asking from the farmer's Soil Conservation Service district. So what are the factors that have contributed to the sorry plight of our nation's soils? Let's examine some of them.

1. *The farmers' independent spirit.* As a result of their fiercely independent nature, farmers will resist applying effective soil conservation measures on a cost-sharing basis with the federal govenment, if in the process they will lose some freedom in the way they operate their farms. They may therefore reject a government-designed plan even though they may realize that it may benefit them financially.
2. *Tenant farming.* The owner-operator might be willing to invest time, energy, and money in effective soil conservation measures, even if the "payoff" in enhanced crop yields may not materialize for several years. However, a tenant farmer, who often rents a given farm on a year-

to-year basis, would obviously not have the same motivation.

3. *Limited federal funding.* Federal funds for cost-sharing programs designed to upgrade soils are shrinking. Take the Agricultural Conservation Program (ACP), for example. It is the oldest, largest, and best known of all such programs. Nevertheless, its annual budget has remained around $200 million for several years despite skyrocketing inflation. And in the early 1980s, President Reagan proposed to slash even these grossly inadequate funds by 25 percent.

4. *Some federal erosion-control programs are not meeting their principal objectives:* curbing soil losses on the most erosion-vulnerable lands. For example, in the early 1980s more than 52 percent of cost-shared erosion control practices were being applied on lands where the erosion rate was *less* than 5 tons per acre per year. Only 20 percent of the funds were being spent on lands that were eroding more than 14 tons per acre per year, and which were responsible for 86 percent of our nation's erosion losses.

5. *Soil conservation measures are expensive.* For example, contour farming requires much more tractor time (as well as costly diesel fuel) than straight row farming. It takes considerably more time (and skill) for the farmer to follow the curving topographical pattern than to plow straight up and down the hills. It is estimated that the application of soil conservation measures may add 10–20 percent to the farmer's operating expenses — and this at a time when the profit margins on most farms are razor-thin.

6. *Soil conservation measures result in a reduced income for the short term.* Suppose, for example, that the farmer were growing wheat on a steep, severely eroding hillside and replaced the wheat with erosion-controlling grass. The annual income for that farmer from the grassed area would be nil.

7. *Modern farm machinery promotes erosion.* Tractors used by today's farmers are big, fast, and impressive. However, they cannot turn on a dime. To be efficient they must work on long, straight rows. In order to accommodate these huge tractors farmers had to combine some of their small fields into one huge field perhaps a half-mile on one side. It is regrettable that such soil conservation applications as terraces and shelter belts get in the way of these large trac-

tors. They also make it inconvenient for the farmer to use modern center-pivot irrigation systems. As a result, thousands of miles of shelter belts and terraces have been sacrificed on the altar of modern farming technology.

8. *American farmers are in the business of feeding the world.* Federal farm policy-makers from time to time put pressure on the American farmer to maximize production so that huge food exports can be made. Such sales, of course, help the United States maintain a favorable balance of trade and are vital to a strong national economy. Major exports, amounting to millions of tons of grain were made to Russia in 1973 and again in 1981. In the early 1980s roughly 40 percent of our nation's farmland was devoted to export production. However, this production is possible only at the cost of considerable abuse to the land. As agricultural expert R. Neil Sampson writes in his highly acclaimed book *Farmland or Wasteland* "If our maximum possible foreign sales were given a value of 100, and the land abuse caused by that level of production suggests that only 50 years of such high intensity production is possible, it is more likely that our *sustainable* level of production is somewhere around 80 or 85. Holding that level of production indefinitely makes a great deal more sense and probably holds the promise to be far more financially rewarding than pushing for all out production that can only last a relatively short time. . . ."

9. *The farmer's pay-off for instituting soil conservation measures is not immediate, but may take years.* Crop yields will not increase until the soil's quality is built up. As a result many farmers will invest in fertilizers which will pay off in increased yields *the same year.* To the average farmer, who is strapped financially, it makes much more sense to spend one dollar on fertilizer in April of 1985 and get a $1.10 return on his investment in September of 1985, than to invest one dollar in soil conservation practices in 1985 and wait until 1995 to get a $1.10 return — maybe.

10. *The farmers may see no future for their farms.* The age of the average American farmer is increasing. At present it is about 50–55 years. And at that age farmers are possibly getting more interested in retirement than in raising the productivity of their soil. In any event, they

may have promised to sell their land to developers or to a mining company interested in the coal underneath the soil. And if this land is going to be covered some day with homes, paved roads and shopping centers, or if it is going to be stripped for coal, the only policy that makes any sense to farmers at all may be to "mine" the soil of its nutrients right up to the day of sale.

11. *Farmers lack appreciation of the gravity of the soil erosion problem.* This was revealed in a recent study in Nebraska. The overwhelming number of Nebraska farmers did not believe that erosion rates of 10–15 tons per acre per year were serious. When questioned by soil conservation researchers as to the reason for their lack of concern they answered something like this: "Even though my farm is experiencing these rates of erosion my crop yields have not declined." And of course they were right. But the only reason their yields remained high was because their increased use of fertilizers, herbicides, and insecticides had *masked* the effect of the erosion losses. (And, of course, such use causes massive water pollution problems downstream from the farm, as will be described in Chapter 8.)

12. *Soil conservation officials simply have not been able to make soil conservation relevant to the modern farmer* — despite the expenditure of roughly $20 billion since the Dust Bowl era. Admittedly, the task is enormous, especially in the face of today's economic pressures. But the job must be done — and soon. As R. Neil Sampson writes: "The fact that the United States Department of Agriculture, after 100 years in business and over 40 years of soil conservation programs, still cannot provide a convincing analysis to demonstrate the full cost of soil erosion to either an individual farmer or to society (in general) is a disgrace. It is proof that such problems have not had a very high priority over the years. . . ."

13. *Political factors.* These are described by Robert B. Delano, president of the American Farm Bureau Federation, in his guest article in this chapter.

What Can Be Done?

Something must be done to halt the degradation of our nation's soil. The USDA must obviously try something new and imaginative. The old methods simply are not working. But what actually can be done? What are some of the policy options?

Political Factors Hampering Proper Soil Management

Robert B. Delano
President, AMERICAN
FARM BUREAU FEDERATION

To a large degree, soil- and water-conservation problems are those of a government working at cross purposes. The Soil Conservation and Cooperative Extension Services are energetic and generally effective. Together they have enlisted the deep concern and practical self-interest of most farmers and ranchers.

But "politics" has been the driving force back of federal farm price support programs, resulting in production incentives for wheat, feed grains, cotton, and rice at high levels completely out of line with market demand. Politically motivated high price supports have encouraged farmers to produce regardless of other considerations, with some production taking place on fragile grasslands highly subject to wind and water erosion.

Farmers suffered terribly from double-digit inflation created by years of federal overspending [and] political and monetary irresponsibility. Embargo attempts to use food as a weapon added further uncertainty and instability. Many farmers perceived increased production as the best route to farm survival.

I agree with University of Minnesota Agricultural Economics Professor Philip M. Raup that inflation and uncertainty are deadly enemies of conservation and that "the most effective expression of a public interest in conservation activities will be to bring inflation under control and reduce uncertainty in agricultural markets."

1. *More research.* Additional research on erosion control methods might result in a technological breakthrough which would be less costly than traditional methods and therefore be more attractive to the farmer.
2. *Focus on the most serious erosion problems.* In this way the limited funds that are available would be used to greater advantage.
3. *Provide strong disincentives to permitting soil quality to deteriorate.*
   a. Laws could be passed that would make it illegal to permit soil degradation.
   b. Fines could be imposed on farmers proportionate to the amount of soil that erodes from their land. They would be fined "by the ton" of erosion loss.
   c. Negligent farmers could become ineligible for federal loans.
4. *Provide strong incentives to maintain and improve soil quality.*
   a. Farmers could be paid a cash bonus in proportion to the amount of soil they "hold" on the land despite the erosive forces of wind and water.
   b. *Green Ticket certification.* Farmers employing sound soil conservation measures on their farms would each be awarded a Green Ticket after their lands had been examined by a certification committee from the local Soil Conservation District. As holders of Green Ticket status the farmers would be eligible for multiple state and federal benefits. Among these benefits might be low-interest loans and breaks on real estate and income taxes. These tax breaks would be based on the premise that the farm operations of the Green Ticket holders were lesser financial burdens to society than that of negligent farmers. After all, erosion causes much off-farm environmental damage such as water pollution, destruction of fish habitat, defilement of scenic beauty, siltation of reservoirs, and so on. Therefore, the Green Ticket farmers should receive financial benefits for preventing such environmental abuse in addition to upgrading their lands. Hopefully, the Green Ticket certification would develop pride in the farmers, attract acclaim from the members of their agricultural communities, and serve as a catalyst in stimulating other farmers to win this award.

The Future

Our nation's agriculture will be in deep trouble — soon. Its ability to produce food and fiber for Americans, let alone for many of the world's hungry, will be in serious jeopardy if current trends continue. You may say: "But how can that be? The supermarkets are jam-packed with attractive fruits and vegetables, meats and fruit juices, pastries, cookies, and milk." True. Right now, in the mid-1980s American farmers are producing more food per acre than ever before. But they are doing it at a price — a price measured in greater vulnerability to erosion, reduced supply of nutrients from natural sources, and reduced ability of the soil to hold water and oxygen. In other words, for a few short years we will be witnesses to a curious paradox: *American farm production is at an all-time high at the same time that our soil resource is deteriorating at record speed.* A growing number of soil scientists firmly believe that if this trend continues, at some point crop yields will drop suddenly — perhaps as much as 40 to 60 percent. It is obvious that such a fall-off of food production would trigger both a national and global calamity.

Again you might raise a question: "But can't we simply put more acres to the plow?" Yes, we can — such a strategy might be a short-term answer to our problem. We do have about 130 million acres of cropland in reserve. But because we are losing roughly three million acres per year due to *buckshot urbanization,* flooding, and erosion, simple arithmetic tells us that in about 40 years, well within your lifetime as a college student, every last acre of that reserve will be put to use. As a matter of fact, that reserve may well be in use much sooner, because the loss of farmland due to urbanization is increasing at an exponential rate. Urban sprawl is not now confined merely to the outskirts of towns, but is now a pervasive pattern throughout much of rural America. And, of course, when every possible food calorie is already being squeezed from every acre, every new shopping center, parking lot, highway or townhouse built over cropland causes a *direct reduction in yield.* And this dilemma may well be facing American agriculture by the year 2000. At that point, the cost of food will skyrocket. "But," you might ask, "can't more food be coaxed from each acre by still more intensive use of pesticides and herbicides, by introducing superior strains of crops, and by using more irrigation water?" Charles

111

E. Little, president of the American Land Forum, an influential organization devoted to upgrading our nation's soil resource, somberly answers that question: "It is possible to substitute fertilizer for land, unless, of course, the next increment of fertilizer costs more than the increased yield will bring in prices. It is possible to substitute pesticides for land, unless it costs more to kill the pests than to lose the crop they destroy. It is possible to substitute water for land, diesel fuel for land, new genetic stocks for land—all of these, but only up to a point. And many believe that industrial agriculture as practiced in the Western nations has reached that point . . ." (18).

A number of historians are of the opinion that the United States is about to lose her position of power and leadership in the world. They list several reasons: lack of abundant oil supplies, lack of nuclear missiles, lack of innovative technology, and lack of devotion to the work ethic. Perhaps another "lack" should be added to the list: the lack of ability to protect and maintain her soil—the greatest food-producing resource ever found on the face of the earth (18).

Rapid Review

1. American farmers must increase their food production to (1) satisfy sharply increasing food needs in the United States, (2) meet a moral commitment to help nourish millions of hungry people abroad, and (3) maintain the economic well-being of our nation.

2. The modern industrialized agroecosystem developed by human beings can be compared with a natural ecosystem, such as a prairie or forest, in terms of such characteristics as elemental cycles, energy inputs, limiting factors, population curves, and ecological succession.

3. A field of corn has many characteristics of the pioneer stage of an ecological succession, including (a) high productivity, (b) simple straight-line food chains, (c) a minimal amount of organic matter, (d) a small number of species, (e) the small size of organisms, (f) the short life cycle of organisms (crops), (g) the poor conservation of nutrients, and (h) poor stability.

4. The agricultural system of civilizations like that in the Middle East and Noth Africa frequently collapsed because of the excessive erosion that followed mismanagement of the land.

5. The severe dust storms that ravaged the Dust Bowl in the 1930s were the product of a combination of factors including severe drought, high-velocity winds, overgrazing, and poor soil management. In one storm alone more than 300 million tons of soil were blown away. Two to twelve inches of topsoil was carried to the Atlantic seaboard. Millions of farmers and ranchers in states like Oklahoma, Colorado, Kansas, and Texas suffered severe economic hardship and were forced to seek employment in urban centers.

6. Even though the federal government has spent about $20 billion on programs to upgrade our nation's soil, it is actually in poorer condition today than back in the Dust Bowl era of the 1930s. Moreover, the annual increase in food production slumped from 2.1 to 1.7 percent between 1939 and 1965. Soil-erosion losses have amounted to almost 4 billion tons annually.

7. Some of our soils are 1,000 times more erodible than others. Erosion losses range from 8 to 200 tons per acre per year.

8. The rate of water erosion is influenced by such factors as (a) volume and intensity of precipitation, (b) topography of terrain, (c) type of vegetational cover, and (d) soil condition.

9. Effective methods of erosion control include (a) contour farming, (b) strip-cropping, (c) conservation tillage, (d) terracing, and (e) shelter belting.

10. More than 3,000 Soil Conservation Districts have been organized. They include over five million farms and about 96 percent of the nation's crop and ranchland acreage. The major function of the districts is to provide technical and financial assistance to the farmer so that he can effectively manage each acre of land according to its capability.

Key Words and Phrases

Accelerated erosion	Haber process
Animal manure	Heterotype
Balanced fertilizer	Inorganic fertilizer
Buckshot urbanization	Legumes
Cobalt	Macronutrients
Conservation tillage	Micronutrients
Contour farming	Methemoglobinemia
Dust Bowl	Milorganite
Energy subsidy	Molybdenum
Geological erosion	Monotype
Guano	Organic fertilizer

Plant manure
Shelter belt
Soil and Water Resources
    Act of 1977

Soil Conservation
    Service (SCS)
Strip-cropping
Terracing

Questions and Topics for Discussion

1. Suppose that a farmer did not harvest his crop of corn but abandoned his farm and let nature take over. Explain the vegetational changes that probably would occur during the next two or three years.
2. Discuss the advantages and disadvantages of removing all energy subsidies from American agriculture.
3. In what ways is a field of corn similar to a pioneer stage in a natural ecological succession? In what ways is it different?
4. Suppose that most Americans raised all the food they required in their own backyard family garden and by keeping a few chickens or pigs. In other words, suppose that the agricultural ecosystem gradually shifted from a few million big farms to thirty million small family farms. Discuss the pros and cons of such a development.
5. Suppose that all commercial fertilizers were banned for agricultural use. Discuss the advantages and disadvantages of such a development.
6. Suppose that all pesticides and herbicides were banned for agricultural use. Discuss the advantages and disadvantages of such a development.
7. Our soil resources are in worse condition today than during the Dust Bowl days, even though roughly $20 billion has been spent by federal and state governments to upgrade this resource. Who is to blame? The farmers? The legislators? The soil scientists? The public? You and me? Discuss your answer.
8. Discuss the advantages and disadvantages of conservation tillage.
9. Some soil scientists project that, by the year 2000, if current trends continue, no further increase in food production by American farmers will be possible. Suppose, however, that the population of the United States and the world continue to increase at present rates. Discuss the probable effect on our economy. What will be the source of the needed food supplies? How will the health of our people be affected? What will be the effect on food prices? What will be

the effect on government stability? On possible international conflict?
10. Discuss the advantages and disadvantages of buckshot urbanization. Are there possible alternatives? If so, what are they? How would they be implemented?
11. Some years ago a distinguished American senator from South Carolina commented on the malnourishment problems in Appalachia and in the ghettos of our big cities with the words: "There has been hunger since the time of Jesus Christ and there always will be." Was he correct? Was his attitude correct? Discuss your answer. Just what are our responsibilities in terms of preventing starvation in the United States? In the world?
12. Compare modern agriculture to the hunting and food-gathering culture of early humans in terms of their disruption of natural ecosystems.
13. Severe drought recurs in the United States at intervals of roughly 21 to 22 years. Were the black blizzards of the Dust Bowl era directly caused by drought? Could they have been prevented despite the drought? Discuss your answer.
14. Discuss the statement: "The only energy an ear of corn on your dinner table represents is the solar energy involved in photosynthesis that made the development of that ear possible."
15. Suppose that the cost of gasoline and diesel fuel became so great that farmers were forced to abandon their power equipment, such as tractors, and once again go back to the horse-and-plow type of farming characteristic of the early part of this century. Would food production increase in the long run? Would it decrease? What would be the overall effects on our economy? What would be the long-range effects on the health of the agricultural ecosystem? What effect would it have on the quality of soil?
16. What could Congress and the state legislative bodies do about buckshot urbanization? Why haven't they done more to date? Discuss the pros and cons of legislation that would outlaw buckshot urbanization completely.
17. Name seven micronutrients and eight macronutrients required by plants.
18. Briefly describe four symptoms in plants that suggest that they are deficient in certain nutrients.

113

19. Compare soil fertility in a state like Pennsylvania today with its fertility before the discovery of America by Columbus.
20. The American Indians put a fish head in each hill of corn. Although they didn't realize it, this practice was beneficial in six different ways. Can you list them?
21. A California irrigation farmer used considerable amounts of the persistent type of pesticide to control an insect infestation on his broccoli crop. During the next few years the crops grown in that same field showed severe symptoms of nutrient deficiency. Could this be a cause-and-effect relationship? Explain your answer.

Endnotes

1. Allen, Shirley W., and Austin W. Leonard. *Conserving Natural Resources.* New York: McGraw-Hill, 1966.
2. Bear, Firman E. *Earth: The Stuff of Life.* Norman: U. of Oklahoma, 1962.
3. Bennett, Hugh Hammond. *Elements of Soil Conservation.* New York: McGraw-Hill, 1955.
4. Coates, R. *Environmental Geology.* New York: Wiley, 1981.
5. Comis. "Research Center Studies Conservation Tillage." *Soil and Water Conservation News,* 2 (Nov. 1981).
6. Commoner, Barry. "Starvation: It's Possible." *The Progressive* (April 1970), 12–18.
7. Cook, R. L. *Soil Management for Conservation and Production.* New York: Wiley, 1962.
8. Costle, Douglas M. "Commonsense Talk About Agriculture and the Environment." Address delivered before American Farm Bureau Federation, April 27, 1977. Washington, DC: Environmental Protection Agency.
9. Dale, Tom, and Vernin G. Carter. *Topsoil and Civilization.* Norman: U. of Oklahoma, 1955.
10. Dasmann, Raymond F. *Environmental Conservation.* New York: Wiley, 1968.
11. Donahue, Roy L., Roy H. Follett, and Rodney W. Tolloch. *Our Soils and Their Management.* Danville, IL: Interstate, 1976.
12. Ehrlich, Paul R., and Anne H. Ehrlich. *Population, Resources, Environment.* San Francisco: Freeman, 1970.
13. Fritschner, Sarah. "Life in the Food Chain." *Washington Post,* November 19, 1981.
14. Herber, Lewis. *Our Synthetic Environment.* New York: Knopf, 1962.
15. Highsmith, Richard M., Jr., Granville Jensen, and Robert D. Rudd. *Conservation in the United States.* Chicago: Rand McNally, 1962.
16. Hill, W. L. "The Need for Fertilizers." *Farmer's World: The Yearbook of Agriculture.* Washington, DC: Department of Agriculture, 1964.
17. Leighton, M. M. "Geology of Soil Drifting on the Great Plains." *Scientific Monthly,* 47 (July 1938), 22–23.
18. Little, Charles E. (ed.) *Land and Food: The Preservation of U.S. Farmland.* American Land Forum Report No. 1, Spring, 1979.
19. Lowdermilk, W. C. "Conquest of the Land Through 7,000 Years." *Agriculture Information Bulletin,* No. 99, Washington, DC: Soil Conservation Service, Department of Agriculture, 1953.
20. Marx, Wesley. *Man and His Environment: Waste.* New York: Harper, 1971.
21. Miller, G. Tyler, Jr. *Living in the Environment: Concepts, Problems and Alternatives.* New York: Wadsworth, 1981.
22. Moran, Joseph M., Michael D. Morgan, and James H. Wiersma. *An Introduction to Environmental Sciences.* San Francisco: Freeman, 1980.
23. *Newsweek,* 5 (March 30, 1935), 5–6.
24. Odum, Eugene P. *Fundamentals of Ecology.* 3rd ed. Philadelphia: Saunders, 1971.
25. Olson, L. "Erosion: A Heritage from the Past." *Agri. Hist.,* 13 (1939), 161–170.
26. Pimentel, David, and John Krummel. "America's Agricultural Future." *Ecologist* 7, No. 7, 254–261.
27. Steinbeck, John. *The Grapes of Wrath.* New York: Viking, 1939.
28. Stout, P. R., and C. M. Johnson. "Trace Elements." In *Soils: The Yearbook of Agriculture.* Washington, DC: Department of Agriculture, 1957.
29. Turk, Amos, Jonathan Turk, and Janet T. Wittes. *Ecology, Pollution, Environment.* Philadelphia: Saunders, 1972.
30. University of Wisconsin Extension Service. "The Soil Survey: A Guide to Rural and Urban Development." *Special Circular, No. 91.* Madison: University of Wisconsin Extension Service, 1964.

Suggested Readings for the Interested Student

Barlow, T. "Solving the Soil Erosion Problem." *Journal of Soil and Water Conservation,* 32 (July–Aug. 1977), 147.
Brady, N. C. *The Nature and Property of Soils.* 8th ed. New York: Macmillan, 1974. This is an authoritative, comprehensive treatment of the subject. It is a classic.

Brill, Winston J. "Agricultural Microbiology." *Scientific American* (Sept. 1981), 199–215.

Brown, L. R. "Vanishing Cropland." *Environment,* **20** (1978), 6–15, 30–34. This is a superb discussion of the many factors contributing to cropland depletion.

Clapham, W. B., Jr. *Human Ecosystems.* New York: Macmillan, 1981, pp. 149–159. This is an excellent middle-level treatment of the characteristics and regulation of agroecosystems.

Dideriksen, Raymond I., and R. Neil Sampson. "Important Farmlands: A National Viewpoint." *Journal of Soil and Water Conservation,* **31** (1976), 196. This is an excellent discussion of the key role of crop-producing soils in the well-being of our nation.

Evans, L. T. "The Natural History of Crop Yield." *American Scientist,* **68** (July–Aug. 1981), 388–397.

Heichel, G. H. "Agricultural Production and Energy Resources." *American Scientist,* **64** (Jan.–Feb. 1976), 64–72. This is a penetrating study of energy subsidies in modern agriculture, combined with recommendations for more effective use of energy in the years ahead.

Little, Charles E. (ed.) *Land and Food: The Preservation of U.S. Farmland.* American Land Forum Report No. 1, Spring, 1979.

Pimental, David *et al.* "Land Degradation: Effects on Food and Energy Resources." *Science,* **194** (October 8, 1976), 149–155. This is an outstanding overview of our nation's soil-erosion problems.

Sanchez, P. A., and S. W. Buol. "Soils of the Tropics and the World Food Crisis." *Science,* **188** (Feb. 21, 1975), 598–603.

Triplett, B., and D. M. Van Doren. "Agriculture Without Tillage." *Scientific American,* **263** (Jan. 1977), 28–33. This is an excellent evaluation of conservation tillage and its role in saving soil, water, and energy in the agricultural ecosystem.

6 Feeding a Hungry Planet

Malthusian Overpopulation and Food Scarcity

Of all the adverse consequences of the current crush of people on planet Earth, undoubtedly the one with the greatest potential for human disaster is widespread hunger and malnutrition. This problem was predicted in 1798 by the British economist Robert Malthus. Malthus argued that the only way the dilemma could ultimately be resolved was by pestilence, warfare, starvation, and other human calamities, which today we would sum up as "environmental resistance" (ER).

Two thirds of the world's population is suffering either from undernutrition or chronic malnutrition, or both. (See Figure 6 – 1.) Undernutrition is a quantitative phenomenon characterized by an inadequate amount of food, resulting in half-empty stomachs and gnawing hunger pains. Nutritionists assume that the average person must have a minimum of 2,200 calories daily. Western Europeans and North Americans get 3,200 calories daily. They are among the fortunate. Have you ever gone to bed hungry? Most Americans are *overfed*. Compare our situation to that of the average Indian, who consumes only 1,600 calories daily — only half of what we're getting. (See Figure 6 – 2.) This 600-daily-calorie deficit undermines strength, causes severe mental and physical lethargy, and weakens resistance to a broad spectrum of diseases. Chronic malnutrition, on the other hand, is a qualitative phenomenon,

characterized by inferior food quality, notably a deficient supply of proteins and vitamins. (See Figure 6 – 3.) Therefore, an African or Asiatic may suffer from chronic malnutrition despite a stomach bulging with high-calorie food. To write glibly about protein hunger is one thing, but to actually witness it firsthand is a distressing, shocking experience. T. A. Nash, a scientist who lived for many years among the natives of West Africa, describes one of his experiences:

Real "meat hunger" is something which should be seen to be believed. In Tanzania, I shot a large zebra near dusk and left two or three men to guard the carcass overnight. On returning next morning with porters, I was amazed to see how little meat was left; the men had eaten and vomited, eaten and vomited, throughout the night. (10)

Millions of children (under six years of age) in the underdeveloped countries are suffering from the protein-deficiency disease kwashiorkor. *Kwashiorkor* is a West African word that means "the disease the child gets when another baby is born" because the mother can no longer feed the older child with her breast milk. Although the disease was first discovered in tropical Africa, it has since been identified among the children of Central and South America, the Caribbean, the Middle East, and the Orient (1). (See Figure 6 – 5.) Symptoms of the disease include malfunction of the digestive system, skin ulcers, swellings, wasting of the limbs, weakness, lethargy, and increasing susceptibility to infectious

116

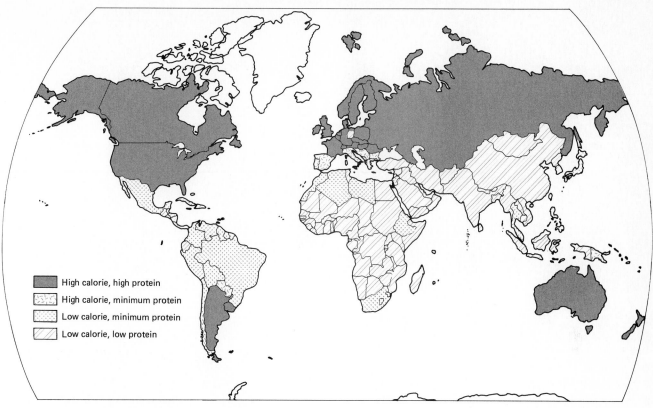

6-1 *The geography of hunger.*

diseases (14). The diseased children frequently have a pot belly because the abdominal muscles are so weak and because of the great amount of water in the tissues. Most serious of all, however, kwashior-kor tends to impede the normal mental development of young children, which cannot be rectified

6-2 *The average American is overfed; the average person living in a poor nation is underfed.*

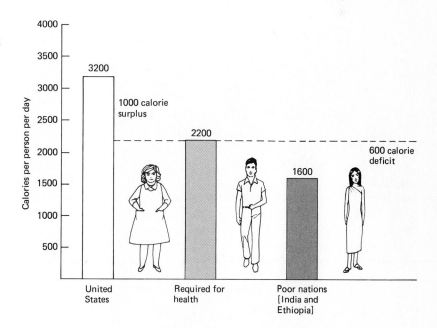

6-3 *One of the world's undernourished children. A mother feeds her child in South India, sitting on the ground outside their straw-thatched hut. Note the small bowl of rice on the "earth" table. Many such children in Asia, Africa, and South America are suffering from the disease kwashiorkor as a result of protein-deficient diets.*

6-4 *Death from starvation. Parvati Pura, India. This village suffered from a local famine because of an extended drought. The two-year-old boy is almost dead from starvation (marasmus).*

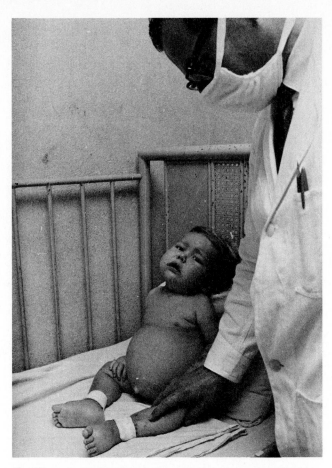

6-5 *A Guatemalan child suffering from kwashiorkor (malnutrition). Note the extreme lethargy and protruding abdomen.*

even if a proper diet is available several years later. It is apparent that these countries — already poorly endowed in many natural resources — are experiencing a lamentable erosion of their human resource as well.

At the time of this writing the food crisis is worsening in Mexico. Food production, once on the rise because of the Green Revolution, has now leveled off. At the same time, however, the population is continuing to zoom upward at a rate of more than 3 percent per year. (At this rate Mexico's population would double in only 23 years.) The undernourishment of Mexican children has made them mortally vulnerable to measles, whooping cough, diarrhea, and parasitic worms. According to Dr. Adolfo Chavez, Mexico's top nutrition expert, "More than 100,000 children die here each year because of the relationship between malnutrition and transmit-

Feeding a Hungry Planet

Georg Borgstrom

Emeritus Professor of
Food Science
MICHIGAN STATE UNIVERSITY

The feeding burden of the Earth, now in excess of 4.5 billion people, is presently increasing by close to 90 million a year. Worldwide this means a new U.S. in added population in less than three years! Before the year 2000 we will exceed 6 billion people. This constitutes a revolutionary development without precedence in history.

The rich well-nourished world, to which we belong, amounts to about one-fourth of humanity. Directly and indirectly we dispose of more than three fourths of world agricultural production and almost two thirds of that of the oceans. We use up much more than our fair share of global natural resources, far in excess of our needs. Three-fourths of mankind have to be content with sharing the remainder. It is in this realm of the majority that undernourishment and water shortage reign and mercilessly exact a huge tribute in human life and suffering, a shocking infant mortality prevails, and poor health impairs productivity. Starvation strikes when drought or large-scale floods occur. Refugees, misery, wars, and strife follow in their wake.

It is high time for us to strike a global balance as to water and plant cover. So far we have created far more deserts than fertile land. Half of currently irrigated lands exhibit declining yields due to salinity, and despite huge new projects the acreage is shrinking. Forest and grazing lands persistently suffer irretrievable losses.

We must immediately start planning for a more equitable utilization of the world's tilled land, water, marine assets, and other natural resources. And not least, we must create a world economy that provides for the basic needs of everyone. The rich, well-fed world must take the lead in this gigantic task. Only then is there a chance for common humanity to meet the next century in somewhat better shape and to progress toward a balance between resources and population as well as between nations. This means in essence a war for human survival, the only kind of war we can afford and the only kind we are justified in launching!

---

table diseases, and of the two million or so which are born each year at least 1.5 million will not adequately develop their mental, physical, and social functions. . . ."*

The food-shortage problem is equally severe in other parts of the world. Indian women have been known to abandon their infants along the roadside because they no longer have enough milk in their breasts to nourish them. Some years ago an American diplomat visiting in Siberia noticed that the bark of many riverside willows along the Volga appeared to have been stripped away as if by some giant rodent. When he questioned his Russian associates as to what animal was responsible, they replied "the human animal." The natives used willow bark as a basic ingredient in a soup that they regularly prepared. During the severe famine of 1974,

*Quoted in a news release from the New York Times *News Service* entitled "Mexico Food Crisis Worsens."

many Africans and Indians stuffed their stomachs with grass, tree leaves, and even mud in a futile attempt to survive. Today 25,000 people will die from hunger worldwide; tomorrow, 25,000 more.

Increasing Food Production

We will now consider some methods by which food production might be increased in a hungry world. (See also Georg Borgstrom's guest article on this page.) They include some novel techniques such as algal culture, yeast culture, and food synthesis, which are of considerable ecological interest but probably will never be of major importance. Other more traditional methods will be considered, such as the extension of agriculture into new regions, drainage, and the increased use of fertilizers, pest control, and agricultural breeding programs. As we

119

examine these methods, however, we must not delude ourselves into believing that hunger will eventually be erased from the face of the earth. *The best these methods can do is buy time*, time to get our rapidly increasing global population under control.

ALGAL CULTURE AND THE SHORTENING OF FOOD CHAINS. (1) Consider the following facts: About 0.1 to 0.5 percent of the solar radiation reaching the earth is converted by crops into chemical energy. (2) Only one calorie of human food is derived for every one million calories of sunshine received by this planet. (3) It takes roughly 100,000 pounds of algae to produce one pound of fish. These facts are explicable in terms of the second law of thermodynamics, as noted earlier. It would seem, therefore, that if humans shortened their food chains and consumed algae directly, a much larger food base would be available to nourish a food-deficient world.

Algal culture has been practiced in the United States, England, Germany, Venezuela, Japan, Israel, and the Netherlands. The alga Chlorella can be grown in ponds about one-half acre in size. Chlorella is rich in proteins, fats, and vitamins and apparently contains all the essential amino acids, especially lysine, which is ordinarily deficient in the human diet. At least 50 percent of the dry weight of the alga is protein. Each acre devoted to algal culture can produce up to forty tons, dry weight, of algae. The protein content in this algal crop is forty times the protein yield per acre of soybeans and 160 times the per acre yield of beef protein. Algal food can be used as a supplement in soups and meat dishes and as livestock feed.

From the foregoing, you might suppose that algal culture would show great promise. Not so, however, according to Georg Borgstrom, a food expert at Michigan State University: "Rarely ever has so much been written about so little." In his opinion the final product is not nearly as nutritious as some would claim; moreover, it has poor keeping qualities. According to Borgstrom, in most cases mass algal culture would be prohibitively expensive. The one exception might be in large urban areas where large quantities of sewage would be available as a nutrient source. Even then, the final product would best serve as food for livestock rather than human beings. In any event, it does not appear that algal culture will be a feasible food-production method in the underdeveloped countries for decades to come (1).

FOOD SYNTHESIS. The technology is available for the laboratory synthesis of the basic sugars, fats, amino acids, vitamins, and minerals of the human diet. Synthetic sources today may provide all the vitamins necessary for vigorous health at a modest annual cost to the consumer of 25 cents to $1. The people in the underdeveloped countries, who rely heavily on cereal foods, frequently are lacking such important amino acids as *lysine, tryptophane,* and *methionine.* Although these can all be synthetically produced, a year's requirement of these three amino acids would cost about $40 and hence would be prohibitively expensive. U.S. food manufacturers have succeeded in producing substitute meats and high-protein breakfast foods and beverages simply by fortifying basic cereals with protein. This process requires an astonishingly small amount of protein. For example, the protein content of a *ton* of wheat can be raised substantially with the addition of a few pounds of lysine. Indians by the thousands are now consuming lysine-fortified bread marketed by Indian government bakeries in Bombay and Madras.

YEAST CULTURE. Much interest has been shown recently in the prospects of yeast culture for alleviating protein-deficient diets. Yeast can be grown on organic substrates such as coal, petroleum, citrus-cannery waste, grain hulls, straw, beet- and cane-sugar molasses, and the black liquor derived from paper-pulp manufacture.

Yeast culture provides a method by which the hitherto inedible crop residues such as corncobs, stalks, stems, and woody fibers can be converted into protein-rich food. In the United States, for example, where a person consumes 0.37-ton of food annually, but where each year almost five times as much inedible corn and wheat residues accumulate per capita, it would be theoretically possible to increase food supplies from 50 to 100 percent. Moreover, yeasts are 65 percent efficient in the conversion of carbohydrate to protein; this compares with the 4 to 20 percent efficiency of livestock. Yeast food has been produced in Africa, Jamaica, Puerto Rico, Australia, Florida, Hawaii, and Wisconsin. A factory in Taiwan produces 73,000 tons of yeast annually, most of which, ironically, is shipped to the United States. Four thousand tons of yeast are produced annually in Green Bay, Wisconsin, as a by-product of the pulp industry. The yeast is used as a supplement in rice dishes, casseroles, soups, and stews (11).

To date yeast has been cultured on only a limited scale and is expensive to produce. Its extensive use in the underdeveloped countries would require the construction of plants and distribution systems and —above all—acceptance by the people. Because of their extremely conservative food habits, many of the very people in greatest need of protein food supplements are least likely to use them.

EXTENDING AGRICULTURE INTO NEW AREAS. In order to be productive, land must embrace the proper combination of soil texture, soil chemistry, temperature, rainfall, growing season, and topography. Of the 12.5 acres of the world's land available per capita, only 1.1 acres are being cultivated. According to a United Nations document, *Statistics of Hunger*, a minimum of 2.65 additional acres per capita have food-production potential. A USDA report states that the world's farmers are now tilling

only 30 percent of the potentially productive land. Note that the key word is potential. In the context of the technology and the social, economic, and political patterns existing in the underdeveloped countries, to believe that the farmers in those countries can actually realize this food production potential is somewhat of a delusion. For example, most of the potentially productive land in Asia requires irrigation, an almost prohibitively costly proposition. The population density per square kilometer of arable land is shown in Figure 6–6.

Tropical Rain Forests. Much publicity has centered around the possibility of establishing agriculture in the tropical rain forests of South America, Africa, and Asia. Would such schemes have much chance for success? Those areas are indeed blessed with an abundance of rainfall, intense sunlight, and a long growing season. The regions have supported dense forest cover for many centuries, so they

6–6 *Relationship between population density and amount of arable land in certain nations. Note the relatively high population density for Egypt, an underdeveloped nation, and the relatively low population density for Canada and Australia, both highly developed nations.*

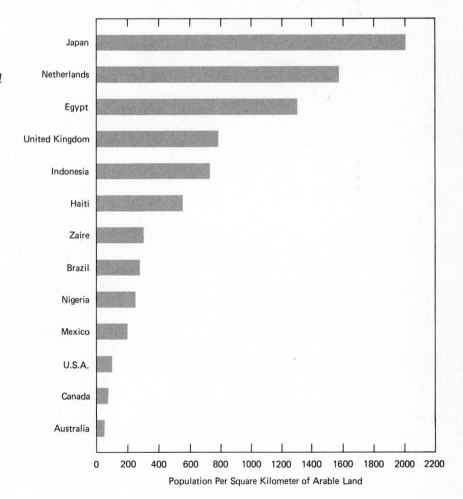

Population Per Square Kilometer of Arable Land

dant bacteria, fungi, insects, and earthworms. The nutrients then are immediately absorbed by root systems to be incorporated into new plant tissue. If the Brazilian settlers were to bulldoze or chop down the forest, the release of nutrients would be so rapid

6–7 *Shifting type of cultivation in central Sumatra. Agricultural land is opened up by cutting and burning the forests. The cleared area will then be intensively cropped for a few years until the fertility has been exhausted; then it will be abandoned and left exposed to erosion by wind and water.*

should be able to produce crops. Unfortunately, there are two unexpected problems: the rapid release of nutrients from the soil and the chemical nature of the soil.

If you were standing in a beech-maple woods during a Michigan summer, the forest floor would be covered with a thick, spongy layer of decomposing leaves, several inches in thickness. Nutrients from those leaves are gradually released to the soil, making the latter a nutrient reservoir. It was this type of soil that was tilled by the colonists of early America and that yielded reasonably good harvests. In Amazonia and many other tropical rain forests, however, a minimum of nutrients are retained by the soil. When leaves and branches fall to the forest floor, the organic matter is rapidly decomposed by the abun-

6–8 *Irrigation made possible in Egypt by the Aswan Dam. An area of one million acres formerly dependent on the annual Nile floods for irrigation is now cultivated under a system of perennial irrigation based mainly on lifting water. The new irrigation system makes possible a 40 percent increase in crop production in Upper Egypt, because at least one additional crop can be grown per year. Photo shows a mechanized irrigation pump at Habu that has replaced the laborious methods of lifting water by a hand-operated or animal-driven waterwheel. Unfortunately, the increased food production can barely keep up with Egypt's population increase.*

that the planted crops would not be able to absorb them quickly enough to prevent the massive nutrient loss caused by the leaching action and erosion from the heavy rainfall.

The second problem has to do with the soil chemistry. The soils, known as laterites, are reddish brown because of their high iron content. After several seasons of cropping, the laterite soil that characteristically underlies much of the tropical rain forest biome, tends to bake brick hard in the oven of the hot equatorial sun. That hardness and durability are good for the construction of buildings but certainly do not facilitate penetration by crop roots. In fact, some historians implicate laterization in the decay not only of the Khmer civilization in Cambodia, for example, but also that of the Mayas in Mexico. In more recent times it caused the failure of the agricultural colony so ambitiously started by the Brazilian government in the heart of the Amazon basin.

Arid Regions. There are rosy-visioned optimists who claim that some day agriculture may even be possible in the Sahara Desert. In 1960 an area of fertile land was discovered in the central Sahara that was equal to the total area of Great Britain. Water might possibly be secured from underground aquifers. For example, in 1950 the Albienne Nappe, a sandstone aquifer, was found. One thousand feet thick in some places, this aquifer now supplies water for an oil town of 30,000 people, for the extension of oases, and for the survival of 50,000 trees. In Egypt the construction of the gigantic Aswan Dam has made possible an increase in crop production because irrigation water is now available on a year-round basis. (See Figure 6 – 8.)

However, many irrigation projects are not so encouraging. For example, salinization and waterlogging as a result of irrigation have virtually destroyed the crop-producing capability of five million acres in West Pakistan alone, with an acre dropping out of production every five minutes (7). Schemes to make the desert "bloom" will never boost world food production to any significant degree. Most of those schemes are either prohibitively costly (about $400 per acre), of too small a dimension, or simply could not become operational soon enough to prevent serious famine. Take the colossal North American Water and Power Alliance project. (See Figure 6 – 9.) Its potential for alleviating world hunger is described by Paul Ehrlich, well-known environmentalist from Stanford University, as follows:

The most ambitious water project yet conceived in this country is the North American Water and Power Alliance, which proposes to distribute water from the great rivers of Canada to thirsty locations all over the United States. Formidable political problems aside, this project would involve the expenditure of $100 billion in construction costs over a twenty-year completion period. . . . To assess the possible contribution to the *world* food situation, we assume that all this water would be devoted to agriculture. Then, using the rather optimistic figure of 500 gallons per day to grow the food to feed one person, we find that this project could feed 126 million additional people. Since this is *less than 8 percent of the projected world population growth during the construction period*, it should be clear that even the most massive water projects can make but a token contribution to the solution of the world food problem in the long term. (8) [*Italics mine.*]

Wetlands. Society has achieved notable success as well as a few infamous failures through drainage schemes. The agriculturally productive fenland of Britain was once a *swamp.* Flourishing Israeli settlements now occupy the site of the former waterlogged Huleh *marshes.* Grain is now abundantly produced in Canada's prairie provinces in areas once dominated by *muskeg.* Drainage has made crop production possible in Italy's Po Valley and in the Yazoo Delta of the Mississippi. Arable land may even be reclaimed to a limited extent from shallow *seas:* in Holland the ingenious Dutch have increased their agricultural area by one million acres by draining the Zuider Zee, once the biggest bay in the Netherlands.

It should be emphasized, however, that marshland habitat, already dwindling throughout the world, is an intrinsically valuable resource in its own right. It provides a unique type of scenic beauty, serves as a natural mechanism for minimizing water-level fluctuations, and is an excellent wildlife habitat.

INCREASED USE OF FERTILIZER. Japan has only 0.166-acre of arable land per capita, only one thirteenth that of the United States. Only with the most intensive agricultural methods has Japan been able to feed her 115 million people. She has achieved amazing success, producing 13,200 calories per cultivated acre per day, almost three times the per acre calorie production of American farmers. One key to Japan's agricultural accomplishments is the large amounts of fertilizer applied to her farms. A great

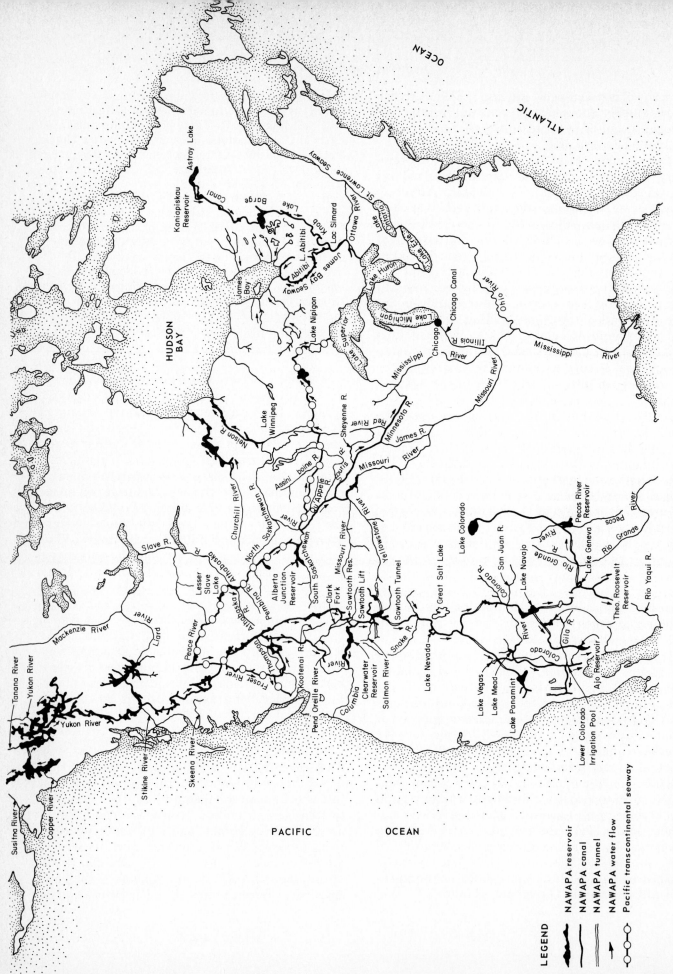

6–9 *Water sources, reservoirs, canals, tunnels, and flow pattern in the North American Water and Power Alliance Plan.*

LEGEND

NAWAPA reservoir
NAWAPA canal
NAWAPA tunnel
NAWAPA water flow
Pacific transcontinental seaway

variety of fertilizers are employed, from sardine-soybean-cottonseed cakes to animal wastes, and from green manure to human dung. Standard commercial preparations are used in addition (11).

It has been shown that Japan's success with soil enrichment can be repeated in many underdeveloped countries, although on a smaller scale. Even without modifying any farm method, 9,500 fertilizer field trials conducted by U.S. agricultural specialists in fourteen less developed countries have shown an overall average yield increase of 74 percent (26). In the late 1960s similar field studies in India showed that for each ton of nitrogen fertilizer applied, at a cost of $150 per ton, the farmer could expect to raise an additional 11 tons of grain worth $1,200 (3).

The preceding data show what can be done in the developing nations on an experimental basis. The sobering truth is that fertilizer application in those countries must be increased sevenfold between 1975 and 2000 if their surging populations are to be properly fed.

The problem may not finally be solved until the governments of the developing nations launch an aggressive program of fertilizer-plant construction. This will require technical assistance, considerable amounts of raw materials, and capital (2). It will also require a great deal of energy for nitrogen fixation and the processing of phosphates. In addition, it will be necessary to construct an extensive transportation system to get the fertilizer to the farmer. It is a tremendous job, and one that has to be done soon. The prospects are not bright. As Michigan State University's Borgstrom states, "The needs are, in the overpopulated parts of the world, so enormous that it is highly unlikely the fertilizer industry will ever catch up with them. . . . India alone would have to invest something on the order of $20 billion in fertilizer factories to achieve parity and balance." Two additional gigantic factories would be required each year merely to feed an annual addition of 15 million stomachs. The rapidly increasing cost of oil compounds the problem, because oil is required in the manufacture of nitrate fertilizer. Thus, India's bill for oil in a given year is about $2 billion, roughly equal to what she earns from all her exports.

China is an exception to the general rule that the poor nations have difficulty becoming self-reliant in terms of fertilizer production. By 1978 China had constructed several gigantic plants to produce an aggregate 2.7 million tons of fertilizer yearly — sufficient to satisfy all of her needs (3).

CONTROL OF AGRICULTURAL PESTS. Roughly 45 of every 100 pounds of food grown throughout the world are destroyed by pests and disease organisms. Rats, insects, and fungi annually destroy 33 million tons of food on a global basis, sufficient to feed one third of the people in India. One of every 14 people in the world will starve because of food deprivation imposed by agricultural pests.

Rodents. The rat is one of man's greatest competitors; just one animal is capable of consuming forty pounds of potential human food yearly. The 120 million rats in the United States alone inflict $1 billion damage yearly (1). In India, where rats may outnumber people 10:1, up to 30 percent of the crops are ravaged by rodents. The crop volume destroyed annually by rats in India would fill a 3,000-mile-long train. Yet India spends 800 times as much money on fertilizer as she does on rat control (2).

Disease-Transmitting Insects. In equatorial Africa, 23 varieties of tsetse fly, the transmitter of the protozoan that causes the dread sleeping sickness in humans and an equally serious disease in livestock, have effectively prevented livestock production in an area larger than the entire United States. (See Figure 6–10.) The microscopic malarial parasite *Plasmodium*, which is injected into the human bloodstream by the bite of a mosquito, has been a scourge to the farmers of southeast Asia. It incapacitates millions of rice farmers at the critical periods of transplanting and harvesting. In an attempt to escape the malarial season in northern

6–10 *Blood sample from a person with sleeping sickness. The dark, elongate cells with a whip at one end are the protozoans that cause sleeping sickness. The victim was injected with the parasites by the bite of a tsetse fly.*

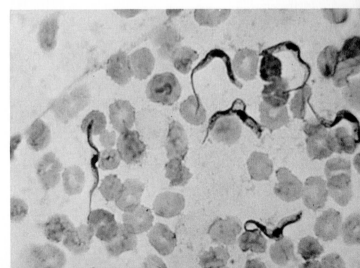

6 – 11 *Locust swarm threatens crops in Hargassa, Somalia. The operator of the spray plane on the left wished to spray this swarm with insecticides but the engine would not start because it was encrusted with locusts. The locusts are so thick that they blot out the terminal building to the right of the picture.*

Thailand, farmers are prevented from raising a second rice crop, one that could be used to great advantage in alleviating hunger elsewhere.

Locusts. Crop destroying insects cause more than $20 billion worth of damage yearly worldwide. Locusts are among the most destructive. By the very extension of his cultivation programs, man has unwittingly improved breeding conditions for locusts. Their migratory hordes have decimated man's grain fields since the time of Moses and are continuing this devastation to the present, as 109 major infestations in India in a single year recently would testify (1). Examples of locust "nurseries" provided by agriculture are the alfalfa fields of Libya and the crop "islands" in Saudi Arabia, Yemen, and the plains of the Red Sea. One locust swarm near the Red Sea, so thick it seemed to blot out the sun, blanketed an area of at least 2,000 square miles. (See Figure 6 – 11.) Because of their great mobility, adult locusts may destroy crops over a thousand miles and several nations away from their hatching sites. Swarms of locusts, for example, are known to have traveled from Saskatchewan all the way to Texas (32).

The effective control of agricultural pests in the developing nations would markedly boost food output. The United States and western Europe have developed sophisticated techniques of pest control. Their control experts now wage war against agricultural pests with a veritable arsenal of weapons, including chemosterilants, gamma radiation, sound waves, sex attractants, resistant mutants, natural predators, and microbial agents, in addition to the more conventional pesticides. (See Figure 6 – 12.) The USDA's Agency for International Development (AID) is currently disseminating some of this know-how to the rural regions of South America, Africa, and Asia.

Plant-Breeding Programs: The Green Revolution

Since the dawn of the human species more than two million years ago, humans have succeeded in domesticating only about eighty species of food plants. The "big three" among food plants are wheat, rice, and corn; over 50 percent of the world's croplands are devoted to them. It is only natural, therefore, that plant geneticists have channeled much of their research into developing superior strains of the three. The progress made within the last decade in this so-called Green Revolution holds some promise for partially closing the gap between food supply and demand in the underdeveloped countries. Plant geneticists have developed high-yield grains with up to 13 percent protein content (8). They have produced wheat that will develop in shorter growing seasons and that are, hence, adaptable to more northern latitudes. They have developed crops with a larger proportion of edible parts

126

or with a greater ability to use fertilizer. Crops have been developed that are resistant to heat, cold, and drought. A variety of grain has been secured that will tolerate the continuous sunlight of the brief Arctic summer.

A few years ago scientists at Purdue University developed a strain of corn bearing large quantities of *lysine* and *tryptophane* (13). Because these two amino acids are essential for normal human growth, nutrition experts agree that this mutant corn may represent a practical approach to alleviating some of the severe protein deficiencies in diets in Africa, South America, and Asia, where meat, fish, eggs, and poultry are prohibitively costly and in short supply.

It is of interest that, although 40 percent of the global corn production comes from the eastern United States, *very little is used directly as human food.* It is fed to pigs and cattle instead, which in turn are ultimately consumed as pork chops and beefsteaks by overfed Americans. As noted in our discussion of energy pyramids, much plant-food energy is squandered when we channel it through livestock instead of consume it directly. In a world where two out of three stomachs are only partly filled or are empty, it seems immoral for Americans to continue to live "high on the hog."

The International Maize and Wheat Improvement Center, sponsored by the Rockefeller and Ford

6–12 *Fighting a locust outbreak in East Africa. In July 1968 more than 40 countries in East Africa were threatened with the most serious locust plague since 1959, a record plague year. International efforts to control the locust swarms were coordinated by the Food and Agriculture Organization of the United Nations. Photo shows field worker dusting crops with benzene hexachloride.*

foundations, was established in Mexico in 1943, at a time when that country was experiencing a critical food scarcity. After 25 years of intensive research, a huge bank of seed varieties has been established. (See Figure 6–13.) When aid is sought by develop-

6–13 *A seed bank to fight global starvations. Scientists at the National Seed Storage Laboratory in Ft. Collins, Colorado, preserve germ plasm to aid the world's plant breeders in improving old crops. This facility also tries to save from extinction seeds of wild and primitive plants that are endowed with irreplaceable traits, such as disease resistance or high protein content. Here technicians are planting seeds on special paper for germination tests. The laboratory stores over 80,000 different kinds of seeds—a living reserve of germ plasm for tomorrow.*

6-14 *One of the architects of the Green Revolution, Nobel Prize-winning Dr. Norman E. Borlaug is shown recording the vigor and stage of growth of wheat plants on a selective breeding plot in Mexico. Dr. Borlaug was successful in developing the so-called miracle wheats that, at least temporarily, greatly boosted wheat production in Mexico and other underdeveloped nations around the world.*

6-15 *Miracle wheats. The six spikes on the right represent recently developed perennials (they grow year after year without replanting) wheat hybrid that have disease and insect resistance, high protein content, and usefulness as forage crops for livestock. The two commercial varieties on the left do not have many of these desirable characteristics and have fewer seeds to the head as well.*

6 – 16 *Women in Bihar, India, harvesting a crop of high-yielding wheat that has been grown with improved irrigation.*

ing nations, this bank can provide a seed variety that is adaptive to that nation's particular combination of soil chemistry, soil structure, climate, rainfall, and growing season. The center has developed strains of rust-resistant beans that have increased yield from 150,000 to 600,000 tons annually. It has produced blight-resistant potatoes that have shown a 500 percent yield increase. Partly as a result of the Improvement Center's work, grain production in Mexico, at least initially, soared from 700 pounds to 4,200 pounds per acre.

Under the leadership of Norman Borlaug, an agricultural geneticist, Mexico's Maize and Wheat Improvement Center developed dwarf varieties of wheat and rice. (See Figure 6 – 14.) These strains

were especially developed for use in tropical and subtropical countries. One big advantage of the new strains is that they utilize much greater amounts of fertilizer and water than traditional strains and therefore have high yields. (See Figure 6 – 15.) In addition, the stems do not topple over as do traditional strains. Instead, the stems remain firm and upright — thus facilitating harvesting of the grain. The new strains are less prone to wind damage. Moreover, because they require only a short growing season, farmers can harvest two to three crops per year. The development of these "miracle" strains was the culmination of nearly thirty years of research. The Nobel Peace Prize was awarded to Norman Borlaug in 1971; it was fitting recognition

129

6–17 *A new rice strain for hungry India: IR5 (left), a new high-yielding variety of rice under test at a research station in Aduthurai. The plant to the right is the traditional variety.*

2. *Lack of top-quality cropland.* Initially only the best-quality cropland was used to grow the miracle crops. This explains, therefore, the initially huge yields for miracle wheat in Mexico and for miracle wheat and rice in Asia. However, any additional planting in the future will have to be made on much less productive land (3). Millions of acres of arable land in Africa and Asia are unsuitable to the new crop varieties because of their adverse soil chemistry: They are either too alkaline — as are more than six million acres in the Middle East, India, and Pakistan — or they are toxic because of their high iron content — as in the humid tropics — or they are deficient in zinc — as is common for lowland soils (3).

3. *Huge water inputs are required.* An abundance of water is essential if the farmers in poor nations are to maximize the potential of the new strains of wheat, rice, and corn. Farmers cannot rely on thunderstorms on a day-to-day basis. Irrigation facilities are a must, in most cases, but unfortunately only a small percentage of these farmers are able to afford them.

4. *Huge fertilizer inputs are required.* The miracle crops require large fertilizer inputs. And the purchase of large amounts of fertilizers, as already

6–18 *Women planting rice in paddies of the Solo River Basin, Java.*

of his service to humankind, especially to the malnourished millions of the tropics and subtropics.

Negative Aspects of the Green Revolution

However, despite the positive aspects of the Green Revolution described here, a growing number of agricultural scientists and economists are of the opinion that the revolution has a number of drawbacks that might sully its otherwise bright promise for the world's hungry. Some of these negative features are discussed here.

1. *Limitations of climate.* Even with the planting of superior seeds, farmers the world over will still be at the mercy of climate. For example, in 1972, 1973, and 1979 many farmers in the underdeveloped world experienced sharply reduced crop yields because of floods and drought.

discussed, is beyond the means of many poor farmers. Without large amounts of fertilizer the yields from miracle crops may actually be less than those from traditional types.

5. *Huge pesticide inputs are required.* Pesticide prices have soared in the last decade. The elevated prices are, in part, the result of global pesticide use having increased at the rate of 20 percent per year. At current price trends, poor farmers will have to reduce their pesticide usage sharply.

6. *Huge energy inputs are required.* Many farm machines, such as planters, cultivators, harvesters, tractors, and irrigation pumps, are powered by gasoline. And gasoline is in extremely short supply in many poor nations. For example, Indian farmers stood, sat, or slept in line *for days* during the Arab embargo of 1973–1974 to obtain a few precious gallons of diesel fuel to run their irrigation pumps (3).

7. *The financial gap between the big and small landowner is accentuated.* Unfortunately, the Green Revolution has been a powerful force in making the rich richer and the poor poorer in many of the underdeveloped countries. This can be easily understood because it is only the wealthier farmer who can afford the technological inputs of fertilizers, pesticides, irrigation equipment, farming machinery, and fossil fuels that are required for the miracle crops to perform their miracles.

8. *The Green Revolution fosters monotypes.* The planting of huge acreages to a single crop carries with it all the potential ecological problems that attend the vegetational monocultures described earlier in this text. The basic problem is that the geneticist, in developing a superstrain for yield, in many cases was not able to build genetic material into the plant that would allow it to resist plant and animal pests. Some ecologists fear that the vast acreages of monotype agriculture ushered in with the Green Revolution might, sooner, or later, result in massive crop failure caused by the rapid buildup of destructive fungi and insect pests. The famine thus triggered could cause more eventual human suffering than occurred before the Green Revolution began.

9. *Loss of genetic diversity.* When farmers in poor nations plant large acreages of a single strain of miracle wheat in place of several varieties of native food plants, they are reducing the *genetic diversity* of their crops. Once such genetic varia-

bility has been lost, it may well be impossible to develop strains of rice and wheat resistant to a new strain of plant disease or the scourge of an insect pest introduced accidentally from abroad.

Livestock Breeding Programs

Of the 24 species of domesticated livestock, only nine (cattle, pigs, sheep, goats, water buffalo, chickens, ducks, geese, and turkeys) provide almost 100 percent of our animal protein. The United States has been foremost in the development of superior livestock strains. In the 1920s the King Ranch in Texas crossed the shorthorn with the Brahman to develop the *Santa Gertrudis.* In the 1930s the *Brangus* strain was produced by Oklahoma breeders by crossing the shorthorn with the Black Angus. Both Santa Gertrudis and Brangus are meaty and resist ticks and heat; both form the basis of livestock production in several tropical countries.

Through Western methods of selection and cross-breeding, a rancher can rapidly develop cattle with meatier carcasses or swine with larger litters and faster growing rates. Cows have been produced with a milk flow vastly superior to that of the dairy cattle of undeveloped nations. For example, American test breeds of Holsteins produce up to 2,000 pounds of milk annually, compared to the 300-pound annual flow from the yellow cattle of China. Chickens with greater egg-laying capacity and more efficient feed-biomass conversions have been developed by American researchers. With the assistance of agricultural specialists from the United Nations, ranchers from underdeveloped countries will gradually acquire the technical assistance required to improve greatly the quality of their livestock.

Wild-Game Ranches

Several years ago a team of wildlife biologists compared the meat-production value of domesticated livestock raised in Africa with an herbivorous wild-game population (antelope, zebras, giraffes, and elephants) maintained in its wild state. Their conclusions, as related by Richard Wagner, environmentalist from the University of Pennsylvania, are most illuminating:

1. *Wild game were very efficient in exploiting the available plant food base.* Cattle were found to be

6-19 *Giraffes and zebras in Southern Rhodesia. Such animals could be raised on large game ranches more profitably and efficiently than traditional livestock such as cattle and goats.*

very selective, however, consuming only certain grasses of high palatability, while other potentially nutritious, although apparently less tasty, forage was neglected. Such a differential feeding response could quickly result in overgrazing in some areas and undergrazing in others, effectively limiting the carrying capacity of a given range acre. On the other hand, a mixed-species population of wild game showed a broad-spectrum utilization of available plant foods: antelopes fed on grasses and low-level foliage, giraffes consumed foliage on the higher branches, and the elephants selected bark and roots.

2. *Wild game were much better adapted to drought than domesticated livestock.* For example, when a given water hole dries out, wild game will move for miles to another water source to satisfy their requirements. Furthermore, they require much less water per pound of biomass than livestock. Thus, a zebra can get along without water for a period of three days, whereas the gemsbok (like the kangaroo rat of the southwestern American desert) does not require drinking water at all, but depends on metabolic water and the water occurring in its plant foods to satisfy its requirements.

3. *Wild game are immune to the potentially lethal sleeping sickness transmitted by the tsetse fly.* On the other hand, introduced livestock are highly susceptible.

4. *Wild-game ranches can expect a profit margin fully six times that of the traditional livestock ranches.* (14)

It might seem that the widespread practice of wild-game ranching would severely deplete and endanger the survival of African game populations. It must be emphasized, however, that in any event, the use of a given range for livestock would preempt its use by wild game.

Donations from Food-Rich Nations

Might the impending starvation in have-not countries be alleviated at least temporarily by food gifts from the nutrient-rich countries, such as the United States and Canada? It certainly does seem that the United States might have a moral obligation to donate food. After all, with only 5 percent of the world population, we consume about 30 percent of the world's resources. Surely it would be better to fill the empty stomachs in Asia, Africa, and South America than to sit by and watch surplus corn and wheat mold in storage bins. However, things aren't quite that simple; they are complicated by the laws of raw economics. Let us look at an example.

In 1969 the world experienced the greatest wheat glut in history. Several factors contributed to the record-breaking harvests: optimal weather, improved agricultural techniques, and the use of superior wheat strains in Mexico, India, and Pakistan. Consider the economic plight of the Canadian wheat farmer, however. Canada's storage bins, already crammed with a record 850 million bushels, now received an additional 650 million bushels, at a time when the price of wheat was falling to bedrock levels. Canadian farmers simply could not afford to give the wheat to Nigeria, Guatemala, Costa Rica, or any other country where the jutting ribs and lethargic behavior of half-starved youngsters are an everyday fact of life. Wheat farmers still owed the Canadian government $65 million in past loans. The government paid out cash advances of $6,000 per farm to compensate for unsold wheat. The Canadians were forced into a financial squeeze; they simply had to get as much money for their wheat as possible. Ironically, and perhaps immorally, the wheat eventually was used, not to assuage the hunger pangs of the malnourished peoples of the world, but to produce more pork chops and beefsteaks for those who were already overfed: the affluent people of America and Europe (4).

High population growth rates also present a problem. Let us consider the hungry nation of Pakistan for a moment. Until very recently it had a population of 131 million and an extremely high birth rate. Unfortunately (or should we say fortunately?), Pakistan also has a rather high mortality rate, which tends to curb its population increase. Let us suppose now that, because of the Green Revolution and/or because of the food donations of the food-rich nations (and the United States did send $15 billion dollars worth of food to hungry nations under Public Law 480), all the men, women, and children in Pakistan eventually will go to bed with a full stomach. What then? The respite from hunger would be brief to say the least. When you consider that within a single century Pakistan's population would increase to 13 billion (almost three times the population on earth today), it is obvious that they ultimately would have bred themselves back to their originally wretched condition or even one infinitely worse.

In fact, this phenomenon is the basis for the curious paradox: *We cause starvation by feeding the hungry.* The editors of the highly respected journal *Bioscience* recognized this dilemma when they wrote, "Because it creates a vicious cycle that compounds human suffering at a high rate, the provision of food to the malnourished populations of the world *that cannot or will not take very substantial measures to control their own reproductive rates* is inhuman, immoral, and irresponsible" (5). [*Italics mine.*]

What of the Future?

Future historians may well speak of the 1980s as the first decade of The Great Hunger. Borlaug himself has predicted that twenty million people in Africa,

Asia, and South America will starve to death annually during this decade. An opinion like this from a world-renowned scientist should give us pause. Considering the *finite* resources of the planet Earth in terms of arable land, water, and soil fertility, we certainly have the innate capacity to breed ourselves into starvation, despite the most advanced agricultural technology and despite food synthesis, yeast and algal culture, drainage schemes, the most effective pest-control programs, and the development of superior plant and animal breeds. Remember that when the Kaibab deer population increased precipitously, the environment eventually deteriorated so severely that it decimated the herd (see Chapter 3). People are not deer, but they are subject to the same basic ecological laws. It could well be that in our intensive efforts to save ourselves, we may destroy ourselves. Perhaps in the long run it would be more humanitarian to permit a relatively small-scale starvation now than to ensure an overwhelming catastrophic food crisis, say, within fifty years. Were you to ask your neighbor this very day what he or she thought of the possibilities of global famine within a century, the answer might be, "Somehow, science and technology will see to that." But that is just the point. Despite all the wonders science and technology have wrought for twentieth-century society, "the population problem cannot be solved in a technical way, any more than can the problem of winning the game of tick-tack-toe" (7). A recognized authority on global food problems, Lester R. Brown of the Overseas Development Council, was once highly optimistic that global food production, with the impetus provided by the Green Revolution, would catch up with the demands of a burgeoning world population. It is of considerable interest, therefore, that his mood has · gradually changed to one of pessimism. For example, even without a drought, Brown believes that Americans now have the choice of either "eating less meat so that more grain will be available for export" or "watching people starve to death on the TV news."

Take another glance at the human population growth curve shown in Figure 3–2. Do you see what part of the J-curve our population is on right now? On the exponential part, where the curve is zooming almost straight up Ehrlich states, "If growth continued at that rate for about 900 years there would be some 60,000,000,000,000,000 people on the face of the earth. Sixty million billion people. This is about 100 persons for each square yard of the earth's sur-

Environmental Problems Caused by Attempts to Feed a Hungry World

1. Erosion of soil that in turn results in a loss of nutrients. Erosion requires more fertilizer, causes siltation of spawning beds of fish, causes siltation of reservoirs, reduces photosynthesis and therefore levels of dissolved oxygen in lakes and streams, demands costly water filtration processes, and requires the costly dredging of harbors and streams so that ships can navigate.

2. Laterization of iron-rich soils in tropical regions where forests were cleared for farming.

3. Overgrazing of pastures. This in turn results in replacing high-quality forage with low-quality weeds and exposes the rangeland to the erosive effects of wind and water.

4. The expansion of deserts.

5. The rapid destruction of forests. This in turn results in the accelerated depletion of wildlife, the extinction of many thousands of plant and animal species, and removal of a ''sink'' for carbon dioxide, which contributes to a global greenhouse effect that may eventually result in the melting of the global icecaps and cause major shifts in the geographic patterns of agriculture, such as a northward shift of the Corn Belt from Iowa into southern Canada. Forest removal may also result in a decrease in the rainfall occurring in the deforested area; it would, of course, eliminate the use of this resource for timber production, control of water flow, recreational use, and scientific study.

6. Accumulation of salt in soil that has been improperly irrigated. The salty soil is virtually useless for the production of most crops. West Pakistan is losing over a million acres per year because of this problem.

7. The overenrichment (eutrophication) of aquatic ecosystems with nutrients from the runoff of fertilizers and animal wastes into lakes and streams. This results in an explosive growth of weeds, reduced levels of dissolved oxygen, and the replacement of high-quality fish with trash species.

8. Pesticide contamination of ecosystems. There may be a buildup of pesticide concentrations in the tissues of fish, birds, mammals, and humans, with such possible harmful effects as sterility, lowered fertility, and behavioral changes. Drastic reduction in the population of predatory birds, such as hawks and eagles, may occur because of the thinning of egg shells. Many species of insects will develop resistance to the pesticides.

9. Replacement of the diversity of natural ecosystems with agricultural monotypes. These, in turn, are very vulnerable to insect and disease outbreaks. Use of some pesticides like DDT would result in a destruction of certain types of soil bacteria that are essential for soil fertility, thus requiring a more intensive use of fertilizers, which in turn cause additional adverse effects.

10. Consumption of increasingly scarce fossil fuels. Coal mining results in ugly strip-mined landscapes and acid mine drainage. The extraction and transport of oil result in oil pollution of the marine environment because of offshore oil-well mishaps and tanker collisions. The actual burning of the fossil fuels (diesel oil and gasoline) results in the release of sulfur and nitrogen. These contaminants in turn may have multiple adverse effects, including acid rain (oxides of nitrogen and sulfur), a greenhouse effect (carbon dioxide), and lead poisoning in children (lead compounds).

11. Reduction of stratospheric ozone. The release of nitrous oxide from the use of nitrogen fertilizers may result in the reduction of atmospheric ozone. As a result, the rate of skin cancers in the human population may rise.

face, land and sea . . ." (6). If the world population continues to increase at its present rate, the world's surface will eventually be saturated with so many people that this planet's life-support systems (air, water, and food) will begin to fail, and population growth will cease.

Is this what we want? To maximize our population on earth? It took the human population one million years before Christ to double from 2.5 to five million. Today, we have a global population of about 4.6 billion; at the current rate of increase it will double in only 41 years.

Borlaug, himself one of the main architects of the Green Revolution, admits that the recent developments in plant breeding, including high-protein strains of rice and wheat, are merely stopgap devices. They serve only to *buy time* against the inevitable catastrophe of global famine, unless the world's nations mount a massive attempt to silence the ominous ticking of the population bomb.

A Master Plan for Feeding a Hungry World

1. Effectively control global population growth by mounting a massive United Nations-sponsored educational campaign — particularly in less developed nations — to demonstrate the function and use of modern birth control techniques, such as delayed marriage, the rhythm method, mechanical and chemical contraceptives, sterilization, legalized abortion, and government permit systems.

2. Launch a United Nations-sponsored, highly coordinated multinational effort to aid less developed nations in building sound, strong economies and viable industrial systems. Eventually, the populations of those developing nations should undergo the demographic transition characterized by a simultaneous reduction of both birth and death rates. The net result should be the end of rapid population growth.

3. Each nation on planet Earth, both rich and poor, should critically examine their projected food needs for the next 25 years, on the basis of realistic, intensively studied estimates of both population and food-production trends.

4. Within the framework of the United Nations Food and Agricultural Organization (UNFAO) provide both the necessary technical and financial assistance (low-interest loans) so that less developed nations can boost their food production by a combination of such methods as hydroponics, algal culture, food synthesis, yeast culture, extending agriculture into arid regions and wetlands (while exerting every effort to keep environmental stress at a minimum), more effectively controlling crop-destroying pests, implementing the Green Revolution, developing livestock breeding programs, establishing wild-game ranches (especially in Africa), upgrading and expanding fish farming, boosting ocean harvests (in part by shifting the emphasis from traditional fishing grounds, which are probably already overfished, to new areas with good potential), and developing a greater social acceptance of nontraditional foods (such as high-protein wheat and corn for rice and fish-protein concentrate instead of whole fish), and adopting nutritionally balanced diets that would include all the essential amino acids despite the absence of meats.

5. Technical and financial assistance must be made available to the poor nations so they can construct their own fertilizer plants.

6. Farmers in both poor and rich nations should be encouraged to make maximal use of organic fertilizers such as animal wastes (cattle, pig, and goat manure). The use of cattle chips as fuel in Africa and Asia should be discouraged.

7. Developed nations, such as the United States, should sharply reduce their use of fertilizer for the median strip in freeway systems, parks, golf greens, and residential lawns. More fertilizer, at lower prices, would then be available for purchase by poor nations.

8. Set up genetic storage banks in each of the developing nations where endangered species of native food plants could be protected and maintained so that their unique germ plasm will be available for developing superior strains of agricultural plants at some time in the future.

9. Establish genetic research stations in the farming regions of each developing nation whose primary function would be the development of crop varieties that would be uniquely adapted to the soil chemistry, soil structure, temperature, rainfall, growing seasons, and solar intensity peculiar to that nation.

10. Establish modern agricultural institutes, sponsored by the United Nations and possibly endowed by grants from the Ford and Rockefeller foundations, in each of the less developed nations. Scholarships would be awarded to superior students so that they might learn the best possible agricultural production and marketing methods. Institute faculty might be made up of both native and foreign personnel. Visiting professors might come from such colleges as Moscow University, the University of Berlin, the University of Illinois, and Cornell University.

11. Establish a 100-day global food reserve that would be administered by the United Nations. This reserve would tend to stabilize food prices and serve as an emergency food supply during periods of drought (such as that experienced in the Sahel of Africa in 1974), hurricanes, crop-damaging floods, and outbreaks of crop-destroying insects and diseases.

12. Industrialized nations should drastically reduce their overconsumption of food (no more diets!). Throwing perfectly good food into a garbage can should be considered morally wrong. Pet populations in nations like the United States, France, and England should be reduced. (Americans alone spend roughly $3 billion per year on pet food — a financial outlay sufficient to feed one third of the world's hungry people.) Surplus pet food could be purchased by underdeveloped nations at more reasonable cost as food for livestock.

13. Farmers' markets should be encouraged in urban areas so that consumers eliminate the costs of wholesalers and retailers and those of the packaging and canning industries as well. The malnourished millions in city slums would benefit greatly were more such market food available. More food should be grown by families in backyard gardens, thus eliminating not only wholesaler, retailer, processing, and packaging costs, but also food-transporting costs. (Remember that the food on the average American's dinner table was grown 1,300 miles away.)

14. Annual global food problem-solving conferences participated in by both rich and poor nations should be held to discuss population-control and food-production strategies and how the two might be integrated on a nation-by-nation basis. The first decade of conferences should be held in the poor nations experiencing the most serious population and food problems. The major functions of such conferences would be the exchange of ideas and expertise by agricultural scientists and population experts.

15. Better long-range forecasting of major changes in climatic patterns (drought, hurricanes, and freezing spells) should be developed by weather experts. In this way advance warnings and alerts can be provided that might prevent massive crop damage or even the planting of the wrong type of crop during a given growing season.

6–20 *Crop-disease detection by aerial photography. To investigate the use of space and aerial photography in crop surveys, the National Aeronautics and Space Administration introduced a blight (fungus infection) into parts of a large potato field. The potato field appears as a large rectangle bordered by light margins, in the upper center. The small dark rectangles are the diseased areas. They were discernible in this infrared photograph several days before the farmer could detect the disease on the ground. Such methods of early detection should enable the farmer to apply disease-control measures earlier and with more effectiveness. Although this photo was made from a plane, similar results can be obtained from spacecraft such as satellites, thus making possible the early detection of crop diseases on a worldwide basis. Such techniques could be used to great advantage in boosting crop production in a food-deficient world.*

16. More effective and widescale use should be made of aerial and space photography for the early detection of crop disease and insect pest problems. (See Figure 6–20.) Using infrared film, the National Aeronautics and Space Administration (NASA) has been able to provide farmers with early warnings of fungus infections in potato and grain fields.

17. Finally, as the recent Presidential Commission on World Hunger emphasized:

The containment of world hunger will require specific responses to problems that arise within diverse countries, cultures and political systems. There is no ideal food, no perfect diet, no universally acceptable agricultural system waiting to be transplanted from one geographic, climatic, and cultural setting to another. Assistance programs from developed countries and international agencies must focus on self-reliant growth, respond to the needs of each country, and not be based upon a predetermined strategy which attempts to generalize needs and requirements.

Rapid Review

1. Malthusian overpopulation is the presence of more people than the available food supply can support.

2. The eighteenth-century British economist Robert Malthus advanced the theory that human populations tend to increase faster than the available food supply. Eventually, therefore, the human population will experience a massive die-off, either from starvation or warfare and disease, until it is reduced to the limits imposed by the food supply.

3. Nutritionists assume that the average person must have a minimum of 2,200 calories daily. The average American receives 3,200 calories; the average Indian consumes only 1,600 calories.

4. Undernutrition is characterized by an insufficient amount of calories. Malnutrition, on the other hand, is caused by a diet deficient in vitamins and proteins.

5. Kwashiorkor is a protein-deficiency disease characterized by disorders of the digestive system, skin ulcers, swellings, wasting of the limbs, weakness, lethargy, and susceptibility to diseases.

137

6. One hundred thousand children die in Mexico each year because of the relationship between malnutrition and infectious diseases.

7. If we shortened our food chains, a much larger food base would be available theoretically to feed a hungry world.

8. The technology is available for the laboratory synthesis of all the basic sugars, fats, amino acids, and minerals in the human diet.

9. Yeast can be grown on organic substrates such as coal, petroleum, cannery waste, straw, and paper pulp wastes.

10. Of the 12.5 acres of the world's land available per capita, only 1.1 acres are being cultivated. At least 2.6 additional acres have food-production potential.

11. Two major problems frequently face the production of food on land that once was covered by tropical forests: the inability of the soil to hold a large supply of nutrients and the tendency for the iron-rich soil to turn brick-hard after a few years of exposure to the tropical sun.

12. Salinization and waterlogging have virtually destroyed the crop-producing capability of 5 million acres in West Pakistan alone.

13. The North American Water and Power Alliance project proposes to transfer water from major Canadian rivers to water-short regions of the United States. The project would cost $100 billion and would require twenty years to complete.

14. Less developed nations will have to boost fertilizer production more than sevenfold in order to meet the food demands of the population increase during the period from 1970 to 2000.

15. Rats, insects, and fungi annually destroy 33 million tons of food throughout the world, sufficient to feed one third of the population of India.

16. Over 50 percent of the world's croplands are devoted to the growing of just three species of plants: wheat, rice, and corn.

17. Under the leadership of Norman Borlaug, agricultural geneticists in Mexico developed superior varieties of high-yielding wheat and other grains. These varieties respond to fertilizer inputs, are less prone to wind damage than traditional strains, and may be cropped several times a year because of the short growing season required.

18. Certain disadvantages of the Green Revolution include (a) the limitations imposed by climate, (b) the lack of high-quality prime land, (c) the huge inputs of water, fertilizer, pesticides, and energy that are required, (d) the accentuation of the gap between the rich and poor farmers, (e) the fostering of monotypes, susceptible to diseases and pests, and (f) the sharp reduction in the genetic diversity of agricultural plants.

19. Fish farming, wild-game ranching, and the selective breeding of livestock have potential for increasing global food production.

20. Providing food to hungry nations that cannot or will not take substantial measures to control their own reproductive rates is inhuman and irresponsible.

Key Words and Phrases

Algal culture
Amino acid
Artificial insemination
Borlaug (Norman)
Chlorella
Extension of agriculture
Fertilizer
Fish farming
Food donations
Food synthesis
Genetic diversity
Green Revolution
International Maize and Wheat Improvement Center
Kwashiorkor
Laterite
Lysine
Malaria
Malnutrition
Malthus (Robert)
Malthusian overpopulation
Miracle grains
Monotypes
North America Water and Power Alliance (NAWAPA)
Pesticides
Salinization
Tsetse fly
Undernutrition
Waterlogging
Wetlands
Wild-game ranches
Yeast culture
Zuider Zee

Questions and Topics for Discussion

1. Discuss the statement: "It is immoral to give food to the starving people of the poor nations." Do you agree? Why or why not?
2. Name the three most important food crops produced in the world.
3. Briefly list six major drawbacks of the Green Revolution.
4. Why is it important to preserve the *genetic diversity* of agricultural plants?
5. Discuss the advantages and disadvantages of algal culture as a method for boosting food production.

6. Give four reasons why, at first thought, the removal of tropical forests and the establishment of farming appear to have great promise.
7. Discuss the statement: "If all the people on earth became strict vegetarians, much more food would be available and malnutrition and starvation problems would be greatly diminished." Do you agree? Why or why not?
8. Describe three advantages that wild-game ranching has over traditional cattle ranching.
9. Why was the Nobel Peace Prize awarded to Norman Borlaug?
10. Discuss the statement: "It is immoral for Americans to be well fed and healthy when 25,000 people are starving to death every day in the poor nations of the world." Do you agree? Why or why not?
11. Discuss the *long-term* food production problems that may be caused by human attempts to boost food production *now*.
12. Sketch the broad outlines of a master blueprint for increasing food production on planet Earth.

Endnotes

1. Borgstrom, Georg. *World Food Resources.* New York: Intext, 1973.
2. Brown, Harrison. "If World Population Doubles by the Year 2000." *U.S. News and World Report* (Jan. 9, 1967), 51–54.
3. Chrispeels, Maarten, J., and David Sadava. *Plants, Food and People.* San Francisco: Freeman, 1977.
4. Davis, Wayne H. "Thoughts on Feeding the Hungry: More or Less People?" *New Republic,* **162** (June 20, 1970), 19–21.
5. Editorial, *Biosciences* (Feb. 1969).
6. Ehrlich, Paul R. *The Population Bomb.* New York: Ballantine, 1968.
7. Ehrlich, Paul R., Anne H. Ehrlich, and John P. Holdren. *Human Ecology: Problems and Solutions.* San Francisco: Freeman, 1973.
8. Ehrlich, Paul R., and John P. Holdren. "Population and Panaceas: A Technological Perspective." *Biosciences,* **19** (Dec. 1969), 1065–1071.

9. Miller, G. Tyler. *Living in the Environment: Concepts, Problems, and Alternatives.* New York: Wadsworth, 1981.
10. Nash, T. A. M. *Africa's Bane. The Tsetse Fly.* London: Collins, 1969.
11. National Academy of Sciences. *Resources and Man.* San Francisco: Freeman, 1969.
12. Oser, Jacob. *Must Men Starve?* New York: Abelard-Schuman, 1957.
13. Paddock, William, and Paul Paddock. *Famine— 1975!* Boston: Little, Brown, 1967.
14. U.S. Department of Agriculture. *Annual Summary 1966. International Agricultural Development.* Washington, DC: Department of Agriculture, 1968.
15. Wagner, Richard H. *Environment and Man.* 3rd ed. New York: Norton, 1978.

Suggested Readings for the Interested Student

Brown, Lester R. *Food or Fuel: New Competition for the World's Cropland.* Washington, DC: Worldwatch Society, 1980. The world's attempt to grow crops for fuel may result in serious food-shortage problems.
———. *World Population Trends: Signs of Hope, Signs of Stress.* Washington, DC: Worldwatch Society, October 1976. This is an outstanding analysis of the global population picture and its associated resource and environmental problems.
———. *The World-wide Loss of Cropland.* Worldwatch Paper 24. Washington, DC: Worldwatch Institute, October 1978. This is a superb discussion of the multiple factors reducing food production.
Gilland, Bernard. *The Next Seventy Years: Population, Food and Resources.* Forest Grove, OR: ISBS, 1979. This is an outstanding projection of the global food and population picture.
Winikoff, B. "Nutrition, Population and Health: Some Implications for Policy." *Science,* **200** (May 26, 1978), 895. The author presents a superb analysis of our planet's food and population dilemma.
Wortman, Sterling, and Ralph W. Cummings, Jr. *To Feed This World: The Challenge and the Strategy.* Baltimore: Johns Hopkins, 1978. This is an excellent overview of the methods by which global food needs might be met.

7 Water

Our Nation's Water Crisis

The United States receives 4.2 trillion gallons (16 trillion liters) of precipitation daily. Sounds like a lot, doesn't it? Nevertheless, authorities warn us that a severe water shortage is the most urgent, long-range, environmental problem facing our nation. How can this be? There are several reasons: (1) a rapidly increasing population, (2) rising demands by agriculture, industry, and cities, (3) flagrant waste, (4) unequal distribution, and (5) pollution.

1. *Agriculture.* Irrigated crop acreage has almost tripled during the last thirty years to about 40 million acres (16 million hectares). The capacity of the Ogallala aquifer, which extends from Nebraska south to Texas, is being strained to the limit because of withdrawals by farmers (as well as industry and cities) — in some areas it has dropped 2 to 5 feet (0.6 to 1.5 meters) per year.
2. *Industry.* Industry uses water to cool equipment and products and to serve as steam to generate electrical power. Its use is highly intensive. For example, electrical power plants in the United States use 89 billion gallons (337 billion liters) a day. It takes 14 gallons of water to make a pound of sugar, 150 gallons for the Sunday newspaper, and 65,000 gallons to manufacture an automobile. One cup of water was needed to make the page you're reading. Our nation is experiencing a fuel-shortage problem. But abundant water is essential to our attempt to solve the energy di-

lemma. For example, it will take 6.5 billion gallons of water annually just to move a coal-water mixture through a pipeline from Wyoming to Arkansas. Moreover, three barrels of water are needed to make a single barrel of synthetic fuel from shale or coal.
3. *Urban use.* Eighty percent of the U.S. population, about 180 million people, depend on 21,000 municipal water systems for their water supply. Sixty gallons (230 liters) are used each day by the average American family. This level of use seems very wasteful in light of the fact that our European counterparts use only half as much. We use water to wash everything from a ten-ton truck to a baby's ear. We use it to douse fires, flush sewage, and clean city streets.
4. *Unequal distribution.* Our water problems are not caused by *absolute* shortages in supply; rather they are problems of *distribution* caused by the intensive concentration of water-using industries and people. The accelerated migration of people to the Southwest, for example, has reduced water supplies in the area to the vanishing point. As a result, water will have to be transported long distances from water-rich regions. For example, in the mid-1980s a $2 billion scheme called the Central Arizona Project will be launched. It will supply Tucson and Phoenix with water from the Colorado River, which is more than 300 miles away. Regrettably, however, by that time if all the Colorado River water that has been legally committed to seven states

140

and Mexico is actually delivered, the Colorado River will be bone dry.

Iowans are up in arms over a plan to channel some water from the Missouri River to Nebraska and Texas. Texas is squabbling with both Nebraska and Arkansas over water rights. Apparently, there just isn't enough of the precious liquid to go around.

5. *The Pollution problem.* Pollution has contributed heavily to our nation's water shortage problems. (See Chapter 8.) For example, some residents in Lake Carmel, New York, have been unable to use their well water for two years because it has been contaminated with gasoline. Lead from old pipes has made water supplies in parts of Boston unfit to drink. According to the EPA, our rivers are so contaminated at 34 sites that public health may be jeopardized. The trouble spots range from the Delaware River near Philadelphia to the bayous near Beaumont, Texas; from the Mississippi River below Minneapolis-St. Paul to the Lake River in Oregon.

The Water Cycle

Because of the cyclical nature of water movement (Figure 7–1), a given water molecule may be used over and over again through the centuries. For example, the bath water used by Cleopatra over 2,000 years ago has flowed to the sea and mixed throughout the oceans. Some has already evaporated and

7 – 1 *The hydrologic cycle.*

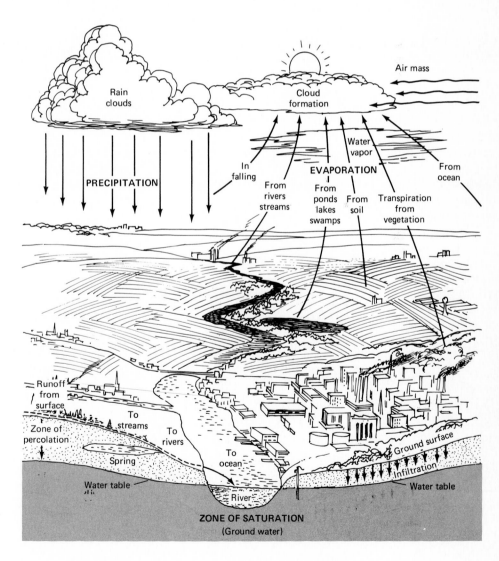

7–2 *North Tongass National Forest, Alaska. Glaciers represent a phase of the hydrologic cycle: about three fourths of the world's fresh water is locked up in glaciers and polar ice caps. They hold as much water as would flow through the world's rivers in about 1,000 years. This is a view of Mendenhall Glacier. Many of the lakes in the northeastern states were originally formed from glacial meltwater.*

fallen on the continents as rain (14). A few molecules from *her* bath may be present in *your* bath next Saturday. In a more serious vein, however, not only bathwater, but *all* water on planet Earth is recycled. Even the 110 pounds of water in the average college student's body is recycled several times during an average school year (21).

Although fluctuations in rate of water movement may occur in certain parts of the cycle, the total water volume involved has remained constant for millions of years. The cycle is powered by solar energy and gravity, the daily energy input being *greater than all the energy utilized by human beings since the dawn of civilization.* Solar energy lifts the water upward from the soil, plants, oceans, lakes, and streams during evaporation, while gravity pulls

Table 7–1 Water Cycle Facts

	Location of Reservoir	Total Water Supply (in %)	Renewal Time
On the land	Ice caps	2.225	16,000 years
	Glaciers	.015	16,000 years
	Freshwater lakes	.009	10–100 years (varies with depth)
	Saltwater lakes	.007	10–100 years (varies with depth)
	Rivers	.0001	12–20 days
Subsurface	Soil moisture	.003	280 days
	Groundwater		
	To half-mile depth	.303	300 years
	Beyond half-mile depth	.303	4,600 years
Other	Atmosphere	.001	9–12 days
	World's oceans	97.134	37,000 years maximum
Total		100.000	

Sources: Moran (22); Miller (21).

it down again as rain or snow (21). In actuality all water is not continuously moving. It may be temporarily stored (for centuries) either within the earth's crust, on the earth's surface as polar ice caps or glaciers, or in the atmosphere. (See Figure 7 – 2.) Only about 0.03 percent of the global water supply actually moves through the cycle in a given year. Familiarity with the water cycle (see Table 7 – 1) is basic to appreciating the nature and complexity of the serious water-conservation problems confronting the United States. Average recycling (replacement) periods range from nine days for water in the atmosphere to 37,000 years for the deep oceans.

OCEANS. When the astronauts peered down at the earth from outer space, it appeared blue, with just a few patches of green. This is understandable, because oceans cover 70 percent of our blue planet. The oceans, parts of which are up to seven miles deep, contain 97.2 percent of the world's total water supply, over 317 million cubic miles. (There are a million million — 1,000,000,000,000 — gallons of water in a cubic mile.) (See Figure 7 – 3.) If the earth were a perfectly smooth sphere, the ocean water would be sufficient to submerge the entire globe to a depth of 800 feet. Water molecules at the ocean's surface are warmed by the sun; they gradually rise into the atmosphere as a gas in a process called *evaporation.* Were the oceans not constantly refilled, they would drop by 39 inches each year (18).

PRECIPITATION. As the water vapor rises, it gradually cools, condenses, and forms clouds. Water that has evaporated from a Louisiana rice field may eventually fall as rain on a college campus in Ohio. Moisture-laden clouds may be carried inland over coastal areas, such as the Gulf or Pacific coasts, and finally, when cooled off sufficiently (as when they pass up the slope of a mountain or when they meet a cold air mass), may release water as rain, snow, hail, or sleet. Our nation's average annual rainfall would be sufficient to cover the entire country (if it were perfectly level) to a depth of 30 inches. In the United States, unfortunately, rainfall is very unevenly distributed, both in time and space. The average annual precipitation per state is shown in Figure 7 – 4. Death Valley receives only 1.7 inches annually, whereas the western slope of the Cascades, not too far from it, receives 140 to 150 inches (18). On one side of Mount Waialeale, Hawaii, annual rainfall is

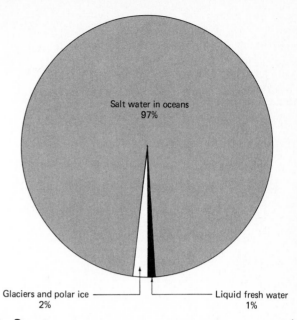

7 – 3 *The oceans represent an enormous reservoir of water, forming 97 percent of all the water passing through the water cycle.*

460 inches, in contrast to a mere 18 inches on the opposite side. A certain town in Florida was deluged with 24 inches of rain in a single day, yet Bagdad, California, once received only 4 inches in five years!

When rain or snow originally forms high above the earth's surface, it is uncontaminated with foreign materials. However, as the raindrops and snowflakes fall earthward they intercept various atmospheric pollutants, such as carbon dioxide, soot, dust, pollen, and bacteria. Where rain falls through atmosphere that is polluted with oxides of sulphur and nitrogen, as is the case in many industrial areas, it is converted into dilute sulphuric and nitric acids. The pH of this rain may be as low as 3, sufficient to corrode water pipes and accelerate the leaching of soil nutrients (22). Eventually all the contaminants in the water are borne to streams, lakes, and finally the ocean, which serves as the ultimate "sink."

The ratio of precipitation to evaporation is of utmost importance in determining the type of biome (ecosystem) occurring in a given region. The higher the ratio, of course, the wetter the area; the lower the ratio, the drier the area. The eastern part of the United States, which represents the deciduous forest biome, has a precipitation-evaporation ratio of about 1.2. The prairie biome has a ratio of 0.4, and the deserts of California, Arizona, and New Mexico

143

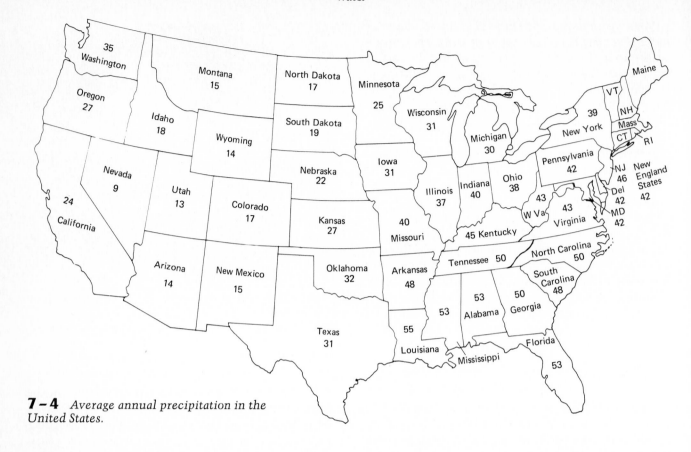

7-4 *Average annual precipitation in the United States.*

have a ratio of 0.2 or less (17). The fate of precipitation in the United States is shown in Figure 7–5.

BODIES OF ORGANISMS.   Plants absorb soil water through their root systems. Animals get their water by direct absorption through their body surfaces (amphibians), by drinking (many birds and mammals), or from the plant tissues (herbivores) and animal tissues (insectivores and carnivores) they consume.

During your lifetime of about seventy years, your body will take in more than 16,000 gallons of water. The body of the average human adult contains 50 quarts (100 pounds) of water. Water has many functions. It serves as a solvent that promotes chemical activity. It serves as a transportation medium for nutrients, hormones, enzymes, minerals, nitrogenous wastes, and respiratory gases. In the form of sweat it has a cooling effect on the body. Human reproduction would be impossible without water. The 300 million sperm that are injected into the female's vagina during intercourse are absolutely dependent on a predominantly aqueous medium for

the 45-minute swim to the egg. The average adult loses 2.5 quarts daily — 1.5 quarts by the excretion of urine, one pint by perspiration, and one pint by exhaling. One and one-half quarts are replaced by drinking and the other quart by eating. Death would result were we to lose more than 12 percent of our body's water content.

EVAPORATION AND TRANSPIRATION.   Of the 30 inches of annual rainfall, about 21 inches (70 percent) pass back into the atmosphere by evaporation and transpiration. *Evaporation* may take place directly from the surface of wet vegetation, moist soil, streams, and oceans or from the bodies of animals and their excreta. Some of the very water molecules that evaporate from your body after a hard game of tennis may some day fall as rain on your backyard vegetable patch. *Transpiration* is the evaporation that occurs through the pores of plant leaves. This process is essential to the plant's survival, for it serves to draw dissolved nutrients from the soil upward through the stem (or trunk) to the leaves. One mature oak tree may transpire *100 gallons per day,*

144

The Water Cycle

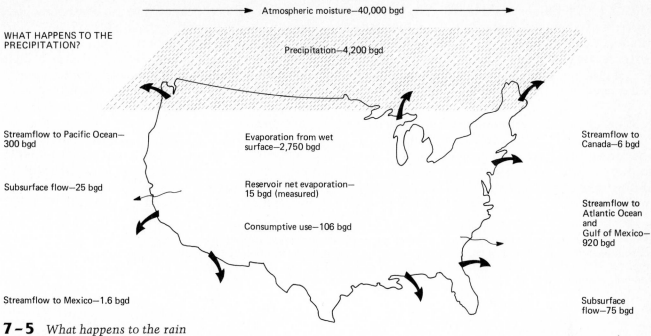

Atmospheric moisture—40,000 bgd

WHAT HAPPENS TO THE PRECIPITATION?

Precipitation—4,200 bgd

Streamflow to Pacific Ocean—300 bgd

Evaporation from wet surface—2,750 bgd

Streamflow to Canada—6 bgd

Subsurface flow—25 bgd

Reservoir net evaporation—15 bgd (measured)

Streamflow to Atlantic Ocean and Gulf of Mexico—920 bgd

Consumptive use—106 bgd

Streamflow to Mexico—1.6 bgd

Subsurface flow—75 bgd

7–5 *What happens to the rain and snow? Water continuously evaporates into the atmosphere, most of it from the oceans. About 40,000 billion gallons per day (bgd) pass over the United States as water vapor, even in times of drought. Roughly 1 gallon in 10—4,200 billion gallons per day — falls to the surface of the conterminous United States. That works out to an average of 30 inches a year, of which 26 inches arrive as rainfall and the rest as snow, sleet, and hail.*

But few places receive the average precipitation, which ranges from less than 4 inches a year in the Great Basin to more than 200 inches a year along the Pacific Northwest coast.

More than two-thirds of the precipitation returns to the atmosphere, but 9 inches (1,300 bgd) either soaks down to the ground-water table or runs into surface water supplies, where it eventually moves to the ocean. Only a fraction—106 bgd—is consumed.

7–6 *Fate of water that has fallen on the ground as precipitation.*

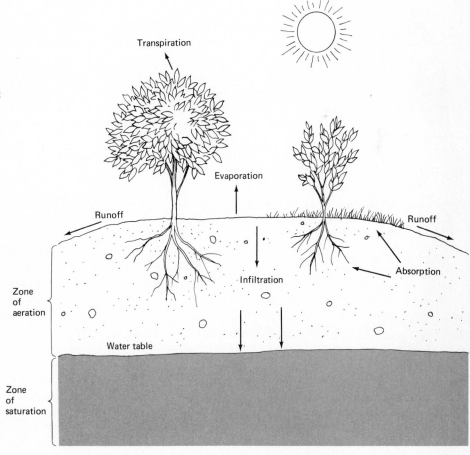

Transpiration

Evaporation

Runoff

Runoff

Absorption

Infiltration

Zone of aeration

Water table

Zone of saturation

145

almost 40,000 gallons in a year (18). The water that passes back into the atmosphere by transpiration cannot be controlled by humans. Nevertheless, this water serves us well in sustaining over 350,000 species of plants, ranging from the regal redwood to the lowly squash.

SURFACE WATER. About nine of the thirty inches of annual rainfall in the United States contribute to the formation of ponds, lakes, and streams and are known as *surface water.* Some may filter downward through the pores and channels of the earth's crust and form groundwater. Surface water and ground-

water are of direct concern to the conservationist, for it is only this portion that yields to human control and is usable for domestic, industrial, agricultural, and recreational purposes. (See Figure 7 – 7.) It is this portion that we pollute with toxic chemicals, pesticides, human waste, and with many other contaminants — a problem we will discuss in the next chapter.

Stream flow in the United States amounts to an average 1,200 billion gallons a day. It may be in the form of a tiny mountain brook or a mighty river such as the Mississippi, which drains 40 percent of the land area in the United States and flows 2,300

7 – 7 *Theoretical scheme showing the fate of 100 units of water withdrawn from a stream to service two farms, a wildlife area, and a city. Although 157 units are actually applied within the service area, because 57 units can be reused, the net water demand for the area is only 100 units.*

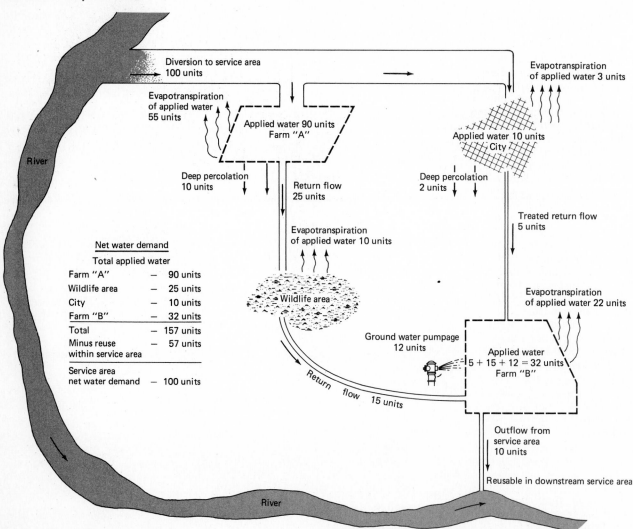

7-8 *Aquifer serves as a source of well water. Continued water withdrawal would eventually deplete the supply if the rate of withdrawal exceeded the rate of recharge.*

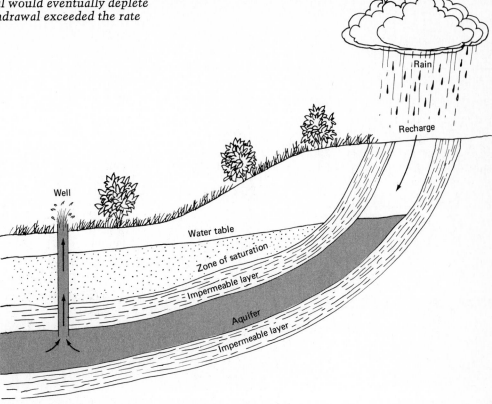

miles across mid-America to the Gulf. Surface runoff water, in the form of streams, ponds, and lakes, satisfies about 80 percent of our water requirements. This water flow can be either destructive (floods and erosion) or beneficial (hydropower, fish habitat, scenic beauty, commercial shipping, and recreation).

GROUNDWATER. Instead of forming surface water, such as ponds and streams, some of the rainfall and snowmelt gradually seeps downward through the soil — a process called *infiltration*. This water first moves through the *zone of aeration*. This zone, which includes both the topsoil and subsoil, is characterized by pore spaces which contain both water and *air*. The soil moisture in this zone is known as *capillary water*. Some of this water is absorbed by plant root systems. It then passes up plant stems and tree trunks to the leaves. Most of this water then evaporates from the leaves into the atmosphere. This process is called *transpiration*. A small amount of the water in the leaves is used as a raw material in photosynthesis.

Much of the soil water continues to filter downward through the zone of aeration into the *zone of saturation*. As the water moves through the soil, many pollutants may adhere to the surfaces of the soil particles. As a result, the water quality is improved. Eventually, the downward movement of the water through the zone of saturation is stopped by a layer of impermeable rock. As a result the water then accumulates in the soil and gravel above the impermeable layer until all the spaces, pores, and cracks become filled with water. The name "zone of saturation" is obviously very appropriate. The upper level of this zone is known as the *water table*. (See Figure 7-8.) The water table may coincide with the surface of the ground and form marshes or springs. In other cases the water table may be more than a mile deep.

Since time immemorial humans have tapped this groundwater by drilling wells deeper than the water table. After heavy rainfall, the water table rises. (An exception would be in the case of flash floods in deserts where most of the water runs off instead of infiltrating.) However, during periods of drought

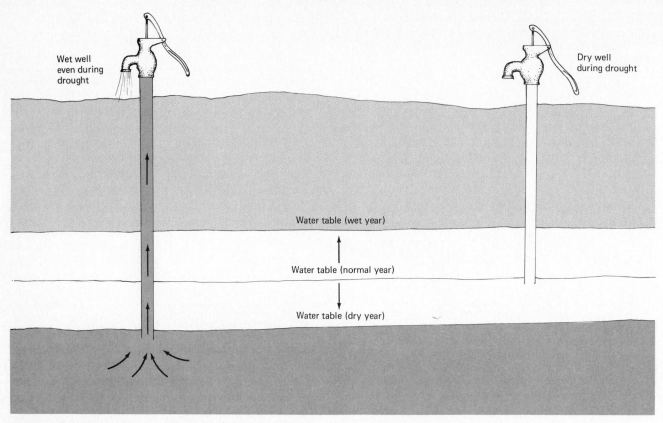

7-9 *Effect of drought on water-table levels and well-water availability.*

the water table drops. In extreme cases, some wells may run dry. (See Figure 7–9.)

Ninety-seven percent of the world's supply of fresh water (two million cubic miles) is held in porous and permeable layers of sand, sandstone, and limestone known as *aquifers*. The water is trapped in these aquifers because both the "roof" and "floor" of the aquifer consist of layers of impermeable rock such as shale and granite. (See Figure 7–8.) In the United States the groundwater in such aquifers in the upper one-half mile of the earth's crust is equal to all the water that will run off into the oceans during the next 100 years!

We are making extensive use of such aquifers. For example, "the sandstones that are yielding . . . great quantities of high-quality water for the city of Chicago got that water from rain that fell on the Great Plains far to the west a million years ago, then slowly trickled through the rocks at rates of a few feet or a few inches a year" (3). The Ogallala aquifer, one of the largest in the United States, spreads under 225,000 square miles of land that ex-

tends through eight states from Nebraska south to Texas. (See Figure 7–10.) This aquifer contains 650 trillion gallons (2.5 million billion liters). It provides drinking water for two million people. In the arid Southwest it makes possible a multibillion dollar economy based on irrigation farming.

Water Problems

Drought

According to the U.S. Weather Bureau, a drought exists whenever rainfall for a period of 21 days or longer is only 30 percent of the average for the time and place. The Great Plains from Texas to Montana, which include the arid part of the grassland biome, average about 35 consecutive drought days each year and 75 to 100 successive days of drought once in ten years. Up to 120 *consecutive rainless days* have been recorded for the southern Great Plains, or Dust Bowl, region. The relative frequency of

148

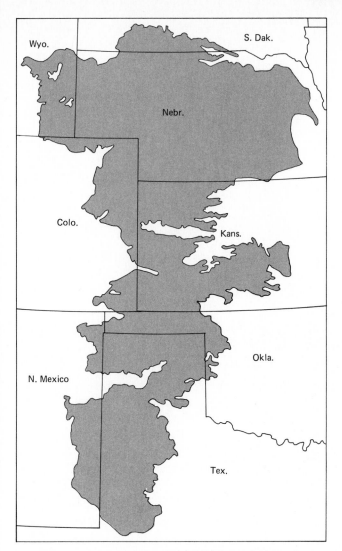

7–10 *Extent of the Ogallala Aquifer.*

fined so that he can predict in what *state* the next drought will occur (5).

THE DELAWARE RIVER BASIN DROUGHT. Twenty-two million people, 13 percent of the nation's population (27), in New York, New Jersey, and Delaware, depend on water drained by the Delaware River and its tributaries. From 1961 to 1965, this region experienced the most devastating drought in the entire history of the Northeast, with the water deficit affecting 300,000 square miles.

The mountain streams of upstate New York were reduced to a trickle. Famous trout streams dried up. Resorts closed in midsummer. Wild game suffered heavy mortality as a result of vanishing food supplies and protective cover. The hunting and fishing vacation lands of thirty million people were so adversely affected that the resort industry alone suffered an annual loss of many millions of dollars.

Saltwater intrusion, advancing at a rate of one-half mile a day, corroded expensive industrial equipment, contaminated the underground aquifers of water-thirsty Camden, and became a threat to Philadelphia.

THE CALIFORNIA DROUGHT. Although many of the central and western states suffered from drought during 1976–1977, the water shortage in California had perhaps the greatest impact. Water levels in some streams were the lowest on record. Rainfall at 19 measuring stations was only 47 percent of normal. Reservoirs contained only 39 percent of their normal supply. Domestic supplies of water ran so low that severe restrictions had to be made on its use. The number of tub baths a person could take was greatly reduced. Sports cars went unwashed, even by college students planning for a Friday night date. Eventually full-scale water rationing was imposed.

The Council on Environmental Quality listed some of the important effects of the drought:

[The city of] Klamath [California] hauled freshwater because saltwater intruded into the aquifer tapped by municipal supply wells. Recreation was also affected. Many reservoir levels fell below the boat ramps, making access impossible. Survival rates for . . . salmon, striped bass, and shad were much lower than normal. Factors responsible were the reduction . . . of fish spawning and nesting habitats, . . . increased temperatures in streams and reservoirs, and low dilution of toxic pollutants. (7)

drought in various regions of the United States is shown in Figure 7–11.

J. Murray Mitchell, a research climatologist with the National Oceanic and Atmospheric Administration, has studied drought patterns as revealed by tree rings. Going all the way back to A.D. 1600 he has found that the western states have experienced a prolonged extended drought about every 22 years. Much to his surprise, Mitchell found that the drought cycle is correlated with the alternate 11-year minimum of sunspots. Such information is extremely valuable for national planning purposes. However, Mitchell's research is not sufficiently re-

149

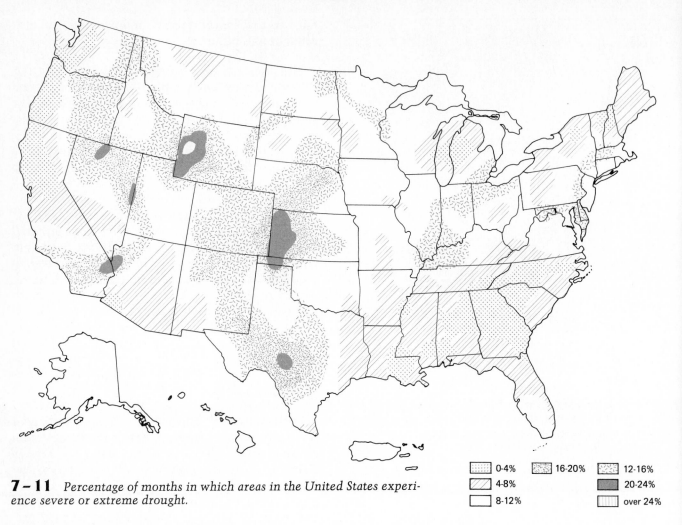

0-4%	16-20%	12-16%
4-8%	20-24%	
8-12%	over 24%	

7 – 11 *Percentage of months in which areas in the United States experience severe or extreme drought.*

Table 7 – 2 Examples of Flood Disasters

Date	Location	Deaths and Injuries	Property Damage
1811	Danube (Germany and Austria)	2,000 drowned	24 villages washed away
1861	Sacramento River (California)	700 drowned	
1877	Hwang Ho (China)	7 million drowned	Destroyed 300 villages; 2 million homeless
1889	Conemaugh River (dam burst) (Pennsylvania)	2,000 drowned at Johnstown, Pa.	$10 million
1900	Galveston, Texas (hurricane-spawned flood waters)	6,000 dead	3,000 buildings destroyed
1936 – 1937	Mississippi River	500 drowned 800,000 injured	$200 million
1942	Columbia River		$100 million
1955	Atlantic Coast (Hurricane Hazel)		$1.6 billion
1965	Upper Mississippi River	16 drowned, 330 injured	$140 million
1979	Zambezi River (Mozambique)	45 drowned	250,000 homeless
1979	Brazos River (West Texas)	22 drowned	
1980	Southeast Brazil	700 drowned	350,000 homeless
1981	Northern India	1,500 deaths	Extensive crop losses

Floods

Not only are we plagued by water scarcity, we also are beset with the equally serious problem of too *much* water from violent rainstorms and floods. Throughout history we have suffered from destructive floods. (See Table 7 – 2.)

How Can We Save Water?

During a recent drought it was reported that one Californian stapled a stamp to an envelope to save saliva (22)! Such extreme measures may be heroic but they are unnecessary. Here is a list of practical measures on how to save water at home that could save our nation billions of gallons of precious water every year.

A. Save in the Bathroom
1. Take shorter showers.
2. Don't use the toilet as a waste basket.
3. Don't let the water run while brushing your teeth.
4. Don't run the water while shaving. Plug and partly fill the basin to rinse your razor.
5. Repair leaks promptly.
6. If you replace your toilet, install a low-flush unit.
7. A few drops of food coloring or dye tablets in your toilet tank can help you spot a leak. If color appears in the bowl, you have a leak. Fix it promptly.
8. The toilet consumes 45 percent of all water used in the home because five to seven gallons of water are lost with every flush. By placing bricks or plastic bottles in your toilet tank you can save up to two gallons per flush. If every toilet in America had such devices, our nation would save millions of gallons per day.
9. Install a low-flow shower head.

B. Save in the Kitchen
1. Wash only full loads in your washing machine and dishwasher.
2. If you wash dishes by hand, don't let the water run.
3. Cool your drinking water in the refrigerator, *not* by letting the water run.
4. Don't use water-wasting garbage disposals.
5. *Stop those leaks* (New York City alone wastes 200 million gallons each day because of them). Leaking faucets and wasteful people are robbing Americans of scarce water supplies. A small leak (eighty drips per minute) wastes seven gallons (26.5 liters) of water daily.

C. Save Water Outside Your Home
1. Use a broom, not a hose, to clean driveways, sidewalks, and steps.
2. Use an "on-off" spray nozzle on your hose.
3. Wash your car with a bucket of water; use a hose only to rinse.
4. Water your lawn and garden only during the cool of the day. Older trees and shrubs often do not require irrigation. Plants are frequently over-watered.
5. Remove water-stealing weeds from lawn and garden.
6. Use less fertilizer; it increases need of plants for water.
7. Add decomposing leaves or peat moss to your soil for improved water-holding capacity.

Source: California Department of Water Resources. *Save Water.* Sacramento, California, 1982.

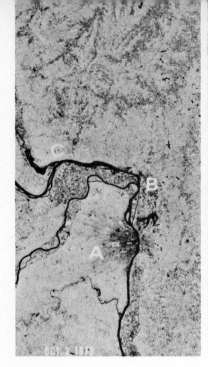

7-12 *Flooding at St. Louis, Missouri, as revealed by NASA's Earth Resources Technology Satellite. In photograph on the left, taken Oct. 2, 1972, St. Louis can be located by the letter A. North of St. Louis, the Missouri River joins the Mississippi River at point B, and further upstream the confluence of the Illinois and Mississippi rivers is noted at C. The photograph on the right was taken of the same region on March 31, 1973. It shows areas under water (D) as a result of flooding. In this near infrared wave-length view, the darkest tones indicate areas of deepest water. The Mississippi River was 38 feet deep at St. Louis, the highest level since 1903. In this photo about 300,000 acres are submerged. The flood wave slowly made its way downstream, threatening cities and agricultural lands along the entire length of the Mississippi River.*

Paradoxically, however, in some parts of the world, our very survival may be dependent on floods. The flourishing agricultural economy of Egypt was sustained for millennia by the recurrent flooding of the Nile. Each inundation was eagerly awaited by floodplain farmers, for when the Nile finally receded, it left behind a bank deposit of extremely fertile topsoil carried from its upstream watershed.

THE UPPER MISSISSIPPI FLOOD. An unusual combination of factors involving excessive rainfall, massive snowmelt, and frozen ground set the stage for a "once-in-a-century" flood in the upper Missis-

sippi River Valley during the spring of 1965. Swollen with spring runoff waters, the Mississippi River surged over its banks from Minneapolis south to its junction with the Missouri at Hannibal, Missouri. Thousands of acres of winter wheat were devastated. More than 90,000 acres of cropland were submerged in Illinois alone. The *Hiawatha*, a crack express train, was forced to halt its Minneapolis–Milwaukee run for the first time in history. At Hannibal, a few resolute shop owners hung out "business as usual" signs, even though much of Main Street was open to motorboat traffic only. At Mankato State College in Minnesota, hundreds of student volunteers erected a sandbag barrier to re-

7-13 *Flood damage in Harrison, Arkansas, caused by the storm of May 7, 1961. Four lives were lost. Damage was estimated at $5,278,000.*

strain the floodwaters. Despite such emergency measures, the rising waters drove 40,000 people from their homes. After a helicopter survey of the stricken area, President Lyndon B. Johnson gave this terse summary: "It was terrible." Eventually the waters receded. A thick, smelly deposit of brownish ooze covered the wall-to-wall carpeting of many riverfront homes. Thousands of fish were stranded in stagnant backwaters. The official toll read: 16 drowned, 330 injured, and $140 million in property damage.

Flood Control

Although we cannot prevent *all* floods, we can prevent some of the lesser ones and can restrict the magnitude and destructiveness of others. Flood-

7 – 14 *Flooding problems as identified by Federal and State regional study teams. The good news is that 1.3 billion acres of nonfederal land are not prone to flooding. The bad news is that damages are expected to increase in the years ahead on the 175 million acres of land that are flood-prone. (A flood-prone area is land adjoining rivers, streams, or lakes where there is a 1 percent chance of flooding in any given year.) Forty-eight million acres of flood-prone land are cropland, 106 million are pasture, range, and forest, and 21 million are other land, including built-up areas.*

Twenty-one thousand communities are subject to floods including 6,000 towns or cities with populations exceeding 2,500. In 1975, the potential damage from floods was $3.4 billion, expressed in 1975 dollars. Because both the number and real value of buildings and their contents are increasing, flood damages also are on the increase.

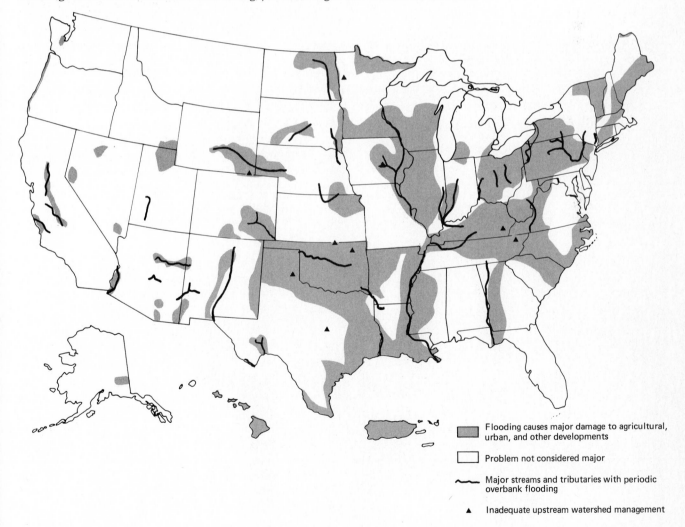

Flooding causes major damage to agricultural, urban, and other developments

Problem not considered major

Major streams and tributaries with periodic overbank flooding

▲ Inadequate upstream watershed management

153

control measures include protecting the watershed, measuring snowpack to predict flood conditions; building levees, and utilizing dredging operations and dams.

PROTECTING THE WATERSHED. A *watershed* is the area drained by a single watercourse. It may range from fewer than 1,000 to more than one million acres. The largest watersheds, such as those of the Ohio, Missouri, Colorado, and Mississippi rivers, are known as *drainage basins*. All watersheds, large or small, have the basic function of converting precipitation into stream flow. Even during a light shower of only 0.1 inch of rain, the water would be converted by a one-square-mile watershed into 1.74 million gallons of stream flow.

Watersheds are protected under terms of the Watershed Protection and Flood Prevention Act. The small watershed program is administered by the USDA's Soil Conservation Service. According to the USDA, 8,000 (61.5 percent) of the 13,000 small watersheds (of less than 250,000 acres) in this country have flood and erosion problems (33). (See Figure 7–14.) Protection of large watersheds is primarily the concern of the Bureau of Reclamation, the U.S. Army Corps of Engineers, and the Tennessee Valley Authority (TVA). Although the primary objective of the act is flood control, it is operated under a multiple-purpose concept, and where possible it embraces problems of erosion, water supply, wildlife management, and recreation.

Any type of vegetational cover on the watershed will impede flow velocity and hence will be of value in flood and erosion control. This is illustrated by the following incident. Some years ago, merry celebrations ushering in the New Year at La Crescenta, California, were abruptly ended. Floodwaters rushed down from the adjacent hillsides of the San

7–15 *Snow surveyors viewing Ward Creek, a tributary to Lake Tahoe.*

Gabriel Mountains, inflicting $5 million in damage and killing thirty people. When flood-control experts investigated the watershed above La Crescenta, they discovered that the floodwaters originated from a seven-square-mile area in the San Gabriel Mountains *that had been burned over only a short time before.* However, the unburned watershed, with its vegetational sponge of chaparral, herbs, and grasses, served to restrain the downhill rush of runoff waters; peak flows were roughly 5 percent of those of the burned areas. Whether it is California chaparral, Alabama alfalfa, or Wisconsin woodlands, any type of vegetational cover is to some degree useful in flood control.

MEASURING SNOWPACK TO PREDICT FLOOD CONDITIONS.   In recent years the U.S. Geological Survey has employed snow surveyors to conduct measurements of the areas and depth of the snowpack at more than 1,000 snow courses in the western mountains. Several years ago such a survey predicted that the imminent spring snowmelt in the Northwest would crest the Kootenai River at 35.5 feet, sufficient to cause extensive flooding at Bonner's Ferry, Idaho. Alerted by this forewarning, federal troops evacuated all residents and reinforced the dikes. On May 21, the river crested at 35.5 feet, as predicted. Flood damage was minimized, however, and not one life was lost.

LEVEES.   Levees are dikes constructed of earth, stone, or mortar that are built at varying distances from the river margin in an effort to protect valuable residential, industrial, and agricultural property from floodwaters. Levees along the Arkansas, Red, White, and Ouachita rivers in Arkansas have given a measure of protection to more than two million acres of fertile alluvial land. During the last 150 years, a mammoth system of over 3,500 levees and dikes has been constructed along the lower Mississippi River.

There are certain negative features associated with levees, however. In some situations, they may actually *increase* flood damage rather than reduce it. This is especially true in the U.S. because the presence of levees encourages people to settle on flood plains. This situation results from pressures exerted by real estate agencies and developers to change zoning on flood plains so that they can reap huge profits. All of this activity takes place in the political arena. (See Figure 7–16.)

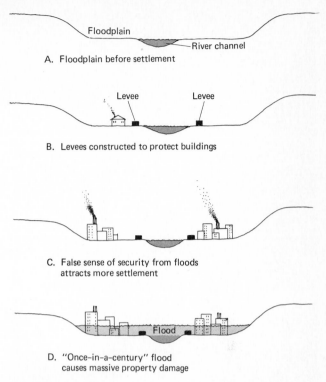

A. Floodplain before settlement

B. Levees constructed to protect buildings

C. False sense of security from floods attracts more settlement

D. "Once-in-a-century" flood causes massive property damage

7 – 16 *Sequence of events on a floodplain that leads to massive flooding.*

DREDGING OPERATIONS.   Because of the huge amounts of soil that are washed into a stream from the surrounding watershed, the channel tends to accumulate sediment, which in turn increases the probability of a flood. The enormity of this problem can be appreciated if we note that the Mississippi River, for example, transports roughly two million tons of sediment daily. To cope with this situation (as well as to deepen the channels for navigation), our major river channels are periodically dredged by the U.S. Army Corps of Engineers.

The importance of periodic dredging is emphasized by the 1852 Yellow River catastrophe in China. As the channel of this river became choked with silt, levees were built higher and higher, until the Yellow River was flowing above the rooftops. Eventually, a massive surge of floodwaters crumbled the retaining walls and drowned two million people.

It should be emphasized, however, that unless they are very carefully planned and executed, dredging operations, may have harmful environmental side effects such as water pollution and wildlife-habitat destruction.

155

7 – 17 *Hoover Dam, one of the world's largest dams. This dam is located on the Arizona-Nevada border, 25 miles southeast of Las Vegas. The electric generators at the dam supply most of the power needs of southern California, Arizona, and Nevada. It restrains the turbulent waters of the Colorado and is valuable in controlling floods downstream. Water from Lake Mead, the 115-mile-long impoundment behind the dam, irrigates one million acres and has increased crop production 120 percent in this region.*

DAMS. Even though there have been serious criticisms because of their expense and siltation-abbreviated life span, the United States has apparently committed itself to a vast program of superdam construction. The largest is the Hoover Dam on the Colorado River. (See Figure 7 – 17.) The Colorado drains almost one thirteenth of the area of the United States. This 6.5-million-ton concrete dam was built to control the river, prevent flooding, and provide irrigation water and cheap electrical power for thousands of farmers in the arid Southwest. The Hoover Dam stands 726 feet high. The impounded water forms Lake Mead, the largest reservoir in the world. One hundred fifteen miles long, it has an area of 246 square miles. Its storage capacity of nearly 30 million acre-feet would be adequate to meet all the water requirements of New York City residents for twenty years.

Are dams effective in flood control? According to Brigadier General W. P. Leber, Ohio River Division Army Engineer, an Ohio River flood of several years ago would have caused additional damage of $290 million had it not been for the coordinated system of thirty flood-control reservoirs, plus 62 floodwalls and levees. He stated that flood crests were reduced by up to 10.5 feet by those flood-control facilities (26). The retention of water by the Shasta Dam and others in northern California aids in preventing the flash floods that formerly plagued the region. Partial flood control is also effected by such dams as the Santee in South Carolina, the Grand Coulee on the Columbia, and the Hoover on the Colorado. Several years ago Los Angeles County, which has experienced repeated floods from rain-swollen rivers, established a coordinated complex of control structures costing nearly $600 million. It involves 60 headwater dams in the mountains, 14 retention reservoirs in the Los Angeles and San Gabriel rivers, and 6 major flood-control dams. This system has proven to be very successful in protecting 325 million acres from flooding.

THE DISADVANTAGES OF DAMS. Despite the value of big dams in flood control and in generating hydroelectric power, some authorities are very critical of big dams. Some of the negative features associated with these dams are listed in Table 7–3. The critics feel that we should increase regulatory measures (keeping buildings and industry off the flood plain) rather than rely on dams and other structural methods of control to reduce flood damage. (See Figure 7–18.)

The Siltation Problem. Another drawback associated with the construction of big dams is the speed with which their reservoirs fill with sediment. The rate of filling depends, of course, on the soil types in the drainage basin, topography, and the degree to which soil erosion is controlled. Because the Columbia River is relatively sediment-free, such dams as the Grand Coulee and Bonneville might have a storage life of 1,000 years. However, the life span of dams constructed across muddier streams may be quite short. For example, the huge Lake Mead Reservoir behind Hoover Dam across the Colorado

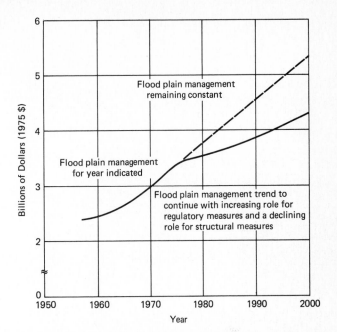

7–18 *Flood damages, historical and projected, in the United States. Note that if there is no increase in floodplain management, by the year 2000, annual flood damage will be about $5.3 billion.*

River in Arizona is filling with silt at a rate of 137,000 acre-feet per year, sufficient to destroy the operation of this multimillion-dollar structure in fewer than 250 years. The death of a Texas reservoir is shown in Figure 7–19. California's Mono Reservoir, which was theoretically designed to provide a permanent water source for the people of Santa Barbara, filled up with sediment within two decades. In addition, biological succession proceeded so rapidly that a thicket of shrubs and saplings became firmly established. For all practical purposes, Mono Reservoir is dead and buried.

Table 7–3 Disadvantages of Big Dams

1. Extremely expensive: hundreds of millions to billions of dollars. (*Example:* Hoover Dam on the Arizona-Nevada border—cost, $120 million.)
2. Prime agricultural land is flooded.
3. Scenic beauty is destroyed. (*Example:* The Rainbow Bridge National Monument in Arizona is threatened by the Glen Canyon Dam on the Colorado River.)
4. The resulting saltwater intrusion in coastal areas destroys cropland and pollutes freshwater aquifers. (*Example:* This has happened in both Florida and California.)
5. Drawdowns periodically eliminate the shallow-water areas where fish frequently spawn.
6. The natural habitat of endangered species is destroyed. (*Example:* The snail darter at the Tellico Dam.)
7. The upstream migration of adult salmon is blocked and therefore reproduction is interfered with.
8. There are excessive water losses from reservoirs because of evaporation. (*Example:* Lake Mead behind Hoover Dam.)
9. The life of a dam is shortened because of the siltation of the reservoir. (*Example:* Mono Dam in California.)
10. The collapse of the dam is possible as a result of faulty construction. (*Example:* Teton Dam in Idaho.)

7–19 *The "death" of a reservoir, Lake Ballinger, Texas. Although the original depth of this lake was 35 feet, it eventually had to be abandoned because of siltation.*

7-20 *The death of a dam: An aerial view of the Teton Dam, Idaho, shortly after its rupture. We are looking upstream. Note the conspicuously white-appearing ruptured portion near the center of the picture. The torrential waters released from the reservoir above the dam caused the death of at least 14 people.*

Reservoir Evaporation Losses. Evaporation losses from reservoirs in hot, arid regions, where winds are prevalent, can be considerable. The top seven feet of Lake Mead, for example, are evaporated annually. About six million acre-feet are lost each year from 1,250 large western reservoirs, sufficient to supply all the domestic needs of fifty million people. Although such losses are reduced on small reservoirs in the West with roofs and floating covers, they still are quite substantial. Although the use of a surface film of hexadecanol will reduce evaporation losses by almost 20 percent, the technique has some drawbacks. First, it is quite costly because the film tends to disperse and therefore must be repeatedly applied. Second, it has adverse effects on fish and other aquatic organisms because levels of dissolved oxygen decline. This is the result of increased water temperatures and of the sealing off of the reservoir from its supply of atmospheric oxygen.

Dam Collapse. On rare occasions a dam will collapse because of faulty design. Such was the case with the mighty Teton Dam in Idaho. (See Figure 7-20.) It was built by the U.S. Bureau of Reclamation, an agency that had compiled an impressive record of technical engineering skill in the successful construction of more than 300 dams, including the world-famous Grand Coulee and Hoover dams. However, on June 5, 1976, the Bureau's record was sullied. Only hours after the first fissure appeared in the dam, the monstrous earthen structure gave way with a deafening roar. A mammoth wall of water surged rapidly down the valley. The resultant destruction was awesome. At least 14 lives were lost. Estimates of property damage, involving demolished homes and barns, approached $1 billion. Shortly afterward, the Secretary of the Interior and the governor of Idaho appointed a panel of distinguished engineers to investigate the cause of the Teton's failure. As reported in *Science*, the panel concluded that "under difficult conditions that called for the best judgment and experience of the engineering profession, an unfortunate choice of design measures together with less than conventional precautions . . . ultimately led to its failure . . . " (24).

The Stream Channelization Controversy

The Soil Conservation Service has built up a splendid reputation during many years of valuable

158

service in the area of soil erosion and flood control. However, in the past few years a storm of criticism has swirled around its recently developed *channelization* program: the deepening and straightening of streams for the purpose of flood control. The stated objective of the program is to prevent the flooding of croplands located in the floodplains of small watersheds. The floodplains, of course, are the low areas on either side of a stream that are frequently subject to spring flooding.

THE METHOD. There are two main steps in channelization. First, all vegetation (including trees) is bulldozed away on either side of the stream to a distance of 100 feet, leaving nothing but bare soil. (By agreement with the landowner, the denuded area is then planted with a cover crop and repeatedly mowed.) Second, bulldozers and draglines then deepen and straighten the channel; in essence the stream is converted into a water-filled ditch.

THE BENEFITS. The actual benefits that result are minimal. First, we must concede that cropland on either side of the channelized portion of the stream is protected from flooding. Second, small lakes with considerable recreational and wildlife potential are constructed by the SCS as an adjunct to the main channelization process.

THE DISADVANTAGES. Unfortunately the disadvantages of channelization are multiple:

1. A picturesque meandering stream is converted to an ugly eroding ditch.
2. Much valuable hardwood timber, already in short supply, is destroyed.
3. With the removal of its food and cover, the diverse bottomland fauna (raccoon, mink, otter, bear, wood ducks, and songbirds) are either eradicated or forced to emigrate.
4. Removal of the overarching trees that formerly intercepted the sunlight results in increased water temperatures (thermal pollution) and a host of associated problems (which will be discussed in detail in the next chapter, on water pollution).
5. Removal of stream-skirting trees means that stream enrichment from leaf fall is considerably reduced.
6. Lowering the water table causes wells to run dry and permits saltwater intrusion in coastal re-

gions. Such intrusion contaminates aquifers and reduces farmland productivity.
7. Stream banks erode because of the removal of the tree roots that formerly stabilized them.
8. The increased speed of the current undercuts stream banks and causes them to slump into the channel.
9. Fish food, in the form of insects that formerly fell into the stream from the overhead tree canopies, is diminished.
10. The deep pools in which game fish take cover and the shallow riffle where valuable fish food in the form of aquatic insects flourishes are eliminated.
11. Many streams may become bone dry during summer drought, when previously their flow was continuous. The effect on aquatic life is highly adverse.
12. Pesticides and herbicides applied to farm crops in the watershed may now drain into the stream more quickly and abundantly. The result is heavy fish mortality downstream.
13. As the river-bottom habitat is removed by channelization, so are opportunities for such recreational activities as canoeing, hiking, swimming, bird watching, and hunting for wildflowers. Such simple pleasures are already becoming less available because of the population crush and land-development squeeze.

It would seem, therefore, in any cost-benefit analysis, that the SCS's channelization program is found wanting. Just why then does the SCS persist in this ecological boondoggle? George W. Folkerts, an aquatic ecologist at Auburn University in Alabama and former consultant to the Natural Resources Defense Council, has suggested that the SCS had done its soil-erosion and flood-control work so well in the past 35 years that it has placed itself in the position where it has to "dream up" projects or find its budget and staff sharply reduced. According to Folkerts, the project should be terminated not only because of its environmental impact, but also because of its profligate use of public funds. He states:

In one Alabama project costing $4,417,312, the cost per acre to reduce flooding amounts to $405.02. The highest value of the land protected was $300 per acre. In other words, money used in the project could have purchased the land and a sizable chunk of funds would have been left. In this project 105 landowners were supposedly ben-

159

efitted. This means that each landowner was, in effect, receiving over $42,000 in tax monies. If this were merely a gravy train it would be disturbing, but when the damages of the project are considered, it becomes appalling. (13)

In their long-range plans, the SCS proposes to channelize (and hence wreak gross environmental abuse on) nearly 9,000 small watersheds by the year 2000. That means degradation of nearly half of our nation's small watersheds. It is inconceivable that the public will permit this bureaucratic ambition to be realized. In the long run, an informed citizenry, mounting pressure on vote-sensitive legislators, most certainly will prevail. There is no time to be lost.

Irrigation

An extensive area of the desert biome and the more arid portion of the grassland biome are character-

ized by more or less permanent drought. There, through eons of interaction with the environment, animal residents have evolved moisture-securing and moisture-conserving adaptations that have promoted their survival. We, however, relative newcomers to this austere region, have not had to depend on long evolutionary processes to "adapt" to the environment. Instead, with the aid of our mental powers, we have "shaped" the environment to fit our design. The most significant and dramatic example of our habitat-shaping talents in this region is modern irrigation.

The History of Irrigation
Perhaps the first use of transported water in arid-land farming in what is now the United States was made in A.D. 700 by Indians living in the valleys of the Salt and Gila rivers of Arizona (3). Employing crude digging tools, they were able to construct 125 miles of canals sufficient to irrigate 140,000 acres of food plots. By A.D. 1400 those early agriculturists, known as the Hohokam ("those who have gone"),

7–21 *Central Valley, California. Aerial view of the Contra Costa irrigation canal. Mount Diablo is on the horizon.*

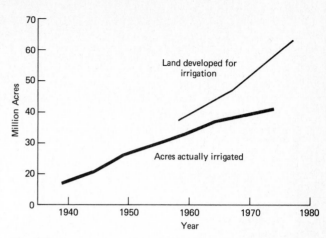

7–23 *Increase in irrigated land in the United States from 1939 to 1977.*

7–22 *Water has transformed this desert. The desert cacti in the foreground contrast sharply with the citrus grove in the background just a few feet away. The citrus crops were made possible with irrigation water taken from the Salt River, Arizona. The productive Salt River Valley, a 250,000-acre area that includes Phoenix, Arizona, would probably still be desert today were it not for the Bureau of Reclamation's first large multipurpose water-resources project completed at the beginning of the century.*

mysteriously disappeared along with their irrigation economy (2). In the seventeenth century, under the influence of Spanish priests, irrigation systems were established in California and Texas adjacent to Catholic missions. In 1847 the Mormons of Utah, faced with possible starvation during the ensuing winter, channeled water from City Creek to their parched potato and grain fields.

THE IMPERIAL VALLEY STORY. The story of the Imperial Valley is one of America's greatest success stories in irrigation. The Imperial Valley, which is 110 miles long and 50 miles wide, lies in the Colorado Desert in southern California, just east of Los Angeles, with San Diego in its southwest corner. Hundreds of thousands of years ago this area was submerged by salt water from the Gulf of California. Gradually, however, it was built up with millions of tons of fertile soil released by overflow of the Colorado River during its flow to the sea. At the

turn of the century this valley was a hot desert wasteland. Annual rainfall, which is almost immediately vaporized because of hot, drying winds, is a paltry 1.5 to 3 inches, hardly enough to settle the dust. The Imperial Valley, however, is no longer a wasteland. Where there were once lizards and cacti, fruit and vegetable farms flourish from which lettuce, tomatoes, watermelons, sugar beets, onions, asparagus, oranges, and dates are shipped to all parts of the United States. This has been made possible by the completion in 1940 of the 200-foot-wide All-American Canal, which conveys water from the Colorado River eighty miles away to 0.5-million acres of fertile valley soil. The potential of this area for crop production was always there. There was an abundance of sunshine and a long growing season (up to ten cuttings of alfalfa have been made). The limiting factor was water, and that was overcome with imagination, resourcefulness, and engineering skill, and, we might add, billions of dollars of taxpayer's money. As shown in Figure 7–23, the amount of irrigated land in the United States is steadily increasing.

Irrigation Problems

Water Loss
Some irrigated fields receive their water from reservoirs or streams located hundreds of miles away. The fruit-raising Central Valley of California, for example, gets its water from the Colorado River, 300 miles to the east. During transit considerable

161

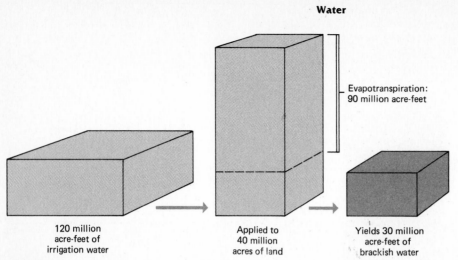

120 million
acre-feet of
irrigation water

Applied to
40 million
acres of land

Evapotranspiration:
90 million acre-feet

Yields 30 million
acre-feet of
brackish water

7–24 *Irrigation of croplands is the biggest consumptive use of water in the United States. It is called* consumptive *because 75 percent of it is lost to transpiration and evaporation. Roughly 120 million acre-feet of water are applied to 40 million acres of land in the western states. This is equivalent to about three feet of water for every irrigated acre. The salts in the original volume become concentrated in the 30 million acre-feet of water that remains. This remaining water may have a salt concentration of more than 2,000 parts per million. It must be drained from the croplands in order to prevent a toxic buildup.*

amounts of water are lost. According to the USDA, only one of every four gallons drawn for irrigation is actually absorbed by crop root systems. The remaining three gallons are lost to evaporation, to water-absorbing weeds, or to ground seepage. In some areas seepage may be sufficient to raise the water table and form a marsh. (Such artificial wet-

7–25 *Delta, Colorado. Irrigating a field planted to sugar beets with siphon tubes drawing water from a concrete head ditch. Seepage losses would be high were this ditch not lined with concrete.*

land habitat has benefits for wildlife but destroys land for crop production.) Systems that transport water to the farms are about 78 percent efficient. The water-carrying systems on the farm itself, however, have an efficiency of only 53 percent. Seepage loss can be minimized by lining canals with water-impervious materials, such as wax coatings or plastic and butyl-rubber membranes. Asphalt and "shotcrete" (cement mortar applied under air pressure) have also proved valuable in reducing seepage. (See Figure 7–25.)

Much water could be saved if the farmers were more efficient in the actual watering of their crops. For example, at least 1.1 million acre-feet could be saved annually nationwide if farmers improved their ability to release water to the root systems of crops at the optimal time and in the optimal amount.

Salinization

Would you believe that bringing fresh water to a desert might be destructive to crops? Sounds incongruous, doesn't it? However, even fresh water is slightly salty, having acquired dissolved sodium, calcium, and magnesium salts as it flowed down mountain slopes and through valley bottoms. When such water is brought by irrigation canals to hot

7-26 *Leemore, California. Note the salt crust on this range caused by excessive evaporation combined with poor drainage conditions. Such land is worthless for crop production or for growing range grasses.*

deserts, where drainage downward through the soil is very poor and the evaporation rate is very high, the water passes into the atmosphere and the salts are left behind on the ground as a white crust. (See Figure 7–26.) Additional salt may be deposited because of the evaporation of groundwater that has been sucked to the surface by capillary action (19). As time passes the salt gradually builds up to the point where it becomes toxic to plants. Even in California's Imperial Valley, where crop harvests have been so bountiful, this process of *salinization* has caused many farms to be abandoned. As ecologist G. Tyler Miller has written, "The All-American Canal, which brings water to the Imperial Valley from the Colorado River also carries about three million tons of salt per year to California's southern coastal plain—equivalent to importing a 210-car

trainload of salts every day. Improperly managed fields produce only one useless crop—'Imperial Valley snow'—a white crust of sodium sulfate. In the San Joaquin Valley it is estimated that 400 tons of salt have built up in its soils and ground water" (11). Salinization also plagues irrigation in Asia and Africa. For example, in the Indus River Valley of Pakistan, the largest irrigated region in the world, salinization has virtually destroyed the crop-producing potential of 23 million acres (16).

Several solutions to the salinization problem in the San Joaquin Valley have been proposed:

1. Construct a system of underground drainage pipes for collecting and disposing of the salty groundwater. (See Figures 7–27 and 7–28.) Those pipes would then connect to a master

7-27 *Typical on-farm subsurface system for draining off salty water from croplands.*

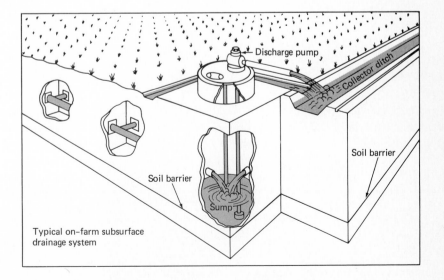

Discharge pump

Collector ditch

Soil barrier

Soil barrier

Sump

Typical on–farm subsurface drainage system

7–28 *Flushing out the salt. These are constructed lakes in Coachella Valley, California to flush salt from the soil by leaching action. Four feet of irrigation water is used to move downward through the soil and flush accumulated salts into drainage pipes buried seven feet below the surface, thus reclaiming the land for farming.*

7–29 *Soil moisture tester. Clyde Reed, irrigation specialist for the Bureau of Reclamation, is shown reading the moisture dial on the speedy moisture tester to determine moisture levels in a citrus grove. The Bureau of Reclamation is concerned with water use, irrigation efficiencies, soil moisture relationships, irrigation timing, and crop yields.*

drainpipe that would extend 290 miles through the length of the valley. The master drainpipe would empty directly into California's wetland ecosystem, the Suisun Bay, northeast of Oakland, where the Sacramento and San Joaquin rivers meet.

2. More efficient irrigation methods would reduce water use, and therefore salinization, from 15 to 20 percent. Accurate soil-moisture testing instruments are available to the irrigation farmer, as shown in Figure 7–29.
3. Salt-resistant strains of crops could be planted in the salty soils.
4. Irrigated crop acreage could be reduced.
5. Areas plagued with salt problems could be converted from cropland into grazing land.

Unfortunately, however, as the Council on Environmental Quality states: "Farmers in the San Joaquin prefer to import more water from northern California, plow up more ground, grow more crops, and pump more water from the aquifers . . ." (11).

The Colorado River receives large amounts of salty water that has been flushed from thousands of irrigated farms. It becomes progressively more salty as it flows southwestward across the border with Mexico toward the Gulf of Lower California. As a result of irrigation, the salinity of the lower Colo-

Federal Subsidies for Irrigation Water

The federal government has pumped tens of billions of dollars into the complex system of dams, reservoirs, canals, and pumps that keep the irrigation economy afloat. The multibillion-dollar irrigation economy in the Southwest is based on multibillion-dollar subsidies from federal coffers. For example, in California's huge Wetlands District, it amounts to $1,500 per acre. A typical 2,200-acre farm receives a subsidy of $3.4 million. And where does this money ultimately come from? From taxes paid by citizens located throughout the fifty states (29).

Fortune magazine puts the problem in historical perspective: ''At the turn of the century, when Congress passed the Reclamation Act, it made sense for the rest of the country to help underwrite development in the Southwest. The region couldn't be opened up without water, and few private groups had the capital to finance projects themselves. But as the recent economic growth suggests, the region no longer needs favored treatment. Subsidies, moreover, are a needless drain on the federal government when it is running huge deficits. And underpriced water, whether from federal projects or any other source, is bad for the Southwest . . .'' (29).

The real cost of irrigation water today includes the cost of constructing dams, reservoirs, canals, pumps, and their maintenance — roughly about $160 per acre-foot. Because of the huge federal subsidies, however, most farmers pay much less. In the Central Valley of California, for example, farmers pay $3.50 per acre-foot, only 2 percent of the water's real cost (29).

Because water is so cheap, farmers do not exert enough effort in its conservation. Reckless waste is everywhere apparent in irrigation country. Relatively large amounts of cheap water are being used to grow low-value crops like alfalfa on inferior soil. Cheap *open-ditch* irrigation is still being extensively used, despite the fact it is the most wasteful method available. It uses 100 times as much water as *drip* irrigation, a method in which precisely controlled amounts of water are applied directly to the root system.

Many irrigation farmers are now clamoring for additional new multibillion-dollar projects to support their water-squandering ways. One such project is a $26-billion scheme to convey water from the Mississippi River to the arid lands of western Texas (29).

---

rado has increased 30 percent in the last twenty years (21). The Colorado's saltiness has jeopardized cotton production in the Mexicali district, where farmers have used the river as a source of irrigation water for decades. The economy of the region was threatened to such an extent that Mexican presidents have frequently conveyed their concern to the American government.

Georg Borgstrom of Michigan State University has described additional problems caused by salinization in this region: ''The salt also goes up in the air in the form of brine spray. The corrosion on agricultural machinery is ferocious. Machines used in the cotton plantations must be greased anew every second hour to avoid their rapid destruction by corrosion'' (6).

Depletion of Groundwater

The number of acres irrigated by American farmers has increased sharply from about 16 million acres in 1940 to about 60 million in 1984. In the High Plains, an area extending from Nebraska south to Texas, more than 75 percent of the irrigation water comes from underground. Much of the water is pumped from the huge underground ''lake'' known as the Ogallala aquifer. In 1946 there were only 2,000 irrigation wells in the entire southern plains region of west Texas (32). Twenty years later the number had increased fifteenfold to 30,000. In 1980 Texas was withdrawing 11 billion gallons per day. The rate of withdrawal in the region around Lubbock, Texas, is fifty times the rate at which the aquifers are naturally recharged (22). Such water-

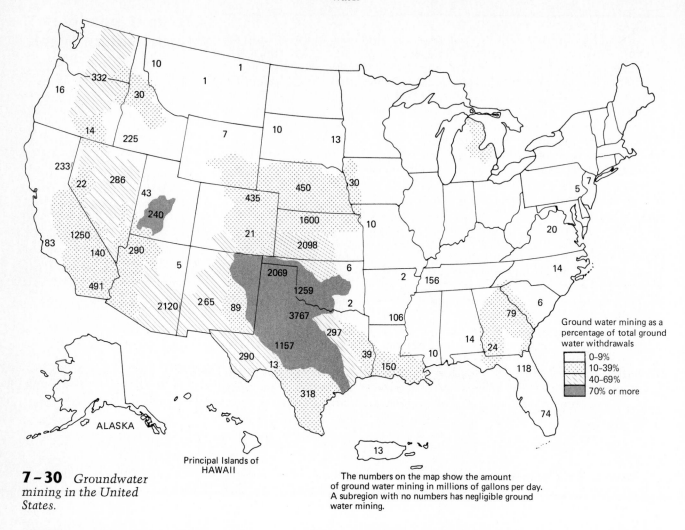

7–30 *Groundwater mining in the United States.*

Principal Islands of HAWAII

The numbers on the map show the amount of ground water mining in millions of gallons per day. A subregion with no numbers has negligible ground water mining.

Ground water mining as a percentage of total ground water withdrawals

- 0–9%
- 10–39%
- 40–69%
- 70% or more

mining is also a serious problem in California, western Kansas, and on the Colorado-Nebraska border. (See Figure 7–30.)

California uses more groundwater than any other state — 16 billion gallons per day. In the San Joaquin Basin of California, the groundwater overdraft amounts to 1.5 million acre-feet per year — about 12.5 percent of the basin's total water supply. Certainly the agricultural prosperity in this region has an uncertain future.

The Future

As a result of the extensive overdrafts, groundwater levels have been dropping rapidly. In one part of Arizona, for example, it has been lowered at least 400 feet. As a result, many wells have to be drilled more deeply, at considerable expense. Once a well is drilled, the water must be pumped out with the aid of costly fossil fuel or electricity. There eventually comes a time when the practice of irrigation is prohibitively expensive. Texas A&M University has reported that crop irrigation in the Texas Panhandle will be in a serious decline in the mid-1980s. By 2015 it is expected that West Texas will have experienced a 95 percent decline in irrigation and a 70 percent decrease in crop production. The outlook for the economy of this area is not bright (22).

Subsidence

As might be expected, when large volumes of water are removed from fine-grained porous aquifers, the weight of the overlying soil and rock occasionally will cause the compression or collapse of the aquifer. As a result, the earth above the aquifer sinks, or subsides. (See Figure 7–31.) Water-mining caused the dramatic appearance of a sinkhole at Winter Park, Florida, in 1981. The huge pit was 37.5 meters deep and 120 meters wide. It swallowed up a house, a swimming pool, six sports cars, and a camper (5). In the San Joaquin Valley, a 4,200-square-mile area sunk more than one foot. Some regions subsided more than 29 feet. Subsidence causes damage to irrigation facilities such as canals and underground pipes. The Department of Interior has spent $3.7 million in a single year to repair the damage caused by subsidence to federal irrigation projects (11). Occasionally, the tilting of the land causes a change in the entire water-flow pattern, so that the farmer has to realign his entire irrigation system — again at considerable expense (11).

Consumptive Use of Water

Some conservationists criticize irrigation in the semiarid West as a profligate use of water. From their viewpoint, irrigation-based crop production is not needed to satisfy America's food requirements. Farmers annually draw four times as much water for irrigation as is used by municipalities. Irrigationists use 60 percent as much water as our nation's industries. Moreover, although almost 97 percent of the water drawn for municipal or industrial use may largely be used again (in some cases only after proper treatment), much irrigation water is consumed and cannot be reused. Over 60 percent of all irrigation water is lost by transpiration, evaporation, and seepage during transit. Furthermore, it is estimated that *10,000 to 50,000 tons of irrigation water must be brought to a farm for every ton of food actually produced* (4). In the opinion of some experts, a higher standard of living might be possible for more people if water currently consumed by irrigation were diverted to industrial and municipal uses. In any event, any new irrigation projects should not be launched without an intensive cost-benefit analysis. This must be done not only in the United States and in other well-fed nations, but even in the underdeveloped nations where hunger is almost a way of life. Charles Warren, former chairman of the Council on Environmental Quality, in an address to the United Nations Water Conference in Argentina emphasized the need for a go-slow policy in starting new irrigation schemes: "Our analysis of crop yields, farming conditions, and water utilization indicates that the overriding focus should not be on the amount of new land and water that might be developed for agriculture, but rather on improving the effectiveness with which water and other production aids are applied and managed *on land already under cultivation . . .*" (10) [Italics mine].

7–31 *Sinkholes are formed when the roof of an underground cavern collapses after the water table has dropped, the result of either severe drought or water mining.*

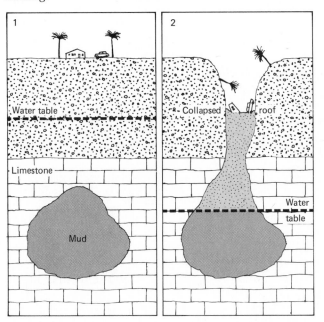

New Sources of Water

Even if per capita use of water *remained the same,* the total water use in the United States by the year 2000 would increase *substantially,* because of our projected population increase of close to 45 million. In actuality, however, our per capita use is rising sharply as well — from 1,500 gallons per day in 1960 to an expected 2,700 by 2000. Total municipal water use will rise from 21 billion gallons per day in 1960 to 43 billion gallons per day by 2000.

Where will this additional water come from? Possible methods for alleviating the impending water-shortage crisis include (1) reclaiming sewage water, (2) developing groundwater sources, (3) using asphalt pavements to catch and retain rainfall in desert areas, (4) desalinizing seawater, (5) eradicating moisture-wasting plants, (6) removing forests, (7) developing drought-resistant crops, (8) rainmaking, (9) "harvesting" icebergs, and (10) transferring surface water to water-deficient areas.

167

Desertification

Definition and Characteristics

DEFINED. Desertification is "a serious degradation of the soil, vegetation, and the ecological resilience of arid and semiarid lands . . . which threatens their long-term productivity and habitability" (11).

CHARACTERISTICS. (1) Lowering of water tables, (2) shortages of surface water, (3) salinization of existing water supplies, and (4) wind and water erosion.

Desertification is not the literal invasion of a desert into a nondesert area. It includes the impoverishment of ecosystems *within* as well as outside of natural deserts. For example, the Sonoran and Chihuahuan deserts of the Southwest are perhaps a million years old as deserts; yet they have become even more barren during the last 100 years. Their animal populations have diminished. Valuable grasses have declined. Invader species such as Russian thistle have multiplied. The original floodplain vegetation has changed beyond recognition in the Santa Cruz River Valley of Arizona (11).

EXTENT IN NORTH AMERICA. One-and-one-tenth million square miles, or 37 percent, of the continent's arid lands have undergone severe desertification marked by (1) the invasion of brush, (2) devegetation by wind and water erosion, or (3) high-salinity buildups that reduce crop yields by more than 50 percent. Some 10,500 square miles of North America have undergone *very severe* desertification characterized by large gullies and sand dunes or salt crusts that have developed on nearly impermeable irrigated soils. In contrast, Africa's *very severe* desertification is less than that in America—only 5,500 square miles. Most of the very severe desertification is in the United States as seen in Figure 7-32. The northernmost area is on the Navajo Indian Reservation. The other two areas bracket El Paso on the

7-32 *Extent of desertification of North America.*

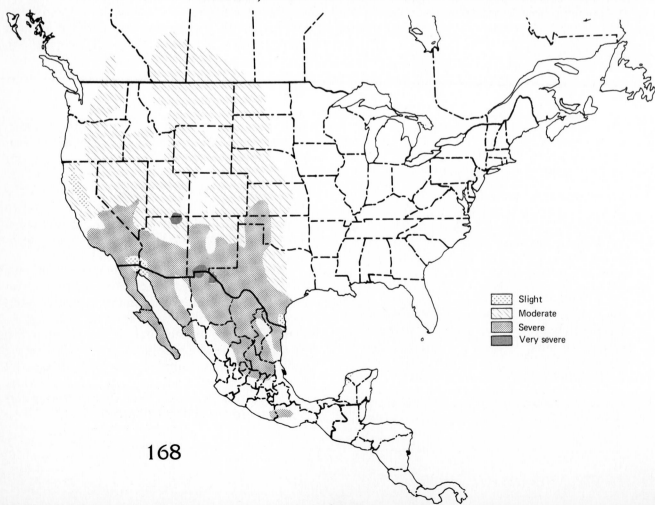

Slight
Moderate
Severe
Very severe

Texas-New Mexico border. As many as 225 million acres *within* the United States, about 10 percent of our nation's land mass, appear to have undergone severe or very severe desertification (11).

ECONOMIC EFFECTS. The United States has already suffered severe economic losses because of desertification. Future losses of far greater magnitude are possible. Costs may be in the form of (1) lower agricultural yields, (2) increased costs of production, (3) increased costs of conservation programs, or (4) ripple effects of cost increases on local, state, and national economic systems. Methods for controlling desertification may add substantial short-term costs to dry-land economies (11).

Case Study: The San Joaquin Basin in California

The San Joaquin Basin is particularly suitable for examination in the context of desertification because all the major desertification causes are involved. They include (1) poor drainage of irrigated land, (2) overgrazing, (3) cultivation of highly erodible soils, (4) overdraft of groundwater, and (5) damage from off-road vehicles.

The San Joaquin Basin comprises the southern half of the Central Valley of California, lying between the coastal mountain ranges and the Sierra Nevadas. (See Figure 7–33.) When irrigated it is one of the most productive agricultural regions in the world.

In 1977 the eight San Joaquin *counties* produced $4.7 billion worth of farm products, more than any *state* except Iowa, Texas, and Illinois. The San Joaquin produces cotton, grapes, tomatoes, alfalfa, sugar beets, walnuts, almonds, oranges, and apricots. It also has a sizable livestock industry (11).

7–33 *The San Joaquin Basin, site of serious desertification.*

1. *Poor drainage of irrigated land.* Of the Basin's 4.8 million acres of cultivated cropland, 4.6 million are irrigated. Twenty percent of the water is obtained from outside the Basin, most of it from northern California. Today about 400,000 acres of irrigated farmland in San Joaquin are affected by high brackish water tables. Unless a means is found to stop the progressive waterlogging and salinization now taking place, the amount of poorly drained land will increase to 700,000 acres by 2000, and the loss in annual crop yield will reach $321 million. Some 1.1 million of the total 18.2 million acres of farmland could become unproductive in 100 years (11).

2. *Groundwater depletion.* Thirty percent of the irrigation water is pumped from aquifers. These supplies are being depleted at the rate of 1.5 million acre-feet per year. This amounts to 12.5 percent of the Valley's water (11).

3. *Overgrazing.* Eighty percent of the four million acres of rangeland in the Valley is seriously overgrazed. As a result, palatable species of grasses preferred by cattle are being replaced by woody vegetation of minimal food value. The removal of plant cover caused by overgrazing has created serious water erosion on 2.2 million acres in the foothills and mountains. The value of the resultant loss in forage is estimated at $1.2 million (11).

4. *Off-road vehicles.* More than one-half-million acres of rangeland have deteriorated as a result of the intensive abuse inflicted by off-road vehicles. This type of recreation has intensified greatly in the last decade. The result has been massive devegetation and erosion (11).

5. *"Buckshot" urbanization.* It is projected that between 1972 and the year 2000 more than 400,000 prime farmland acres in the San Joaquin Valley will have been converted to urban use. Much of this will be caused by the rapid growth of such towns as Bakersfield, Fresno, and Modesto (11).

Reclamation of Sewage Water

Sewage effluent is 99 percent water, and when the one percent of pollutant is removed, the final water product may be purer than the original substance (20).

Processed sewage water is already being utilized for a variety of functions. The Bethlehem Steel plant at Baltimore, Maryland, employs 150 million gallons of sewage effluent daily for steel-cooling purposes (15). Golf links are sprinkled with it in San Francisco, Las Vegas, and Santa Fe. Treated sewage water is used to irrigate crops in the San Antonio area (20). Ornamental shrubs along highways in San Bernardino, California, are watered with it (2).

Los Angeles daily discharges 17 million gallons of processed sewage water over sewage-spreading beds at the edge of town. Eventually, this water seeps into aquifers that supply the town's wells. This water is of higher quality than the water piped 200 miles from the Colorado River. Treated wastewater has also been employed in southern California to form a barrier to saltwater intrusion from the ocean. By the early 1960s water-table levels had been dropping steadily in the coastal region, in some areas to a point 25 feet below sea level. As a result, saltwater encroachment progressed at the rate of one mile per year. To check this invasion, a freshwater barrier was formed by injecting treated wastewater into a series of coastal wells (2). The use of reclaimed sewage water in Los Angeles is expected to quintuple during the period 1970–1990.

Developing Groundwater Resources

There are 53,000 cubic miles of fresh water in the aquifers located in the upper half-mile of the earth's crust. In an effort to alleviate the impending water deficit, aquifers will be tapped to depths of 500 to 2,000 feet. Utilization of the increased supplies must be carefully planned from the long-range economic viewpoint. In some situations the proper decision may be to "mine" the water until the supply is exhausted; in other cases, it may be better to draw the water on a sustained-yield basis (22).

Intensive efforts are being made by the U.S. Geological Survey to locate and develop new aquifers. Radioactive-tracer techniques are being used to determine the pattern and rate of aquifer water flow. Such data will enable scientists to predict how withdrawal from one site will affect water tables at other points. These studies are already yielding results. One water-rich layer was found at Salisbury, Mary-

land. An aquifer was recently found in northern New Jersey that is capable of yielding 30 million gallons daily.

Using Asphalt Coatings in Desert Regions

Many desert plants possess remarkable flattened root systems that lie just a few inches below the desert floor. As a result, they are able to use rainfall before it vaporizes. Recently, the U.S. Geological Survey developed a "human adaptation" that might be equally efficient in securing rainfall in desert regions. The technique involves coating the desert floor with water-impervious asphalt. Collected rainfall could then be channeled into large water-holding pits from which it could be drawn off periodically either for irrigation or to raise the water table.

Desalination

"Water, water everywhere, but not a drop to drink" wailed the sailor in "The Ancient Mariner." It is a curious paradox that 70 percent of the earth's surface is covered by oceans, in some places up to six miles deep, yet a water shortage harasses civilization from New York to New Delhi. The problem, of course, is that seawater is salty. Deeply concerned with this dilemma, Congress has authorized a research-and-development program for improving *desalination* processes. As a result, a number of American communities are now operating desalination plants. The nation's first desalination plant was set up in California. It produces 28,000 gallons of fresh water daily. About 75 installations have been established on the west coast of Florida alone. These plants, in aggregate, are capable of producing 114 million gallons per day of fresh water.

Unfortunately, however, desalination is a rather expensive process. According to the U.S. Office of Water Resources and Technology, the four major factors contributing to the cost are (1) the salt concentration in the water, (2) the cost of the energy (electricity or fossil fuel), (3) the distance between the plant and the site of freshwater use, and (4) the capital interest rates. The cost of desalting is about $5 per 1,000 gallons for a medium-sized plant. In general, it is much cheaper to pump fresh water — if it's available. However, if the freshwater source is more than 150 kilometers away from the site of consumption, desalination then becomes economically feasible (5).

Eradicating Moisture-Wasting Plants

Phreatophytes cover about 16 million acres in the arid Southwest. They are plants that absorb and transpire exceptionally large volumes of water, roughly 50 to 100 percent more than agricultural crops per pound of biomass (23). Among the most important phreatophytes are salt cedar, cottonwood, willow, greasewood, rabbit brush, and cattail. One species alone, the salt cedar, whose roots extend down to the water table, inflicts a 20-trillion-gallon water loss in a 900,000-square-mile area of the western United States (18).

One to six million acre-feet of water can be saved annually if the phreatophytes are properly controlled. This salvaged water could then be pumped into irrigation systems (2).

It must be emphasized, however, that many phreatophytes are not only aesthetically satisfying, but serve a beneficial function as food and cover for wildlife, such as mule deer, black-tailed deer, rabbits, and quail. Therefore, before this type of vegetation is removed, it must be determined whether the trade-off of aesthetics and wildlife for water is desirable.

Forest Removal

It has been estimated that the daily domestic requirements of 100,000 people can be satisfied with 12 million gallons of water. Were this water spread over a ten-square-mile watershed, it would form a layer only 0.1-inch deep. However, in a single day the root systems of a growing stand of timber on that same ten-square-mile watershed could absorb twice this amount of water. It is apparent, therefore, that as water demands increase, responsible officials must eventually determine whether a given watershed acreage is more valuable for water collection and storage than for timber, wildlife habitat, scenic beauty, or some other function. It could well be that in some areas timber, with its high water requirements, should be replaced with grass or some other vegetation with lesser water needs. Watershed research in humid West Virginia and North Carolina has shown that clear-cutting has produced maximal annual increments of 12 to 16 inches, or 434,000 gallons per acre. Increases were smaller in partial cuttings. In North Carolina the clear-cutting of oak stands growing in deep soil resulted the following year in sufficient water increment per square mile to supply the water needs of 6,800 people (15).

Developing Salt-Resistant Crops

After six years of research two scientists from the University of California-Davis announced the development of a new strain of barley that will grow well even though irrigated with *seawater*. The plants were grown on a tiny windswept beach at Bodega Bay in northern California. They have achieved yields of 1,320 pounds per acre, equal to the average global per acre yield of barley provided with fresh water. As one of the researchers, Emanuel Epstein, noted: "We have shown that sea water is not pure poison to crops. . . ." Their success is highly significant. Millions of acres of once-prime agricultural land the world over (4.5 million acres in California alone) have been rendered worthless because of salinization—an unfortunate condition resulting from improper irrigation practices or from the intrusion of seawater because of the intensive mining of groundwater supplies. Until now farmers have been advised to cease cropping salinized soils or else flush out the salt at considerable expense with huge volumes of fresh water. It would seem, however, that the new "saltwater barley" would do quite well in this type of soil.

Developing Drought-Resistant Crops

Even if we are unable to increase water supplies for agriculture, we could nevertheless increase food production if we could develop new varieties of crops that would be *resistant to drought*. Gerald G. Still, a scientist for the USDA, is optimistic about the water-saving potential of such plant-breeding projects: "Sorghum is a very important grain crop in the arid portion of the Third World. . . . There is something inherent in the plant, the germ plasm or the genes, that causes sorghum to put itself on 'idle' during a dry spell and then go on and yield a crop when the rains come." Certainly, one of the most promising strategies for fighting water shortages is intensified study of the effects of drought on plants. With the aid of recently developed techniques in genetic engineering, it may be possible to breed plants that require considerably less water. To this end the USDA plans to set up a $21-million research laboratory in Lubbock, Texas (5).

Rainmaking

Rainmaking is a novel approach to increasing the water supply. One technique involves seeding clouds with crystals of dry ice and silver iodide, with the hope that the crystals will serve as *condensation*

171

nuclei around which moisture will collect until raindrops are formed (26). The Bureau of Reclamation is confident that the weather-modification techniques now available could substantially increase the water supply in the San Joaquin River Basin by 25 percent, the Upper Colorado River Basin by 44 percent, and the Gila River Basin (Arizona) by 55 percent. Nevertheless, the Bureau is moving very cautiously with its Project Skywater Program because of the serious political and legal problems involved. Another drawback is the high cost. Still another disadvantage is the lack of control over the volume and distribution of induced precipitation. For example, a late-July rainfall might benefit the corn farmer but might be damaging to cut alfalfa awaiting the baler (12). Increased rainfall may improve forage for cattle but may be harmful to fruit orchards. Even more serious, such artificially induced rainfall might contribute to flooding, as has been suggested by environmentalist Virginia Brodine:

The danger of an experiment at the wrong time and place was demonstrated when a rainmaking experiment in the summer of 1972 was carried out near Rapid City, South Dakota, while a storm was gathering. Experimenters claimed that the cloud-seeding had no effect on the subsequent 14-inch rain and flood that followed, but this is impossible to prove. It is clear, however, that there was inadequate understanding of the weather conditions and poor judgment in seeding clouds which *could* contribute to the severity of the rainfall. (7) *[Italics mine.]*

Harvesting Icebergs

Many billions of gallons of fresh water are locked up in Antarctic icebergs. Some day you may be taking this iceberg water into your body in the form of a grape or watermelon grown in California. Researchers for the Rand Corporation found that the use of the extensive iceberg resources in the Antarctic's Ross Sea to support crop yields in our southwestern states is realistic from both a technical and economic standpoint. In Rand's imaginative scheme a number of iceberg blocks could be harvested and cabled together to form "trains." The trains would then be pushed into suitable ocean currents and guided northward for more than 6,000 miles to a "parking" area off Los Angeles. Warm-water discharges from electric power plants along the coast would speed up the meltdown of the "bergs." The water would then be piped inland for either domestic, industrial, or agricultural use. The

water would actually be much less salty than that of the Colorado River—which is being intensively tapped for irrigation farming today. By using such iceberg water southern Californians could reduce their highly expensive withdrawals from the Colorado River by at least one million acre-feet per year. The estimated cost per acre-foot would be less than if the water were obtained by desalination or from the Colorado River. Sounds attractive and exciting, doesn't it? However, before a single iceberg is guided northward, the environmental effects of those icy mountains on coastal water temperatures, fish reproduction and migration, as well as on climatic patterns, must be thoroughly studied (25).

Long-Distance Transport: The California Water Project

Looking down on the planet Earth, a shrinking bluish sphere far below, America's moonbound astronauts could identify only two man-made structures: the Great Wall of China and the main aqueduct of the California Water Project (CWP). California has long been victimized by the curious fact that 70 percent of its potentially usable water has its source in the northern third of the state (in the form of relatively abundant rainfall and the snowmelt of the High Sierras), while 77 percent of the demand is located in the semiarid southern two thirds, occupied by ten million people, where only five inches of rain falls per year. The CWP was completed in order to rectify this problem. The most complex and expensive water-moving project in the history of the world, the CWP includes 21 dams and reservoirs, 22 pumping plants, and 685 miles of canals, tunnels, and pipelines. (See Figure 7–34.) A pretty expensive "faucet," the project cost well over $2 billion—enough money to build six Panama Canals (8).

The keystone to the system is the Oroville Dam (as tall as a 77-story skyscraper), which blocks northern California's Feather River to form the 15,800-acre Lake Oroville. With a depth of 700 feet, the lake could feed all the household faucets in California for a full year before finally going dry. The water is alternately moved by pumps and gravity toward southern California, the main aqueduct being sufficiently wide and deep to float an ocean-going steamship. Eventually, the water is channeled to the foot of mile-high Tehachapi Mountain, a seemingly impossible barrier. However, with the

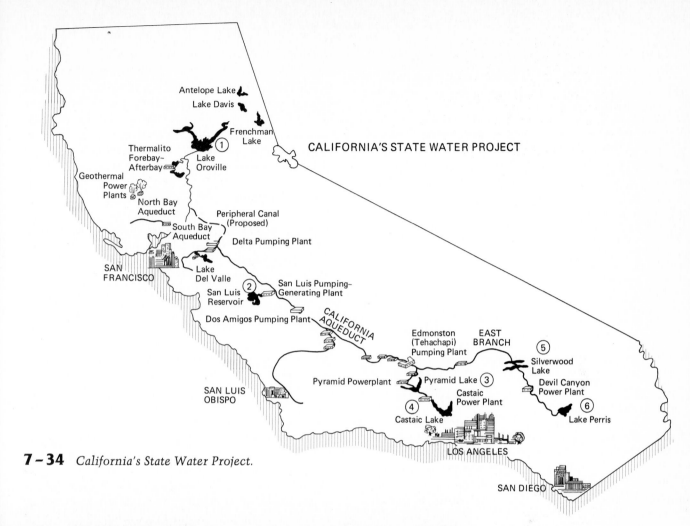

CALIFORNIA'S STATE WATER PROJECT

Antelope Lake
Lake Davis
Frenchman Lake
①
Thermalito Forebay–Afterbay
Lake Oroville
Geothermal Power Plants
North Bay Aqueduct
Peripheral Canal (Proposed)
South Bay Aqueduct
Delta Pumping Plant
SAN FRANCISCO
Lake Del Valle
San Luis Pumping–Generating Plant
②
San Luis Reservoir
Dos Amigos Pumping Plant
CALIFORNIA AQUEDUCT
Edmonston (Tehachapi) Pumping Plant
EAST BRANCH
⑤
Silverwood Lake
Pyramid Powerplant
Pyramid Lake ③
Devil Canyon Power Plant
SAN LUIS OBISPO
Castaic Power Plant
④
Castaic Lake
⑥
Lake Perris
LOS ANGELES
SAN DIEGO

7–34 *California's State Water Project.*

7–35 *Focal point of the California Water Plan System is Oroville Dam and Lake pictured here. The lake provides multiple benefits, including recreational facilities such as swimming, boating, and fishing; scenic beauty; waterpower for producing electrical power; and release to arid regions for irrigation purposes.*

173

Table 7-4 Summary of Methods for Conserving and Increasing Our Nation's Water Supply

1. Move people, agriculture, and industry from water-short to water-abundant regions.
2. Transfer water long distance from water-abundant to water-poor regions (California Water Project).
3. Dam rivers to form reservoirs of water (Hoover Dam and Lake Mead).
4. Reduce evaporation losses from reservoirs and irrigation canals.
5. Employ rainmaking.
6. Harvest icebergs.
7. Use more efficient irrigation methods, such as *drip irrigation*.
8. Line irrigation canals with plastic or concrete to prevent seepage losses.
9. Recharge groundwater supplies.
10. Desalinate seawater and brackish water.
11. More effectively control water pollution.
12. Reclaim wastewater for industrial and agricultural use.
13. Reduce domestic, agricultural, and industrial water waste.
14. Locate and use new aquifers.
15. Use water-holding pits in desert regions.
16. Remove moisture-wasting vegetation.
17. Replace forests with their high water demands with low water-demanding vegetation such as grasses.

aid of fourteen 80,000-horsepower pumps, the water is pushed up to the 3,000-foot level. From there it rushes downslope to the fertile San Fernando Valley and the densely populated cities of Los Angeles and San Diego. From beginning to end the system extends a distance equal to that from New York to Columbia, South Carolina (8).

The CWP provides water for the lower San Joaquin Valley, converting a 250,000-acre cactus-jackrabbit-rattlesnake desert into productive farmland that may eventually gross $75 million per year. It was estimated that in a single year the crop production made possible by CWP produced 800,000 tons of oxygen, sufficient to supply the annual requirement of one million people. In addition, it has at least temporarily slowed down the lowering of the water table that had been caused by the mining of groundwater.

Despite the obvious benefits derived from this colossal project, certain aspects have drawn heated criticism from environmentalists. They claim that the CWP was built at an excessive cost, not only in tax dollars, but in energy costs, losses in scenic beauty, and the destruction of fish and wildlife habitat as well. Environmentalists also criticize the proposal to dam up other free-flowing "wild" rivers in

northwestern California, such as the Eel, Klamath, and Trinity. In their view too many of such unharnessed streams have already been sacrificed on the altar of irrigation and power production.

Notwithstanding these criticisms, and the enormous cost to the people of California, the CWP is an accomplished fact and is helping to alleviate southern California's recurring water-shortage problems.

Rapid Review

1. A severe water shortage is the most severe, long-range environmental problem facing our nation. The causes of the shortage are (a) a rapidly increasing population, (b) increasing demands by agriculture, cities, and industry, (c) flagrant waste, (d) unequal distribution of water, and (e) pollution.

2. Water continuously moves from oceans-to-air-to-land-to-rivers-to-oceans in what is known as the *water cycle*. This cycle is powered by solar energy and gravity. The oceans contain more than 97 percent of the world's total water supply. On the average, the United States receives 30 inches of rainfall annually. Much water filters down into the soil and rocks to form *groundwater*. The uppermost level of the zone that is *saturated* with groundwater is called the *water table*. Ninety-seven percent of the world's supply of fresh water is held in porous layers of sand, gravel, and rock known as *aquifers*. The Ogallala aquifer, which extends from Nebraska south to Texas, provides drinking water for two million people and irrigation water for many thousands of farms.

3. A *drought* exists whenever rainfall for twenty-one days or longer is only 30 percent of the average for time and place. Two of the most serious droughts in our country in recent years were the Delaware Basin drought (1961-1965) and the California drought (1976-1977).

4. The Upper Mississippi River flood (1965), a "once-in-a-century" flood, caused the death of 16 people, injured 330, and inflicted $140 million of property damage.

5. Floods can be controlled by (a) protecting the watersheds, (b) measuring snowpack to predict flood conditions, (c) building levees, (d) building dams, and (e) undertaking dredging operations.

6. Big dams have several disadvantages. Among them are (a) high costs, (b) possible dam collapse, (c) reservoir evaporation losses, (d) flooding of prime

agricultural land, (e) siltation of reservoirs, (f) salt-water intrusion in coastal areas, (g) destruction of scenic beauty, and (h) destruction of habitat for rare aquatic species, such as the snail darter.

7. Stream channelization has multiple disadvantages: (a) wildlife habitat is destroyed, (b) stream-bank erosion is accelerated, (c) the water table is lowered, (d) severe aesthetic losses are inflicted, (e) the recreational functions of streams are lost, and (f) the projects are excessively costly to the taxpayer.

8. Irrigation permits the establishment of a flourishing agricultural economy in arid portions of the Southwest that were once relatively nonproductive.

9. Serious problems associated with irrigation include (a) water loss during transit along canals, (b) inefficient practices during the application of water to the crops, (c) salinization of the soil, and (d) the depletion of groundwater.

10. Desertification is "a serious degradation of the soil, vegetation, and ecological resilience of arid and semiarid lands that threatens long-term productivity and habitability." It is characterized by (a) lowered water tables, (b) a shortage of surface water, (c) salinization, and (d) wind and water erosion. Some 10,500 square miles of North America have undergone very severe desertification characterized by large gullies and sand dunes or salt crusts. In the San Joaquin Basin of California all the major causes of desertification are at work. They include (a) poor drainage of irrigated land, (b) overgrazing, (c) cultivation of highly erodible soils, (d) mining of groundwater, and (e) damage from off-road vehicles.

11. Possible methods for alleviating the crisis of water scarcity are the following: (a) reclaiming sewage water, (b) developing new sources of groundwater, (c) using asphalt pavings to catch rainfall in desert regions, (d) desalinizing sea water, (e) removing moisture-wasting plants, (f) removing forests, (g) developing drought-resistant and salt-resistant crops, (h) rainmaking, (i) harvesting of icebergs, and (j) transferring surplus water to water-short areas.

12. The California Water Project (CWP) serves multiple functions: (a) it provides irrigation water for arid regions, (b) it generates electrical power, (c) it provides flood control, and (d) it provides recreational activities such as fishing, swimming, and boating.

Key Words and Phrases

Aquifer	Levee
California Water Project	Mono Reservoir
Central Arizona Project	Ogallala aquifer
Delaware River Basin drought	Open-ditch irrigation
	Phreatophytes
Desalination	Rainmaking
Desertification	Salinization
Dredging	Salt-resistant crops
Drip irrigation	Saltwater intrusion
Drought	Seepage
Drought-resistant crops	Snowpack
Ground subsidence	Spray irrigation
Ground water	Stream channelization
Hoover Dam	Teton Dam
Hydrologic cycle	Transpiration
Imperial Valley	Upper-Mississippi
Irrigation	River flood
Irrigation water subsidies	Water-mining
	Water table
Lake Mead	Watershed

Questions and Topics for Discussion

1. Discuss four factors that have contributed to our nation's water crisis.
2. Discuss the movement of water through the water cycle. What powers the water cycle? What are the main water reservoirs? What are the renewal times for atmosphere, rivers, lakes, glaciers, and oceans?
3. Is water ever lost from ecosystems as is energy?
4. Discuss the statement: "The United States does not really have a water *shortage*; it is plagued with a water *distribution* problem."
5. Trace the water in the food (soup, milk, hamburger, salad, and apple pie) you had in your last meal at the college cafeteria "backward" in time and place through the water cycle as far as you can.
6. Trace a water molecule in a raindrop falling on your college campus through your own body and finally into another rain drop.
7. Discuss the relationship between periods of drought and the sunspot cycle.
8. Drawing from your knowledge of ecological concepts, discuss the effect of floods on an aquatic ecosystem; on a woodland ecosystem.

9. Discuss the effects of drought on an aquatic ecosystem; on a woodland ecosystem.

10. Consider some of the negative effects of dredging operations.

11. Discuss the statement: "Big dams, like the Hoover, are engineering masterpieces that have been unqualified successes in boosting human welfare."

12. Suppose that the dams that now occur in the United States were never built. What would have been the disadvantages? Would there have been any advantages? Discuss your answer in terms of the American economy, human safety, agricultural production, wildlife preservation, scenic beauty, and endangered species.

13. With another student in your class, debate the statement: "Egypt would be better off today if the Aswan Dam were never built."

14. List disadvantages of stream channelization to the agricultural ecosystems; to the stream ecosystem.

15. With another student in your class, debate the statement: "The American economy, overall, would be better off if irrigation were completely eliminated."

16. What causes salinization? Briefly describe five ways in which salinization could be controlled.

17. Does iceberg harvesting seem feasible to you? Why or why not?

18. Discuss the pros and cons of forest removal to increase water supplies. Under what circumstances might it be advantageous? Disadvantageous?

19. Discuss the pros and cons of removing moisture-wasting plants to increase water supplies. Is the term *moisture wasting* a good one? Why or why not?

20. With another student in your class, debate the statement: "The California Water Project is an unqualified success in providing southern California with more water." Suppose that you are an environmentalist; can you think of possible drawbacks to the project?

Endnotes

1. Ackerman, Edward A., and George O. G. Lof. *Technology in American Water Development.* Baltimore: Johns Hopkins, 1959.

2. Allen, Shirley W., and Justin W. Leonard. *Conserving Natural Resources.* New York: McGraw-Hill, 1966.

3. Barnes, Kenneth K. "Water Makes the Desert Bloom." *Outdoors USA: The Yearbook of Agriculture.* Washington, DC: Department of Agriculture, 1967.

4. Bernarde, Melvin A. *Our Precarious Habitat.* New York: Norton, 1970.

5. Bodde, Tineke. "Quality vs. Quantity: Is a U.S. Water Crisis Imminent?" *Bioscience,* **31** (July – Aug. 1981).

6. Boffey, P. M. "Teton Dam Collapse: Was it a Predictable Disaster?" *Science* (July 2, 1976), 30 – 32.

7. Borgstrom, George. *World Food Resources.* New York: Intext, 1973.

8. Brodine, Virginia. *Air Pollution.* New York: Harcourt, 1973.

9. California Department of Water Resources. *The California Water Plan.* Sacramento: California Department of Water Resources, 1973.

10. Clark, George L. *Elements of Ecology.* New York: Wiley, 1954.

11. Council on Environmental Quality. *Environmental Quality.* Ninth Annual Report. Washington, DC: Government Printing Office, 1978.

12. Council on Environmental Quality. *Environmental Quality.* Eleventh Annual Report. Washington, DC: Government Printing Office, 1980.

13. Cunningham, Floyd F. *1001 Questions Answered About Water Resources.* New York: Dodd, 1967.

14. Folkerts, George W. "Stream Channelization: How a Bureaucracy Destroys a Resource." In William H. Mason and George W. Folkerts, eds. *Environmental Problems.* Dubuque, IA: Brown, 1973.

15. Hunt, Cynthia A., and Robert M. Garrels. *Water: The Web of Life.* New York: Norton, 1972.

16. Jones, E. Bruce, Richard Lee, and John C. Frey. "Land Management for City Water." *Outdoors USA: The Yearbook of Agriculture.* Washington, DC: Department of Agriculture, 1967.

17. Keeton, William T. *Biological Science.* 2nd ed. New York: Norton, 1972.

18. Kormondy, Edward J. *Concepts of Ecology.* 2nd ed. Englewood Cliffs, NJ: Prentice-Hall, 1976.

19. Leopold, Luna B. *Water.* New York: Time, 1966.

20. Lull, Howard W. "How Our Cities Meet Their Water Needs." *Outdoors USA: The Yearbook of Agriculture.* Washington, DC: Department of Agriculture, 1967.

21. Mattison, C. W., and Joseph Alvarez. *Man and His Resources in Today's World.* Mankato, MN: Creative Educational Society, 1967.

22. Miller, G. Tyler, Jr. *Living in the Environment: Concepts, Problems and Alternatives.* New York: Wadsworth, 1980.
23. Moran, Joseph M., Michael D. Morgan, and James H. Wiersma. *An Introduction to Environmental Sciences.* San Francisco: Freeman, 1980.
24. Peterson, Elmer T. "Insoak Is the Answer." *Land,* 11 (1952), 83–88.
25. Sheridan, David. "The Underwatered West." *Environment,* 23, (March 1981), 7–13, 30–32.
26. Smith, Guy-Harold, ed. *Conservation of Natural Resources.* New York: Wiley, 1965.
27. Smith, Robert L. *Ecology and Field Biology.* New York: Harper, 1966.
28. Turk, Amos, Jonathan Turk, and Janet T. Wittes. *Ecology, Pollution, Environment.* Philadelphia: Saunders, 1972.
29. "The Whence and Whither of One State's Water." *Fortune,* 103 (Feb. 23, 1981), 96, 100, 104.
30. Van Riper, Joseph E. *Man's Physical World.* New York: McGraw-Hill, 1971.
31. Vitallo, Martin. "Ending Southwest's Water Binge."
32. Walton, Susan. "Aswan Revisited: U.S. — Egypt Nile Project Studies High Dam's Effects." *Bioscience,* 31 (Jan. 1981), 9–13.
33. White, Gilbert F. "Flood Plain Safeguards: A Community Concern." *Outdoors USA: The Yearbook of Agriculture.* Washington, DC: Government Printing Office, 1967.

Suggested Readings for the Interested Student

Bodde, Tineke. "Quality vs. Quantity: Is a U.S. Water Crisis Imminent?" *Bioscience,* 31 (July–Aug. 1981). This is a very readable discussion of factors (water mining and pollution) that are edging our nation toward a water emergency.

Boffey, P. M. "Teton Dam Collapse: Was it a Predictable Disaster?" *Science* (July 2, 1976), 30–32.

Council on Environmental Quality. *Environmental Quality.* Eleventh Annual Report. Washington, DC: Government Printing Office, 1980. This has a comprehensive report on the nation's water crisis.

Sheridan, David. "The Desert Blooms at a Price." *Environment,* 23 (April 1981), 6–20, 38–39. This is a well-written discussion of the economic and environmental effects of water use in the arid lands of the Southwest.

Soil Conservation Service. *America's Soil and Water: Condition and Trends,* Washington, DC: Department of Agriculture, December, 1980. This is authoritative, concise, and beautifully illustrated.

Vitallo, Martin. "Ending Southwest's Water Binge." The author considers the seriousness of excessive water use by irrigation farmers in the Southwest.

Walton, Susan. "Aswan Revisited: U.S. — Egypt Nile Project Studies High Dam's Effects." *Bioscience,* 31 (Jan. 1981), 9–13.

"The Whence and Whither of One State's Water." *Fortune,* 103 (Feb. 23, 1981), 96, 100, 104.

8 Water Pollution

The Effects of Water Pollution

A high frequency of illness in Jackson Township, New Jersey, ranging from skin rash and kidney malfunction to premature death; a once-clear lake near Chicago converted to pea green "soup"; the skeleton of a perch loaded with radioactive strontium; a stream bottom near Baltimore blanketed with sludgeworms at a density of 20,000 per square foot;

8–1 *A sign of the times. Throughout America swimming beaches have been closed because of pollution, as was this lake-front beach.*

maggot-infested fish rotting on a Lake Erie beach; eight youngsters coming down with typhoid fever after eating a watermelon they found floating in the Hudson River; 140 million fish deaths in our nation's waters in a single year; the Cuyahoga River (Ohio) bursting into flames; 18,000 people in Riverside, California, stricken with fever and vomiting; the Mahoning River in Ohio heated up to 140° F; 400 million tons of mud washed into the Gulf of Mexico by the Mississippi each year; a high frequency of earth tremors near Denver; an outbreak of hepatitis in New York and New Jersey; thousands of fish floating belly up in the Potomac River just below our nation's Capitol; the premature "death" of the Mono Dam Reservoir near Santa Barbara, California — all these seemingly diverse events have one thing in common: they were caused by water pollution.

Kinds of Water Pollution

Water pollution can be defined as *any contamination of water that lessens its value to humans and nature.* In the context of ecosystem function, pollution represents an imbalance of one or more elemental cycles. There are two broad classes of water pollution facing our nation. One is *point pollution.* It has its source in a well-defined location, such as the pipe through which a factory discharges waste into a stream. Although such pollution may be very serious, it usually can be effectively controlled with

☆ Surface water shortage
★ Ground water shortage
○ Salt water seepage
□ Silting of reservoirs
■ Increasing salinity from evaporation

▨ Serious pollution

▨ Less serious but important pollution

8-2 *Water problems in the United States.*

current technology if industry and/or local, state, and federal governments are willing to finance the appropriate measures. The other broad class of water pollution is *nonpoint pollution*. It has its source over large areas such as farms, grazing lands, logging roads, construction sites, abandoned coal mines, and the gardens, lawns, streets, and parking lots of cities. The proper control of nonpoint pollution can be exceedingly difficult.

Even though they are not all mutually exclusive, for purposes of simplification we will consider water pollutants in this chapter under the following six categories: (1) sediments, (2) nutrients (eutrophication), (3) oxygen-demanding organic wastes, (4) thermal pollution, (5) disease organisms, and (6) toxic organic wastes.

Sediment

America's aquatic ecosystems are polluted with one billion tons of sediment annually. It is a curious paradox that the very soil that makes the production of life-sustaining food possible, when washed into a lake or stream, suddenly becomes our nation's most destructive water pollutant.

Silt concentrations of up to 270,000 parts per million have been recorded in certain muddy Iowa streams. According to the Soil Conservation Service (SCS), which made a survey of 157 watersheds, 70 percent of the silt is the result of sheet erosion, 10 percent of gully erosion. The Mississippi River alone washes 400 million tons of sediment into the Gulf of Mexico each year. To freight one year's load would require a train of boxcars 63,300 miles long

—long enough to encircle the world two and one-half times at the equator. As Spencer Havlik, ecologist at San Jose State University, writes: "Soil has been listed as a renewable, replenishable resource, but the living soil community is very hard to reestablish . . . once it is deposited as a sloppy sediment in a Louisiana delta or carried off in a Gulf Stream current . . ." (6).

Negligent land-use practices at urban-suburban construction sites have resulted in the severe sedimentation of nearby streams. While this writer lived in Gaithersburg, Maryland, in 1981, only 25 miles from Washington, D.C., the roar of bulldozers filled the air all day long. During this period of intense "buckshot" urbanization, the sediment load washed from each bulldozed acre per year was a startling 73 tons. The turbidity of nearby Mill Creek rose from 11.5 to 13,000 parts per million within one hour after the start of a thunderstorm. Sediment loads washed from construction sites are roughly 2,000 times greater than from the wooded land where the construction (destruction?) began.

HARMFUL EFFECTS. Every day the American people lose about $1 million as a result of silt-polluted water. Silt inflicts damage on our public water supplies, our reservoirs, and on our hydroelectric plants. It clogs irrigation canals and slows up barges on the Mississippi. Harbors must be routinely dredged at great expense because of sedimentation. Soil particles are carriers of nutrients and toxic chemicals that in turn inflict their own distinctive form of pollution on aquatic ecosystems.

Suspended soil clouds the water to such a degree that millions of algae, an important producer base for aquatic food chains, die because of their inability to carry on photosynthesis. This in turn reduces the levels of dissolved oxygen in the water and results in extensive fish kills. Wastes discharged from canneries, slaughterhouses, and pulp mills tend to accumulate instead of being decomposed by bacteria. Beds of aquatic vegetation in Lake Erie that were once important spawning grounds for fish have been smothered under blankets of silt. In the Pacific Northwest sedimentation is the major form of water pollution. Much of it is the result of poor logging practices, such as clear cutting on steep slopes.

Over 2,000 billion gallons of silt-polluted water must be filtered annually so that Americans can draw drinking water that is clear rather than the color of diluted mud. The life span of thousands of reservoirs throughout the United States has been shortened as a result of sedimentation. The Mono Dam Reservoir near Santa Barbara was given a muddy burial a relatively short time after its construction.

Nutrients and Eutrophication

All aquatic organisms require carbon, hydrogen, oxygen, nitrogen, phosphorus, sulfur, and many other elements for survival. As we discussed earlier in our study of ecological principles, when any essential element occurs in minimal amounts, it forms a *limiting factor*—that is, it restricts the population growth of the organism concerned. Of those elements, nitrogen and phosphorus are most frequently found to be limiting. Nitrogen usually becomes available to the aquatic ecosystem in the form of nitrate ions (NO_3^{2-}); phosphorus usually becomes available as phosphate ions (PO_4^{3-}). Because phosphorus is usually less abundant, it is more important as a limiting factor than nitrogen.

On the basis of *productivity*, the ecologist recognizes two major types of lakes: the *oligotrophic* (nutrient poor) and the *eutrophic* (nutrient rich). A summary of the characteristics of each lake type is found in Table 8–1. The oligotrophic type is represented by Lake Superior, Lake Huron, the Finger Lakes of central New York, and many glacial lakes in northern Minnesota, Wisconsin, Michigan, and New York. Tributary streams gradually increase lake fertility by washing in nutrient-rich loads of sediment. This permits the production of larger quantities of phytoplankton and other aquatic vegetation, which in turn provide a more ample food supply for herbivorous crustaceans, insects, and fish. When these plants and animals die, their bodies settle to the lake bottom and accumulate along with the stream-borne sediment. The plant and animal remains then gradually decompose, thus releasing nutrients that could be channeled into the living bodies of future generations of organisms. It is apparent that in this way the original oligotrophic lake is gradually converted into a eutrophic lake. This process of aging characterized by enrichment is known as *natural eutrophication*.

When this process is speeded up by human activity, it is called *cultural eutrophication*, a condition that represents one of the more serious and exten-

Table 8 – 1 Comparison of the Characteristics of Oligotrophic and Eutrophic Lakes

Oligotrophic Lake	Eutrophic Lake
1. Poor in nutrients	1. Rich in nutrients
2. Deep basin	2. Shallow basin
3. Gravel or sandy bottom	3. Muddy bottom
4. Clear water	4. Turbid water
5. Plankton scarce	5. Plankton abundant
6. Rooted vegetation scarce	6. Rooted vegetation abundant
7. Cold water	7. Warm water
8. Characteristic fish: lake trout, whitefish, ciscoes	8. Characteristic fish: sunfish, yellow perch, carp, bullheads

sive forms of water pollution besetting us today. Such cultural eutrophication caused Lake Erie to age 15,000 years in only 25 years between 1950 and 1975. Lake Mendota (near Madison, Wisconsin) and Lake Washington (near Seattle, Washington) have also undergone rapid eutrophication as a result of human activities. Roughly 80 percent of the nitrogen and 75 percent of the phosphorus added to lakes and streams in the United States has its source in human activities. This human-generated nu-

trient input is derived from several sources, including domestic sewage, livestock waste, agricultural fertilizer, detergents, and industrial waste. When the average concentration of soluble inorganic nitrogen exceeds 0.30-part per million and the soluble inorganic phosphorus content exceeds 0.01-part per million, algal populations may explode. Usually during the summer, such algal blooms convert once-clear water into "pea soup," with visibility frequently being restricted to a depth of one foot.

The Algal-Bloom Problem

The bad effects of such a bloom are multiple. First, it destroys the aesthetics of the lake, rendering it repulsive to swimmers and other sports enthusiasts. Canoe paddles, motorboat propellers, water skis, and fishing lines (as well as human arms doing the crawl stroke) get fouled up in the green slime. Second, the bloom impairs water quality by giving it a bad taste and odor. If the lake is a source of drinking water, considerable expense may be involved in improving its quality. Third, as a result of wind and wave action, huge masses of algae (and even rooted plants that have been torn loose from the lake bottom) will pile up along the shore and decompose. Hydrogen sulfide (H_2S) gas is given off. Not only does this gas smell like rotten eggs, but it is also toxic. Fourth, some of the blue-green algae release

8 – 3 *Eutrophication caused this dense growth of algae in Lake Tahoe, Nevada, May 1972.*

chemicals that are poisonous to both fish and humans. Fifth, the dense algal blooms near the surface prevent sunlight from reaching the billions of algal cells at lower depths. As a result, the sunlight-deprived algae eventually die off, sink to the lake bottom, and form a dense organic ooze. (See Figure 8–4.) The billions of bacteria that then decompose this material use the oxygen dissolved in the surrounding water. As a result, the oxygen concentration in the deep water (hypolimnion) may be severely depleted, dropping rapidly from seven to two parts per million or less. Consequently, any fish adapted to cold water, such as lake trout, would be in danger of asphyxiation. Eventually the dead fish float to shore, decompose, begin to smell, and attract flies.

The Rooted-Weed Problem

Eutrophication is characterized not only by algae growths, but by excessive populations of rooted weeds as well. Turk, Turk, and Wittes (16) have summarized this problem not only for the United States, but for the entire world:

In many areas of the world, especially in the great rivers and lakes of the tropical and subtropical regions, aquatic weeds have multiplied explosively. They have interfered with fishing, navigation, irrigation, and the production of hydroelectric power. They have brought disease and starvation to communities that depended on these bodies of water. *Water hyacinth* in the Congo, Nile, and Mississippi rivers and in other waters in India, West Pakistan, Southeast Asia, and the Philippines, the *water fern* in southern Africa, and the *water lettuce* in Ghana are a few

8–4 *Fish mortality caused by oxygen depletion in lake bottom (hypolimnion) in late summer because of overenrichment (eutrophication) and excessive algae growth.*

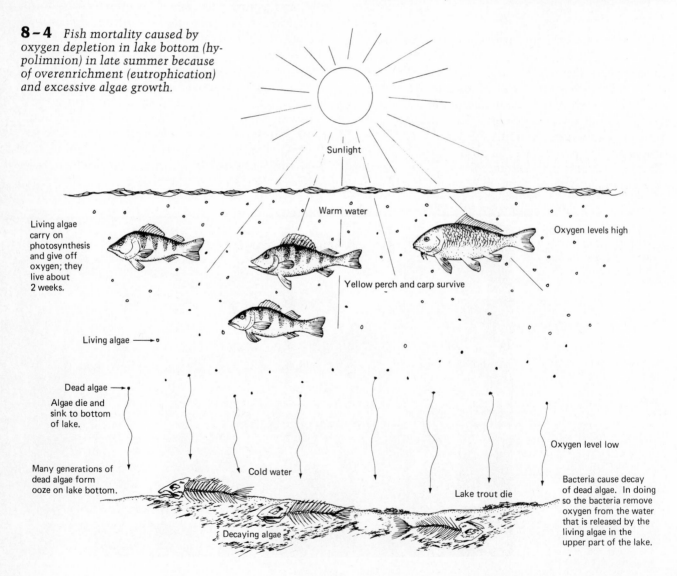

Sunlight

Warm water

Living algae carry on photosynthesis and give off oxygen; they live about 2 weeks.

Oxygen levels high

Yellow perch and carp survive

Living algae ⟶ ∘

Dead algae ⟶ •

Algae die and sink to bottom of lake.

Oxygen level low

Cold water

Many generations of dead algae form ooze on lake bottom.

Lake trout die

Decaying algae

Bacteria cause decay of dead algae. In doing so the bacteria remove oxygen from the water that is released by the living algae in the upper part of the lake.

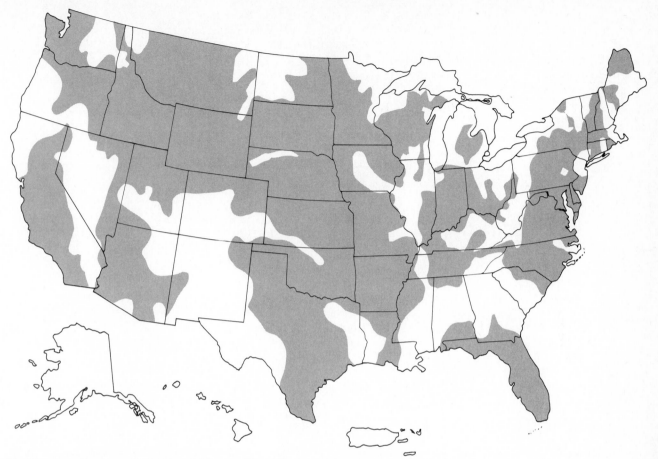

8 – 5 *River basins in the United States polluted by nutrients.*

examples of such catastrophic infestations. Man has always loved the water's edge. To destroy the quality of these limited acres of the earth is to detract from his humanity as well as from the resources that sustain him. (16) [Italics mine.]

Stream Eutrophication

Although eutrophication can occur in streams as well as lakes, the effects are usually not quite so severe. Many rivers are naturally oligotrophic at their headwaters, where the waters flow clear and cold and probably support trout. Such is the case of the small northern streams feeding into the Mississippi. However, by the time the water has neared the stream's mouth, it has received such a cumulative load of nutrients, either from natural or human-generated sources, that it becomes turbid, warm, muddy, and weedy, harboring bullheads and carp rather than trout. (See Figure 8 – 5.) Stream eutrophication is more easily reversed than lake eutrophication, because once the nutrient input is

Table 8 – 2 Adverse Effects of Nutrient Pollution on a Lake

1. Lake aesthetics are destroyed.

2. The recreational values of a lake are destroyed.

3. Water quality is impaired by foul tastes and odors.

4. Gases that emanate from rotting algae have foul odors, tarnish silverware, and discolor painted houses.

5. Toxins given off by algae result in gastric disturbances if ingested.

6. Dense algal blooms at the surface reduce penetration of sunlight to the lake bottom.

7. Decomposing algae at the lake bottom represent a high BOD load. (i.e., a high biological oxygen demand).

8. Contributes to the winter kill of fish in northern lakes.

9. Rooted weeds interfere with navigation and recreation.

10. Game fish are replaced with trash fish.

11. Lake basins are gradually filled in and the lake becomes "extinct."

183

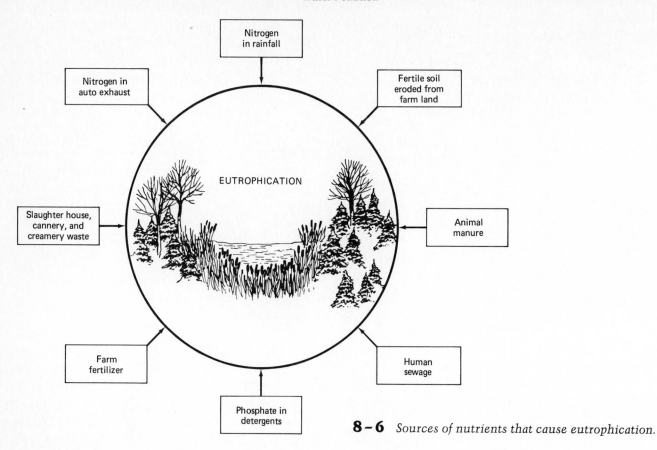

8 – 6 *Sources of nutrients that cause eutrophication.*

Sources of Nutrients

stopped, the current will eventually wash the nutrient-rich sediments into the ocean.

Obviously, human-accelerated eutrophication is highly objectionable. What are the sources of the added nutrients for which we are responsible? There are four major sources: (1) agricultural fertilizers, (2) domestic sewage, (3) livestock wastes, and (4) phosphate detergents. (See Figure 8 – 6.)

AGRICULTURAL FERTILIZERS. Commercial fertilizers effectively promote crop production because they are rich in nitrates and phosphates. Regrettably, however, as our nation's farmers strive to feed a rapidly increasing human population, they inadvertently also feed a population explosion of aquatic plants. The amount of agricultural fertilizer used in the United States has increased more than 15 times since 1945. Much of the fertilizer, which is not absorbed by crop roots, is washed by runoff waters into lakes and streams. (See Figure 8 – 7.) It is estimated that over one billion pounds of agriculture-generated phosphorus enters America's aquatic ecosystems yearly (6). Donald E. Wilkinson, when secretary of the Wisconsin Department of Agriculture, suggested that the use of high-phosphate and nitrate fertilizers by Wisconsin farmers should be restricted in the near future to "alleviate the algae problem in our waters," even though the fertilizer curb would temporarily reduce crop yields.

DOMESTIC SEWAGE. Domestic sewage containing human wastes and household detergents contributes an estimated 200 to 500 million pounds of phosphorus to aquatic ecosystems yearly (8). Most sewage treatment plants remove only about 50 percent of the nitrogen and 30 percent of the phosphorus from domestic sewage. The rapid increase of water milfoil, sea lettuce, and algae in the lower Potomac River below Washington, D.C., several years ago was attributed to the 45 tons of nitrogen and phosphorus compounds contained in the domestic sewage it received daily.

ANIMAL WASTES. Each of the more than twenty million cattle in the United States produces ten times as much waste per day as a human being. In other words, our country's cattle alone produce the waste-equivalent of 200 million people. That does not even include the waste produced by all other types of livestock, including horses, sheep, pigs, goats, chickens, ducks, and turkeys, or the waste left on city lots by 200 million pet cats and dogs. It is apparent that if all this waste were washed into lakes and streams, its eutrophication potential would be enormous. During the winter it has long been the farmer's custom in the northern states to spread animal manure on the frozen ground. When spring comes, of course, some of the nitrogen and phosphorus is absorbed by crop root systems. Unfortunately, however, almost half of this manure may be washed by spring runoff into aquatic ecosystems.

The problem has been accentuated by the recent trend to crowding livestock in feedlots where food is brought to the animals, instead of permitting them to forage for their own food in the open pas-

8-7 *Concentration of phosphorus and nitrogen in streams flowing through forest and agricultural land. Note that streams flowing through land that is about 90 percent agricultural contain about nine times as much phosphorus and about eight times as much nitrogen as streams flowing through land that is about 90 percent forested.*

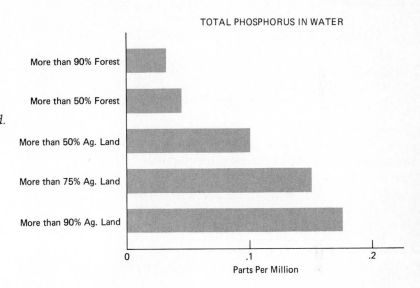

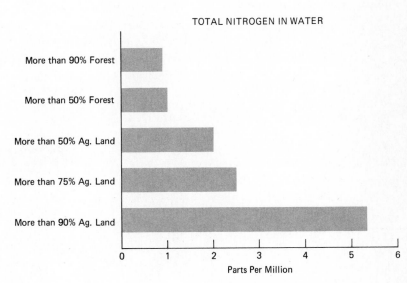

8-8 *Aerial view of huge cattle feedlot at Coalinga, California, May 1972. Runoff from such feedlots contributes to the eutrophication of American lakes and streams.*

ture. (See Figure 8–8.) More than ten million cattle, more than half of our nation's cattle population, are maintained in such feedlots. One large lot, accommodating 10,000 cattle, yields 200 tons of cow ma-nure daily. Without proper control measures, much of this manure eventually contributes to eutrophication. One control method, the *catch basin*, is shown in Figure 8–9.

8-9 *Control of feedlot runoff, Boystown, Nebraska. This basin catches the manure and urine that ordinarily drains into a stream after a rainstorm. The effluent that accumulates in the basin eventually is pumped to nearby croplands with irrigation pipes.*

Detergents: A Story of Clean Clothes and Dirty Lakes

The Problem

Prior to World War II most housewives used old-fashioned natural soaps, made from animal fats, for cleaning purposes. The soaps were inexpensive and performed reasonably well. Moreover, they were biodegradable. In other words, they would quickly decompose and therefore, did not accumulate in the aquatic environment. One big disadvantage, however, was that they did not work well in hard water. However, after World War II those soaps were quickly replaced by synthetic detergents, whose big advantage was that they were equally effective in hard or soft water. The reason for their effectiveness is in their basic components. One component, known as the *surfactant*, does the actual cleaning: it dissolves the dirt. The second component, known as the *builder*, makes possible the high performance of the detergent in hard water. Hard water contains calcium and magnesium ions, which tend to block the cleansing action. The *builder* combines chemically with the ions, thus effectively "locking them up," so that the cleansing action can proceed without interference. Of course, the merits of the new detergents were proclaimed across the land by high-pressure, aggressive multimillion-dollar advertising campaigns. Soon the old-fashioned natural soaps were, in most homes, a thing of the past. Unfortunately, the detergents proved to be nonbiodegradable. As a result, they frequently formed clouds of foam in the lakes and streams into which they were discharged. (See Figure 8–10.) In some areas water would actually foam up like beer when drawn from the tap. Eventually, during the 1960s, under mounting pressure from an indignant public and scathing indictments from environmentalists and several legislators, the detergent industry switched to a biodegradable detergent. Unfortunately, the builder in the new detergents was a phosphorus-containing compound known as STP (sodium tripoly phosphate). That was, indeed, bad news for the state and federal agencies —as well as environmentalists, in general—committed to the battle against eutrophication. By the early 1970s the detergent industry was producing five billion pounds of phosphate annually and accounted for fully half of the phosphorus load in domestic sewage.

Possible Solutions

There have been three basic approaches to solving the problem caused by phosphorus-containing detergents:

8–10 *Sandy Run Creek in Montgomery County, Pennsylvania, forms foamy clouds because of its heavy detergent load.*

1. *Upgrading sewage plants for phosphorus removal.* The detergent industry, as might be expected, strongly suggests that upgrading sewage plants to remove phosphorus is the most effective method for solving the problem. The big drawback, however, is that the large majority of sewage-treatment plants do not have the capability for phosphorus removal. Their upgrading for this purpose would be costly.

2. *Banning phosphorus-containing detergents.* By 1980 a number of communities (Akron, Chicago, Miami, and Syracuse) and states (Minnesota, Wisconsin, Michigan, Indiana, New York, and Vermont) passed laws banning phosphorus-containing detergents (10). Several other states limited the phosphorus content in detergents to 8.7 percent. The result was a dramatic improvement in water quality in some regions. Take Lake Onandaga in New York as an example. For many years it served as a "liquid container" for the sewage of Syracuse. As might be expected, the once-beautiful lake gradually took on the pea-green color of eutrophication. The outraged city fathers met the problem head on. They passed an ordinance banning the use of phosphorus-containing detergents. In only one and one-half years phosphorus levels in the lake were reduced by 57 percent, the frequency of algal blooms decreased, and dissolved oxygen levels suitable for game fish were restored (10, 12).

   Unfortunately, that method of control, attractive as it might appear, may have been a mixed blessing. The trouble lies with the substitutes for the phosphate builder. Several substitutes, which at first seemed promising, have certain highly undesirable features. For example, one of them (carboxy methyl cellulose) appears to be nonbiodegradable. A second (sodium carbonate) causes skin burns. In addition it would increase the solubility of phosphates that hitherto had been locked up in the mud of lake bottoms. As a result they would become available for promoting the growth of weeds and algae. A third proposed substitute (borax) is toxic to aquatic plants even at concentrations as low as one part per million (12). A fourth substitute, NTA (nitrilo triacetate), is suspected of causing deformities in human embryos (7).

   The detergent industry points to still another problem caused by a phosphorus detergent ban: increased costs to the consumer. It contends that the average household would spend an additional $11 per year on additional hot water and laundry aids simply because of the reduced cleansing performance of the nonphosphorus detergents. On the other hand, according to the industry, the cost for removing phosphate from wastewater is only about $1.50 per year per family. In essence, the industry asks American families: "Why switch to nonphosphorus detergents and lose money in the process?" (11).

3. *Using newly developed phosphate-free natural detergents.* Perhaps the ultimate solution to the phosphate detergent problem is the phosphate-free natural soaps and detergents developed recently by the USDA. Because they are made from beef fats, they are to some degree similar to the old-fashioned soaps used before World War II. They perform as well or better than the phosphorus detergents, in hot or cold or soft or *hard* water. Moreover, they are relatively inexpensive, are biodegradable, and of course, do not cause eutrophication. The natural detergents have already seen wide acceptance in Japan. For some reason, however, American manufacturers have been slow to produce a product that would seem to solve the detergent-caused eutrophication problem once and for all (10, 11).

Oxygen-Demanding Organic Wastes

We are well aware that if the garbage collector fails to make a pickup for several days, the accumulating debris will begin to decay and give off vile odors. The same would be true of the rabbit remains left by a fox. What is happening? Bacteria are at work, using oxygen from the air to break down (oxidize) the complex, energy-rich compounds in the garbage. The energy that is released during decomposition is then used by the bacteria to sustain life. Because there is a superabundance of atmospheric oxygen, bacteria do not compete for oxygen with other terrestrial organisms.

Organic matter, however, may also accumulate in aquatic environments, as, for example, when an autumn-leaf fall almost blankets a woodland stream, when a massive fish kill occurs, or when slaughterhouse debris is discharged.

The process by which such organic material is eventually decomposed by bacterial action may be summarized as shown at the bottom of this page.

However, the amount of dissolved oxygen (DO) in the *water* is not nearly as abundant as *atmospheric* oxygen. As a result, the bacteria actively *compete* with other oxygen-demanding aquatic organisms (fish, crustaceans, insect larvae, and so on). If sufficient organic food is available, and if other conditions such as water temperature are favorable, the oxygen-using bacteria will multiply rapidly. Levels of dissolved oxygen will, of course, decrease proportionately, sometimes from ten parts per million down to less than three parts per million, to the detriment of aquatic insects, crustaceans, and fish. The federal government maintains a network of stream-monitoring sites at which dissolved oxygen levels are checked on a systematic basis. Of the many thousands of measurements taken in the past few years, fewer than 5 percent were below five parts per million of dissolved oxygen — the minimal level required for quality fish populations. Although it would appear that our streams are in relatively good condition, we should remember that a *single* decline of dissolved oxygen down to one part per million could destroy every fish in that stretch of stream. For example, the massive discharge of sewage into the Potomac River below Washington, D.C., in recent years has reduced dissolved oxygen levels to less than one part per million. As a result, extensive fish kills occur each May when several species of fish move through the oxygen-depleted waters during their spring spawning runs (14).

The biologists refer to the oxygen used by bacteria in decomposing organic waste in bodies of water as the *biological oxygen demand*, or BOD. This term has also been transferred to the waste itself — in other words it is customary to speak of the BOD of human sewage, or of slaughterhouse wastes, and so on. Every time you flush your toilet you are making it a bit tougher for scrappy game fish in the stream or lake near your home to survive, for there are about 250 parts per million of BOD in the wastewater going down the pipe.

Many of the wastes from canneries, cheese factories, dairies, bakeries, and meatpacking plants have BOD levels ranging from 5,000 to 15,000 parts per million. (See Figure 8–11.) In the late 1960s seven paper and pulp mills in the state of Washington discharged 210 million gallons of mill waste into Puget Sound. In terms of BOD, this was equal to the domestic sewage from a population of 814 million people, which is remarkable when we consider that there are only 2.8 million people in the entire state of Washington (18).

high-energy organic molecules + oxygen → low-energy carbon dioxide + energy
(fats, carbohydrates, and proteins)
$$+$$
low-energy water
$$+$$
nitrate ions (NO_3^{2-})
$$+$$
phosphate ions (PO_4^{3-})
$$+$$
sulphate ions (SO_4^{2-})

(used by bacteria to sustain life

189

8–11 *Biologists examining fish destroyed by oxygen-demanding cheese-factory wastes discharged into stream near Loganville (Sauk County), Wisconsin.*

8–12 *Effect of sewage with a high level of BOD on the oxygen levels and aquatic life of a stream.*

Dominant fish	Game fish: Trout Black bass, etc.	Trash fish: Bullheads Carp Garpike, etc.	Fish absent	Trash fish: Bullheads Carp Garpike, etc.	Game fish: Trout Black bass, etc.
Index animals present on river bottom	May fly larvae Stone fly larvae Caddis fly larvae	Black fly larvae Bloodworm	Sludge worms Bloodworms Rat-tailed maggot	Black fly larvae Bloodworms	May fly larvae Stone fly larvae Caddis fly larvae
Dissolved oxygen (ppm) 8 6 4 2 0	8 ppm	Oxygen sag	2 ppm		8 ppm
	Clean water A	Decline B	Severe damage Decomposition C	Recovery D E	Clean water
		Discharge of sewage with high BOD			
Physical features	Clear water; no bottom sludge	Cloudy water; bottom sludge	Cloudy water; bottom sludge, bad smelling gases	Clear water; bottom sludge	Clear water; no bottom sludge

The BOD Test

Now how do we measure the BOD of organic waste? Let us suppose that the health authorities of a certain town are suspicious that the effluent from the local sewage-disposal plant has an excessive BOD. It might be assumed that the easiest and most direct procedure is simply to filter the organic material from the water or scoop it from the stream or lake bottom and weigh it. Then it might be determined that there are x number of pounds of organic matter in y gallons of sewage effluent or z gallons of river water. Unfortunately, some organic material (fish carcasses, human feces, an so on) decomposes rapidly and some (pesticides, such as DDT) is virtually nonbiodegradable. It is apparent, therefore, that the direct method of measuring the degree of organic pollution will not work. The degree of pollution can also be measured by the BOD test, in which a sample of polluted water whose dissolved oxygen content has been determined is placed in a container from which all air and light is excluded and incubated for five days at 20° C. The amount of oxygen consumed is then determined by comparing the amounts present before and after incubation.

The Effect of a High BOD on Stream Animals

Does sewage effluent with a high BOD have any noticeable effect on aquatic animal populations? The answer, of course, is of vital interest to fishermen, nature lovers, streamside property owners, and resort operators, as well as to biologists. The answer to such a question is frequently sought by an aquatic biologist working for a state environmental protection agency. He or she could get the answer simply by determining the kinds and numbers of organisms occurring immediately above and at several sites below the point of sewage discharge. Note that in Figure 8–12, site A, just above the outfall, the river is characteristic of an unpolluted stream. The high levels of dissolved oxygen at eight parts per million, and the abundant food in the form of may-, stone-, and caddis-fly larvae, make possible the survival of highly prized game fish such as bass and trout. (See Figure 8–13.) However, at point B, in the Zone of Decline, immediately below the outfall, dissolved oxygen levels drop rapidly because of the high organic component of the waste. In some streams the dissolved oxygen may drop to three parts per million or less, which is insufficient to

INDICATORS OF CLEAN WATER

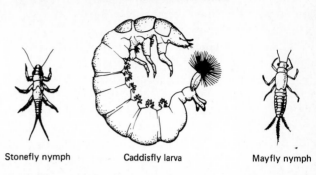

Stonefly nymph   Caddisfly larva   Mayfly nymph

8–13 *Insect larvae that can be used as indicators of clean water.*

INDICATORS OF POLLUTED WATER

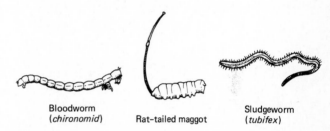

Bloodworm (*chironomid*)   Rat-tailed maggot   Sludgeworm (*tubifex*)

8–14 *Insect larvae that can be used as indicators of sewage-polluted water with low oxygen levels.*

support the oxygen requirements of *quality fish*, such as black bass, walleyes, and trout. Instead, only *trash fish*, such as carp and bullheads, which have low oxygen requirements, can survive. The larvae of mayflies, stoneflies, and caddis flies, which require higher oxygen levels, are virtually absent. The dissolved oxygen concentration is so drastically reduced in the Damage Zone that even carp and bullheads cannot survive. The most typical bottom-dwelling animals in this zone are reddish sludgeworms, of which there may be 20,000 per square foot of stream bottom; bright-red midge larvae; and the reddish rat-tail maggot.* (See Figure 8–14.) These animals are sometimes used as *index organisms:* their occurrence indicates that a particular stretch of stream is highly contaminated with organic waste. Unpolluted aquatic ecosystems usually have a much greater species diversity than

* The reddish color of these organisms is caused by the large amounts of oxygen-carrying hemoglobin just under their body surface. The rat-tail maggot, in addition, takes in oxygen through a long tube that extends to the water surface.

191

their polluted counterparts. Rather surprisingly, however, the total *biomass* in severely deoxygenated areas might approach that of unpolluted water. The reason is that each of the few highly specialized species that *can* survive, such as the sludgeworms, are represented by huge populations (11).

Beginning at point *D* in the Recovery Zone, the amount of oxygen removed by the sewage bacteria is more than counterbalanced by the oxygen entering the stream from the atmosphere because of wind action or the stroke of a canoe paddle, or being generated by the photosynthesis of stream-dwelling plants. As a result, the dissolved oxygen level rises, permitting once again the occurrence of carp and garpike. Finally, still farther downstream at point *E*, most of the organic material discharged from the sewage plant has been decomposed; consequently the dissolved oxygen curve rises to its original level and permits the occurrence of animals characteristic of a nonpolluted stream (11).

The characteristic dip of the oxygen curve at points *B* and *C* is known as the *oxygen sag*. The slope of the dissolved oxygen curve, which is highly variable, is dependent on the amount of BOD in the sewage, the rates at which oxygen enters the stream, and the water temperature.

Thermal Pollution

Biscayne Bay, Florida, is an unusually productive ecosystem, having great numbers of species of aquatic organisms such as lobsters, crabs, fish, and wading birds. More than 600,000 pounds of seafoods are harvested annually from the Bay. It was, thus, of considerable significance when biologists in the early 1970s found a 75-acre region that was virtually lifeless — a biological desert. What happened there? Thermal pollution. The scarcity of life was caused by the discharge of heated water directly into the Bay from the Florida Power and Light Company's plant. This is a dramatic example of the harmful effects of thermal pollution on an aquatic ecosystem (12). Let's look at this form of pollution more closely.

An acceptable definition for *thermal pollution* is *"the warming up of an aquatic ecosystem to the point where desirable organisms are adversely affected."* Although thermal pollution may result

8–15 *Nuclear reactor cooling system. Note the 1,000-foot zone of thermal pollution caused by the discharge.*

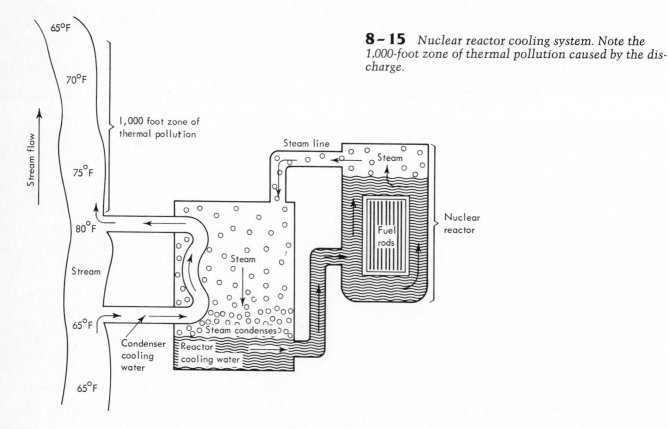

from both natural (excessive heating by the summer sun) and industrial causes, the latter are by far the most significant. Many industries take water from a lake or stream to cool equipment or products. By the time the water is returned, it may have warmed up considerably. The electric-power, steel, and chemical industries are the most important users of cooling water. A single 1,000-megawatt power plant may use one-half-million gallons of cooling water every minute, equal to the gross water use of the entire city of Chicago, with a population of more than 3.3 million people (9).

Remember the *second law of energy?* It states that whenever energy is converted from one form to another, a certain amount is lost as heat. There are several energy conversions involved in a power plant fired by fossil fuel. The chemical energy in coal or oil, or the nuclear energy in radioactive fuels, is converted into heat to generate steam to turn the blades of the turbine. That mechanical energy is then converted into electrical energy by the generator. In order to condense the steam back to water to return it to the boiler, the steam is passed over coils that carry cold water drawn from a stream or lake. (See Figure 8–15.) As a result, the steam is condensed and heat is transferred to the cooling water. The temperature of the cooling water may be raised 20° F.

By the year 2000 our industries will have to dispose of about 20 million billion BTUs* of waste heat per day. To accomplish this they will have to use fully one half of our nation's dry-season stream flow for cooling purposes exclusively. It has been estimated that the waste heat discharged into Lake Michigan from industrial, nuclear, and coal-fired power plants by the year 2000 will be 16 times as much as in the late 1960s. The volume of heated water will be sufficient to cover Lake Michigan's 14.3 million acres with a 4.6-foot-thick sheet of water heated 20° F above normal lake temperature (9).

Harmful Effects

Thermal pollution has many adverse effects on aquatic ecosystems. Let us consider some of them.

* BTU — British Thermal Unit — is the amount of heat required to raise the temperature of one pound of water from 63° to 64° F. One BTU is equal to 252 calories.

REDUCTION IN DISSOLVED OXYGEN. When water is warmed, its capacity for dissolving oxygen is *decreased.* For example, at a temperature of 32° F, water that has been thoroughly mixed with oxygen has an oxygen content of 14.6 parts per million, but at 104° F it contains only 6.6 parts per million (15). Unfortunately, this decrease occurs at the same time that the need for oxygen by aquatic organisms (fish, crustaceans, and so on) increases. For example, even the lowly carp, which requires only 0.5-part per million of oxygen at 33° F, needs at least 1.5 parts per million at 95° F if it is to survive (5). It is apparent that cold-water fish such as trout and salmon, which require about six parts per million to survive, could not tolerate the high water temperatures that would prevail at the point where the warmed-up coolant water is discharged. If they remained in the area they would die from oxygen starvation.

INTERFERENCE WITH REPRODUCTION. Fish are cold-blooded animals whose body temperatures (and activity levels) vary with that of the external environment. Some fish have been able to survive even after being frozen solid in the Arctic ice. Other species of fish can live in the hot springs of Yellowstone National Park. Most fish, however, are extremely sensitive to slight thermal changes. Some species, in fact, can detect water-temperature shifts of only 0.05° F. Many kinds of fish are instinctively "tuned" to certain thermal signals that trigger such activities as nest building, spawning, and migration. For example, the maximum temperature at which cold-water fish such as lake trout will successfully spawn is 48° F (8.9° C). The corresponding temperature for large-mouthed black bass is 80° F (26.7° C). Not only will warmed water disturb spawning, and in some cases prevent it altogether, but it may also destroy the eggs once they are laid. Thus, according to the Oregon Fish Commission, a mere 5.4° F increase in temperature of the Columbia River could have disastrous effects on the eggs of the Chinook salmon (13).

INCREASED VULNERABILITY TO DISEASE. The ability of some bacteria such as *Chondroccus* to penetrate the body of a fish is poor at 60° F, but it gradually increases with rising water temperatures. *Chondroccus* is believed to be responsible for the massive kills of blueback salmon on the Columbia

193

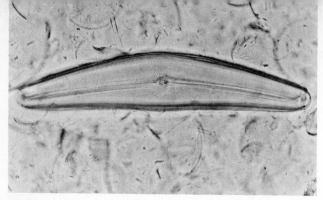

8-16

A. A diatom. This alga prefers a water temperature of about 58° F. It is an important initial producer link of the food chains of fish. Note the exquisitely sculptured "case" of silica which encloses this single-celled creature.

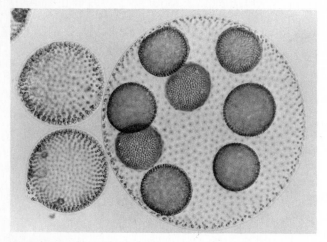

B. A green alga. This is Volvox, *which prefers water temperatures of about 90° F. It is a beautiful spherical colonial form. Shimmeringly beautiful in the sunlight, it drives itself through the water by means of hundreds of tiny whiplike "oars."*

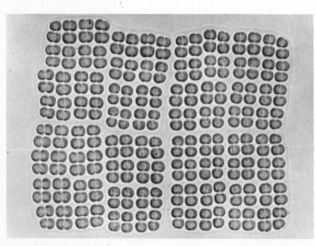

C. A blue-green alga. This is Merismopedia, *a colonial form that prefers a water temperature of about 104° F. A predominance of blue-green algae may be a sign of thermal pollution. In general, blue-green algae are not important links in fish food chains. Moreover, some species of blue-green algae may give off toxic wastes.*

River in 1946. Thermal pollution of the Columbia was undoubtedly a contributing factor.

DIRECT MORTALITY. The body temperature of fish is determined by the temperature of the water in which it lives. A lake trout will perish if the water temperature is much higher than 50° F. The lethal temperature for trout in Minnesota and Wisconsin is 77° F; for walleye, 86° F; and for yellow perch, 88° F. It is apparent that because the discharge of warmed-up cooling water may raise stream temperatures 20° F above normal (in other words, well into the 90° F range in summer) any cold-water fish would have to emigrate in order to survive. Several years ago the heated water from power plants and other industries raised the temperature of a stretch of the Mahoning River in Ohio to 140° F (24). Although no data are available, we can logically assume that at that temperature the Mahoning River was beyond the heat tolerance range for all species of fish in the area.

THE INVASION OF DESTRUCTIVE ORGANISMS. Thermal pollution may permit the invasion of organisms that are tolerant to warm water and highly destructive. A good example is the invasion of *ship-worms* (highly specialized relatives of clams and oysters) into New Jersey's Oyster Creek. A few years ago shipworms were absent from Oyster Creek apparently because they could not tolerate the cold water. (Remember the law of tolerance.) However, thermal discharges from the New Jersey Central Power and Light Company power plant gradually warmed up the creek. One result was the shipworm invasion. They burrowed into wooden docks and the hulls of ships, wreaking considerable damage. During the burrowing (and feeding) process they grew rapidly in size from a fraction of an inch to more than two feet (12).

UNDESIRABLE CHANGES IN ALGAE POPULATIONS. Each of the three major groups of algae—diatoms, green, and blue-green—have distinct tolerance ranges for water temperature. (See Figure 8–16.) Thus, the greatest species diversity for diatoms, green algae, and blue-green algae occurs at 58°, 90°, and 104° F, respectively. The most valuable algae, as far as fish and human food chains are concerned, are the diatoms that prefer cool water. On the other hand, those that prefer warm water—the blue-green algae—are the least desirable as

8-17 *Wet cooling towers in operation. Note the clean water vapor being discharged into the atmosphere by one of the twin wet cooling towers. This $260-million power plant, located near Danville, Pennsylvania, has a 1.5-million-kilowatt capability.*

aquatic animal food. Not only that, they give off toxic substances and cause the multiple problems already discussed under nutrient pollution. Along with nutrients, high water temperature is an important factor in promoting blue-green algal blooms. It is easy to see how aquatic food chains could be disrupted by discharges of heated water effluents. As Richard Wagner, environmentalist at the University of Pennsylvania, states: "A water flea, for example, which might be able to tolerate the thermal extreme of 95° F, would probably starve to death if the diatoms on which it fed were unable to survive at that temperature. In turn, fish feeding on water fleas would be similarly hard pressed to survive, regardless of their tolerance or adaptibility to the high temperature" (17).

THE DESTRUCTION OF ORGANISMS IN COOLING WATER. The volume of water removed from a stream for cooling purposes is enormous, sometimes involving a substantial part of a stream's total flow. A large power plant will withdraw *500 million gallons per day*. Unfortunately, many of the plankton, insect larvae, and small fish that are sucked into the condenser along with the cooling water are destroyed by the thermal shock, as well as by water velocity and pressure.

Control

After much prodding by state and federal environmental protection agencies, the power industry has tried to control the thermal-pollution problem with *cooling towers* and *lagoons*. Cooling towers

are mammoth structures about thirty stories tall. (See Figure 8-17.) They are large enough at the base to cover a football field. In the *wet* cooling tower illustrated in Figure 8-18, the heated water is piped to a high level in the tower and then directed downward in a thin sheet over a series of baffle plates.

8-18 *Natural-draft on "wet" cooling tower removes heat from condenser water by evaporation on direct contact with air rising up through the hollow concrete shell. Its large size is necessary to provide sufficient surface area and draft to cool thousands of gallons of water each day. The distinctive shape channels the airflow and yields great structural strength with less material.*

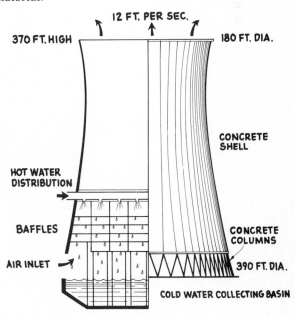

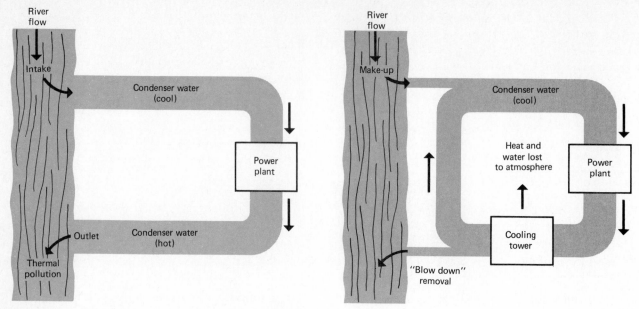

8 – 19 *Comparison of closed-cycle and open-cycle cooling.*

Cooling Cycles

Power plants use two basic methods for steam-condensing purposes: open and closed cycles. (See Figure 8 – 19.)

Open Cycle

In the open cycle (Figure 8 – 22) cold water is withdrawn from a nearby lake, stream, or bay for steam-condensing purposes; then, with its temperature increased about 15° F, the water is discharged back to the lake or stream from which it came. Most of the thermal-pollution problems described here were caused by this type of cooling cycle. Open cycles on new plants were banned by the EPA in 1974 (12).

Closed Cycle

In the closed cycle the warmed-up cooling water is pumped to a *cooling tower* or a *cooling pond*, where the heat is removed. The cooled water is then recirculated through the condenser. This cycle is repeated over and over. Unfortunately, despite its name, this system is not completely closed. A small percentage of water is lost by evaporation and a small amount, known as *blow-down water*, is discharged. The water that leaves the system in this way must be made up by an equal volume of intake. All new steam electric plants, with few exceptions, are required by the EPA to use closed-cycle systems. As the older open-cycle power plants are phased out, the thermal-pollution problem should gradually be reduced (12).

During this time about 2.5 percent of the water evaporates, a process facilitated by the upward flow of fan-propelled air. The coolant water is then either (1) discharged into the stream, lake, or ocean from which it was drawn, (2) directed into a lagoon for further cooling, or (3) cycled back to the plant's condenser.

Although cooling towers reduce the thermal-pollution problem somewhat, they do have certain undesirable features. First, when the air temperature is

32° F or lower, the towers generate a considerable amount of fog; further, if the fog comes in contact with a solid surface, a thin layer of ice is formed. As a result, cooling towers, when located near highways, could greatly increase traffic hazards during their periods of operation. Second, the water that is evaporated, amounting to 25,000 gallons per minute for a 1,000-megawatt plant, is *consumed.* In other words, it is lost to the aquatic ecosystems (rivers and lakes) from which it came. This water loss is equal to a daily rainfall of one inch on a two-square-mile area. Third, toxic materials such as chlorine, used to prevent pipe-clogging bacterial slimes, must be removed from the cooling water before it re-enters lakes or streams. Fourth, although the towers are remarkable engineering accomplishments, they are 400-foot-tall masses of concrete and steel that dominate the skyline and detract from environmental aesthetics. Fifth, the towers are very expensive, costing about $2 million each. Such an expenditure, of course, is eventually passed along from the utility to the consumer in the form of increased electric rates, adding perhaps 1 percent to a customer's annual bills. This cost, however, is tolerable, when weighed against the advantages of thermal reduction in our aquatic ecosystems.

The Beneficial Effects of Heated Water

Artificially heated water is usually considered harmful to aquatic ecosystems. Nevertheless, under certain circumstances, it may have a beneficial effect. Let's briefly consider some of them:

1. In some farming regions heated cooling water from power plants has been distributed through underground pipes in early spring and late fall to raise average soil temperatures. The warmed-up soil makes possible a prolonged growing season and double harvests of some crops.
2. In Eugene, Oregon, heated water from a paper mill was sprayed on fruit trees to prevent frost damage.
3. In Vineyard Haven, Massachusetts, heated cooling water is used by a hatchery to speed up the growth of lobsters to a marketable size. The time required has been reduced from eight to only two years (12).
4. Researchers in Georgia have found that thermal pollution of the Savannah River resulted in increased growth rates in black bass. The warmed-

up water also attracted fish to the area; as a result, fishermen enjoyed huge catches.
5. It has been suggested that cooling water, bearing a thermal load, and domestic sewage effluent, bearing a nutrient load, might be combined in specially created lagoons (5). In this scheme, *both the nutrient and thermal pollutants could be put to constructive use.* For example, fast-growing Asiatic milkfish could be stocked in the lagoons. Because they are of tropical origin and adapted to warm waters, the relatively high lagoon temperatures would pose no problems. Moreover, during winters in the northern states, the warm water would prevent ice from forming and permit the milkfish to feed and grow on a year-round basis. Furthermore, because the fish are plant eaters, not only would the nutrients be efficiently converted into fillets, but the weed problem commonly associated with eutrophic ponds would be under control. Milkfish have extremely rapid growth rates, increasing in length from 5 to 25 inches a single year. As a result, thousands of such "fish factories" distributed throughout the country might partially compensate for the progressive loss of prime food-protein-producing land to highways, parking lots, and shopping centers.
6. Warmed-up cooling water may also be useful in heating homes. A study is being conducted in West Germany to determine whether such a scheme is feasible for cities of more than 40,000 people. Because pipes required for conducting the heated water are very expensive, the power plants and the homes that are to use the water must be designed with this heating scheme in mind (12).

Disease-Producing Organisms

Water pollution is responsible for more cases of human illness the world over than any other environmental factor. Among the diseases it causes are *cholera, typhoid fever, dysentery, polio,* and *infectious hepatitis.* Most of these diseases occur in the underdeveloped nations of South America, Africa, and Asia. Here in the United States the death rate from such illnesses has dropped dramatically in the last century. For example, in the 1880s the death rate from typhoid was 75 to 100 per 100,000 people per year; today it is a mere 0.1 per 100,000 people per year. In other words, the death rate in the 1880s was 750 to 1,000 times greater than it is today. Nevertheless, American waters are not exactly germ free.

Don't be startled, but that last glass of water you drank may already have passed through the bodies of eight people, especially if you live in a densely populated region. Our use and reuse of sewage-contaminated streams throughout urbanized America today is intensive. Such recycling of precious water supplies will probably become more and more necessary in the future, because there will be a simultaneous increase in population and per capita use. It is apparent, however, that such reuse will depend on extremely effective fail-safe water-treatment methods to reduce harmful micro-organisms to a very low level. Without such methods the incidence of infectious, waterborne diseases in our nation will most certainly increase.

Let us briefly examine some typical disease outbreaks caused by waterborne micro-organisms.

1. From May to July 1965, 18,000 of the 130,000 residents of Riverside, California, were stricken with fever, diarrhea, and vomiting. Three died. The organism responsible was *Salmonella typhimurium*, a bacterium related to the one that causes typhoid. Intensive chlorination of the city's water supplies eventually brought the epidemic under control.
2. In 1916, and again in 1924, two major typhoid epidemics along the Atlantic coast were traced to contaminated clams and oysters. Fifteen hundred people were infected; 150 people died in the 1924 epidemic. After the 1924 outbreak, the shellfish companies formed a compact with the U.S. Public Health Service whereby interstate health controls and standards were established (18).
3. In the early 1960s some children were playing along the Hudson River, into which 400 million gallons of human sewage were being discharged daily. After retrieving a watermelon they had spotted floating downstream, they sliced it up and had a feast. Soon thereafter, eight of those youngsters came down with typhoid fever.
4. In 1933 an outbreak of dysentery occurred in Chicago during the World's Fair. This disease is caused by a one-celled animal, the amoeba. It is characterized by extreme weakness and diarrhea.

Most of the sick people were visitors to the fair who had stayed in two first-class hotels. In the investigation that followed, it was discovered that the drinking water in those hotels had been contaminated with human sewage because of faulty plumbing (12).

State and municipal health departments take frequent samples of drinking-water supplies to ensure that disease-causing bacteria are held to an absolute minimum. Because the number of kinds of pathogenic bacteria is so numerous, however, it is not practical to make counts of each type. Instead, counts are made of the *coliform bacteria*, the relatively harmless organisms that live in the human gut. (See Figure 8 – 20.) These bacteria pass from the human intestines along with the feces and, therefore, occur in sewage-contaminated waters. A low coliform count indicates a low number of pathogenic bacteria in the water. A high coliform count indicates the presence of a high number of disease-causing bacteria. The EPA has ruled that whenever drinking water has four or more coliform bacteria per 100 milliliters, this fact must be reported to state health authorities. Corrective action must then be taken. One drawback to this method is that it is rather difficult to distinguish *human coliforms* from those occurring in the digestive tracts of other mammals, such as muskrats, sheep, and cattle.

Nevertheless, despite these water-testing methods over 46,000 Americans *did* get sick from contaminated drinking water between 1961 and 1970. In 1971 a Public Health Service survey of 969 community water systems revealed that 36 percent of the water systems contained bacteria exceeding safe limits.

Viruses

Have you ever complained of vague pains, headache, nausea, and muscular stiffness? Of course. Perhaps you went to the doctor for a diagnosis, only to have him say, almost evasively, "You must have some kind of virus." But just what kind of virus was it? And where did it come from? It is quite possible, that water may be implicated in viral disease *as yet unrecognized.* One well-known viral disease that can be lethal to humans is *infectious hepatitis.* The virus causes damage to the liver. Symptoms include fever, extreme weakness, vomiting, yellow skin, and coffee-colored urine. Between 1844 and 1956

198

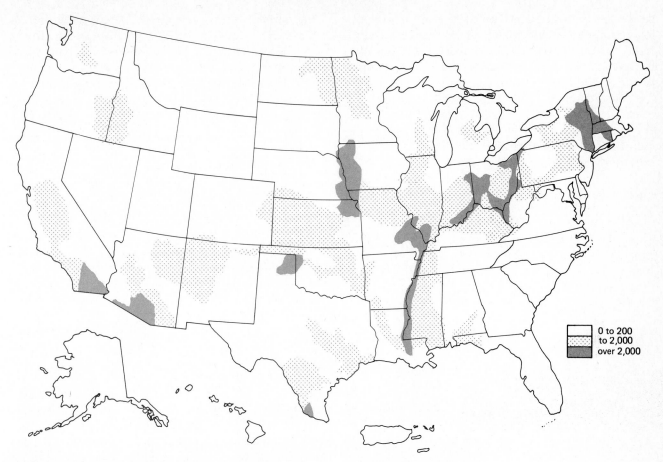

8–20 *Levels of fecal coliform bacteria in U.S. rivers and streams in 1976. Annual mean values are the number of coliform bacterial colonies per 100 milliliters of water. Water is considered unsafe for drinking when coliform counts are over 100 and unsafe for swimming when over 200.*

0 to 200
to 2,000
over 2,000

there were at least six outbreaks of waterborne infectious hepatitis in the United States. Another extensive outbreak of the disease occurred in 1961 in New York and New Jersey. During an ensuing investigation, it was revealed that each disease victim had eaten clams harvested from Raritan Bay, off the New Jersey coast. The clams had taken the virus into their bodies during the process of filtering food from the sewage-contaminated water (15).

Public-health workers are hampered by the limited knowledge of the movements of viruses in aquatic ecosystems. How fast are they transported? At what densities? Are viruses present in aquifers? If so, how did they get there? How effective are water-treatment methods in destroying or neutralizing viruses? Would ozone be more effective than chlorine? Much more research is needed before satisfactory answers are forthcoming.

Chlorine: A Mixed Blessing

The use of chlorine in destroying disease-causing bacteria in drinking water has probably saved the lives of millions of people in the United States. But is chlorine a mixed blessing? In recent years there has been considerable concern that it might actually be the cause of serious human illness and even death.

The year was 1967. The place was New Orleans. The drinking water tasted terrible. Besides, it had a fishy smell. EPA scientists were called in to investigate. Their conclusion was that something more serious than taste or odor was involved. In 1972 the EPA published its findings: the chlorine was combining with organic compounds in the water to form chlororganic compounds. Among those identified were *chloroform* and *carbon tetrachloride*. In laboratory tests both of those chemicals have caused cancer in rats and mice. The EPA then made a follow-up survey of chlorine-treated drinking water in more than 120 cities (12). *Traces of chlororganic compounds were found in almost every case.* People drinking chlorinated water, of course, have reason for some concern. They might well reason: "I've been drinking chlorinated water all my life. Will I come down with cancer some day because of the chloroform and carbon tetrachloride I have taken into my body with each swallow?" The EPA is studying the problem closely. In the near future it may well order all plants that chlorinate their drink-

ing water to filter it through *activated carbon*. In this way the level of chlororganic compounds would be sharply reduced. Unfortunately, activated carbon filtration is expensive. It would cost a family of four about $35 per year, and close to $1 billion for the entire nation (11). So the question comes down to either having people die of cancer caused by excessive clorine or protecting people by installing expensive filters of activated carbon. In America, we have a penchant for placing an economic value on everything. How many cancer deaths will we accept as the price for chlorinated water?

8–21 *Sources of ground water contamination.*

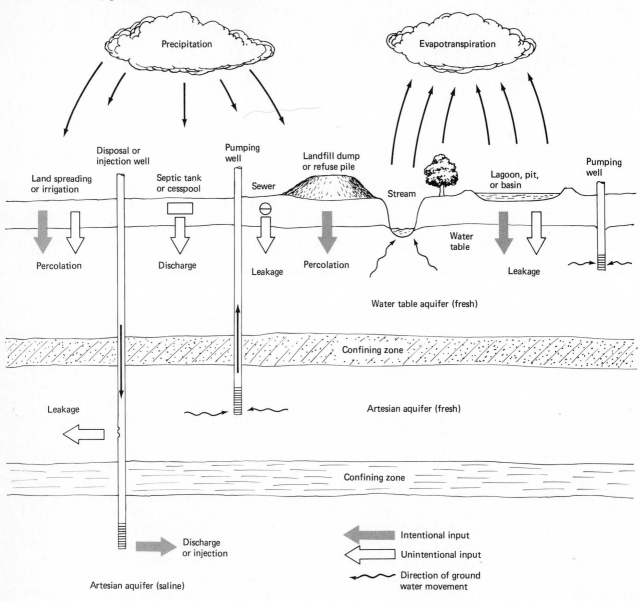

**An Underground
Threat: Toxic
Organic Chemicals**

It is easy to ignore groundwater because we cannot see it. It moves slowly through stone and gravel aquifers far beneath our feet. Yet, within only one-half mile of the earth's surface, this vast water resource has a volume equal to that of the Great Lakes — about 40 quadrillion gallons. More than one-half of the people in the United States depend on this unseen resource for drinking water, consuming more than eight trillion gallons yearly. These statistics cause considerable concern among public-health officials. Since the late 1970s they have become increasingly aware that much of our drinking water is polluted with *toxic organic chemicals.* (All organic compounds contain both the elements carbon and hydrogen.)

Sources of Groundwater Pollution

Groundwater contamination with toxic organic chemicals originates in a number of sources: surface impoundments, land disposal of wastewater, underground injection wells for waste disposal, municipal landfills, septic tanks, leaks and spills, agriculture, mining activities, and petroleum production. (See Figure 8–21.) Because water flows so slowly through an aquifer, it may take decades for a contaminant to move a mile or two from the original point of contamination (2).

INDUSTRIAL LANDFILLS AND LAGOONS. Many industrial plants dispose of their wastes in trenches or pits. The waste is then covered with soil. Such disposal sites are *landfills.* More than 50,000 industrial landfills may contain hazardous wastes in potentially dangerous amounts. A survey of 8,163 industrial disposal sites revealed the following disturbing facts:

1. Fifty percent may contain hazardous liquid waste.
2. Seventy percent do not have a lining that would prevent pollutants from seeping downward and contaminating groundwater.
3. Ten percent are not only unlined but are located within one mile of a water well that could easily become contaminated.
4. Ten percent do not have monitors to check groundwater for the presence of pollutants.
5. A 1977 survey of groundwater quality below fifty industrial landfills revealed that forty were contaminated with toxic organic wastes, forty-nine with heavy metals, and thirty-seven with selenium, arsenic, or cyanide.

MUNICIPAL LANDFILLS. In 1976 only about one in three of the 16,000 municipal landfill sites that were active were in compliance with state regulations.

SEPTIC TANKS. About twenty million homes rely on septic tanks for waste disposal. These systems discharge more than one trillion gallons of waste into the ground annually. Families using septic tanks usually rely on private wells for drinking water. Unfortunately, those wells frequently become contaminated with toxic organics that have leached from the septic-tank system.

Groundwater contamination with synthetic organics is frequently ten to twenty times greater than in the most badly polluted surface-water sources, such as the lower Mississippi River in Louisiana or the Kanawha River in West Virginia. Some examples follow:

1. *San Gabriel Valley, California.* In 1980, thirteen cities in the San Gabriel Valley, with a total population of more than 400,000 were shut off from badly needed water supplies because public health authorities closed

thirty-nine community wells. The reason was contamination of the wells with TCE (trichloroethylene), an organic chemical known to cause cancer in mice. In one well the TCE concentration was 600 parts per billion, a much higher level than is considered acceptable (2).

2. *Jackson Township, New Jersey.* In 1980 more than 100 drinking-water wells became contaminated and were closed in Jackson Township in New Jersey because of the apparent illegal disposal of chemicals in a landfill. Residents in the area believe that a number of illnesses, ranging from infections to kidney disorders, and from skin rashes to premature deaths, were directly caused by the polluted well water (2).

3. *Bedford, Massachusetts.* For many years the city of Bedford, Massachusetts, was supplied with drinking water from four large wells. In 1978 a resident engineer routinely tested the water for a paper he was writing. Much to his surprise and dismay, he found the water seriously polluted with toxic organic chemicals. Levels of dioxane reached 2,100 parts per billion. As a result, Bedford was forced to close its wells and purchase water at considerable expense, from four nearby communities — until one of these towns in turn had to close two of its wells. Bedford is not an exception. Public and private wells have been restricted or closed in at least 22 Massachusetts communities (2).

4. *Nassau and Suffolk Counties, New York.* Water testing in 1978 resulted in the closing of 23 community wells in Nassau county and 13 in Suffolk county. More than two million people were affected by the closings. Thirty-nine additional wells were tested in other parts of the state. All were contaminated with synthetic organic chemicals (2).

Table 8–3 Effects of Toxic Organic Chemicals on the Health of Occupationally Exposed Workers

Chemical	Exposure	Effects*
Carbon tetrachloride	Inhalation; absorption through skin	Liver and kidney damage Vomiting Abdominal pain Diarrhea Jaundice Red and white blood cells in urine Coma Death
Chloroform	Inhalation	Anesthetic effect Dizziness Mental dullness Kidney damage Liver enlargement Digestive disturbances Coma Death
Vinyl chloride		Chromosome abnormalities Increased spontaneous abortions (in the opinion of exposed workers)
Ethylene dibromide		Decreased fertility
Benzene		Prolonged menstrual bleeding Leukemia (blood cancer)

* All of these chemicals have caused cancer in laboratory rats and mice.
Source: Council on Environmental Quality, *Contamination of Ground Water by Toxic Organic Chemicals.* Washington, DC: U.S. Government Printing Office, 1981.

EFFECTS ON HUMAN HEALTH.   As yet scientists do not know what effect the daily *consumption* of one or more of the 33 toxic organic chemicals found in drinking-water wells would have on human health. However, a number of people who have been occupationally exposed to those compounds have either inhaled the chemicals or absorbed them through the skin. Nevertheless, no matter how the chemicals enter the body, their effects should be similar. In the occupationally exposed people the organic compounds caused dizziness, fatigue, and vomiting. Some caused damage to the kidneys and liver. At high concentrations some chemicals caused decreased fertility and spontaneous abortions. Table 8–3 lists the health effects of some organic chemicals currently being found in our nation's drinking-water wells (2).

PREVENTION.   Unlike a flowing river, groundwater has virtually no natural cleansing or diluting mechanisms. As a result, once it becomes contaminated it may remain so for thousands of years. It is obvious, therefore, that pollution *prevention* is of utmost importance in groundwater management.

Sewage Treatment and Disposal

All the types of water contaminants described thus far — sediments, infectious organisms, detergents, human excrement, and organic material — are components, to a greater or lesser degree, of municipal sewage. In order to minimize the potentially harmful effects of these pollutants, municipal sewage is usually treated at *sewage-treatment plants* before it is discharged into a lake, stream, or ocean.

During the Middle Ages, in some of the densely populated cities of Europe such as London and Paris, human waste was often disposed of simply by opening a window and sloshing it into the street below. The stench that assaulted the nose of passersby along those streets was so vile that refined gentlemen carried sweet-smelling spices as deodorants. Before the advent of indoor plumbing in the United States, human waste was crudely disposed of by means of the backyard privy — a method still in use today in some rural areas and in poverty-stricken regions such as Appalachia. (See Figure 8–22.)

8–22 *"The solution to pollution is dilution" is the false concept shown here. Water pollution in Yancey County, North Carolina, May 15, 1969. Note the privy that has been built over the edge of this mountain stream, an extremely primitive method of disposing of human wastes.*

Sewage-Treatment Methods

SEWAGE TREATMENT IN THE U.S.

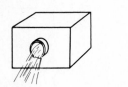

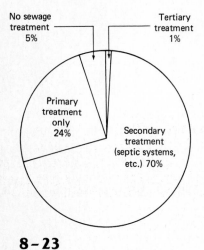

No sewage treatment 5%

Tertiary treatment 1%

Primary treatment only 24%

Secondary treatment (septic systems, etc.) 70%

8-23

Domestic sewage treatment may be primary (rudimentary), secondary (more effective), or tertiary (most effective but rather expensive). (See Figure 8–23.) We will briefly examine these methods.

Primary Treatment

About 30 percent of our nation's sewage receives primary treatment. It is mainly a mechanical process. Domestic sewage (from homes, schools, hospitals, and stores) containing human waste, ground-up garbage, waste toilet paper, soap, toothpaste, detergents, and a variety of debris, flows through a network of street sewer pipes. On its way to the sewage-treatment plant this sewage may be joined by rainstorm runoff (which has flowed down street gutters into storm-sewer pipes) carrying sediment, leaves, gravel, sticks, lawn fertilizer, and even wastes from cats and dogs. The combined flow of domestic sewage and storm runoff eventually enters the sewage plant.

With an occasional reference to Figure 8–24, the major steps in primary treatment will be described here. The major function of primary treatment is to remove the solids.

1. *Screening.* A series of screens removes large objects from the inflowing sewage, everything from rocks to rats and baseballs to bananas.
2. *Grit chamber.* Any fairly large objects that may have gotten through the screen are ground up to facilitate their processing.
3. *Settling tank.* The sewage is then piped into settling tanks, where it is detained for several hours so that sand, silt, and suspended organic (BOD) material can settle to the bottom. (See Figure 8–24.) The fluid that is left is removed from the tank, chlorinated to kill disease organisms, and discharged into a lake or stream.
4. *Sludge digester.* The sedimented solids are then piped to a sludge digester, where the organic material is decomposed by bacteria in the absence of oxygen. One decomposition product, methane gas, is frequently used by the plant to serve up to 90 percent of its power needs (a highly desirable use in this era of fuel scarcity).

Primary treatment removes about 60 percent of the solids and about 33 percent of the oxygen-demanding waste (10). (See Figure 8–25.)

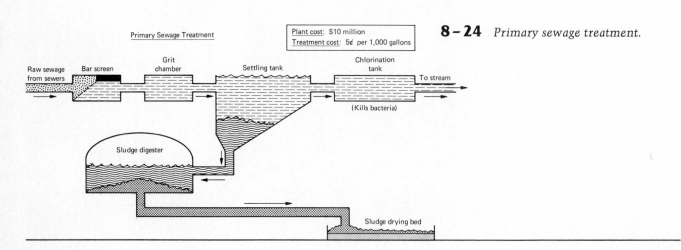

Primary Sewage Treatment

Plant cost: $10 million
Treatment cost: 5¢ per 1,000 gallons

8-24 *Primary sewage treatment.*

Raw sewage from sewers — Bar screen — Grit chamber — Settling tank — Chlorination tank — To stream

(Kills bacteria)

Sludge digester

Sludge drying bed

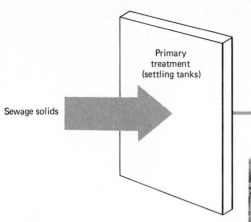

8-25 *Effect of primary treatment on sewage.*

8-26 *Close-up of settling tanks at a New York state sewage-treatment plant. The sewage is detained in these tanks for several hours. The heavier material settles to the bottom and forms a sludge, which is removed from the tanks. The lighter greasy materials that rise to the surface are eventually skimmed off the top.*

8-27 *Secondary sewage treatment.*

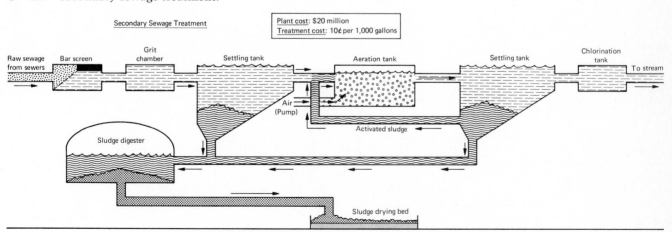

205

About one third of the plants in the United States provide primary treatment only, in which most of the settleable solids are removed. However, although it makes the sewage look a lot better, primary treatment still leaves a substantial amount of organic material, nitrates, phosphates, and bacteria, some of which may cause human disease. Federal and state governments, with the aid of cost-sharing grants to municipalities, are striving to replace primary-treatment plants with secondary plants as soon as possible.

Secondary Treatment

About 60 percent of the municipal sewage-treatment plants in the United States provide secondary treatment. (See Figure 8–27.) It is a more advanced treatment, primarily biological in nature, that involves intensive use of bacterial activity. Its main function is to remove much of the suspended organic material that remains in the effluent after primary treatment.

ACTIVATED SLUDGE PROCESS. Figure 8–28 indicates that fluid from the first sedimentation tank is piped to an aeration tank in which air is bubbled to provide a maximal supply of oxygen. This enables the aerobic (oxygen using) bacteria to act with optimal efficiency in decomposing the organic compounds. It is apparent that the greater the amount of atmospheric oxygen used here in oxidizing this material, the less the demands on the limited supply of dissolved oxygen in the stream once the effluent is discharged. In other words, the BOD of the sewage is being greatly reduced. The liquid that accumulates at the top of the second sedimentation tank is then chlorinated and discharged. However, the sludge that settles to the bottom of the second tank is then called *activated sludge* because it bears a high number of bacteria that have become conditioned to the unique environment of the system. Only a part of this activated sludge is piped to the sludge digester. The remainder is recycled back to the aeration tank and the second sedimentation tank, where it in turn activates the inflowing nonactivated effluent.

Secondary treatment removes 90 percent of the BOD and 90 percent of the suspended solids. However, fully 50 percent of the nitrogen compounds and 30 percent of the phosphorus compounds (the chemical culprits responsible for eutrophication) still remain.

TRICKLING FILTER. A second form of secondary treatment that is widely used is the trickling filter process in which the sewage is sprayed by the arms of a slowly rotating sprinkler onto a filter bed made up of stones. The filter bed may be about six feet thick and up to 200 feet in diameter. The stones

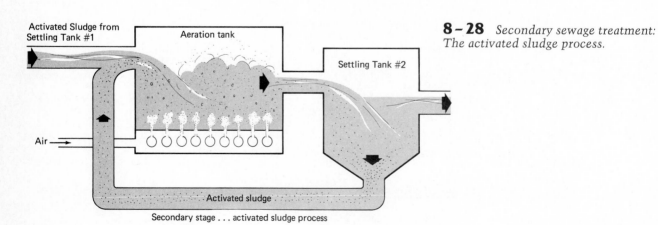

Activated Sludge from Settling Tank #1

Aeration tank

Settling Tank #2

Air →

Activated sludge

Secondary stage . . . activated sludge process

8–28 *Secondary sewage treatment: The activated sludge process.*

8-29 *Secondary treatment of sewage at Sacramento, California. This rotary trickling-filter device handles four million gallons of liquid waste daily. After chlorination it is passed into the American River.*

are coated with a slime of bacteria that has accumulated during the operation of the filter. The sewage, containing a load of dissolved organic compounds, gradually trickles downward through the stones. Some of the bacterial slime enters the trickling waste water. Just as in the case of activated sludge treatment, the bacteria now decompose the dissolved organics and remove nutrients and energy for their growth and reproduction. Any solids present are piped to a settling tank and later transferred to a sludge digester (11). (See Figure 8-30.)

Also left in the waste stream are most of the dissolved organic compounds, such as pesticides. The removal of these materials depends on still another process called *tertiary treatment.*

Tertiary Treatment

Tertiary treatment is the most advanced phase of sewage treatment. The water quality of our streams and lakes would be very good if all sewage were given tertiary treatment. Unfortunately, these plants are twice as expensive to build as secondary sewage plants and four times as expensive to operate. Tertiary treatment involves several steps.

8-30 *Effect of secondary treatment in removing dissolved organics from sewage.*

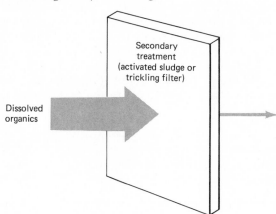

8-31 *Effect of tertiary treatment in the removal of nitrogen and phosphorus.*

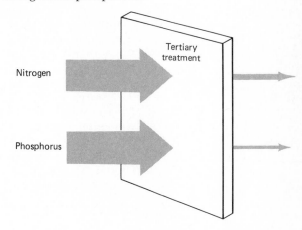

207

1. PRECIPITATION. The waste stream is mixed with lime (calcium oxide). The lime then reacts with phosphorus-containing compounds in the waste stream to form insoluble calcium phosphate, which then settles to the bottom of the settling tank and is removed.
2. NITROGEN STRIPPING. Nitrogen is usually present in the waste water as ammonia gas (NH_3) nitrites ($—NO_2$) and nitrates ($—NO_3$). We already know, of course, that the nitrogen in the ammonia may eventually (as nitrites or nitrates) contribute to eutrophication. But ammonia is undesirable for another reason. It is highly undesirable in lakes and streams because it is harmful to fish (12). The ammonia-containing wastewater is directed into a metal tower. As this water slowly flows downward over a series of small plastic baffle plates, air is forced upward through the waste stream and strips the ammonia gas from the water (12). (See Figure 8–31.)
3. CARBON ABSORPTION. The purpose of this process is to remove dissolved organic compounds, from the waste stream. This is done by passing the water through a tower packed with small particles of carbon. The dissolved organics stick to the carbon particles — a process sometimes referred to as carbon polishing.
4. CHLORINATION. After the phosphorus, nitrogen, and dissolved organic compounds are removed, the waste stream is chlorinated again to destroy any disease-causing organisms that might remain.

An Example of the Effectiveness of Tertiary Treatment

Lake Tahoe, an isolated beauty spot in the High Sierras on the California-Nevada border, is a classic example of the effectiveness of tertiary treatment in reducing the eutrophication problems caused by sewage. Once it was an aquatic jewel, with a gravel bottom, clear cold water, and abundant trout populations — a swimmers', anglers', and tourists' delight. However, in the early 1960s definite symptoms of eutrophication appeared: weedy growths, slimy algal mats, bottom ooze, increased turbidity, declining game fish, and all the rest. (See Figure 8–32.) Eutrophication was a direct result of the accelerated influx of both tourist and permanent residents to the area. An increase in people meant an increase in the amount of inadequately treated sewage discharged into the lake. Alarmed at seeing their jewel tarnished, the residents, who fortunately were rather affluent, decided to do something about their effluent. With the aid of expert technical advice, they installed a 7.5-million-gallon tertiary treatment plant that incorporates the most sophisiticated developments in treatment technology. In a few years the eutrophication problem gradually lessened, and the original beauty of the lake has been restored. What happens to the effluent? Instead of being discharged into the lake it is piped over the mountains rimming the lake to Indian Creek Reservoir, 27 miles away, where it is available for watering crops.

Although it is theoretically advisable for all communities in the United States to follow Tahoe's example and provide tertiary treatment, the financial burden for the taxpayer would be increased. However, here again, as in other environmental dilemmas, we must do a cost-benefit analysis. A few extra pennies on our yearly tax bill might mean the difference between an unsightly, smelly, carp-infested river or lake and an attractive aquatic resource. Are the extra pennies worth it? A summary of the effects of primary, secondary, and tertiary treatment is presented in Figure 8–33.

8-32 *"Scenic" Lake Tahoe. Note boatmen trying to make headway through barrier of algal growths caused by eutrophication.*

8-33 *Summary of the effects of primary, second- ary and tertiary treatment on sewage.*

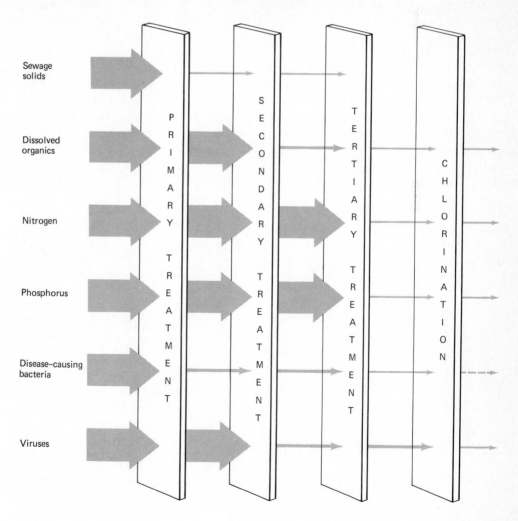

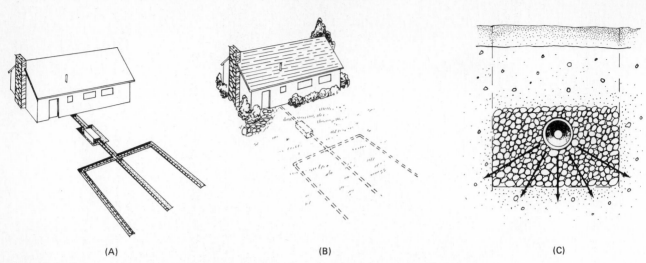

(A)   (B)   (C)

8–34 *In a conventional septic-tank drain field, drain tile is laid in trenches (a). The tank and tile are covered with soil, and the area is planted with grass (b). The effluent from the tank is carried through the drain tile to all points of the field, where it is absorbed and filtered by the surrounding soil.*

Septic Tanks

Many rural and suburban families are not served by sewer systems. They use *septic tanks* to process their waste. (See Figure 8–34.) Septic tanks are underground sewage containers made of steel or concrete. Solids settle to the bottom of the tank and form sludge. (See Figure 8–35.) The fluids flow from the tank into a system of perforated pipes. The waste stream then passes through the holes in the pipes and slowly filters through the soil. Soil bacteria then break down any organic wastes that might be present. The sludge that accumulates at the bottom of the septic tank is slowly digested by the bacteria present in the sewage. The sludge must be periodically pumped out by a "honey wagon" and hauled to a sewage treatment plant for final disposal.

Sludge Disposal

The solid material that remains after sewage treatment is collectively known as *sludge.* The dried sludge is used as soil conditioner in lawns and flower gardens. The Milwaukee municipal sewage plant processes its sludge and sells it as the commercial product called Milorganite.

The handling and disposal of sludge can be a costly headache for many treatment-plant operators, sometimes using up almost 50 percent of the budget. Another problem is the "simple" question of where to put the mounting piles of material. Take

8–35 *Cutaway view of septic tank.*

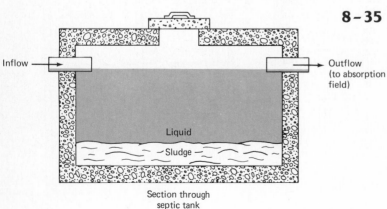

Inflow

Outflow
(to absorption field)

Liquid

Sludge

Section through
septic tank

210

Chicago, for example. Its sewage plants generate *1,000 tons of sludge daily*. Until recently about half of that material was dumped into huge excavations near the plant at a cost of $60 per ton; the remainder was sold to fertilizer companies and to citrus ranchers in Florida. In the 1970s, however, the plant experienced a dire shortage of suitable disposal sites. Faced with this dilemma, Vincent Bacon, the sanitary-district superintendent, conceived an ingenious scheme that would not only solve the disposal problem and reduce costs, but would also reclaim nonproductive Illinois land as well. The sludge would first undergo bacterial digestion to remove odors and eliminate the health hazard. It would then be pumped through a 24-inch pipe to strip-mined barrens and marginal farmlands 60 miles southwest of Chicago. As Bacon says, ''It's the perfect marriage. That land needs our sludge as much as we need the land.'' The most astounding feature is that the disposal cost comes to only $20 per ton, one third the cost of the original disposal method.

Water Pollution and Industry

Industry's water use is increasing daily. It is estimated that the 360 billion gallons per day used in 1980 will increase 100 percent by the year 2000. Water is industry's most important raw material. It is used as a *solvent*, as a *cleansing agent*, as a *mineral extractant*, as a *coolant*, and as a *waste-removal agent*.

In the early 1970s industrial pollution of water was much in evidence. Dyes from a factory stained a Mississippi tributary green. Oily scums spread over the Rouge River near Dearborn, Michigan. The Merrimack River in Connecticut bubbled with nauseating gases. Water from a Minnesota iron mine stained a trout stream reddish brown. Partly because of industrial pollution the Niagara Falls emanated foul odors. Parts of the Missouri ran red with slaughterhouse blood. Because thousands of industrial plants were employing the Mississippi River as an open sewer, conservationists renamed it the ''colon of mid-America.'' There was certainly little resemblance between its clear, sparkling headwaters at Lake Itasca in Minnesota and the foul-smelling broth of domestic and industrial waste that spewed into the Gulf at New Orleans. Since the early 1970s, fortunately, the pollution of surface waters has lessened somewhat, due to state and federal control programs.

Industrial wastes are destructive in many ways. Some have a high BOD, some have foul odors, some impart an ugly appearance to a stream, some are toxic to aquatic life, some curtail photosynthesis, and of course all industrial wastes reduce the quality of a stream for human use.

The effective treatment of industrial wastes, in particular those from chemical industries, is exceedingly complex and in many cases methods of treatment are unknown. Thanks to the Clean Water Act of 1977, which now provides more muscle than ever before to bring industrial offenders in line, a number of plants are studying possible methods of either reducing the amount of discharged waste or at least rendering it less toxic before it is released. Although grudgingly, in some cases they have finally accepted the principle advanced by the EPA that pollution control is part of the expense involved in operating their plants. Some industries have effectively reduced pollution by converting their waste into commercially valuable by-products. Thus, the sugar-beet industry has found a market for dried pulp. One company received a gross return on a single by-product that amounted to one tenth of the payment received for the beets. Tanneries have similarly discovered that hair and fleckings have value and that their reclamation increases stream quality.

A few years ago an American-Canadian International Joint Commission reported that pollution in the Rainy River at International Falls, Minnesota, was a menace to health. It further stated that the pollution was largely caused by the effluent from a large paper and pulp plant located on the river's shore. Twelve years of dealing with the plant by the Minnesota Water Pollution Control Commission had produced no improvement in the situation. Eventually, however, several studies were launched by the company to abate pollution. One of them involved a ''dry-barking'' process, in which the bark from poplar and aspen trees is removed without water.

The Kimberly-Clark Corporation planned to construct a giant pulp and paper mill in northern California. However, a state statute required that the waste stream discharged into the Sacramento River have no poisonous effect on newly hatched salmon and steelhead trout. Those fish are an important wildlife resource that attract anglers to California from all over the United States. The problem was finally solved after many technical difficulties; a $2 million waste-purifying plant capable of treating 12 million gallons of mill waste daily was constructed.

Plant fiber waste from food-processing plants poses a special problem. It is rich in organic content and has an extremely high BOD. One of the most successful techniques for removing that type waste has been developed at Seabrook, New Jersey, where wastes are sprinkled on the floor of a forest. Some areas of the forest have received up to 4,000 inches of water in four years, with no apparent reduction in infiltration capacity.

On the other hand, some of the waste-disposal schemes employed by industry have not been so well conceived. Take *injection wells*, for example. Certain wastes, such as arsenic compounds, cyanides, and radioactive materials, are potentially so harmful to humans that to discharge them directly into lakes and streams would be unthinkable. Furthermore, those wastes are not amenable to treatment by conventional waste-disposal plants. Instead, many industries (oil refineries, pharmaceutical plants, chemical-manufacturing companies, uranium mills, and photographic-processing plants)

have injected these wastes into wells ranging from 300 feet to over two miles in depth. For example, in order to dispose of the strong acid wastes that result from a steel-cleaning process, one company drilled a well 0.80-mile deep into a 1,800-foot-thick layer of porous sandstone. In theory the wastes would then "stay put" because the waste-holding sandstone was completely walled off by impervious rock. However, if there were earthquakes, the wastes might be released from their sandstone "prison," move laterally, and eventually contaminate an aquifer used by a community as a source of drinking water.

In fact, there is evidence to suggest that the deep-well-injection technique may actually cause earthquakes. Scientists have demonstrated a well-defined correlation between the volume of waste injected by the U.S. Army chemical plant near Denver, Colorado, and the frequency of earthquakes in the immediate region (17). Certainly, the injection-well technique is similar to "sweeping pollution under the rug." It may be a stopgap answer for our generation, but the final effective solution is simply being postponed for our descendants, who might have a dire need for these aquifers in the next century.

Understanding Political Roadblocks to Water-Quality Improvements

Howard Eastin

Acting Director
CALIFORNIA DEPARTMENT OF
WATER RESOURCES

Water-quality problems come in many different forms. Their solutions, too, can vary with different alternatives, each with its own set of political, social, and economic impacts. When we understand the physical problem and determine the alternative solutions, we can begin to understand socio-economic and political implications of each solution. Whether or not we attempt improving water quality, there will be individuals who stand to gain or lose from our actions. By understanding this concept, we begin to see the types of political roadblocks which hamper our nation's efforts at improving water quality.

Political roadblocks will stem from three general areas:

1. adverse public perceptions of the solution or lack of adequate understanding of the problem;
2. inability to obtain cooperation between government agencies; and
3. perhaps most importantly, the actual cost of the solution.

For a specific water-quality problem, any combination of the above general roots of political roadblocks can be observed.

As in any decision that must be made in a political arena, improvements in water quality will succeed when the political roadblocks are anticipated and political coalitions are formed to countervail. In forming coalitions, and especially in analyzing the problem and solutions, I cannot emphasize enough the value of determining who stands to gain and lose.

Table 8–4   Water Pollution: Sources, Effects, and Control

Contaminant	Source	Effects	Control
Oxygen-demanding waste	Soil erosion. Autumn leaf fall. Fish kills. Human sewage. Domestic garbage. Remains of plants and animals. Runoff from urban areas during storms. Industrial wastes (slaughterhouses, canneries, cheese factories, distilleries, creameries, and oil refineries).	Bacteria that decompose the organic matter will deplete the stream of oxygen. Game fish are replaced by trash fish. Valuable food for game fish (may flies, etc.) is destroyed. Foul odors.	Reduce runoff from barnyards. Reduce BOD of sewage with modern secondary-sewage-treatment plants. Reduce runoff from feedlots with catch basins.
Disease-producing organisms	Human and animal wastes. Contaminated aquatic foods (clams, oysters).	High incidence of water-borne diseases such as cholera, typhoid fever, dysentery, polio, infectious hepatitis, fever, nausea, and diarrhea.	Reduce runoff from barnyards and feedlots. More effective sewage treatment. Proper disinfection of drinking water.
Nutrients	Soil erosion. Food-processing industries. Runoff from barnyards, feedlots, and farmlands. Untreated sewage. Industrial wastes. Household detergents. Exhaust of motor cars.	Eutrophication. May cause methemoglobinemia in infants. Foul odors. Decreased recreational and aesthetic values.	Tertiary sewage treatment. Reduce use of commercial fertilizers. Change detergent formula. Control soil erosion with strip-cropping, contour plowing, and cover cropping. Control feedlot runoff with catch basins.
Sediment	Soil erosion from farmland, strip-mined land, logged-off areas, and construction sites (roads, homes, and airports).	Fills in reservoirs. Clogs irrigation canals. Increases probability of floods. Impedes progress of barges. Interferes with photosynthesis—therefore, DO is reduced. Destroys freshwater mussels (clams). Fish die from asphyxiation. Destroys spawning sites of game fish. Necessitates expensive filtration of drinking water.	Employ erosion-control practices on farms such as contour plowing, cover cropping, and shelter belting. Employ erosion-control practices at construction sites: sodding, use of catch basins, etc. Use mulching and jute matting on seeded road banks. Establish temporary cover, such as rye and millet, at construction sites.
Heat	Midsummer heating of shallow water by the sun. Discharge of warm water from electrical power, steel, and chemical plants.	Disrupts structure of aquatic ecosystems. Causes shift from desirable to undesirable species of algae and fish. Kills cold-water fish such as salmon and trout. Blocks spawning migrations of salmon. Interferes with fish reproduction. Increases susceptibility of fish to disease and to the toxic effects of heavy metals such as zinc and copper.	Reduce the nation's energy demands for electricity. Use closed cooling systems exclusively. Instead of discharging heated water to streams, use it to heat homes, extend growing seasons on cropland, increase growth rate of food fish and lobsters, and prevent frost damage to orchards.

213

The Serious Water-Pollution Problems Facing Us in the Decade Ahead

Robert A. Canham

Executive Director
WATER POLLUTION CONTROL
FEDERATION,
WASHINGTON, D.C.

Much has been accomplished in the years since the Clean Water Act of 1972, but much remains to be accomplished.

The 1972 act did not address some important water-quality problems. The act focused on the immediate pollution problems of getting an enforceable law passed and providing enough funding to towns and cities to address the conventional pollutants.

The goals represented more of a statement of changed purpose than of unrealistic dreams. Congress looked at the act in 1977, found it basically workable, and reauthorized the act for another five years. In 1982, Congress looked again, and couldn't agree on changes. The forecast, however, is for few substantive changes other than delaying some of the early requirements. One requirement, for "fishable, swimmable" waters throughout the nation by 1983, will be met in many places, but not nationally.

As for results, we'll continue to see improvements in the conditions of our rivers, but pollutants and problems have cropped up that we didn't even dream about in the 1970s: dioxins, radioactivity, minute levels of exotic chemicals. And there are other challenges as well — challenges that have little to do with exotic pollutants.

The national program of water-pollution control faces an uncertain future. Changes in the law in 1981 recognize a trend apparent in the late 1970s and early 1980s: that the financial resources of the federal government are not a bottomless well. It is likely that the federal grant program will end sometime in the next ten years. State and local governments will have to shoulder a growing percentage of the work to be done, and they have been having problems with funding as well.

Operation and maintenance of treatment plants built during the last decade — and before — will become a crucial factor in the next decade. Many of the plants were built using new technology. Operating these plants requires highly trained individuals, sensitive not only to the way the plants work, but also to the way they effect streams and rivers. Other communities haven't yet reached minimal levels of treatment; some face mounting sludge disposal and nonpoint pollution problems. In some river basins, pollution from diffuse sources such as farms, city streets, and construction sites often exceeds the load from treatment plants and industry. Techniques for controlling this nonpoint pollution are still being developed.

Industries, which were the focus of much of the 1972 Clean Water Act, had far more success in reaching federal deadlines than have municipalities. But industries face new challenges as the Environmental Protection Agency completes its long-delayed effluent guidelines. These guidelines, written for more than two dozen industries, specify the "best available technology" (BAT) and other new requirements for clean-up.

Water-pollution control facilities are included in America's infrastructure — the network of roads, bridges, and other public facilities that help our society function. New legislation aimed at repairing public works was signed into law in early 1983 and signals the beginning of perhaps our greatest challenge.

Legislating Water-Pollution Control

The federal Water Pollution Control Act of 1972 is one of the most important pieces of environmental legislation passed by Congress. Under terms of the Act (1) minimal water-quality standards were set, (2) deadlines were established for industries and cities to clean up their wastes, (3) pollutant discharges from point sources were banned without

EPA-approved permits, (4) cities were required to provide at least secondary sewage treatment, (5) our nation's waters should be fishable and swimmable (6) repeated violations of the Act would result in fines of up to $50,000 per day and jail sentences of up to two years.

By the early 1980s roughly 98 percent of all point pollution sources had cleaned up their sewage wastes in compliance with the law. In 1977 the Water Pollution Control Act was amended by the Clean Water Act. The latter act made it mandatory that cities and industries use the best available technology for sewage waste clean-up by 1984. It also made $24.5 billion available for the upgrading of sewage treatment plants during the period 1977–1982.

The Toxic Substances Control Act of 1976 was another landmark piece of environmental legislation. The law makes it mandatory for a manufacturer to inform the EPA 90 days before it intends to manufacture a new chemical. If, in the EPA's opinion, the chemical would pose a health risk, or cause environmental harm, the manufacturer would not be permitted to produce the chemical.

The pollution of our waterways with industrial waste was reduced by more than 50 percent between 1972 and 1980, largely as a result of the preceding laws. The quality of our nation's water is slowly improving. Outstanding examples are the Detroit River in Michigan, the Willamette River in Oregon, and Lake Washington near Seattle.

At the time of this writing the Clean Water Act has come up once again for review by Congress. The EPA wants to make some changes in the law. Its proposals would postpone the date when toxic waste would have to be controlled with the "best available technology," exempt dams from the act's requirements (even though dams often cause such problems as sedimentation, low levels of dissolved oxygen, and water temperature increases), slash the federal budget for water pollution control by 17 percent, and relax rules on thermal discharges. The proposals have enraged environmentalists. According to the Natural Resources Defense Council, a private environmental group, the proposed changes would cripple the water-pollution control program. The national Audubon Society has also been very critical of the EPA. In the Audubon view the best way to control water pollution is the "prompt, vigorous implementation of the law we already have. If EPA really wants to do something about water pol-

lution, it should tackle two problems it has never really confronted: nonpoint pollution, such as run-off from agricultural fields and city streets, and contamination of the groundwater that constitutes half the nation's drinking water supply (3)."

See Howard Eastin's guest article in this chapter concerning political roadblocks to water quality improvement.

Rapid Review

1. Water pollution can be defined as "any contamination of water that lessens its value to humans and nature."

2. Two broad classes of water pollution are *point* and *nonpoint.*

3. Point pollution has its origin in specific, well-defined sources such as the discharge pipes of sewage-treatment plants; nonpoint pollution stems from widespread sources such as the run-off from agricultural lands or urban areas.

4. *Natural* eutrophication is a slow process measured in thousands of years.

5. *Cultural* eutrophication is caused by human activities and may age a lake 25,000 years in only 25 years.

6. The amount of agricultural fertilizer used in the United States increased twelvefold during the period 1945–1970.

7. Many of the twenty million cattle in the United States are crowded into feedlots, where food is brought to them.

8. Old-fashioned soaps, which were biodegradable, were made from animal fats.

9. Synthetic detergents consist of two main components: (a) the *surfactant*, which does the actual dissolving of the dirt, and (b) the *builder*, which enables the detergent to be effective in hard water.

10. Recently the USDA developed a type of phosphorus-free detergent that is not only biodegradable, but is fully as effective as synthetic detergents.

11. Good examples of oxygen-demanding organic wastes are those from (a) fruit and vegetable processing industries, (b) cheese factories, (c) creameries, (d) distilleries, (e) pulp and paper plants, (f) slaughterhouses, and (g) bakeries.

12. The discharge of organic waste with a high BOD into a stream causes a reduction of the dissolved oxygen in the stream and is expressed in the occurrence of trash fish rather than game fish.

215

13. By the year 2000 our nation's industries will require the disposal of 20 million billion BTUs of waste heat per day.

14. Thermal pollution has multiple adverse effects: (a) fish mortality resulting from the reduction of dissolved oxygen, (b) the direct mortality of fish because of the heat, (c) the replacement of beneficial diatoms with undesirable blue-green algae, (d) the acceleration of the process of eutrophication, and (e) the destruction of plankton in the cooling waters of power plants.

15. Undesirable features of large cooling towers are that (a) 25,000 gallons of water may be lost per minute from evaporation, (b) their ugliness dominates the skyline, and (c) they are expensive, adding $5 per year to an average customer's electric bill.

16. Thermally polluted (enriched?) water may be beneficial in several ways: (a) it provides ice-free areas for waterfowl during the winter, (b) it prolongs the crop-growing season, (c) it prevents frost damage to fruit trees, (d) it increases growth rates in game fish and lobsters, and (e) it can be used to heat homes.

17. Disease outbreaks caused by waterborne organisms include the *Salmonella* outbreak in Riverside, California, in 1965, and the typhoid outbreak along the Atlantic Coast in 1916 and 1924.

18. A high *coliform bacteria* count indicates that the water sample may contain high levels of microorganisms capable of causing disease.

19. Sediment pollution has many adverse effects: (a) silt in reservoirs, (b) damage to hydroelectric plants, (c) the clogging of irrigation canals, (d) interfering with barge traffic along the Mississippi River, (e) destroying fish spawning grounds, (f) reducing the photosynthetic activity of aquatic plants, and (g) making necessary the costly filtration of drinking water.

20. Thirty percent of our nation's sewage-treatment plants provide primary treatment; 60 percent provide secondary treatment.

21. Primary treatment is mainly a *physical* process in which solids are removed by sedimentation.

22. Secondary treatment is primarily a *biological* process in which organic wastes are decomposed by bacterial action.

23. The bacterial decomposition of organic waste during secondary treatment can be accomplished either by the *activated sludge* process or by *trickling filters.*

24. Tertiary sewage treatment, which is rather expensive, removes most of the nitrogen and phosphorus from the waste.

25. Many industries have curbed water pollution by converting their waste into commercially valuable by-products.

26. Our nation's groundwater supplies amount to 40 quadrillion gallons—equal to the volume of the Great Lakes.

27. More than 50 percent of the people in the United States depend on groundwater for drinking purposes.

28. Sources of groundwater contamination with toxic organic compounds are (a) industrial landfills and lagoons, (b) municipal landfills, and (c) septic tanks.

29. The groundwater contamination of drinking-water wells has been severe in many regions of the United States, including: (a) San Gabriel Valley, California, (b) Jackson Township, New Jersey, (c) Bedford, Massachusetts, and (d) Nassau and Suffolk counties, New York.

30. People who have been occupationally exposed to some of the same toxic organic compounds occurring in ground water have experienced a variety of symptoms, including: dizziness, fatigue, vomiting, kidney and liver damage, reduced fertility, and spontaneous abortions.

31. Important water-pollution control legislation at the federal level includes the (a) Federal Water Pollution Control Act of 1972, (b) Clean Water Act of 1977, and (c) Toxic Substances Control Act of 1976.

32. The chlorine used to disinfect drinking water has been found to react with organic compounds to form chlororganics such as *chloroform* and *carbon tetrachloride;* both of these compounds will cause cancer in laboratory animals.

33. The level of chlororganics in drinking water can be greatly reduced with *activated carbon treatment*—an expensive method that will cost American taxpayers about $1 billion yearly.

Key Words and Phrases

Activated carbon process	Biodegradable
Activated sludge process	Biomass
Algal blooms	Biscayne Bay
Amebic dysentery	Blue-green algae
Animal wastes	Caddis flies
Bedford, Massachusetts	Carbon absorption

Chlorination
Chloroform
Chlororganics
Cholera
Clean Water Act of 1977
Closed-cycle cooling system
Cold-blooded animal
Cooling tower
Cultural eutrophication
Detergents
Dry cooling tower
Dysentery
Eutrophication
Eutrophic lake
Federal Water Pollution Control Act
Feedlot
Game fish
Green algae
Groundwater
Industrial landfill
Industrial sewage
Infectious hepatitis
Injection wells
Jackson Township, New Jersey
Lake Tahoe
LAS detergents
Laws of energy
Mayflies
Milkfish
Milorganite
Municipal landfill
Nassau County, New York
Natural detergents
Natural eutrophication
Nitrogen-stripping
Nonpoint pollution
NTA detergents

Oligotrophic lakes
Open-cycle cooling system
Oxygen sag curve
Parts per billion (ppb)
Parts per million (ppm)
Point pollution
Polio
Precipitation process
Primary sewage treatment
Quality fish
Rooted weeds
San Gabriel Valley, California
Secondary sewage treatment
Sediment pollution
Settling tank
Sludge
Sludge digester
Sludge worms
Species diversity
Stone flies
STP (sodium tripolyphosphate)
Stream eutrophication
Suffolk County, New York
Surfactant
Tertiary sewage treatment
Thermal enrichment
Thermal pollution
Toxic organic chemicals
Toxic Substances Control Act (TSCA)
Trash fish
Typhoid fever
Viruses
Water pollution
Wet cooling tower

Questions and Topics for Discussion

1. Define *water pollution.*
2. Briefly list seven basic types of water pollution.
3. Briefly list eight differences between oligotrophic and eutrophic lakes.
4. Distinguish between *natural* and *cultural* eutrophication.

5. You might think that, because photosynthetic activity levels are high in eutrophic lakes, the water would contain a high level of dissolved oxygen. Does it? If not, why not? Discuss your answer.
6. Briefly list five adverse effects of algal blooms.
7. Briefly list three adverse effects of rooted weeds in eutrophied lakes and streams.
8. Explain the role of synthetic detergents in eutrophication. In your opinion should phosphorus-containing synthetic detergents be banned? Why or why not? Debate this question with one of your classmates.
9. Describe the effects of a high level of BOD waste on the aquatic life of a stream.
10. Roughly what levels of dissolved oxygen does a particular stretch of stream have if one of the dominant organisms found in it is (a) a carp, (b) a trout, (c) a sludgeworm, (d) a mayfly larva?
11. Draw labeled diagrams of open- and closed-cycle cooling systems.
12. Could thermal pollution cause a species of fish to be eliminated from a lake even if the actual fish living in the stream at the time of the pollution are not harmed in any way?
13. What does the phrase "biological oxygen demand" (BOD) mean?
14. Some manufacturers feel that the term *thermal pollution* should be replaced with the term *thermal enrichment.* Are there valid reasons for such a shift in terminology? Discuss your answer.
15. List some of the gaps in our knowledge concerning the role of viruses in water-borne disease.
16. What is the importance of coliform bacteria to public health?
17. In your opinion what would be four effective methods for controlling sediment pollution?
18. Summarize the main benefits derived from (a) primary sewage treatment, (b) secondary sewage treatment, and (c) tertiary sewage treatment.
19. Why is the contamination of groundwater much more serious than the pollution of surface water such as a stream?
20. In addition to the material in this text, consult recent periodicals and newspapers so that you can present a ten-minute talk on the subject: "Groundwater contamination and human health."

217

21. Discuss the statement: "The use of chlorine in disinfecting drinking water supplies should be banned in order to prevent cancer."
22. Name five human diseases that are caused by waterborne organisms.
23. List six harmful effects of sediment pollution.
24. Discuss the validity of the statement: "Sewage sludge is one of our nation's valuable resources."

Endnotes

1. California Department of Water Resources. *Save Water.* Sacramento: California Department of Water Resources, 1982.
2. Council on Environmental Quality. *Contamination of Groundwater by Toxic Organic Chemicals.* Washington, DC: Government Printing Office, 1981.
3. "EPA Proposed Amendments to Clean Water Act Crippling National Resources Defense Council Charges." *Ecology USA,* 11 (June 21, 1982), 96.
4. Ehrenfeld, David W. *Biological Conservation.* New York: Holt, 1970.
5. Ehrlich, Paul R., and Anne H. Ehrlich. *Population, Resources, Environment.* San Francisco: Freeman, 1970.
6. Havlick, Spenser W. *The Urban Organism.* New York: Macmillan, 1974.
7. Hodges, Laurent. *Environmental Pollution.* 2nd ed. New York: Holt, 1977.
8. Leopold, Luna B. *Water.* New York: Time, 1966.
9. McCaull, Julian, and Janice Crossland. *Water Pollution.* New York: Harcourt, 1974.
10. Miller, G. Tyler, Jr. *Living in the Environment.* 3rd ed. New York: Wadsworth, 1982.
11. Moran, Joseph M., Michael D. Morgan, and James H. Wiersma. *An Introduction to Environmental Sciences.* San Francisco: Freeman, 1980.
12. Revelle, Penelope, and Charles Revelle. *The Environment: Issues and Choices For Society.* New York: Van Nostrand, 1981.
13. Smith, Robert L. *Ecology and Field Biology.* 3rd ed. New York: Harper, 1980.
14. Southwick, Charles H. *Ecology and the Quality of Our Environment.* 2nd ed. New York: Van Nostrand, 1976.
15. "Spectrum." *Environment,* 20 (Oct. 1978), 23.
16. Turk, Amos, Jonathan Turk, and Janet T. Wittes. *Ecology, Pollution, Environment.* Philadelphia: Saunders, 1972.
17. U.S. Department of the Interior. *The Third Wave.* Washington, DC: The Department of the Interior, 1967.
18. Wilson, Ralph C. "Small Watersheds Make a Big Splash." *Outdoors USA: The Yearbook of Agriculture.* Washington, DC: Department of Agriculture, 1967.

Suggested Readings for the Interested Student

Ambroggi, R. P. "Underground Reservoirs to Control the Water Cycle." *Scientific American,* 236 (May 1977), 21–27. The author explains methods for managing water supplies in aquifers so that arid regions will benefit.

Barrett, B. R. "Controlling the Entrance of Toxic Pollutants into U.S. Waters." *Environmental Science and Technology,* 12 (Feb. 1977), 154–162. This is a comprehensive look at the federal laws dealing with water-pollution control.

Bodde, Tineke. "Quality vs. Quantity: Is a U.S. Water Crisis Imminent?" *Bioscience,* 31 (July–Aug. 1981), 485–488. The twin stresses of pollution and groundwater "mining" may cause a major water crisis in the United States in the near future. This discussion is nontechnical and well written.

Council on Environmental Quality. *Annual Reports.* Washington, DC: Council on Environmental Quality, 1970–1981. This is excellent material; it is nontechnical and well illustrated. It shows general trends of water quality in the United States. There is a sharp focus on trouble spots.

———. *Contamination of Groundwater by Toxic Organic Chemicals.* Washington, DC: Government Printing Office, 1981. This is a nontechnical discussion of public-health implications.

Environmental Protection Agency. *A Primer on Waste Water Treatment.* Washington, DC: Government Printing Office, 1971. This is nontechnical and well written. It describes in simple language the major steps in sewage treatment. The drawings are effectively done.

Gibbons, J. Whitfield, and Rebecca R. Sharitz. "Thermal Ecology: Environmental Teachings of a Nuclear Reactor Site." *Bioscience,* 31 (Apr. 1981), 293–297. This is an excellent study of the long-term effects of the thermal pollution of the Savannah River in Georgia. Surprisingly, some of the effects reported were desirable ones.

Woodwell, George M. "Recycling Sewage Through Plant Communities." *American Scientist,* 65 (1977), 556–562. The author discusses a unique method of sewage disposal that makes use of the natural cleansing action performed by the soil and vegetation.

9 Lakes, Streams, and Fish

Fishing is certainly one of our most ancient forms of recreation and food getting. Human beings scooped fish from shallow streams with their bare hands even, perhaps, before the Stone Age. Egyptian tombs built 2,000 years before Christ show scenes of netting fish from boats. A number of American presidents, including Cleveland, Coolidge, Hoover, Franklin D. Roosevelt, and Eisenhower sought respite from the tensions of their office by "wetting a line."

In a typical year more than forty million anglers pit their luck and skill against the scaly denizens of our lakes, streams, farm ponds, mountain brooks, and impoundments. (See Figure 9–1.) They spend over $3 billion, averaging about $100 per fisherman. The average angler travels about 800 miles to and from his fishing haunts. Transportation media include the motorcar, bus, train, airplane, helicopter, mule, and snowmobile. In aggregate, our nation's fishermen, whose numbers have increased over 100 percent since 1955, travel about 25 billion passenger miles yearly in order to fish.

The Lake Ecosystem

Fish occur in a great variety of freshwater habitats, from rushing mountain streams to sluggish rivers, from tiny farm ponds to large natural lakes. In order to develop an appreciation of the general features of aquatic habitats and to provide some background for our later discussion of fish conservation and management, the major features of a lake ecosystem will be briefly described here. Ecologists usually recognize three major lake zones: the *littoral, limnetic,* and *profundal.*

9–1 *"Just fishin'." Copper Falls State Park, Wisconsin.*

219

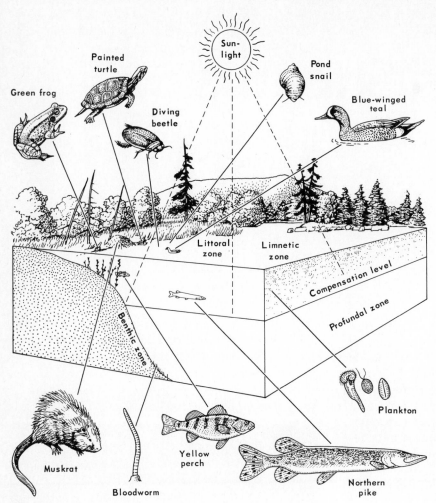

9–2 *Stereo view of a lake ecosystem in midsummer showing littoral, limnetic, and profundal zones. Observe rooted vegetation in the littoral. The level at which there is insufficient sunlight penetration to sustain photosynthesis is known as the compensation level.*

The Littoral Zone

The littoral zone is the shallow, marginal region of a lake that is characterized by rooted vegetation. (See Figure 9–2.) The rooted plants usually are arranged in a well-ordered sequence, from shore toward open water, as emergent, floating, and submergent. Representative emergent plants include cattails and bulrushes. Characteristic floating plants include water lilies and duckweed. Among typical submergents are pondweed and pickerel weed. Because sunlight penetrates to the lake bottom, this zone sustains a high level of photosynthetic activity. The swarming, floating micro-organisms known as plankton frequently impart a faint greenish-brown cast to the water. The term means "the wanderers"; it is quite appropriate, because they are largely incapable of independent movements through the littoral zone and are passively transported by water currents and wave action.

Plankton are divisible into plants (chiefly algae), known as phytoplankton, and animals (primarily crustaceans and protozoa), known as zooplankton. The littoral zone provides suitable food, cover, and/ or breeding sites for an abundance and variety of aquatic life, including both invertebrates (diving beetles, dragonflies, damselflies, crayfish, mussels, clams, and snails) and vertebrates (pickerel, sunfish, yellow perch, frogs, salamanders, turtles, ducks, herons, and muskrats). Per unit volume of water the littoral zone produces more biomass than either the limnetic or profundal zones. A small pond may consist *entirely* of littoral zone; however, a deep lake with an abruptly sloping basin may possess an extremely reduced littoral zone (19).

The Limnetic Zone

The limnetic zone is the region of open water beyond the littoral down to the maximum depth at which there is sufficient sunlight for photosynthesis. (See Figure 9–2.) This is the depth at which phytosynthesis balances respiration. It is known as the *compensation depth*. The light intensity here is about 100 footcandles, or 1 percent of full sunlight. Although rooted plants are absent, this zone is frequently characterized by a great abundance of phytoplankton (plant plankton), dominated by algae. In large lakes this phytoplankton may play a much more important role as producer than the more conspicuous rooted plants of the littoral zone. In spring, when nutrients and light are optimal, phytoplankton populations increase rapidly to form blooms. The limnetic zone derives its oxygen content from the photosynthetic activity of phytoplankton and from the atmosphere immediately over the lake's surface. The atmospheric source of oxygen becomes significant primarily when there is some surface disturbance of water caused by wind action, a canoe paddle, or the propeller of a speedboat. Fish are the most characteristic vertebrates. Suspended among the phytoplankton are the zooplankton (animal plankton), primarily tiny crustaceans (copepods) that form a trophic link between the phytoplankton food base and the higher aquatic animals (19). (See Figure 9–3.)

The Profundal Zone

The profundal zone embraces the area beneath the limnetic zone and extends downward to the lake bottom. (See Figure 9–2.) Because of the limited penetration of sunlight, green-plant life is absent. In north-temperate latitudes, where winters are severe, this zone has the warmest water (4° C) in the lake in winter and the coldest water in summer. Large numbers of bacteria and fungi occur in the bottom ooze, sometimes up to one billion bacteria per gram. Those bacteria are constantly bringing about the decomposition of the organic matter (plant debris, animal remains, and excreta) that accumulates on the bottom. Eventually the organic sediments are mineralized, and nitrogen and phosphorus are put back into circulation in the form of soluble salts. In winter, because of the reduced metabolism of aquatic life and the greater oxygen-dissolving capacity of colder water, oxygen ordinarily is not an important limiting factor for fish if the ice cover remains clear of snow. In midsummer, however, when the metabolic rates of aquatic organisms are high, the oxygen-dissolving capability of the warm water is relatively low, and the oxygen-demanding processes of bacterial decay proceed at high levels. Under these conditions oxygen depletion, or stagnation, of the profundal waters may result in extensive fish mortality.

Thermal Stratification

In temperate latitudes lakes show marked seasonal temperature changes.

Winter. The coldest water forms ice at 0° C (32° F) and floats at the surface. The water at increasing depth below the ice is progressively warmer and

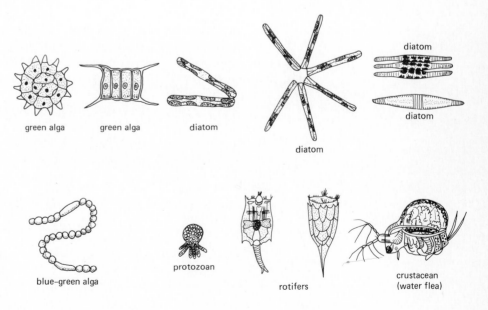

9–3 *Plankton occurring in the limnetic zone of lakes.*

green alga   green alga   diatom   diatom   diatom   diatom

blue–green alga   protozoan   rotifers   crustacean (water flea)

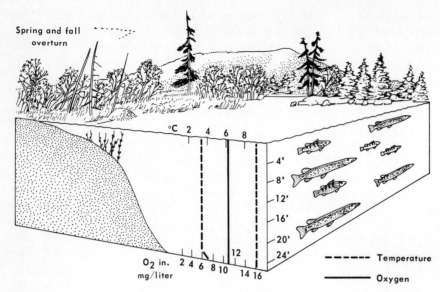

9–4 *Spring and fall overturn in a lake ecosystem. Note that uniformity of temperature and oxygen distribution are expressed in dispersal of fish through much of the lake from surface to bottom.*

more dense. The heaviest water, at the bottom of the lake, has a winter temperature of 4° C. All winter the water remains relatively stable.

Spring. Following the ice melt, the surface water gradually warms to 4° C. At this point all the water is of uniform temperature and density. (See Figure 9–4.) Hence, the strong spring winds cause considerable stirring, which results in a complete mixing of water, dissolved oxygen, and nutrients from the lake surface to the lake bottom, a phenomenon known as the *spring overturn.* As spring progresses, however, the surface waters become warmer and lighter than the water at lower levels. As a result, the

lake becomes thermally stratified. The upper stratum, which usually has the highest oxygen concentration and is characterized by a temperature gradient of less than 1° C per meter of depth, is the *epilimnion* ("upper lake"). The middle layer of the lake, typified by a temperature gradient of more than 1° C per meter is the *thermocline.* The bottom layer of water, the *hypolimnion* ("bottom lake"), has a temperature gradient of less than 1° C per meter.

Summer. Unless the lake is exceptionally clear and permits phytoplanktonic photosynthesis, the hypolimnion frequently becomes depleted of oxy-

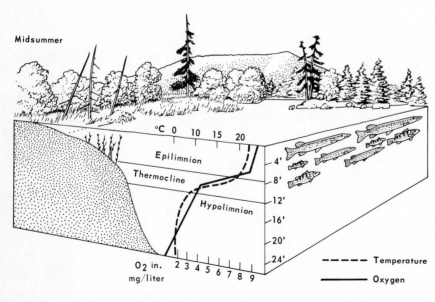

9–5 *Midsummer distribution of oxygen and temperature in a lake ecosystem. Note the stratification.*

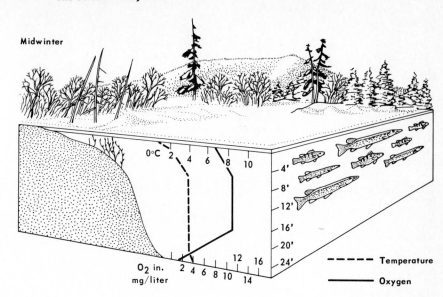

9 – 6 *Midwinter distribution of oxygen and temperature in a lake ecosystem. Note influence on fish distribution.*

gen in summer because of the *biological oxygen demand* (BOD) of bacterial decomposers, the reduced or nonexistent photosynthetic activity, and the minimal mixing with upper waters as a result of density differences (19). (See Figure 9 – 5.)

Autumn. The surface waters gradually cool, as a result of conduction, evaporation, and convection. Eventually a point is reached where the lake attains temperature uniformity from top to bottom. Because the water is now also of uniform density, it becomes well mixed by wind and wave action in what is known as the *fall overturn.* (See Figure 9 – 4.) Nutrients, dissolved oxygen, and plankton become uniformly distributed.

Winter. As winter approaches, the lake gets colder until the water attains a uniform temperature of 4° C, at which it has maximal density. As the surface cools below 4° C it becomes lighter. Eventually the surface water may freeze at 0° C. During the winter season, in ice-bound lakes there exists an inverted temperature stratification, with the coldest water (ice) at the surface and the warmest water (4° C) on the bottom (19). (See Figure 9 – 6.)

The Stream Ecosystem

Although lakes and streams are both aquatic habitats and, of course, have many characteristics in common, they are, nevertheless, quite distinctive in many aspects. Therefore, the problems facing the fisheries biologist in a lake may be quite different

from those demanding his attention in a stream. Let us examine a few of the basic characteristics of a stream.*

Current

Water flow is the most important factor determining the kinds of organisms present. Current velocity is determined by stream gradient. Fish distribution is frequently correlated with gradient flow. For example, George Trautman, of Ohio State University found that black bass were virtually absent from Ohio streams where the gradient is below three or above twenty-five feet per mile. On the other hand, the highest bass populations occurred in stream stretches where the gradient was from seven to twenty feet per mile (34).

Land – Water Interchange

The amount of land-water interface is much greater per unit volume of water in a stream than in a lake. (See Figure 9 – 7.) Therefore, the stream is a rather open ecosystem in which materials are constantly being received from the terrestrial ecosystems that border it. For example, a stream receives a considerable portion of its basic energy supply from materials originating on land — leaves that fall into the water in autumn or organic debris (stems, nuts, twigs, seeds, dead weeds, cow manure, and the bodies of insects, worms, and mice) that is washed

* Much of the material in this section is derived from *Fundamentals of Ecology*, by Eugene P. Odum of the University of Georgia (Philadelphia: Saunders, 1971).

9–7 *A stream ecosystem. Note that the water is usually well aerated because of the large air-water interface per unit volume of water and also because of the turbulence of the stream. Leaf fall from the overhanging branches provides an important source of organic material and energy. This stream has been improved for fish production by the establishment of three straight-log dams. Water accumulates behind the logs and forms "cover" for game fish.*

into the stream during the spring runoff. In fact, many of the primary consumers living in a stream feed on such *detritus* (decomposing organic material) rather than on living green aquatic vegetation. This is not to say that a stream does not have its own distinctive population of producer plants. It does, in the form of specialized *diatoms* that form a crust on rocks and plants and *water moss*, which sometimes forms a bright-green slippery covering on a stream bottom (to the distress of the wading trout fisherman). However, the characteristic producer population of a stream can supply only a fraction of the energy required by its animal population.

Oxygen

Streams are usually very well aerated. The reasons for this are multiple: flowing water, the relative shallowness of the stream, and the large surface area exposed to the atmosphere. All things being equal, the waters of shallow, fast-moving streams have much higher oxygen levels than deep, sluggish streams. The photosynthetic production of oxygen is not nearly as important as it is in a pond or lake. Because of the thorough mixing of stream water, the oxygen-starvation problems that occur in the hypolimnion of deep lakes is less frequent. However, stream fish are very sensitive to even slight reductions of oxygen levels. Therefore, if a stream becomes polluted with oxygen-demanding organic material, such as human sewage or the waste from slaughterhouses, pulp mills, and canneries, the oxygen reduction that results may trigger a massive fish kill.

Longitudinal Zonation

Ecologist Eugene P. Odum describes the linear differentiation of the stream ecosystem:

In lakes and ponds the prominent zonation is *horizontal*, whereas in the streams it is *longitudinal*. Thus, in lakes, successive zones from the middle to the shore represent, as it were, successively older geological stages in the lake-filling process. Likewise in streams we find increasingly

224

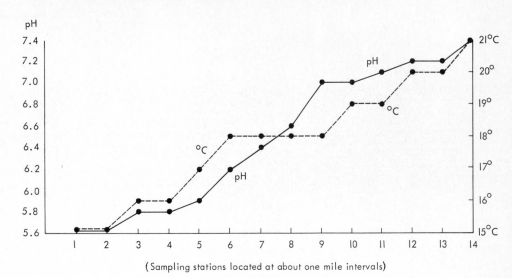

9 – 8 *Longitudinal differences in temperature and pH along a 14-mile stretch of Little Stony Creek, Virginia.*

(Sampling stations located at about one mile intervals)

older stages from source to mouth. Changes are more pronounced in the upper part of streams because the gradient, volume of flow, and chemical composition change rapidly. The change in composition of communities is likely to be more pronounced in the first mile than in the last fifty. (17) *[Italics mine.]*

9 – 9 *Bluegill spawning on nest. Most panfish spawn each year in such community spawning areas, which sometimes include 50 to 100 nests. The advantages of such social behavior are the sharing of ideal spawning habitat by a large number of individuals, and protection. It does promote hybridization between similar species, however, such as bluegill and sunfish.*

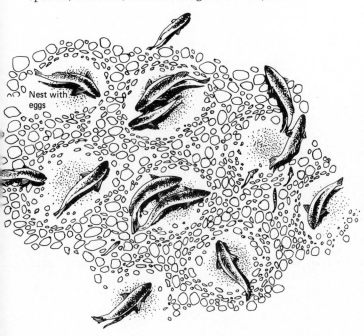

Nest with eggs

Fish populations frequently reflect the changing physical (chemical, thermal, and so on) character of the stream. A study was conducted by Burton and Odum of the fish distribution in Little Stony Creek near Mountain Lake, Virginia. It showed that a species distribution was correlated with changes in pH, water temperature, and velocity of the current. (See Figure 9 – 8.) Thus, the colder (15° C), more acid (pH 5.6) upper stretches of the creek were populated only by brook trout. In the warmer (21° C), more alkaline (pH 7.4) lower stretches, the brook trout were missing, but seven other species were represented, including the rainbow trout, several kinds of minnows, and the common sucker (3, 17).

The Biotic Potential of Fish

As with most organisms, freshwater fish have an extremely high reproductive capacity. Thirteen thousand eggs were found in the ovaries of a brown bullhead only one foot long. Some bass nests in Michigan have had up to 4,000 young fish per nest. A ten-pound female northern pike may deposit 100,000 eggs at spawning time. A 35-pound female muskellunge may bear 225,000 eggs in her ovaries. Some species, such as bluegill, have a well-developed community behavior which promotes reproduction. (See Figure 9 – 9.) It is apparent that were it not for the negative effects of environmental resistance, these species would soon choke river channels and lake basins with their aggregate biomass.

225

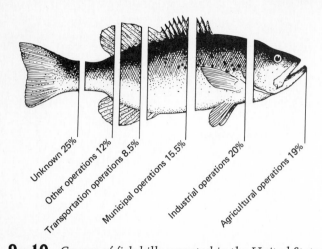

9-10 *Causes of fish kills reported in the United States.*

Unknown 25% · Other operations 12% · Transportation operations 8.5% · Municipal operations 15.5% · Industrial operations 20% · Agricultural operations 19%

The Environmental Resistance Encountered by Fish

Tagging studies have revealed that the environmental resistance operating on fish populations is fully as impressive as their reproductive capacities, for roughly 70 percent of a given fish population dies each year. Thus, if a million young of a given species hatch, 300,000 will survive by the end of the first year, 90,000 by the end of the second, but only 6 by the end of the tenth. Some years ago an analysis was made in Minnesota of 15,000 perch caught in Ottertail Lake. Few were more than one-year old. Age-class analysis indicated that only 2.8 percent survived to the second year, and only 1 percent reached

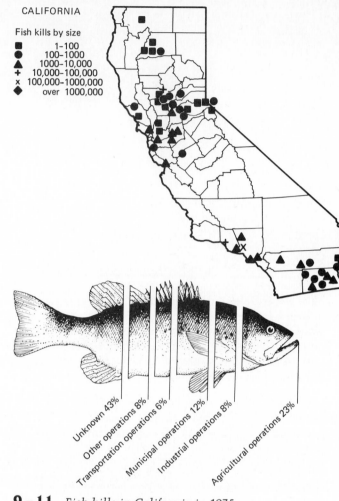

CALIFORNIA

Fish kills by size

- ■ 1-100
- ● 100-1000
- ▲ 1000-10,000
- + 10,000-100,000
- x 100,000-1000,000
- ◆ over 1000,000

Unknown 43% · Other operations 8% · Transportation operations 6% · Municipal operations 12% · Industrial operations 8% · Agricultural operations 23%

9-11 *Fish kills in California in 1975.*

9-12 *Fish kills reported in Ohio, 1975.*

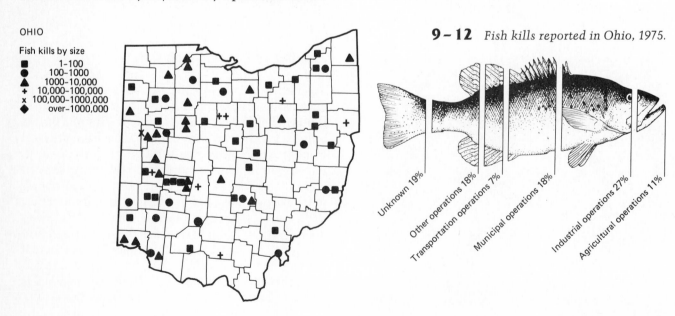

OHIO

Fish kills by size

- ■ 1-100
- ● 100-1000
- ▲ 1000-10,000
- + 10,000-100,000
- x 100,000-1000,000
- ◆ over-1000,000

Unknown 19% · Other operations 18% · Transportation operations 7% · Municipal operations 18% · Industrial operations 27% · Agricultural operations 11%

9 – 13 *"A tight squeeze"—a symbol of the impact of technology on fish life. This 5½-inch brook trout was taken from the Au Sable River in Michigan. Note the metal ring from a beer can around the middle of the trout. The fish is permanently deformed.*

the age of four (13). A similar study of brook trout showed that of every 182,000 eggs laid, only 0.6- fish survived at the end of five years.

Water Pollution

In 1980 water pollution caused the death of more than 30 million fish in the United States. The percentage of fish kills in the United States, by cause, is shown in Figures 9 – 10 to 9 – 12. Some of the harmful effects of water pollution on fish are summarized here:

1. *Silt* (a) causes suffocation by clogging the gills (see Figure 9 – 14); (b) smothers spawning beds; (c) reduces photosynthesis by blocking sunlight, and as a result levels of dissolved oxygen drop; and (d) destroys the proper habitat for fish-food organisms such as insect larvae.
2. *Thermal pollution* (see Figure 9 – 15) (a) reduces levels of dissolved oxygen; (b) increases suscepti-

9 – 14 *Fish kill caused by sediment. These fish were choked to death when sediment clogged their gills during a flooding of the Iowa River in New Mexico.*

9 – 15 *Researchers from the Argonne National Laboratory seine for fish in Lake Michigan near the warm-water discharges of a power plant. They are attempting to find what effect heated water has on the numbers and kinds of fish in a region of thermal pollution.*

227

bility to disease; (c) increases the toxic effects of heavy metals such as zinc and copper; and (d) causes the death or mass emigration of cold-water fish.

3. *Oxygen-demanding organic waste* reduces the levels of dissolved oxygen.
4. *Strong acids* cause suffocation by eroding gill membranes.

Lake-Renewal Projects

As described in the chapter on water pollution, the waters of our lakes and streams have become increasingly polluted during the last fifty years, especially with such contaminants as nutrients, bacteria, oxygen-demanding organic wastes, and sediments. The question naturally arises: Are such lakes "doomed" or can they be renewed? Can the pollution process be reversed?" Fortunately, the answer, in the case of many smaller lakes, at least, is "Yes."

Under Section 313 of the Clean Water Act of 1977, known as the Clean Lake Program, the EPA has funded several lake-renewal projects throughout the nation. Let's examine some of them.

LAKE TEMESCAL.   Lake Temescal, in Oakland, California, is located fewer than three miles from the skyscrapers of downtown Oakland; it is a man-made ten-acre lake used intensively for swimming and fishing. The lake's problems were:

1. *Sedimentation* from runoff from nearby construction sites.
2. Intense *eutrophication* caused in part by the nutrient load in the sediments.
3. Health-threatening concentrations of *bacteria* that entered the lake via two tributary streams.

The solutions to its problems were undertaken with the aid of a Clean Lake Act grant of $488,972 from the EPA. Several management methods were put into effect:

1. The related problems of sedimentation and eutrophication were (?) solved by scooping out 57,000 cubic yards of nutrient-rich mud from the lake bottom.
2. The bacterial concentrations were reduced by building a series of basins for temporarily catching and holding some of the flow from the two tributary streams. (The basins were designed to look like natural ponds.) Such basins will increase the time during which the coliform bacteria are exposed to water. As a result, their die-off rate will be increased. In addition, the stream flow can be pumped *around* Lake Temescal if the bacterial counts occasionally get too high (6).

LITTLE POND.   Little Pond is in Damariscotta, Maine. Most of the residents of Damariscotta and New Castle, Maine, get their drinking water from this seventy-acre lake. The lake's problem was bad-tasting water caused by dense populations of water fleas (tiny crustaceans). For many years water fleas were controlled with the use of copper sulfate. However, the procedure was discontinued when high levels of the chemical caused severe fish kills. The solution to the problem was initiated during the spring of 1976. The Maine Department of Environmental Protection stocked the lake with thousands of *alewives* — small, silvery fish with an enormous appetite for water fleas. The alewives fed on the crustaceans all summer long. As a result, the water-flea population was drastically reduced and the taste of drinking water in Damariscotta and New Castle was much improved (6).

Lake Erie: A Case Study of Eutrophication

Lake Erie lies astride the border between the United States and Canada. It has been polluted with almost every imaginable type of contaminant. Our major interest here, however, is eutrophication, caused by excessive inputs of nitrates and phosphates. Let's list the sources of these nutrients:

1. The untreated or partially treated sewage of roughly 11 million people living in Cleveland, Toledo, Erie, Detroit, and other cities. (See Figure 9–16.)
2. Fertilizer runoff from 30,000 square miles of agricultural lands.
3. The exhaust pipes of millions of motor cars. The nitrogen-containing gases react with water to form nitric acid. This acid in turn, is washed into the lake by rain or snow. It then reacts with other chemicals to form nitrates.
4. Eroded soil that is carried into the lake by runoff. Accelerated erosion has occurred because of construction activities, mining, and improper soil management by farmers.

9–16 *Lake Erie. Note the heavily industrialized communities, such as Detroit. Toledo, Sandusky, Cleveland, Ashtabula, and Erie, which contributed greatly to the lake's pollution, as a result both of industrial waste and municipal sewage.*

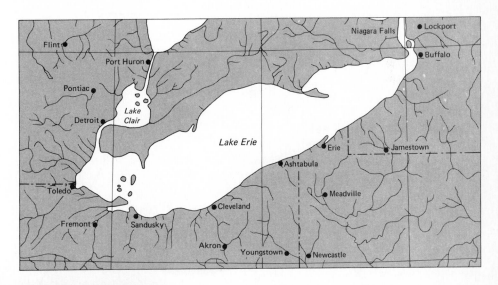

9–17 *These white bass died from suffocation after algae clogged their gills. The dense algal population was caused by eutrophication. High Cliff State Park (Calumet County), Wisconsin.*

229

Effects of Eutrophication
   Between 1919 and the mid-1970s the production of algal biomass increased twenty times. Waters turned to pea soup. Beaches became fouled
with thick mats of algae. Massive quantities of dead algae and mud accu-

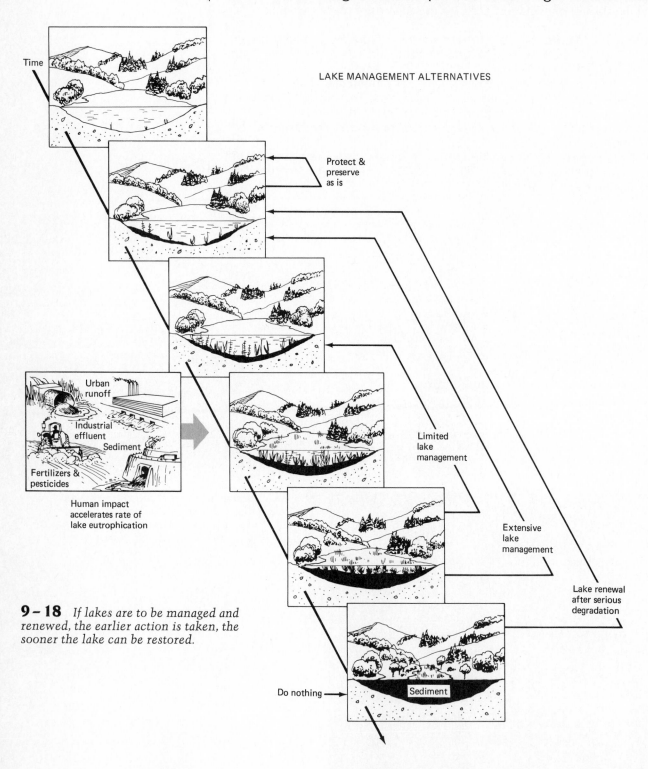

Time

LAKE MANAGEMENT ALTERNATIVES

Protect &
preserve
as is

Urban
runoff

Industrial
effluent

Sediment

Fertilizers &
pesticides

Human impact
accelerates rate of
lake eutrophication

Limited
lake
management

Extensive
lake
management

Lake renewal
after serious
degradation

9–18 *If lakes are to be managed and
renewed, the earlier action is taken, the
sooner the lake can be restored.*

Do nothing

Sediment

mulated on the lake bottom to form an ooze up to 120 feet thick. The more pessimistic lake experts suggested that the layer of muck contained such an enormous quantity of nutrients that, even if all inputs of nitrogen and phosphorus were shut off immediately, the continuation of anaerobic conditions on the lake bottom would ensure severe eutrophic conditions for many years to come.

The depletion of dissolved oxygen during the summer caused a severe reduction of high-oxygen demanding insects and fish. In 1953 oxygen levels in some areas were reduced to one part per million. That caused the virtual disappearance of the oxygen-demanding mayfly, a valuable fish food. The mayfly was replaced by bottom-dwelling sludgeworms, uniquely adapted to live under the low-oxygen conditions.

The composition of Lake Erie's fish population has changed drastically since 1920. To a considerable degree these changes were caused by the accelerated pollution of the lake. Before 1920 such highly edible fishes as lake trout, whitefish, blue pike, and walleye supported a multimillion-dollar commercial and sport fishery. Unfortunately, all of those species are adapted to cold water, so they remain deep in the hypolimnion during the warm days of late summer. Moreover, they are fish that require high levels of dissolved oxygen. The decline of these species, therefore, was predictable. Heavy predation by commercial fishermen contributed to their reduction. A comparison of prepollution and postpollution fish-catch figures is revealing. For example, in 1920 the catch of those fishes was about 50 million pounds, but by 1970 it had dropped to a mere 1,000 pounds — a decrease of more than 99.99 percent.

In the early 1970s many popular writers referred to the "death" of Lake Erie. Actually, Lake Erie was very much alive. The trouble was that the *valuable* species were replaced by less desirable species (*rough* fish). Thus, the lake trout, blue pike, and whitefish were replaced with carp, smelt, drum, and alewives. The total fish biomass, however, rather surprisingly, remained the same — at about 50 million pounds.

The Future

Environmentalists began asking the question: Is it possible to resurrect Lake Erie from its pollution-inflicted death? Some scientists were rather pessimistic. Most, however, felt that if the nutrient inputs were sharply reduced, considerable recovery could be made within ten years. Arthur Hasler of the University of Wisconsin, an international authority on eutrophication, was cautiously optimistic. See W. T. Edmonson's guest article on the reversal of eutrophication in this chapter.

In the spring of 1978 Canada and the United States initiated a series of joint studies of the lake's ecological problems. As a result of those continuing investigations, a systematic management of the lake's water quality was made possible. The control of nutrient-loaded sewage inputs to the lake has received top priority, and the lake has responded. The weeds and algal mats that once choked its shores are thinning out. The "No Swimming" signs are being taken down at beaches that had been closed for thirty years. Once again sport fishermen thrill to the catch of lake trout. The eventual complete resurrection of Lake Erie from its pollution-imposed death now seems possible.

Unbridled optimism, however, is not yet warranted. For example, within the past few years the levels of toxaphene and PCB's, chemical "cousins" of DDT, were so high in some Lake Erie fish that the public was warned to minimize its consumption of them.

How Eutrophication Can Be Reversed

W. T. Edmondson
UNIVERSITY OF WASHINGTON

A eutrophic lake is one that has a relatively high rate of input of nutrients, whether from natural or man made sources. The usual consequence is high productivity and dense populations of algae (phytoplankton) in the open water. Often the populations are dominated by so-called blue-green algae with unpleasant characteristics: they float in calm weather, forming scums of decaying matter that smell bad and interfere with use of the lake. Such conditions are called algal nuisances, but they can cause more than trivial trouble. In contrast, an oligotrophic lake has a relatively small nutrient supply and is unlikely to support dense populations of phytoplankton for long times.

Eutrophication refers to an increase in the nutrient supply, often with consequent deterioration of the lake because of development of algal nuisances. Most known cases of genuine eutrophication result from inputs from human activity, usually raw or treated sewage. In many lakes phosphorus is naturally scarce relative to nitrogen and carbon and an excess supply of phosphorus is therefore likely to be the most damaging factor of the three. For that reason, the kinds of detergents that contain phosphorus have attracted much unfavorable attention. This concept of eutrophication is the basis for the following comments. The word has been used by others to cover somewhat different concepts.[1]

When a lake is observed to deteriorate from an acceptable condition to one that produces algal nuisances at the same time that it has been receiving increasing quantities of waste, the chances are good that it is showing signs of eutrophication. This idea can be checked by appropriate experiments. One must be sure that some other important influence has not been changing at the same time. For instance, as a lake ages it fills in with sediment and becomes shallow enough to support a jungle of rooted plants across the bottom. This will happen even if the lake is not receiving sewage.

The most direct way of truly reversing eutrophication is to divert the waste somewhere else where it will not create the same problem, as was done with Lake Washington. When that is not possible there are other techniques that may be at least partly effective in some lakes. One is to put the sewage through an additional treatment that removes the phosphorus. In some situations an effective reduction of phosphorus could be made by stopping the use of phosphate detergents. Another is the binding of phosphorus in the bottom sediments by adding alum, although this is not a permanent solution in the face of continued input. It is sometimes possible to reduce recycling of nutrients by draining water from the hypolimnion. Control of input is not likely to help the weed problem in shallow lakes, but harvesting weeds or dredging the sediments has been effective in some situations.

Considerable hope has been expressed for biomanipulation, changing the abundance of animals that eat algae and make a lake more transparent.[2] In some cases this requires decreasing the abundance of some kinds of desirable fish. Thus, in this field as in so many, we have to deal with scientific knowledge and concepts in a context of conflicting values and priorities that involve other than scientific judgements.

---

[1] Edmondson, W. T. 1974. Review of The Environmental Phosphorus Handbook. *Limnol. Oceanogr.* 19:369–375.
[2] Shapiro, J., V. Lamarra, and M. Lynch. 1975. Biomanipulation: an ecosystem approach to lake restoration. pp. 85–96 in *Proc. Symp. Water Quality Management Through Biological Control*. Univ. Florida Dept. Env. Engineering.

Acid Rain

Can the burning of coal in an Ohio steel plant cause the death of trout high in the Adirondack Mountains of New York? Although it seems highly improbable, the answer is "Yes." The sulphur dioxide gas that is released from the smokestacks undergoes chemical reactions to form sulphuric acid. Prevailing winds carry the acid droplets northeastward to a point high over the Adirondacks. The rain (or snow) then washes the acid into the lakes. Normal, unpolluted rain has a pH of 5.6 — slightly acid because carbon dioxide is dissolved in it to form carbonic acid. (The chemistry of pH is discussed in Chapter 4.) However, much of the acid rain in the eastern states has a pH below 4 — more than one hundred times as acid as normal rain. The role of acid rain in causing massive fish mortality was not fully appreciated until the 1970s. When the lake water pH gets as low as 5, fish survival is threatened. The pH of many Adirondack lakes is below 5. Under those conditions lake trout become deformed and embryos suffer high mortality. The acid rainfall releases aluminum from the soil. After being washed into a lake, the aluminum causes fish to suffocate by interfering with normal gill function. A recent survey conducted by the New York State Bureau of Fisheries revealed that 50 percent of 2,877 Adirondack lakes above 2,000 feet in elevation were devoid of fish. Lakes like Avalanche and Coldman were once famous for their brook trout. Today not one trout is swimming in their waters. The Adirondack lakes are not exceptional. Many lakes in the northern parts of Minnesota, Wisconsin, and Michigan are also threatened. Acid rain has caused the disappearance of fish from lakes in Scandinavia and Canada as well. It is estimated that fish populations may vanish from 40,000 lakes in Canada by the end of this century if present trends continue (5, 7, 12).

Winterkill Resulting from Oxygen Depletion

During the long winters of the northern states, an icy barrier may effectively seal lakes off from their summer source of atmospheric oxygen. However, as long as the ice remains clear of snow, sufficient sunlight may filter down through the ice to sustain photosynthesis. (See Figure 9–19.) As a result, oxygen levels remain adequate. Snow, however, forms an opaque barrier that prevents sunlight penetration. The resultant cessation of photosynthesis and reduction in oxygen levels often result in heavy fish kills, especially if the lake is fertile and shallow. The decay of dead vegetation, with its high BOD, accentuates the problem. As winter progresses, oxygen levels may drop to five parts per million, at which point many of the more sensitive game species succumb; the more resistant rough fish, such as carp and bullheads, capitulate somewhat later, when levels drop to about two to three parts per million.

In a lake supporting a mixed population of game and rough fish, a complete winterkill is more desirable than a partial kill. A partial kill is selective, eliminating only the preferred game fish, and necessitates costly and time-consuming rough-fish removal operations (poisoning and seining) before game-fish restocking can be initiated. On the other hand, if all the fish die, fishery biologists can begin stocking immediately.

In their excellent book *Northern Fishes* (4), Samuel Eddy and Thaddeus Surber describe a classic example of winterkill in a shallow southern Minnesota Lake that had a dense population of bullheads. Although the ice cover that formed in November ultimately became 20 inches thick, oxygen levels initially were adequate. During the second week of January, however, a storm covered the ice with a 6-inch layer of snow. Only two days later, tests revealed that oxygen was severely depleted. After the ice melted in spring, thousands of dead bullheads littered the shore. Not one fish survived (4).

Summerkill Resulting from Oxygen Depletion

Oxygen depletion frequently occurs in the hypolimnion of thermally stratified lakes in late summer. A Kansas study showed that the growth of channel catfish in 0.1-acre earthen ponds was retarded as a result of stress caused by critically low oxygen levels of less than three parts per million. When ponds were aerated, however, the affected fish resumed rapid growth. Fish mortality from oxygen depletion may be caused accidentally by the use of chemicals to control heavy plankton blooms. The sudden death and decay of the plants results in a sharply increased BOD and extensive fish kills. Oxygen depletion is usually less common in streams than in lakes and ponds because the rapid movement of the water promotes aeration. Nevertheless, under some conditions stream mortality may be high. For example, a study was made in three Alaskan streams that revealed that low dissolved oxygen levels in late summer after the spawning period

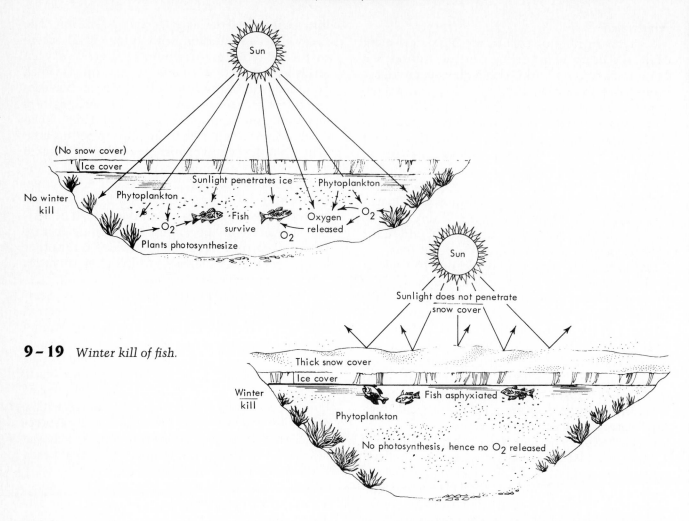

9-19 *Winter kill of fish.*

caused the death of 60 to 90 percent of the young salmon.

Predation

Fish are subjected to intense predatory pressure from members of all vertebrate classes, including other fish, amphibians, reptiles, birds, and mammals. Predation has the greatest impact when fish populations are high.

Fish. Game fish show increased vulnerability to predation when starving, parasitized, or diseased. A six-inch muskellunge will consume 15 minnows daily. A walleye may consume up to 3,000 fish by the time it is three years old. When other food is scarce, many fish will resort to cannibalism. Smaller species may prey on the eggs of larger species that as adults regularly feed on the smaller forms.

Reptiles. Unusually low water levels may render fish especially vulnerable to predation by osprey,

terns, and mink. Garter snakes devour great numbers of smaller fish while they are stranded in shallow pools during summer drought. Game fish make up one third of the food of Michigan snapping turtles, for example.

Birds. Kingfishers may pose serious problems at hatchery rearing ponds. Egrets, herons, and mergansers (a diving duck) consume large numbers of fish. A single merganser may consume over 35,000 fish annually. The famous ornithologist John Audubon found over 9.5 pounds of fish in the stomach of one American merganser!

Mammals. Among mammals, the bear, otter, fisher, and mink have exerted considerable environmental resistance on fish populations, especially during periods of drought, when unusually low water levels leave the fish vulnerable. Of course, the most destructive of all fish predators are human beings.

Salmon Mortality During Migration

The salmon is an *anadromous* fish — it spends most of its growing years in the ocean and, after attaining sexual maturity, ascends freshwater streams in order to spawn. The chinook, or king salmon, is a handsome Pacific species that may attain a weight up to 100 pounds. On the breeding grounds the female excavates a shallow trough, the *redd,* in the sandy or gravelly bed of some swiftly flowing stream emptying into the Pacific Ocean, such as the Sacramento in California, the Fraser in British Columbia, or the Columbia bordering Oregon and Washington. (See Figure 9–20.) The female may deposit several thousand eggs in the redd. After the male has fertilized them, they are covered with a protective layer of gravel. Following a two-month incubation period, the eggs hatch, and the young gradually move downstream. However, only 10 percent of the salmon fry ultimately reach the ocean. They suffer heavy losses from predation by fish, birds, and mammals. In some streams, such as the Columbia, many young salmon are killed by *nitrogen intoxication,* resulting from the high levels of nitrogen occurring in the turbulent waters below dams.

9–20 *The natural life cycle of the Pacific salmon (left). Fisheries biologists at the Feather River Hatchery in California have modified this natural cycle as shown.*

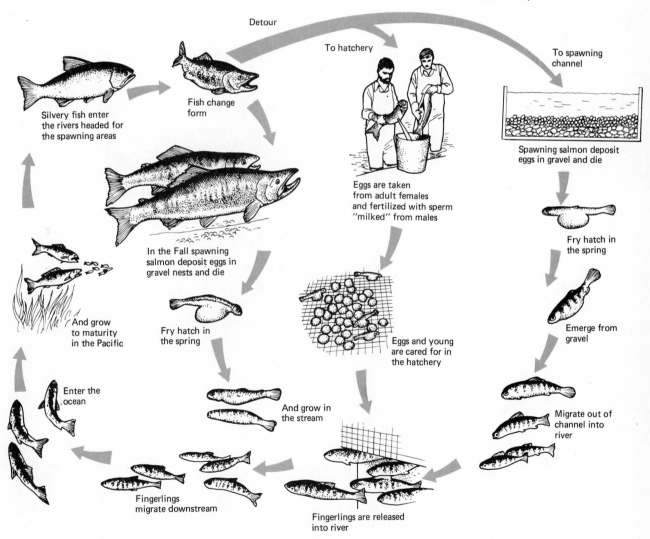

Detour

To hatchery

To spawning channel

Silvery fish enter the rivers headed for the spawning areas

Fish change form

Spawning salmon deposit eggs in gravel and die

Eggs are taken from adult females and fertilized with sperm "milked" from males

Fry hatch in the spring

In the Fall spawning salmon deposit eggs in gravel nests and die

Eggs and young are cared for in the hatchery

Emerge from gravel

And grow to maturity in the Pacific

Fry hatch in the spring

Enter the ocean

And grow in the stream

Migrate out of channel into river

Fingerlings migrate downstream

Fingerlings are released into river

235

9-21 *Salmon jumping Brooks Falls, Alaska, during migration to spawning grounds.*

9-22 *King (chinook) salmon leaps up the top step of a fish ladder at the Red Bluf Diversion Dam during a late-spring spawning run. This fish ladder enables salmon to move upstream beyond the dam and eventually spawn in the Sacramento River in California.*

236

The salmon remain in the Pacific Ocean for four to seven years, feeding ravenously on small fishes such as herring and anchovies. Many move a long way from the mouth of their native stream. Thus, adult salmon tagged off Baranof Island, Alaska, were recovered in the Columbia River of Washington, a distance of about 2,000 miles. Upon attaining sexual maturity, the salmon ascend the mouths of their native streams, apparently recognizing them by their distinctive smell. They gradually make their way to the shallow headwaters near the site of their hatching. This is accomplished only after they have negotiated all sorts of obstacles, including rushing cataracts, a variety of predators (gulls, ospreys, and bears), fishermen, pollution (silt, heated waters, radioactive materials, and chemicals), the nets of research biologists, and big dams. (See Figure 9–21.) Once they arrive at the headwater, they immediately spawn and die, thus completing their life cycle.

Some years ago railroad builders accidentally set off an avalanche of rock and rubble that clogged up the narrow channel of the Fraser River at Hell's Gate. As a result, the sockeye-salmon run was hopelessly blocked, and countless thousands of fish, loaded with eggs and sperm, died below the rockslide, unable to press on to their spawning grounds.

The erection of dozens of power dams (such as the 550-foot-tall Grand Coulee on the Columbia) across the migration path of the Pacific salmon has effectively cut off considerable numbers from their spawning grounds. In order to insure the survival of Pacific salmon runs in the Columbia River the young salmon are netted far upstream, transported downstream by tank truck, and then released into the river below the Bonneville Dam. In some other rivers, fish ladders have been constructed to enable the fish to reach their spawning grounds. (See Figure 9–22.) High water temperatures may be just as effective as a high dam. Thus, water temperatures of 70° F or above block the movement of sockeye salmon from the Columbia River into the tributary Okanogan River (14). When temperatures drop below 70° F, however, the migration is quickly resumed. In recent years there has been a marked decline in the once-abundant Columbia River salmon harvest. Thermal and concrete barriers to migration, together with overfishing, have been important factors in the decline.

Fishing Pressure

Overfishing undoubtedly has been a major factor in the decline of many of our freshwater commercial and game fishes. The classic example of extreme fishing pressure is afforded by trout fishermen on the opening weekend of the trout season. During their enthusiastic quest for the king of American game fish, they frequently become crowded shoulder to shoulder along stream margins. Fishing pressure is increasing. The number of licensed anglers has increased from ten to thirty million within the last three decades. One of every eight Americans tries his or her luck with hook and line. And with the nation's increasing population, the increase in leisure hours and mobility, and the desperate need for a release from urban pressures afforded by the wilderness, the pressure of the human predator on fish populations is bound to intensify.

Fisheries Management

Fisheries management is *the manipulation of fish populations and their environment to increase sport and commercial fish harvests.* In its broadest sense, fisheries management embraces all the laws, policies, research, and techniques that have as their ultimate objective the enhanced value of the fisheries resource for the greatest number of people over the longest period of time. The *sustained-yield concept* is implicit in all sound fish-management activities.

To manage a fish population effectively, the

fisheries biologist must understand the dynamics of the fish population. He or she must be able to predict the overall effect of a specific level of fishing pressure and be prepared to cope with the adverse environmental factors of disease, competition, parasites, pollution, drought, and oxygen depletion. Ordinarily the fisheries biologist draws on knowledge derived from life-history studies of the species. From such studies data are secured on food habits, longevity, mortality factors, growth rates, sex and age ratios, breeding behavior, and spawning habitat. The following fish-management procedures will be discussed briefly: restrictive laws, artificial propagation, introductions, habitat improvement, natural and artificial selection, and managing endangered species.

Restrictive Laws

As in the case of wild game, an early step taken in fisheries restoration was the establishment of protective laws. Closed seasons were established during the breeding period of a species. It was apparent that when a female bass or walleye was taken when swollen with eggs, the angler was removing much more than a single adult; he or she was also removing thousands of future young fish. Creel limits were imposed. Certain fishing techniques were outlawed, such as seining, poisoning, dynamiting, spearing, and using multiple-hook lines for taking game fish. It was felt that if the activities of the human predator were effectively controlled, fish populations inevitably would assume their original abundance.

In recent years, fisheries biologists have been experimenting with more liberalized regulations on many species of warm-water fish. In many states size limits on panfish (sunfish, bluegills, rock bass, and crappies) have been lifted, permitting fish of any size, from runts to giants, to be taken. On the other hand, minimum-size limits have been placed on predatory species such as bass and pike. The main objective of these regulations is to insure the presence of large predators which will be effective in controlling populations of panfish (bluegills, sunfish, rock bass). Stuntedness of the latter fish would thus be prevented. Incidentally, of course, such regulations provide more opportunity for anglers to land a lunker bass or pike. However, in some species it has been shown that size limit regulations have no effect on the total number of that species surviving in a given year. (See Figure 9–23.) The effects of creel limits, varying fishing methods and gear, open and closed seasons, and winter fishing on fish populations are continuously being evaluated (2).

Legislation in relation to fish management is discussed by Karl Lagler of the University of Michigan in his book *Freshwater Fishery Biology* (13). In his view there is a cause for both pessimism and optimism. The negative features of fisheries legislation include (1) the multiplicity of restrictions, which make it difficult for even the well-informed angler to refrain from committing occasional violations; (2) the setting up of different regulations for two species that are closely related and extremely difficult to tell apart in the field, such as the white-fish and cisco, the northern pike and grass pickerel, and the bluegill and green sunfish; and (3) the establishment of different regulations for two margins of a river that serves as the common boundary of two states, for example, the Mississippi River between Wisconsin and Minnesota.

REGULATING FISHING PRESSURE. *Fishing pressure* is the number of hours of fishing done per unit (for example, 1,000 acres) of lake area. The intensity

9–23 *Size limits on northern pike have very little, if any, effect on the number of northerns that die during a given year. Even if no fishing at all is permitted, the mortality of a given northern-pike population will be the same.*

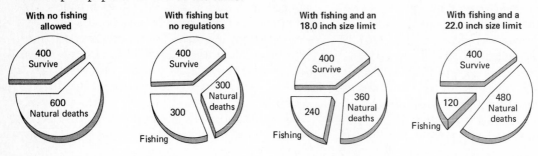

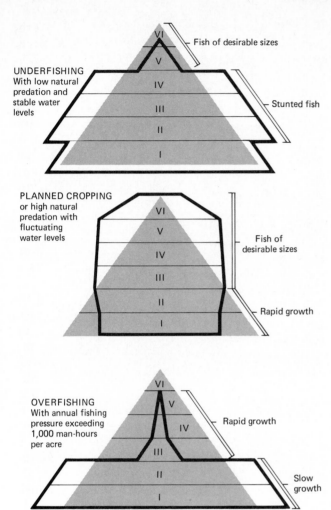

9 – 24 *Differential effects of underfishing, planned cropping, and overfishing on year classes and numbers of fish that are of desirable size.*

of such fishing pressure is an important factor in determining the number of good-sized fish that are prized by the angler. Figure 9 – 24 illustrates the effects of three different levels of fishing pressure on fish size in a theoretical lake (1). The segmented triangles represent the first six year classes of the fish population, assuming 50 percent mortality each year. In other words, if we begin with 1,000 fish of Age I, the lake will have 500 fish of Age II, 250 fish of Age III, and so on. Suppose now that we expose such a hypothetical fish population to three different levels of fishing pressure. Which level of fishing pressure, if long sustained, would provide anglers with the best sport — catching a sizable

number of big fish? The effects of each level of fishing pressure are indicated by the heavy black diagram superimposed on the triangles. The wider the age class, the greater the number of fish in that class.

1. *Underfishing.* If the lake is underfished, there will be high survival in all year classes. However, fish of Age I through IV will be stunted and therefore hardly worth catching. Only the five-year-old fish will be of desirable size.
2. *Overfishing.* If the lake is overfished, the one- and two-year-old fish will be very abundant but will also grow very slowly because of the intense competition for food. The three- to six-year-old fish will grow rapidly but will be small in number.
3. *Moderate Fishing (Planned Cropping).* When the lake is carefully managed so that fishing pressure is moderate, all fish in the lake — from age one to age six — will grow.

Now suppose that fishing pressure is maintained at a moderate level of intensity (planned cropping). The result will be rapid growth in fish of age one and two. The reason is that because overpopulation is prevented, an abundance of food is available. Growth continues as the fish get older. Eventually the fish population contains a sizable number of large fish to provide anglers maximum sport on a long-term basis (1).

Artificial Propagation

In the early history of fish management it seemed logical to biologists and anglers alike that if human beings could supplement the natural reproduction of a given fish species by artificial methods and introduce those artificially propagated fish into a given habitat, the fish population of that area would be augmented and the angling success of fishermen virtually assured. Since about 1935, however, on the basis of intensive studies of population dynamics, it has become apparent that this technique frequently results in dismal failure, especially if the objective is to increase the numbers of an already well-established species. Moreover, the cost of artificial propagation in terms of facilities, maintenance, staff, rearing, and eventual distribution of the young fish is almost prohibitive. For these reasons, artificial propagation is not well regarded by some fisheries biologists. Fish stocking, may have various objectives: it may re-establish a fish popula-

239

9–26 *Salmon eggs reared in a hatchery. The white eggs are dead and will be removed from the egg tray.*

9–25 *Superintendent checks salmon eggs at the Platte River (Michigan) hatchery. Note the light-colored eggs in the egg tray in the foreground. The embryos in those eggs have died; the eggs will be removed from the tray to prevent contamination of the water supply.*

9–27 *Fisheries biologists handling salmon at the Lake Oroville Fish Hatchery, California.*

9–28 *Fingerling rainbow trout are planted by air in Lake Powell behind Glen Canyon Dam on the Colorado River.*

tion that has been destroyed by predators, drought, pollution, disease, or some other environmental factor. A fisheries biologist may want to stock a southern farm pond with tilapia in order to get rid of excess aquatic vegetation. He or she may want to stock a reservoir with a predatory species in order to reduce an overpopulation of stunted bluegill. Impoundments may be stocked with rainbow, brook, or brown trout if the water temperature does not exceed 65° F. Largemouth bass may be stocked in reservoirs and farm ponds where water gets too warm for trout. Bass ponds are frequently stocked with food fishes such as bluegills, crappies, and minnows (13).

Stocking is one of several useful techniques that must be used if salmon and trout populations are to be maintained at reasonably high levels. (See Figures 9–25 and 9–26.) The U.S. Fish and Wildlife Service maintains a number of salmon hatcheries along the Columbia and Sacramento rivers. (See Figure 9–27.) Without the artificial propagation of trout, the thrill of hooking one of those scrappy fish would soon be nothing but a memory for most anglers, despite the most ingeniously tied fly and the most sophisticated arch of a bamboo rod. Currently both federal and state fish hatcheries rear brook, brown, cutthroat, rainbow, and lake trout. In mountainous areas of Wyoming and Colorado, trout fingerlings

may be stocked by means of aerial drops (2). (See Figure 9–28.)

The official policy of federal hatcheries is to propagate trout to fill the following needs: (1) To stock trout in suitable waters in which they do not occur. Such waters may be newly created reservoirs or may be waters from which competitive rough fish have been eradicated; (2) To stock trout in waters where conditions for growth are good but where natural spawning sites are inadequate. Growth usually is rapid. Nevertheless, such streams must be restocked at intervals of one to three years; (3) To stock trout in waters where fishing pressure is too great to be sustained by natural reproduction. This is sometimes known as put-and-take stocking. The trout planted are of catchable size. Most of them are caught the same season they are planted. (See Figure 9–30.) Several of our nation's sportsmen-presidents, such as Dwight Eisenhower and Lyndon Johnson, have waxed eloquent about the fishing potential of a particular trout stream, on the basis of the lunkers they hooked only minutes after strategic stocking by publicity-sensitive conservation officials.

Local sportsmen's groups can greatly increase trout populations in their favorite streams by using a simple, but ingenious, device called a *Vibert Box*. (See Figure 9–31.) The Vibert Box is a plastic box

9–29 *Stocking young trout in a Wisconsin lake.*

9 – 30 *Opening day of the New Jersey trout season on the Musconetcong River near Hackettstown. These anglers hope to catch trout stocked on a "put-and-take" basis.*

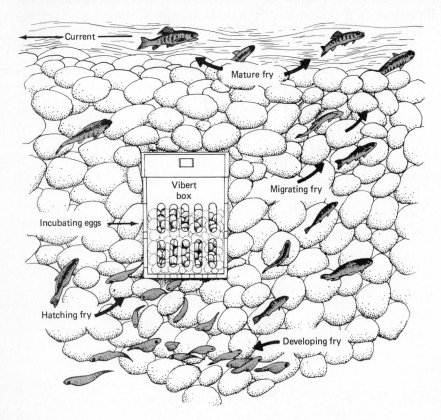

9 – 31 *Stream-planted Vibert box. View is a section through the gravel on the stream bottom. All stages of fry development are shown.*

that is slotted on all sides to permit the free flow of stream water. About 100 trout eggs are placed in the box, which is then planted in the gravel bed of the stream. The Vibert Box has many advantages: (1) It permits the eggs to develop under natural conditions. (2) It protects the eggs from predation. (3) The technique is inexpensive. (One trout fishermen's club planted 50,000 brown trout eggs by this method at a cost of only $300. Hatchery production methods would have been ten times as expensive.) (4) Ninety percent of the eggs actually hatched, compared to a natural hatching success of only 15 percent. (5) The newly hatched fish (fry) are immediately conditioned to their immediate environment, in terms of dissolved oxygen, water temperature, water chemistry, and stream flow. They, therefore, have greater ability to resist environmental stress than hatchery-reared stock (15).

New Introduction

An *introduction* is the stocking of an animal in a new region. The introduced species may be native to the United States, or it may be an exotic.

Native Introductions.

1. *Coho Salmon.* In 1966 the Conservation Department of Michigan introduced about 800,000 *coho salmon* from the Pacific coast into streams that are tributaries to Lake Michigan and Lake Superior. Those salmon have provided excellent sport and commercial fishing. (See Figure 9–32.) They have served as effective agents of biological control by feeding on exploding populations of alewife—a nondesirable species that competes with more desirable fish. Because the coho has a short life span, an abundant food supply is essential for appreciable growth. The Michigan Conservation Department has also introduced the chinook salmon into Lake Michigan.

2. *Walleye.* The Minnesota Conservation Department has enjoyed a great deal of success with walleye introductions. For example, only three years after walleye fry were introduced into 4,000-acre Brule Lake (Cook County, Minnesota), it was possible to catch legal limits of walleyes in any part of the lake.

3. *Smelt.* American smelt were successfully introduced into the Great Lakes region from the Atlantic and Pacific coasts. During the spawning run of the smelt in early April, fishermen come

9–32 *Native introduction: coho salmon. Wisconsin angler with good-sized coho salmon stocked in Lake Michigan. The coho grow rapidly because of the superabundance of alewives, on which they feed.*

from all over Michigan and Minnesota to net or seine the silvery little fish as they ascend tributary streams. During a good run it is not uncommon for smelt fishermen to catch a tubful of fish in half an hour.

Habitat Improvement

In recent years many fisheries biologists have come to the conclusion that the most effective long-range measure for improving sport and commercial fishing is *improving the carrying capacity of fish habitat.* They have seen fishing in a particular lake or stream deteriorate despite the most stringently enforced restrictive laws (closed seasons, creel limits, and so on) and despite the most intensive and carefully supervised programs of propagation and stocking. They believe that if the carrying capacity of the lake or stream is good (in terms of food supply, cover, unpolluted water, abundance of breeding sites, proper oxygen levels, and suitable water temperatures), some of the other fish management measures may be de-emphasized or, in some situations, even abandoned completely.

243

Introduction of Exotics: For Better or for Worse?

The U.S. Fish and Wildlife Service is increasingly concerned with the "biological pollution" of native fish populations with exotic species. Some of the foreign fish were deliberately introduced by fisheries biologists either to provide a desirable game or food fish or to aid in controlling some environmental problem. On the other hand, many exotics have been accidentally introduced. In either case, a number of the introductions have been highly destructive. Thirty-nine of the 84 exotic species of fish occurring in our lakes and streams have been able to reproduce successfully. Even more significant, six of those exotics are rapidly expanding their ranges.

Beneficial Introduction: The Brown Trout

The introduction of the European brown trout roughly one hundred years ago was highly successful. (See Figure 9 – 33.) This species has been able to establish itself in waters either too warm or too badly polluted for the survival of native trout. As a result, the brown trout has provided angling thrills for the sport fisherman even in urban areas. The brown trout is able to survive in the relatively warm, somewhat muddy waters of Lowes Creek, for example, which is only a stone's throw from the city limits of Eau Claire, Wisconsin, a bustling city of 45,000.

Harmful Introduction

EUROPEAN CARP. The European carp has been the most destructive exotic fish ever introduced to the United States. (See Figure 9 – 34.) It was originally introduced to California (1872), the Great Lakes (1873) and Washington, D.C. (1877). The objective was good: to provide Americans with a valuable source of food. The carp proved to be an extraordinarily adaptable fish. The introduced populations grew rapidly, following the characteristic S-shaped growth curve. Only twenty years after the introduction of European carp to Lake Erie, fishermen were able to harvest 3.6 million pounds in a single year from that lake. Soon, however, the carp were affecting aquatic ecosystems in ways that had not been predicted. For example, they uprooted aquatic vegetation during their bottom-feeding activities. The results have been exceedingly harmful to game-fish populations because (a) their spawning grounds were destroyed, (b) their food supplies were diminished, and (c) levels of dissolved oxygen were reduced as a result of the interference with photosynthesis caused by the muddying of the waters.

WALKING CATFISH. The walking catfish was accidentally released from the holding ponds of exotic fish dealers in Florida. It is an air-breathing fish that is able to "walk" over land by means of highly specialized front fins. Auto traffic may actually be halted when swarms of these fish wriggle their slimy way across Florida highways. Even worse, the walking catfish competes aggressively for common food supplies with desirable game species such as the black bass and blue gill. As a result, populations of the latter fish have been reduced. Because it has no natural predators in this country, and because fishermen consider it useless either as sport or food, its populations have exploded, especially in Florida (8).

WHITE AMUR. The white amur or grass carp, was introduced from Malaysia in 1963. (See Figure 9 – 35.) The objective was to control the aquatic weeds that choke many lakes, streams, and irrigation canals as a result of eutrophication. The white amur has an enormous appetite for aquatic plants. As a result, it grows rapidly, some specimens reaching a length of 20 inches in their first year. It is hoped that the white amur will eat its way through the weedy barriers that interfere with boating, swimming, fishing,

244

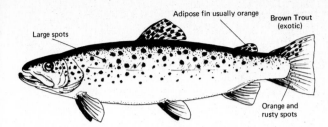

Large spots

Adipose fin usually orange

Brown Trout
(exotic)

Orange and
rusty spots

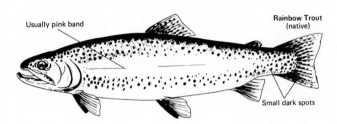

Usually pink band

Rainbow Trout
(native)

Small dark spots

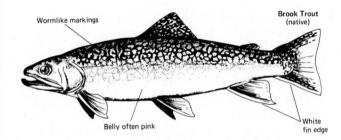

Wormlike markings

Brook Trout
(native)

Belly often pink

White
fin edge

9-33 *Field marks for identification of three common species of trout occurring in the United States. The brown trout was introduced from Europe. The rainbow and brook trout are native to this country.*

9-34 *The carp, an exotic that was introduced from Europe to the United States in the nineteenth century. Its effect on lake and stream ecosystems has been highly adverse.*

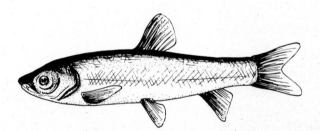

9-35 *The white amur—for better or worse? This exotic species was introduced to the United States from Malaysia in 1963. It has been employed by several states, such as Arkansas and Iowa, for the purpose of weed control. On the other hand, Wisconsin has placed a ban on the fish, because it is feared that it might have an undesirable impact on the habitats of more desirable fish such as bass and pike.*

and irrigation. The white amur has become well established in the central portion of the Mississippi River drainage, much to the distress of waterfowl biologists and duck hunters. It is feared that a rapid decline in aquatic vegetation, which will most certainly occur, will have serious consequences for the plant-feeding waterfowl that concentrate along the Mississippi River by the tens of thousands during their migrations. Commercial fisheries in this region may also be harmed. Unfortunately, the white amur has spread through 34 states, even to Wisconsin, where it has been banned. It is apparent, then, that whether the white amur's plant-eating activity is beneficial or harmful depends on *where* it takes place (8).

245

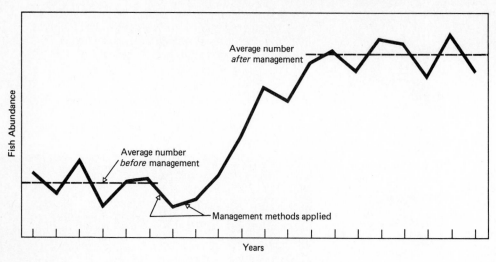

Fish Abundance

Average number
after management

Average number
before management

Management methods applied

Years

9 – 36 *Trout populations respond readily to stream habitat improvements.*

HABITAT IMPROVEMENT FOR TROUT. Wild trout populations may increase considerably when the carrying capacity of their environment is raised. (See Figure 9 – 36.) Various methods are available to improve stream habitat for trout. The components of the habitat that can be effectively managed are (1) water flow, (2) space, (3) cover, and (4) food. Some methods of stream improvement are shown in Figures 9 – 37 and 9 – 38. Each management method will have a positive effect that in turn may result in other positive effects. For example, let us suppose hiding cover is increased by the introduction of brush shelters. (See Figure 9 – 38.) The cover will protect the trout from predation by mink, otters,

9 – 37 *Improving fish habitat. Personnel for the New York State Conservation Department are constructing a dam across a trout stream. Fish will use the deep water behind the dam as a refuge from predators or as a relatively cool loafing site.*

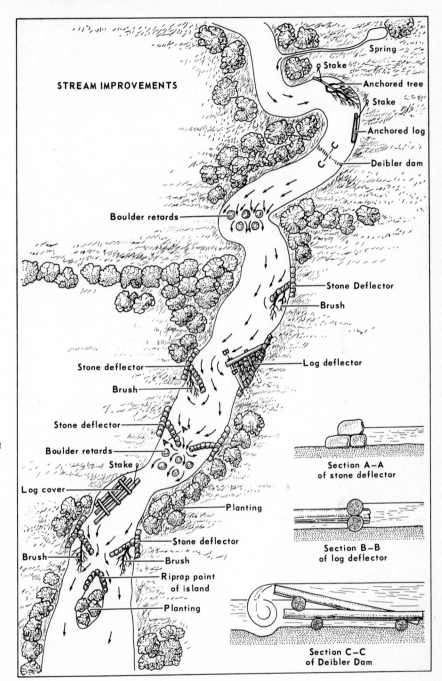

STREAM IMPROVEMENTS

Spring
Stake
Anchored tree
Stake
Anchored log
Deibler dam
Boulder retards
Stone Deflector
Brush
Stone deflector
Log deflector
Brush
Stone deflector
Boulder retards
Stake
Log cover
Planting
Brush
Stone deflector
Brush
Riprap point of island
Planting

Section A–A of stone deflector

Section B–B of log deflector

Section C–C of Deibler Dam

9–38 *Methods of improving stream habitat for fish. On hard-bottom streams spawning and refuge pools may be established by erecting low dams constructed of either logs or boulders. In sand-bottom streams use of properly situated deflectors will result in the buildup of a silt bank and weed bed (essential substrates for many fish food organisms) on the downstream side. In shallow streams the shelter area can be enlarged by the introduction of streamside shrubs and trees. Note riprap at point of island to prevent erosion. Shrubs may be planted to intercept sunlight and prevent critical warming of water during midsummer. Note plunge basin and shelter formed by Deibler dam.*

bear, fish hawks, and herons. As a result, trout will become more numerous. But the shelters will have an additional positive influence: As shown in Figure 9–38, the twigs and branches of the shelter serve as attachment sites for insect larvae, snails, and crustaceans. Those organisms serve as food for the growing trout populations. As a consequence, the growth rates of trout will increase, which in turn results in bigger fish. Such shelters also provide shaded areas where fish may retreat during the heat of the day. The cooling effect on the water enables it to dissolve more oxygen. The increased levels of

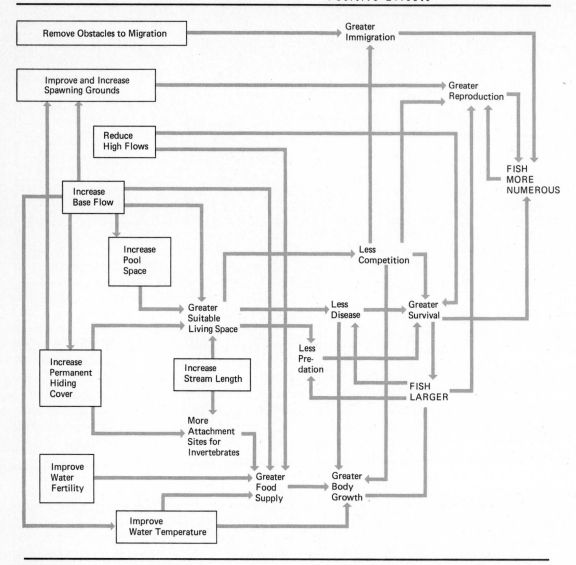

9 – 39 *"Chain responses" resulting from the application of various habitat-management methods to trout streams. The management methods are shown in the rectangles.*

oxygen enable the trout to swim faster in escaping predators or in pursuing prey. Figure 9 – 39 shows the pathways of effect for several other stream-management methods such as cover, the increase of flow, and the improvement of water fertility (18).

A series of brush shelters may be anchored along the inner margin of a lake's littoral zone with great effectiveness. In the winter season brush piles can be set up on the ice cover in strategic areas and weighted with bags of stones; they will gradually

sink to their proper place on the lake bottom as soon as the ice melts in spring (13).

WEED CONTROL. A certain amount of aquatic vegetation is useful to fish populations as cover, refuge sites, spawning sites, food, and as a source of oxygen released during photosynthesis. Nevertheless, when vegetation becomes too thick, it may be more destructive than beneficial because it competes for nutrients with phytoplankton, utilizes too much water space, and permits escape from predators to such an extent that overpopulation and stunting result. Moreover, in late summer the decomposition of the accumulated vegetation on the lake bottom exerts a high BOD, which may result in serious oxygen depletion. Under such conditions the weeds must be removed, either by weed-cutting machines, by biological methods, or by species-specific herbicides.

At least 27 major weed-control programs have been conducted in 15 states and Puerto Rico, with the aid of $400,000 in federal funds. The experimental control of algae and submerged plants has been achieved with copper sulphate. Great caution must be exercised in the selection of such chemicals, however, for they may affect both fish food organisms and fish adversely. Considerable research is currently being conducted to determine the total impact of herbicides on the entire aquatic ecosystem, whether stream, lake, or reservoir.

Among the more serious water-weed pests in the United States are the lotus (Texas and Tennessee), water chestnut (New York), and water hyacinth (Texas, Florida, and Louisiana). Much interest has been generated in recent years in the possibility of controlling such weeds with *tilapia*, a fish introduced from Africa. In an experimental study it was found that a population density of 1,000 tilapias per acre will eliminate rooted submergent vegetation and algae. Tilapia might be useful as a weed-control agent in artificial lakes and ponds and where aesthetic values are of consideration. Its use would be restricted to southern lakes because the subtropical tilapias cannot tolerate water temperatures below 55° F for extended periods.

SPAWNING SITES. The fish production of a body of water may be increased by providing artificial spawning substrates where suitable natural ones are lacking. Thus, sand or gravel might be introduced on the otherwise muddy bottom of a lake or stream to enhance bass or trout production. The use of nylon as an artificial spawning substratum for largemouth bass was tested in five ponds. Spawns were observed on 68 of 90 (75.5 percent) mats over a two-year period. Transferring those spawn-laden mats to rearing ponds for incubation and growth was moderately successful. One trial resulted in a per acre production of 54.3 pounds of biomass made up of 37,600 two-inch fingerlings.

Spawning habitat may be increased or decreased by manipulating the water levels of reservoirs. Intensive study of the breeding behavior of the northern pike has revealed that shallow marshy fringes of the littoral zone are the preferred spawning habitat. Flooding marshes with the aid of low dikes may enhance spawning conditions for this species (13). In recent years suitable spawning sites for the northern pike have been greatly reduced as a result of real-estate developments, marina construction, and industrial expansion. State fish and game departments are attempting to correct the situation. Wisconsin, Iowa, and Minnesota acquired thousands of acres of marshes for developing northern-pike breeding and spawning habitat (2).

FERTILIZATION. Just as the abundance of a farmer's corn crop depends largely on the fertility of the soil, so the black bass or pike crop of a lake or stream depend on the fertility of the water. Water fertility (that is, the concentration of dissolved salts such as carbonates, nitrates, and phosphates) in turn ultimately depends on the soil fertility of the watershed. Water fertility determines the abundance of phytoplankton, which forms the base of fish food chains.

Many lakes in central Minnesota, occupying a region of fertile soil, produce up to 80 pounds of animal food (dry weight) per acre compared to .2 pound per acre by lakes in the infertile watersheds of northeastern Minnesota. It is apparent, therefore, that the use of artificial fertilizers can increase fish production in a lake or farm pond just as it can on a farmer's fields. It would, of course, be prohibitively expensive in a lake of any considerable area. Moreover, most lakes in the United States are already too rich in nutrients (eutrophied). Russian researchers have found that pond fertilization with phosphate, nitrate, and manure increased the production of both phytoplankton and zooplankton, and fish biomass was increased two to three times. There is great variation in the efficiency with which various species of fish convert the available food to biomass. As shown in Figure 9–40, fish biomass per acre in North American ponds, lakes, and reservoirs varies from four pounds in trout to 180 pounds in the gizzard shad.

Wild birds, of course, may assist humans in fertilizing lakes. Immense quantities of droppings are voided by birds in the vicinity of their nesting areas.

249

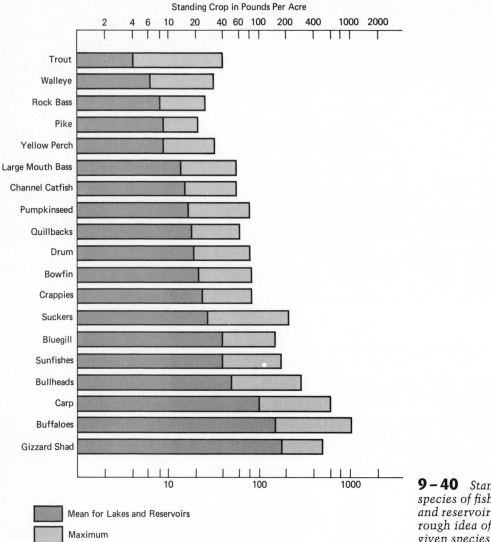

9 – 40 *Standing crops of various species of fish in North American lakes and reservoirs. These figures furnish a rough idea of the relative efficiency of a given species to exploit its habitat.*

Some of this nitrate- and phosphate-rich material falls into the water, heightening its fertility. This may result in increased phytoplankton production, which will permit higher densities of the small aquatic invertebrates utilized as food by fish. Recently, fish and duck farms have been established in Russia, in which the ducks not only increase fish productivity by fertilizing the water, but serve to control excessive aquatic weeds as well.

PREDATOR CONTROL. Just as many deer hunters feel that any deer-eating wolf should be shot on sight, so the angler becomes equally upset over the fish-eating activities of herons, mergansers, pelicans, loons, mink, otter, and bear. However, most fish-eaters may be performing a beneficial population-control function that may minimize the stuntedness food shortages cause, as well as reducing the occurrence of epidemic diseases. The absence of this predatory pressure might leave more fish for the angler, but many would be so small as to be hardly worth catching. In any case, when food-analysis studies are made, the accusations of sportsmen frequently appear unfounded. Thus, a study of digestive tracts of otters from Wisconsin, Michigan, and Minnesota revealed that, although fish were indeed the otter's main prey, game fish were seldom taken.

The Sea Lamprey Story

Although most predators and parasites do not affect the fish population appreciably, on occasion a specific predator may cause a drastic population reduction. A classic example is the havoc wrought in the Great Lakes by the *sea lamprey* on the lake-trout population. The lamprey is a primitive jawless vertebrate with a slender, eelike body. The muscular funnel around its circular mouth enables it to attach firmly to its prey. Its pistonlike tongue, which is armed with numerous hard, rasping teeth, is moved back and forth through the lake trout's tissues, tearing both flesh and blood vessels and causing severe bleeding. After gorging itself on a meal of blood and body fluid, the predator may drop off its host and permit it to swim weakly away. However, if the trout does not eventually die from the direct predatory attack, it may succumb secondarily to bacterial and fungal parasites that can freely invade the body through the open wounds. Even if a lake trout survives, the ugly scar left on its body would scarcely be admired by the grocery-buying housewife (see Figure 9–42).

Originally, the lamprey was primarily an anadromous fish, spending its adult life in marine habitats but ascending freshwater streams to spawn. (Apparently small populations, however, also occurred in Lake Ontario.) Today, the lampreys along our Atlantic Coast retain this anadromous behavior. However, the Great Lakes lampreys spend their entire life cycle in fresh water. The fasting adults migrate up tributary streams to mate, spawn, and die. The adults usually build a shallow nest on a gravel or sand bottom into which they deposit their eggs. A 15-inch female may produce 60,000 eggs. After hatching from the eggs, the larval lampreys drift downstream until they come to a muddy bottom. They then burrow tail first into the mud, allowing only their heads to remain exposed to the swiftly moving current. During this time they feed on small algae, insects, worms, and crustaceans. After several years, they acquire the muscular funnel and rasping tongue of the adult, emerge from their burrows, swim into the open waters of the lake, and assume the predatory behavior of their parents.

The lamprey originally occurred in the shallow waters off the Atlantic seaboard from Florida to Labrador, in the waters of the St. Lawrence River, and also in Lake Ontario at the eastern end of the Great Lakes chain. For many centuries the westward extension of the lamprey's range into Lake Erie was blocked by Niagara Falls. However, in 1833 human beings unwittingly provided an invasion pathway by constructing the Welland Canal to benefit commercial shipping. The spread of the lamprey through Lake Erie

9–41 *An adult lamprey tenaciously attached to a boulder by means of its suctorial funnel. The eye and seven openings to the gill pouches are clearly visible.*

9–42 *Lamprey-scarred lake trout. Note the lamprey hand-held at the upper right.*

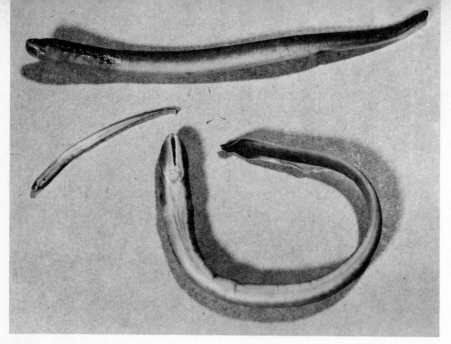

9–43 *Stages in the development of the sea lamprey. Center: About one year old and still nonparasitic. Early eyeless state, about two inches long. Upper: Three-year-old larva, still nonparasitic. about four and a half inches long. Lower: Recently transformed larva almost ready to assume parasitic life. Ventral view showing transformed mouthparts.*

was relatively slow. It was not taken in the Detroit River until the 1930s, possibly because of a lack of suitable spawning streams. However, once it invaded Lake Huron it spread rapidly through the remainder of the Great Lakes chain, and by the 1950s it had reached western Lake Superior. Its predatory activity soon threatened the multimillion-dollar Great Lakes trout-fishing industry with total collapse. The annual catch declined from ten million pounds in 1940 to one-third million pounds in 1961, a 97 percent reduction in 21 years.* Idle nets rotted along the waterfront. Veteran fishermen, too old to acquire new skills, went on relief. Many of the younger men emigrated to Minneapolis, Milwaukee, Chicago, and Detroit to seek employment.

Confronted with this economic and biological dilemma, research teams of the lakes states' fisheries departments and the U.S. Fish and Wildlife Service collaborated in an intensive effort to eradicate the predator. Various stratagems were employed. Adults were netted, seined, and taken in electric fences as they attempted to ascend their spawning streams. Those methods, however, met with only partial success, so from 1951 to 1959 over 6,000 chemicals were tested by biochemists to determine their suitability as agents of lamprey control. Finally, a selective poison (3,4,6-trichloro-2-nitrophenol), known by its trade name Dowlap, was developed. A concentration of 12 parts per million destroyed all lamprey larvae within 16 hours. A 24-hour exposure of 36 parts per million had no adverse effect on game fish such as trout, sunfish, and rock bass. Moreover, it proved to be harmless to fish food organisms such as creek chubs and aquatic insect larvae (16).

As a result of these encouraging findings, the Great Lakes Fishery Commission employed Dowlap and related nitrophenols on all lamprey-spawning streams tributary to the Great Lakes. By 1962 the lamprey had been reduced to 20 percent of its peak numbers. In 1960 almost a million lake trout were stocked in Lake Superior; later stockings were made in Lake Huron and Lake Michigan. It is hoped that the combination of restocking and the continued chemical treatment of lamprey-spawning streams will gradually restore the lake-trout fishery (16).

* Some fisheries experts, however, attribute the decline in the lake trout population to overfishing rather than the predatory activities of the lamprey.

9 – 44 *Chemical being sprayed on lake surface in order to control rough (trash)-fish populations.*

THE REMOVAL OF TRASH FISH. Because of their destructiveness to game fish, trash fish such as *carp*, *bowfins*, and *gar* are frequently the focus of intensive eradication projects. Even *gizzard shad* and *panfish*, ordinarily valuable as forage for game fish,

may require control if they become abundant. However, eradication of any of these species from a given body of water would be enormously difficult to accomplish. Various control methods under study currently involve chemicals, seining, commercial fishing, manipulation of water levels, and fish-spawning control. Before state or federal biologists may employ a specific chemical, it must first be registered with the USDA and approved not only by state health and pollution agencies, but also by the Federal Committee on Pest Control (2). Carp probably could not be completely eliminated unless dynamite or a chemical were employed. The gizzard shad, a forage fish that has become excessive in some Texas reservoirs, can be eliminated by the precise application of selective chemicals released from low-flying helicopters (2). *Rotenone*, a chemical derived from the roots of an Asiatic legume, will kill fish at a concentration of only one part per million within minutes, at water temperatures of 70° F. Unfortunately, both dynamiting and massive poisoning with rotenone would be unselective, resulting in the indiscriminate death of many species. The chemical control agent known as *antimycin* kills carp more readily than it does most other fish and does not appear deleterious to invertebrates. In 1972 – 1973 the Wisconsin Department of Natural Resources made extensive use of antimycin in an attempt to reduce the carp population in the Rock River drainage system of southeastern Wisconsin. The project triggered a storm of controversy. Oppo-

9 – 45 *Fisheries biologists removing many pounds of carp from a New York lake by seining. The fish may be sold as food for eastern markets or converted into fertilizer.*

nents of the program believed that irreparable damage would be inflicted on the ecosystem and that certain rare species of fish might be eliminated along with the carp. Moreover, suppose that some fishermen came along some time later and dumped their surplus carp-bait minnows into a stream that had just been "decarped." With the aid of its tremendous reproductive capacities, the carp would soon be just as numerous as before the eradication project was launched. According to the opponents of the project, more acceptable methods would have been to keep the carp population down to reasonable levels either by trapping them on their spawning grounds or by periodic seining. Thousands of pounds of carp have been removed from certain shallow lakes in southern Minnesota and Wisconsin in a single day by these methods.

CONTROL OF OXYGEN DEPLETION IN WINTER. There are various methods of alleviating winterkill of fish from oxygen depletion. If the lake is small, the opaque snow blanket can be removed with snowplows to permit sunlight to penetrate to the aquatic vegetation. Parts of the frozen lake can be blasted with dynamite to expose surface waters to atmospheric oxygen. Oxygen can be introduced

9–46 *Aerating oxygen-depleted hypolimnion in late summer.*

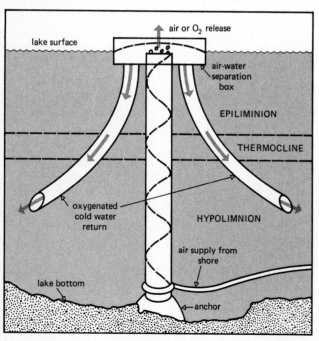

through ice borings by means of motorized aerators. However, such an operation would require several dozen aerators and would be prohibitively expensive, except on a small lake or under special situations where the improved fishing justified the investment. Finally, because winter depletion of oxygen is aggravated by the aerobic decomposition of aquatic vegetation on the lake bottom, removal of excess weedy growth in the littoral zone before the freeze-up might lessen the winterkill.

CONTROL OF OXYGEN DEPLETION IN SUMMER. Oxygen depletion, which frequently occurs during midsummer in the hypolimnion of thermally stratified lakes, can limit game fish distribution and abundance. For example, only 15 percent of the volume of a certain western lake was used by coho salmon during late summer, as a result of the combination of high surface temperatures and oxygen depletion in the hypolimnion. The introduction of compressed air into the hypolimnion aerated the water and made possible a much broader distribution of coho salmon in the lake. It also mixed the water, bringing nutrients from the hypolimnion up into the epilimnion. As a result, phytoplankton, and ultimately crustaceans and insect larvae, increased in numbers. With greater quantities of food available, the salmon biomass production of the lake was increased by 300 percent.

CONSTRUCTING FARM PONDS AND RESERVOIRS. Constructing farm ponds, artificial lakes, and reservoirs is the most effective means of providing adequate fishing opportunities for the burgeoning recreational needs of our nation's growing population. (See Figure 9–47.) The United States has more than 1,000 reservoirs of over 500 acres, embracing roughly ten million acres (2). The physical, chemical, and biological characteristics of many new impoundments are being scrutinized with respect to their potential as suitable fish habitat. It is expected that by the end of this century three million farm ponds with total area of 2.2 million acres will be contributing about 160 million pounds of fish to American dinner tables each year.

Natural and Artificial Selection of Superior Fish

For several years the Mississippi River has been heavily contaminated with pesticides borne by agricultural runoff waters. Surprisingly, several species

9 – 47 *Fishing on a 20-acre Georgia farm pond. A good program of pond management has provided excellent fishing. Watershed above pond is fully protected with cover.*

of fish in the Mississippi have developed some resistance to the potentially toxic pesticides. (This is reminiscent of the DDT resistance genetically acquired by houseflies and mosquitos.) It is supposed that the selection for resistance-contributing genes probably operates at the highly sensitive embryonic or larval stage. Fisheries biologists hope to accelerate this process. Scientists at the Federal Fish Genetics Laboratory at Beulah, Wyoming, are exploring the possibility of developing pesticide-resistant strains of trout by selective breeding experiments. (Of course, it must be emphasized that a far better strategy would be to prevent contamination of the aquatic ecosystem in the first place!)

Larger and higher-quality fish for stocking southern fishponds are being developed at the Federal Fish Farming Station at Stuttgart, Arkansas. A rapidly growing hybrid catfish has been produced by crossing a channel catfish with a blue catfish (9). Measurements taken in August after the second season of growth showed the hybrids to have a weight increment 32 percent greater than that of the blue catfish and 41 percent larger than the channel catfish. Fisheries geneticists in New York have successfully developed strains of trout which can survive in waters with a very low pH. It is hoped that

they can be used to stock Adirondack lakes where fish have disappeared due to acid rain. Such progress in the selective breeding of superior strains of fish should be encouraging news to the increasing numbers of people in the United States who rely on our fish resource as a source of food and recreation.

Rapid Review

1. Ecologists recognize three major lake zones: littoral, limnetic, and profundal.

2. The littoral zone is the shallow marginal region of a lake that is characterized by rooted vegetation.

3. The suspended, floating micro-organisms in a lake are known as *plankton.*

4. The limnetic zone is the region of open water beyond the littoral zone down to the maximum depth at which there is sufficient sunlight for photosynthesis.

5. In spring and autumn the lakes in the temperate zone undergo a thorough mixing that is known as the *spring* and *fall overturn.*

6. The *current* is the most important factor in determining the kinds of organisms present in streams.

7. A stream receives a considerable portion of its energy supply from materials like leaves and twigs that originate on land.

8. The distribution of the kinds of fish in a stream is correlated with changes in pH, temperature, and the velocity of current.

9. Roughly 70 percent of a given fish population dies each year.

10. Severe winterkills of fish caused by oxygen starvation occur in shallow lakes when snow cover prevents aquatic plants from getting sufficient sunlight for photosynthesis.

11. Summerkills caused by oxygen starvation may occur in the hypolimnion of thermally stratified lakes in late summer.

12. The salmon is an andromous fish—one that spends most of its life in the ocean; then, after becoming sexually mature, it swims up its native freshwater stream to spawn.

13. Some Columbia River salmon must negotiate a number of hazards, such as rushing cataracts, predators, fishermen, pollution (silt, heated water, radioactive materials, and chemicals) and big dams.

14. Fisheries management is the manipulation of fish populations and their environment to increase both sport and commercial fish harvests.

15. Techniques of fisheries management include restrictive laws, artificial propagation, introductions of both native and exotic species, habitat improvement (weed control, artificial spawning-site development, fertilization, predator control, removal of trash fish, control of oxygen depletion, and farm pond and reservoir construction), and the selective breeding of superior fish.

16. Predation by the sea lamprey caused the annual lake-trout harvest in the Great Lakes to drop from ten million pounds in 1940 to one-third million pounds in 1961—a 97 percent reduction in only 21 years.

17. Lamprey populations in the Great Lakes have been controlled by treating their spawning streams with the chemical Dowlap.

18. Carp populations have been brought under partial control, in some regions, by periodic seining and the use of selective chemicals such as antimycin.

19. Levels of dissolved oxygen in snow-covered northern lakes can be increased by snow removal, opening the ice cover with dynamite, and using motorized aerators.

20. By the year 2000 it is expected that almost three million farm ponds will be yielding 157 million pounds of fish annually.

21. Selective breeding has resulted in the development of superior strains of fish that have better sporting qualities and are more resistant to disease and pollution.

22. Fish habitat can be improved by such methods as weed control, spawning, site development, fertilization, predator control, removal of trash fish, farm pond construction, and the use of brush shelters.

Key Words and Phrases

Acid rain
Aeration
Algae bloom
Anadromous fish
Antimycin
Artificial propagation
Artificial selection
Biological control
Biological oxygen
    demand (BOD)
Biotic potential
Brown trout
Carp
Carrying capacity
Catadromous fish
Coho salmon
Detritus
Dowlap
Emergent vegetation
Environmental
    resistance
Epilimnion
Eutrophication
Exotic species
Farm ponds
Fisheries management
Fishing pressure
Habitat improvement
Hybrid fish
Hypolimnion
Introduction
Lake Erie
Lake renewal
Lake Temescal
Lake trout
Limnetic zone
Littoral zone

Longitudinal zonation
    (streams)
Mayfly
Native species
Natural selection
Nitrates
Nitrogen intoxication
Oxygen depletion
Phosphates
Phytoplankton
Plankton
Predator control
Profundal zone
Put-and-take stocking
Redd
Restrictive laws
Rotenone
Rough fish
Salmon migration
Sea lamprey
Smelt
Spawning sites
Spring overturn
Stagnation
Submergent vegetation
Summerkill
Sustained yield
Thermal stratification
Thermocline
Tilapia
Vibert Box
Walleye
Welland Canal
White amur
Winterkill
Zooplankton

Questions and Topics for Discussion

1. Describe the characteristic distribution of rooted plants in the littoral zone.
2. Identify three insects, three fish, and three birds that are characteristic of the littoral zone.
3. Suppose that the light intensity on the bottom of a lake is 10 percent of that at compensation depth. What percentage of full sunlight would that be?
4. Identify two sources of the dissolved oxygen present in a lake.
5. Give three reasons why oxygen might not be a limiting factor for fish in northern states during the winter season.
6. Describe the vertical temperature pattern of a northern lake in summer; in fall; in winter; in spring.
7. What causes the *fall turnover*? What causes the *spring turnover*?
8. Do the *fall* and *spring turnovers* have any significance for the survival of aquatic organisms? Explain your answer.
9. Suppose that a given lake has 100 black bass. If no reproduction occurred, how many bass would you expect the lake to have one year later?
10. What is the source of acid rain? What is its effect on fish?
11. What causes the *winterkill* of fish in northern lakes? How can it be prevented?
12. Describe three activities of carp that are harmful to game-fish populations.
13. Describe the life cycle of the Pacific salmon.
14. List six adverse environmental factors that may be encountered by Pacific salmon as they swim to their spawning grounds.
15. Discuss the pros and cons of artificial propagation.
16. Name three native fish that have been successfully introduced into new bodies of water in the United States.
17. How can stream habitat be improved for fish?
18. Discuss the statement: "Predator control is an effective method for increasing game-fish populations in the United States." Is it valid? Why or why not?
19. Describe the life cycle of the sea lamprey.
20. Human activities frequently have harmful effects on wildlife. Was this true in the case of the sea lamprey? Discuss your answer.
21. Describe efforts to control the sea lamprey in the Great Lakes.
22. Discuss four methods that might be used to prevent winterkills of fish in northern lakes.
23. If you were in charge of a selective breeding program to develop a "supersalmon," in what structural, physiological, and behavioral traits might you be interested?

Endnotes

1. Bennett, George W. *Management of Lakes and Ponds.* New York: Van Nostrand, 1971.
2. Bureau of Sports Fisheries and Wildlife. *Fifteen Years of Better Fishing.* Washington, DC: Fish and Wildlife Service, 1967.
3. Burton, G. W., and Odum, Eugene P. "The Distribution of Stream Fish in the Vicinity of Mountain Lake, Virginia." *Ecology,* **26**(1945), 182–193.
4. Eddy, Samuel, and Thaddeus Surber, *Northern Fishes.* Minneapolis: University of Minnesota, 1947.
5. Ember, Lois R. "Acid Pollutants: Hitchhikers Ride the Wind." *Chemical and Engineering News,* **59**(1981), 20–30.
6. Environmental Protection Agency. *Clean Lakes and Us.* Washington, DC: Government Printing Office, 1979.
7. ———. *Research Summary: Acid Rain.* Washington, DC: Government Printing Office, 1979.
8. "Exotic Fish Species Causing Increased Environmental Concern." *Ecology USA,* **9**(1980), 60–61.
9. Guidice, John J. "Growth of a Blue X Channel Catfish Hybrid as Compared to Its Parent Species." *Progressive Fish-Culturist,* **28**(1966), 142–145.
10. Hessler, Thomas J., John M. Neuhold, and William F. Sigler, "Effects of Alkyl-Benzene-Sulfonate on Rainbow Trout." *Bureau of Sport Fisheries and Wildlife Technical Paper.* Washington, DC: Government Printing Office, 1967.
11. King, Dennis R., and George S. Hunt. "Effect of Carp on Vegetation in a Lake Erie Marsh." *Journal of Wildlife Management,* **31**(1967), 18.
12. Kish, Tony. "Acid Precipitation: Crucial Questions Still Remain Unanswered." *Journal of Water Pollution Control Federation,* **53**(1981), 518–521.
13. Lagler, Karl. *Freshwater Fishery Biology.* Dubuque, Iowa: Brown, 1956.
14. Major, Richard L., and James L. Mighell. "Influence of Rockly Reach Dam and the Temperature of the Okanagen River on the Upstream Migration of Sockeye Salmon." *U.S. Fish and Wildlife Service Bulletin,* **66**(1947) 131–147.
15. Migel, J. Michael (ed.) *The Stream Conservation Handbook.* New York: Crown, 1974.

16. Milne, Lorus J., and Margery Milne. *The Balance of Nature.* New York: Knopf, 1961.

17. Odum, Eugene P. *Fundamentals of Ecology.* 3rd ed. Philadelphia: Saunders, 1971.

18. *Proceedings: Upper Midwest Trout Symposium I and II.* St. Paul: Agricultural Extension Service, University of Minnesota, 1978.

19. Smith, Robert L. *Ecology and Field Biology.* 3rd ed. New York: Harper, 1980.

Suggested Readings for the Interested Student

Clean Lakes and Us. Washington, DC: Government Printing Office. This is a nontechnical discussion of several lake-restoration projects.

Edmondson, W. T. "Fresh Water Pollution." In William W. Murdoch, ed. *Environment: Resources, Pollution and Society.* Sunderland, MA: Sinauer, 1975. This is a superb analysis of the causes and effects of eutrophication.

Edmondson, W. T. "Lake Washington." In Charles R. Goldman *et al.,* eds. *Environmental Quality and Water Development.* San Francisco: Freeman, 1973. An expert discusses how eutrophication was reversed in Seattle's Lake Washington.

Kish, Tony. "Acid Precipitation: Crucial Questions Still Remain Unanswered." *Journal of Water Pollution Control Federation,* **53** (1981), 518–521. This is a fine discussion of the causes and effects of acid rain, with regard to freshwater ecosystems.

Lee, G. Fred, et al. "Eutrophication of Water Bodies: Insights for an Age Old Problem." *Environmental Science and Technology,* **12** (1978), 900–908. This is an excellent discussion of the mechanism leading to eutrophication and of promising methods of control.

Smith, Robert L. *Ecology and Field Biology.* 3rd ed. New York: Harper, 1980. In Chapter 7, "Freshwater Ecosystems," there is a very fine description and analysis of lake ecosystems. There are excellent line drawings.

10 The Ocean– Our Last Frontier

Everyone is familiar with the feeling of fear that a storm-driven ocean can cause. In the context of human ecology, however, the ocean deserves our appreciation and gratitude as well as our respect. From Stone Age to Space Age it has served our needs:

1. By way of the hydrologic cycle its 31.7-million-cubic-mile volume represents a virtually limitless water supply for both humans and all other organisms, from bacteria to the whale.
2. For eons the teeming trillions of tiny algae in its sunlit waters have aided in replenishing the oxygen supply of the earth's atmosphere.
3. For millennia it has served as a highway for international transport.
4. Ever since primitive human beings scooped fish from its tidal pools with their bare hands, it has provided abundant supplies of essential protein. (See Figure 10-1.)

Let us now examine this unique ecosystem, so that we can develop some insight into the nature and interactions of its physical and organismal components; the source, possible effect, and control of its pollutants; and, finally, its significance as a food source for a malnourished world.

Major Features of the Marine Ecosystem

Some of the major ecological features of the oceanic environment follow:

10-1 *Protein from the sea. Nice catch of menhaden off Southport, North Carolina.*

259

1. It covers 70 percent of the earth's surface.
2. It extends to depths of up to 6.5 miles (Mariana Trench) and hence has a much greater vertical dimension, or "thickness," than the terrestrial or freshwater environment.
3. The ocean is about seventy times as salty as a lake or stream.*
4. The ocean is continuously circulating. (See Figure 10-3.) The Alaskan Current brings cold water down the Pacific coast; the Gulf Stream brings water upward along the Atlantic coast. These currents move water masses horizontally and modify the temperatures of nearby coastal regions. (As a result, New York City has a relatively moderate climate even in winter, whereas summer evenings in San Francisco may be quite

chilly.) There are also vertically moving currents. Upwelling, for example, brings nutrient-rich cold water from the ocean bottom to the surface.
5. The sea is relatively infertile compared to fresh water. Nitrates and phosphates are extremely scarce. Two exceptions to this are the areas of upwelling and the coastal areas, where tributary streams discharge massive loads of sediment (24).

* The ocean has an average salinity of 35 parts salts (by weight) per 1,000 parts water; in contrast, fresh water usually has a salinity of less than 0.5 part per 1,000 parts water.

The Zonation of the Ocean

The oceanic environment can be divided into five basic ecological regions, as indicated in Figure 10-4A. In the context of this book it will be necessary to describe only the *neritic, euphotic,* and *abyssal zones.*

10-2 *Composition of seawater.*

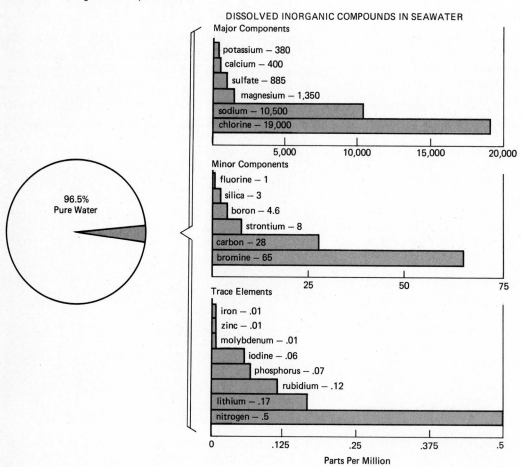

DISSOLVED INORGANIC COMPOUNDS IN SEAWATER

Major Components

potassium — 380
calcium — 400
sulfate — 885
magnesium — 1,350
sodium — 10,500
chlorine — 19,000

5,000   10,000   15,000   20,000

Minor Components

fluorine — 1
silica — 3
boron — 4.6
strontium — 8
carbon — 28
bromine — 65

25   50   75

Trace Elements

iron — .01
zinc — .01
molybdenum — .01
iodine — .06
phosphorus — .07
rubidium — .12
lithium — .17
nitrogen — .5

0   .125   .25   .375   .5

Parts Per Million

96.5% Pure Water

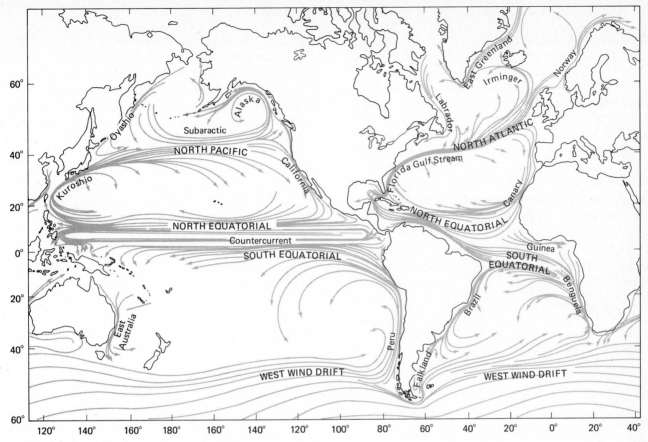

10-3 *Major ocean currents. Where flow lines are together, a strong current is indicated.*

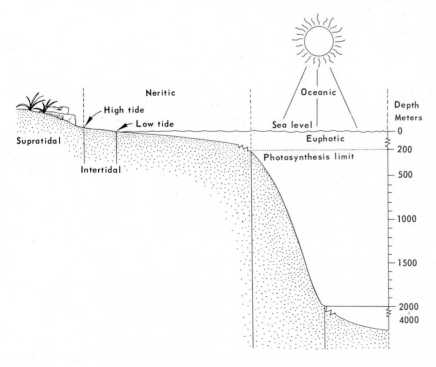

10-4A *Zonation of the marine ecosystem. The neritic, euphotic, and bathyal zones roughly correspond to the littoral, limnetic, and profundal zones of the lake ecosystem. Because of the high levels of dissolved nutrients and solar radiation, gross production, and hence plant and animal abundance and diversity, is greatest in the neritic zone.*

The Neritic Zone

The neritic zone is the marine counterpart of the littoral zone of a lake. It is a relatively warm, nutrient-rich shallow-water zone overlying the continental shelf. Occurring along our Atlantic, Pacific, and Gulf coasts, it has an average width of 10 to 200 miles and extends to depths of 200 to 600 feet. The neritic zone ends where the continental shelf abruptly terminates and the ocean bottom plunges to great depths. The fertility of the neritic zone is supplied primarily by upwelling and the sedimentary discharge of tributary streams. (The Missis-sippi River washes almost two million tons of nutrient-rich mud into the Gulf of Mexico daily.) Sunlight normally penetrates to the ocean bottom, thus permitting considerable photosynthetic activity and the presence of a vast population of anchored and floating plants. Animal populations are rich and varied. (See Figure 10–4B.) Oxygen depletion is not a problem because of photosynthetic activity and wave action. The total amount of biomass supported by the neritic zone is greater per unit volume of water than in any other part of the ocean.

10–4B *Communities occupying the neritic zone. Seaweeds and algae are the producers. They form the base of the food chain and webs. Tiny zooplankton feed on the producers and in turn are consumed by fish, lobsters, crabs, and whales. The top consumers are the sea birds, tuna, swordfish, and humans. The bottom dwellers, which cling to rocks or are buried in the mud, include clams, snails, crabs, and bacteria. These bottom dwellers feed on detritus. Note the arrows on the left indicating the upwelling of nutrients from the ocean bottom.*

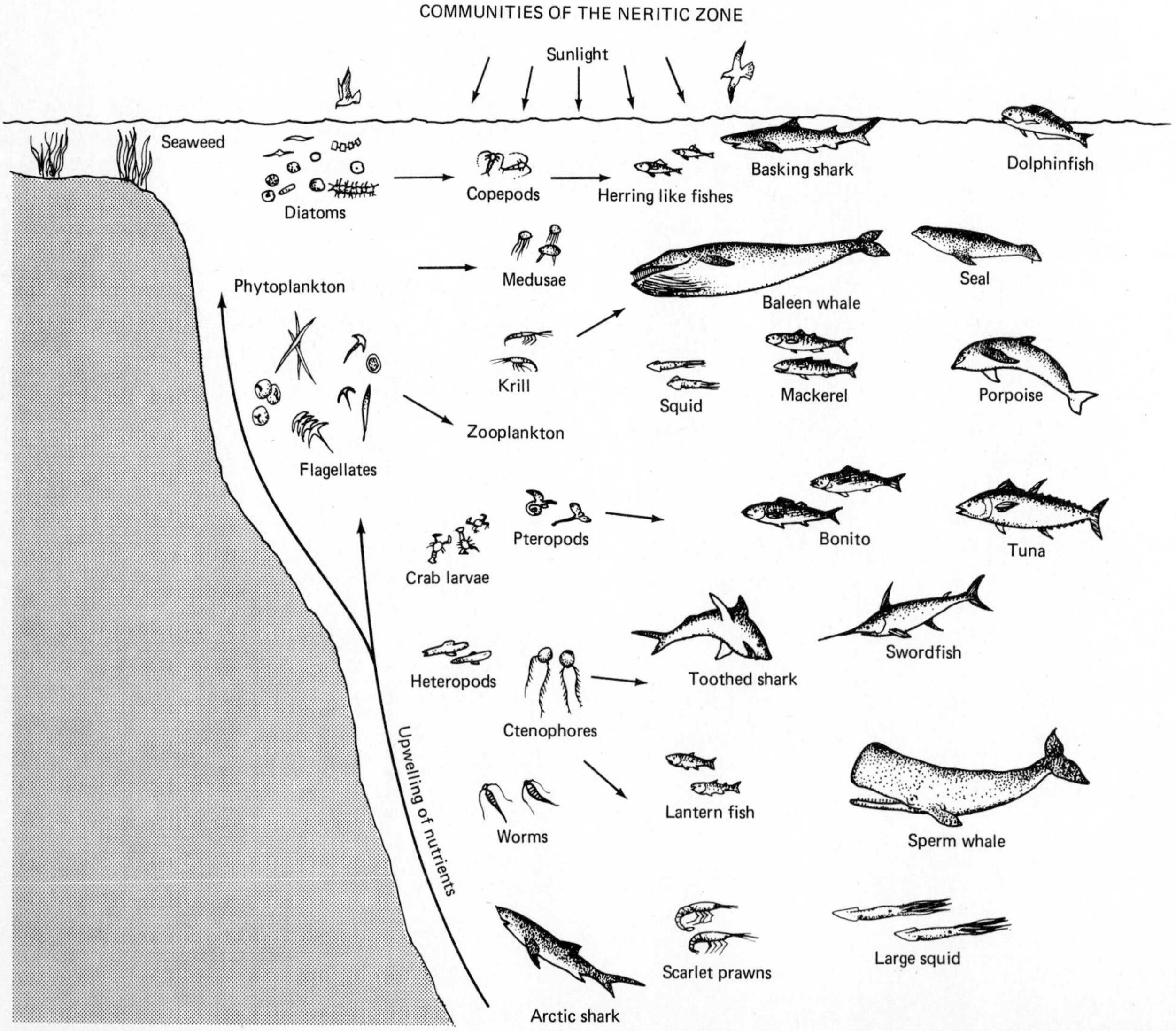

COMMUNITIES OF THE NERITIC ZONE

The Euphotic Zone

The euphotic zone is the open-water zone of the ocean, which corresponds to the limnetic zone of a lake. The term euphotic, which literally means "abundance of light," is appropriate to this zone, for it has sufficient sunlight to support photosynthesis and a considerable population of phytoplankton. In turn, the phytoplankton support a host of tiny "grazing" herbivores, such as the small crustaceans. The total energy made available to animal food chains by euphotic phytoplankton is much greater than that made available by plants of the neritic zone; this is largely because of the vast area of the euphotic zone, which extends for thousands of miles across the open sea. The degree to which light penetrates of course depends on the transparency of the surface waters. Because sunlight cannot penetrate deeper than 650 feet in most marine habitats, this is frequently considered the lower limit of the euphotic zone.

The Abyssal Zone

The abyssal zone is the cold, dark-water zone of the ocean depths that roughly corresponds to the profundal zone of the lake habitat. It lies immediately above the ocean floor. Animal life is rather sparse there. Any animal living in the abyssal zone must be highly specialized to adapt to the extreme conditions. It must adapt to darkness, to intense cold (because the abyssal water frequently approaches the freezing point), to greatly depleted levels of dissolved oxygen (because no photosynthesis can occur here), to water pressures over thousands of pounds per square inch, and to scarcity of food. There may be an abundance of nutrient-rich sediments on the ocean floor that may have come from the decaying bodies of marine organisms drifting down from the sunlit waters far above or that may have been derived from the excretions of animals living at upper oceanic levels. For example, in certain areas of the western Atlantic the concentration of phosphates at a depth of 3,000 feet may be ten times the concentration at 300 feet. Because neither phytoplankton nor herbivorous animals can exist in the abyssal zone, most consumers are either predators or scavengers. A number of the deep-sea fish of the abyss have evolved luminescent organs that may aid them in securing food and mates.

The Estuarine Ecosystem

Estuaries are transitional zones between coastal rivers and the sea. In one sense they represent a river-ocean "hybrid," in that they possess some of the characteristics of each ecosystem. Nevertheless,

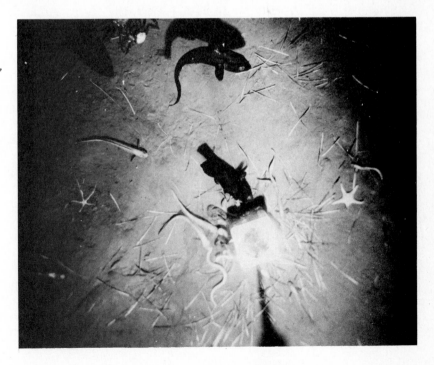

10–5 *Life in the abyss. Through the use of a camera developed by the Scripps Institute of Oceanography (La Jolla, California) of the University of California, pictures have revealed fish populations at least ten times greater than were thought to exist in deep water. In this photo, taken at a depth of 6,588 feet, a variety of fish are seen (grenadier, eel pout, hagfish) as well as tubeworms, starfish, and crabs. The bait can is 9.5 inches wide. (University of California)*

10-6 *Estuary of the San Joaquin River, California.*

the estuary has some distinctive properties in its own right and therefore must be considered a unique ecosystem.

Major Characteristics

1. The estuarine ecosystem contains brackish water, a mixture of freshwater flow from the stream and salt water from the ocean. The salinity of estuarine water is highly variable, changing by a factor of 10 within a 24-hour period, the salinity being higher when the tide comes in, lower when the tide moves out.
2. The water density is intermediate between that of fresh (1.00) and salt (1.03) water. The actual density, however, depends on the incoming and outgoing tides.
3. The water level rises and recedes in synchrony with the tides.
4. The concentration of dissolved oxygen is relatively high because of the shallow basin and the turbulence of the water.
5. The turbidity is characteristically high because of the stirring action of the tides. Phytoplankton populations, therefore, are limited because of the restricted penetration of sunlight.
6. The estuary is extremely rich in nutrients because the tides tend to concentrate those nutrients carried "down" to the estuary by stream flow and carried "up" from the ocean by the incoming tides. As W. B. Clapham states:

The mechanism of concentration is quite simple: particulate nutrient material enters the estuary at its upper end, is carried seaward by the falling tide, and so on for several cycles. The length of time it takes for a nutrient particle to traverse the estuary is substantially longer than it would be for it to traverse a similar length of even the most slowly flowing river. Thus, the estuary acts as a *nutrient trap*, with an average nutrient level significantly higher than either the river or the sea that it connects. In a like manner the concentration of nutrient and energy-rich organic material is very high. (3) *[Italics mine.]*

The accumulating load of nutrients can be channeled into the biomass of organisms in two ways: by nutrient absorption on the part of both phytoplankton and rooted vegetation, after the nutrients have been released from organic material by bacterial decomposition, and more importantly, by the inert organic material (decayed bodies of marsh grasses, crustaceans, worms, fishes, bacteria, and algae), known as *detritus*, being consumed directly by *detritus feeders*, such as clams, oysters, lobsters, and crabs.

7. Because of the extremely abundant supply of nutrients and the high oxygen levels (among other factors), the estuarine habitat is more productive than any other ecosystem known except the coral reef.
8. Sixty percent of the marine fish harvested by American fishermen spend part of their life cycle in the estuarine environment. Many marine species use the estuary as a "nursery" in which they spend the larval period immediately after hatching from the egg. Other species, such as the Pacific salmon, pass through estuaries twice during their stream-ocean-stream migration.

Harmful Effects Caused by Humans

In the last twenty years many of the original estuarine habitats along our coasts have either been destroyed outright or have been harmed by such human activities as dam construction, ocean dumping, or real-estate development. (See Figure 10-7.) Rezneat M. Darnell, an ecologist at Texas A&M, has described the dilemma facing an estuarine fish, the Atlantic croaker, a valuable game and food species, in "attempting" to complete its life cycle.

Through millions of years of evolution, the larval croaker has become exquisitely adapted to precise environmental cues of water temperature, salinity

10-7 *Earth satellite photo of Delaware Bay and the adjacent Atlantic coast. The light gray areas indicate sediment-polluted waters. The muddy waters of the Delaware River (center top) interact with clearer ocean water as the river enters the bay (center). A significant amount of sediment is maintained in suspension for several miles offshore along the Maryland-Delaware coast. Note also the great amount of sediment pollution in Chesapeake Bay (left). Satellite photos such as this can help assess topsoil erosion and changes in water quality caused by processes such as heavy rainfall, urbanization, and construction activities in coastal areas. Photo released June 7, 1973.*

gradients, water currents, and estuarine "odors" that trigger, direct, and regulate behavioral patterns. Those behavior patterns enable it to move from the shallow coastal waters, where it was hatched, into the estuary where it will feed and undergo its early development and then return to the ocean where it eventually will grow to sexual maturity. Of the many thousands of eggs hatched, under even the most favorable conditions, probably less than 1 percent would finally develop into mature fish. Over 99 percent of the hatch would have been destroyed as a result of some sort of environmental resistance, including disease, predation, toxic pollutants, and so on. In recent years, however, human activities have drastically modified the estuary — to the disadvantage of the croaker. Darnell writes:

The subtle odors of the natural estuarine water are now masked by a thousand exotic chemicals which have entered the stream through the activities of streamside farmers and manufacturers and by city sewage disposal plants. The tiny crustaceans upon which the fish normally feeds have been greatly reduced by pesticides. Food is . . . charged with exotic chemicals which . . . reduce the vitality of the little fish. With the journey thus slowed . . . vulnerability to predation is correspondingly increased. Furthermore, many of the marshes and mud flats no longer support the luxurious plant and bacterial growths upon which the fish used to feed; instead they are now surrounded by concrete walls and filled in for housing developments and boat marinas. From time to time the local power plant . . . releases "slugs" of hot water into the estuary. If not killed outright by the heated water, the fish is placed under great stress . . . [the heat] increases the fish's food and energy requirements at a time when it is killing the food supply. . . . Year after year, generation after generation, civilization adds burden upon load, stress upon strain, which, in total, poses a many-horned dilemma in the fish's struggle to survive. (7)

Marine Food Chains

Food Chains Based on Algae

Because the ocean covers 70 percent of the earth's surface, it obviously also receives 70 percent of the earth's solar energy. Except for the anchored green plants of the neritic zone, this solar energy is trapped primarily by the phytoplankton producers swarming in the open waters of the sea. It has been estimated that 19 billion tons of living plant matter (mostly phytoplankton) are produced annually, which in turn support five billion tons of zooplankton biomass. Marine zooplankton may be consumed by a variety of filter feeders, including shrimp, herring, anchovy, and blue whale. The terminal link of the marine food chain is represented by fish-eating predators such as the shark, barracuda, cod, and salmon. As in the case of terrestrial food chains, the shorter the chain, the more efficient the production of terminal-link biomass. Thus, the three-link food chain of phytoplankton-zooplankton-herring that occurs off the California coast is much more efficient in the production of human food than the six-link food chain of phytoplankton-zooplankton-shrimp-lance-small fish-cod that occurs off the Grand Banks of Newfoundland.

265

Chesapeake Bay: A Case Study of an Estuary

Chesapeake Bay is a long narrow arm of the Atlantic Ocean that reaches northward into Maryland and cuts the state into two parts. (See Figure 10–8.) It is more than 190 miles long, has 4300 square miles of water surface, and has a shoreline of more than 8000 miles. More than 150 rivers feed into it, including the Susquehanna, Potomac, Rappahannock, York, and James. The Bay has supplied an abundance of protein as well as shipping and recreational resources for Americans for almost two centuries. Stresses on this vast ecosystem are already formidable and will intensify in the near future. For example, by the year 2020 the Bay area population will be 40 percent greater, cargo transport will have doubled, recreational boating will have increased threefold, and fishing pressure on the Bay will have risen sharply (11).

The Bay is the largest producer of blue crabs in the world. It yields more oysters and soft-shelled clams than any other region in the United States. It provides wintering grounds for more than one-half-million Canada geese. Important food fishes, such as striped bass, white perch, and shad spawn in its tributaries. The Bay's annual fish harvest is worth more than $100 million — a valid reason for calling the Bay "one vast outdoor protein factory," as Baltimore's sage, H. L. Mencken did some years ago.

In 1976 the EPA was directed by Congress to conduct an intensive study of the Bay's resources and how they might best be managed. Listed in descending order of importance are major environmental-resource problems identified by the EPA: (1) decline in submerged aquatic vegetation (SAV), (2) eutrophication, (3) accumulation of toxic chemicals in food chains, (4) dredging, (5) closure of oyster beds, (6) decline of fisheries, (7) filling in and drainage of wetlands, (8) shoreline erosion, and (9) the effects of shipping and recreational boating on water quality (11). (See Figure 10–9.)

Let's look at a few of those problems.

Decline in Submerged Aquatic Vegetation (SAV)

Rooted bottom vegetation has multiple values: it provides food, shelter, and breeding habitat for shrimp, snails, clams, oysters, fish and waterfowl, and it reduces shoreline erosion and water turbidity by diminishing the force of waves. The seriousness of the decline in SAV is exemplified by one area of 241 hectares that was covered with SAV in 1953 but is now completely bare. Since the late 1960s the once abundant SAV has been reduced by 80 percent.

EPA scientists are trying to determine historical trends in SAV abundance by comparing aerial photos of years past with recent photos. Another method being employed is to take core samples from the bottom of the Bay and analyze them for seeds and pollen of SAV. In this way fluctuations in SAV abundance and distribution can be charted backward in time for several centuries. Increased turbidity and herbicide pollution may have contributed to the SAV decline. The major cause, however, appears to be eutrophication.

Eutrophication

Nutrients responsible for eutrophication of the Bay have their origin in farm runoff; in discharges from food-processing and sewage-treatment plants; in construction activity along the shoreline that causes the erosion of nutrient-containing organic matter; and in atmospheric fallout. The frequent algal blooms in the Bay ecosystem are, of course, a symptom of eutrophication. Fortunately, with appropriate attention to the reduction of nutrient

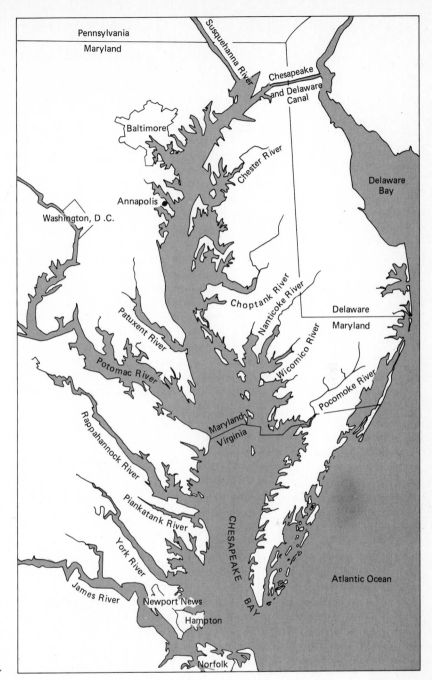

10-8 *Chesapeake Bay.*

10-9 *Major problem areas in Chesapeake Bay.*

Major Problem Areas			
Priorities			
high	submerged aquatic vegetation	eutrophication	toxics accumulation in the food chain
medium	dredging and dredged material disposal	shellfish bed closures	fisheries modification (biological resources)	hydrologic modification
low	wetlands alteration	shoreline erosion	water quality effects of boating and shipping

267

inflow, the problem probably can be controlled. For example, the construction of new sewage-treatment plants along the Potomac estuary in the 1970s has reduced phosphorus levels and the algal growths considerably (12).

Contamination of the Bay Food Web with Toxic Substances

The major stands of the Bay food web are shown in Figure 10–10. Poisonous chemicals which adversely affect this web are entering the Bay from multiple sources. Point sources include industrial discharges and accidental oil spills. Nonpoint sources include agricultural runoff, urban runoff, atmospheric fallout, and rainfall. Among the toxic substances are metals such as cadmium, chromium, copper, lead, nickel, and zinc. Most of the toxic substances persist in the environment for many years. During the feeding process, burrowing clams will nose their way through the bottom muds, where they take in considerable amounts of toxic materials. A mechanism is thus provided by which toxic chemicals enter human food chains. The contaminated clams may be eaten directly by humans, or by the ducks or fish that eat the clams and are in turn eaten by humans. The massive release of the toxic pesticide Kepone into the James River at Hopewell, Virginia, in 1975, was perhaps one of the most serious toxic insults suffered by the Bay ecosystem.

Toxic chemicals may be the cause of the drastic population decline of the striped bass in the Bay. By 1978 the population dropped to a 21-year low. U.S. Fish and Wildlife Scientists have found high levels of lead, zinc, arsenic, and selenium in young fish taken from the Potomac River. Moreover, the

10–10 *The food web of Chesapeake Bay.*

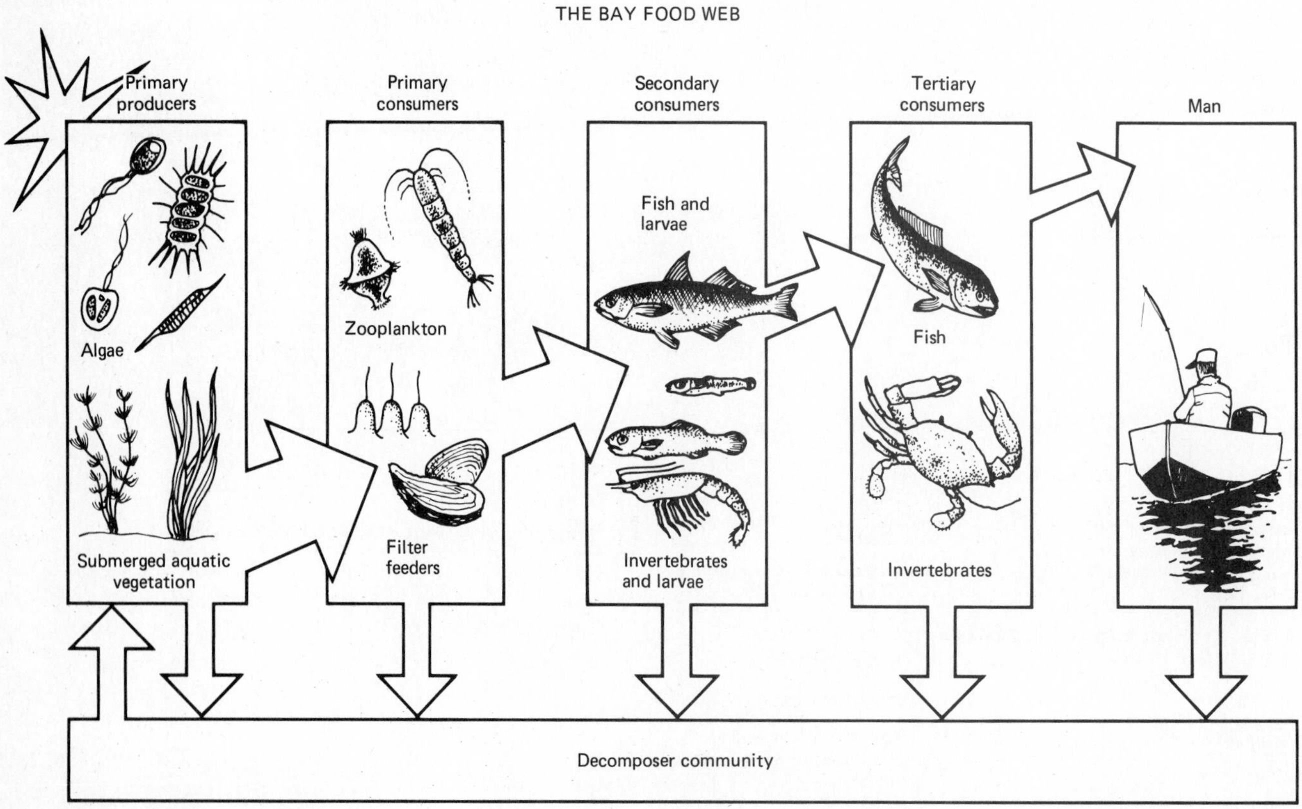

THE BAY FOOD WEB

backbones of these fish were 20 percent weaker than normal. As biochemist Paul Mehrle has stated: "A weakened backbone would certainly reduce the ability of striped bass to compete for food, avoid predators, or endure the stresses of migration and reproduction." Fish and Wildlife Service biologists believe that the toxic chemicals cause abnormal development of the backbone even before the fish are three months old. At present, the eggs and young of this fish, as well as bottom sediments in six tributaries of the Bay, are being intensively monitored to determine the kinds and concentrations of the toxic chemicals present (32).

Erosion and Sedimentation

The related forces of erosion and sedimentation are constantly reshaping the Bay for better or for worse. The EPA vividly describes this problem: "The speed at which these modifying processes progress is determined by a multitude of factors, including weather, currents, composition of the affected land, tides, winds, and human activities. The story of Sharp's Island, off the eastern shore of the Chesapeake, provides a telling example of the power and swiftness of erosion in the Bay area. In colonial times the island was a rich plantation of six hundred acres. Today, it is *completely submerged*, a victim of erosion. Sharp's Island disappeared so quickly that some longtime residents of the eastern shore can still remember seeing the white frame hotel that was situated on it" (12).

Historical trends in sedimentation rates are being determined with the aid of core samples taken from the bottom of the Bay. Sources of sedimentation are multiple and diverse. Bottom sediments are stirred up by the burrowing activities of clams, by water currents, and by storms. Hurricane Agnes in 1972 delivered 100 years of sediment to the Bay in only three days (12). Dredging operations, construction projects, and improper soil management by farmers have also contributed significantly to sediment loads. Such erosion-sedimentation problems are not restricted to Chesapeake Bay, but occur all along the Atlantic and Pacific coasts. Long shore drift redistributes sand into spits and forms barriers to the mouths of bays which cause navigational hazards. The construction of jetties — walls of stone and timber to reduce the erosive force of waves and currents — affords only a temporary abatement of the problem.

Food Chains Based on Rooted Plants

In the shallow waters of the neritic zone, anchored green plants convert much more solar energy into chemical energy than the phytoplankton. However, the efficiency of energy conversion for food chains based on the rooted vegetation is not very great. Thus, it has been estimated that 24 million tons of eelgrass *(Zostera)* off the Danish coast is the primary food source of *five million tons of waterfowl*. It is also the primary food source of one million tons of small herbivores that in turn would be eventually consumed by 11,000 tons of food fishes (halibut and cod), that in turn would be eaten by humans. Here, the ratio of eelgrass crop to the ultimate food crop of fish usable by humans is 2,400 to 1. Obviously this represents a high degree of wasted energy.

Pollution of the Ocean

In a very real sense, the ocean is our last frontier — *the last reasonably uncontaminated environment remaining on planet earth*. However, despite the multiple benefits derived from the ocean, it almost seems as though we are ready to abandon it — to write it off as expendable. In recent years we have been using it more and more extensively as the world's largest sewer; we dump into it the assorted garbage that unfortunately accumulates as a by-

269

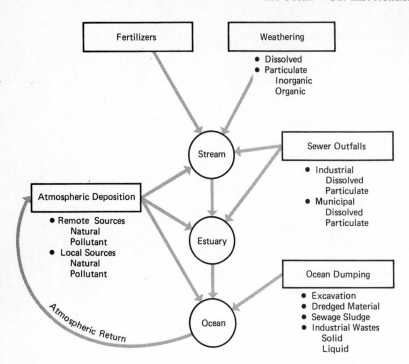

10-11 *Sources of chemicals discharged into the ocean.*

product of our technological and cultural "progress." (See Figure 10-11.) Into this last frontier we have discharged a bewildering variety of contaminants from raw human sewage to toxic industrial poisons, from household detergents to pesticides, from agricultural fertilizers to radioactive materials. Our chemical industry is developing thousands of new compounds yearly, many of which eventually find their way to the sea. Some of their effects are predictable; there are many others, however, that marine ecologists do not even pretend to understand.

Virtually every river on this planet carries a pollutant burden that eventually is washed into the ultimate oceanic sink. Pollutants such as pesticides, lead, acids, and radioactive materials also find their way into the sea as fallout from the air or as washings from the atmosphere by way of rain and snow. Such marine contamination is inadvertent. In addition, however, there is the regrettable deliberate dumping of waste into the ocean. Here we seem to be operating on the "out of sight, out of mind" philosophy.

Thor Heyerdahl is the celebrated Norwegian who sailed from Peru to the Polynesian Islands in a balsawood raft in 1947. He has written: "We treat the ocean as if we believed that it is not part of our own world, as if the blue water curved into space somewhere beyond the horizon and our pollutants would fall off the edge, as ships were believed to do before the days of Christopher Columbus . . . " (13).

Oil Pollution

While sailing through the Sargasso Sea some years ago, Heyerdahl was dismayed to find a melange of human-generated litter floating on the surface of the placid sea, hundreds of miles from land. As reported in *Time* magazine:

Almost every day, plastic bottles, squeeze tubes and other signs of industrial civilization floated by the expedition's leaky boat. What most appalled Heyerdahl were sheets of "pelagic particles." At first he assumed that his craft was in the wake of an oil tanker that had just cleaned its tanks. But on five occasions he ran into the same substances covering the water so thickly . . . that it was "unpleasant to dip our toothbrushes into the sea." . . . Oily and sometimes encrusted with barnacles, they smell like a combination of putrefying fish and raw sewage. (28)

SOURCE OF OIL POLLUTION. Oil has always reached the sea, even before humans inhabited this planet, by way of seepage through cracks and fissures in the ocean floor. But most of the oil contamination has been the result of human activities. In a very real sense we are now "pouring oil on troubled waters," the waters being the world's oceans, which

Source	Percent of Total Volume
Marine transportation	34
River runoff	26
Atmospheric rainout	10
Natural seeps	10
Municipalities	10
Industrial wastes	8
Offshore production	2

10 – 12 *Sources of oil in the oceans. Note that although offshore oil blowouts, such as occurred at Santa Barbara, are very dramatic and cause headlines, nevertheless only a small percentage of marine oil pollution comes from this source.*

are already severely "troubled" with thermal pollution, sewage, industrial waste, farm runoff, discarded military chemicals and explosives, radioactive wastes, pesticides, and lead fallout. Each year we contaminate the ocean with at least seven million tons (six billion kilograms) of oil. Not only does oil pollution have an adverse effect on ecosystems,

it represents a waste of a precious fuel and is expensive to clean up — roughly $28,000 for every 1,000 gallons spilled (21). This oil is coming from a number of sources (see Figure 10 – 12).

Oil-Tanker Accidents. Although oil-tanker accidents are the most dramatic source, they account for only 5 percent of the oil that enters the ocean (21). Tanker accidents are widely publicized by the press, radio, and TV. (See Figure 10 – 13.) In fact, it was the breakup of the *Torrey Canyon* off the British coast in 1968 (during which over 36 million gallons of oil were lost) that first alerted the general public to the problem. On December 21, 1976, the tanker *Argo Merchant* broke apart on the Nantucket Shoals, 24 miles off the coast of Massachusetts, and polluted the seas with 7.7 million gallons of heavy fuel oil. (See Figure 10 – 14.) On March 17, 1978, the world's most serious tanker spill occurred. The Council on Environmental Quality describes the episode: "The oil tanker *Amoco Cadiz* went aground two kilometers off Portsall on the . . . coast of France. Efforts to stop the spill or contain it were unsuccessful. The ship broke apart and high winds and seas made it impossible to transfer oil to other tankers, with the result that the entire cargo of 60 million gallons of crude oil was spilled, polluting the waters and shoreline along 124 miles of the coast and 37½ miles out to sea. . . ."

Roughly 80 percent of tanker accidents involve

10 – 13 *Major oil spills resulting from tanker accidents.*

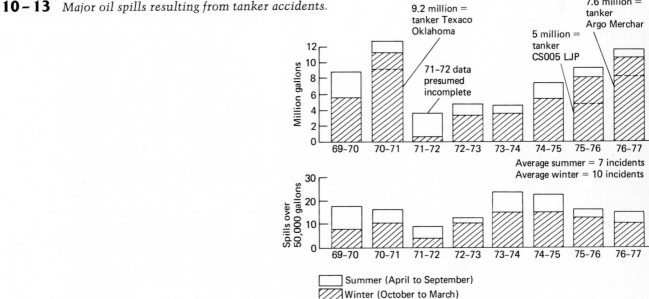

271

10 – 14 *Oil tanker breaks up. Aerial view of the ill-fated oil tanker* Argo Merchant, *which broke in two off Nantucket Island near Massachusetts on December 16, 1976. As a result of the accident, 7.7 million gallons of oil were released, more than half of the oil spilled in United States waters in 1976–77. This one spill released a greater volume than the combined spillage from 10,553 lesser incidents during 1976.*

vessels that are registered in nations such as Liberia and Panama, whose ocean shipping standards are lower than those of the United States, Japan, and other highly industrialized seafaring nations (46). This procedure is both convenient and profitable for the company that owns the tanker, for it does not have to keep its vessels shipshape, nor purchase expensive modern navigational instruments. Moreover, such companies do not have to employ well-trained crew members who would command relatively high union-scale wages. Of course, if the high rate of tanker accidents continues, those companies probably would be better off economically over the long run if they upgraded both their tankers and the caliber of their crews (33).

Offshore Oil-Well Accidents. In 1969 a major oil well off the coast of Santa Barbara, California, accidentally released many thousands of gallons of oil because of a faulty drilling technique. (See Figure 10 – 16.) However, the spill was a mere grease spot compared to the oil well blowout that occurred in June, 1979, in the Bay of Campeche off Mexico's east coast. The oil continued to escape into the sea for several *months.* It eventually even threatened marine life along the Texas shore, several hundred miles to the north. This source of marine pollution will certainly become more important in the future, for it has been estimated that in the 1980s something like 4,000 new offshore wells will be drilled worldwide every year. It is imperative that the offshore oil platforms be equipped with effective devices for oil pollution control. (See Figure 10 – 17.)

Disposal of Waste Crankcase Oil. Remember the last time you drove up to a service station and asked

10 – 15   MAJOR OIL SPILLS

Amoco Cadiz
60 million gallons
(coast of France, 1978)

Torrey Canyon
36 million gallons
(coast of Great Britain, 1967)

Argo Merchant
7.5 million gallons
(off Nantucket, Massachusetts, 1976)

Sealift Pacific
1.3 million gallons
(off Cook Inlet, Alaska, 1976)

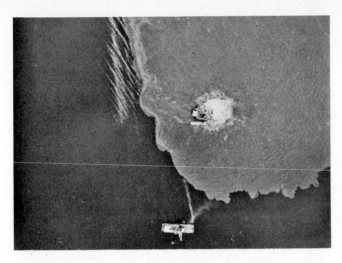

10-16 *Santa Barbara oil spill. A view from 1,800 feet, showing the spreading oil leak from the well at the bottom of Santa Barbara Channel, as made in February 1969. At the bottom of the photo is a barge that put down a pipe to the well in an effort to lessen the outpouring of oil from under the Union Oil Company rig (center). Thousands of gallons of oil covered the channel and floated to and polluted nearby shores before the leakage stopped.*

10-17 *Major safety devices and pollution controls on an offshore oil platform.*

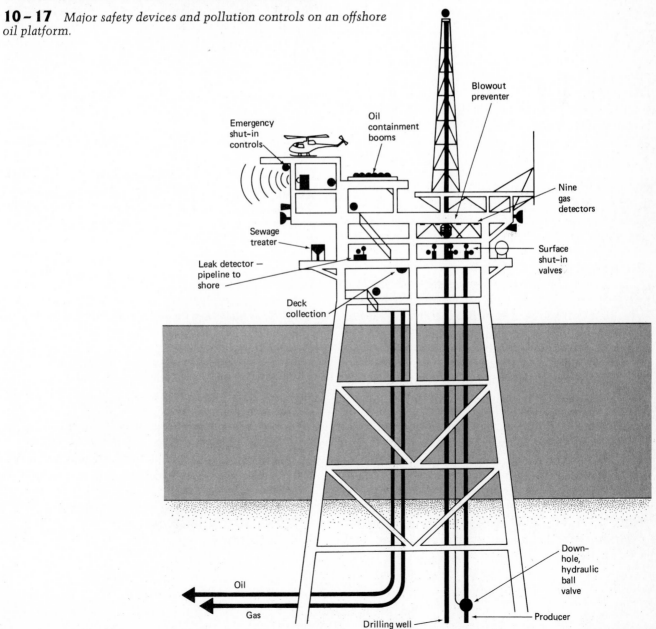

for an oil change? Did you ever wonder what happened to the old oil? Well, it is likely it was discharged into a river and eventually flowed to the sea. Now, two or three quarts of oil doesn't seem like such a big deal. But how about *billions* of quarts? In fact, millions of motorists throughout the world are indirectly responsible for a much greater volume of oil pollution of the oceans than is caused by the more spectacular tanker breakups and oil-well blowouts.

Airborne Hydrocarbons from Factories, Service Stations, and Vehicles. Maybe you fill up at a self-service pump. If so, you are well aware of the pungent odor of evaporating gasoline. Obviously not all of the gasoline went into your tank. Much of it escapes into the air. Much unburned gas similarly escapes from your exhaust pipe and becomes airborne. Such evaporation of petroleum also occurs at thousands of industrial plants throughout the world. The net result was contamination of the oceans with at least twenty million metric tones of airborne petroleum hydrocarbons annually during the 1980s. This represents roughly 80 percent of the total oil pollution of the marine environment caused by humans (20).

ADVERSE EFFECTS OF OIL POLLUTION. Just how a given oil spill will affect marine life is exceedingly difficult to predict. The reason is that effects depend on a number of highly variable factors such as the amount and type of oil (crude or refined), nearness to the organisms, season of the year, weather, ocean currents, and wind velocity.

Reduction of Photosynthetic Rates. Because a heavy oil slick is opaque, it effectively blocks sunlight penetration. Photosynthetic activities of the marine algae below the oil barrier are sharply reduced, if not arrested completely. Such diminished rates of food production restrict the growth and reproduction of all organisms directly or indirectly dependent on those marine algae for food.

Concentration of Chlorinated Hydrocarbons. An oil spill may greatly increase the concentration of chlorinated hydrocarbons, such as the pesticides DDT, dieldrin, and toxaphene and the PCBs. The reason is that those compounds are highly soluble in oil. In fact their concentration in the oil slick may be many times their concentration in the surrounding water. As a result, such marine organisms as phytoplankton, as well as animals such as crustaceans and larval fishes, which make vertical migrations to the

sea surface at night, would be adversely affected. Even if those organisms are not killed directly, their physiology, growth, reproduction, and behavior may be impaired. (See Chapter 14 for more details.)

Mortality of Marine Animals. The heaviest influx of oil occurs in the neritic zone, near the continental margins — the zone where virtually all of our shellfish (oysters, lobsters, and shrimp) and over half of our commercial fish crop are produced. Scientists at the Woods Hole Oceanographic Institution in Massachusetts made a study of the effects of 700 tons of number 2 fuel oil released from an oil barge that was grounded in Buzzards Bay, off West Falmouth, Massachusetts, in 1969. They report:

Massive, immediate destruction of marine life occurred offshore during the first few days after the accident. Affected were a wide range of fish, shellfish, worms, crabs, other crustaceans, and invertebrates. Bottom-living fish and lobsters were killed and washed up on the shores. Trawls made in ten feet of water soon after the spill showed that 95 percent of the animals recovered were dead and others were dying. The bottom sediments contained many dead snails, clams, and crustaceans. (2)

Damage to marine life was still being detected in 1979, ten years after the spill.

In a single winter more than 250,000 murres, eiders, and puffins died off the Newfoundland coast because of oil pollution. Many thousands were destroyed by the Santa Barbara spill. (See Figure 10–18.) The number of seabirds annually killed

10–18 *A dead, oil-soaked bird—one of the many victims of the oil leak in Santa Barbara Channel in January–February 1969. The leak started several miles offshore, at the site of the Union Oil Company's drilling rig.*

worldwide by oil is enormous. The insulative function of the bird's feathers is lost when they become soaked with oil. (See Figure 10–19.) As a result, the body temperature drops. The matted feathers prevent the birds from swimming, diving, or flying to search for food. The ultimate result is death from accelerated starvation.

Food-Chain Contamination with Carcinogens. Crude oil is not just a single compound but a complex mixture of dozens of different hydrocarbons, such as benzopyrene, an acknowledged cancer-inducing chemical, or carcinogen. Unfortunately, the carcinogenic components of crude oil resist decomposition and hence persist in the marine environment long after more harmless components have been broken down. Body-tissue analysis of sea cucumbers ("pickle-like" relatives of the starfish that live on the ocean floor) indicates substantially higher concentrations than in the surrounding ocean waters. Although it is not as yet definitely established, it is possible that these carcinogens may also be concentrated in marine organisms consumed by humans, such a shrimp, lobsters, and fish. The implications are not pleasant to contemplate.

The Disruption of Chemical Communication in Marine Animals. Several of the hydrocarbons in crude oil mimic certain chemicals used by marine animals as cues in guiding them during such activities as mating, feeding, homing, and migrating. For example, the males of some species may find a suitable female with which to mate by following a scent trail emitted from the female's body. Such chemical stimuli may also aid in food location. For example, certain chemicals in concentrations of only a *few parts per billion* may attract the predatory starfish to its oyster prey (16). Under laboratory conditions it has been shown that, at extremely low concentrations — parts per billion — kerosene is very attractive to lobsters. Therefore, possible effects of kerosene in the marine environment might be not only to draw lobsters away from their natural food sources but, even worse, to attract them to an oil spill where they could become grossly contaminated. It is apparent that the flooding of the oceanic environment with pseudosignals as a result of oil spills might greatly derange the marine animal's behavior patterns, causing it to expend valuable energy in nonadaptive pursuits. The eventual decline in vitality and numbers of the species would seem assured.

10–19 *"Operation Pelican Wash." Coast Guardsmen bathe one of some 500 pelicans that were coated with oil in the aftermath of the Ocean Eagle wreck off Puerto Rico. The pelicans were washed with an oil-dissolving solution. Unfortunately, the percentage of birds actually saved by these heroic measures was small.*

Harmful Effects from Long Exposure to Low Levels of Oil. Even "captive" scientists working for oil companies will admit that a massive oil spill will cause heavy mortality in marine organisms. The big question, however, is this: "Will *low* levels of oil contamination have any harmful effect on marine organisms that are exposed over *long periods of time*?" Until recently a definite answer to this question was unavailable. In 1980, however, scientists with the National Oceanic and Atmospheric Administration reported on an intensive and highly authoritative five-year study conducted in Puget Sound that indicates that such long-term exposure can indeed be highly destructive to marine life. Some of the results of their studies follow:

1. It is likely that oil interacts with several hundred other substances in the marine environment and that the combined effects may be more severe than that of the oil alone.

275

2. The feeding behavior of shrimp was adversely effected by exposures of only 15 parts per *billion* of a water-soluble fraction of Alaskan oil.

3. The eggs of several species of flatfish (sole, flounder, and halibut), which float on the ocean surface, either did not hatch at all or had highly abnormal development when exposed to Alaskan crude oil.

4. Upstream migration of salmon past a dam was completely blocked by hydrocarbon concentrations of only 203 parts per million.

5. Petroleum undergoes a considerable degree of biological magnification in flatfish. The concentrated hydrocarbons may then be converted to toxic substances that are stored in the liver and skin. Eight types of liver abnormalities were found in fish. The question naturally arises: Suppose those fish were consumed by humans — would human health suffer? (36)

Control of Oil Pollution

Let us examine some methods by which the oil pollution problem might be brought under reasonable control.

International Regulations. The world's energy demands will increase sharply in the foreseeable future. Much of this energy will be derived from oil that will be shipped via supertankers with up to 400,000-ton capacities. Some of these giant tankers are much larger than the luxury passenger liner *Queen Elizabeth II*, being over one-quarter-mile long and fully as wide as a football field (21). It would seem, therefore, that the potential of oceanic oil pollution will become greater than it has been in the past. Because the routes of oil-bearing tankers belonging to several dozen different nations intersect on the global seas, it is unrealistic to assume that the individual nations involved will develop a strong sense of responsibility to prevent further oil spillage. The reasoning goes something like this: because the ocean belongs to *all* nations, it belongs to no single nation in particular; therefore, no single nation has a well-defined responsibility to prevent marine pollution. Perhaps reasonable regulations have to be formulated and enforced by an international body such as the United Nations. A nation whose tankers were guilty of flagrant violations would be subject to censure and possible economic sanctions.

Fingerprinting. The EPA's research laboratory at Athens, Georgia, is perfecting techniques by which a given oil sample can be identified by its *"fingerprints."* The distinctive fingerprints are recorded with the aid of a sophisticated instrument known as a gas-liqiuid chromatograph. By means of this technique investigators who are trying to locate the source of an oil slick can determine with certainty whether the oil had its source in a natural oil seep, a particular pipeline, a certain offshore oil well, or a tanker transporting oil from, say, Kuwait or Alaska. Once the source is identified, appropriate legal action can be taken against the parties responsible for the spill (10).

Oil-Pollution-Abatement Techniques. International regulatory authority would serve only to keep the number of spills down to a minimum. Once a spill actually occurred, the volatile component would rapidly evaporate, causing a 25 percent volume reduction within a few days. After several months bacterial decomposition would degrade the oil to a point where only 15 percent of the original volume was left — most of it in the form of black balls of tar.

Such natural processes of oil reduction, however, must be supplemented by control methods devised by human beings. Techniques that were employed after the breakup of the 200,000-ton oil tanker *Torrey Canyon* off the British coast in 1968 included (1) soaking up the oil with straw (see Figure 10–20), (2) absorbing it with powdered chalk, (3) burning it, and (4) emulsifying it with the aid of detergents. The French were moderately successful in attempting to abate the oil problem with powdered chalk. Once absorbed by the chalk, some of the oil gradually sank to the ocean bottom. The British tried to burn the oil after applying aviation gasoline delivered by helicopter. When this proved ineffective, they scattered detergent in order to *emulsify* the oil, to break the huge globules into smaller ones so that a larger surface area would be exposed to bacterial action and thus hasten decomposition. Although the idea was theoretically sound, the results were disappointing. Moreover, the "cure was worse than the disease," in terms of the harmful effects on marine organisms (50).

Decomposition of Oil by Bacteria. In the spring of 1973 two Israeli scientists developed a technique whereby bacteria are used to break down the oil in the ballast water that is used to fill tankers after the oil has been removed at some port facility. This ballast water later is discharged when the tanker is ready to receive another load of oil. Theoretically,

10–20 *Spreading chopped straw to contain the oil spill at Santa Barbara, February 7, 1969.*

10–21 *Beach cleanup after the Santa Barbara oil spill, February 7, 1969.*

Sludge Dumping in the New York Bight

In their book *Water Pollution,* Julian McCaull and Janice Crossland describe the intensive studies of the effects of waste dumping conducted by M. Grant Gross in the waters of the New York Bight, a relatively shallow area over the continental shelf opposite New York Bay. This region has been used as a dumping ground for fly ash, dredging wastes, and sewage sludge for many years. In 1970, over 1.8 billion gallons of sewage sludge from the New York metropolitan area spewed through 130 discharge pipes directly into the Bight. Most regrettably, more than 16 percent of this sewage received no treatment whatsoever. Moreover, raw sewage generated by 23 New Jersey towns entered the Bight through pipes extending 1,000 feet into the ocean. On the basis of the wastes disposed in the Bight during the period from 1964 to 1968, Gross estimated that at least 100,000 metric tons of oxidizable carbon were introduced to the ocean every year. He considered this vast amount of carbon to have 19 times more oxygen demand than all the dead organisms in the study area for the same time period. The high BOD would be especially serious in the New York Bight because it is relatively shallow except for the Hudson Canyon, which has been carved from the ocean bottom by the water flow from the Hudson River. An extremely distressing aspect of the problem is the *mobility* of the waste once it has been dumped. Thus, the sewage sludge dispersed northward a considerable distance from the dumping point until it covered an area of 14 square miles. The Sandy Hook Marine Laboratory in New Jersey found that this dumpage had serious adverse effects on marine life. The oxygen concentration in waters above the sludge-dumping site was frequently lower than two parts per million in late summer. Small marine plankton, such as algae, protozoans, and crustaceans, showed sharply reduced populations or were completely absent. Adult crabs removed from the study area were either very sick or dead (20).

McCaull and Crossland report on the detrimental effects of the sludge on marine fish:

Flounder and ling (bottom-dwelling fish) caught in the vicinity of the sewage sludge disposal area had been feeding on smaller bottom organisms. Stomach analysis showed that the fish also had taken in hair, bandaids, seeds, and cigarette filters from the sludge. Some flounders had black gills, a condition that was reproduced experimentally in healthy fish kept in aquaria with sludge. Levels of nickel, chromium, and lead in several fish exceeded amounts considered normal for marine animals — possibly an indication that metals from the dumping sites had been concentrated in the fish through the food chain. . . . (20)

There are other problems. For example, federal scientists detected a high rate of *chromosome damage* in mackerel eggs taken from sludge dump sites. Under the 1972 Marine Protection, Research and Sanctuaries Act, the EPA is charged "with the regulation of ocean dumping to protect human health and the marine environment" (9). The most severe enforcement action under the act occurred in 1978 when the city of Philadelphia was fined $225,000 for committing 32 violations of its annual permit.

By congressional mandate all ocean dumping was halted on December 31, 1981. As a result, alternative disposal programs had to be started. For example, New York City is now barging its daily sewage sludge production of 300 tons to Ward Island off Long Island Sound. Philadelphia, on the other hand, is trucking most of the 65,000 tons of sludge it generates each year to southwestern Pennsylvania. Here it is applied to strip-mined land so that vegetation can be established.

278

In late 1980, to the surprise and dismay of many antiocean dumping advocates, a National Advisory Committee, appointed by President Reagan, criticized the EPA and Congress' strict regulation of ocean dumping as "highly irrational." According to the committee the oceans "have assimilative capacity to take organic- and metal-rich wastes and we should be using that. We are not calling for a return to wholesale dumping. We are calling for careful consideration of what can be placed in the ocean and where" (26). Apparently, the ocean dumping issue has not been "disposed of" and will be the subject of considerable controversy in the years ahead.

an oil slick could be "seeded" by helicopter with the bacterial powder, thus accelerating the rate of decomposition and ultimate oil-slick breakup. In the process of breaking down the oil, the bacterial population multiplies rapidly to the point where it can be used as protein feed for livestock. The Israeli scientists estimate that 300 tons of animal food could be obtained by processing ballast water from a 200,000-ton tanker.

Biological Monitors: "Oyster Watch." Oysters and other shellfish have the capability of storing and concentrating petroleum hydrocarbons in their tissues even though the levels in seawater are exceedingly low. As a result, these organisms can be used as *living monitors* of oil pollution in a given coastal region. At the present time the Scripps Oceanographic Institute at La Jolla, California, is coordinating just such a monitoring program, "Oyster Watch," which involves one-hundred stations distributed along the Pacific, Gulf and Atlantic coasts. The program has received considerable attention and acclaim from the international scientific community (10).

Fisheries Decline from Overfishing

Pacific Sardine Fishery

The sea is the world's biggest commons — a public area over which no single nation has sovereignty. The tragedy of such a commons, however, as pointed out by Garett Hardin of the University of California – Santa Barbara, is that its resources are ruthlessly plundered. After all, with no restrictions on the "take," it would seem foolish and downright naive for a country bordering the ocean not to "get what it can while the getting is good." This sort of

attitude has dominated the fishing industries of seaboard nations for years. As a result, many fishing stocks have become severely depleted.

A classic example of the collapse of a once major fishery caused by intense human predation is that of the Pacific sardine (*Sardinops caerulea*). (See Figure 10–22.) The sardine story is aptly described by ecologist Robert Leo Smith.

10–22 *Pacific sardine catch, 1916–1963.*

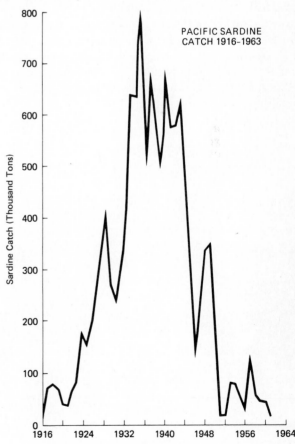

279

The Pacific Coast sardine industry had its beginnings back in 1915 and reached its peak in 1936–1937 when the fishing netted 800,000 tons. It was first in the nation in number of pounds of fish caught, and ranked third in the commercial fishing industry, grossing $10 million annually. The fish went into canned sardines, fish bait, dog food, oil, and fertilizer. The prosperity of the industry was supported by overexploitation. The declines in the catch per boat and success per unit of fishing were compensated for by adding more boats to the fleet. The fishing industry rejected all forms of regulation. In 1947–1948 the Washington-Oregon fishery failed. Then, in 1951, the San Francisco fleet returned with only eighty tons. The fishery closed down and has never recovered. . . . " (30)

Collapse of Other Fisheries

Unfortunately, the sardine fishery is only one among many that have been going downhill in the past few years. Others include the Barents Sea cod, the Peruvian anchovy, the Atlantic herring, and the Pacific salmon. It is highly probable that unless future harvests are made on a sound biological basis, the same fate awaits such highly palatable species as the yellow-finned tuna, haddock, Bering Sea flatfish, British Columbia herring, and the Newfoundland cod (30). (See Figure 10–23.) In the early 1960s the fisheries located between the Hudson Canyon (just opposite the mouth of the Hudson River) and the Nova Scotia Shelf yielded over one million tons of fish. However, the harvest from this region has declined steadily ever since (35).

Marine-Fisheries Management

The following phase of marine-fisheries management will now be briefly described in the following paragraphs.

INTRODUCTIONS.   One aspect of marine-fisheries management is the introduction of food and game fishes into new suitable areas for the purpose of establishing or improving the commercial or sport-fishing resource. Such introductions began in the late nineteenth century and are continuing today. The commercially profitable striped-bass (*Roccus saxatilis*) industry that prevails along the Pacific coast (from Washington to southern California) and the Atlantic coast is a notable result of introductions. This species was originally distributed along the Atlantic coast from northern Florida to the Gulf of Saint Lawrence. However, in 1879 and 1882 a total of 432 individuals were planted off the California coast near San Francisco (21). Responding to a suitable physical and biotic environment, with abundant food and satisfactory breeding areas, the striped-bass population increased so rapidly that commercial harvesting was possible in fewer than ten years. The striped bass has provided millions of pounds of seafood to commercial fisheries as well as recreation for Pacific coast anglers (5).

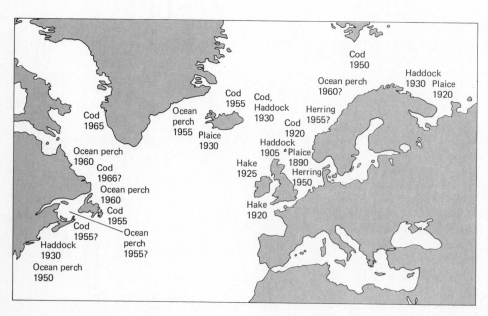

10–23 *Overfishing in the North Atlantic. The exhausted stocks of plaice (flatfish) in the North Sea became obvious in 1880. Since that time stocks of many other species have become severely depleted. Note the decline of cod, ocean perch, and haddock off Labrador and Newfoundland.*

CONSTRUCTION OF ARTIFICIAL REEFS. Considerable interest has been shown recently by marine-fisheries biologists in the potential of artificial reefs in providing food and cover for game and commercial species. Artificial reefs are especially functional in raising the carrying capacity of otherwise flat, sandy coastal plains. Venice Pier in Los Angeles County is surrounded by artificial reefs constructed for the benefit of salt-water anglers. A reef composed of large boulders and building rubble was started in 70 feet of water off Fire Island, New York. When three years old, it was already frequented by large numbers of sea bass, hake, and flounder. The Sandy Hook Marine Laboratory has constructed an artificial reef of sixteen junk automobile bodies sunk to a depth of 55 feet, two miles of Monmouth Beach, New Jersey. Monthly observations by scuba divers have revealed its attraction for sea bass, flounder, and mackerel. The presence of a number of juvenile fishes generated speculation that such reefs may eventually function as nursery habitats.

Marine scientists at the State University of New York at Stony Brook have constructed a reef from blocks of compacted sludge and fly ash waste — materials that form a major disposal problem for coal-fired power plants. In 1980 the researchers formed a 500-ton reef by dumping 18,000 of those blocks in the Atlantic Ocean, 2.5 miles south of Saltaire, Long Island. It is hoped that such reef construction will enhance sport and commercial fishing in an area of high human-population density. It should also serve to help solve an increasingly serious waste-disposal problem experienced by power-plant operators as they switch from oil to coal. This problem is especially acute on Long Island because of the scarcity of land disposal sites.

MAN-CAUSED UPWELLING. Upwelling and the resultant mineral enrichment of the important euphotic zone can be induced by artificial methods in the opinion of some authorities. It has been suggested, for example, that compressed air bubbling through perforated pipes laid on the ocean bottom enhances the vertical movement of water sufficiently to fertilize relatively shallow regions of the ocean. If the ocean bottom between Cuba and Florida cold be adequately roughened (possibly by dumping gravel, rubble, or junk), the resultant turbulence generated by the Gulf Stream might ultimately be carried into the Atlantic off the southeast

Florida coast and increase fish harvests. Oceanographic experts from the National Academy of Science are of the opinion that nuclear reactors placed on the ocean bottom in areas of deep-lying stagnant waters might produce sufficient heat to cause bottom waters to rise and bring dissolved minerals to upper levels, where they might be utilized by phytoplankton and ultimately by fishes.

REGULATION OF FISHING PRESSURE. In an attempt to appreciate the various positive and negative factors that determine the optimal yield of a fish stock during given year, it would be helpful to express the pertinent relationships in the form of an equation:

$$S_2 = S_1 + (A + G) - (C + M)$$

S_1 is the harvestable stock at the beginning of the fishing year. In commercial fisheries it would represent the fish large enough to be taken by certain trawls and nets; they would be too large to slip through the meshes of the nets. In the context of sport fishing we might consider all legal-sized fish as S_1. The weight of harvestable stock at the termination of the fishing year is signified by S_2. A represents the *addition of young fish to the harvestable stock as a result of the growth* during the year. G represents the *weight increase during the year* as a result of the growth of A (after entering the harvestable stock) and S_1. C is the *total weight of fish harvested during the year*. M represents the *weight of catchable stock that died as a result of all causes* (both physical and biotic), *except those associated with fishing*. A obviously depends to some degree on food conditions spawning success, and population density; G depends on the abundance of food and suitable temperatures; C, of course, is variable, depending on fishing pressure and the nature of fishing regulations; and M is based on such factors of environmental resistance as parasites, competitors, disease organisms, predators, pollution, oxygen depletion, adverse winds, and thermal changes. An important point to remember in terms of optimal fishing pressure is that *young fish are more efficient in converting food to biomass than older fish*. Fishing pressure on an old, slow-growing stock may be beneficial up to a critical point — beyond which the stock will be overfished — to permit younger age classes to become established (13). The optimal

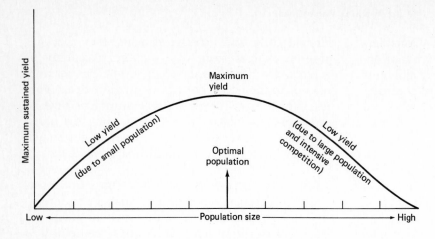

10–24 *The dynamics of maximum sustained yield of marine fishes.*

10–25 *In 1977 the United States extended its territorial limits from 3–12 miles to 200 miles. This reduced much of the area of the international fishing "commons" and enabled American fishermen to boost their harvests.*

population size for maximum sustained yield is shown in Figure 10–24.

In summary, for optimal sustained fishing harvests, fisheries biologists must establish regulations that tend to ensure the most effective fishing pressure (or rates). To this end, restrictions might be made on type of gear, seasons, regions, fish size, and even the number of fisheries.

ESTABLISHMENT OF THE 200-MILE FISHING ZONE. One important result of the recent United Nations Conference on the Law of the Sea, was the agreement that each nation would have economic jurisdiction over a 200-mile belt of sea space bordering its coasts. (See Figure 10–25.) Each such area has been termed an Extended Economic Zone, or EEZ. It is estimated that 95 percent of the world's living marine resources are contained within these EEZs. Certainly maritime nations all over the world now have a much stronger incentive to manage their marine resources on a long-term sustained-yield basis. The establishment of the 200-mile zone should be especially welcome to an underdeveloped nation like Indonesia, which derives more than 70 percent of its animal protein from its coastal waters (1). (See John E. Bardach's guest article on world fisheries in this chapter concerning the significance of the EEZs.)

Prior to the formation of the EEZs, the far-flung fishing fleets of foreign nations such as Japan and the USSR would aggressively compete with American fishers for limited stocks of salmon, haddock, and cod only 12 miles or so from the American coast. (See Figure 10–26.) Today, however, for-

10–26 *Foreign fishing vessels off southern New England and the Georges Bank, September 1969. In the 1960s and early 1970s these waters were invaded by a large number of Russian and other European vessels that competed intensively with American boats for the available fish stocks. The establishment of the 200-mile zone (EEZ) has substantially reduced this foreign competition.*

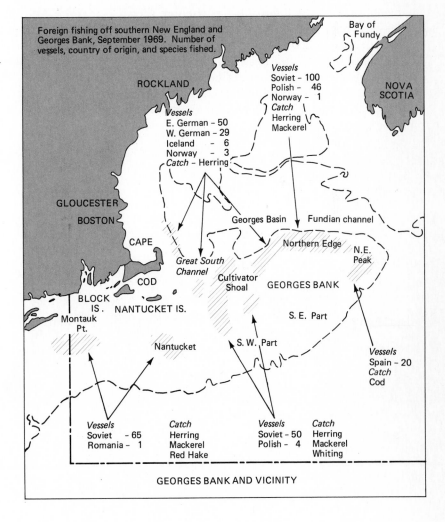

eigners are banned from fishing in America's EEZ without a special permit. Certainly, Japan, with its penchant for exploiting fish stocks up to a "net's throw" of the shores of other nations, has the greatest to lose from the new law. On the other hand, countries with extensive continental shelves, such as the United States and Canada, have the greatest to gain. America's commercial fishers have greeted the new law with jubilation. From the Gulf of Alaska to New England's George's Bank, they are catching more fish off their own shores than foreign fishers — something that has not happened for a long, long time (1). For example, in 1981, American fishers caught 5.9 billion pounds in the EEZ compared to only 3.6 billion pounds caught by their foreign counterparts.

International Regulations. It is simple for nations to adopt the philosophy that because the open sea belongs to all nations, the responsibility for their management belongs to no one in particular. Nevertheless, within the last few decades the phenomenon of decreased harvests of a particular species, such as halibut and tuna, despite intensified fishing effort, has caused concerned nations to form international conventions in which they agree to cooperate in halting further decline and in eventually re-

storing the fishery to a basis of maximum sustained yield. At present the United States is a member of several international commissions regulating fisheries in the north Pacific (salmon), the northeast Atlantic (cod, haddock, and halibut), and the tropics (tuna). In spite of such international efforts, however, the overfishing of most major species has not been brought under control.

Ocean Harvests and Global Food Needs

Many authorities regard the ocean (our planet's last frontier) as an abundant future source of animal protein that can be harvested in sufficient quantities to help forestall the threat of global famine posed by the human population surge. There seems to be some basis for this hope: first, the oceans cover 70 percent of the earth's surface and, hence, receive the same percentage of the earth's incident solar energy; second, the marine phytoplankton are efficient photosynthesizers; and third, the oceanic environment is as yet *relatively* uncontaminated with pollutants, although it is true that oil, pesticides, sewage, and industrial chemicals are of increasing concern in the neritic zone.

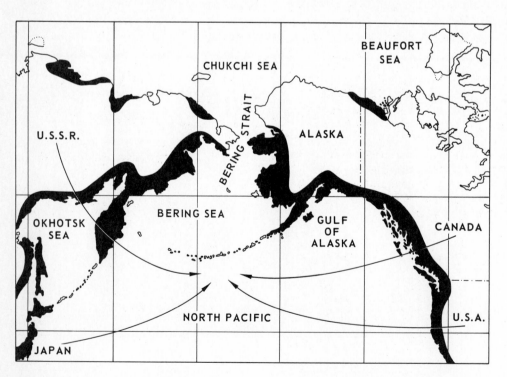

10-27 *International competition for the North Pacific fishery resource. The interests of the United States, Canada, the Soviet Union, and Japan conflict in this region. The areas indicated in black include the best salmon rivers in the world. International fishing agreements must be formulated if the resources of the North Pacific are to be most effectively managed and harvested.*

United States and World Fisheries

John E. Bardach
East-West Resource Systems
Institute, Honolulu,
Hawaii

As of March 10, 1983, the date of the proclamation for the United States of a 200-mile Extended Economic Zone — EEZ for short — by President Reagan, this country had the largest area of fishing real estate of any nation. This position is, of course, due to our very long Atlantic and Pacific coastlines and Hawaiian and Guam waters; Australia, Indonesia with her many thousand islands, and New Zealand are next in this ranking.

Granted both that 95 percent of all economically harvestable living resources occur within coastal and continental shelf areas (that is, within 200-mile EEZs) and that various ocean spaces differ greatly in their productivity, it is still likely that the U.S. now has in her waters a greater absolute fishery potential than any other nation. She does, however, only rank fourth in tonnage produced with her own vessels, 3.635 million metric tons — MMT, in 1980, the reference year of all figures to follow. In the same year Japan brought in 1,040 MMT and the Soviet Union fished 9,412 MMT in various oceans, including some parts of the U.S. EEZ. The No. 3 fishing nation, the People's Republic of China, lists 4,240 MMT as its annual catch with about 30 percent thereof coming from fresh water and aquaculture rather than from worldwide fishing operations.

The world total aquatic harvest was 72.2 MMT, of which 66 MMT came from the seas proper while 6.2 MMT were of fresh water provenance. There are twenty nations with harvests of over 1 MMT but none reach the take of the first fishing giants, Japan and the USSR. Reasons for this ranking are historic, geographic, and economic and long antedate the recent conclusion of UNCLOS III (the Third United Nations Conference on the Law of the Sea), which established 200-mile-wide ownership of fishery resources by coastal nations among other new factors in ocean governance. Worldwide fishing was based on the age-old concept that fish belong to those who catch them; with the UNCLOS III treaty now in the process of becoming customary international law, distant water fishing is becoming more constrained. Still there are, in the treaty, provisions for the sharing of such fish surplus as may exist in the EEZ of any coastal state and for the setting up of regional management instruments and organizations.

But to get at the real fishing position of a nation one must consider, in addition to direct harvest, such foreign fishing as may be licensed in respective EEZs as well as the flow of imports and exports of fishery products. (We annually bring in around three billion dollars' worth of them and export around a billion dollars' worth). Foreign catches in our EEZ, mainly by Japan, and mainly in Alaskan waters (1,169 MMT) amounted to a total of 1,627 MMT; the Republic of Korea, Poland, the USSR, Canada, and a few Western European nations also fished in our EEZs, roughly in this order of importance. Alaskan pollock, flounders and cod predominated in these catches; tonnages such as these, then, must really be added to direct catches when one considers biologic and economic marine fishery potentials of our — and for that matter any — nation.

Another way to gauge the national importance of fisheries is to look at the place of proteins of aquatic provenance in the national diet: our direct seafood consumption, on a per capita basis (not accounting for obvious differences between, say, Massachusetts and Kansas) changed from 11.8 lbs (5.36 kg) in 1950 to 12.8 lbs (5.81 kg) in 1980 while total per capita fish use for animal feed, oils, etc., rose from 43 lbs (19.54 kg) to just under 50 lbs (ca. 22.5 kg) during that same period. Prorating these figures for population increases (152.3 to 227.7 million) absolute tonnages involved here have risen by well over a third.

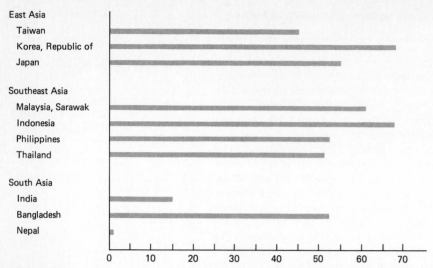

Figure 1

Figure 2

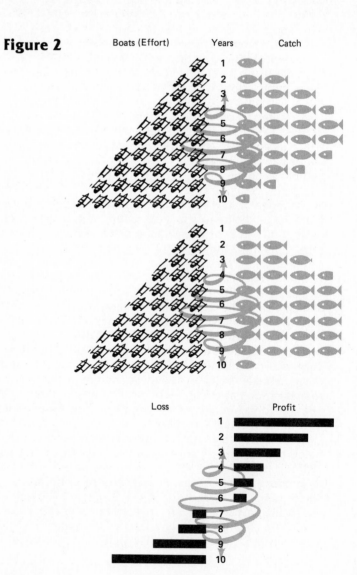

286

Yet fish only make about 6 percent of our direct meat consumption; we are, after all, renowned meat eaters, a fact not unrelated to our high per-capita GNP. In other nations such as Korea, Indonesia, China, India, and Bangladesh, fish are and will remain far more important (Figure 1). Since it is in these nations and not in the Northern Hemisphere that the brunt of the population explosion will be felt, it is germane to speculate if and how fish supplies of the future can feed more and more hungry mouths. One needs to note in this context that the oceans of the Northern Hemisphere, where by and large the rich nations live, produce near 80 percent of the total marine tonnage now taken. This is not only because of more advanced fisheries technologies and more available capital but also because of the plain fact that tropical marine waters (with some exception like shallow inland seas, the mouths of giant rivers, and unspoiled coral reefs) are just not as rich in aquatic life as temperate seas.

Before one hopes to count on now unexploited segments of the aquatic foodchain to satisfy future fish needs in a substantial way one has to consider the costs of getting them onto people's plates, especially the plates of the poor in the Third World. Antarctic krill is a good case in point; there is much of it but only in hostile waters far away where only technically advanced vessels can operate. Also krill is more pivotal in the Antarctic food web than other plankton feeders anywhere; early conservation measures may well be in order. Similar economic, if not conservation, considerations apply to midwater squid and fishes, at one time considered candidates to help to satisfy future world food needs.

Even where fish abound in the tropics, there tends to be more overfishing there than in more temperate seas (Figure 2). The solutions (if any) here are not technical but social and economic and indeed are hard to devise, let alone implement.

Does aquaculture offer a partial solution? It may, but the fact that the 50-kilometer coastal strip of India, for instance, will be settled solidly by 2010 suggests that there will be competition for site and water use, sooner rather than later. In the meantime aquaculture needs greater emphasis than it receives at present on semi-intensive techniques of recycling polyculture, even in combination with small-animal rearing and horticulture.

Some nations, big (for example, the U.S.) and small (for example, New Zealand) will have a good chance to augment their own fish takes, and of various species at that. Others will rely for substantial earnings on licensed or joint venture fishing in their EEZs, such as in cooperation with the new Pacific Island nations that have skipjack tuna as a main resource. But because more people will settle in coastal zones than elsewhere in Third World nations, there will be further increasing pressure, especially on near-shore stocks. Pollution control and overfishing will be more and more severe threats — all the harder to counter because they stem from social and economic problems. Where food from the sea will be most needed, then, production is hardly likely to keep up with the inevitably increasing demand for it.

Food and Agriculture Organization of the United Nations. *Yearbook of Fishery Statistics 1979,* Vol. 48. Rome: FAO, 1980.

U.S. Department of Commerce, National Oceanic and Atmospheric Administration. *Fisheries of the United States, 1981.* Washington, DC: U.S. Department of Commerce, 1982.

Farming the Seas

For many thousands of years human beings obtained their food by hunting game and gathering eggs, fruits, berries, nuts, and seeds — a rather inefficient process that was not able to support more than a few million people the world over. Eventually, humans invented agriculture — the controlled rearing of plants and animals — a much more efficient process that has been able to feed many more people. In a similar fashion humans have for many years harvested fish from the sea by a relatively inefficient hunting-and-gathering technique: fishing vessels move to fishing grounds where the harvest is unpredictable and then transport the catch back to market. Certainly the controlled rearing, or culturing, of fish and other aquatic food organisms is potentially a much more efficient process. When this technique is practiced in land-based ponds it is *aquaculture;* when practiced in shallow bays or in estuaries, it is *mariculture.*

Many authorities agree that aquaculture holds considerable promise for boost in the meat protein in the otherwise starch-heavy diets of millions of malnourished poor in the underdeveloped nations of the world. Various organizations, such as the United Nations Food and Agricultural Organization (FAO), the World Bank, and the United States Agency for International Development (AID) are optimistic concerning mariculture's role in alleviating the protein deficiency problem.

The basic principles of mariculture, according to J. H. Ryther of the Woods Hole Oceanographic Institution, are the following:

1. Cultivate a species that is low on the food chain, such as a producer, an herbivore, or a detritus feeder. Ideally, of course, humans would consume the producers directly, thus minimizing the energy losses that always occur between successive food chain links. The next best strategy would be for humans to culture herbivores, somewhat analogous to our raising of herbivorous livestock such as cattle, sheep, and goats in land-based agriculture (27).
2. Productivity of the water should be increased by providing nitrogen and phosphorus nutrients in the form of plant, animal, and even human waste (27).
3. Use a technique known as *polyculture.* This involves the culture of several species of marine organisms, each with *different* food and habitat preferences *simultaneously.* For example, if the food base is represented by both algae and detritus, two species of herbivores would be cultured, one adapted to feed on algae, and the other specialized to feed on detritus. The two species probably would stratify themselves in the water column, the algae-eater feeding normally at a higher level than the detritus feeder. Examples of species that are likely candidates for polyculture are seaweeds, crabs, shrimp, and fish such as tilapia, mullet, and milkfish (27).
4. The site of mariculture should be located as close as possible to the potential consumers of the organisms being raised — in other words, near big cities — in order to minimize the energy costs involved in transporting the "crop" (27).

Seaweed Culture

As yet Westerners have not enthusiastically accepted the potential of seaweed as nutritious food. Many seaweeds, however, have as much protein and caloric content as terrestrial plants. Moreover, their mineral and vitamin content in many cases exceeds that of land-grown vegetables and grains. Seaweed culture consists in part of rearing seedlings in marine

288

greenhouses, often a complex, multistage process. The seedlings may then be set in the open ocean where they grow from rafts, net frames, and moored longlines. The young seaweed plants must be carefully protected from fish and other predators. At the present time China, Japan, Korea, and Taiwan produce more than one million metric tons of edible seaweed annually. This makes seaweed the world's most important produce of mariculture.

Oyster Culture

The public abuse of the oyster resource, which continued unabated for much of this century, has largely been replaced by the farsighted responsible programs of private commercial interests. (See Figure 10–28.) The commercial fishermen, who lease barren, unused areas of the ocean floor, have developed a type of oyster culture in which they provide a suitable substratum upon which the motile oyster larvae can attach themselves and grow into adults. This surface may be in the form of old mollusk shells, gravel, or even slag from blast furnaces. Once the larvae have become affixed to the substrate, they may be transported by the fishermen to food-rich waters that permit a faster growth rate than the nursery grounds. The emphasis is on maximum production per unit of cost, time, and area. These culture methods are practiced primarily in the Chesapeake and Delaware bays and along the Louisiana coast. Oyster fishermen may harvest a crop of 100 bushels per acre under satisfactory conditions.

Because the adult oyster is immobile and therefore has an extremely limited "home range," it is more readily domesticated than forms, such as fish, that are highly mobile. Researchers of the National Marine Fisheries Service have been experimenting with a mode of oyster culture adapted from the Japanese. The service has established a series of artificial, brackish-water ponds. (See Figure 10–29.) Racks placed in the ponds bear thousands of clamshells strung on submerged wires. (See Figures 10–30 and 10–31.) In this way the researchers utilize the vertical dimension of the habitat as well as the two-dimensional ocean floor in providing suitable substrata on which oyster larvae can become established. This technique substantially increases the carrying capacity of a given volume of oyster habitat. Burial of oysters by sediment is also avoided. Three-dimensional raft culture permits yields that are ten to twenty times greater than those obtained from traditional methods employing the ocean floor. In Japan oyster culturists suspend shells from mobile rafts that can be towed to "plankton pastures" of suitable density for maximal oyster growth. Much of the environmental resistance that normally confronts oyster populations

10–28 *The oyster in its shell. These animals strain out plankton from the surrounding water. Therefore, any pollutants, such as toxic pesticides, that would decrease plankton populations would depress oyster numbers as well.*

10-29 *Experimental oyster ponds at the National Marine Fisheries Service Laboratory at Oxford, Maryland.*

10-30 *Oyster culture. The productivity of inshore culturing areas could be increased in a number of ways. Here deep nutrient-rich water enhances the growth of algae. Because the oysters either feed on the algae directly or on crustaceans that feed on the algae, oyster production on inshore rafts is increased significantly.*

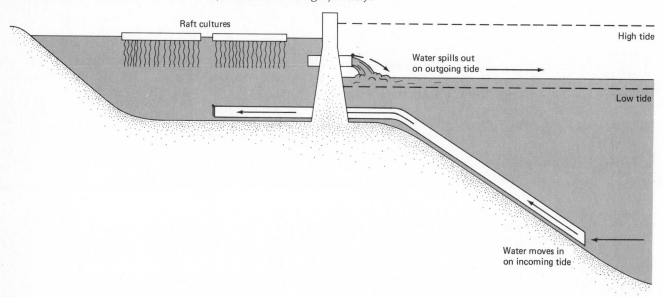

Raft cultures

High tide

Water spills out
on outgoing tide

Low tide

Water moves in
on incoming tide

10-31 *Experimental oyster raft. Mollusc shells are attached to the submerged ropes, thus providing an optimal substratum for oyster-larvae establishment. Bureau of Commercial Fisheries Biological Laboratory, Oxford, Maryland.*

under natural conditions is reduced by this type of culture. The ravages of bottom-dwelling predators, such as starfish, are minimized. By such methods Japanese culturists, for example, have been able to secure an annual yield of 13,000 pounds of oyster meat per acre. Such a high meat yield cannot even be matched by livestock ranchers on land, except under the most optimal conditions.

The potential for boosting mollusc protein production in underdeveloped countries is very great. Oysters, clams, mussels, scallops, and abalone can be easily raised in simple hatcheries. Organisms can be sent by airplane anywhere in the world.

Hatchery rearing of molluscs makes possible the improvement of the stock by selective breeding. In U.S. hatcheries, for example, strains of oysters have been developed that are resistant to disease or that grow so rapidly they are harvestable one year earlier than normal.

The location of mollusc culture beds near urban areas obviously has great economic advantages because the energy costs of transport to the consumer are minimized. On the other hand, those same urban areas usually represent a source of pollution from the discharge of domestic and industrial waste. More than 30 percent of the shellfish beds in the United States are now closed because the food organisms may be contaminated with disease-causing bacteria or toxic heavy metals. (See Figure 10–32.)

10–32 *The percentage of shellfish-harvesting areas that were closed to commercial shellfish harvesting in 1979–80.*

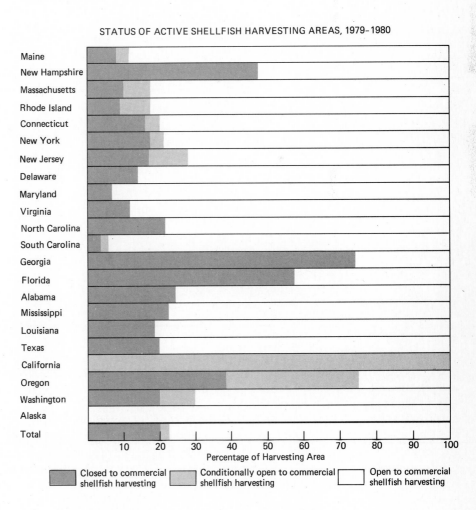

STATUS OF ACTIVE SHELLFISH HARVESTING AREAS, 1979-1980

The Salmon Culture

Net cage culturing of salmon in the United States and Norway is a very intensive form of mariculture. The cages holding the fish are placed in estuaries and protected bays. The fish have continuous access to clean, aerated water because of the action of natural currents and the tides. Predation and net fouling are the disadvantages of the technique, however.

Brackish pond aquaculture has great potential for boosting meat-protein supplies in the underdeveloped nations of Southeast Asia and India. India alone has a potential area of over four million acres that could be effectively used in brackish pond culture. With the technology already available, the production of marine foods could be increased in this region by at least ten million tons annually.

Total Mariculture Production in the World

The estimated total maricultural production in the world at present is 3.11 million metric tons per year. Of this production 38 percent is represented by seaweeds, 33 percent by oysters and mussels, and 23 percent by finfish. (See Table 10–1.) For the sake of the millions of malnourished poor in Asia, South America, and Africa, let us hope that the optimistic goal of an annual aquaculture (marine and fresh water) harvest of fifty million tons by the year 2000 will be met.

Table 10–1 World Mariculture and Ocean-Ranching Yields for 1975

Species	Yield (in million metric tons)
Marine finfish	
milkfish (Philippines, Indonesia, Taiwan)	.207
yellowtail (Japan)	.052
salmon (net cage culture)	.100
salmon (ocean ranching) (USA, Japan, USSR)	.200
Others	.100
Oysters	.652
Mussels	.591
Clams, scallops, and other molluscs	.132
Shrimp and prawns	.016
Seaweeds	1.055
Total Marine	3.115
Freshwater fish culture	2.528

Source: J. H. Ryther. "Mariculture, Ocean Ranching, and Other Culture-Based Fisheries." *Bioscience,* **31** (Mar. 1981), 223–229.

Global fish harvests increased from 21 million metric tons in 1951 to 66 million metric tons in 1980. These gains have been possible only under extremely heavy fishing pressure, and the use of such sophisticated techniques as sonar and aerial surveillance. The distribution of the global fish catch is shown in Figure 10–33. Some experts believe that the maximum sustained yield for our global fisheries is about 100 million metric tons annually. It appears that it will be some time before that level of harvest will be attained. But even if it is eventually attained, would that mean that the poor people on this planet would no longer suffer from protein deficiencies? Not at all. Remember that the global population is still riding the J-curve. And even if we could increase our global fish catch to 200

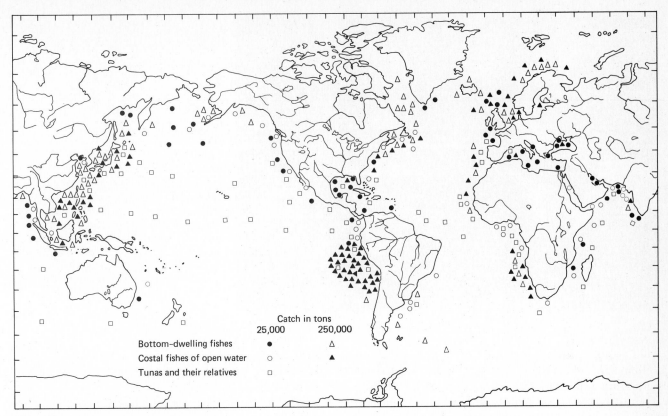

10-33 *The global fish catch, 1972.*

million tons by the year 2030, which would be almost three times our present harvest, the amount of fish protein available per person would actually be *less* than it is today (21).

It may be possible to increase our fish harvest somewhat by shifting attention from traditional fishing areas like the North Sea, the Grand Banks of Newfoundland and the Pacific coast of California, which are already overfished, to virtually unexploited fisheries in the Indian Ocean and the southwest Atlantic. Although stocks of cod, tuna, haddock, and salmon are largely overfished, there are still a few species that could withstand a more intensive fishing effort. Good examples are anchovies off the coast of West Africa and squid in the eastern Pacific (Moran, 1980). Another strategy that might improve the amount of fish protein available to humans simply involves a shift in food preferences. For example, more than 20 million tons of rough fish, such as skate and dogfish, which are high in protein value, are caught, almost accidentally, every year. There is no reason why they, with some culinary tricks, cannot be made reasonably acceptable to the human palate (22).

Millions of malnourished people in the underdeveloped nations of South America, Africa, and Asia are suffering from a protein-deficiency disease called *kwashiorkor*. It causes irreversible mental retardation in young children, along with a host of other afflictions. The average adult requires a minimum of 36 grams of animal protein daily. But most animal protein, when derived from land animals such as cattle, sheep, or swine, is very expensive. On the other hand, protein from the sea in the form of fish is relatively cheap. We might expect that at least the poor people living close to the ocean would receive an adequate supply. Regrettably, nothing could be further from the truth. (See Figure 10-34.) For example, for several years the Peruvian anchovy fishery yielded more than 12 million metric tons annually. Where did most of the fish wind up? Not in Peruvian or Chilean stomachs. Most of the fish were shipped to the already overfed countries of western Europe and the United States, not to be

293

10-34 *Chilean fisherman with a big haul off the coast near Valparaiso. Many of these fish will be ground into fish meal. Just south of Valparaiso is the largest fish-meal factory in South America. An average of 600,000 pounds of fish fillets are processed monthly and are mostly exported.*

used as human food, but to be processed into food pellets for cattle, swine, cats, and dogs. Perhaps the next time you savor that pork chop, or watch Fido devouring his chow, you might soberly reflect on the tragic inequalities of human existence.

Decline of the Whale Population

The world's original whale population of over four million has slowly but surely been depleted by the human predator to a current level of only several hundred thousand. For example, the blue-whale population, which prior to 1920 numbered more than 200,000 animals, has been reduced to a mere 300 animals—a 99.9 percent reduction. Each year since 1956, despite the most advanced techniques of locating and killing, there has been a steady decline in the total whale harvest. This decline has continued despite the protective regulations formulated and accepted by the seventeen nations of the International Whaling Commission (IWC), which was organized in 1946.

The IWC attempts to regulate whale catches and to protect endangered species. Some of the IWC's regulations follow:

1. The killing of whales that have not attained a minimum length is forbidden. The minimum length, of course, varies with the species (52).

2. It is illegal for factory ships to operate on the high seas except to harvest the relatively abundant minke whale.
3. The killing of calves and nursing cows is forbidden.
4. The killing of blue, gray, humpback, right, and killer whales is banned and has sharply reduced the quota for killing sperm whales.
5. A restriction is imposed on the total number of whales killed during a single whaling season.

Notwithstanding these regulations, the future is grim for the goliaths of the sea. There are several factors involved. First, *whales have an extremely low reproductive potential.* The female blue whale, for example, is not capable of giving birth until she is four to seven years old. Moreover, because the gestation period of the blue whale lasts 12 months, and the nursing period is seven months, the average cow gives birth to a maximum of one calf every two years. Many ten-year-old cows probably have given birth to no more than two young (12). Second, *many whales tend to concentrate in the summer waters of the Antarctic, where the whales become highly vulnerable* to the explosive harpoon of the whaler. Third, and most important, *the rules of the IWC are not always respected.* Russian and Japanese whalers frequently pursue their short-term "quick-buck" interests not only at the sacrifice of their future long-term gains (based on sustained-yield harvest-

10 – 35   *The gray whale. The head is at the left. Notice the region of the blowhole in the center of the highest part of the head. The gray patches on the whale's body are caused by growths of barnacles, small marine organisms related to crabs and lobsters. The gray whale attains a length of 50 feet and a weight of 40 tons.*

10 – 36   *White whales. These whales are being hunted for "sport" in Hudson Bay at a license fee cost of $350 per whale. The "bag limit" is one whale per day and two per season. The whales weigh up to 1,300 pounds and attain a length of fourteen feet. They are run down with motorboats, harpooned, and then shot with a high-powered rifle.*

295

Controversy: The Whale War

The battle lines are drawn. On one side are the antiwhaling nations led by the United States. On the other side are Japan, Russia, and a few lesser whaling nations. What are the basic arguments of the opposing sides? Let's see.

Estimates of Whale Populations

The antiwhaling nations assert that the blue, humpback, sperm, and several other species are dangerously close to extinction. On the other hand, Japan, who has assumed the "spokesman" role for the prowhaling nations, maintains that most whale species are not in immediate danger. Japanese scientists have identified a pygmy blue whale, which they claim is a distinct species from the blue whale. (The antiwhaling nations argue that this pygmy species was "invented" by the Japanese to justify their persecution of immature blues.)

Sperm-Whale Quotas

During the 1980 meeting of the International Whaling Commission (IWC), the harvest quota for the sperm whale was reduced to only 890 for 1981. This is a drastic quota reduction from 1978, when more than 10,000 sperm whales were killed. The verbal skirmishing on the sperm-whale issue was very fierce. According to American delegate Richard A. Frank: "We would have preferred a total ban on killing sperm whales." On the other hand, his Japanese counterpart, Kuneo Yonezawa, heatedly fumed: "This is a very serious situation for us. We deeply resent the decision. It will mean we have to lay up two of the seven ships we currently have whaling." (18)

The Morality Issue

The antiwhaling nations claim that it is downright immoral for the Japanese to feed on the flesh of animals whose intelligence may very well be second only to that of humans. On the other hand, the Japanese state that this argument slips on the ham sandwich and pork chops so popular in the United States. After all, they contend, the pig is a mighty brainy animal in its own right. Moreover, the American appetite for beefsteak causes the butchery of thousands of cattle which are worshipped in India as living gods.

Responsibility for Shrinking Whale Populations

Antiwhaling nations claim that the relentless commercial harvesting by Japan and Russia is threatening several species of whales with extinction. The Japanese contend that the United States and other western nations are not exactly guiltless. After all, during the nineteenth century their own whaling fleets were largely responsible for the whale's initial decline. They also point out that during the early 1970s American tuna fishermen were annually destroying 100,000 porpoises (small whales) that got caught accidentally in their nets.

Japan's Need for Food

According to the antiwhaling nations, Japan can get sufficient protein from fish, chickens, soybeans, and other foods. After all, 40 percent of the Japanese whale harvest is made up of sperm whales, which are useless for human consumption. On the other hand, the Japanese assert that a significant 9 percent of their meat protein is derived from whales. Moreover, one of their major alternative sources, beef, must be imported from the United States or Argentina, and is very costly. They state that whale steaks are relatively cheap, costing the Japanese consumer one fourth as much as beef.

Japan's Economic Interests

The antiwhalers argue that the extensive Japanese fishing industry could easily absorb any Japanese whalers that might be thrown out of work because of a ban on whaling. In their view, crass economic considerations are less important than the survival of whales — the unique end products of millions of years of evolution. The Japanese contend, however, that many ex-whalers would be permanently unemployed. Employment in their whaling industry has plummeted from 15,000 in the 1960s to a mere 1,000 today.

What Lies Ahead?

So the whale war continues to be waged, with great intensity on both sides. What does the future hold? Bradley K. Martin of the *Baltimore Sun* points out: "The Japanese may not give up. The minister of agriculture and fisheries is on record as saying that Japan is determined to retain one factory ship fleet. And there is talk that Japan and the other countries still whaling might break away from the commission and form their own regulatory body" (18). The antiwhaling nations, led by the United States, are determined to attain their ultimate goal: the complete banning of all commercial whaling for a period of at least ten years so that whale stocks can recover.

So what's all the hassle about anyway? Is the whale really worth the war? To the antiwhalers the whale is more than just a few thousand pounds of bone, blood, and blubber — much more than a chicken, pig, or cow. What whales really mean to them has been eloquently expressed by marine biologist Victor Scheffer: "Whales have become symbolic of life itself. . . . They live in families, they play in the moonlight, they talk to one another, and they care for one another in distress. They are awesome and mysterious. . . . They deserve to be saved, not as potential meatballs, but as a source of encouragement for mankind . . ." (8).

What do you think? Which side would you take in this controversy?

---

ing), but also at the sacrifice of the largest and most fascinating mammals the human eye has ever seen.

Whales have been hunted for at least 1,000 years, ever since the Basques pursued them in the Bay of Biscay. However, unless stringent conservation measures are both formulated and enforced, several whale species may well go the way of the dinosaur and saber-toothed cat.

Rapid Review

1. The ocean covers 70 percent of the earth's surface, is characterized by both horizontal and vertical currents, is about seventy times as salty as a lake or stream, and is relatively infertile.

2. The three major zones of the ocean are discussed in this chapter: the neritic, euphotic, and abyssal.

3. A typical estuary has the following features: (1) it contains brackish water, (2) its density is intermediate between that of fresh and salt water, (3) the water level rises and falls with the tides, (4) dissolved oxygen levels are high, (5) turbidity is relatively high, and (6) it acts as a nutrient trap.

4. Estuaries serve as spawning and nursery grounds for many valuable species of shellfish and fish.

5. In areas of upwelling, fish production is highly efficient because many of the food chains have only two links: the producer phytoplankton and the consumer fish. In the deep waters of the open sea, however, fish production is much less efficient because the food chains may have as many as six links.

6. The oxygen demand of the sewage sludge

dumped into the New York Bight during the 1970s was roughly 19 times greater than that of the decaying bodies of plants and animals.

7. The main sources of oil in the marine environment, in order of total volume, are (1) marine transportation, (2) river runoff, (3) atmospheric rainout, (4) natural oil seeps, (5) municipalities, (6) industrial wastes, and (7) offshore oil production.

8. Oil pollution has a number of adverse effects on the marine ecosystem. They include: (1) reduction of photosynthetic rates in marine algae; (2) concentration of chlorinated hydrocarbons, such as pesticides; (3) contamination of human food chains with carcinogens such as benzopyrene; (4) disruption of chemical communication in marine organisms that adversely affects such activities as feeding, reproduction, and escape from predators; (5) outright mortality, as in the case of an estimated million seabirds each year, and (6) long-term effects such as liver cancers resulting from chronic exposure to low levels of oil.

9. Management methods employed to increase the production of marine fish include (1) introductions, (2) construction of artificial reefs, (3) the artificial induction of upwelling, and (4) regulation of the harvest.

10. Some authorities believe that the maximum sustained yield from the sea of 100 million tons will be realized by the year 2000.

11. Shrimp represent our most valuable marine fishery: 240 million pounds worth more than $70 million are being taken every year.

12. Our nation's oyster beds have been adversely affected by a variety of human activities in the last few decades, including (1) the establishment of marinas; (2) the filling in of marshes for industrial development and real estate projects; (3) using oyster habitat as dumping grounds for dredge spoils, sewage and other forms of solid waste; and (4) smothering the beds with silt because of poor erosion-control practices.

13. The practice of oyster culture may theoretically result in an annual yield of 13,000 pounds of oyster meat per acre.

14. Despite harvest restrictions formulated by the IWC, several species of whales, such as the blue, are on the verge of extinction. There are several factors involved. Among them are (1) the extremely low reproductive potential of whales; (2) the tendency for some species to congregate in the vicinity

of their crustacean food supplies, a characteristic that makes them more vulnerable to capture; and (3) the limited recognition given to the regulations of the IWC by Russia and Japan, the two most important whaling nations.

15. Among the oil-pollution-abatement methods that can be used are the following: (1) soaking up the oil with straw, (2) absorbing it with powdered chalk, (3) burning it, (4) employing detergents so that the oil is emulsified and bacterial decomposition of the oil is facilitated, (5) seeding the oil slick with special strains of "oil-eating" bacteria, and (6) coating the beaches with a protective film that prevents the incoming oil slick from adhering to the sand and gravel.

Key Words and Phrases

Abyssal zone
Alaskan current
Amoco Cadiz
Argo Merchant
Artificial Reef
Baleen
Benzopyrene
Biological magnification
Detritus feeder
El Nino
Emulsification
Estuary
Euphotic zone
Extended Economic Zone (EEZ)
Factory ship
Fingerprinting
Gulf Stream
Indicative World Plan

International Whaling Commission (IWC)
Introduction
Killer boat
Kwashiorkor
Maximum sustained yield (MSY)
Natural oil seep
Neritic zone
Ocean dumping
Oyster culture
Oyster Watch
Santa Barbara oil spill
Supertanker
Thor Heyerdahl
Torrey Canyon
Two-hundred-mile fishing zone
Upwelling

Questions and Topics for Discussion

1. In your own words, define the key words or phrases in the list on the preceding page.
2. Describe three methods by which *upwelling* might be induced in order to increase ocean productivity in a given area.
3. In what ways does an estuary differ from an

298

ocean? From a river? Why are estuaries so highly productive?

4. Briefly list seven environmental problems, in order of their seriousness, that are threatening the stability and productivity of the Chesapeake Bay estuary.

5. Why is the decline of submerged vegetation in the Chesapeake Bay of such serious concern to EPA scientists? What is being done to rectify the problem?

6. In order of importance, list five sources of the oil that contaminates the marine ecosystem.

7. Discuss five adverse effects that oil spills have on marine organisms.

8. Discuss three approaches to *preventing* oil pollution. Discuss three methods by which oil pollution might be *controlled* after it has occurred.

9. Trace a given molecule of the carcinogen *benzopyrene* from an oil deposit in Kuwait to the living tissues of *your* body.

10. Discuss the events leading to the collapse of the anchovy fishery off the coast of Peru. Can such a collapse be prevented in the future? Why or why not?

11. At its peak, the anchovy fishery yields 12 million tons per year. Discuss the relative importance of this harvest in supplying valuable protein food to the people of Peru and neighboring South American countries.

12. Discuss the relationship between the current pet "explosion" in the United States and the incidence of kwashiorkor in the underdeveloped countries.

13. Discuss the importance of the newly established 200-mile fishing zone.

14. Suppose that all the oceans on planet Earth disappeared. What would be the effect on climate? On agriculture? On the water, carbon, and phosphorus cycles? On our life-style?

15. Discuss the ecological problems associated with sludge dumping in the New York Bight in the 1970s. Sludge dumping in the ocean is now prohibited, although such cities as New York, Philadelphia, and Camden, New Jersey, are still generating more than 100,000 tons yearly. How is this sludge being disposed of now?

16. In this chapter we have briefly discussed the neritic, euphotic, and abyssal zones. Which of the three would you conclude is the most important to human welfare? Why? Suppose that the abyssal zone did not exist. What effect would this have on the structure and operation of the marine ecosystem?

Endnotes

1. Bardach, John E. "Living Marine Resources and the Law of the Sea." *Bioscience*, **31** (Mar. 1981).

2. Blumer, Max, Howard L. Sanders, J. Fred Grasole, and George R. Hampson. "A Small Oil Spill." *Environment*, **13** (Mar. 1971), 2–12.

3. Clapham, W. B., Jr. *Natural Ecosystems.* New York: Macmillan, 1973.

4. Clark, John R. "Thermal Pollution and Aquatic Life." *Scientific American*, **220** (Mar. 1969), 18–27.

5. Cromie, William J., *The Living World of the Sea.* Englewood Cliffs, NJ: Prentice-Hall, 1966.

6. Curry-Lindahl, Kai. *Let Them Live.* New York: Morrow, 1972.

7. Darnell, Rezneat M. *Ecology and Man.* Dubuque, Iowa: Brown, 1973.

8. Ehrlich, Paul R., Anne H. Ehrlich, and John P. Holdren. *Ecoscience: Population, Resources, Environment.* San Francisco: Freeman, 1977.

9. Environmental Protection Agency. *Environmental News.* Washington, DC: Government Printing Office, December 9, 1976.

10. ———. *Research Summary: Oil Spills.* Washington, DC: Government Printing Office, 1979.

11. ———. *Research Summary: Chesapeake Bay.* Washington, DC: Government Printing Office, May 1980.

12. ———. *Chesapeake Bay: Introduction to an Ecosystem.* Washington, DC: Government Printing Office, January 1982.

13. Hardy, Alister C. *Fish and Fisheries.* Boston: Houghton, 1959.

14. Herald, Earl S. *Living Fishes of the World.* Garden City, NY: Doubleday, 1961.

15. Heyerdahl, Thor. "How to Kill an Ocean." *Saturday Review* (Nov. 29, 1975), 12–18.

16. Holcomb, Robert. "Oil in the Ecosystem." *Science*, **166** (Oct. 10, 1969), 204–206.

17. "International Whaling Commission Reduces World's Whaling Quota by 9 Percent." *Ecology USA*, (Aug. 11, 1980), 123.

18. "Japan to Stand Firm Against Anti-Whaling Drive." *Ecology USA*, **8** (Dec. 17, 1979), 194.

19. Krebs, Charles J. *Ecology: The Experimental Analysis of Distribution and Abundance.* 2nd ed. New York: Harper, 1978.

20. McCaull, Julian, and Janice Crossland. *Water Pollution.* New York: Harcourt, 1974.

21. Miller, G. Tyler. *Living in the Environment.* 3rd ed. New York: Wadsworth, 1982.
22. Moran, Joseph M., Michael D. Morgan, and James H. Wiersma. *An Introduction to Environmental Sciences.* San Francisco: Freeman, 1980.
23. Moriber, George. *Environmental Science.* Boston: Allyn, 1974.
24. Odum, Eugene P. *Fundamentals of Ecology.* 3rd ed. Philadelphia: Saunders, 1971.
25. Polycarpov, G. G. *Radioecology of Aquatic Organisms.* 1966. (Translated by S. Technica and edited by Vincent Schultz and A. W. Klement.) Circular No. 275, Washington, DC: Bureau of Commercial Fisheries, 1967.
26. "Presidential Commission Leaning Toward Ocean Dumping." *Ecology USA* (Nov. 17, 1980), 181.
27. Ryther, J. H. "Mariculture, Ocean Ranching, and Other Culture-Based Fisheries." *Bioscience,* **31** (Mar. 1981), 223–229.
28. "Shock at Sea." *Time,* **94** (Aug. 15, 1969), 40.
29. Smith, Robert L. *Ecology and Field Biology.* New York: Harper, 1966.
30. ———. *The Ecology of Man: An Ecosystem Approach.* New York: Harper, 1976.
31. "Spectrum." *Environment* (Jan.–Feb. 1981), 24.
32. "Toxic Chemicals May be Cause of Striped Bass Decline, FWS Reports." *Ecology USA,* **11** (Sept. 13, 1982), 140.
33. Turk, Amos, Janet T. Wittes, Jonathan Turk, and Robert E. Wittes. *Environmental Science.* 2nd ed. Philadelphia: Saunders, 1978.
34. *U.S. News and World Report.* "The 200 Mile Fishing Limit Hits a Snag." (Apr. 24, 1978), 42.
35. Wagner, Richard H. *Environment and Man.* New York: Norton, 1971.
36. Walton, Susan. "Academy Looks Again at Petroleum in the Marine Environment." *Bioscience,* **31** (Feb. 1981), 93–96.
37. Warinner, J. E., and M. L. Brehmer. "The Effects of Thermal Effluents on Marine Organisms." *International Journal of Air and Water Pollution,* **10** (1966), 277–289.
38. *World Book Encyclopedia.* "Whales." Chicago: Field Enterprise Educational Corporation, 1976.

Suggested Readings for the Interested Student

Bardach, John E. "Living Marine Resources and the Law of the Sea." *Bioscience,* **31** (Mar. 1981).

MacLeish, William H. "Oil, Fish and Georges Bank." *The Atlantic,* **238** (Sept. 1981), 18–21. This article explores the effects of offshore operations on fish stocks on the Georges Bank, 150 miles east of Cape Cod.

Rhoads, Donald, C., Peter L. McCall, and Josephine Y. Yingst. "Disturbance and Production on the Estuarine Sea Floor." *American Scientist,* **66** (Sept.–Oct. 1978), 577–586. The authors discuss managing the disposal of dredged material in Long Island Sound.

Rothschild, B. J. "More Food From the Sea?" *Bioscience,* **31** (Mar. 1981), 216–220. The author describes the factors controlling the marine fish catch and considers methods by which the harvest can be increased.

Ryther, J. H. "Mariculture, Ocean Ranching, and Other Culture-Based Fisheries." *Bioscience,* **31** (Mar. 1981), 223–229. This is an excellent, authoritative discussion of current techniques for farming the oceans.

Steele, J. H. "Living Marine Resources: A Personal View." *Bioscience,* **31** (Mar. 1981), 205. The author considers the adverse effects of climatic changes, pollution, and overfishing on our living marine resources.

Thayer, Gordon W., Douglas A. Wolfe, and Richard B. Williams. "The Impact of Man on Seagrass Systems." *American Scientist,* **63** (May–June 1975), 288–295. The authors discuss the importance of seagrass communities to the productivity of estuaries.

U.S. News and World Report. "The 200 Mile Fishing Limit Hits a Snag." (Apr. 24, 1978), 42. This article describes an adverse effect of the 200-mile fishing zone on American fishermen.

Walton, Susan. "Academy Looks Again at Petroleum in the Marine Environment." *Bioscience,* **31** (Feb. 1981), 93–96. The National Academy of Science examines recent oil-pollution research in Puget Sound.

———. "Chesapeake Bay Blues — Resources Threatened by Overuse." *Bioscience,* **31** (Mar. 1981), 358–360. This is a description of the Chesapeake Bay's "battle" for biological survival.

11 Forest Management

From early colonial days, when the straight, sturdy trunks of New England spruce and pine were fashioned into masts for the Royal Navy, until today, fully three centuries later, American forests have been the source of a variety of products useful to humans. Today our forests provide the raw materials for over 5,000 products worth $23 billion annually. They support an industry that employs 1.4 million people and has an annual payroll of over $6 billion.

To help maintain the world's highest standard of living, the United States uses more wood per capita than any nation on earth. Each year, every American man, woman, and child uses about 204 board feet* of lumber, much of it imported from Scandinavia and Canada. In 1962 Americans used 37.3 billion

* A board foot is a unit of measurement used in the lumbering industry to refer to a volume of wood one-foot square and one-inch thick.

11-1 *Felling a large Western red cedar in the Wenatchee National Forest, Washington. A wedge is employed to prevent the tree from binding the chain saw.*

11–2 *Gun stocks, samples of veneer, and other products derived from walnut.*

board feet, enough to build 3.5 million six-room cottages or build a four-foot-wide boardwalk long enough to bridge the distance to the moon at least seventy times. Americans eat, sleep, work, and play in a world of wood. Whether it is toothpicks, telephone poles, photographic film, maple syrup, acetic acid, or cellophane, we depend heavily on wood and

wood-derived products. Each year we use over 0.5 million barrels of turpentine to thin our paints, over 30 million railroad ties to cushion our trains, over 200 million fence posts to fence our lands. Each year, well-fed Americans use over 232,000 tons of napkins, buy over one million tons of paper bags, use two million tons of newsprint, and purchase two million tons of writing paper.

The Forest Ecosystem

The forest ecosystem is essentially a *community* of organisms, the members of which *interact* with the living and nonliving components of this environment. We shall briefly consider the structure and function of the *deciduous forest*.

1. *Structure.* Physical components include solar energy, precipitation, soil, lightning, wind, fire, and so on. Plant components consist of trees, shrubs, ferns, mosses, and so on. The mature forest usually has a well defined layering or *stratification* which includes the canopy, shrub, and

11–3 *"Mountain" of pulp logs at a pulp mill.*

ground strata. Animal components include earthworms, millipedes, centipedes, insects, frogs, birds, and animals and rodents.

2. *Function.* A few of the activities or functions of the forest ecosystem follow:

   a. Solar energy powers the process of photosynthesis which occurs in all the green leaves and stems. The intensity of solar radiation on the ground stratum is only a small fraction of the intensity in the upper canopy.

   b. The food energy in plant tissues made available by photosynthesis is exploited by such herbivores as bark beetles, caterpillars, grouse, mice, flying squirrels, deer, and so on.

   c. The herbivores in turn are consumed by insect-eating birds, and carnivores such as owls, foxes, skunks, and racoons.

   d. Fungi and bacteria cause the decomposition of dead trees and shrubs, fallen leaves, and the remains and excreta of forest-dwelling animals. These nutrients are temporarily stored in the soil, only to be rapidly absorbed by plant roots. The circular "flow" of a given nitrogen atom from a poplar tree leaf to the soil and then back to a tree (possibly the same one), may be completed in less than a year.

   e. Strong winds may blow down diseased trees. As a result the canopy in that localized area will temporarily be opened up, allowing more sunlight to "bathe" the forest floor. This, in turn, will permit sunloving aspens to become established in the windfall area. Several years later the aspen buds will serve as winter food for grouse. In a sense, the wind storm "pushed" the ecological succession back to an earlier stage.

   f. A woodpecker such as the yellow-bellied sapsucker may drill dozens of neatly arranged holes in a maple tree. The bird then feeds on the sap which rises in the well holes. Concentrations of insects may be attracted to the sap, and may in turn be consumed by other species of birds, such as warblers. Eventually a fungus may invade the tree via one of the well holes and ultimately cause the death of the tree.

   g. Forest fires may be very destructive to trees. However, other forest organisms may benefit from fire. For example, bark beetle larvae will feed on the dead wood and in turn be consumed by woodpeckers. The woodpeckers may excavate nesting cavities in the dead trunks, which, some time later, may be taken over by flying squirrels and even wood ducks.

   h. The feeding activities of woodland animals may play an important role in extending the distribution of certain species of plants. Young oaks may develop from acorns buried by squirrels. The seeds of species like sumac, cherry, and grape may be excreted by a robin many miles from the spot where the bird had been feeding. Exposure to the digestive juices of the bird will actually increase the germination success of the seeds.

The U.S. Forest Service

Four federal bureaus are charged with administering and managing our nation's forested areas: the Soil Conservation Service (SCS), which is concerned with farm-management-associated forests; the Tennessee Valley Authority (TVA), charged with timberland management in the vicinity of the numerous dam-reservoir sites along the Tennessee River and its tributaries; and the Fish and Wildlife Service, which is interested in improving forest habitat for game and fish. However, the Forest Service, a bureau of the Department of Agriculture, has the primary responsibility for managing our nation's forests to promote "the greatest good for the most people" over the long run. (Major forest regions of the United States are shown in Figure 11–4.)

The U.S. Forest Service was established in 1905. President Theodore Roosevelt appointed Gifford Pinchot to be its first chief forester. (Figure 11–5.) As a forestry professor at Yale University, Pinchot promoted the use of several forest-management methods he had learned in Europe. Pinchot was a zealous crusader for resource conservation.

The Forest Service divides its attention now among three major areas: (1) administering and protecting the national forests; (2) doing research on forest, watershed, range, and recreation management; on wildlife-habitat improvement; on forest-product development; and on fire and pest control; and (3) cooperating with the state and private forest owners in the fifty states, Puerto Rico, and the Virgin Islands to promote sound forest management.

The Forest Service protects and manages 154 national forests and grasslands, embracing 182 million acres with 990 billion board feet of timber. Included under its supervision are the grazing lands of

303

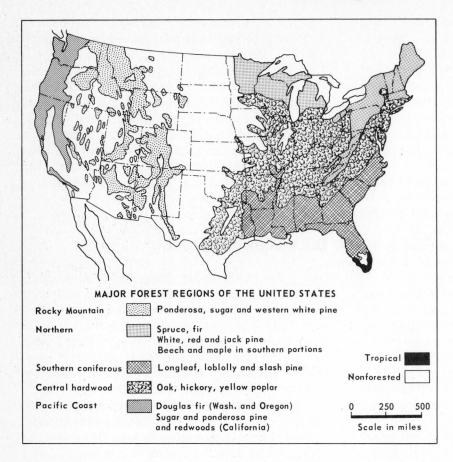

MAJOR FOREST REGIONS OF THE UNITED STATES

Rocky Mountain — Ponderosa, sugar and western white pine

Northern — Spruce, fir
White, red and jack pine
Beech and maple in southern portions

Southern coniferous — Longleaf, loblolly and slash pine

Central hardwood — Oak, hickory, yellow poplar

Pacific Coast — Douglas fir (Wash. and Oregon)
Sugar and ponderosa pine
and redwoods (California)

Tropical

Nonforested

0   250   500
Scale in miles

11–4 *Distribution of major forest types in the United States.*

six million head of livestock and habitat for one third of America's big-game animals. In a single year the Forest Service extinguishes almost 10,000 fires.

Criticisms of the U.S. Forest Service

The reader must not get the idea that the Forest Service is a *model* agency and can do no wrong, that it is staffed by scientists and administrators so knowledgeable that they have an instant answer for every forest management problem that develops. This is not correct. In recent years, in fact, the bright shining image that the Forest Service once enjoyed as the steward and protector of our National Forests has been sullied. Some of the Service's recent policies have caused storms of protest, not only in scientific circles but in the halls of Congress as well. Consider a few examples:

1. The Service recently advocated the intensive use of herbicides and fertilizers so that young forest trees would respond with accelerated growth. Operating on this premise the Service then per-

mitted a greater volume of timber to be harvested from our National Forests than ever before. This policy has engulfed the Service in lawsuits and public censure.

11–5 *Theodore Roosevelt and Gifford Pinchot (to left of Roosevelt) standing at the base of a giant redwood called "Old Grizzly." Pinchot was America's first Chief Forester.*

304

2. In 1982 the Service proposed to make changes in the National Forest Management Act. This action stirred up a hornet's nest of criticism. One scientist writing for the Sierra Club stated: "The proposed changes create a document that I seriously doubt meets the intent of Congress in many key areas." Peter Kirby, spokesman for the Wilderness Society, was equally concerned: "The proposed changes would weaken protection for fish and wildlife, further reduce study of the impact of mineral development on federal lands, contribute to the subsidization of timber sales, and allow overcutting of the remaining old-growth (350–1,000 years) timber in the Pacific Northwest."

3. In the early 1970s the Forest Service planned to build a paved road through National Forest land in northern California. The official objective of the plan was to provide loggers easier access to timber in Humboldt County. This project has been the object of scathing criticism from a coalition of environmental groups including the Siskiyou Mountains Resources Council, the Sierra Club, Friends of the Earth, and the National Audubon Society. This coalition believed that the project would destroy the wilderness character of the forest, would invade and desecrate the sacred High Country of Indians living in the area, and would cause serious erosion and stream pollution. Construction was started by the Forest Service in the early 1970s even though it had not yet prepared the legally required Environmental Impact Statement. It was only after a suit was brought against the Service by the Sierra Club that the Statement was finally prepared. During the legal skirmish the U.S. District Court commented that the Service had manipulated and suppressed pertinent data in the case. In his article "Stop the GO Road" which appeared in *Audubon*, novelist and nature writer Peter Mathiessen comments:

One report (ordered destroyed by a Forest Service officer) clearly supported the Sierra Club's position that the GO Road would cause massive landslides and destruction of the watersheds. Another report estimated that proposed road-building and logging in the Siskiyous would increase sedimentation by 1500 percent. . . . Despite all the Forest Service rhetoric about "multiple use" (known locally as "multiple abuse") the GO Road has no serious purpose besides expediting swift access to the Six Rivers National Forest, not for the benefit of the Americans, present and future, who own it, but for lumber corporations, which will have a "glorified logging road" at the taxpayers' expense.

Forest Management

A forest is a complex ecosystem. It is composed of both living (trees, herbs, shrubs, weeds, soil bacteria, fungi, viruses, earthworms, caterpillars, moths, bark beetles, grouse, bear, deer) and non-living (water, rock particles, solar radiation, wind, and so on) components. As in all other ecosystems interactions occur between the living and nonliving components. As we discuss various aspects of forest management, we shall consider some of the ways in which these interactions are affected.

Not all forests are managed in the same way. The type of management depends upon the main function of the forest — whether it be commercially valuable wood, wildlife, aesthetics, recreation, flood control, grazing, or another use. Depending upon the particular function or combination of functions of the forest, the forest manager will try to establish and maintain a unique stand with regard to species composition, species distribution, and age of trees. If the main function of the forest is to be the production of wood, it can be managed very efficiently. However, if the forest is to have multiple functions, as is the case in many of our national forests, then there will inevitably be some loss in efficiency for any one use. For example, clear cutting might be the most advantageous method to harvest wood, but it might also cause visual pollution, destroy wildlife habitat, and accelerate erosion.

Constraints

The forest manager must always consider the managerial, ecological, social, and legal constraints under which he operates.

1. *Managerial constraints* include such items as the overall cost of the management plan, as well as the limitations of the equipment available for harvesting, thinning, seeding, fertilizing, and planting, and so on.
2. *Ecological constraints* would include such conditions as the slope of the land, the fertility and depth of the soil, the age-species composition of the original vegetation, the micro-environment within the forest (light intensity, wind velocity,

temperature, evaporation rate, rate of water run-off, and so on). It would also include the potential for buildups of insect and disease pests.

3. *Social constraints.* In the past forest managers have too often lightly disregarded social pressures. However, this can be done no longer. Hunters, fishermen, nature lovers, wilderness seekers, tourists, ecologists, environmental organizations, and so on, have become increasingly vocal and political in their effort to influence the direction of forest management.

4. *Legal constraints.* The forest manager, of course, must operate within a legal framework composed of federal acts (such as the National Forest Management Act of 1976), as well as state laws and county ordinances, all of which establish certain standards for forest management.

We shall now consider the various aspects of forest management practiced by the Forest Service, many state forestry departments, and an increasing number of enlightened private owners, with respect to sustained yield, clear cutting, selective cutting, fertilization, reforestation, selective breeding of superior trees, multiple-use management, and pest and fire control.

Sustained Yield

Today's lumbermen are a different breed from the "cut-out-and-get-out" loggers of the late nineteenth and early twentieth centuries. After studying German silvicultural techniques, American foresters learned that a forest can be managed in such a way that a modest timber crop can be harvested indefinitely year after year if annual decrements are counterbalanced by annual growth increments. This is called the *sustained-yield* concept. (See Figure 11–6.) Under terms of the Multiple Use-Sustained Yield Act of 1960, foresters have a mandate from Congress to employ the principle of sustained yield in their operations. (See the guest article "The Meaning of Sustained Yield" by forest policy analyst B. Thomas Parry, in this chapter.)

Harvest Methods

CLEAR CUTTING. The clear-cutting method of timber harvest, which is the standard logging practice in the Northwest in both private and public forests, is employed on even-aged stands composed of only a few species and is applicable only to trees whose seedlings thrive best in full sunlight. The Douglas fir on the Pacific coast is harvested by this method. Perhaps the most valuable timber species

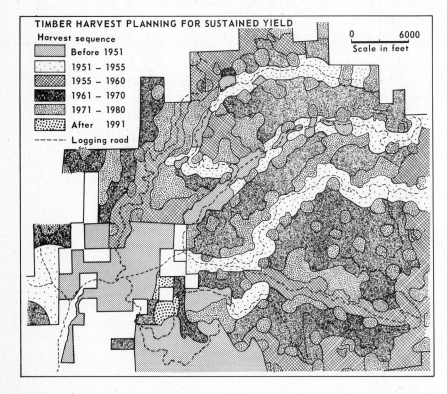

11–6 *Sustained-yield plan. This map of a timber tract owned by the Weyerhaeuser Company demonstrates the type of long-range planning required for successful sustained-yield forestry. Symbols indicate areas that will mature and should be harvested within a given decade. Note the large number of well-distributed logging roads providing fire protection and serving as logging facilities as well.*

11-7 *Clear cutting of old-growth Douglas fir in the Gifford Pinchot National Forest, Washington. Mt. St. Helens is in the background.*

in the world, it has been exported to Europe, where it has proved superior to native species. Some Douglas fir in Washington and Oregon stand over 200 feet high and are over 1,000 years old.

A Douglas fir, unlike a beech or maple, is not a climax tree and is not shade-tolerant as a seedling. Therefore, the species would not be amenable to selective cutting; its seeds would not germinate in the shade of the forest floor. Moreover, its place in the forest would rapidly be appropriated by shade-tolerant species. In addition, a 100-foot Douglas fir weighing several tons could not be removed without badly bruising and killing younger growth. With the clear-cutting technique, an entire patch of evenly aged mature trees, 40 to 200 acres in area, is removed, leaving an unsightly rectangular "scar" in the midst of the forest. (The maximum size of the area that may be clear cut is as follows: 100 acres for spruce and hemlock in coastal Alaska; 80 acres for yellow pine in some southern states; 60 acres for Douglas fir in the Pacific Northwest; and 40 acres for all other forest types.) Because a large number of such blocks may be removed, when viewed from the air a clear-cut forest resembles a giant green-and-brown checkerboard. (See Figures 11-7 and 11-8.)

11-8 *The slash in this clear-cut area in the Kootenai National Forest, Montana, has been piled in windrows by a bulldozer to reduce the fire hazard.*

307

The Meaning of Sustained Yield

B. *Thomas Parry*
CENTER FOR NATURAL
RESOURCE STUDIES
BERKELEY, CALIFORNIA

Sustained yield has been a cornerstone of conservation policy on America's national forests for over three-quarters of a century. Yet, close scrutiny shows that the very definition of sustained yield has changed substantially since the U.S. Forest Service began managing the national forests in the early 1900s. The historical context in which the policy has developed and changed is crucial in examining the validity of the current interpretation of sustained yield.

Early Forest Service sustained-yield policy, a legacy from European forestry of the nineteenth century, limited the amount of timber cut from the national forests to the amount grown. However, this conception of sustained yield rested on the assumption that the forests had a particular structure, called *fully regulated,* in which age and size classes of trees existed in such proportion and were growing at such rates that an equal annual amount of timber could be cut in perpetuity without depleting the growing stock. In this way, timber supply could be ensured forever.

By the early 1920s, however, the Forest Service had collected data on the timber resource in the national forests and realized that, instead of the forests being in a regulated condition, they were dominated by very large old trees that were growing very slowly, if at all. This situation caused the agency to change its sustained-yield policy and to begin to harvest trees in such a way that a regulated forest would be created as soon as was practical. No longer was cut limited to the amount grown, simply because so little net growth was being produced by the old forests of the day. The Forest Service's sustained-yield policy provided for harvesting more timber than was being grown at the time.

In the 1920s and 1930s, as part of a strategy by some members of the timber industry to increase sagging prices for timber by reducing overcutting on industry lands, a new conception of sustained yield was introduced: harvest at the capacity of the land to produce timber. These individuals argued that the relatively even annual volume of timber produced under such a policy would stabilize local communities by providing a continuous flow of wood to local industry. By the middle of the 1940s, even though the national forests were not yet regulated and there was little evidence that a continuous wood supply would be sufficient to stabilize local communities, the Forest Service adopted this new definition of sustained yield.

Prior to World War II, very little of the timber harvested in this country came from the national forests. As the American economy expanded after the war, however, the timber industry in the West began to rely heavily on national forests as sources of timber. Since timber on the national forests had not been previously harvested anywhere near productive capacity, national forest timber cuts increased dramatically in the 1950s and 1960s. In the late 1960s, however, the Forest Service realized that it could not indefinitely continue this new level of cutting in some parts of the country. The Forest Service's sustained-yield policy was in doubt.

During this era, environmentalists became an important political force and pressed the Forest Service to ensure that all forest resources were protected. In 1973, facing rising environmentalism and a western timber industry that had become dependent on national forest timber, the Forest Service adopted its most restrictive definition of sustained yield: nondeclining even flow. Under this conception, a national forest could not harvest timber at a level that could not be maintained well into the twenty-first century. This new view led to immediate reductions in timber harvests on many western national forests.

National forests are still not in a regulated condition. No hard evidence exists to support the claim that nondeclining even flow necessarily ensures stable communities or resource protection. The question that conservationists now face is: "How should this most important conservation policy be defined for the future management of the national forests?"

In addition to its use on Douglas fir in Oregon and Washington, the clear-cutting method has been used effectively in harvesting even-aged stands of Southern pine; aspen forests in northern Minnesota, Wisconsin, and Michigan; and coniferous forests in the West.

Let us see now why this method of harvest may result in a *sustained yield*. Suppose that a Wisconsin farmer who owns twenty acres of aspen woods wants a yearly harvest of pulpwood logs. He could log off a one-acre block year after year for twenty successive years. At the end of the period, if each block removed had been successfully reseeded, he would have twenty age classes, each one acre in area, ranging from one to twenty years in age. At the end of this twenty-year period, he could harvest one acre of twenty-year-old pulpwood stock, year after year for an indefinite period, as long as he ensures successful reseeding. The length of the cutting cycle, or rotation, depends on the species of tree and on its intended commercial use. For aspen and birch to be used as pulpwood, it varies from 10 to 30 years; on the other hand, the rotation for Douglas fir to be used as lumber may be up to 100 years.

The Clear-Cutting Controversy. The clear-cutting practices of the Forest Service became a storm center of considerable controversy in 1971. Much of the criticism focused on the ponderosa-pine logging in the Bitterroot National Forest of Montana. Let us examine some of the criticisms:

1. Clear cutting resulted in accelerated water runoff. Theoretically, this water could be used for irrigation and for watering livestock in nearby valley ranches. However, as one rancher from Sleeping Child, Montana, stated, "Nature previously controlled the runoff and regulated it naturally. Now the water is coming down in early spring, at the least desirable time. . . . if they keep this up we might as well forget about farming . . ." (2).
2. The wildlife-carrying capacity of an area that has been clear cut is greatly diminished, at least temporarily.* How many grouse or deer can be supported by a bare patch of ground?

---

* It is true that, in the third or fourth year after clear cutting, such early successional species as aspen, birch, and various shrubs may provide more wildlife food than was actually available in the mature forest before the clear cutting.

3. Clear cutting destroys the scenic beauty of a region, converting it into ugly, desolate scars.

Perhaps some of this criticism is valid. In any event, it certainly has served as a catalyst for a series of self-examination studies on the part of the Forest Service. The chief of the Service has emphasized that in the future the service will make more strenuous efforts to protect environmental quality. The record of the Forest Service, over the long haul, has been an admirable one. It has been vigorously defended by William E. Towell, in *American Forests*, the official magazine of the American Forestry Association, as follows:

Clear cutting most certainly has been abused in some areas. But it is a necessary tool in the professional forester's kit. It is the only way of regenerating forests of desirable species in certain regions. It is the only way to control some diseases and insects that can destroy the forest in a much more unsightly way. Clear cutting can be just as important to the forester as amputation is to the surgeon who must use it to save a life, but unlike human amputation, the forest will grow again. Foresters are learning to use the clear cut more sparingly, in smaller units, and away from public view, just as they are giving greater priority to aesthetics, to recreation, to wildlife, to water quality, and other amenities of forest lands. Let's not rob him of the essential tools of his profession, but rather demand that they be used with greater discretion in the public interest. The forester is a professional who will rise to the challenges of today as he has in the past. Let's give him that chance. . . . (14)

STRIP CUTTING. This method of harvesting timber has been used effectively in the forests of northeastern United States. You recall in our discussion of erosion control on farmland that strip cropping on the contour was a highly desirable technique. Strip logging is somewhat similar. It is usually employed in hilly terrain where clear cutting might result in massive pollution of streams just below the logging site.

Strip cutting involves the removal of trees along narrow strips of forest at intervals of several years. The strip cutting method has several advantages over clear cutting: a) it minimizes the loss of soil nutrients from the forest; b) it curbs the pollution of mountain streams with sediment (thus preventing the destruction of spawning sites for trout); c) it minimizes the ugliness associated with much larger clear cut areas; and d) it permits for more effective reforestation by natural mechanisms.

SELECTIVE CUTTING. It is apparent that clear cutting will not work in timber stands composed of unevenly aged trees, or in mixed stands composed in part of valuable timber species and in part of trash species. Under such conditions trees are harvested by *selective cutting*, a sort of hunt-and-pick method in which mature trees of quality species are harvested after being marked in advance with spray paint or some other method. Selective cutting has been employed extensively in mixed coniferous-hardwood stands and in deciduous forests (oak, hickory, butternut, and walnut). It is obviously a more costly and time-consuming method than clear cutting. However, such environmental abuse as land scarring, accelerated runoff, soil erosion, and wildlife depletion is reduced to a minimum.

Selective cutting on a given stand is often done on a ten-year rotation. Sustained-yield management is practiced — the volume of wood harvested during a given year being equal to the volume grown since the previous cutting. A small number of trees is re-moved per acre. They are eventually replaced by natural reproduction. The selective-cutting method can be used only on species such as maple, beech, and hemlock, whose seedlings can germinate in the shade of the forest floor.

Audubon magazine has reported on a case where selective cutting was carried to extremes:

Walnut veneer is so popular that tree "rustlers" range the Great Plains states, making off with any rare old black walnuts that remain. One thief sawed down and carried off a handsome specimen from a city park in broad daylight. Another took a prized tree from a farmer's front yard while he was attending church services! The best old trees can be sold for up to $25,000 and buyers come all the way from West Germany and Japan to bid for them. . . . (12)

FERTILIZATION. The fertilization of a forest site has four main objectives:

1. The accelerated growth of commercially valuable wood.

The Role of Clear Cutting in Forest Management

John E. Benneth
Western Regional Manager
AMERICAN FOREST INSTITUTE

Clear cutting is the practice of harvesting all of the trees in a stand of timber in one cutting. Though the result isn't pretty, it's a temporary condition and it's good forestry when applied correctly.

The role of clear cutting in forest management becomes understandable when seen in terms of forest ecology. The forests of nearly all of North America, unlike tropical forests, renewed themselves periodically over the millenniums of time by disruptive events such as fire or windstorm. These were nature's own "clear cuts," and man drastically altered this historic process through his recent substantial success in controlling wildfire. Clear cutting became the forester's way of replicating nature's process of renewal.

The Douglas fir forests of western Oregon and Washington are an example of the necessary role of clear cutting when wildfire is controlled. In natural stands of Douglas fir, the trees are found to be even-aged, evidence of a cataclysmic event in the past. There are no young fir seedlings growing in such stands because young Douglas fir requires open sunlight for growth. Only other shade-tolerant species exist there. Yet the forests of that region have remained predominantly Douglas fir — further evidence of the fact that huge forest fires over the ages periodically wiped out the old stands and created openings for the new young Douglas firs.

In modern forestry, clear cuts are virtually always planted immediately with two-year-old seedlings to put the land back to work growing more trees.

2. The establishment of a young forest which might be getting a "root-hold" in an area which had been clear cut.
3. The rapid development of vegetative cover, which will protect a burned-off or logged-off area from erosion.
4. Raising the carrying capacity of the forest for wildlife such as grouse and deer by increasing the abundance and the quality of both food and cover.

Nitrogen is the most important element required for the vigorous growth of trees. However, nitrogen requirements vary, depending upon the species. For example, maple, oak and aspen need rather small amounts. Basswood, ash, and tulip poplar, on the other hand, require relatively large amounts of nitrogen. Nitrogen is usually applied in the form of urea pellets from low-flying helicopters. One fertilizer application of about 200 kilograms per hectare is adequate for about a six-year period. Nitrogen fertilization is most effective on sites that are nitrogen deficient. In northern hardwoods tree growth may be increased by 80 percent; on the other hand in the Douglas fir forests of the Pacific Northwest the maximal growth response to fertilization is about 18 percent.

Effect on Insect Pest Populations. Fertilization will result in changes in the mineral, sugar, and amino acid content of the leaves on which pest insects feed. These changes may have either positive or negative effects on insect pest populations, depending upon the species involved. Fertilization will certainly increase the *volume* of plant food available to insect pests. On the other hand, it may also alter the *texture* of the leaves so that they are less desirable as a food supply to herbivorous insects.

Effect on Wildlife (Game) Populations. Fertilization of forest sites usually has a beneficial effect on wildlife populations. Game animals such as deer, elk, and grouse require certain essential amino acids that they can get only from their plant foods. These amino acids are more highly concentrated in the stems, buds, and leaves of trees and shrubs that have had an adequate supply of nutrients, including nitrogen. Numerous studies have shown that deer will browse preferentially on plant tissues containing high levels of amino acids and virtually ignore other vegetation that is deficient in amino acids.

Effects on Water Quality of Lakes and Streams. The runoff of excess nutrients into lakes and streams after fertilization may result in eutrophication problems. This is especially true when very young stands in the seedling stage are fertilized, since runoff is relatively considerable. Another negative feature is that fertilization may indirectly cause decreased water levels. This is due to the increased amount of water that is absorbed from the soil and later transpired by rapidly growing trees. The declining water levels may then result in elevated water temperatures, which might exceed the temperature tolerance range for cold-water fish such as trout and salmon.

Reforestation

The sustained-yield concept dictates that, whenever timber is removed, either by clear cutting or by selective cutting, the denuded area must be reforested. This may be done by natural or artificial methods. Similarly, any forested land that has been destroyed by fire, insects, disease, hurricanes, or strip-mining activities also should be reforested, even though timber may not be its ultimate primary use.

After clear cutting, a few mature, wind-firm trees on a ridge may be left intact as a seed source within the otherwise logged-off site. Scattered by wind and to a lesser degree by birds, rodents, and runoff water, the seeds will eventually become dispersed throughout the denuded area. Natural reseeding, however, is usually not completely adequate. One reason is that some tree species, such as loblolly pine, may have only one good seed-producing year out of every two- to five-year period. (In a good year seed production may be ten times what it is in a poor year.) Another reason is that the dispersed seeds must reach mineral soil to develop properly. Because of these drawbacks, natural reseeding is usually combined with aerial, hand, or machine seeding.

In rugged terrain aerial seeding is the best method. Seeds are sown from planes flying slowly just above treetop level. Unfortunately, many of these seeds fall on infertile soil or are consumed by birds and rodents. To minimize loss to animals, the seeds are frequently coated with a toxic deterrent. Except in the case of exceptionally small seeded trees, such as hemlock and spruce, rodent eradication is virtually a prerequisite to successful seeding.

If the logged-off site has an even topography, power-driven seeding and planting machines may be advantageously employed, as has been done in the cutover land of Wisconsin and Michigan. These machines are not only capable of planting up to eight acres per day, but simultaneously fertilize the soil and apply a herbicide to prevent weed encroachment.

In addition to the bird and rodent problem, a major disadvantage to seeding is the high number of first-year seedlings killed by frost, drought, hot weather, insects, and autumn leaf fall. As a result, seeding, even by artificial methods, is less effective than planting young trees from plantation stock. In the South and in the Great Lake states, trees can be planted at a rate of 150 per worker-hour. Open fields in the Midwest have been planted with the aid of an ordinary moldboard plow. On flatland, three workers, a tractor, and a planting machine can set 1,000 to 2,000 trees per hour.

TREE FARMS.   A tree farm is a private land area used for growing timber for profit. The tree-farm movement was started by the Weyerhaeuser Company at Montesand, Washington, in 1941. It is currently sponsored by the American Forest Products Industries, which is composed of the timber, paper, pulp, and plywood industries and private owners of forest lands. In applying for certification the owner must demonstrate to an inspecting forester that he or she is employing sound forest-management practices, such as sustained yield and effective pest and fire control. When a state tree-farm certification committee has approved the forester's report, the tree-farm owner is awarded the official roadside tree-farm sign as recognition of achievement. This movement has grown from 8,086 tree farms embracing 39 million acres in 1956 to 35,000 farms covering 75 million acres in the early 1980s.

Development of Genetically Superior Trees

Forest genetics is a young, vigorously growing science that holds great promise for the forest manager. Results of numerous breeding experiments have indicated that a large number of economically significant tree characteristics may be enhanced by selective breeding. Among these characteristics are growth rate, wood density, shape of trunk, and resistance to drought, cold, insect pests and diseases. Foresters usually are able to visually identify supe-

11–9 *Reforestation. A contract planter for the Crown-Zellerbach Corporation puts a fir seedling in the ground on a managed forest area near Seaside, Oregon.*

rior trees that can be used as the parents in the production of superior seedlings.

HYBRIDIZATION.   The crossing of two species of trees, known as *hybridization*, may result in offspring that combine the best traits of the parents.

For example, in northern California plantations of Jeffrey pine were formerly very vulnerable to the attacks of the pine weevil. Economic damage was severe. The problem has been somewhat reduced, however, by the hybridization technique. Thus, the cold-resistant Jeffrey pine was crossed with the weevil-resistant Coulter's pine. The resultant hybrids were resistant to both cold and the pine weevil. The timber-valuable Western Red Cedar is susceptible to needle-spot disease caused by a fungus. By crossing it with another species of cedar which is less valuable as a timber source but is resistant to needle spot fungus, a hybrid was developed which combines the good traits of the parent types.

It has been shown that in southern pine stands selective breeding techniques may improve wood volume by 9.9 percent, straightness of trunk by 9.3 percent, wood density by 4.8 percent, and rust resistance by 4.2 percent. The economic gains resulting from applied forestry genetics may be considerable. A forest breeding program in California, for example, resulted in an increased return of $27.37 per acre.

Multiple-Use Management

A primary objective of the U.S. Forest Service is to make the greatest number of forest resources available to the greatest number of Americans. Under terms of the Multiple Use-Sustained Yield Act of 1960 the Forest Service, as well as the forest industry, has been committed to this concept in its operations.

The multiple-use management of forests looks simple on paper. In actual operation, however, it is an extremely complex ecological problem with a veritable "thicket" of cause-and-effect relationships. For example, the Forest Service is frequently forced to utilize a given forest acre primarily for one resource while sacrificing its potential for other values. A given acre of forest cannot be all things to all people. If a given acreage of Douglas fir is to be developed for high-quality timber, then clear cutting this acreage would certainly be a perfectly valid management procedure. However, at the same time, the wholesale removal of a timber block would greatly impair the value of that particular acreage in terms of flood and erosion control, wildlife habitat, and recreation. Sound multiple-use management must weigh the needs of the people, and these vary both in time and place. Thus, timber production may have top priority in the valuable

Douglas fir and Western-hemlock stands of Washington and Oregon, but in the low-value second-growth forests of populous New York, where many city dwellers require occasional doses of "wilderness tonic," recreational values would have high priority.

We will now briefly examine some examples of how the Forest Service has managed our forests in terms of flood and erosion control, rangeland, and wildlife habitat.

THE USE OF FORESTS IN FLOOD AND EROSION CONTROL. Ever since the late nineteenth century, many of our Western valley towns situated at the base of steep mountain slopes have been periodically battered by brief but damaging flash floods spawned by sudden summer storms. A valley

11–10 *Multiple use of the forest. A logger and a fisherman greet each other along the Santeetlah Creek in North Carolina's Nantahala National Forest. The logger is transporting part of the timber harvested annually from the surrounding watershed, and the angler is anxious to fill his creel.*

The Monoculture Controversy

Monoculture is the practice of growing trees as crops, much like the farmer grows a crop of corn or oats. It involves planting and raising a single-species stand of trees, with all individuals in the stand being of the same age and size. Monoculture has been firmly espoused by some forest managers and big forest-products corporations and economists on the one hand, but it has been sharply criticized by other professional foresters and, more significantly, by eminent ecologists as well. In heated controversies such as this, it is instructive to list objectively the major points both for and against monoculture (9, 10).

Arguments for Monoculture

1. It is an efficient method of growing and harvesting a large volume of timber.
2. Because growth is rapid, harvesting (by clear cutting) can be done on a relatively short rotation.
3. It is amenable to the intensive application (frequently by air) of fertilizers, herbicides, fungicides, and insecticides.
4. It makes possible maximal use of such recent technological developments as machine seeders, tree-planting machines, the "tree monkey" (which climbs and prunes trees simultaneously), the chip harvester, the one-man logger, and the crusher (which can clear 600 acres of forested land in only one month).
5. Monoculture is tailor made for harvest by clear cutting — a relatively inexpensive method.
6. If the forestry profession is to meet America's growing demands for wood products, it must rely more and more on the practice of monoculture.
7. It makes possible the establishment of sun-loving (shade-intolerant) seedlings of such economically valuable species as Douglas fir, redwood, longleaf pines, ponderosa pine, yellow poplar, red oak, cherry, and black walnut.

Arguments Against Monoculture

1. A forest under monoculture is an artificial, man-made, simplified ecosystem. As such it lacks the built-in balancing mechanisms incorporated in the more complex natural ecosystem represented by the multiaged, multispecies forest.
2. Although monoculture admittedly grows wood faster, it is inferior in quality when compared to the more slowly growing wood of the mature trees in a natural forest.
3. The intensive use of fertilizers results in nutrient runoff, which eventually contributes to the eutrophication and degradation of lakes and streams.
4. The intensive use of insecticides will contribute to the pollution of both aquatic ecosystems and the atmosphere. Pesticide contamination of food chains may have adverse effects on wildlife and humans. (See Chapter 12.) Continuous use of insecticides will result in the development of insecticide-resistant strains of forest insects.
5. The practice of monoculture depends on intensive inputs of energy derived from fossil fuels. This energy may be used directly — as in the consumption of gasoline by tree planters, pruners, chain saws, helicopters, and airplanes (used in seeding and in applying fertilizers and insecticides) — or indirectly — by being consumed in the manufacture of

the heavy forest-planting and harvesting machinery or in the production of fertilizers and pesticides.

6. The single-species, single-aged forest primarily serves one function: wood production. But other functions, such as erosion and flood control, provision of wildlife habitat, scenic beauty, and recreational opportunities, are much better served by the naturally developed multispecies, multiaged forest.

7. Because of the relative scarcity of moisture-absorbing organic material on the floor of the monoculture forest, the forest floor tends to be drier and warmer than that of the "natural" forest. As a result, the monoculture forest is more susceptible to fires.

8. A forest monotype is very vulnerable to destructive outbreaks of insects and disease organisms.

9. Eventually, of course, the monoculture forest will be clear cut — a harvesting method that results in a whole complex of environmental problems.

To The Student: After weighing the arguments for and against monoculture, what opinion do you have? Prepare to discuss this issue with your instructor and classmates.

stream would be placid for one hour, but the next it might be transformed into a churning torrent, bearing soil, rocks, uprooted shrubs, and debris washed from the slope of a mountain. Surging down the valley, the swollen stream might cause considerable property damage and loss of life.

One of the regions hardest hit by this type of flash flood a number of years ago, was Davis County, Utah, at the eastern margin of Great Salt Lake. Harried citizens, beleaguered by recurring disasters, finally asked Congress for federal assistance. In his book *Land, Wood and Water,* the late Senator Robert S. Kerr of Oklahoma described the work of the Forest Service in dealing with the problem (6). During their survey, Forest Service investigators discovered that much of the flood-triggering runoff originated from areas that had been depleted of their vegetational cover. Those denuded parts of the watershed had either been burned over, overgrazed, or plowed up and converted into marginal croplands. In some areas the runoff waters carved gullies 70 feet deep. During one rainy period, up to 160 times as much water ran off an abused plot than ran off an undisturbed one. With the aid of bulldozers, the gullies were filled in, slopes were contoured, and the bare soil was carefully prepared as a seedbed and planted with rapidly growing shrubs and trees. Only 11 years later, severe August rainstorms put the rehabilitated watershed to the test. An investigation

revealed that fully 93.5 percent of the rainfall was retained by the newly forested area. Moreover, soil erosion was reduced from the pretreatment figure of 268 cubic feet per acre to a mere trace (7).

THE USE OF FORESTS AS RANGELANDS. In addition to timber, our forests frequently include considerable areas of high-quality livestock forage. Thus, of the 186 million acres comprising our national forests and national grasslands, 100 million acres (over 53 percent) provide forage for six million cattle and sheep belonging to 19,000 farmers and ranchers. (Most of this is in the West. In the lake and central states most forest grazing occurs on farm woodlots.) Graziers pay fees for the privilege of grazing their livestock in national forests. (See Figure 11–11.) In a typical year, grazing-fee receipts amount to $4 million, of which 25 percent is returned to the state coffers for the improvement of highways and schools in the counties where the fees were levied (19).

THE USE OF FORESTS AS WILDLIFE HABITAT. Our 154 national forests and nineteen national grasslands embrace 186 million acres, almost one acre for each American. Two thirds of the sportsmen visiting this vast public hunting ground seek big game; the remainder seek upland game and waterfowl. In a typical year, hunters spend about 15 million visitor

11-11 *Sheepherder and two sheepdogs watch over sheep grazing in a high meadow within the Plumas National Forest, California. Some 18,000 sheep graze the summer ranges of the Plumas under paid permit.*

days in the national forests and grasslands and bag about 600,000 big-game animals, 95 percent of which are deer and elk.

The Forest Service attempts to manage our national forests to provide the best possible habitat for wildlife. Sometimes the best management involves increasing the "forest-edge" habitat frequented by many game animals such as deer, rabbit, and pheasant. Forest-edge improvement for game may be integrated with timber harvesting and the construction of fire lanes and logging trails. Because game food and cover are more abundant in early stages than in climax stages, the retardation of succession by prescribed burning may be beneficial to wildlife. In a typical year the Forest Service seeds and plants game food on 45,000 acres, protects 35,000 acres of key wildlife habitat, and employs regulated burning to improve the wild-game-carrying capacity of 45,000 acres (20).

THE USE OF FORESTS AS RECREATIONAL, WILDERNESS, AND SCIENTIFIC AREAS. In this polluted age, when urban dwellers from Seattle to Miami and from San Diego to Boston are being crowded together shoulder to shoulder, when air is weighted with soot and odious with industrial gases, when drinking water tastes of chlorine, and when the tyranny of noise assaults the ears from all compass points, it is somehow reassuring to know that "way out there," somewhere in the great forests of Amer-

ica, is wilderness country. And once you get there, you can hike or canoe for miles without even getting near a human shoulder; you can actually inhale unadulterated fresh air; you can drink clear, cold water from a tumbling brook, and the only sounds are pine boughs sighing in the evening breeze or the dusk chant of a whippoorwill.

Of the 188 million acres of National forests in the United States, only about 110 million acres (58.5 percent) have roads. About 15.6 million acres of the roadless forests were included under the National Wilderness Preservation System as of 1977. However, an ongoing controversy has been raging concerning the designation of the remaining 62 million roadless acres. On the one hand private timber interests would like to lease or purchase some of this land and log it. (Almost incredibly, these interests have actually received some support for their position from no less than Secretary of the Interior James Watt!) On the other hand environmentalists, led by such organizations as the Sierra Club, the National Audubon Society, and the Wilderness Society, would like most or all of this acreage to be included under the National Wilderness Preservation System. In the name of "progress," wilderness country has gradually receded under the onslaught of timber and mining interests, highway engineers, and land developers. Even the U.S. Navy has gotten into the act with its controversial Project Sanguine, an electronic system for communicating with submarines that, as initially proposed, would have converted 20,000 square miles of Wisconsin backwoods country into a gigantic "electric waffle."

Among the officially designated wilderness areas are the Boundary Waters Canoe Area in northern Minnesota. Under the terms of this act, such obtrusive activities as logging, mining, and the use of automobiles, motorboats, and snowmobiles are prohibited. In some areas even aircraft are not permitted to descend below a designated altitude. In the officially designated wilderness area, every attempt is made to permit the forest ecosystem to operate without human interference. If an overmature pine, riddled with bark-beetle galleries, blows down during a windstorm, it remains where it falls. Barring a major catastrophe, such as a crown fire, the official policy is, "Let nature take its course." As a result, these areas have considerable scientific as well as recreational value. In such an area, many a university researcher can make observations, collect data, and formulate hypotheses, and many an eager college student can acquire valuable field experiences in geography, entomology, mammalogy, ornithology, ecology, field natural history, and game management, as well as forestry.

USE OF FORESTS AS A SOURCE OF FUEL. The supply of fossil fuels (other than coal) is rapidly becoming exhausted. As a result, alternative sources of energy are being explored. One such source is the biomass represented by trees. Of course, the great advantage of wood as a fuel source is that, unlike fossil fuels, it is renewable.

At the present time, wood and wood products provide 1.3 quads* or 1.5 percent of the 80 quads of

* One quad equals one quadrillion, which equals 1×10^{15}, which equals 1,000,000,000,000,000 BTUs (British Thermal Units). One BTU equals the quantity of heat required to raise the temperature of one pound of water one degree Fahrenheit at 39.2° F.

11–12 *Use of forests as wilderness areas. Large redwoods in Del Norte State Park, California. Interesting light patterns are created by sunlight filtering through dense fog. Some California redwoods are more than 3,000 years old.*

energy consumed in the United States each year. However, in its National Energy Program for Forestry, the Forest Service hopes to increase the amount of wood-derived energy from 1.3 quads to 5 quads annually by 1990. This goal, according to the Service, may be realized, in part, by adopting the following strategies:

1. Develop management techniques for maximizing biomass production in natural forest stands.
2. Identify the species of trees that can be grown under relatively crowded conditions, yet grow very rapidly in volume.
3. Set up experimental tree plantations of the selected species of "energy" trees.
4. Encourage the wise production of fuel wood on private stands, including those on small woodlots.
5. Develop new harvesting equipment that can handle small trees as well as wood residues, such as branches, that accumulate on the forest floor.
6. Develop improved methods for producing alcohol (a possible motor fuel), oil, and natural gas from wood (15).

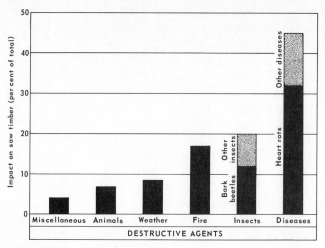

11 – 13 *Impact of destructive agents on sawtimber (indicated in percent of total impact).*

Forest Pests

The most serious agents of forest destruction are disease and insect pests. (See Figure 11 – 13.) Under the authority of the Forest Pest Control Act of 1947,

Chestnut Blight

At the turn of the century, the American chestnut was a conspicuous, attractive, and valuable member of the deciduous forest in the eastern United States; in some areas, such as the Appalachians, it formed over 50 percent of the stand. (See Figure 11 – 14.) Both humans and beasts found its nuts nutritious and palatable. Tannin, a substance of prime importance in the leather-tanning process, was derived from its bark; from its straight trunk durable fence posts and rails were fashioned. Today, however, only the leafless skeletons of those trees remain. You can tramp the Appalachians for weeks without finding a single living mature tree. In New England a few living sprouts from native stumps may be found.

The near extinction of the once-abundant chestnut was caused by a parasitic fungus, inadvertently introduced along with nursery stock from China. The parasite was first reported in New York City in 1904. Once established, the fungus spread rapidly, virtually eliminating the chestnut as a commercial species by 1914. After gaining access through a bark wound (possibly caused by fire, insects, or rodents), the fungus invades the cambium and phloem, spreads rapidly, and ultimately plugs the food-conducting phloem tissue, causing the leaves to turn brown and wither. Eventually, when the malnourished roots no longer can absorb soil moisture and nutrients, the tree dies. (See Figure 11 – 15.) Trunk and branches swell at the foci of infection and form cankers that produce tiny reproductive spores. During dry seasons light spores are formed that are wind disseminated. During wet seasons, heavy, sticky yellowish-brown tendrils of spores ooze from the cankers and adhere to the bodies of bark beetles and squirrels and the bills and feet of woodpeckers. (Up to one billion spores have been washed from

11-14 *Original distribution of the American chestnut tree.*

11-15 *These American chestnut trees in the mountains of North Carolina have been killed by the chestnut blight.*

the feet of one woodpecker.) During migrations woodpeckers may fly twenty miles or more daily, thus serving as superb dispersal agents.

In recent years Oriental chestnuts, which are quite resistant to the blight, have been introduced. Although these trees do well when given solicitous care under nurserylike conditions, they are unable to survive in the wild. Forest geneticists have been crossing the resistant Oriental chestnut with the American chestnut in an attempt to develop a blight-resistant hybrid. If successful, the chestnut may yet again be an important component of our deciduous forests.

319

surveys are annually conducted in both private and public forests to permit the early detection of pest population increases so that they can be arrested before they reach disastrous levels. In a typical year Congress appropriates $10 million for pest control and an additional $3 million for research.

Diseases

Forest diseases cause roughly 45 percent of the total saw-timber destruction. Heart-rot fungus alone is responsible for about 33 percent of the total forest damage. (This fungus, however, may be beneficial as an important agent in the decay of fallen logs, dead stubs, and slash, thus recycling elements and removing flammable debris.) The remaining disease damage can be attributed primarily to white-pine blister rust, dwarf mistletoe, and Dutch elm disease. The most injurious disease pests are exotics, accidentally introduced to the United States, that have suddenly been released from environmental factors that ordinarily keep them in check.

WHITE-PINE BLISTER RUST. The blister-rust parasite has primarily infected the white pines of New England and the lake states and the western white pine and sugar pine of the Pacific Coast. Many of these stately trees, over 200 years old and 150 feet

11 – 16 *Tree infected by white pine blister rust.*

tall, have withstood wind, storm, hail, sub-Arctic cold, drought, fires, and insect attacks, only to succumb to this microscopic fungus. The blister rust was introduced accidentally from Germany; it was first found in North America at Geneva, New York, in 1906. When new infections were introduced on the West Coast, hope for its eradication was abandoned.

Control Methods

REMOVAL OF HOST. The White-pine blister rust requires two alternative hosts to complete its lifecycle: one is the white pine, the other is either gooseberry or currant bushes. It can be controlled, therefore, simply by depriving the rust of one of them. White-pine timber is much more valuable than jam; hence, all gooseberry and currant bushes within a 1,000-foot radius of a white-pine stand are destroyed. (See Figure 11 – 17.) These thorny shrubs may be bulldozed, burned, or treated with a herbicide. The Forest Service surveys about three million acres in its blister-rust control operations and removes gooseberry and currant bushes from about 240,000 acres annually.

USE OF ANTIBIOTICS. Several antibiotics have been developed recently that have proved effective in blister-rust control. One, phytoactin, has been successfully used on infected western white pine. (See Figure 11 – 18.) Another, cyclohexamide, has given promising results on infected white-pine seedlings (20). The Forest Service treats over 100,000 acres of infected pine with rust-killing antibiotics annually.

DEVELOPMENT OF RESISTANT PINES. In recent years Forest Service geneticists have succeeded in developing rust-resistant hybrids. A 100-acre seed orchard of resistant hybrids has been developed. As a result, a mass quantity of seeds is now available for planting several hundred thousand acres to rust-resistant pine (17). The extension of this program of genetic control may ultimately eliminate blister rust as a major agent of forest destruction in this country.

Insects

Insects account for 20 percent of all timber destroyed, ranking second only to diseases as a destructive agent. Each year insects ruin five billion board feet of timber, roughly equivalent to 10 per-

11 – 17 *Dissemination of blister-rust spores. Because the spores can be dispersed a maximum of 1,000 feet from the currant or gooseberry hosts, removal of all such hosts within a radius of 1,000 feet from a stand of white pine would protect the pine from infection with blister rust.*

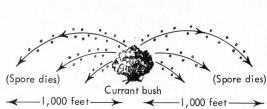

White pines (Spore dies) Currant bush (Spore dies) White pines

←—— 1,000 feet ——→ ←—— 1,000 feet ——→

11 – 18 *A young Western white pine stand in the St. Joe National Forest in Idaho is being sprayed with the antibiotic fungicide phytoactin to arrest the damage being caused by the white pine blister rust.*

11 – 19 *Aerial photo taken with infrared film readily reveals the extent of an insect infestation of Oregon timber. Damaged trees appear darker.*

cent of our total annual timber harvest. Each tree species has its own unique assemblage of insect pests. An oak tree may be ravaged by over 100 species. No part of a tree's anatomy is spared.

BARK BEETLES. Almost 90 percent of insect-inflicted timber mortality is caused by bark beetles. They destroy roughly 4.5 billion board feet annually. Adult beetles attack a tree by boring through the bark and then tunneling out egg chambers and galleries with their powerful jaws. The tiny grubs that hatch from the eggs consume the soft inner bark, and if sufficiently numerous (1,000 per large tree) may actually girdle the tree and kill it within a month. The bark-beetle group includes a large number of destructive species. The Western pine beetle killed 25 billion board feet of ponderosa pine along the Pacific coast between 1917 and 1943. (See Figure 11–20.) The mountain pine beetle has killed an aggregate 20 billion board feet of sugar pine, Western white pine, and lodgepole pine in California alone.

The fluctuating populations of the Englemann-spruce beetle in the higher elevations of the Rockies form an interesting ecological study. (See Figure 11–21.) For many years before 1942, these beetles were at least partially held in check by predatory insects and birds; woodpeckers were especially well adapted for feeding on them. Woodpeckers have extremely long, sticky tongues with which they can probe the beetle galleries and snare their bean-sized prey. Whenever the beetle population increased, an influx of woodpeckers would soon check the incipi-

11–21 *Englemann spruce bark-beetle larvae located just under the bark of a tree in the White River National Forest, Colorado. These beetles have destroyed over two billion feet of Englemann spruce timber on the White River.*

ent buildup, thus keeping the population in dynamic equilibrium. During this pre-1942 period, the spruce beetles had concentrated on moisture-deficient trees or on trees in which the sap flow was not sufficiently vigorous to protect them from beetle intrusions. However, in 1942, a violent windstorm uprooted thousands of spruce. The fallen trees formed a food bonanza for the spruce beetles. Because they were protected from woodpeckers by the interlocking branches of the prostrate trunks, and probably also as a result of the superabundant food supply, the beetle population increased sharply. They now could more fully realize a reproductive potential in which a single pair could theoretically give rise to 10,000 progeny in a single breeding season. In 1949 a portion of the beetle population drowned in a small lake and drifted ashore, forming a solid drift of beetles one foot deep, six feet wide, and two miles long (15). The beetle hordes

11–20 *Adult western pine beetle* (Dendroctonus brevicomis).

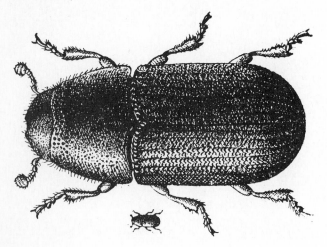

322

were then so numerous that they successfully attacked even young, vigorously growing trees (heretofore protected by their sap flow), as well as overmature trees and windblown timber. Within a six-year period (1940 to 1946), the spruce beetles had destroyed 20 percent of the Engelmann spruce in Colorado, a volume of three billion board feet — sufficient to provide homes for two million people. The rate of timber destruction by beetles in the region was 75 times the rate of destruction by fire.

Various methods have been used to control bark beetles. On a long-term basis, perhaps the best method of "control" is to prevent infestations from occurring in the first place. This may be done by using *sanitation techniques:* by burning all potential bark-beetle breeding sites, such as senile and windblown trees, and by logging accumulated slash and debris and the broken-off trunks of lightning- and fire-killed trees. (In removing those trunks, however, the forester is also removing the potential nesting cavities of beetle-eating woodpeckers, so a cost-benefit analysis would have to be made.) Insecticides can be applied by planes that fly low over the infected area.

Integrated Pest Management (IPM)

In the late 1970s certain environmental groups, notably the National Audubon Society, became

Controlling Insect Outbreaks with Heterotypes

Insect-pest populations sometimes build up to impressive densities. Charles Kendigh, an ecologist at the University of Illinois, was making a study of a severe spruce budworm outbreak in Ontario. The larvae, which were feeding on coniferous foliage, occurred in such vast numbers that their excreta made sounds like drizzling rain as they fell on the forest floor. More recently, a population "explosion" of forest tent caterpillars virtually destroyed 26,850 acres of water tupelo in the region of Mobile Bay, Alabama (23). Aerial photographs revealed almost complete defoliation of extensive stands of once-healthy trees.

Now the question is, is it possible to control such outbreaks without resorting to expensive insecticides that may have subtle adverse effects on the forest ecosystem? One possible alternative method is establishing forest *heterotypes,* as suggested by Kenneth Watt, an ecologist at the University of California, Davis. When monoculture is practiced in a large contiguous area, populations of insect pests tend to fluctuate violently. Over a long period of evolution involving millions of years, certain species of insects have developed that not only have become specialized to feed on a *particular species* of tree (spruce budworm on balsam fir, larch sawfly on larch, gypsy moth on oak, pine-bark beetle on pine, and so on), but also to feed on that kind of tree at a *particular stage* (seed, seedling, sapling, or mature tree) in its life cycle. In natural forest ecosystems, the particular food tree to which a species of insect has become adapted may be widely dispersed. An insect, such as a pine-bark beetle, for example, might have to creep, crawl, or fly a considerable distance from one food tree until it finds another. In the process, of course, such an insect becomes vulnerable to predation, windstorms and rainstorms, fire, and other mortality factors. Even if it survives these factors, it may eventually starve to death before it is able to find another food tree. Conversely, in an artificial forest ecosystem, as represented by a monotype, the pine-bark beetle is not only surrounded by the right species of food tree, say white pine, but also by white-pine trees of the precise age that the pine-bark beetles can most effectively exploit as a food source. Watt has shown that the severity of forest-insect outbreaks can be substantially reduced simply by breaking up the large contiguous stands of single-age, single-species trees into a number of small isolated stands, interspersed with trees of different kinds and ages (23).

very concerned with the large amounts of chemical pesticides used by the Forest Service to control insect outbreaks. This criticism reached a peak of intensity when the Forest Service used DDT (banned except for emergencies) to control an explosion of tussock moths in conifer stands of the Northwest. Ecologists considered this strategy particularly questionable because ordinarily the tussock moth population is "knocked down" anyway, after a period of time, by a death-causing virus, which acts as a density-dependent agent of control. Eventually the Forest Service, stung by criticism from many quarters, decided to adopt the integrated pest management (IPM) policy, under which the use of chemicals in insect control is sharply reduced. Among the IPM strategies now employed by the Forest Service are the following:

1. Biological control agents, such as predators and parasites, are used whenever feasible.
2. Selective cutting methods are used in preference to clear-cutting methods (since even-aged trees are highly vulnerable to insect attacks).
3. Bark-damaged trees are removed because they serve as focal points of insect infestation.
4. Heterotypes are favored over monotypes whenever feasible.

Fire Control

Even before the white man's coming, North American forests had been consumed by flames. Annual ring-sequence studies on giant redwoods indicate that those trees have been exposed to fire about once every 25 years over the last ten centuries. Early Spanish and French explorers wrote of traveling through dense clouds of smoke issuing from flaming forests. Every three minutes a forest fire starts somewhere in the United States. Not too long ago there were more than 100,000 forest wildfires in the United States in a single year. They burned more than 10,500 square miles of forest, equivalent to sending the entire state of Maryland up in smoke. Although fire may not kill a tree outright, it may cause distorted growth and impair its timber value. Fire annually is responsible for 17 percent of sawtimber destruction from all causes. (See Figure 11–13.) Because of the better fire-control techniques that have been developed recently, the total acreage of destroyed timber has been sharply re-

duced. For example, the forest fires that broke out in 1979 succeeded in burning only about three million acres, roughly 6 percent of the high of 50 million acres in 1931.

Fire Classes

Forest fires are classified as surface, soil, or crown.

SURFACE FIRES. The surface fire is the most common type of fire. It moves along the forest floor, fed by tinder-dry pine needles, crisp leaf litter, twigs, vines, shrubs, logs, leathery mushrooms, and the leaf-woven homes of ground-nesting birds. Driven by the wind, these fires may burn intensely but are of short duration. An occasional tree will have its bark singed, making it susceptible to insects and fungus growths. The most destructive aspect of the surface fire is that, in consuming millions of germinating seeds and seedlings, it destroys the forest of the future.

SOIL FIRES. Surface fires may develop into *soil fires*, which consume the organic content of the forest soil just below the leaf litter. Some penetrate to a depth of six feet. Because soil-fire fuels rarely dry sufficiently to burn, they are uncommon. Largely deprived of access to oxygen and wind, the soil fire burns slowly but continuously, sometimes for months, producing a considerable amount of smoke but little flame. The tremendous heat generated by soil fires may destroy timber in an insidious, underground attack on their heat-sensitive roots. Low-lying smoke clouds from soil fires may form serious traffic hazards. In October 1966, smoke-blinded motorists speeding along a Wisconsin freeway near Mauston were involved in a chain-reaction wreck that claimed four lives and destroyed several cars.

CROWN FIRE. The highly spectacular and destructive *crown fire* may also originate from a surface fire. The crown may be ignited by windblown sparks. Flames from burning litter may find a combustible pathway to a forest canopy by way of dried moss streamers or by resin flowing down a pine trunk. (See Figure 11–22.) Heat from a surface fire may ignite dry crown needles. In a strong wind the crown fire may jump from crown to crown with a speed of up to 40 miles per hour. Wind-driven sparks and brands may be carried far in advance of the original fire and ignite spot fires, thus making it

11-22 *Crown fire. Ochoco National Forest, Oregon. Forest fires burned approximately 100 acres in August 1951.*

11-23 *Payette National Forest, Idaho. The aftermath of a forest fire. Much life is destroyed, even many of the soil organisms.*

325

11-24 *Forest-fire victim. Charred carcass of deer provides mute testimony of the wildlife-destroying potential of a forest fire. Although deer can attain speeds of about 35 miles per hour, a raging forest fire can move even faster.*

extremely hazardous for humans or animals to remain in the crown fire's path. (See Figure 11-24.) A crown fire at Freeman Lake, Idaho, devastated 20,000 acres within a 12½-hour period. Although the wind was of only moderate velocity, a 350-acre spot fire was ignited fully three miles ahead of the parent blaze (6).

Causes of Wildfires

Roughly 10 percent of our nation's forest fires are caused by lightning. Even before the Pilgrims settled at Plymouth Rock, many destructive forest fires had been ignited during electrical storms. Lightning started over 18,000 forest fires in the United States in 1977. Until recently not much could be done to prevent these "acts of God." Recent research, however, has shown that the number of such fires will be substantially reduced by seeding thunderclouds with crystals of silver iodide at the right time and place.

On the other hand, 90 percent of our forest wildfires are caused by people. In 1977 120,000 forest fires were caused by people in the United States. As John D. Guthrie, a former fire inspector for the U.S. Forest Service, has written: "To stage a forest fire you need only a few things—a forest, the right atmospheric conditions, and a spark either from a lightning bolt or a match in the hands of a fool or a knave. The formula is simple . . . the larger the

forest, the drier the air, the bigger the fire you will have."

Sad to say, roughly 30 percent of our nation's wildfires are started deliberately by "firebugs," or incendiaries. Up to 94 percent of such incendiary fires during the last twenty years have occurred in our southern forests (5). Sometimes they are started "just for fun," sometimes they are employed as a weapon to "get even with someone," possibly a big timber company that would not permit a neighboring farmer to graze his cattle on company land. Incendiary-caused fires have burned more than 1,000 square miles yearly in the United States—an area the size of Rhode Island.

Firefighting

Even during the first three decades of this century, firefighting was a poorly organized, haphazard operation that relied primarily on hand tools and the ineffectual efforts of bucket brigades. The technique of modern forest-fire suppression, however, is an intensively organized, well-coordinated operation that employs the latest technological developments, from infrared scanners to helicopters (16). So effective are modern fire-suppression techniques that in recent years only one acre of protected forest has been burned for every 34 acres of unprotected forest.

FIRE DETECTION. Fire detection is frequently made by observers stationed in lookout towers. Most well-forested states have a network of such spotting towers in operation. During seasons of severe fire hazard, this detection work is frequently supplemented with airplane patrols. The potential for the occurrence of forest fires is measured by forest fire meters, such as that shown in Figure 11-25. Once the fire is spotted, the precise position is determined and radioed to the dispatcher. (See Figure 11-26.)

USE OF SMOKE JUMPERS. Over 2,000 firefighters have been used in major conflagrations. The fighters rush to the scene of the fire by truck or jeep if roads are accessible. In rugged mountainous country, "smoke jumpers" may parachute into the fire area. (See Figure 11-27.) The national forests of mountainous regions in Washington, Oregon, California, Montana, Idaho, and New Mexico are protected by a corps of 350 Forest Service smoke jumpers. Forest-fire suppression is most effective at

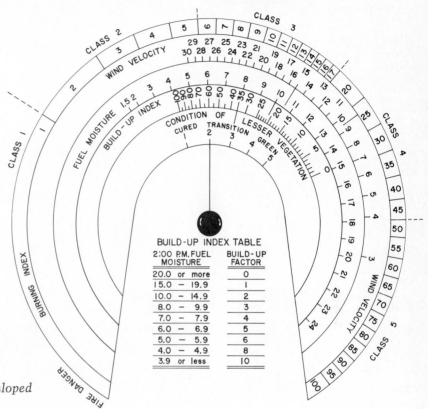

FOREST FIRE DANGER METER TYPE 8-100-0

BUILD-UP INDEX TABLE

2:00 P.M. FUEL MOISTURE	BUILD-UP FACTOR
20.0 or more	0
15.0 — 19.9	1
10.0 — 14.9	2
8.0 — 9.9	3
7.0 — 7.9	4
6.0 — 6.9	5
5.0 — 5.9	6
4.0 — 4.9	8
3.9 or less	10

11–25 *Forest-fire-danger meter developed by the U.S. Forest Service.*

night, when fire intensity is reduced and fighters find the heat less oppressive. With the help of smoke jumpers, many remote blazes that in 1930 might have flamed out of control may now be extinguished within a matter of minutes.

FIRE SUPPRESSION. The actual suppression or attack pattern employed by fighters varies greatly, depending on the size of fire, terrain, fire class, wind direction, location of roads, availability of water supplies, and relative humidity.

11–26 *A fire-control worker employs the fire-finder alidade to make a fix on smoke. Olympic National Forest, Washington.*

11 – 27 *Smoke jumpers in action. Some 35 miles north of the Arctic Circle, three smoke jumpers drift toward a spruce forest far below. The fire, racing through moss-laden spruce and parched peat, had a headstart.*

Fire Lanes. The fire lane is a ten-foot-wide strip that is plowed up around the periphery of the fire. In well-managed forests these lanes usually have already been systematically carved out of the forest at regular intervals. Because a fire lane is denuded of all combustible material, it effectively checks the fire's advance.

Back Fires. Occasionally, in an effort to head off an advancing fire, the intervening forest between the fire head and a fire lane may be set on fire. If wind conditions are right, the back fire will burn its way toward the major fire; when both fires meet, they will die from lack of fuel. This technique can boomerang if the wind suddenly shifts direction.

11 – 28 *Helicopters are employed to scout fires, transport men, and deliver urgently needed supplies to firefighters.*

328

11 – 29 *Fire suppression in the Angeles National Forest, California.*

Water. Water may be sprayed from a portable back-tank or tank truck. Portable motor pumps may take water from a nearby stream or lake. Some fighter teams have special well-drilling equipment with which they can sink a shallow well shaft within 15 minutes. In rough country, helicopters have laid 1,500 feet of fire hose in less than a minute. Some planes have special water tanks that can skim water from a lake for use in dousing a fire.

Fire-Retardant Chemicals. Fire-retardant chemicals can be sprayed from a back-tank and tank truck or dropped on the blaze from a plane in the form of chemical bombs. Huge air tankers with up to a 4,000-gallon capacity have been used.

Aerial Photography. Aerial photographers may take pictures of the fire, develop them in a dark-room aboard the plane, and within minutes parachute them down to the firefighters. The pictures will show the fire boss the overall pattern and status of the fire. They may suggest to him or her how best to deploy the fighters, not only for the most effective suppression, but also to prevent their possible encirclement by flames.

The Use of Controlled Fires in Forest Management

Ever since the 1930s, the U.S. Forest Service has used the symbol of "Smokey the Bear" to alert the American public to the highly destructive effects of wild forest fires. In recent years, however, the ser-

vice, with some chagrin, has come to the conclusion that at least some wild fires, from an ecological standpoint, are actually beneficial. In fact, it is now believed that a number of our nation's most valu-

11 – 30 *Ozark National Forest, Arkansas, April 1966. A U.S. Forest Service plane drops a chemical slurry to suppress a fire.*

11–31 *Marion County, South Carolina, February 1969. The prescribed (controlled) burning of a 28-year-old stand of slash pine.*

able timber stands may be established and maintained *because of fire.* Examples include the giant sequoias in California and the old-growth, even-aged stands of Douglas fir in the Northwest, of red pine in northwestern Minnesota, and of white pine in northwestern Pennsylvania and southwestern New Hampshire. Certain less valuable species, such as pitch pine on sandy soils near the mid-Atlantic coast and jack pine in the lake states, are also considered to be "fire types" or "fire climaxes."

Today foresters employ *controlled burning* to improve the quality of timber, livestock forage, and wildlife habitat. (See Figure 11–31.) Controlled burning is surface burning according to a plan in which the utmost precaution is taken in terms of (1) dryness of the fuel, (2) wind velocity (three to ten miles per hour is preferred) and direction, (3) relative humidity, (4) type of fire (head, flank, or back), and (5) composition and combustibility of fuel. The long-term effect on the forest in terms of multiple use receives top priority. Controlled burning has been employed with considerable success in southern stands of longleaf-slash pine and more limited success on shortleaf-loblolly hardwood stands. At

the Alapaha Experimental Range in Georgia, controlled burning is conducted only in the afternoon under damp conditions, and the low fire is usually extinguished by ensuing night dewfall. Any pine stand 8 to 15 feet tall can be controlled burned, whereas the highly fire-resistant longleaf pine (whose terminal bud is protected by a group of long needles) can be burned without ill effect when the seedlings are only six inches high.

In the longleaf slash-pine stands of the South, controlled burning serves to (1) reduce crown-fire hazard by removing highly combustible litter, (2) prepare the forest soil as a seedbed, (3) increase the growth and quality of livestock forage, (4) retard a forest succession leading to a low-value scrub-oak climax and maintain the high-timber-value pine subclimax, (5) promote legume establishment and resultant soil enrichment, (6) increase the amount of soluble mineral ash (phosphorus and potassium) available to the forest plants, (7) stimulate the activity of soil bacteria, (8) control the brown-spot needle blight *(Scirrhia acicola)* of seedling longleaf pines, and (9) improve food and cover conditions for wild turkey and quail.

330

Ecologist Richard J. Hartesveldt and his co-workers at San Jose State College in California have found that recurrent fires are absolutely essential to the successful regeneration of the magnificent sequoias. (Several of those now standing developed from seeds that fell on the forest floor at the time of the Roman Caesars!) In the event that fires do not periodically occur, plant succession progresses to the point where it is almost impossible for sequoia seedlings to become established. White fir, for example, will shade out the seedlings. The San Jose group found that sequoia reproduction in burn areas was best where high temperatures penetrated deeply into the soil. The researchers think that the elevated soil temperatures "probably aided in sterilization against pathogenic fungi, reduced competition with established plants, [and] improved the soil wettability and structure . . ." (4). As Hartesveldt et al. observe:

The concept of fire as a natural environmental factor before the advent of man has been a most difficult one to establish. Perhaps this has been due to man's role in starting forest fires and perhaps to the fact that man has too long been inclined to see trees as *individuals* rather than dynamic *communities* in which fire has always played a significant role. . . . (4) *[Italics mine.]*

The National Park Service now utilizes wildfires that result from lightning strikes, as well as controlled burns (purposely ignited by highly trained personnel), in a rapidly expanding forest-management program in 17 National parks, including Grand Teton (Wyoming), Rocky Mountain (Colorado), Sequoia (California), Yosemite (California), and Yellowstone (Wyoming). For example, wildfires, under careful surveillance, are permitted to burn on 77 percent of Yellowstone's 2.2 million acres. Controlled burning was recently used in Rocky Mountain National Park to contain a pine-beetle outbreak that had ravaged a 30-acre stand of mature timber. All this is quite a turnabout, indeed, from only forty years ago, when fire was considered to be the forest's "prime evil."

Small Woodlots and Their Management

The large forested tracts, numbering many thousands of acres in size, which are owned by large lumber industries, such as Weyerhauser or Kimberly-Clark, are managed very efficiently. They have to be. The economic survival of these companies demands nothing less. On the other hand, the small wooded acreages, owned by farmers or suburbanites, ranging from one to 100 acres in size, are frequently managed very poorly. After all, the farmer's expertise is in the area of agriculture rather than forestry. Similarly, the surburbanite, with perhaps 20 wooded acres on an estate, may be a banker, lawyer, or doctor, with barely enough knowledge of trees to tell the difference between a pine and a spruce. As a result most trees in these small private woodlots get old and die, their once valuable wood eventually either decaying or being consumed by insects without ever directly contributing to human welfare in the form of timber or paper pulp. This is indeed a deplorable situation since about 60 percent of our nation's forested acreage consists of such small rural and suburban tracts.

Fortunately, both financial and technical assistance is available to the owners of these small patches of woodland. The federal government, for example, will share up to 75 percent of the management costs. This financial assistance has been available since 1973 under the Forestry Incentives Program established by Congress in 1973. Technical assistance, in most states, is available from state conservation departments.

Forest Conservation by Efficient Utilization

During the cut-out-and-get-out logging operations of the 1890s, lumbermen were interested only in logs. The rest of the tree — stump, limbs, branches, and foliage — was left in the forest as worthless debris that frequently served as tinder for a catastrophic fire. Further waste occurred at the sawmill, where square timbers were fashioned from round logs. Slabs, trimmings, bark, and sawdust were hauled to the refuse dump and burned. Even today, three quarters of a century later, too much of the forest harvest is squandered. It is apparent that unless we also practice conservation *after* a tree is finally harvested and removed from the forest, all the solicitous effort devoted to protecting it from destructive diseases, insects, and fires during the thirty to one hundred years before the harvest seems futile.

Although we are still much too wasteful of our

timber resource, a definite trend toward more efficient utilization is under way. (See Figure 11–32.) The U.S. Forest Products Laboratory at Madison, Wisconsin, is the world's largest institution dedicated to studying the mechanical and chemical properties of wood and how this resource can most effectively be used by society. Whereas early in the timber industry wood had only two primary uses, as lumber or as fuel, through the efforts of the Forest Products Laboratory and similar research centers, a number of ingenious methods have been developed for utilizing almost every part of the tree, including the bark.

The forest industry has become much more diversified. Whereas in 1890 almost 95 percent of the forest harvest was converted into lumber, today only about 30 percent of the harvest consumed by the American people is fashioned into boards and timbers. In the last few years techniques have been developed for making extremely useful products from scrap boards, shavings, wood chips, bark, and sawdust. For example, years ago extremely short boards went to the scrap heap. Today, however, with the development of superior waterproof glues, such boards can be joined to form structural beams

11–32 *A single man here operates equipment that cuts and removes a number of pulpwood trees and then places them in a chipper machine. The chips can then be trucked to a plant and converted into paper pulp or chipboard.*

of almost unlimited length. Techniques have been developed for compressing small chips into chipboard or hardboard.

Meeting Future Timber Demands

According to the National Association of Home Builders, there will be a serious housing crunch in the 1980s. One big reason is that there will be 25 percent more families than in the 1970s. Moreover, during the decade of the 1980s, 41 million Americans will become thirty years old — the age at which most home-buying occurs. The association strongly feels that our nation's timber supply will be inadequate to meet this housing demand.

Using consumption figures for 1970 as a benchmark, by the year 2020 we will be using 27.3 billion cubic feet of timber — a 114 percent increase over the 11.7 billion cubic feet consumed in 1970 (1). Because our projected annual supply of timber for the year 2020 will be only 18 billion feet, we will be faced with an *annual deficit of 9.3 billion cubic feet.* (See Figure 11–33.)

Theoretically, there are several ways in which these demands may be satisfied. Unfortunately, some of the "solutions" are fraught with economic or ecological problems. Among them are the following:

1. *By upgrading and extending forest management in all forests, public and private, large and small.* Where can the greatest gains be made? Primarily on small, privately owned woodlots. Of the 4.5 million small-forest ownerships in the United States, over 50 percent are under thirty acres each. Yet these small owners control over three times as much timberland as is included in the entire National Forest System. Until now, the small-forest owners have sadly botched their forest-management responsibilities.

2. *By more effective use of wood residues and "weed" species of trees.* In a given year about 1.6 billion cubic feet, roughly 11 percent of the total volume of wood taken from the forest, is left as unused residue. (Of course, eventually this material will decompose and the resulting nutrients will serve to enrich the soil for the growth of future generations of trees.) Another billion cubic feet of wood is left as milling residue (1). It may well be, however, that the value of such resi-

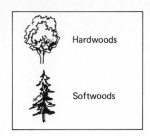

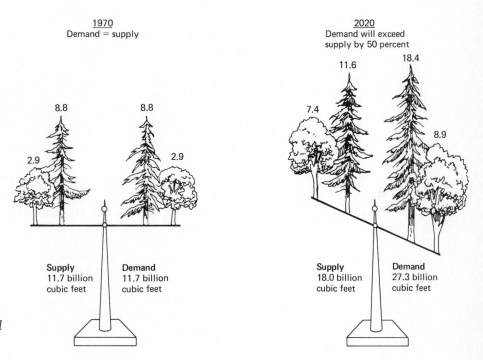

11-33 *Note that in 1970 timber demand in the United States equaled supply. However, by the 2020 timber demands will exceed supply by 50 percent.*

dues and weed species as a source of fuel will exceed their value as wood products.

3. *By developing superior (faster growing, better grained, and disease, insect, fire, and drought resistant) trees through the techniques of grafting and hybridization.*

4. *By increasing the use of wood substitutes.* Plastics and aluminum foil might be substituted for wood in packaging; fiberglass, concrete, bricks, and aluminum might replace construction timber; bagasse from sugarcane could be employed instead of pulp in paper manufacture (8). It must be emphasized, however, that the manufacture of some of these substitutes depends on the intensive use of energy derived from fossil fuels—a source that is already in extremely short supply. Moreover, the extensive use of plastics is frowned on by environmentalists be-

cause plastics do not decompose easily and therefore pose a formidable waste-disposal problem.

5. *By increasing imports.* By the year 2000 it is estimated that we will have to import 5.0 billion cubic feet of roundwood—108 percent more than the 2.4 billion cubic feet imported in 1970 (1). The best we can expect from our Canadian source by 2000 is about three billion cubic feet of softwood annually. In addition we will import Canadian newsprint and woodpulp. This will tax Canadian supplies to the limit. Current imports of hardwood plywood from Japan and the Philippines might be expanded. In addition by 2000 the tropical and subtropical hardwood forests of South America and Africa might be tapped (11). Of course, this last option would not be justified on an ecological basis, unless those forests are by then managed on a sound sustained-yield basis.

333

The Tropical Forests: Is Survival Possible?

Some have called it a green hell, others a green cathedral. Whatever its name, the world's tropical rain forests, which once covered much of the earth like a thick green blanket, are rapidly being reduced to shreds. And you say: "So what?" "You say," I could care less. After all, what is a tropical forest good for, anyway? Good for snakes, and squawking parrots and monkeys, maybe. But what about me? What's it got to offer me?" The answer is, "Plenty. From the medicine you took for your last illness, to the rubber tires on your sports car, tropical forests have a lot to do with you." And they have significance to the well-being of nations as well as individuals. For example, a favorable trade balance for the United States may well depend on tropical forest survival. Those forests may be important factors in international politics and world peace as well.

Description

You may recall that the tropical rain forest represents one of the world's great biomes. Rainfall may exceed 160 inches annually. Rates of tree growth, soil-tree-soil nutrient flow, and ecological succession following forest removal are very high. Nutrients have little chance to build up in the soil. Instead, they are almost immediately taken up by plant root systems. The diversity of life is enormous.

Forest Values

Tropical forests represent a rich source of food, fiber, fuel, timber, and medicines — all essential to human well-being. In addition, they provide habitat for wildlife and native human populations. By regulating water flow they control flooding and soil erosion.

1. Nearly two billion people living in the tropics now depend on food supplies grown in soil whose development was made possible by tropical forests. The agriculture dependent on those soils is equal to the amount of agriculture in the United States and Canada combined (22).
2. Rice production and irrigation farming in the tropics is dependent on water supplies slowly released from tropical forests.
3. More than one billion cubic meters of wood is removed from the world's tropical forests for human use each year. Tropical nations receive about $4.7 billion annually for the export of wood obtained from these forests. Brazil, for example, exports much of its wood to the United States. The economic potential of the tropical forests is enormous. For example, the hardwoods in the Amazon of Brazil alone are estimated to be worth $1 trillion (U.S. money) (22).
4. Tropical forests provide habitat for more than three million species of plants and animals — the greatest variety of life occurring anywhere on this planet.
5. More than 80 percent of the wood harvested is used as cooking fuel. Such use is keeping pace with population growth — which is rising sharply.
6. On a global basis, the tropical forest biome has unsurpassed scientific and educational values. For example, the raw material for productive studies of plant and animal ecology is almost unlimited.
7. Tropical forests influence the weather and the climate in important ways that scientists do not as yet perfectly understand. By means of transpiration in densely forested areas, such as the Amazon, large amounts of moisture are released into the air; that moisture will later fall as rain (22).

Removal of the Tropical Forests

Human activities have already reduced closed tropical forests by more than 40 percent. At present rates of destruction nothing but scattered remnants will remain by the year 2025, except for parts of the Amazon Basin and Central Africa. One to 2 percent is being cleared annually. The Ivory Coast and Costa Rica lost one third of their forest cover in eight and ten years, respectively. Thailand's forests were reduced by 25 percent in a single decade. The causes of tropical forest removal, which are multiple, are discussed here (22).

CONVERSION AND USE FOR AGRICULTURE. In Central America, Indonesia, the Philippines, and Thailand alone, forest farming is clearing a forested area the size of Great Britain for farming each year. Much forest loss can be blamed on "slash and burn" or "shifting" agriculture. Shifting agriculture is used on upland soils that cannot retain their fertility under continuous cropping. The farmer crops the land for a few years and then temporarily abandons it — in other words, leaves it fallow — for up to seven years. During the fallow period the forest begins to regenerate. The deeper root systems of the trees pump up nutrients from the subsoil. If the fallow period is long enough, soil fertility will slowly be restored. This system, in theory, at least, is ecologically sound. However, because of the pressures of increasing food demands caused by a rapidly growing human population, the fallow period, in many cases, is actually too short for the proper restoration of soil fertility. Shifting agriculture is employed on one of every five acres in the tropical rain forests.

FIRE. Fire is used as a tool in shifting agriculture to dispose of felled trees and to prevent the invasion of weeds and shrubs into the crop area. In the drier tropical forests, fires that get out of control have been extremely destructive. They have converted millions of hectares of forest into savannahs.

CATTLE RANCHING. The American appetite for beefsteak has indirectly contributed to the tropical forest dilemma. At present the international demand for beef is very strong, and beef prices are correspondingly high. As a result, it is very profitable for a cattle rancher to remove tropical forest cover and convert it to grazing land.

GATHERING FUEL WOOD. More than one billion cubic meters of wood are harvested for fuel in the tropics. This wood is either used directly for firewood or is converted to charcoal. In Haiti the production of charcoal is big business. Unfortunately, the resulting forest destruction in this country is also immense.

INDUSTRIAL LOGGING. Commercial logging in tropical regions is frequently very wasteful and inefficient. For example, during a logging operation in Malaysia, more than 55 percent of the trees were either severely damaged or destroyed. Until recently, commercial logging employed selective cutting. The only trees taken were mature specimens of the most valuable species, such as teak, mahogany, and rosewood. Today, however, any tree has potential value if it can be reduced to wood chips. As a result, clear cutting is being more widely used (3). Unfortunately, most clear-cut areas do not become reforested by natural means. They must be replanted by people. Frequently, however, the forestry people either do not have the know-how for effective reforestation, or they simply refuse to use it. Moreover, land-starved squatters move in to squeeze out an existence based on slash-and-burn agriculture.

The Harmful Effects of Forest Destruction

EROSION AND SILTATION. The problem of erosion and siltation is especially severe in mountainous Nepal. There, 87 percent of the wood consumed comes from the forests. As Lawrence S. Hamilton, an authority on tropical forest ecology has written: "As the trees disappear, the soil is being washed down into the Ganges, Indus, and Brahmaputra rivers, which carry it with it to the plains of India, Bangladesh, and Pakistan. There it pollutes drinking water, kills food fish, and silts up reservoirs, thus lowering the generating potential for hydropower, reducing irrigation-water storage, and decreasing flood control capacity. . . . For example, the Mangla Reservoir in Pakistan, completed in 1967, was designed to last for 100 years. However, about 100 million short tons of sediment now collect in it yearly. At this rate the reservoir will probably lose its capacity in fifty years . . ." (3).

FIREWOOD SCARCITY.   Because of the severe firewood shortages in India, Haiti, and Nepal, hot meals are almost a thing of the past. Eric Eckholm, a research ecologist with the Worldwatch Institute in Washington, has pinpointed the problem for the natives: "For one third of the world's people, the energy crisis does not mean . . . high prices of petroleum. . . . It means something much more basic — the daily scramble to find the wood needed to cook dinner . . ." (3). As a result of increasing wood scarcity, the poor are now shifting from wood fuel to animal dung. Unfortunately, however, dung is also valuable as fertilizer. An additional twenty million tons of grain could be produced if the cow dung now being burned as fuel in Africa, Asia, and the Near East were used as fertilizer instead.

CLIMATIC CHANGES.   Because when a tropical forest is removed the radiation of heat from the denuded area is greatly increased, the pattern of global climate may be adversely affected. The intensive burning of wood releases fully as much carbon dioxide into the atmosphere as does the burning of fossil fuels in industrialized countries. The result of that increased heat radiation and increased levels of carbon dioxide may well result in a progressive warming of the earth. That, in turn, will necessitate radical shifts in agricultural and settlement patterns. According to some experts, increased global temperature could cause the polar icecaps to melt and the major cities on our coasts to be destroyed by floods.

LOSS OF GENETIC "POOLS."   The irreplaceable gene pools of many kinds of organisms are rapidly being diminished. The tropical forests contain the parental species from which many of our present agricultural crops were derived. Those species may be needed as genetic reservoirs from which new varieties of disease- and pest-resistant crops are developed.

THE EXTINCTION OF SPECIES.   Although the tropical forests are rich in numbers of *species,* they are very poor in numbers of *individuals.* As a result, forest removal is critical to their continued existence. For example, in Columbia and Venezuela alone, such species as the jaguar, spectacled bear, and silky anteater, are walking the tight rope of survival. The National Academy of Science projects that, at present rates of tropical forest destruction, more than one million species of tropical organisms will be extinct by the year 2000 (22).

What Can Be Done to Save the Tropical Forests?

Despite the fact that only 0.5 percent of the tropical forests are found in the United States, our nation must assume leadership in coordinating an international program to save them. To this end, the U.S. Inter-Agency on Tropical Forests identified several goals that should be met by the international community by the year 1995.

1. Significant reduction in the rate of deforestation.
2. Any large-scale removal of tropical forests will be the result of deliberate, enlightened decisions of governments and communities.
3. Establishment by nations with tropical forests of revised laws, policies, and national planning priorities that are dedicated to sound forestry management.

Rapid Review

1. Our nation's forests provide the raw materials for more than 5,000 wood products worth more than $23 billion annually.

2. Our national forests are administered and managed by four federal agencies: the Forest Service, the Soil Conservation Service, the Tennessee Valley Authority, and the Fish and Wildlife Service.

3. President "Teddy" Roosevelt appointed Gifford Pinchot to be the first chief forester of the newly created U.S. Forest Service.

4. Sustained-yield management ensures that annual forest harvests are balanced by annual timber growth.

5. Clear cutting is employed on even-aged stands composed of only a few species and is applicable only to species whose seedlings thrive in full sunlight.

6. The Douglas fir of the Pacific Coast is probably the most valuable timber species in the world.

7. Opponents of clear cutting criticize it for the following reasons: (a) it results in accelerated water runoff, flooding, and soil erosion; (b) wildlife-carrying capacity is sharply reduced, at least temporarily; and (c) scenic beauty is destroyed.

8. Supporters of clear cutting claim that it has many advantages: (a) it is an essential tool in the kit of the professional forester, (b) it is the only way to regenerate forests in some areas, (c) it is the only way to control certain disease and insect outbreaks, (d) it is cheaper than selective cutting, and (e) timber grows faster on clear-cut areas than on areas that are selectively cut.

9. Selective cutting is used on mixed-species stands of unevenly aged trees.

10. Selective cutting is a more costly and time-consuming method than clear cutting; however, it reduces land scarring, accelerated runoff, soil erosion, and wildlife depletion to a minimum.

11. Selective cutting can be used only on such species as maple, beech, and hemlock, whose seedlings are tolerant of the shade on the forest floor.

12. The sustained-yield concept dictates that whenever timber is removed the denuded area must be reforested, either by natural or artificial means.

13. A tree farm is a private land area that is used for growing trees for profit under sound management principles.

14. Arguments for monoculture are that it: (a) takes optimal advantage of fertilizer and pesticides; (b) is rapid and efficient; (c) makes maximal use of modern tree-planting and harvesting methods; (d) is needed to satisfy America's growing demand for lumber and wood products; and (e) makes possible the establishment of sun-loving seedlings of timber-valuable species such as Douglas fir, redwood, and ponderosa pine.

15. Arguments against monoculture are that: (a) it is an artificial system made by humans that lacks the built-in balancing mechanisms of a multispecies, multiaged forest; (b) the fast-growing wood is inferior in quality; (c) intensive fertilization causes the eutrophication of lakes and streams; (d) intensive use of pesticides may contaminate wildlife and human food chains; (e) it requires intensive inputs of costly energy derived from fossil fuels; (f) the monoculture forest is more susceptible to fires than the natural forest; and (g) the monoculture forest is highly susceptible to destructive disease and insect outbreaks.

16. Under the terms of the Multiple Use-Sustained Yield Act of 1960, natural forests must be managed for many uses in addition to timber. Among them are: (a) flood and erosion control, (b) grazing land, (c) wildlife habitat, (d) biomass fuel, and (e) scientific, educational, wilderness, and recreational areas.

17. The Boundary Waters Canoe Area in northern Minnesota was officially designated a wilderness area under the National Wilderness Preservation Act of 1965.

18. Forest diseases such as heart rot and white-pine blister rust cause 45 percent of saw-timber destruction.

19. The American chestnut was eliminated from the eastern United States by the chestnut blight that was accidentally introduced from China in 1904.

20. White-pine blister rust, which was accidentally introduced from Germany in 1906, can be controlled by destroying its alternate host (gooseberry and currant bushes) or by using antibiotics.

21. Insect pests, such as bark beetles, gypsy moths, and tussock moths, account for 20 percent of all saw-timber destruction. This amounts to five billion board feet annually — roughly 10 percent of our annual timber harvest.

22. Insect pests can be partially controlled by using insecticides; by clear cutting the infested area; by using biological control agents such as viruses, parasites, and predators; and by replacing monotypes with heterotypes.

337

23. Fire accounts for 17 percent of our saw timber destruction.

24. Forest fires are classified as surface fires, soil fires, and crown fires.

25. Thirty percent of the wildfires are caused by "firebugs" or incendiaries.

26. Forest fires are detected by the use of lookout towers and by airplane surveillance.

27. Fires are controlled with the use of backfires, fire lanes, fire-retardant chemicals released from planes, and water pumped from tank trucks and released from tanker planes.

28. Forest-fire boundaries are determined with the aid of infrared scanners and aerial photographs.

29. The idea that every forest fire is a destructive fire has been replaced with the concept that occasional fires are a natural and beneficial feature of the forest ecosystem and are actually needed to maintain the forest in a condition where it best serves society's needs.

30. Controlled fires, purposely started by highly trained personnel, serve many functions. They: (a) reduce crown-fire hazard, (b) prepare soil as a seed bed, (c) maintain a subclimax that is valuable as timber and as a wildlife habitat, (d) control insect and disease outbreaks, (e) stimulate soil bacteria activity, and (f) increase the quality of livestock forage.

31. The timber industry and the U.S. Forest Service have developed techniques by which almost every part of the tree, including the bark, can be put to use.

32. The economic potential of the world's tropical forests is enormous: the hardwoods of the Amazon region in Brazil alone are worth more than $1 trillion (U.S. money).

33. Tropical forests have multiple values: (a) erosion and flood control, (b) timber and forest products, (c) medicines, (d) wood fuel, (e) outdoor "laboratories" for scientific research, (f) the habitat of more than three million species of plants and animals, and (g) recreational functions.

34. Tropical forests have been greatly reduced because of: (a) slash-and-burn agriculture, (b) conversion to grazing land, (c) industrial logging, and (d) fuel-wood gathering.

35. Under the leadership of the U.S. Interagency Task Force on Tropical Forests, it is hoped that the international community will establish and implement long-range goals that will eventually result,

not only in the survival, but also in the expansion, of the unique tropical-forest biome.

36. Projections indicate that by the year 2020 our nation's timber demand will exceed supply by roughly 50 percent. This increased demand may be met by: (a) upgrading our small private forests, (b) more effectively controlling the agents of forest destruction (diseases, insects, and harmful wildfires), (c) developing superior (faster growing, better grained, and insect, disease, and drought resistant) trees through the techniques of grafting, hybridization and cloning, (d) increasing the use of wood substitutes, and (e) increasing imports.

Key Words and Phrases

Alternate host	Multiple Use-Sustained
Back fire	Yield Act
Bark beetle	National Wilderness
Board feet	Preservation Act
Boundary Waters Canoe	Pest control
Area	Phytoactin
Brown-spot needle	Pinchot, Gifford
blight	Project Sanguine
Chemical bomb	Recreational areas
Chestnut blight	Reforestation
Clear cutting	Roosevelt, Teddy
Controlled burning	Rust-resistant hybrids
Crown fire	Scientific areas
Cyclohexamide	Shifting agriculture
Engleman spruce beetle	Slash-and-burn
Erosion control	agriculture
Exotic	Smoke jumpers
Federal Forest Reserve	Smoky the Bear
Acts	Soil Conservation
Fire bug	Service
Fire climax	Soil fire
Fire control	Surface fire
Fire detection	Sustained yield
Flood control	Tennessee Valley
Forest conservation	Authority (TVA)
Forest Pest Control Act	Tree farm
Hartesveldt, Richard J.	U.S. Forest Service
Heart rot	U.S. Interagency Task
Heterotype	Force on Tropical
Incendiary	Forests
Longleaf pine	White-pine blister rust
Monoculture	Wilderness area
Multiple use	Wildfire

Questions and Topics for Discussion

1. Discuss the economic importance of our nation's forests.
2. Discuss the statement: "Clear cutting is the best harvesting method for our nation's forests."
3. Describe six advantages and six disadvantages of the practice of monoculture.
4. What type of forest is most suitable for clear cutting?
5. List four factors that make reforestation by seeding rather difficult.
6. Describe the functions of our nation's forests in terms of: (a) flood and erosion control, (b) rangeland, (c) wildlife habitat, (d) wilderness area, and (e) source of fuel.
7. How was it possible for the chestnut blight to spread so rapidly through the Appalachian forests?
8. Describe two methods by which white-pine blister rust can be controlled.
9. Can you think of any reason why so many of our forest pests are exotics?
10. Discuss the ecological factors involved in the population explosion of the Englemann spruce beetle in the Rockies in 1942.
11. Discuss the factors that make heterotypes resistant to violent outbreaks of insect pests.
12. Suppose a forest fire breaks out high in the Rockies. Wind velocities are high. The nearest ranger station is one hour away. Discuss methods that might be used to bring this fire under prompt control.
13. List eight functions of controlled burns in the longleaf pine stands of the South.
14. Describe six methods by which our nation's future timber needs might be satisfied.
15. Where are the world's major tropical forests located?
16. Suppose that tomorrow all the tropical forests in the world were suddenly destroyed. Discuss the aftermath of such a catastrophe. What might be the long-range climatic effects? The biological effects? The social and economic effects? The effect on world peace?

Endnotes

1. Council on Environmental Quality. *Environmental Quality.* The Seventh Annual Report. Washington, DC: Government Printing Office, 1976.
2. Craig, James B. "The Clearcut Crisis." *American Forests,* 77 (Mar. 1971), 11.
3. Hamilton, Lawrence S. "Pondering the Fate of the Forests." *The 1981 World Book Year Book.* Chicago: World Book-Childcraft International, 1981.
4. Hartesveldt, Richard J., H. Thomas Harvey, Howard D. Shellhammer, and Ronald E. Stecker. "Sequoia's Dependence on Fire." *Science,* **166** (Oct. 31, 1969), 552–553.
5. Havlik, Spenser W. *The Urban Organism.* New York: Macmillan, 1974.
6. Hawley, Ralph C., and Paul W. Stickel, eds. *Forest Protection.* New York: Wiley, 1948.
7. Kerr, Robert S. *Land, Wood and Water.* New York: Fleet, 1960.
8. Landsberg, Hans H., Leonard L. Fischman, and Joseph L. Fisher. *Resources in America's Future.* Baltimore: Johns Hopkins, 1962.
9. Miller, G. Tyler, Jr. *Living in the Environment: Concepts, Problems and Alternatives.* New York, Wadsworth, 1975.
10. Northern, Henry T. *Introductory Plant Science.* New York: Ronald, 1953.
11. Parson, Ruben L. *Conserving American Resources.* Englewood Cliffs, NJ: Prentice-Hall, 1956.
12. Sayre, Roxanna. "Econotes." *Audubon* (May 1972), 103.
13. ———. "Econotes." *Audubon* (Sept. 1972), 110.
14. Towell, William E. "Let's Not Scuttle Professional Forestry." *American Forests* (Mar. 1971), 10.
15. U.S. Department of Agriculture. *Insects: The Yearbook of Agriculture.* Washington, DC: Government Printing Office, 1952.
16. U.S. Forest Service. *A National Energy Program for Forestry.* Miscellaneous Publication No. 1394. Washington, DC: Government Printing Office, 1980.
17. ———. *Annual Report.* 1962. Washington, DC: Government Printing Office, 1963.
18. ———. *Annual Report.* 1963. Washington, DC: Government Printing Office, 1964.
19. ———. *Annual Report.* 1964. Washington, DC: Government Printing Office, 1965.
20. ———. *Annual Report.* 1965. Washington, DC: Government Printing Office, 1966.
21. ———. *Multiple Use Management.* Washington, DC: Government Printing Office, 1966.
22. U.S. Interagency Task Force on Tropical Forests. *The World's Tropical Forests: A Policy, Strategy and Program for the United States.* Department of State Publication No. 9117. Washington, DC: Government Printing Office, 1980.
23. Watt, Kenneth F. *Principles of Environmental Science.* New York: McGraw-Hill, 1973.

Suggested Readings for the Interested Student

Ahlgren, I. F., and C. E. Ahlgren. "Ecological Effects of Forest Fires." *Botanical Review*, **26** (1960), 483–533. The authors review many of the beneficial effects of forest fires.

Brown, Thomas C., and D. Ross Carder. "Sustained Yield, of What?" *Journal of Forestry*, **75** (1977), 722–723. This is a critical examination of the sustained-yield aspect of forest management.

Hartesveldt, Richard J., H. Thomas Harvey, Howard D. Shellhammer, and Ronald E. Stecker. "Sequoia's Dependence on Fire." *Science*, **166** (Oct. 31, 1969), 552–553. This is a convincing statement that without fire the sequoias would be eliminated by natural succession.

Likens, G. E., F. H. Bormann, R. S. Pierce, and W. A. Reiners. "Recovery of a Deforested Ecosystem." *Science*, **199** (1978), 492–496. This is an excellent description of the process of reforestation.

Maisurow, D. K. "The Role of Fire in the Perpetuation of Virgin Forests in Northern Wisconsin." *Journal of Forestry*, **39** (1941), 201–207. This is a superb analysis of fire's role in maintaining quality timber.

McArdle, R. E., W. H. Meyer, and D. Bruce. "The Yield of Douglas Fir in the Pacific Northwest." Dept. of Agriculture Technical Bulletin No. 201. Washington, DC: Government Printing Office, 1949. This is a splendid treatment of Douglas fir as a high-quality timber species.

Richards, P. W. "The Tropical Rain Forest." *Scientific American*, **229**: 58–61. The author describes the unique characteristics of the rain-forest biome.

Smith, Robert Leo. *Ecology and Field Biology.* 3rd ed. New York: Harper, 1980, pp. 310–336. This is an outstanding treatment of the structure and function of the forest ecosystem.

Steen, H. K. *The U.S. Forest Service: A History.* Seattle: University of Washington, 1976. This is a superb study of the origins and operations of the U.S. Forest Service.

U.S. Interagency Task Force on Tropical Forests. *The World's Tropical Forests: A Policy, Strategy, and Program for the United States.* Department of State Publication, No. 9117. Washington, DC: Government Printing Office, 1980. This is an outstanding review of the causes and effects of the tropical forest's progressive reduction. It considers essential goals that must be accomplished by the international community if these forests are to survive.

12 Wildlife Extinction

The quavering howl of a wolf, the plunge of a fish hawk, the rhythmic murmur of the insect chorus on a summer's night — these are the sights and sounds of wildlife. These are rewards for the human spirit that cannot be bought at a supermarket or discount store. They represent aesthetic values. But this is just the beginning. Wildlife has recreational value for the fishermen, hunter, and photographer. It has medicinal value, representing as it does a potentially rich source of skin ointments, antibiotics, and a variety of drugs to combat everything from heart disease and malaria to cancer. Wildlife, of course, has food value, as anyone who has feasted on rabbit stew, broiled trout, or venison steak knows. Wildlife has economic value — more than $1 billion is spent annually by our nation's hunters. The sporting firearms industry alone has over 20,000 employees and a payroll of more than $100 million. Our wildlife represents a resource of genetic diversity from which superior varieties of food crops, game, and livestock can be derived. Wildlife has scientific values. This is obvious simply from the science course offerings listed in your school's catalogue — everything from Animal Behavior to Zoology. And finally, it is the numerous types of wildlife, from prairie grasses to oak trees, from earthworms to antelopes, that make ecosystems function in a manner which supports the ultimate form of wildlife: human beings.

The Biotic Potential of Wildlife

Biotic Potential (BP) is the theoretical maximum population growth rate of a species. Let us take a hypothetical case. Suppose all American robins lived to be ten years old and that each adult female annually fledged eight young. If the robin population started in 1970 with only a single breeding pair, there would be 1,200 million million million robins by 2000 — a population so enormous that 150,000 additional planet Earths would be needed to accommodate it.

A bird's clutch is the number of eggs she broods at one time. Clutch size in birds, which is primarily determined by heredity, varies greatly with the species. One-egg clutches were characteristic of the now-extinct great auk and passenger pigeon and may have been a factor in their extinction. Thrushes, sparrows, and blackbirds lay four to six eggs per clutch; eight- to fifteen-egg clutches are representative of ducks, pheasants, and grouse. A gray partridge hen may produce twenty eggs per clutch. The number of eggs laid is probably determined by the maximum number of young the parents can adequately nourish.

Because it is exceedingly difficult to find mammalian litters, data are frequently indirectly determined by counting embryos in the uteruses of collected specimens. The number of young per litter is

341

limited by uterine size and the number of mammary glands in the female.

Reproduction in the whitetail deer has been studied intensively. A doe usually gives birth to a single fawn after her first pregnancy and to twin fawns thereafter. In addition to age, the health of a doe may influence the number of young she produces. An experimental dietary study on a captive whitetail herd in Michigan revealed that the reproductivity of well-fed does was three times that of poorly nourished animals.

When mortality factors are minimized, whitetail populations may increase rapidly. A Maryland herd of three bucks and three does increased to an estimated 1,000 head in only 16 years. Under optimal conditions a deer herd could double its population annually.

Population Growth Curves

The population of any organism will be the result of the interaction of the two antagonistic forces of the environmental resistance (ER) and the biotic potential (BP), with the BP tending to "push" the population upward and the ER tending to push it downward. It is apparent, then, that the increase, decrease, or stability of a given population depends on the values of ER and BP. When the BP is greater than the ER, the population rises. Conversely, when the ER is greater than the BP, the population declines. When both values are the same, the population attains a stability in the form of a dynamic equilibrium.

Whenever a species becomes established in a new habitat with good carrying capacity, its population will show a characteristic S-shaped, or sigmoid, growth curve. Such a curve usually has four phases, known in chronological sequence as (1) the establishment phase, (2) the explosive (or logarithmic) phase, (3) the deceleration phase, and (4) the dynamic equilibrium phase. Once the population has reached the equilibrium phase, no further substantial population surges are possible, for at this point in its growth the population has attained the so-called carrying capacity of the habitat. In other words, it has reached the maximum population that the habitat will support under prevailing conditions over a long period of time.

A number of exotics introduced into the United States from abroad — such as the English sparrow, European starling, and German carp — have followed S-shaped growth curves. Thus, a few pairs of house sparrows were introduced to the United States in 1899 and within ten years the sparrow population had increased to many thousands of birds. Although introduced with good intentions (the sparrow was brought over from Europe to control insect pests), many exotics have destroyed wildlife habitat, disseminated disease, or aggressively competed with more valuable wildlife species for food, cover, and breeding sites.

The population growth of pheasants on Protection Island, off the west coast of Washington was followed after an initial 1937 stocking of two cocks and six hens. Careful censuses were taken yearly from 1937 until 1942, when the study was abruptly halted by World War II. When servicemen were stationed on the island they promptly applied rather intensive "environmental resistance." Up to this time, however, the pheasants had closely followed the sigmoid growth curve and had increased to 1,898 birds, a 230-fold increase over the original population (4).

A given crop of pine trees, bluegills, or deer may be periodically harvested to give a *yield.* One of the most important problems facing scientists in the fields of forestry, wildlife management, agriculture, livestock ranching, and fisheries is how to secure the maximum sustained yield, or optimum yield, from a given resource. In these cases humans are interested in harvesting *net production* for their economic gain. If the yield is *greater* than net production, it may so greatly reduce a given population as to depress its reproductive potential. On the other hand, if the harvest is *less* than the net production, the resource is not being managed for maximum economic return. Moreover, when population density rises, such factors as competition, disease, and predation affect the yield adversely. There is a point in the growth curve of any species where productivity is highest. This point is between the accelerating and decelerating phases of the curve. Research has revealed that in most species this point is attained when the population is at roughly 50 percent of the carrying capacity of the habitat (6).

The Control of Populations

Population Regulation by Density-Independent Factors

The population of an organism is controlled in part by *density-independent factors.* These are factors such as heat, cold, drought, and tornadoes whose effect on the individual organism is the same regardless of the number of organisms present in the population. A late freeze in spring, for example, will have the same effect on a robin's egg — it will kill the embryo — regardless of whether it is the only egg in the nest or if four other eggs are present. Hurricanes and tornadoes can level vast acreages of valuable spruce and pine. A severe spell of cold weather along the Texas coast in January 1940 inflicted considerable fish mortality; the percentage decline in the catch of flounders, a fish highly vulnerable to cold, was 92.6 percent at Laguna Madre, 93.6 percent at Matagorda, and 95.4 percent at Arkansas. Thus, the percent of flounders that were killed was roughly the same in all three areas, even though the flounder populations in those areas varied greatly. Many human activities are density-independent with respect to their affect on wildlife. Thus, marsh drainage has severely depleted waterfowl populations. The discharges of heated water from power plants have either killed game fish or caused them to migrate. Pesticide-contaminated food supplies may cause direct mortality among songbirds or reduce their reproductive success. Robin populations in certain DDT-sprayed areas in Wisconsin were reduced by 69 to 98 percent. The passenger pigeon's extinction was caused in part by the removal of its deciduous-forest-breeding habitat by the farmer and logger. In summary, climatic factors and human activities frequently operate as density-independent factors in regulating populations. Some human influences, however, have resulted in population increments rather than decrements. For example, house-sparrow populations have flourished because of the abundance of suitable nesting sites and food (waste grain and manure) associated with human settlement. Similarly, the removal of forests in the eastern United States has permitted the eastward extension of the coyote, a brushland species now found within a stone's throw of New York City.

Population Regulation by Density-Dependent Factors

Density-dependent factors are those whose influence in controlling a population either increases or decreases depending on the *size* (density) of the population. An example of such a factor is *competition* for a limited supply of food. Suppose there are only ten earthworms in your yard for robins to eat. If there is only one robin feeding on those worms, the limited supply of worms, at least temporarily, will have little effect on that one robin. However, if 100 robins were depending on those ten worms for food, the competition for the limited supply of worms would be so intense that some robins would starve to death.

When the number of oaks on an acre increases, competition for sunlight, soil nutrients, and moisture increases proportionately. Individuals with less extensive root systems may die as a consequence of nutrient and moisture deficiencies. Stunted individuals may die because they are shaded out by taller trees.

Among animals it is apparent that when food, water, cover, nesting sites, breeding dens, and space are in limited supply, any population increase will intensify competition. Inevitably this competition will have adverse effects on the physically unfit. Even if they do not suffer injury or death because of fighting, they may spread out to poor habitats where death from starvation or predation may await them.

The percentage of diseased or parasitized organisms in a population increases with population density, presumably as a result of the increased possibilities of transmission. With large plots planted to a single crop species such as corn or wheat, farmers have unwittingly increased the possibilities for the infection of their crops with parasites and disease organisms. The population-reducing effects of wheat rust, corn smut, and Dutch elm disease are widely known. The incidence of infectious diseases in humans also increases with population density. This was well demonstrated by the massive mortality caused by the influenza virus among our soldiers when they were crowded, shoulder to shoulder, in barracks and trenches during World War I. Because the causative organisms of infectious disease (viruses, protozoa, and bacteria) can be transmitted by contact, by eating contaminated food, and by animals (malaria and the mosquito), it is readily apparent that their influence is directly proportional to host density, whether that host is plant, animal, or human being.

Although we have segregated population-regulating mechanisms into two groups, density-independent and density-dependent, it is actually exceedingly difficult to distinguish one from the other in the field because a given organism's density at a given moment is the result of a combination of both density-independent and density-dependent factors acting at the same time.

343

Wildlife Populations Patterns

Stable Populations

Stable populations are characterized by a saw-toothed pattern as a result of small, irregular increases and decreases. (See Figure 12–1.) However, from a long-range standpoint, the population remains at a rather constant level. Most wildlife populations become stable once they have reached the plateau of the S-shaped curve or, in other words, have reached the carrying capacity of the habitat. Factors such as disease, predators, climate, cover, and food availability may vary, resulting in the slight upward or downward population swings.

Irruptive Populations

After fluctuating mildly for many years, some populations, such as those of deer and house mice, may suddenly increase sharply, or *irrupt*, and then suddenly crash to a very low level. Irruptions are highly erratic and unpredictable. In some cases they occur when there is an unusually favorable climate for reproduction or an unusually abundant, though temporary, food supply.

Perhaps the most celebrated example of an irrup-tion involves the mule-deer herd of the Kaibab National Forest in the Grand Canyon region of Arizona. (See Figure 12–2.) A deer population of about 6,000 head lived there for many years in the late nineteenth century in dynamic equilibrium with a biotic environment that included a variety of predators, such as the wolf, coyote, cougar, and bear. However, in 1906, the same year the area was proclaimed a national forest by Theodore Roosevelt, an all-out predator-control campaign was launched in a naive attempt to increase the deer herd for the combined benefit of tourists and hunters. All predators were drastically reduced in numbers. The wolf was eradicated. With environmental resistance reduced, the deer population's biotic potential attained full expression: the herd population climbed to 100,000 by 1924, *a sixteenfold increase within sixteen years.* Unfortunately, however, the herd had increased beyond the carrying capacity of its range. A browse line became well-defined on palatable shrubs and trees, such as aspens and conifers. Herbs were grazed down to the bare ground. Thousands of valuable seedlings, representing the timber of the future, were destroyed. Then came the inevitable "crash." Saved from a quick, sudden death from

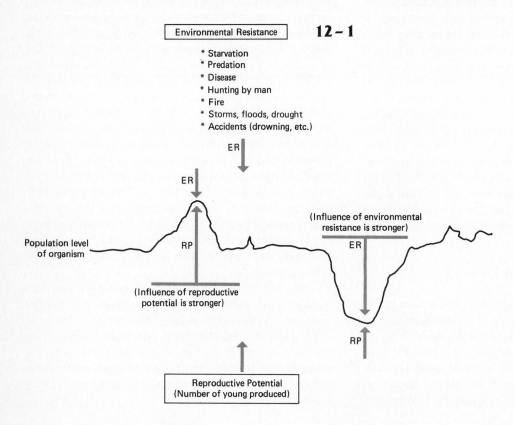

Environmental Resistance

12–1

* Starvation
* Predation
* Disease
* Hunting by man
* Fire
* Storms, floods, drought
* Accidents (drowning, etc.)

ER

ER

Population level of organism

RP

(Influence of environmental resistance is stronger)

ER

(Influence of reproductive potential is stronger)

RP

Reproductive Potential
(Number of young produced)

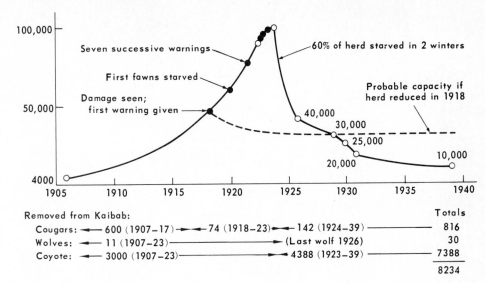

12-2 *This classic example of a deer irruption occurred in a herd of mule deer on the Kaibab Plateau on the north edge of the Grand Canyon, Arizona. It was caused by an intensive predator-removal campaign. Note that repeated warnings of impending disaster were ignored.*

predators, deer now began to succumb to slow, agonizing death by starvation. Within the six-year period from 1924–1930, 80,000 deer starved, their scrawny carcasses bearing eloquent testimony to our heavy-handed and simple-minded solution to an extremely delicate and complex ecological problem.

Cyclic Populations

Cyclic populations show sharp increases, followed by crashes, at rather regular intervals. To some degree the population peaks and troughs can be predicted.

THREE- TO FOUR-YEAR CYCLES. The three- to four-year cycle is characteristic of the brown lemming of the North American tundra biome. Other species in which this cycle has been observed include the red-tailed hawk, meadow mouse, and sockeye salmon. The lemming forms the principal food of the Arctic fox and snowy owl. Therefore, the populations of those predators vary with that of their prey. Apparently the predators have few alternative prey on which to feed. Many snowy owls starve during winters when there is a scarcity of lemming. On the other hand, large numbers will emigrate from the tundra to the United States, some moving as far south as North Carolina. In a study of brown-lemming "crashes" in northern Alaska, it was found that the peak lemming population overgrazed vegetation that had served as protective cover (7). During the following spring snowmelt,

therefore, the lemmings became highly exposed to predators and their numbers were drastically reduced.

THE TEN-YEAR CYCLE. The ten-year cycle is not understood well. It is characteristic of the snowshoe hare, an occupant of the northern coniferous forest. It has also been reported for the muskrat, grouse, and pheasant. The lynx, which preys largely on the snowshoe hare, has a ten-year cycle that lags just behind the hare's. The lynx cycle was revealed by examination of the Hudson Bay Company's lynx-pelt returns (5). (See Figure 12-3.)

Some scientists believe that shock disease may be responsible for some population cycles. This disease is characterized by a hormone imbalance. The theory is that when there is a population "high," the increased competition for food, mates, and breeding sites results in much fighting and body contacts. As a result the animal suffers from stress. The stress in turn causes an oversecretion of certain hormones. The result is that reproduction stops and eventually the animal dies. Shock disease, of course, would cause the population to crash. During the ensuing population "low," of course, stress would be minimized. The animals therefore would be able to reproduce normally, and the population would increase once again.

A number of other theories has been advanced to explain the immediate cause of the nine- to ten-year cycle. They include variations in weather, fluctua-

345

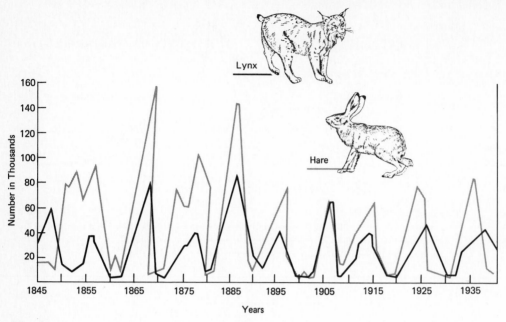

12 – 3 *An example of a wildlife population cycle, based on pelt records of the Hudsons Bay Company. Note the approximate ten-year interval.*

tions in solar radiation, depletion of food supply, disease, and changes in nutrient levels of plant foods. It may be that several of these in combination are responsible for the cycles. As yet, however, much of the underlying mechanism remains to be defined.

The Extinction of Wildlife

Extinction is the rule rather than the exception in nature. Perhaps 99 percent of all the plant and animal species that ever existed are now extinct. It has been estimated that the average life span of an avian species is about two million years; that of a mammal is six million years. It is assumed that many prehistoric organisms, such as the dinosaur Tyrannosaurus rex and the saber-toothed cat, became extinct because of overspecialization or inflexibility; once their environment changed, they were unable to adjust to the new conditions.

Theoretically, it could be said that all of the organisms on earth today will some day become extinct, including us. (See Figure 12 – 4.) This point is, however, that since *homo sapiens* appeared on the scene about two million years ago, and especially since the

dawn of the Industrial Age in about 1850, we have unwittingly accelerated the process — more than 75 species of birds and mammals have gone down the road to oblivion. Recently the International Union for Conservation of Nature and Natural Resources listed 359 species of birds and 297 species of mammals as "endangered" (threatened with extinction) the world over. Within the United States, 172 species of wildlife are listed as endangered by the U.S. Fish and Wildlife Service. Several American species have had their ranks severely depleted. Thus, according to the Fish and Wildlife Service, there are fewer than 100 individuals of the Ipswich sparrow left in the world, only 70 whooping cranes, about 40 California condors, 10 Florida Everglade kites, and 10 ivory-billed woodpeckers.

"So what?" you may ask. "What if a few more species of wildlife become extinct — what is that to me? A few less of the 1.5 million kinds of animals and the 450,000 kinds of plants will not affect me one iota." Or will it? Suppose that organism X became extinct. What possibly could be the loss to you and the rest of society?

First, the extinction of an organism like the California condor would be an awesome loss to science. The condor represents the end product of many

346

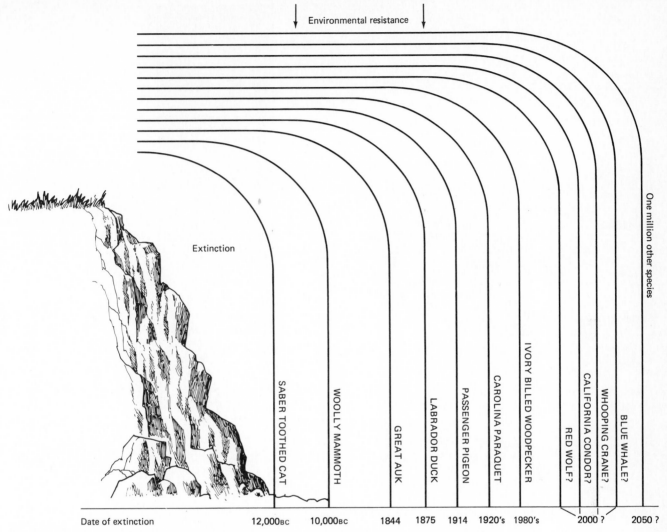

Environmental resistance

Extinction

One million other species

SABER TOOTHED CAT

WOOLLY MAMMOTH

GREAT AUK

LABRADOR DUCK

PASSENGER PIGEON

CAROLINA PARAQUET

IVORY BILLED WOODPECKER

RED WOLF?

CALIFORNIA CONDOR?

WHOOPING CRANE?

BLUE WHALE?

| Date of extinction | 12,000 BC | 10,000 BC | 1844 | 1875 | 1914 | 1920's | 1980's | 2000 ? | 2050 ? |

12–4 *Some notable cases of extinction. The red wolf, California condor, whooping crane, and blue whale are future extinction candidates.*

millions of years of evolution. It represents a constellation of genes found nowhere else in the universe. Its anatomy, physiology, and behavior patterns are quite unique and not duplicated in any organism on earth.

Second, wild plants and animals are integral components of the human ecosystem. We still do not fully understand just how all the living parts of the human ecosystem relate to each other. However, from what we have learned in Chapter 2 on ecological concepts, it appears that almost every organism on earth exerts a greater or lesser effect on every other kind of organism. Thus, when we cause the extinction of an organism, we may be removing an important cog in the ecological "machine" to which we belong. And without that cog, the machine may break down or at least not work quite as well as before.

Third, we never know in what way some obscure plant or animal may be of *direct* value to humans. Consider some examples. (1) Today we take the miracle antibiotic *penicillin* for granted. It has saved the lives of millions from death from infection. What is its source? A slimy greenish mold com-

347

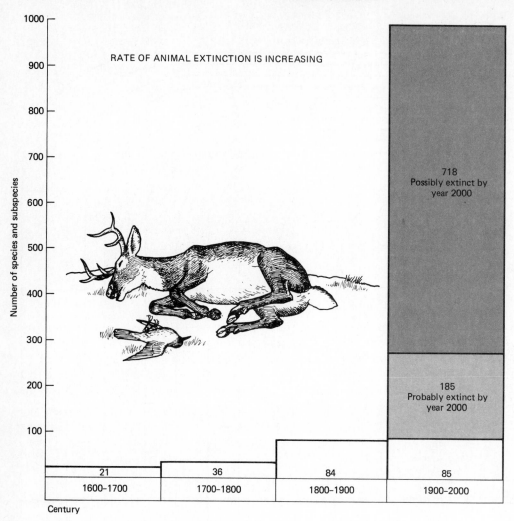

RATE OF ANIMAL EXTINCTION IS INCREASING

Number of species and subspecies

718
Possibly extinct by
year 2000

185
Probably extinct by
year 2000

| 21 | 36 | 84 | 85 |
| 1600–1700 | 1700–1800 | 1800–1900 | 1900–2000 |

Century

12–5 *The rate of animal extinctions is increasing.*

monly found on rotting oranges. (2) Many plants serve as *indicators,* or *biomonitors,* of subtle forms of pollution. Several species of plants, such as soybeans and lichens, will become badly discolored when even the slightest trace of sulphur dioxide is in the air. The Exxon oil company uses these plants as biomonitors of atmospheric pollution around its Alabama oil refineries. They react to sulfur dioxide by leaf-yellowing, long before it is discerned by human senses. (3) Suppose that the snakeroot shrub (*Rauwolfia serpentina*) of southeast Asia became extinct? Would it be missed? Most certainly. From its juices is extracted a drug, *reserpine,* which is used effectively on thousands of mental patients throughout the world to calm them and make them more amenable to treatment. (4) Billions of dollars

are being spent worldwide to find a method for controlling cancer. The search has led to the bottom of the sea. At least 500 little-known, seldom-seen organisms live there from whose bodies cancer-fighting extracts have been derived. (5) In Mexico there survives an extremely rare native plant called *teosinte,* closely related to corn. However, it has many desirable traits that are lacking in corn. It can grow in wet soil. It is resistant to viral diseases. Most important, it is a perennial — it grows year after year instead of living only one season, like corn. Plant geneticists believe that it may be possible to cross teosinte with corn and develop a supercorn hybrid. Such a crop would save farmers billions of dollars in seeding and planting costs. Yet it could easily have become extinct. As the Council of Envi-

348

ronmental Quality reports: "Only a few thousand of these plants exist, occupying three minute sites in a mountain range now being developed. A bulldozer could have destroyed them all in an hour. It will never be known how many other multibillion dollar plants will be clear cut, paved over, plowed under, nibbled by goats, or poisoned into extinction before their value is recognized."

Traits of Vulnerable Species

Some species are prime candidates for extinction because of certain characteristics: (1) restricted range, (2) low biotic potential, (3) nonadaptive behavior, (4) a low tolerance range to stress, and (5) a specialized diet.

RESTRICTED RANGE AND HABITAT. The Kirtland's warbler is a diminutive blue-gray and yellow creature, small in size (4.5 inches) but large in song. (See Figure 12–6.) The entire world population of this species, which amounts to only about 400 individuals, could be held in a gunny sack. It has perhaps the smallest breeding range of any North American bird—an 85-by-100-mile area in the northcentral part of Michigan's lower peninsula. (However, in June 1978, two males were observed in west-central Wisconsin, presumably in breeding territories. They were discovered by Nancy Tilghman, a field biologist for the Wisconsin Department of Natural Resources.) Not only does the Kirtland's warbler nest exclusively in jack-pine-barren habitat, but

more particularly in pine stands *ranging in age from six to fifteen years and from five to twenty feet in height.* In pines under six years of age the lower branches do not provide adequate nesting cover; in pines older than fifteen years, the bottom branches become shaded out and die, again not serving as suitable cover. The natural growth of the pine stand poses a survival threat for the warbler. When the pines mature, the warbler is forced to move out. Michigan conservation officials and the U.S. Forest Service have been employing prescribed burning to increase the amount of suitable habitat. The fire destroys the mature pines, and many young pine seedlings eventually become established from the seeds that are released when the seared pine cones "pop" open. Burnings are made in patches of forty acres or more, because that is the size of the warbler's breeding territory.

LOW BIOTIC POTENTIAL. Some animal species are extremely vulnerable to environmental stress (storms, drought, and disease) because of their low reproductive potential. The female polar bear, for example, breeds only once in three years and then gives birth to only two cubs. The female California condor, of which there are only about 24 individuals left in the world, lays only a single egg every other year. Because there are only about 12 females left, even if all of them bred successfully, the world total annual egg production for the species would be six eggs, and probably not all of them would hatch.

12–6 *Kirtland warbler at nest. Nests are located on the ground beneath the protective lower branches of a jack pine which is 5 to 20 feet in height.*

NONADAPTIVE BEHAVIOR. The Carolina parakeet, the only parrot native to the United States, became extinct in 1914 when the last survivor died in a zoo. The parakeet was hunted extensively by fruit ranchers because it descended on their orchards in huge flocks and ravaged the fruit. However, we might still be able to see this fascinating red-yellow-green "paint pot" were it not for a peculiar behavioral trait: when one member of a flock was shot and fluttered to the ground mortally wounded, the remaining birds would fly toward the dying bird and hover over its body, thus forming ridiculously easy targets for the gunners. Of more recent interest, the red-headed woodpecker, whose population has undergone drastic reduction in the last few decades, has the curious tendency to fly along a highway directly ahead of a motorcar, with the latter frequently winning the race.

SPECIALIZED DIET. The gracefully soaring hawk known as the Florida Everglade kite is truly among the rarest species of bird in the United States. There are only about ten individuals left. (The species is well represented in Mexico and South America, however.) An important factor contributing to its plummeting numbers has been its highly specialized diet: it feeds almost exclusively on snails. The kite's hook-shaped bill is adapted to remove the snail from its shell. Now that real-estate developers are draining much of the snail's marshy habitat, both snail and kite populations are declining rapidly.

Causes of Extinction

Now let us consider some of the major factors contributing to the decline (and possible ultimate extinction) of wildlife today.

GENETIC ASSIMILATION. The red wolf (*Canis niger*) and the coyote (*Canis latrans*) are closely related brush wolves. (See Figure 12–7.) The highly adaptable coyote is one of the few animals that has actually benefited from the human alteration of terrestrial ecosystems because its preferred habitat, brushlands, has increased extensively in the wake of logging and forest clearing for agriculture. At one time the coyote was found primarily west of the Mississippi; however, it has now extended its range eastward to within a stone's throw of New York City. The red wolf, on the other hand, is on the verge of extinction, there being only 150 animals left, all of them in Texas (3). Now there are reports that the

12–7 *The red wolf, a species that will probably be extinct by the year 2000 as a result of genetic assimilation.*

coyote is crossing with the red wolf to form coyote-red-wolf hybrids. It is apparent that if such hybridization continues, the red wolf's unique group of genes will probably be eventually absorbed into the coyote gene pool. At that point the species *Canis niger* will have ceased to exist (2).

PET TRADE. Wasn't it fun taking your little sister and brother to the five-and-dime store and buying them a pet — maybe a white Easter bunny or turtle or baby alligator or even a horned lizard? That is, it was fun until the time came to take care of it. William G. Conway, general director of the New York Zoological Society, looks at the animal-pet trade in general and the horned-lizard traffic in particular with a jaundiced eye:

The trade in horned lizards has been going on for decades. . . . The unforgivably immoral nature of this piece of commercialization is that horned lizards almost invariably starve to death after a few weeks in captivity. This tells us something about the character of the exotic pet trade, for it is well known that horned lizards have highly specialized and poorly understood food and temperature requirements, which few pet buyers could hope to meet. (3)

The horned lizard is not alone. Many dozens of sensitive species, including the three-toed sloth, Saki monkey, South American parrot, and arboreal anteater, with highly exacting temperature-humidity-dietary-spatial requirements, are imported from abroad and end up in ordinary pet shops where their survival is threatened. It is estimated that South American parrots are given such rough treatment during their transport from the Amazon rain forests to New York and Chicago pet shops, that only one of fifty birds survives the trip. In other words almost 0.5-million parrots died to supply the 10,000 sold by American pet shops in one year.

According to the U.S. Fish and Wildlife Service, in a single year recently the American pet trade imported 74,304 mammals, 203,139 birds (not including parrots and canaries), 405,134 reptiles, 137,697 amphibians, and 27,759,332 fish (6). How many of those unfortunate creatures are still alive is food for thought.

THE INTRODUCTION OF EXOTICS. Although with the best of intentions, we have all too many times introduced *exotic* species of animals only to discover, too late, that the beneficial objective, such as increased game for the hunter or the effective control of insect pests, never actually materialized. Instead, the ultimate result was the serious depletion of native wildlife. A classic example of this phenomenon was the introduction of the Indian mongoose (a fierce, quick-moving, weasel-like predator) to Hawaii and Puerto Rico. The purpose was to control rats that had been causing extensive damage to the sugarcane crop. Unfortunately, the people in charge of the mongoose's introduction had not studied its behavior patterns very carefully: The mongoose hunts prey primarily in the daytime, while the rat is a nocturnal animal. As a result, mongoose-rat encounters were relatively few. Although the mongoose did kill a few rats, it soon began to destroy many ground-nesting birds to the point where some of them became quite scarce. It eradicated the Newell's shearwater and the dark-rumped petrel from the island of Molokai.

KILLING GAME FOR NOVEL USES. Have you ever swatted a fly with the tail of a gnu? Or worn a necklace made of lion's teeth "beads"? Or carried your money in a purse made from an elephant's ear? Or taken an afternoon stroll in a pair of zebra-skin sandals? Until recently you could purchase those items in any one of the 298 curio shops of Nairobi — a major city in Kenya, Africa. As Wagner has so aptly stated:

Killing wild animals for food or for their skins can perhaps be rationalized, but killing a gnu to make a flyswatter out of its tail or an elephant to convert its feet into waste paper baskets is perverse. In the United States mummified baby alligators or baskets made of armadillo's "shells" are as tasteless as a cookie jar made out of a human skull. . . . (8)

At the turn of the century it was fashionable for ladies to wear immense hats decorated with egret plumes. The feathers came from the American egret, a tall, long-legged, snow-white wading bird. The plumes brought a price of $500 per pound. Market hunters shot the egret to a feather's breadth from extinction. Fortunately, however, when restrictive laws were passed early in this century, the population responded, and the species is no longer endangered.

Superstitious people have for millennia ascribed magical healing powers to portions of the bodies of wild animals. The use of albino buffalo hides as "big medicine" by the Plains Indians is an example. (See

351

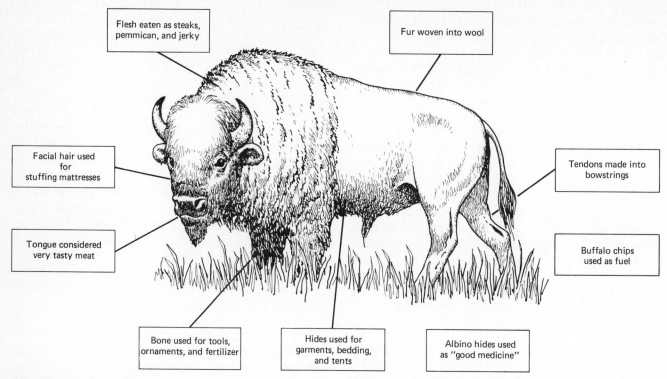

Flesh eaten as steaks, pemmican, and jerky

Fur woven into wool

Facial hair used for stuffing mattresses

Tongue considered very tasty meat

Tendons made into bowstrings

Buffalo chips used as fuel

Bone used for tools, ornaments, and fertilizer

Hides used for garments, bedding, and tents

Albino hides used as "good medicine"

12 – 8 *The bison, a multiple-use species. It formed an important base for the culture of the Great Plains Indians.*

Figure 12 – 8.) Perhaps the most "curative" animal in history, however, was the wild mountain goat (ibex) of the Swiss Alps. According to Vinzenz Ziswiler (as quoted by Wagner), the hairy balls rarely found inside the animal's stomach were reputedly "effective against fainting, melancholy, jaundice, hemorrhoids, hemorrhagic diarrhea, pestilence, cancer, and other ills. The ibex's blood was considered a cure for bladder stones; the heelbone helped combat spleen diseases; the heart yielded a strength-giving tonic; and even the droppings were utilized as medicine against anemia . . . " (8). All those supposed medicinal values, however, did not help the health of the ibex; in fact, they hastened its ultimate extinction in the Swiss Alps by the seventeenth century (8).

THE FRAGMENTATION OF HABITAT.   Urban expansion, logging, mining, and construction activities (highways, railroads, pipelines, and dams) obviously destroy wildlife habitat simply by replacing it with concrete, steel, bricks, and tar. Such activities, however, also have a *more subtle effect* that is

equally harmful to wildlife: the *fragmentation of habitat* into small patches, or ecological islands. (See Figures 12 – 9A and 12 – 9B.) The degree of wildlife diversity on oceanic islands of different sizes recently captured the attention of the ecologist Robert Macarthur of Princeton University. On the basis of his studies he made the generalization that, all other things being equal, a *larger number of terrestrial species can be supported on large islands than on small ones.* Observations by other scientists demonstrated that Macarthur's theory was valid not only for species occupying oceanic islands, but also for those living on such ecological islands as mountain tops, lakes, or small patches of woodlot and prairie cut off from similar vegetation by home or highway construction.

There are several reasons for the reduction in the number of species:

1. The ecological island may be too small to sustain the minimal number of individuals necessary for reproduction. Some animals need much visual and auditory stimulation from a number of indi-

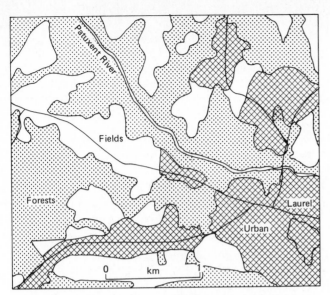

12–9A *Before forest fragmentation. Vicinity of Laurel, Maryland in 1951, showing forest cover (dots), fields (white), urban areas (squares), and main highways (black lines).*

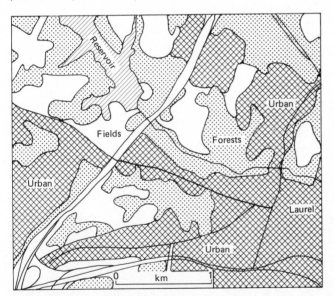

12–9B *After forest fragmentation. Same area as in Figure 12–9A. Construction activities have carved the forest habitat into small pieces. Note the Rocky Gorge Reservoir, Interstate Route 95, and Maryland Route 198 (bottom).*

viduals of their own species before they are psychologically and physiologically ready to mate.
2. Too much inbreeding — that is, mating with close relatives — may result in inferior offspring.
3. Large predatory species, such as lynx, wolves,

bear, and hawks, may not be able to find sufficient food for survival.

Recently this writer discussed fragmentation of habitat with researcher Chandler Robbins at the U.S. Fish and Wildlife Service's Research Center at Laurel, Maryland. According to Robbins the fragmentation of deciduous forests into ecological "islands" has caused a drastic reduction in the number of breeding bird species in the northern states — Maryland, New York, and Pennsylvania. For reasons still unknown, the long-distance migrants, such as the vireos, tanagers, and orioles, who winter in South America, have been most vulnerable.

POLLUTION. Thousands of new chemicals are being synthesized each year. A number of them are eventually discharged into lakes and streams, released into the air, or dumped on land. Invariably their effect on wildlife is adverse. The accidental release of oil into the ocean is also very destructive. Hundreds of thousands of sea birds may be destroyed in a single oil spill. Populations of Africa's black-footed penguin, for example, have sharply declined as a result of this problem. The role of chlorinated pesticides such as DDT, dieldrin, and endrin in decimating wildlife populations is described in detail in Chapter 14. The point here is that the decline of the osprey (fish hawk), the Southern bald eagle, and the brown pelican in the 1960s and 1970s was largely attributed to chlorinated pesticides. Not only do they impair gonadal function, but they also apparently cause the production of extremely thin-shelled eggs. The eggs are destroyed, along with the contained embryo, by the weight of the incubating female. However, since the banning of many of those pesticides, the species appear to be slowly recovering.

Methods for Preventing Extinction

Three major methods are presently used to prevent rare species from becoming extinct: the zoo-botanical garden approach, the species approach, and the ecosystem approach.

THE ZOO-BOTANICAL GARDEN APPROACH. The survival of some species of trees such as Wood's cycad (South America) and Cooke's kokio (Hawaiian Islands) is possible only because of botanical gardens, where they are carefully nurtured by

353

An Extinction Case History: The Passenger Pigeon

The passenger pigeon *(Ectopistes migratorius)* was once the most abundant bird on earth. Early in the nineteenth century the renowned ornithologist Alexander Wilson observed a migrating flock that streamed past him for several hours. Wilson estimated the single flock to be one mile wide and 240 miles long and composed of about two billion birds. (The population of this flock was roughly ten times the total North American waterfowl population today.) Yet not one passenger pigeon is left.

What factors contributed to the passenger pigeon's extinction? First, many potential nest and food trees (beech, maple, and oak) were chopped down or burned to make room for farms and settlements. The pigeon fed extensively on beechnuts and acorns; the single flock observed by Wilson could have consumed 17 million bushels per day.

12 – 10 *Shooting "wild pigeons" in Iowa. Copied from Leslie's* Illustrated Newspaper, *21 September, 1867. Note the gunner firing point blank into the densely massed birds. Over 100 birds are resting on the bare branches of the oak in the background.*

12 – 11 *Extinction. When the last living passenger pigeon, Martha, died at the Cincinnati Zoo, on September 14, 1918, a unique organism was removed from the human ecosystem forever.*

Second, disease may have taken a severe toll. The breeding birds were susceptible to infectious-disease epidemics because they nested in dense colonies. In 1871 a concentration of 136 million pigeons nested in an 850-square-mile region in central Wisconsin. Up to 100 nests were built in a single tree.

Third, many pigeons may have been destroyed by severe storms during the long migrations between the North American breeding grounds and the Central and South American wintering region. Cleveland Bent cites a record of an immense flock of young passenger pigeons that descended to the surface of Crooked Lake, Michigan, after becoming bewildered by a dense fog. Thousands drowned and lay a foot deep along the shore for miles.

Fourth, the low biotic potential may have been a factor in their extinction. Although many perching birds, such as robins, lay four to six eggs per clutch, and ducks, quail, and pheasants lay eight to twelve eggs, the female pigeon produced only a single egg per nesting.

Fifth, the reduction of the flocks to scattered remnants possibly deprived the birds of the social stimulus requisite for mating and nesting.

Sixth, the bird's decline was hastened by persecution from market hunters. They slaughtered the birds on their nests. Every imaginable instrument of destruction was employed, including guns, dynamite, clubs, nets, fire, and traps. Over 1,300 densely massed birds were caught in one pass of the net. Pigeons were burned and smoked out of their nesting trees. Migrating flocks were riddled with shot. Over 16 tons of shot were sold to pigeon hunters in one small Wisconsin village in a single year. Pigeon flesh was considered both a delectable and fashionable dish in the plush restaurants of Chicago, Boston, and New York. Sold for two cents per bird, almost 15 million pigeons were shipped from a single nesting area at Petoskey, Michigan, in 1861. The last wild pigeon was shot in 1900. Martha, the last captive survivor, died on September 1, 1914, at the age of twenty-nine, in the Cincinnati Zoo. (See Figure 12–11.)

humans. Not a single specimen of either tree now exists in the wild. Similarly, Pere David's deer (China) continue to exist only in zoos.

This approach, however, is not without its problems. Thus, the Council on Environmental Quality reports:

Many organisms . . . do not fare well in captivity. In the poorest zoos, jaguars, which once ranged over tens of square miles, may be confined to tens of square feet. Instead of the countless visual, auditory, tactile [touch], and chemical stimuli from encounters with other jaguars, prey, and other species, there are concrete walls, bars, a wooden platform for resting, and perhaps a scratching post, with a daily horsemeat ration at a scheduled hour. Under such conditions it is not surprising that many zoo organisms behave abnormally. Failure to mate or care for young is all too common.

THE SPECIES APPROACH. The species approach technique focuses on a few species that are of particular interest to society. They may be valuable as food (wild rice), as game (largemouth bass and whitetail deer), or have great aesthetic value (polar bear, California condor, and whooping crane). An intensive study is made of the biology and ecology of the species. Efforts are made to boost reproductive success, enhance food supplies, and control predators and diseases. Sometimes certain species are even transplanted from a less favorable to a more favorable habitat. Attempts at preserving the bison and the sea otter succeeded very well with this approach.

One major problem with this method is the selection of the species to be preserved. It is quite possible, for example, that the species that might, in the long run, be most valuable to society will be neglected in favor of species that may be of much less importance to it but that happen to be visually appealing. For example, many people who enthusiastically support efforts to preserve the tiger or polar bear would snort in disgust at similar efforts in behalf of the Furbish lousewort or some bug.

THE ECOSYSTEM APPROACH. The ecosystem approach to preservation is perhaps the most effective, as well as the least costly, in the long run. In essence, it simply involves setting aside a large area of natural habitat (woods, prairie, or marsh) that is populated with a number of different species and letting "nature take its course." As long as the populations of the species are not too low, the assumption is that the natural adaptations of the organisms will enable them to survive during their complex interaction with both the physical and biotic components of their ecosystems.

One problem with the ecosystem approach is in determining the minimal area required by a given species. The space requirements for herbivores such as prairie dogs and antelope are much less than for carnivores like grizzly bears and mountain lions. Environmental resistance, of course, will occasionally "knock populations down." Inevitably, natural environmental stresses such as drought and disease will take their toll of wildlife. Pollutants may have their origin from sources hundreds of miles from the ecosystem preserve. Acid rain, originating in Ohio, for example, has converted many Adirondack lakes into biological deserts.

Managing an Endangered Species: The Whooping Crane

The four-foot whooping crane (*Grus americana*) is the tallest bird on the North American continent. Snow white, except for its scarlet crown and black wing tips, it resembles a flying cross as it passes overhead, with its graceful neck projecting forward and sticklike legs trailing behind. In the early nineteenth century its breeding range extended throughout the grassland biome from the prairie provinces of Canada south through the Dakotas to Iowa. It wintered along the Gulf Coast from Mexico east to Florida. It wasn't until 1954 that its nesting ground was discovered in Wood Buffalo National Park in northern Alberta, Canada. The wintering area is restricted to the Aransas Wildlife Refuge on the Texas coast. Although the species is very slowly increasing in numbers, only about 87 wild whooping cranes survived as of 1980—a drastic decline from an estimated population of 1,500 in 1870.

Among the factors that have contributed to the endangered status of this strikingly handsome bird are the following: low biotic potential, appropria-

12–12 *Courtship dance of the whooping crane.*

Habitat Loss: A Major Problem in Wildlife Management

Robert A. McCabe

Department of Wildlife Ecology
UNIVERSITY OF WISCONSIN, MADISON

Identifying a problem in wildlife management is infinitely easier than resolving it or even recommending an untried solution. The major problem among many in wildlife management that await resolution is *the continuing loss of wildlife habitats.* The problem is generic and underlies a family of related problems. When wildlife habitats are encroached upon by the activities of people seeking to feed, clothe, house, and enjoy themselves, the justification to hold intact such habitats becomes difficult. World agriculture, forestry, mineral exploitation, industry, and urbanization each in its own way contributes to habitat loss or degradation and each often considers the "other" land exploiters the prime culprit.

Aquatic and wetland habitats are particularly vulnerable. Ocean, lake, and stream eutrophication can be laid at the doors of agriculture as a result of soil erosion and other nonpoint pollution; to mining due to waste dumping; to industrial forestry, and other industries; and to urbanization because of storm sewer runoff, sewage outlets, and garbage dumping.

Eutrophication destroys habitats for most fish, mammals, birds, reptiles, and amphibians and the invertebrates that are vital to the respective food chains to which they are vital. Aquatic plants are also lost as an integral part of the habitat.

The rate of land misuse and degradation outspeeds the ability of people everywhere to comprehend and react to a land ethic. Therefore, we must adapt the Leopoldian land-man ethic. This states in essence that the attitude of people toward land is, ". . . right when it tends to preserve the integrity, stability, and beauty of the biotic community. It is wrong when it tends otherwise." So long as land is violated by human exploitation without direct and horrifying consequences to individuals and society we blunder along in the idle hope that technology can render obsolete a land-man ethic and save us and our natural resources from our own excesses.

The encroaching of private interests on public lands is also an economic malady of our time and it is often sanctioned by government itself. Unless the self-interest of individuals or of political units within government can be subordinated for a common good, land and its wildlife environments are in jeopardy.

Overprotection is as detrimental as overexploitation, for it relies on the misconception that protection will solve resource ills. Limiting the manager to only one tool (total nonuse) does a disservice, particularly when several approaches would best serve the welfare of the resource in question. Total protection may be its own worst enemy and a denial of scientific management.

However, one example of where complete protection is worthy of consideration, although it flies in the face of some sportsmen, government, and industry, is a total closure of waterfowl hunting for at least one year. Such complete protection in certain segments of the United States (for example, the Atlantic and Mississippi flyways) might allow our greatly diminished waterfowl resource to recoup in order to preserve the resource and assure the survival of waterfowl hunting. I regard this move as imperative for the welfare of waterfowl and sport hunting.

We have approached an impasse where today dwindling resources (including wildlife habitats) must be divided among accelerating user publics. Quality use, passive or consumptive, relies on quality wildlife habitat.

357

12 – 13 *Whooping crane at nest in Wood Buffalo National Park, Alberta, Canada. Note egg.*

12 – 14 *Young whooping crane. Although two eggs are laid by the female, usually only a single young survives because of fighting between the two chicks.*

tion of its prairie nesting habitat by ranchers and farmers, intensive shooting, severe storms during migrations, and coyote predation on chicks.

Under the terms of the Endangered Species Act of 1973, a whooping crane recovery team (WCRT) was established in 1975. The primary goal of the WCRT is to remove the whooping crane from its endangered status. To attain this goal, the WCRT hopes to (1) increase the Wood Buffalo-Aransas National Refuge population to at least forty nesting pairs and (2) establish two additional but separate self-sustaining populations consisting of at least twenty nesting pairs.

Although the female whooping crane normally lays two eggs per clutch, usually only one young fledges per nest. Research biologists with the Fish and Wildlife Service have capitalized on this fact in an ingenious approach that not only increases the whooper population but extends its range as well. For example, researchers have carefully removed the second egg from a number of nests at the Wood Buffalo National Park in Canada. The eggs were then put in incubators, flown to Idaho, and carefully placed in the nests of incubating sandhill cranes (a much more abundant species). As was hoped, the foster parent completed the incubation of the eggs and raised the young whoopers. During the ensuing fall migration, the young birds followed their foster parents to the sandhill crane wintering grounds in New Mexico. By 1980 the foster-reared population had increased to eleven birds. None of those whoopers have nested. Two five-year-old males have established territories, however, an indication that they were ready to start breeding activity — if they could find a mate. If indeed two separate populations can be established, the whooping crane's chances for survival will be greatly enhanced. Even though a natural disaster, such as fire, high water levels, unseasonable cold, or infectious disease epidemics, might wipe out one population, the other probably would be able to survive.

The Endangered Species Act

In 1973 Congress passed the Endangered Species Act. It has proven effective in promoting the survival of many species of plants and animals that had been crowded to the very edge of extinction. The main provisions of this act follow:

BOX SCORES OF SPECIES LISTINGS

Category	Endangered U.S.	Endangered Foreign	Threatened U.S.	Threatened Foreign	Species Total
Mammals	32	241	3	21	279
Birds	66	159	3	0	214
Reptiles	13	61	10	4	75
Amphibians	5	8	3	0	16
Fishes	34	15	12	0	57
Snails	2	1	5	0	8
Clams	23	2	0	0	25
Crustaceans	1	0	0	0	1
Insects	7	0	6	1	13
Plants	51	2	8	3	60
Total	234	489	50	29	750

Number of species currently proposed: 17 animals
10 plants
Number of Critical Habitats listed: 48
Number of Recovery Teams appointed: 68
Number of Recovery Plans approved: 39
Number of Cooperative Agreements signed with States:
37 (fish & wildlife)
8 (plants)

12–15 *Box score of endangered and threatened species, U.S. and foreign.*

1. The Department of the Interior is charged with the responsibility of identifying species of wildlife that are in imminent danger of extinction. Such species are officially designated as *endangered.* As of 1980 about 182 species of animals in the United States, such as the manatee, red wolf, peregrine falcon, California condor, black-tailed ferret, bobcat, and snail darter have been so designated. Species whose populations have been declining rapidly but are not yet in imminent danger of extinction are classified as *threatened.* (See Figure 12–15.)
2. The act prohibits the hunting and killing of the endangered species as well as the selling, exporting, or importing of their hides, pelts, and feathers.
3. The act charges the department of the Interior to identify the habitats of the endangered species and to map the distribution of those habitats.
4. The act forbids any private, state, or federal agency from destroying such habitats, by any means in particular, as a result of building projects for dams, highways, housing, or airports.
5. Violators of the act are liable to fines up to $20,000 and one year in federal prison.

Congress passed the Endangered Species Act at the height of the environmental movement in 1973.

How Can We Make the Endangered Species Act Do a Better Job?

Russell W. Peterson

President
NATIONAL AUDUBON SOCIETY

Congress passed the Endangered Species Act at the height of the environmental movement in 1973. Yet we now know that this landmark conservation law, which is intended to protect imperiled species of animals and plants and the habitat on which they depend, is more important than even its most enthusiastic sponsors then recognized.

Two years ago the President's Council on Environmental Quality estimated that as many as one million species may become extinct by the year 2000. Even if "only" half a million species are lost in that brief time, we face an ecological threat of unprecedented scope.

The Endangered Species Act has been reasonably successful in limiting federal actions that endanger species. But the act fails to address the threat of extinction where it is greatest: in the undeveloped world. And it lacks government funding to meet even a small percentage of the recovery and land-acquisition needs of the species now listed in this country alone.

Question: How can we make the Endangered Species Act do a better job?

Answer: By writing, calling, and visiting our U.S. senators and representatives and insisting politely that *they* do a better job by authorizing adequate funding for the act and extending it to deal with the plight of species worldwide — many of which are jeopardized by actions originating with American agencies, corporations, and individuals.

Dam Versus Darter: A Classic Confrontation

In 1973 David Etnier, a fish expert at the University of Tennessee, discovered a new species of fish in the Little Tennessee River. The tiny fish, only three inches long, was given the name snail darter *(Percina tanasi)*. According to Etnier the entire world population of this species, numbering about 1,400 individuals, was confined to a 15-mile stretch of the Little Tennessee River. Obviously, the species qualified as endangered, under the criterion of the Endangered Species Act. It was most unfortunate, however, that the fish's habitat would soon be destroyed because the Tennessee Valley Authority, a federal agency, was constructing the $116 million Tellico Dam in the Little Tennessee, a short distance from where the darter was discovered. The resulting reservoir, impounded behind the dam, would replace the shallow, fairly rapidly flowing water essential for snail-darter survival with deep quiet water — a completely different type of aquatic habitat.

The discovery of the tiny fish, therefore, set the stage of a classic confrontation between technology and a powerful federal agency (the TVA), on one hand, and a vanishing species, supported by a few dedicated environmentalists, biologists, and nature lovers on the other. In a letter to this writer, Etnier described the confrontation:

The story is an interesting one that involves a small fish and a group of little people with virtually no resources attempting to force a governmental agency to comply with federal law. The number of participants has been immense, on both sides. Our side fought with money from the sale of snail darter T-shirts. TVA's efforts to thwart us have probably cost that agency well in excess of a million dollars in lobbying and expenses associated with their staff of lawyers, biologists, and administrators working on the case. Virtually every newspaper, press service, and TV network has devoted some time or space to the issue and magazines such as *People, The New Yorker, Time,* etc. have carried lengthy articles. . . .

Eventually the case was brought to the courts. In early 1977 a federal appeals court ruled that the TVA would have to terminate construction on the Tellico Dam. But the prodam people did not give up easily. In April 1978 no less an official than U.S. Attorney General Griffin Bell himself asked the U.S. Supreme Court to spare the dam and scrap the darter. But to no avail. In June 1978 our nation's highest court ruled in favor of the three-inch fish.

However, legislators began pondering the question: "When we formulated and enacted the Endangered Species Act, were we really concerned about saving tiny fish, or were we thinking of eagles and moose?" As one scientist wrote: "Congressmen are now finding themselves confronted with a Pandora's box containing infinite numbers of creeping things they never dreamed existed." (9)

Nevertheless, in 1978, when the Tellico Dam was 90 percent finished, the Supreme Court ruled that the Tellico Dam project had to be stopped because it did indeed violate the provisions of the Endangered Species Act. The court ruled that the act made any federal construction project illegal if it jeopardized the survival of any organism that had been formally classified as endangered under provisions of the act.

A storm of controversy raged in Congress for many months concerning the act. Verbal battles were waged. Congressman were heavily pressured by lobbyists. The construction industry naturally as interested in weakening the Endangered Species Act so that federal projects could be exempted. Environmentalists, on the other hand, were steadfastly opposed to any modification of the act that would lessen its influence in preserving endangered organisms. Eventually the act was amended. Under the amendment any requests for exemptions from the act were to be considered by a special high-level review committee. In 1979 the committee ruled to block any further construction of the Tellico Dam on the grounds that the economic benefits resulting from its construction did not justify its costs — in addition to threatening the survival of the snail darter. However, special-interest groups with a vested financial interest in such multimillion dollar projects as dams, levees, reservoirs, and highways refused to conceed defeat. They succeeded in convincing legislators to amend a public works bill that would permit the completion of the Tellico Dam after all. The prodarter people were understandably dismayed. However, they did the best they could, under the circumstances, to preserve the fish. The entire snail-darter population was removed from the Little Tennessee and introduced in the Hiwassee River nearby. Because the Hiwassee River appears to have all the essential habitat features of the Little Tennessee, such as a gravel bed and free-flowing cool water, it is hoped that the transplants will be able to persist. A delightful and rather surprising sequel to the story was David Etnier's 1980 discovery of six snail darters in the South Chickamauga Creek in Chattanooga, roughly 80 miles from the Tellico Dam. Researchers are now trying to determine whether South Chickamauga Creek has always been populated by snail darters or whether these fish migrated from the transplantation site in the Hiwassee River, some 50 river miles away. As one spokesman for the Fish and Wildlife Service has stated: "Until more information is collected, the implications of the discovery to the species' endangered status cannot be assessed (13)." The saga of the snail darter continues. (See David Etnier's guest article on the darter/dam controversy.)

The Snail Darter/ Tellico Dam Controversy Evaluated with Several Years of Hindsight

David A. Etnier

Department of Zoology
UNIVERSITY OF TENNESSEE
AT KNOXVILLE

Tellico Dam is a reality. The snail darter is not extinct and has recently been found in fair numbers in lower South Chickamauga and Big Sewee creeks, Tennessee; and in lesser numbers in the lower Sequatchie and Little Rivers, Tennessee, and lower Paint Rock River, Alabama. The population transplanted by TVA into the Hiwassee River in early 1976 still appears to be thriving.

The controversy surrounding Tellico Reservoir would have died an early death had the presence of these populations been known prior to litigation. Opponents of the project optimized their chances to preserve the Little Tennessee River ecosystem by relying on the most powerful piece of substantive law available — The Endangered Species Act (ESA). There were cultural, recreational, aesthetic, ecological, and economic reasons for fighting the project, but none carried the potential, but untested, legal clout of the ESA. The soundness of this strategy was apparent when opponents of the dam won decisions in both the Federal Circuit Court and the U.S. Supreme Court. The validity of the other reasons for fighting the project became apparent when first a joint Tennessee Valley Authority (TVA)/ Department of the Interior (USDI) team, followed by the cabinet-level Endangered Species Committee, concluded that alternatives to Tellico Reservoir had potentially equal or greater economic, aesthetic, and recreational benefits and were also compatible with preserving the ecology and past and present cultural heritage of the valley, while ensuring the survival of the snail darter.

Had presently known snail-darter populations been found earlier (a subtle reminder of the continued need for basic research), there would have been at best a feeble lawsuit, and tax dollars would have been saved. But perhaps more tax dollars would have been saved by abandoning the project even late in the controversy, according to the earlier mentioned TVA/USDI and Endangered Species Committee reports.

Garrett Hardin's essay on "The Tragedy of the Commons" is certainly pertinent to this study. In the final reckoning, the Tennessee congressional delegation, in an apparently logical attempt to maximize the return of federal tax dollars to Tennessee, attached to a large appropriations bill a rider exempting the project from *all federal law*. The bill passed both the House and the Senate (with little if any discussion of the rider), and just one more federal "boondoggle" was finally cleared for completion. Clearing this final hurdle for completion probably reflects the reluctance of the Congress to admit their [sic.] past errors in appropriating funds for an economically unsound project, but it is also obvious that our system of federal government continues to be ill-equipped to prevent "pork barrel" projects. As opponents projected, and contrary to TVA's optimistic guesses, there has been no industrial development in the valley as of yet, and a generous description of the recreational fishery created would be "average."

African Elephants and White Gold

Africa's elephant population of 1.3 million animals is scattered through 35 nations over an area of 2.8 million square miles. Although the number seems large, the survival of the species will soon be in jeopardy if present trends continue. One reason is the demand for curios — such as wastebaskets made out of an elephant's feet. The curio demand has been especially heavy in Kenya, even though hunting there was declared illegal in 1977. The ban "ended the era of the White Hunter — of big game safaris that attracted European royalty, American millionaires, and authors like Ernest Hemingway . . ." (1). Another big reason for the plummeting elephant population is the price of ivory. It has increased fifteenfold in the last decade and is now selling for $35 per pound. At that price an average tusk, weighing 20 pounds, would be worth $700. No wonder ivory is called white gold.

To get the "gold" poachers have used almost every conceivable method — from poisoned arrows, traps, and automatic rifles, to poisoning water holes with battery acid. Even rocket-propelled grenades have been employed. Armed with rifles and grenades four poachers can destroy 29 elephants in fewer than three minutes. A former government official has described the poachers' methods:

Poaching in the parks is a constant threat every day. . . . A large gang of poachers will break up into small gangs, supplied with poisoned arrows or automatic rifles. They make a little camp under a bush . . . then look for signs of elephants where they've been drinking regularly. They fire, then follow . . . the fleeing, wounded animals and look for vultures to guide them to their corpses. One group may shoot ten or twelve elephants and may find only one or two. . . . (1)

The ivory-seekers are killing about 100,000 elephants per year. According to elephant expert Ian Douglas-Hamilton: "By protecting the elephant one protects the whole ecosystem. By killing it . . . we are putting an end to a species that has been perfecting itself for 40 million years."

Despite the severe decline in numbers, wildlife organizations feel that the African elephant can still be saved. To this end the World Wildlife Fund has proposed an African Elephant Action Plan. The $1.1 million project would include four major features:

1. A conservation program to protect the elephant and its prime habitat.
2. An economic program that would attempt to control the illegal traffic in white gold.
3. An education program to develop ecological awareness among the natives.
4. A research program that would keep close watch on the animal's reproductive success, mortality rates, and overall population trends.

Let us hope that the African Elephant Action Plan will succeed. If it doesn't, this mighty species may continue to exist in the form of mounted heads, carved tusks, and wastebasket feet, but the living, breathing, trumpeting "king of the savannah" will have vanished forever.

Rapid Review

1. America's wildlife resources have multiple values for society: aesthetic, nutritional, recreational, economic, and scientific.

2. The biotic potential is the theoretical maximum population growth rate of a species.

3. Clutch size in birds varies from one in the extinct passenger pigeon to twenty in the gray partridge.

4. Under optimal conditions a deer herd can double its population annually.

5. Density-independent factors such as heat, cold, and drought affect the individual organism in the same degree — regardless of the number of organisms present in the population..

6. Density-dependent factors are food competition and disease; their influence in controlling a population depends on the size (density) of the population.

7. Three major types of population curves are stable, irruptive, and cyclic.

8. Irruptions are highly erratic and unpredictable. A good example was the Kaibab deer irruption in the Grand Canyon region of Arizona.

9. Three- to four-year cycles are characteristic of the brown lemming, meadow mouse, and salmon. Ten-year cycles are characteristic of the snowshoe hare, lynx, and grouse.

10. Perhaps 99 percent of all plant and animal species that ever existed are now extinct.

11. In the United States about 172 species of wildlife are listed as endangered.

12. The extinction of an organism would be an awesome loss to science. It represents a group of genes found nowhere else in the universe. Its anatomy, physiology, and behavior are not duplicated in any organism on earth.

13. When organisms become extinct, the normal functioning of the ecosystem to which they and we belong does not function as well as before.

14. Even obscure organisms, little known by humans, may have importance to our well-being. Thus, a mold is the source of penicillin, lichens serve as early monitors of air pollution, a tranquilizing drug is derived from the roots of the snakeroot shrub, and anticancer extracts have been obtained from organisms living on the bottom of the sea.

15. Among the traits of species that make them vulnerable to extinction are (a) restricted range and habitat (Kirtland's warbler), (b) low biotic potential (polar bear and California condor), (c) nonadaptive behavior (Carolina parakeet and red-headed woodpecker, and (d) specialized diet (Florida Everglade kite).

16. Among the causes of extinction are (a) genetic assimilation, (b) the pet trade, (c) the introduction of exotics, (d) killing game for novel uses, (e) pollution, and (f) habitat destruction and fragmentation.

17. Among the factors that contributed to the extinction of the passenger pigeon were (a) the destruction of nest and food trees, (b) disease, (c) storms during migration, (d) low biotic potential, (e) lack of the social stimulus necessary for breeding, and (f) intensive killing by market hunters.

18. Researchers have succeeded in establishing a second flock of whooping cranes that migrate between a wintering ground in New Mexico and a summer area in Wyoming and Idaho.

19. Methods for preventing the extinction of endangered species include (a) the zoo approach (Pere David's deer) and botanical garden approach (Wood's cycad), (b) the species approach (whooping crane and elephant), and (c) the ecosystem approach.

20. In the late 1970s a classic confrontation took place between an endangered fish known as the snail darter and the $116 million Tellico Dam.

21. After many court battles between environmentalists and pro-dam people, the Supreme Court permitted the dam's construction to be completed.

22. In 1980 six snail darters were discovered in the South Chickamauga Creek in Chattanooga, thus strengthening hopes that this fish will be saved from extinction.

23. Africa's elephant population is decreasing rapidly, largely as a result of illegal hunting by poachers armed with automatic rifles and even grenades. Most of those elephants are being hunted for their tusks, which are worth $35 per pound.

24. To save the African elephant from extinction, the World Wildlife Fund has proposed an African Elephant Action Plan that embraces conservation, economic, educational, and research programs.

Key Words and Phrases

African elephant	Bird banding
American egret	Botanical garden
Biomonitor	California condor
Biotic potential	Carolina parakeet

Clutch
Coyote
Cyclic curve
Density-dependent
 factor
Density-independent
 factor
Endangered species
Endangered Species Act
Everglade kite
Extinction
Four-year cycle
Genetic assimilation
Habitat fragmentation
Ibex
International Union for
 the Conservation of
 Nature and Natural
 Resources
Irruption
Kaibab deer
Kirtland's warbler
Lemming

Lynx
Non-adaptive behavior
Oil spill
Passenger pigeon
Pet trade
Prescribed burning
Red wolf
Reproductive potential
Restricted range
Shock disease
Snail darter
Snowshoe hare
Specialized diet
Stable population
Tellico Dam
Ten-year cycle
Teosinte
Waterfowl flyways
Waterfowl manage-
 ment
Whooping Crane
 Recovery Team

Questions and Topics for Discussion

1. Suppose that a classmate of yours made the statement: "I could care less about the extinction of some weed or bug in Africa, Asia, or some other far corner of the world." Do you consider such an attitude appropriate? Why or why not? Discuss your answer.

2. Describe four traits that make organisms vulnerable to extinction.

3. Discuss the following causes of extinction: (a) introduction of exotics, (b) pet trade, and (c) habitat fragmentation.

4. Do you consider it inevitable that humans will someday become extinct? Why or why not? Discuss this matter with other members of your class.

5. Suppose that fire were excluded from the Kirtland's warbler habitat. Would this promote the bird's survival? Why or why not?.

6. Discuss six factors that contributed to the extinction of the passenger pigeon. Suppose that at this moment there were still 100 passenger pigeons left somewhere in the United States. Do you think we could prevent their extinction? Why or why not?

7. Discuss the methods currently being employed to prevent the extinction of the whooping crane.

8. List four major provisions of the Endangered Species Act.

9. Since robins, deer, and almost all other species of organisms have such a high reproductive potential, why don't they overrun the earth?

10. List three factors controlling the numbers of organisms that are density dependent; list three that are density independent.

11. Name four animals that have three-year cycles; name three that have ten-year cycles.

12. Give a possible explanation for the four-year cycle of the lemming.

13. Discuss the Kaibab deer irruption. What caused it? Do you suppose that an irruption like this may have occurred even before human beings appeared on the scene? Discuss your answer.

14. Is it possible that the human species might undergo an irruption? Why or why not? Discuss the possibility with members of your class.

15. Discuss the Tellico Dam-snail darter controversy. If all the snail darters in the world were filetted and deep fried, their value would still be less than one millionth of that of the Tellico Dam. Were the prosnail-darter people fighting for more than just the tiny three-inch fish? If so, what was it?.

16. Exactly what is meant when we say that wildlife has aesthetic value? Have you perhaps been exposed to the aesthetic values of wildlife when you were camping, hiking through wilderness country, or just walking to your 8:00 class this morning? Share your experiences with your classmates.

17. Discuss the African Elephant Action Plan. What is its purpose? Who sponsored it? Identify four types of programs included in the plan. If you had the money, the time, and the inclination, would you go on an elephant-hunting safari in Africa some day? Why or why not?

Endnotes

1. Clark, Fran. *The Milwaukee Journal*, March 26, 1978.
2. Dasmann, Raymond F. *Wildlife Biology*. New York: Wiley, 1964.
3. Ehrenfeld, David W. *Biological Conservation*. New York: Holt, 1970.

4. Einarsen, A. S. "Some Factors Affecting Ring-necked Pheasant Population Density." *Murrelet,* **26** (1945), 39–44.
5. Elton, Charles, and M. Nicholson. "The Ten Year Cycle in the Numbers of the Lynx in Canada." *Jour. Anim. Ecol.,* **11** (1942), 215–244.
6. Kendeigh, S. Charles. *Animal Ecology.* Englewood Cliffs, N.J.: Prentice-Hall, 1961.
7. Pitelka, F. A. "Population Studies of Lemmings and Lemming Predators in Northern Alaska," *15th Int. Cong. Zool.,* Sect. X, Paper 5 (1959).
8. Wagner, Richard H. *Environment and Man.* New York: Norton, 1971.

Suggested Readings for the Interested Student

Bollengier, Rene M., *et al. Eastern Peregrine Falcon Recovery Plan.* Washington, DC: Government Printing Office, 1979. The authors describe efforts to restore a new self-sustaining population of peregrine falcons in the eastern United States. It is fascinating and highly readable.

Council on Environmental Quality. *Environmental Quality.* (Chapter Two: "Ecology and Natural Resources — Biological Diversity.") Washington, DC: Government Printing Office, 1980. This is an extremely well-written account of the multiple values of biological diversity to human beings and of the environmental stresses to which it is exposed.

Ehrlich, Paul, and Anne Ehrlich. *Extinction: The Causes and Consequences of the Disappearance of Species.* New York: Random, 1981. This is an absorbing documentation of the multiple scientific and economic values of wild plants and animals. The stresses that have edged many species closer to extinction are explored with precision and impressive statistics.

Holden, C. "Endangered Species: Review of Law Triggered by Tellico Impasse." *Science,* **196** (June 24, 1977), 1427. The confrontation between the snail darter and the Tellico Dam caused a re-examination of the implications of the Endangered Species Act.

Shaffer, Mark L. "Minimum Population Sizes for Species Conservation." *Bioscience,* **31** (Feb. 1981), 131–134. The author explains why the most pressing need facing wildlife biologists is to understand the relationship between the population size of a species and the probability of its extinction.

U.S. Interagency Task Force on Tropical Forests. *The World's Tropical Forests: A Policy, Strategy and Program for the United States.* Washington, DC: Government Printing Office, 1980. This discussion explores the multiple causes of tropical forest destruction and the implications for wildlife survival. An international program to reverse this trend is described

Walton, Susan. "Bailing out the Ark: Norman Myers Discusses Saving Threatened Species." *Bioscience,* **30** (Aug. 1980), 553–556. This is a highly readable, but grim account that describes the basic causes of the current "wildlife crisis." The question-answer format of the article is very effective.

13 Wildlife Management

The Habitat Requirements of Wildlife

Habitat is the general environment in which an organism lives — its natural home. The habitat of a wild animal provides certain essentials: shelter, food, water, breeding sites (den, nest, or burrow), and a fairly well-defined area called the *territory*, in which an animal has psychological dominance over intruders.

Cover

Cover may serve to protect an animal from adverse weather conditions. Good examples are the dense cedar swamps that protect whitetail deer herds from winter winds and drifting snow and the leafy canopies of apple trees that shield nestling robins from the heat of the midday sun. Cover may also protect wild animals from predators. (See Figure 13–1.) Representative of this function is the thicket into which a cottontail plunges when eluding a fox or the marsh grasses that conceal a teal from a hawk. Even water may serve as cover, as for a muskrat or beaver, providing relative security from all landbound predators, from wolves to humans.

Food

On the basis of food habits, vertebrate animals may be classified as herbivores, spermivores (seed eaters), frugivores (fruit eaters), carnivores, insectivores, omnivores, and so on. The tendency to eat

13–1 *Long grasses form protective cover for ground-nesting bobwhite quail.*

367

certain basic food types is inherited but is subject to modification on the basis of experience. There may be considerable variation in food habits within the species, and even in the same individual, depending on such variables as health and age of the animal, season, habitat, and food availability. An animal's access to adequate food may be influenced by many factors, including population density, weather, habitat destruction (by fire, flood, or insects), plant succession, and type of habitat. (See Figure 13–2.)

Because mammals (and presumably birds) must spend 90 percent of their waking hours searching for food, the importance of food availability is emphasized. Occasionally, when a food occurs in superabundant quantities, an animal will exploit the source, even though it is not a usual dietary item. Consider some examples: even though the green-winged teal's diet is 90 percent vegetation, it avidly consumes the maggoty flesh of rotting Pacific salmon. Although the lesser scaup is not normally a scavenger, the stomachs of ducks that had been feeding at the mouth of a sewer were filled with slaughterhouse debris and cow hair (as well as rubber bands and paper). A house wren, usually insectivorous, fed its nestlings large quantities of newly hatched trout from an adjacent hatchery (41). A study of winter mink diets in Missouri, revealed that the volume percentage of fish increased from 11.9 in 1951 to 27.4 in 1953, apparently because low water levels increased the vulnerability of the prey. Similarly, during periods of drought or high muskrat-population densities, muskrat may become the principal mink food, although at other times it forms only 1 or 2 percent of the mink diet.

Dietary changes are frequently seasonal in character. Thus, although the red fox consumes mice throughout the year, Hamilton decribes the following shifts in its diet: *winter* — carrion, offal, and frozen apples; *spring and summer* — snakes, turtles, eggs, an occasional fawn, blackberries, and raspberries; *autumn* — wild cherries, grapes, and grasshoppers (16). Joel Welty, bird specialist at Beloit College, Wisconsin, reports that barn owls near Davis, California, that had subsisted primarily on house and deer mice during spring and summer shifted to gophers and moles during autumn and winter (40).

Animals that consume a great variety of foods are *euryphagous*. The omnivorous opossum is a classic example. It consumes fruits, blackberries, persimmons, corn, apples, earthworms, insects, frogs, snakes, lizards, newly hatched turtles, bird eggs, young mice, and even bats. It is apparent that during critical periods when usual foods are scarce, the euryphagous animal is well adapted to survive. Thus, although the usual foods for the ring-necked pheasant are corn, sorghum, rye, wheat, barley, soybeans, lesser ragweed, and pigeon grass, when these foods are covered with ice and snow, the bird shifts to the seeds of bittersweet, sumac, and black locust.

A *stenophagous* animal, maintains a *specialized* diet. It is more vulnerable to starvation when its usual foods are scarce. For example, a spell of freezing weather in late April that causes a dearth of flying insects will frequently result in considerable starvation losses to chimney swifts and swallows. In 1932 a blight caused a 90 percent destruction of the eelgrass along the Atlantic coast. As a result, the wintering population of brants (small geese), which depend on eelgrass for food, almost exclusively, was reduced by 80 percent (30).

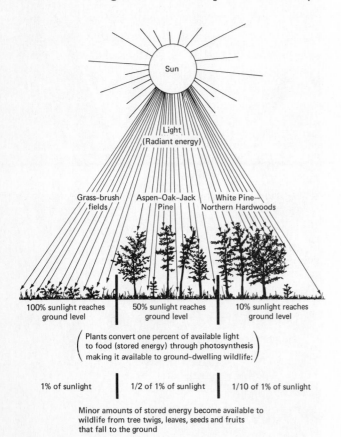

13–2 *The amount of food energy available to ground-dwelling wildlife on the floor of a dense forest is much less than is available in an open woods or a grassy field.*

13 – 3 *Parent bluebird bringing bill full of insects to hungry young. A young bluebird will eat half its weight in insects in one day.*

Water

Roughly 65 to 80 percent of wild-animal biomass is composed of water. It serves many functions. It flushes wastes from the body. As a major blood constituent it transports nutrients, hormones, enzymes, and respiratory gases. Animals can survive for weeks without food but only a few days without water. Buffalo herds living in arid western grasslands in the 19th century traveled many miles to waterholes, leaving trails that are visible to this day. Mourning doves may fly up to 30 miles from nesting site to watering place. Dove and quail populations have been increased in the Southwest by the installation of "guzzlers"—devices that collect rainwater (10). (See Figure 13–5.) Some herbivores (for example, wild donkeys) may recover up to 25

percent of water loss in less than two minutes, thus minimizing the predator hazard (12). Birds and mammals may secure their water from dew or may drink it as it drips from foliage and tree trunks after a shower. During the northern winter, when liquid water is scarce, this writer has observed English sparrows and starlings eating snow. The versatile Adelie penguin may drink salt water or fresh water as well as eat snow. Many animals living in arid regions satisfy their water requirements by consuming water-containing foods. Desert carnivores, such as the rattlesnake, desert fox, prairie falcon, and bobcat, may secure water from the blood and body fluids of prey. The desert-dwelling grasshopper mouse feeds extensively on insects having a 60 to 85 percent water content (11). Forty-four percent of the white-throated wood rat's desert diet consists of cacti and other succulent plants. The kangaroo

13 – 4 *The anhinga—a classic example of a stenophagous species. This bird is structurally and behaviorally specialized for preying on fish. Its bill is long and slender and twice as long as its head. The margins of the bill are saw-toothed to prevent loss of the slippery prey. The habit of swimming around almost totally submerged with its long snaky neck sliding above water like a periscope has won the anhinga the nickname "snake bird." A skilled fisherman, this beautiful large bird seeks its quarry by swimming underwater, spearing the fish with its beak, then tossing it into the air, catching it, and gulping it down in one fell swoop.*

13–5 *Wildlife habitat improvement. Chukar partridge (introduced from Asia) attracted by a "guzzler," a recently developed watering device employed in arid regions.*

rat may not require ingested water during its entire life span because it can make effective use of the metabolic water synthesized within its tissues from the breakdown of fats and proteins (33).

Home Range

Ecologist Robert L. Smith defines a home range as "the area over which an animal habitually travels while engaged in its usual activities" (35). Home range can be determined by marking, releasing, and recapturing an animal. Animals can be tracked with Geiger counters after having been fed radioactive materials. Dyed foods will result in colored feces; the home range can then be determined on the basis of dropping distribution (12). Birds can be individually marked with a colored leg band or spray paints. Small mammals can have their ears notched or toes clipped. Large animals (buffalo and elk) can be tattooed or marked with colored plastic collars so that visual identification is possible at a distance. (See Figures 13–6 and 13–7.)

Herbivores usually have smaller home ranges than carnivores. Animals occupying a deteriorated habitat maintain larger home ranges than those in a good habitat. A few home ranges for herbivorous mammals are as follows: field mouse, 0.5-acre; deer mouse, 0.5-acre (good habitat) or 5 acres (poor habitat); porcupine, 1 kilometer; and beaver, under 1 kilometer. In one study 70 percent of the released muskrats were retaken within 160 feet of their original capture (12). Bull moose may have a summer

13–6 *Home Range in deer. This mule deer will soon be "reporting" its location. This deer, which lives on a range near the Los Alamos Scientific Laboratory in New Mexico, was trapped in a live trap seen in the background. It is being marked with colored ear streamers and a numbered ear tag and fitted with a radio transmitter (contained in a colored neck band). The transmitter will permit accurate tracking of the animal. The tag and colored streamers will aid in identification if the deer is sighted by the public or scientific personnel. By such methods the home range of this individual will be determined.*

370

13-7 *Home range in deer. Group of twelve deer photographed from a plane during an aerial census in the Upper Souris Refuge, Foxholm, North Dakota.*

home range of only 100 acres of swamp. After attaching miniature radio transmitters to the bodies of eastern wild turkeys, Missouri researchers acquired telemetric data indicating an annual average home range of 1,100 acres for four adult gobblers (14). Although more data are required, the mink appears to occupy a home range embracing 15 to 100 miles of lake or river shoreline. Timber wolves have circular runways 20 to 60 miles in diameter (4).

Territory

A *territory* is any defended area. Territories are usually defended against individuals of the same species. Margaret Nice set up the following classification of avian territories in terms of areas defended: Type A—entire mating, feeding, and breeding area; Type B—mating and nesting area; Type C—mating area; Type D—nest only; and Type E—nonbreeding areas such as feeding and roosting sites (See Figure 13–8.) In many species of birds, territory is "defended" by display and/or song rather than fighting. (See Figure 13–9.)

Territorialism in birds may serve the following functions: provision of adequate food; a mechanism for establishing and maintaining the pairing bond; regulation of population density (territories are on the average smaller where food is superabundant); reduction of interference with breeding activities (copulation, nest building, and incubation); reduction of predation losses (resulting from familiarity with refuge sites as well as from the population dispersion); and reduction of infectious-disease transmission (little evidence) (39).

Average territorial areas (in square meters) for certain avian species follow: black-headed gull in England, 0.3; eastern robin in Wisconsin, 1,200; red-winged blackbird in Wisconsin, 3,000; black-capped chickadee in New York, 53,000; great horned owl in New York, 500,000; and golden eagle in California, 93 million (41). (See Figure 13–11.) Territorial size depends partly on function and partly on the size of the bird. The black-headed gull's territory is so small because it is concerned

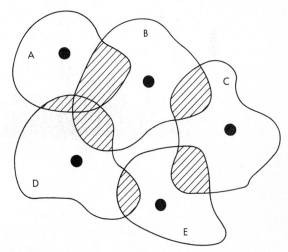

13-8 *Home range compared with territory. A diagrammatic representation of five home ranges and territories. The large clear areas (A, B, C, D, E) are home ranges. Note the diagonally hatched areas where two adjacent ranges overlap. Territories are indicated by the black spot in the center of each home range. Note that territories never overlap.*

371

13-9 *Territorial defense. Ruffed grouse drumming on log. Drumming sound is caused by the rapid series of air-mass compressions resulting from the beating wings. The drumming not only serves as territorial advertisement to competitive males, but also as an attractant to prospective mates. A suitable drumming log (partially decomposed) is an essential component of the ruffed grouse's territory.*

13-10 *Black-capped chickadee feeding from hand. These birds respond so readily to human imitation of their territorial song that they will perch on one's hand.*

13-11 *The golden eagle, like most carnivorous birds, maintains an extremely large territory—in some cases up to 93 million square meters.*

only with nest defense. On the other hand the territories of the great horned owl and the golden eagle are so large because the birds are concerned not only with the provision of nesting areas, but also with mating and feeding areas.

Territorial behavior is well developed in many species of fish, including the sunfish, bass, and many kinds of minnows. Male black bass and sunfish will defend their nests by rushing directly at an intruder.

Animal Movements

The large-scale movements of animals serve functions for both the individual and the species. Individuals may secure more favorable food supplies, breeding facilities, climate, or simply more living room. A species may benefit if movements result in establishing a new habitat where the species can persist in the event that formerly occupied habitats are destroyed. Movements may also aid the species by increasing the amount of genetic variability on which natural selection can operate. Three basic types of movements among vertebrates are dispersal of the young, mass emigration, and migration.

Dispersal of Young

The phenomenon of dispersal occurs in the young of many birds (gulls, herons, egrets, grouse, eagles, and owls) and mammals (muskrats, fox squirrels, and gray squirrels). In a pine-oak habitat in central Pennsylvania, up to half of the juvenile ruffed grouse emigrated from their nesting areas to all points of the compass, some up to a distance of 7.5 miles (7). Charles Broley reports that young bald eagles banded in Florida moved northward immediately after nesting, some arriving 1,500 miles distant in Maine and Canada by June (3). Some scientists believe that the eagle was a bird of more northern origin whose establishment in Florida may have been relatively recent (39). If so, dispersal was adaptive because it enabled eagles to escape the intense heat of the Florida summer. Up to 40 percent of a wintering muskrat population may disperse in spring. They are primarily young animals who have been ejected by the established, more aggressive adults. Such dispersal apparently is an important mechanism for controlling population densities. Many of the dispersed young move into marginal habitats, where they incur heavy mortality from predation and accidents.

Mass Emigration

Mass emigrations frequently occur when a population has peaked because of extremely favorable conditions (e.g., food or weather) and then experienced a greatly reduced food supply. Under such conditions the alternatives to starvation are summer dormancy, hibernation, or emigration. Emigrations of crossbills into the United States from Canada's coniferous forests result from pine-seed crop failure. Crossbills are highly erratic in their movements, in terms of season and direction; even time and place of nesting are apparently determined by the availability of an adequate seed supply. Snowy-owl emigrations into the United States from the Canadian tundra are correlated with the population crash of their lemming prey. Ornithologists recorded 13,502 snowy owls during the 1945–1946 emigration, which extended as far south as Oregon, Illinois, and Maryland. Twenty-four were observed out over the Atlantic. Some were even seen in Bermuda (34).

The huge owls frequently perch on such unlikely sites as telephone poles, fence posts, television antennae, and the window ledges of downtown skyscrapers. It is believed that very few of these owls live long enough to make the return flight to the Canadian tundra the following spring. Many are shot illegally by so-called sportsmen and wind up stuffed with cotton on someone's mantlepiece.

Latitudinal Migrations

Winter bird densities in the southern latitudes of the United States are high, not only because of the permanent residents, but also because of the many individuals that breed in more northern latitudes. For the most part territorialism is relaxed — many species traveling, feeding, and roosting in flocks. Food supplies, such as insects, fruits, and seeds, are more readily available than in northern latitudes. In spring, however, the lengthening photoperiod eventually triggers a neuroendocrine mechanism that causes some birds to migrate northward. Presumably the northern habitats have a higher carrying capacity for the migrants and their future broods. In far northern latitudes during the summer, there is more time in one 24-hour cycle for feeding the young. For example, in northern Alaska (69° north latitude) a robin brood was fed 21 hours a day by the

373

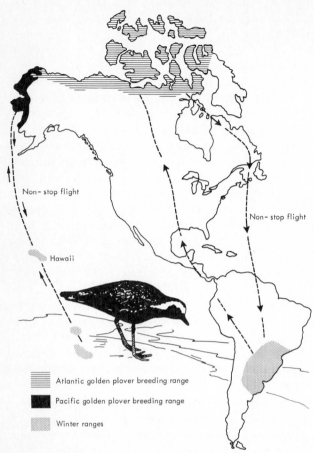

moving thousands of miles to the south, are secured by altitudinal migrants simply by moving a few miles down the mountainside (22). (See Figure 13–13.) The elk herds of the Jackson Hole country in Wyoming ascend the mountains in spring, keeping pace with the receding snow line, and spend the summer at relatively cool upper levels. Only when the first snows cover their food supplies, whether in September or November, do the elk move down to the sagebrush valleys for the winter (32). The bighorn sheep of Idaho make similar migrations (in herds of five to fifty animals), which may be up to 40-miles long. Altitudinal migrations are characteristic of several birds breeding in the Colorado Rockies. Thus, the pine grosbeak, black-capped rosy finch, and gray-headed junco all nest at higher altitudes than those at which they winter. Curiously, the blue grouse reverses the usual altitudinal migration; it winters at higher levels than it breeds.

13–13 *An altitudinal migrant—the Dall's sheep. Occurring in the Mt. McKinley region of Alaska, these sheep move to higher elevations in spring as the snow and ice melt on the mountain slopes but return to lower levels with the approach of winter.*

Atlantic golden plover breeding range

Pacific golden plover breeding range

Winter ranges

13–12 *Distribution and migration of the golden plover. Adults of the eastern form migrate across northeastern Canada and then, by a 2,400-mile nonstop flight, reach South America. In the spring they return by way of the Mississippi Valley. Their entire route is in the form of a great ellipse with a major axis of 8,000 miles and a minor axis of about 2,000 miles. The Pacific golden plover, which breeds in Alaska, apparently makes a nonstop flight across the ocean to Hawaii, the Marquesas Islands, and the Low Archipelago, returning in the spring over the same route.*

female parent. Joel Welty has suggested that the exploitation of two different habitats (winter and summer) may ensure a more balanced supply of vitamins and minerals (41). The unique "loop" migration of the golden plover is shown in Figure 13–12.

Altitudinal Migrations

As Kendeigh has pointed out, the conditions of less snow, higher temperatures, and more available food supplies, which latitudinal migrants secure by

It has been postulated that this arrangement perhaps lessens winter competition with other species for buds and conifer needles (34).

Factors Depleting Waterfowl Populations

A variety of factors, both biological and physical, prevent waterfowl from realizing their high biotic potential. Among those discussed here are pothole drainage and drought, appropriation of duck habitat for recreation, habitat destruction by carp, oil pollution, lead poisoning, and botulism.

Pothole Drainage and Drought

The most productive duck factory on the North American continent is located in the grassland biome of Manitoba, Saskatchewan, Alberta, the Dakotas, western Minnesota, and northwestern Iowa. (See Figure 13–14.) This region produced 53 per-

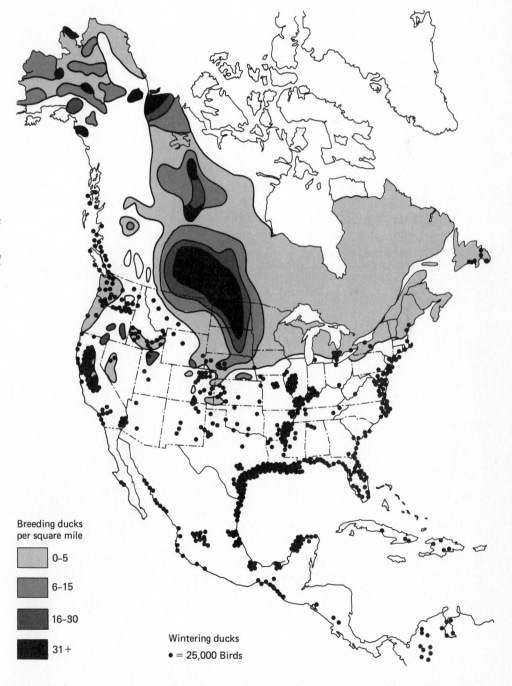

13–14 *Distribution of North American breeding and wintering ducks. Over 50 percent of the ducks raised in the North American continent are produced in the duck factories of Manitoba, Saskatchewan, Alberta, the Dakotas, western Minnesota, and northwestern Iowa. The major wintering areas are the Atlantic, Gulf, and Pacific coasts; the lower Mississippi River Valley; and California. Many ducks that migrate through the United States winter in Mexico. Effective waterfowl management obviously depends on cooperative actions of Canada, the United States, and Mexico.*

Breeding ducks
per square mile

- 0–5
- 6–15
- 16–30
- 31+

Wintering ducks
• = 25,000 Birds

cent of the continent's waterfowl from 1950–1957 (27). The ducks are raised primarily on tiny *potholes*, one or two acres in size, where all the basic waterfowl-habitat requirements of food, cover, water, and nesting sites are usually met. However, the drainage of considerable pothole acreage for agricultural purposes, some of which, inexplicably, was actually subsidized by the federal government, has long posed a critical habitat-impairment problem. In 1948 the government paid $17,285 to 350 farmers of Day County, South Dakota, to dig 43 miles of drainage canals (5). As a result 1,400 potholes, representing 6,285 acres, were eliminated as duck-nesting areas. From 1949 to 1950 in Minnesota, North Dakota, and South Dakota 64,000 potholes were destroyed, representing a loss of 188,000 acres of waterfowl habitat (27). In 1955 only 56,000 of the original 150,000 square miles of pothole habitat still remained. In Iowa alone, over the last sixty years, the number of potholes has been reduced by at least 90 percent. Regrettably, despite the widely known seriousness of the problem relative to waterfowl depletion, wetland drainage in the United States continues virtually unabated, 600,000 acres having been lost in 1977 alone.

In 1977 a federal agency proposed a multimillion dollar ditching program in the Cache River basin of Arkansas — a project that would have adversely affected the survival of the largest concentration of wintering mallards on the North American continent. Waterfowl biologists breathed a collective sigh of relief when the project was at least temporarily halted, pending the completion of an environmental-impact study.

Severe drought in the 1930s and early 1960s compounded the problem by drying up many potholes that hiterto had escaped drainage. During drought conditions, the number of potholes in Canada may be reduced from a wet-season peak of 6.7 million to 1.7 million, with a corresponding reduction in waterfowl populations (36). During the extremely dry spring of 1977, many ducks migrating northward along the Pacific Flyway apparently deliberately "overshot" their usual nesting grounds because of the low water levels and nested in Alaska and northern Canada instead. As a result, the 1977 duck population in Alaska alone reached a peak of seven million birds – the highest number recorded there in 22 years.

It should be mentioned that some drainage has not only benefited agriculture, but also some game other than waterfowl. Thus, the Black Swamp in

13–15 *Aerial view of dried-up potholes near Antler, Saskatchewan, Canada.*

376

Wood County, Ohio, which was converted into a profitable agricultural region by drainage, now affords some of the best pheasant hunting in the state.

Appropriation of Duck Habitat for Recreation

For many centuries the weed beds and marshes along the western end of Lake Erie provided optimal habitat for thousands of waterfowl to swim, feed, and nest. Today, as a result of a mushrooming human population with increasing amounts of leisure time, the area's waterfowl carrying capacity has been severely impaired. Where mallards once paddled, motorboats churn. The scuba diver has replaced the scaup; the marsh has given way to the marina. Over 3,000 boats are berthed along a 0.5-mile shoreline of Lake St. Clair. They appropriate space once used by waterfowl. During the summer large numbers of motorboats trim the tops of emergent food plants with great efficiency. We would not expect a field of daisies to be capable of reproduction were we to go through them with a power mower; neither can duck-food plants survive unless they are permitted to keep their reproductive heads above water to effect pollination. It is apparent that in this confrontation of ducks — concerned with survival itself — and humans — concerned only with weekend water fun — the interests of the latter have been served, with catastrophic effects on the waterfowl.

Habitat Destruction by Carp

To many a barefooted youngster armed with cane pole and worms, a carp might seem a prize, but to the sophisticated duck hunter, it is a notorious destroyer of waterfowl habitat. Carp can eradicate dense growths of sago pondweed, water milfoil, and coontail, all favored duck foods (31). By means of enclosure experiments, Threinen and Helm of the Wisconsin Department of Natural Resources showed that carp could quickly devastate growths of floating-leaf pondweed. Lake Koshkonong in southern Wisconsin was once almost blanketed with rafts of canvasbacks, which consumed the abundant wild celery buds and pondweed nuts. Late in the nineteenth century, however, carp were introduced to Lake Koshkonong. In a brief time the fish uprooted the choice waterfowl food plants, and the thrilling panoramas of rafting "cans" quickly vanished, except in memory. Hundreds of waterfowl feeding areas throughout the United States have shown that young carp will compete directly

with ducklings for protein-rich invertebrates, so essential for growth and development. Small crustaceans are preferred by carp under five inches long, five-inch to eleven-inch carp prefer aquatic insects (31).

The turbidity caused by carp, which stir up the bottom muds while searching for plant rootstocks and invertebrates, may restrict photosynthesis sufficiently to eliminate certain duck-food plants not actually directly killed by the fish. This factor was partially responsible for the impaired waterfowl-carrying capacity of the Potomac River and the Susquehanna Flats some years ago (28).

Carp are extremely difficult to eradicate. Once under control, however, a given site may recover its original ability to support waterfowl. This was demonstrated at the Lake Mattamuskeet Wildlife Refuge in North Carolina, where carp had infiltrated from brackish coastal waters in the 1930s. Because of their deleterious impact on waterfowl, refuge personnel launched an intensive carp-control campaign in 1945. It included the erection of a barrier to prevent further infiltration and an extended seining operation that netted 2.4 million pounds of carp from 1945 to 1960. Already by 1952, water turbidity was markedly reduced and duck-food plants were becoming established on the formerly barren lake bottom. As a result, Lake Mattamuskeet once again is a celebrated water-fowl wintering ground, currently being utilized by 60,000 to 80,000 Canada geese, 80,000 to 150,000 ducks and teal, and hundreds of whistling swans annually (6).

Oil Pollution

An excess of 100,000 waterfowl are destroyed annually by oil pollution. One-quarter-million murres, eiders, razorbills, and puffins died off Newfoundland because of jettisoned oil during the winter of 1960. Oil killed 4,000 ducks in Long Island Sound in December 1960. Another 4,000 ducks, almost 20 percent of the wintering population in Narragansett Bay, were destroyed by an oil spill in 1961. More than 20,000 ducks died moving northward along the Mississippi River in 1963. (See Figure 13–16.) In 1969 thousands of waterfowl were destroyed off Santa Barbara, California, because of an oil spill resulting from faulty drilling operations.

Oil hazards for marine birds developed in about 1925, when oil-burning ships replaced those utilizing coal as fuel (29). Much of this pollution occurs in

13–16 *Spring Lake, Minnesota. Oil-coated ducks are piled up on the shore of the Mississippi River, near Spring Lake, victims in 1963 of petroleum- and soybean-oil-polluted waters. Collected in 20 minutes, these were a few of the 20,000 ducks killed by the oil.*

Atlantic coastal waters. Oil kills ducks by matting their feathers and impairing their insulative function. An oil-soaked area the size of a quarter will kill a murre. Oil may also prove lethal if swallowed accidentally during preening and drinking. Accelerated starvation may frequently occur when oiled ducks exhibit a greatly increased metabolic rate in conjunction with a retarded food intake (18).

Lead Poisoning

Hunters deposit more than 3,000 tons of spent shot on our nation's lakes, rivers, and marshes annually. Because there are 280 pellets of #6 shot in one shell, and the average hunter requires five shots to kill one duck, he deposits 1,400 pellets on waterfowl habitat for each bird taken. Sixty thousand pellets per acre were counted in the San Joaquin River marshes of California; 118,048 per acre were recorded from the bottom of Wisconsin's Lake Puckaway (1). Species incurring the heaviest losses have been the bottom feeders, such as mallards and pintails, which ingest the shot inadvertently along with food and grit. Nevertheless, up to 179 pellets have been recovered from a pintail and 451 from a trumpeter swan (1).

After ingestion of the shot, chemical reactions within the digestive tract cause the release of soluble lead salts, which may paralyze the gizzard and cause starvation in a month. In acute cases poisoning of the liver, blood, and kidneys may cause death in one to two weeks. Symptoms include extreme emaciation, protruding breast bone, absence of fat deposits in the body cavity, much enlarged gallbladder, and characteristically green-stained gizzard lining and vent (1).

The average hunter is not aware of the high rate of lead poisoning. One reason is that the intact lead pellets are not often found in the gizzard of the duck; they are rapidly ground up into small particles and cannot be detected. Furthermore, a duck suffering from lead poisoning will frequently hide in the vegetation of the marsh, or it might be eaten by predators.

Lead poisoning resulting from the swallowing of spent shot causes an estimated 2 to 3 percent annual waterfowl loss in the United States, almost equivalent to the combined duck production of North and South Dakota (1). (Nearly 25 percent of 8,000 waterfowl investigated in southern France contained lead shot.) From 1940 to 1963, over 1,500 Canada geese died in Wisconsin from lead poisoning. The heaviest duck mortality from lead poisoning has oc-

378

curred along the Mississippi flyway, especially in Louisiana, Illinois, Missouri, Indiana, and Arkansas.

In order to terminate heavy duck mortality from lead poisoning — amounting to at least two million ducks per year, or one duck per hunter — the U.S Fish and Wildlife Service began phasing out lead shot and replacing it with steel shot in 1976. The mandatory use of steel shot has caused a considerable amount of controversy among duck hunters and waterfowl biologists. The advantages of shifting to steel shot follow:

1. Saving the lives of over two million ducks per year.
2. At a distance of more than 45 yards, steel shot does not cripple as many ducks as lead shot.

The disadvantages of steel shot are

1. Steel shot is more expensive than lead shot.
2. Steel shot will not kill at a distance of more than 45 yards; the hunter might as well point his gun at the water.
3. Steel shot will ruin outdated shotgun barrels made of soft steel.

Regardless of the negative features, steel shot is here to stay.

Botulism

The prostrate bodies of dead and dying ducks littered the mud flats of a western marsh. A mallard feebly fluttered its wings and voided bright green droppings; a widgeon struggled vainly to lift its head out of the stagnant ooze; a Canada goose was blinded by the yellowish slime that covered its eyes; a blue-winged teal gasped and died. What had happened to those birds? They were the victims of *botulism*, a disease caused by the toxic metabolic wastes of the anaerobic bacterium *Clostridium botulinum*, Type C. Although most prevalent in the West, it has been recorded from Canada to Mexico and from California to New Jersey. During the summer of 1910 this microscopic organism was responsible for millions of waterfowl deaths. In 1929 and again in 1932, an estimated 100,000 to 300,000 waterfowl in the Great Salt Lake (Utah) died from botulism (19). In 1965 botulism claimed the lives of 20,000 birds in Utah's Bear River Migratory Bird Wildlife Refuge.

The optimal environmental conditions for a population buildup of *Clostridium* include (1) exposed stretches of stagnant alkaline flats, (2) an abundance of trapped organic matter such as dead aquatic vegetation, to serve as food, and (3) high water temperatures. These conditions are most likely to occur in

13–17 *Botulism at the Bear River Migratory Bird Refuge. Biologist picks up sick and dead birds. Sick birds are given antitoxin treatments at the duck hospital. Since the hospital was established, the loss of waterfowl from this disease has dropped off greatly in the refuge.*

13–18 *Unloading botulism-stricken ducks at the Bear River Migratory Bird Refuge, Utah. They will be given antitoxin shots at the duck hospital. A very high percentage of treated birds recovers.*

the late summer during periods of protracted drought. The shallow-feeding dabbling ducks are especially vulnerable because they accidentally swallow the toxic material along with aquatic plants and their invertebrate foods. Apparently insect larvae serve as a specialized microhabitat for bacteria where growth and reproduction are favored (19). Once absorbed by the bloodstream of the waterfowl, the toxin affects the nervous system, rendering the birds flightless and eventually causing death by paralysis of the breathing muscles. At the Bear River Wildlife Refuge many thousands of sick ducks have recovered after receiving antitoxin shots. Such treatment, however, would be prohibitively costly and time consuming in the event of a major outbreak. Thus, *prevention* seems to be the answer. This can be done by rapidly raising the water level of the marsh or mudflat so that *Clostridium* no longer has optimal conditions for reproduction (21). Such flooding would both lower the water temperature and dilute the toxin. Research is currently being conducted to determine whether botulism can be controlled indirectly by reducing the invertebrate populations (20).

Factors Depleting Deer Populations

Malnutrition

Winter is a critical season for deer survival in the northern states because available food is extremely limited. Much potential food, such as herbs, mosses, fungi, seedlings, low-growing shrubs, and stump sprouts, is frequently covered with snow. Under such conditions the only available plant materials are buds, twigs, and the foliage of shrubs and trees. (See Figure 13–20.) If the deer population exceeds the carrying capacity of the habitat (as it has in many of the lake states in the last few decades), deer will consume all the available browse up to the height they can reach when rearing up on their hind legs. As a result, a conspicuous *browse line* will form at a height of 4.5 to 5 feet, a definite warning to the biologist of deteriorating range. Under these conditions fawn mortality is high, not only because of their restricted reach, but because the young rank at the bottom of the buck-doe-fawn social hierarchy. During the winter of 1955–1956, game wardens in Michigan found large numbers of deer floundering in snowdrifts, severely weakened from

13–19 *Michigan deer yard. During the winter season deer tend to congregate in deer yards. These yards frequently are located in cedar swamps where the animals are protected from wind and blowing snow. The compaction of snow in a yard facilitates movement to and from feeding areas. When deer are alerted to possible danger, they lift their tail erect; it looks like a white "flag" as the animal bounds away.*

malnutrition. Over 115,650 deer died that year, at least one third perishing directly from starvation, the remainder from predators and disease that merely finished off the deer after starvation had set the stage.

Emergency feeding of starving deer is not considered sound management by most game biologists. They argue that it permits the survival of deer whose future progeny will exert even greater demands on the available natural browse, thus aggravating the problem. Artificial feeding also may facilitate the spread of disease by promoting concentrations of highly susceptible animals. Moreover, it is expensive. During the period from 1934 to 1956, Wisconsin spent over $0.5-million on the purchase and distribution of 7,000 tons of artificial feed. To feed the Michigan deer herds properly for one winter would cost $800,000, or roughly $16 to $40 per head.

Accidents

At least thirteen types of fatal deer accidents have been recorded in Wisconsin (9). They include death by auto and train, entanglement in browse trees, falling over a cliff, enmirement in muck, drowning,

13–20 *Note how deer have browsed and twigs of this young pine. When deer populations are dense in winter deer yards, damage to pine stands may be severe.*

13–21 *Just a small sample of the thousands of white-tailed deer that starve annually during severe winters (with deep snow cover) in Wisconsin, Minnesota, Michigan, New York, and Pennsylvania.*

lightning strike, herbicide poisoning, and antler locking while fighting. A speeding convertible can be a more significant mortality factor than a wolf. Over a 16-year period, Minnesota game wardens found that 7,937 (79.39 percent) of 9,991 deer deaths were caused by motorcars, as compared to only 457 (4.57 percent) fatalities caused by predation. In a single year cars have killed 1,093 deer in Wisconsin. Currently an estimated 3,000 deer are killed annually by Minnesota motorists. Most accidents to the black-tailed deer of California's chaparral range are experienced by male fawns (37).

Predation

Among deer predators may be listed wolves, cougars, bobcats, coyotes, and domestic dogs. From 1951 to 1960, wolves in the wilderness of the Superior National Forest destroyed 1.5 deer per square mile annually. In 1950 wolves killed 6,000 (17 percent) of the 37,000 deer in the forest. Ninety-seven percent of 435 wolf scats (deposited fecal matter) collected in northern Wisconsin from 1946 to 1948 contained the remains of deer. Despite much contrary opinion, wolves do not cull the weak, sickly,

crippled, or senile individuals but simply take any deer regardless of sex, age, or physical condition. However, because hunting pressure in the remote backwoods country of the Superior National Forest is extremely light, accounting for only 0.65-deer per square mile, wolf predation might help control a deer herd that is often on the verge of exceeding the carrying capacity of the range. Because there are only about 800 timber wolves in the entire state of Minnesota, the impact of wolf predation on deer in that state must be negligible. Wisconsin has about 20 timber wolves; Michigan has a few.

Although one cougar may kill an estimated fifty or more deer annually, cougars are unimportant as regulators of deer populations because of their scarcity, except in localized areas of Arizona and other parts of the Southwest. One observer reports seeing a black bear killing a black-tailed fawn and consuming the entire carcass (23). Bobcats weighing 25 pounds can kill deer weighing 175 pounds, usually attacking when the latter are lying down. Deliberate aggressive responses of mule-deer does toward bobcats that have approached fawns have been observed (17). Deer remains were found in only 3.5 percent of

382

300 bobcats scats collected in Michigan. Surprisingly, the most serious deer slayer other than humans is the dog. Beagles, German shepherds, and Airedales have been implicated. Pregnant does and young fawns are especially vulnerable. Dogs killed 43 deer in one month on the Carlos Avery Game Refuge in Minnesota. During one January dogs killed 1,000 snowbound deer in New York. In summary, over most of the whitetail deer's range, domestic dogs that have gone astray are the most significant predators; except in local situations, wild predators are of little consequence. In remote hunting areas where hunting pressure is light, a higher predator population might be advantageous in preventing disastrous irruptions.

13-22 *Deer killers. Minnesota conservation officer holding two dogs responsible for killing more than 50 deer in St. Croix State Park in one winter.*

Wildlife Management

Through the years American biologists and legislators have employed a number of techniques for restoring, maintaining, and increasing game populations. They include protective laws, wildlife refuges, the introduction of exotic species, predator control, and most recently development of habitat.

Game Laws

Throughout human history there have been a few farsighted citizens aware of the importance of wildlife to our happiness and welfare and of the ease with which the resource can be depleted, if not exhausted, by the unrestrained human "predator." Thus, as early as 700 B.C., Moses decreed (Deuteronomy 22:6) that, although eggs and nestling birds could be taken for food, the adult breeding stock should be spared "that it may go well with you and that you may live long."

Although game was generally abundant during early colonial times, the constant hunting for a few species such as the whitetail deer prompted some states to enact protective laws. Thus, in 1646 Rhode Island established the first closed season on deer, and by 1694 Massachusetts was also protecting this popular game species. The first law to protect does was enacted by Virginia in 1738; in 1788 the state prohibited the use of hounds in hunting deer. In 1874 the American people became so aroused over the near extermination of the buffalo that Congress was prodded into passing a protective law; unfortunately, it was vetoed by President Grant.

During most of the nineteenth century, however, protective game laws were poorly enforced. Very few officials were sufficiently courageous to punish the numerous violators. Nevertheless, greater respect for restrictive game legislation developed by 1878, when New Hampshire and California employed game wardens charged with the responsibility of law enforcement. By the turn of the century, 31 states employed wardens.

In 1894, just three years before the last wild bison was shot in Colorado, a bison law was passed that made poaching in Yellowstone Park punishable by fine or imprisonment. Several states in the late 1890s tried to protect vanishing passenger pigeons by enacting appropriate laws. But by the time the laws were passed, the buffalo herds had been reduced to remnants, and the pigeon was well on the road to oblivion.

Current hunting, trapping, and fishing regulations place restrictions on the species and number of individuals taken; on the season and/or time of day; and the type of firearm, trap, or fishing equipment used. The severity of such restrictions as bag limits frequently depends on the population status of the animal in question. When a game animal is abundant, the laws are more liberal; when the target species declines in number, the regulations become more severe.

Regulation of the Deer Harvest

One of the primary objectives of deer management is to provide a *shootable surplus* for the hunter. Several decades ago, when deer were relatively scarce, state legislatures restricted hunting by closing or abbreviating the season, by timing the season to ensure an absence of tracking snow, by restricting firearms to shotguns, and by restricting the kill to one per hunter. The doe was afforded special status. The deer-herd buildup was further implemented by winter feeding, introductions, predator control, and the establishment of refuges.

In response to these measures, as well as to the great abundance of edge and food available in the wake of extensive fires and logging, the herd increased rapidly — too rapidly. In only thirteen years the whitetail population credited to forty-five states increased from 3,181,675 in 1937 to 5,135,040 in 1949, a gain of 61 percent. It soon exceeded the range's carrying capacity, browse lines appeared, winter starvation was common, and the range rapidly deteriorated.

Many state game departments advised legislators to reverse the trend by liberalizing hunting regulations. After much prodding from professional game biologists, herd reduction was implemented by opening and extending seasons, timing the seasons with the occurrence of tracking snow, legalizing the use of rifles, lifting the ban on does, establishing bow seasons, and removing bounties on predators. Access roads were built to facilitate hunter movement in backcountry.

The overpopulation problem is far from solved. Despite liberalized laws, hunters rarely harvest more than 10 percent of herds. One reason is the deer's secretive behavior; the animals rarely emerge from protective cover during daylight hours of the hunting season. Hunters sometimes are unable to see a single deer in an area supporting a population density of 100 per square mile (10). A 10 percent annual harvest is simply not enough to appreciably check herd increase (see Figure 13–23). According to Taylor:

Annual removal of deer (by hunting, transfer, or otherwise) should be based on actual yearly increase in numbers as related to available deer foods. Usually at least one third of a fall population of deer can be taken, year after year, if both sexes are removed in equal numbers. Ordinarily, the game manager does not need to be concerned either with inbreeding or with an overwide buck-doe ratio (38).

13–23 *Annual population fluctuation in a deer herd occupying a range with a carrying capacity of 440 head. Note that even during a closed season the various agents of ER (starvation, parasites, predation, disease, and accidents) will reduce the herd to the carrying capacity of the range. It is apparent that a considerable surplus may be safely harvested by hunters. With or without an open season, the population of the herd by the end of the winter-spring hardship period will be virtually the same.*

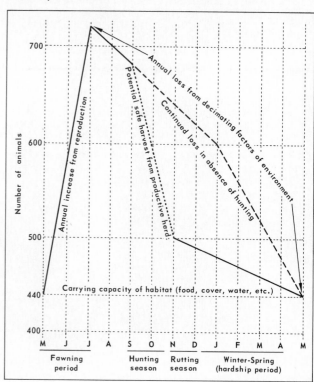

Deer populations frequently vary from region to region within a single state, being high perhaps in semiwooded agricultural regions and low in climax forests and near urban centers. Therefore, a state may be divided into a number of zones, each with its own set of regulations. (One state has had sixty zones.) In zones where herds are at low levels, the season may be closed completely or may be open to bow hunters only. In overpopulated zones, the season may be opened on bucks, does, and even fawns. In some states, game managers are not permitted to practice what they preach because their technical knowledge in game management is far in advance of a receptive public or political climate. Too often the framers of our hunting laws yield to pressures exerted by hunters, misguided nature lovers, and resort owners, to whom the essence of game management is "more deer." Only when regulations are formulated in accordance with the advice of professionally staffed conservation departments will hunting regulations serve as an effective management tool.

The Introduction of Exotics

Another phase of wildlife development and management involves the introduction of *exotic* species. They may be brought over to provide game, to serve as predators in controlling some pest, or simply to add color to the native wildlife community. In the late nineteenth century several societies were organized for the explicit purpose of introducing and dispersing exotic species of birds (41). Most of those efforts failed, despite an extensive program in which hundreds of thousands of individuals, representing over one hundred foreign species, were released. The U.S. Fish and Wildlife Service has the responsibility of permitting or barring such imports. Several years ago, a would-be smuggler tried to bring four exotic finches into the country by tying them around his ankles inside his socks (15). In recent years fourteen exotic species of game birds were being reared in twenty-one states with the objective of ultimate release. A few introductions have been successful, notably that of the ring-necked pheasant, which was originally introduced to Oregon from Asia in the late nineteenth century. After several additional "plantings" elsewhere in the United States, it became the most important upland game bird in much of the agricultural Midwest. (See Figure 13–24.) South Dakota prides itself on being the "pheasant capital of America." Our experience with the ring-necked pheasant is a convincing demonstration that the right exotic in the right habitat may ultimately form an important component of our wildlife resource.

Before spending a lot of time, effort, and money on the introduction of an exotic species, game-management officials, of course, would like to have some evidence that the introduced species would successfully adjust to its new home. For example, it would be important to make sure that the climatic conditions at the release site closely match those of

13–24 *Flushing a pheasant on an Indiana hunting preserve. The game-farm-reared birds were released in patches of good wildlife cover, such as the sargo in this picture.*

the species' native haunts. For this purpose use can be made of *climographs*—"pictures" of the climate of a given region in which temperature is plotted against rainfall. Each point in a climograph could represent average temperature and rainfall for a given month. Back in the 1920s, the gray partridge was introduced into several regions of the United States, including Missouri and Montana. Although the Montana venture was highly successful, the Missouri project failed miserably. Biologists were puzzled by the highly diverse results. However, when they compared the climographs of Montana and Missouri, a possible reason for the Missouri failure was suggested. During the breeding season (May and June) when eggs and young are highly vulnerable to climatic extremes, the introduction site near Columbia, Missouri, was considerably warmer and wetter than in the partridge's optimal European range. Of course there are many other environmental factors, such as predators, disease, food, soil nutrients (calcium), atmospheric pollution, availability of protective cover, and so on, that also determine the success or failure of an introduction.

It is apparent, however, that if climographs of the native range and the range of introduction are grossly mismatched, the proposed introductions should probably be abandoned.

Some introductions have had an adverse effect on the native wildlife community. Notable among such unfortunate importations is that of the English sparrow in 1865 and the European starling in 1880. Both of those aggressive and noisy species have appropriated breeding habitat formerly utilized by more attractive and/or melodic native species such as the bluebird, purple martin, and red-headed woodpecker. It is apparent, therefore, that all aspects of the ecology of the proposed exotic must be thoroughly studied before it is released. With such investigations, future harmful introductions will be held to a minimum.

Predator Control

The control of predators assumed a popular and conspicuous role early in wildlife management history. It was only natural for the hunter, tired and disappointed after tramping the fields in fruitless

13-25 *Wanted: dead—or alive! Red-fox pup peers out from behind a rock at Kettle Moraine State Forest, Wisconsin. Predators add interest and sparkle to the out-of-doors, well worth the few rabbits and other small game they may take.*

quest of elusive quail or cottontail, to vent his frustration by blaming the hawk or fox. His thesis was based on grade-school arithmetic. If a fox in a certain meadow eats thirty rabbits a year, a rifle bullet through that fox's brain will mean thirty additional cottontails available for hunters. In the past, pressure has been exerted by sportsmen's organizations on state legislators to enact bounty laws, resulting in the expenditure of funds that could have been used to greater advantage in the acquisition and development of wildlife habitat. Money paid by a state for bounties may be considerable, ranging from $2 for a fox and $15 for a bobcat, to $25 for a coyote and $35 for a timber wolf. Game officials in many states, however, have been re-examining predator control in the last few years. The bounty system has been criticized for several reasons.

The possibility for fraudulent bounty claims is well pointed up in the following account. Some years ago, a midwestern state had placed a bounty on squirrels. To claim the bounty, all that was required was to turn in the squirrel's tail. Some quick-witted youngsters devised a scheme whereby they live-trapped a number of squirrels, cut off their tails, released the animals, and turned in their tails for payment. Because the de-tailed squirrels suffered no reduction in biotic potential, the squirrel population remained at a relatively high level, thus assuring a continuous supply of tails (and bounty payments) for the enterprising youths (15).

Many accusations against predators are ill founded. For many years the coyote has been accused of killing calves and sheep by western ranchers. As a result these "brush wolves" have been shot, trapped, and poisoned with great intensity and zeal by the outraged livestock owners for 150 years. Many wildlife biologists, however, doubt very much that such predator control campaigns are justified on either economic or ecological grounds. First of all, in many cases the killings may have been caused by predators (grizzly bear, wolves, cougar, and so on) other than the coyote. Secondly, the coyote frequently merely "finishes off" an animal that is ill or crippled, or else it feeds on the carcasses of animals that have died recently from other causes. Thirdly, despite these long-sustained control attempts, the coyote population has remained steady while doubling its geographic range. Fourthly, the coyote may actually be valuable to the rancher because it destroys many mice, ground squirrels, and rabbits that would otherwise compete with sheep and cattle for forage grasses. An unbiased cost-benefit analysis might well show that the rancher would be in better financial shape if he or she left the coyote alone—even if it did take an occasional sheep or calf.

Let us consider another example. The barn owl is frequently persecuted by the harried farmer for raiding his chicken yard or by the irate hunter for seizing quail and rabbits. However, a three-year investigation by Michigan state biologists has revealed the misdirection of their control efforts. An examination of 2,200 barn-owl pellets (regurgitated masses of indigestible bones and fur) showed absolutely no trace of poultry or game birds. Although 1.07 percent of the owl's diet was indeed made up of birds, the great majority of them were the pestiferous starlings and English sparrows. Furthermore, over 90 percent of the mammals represented in the pellets were mice, primarily the meadow mouse, a species capable of inflicting serious crop damage.

Most ecologists consider the predators as forming an essential part of the ecosystem. As Dasmann has pointed out, the number of predators at the apex of a food pyramid is dependent on the number of prey animals at the lower levels, and *not the reverse* (10). Thus, in an analysis of data provided by a 15-year study of Wisconsin quail, it has been shown that the greater the quail population in spring, the heavier the mortality (including predation) the following fall (25). In some cases, paradoxical as it may seem, predators may actually promote the welfare of the prey species by culling the aged, crippled, and disease-ridden individuals from the population. Moreover, predators may serve a useful role in keeping the resilient prey population within the limits imposed by the carrying capacity of its habitat. A lack of predatory pressure might release a population explosion resulting in habitat deterioration and culminating in massive death caused by starvation and disease.

Habitat Development

Currently, the best prospect for increasing wildlife populations is to increase the amount and quality of suitable habitat. Many game biologists consider habitat development absolutely indispensable. In other words, even with protective game laws, predator control, exotic introductions, transplantations, and artificial propagation, wildlife populations will nevertheless be in jeopardy if at the same time their habitat is usurped, destroyed, or permitted to deteriorate. Conversely, if an abundance of high-quality wildlife habitat is available, game populations will remain relatively high, regardless of the lack of predator control, artificial propagation, introductions, and transplantations. (See Figure 13–26.)

It is not surprising, therefore, that habitat acquisition and development programs are receiving high priority among many state game divisions, as well as in wildlife-research units administered by the U.S. Fish and Wildlife Service.

Because over 85 percent of the hunting lands in the United States are privately owned or controlled, and because it is on the private farms, ranches, and woodlots that most of the grouse, quail, doves, pheasants, and rabbits are produced, the biggest contribution to an abundant and varied game resource (as in the case of forest development) can be made by the private citizen. Fortunately, many of the land practices that are effective in soil and water management can be simultaneously applied toward the goal of wildlife-habitat improvement. (See Robert A. McCabe's guest article concerning habitat loss as a major problem in wildlife management.)

Living Fences

Before the advent of barbed wire in 1874, ranchers and farmers resorted to other devices for separating woodlot from pasture and cropland from marsh. In much of the deciduous-forest biome, split-rail fences were used; in rocky New England, crude fences were constructed from boulders removed from the path of the plow; and in the lake states rows of pine stumps were employed. Osage orange was used in midwestern prairies as a "living fence." None of these fences was as neat as the barbed-wire fences that replaced them; nevertheless, they were much more picturesque, and they reserved more land between boulders, trunks, stumps, and zigzagging rails for potential use as wildlife habitat. The barbed-wire fence reserved *nothing* for wildlife. Because the farmer could now plow to within inches of his fences, results for upland game were disastrous.

In recent years game biologists have encouraged landowners to replace barbed-wire fences with living fences composed of native or exotic shrubs (such as the *multiflora* rose), which provide food, cover, and travel lanes for pheasants, quail, and cottontails. (See Figure 13–27.) To date, an encouraging 2,000 such fences are being constructed annually. When planted at one-foot intervals, the exotic *mul-*

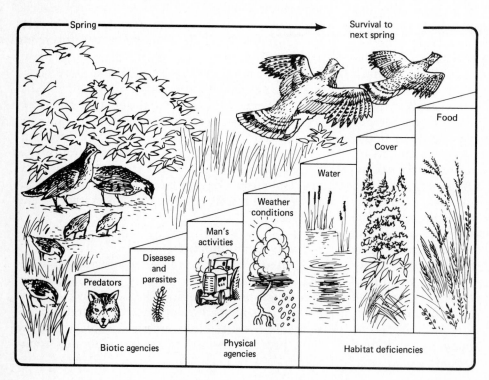

13–26 *Habitat development is of basic importance in game management. This figure depicts the* biotic potential *of grouse versus their* environmental resistance. *Factors that hold down game populations are represented as hurdles over which the young hatched in spring must fly in order still to be around next spring. Humans can control some of these limiting factors. For the most part predator control is not effective or justified. It is difficult to control disease and parasites. Successful game management depends primarily on improving wildlife habitat in terms of food, water, breeding sites, and shelter from predators and the severities of weather.*

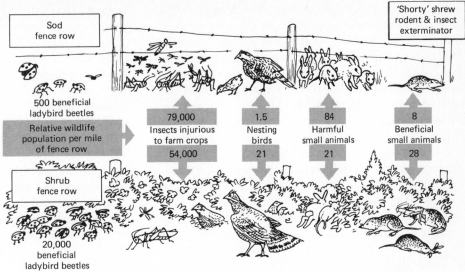

13–27 *Wildlife habitat potential of a shrub fence row is far superior to that of a sod-and-barbed-wire fence row.*

tiflora rose, introduced from Asia, produces a thorny livestock barrier in within three to five years. Not only is it attractive, but it provides cover for rodent-destroying skunks and weasels. Songbird density in such a fence, according to an Ohio study is 32 times that in open crop fields. Other fence shrubs suitable for game use are bayberry, tartarian honeysuckle, silky cornel, and highbush cranberry.

The Manipulation of Ecological Succession

In our earlier discussion of ecological succession, we indicated that both plant and animal communities change as the physical environment (available sunlight, moisture, wind velocity, and soil fertility) changes. Dasmann (18) has classified as follows a number of game species according to the successional stage of which each is characteristic: *climax species:* bighorn sheep, caribou, grizzly bear, musk-ox, and passenger pigeon; *mid-successional species:* antelope, elk, moose, mule deer, pronghorn antelope, ruffed grouse, sage grouse, and whitetail deer; *low-successional species:* bobwhite quail, dove, hare, rabbit, and ring-necked pheasant. From the preceding classification, it is apparent that the game biologist can regulate the abundance of these species by manipulating ecological succession. Thus, he or she could permit a succession to proceed on its natural course to a climax or, by employing such artificial devices as controlled (prescribed)

burning, controlled flooding, herbicides, plowing, and logging, he or she could retard the succession or even revert it to the pioneer stage. Way back in 1936 Herbert Stoddard, a pioneer in game management, reported on his use of prescription burns in main-

13–28 *Prescribed burn area at the Agassiz Wildlife Refuge in Minnesota for the purpose of developing suitable habitat for sharp-tailed grouse.*

taining high-quality quail habitat in Georgia. If the natural succession in Stoddard's study area had been permitted to "move" to the climax, the ground-scratching quail would have experienced considerable difficulty in securing adequate food (acorns, nuts, and seeds) on the forest floor because of the dense tangle of wire grass and shrubs. However, if that same habitat were to be periodically burned "by prescription," the vegetation on the floor would remain sufficiently open to permit both mobility and effective utilization of available foods.

Because *climax-associated* or *wilderness* species such as caribou, bighorn sheep, and grizzly bear will flourish only in relatively undisturbed climax communities, their survival depends to a large degree on the establishment of state and national refuges. Without such protected "islands" in the "oceans" of successional disturbance caused by man, these climax-associated species would face decline and extinction — a fate already met by the passenger pigeon.

Mid-successional species such as the moose, whitetail deer, and ruffed grouse, must be regarded as purely *temporary* phenomena, as temporary as the plant community on which these herbivores depend for food. In northern Minnesota, for example, moose are not found in the dense, well-shaded spruce-fir climax forest, but in midsuccessional thickets of willow, aspen, and birch. Inevitably, when these thickets are shaded out by climax spruce and fir, the local moose, a highly sedentary species, will gradually decline in numbers and disappear. On the other hand, such management techniques as logging or controlled burning may open up a dense climax forest and permit the eventual establishment of sun-tolerant birch and aspen trees as well as the moose that feed on them. In any event, these mid-successional species are disturbance-dependent, and without the intervention of game biologist, lumberman, or forest fire (ignited by lightning or man) they will vanish.

The *early-successional species* such as the rabbit, quail, and dove are greatly dependent on major disturbances of the ecological succession by man. All these species, for example, find food and cover in the weedy pioneer plants that invade an area that has been denuded by human activity. Such vegetation may become established when farmland is abandoned and a pioneer community of invading weeds and shrubs becomes established.

In many southeastern states the natural climax is composed of oak-dominated hardwood stands, a community of inferior timber value and poor carrying capacity for quail. Controlled burnings have been used periodically in this region to hold the succession in a subclimax stage. These fires effectively destroy the heat-vulnerable oak seedlings, but promote the establishment and survival of fire-tolerant and timber-valuable longleaf pine, as well as a great variety of herbs and shrubs that provide top-quality food, cover, and nest sites for quail. Here, then, we have a good example of how succession can be effectively regulated by a single management method, controlled burning, to promote the twin objectives of high-value timber and wildlife.

Habitat Development for Waterfowl

Waterfowl habitat can be improved by creating openings in dense marsh vegetation, constructing artificial ponds, developing artificial nests and nest sites, and establishing waterfowl refuges.

CREATING OPENINGS. Although waterfowl require cover for protection from both weather and predators, they also require channels and openings through which they can paddle or waddle (between nest site and feeding area, between feeding and loafing area) or that serve as areas where the birds can secure aquatic food supplies. These essential openings may be the result of such natural agencies as hurricanes and lightning-triggered fires, or they may be developed by humans by controlled burning and the use of explosives.

CONSTRUCTING ARTIFICIAL PONDS. Where sloughs and potholes are scarce, waterfowl habitat can be created by the construction of *artificial ponds* (13). Between 1936 and 1980 the USDA assisted Soil Conservation District farmers in building almost 3.5 million farm ponds. Roughly two thirds of those ponds are usable by waterfowl, either as nesting, feeding, and loafing areas by resident birds, or as rest areas where migrating waterfowl can touch down for a brief respite before resuming their strenuous journeys. The farmer can increase the carrying capacity of a pond by erecting artificial nest boxes for mallards and wood ducks; by dumping piles of rocks or anchoring logs and bales of hay

13–29 *Taylor County, West Virginia. The waterfowl productivity of this farm pond could be increased by fencing portions of it from livestock, by providing anchored logs and gravel piles for sunning and preening sites, and by seeding the pond with choice food plants.*

in the open water to serve as preening and sunning areas; by periodically draining the pond to promote the mineralization of organic matter and the release of nutrient elements, which can then be recycled into the waterfowl food chain; and by seeding the pond with choice duck-food plants. With the extensive employment of such pond-management procedures, the 3.5 million farm ponds of 1980 will provide at least partial use for an estimated ten million birds.

CONSTRUCTION OF ARTIFICIAL ISLANDS.   In recent years society has destroyed much valuable wildlife habitat in its attempts to promote its own welfare. As a result, wildlife populations have frequently been decimated. And for years it has been assumed, by at least a few biologists, that virtually all human-induced changes of the natural environment were detrimental to wildlife. That this type of thinking is manifestly erroneous is shown by the effect man-made islands have had in boosting waterbird populations. For example, in 1977 the Bureau of Reclamation (frequently assailed by environmentalists because of its obsession with big dam construction) used fill material to form 62 artificial nesting islands for Canada geese in Canyon Ferry Lake near Townsend, Montana. (See Figures 13 – 30 to 13 – 32.) Since the construction of these artificial islands, biologist Robert Eng of Montana State University has noted a threefold increase in Canada goose production in the region.

For a number of years the U.S. Army Corps of Engineers has constructed "dredge islands" from the sand, mud, and shells it removes during dredging operations. More than 2,000 of those islands are scattered along the nation's coast from Long Island, New York, to Brownsville, Texas. Some have also been formed in the Mississippi River, the Great Lakes, and along the Pacific coast. They are usually located far enough from shore to afford protection from such predators as raccoons, foxes and free-running dogs. Moreover, because the dredge islands are frequently from five to ten feet in elevation, they are not as susceptible to immersion during high tides, as are many of the low-lying natural islands near shore. Sidney Island, now administered by the

13–31 *Artificial nesting island for Canada geese. A pair of Canada geese chooses a nesting site on one of the artificial islands in the Westside Pond of Canyon Ferry Lake. Territorial behavior at the beginning of the nesting season is intense.*

13–30 *Artificial nesting islands for Canada geese. Aerial view of the newly completed (1977) Westside Pond in Canyon Ferry Lake, near Townsend, Montana. About 62 artificial nesting islands (appearing as light-colored areas in the pond) were formed with fill material.*

392

13-32 *Artificial nesting islands for Canada geese. Dr. Robert Eng of the Montana State University Biology Department and a clutch of Canada goose eggs on one of the islands. The Bureau of Reclamation constructed 82 of these islands in ponds on Canyon Ferry Lake. The ponds were created for dust abatement as well as for wildlife habitat. Goose production trebled in the first three years since the installation of the island.*

National Audubon Society, was formed from spoil resulting from the dredging of the ship channel at Orange, Texas. As Richard C. Davids writes: "when your boat touches the beach the island is instantly beautiful. Clouds of herons and ibises leave their nests and circle above, their wings flashing in the sun. Roseate spoonbills fly over with a soft whoosh-whoosh. A little blue heron flaps away, croaking hoarsely . . . " (11). In 1978, according to Audubon Society counts, Sidney Island provided food, cover, and breeding sites for 20,600 egrets, almost 8,000 herons, 2,200 ibises, 1,400 roseate spoonbills and 380 cormorants—including several species whose populations in other areas had been in serious decline (11).

DEVELOPING ARTIFICIAL NESTS AND NEST SITES. Through the process of natural selection operating for millions of years, each species of waterfowl has evolved its own unique instinct for nest-site selection and nest construction. It would appear almost impertinent, therefore, for humans to attempt to improve on nature by constructing *artificial* nests and sites for waterfowl. However, game biologists have done precisely this and with encouraging success. (See Figure 13-33.) Moreover, not only do these man-made nests serve the reproductive function as well as natural nests, but they may be even *more* effective in minimizing mortality caused by mowing machines, predators, and nest-site competitors.

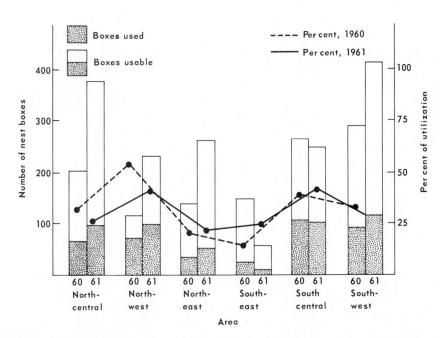

13-33 *Wood-duck nest-box utilization in Ohio, 1960 and 1961. The Ohio Department of Natural Resources erected nest boxes in an attempt to augment wood-duck production. In 1960, 373 of 1,176 (31.7 percent) were utilized, and 461 of 1,569 (29.4 percent) were occupied in 1961.*

393

Problems Facing the Waterfowl Manager

Paul Springer

Biologist-in-Charge
U.S. Fish and Wildlife
Service
Arcata, California

The forty-five species of waterfowl regularly inhabiting the United States provide observation and hunting opportunity for millions of Americans. Unfortunately, the waterfowl manager is faced with a number of serious problems in maintaining this valuable resource.

Foremost among these is habitat destruction. Of the estimated 215 million acres of wetlands originally found in the United States, approximately half have been destroyed and a substantial portion of the remainder have been lowered in value by pollution, siltation, and other influences. Even today, losses continue at the rate of 450,000 acres annually. The main destructive factors have been drainage, filling, and interruption of natural run-off by dikes and dams. Other factors affecting upland as well as wetland nesting habitats are plowing, burning, and clearing of bottomland hardwoods.

Habitat loss has not only reduced waterfowl numbers, but has concentrated the remaining populations. This has increased their vulnerability to shooting, predation, disease, and environmental contaminants. In addition, it has caused crop depredations and nuisance problems, with wild birds fouling shorelines, docks, and golf courses.

At times man has unintentionally developed habitat that waterfowl have found attractive. For example, damming rivers to form reservoirs and clearing and plowing land for agriculture have provided roosting and feeding areas for adaptable species such as Canada geese and mallards. However, these new habitats can disrupt normal migratory patterns or "short-stop" birds north of their usual wintering quarters. Not only does this reduce the use of traditional areas, but short-stopping can cause thermal stress and may affect reproduction by lowering the birds' physical condition.

During the last two decades most waterfowl populations in the United States and Canada have remained fairly constant. Certain species, however, such as the black duck and the Pacific Flyway white-fronted and cackling Canada geese, have declined. Among the various factors involved, over-hunting is thought to be significant.

Wildlife Refuges

Our system of national refuges was launched in 1903 when Theodore Roosevelt established the Pelican Island Refuge in Florida's Indian River to protect the rapidly depleting population of brown pelicans. From this modest beginning the federal refuge system has grown to more than 350 refuges covering about 30 million acres. Of these, 229 (77.4 percent) were primarily established to provide a suitable habitat for waterfowl for nesting purposes, as wintering grounds, or as stopover areas for migrants. In 1934 Congress passed the Migratory Bird Hunting Stamp Act, which authorized that funds for the acquisition, maintenance, and development of waterfowl refuges be derived from the sale of "duck stamps." The stamps must be purchased by each waterfowl gunner at the start of the hunting season. From 1937 to 1968, close to 90 million stamps were sold. Our national waterfowl refuges annually provide over 1.25 billion waterfowl-use days. (One waterfowl-use day is one day's use by one duck, coot, swan, or goose.) Our refuges produce over 500,000 ducklings each year. The Tule Lake (California) and Agassiz (Minnesota) refuges each produce 30,000 ducks yearly, and the Malheur (Oregon) Refuge produces 40,000 annually (24). Huge concentrations of ducks and geese utilize some of the refuges during the fall migration. For example, in the Klamath Basin Refuge on the California-Oregon border, where considerable acreages of wheat and barley are grown exclusively as waterfowl food, a peak of 3.4 million ducks and geese was recorded in 1964. Similarly, during the fall of 1966 up to 147,000 Canada geese stopped over at the Horicon National Wildlife Refuge in southern Wisconsin — the greatest concentration of this species ever re-

13–34 *Our National Wildlife Refuge system includes more than 350 refuges embracing about 30 million acres (12 million hectares).*

13–35 *Sky darkened with thousands of pintail ducks at the Sacramento National Wildlife Refuge in California.*

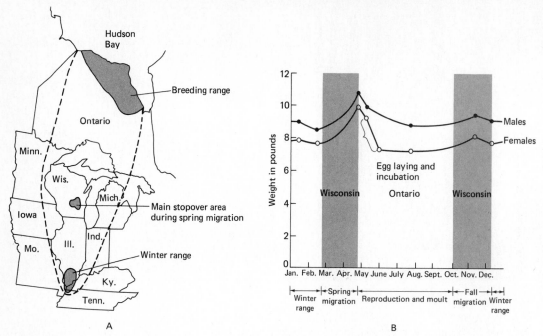

13–36 *The value of "stopover" refuges in Wisconsin for the Mississippi Valley population of the Canada goose. The geese fly 450 miles nonstop to stopover refuges like Horicon Marsh in southeastern Wisconsin. There they find an abundance of food, which enables them to acquire the fat needed to fuel their 850-mile nonstop flight to their breeding ground in northern Ontario.*

corded in the United States (42). The geese fatten up or "refuel" at these stopover refuges before continuing their migration. (See Figure 13–36.)

Migration Studies of Banded Waterfowl

Waterfowl may be captured for banding purposes by a variety of baited traps. Canada geese are effectively taken with nets that are shot over the baited birds with miniature cannons. (See Figures 13–37 and 13–38.) During the late summer molting period, when ducks are temporarily flightless, thousands of adults and juveniles may be corralled in huge drives. Recently, tranquilizers have been employed. One biologist captured 573 Canada geese and five blue geese in Florida by adding one-fourth gram of the tranquilizer alpha-chloralose to each cup of bait (8).

Scientific bird banding had its inception with the work of a Danish schoolmaster, Christian Mortensen, who marked storks, hawks, and starlings as well as waterfowl. The American Bird Banding Association, which was organized in 1909 in New York City, conducted pioneering studies in the

United States (26). Since 1920, over 11 million birds (of all species in addition to waterfowl) have been leg-banded in the United States with serially numbered metal bands. These banding operations are conducted, with the aid of 100,000 volunteer banders, by the U.S. Fish and Wildlife Service. Records of the species, age, sex, weight, date, and banding locality are filed in the Bird Banding Laboratory at the Patuxent Wildlife Research Center at Laurel, Maryland. About 8 million waterfowl had been banded by 1980. Each year, roughly 300,000 ducks, geese, and swans are banded primarily in waterfowl refuges. About 32,000 waterfowl bands are recovered annually. Although most recoveries are made by hunters, a considerable number are also recovered by biologists, bird watchers, and interested amateur naturalists who retrieve bands from birds killed by storms, pollution, predators, and disease.

Analysis of recovery data provides waterfowl biologists with information concerning growth rate, longevity, and hunting pressure, as well as the length, speed, and route of migration. From banding

13–37 *Close-up of cannon showing firing mechanism on right and three ropes attached to a heavy metal piston that, when fired, carries the net out over the waterfowl.*

13–38 *Waterfowl biologists removing Canada geese trapped under cannon net. Note corn used to bait the geese.*

397

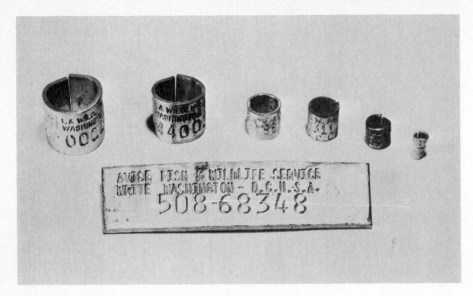

13-39 *Bird bands contain a serial number and directions for returning them to the Fish and Wildlife Service, Washington, D.C. The straightened band is used on Canada geese. Fourteen different sizes are used to band any species of North American bird from swans to hummingbirds.*

studies we know that some snow geese may travel 2,000 miles nonstop from James Bay, Canada, to the Texas coast in two days. Several years ago the Patuxent Wildlife Research Center received a letter from Rodolfo Marino, a pharmacist, who shot a blue-winged teal in a marsh two miles from his home in Peru. The serial number on the enclosed band revealed that the bird had been banded only six months previously in Saskatchewan, fully 7,000 miles distant! Even more remarkable was the record of a pintail recovered in England only eighteen days after being banded in Labrador. Another pintail, banded in northwestern California, was taken at Baykal Lake, Russia (43). Still another pintail banded in California turned up three months later in New Zealand after a transoceanic flight of over 7,000 miles.

From the practical standpoint of waterfowl management, however, the most significant information accruing from waterfowl-banding studies is that most migratory waterfowl breeding in the northern states and Canada funnel into four rather well-defined flyways on their way to their southern breeding grounds. Known as the Atlantic, Mississippi, Central, and Pacific flyways, they have served as operational units in the formulation and administration of hunting laws by state and federal governments. It should be emphasized, however, that these flyways are not mutually exclusive. Thus, many mallards that nest in the prairie provinces of Canada begin their fall migration by moving southward along the Central Flyway into South Dakota; eventually, however, they swerve southeastward,

switching to the Mississippi Flyway in Minnesota and continuing along that flyway to their wintering ground. Apparently, these birds do not consult the

13-40 *Banding Canada goose at the Blackwater National Wildlife Refuge, Cambridge, Maryland. Note band dispenser. Cannon net is in background.*

13-41 *Major waterfowl flyways. Recovery data on many thousands of waterfowl have revealed that four major flyways are followed during migration: (1) Pacific, (2) Central, (3) Mississippi, and (4) Atlantic. Note that flyways are not mutually exclusive. For example, ducks reared in Alberta and Saskatchewan might initially move down the Central Flyway and later switch over to the Pacific Flyway to complete their fall migration to wintering grounds in California or Mexico. Species like mallard, baldpate, and scaup might use all four flyways.*

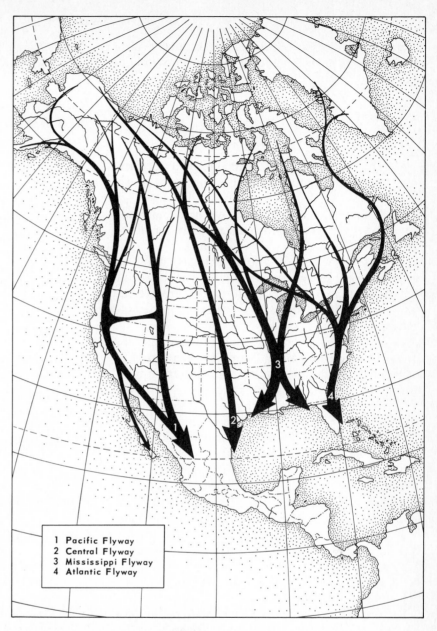

1 Pacific Flyway
2 Central Flyway
3 Mississippi Flyway
4 Atlantic Flyway

13-42 *End of a good day's hunting.*

399

flyway maps! (See Paul Springer's guest article concerning major problems facing the waterfowl manager.)

Rapid Review

1. The habitat of a wild animal provides certain essentials: shelter, food, water, breeding sites, and a territory.

2. A home range is the area over which an animal habitually travels while engaged in its usual activities.

3. The dispersal of young animals, such as muskrats and grouse, apparently is a mechanism that reduces population density and therefore reduces competition for food supplies and other essentials.

4. Four types of movements in wild animals are (1) dispersal of the young, (2) mass emigration, (3) latitudinal migrations, and (4) altitudinal migrations.

5. The biotic potential of a species is its theoretical maximum population growth rate.

6. Wildlife populations may show various patterns: stable, irruptive, and cyclic.

7. Waterfowl populations are controlled by a number of factors, including drought, pothole drainage, oil pollution, lead poisoning, and botulism.

8. When deer populations get too high for the carrying capacity of the range, a conspicuous browse line will form at a height of 4.5 to 5 feet.

9. Among deer predators are wolves, cougars, bobcats, coyotes, and dogs.

10. Important wildlife-management techniques include (1) protective laws, (2) wildlife refuges, (3) introduction of exotic species, (4) predator control, and (5) habitat development.

11. Effective habitat development techniques for enhancing wildlife populations include (1) establishing "living" fences, (2) manipulating ecological succession, (3) creating openings in marshes for waterfowl, (4) constructing artificial ponds for waterfowl, and (5) developing artificial nest sites for waterfowl.

12. Our national waterfowl refuge system annually provides over 1.25 billion waterfowl-use days.

13. Analysis of recovery data from banded waterfowl provides information concerning growth rates, longevity, hunting pressure, and length, speed, and route of migration.

Key Words and Phrases

Altitudinal migration
Artificial islands
Artificial nest sites
Artificial ponds
Biotic potential
Bird banding
Botulism
Climax species
Cover
Cyclic population
Density-dependent factor
Density-independent factor
Dispersal of young
Euryphagous species
Exotic species
Habitat development
Home range
Irruption
Latitudinal migration
Lead poisoning
Living fence
Low-succession species
Malnutrition
Mass emigration
Mid-successional species
Multiflora rose
Pothole
Predator control
Stable population
Stenophagous
Territory
Waterfowl flyway
Wildlife refuge

Questions and Topics for Discussion

1. Compare stenophagous and euryphagous species. Give an example of each type.
2. Discuss the function of territory. Is there any correlation between food habits and territorial size? Discuss your answer.
3. Discuss the advantages and disadvantages of latitudinal migrations.
4. Describe the Kaibab deer irruption episode. What lessons can the modern game manager derive from the incident?
5. Suppose that you were the chief waterfowl biologist on a wildlife refuge. What measures could you employ to prevent or alleviate the botulism problem?
6. What causes lead poisoning in waterfowl? What can be done to control the problem?
7. Discuss the pros and cons of predator control.
8. Briefly discuss the history of wildlife legislation in the United States.
9. In what way can a game biologist make effective use of climographs?

10. Discuss the manipulation of ecological succession in improving habitat for wildlife.
11. Name the major waterfowl migration flyways.

Endnotes

1. Bellrose, F. C. "Spent Shot and Lead Poisoning," *Waterfowl Tomorrow.* Washington, D.C.: U.S. Fish and Wildlife Service, 1964.
2. Bourlière, François. *The Natural History of Mammals.* New York: Knopf, 1956.
3. Broley, Charles L. "Migration and Nesting of Florida Bald Eagles." *Wilson Bull.,* **59** (1947), 3–20.
4. Burt, William Henry. *Mammals of the Great Lakes Region.* Ann Arbor: University of Michigan, 1957.
5. Burwell, Robert W., and Lawson G. Sugden. "Potholes—Going, Going . . . ," *Waterfowl Tomorrow.* Washington, D.C.: U.S. Fish and Wildlife Service, 1964.
6. Cahoon, W. G. "Commercial Carp Removal at Lake Mattamuskeet, North Carolina." *Jour. Wild. Mgt.,* **17** (1953), 312–317.
7. Chambers, R. E., and W. M. Sharpe. "Movement and Dispersal Within a Population of Ruffed Grouse." *Jour. Wild. Mgt.,* 22 (1958), 231–239.
8. Clarke, George L. *Elements of Ecology.* New York: Wiley, 1954.
9. Dahlberg, Burton L., and Ralph C. Guettinger. "The White-tailed Deer in Wisconsin," *Tech. Wild. Bull.,* No. 14. Madison, Wis.: Wisconsin Conservation Department, 1956.
10. Dasmann, Raymond F. *Wildlife Biology.* New York: Wiley, 1964.
11. Davids, Richard C. "Managing America's Man-Made Islands." *Exxon-USA.* Fourth Quarter, 1978, Public Affairs Dept., Exxon Company, U.S.A., pp. 16–21.
12. Davis, David S., and Frank B. Golley. *Principles in Mammalogy.* New York: Reinhold, 1963.
13. Edminster, Frank C. "Farm Ponds and Waterfowl," *Waterfowl Tomorrow.* Washington, D.C.: U.S. Fish and Wildlife Service, 1964.
14. Ellis, James E., and John B. Lewis. "Mobility and Annual Range of Wild Turkeys in Missouri." *Jour. Wild. Mgt.,* 31 (1967), 568–581.
15. Gustafson, A. F., C. H. Guise, W. J. Hamilton, Jr., and H. Ries. *Conservation in the United States.* Ithaca, N.Y.: Comstock, 1949.
16. Hamilton, William J., Jr. *The Mammals of Eastern United States.* Ithaca, N.Y.: Comstock, 1943.
17. Hansen, William R. "Aggressive Behavior of Mule Deer Toward Bobcat." *Jour. of Mamm.,* **37** (1956), 458.
18. Hartung, Rolf. "Energy Metabolism in Oil-Covered Ducks." *Jour. Wild. Mgt.,* **31** (1967), 769–777.
19. Hawkins, R. E., D. C. Autry, and W. D. Klimstra. "Comparison of Methods Used to Recapture White-tailed Deer." *Jour. Wild. Mgt.,* **30** (1967), 460–464.
20. Jensen, Wayne I., and Cecil S. Williams. "Botulism and Fowl Cholera," *Waterfowl Tomorrow.* Washington, D.C.: U.S.Fish and Wildlife Service, 1966.
21. Kabat, C., N. E. Collias, and Ralph C. Guettinger. "Some Winter Habits of White-tailed Deer and the Development of Census Methods in the Flag Yard of Northern Wisconsin," *Tech. Wild. Bull.,* No. 7. Madison, Wis.: Wisconsin Conservation Department.
22. Kendeigh, S. Charles. *Animal Ecology.* Englewood Cliffs, N.J.: Prentice-Hall, 1961.
23. King, David G. "A Black Bear Kills a Fawn." *Can. Field Nat.,* 81, No. 2 (12967), 149–150.
24. Kolenosky, George B., and David H. Johnston. "Radio-tracking Timber Wolves in Ontario," *Ecology and Behavior of the Wolf.* College Park, Md.: Animal Behavior Society, 1966.
25. Lack, David. *The Natural Regulation of Animal Numbers.* New York: Oxford U.P., 1967.
26. Laskey, Amelia R. "A Study of Nesting Eastern Bluebirds." *Bird Banding,* **10** (1939), 23–32.
27. Lee, Forrest B., et al. "Waterfowl in Minnesota," *Tech. Bull.,* No. 7. St. Paul: Minnesota Department of Conservation, 1964.
28. Lincoln, Frederick C. "The Future of American Waterfowl," in Eugene Connett, ed., *Duckshooting Along the Atlantic Tidewater.* New York: Morrow, 1947.
29. Milne, Lorus J., and Margery Milne. *The Balance of Nature.* New York: Knopf, 1961.
30. Moffit, J., and C. Cottam. "The Eel-Grass Blight and Its Effect on Brant." *U.S. Fish and Wildlife Service Leaflet,* **204** (1941), 1–26.
31. Moyle, John B., and Jerome H. Kuehn. "Carp, a Sometimes Villain," *Waterfowl Tomorrow.* Washington, D.C.: U.S. Fish and Wildlife Service, 1964.
32. Murie, Olaus J. *The Elk of North America.* Harrisburg, Pa.: Stackpole, 1951.
33. Odum, Eugene P. *Fundamentals of Ecology,* 3rd ed. Philadelphia: Saunders, 1971.
34. Orr, Robert T. *Vertebrate Biology.* Philadelphia: Saunders, 1961.
35. Smith, Robert L. *Ecology and Field Biology.* New York: Harper, 1964.
36. Studholme, Allan T., and Thomas Sterling. "Dredges and Ditches," *Waterfowl Tomorrow.* Washington, D.C.: U.S. Fish and Wildlife Service, 1964.
37. Taber, R. D., and Raymond F. Dasmann. "The Black-tailed Deer of the Chaparral." *Game Bull.* No. 8. Sacramento: California Department of Fish and Game, 1958.
38. Taylor, Walter P., ed. *The Deer of North America.* Harrisburg, Pa.: Stackpole, 1956.

39. Van Tyne, Josselyn, and Andrew J. Berger. *Fundamentals of Ornithology.* New York: Wiley, 1959.

40. Wagner, Richard H. *Environment and Man.* New York: Norton, 1971.

41. Welty, Joel Carl. *The Life of Birds.* Philadelphia: Saunders, 1962.

42. *Wisconsin State Journal* (April 22, 1969).

43. Yocum, Charles F. "Pintail Banded in Northwestern California Taken at Baykal Lake, Russia *(Anas acuta).*" *Condor,* **69** (1967), 205–206.

Suggested Readings for the Interested Student

Amman, G. A. *The Prairie Grouse of Michigan.* Lansing, Mich.: Department of Conservation, 1957.

Beckwith, S. L. "Ecological Succession on Abandoned Farmlands and Its Relationship to Wildlife." *Ecological Monograph,* **24** (1954), 349–376.

Bond, R. R. "Ecological Distribution of Breeding Birds in the Upland Forests of Southern Wisconsin." *Ecological Monographs,* **27** 351–384.

Brown, E. R. *The Black-tailed Deer of Western Washington.* Biological Bulletin No. 13. Olympia, Wash.: Washington State Game Department, 1961.

Burger, G. V. "Response of Gray Squirrels to Nest Boxes at Remington Farms, Maryland." *Journal of Wildlife Management,* **33** (1969), 796–801.

Crosby, G. T. "Spread of the Cattle Egret in the Western Hemisphere." *Bird-banding,* **43** (1972), 205–212.

Johnston, D. W., and E. P. Odum. "Breeding Bird Populations in Relation to Plant Succession on the Piedmont of Georgia." *Ecology,* **37** (1956), 50–62.

Leopold, Aldo. *Game Management.* New York: Scribner, 1933.

Lord, R. D. "A Population Study of the Gray Fox." *American Midland Naturalist,* **66** (1961), 87–109.

Myers, Norman. "An Expanded Approach to the Problem of Disappearing Species." *Science,* **193** (July 16, 1976), 198–202.

Schoener, T. W. "Sizes of Feeding Territories Among Birds." *Ecology,* **49** (1968), 123–141.

Wing, L. D., and I. D. Buss. "Elephants and Forests." *Wildlife Monograph,* Number 19 (1970).

14 The Pesticide Problem

Causes of Pests

In undisturbed ecosystems there exist naturally occurring regulatory mechanisms (see Chapter 2) that keep population levels of a species at a point of equilibrium. However, whenever the original ecosystem becomes restructured by humans, it tends to become simplified, with a resultant disruption of the stabilizing influences of density-dependent regulatory factors. The removal of forests to make way for freeways; the conversion of a swamp into a parking lot or a prairie into a golf course; the establishment of monotypic agriculture fields composed of a single species where originally there existed a natural ecosystem including several dozen plant species — all are examples of human intervention that tends to simplify the ecosystem. (See Figure 14 – 1.) The net result is a man-made ecosystem characterized by large populations of a few species, in marked contrast to the original ecosystem, which was characterized by smaller populations of many species.

In such biologically simplified ecosystems, a given organism may achieve *pest* status even though in the original diversified ecosystem it was never of economic concern. Let us use an exaggeratedly simple example. In the simplified ecosystem, organism X may be controlled by only one important predator, A. Any environmental change that would depress the population of predator A would, of course, result in a population surge of organism X. In the event that X attains a population level where it be-

comes detrimental to humans, for example, as a transmitter of disease or as a destroyer of crops, it then may be classified as a pest. On the other hand, in the original biologically diversified ecosystem, relatively unaltered by humans, organism X might well have been controlled not only by predator A, but by predators B and C and a number of parasites and competitors as well. In the more diversified ecosystem, it is readily apparent that a decrease in predator A might conceivably be countered by a concurrent increase in predator B, especially if they were competitors, so that regulatory pressure on species X would be maintained. As a result of the dynamic interaction of species populations, fluctuations within simplified (disturbed) ecosystems tend to be intensified, whereas those within a diversified ecosystem tend to be dampened.

In addition, pests may become established in an ecosystem simply because they have been introduced from abroad. In doing that, humans unwittingly release them from their usual agents of control, such as predators and parasites. As a result, populations of such exotic pests may increase explosively when climatic and other conditions are optimal. More than half of the weeds in the United States, and many of the most destructive insect pests, such as the cotton boll weevil and Mediterranean fruit fly, are of foreign origin.

Finally, an organism may achieve pest status as a result of society's changing cultural patterns. For example, the lygus bug is considered a major pest to

403

14 – 1 *Monotype: a pest's paradise. Modern agriculture is based on the planting of monotypes—a vegetational plot made up of a single species of plant, such as the citrus trees shown in this photo of the irrigated Gila River Valley in Arizona.*

the lima-bean industry because of the blotches it leaves on an occasional bean. Today's shoppers demand beans that look perfect and will reject others regardless of their food value. Fifty years ago American consumers were not so fussy, and therefore lygus bugs were not considered serious pests.

The Manufacture and Use of Pesticides

Before World War II most organic pesticides were primarily derived from plant tissues. Thus, pyrethrum was obtained from chrysanthemums, nicotine from tobacco, and rotenone from the roots of tropical Asiatic legumes. Since World War II, however, the great majority of pesticides have been organic compounds synthesized in chemical laboratories. Many of them, such as the chlorinated hydrocarbons, are *persistent*—they may remain intact for many years in either water or soil (7).

The organic pesticide industry grew at a fantastic rate during the immediate postwar years. Sales in the United States mushroomed from $40 million in 1939 to more than $4 billion today. By the early 1980s more than four billion pounds of pesticides were being used worldwide. This amounts to about one pound of pesticide for each person on earth. In 1981 the United States produced 1.4 billion pounds of synthetic organic pesticides. Escalating sales can be attributed to the increased need for pest control because of agricultural monotypes, but also to an aggressive multimillion-dollar advertising assault

and brainwashing via all the communications media employed by big business. (See Figure 14–3.) On a global basis, the use of pesticides will probably continue to expand because of the food requirements of

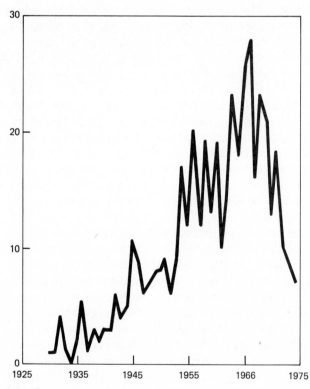

14 – 2 *Number of pesticides introduced each year since 1930.*

404

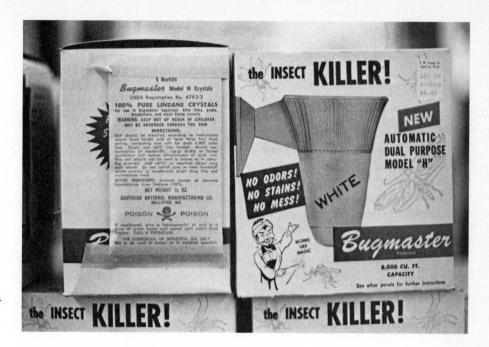

14–3 *A commercial insecticide employing lindane as the active ingredient. Note the warning on back of package: "Keep out of reach of children—may be absorbed through the skin."*

a sharply increasing world population, as well as intensified efforts to control disease-transmitting insects.

In a mere five pest-control campaigns against the spruce budworm, gypsy moth, Japanese beetle, Dutch elm disease, and the fire ant, pesticides were applied to almost five million acres (27). In addition, they are liberally applied to forests, rangeland, residential lawns and gardens, golf links, and parks. Enough pesticides are made each year in the United States to cover each square mile with a 275-pound application (21). However, some fields receive heavy dosages, and some none at all. As a result, only about 9 percent of our cropland receives pesticide treatment (21).

The Classification of Major Pesticides

Insecticides

ORGANIC PHOSPHATE COMPOUNDS. Examples of organic phosphate compounds are *parathion* and *malathion*. These chemicals inhibit the production of cholinesterase at the junctions between adjoining nerve cells. Because cholinesterase normally has the function of breaking down acetylcholine, a substance normally secreted by nerve-cell axons when they are "fired," organic phosphate pesticides cause an excessive accumulation of acetylcholine, which tends to interfere with impulse transmission. Extreme muscular weakness, tremors, and dizziness

are common symptoms in poisoned mammals. Fish and other aquatic organisms are apparently little affected.

CHLORINATED HYDROCARBONS. Examples of chlorinated hydrocarbons are DDT, endrin, and Kepone. The effects of these pesticides on animals are quite varied. However, DDT, employed the most extensively and abundantly worldwide, primarily affects the central nervous system. Symptoms in poisoned animals include increased excitability, muscular tremors, and convulsions. DDT residues frequently accumulate in fatty tissue (subcutaneous fat and fatty tissue of the mesenteries, heart, liver, thyroid gland, and gonads). With the continued ingestion of contaminated foods over a long period of time, the DDT concentration in the fatty depots gradually increases. Residues may be released from those storage areas when the stored fat is required as an energy source during periods of stress, as when the animal is engaged in strenuous physical activity (as a migration) or faced with food deprivation. Fish and other aquatic organisms are killed by chlorinated hydrocarbons because of impaired oxygen diffusion through gill membranes. Chlorinated hydrocarbons are quite resistant to biological disintegration by bacteria in either water or soil—in other words, they are *persistent*. It has been suggested by some authorities that some DDT molecules may remain intact in ecosystems for 25 years. In clay-rich soils both DDT and dieldrin are less liable to

405

contaminate food chains because they tend to be fixed by being bound to clay particles (22).

Rodenticides

Sodium fluoroacetate is an extremely hazardous rodent killer that results in hyperstimulation of the central nervous system (brain and spinal cord) and interferes with heart action. Because it is highly stable in protoplasm, it can be transferred in food chains. Warfarin is rather safe to use; it acts as an anticoagulant, depressing levels of prothrombin, a blood protein essential for blood clotting. Repeated intake of warfarin, therefore, eventually results in death from internal hemorrhaging.

Herbicides

The most extensively employed of the herbicides, or "plant killers," is 2,4-D, which causes the death of weeds by accelerating growth rates. 2,4-D can be quite selective because it is much more effective on broad-leafed weeds (such as plantain) than on narrow-leafed crops (wheat and barley). 2,4,5-T was used by the United States as a defoliant in Vietnam. The effects of its use on the environment have been highly adverse.

The Effect of Pests on Human Welfare

Pests cause economic damage, irritation, mental anguish, pain, sickness, and even death. Consider these items: the annual economic costs caused by rodents, weeds, and insects in the United States are $2, $5, and $7 billion, respectively. Plant and ani-

14–5 *Cotton boll weevil attacking cotton boll. Ten percent of the average cotton crop in the United States is destroyed by this weevil. Pesticides have been employed to control its populations.*

mal pests cause the destruction of 40 percent of the food crops grown in the United States annually. Ten percent of the average annual cotton crop in the United States is destroyed by a single insect species, the cotton boll weevil. (See Figure 14–5.) The U.S. Forest Service reports that insects inflict mortality losses of five billion board feet annually.

Mosquito borne diseases alone are annually responsible for more than 100 million cases of illness throughout the world (24).

Benefits Derived from Insecticides

It is no wonder, therefore, why mankind hailed the insecticidal properties of DDT during the years immediately after World War II. It is an excellent insect killer, as are many other insecticides. Undoubtedly their use has been a boon to the farmer and orchardist, for the most part. The use of pesticides to boost crop yields in underdeveloped nations in Asia, Africa, and South America has prevented millions of starvation deaths annually. The U.S. Department of Agriculture has estimated that if American farmers suddenly discontinued the use of pesticides food production would be reduced 25 to 30 percent. The result would be that we would be paying 50 to 75 percent more for a loaf of bread, a bag of potatoes, or a pound of ham.

14–4 *Rice weevils in wheat. The USDA is investigating the possibility of eradicating weevils and corn borers from stored grains by the process of irradiation. The point of an ordinary lead pencil is used here to show the actual size of the wheat grains and weevils.*

14-6 *Benefits derived from insecticides. Untreated cotton on the left yielded only one-tenth bale per acre. Cotton on the right, treated with insecticide, yielded one bale per acre.*

14-7 *Aerial spraying of sulfur, a fungicide, in order to check mildew on grapevines, twenty miles south of Fresno, California, May 1972.*

14-8 *Mosquito taking blood from a human arm. About 145 kinds of mosquitoes inhabit the United States. Their host preferences and life patterns vary so that a control method devised for one species may be futile against another. Entomologists therefore do not envision a single major defense against mosquitoes. USDA scientists have pioneered in developing mosquito-control methods including new repellents, better techniques for applying pesticides, and ways to enlist allies from among the natural enemies of mosquitoes— parasites, predators, and disease organisms.*

407

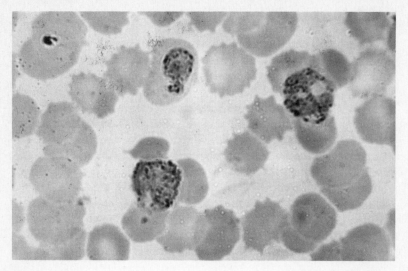

14–9 *Malaria organisms in human blood cells. The two dark cells have been invaded by the parasitic protozoan Plasmodium. It multiplies inside the cell and gives off toxic wastes that cause chills and fever. The human host becomes infected with the microscopic killer when bitten by a mosquito that harbors the protozoans.*

14–10 *Insecticides are employed against the harmful species of insects shown here. Only 0.1 percent of the 800,000 species of insects in the world are considered harmful to humans.*

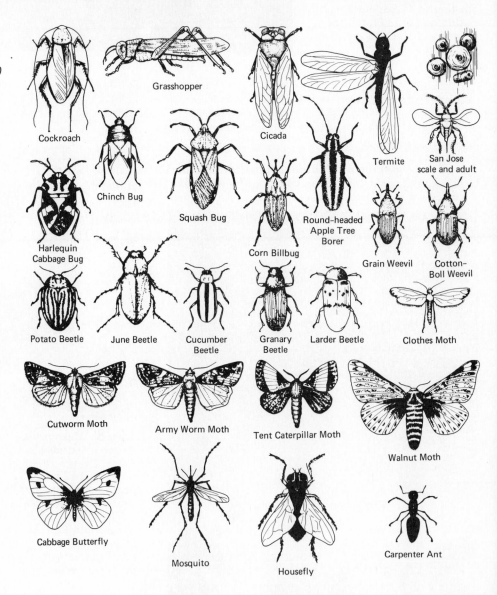

Cockroach

Grasshopper

Cicada

Termite

San Jose scale and adult

Chinch Bug

Squash Bug

Round-headed Apple Tree Borer

Harlequin Cabbage Bug

Corn Billbug

Grain Weevil

Cotton-Boll Weevil

Potato Beetle

June Beetle

Cucumber Beetle

Granary Beetle

Larder Beetle

Clothes Moth

Cutworm Moth

Army Worm Moth

Tent Caterpillar Moth

Walnut Moth

Cabbage Butterfly

Mosquito

Housefly

Carpenter Ant

When the United States Army entered Naples, Italy, in 1943, both American soldiers and native Italians became highly vulnerable to an epidemic of death-dealing typhoid fever—a disease transmitted by lice. DDT was used liberally. The result: virtual eradication of the louse population in Naples. Certainly many thousands of lives were saved by this "miracle" insect killer. DDT and other insecticides have sharply reduced mortality caused by other insect-transmitted diseases such as malaria (mosquito), sleeping sickness (tsetse fly), bubonic plague (rat flea), and Chaga's disease (kissing bugs). During the twenty-three-year period from 1947 to 1970 alone it is estimated that at least five million people the world over were saved from malaria deaths due to the use of DDT and dieldrin (13).

The Harmful Effects of Pesticides on the Ecosystem

Negative Features of the Persistent Pesticides

Unfortunately, the use of modern pesticides is a "mixed" blessing, at best. A number of undesirable characteristics are associated with the persistent

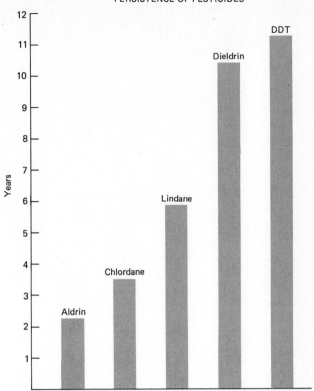

PERSISTENCE OF PESTICIDES

14 – 11 *Average persistence of pesticides in the soil.*

14 – 12 *River basins in the United States having pesticide pollution problems.*

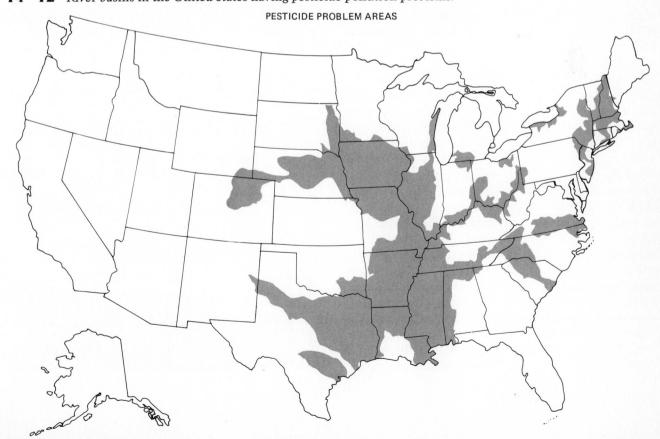

PESTICIDE PROBLEM AREAS

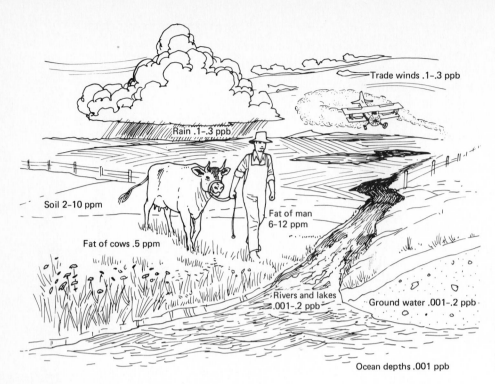

14–13 *Avenues for the dispersal of pesticides, such as DDT, once they are released. Average values for DDT concentrations are indicated.*

Trade winds .1–.3 ppb

Rain .1–.3 ppb

Soil 2–10 ppm

Fat of man 6–12 ppm

Fat of cows .5 ppm

Rivers and lakes .001–.2 ppb

Ground water .001–.2 ppb

Ocean depths .001 ppb

pesticides, such as DDT. Among them are the following:

RAPID DISPERSAL THROUGH THE ENVIRONMENT. DDT and other chlorinated hydrocarbon pesticides are highly *mobile;* that is, they can move rapidly and easily through a single ecosystem (cornfield) or from one ecosystem (river) to another (ocean). For example, DDT may be washed from a sprayed cotton field by runoff waters and eventually be carried to a river and finally to the ocean. According to the U.S. Public Health Service, all major river basins in North America are polluted with dieldrin, endrin, and DDT. These pesticides may also gradually seep downward into groundwater aquifers and eventually contaminate public drinking water supplies. When water evaporates from an irrigated field or from a river or lake, the chlorinated hydrocarbon molecules may *codistill* —be carried into the atmosphere along with the evaporating molecules of water. DDT and the other chlorinated hydrocarbons may adhere to the soil particles of a sprayed field, be wafted aloft during a dust storm, and then eventually be washed to earth, lake, or ocean, many thousands of miles from the point of its original release. The Gulf Stream, for example, might transport pesticide molecules that were sprayed on a Georgia cotton field all the way to the west coast of Europe. The marine ecosystem has

apparently been widely contaminated. Trace amounts (parts per billion) have even been found in the fatty tissues of seals and penguins in the Antarctic (22). State and federal environmental agencies constantly monitor the levels of pesticides occurring in the soil, water, and the bodies of organisms as shown in Figures 14–16 and 14–17. (See Milton D. Hakel's guest article on how to minimize pesticide pollution on the farm.)

14–14 *Crop dusting with pesticide near Calipatria, California. Unless the crop duster is highly trained and uses good judgment, almost half of the pesticide will never get to the target crop. Strong winds may blow the chemical to nearby forests, pasture land, or residential areas. Much of it may eventually drain into a stream and be carried miles from the point of its original release.*

14–15 *Plane spraying DDT (one pound per acre) in a gypsy-moth control project in the area of Lansing, Michigan. Spraying was done prior to the banning of DDT.*

14–17 *Sediment and soil samples are collected in the monitoring area here with a hand-operated corer to help scientists of the Agricultural Research Service, U.S. Department of Agriculture, study the impact of pesticides on the environment. Twenty-five cores are collected in a bucket and mixed together by a sifting process. One gallon of the mixture is then shipped to a laboratory at Gulfport, Mississippi, in a sealed can for analysis.*

14–16 *Two team members study a map of a pesticide-monitoring area where scientists of the Agricultural Research Service, USDA, are studying the impact of pesticides on soil organisms, fish, birds, and mammals. In the background, members of a field team are bringing in a fish trap.*

411

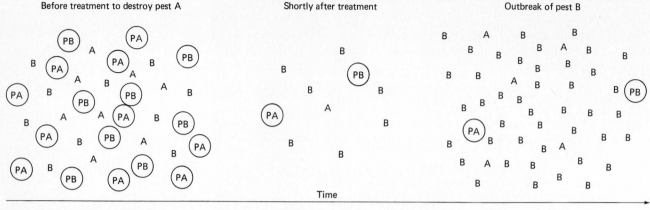

14–18 *How use of a pesticide against pest A may cause an outbreak of pest B, due to the destruction of B's predator.*

DESTRUCTION OF INSECT PREDATORS. Another deleterious aspect of broad-spectrum pesticides such as DDT, endrin, dieldrin, and many other chlorinated hydrocarbons is that their use may kill not only the target insect, *but also the predatory species that may have been keeping the pest species at reasonably low levels.* (See Figure 14–18.)

A classic example of this problem involves the citrus industry in California, which was well established by the end of the nineteenth century. At about the same time, a strange-looking flattish, snow-white insect, called the *cottony-cushion scale,* was accidentally introduced from Australia. The scale insects immediately began attacking the superabundant food source represented by the orange trees, which, of course, were neatly lined up in rows, almost inviting such an invasion. The insects pierced the tender bark of the orange trees with their sharply pointed mouthparts and then rapidly sucked up the tree's sap. Even if the scale insects did not kill the host trees outright, they reduced the tree's ability to produce marketable fruit. With its only natural predators 7,000 miles away back in Australia, the scale-insect population surged upward. (See Figure 14–19.) Many an orange rancher became threatened with economic collapse. Finally, after many attempts to control the pest met with failure, a natural predator, the *vedalia beetle* (a type of ladybug), was introduced from Australia by C. M.

Riley, an early advocate of biological control. With such an abundant supply of prey scale insects available as a food source, the vedalia-beetle population

14–19 *Fluctuations in population density of the cottony cushion scale on citrus trees in California. The scale pest, which was introduced accidentally in 1868, increased explosively until 1889, when species of predator ladybugs were released to control the scale insects. Unfortunately, when DDT was used on citrus trees in 1947, the scale populations again increased dramatically as a result of the destruction of ladybug populations.*

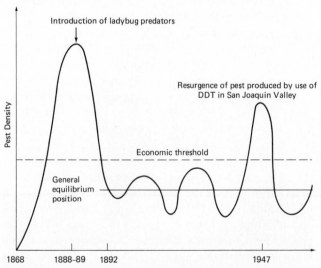

How to maintain the ability of American farmers to produce needed quantities and qualities of food while avoiding pollution of our environment from such agricultural sources as pesticides, fertilizers, animal wastes, and sedimentation raises perplexing, sometimes controversial, questions for our society.

If agriculture were asked to produce without pesticides, chemicals, and fertilizer, or with significantly smaller quantities of them, farm output would be sharply reduced in volume and quality. This will be true at least until such time as effective biological controls and other environmentally safe strategies are available.

In the meantime, however, the nation does have acceptable alternatives to continued pollution at current levels.

The National Farmers Union believes that family-scale farmers are the best guardians of a livable environment, while substantial damage to the ecology can be expected from large-scale, corporate, industrialized agricultural enterprises.

The Farmers Union also urges better testing and evaluation of pesticides and chemicals before they are allowed into use. We ask this for the sake of the farmer, who gets the first exposure if materials are toxic, and for the eventual consumer.

We point out that most of the difficulty with agricultural pollution can be avoided if soil erosion can be minimized. The contaminants cannot move unless they have a carrier. If the soil can be kept in place, the spread soil particles carrying pesticides, chemicals, and farm wastes will be reduced. Good conservation strategies can reduce 85 to 90 percent of current rates of soil erosion. Having done that, remaining pollution problems become more readily manageable.

Unfortunately, however, in today's era of budget stringency, far too little public investment is being made in erosion control.

A Simple Formula for Minimizing the Risks of Farm Use of Pesticides

Milton D. Hakel
NATIONAL FARMERS UNION

soon flourished. Under this predatory curb, the scale insects were kept at relatively harmless levels for almost seventy years.

Shortly after World War II, however, the insect-destroying virtues of DDT were proclaimed across the land of America by aggressive, fast-talking pesticide salesmen. Citrus ranchers responded by making liberal and systematic applications of DDT to their orchards. In the excitement of using the new "wonder bug killer," they pretty much forgot about the vedalia beetle and its seventy-year record of scale-insect control. True, the DDT did kill some scale insects, but it also destroyed large numbers of vedalia beetles. In fact they appeared much more vulnerable to DDT than the target insect itself. Released from predatory pressure, the scale population increased dramatically to levels reminiscent of the prevedalia years (26).

DEVELOPMENT OF RESISTANCE IN INSECTS. Another negative aspect of insecticide use is that repeated applications of a given insecticide may result in the development of *resistant* or *immune* strains of the target pest. It would almost appear as if the insecticide were losing its potency. How is such resistance acquired? First of all we must appreciate that in all animal populations, whether mosquitos or humans, there exists a great deal of genetic variability. In fact, even before a population of, say, houseflies, is sprayed with insecticide X, perhaps 1 percent of the population will have genes that make them resistant to insecticide X; the remaining 99 percent will not have that special type of gene and hence will be susceptible. How did the resistant flies acquire that resistance? They acquired it purely as a result of a chance change in the chemical structure of the sperm and/or egg cell from which they devel-

413

oped. Such a gene change is a *mutation* and represents the "raw material" by which organisms, through eons of time, have been able to adapt to their particular environment—in other words, to be biologically successful in growing, feeding, escaping predators, mating, reproducing, and, in the present example, escaping the deleterious effects of insecticides. Let us suppose now that pesticide X is repeatedly sprayed on a given housefly population and that more and more of the susceptible population is destroyed, while the resistant flies—those bearing the "resistant" mutation—survive. Eventually you may eliminate 99 percent of the original fly population. You might think that a 99 percent reduction is cause for jubilation. Not so. Remember that the 1 percent remaining are all resistant. Furthermore, because the housefly has an extremely high reproductive potential (producing ten generations yearly), within five years the resistant housefly population will have "bounced back" to its original population level before the use of pesticide X. (The reason for this rapid increase in numbers of resistant individuals is partly because they no longer have to compete with the nonresistant flies, and partly because many of their insect predators were also destroyed by the same insecticide.)

The development of such resistance in pest populations is well documented. Since DDT-resistance* in the housefly was first reported in Italy and California in 1947, resistance has also been noted in malaria-transmitting mosquitos and disease-carrying lice (typhus) and fleas (plague). By the early 1980s more than sixty species of malaria mosquitos had developed resistance to DDT and other chlorinated hydrocarbon insecticides. The unfortunate

result was that in many nations the incidence of malaria increased thirty to forty times. The development of DDT-resistance in malaria-transmitting mosquitos has seriously jeopardized malaria-control campaigns in Central America and Indonesia. In 1943 only 12 species of insects had acquired resistance to one or more insecticides. By 1960 the number had risen to 137. Today more than 305 are resistant. (See Figure 14–20.) Among highly destructive agricultural pests that have developed resistance to chlorinated hydrocarbons are the alfalfa weevil, cabbage maggot, Colorado potato beetle, boll weevil, cotton bollworm, northern corn rootworm, and the sheep blowfly.

Of great significance is the fact that this resistance is passed on from generation to generation. Such an inheritance of resistance means that progressively more toxic concentrations of the original pesticide must be employed or otherwise a new pesticide Y must be tried to replace X. However, the repeated use of Y will eventually result in a Y-resistant population, requiring still a third pesticide, Z, to keep it under (temporary) control. J. Moran, M. Morgan, and J. Wiersma describe a classic example of such multiple-pesticide failure in the case of California's pasture mosquito:

When DDT was first employed in 1945 the pasture mosquito population appeared to be under control. Within seven years, however, a DDT-resistant population developed, so a new chemical, *ethyl parathion*, was applied. By 1961, ethyl parathion was no longer effective, so *methyl parathion* was introduced; but it also became ineffective in 1963 as did *flenthion* in 1968. Presently there is no insecticide that can be used in safe dosages that will kill the pasture mosquito. (26) [*Italics mine.*]

In some agricultural areas, especially where the economy is based primarily on a single crop plant,

---

* DDT resistance in the housefly is the result of an enzyme that breaks down the DDT molecules.

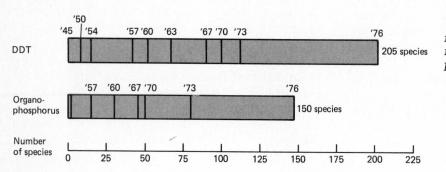

14–20 *Numbers of species of insects and mites that have developed resistance to DDT and organic phosphorus insecticides.*

the development of resistance to insecticides among insects adapted to feed on that particular crop plant can cause severe and extensive hardship. An example is described by the Council on Environmental Quality: "In the late 1960s, after an eight-year exposure, the tobacco budworm in Texas and northern Mexico suddenly became extremely resistant to methyl parathion. This cotton pest could no longer be economically controlled with insecticides. So severe was the damage in northern Mexico that the entire cotton industry collapsed. The region had been almost totally dependent on cotton; the collapse forced the migration of many farmworkers and disrupted the economic and social structure of the area's small villages . . . " (11).

BIOLOGICAL MAGNIFICATION. Perhaps the most serious trait of the persistent pesticides such as DDT, aldrin, dieldrin, and endrin is that their concentrations are progressively increased as they move through the successive links of the food chain. (See Figure 14–21.) This increase results from the fact that each organism in the food chain takes in

more of the pesticide in its food than it excretes as waste. Thus, even though the initial pesticide concentration, when released in the environment (cotton field, city park, and lake) may appear relatively harmless to wildlife (and humans), by the time the pesticide has been channeled into the terminal link, the concentration may be *lethal*. A classic example of such biological magnification occurred in the marshlands of Long Island during twenty years of mosquito control involving the use of DDT. (See Figure 14–22.) It had been assumed that the DDT would eventually be carried out to sea, be diluted, and be rendered perfectly harmless. After twenty years of control measures, samples of marsh water showed a DDT concentration of only 0.00005-part per million. Unfortunately, however, the DDT was absorbed by algae, phytoplankton, and other marsh plants, stored in their cellular fat bodies, and then, by a series of ingestion-reingestion processes, eventually were so highly concentrated that the level in the terminal links, such as fish-eating birds, was 500,000 times the original concentration in the seawater (26).

14–21 *Biological magnification: the increasing concentration of toxic chemicals, such as DDT, in the food chain. A given organism takes in large amounts of contaminated food. Much of the food may not be converted into protoplasm but may be burned up as fuel during respiration, or may be excreted as waste. However, the load of pollutant, such as DDT, that was taken into the body along with the food may remain inside the cells of the organism's body. As a result, the concentration of the pollutant increases progressively from link to link in the food chain.*

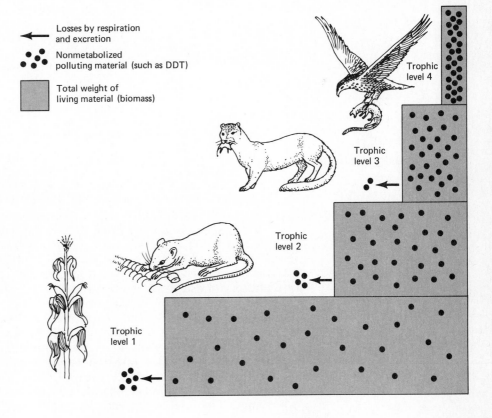

415

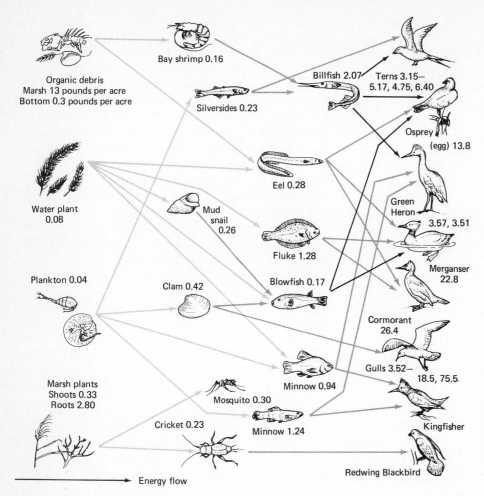

Organic debris
Marsh 13 pounds per acre
Bottom 0.3 pounds per acre

Bay shrimp 0.16

Billfish 2.07   Terns 3.15—
5.17, 4.75, 6.40

Silversides 0.23

Osprey
(egg) 13.8

Water plant
0.08

Eel 0.28

Mud
snail
0.26

Green
Heron
3.57, 3.51

Fluke 1.28

Plankton 0.04

Clam 0.42

Blowfish 0.17

Merganser
22.8

Cormorant
26.4

Marsh plants
Shoots 0.33
Roots 2.80

Minnow 0.94

Gulls 3.52—
18.5, 75.5.

Mosquito 0.30

Cricket 0.23

Minnow 1.24

Kingfisher

Redwing Blackbird

Energy flow

14–22 *Food web of the marsh ecosystem off Long Island, which had been sprayed with DDT for mosquito control. Note the biological magnification of DDT as it moved up the food web. The greatest concentrations were found in the fatty tissues of fish-eating birds, such as gulls and mergansers.*

Case History: Controlling Dutch Elm Disease

The American elm is a stately tree; it provides beauty and shade for countless urban dwellers; graces parks, boulevards, and college campuses; and supplies cover, food, and nesting sites for many species of birds. Today, throughout the nation many elms are either dead or dying because of an exotic fungus accidently introduced from Europe in about 1933. (See Figure 14–23.) The disease has caused billions of dollars of direct losses in America and Europe. The aesthetic losses are beyond estimation. The fungus (Figure 14–24.) apparently gives off a toxin that interferes with water movement through the xylem from the roots to the leaves (27). As a result, photosynthesis stops and the tree dies. The spores of the fungus are effectively spread from diseased to healthy trees by tiny brown bark beetles. (See Figure 14–25.) The fungus that causes the disease can also spread through root grafts or fusions of roots from adjacent trees. Because it has been customary to plant elms in rows (monotypes) along residential streets, the fungus infection in one tree may spread rapidly by means of such root grafts through all the elms in the row, in a sort of domino effect. (See Figure 14–26.) The first indications that elms are afflicted are premature (midsummer) leaf yellowing and defoliation. Sanitary measures, such as the

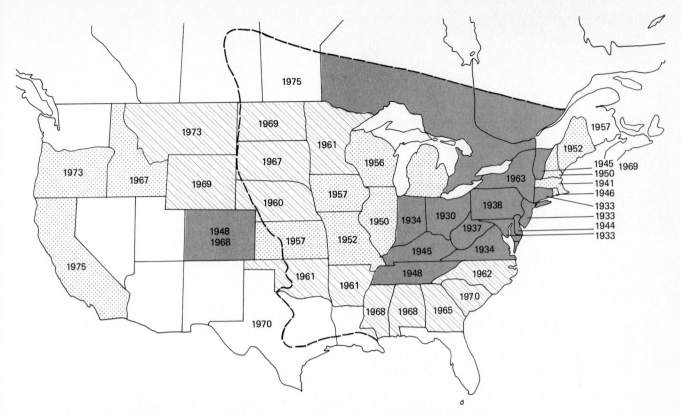

14–23 *Spread of Dutch elm disease across North America is recorded on this map. The dates mark the first appearance of the infection in each state and province. The broken black line traces the limit of the natural range of the American elm.*

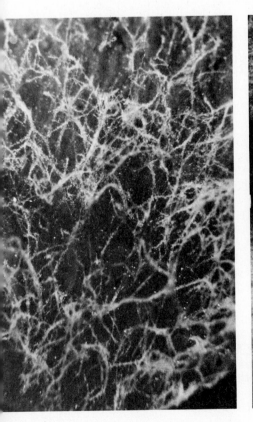
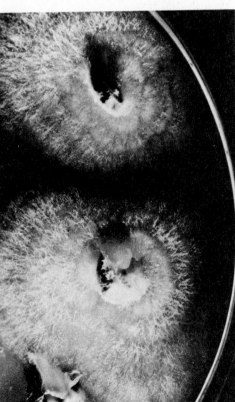

14–24 *(Left) Mycelium growing from spores of Dutch elm disease over surface of agar in a Petri plate. (Right) Chips of wood infected with Dutch elm disease in agar culture in a Petri plate, with fungus growing on them.*

417

14–25 *European elm bark beetle many times enlarged. This insect may transmit the spores of the fungus that causes Dutch elm disease in healthy trees.*

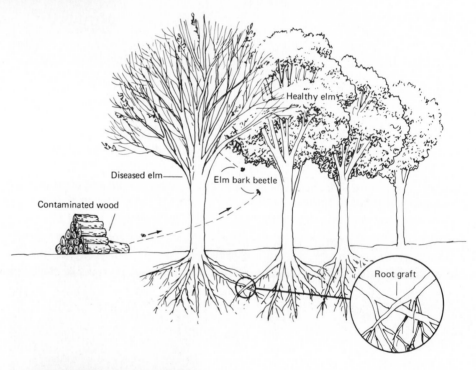

14–26 *Two methods by which Dutch elm disease can be transmitted: (1) by bark beetles from diseased to healthy trees, and (2) by root grafts from diseased to healthy trees.*

14–27 *Washington, D.C. The work of the elm bark beetle is visible (short dark veins) where the bark has been cut from a tree.*

removal and burning of dead and diseased trees, would slow the spread of the disease. However, they are laborious, costly, and time consuming.

Under early recommendations from both federal and state agencies, thousands of municipalities initiated intensive DDT spray campaigns to control the elm disease. About two to three pounds of DDT were employed per tree, usually as a "slurry" (wettable DDT powder suspended in water), by means of spray trucks that projected streams of the insecticide into elm canopies. Because DDT is lethal to the elm bark beetles, this method would seem excellent for halting the spread of the disease across mid-America. On the contrary, however, although such control campaigns were mounted vigorously, by 1976 the disease had spread from Massachusetts south to Virginia and west to California. More than one million of our nation's elms are dying annually. In many smaller cities only the stumps remain. The lovely elms of Rosa, California, once a tourist attraction, are now succumbing rapidly. In St. Paul and Minneapolis, authorities predict a 100 percent kill by 1989. Even the elms on the White House lawn are dying.

In the wake of Dutch elm disease control, communities throughout the elm's range in the late 1950s and 1960s not only experienced "silent springs," but silent summers, autumns, and winters as well. Although it is extremely difficult if not impossible to prove (dead wild animals are rarely found), a number of scientists are of the firm opinion that literally millions of birds in the United States have been destroyed by DDT sprays intended for elm bark beetles.

In 1950 R. J. Barker and his colleagues began studies on the University of Illinois campus that showed how DDT is progressively concentrated as it is transferred from link to link of avian food chains (3). The data from his studies and from those of George Wallace on the Michigan State University campus showed that bird mortality could be either *immediate* or *delayed*. First, the concentration of DDT on leaves and the area under elm trees was so

14–28 *Washington, D.C., near the Jefferson Memorial. The branches of an American elm tree are cut off as the first step in destroying the tree, which is infected with Dutch elm disease. The tree has witnessed the passing of 12 Presidents and several generations of Washingtonians. It will take 80 years to grow another tree of this size.*

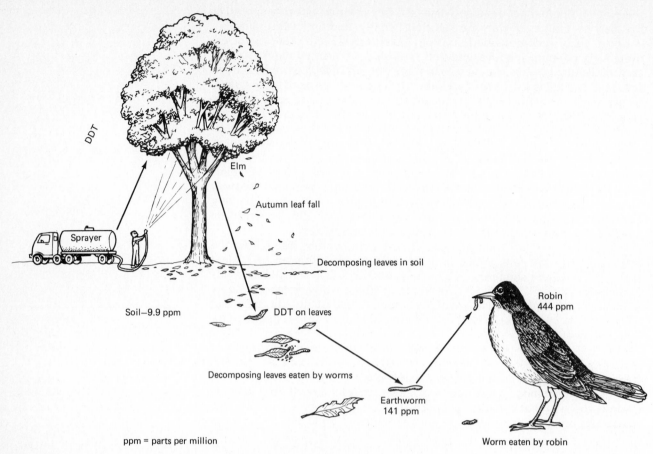

DDT

Elm

Autumn leaf fall

Decomposing leaves in soil

Sprayer

Soil—9.9 ppm

DDT on leaves

Robin
444 ppm

Decomposing leaves eaten by worms

Earthworm
141 ppm

ppm = parts per million

Worm eaten by robin

14-29 *Movement of DDT from sprayer to elm to earthworm to robin.*

high immediately after spraying (remember that two to three pounds were used per tree) that many birds died shortly thereafter from eating DDT-contaminated foods, such as insects, worms, and buds. Bird watchers and biologists frequently observed the tremors and convulsions of dying birds in the wake of control programs.

Second, more subtly but perhaps more significantly, bird mortality results from the delayed expression of the pesticide. DDT remained on the elm-leaf surface all summer long, despite intermittent showers. After leaf fall in autumn the DDT, which is extremely stable, gradually became incorporated into the soil as the leaf fragments were decomposed by soil bacteria and fungi. (See Figure 14–29.) Earthworms subsequently became contaminated by feeding on leaf fragments. Tissue analysis of earthworms collected shortly after summer spraying revealed that all worms contained residues ranging from four parts per million in the nerve cord to 403 parts per million in the crop and gizzard.

Shortly after migrant birds returned in the spring from their wintering grounds, they began consuming DDT-contaminated worms. It has been estimated that feeding on only 11 contaminated worms might be fatal to an adult robin — a quantity easily consumed by a hungry bird in less than an hour. The DDT was stored and eventually concentrated in the animal's fatty tissues. Up to 744 parts per million of DDE (a breakdown product of DDT) have been found in the heart, brain, and liver, respectively, of dead robins. If stored in the gonads, DDE may interfere with gonadal development and function. The reproductive capacity of the bird may be lowered by impaired fertility, hatching success, or vigor of the nestling.

420

Current Methods of Control

Since the ban of DDT, scientists have developed a number of strategies for controlling, or at least slowing down, the spread of Dutch elm disease.

1. *Chemical.* (a) The insecticide *methoxychlor* has been employed on the elm bark beetles. Although it is a chlorinated hydrocarbon like DDT, it breaks down more rapidly and appears to be much less destructive to wildlife. (b) The use of a chemical *repellant* would cause the bark beetles to avoid individual elm trees to which it had been applied.
2. *Cultural.* Instead of planting elms in solid rows (monotypes), it has been suggested that elms be alternated with such species as sugar maple and ironwood, thus forming *heterotypes.* This pattern of tree planting along boulevards, for example, would prevent the spread of the fungus by the root grafting of adjacent elm trees.
3. *Biological.* (a) *Resistant* hybrids can be developed from crossing resistant Siberian elms with the nonresistant American elms. (See Figure 14–30.) (b) *Parasitic wasps* lay their eggs in the larval bark beetles. The larval wasps hatching from the eggs would then consume the larval bark beetles. (See Figure 14–31.) (c) In the early stages of the disease the elms can be innoculated with a *bacterium (Pseudomonas)* that would inhibit the

14–31   *Biological control. The larva of the wasp* Dendrosoter protuberan *feeds on the larva of an elm bark beetle here. Although much smaller than its host, it will suck the body juices of the beetle larva and eventually kill it.*

growth of the fungus inside the tissues of the elm.

The Future

What does the future hold for the American elm? Gary Strobel of Montana State University and Gerald N. Lanier of the University of Syracuse are cautiously optimistic that the elm can be saved from extinction. They write: "One can rest assured that substantial numbers of elms will be preserved by various control programs. Its tremendous power of reproduction will surely save it. In the longer run, one can also hope that natural selection or breeding programs will some day create an American elm able to ward off the fungus (27).

14–30   *Dr. Curtis May, researcher with the U.S. Department of Agriculture at Beltsville, Maryland, holds a Siberian elm. It is hoped that the resistance of the Siberian elm to Dutch elm disease will be transmitted to hybrids resulting from crossings with the American elm.*

Case History: The Kepone Story in Virginia

As previously described, extensive contamination of the ecosystem with pesticides has occurred as the result of their agricultural use. Occasionally, however, gross contamination results from the ignorance, mismanagement, or irresponsibility of the pesticide producers. In July 1975, Kepone, a previously little-known insecticide, became almost a household word. Newspapers, radio, and television highlighted accounts of an environmental disaster that resulted from the discharge of Kepone waste into the James River in Virginia and ultimately into the richly productive estuarine habitat of Chesapeake Bay. The Kepone originated at Hopewell, Virginia, in a small, makeshift plant operating in a crudely converted gas station. There the Life Science Products Company, a subsidiary of Allied Chemical, produced over 1.7 million pounds of the extremely toxic chemical over a period of 16 months (1). Kepone was being used in ant and roach bait and to destroy pests of bananas. Most of it was exported.

Kepone is a chlorinated-hydrocarbon insecticide, closely related to DDT. As expected, it has many of DDT's undesirable properties, such as persistence, mobility, biological magnification, and fat solubility.

Kepone-contaminated waste was discharged from the plant into Hopewell's municipal sewage system. Sewage containing relatively high levels of Kepone was released into the James River in this manner for a period of nine years, first by Allied Chemical and later by Life Science Products Company (1). Environmental authorities first became aware of the slipshod operation of the Life Science plant shortly after a local physician discovered that one of the plant employees was suffering from a nervous disorder that caused him to tremble uncontrollably. Analysis of this worker's blood showed a high level (7.5 parts per million) of Kepone. Of the 150 employees who were later examined by the Virginia State Health Department, 50 showed Kepone-related toxicity symptoms, such as blurred vision, loss of memory, and chest pains. Eventually, after investigators found Kepone dust almost everywhere in the plant, Life Science Products closed its doors forever (1).

The discharge of 100,000 pounds of Kepone waste into the James River contaminated a 100-mile stretch of the river downstream from Hopewell and much of the Chesapeake Bay area near the river's mouth. Because Kepone, like DDT, is not very soluble in water, it accumulated in the mud of the river bed. Kepone was gradually released from this stream-bottom reservoir, taken up by the bodies of plankton, and then moved up the food chain to contaminate commercially valuable fish, crabs, and oysters. A two-year fish-monitoring program (1978–1980) conducted by Virginia health officials, indicated that Kepone levels were gradually dropping. As a result, the five-year ban on commercial fishing in the James River was lifted by the Virginia Board of Health. Heavy pressure from the seafood industry may have been a factor in the decision. Nevertheless, there were still some unanswered questions about the safety of eating James River fish. For example, David Stroube, Virginia's director of health protection, cautioned pregnant women against including the fish in their diet.

Many lawsuits relating to the Kepone pollution episode made their way through the courts. Allied Chemical received the stiffest federal penalty ever levied in the United States for the violation of antipollution laws: a fine of $13.2 million. The State of Virginia fined Allied Chemical $5.2 million. But that is not all. More than 10,000 fishermen, restaurant owners, resort proprietors, commercial oyster farmers, and others whose financial interests were damaged by the Kepone contamination sued Allied Chemical for $8 billion in damages in a mammoth collective-action suite (1). The courts, however, required Allied Chemical to pay only $500 million. The irony is that a modest expenditure of only $200,000 by the company could have prevented the incident in the first place (1).

"As the first clouds of malathion droplets descended on the cars, sidewalks, and fruit trees of northern California last week, physicians, toxicologists and health officials in the San Jose area, and across the nation, held their collective breath." So reported *Science News* on July 18, 1981, of a last-ditch attempt to control one of the most destructive agricultural pests in California's recent history, the Mediterranean fruit fly, popularly known as the Medfly.

The Medfly has high a reproductive potential. The female deposits her eggs in at least 200 kinds of fruits and vegetables, such as peaches, tomatoes, melons, oranges, lemons, and grapefruits. In a few days the eggs hatch into maggots that rapidly convert the once valuable fruit to a worthless pulp.

For several days a controversy had raged concerning the advisability to spray or not to spray. There was much heated argument for both points of view. Let's briefly consider some of them:

Arguments Against the Aerial Spraying of Malathion

1. Some skeptics fretted that California agriculture was "running on a treadmill of chemicals." Average crop losses to insects, for example, remained the same despite a tenfold increase in pesticide use in recent years (7).
2. Aerial spraying is expensive.
3. Aerial spraying in a residential area will be nonselective, with much of the spray landing on roads, rooftops, patios, backyards, sport cars, and swimming pools — as well as fruit trees.
4. Standford University's Sumner Kalman pointed out that there is strong evidence that malathion can cause harmful mutations in laboratory animals.
5. Frank H. Duffy of the Harvard Medical School said that malathion can be dangerous to humans if dosages are sufficiently high: "The effects of taking micrograms of nerve gas and a coffee cup of malathion are identical" (17).
6. The aerial spray program was branded a "cruel biological experiment" by no less than Dr. Theodore Feinstadt, professor of obstetrics at the Stanford University Medical School. Feinstadt warned that the spray might cause "cellular poison" in newborns (20).

Arguments for the Aerial Spraying of Malathion

1. Aerial spraying is fast.
2. Aerial spraying can be employed over an extensive area.
3. According to Eliot Marshall, writing in *Science* magazine: "With aerial spraying, the pest fighters can move farther and faster against the Medflies, covering a 120-square-mile area (as they hope to do) with six fresh blankets of (poisoned) bait in one hatching period. The poison must be fresh because it loses its potency after a few days in the sun . . . " (18).
4. In the opinion of Stanford University's Kenneth Melman, the proposed aerial treatment was even safer than routine spraying in Texas and Florida. The reasons were that small doses of only 1.6 milligrams per square foot were used, and that the pesticide was applied in 500-micron particles, assuring that it would sink to the ground faster and could not be easily inhaled.
5. Kim Hooper, a state geneticist for California, was of the opinion that the aerial spraying of malathion would not be any more harmful for San Jose residents than the air pollution they were breathing in every day (18).

6. The aerial spray program was given the blessing of both the National Cancer Institute and the EPA. According to one EPA spokesman: "Malathion is perfectly safe to be used as directed and has never been on one of our hazardous chemical lists" (18).
7. The alternative to aerial spraying would be to fumigate all fruit and vegetables in the area of infestation with ethylene dibromide, a proven cancer-causing chemical (17).

Governor Brown had been firmly opposed to aerial spraying of malathion early in the Medfly crisis. In fact, he stoutly maintained this position, despite the recommendations of technical experts, the majority of fruit and vegetable growers, and both state and federal agriculture departments. On July 10, however, he yielded to an ultimatum from Washington, D.C., that he either give aerial spraying the green light or risk the quarantine of California's entire fruit and vegetable crop. Brown grumbled that the federal authorities "put a gun to my head" (7). So the aerial spraying began, and eventually the Medfly outbreak in Santa Clara and Alameda Counties was brought under control.

To the Student: What stand do you take in this controversy? Would you support Governor Brown's early decision not to release malathion from planes over a heavily populated area? Or would you align yourself with the advocates of aerial spraying? Perhaps you would like to discuss this matter with your classmates. If so, why don't you fortify your position by gathering more information on the topic in your university library. Several informative books and articles are listed at the end of this chapter.

Controversy Over TCDD: Is It a Boon or a Bane?

The release of chemical "bombs" by American planes during the Vietnam War; an explosion in an industrial plant at Seveso, Italy; the control of brush in an Oregon forest — these are seemingly unrelated events. But they are united by a common chemical bond, TCDD, considered to be the most poisonous compound ever synthesized.

TCDD, technically known as 2,3,7,8-tetrachlorodibenzo-p-dioxin, is only one of a group of 75 different molecules, known as *dioxins,* that is distinguished by the number and position of the chlorine atoms in the molecule. Although never intentionally manufactured, they are formed *incidentally* during the production of other chemicals. As a result, dioxins have become widely dispersed in the human environment. A once widely used weed killer, known as 2,4,5-T, invariably contains traces of TCDD, although usually in concentrations of less than .03-part per million.

TCDD tends to accumulate in the soil because it is only slightly soluble in water. In typical studies about 50 percent of the TCDD is still present after one year. TCDD is not readily decomposed by bacterial action. Under certain conditions, however, sunlight will cause it to break down. In one experiment TCDD was applied to sand at the bottom of an aquarium that contained several different aquatic organisms, including larval mosquitos. Although the TCDD concentration in the water was only 1.3 parts per billion, the concentration in the mosquitos at the upper end of the food chain was 3,700 parts per billion. In Vietnam the tissues of carp and catfish that were taken downstream from areas that had been sprayed previously with 2,4,5-T contained traces of TCDD. Because TCDD is somewhat soluble in fat, like DDT it tends to accumulate in the fatty tissues of both animals and man.

Release of TCDD into the Human Environment

INDUSTRIAL ACCIDENTS.   Dioxins, such as TCDD, have been released into the human environment as a result of industrial accidents. This was the case, for example, at the Monsanto Chemical Plant at Nitro, West Virginia, in

1949. In 1976 an explosion in a chemical plant in Seveso, Italy, released about four pounds of pure TCDD into a densely populated area. The TCDD caused the death of thousands of wild and domesticated animals. During the year that followed the incident, there was apparently an increase in the rate of birth defects in the human population exposed to the TCDD. There is always the possibility that delayed effects might also appear some time in the future.

THE DEFOLIATION PROGRAM IN VIETNAM. In 1962 the United States began a massive campaign to defoliate large sections of Vietnam with the aid of several different herbicides. One type of spray employed was known as Agent Orange — a half-and-half mixture of two weed killers commonly used back in the states, 2,4-D and 2,4,5-T. The purpose of the project was to clear jungle growth and lessen the hazards of ambush by the Viet Cong (Communist) forces. Defoliation would also enable American forces to follow the movements of the enemy.

In 1967, when the herbicide assault was at its peak, a relatively high incidence of unexplained birth defects appeared in South Vietnam. Experiments being conducted back in the United States revealed that injections of 2,4,5-T into pregnant female mice caused a variety of birth defects such as cleft palate, abnormal kidneys, and deformed spinal cord and brain. In light of those findings, concerned scientists began to ask whether there was a cause-and-effect relationship between the massive spraying of Agent Orange, which was 50 percent 2,4,5-T, and the high rate of birth defects. About this same time it was determined that the toxic effects of 2,4,5-T were actually caused by TCDD, an unavoidable contaminant which was incidentally produced during the manufacture of the herbicide. Under considerable pressure from the scientific community, the Army eventually banned the use of 2,4,5-T in the defoliation program in 1970.

When the Vietnam War finally ended, the U.S. military was ready to forget the entire Agent Orange fiasco. But newscaster Bill Kurtis of station WBBM-TV in Chicago would not let the American public forget. On his news program Kurtis alleged that a number of Vietnam veterans living in the Chicago area were showing some of the classic symptoms associated with TCDD poisoning: memory loss, depression, irritability, a peculiar tingling and numbness of hands and feet, and vision problems. In addition, the children of some of the veterans were deformed. The television program received widespread publicity. In a short time Vietnam veterans throughout the country reported similar symptoms. At least 1,200 applied for disability payments from the U.S. Veterans Administration. The Veterans Administration found that some of the veterans carried TCDD concentrations of 57 parts per trillion in their body fat. However, as of 1980 only *three* veterans were awarded compensation — and these for scars left by a skin rash which sometimes develops after exposure to TCDD (3).

BRUSH CONTROL IN FORESTS NEAR ALSEA, OREGON. Bonnie Hixl is a young mother who lives in Alsea, a small town in the heavily forested mountains of western Oregon. The forests in that region were routinely sprayed with 2,4,5-T to control brush. In April, 1978, Bonnie wrote a letter to the EPA in which she complained that she and seven other women from Alsea had suffered a total of ten spontaneous abortions from 1973 to 1978. The EPA registered proper concern. It commissioned Colorado State University and the Miami Medical School to study the problem. The resulting investigations showed that the rate of spontaneous abortions among women in the Alsea area rose sharply from about 60 per month per 1,000 live births during most of the year to 130 in June, a few weeks after the surrounding forests had been routinely sprayed with 2,4,5-T. The studies thus showed a strong correlation between the spraying of 2,4,5-T and the number of abortions. They did not, however, actually prove that the 2,4,5-T (and its TCDD contaminant) actually caused the increase in abortion rates. On the basis of the studies, the EPA finally decided to suspend the use of 2,4,5-T in brush control.

DDT: Harmless or Harmful to Human Health?

In 1980 the Federal Center for Disease Control reported that most of the people living in Terance, Alabama, had DDT levels in their bodies that were ten times higher than the levels in the general population. The reason was that they were eating DDT-contaminated fish from a stream located near an insecticide-manufacturing plant owned by the Olin Corporation. The blood level found in an eighty-five-year-old retired farmer of 3,500 parts per billion was considered the highest ever recorded for any person in the United States.

The average person in the United States, such as the student, housewife, or businessman, who is not occupationally exposed to DDT, takes DDT into his or her body when eating DDT-contaminated foods. DDT levels in food are closely monitored and regulated by the Food and Drug Administration (FDA). In the case of milk, the FDA has set the tolerance level at 0.05-parts per million. Studies have indicated that the daily intake of DDT by adult Americans in the early 1980s was about 3 micrograms. Roughly 90 percent of the DDT intake is ingested with food; much of the remainder has its source in DDT-contaminated air and water (25).

Now what happens to this DDT once it gets inside our body? The key to the answer is in the solubility of DDT. As already mentioned, DDT is very insoluble in water; dissolved concentrations in water only reach a maximum of two parts per billion. This is unfortunate, for the human body is essentially a water system, and if the DDT were highly soluble in water, much of it could dissolve in the blood plasma, be filtered from the blood by the kidneys, and eventually be excreted from the body with the urine. On the other hand, DDT is extremely soluble in fat. As a result, it tends to accumulate in the fatty tissue of the body. (See Figure 14–32.) The average American adult is storing about three parts per million of DDT in his or her fatty tissues (25). However, the amount stored varies with the sex, age, race, and health of the individual as well as with the amount of DDT taken into the body. Therefore, the absolute amount of DDT in fat storage varies from 0.0 parts per million in some individuals to 90 parts per million in others (27). Although most Americans are probably taking DDT into their bodies every day with the food they eat and the air they breathe, the amount of DDT stored in body fat does not continue to increase indefinitely. Eventually a "plateau" or "steady state" is reached, at which point the amount ingested during a 24-hour period is exactly counterbalanced by the amount excreted or broken down by the body cells (25).

DDT may be stored in other tissues besides fat, but in much lesser amounts. Thus, it is stored in liver tissues at concentrations roughly 10 percent of that in fat and in the tissues of gonads, brains, kidneys, and blood at concentrations of only 1 percent of that in fat (27).

There is no doubt that a persistent chlorinated hydrocarbon pesticide, such as DDT, may cause

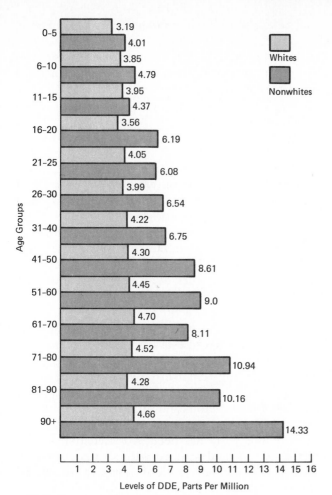

Whites

Nonwhites

14–32 *Levels of DDE, a breakdown product of DDT, in the fat of people in the United States.*

levels of DDT that we carry in our bodies sooner or later may cause cancer (9). A study by the National Academy of Sciences showed that human cancer could be caused by at least 350 of the 1,400 (25 percent) chemicals used in pesticides in the United States (21). Dr. Malcolm M. Hargraves, senior consultant at the Mayo Clinic, is of the belief that *more fatalities are caused by pesticides in the United States than are caused by car accidents.* If he is correct, this means that pesticides are killing about 60,000 Americans yearly—roughly 14 times the mortality rate for American soldiers killed in action during the Vietnam War. A commission on pesticides and health appointed by the U.S. Department of Health, Education, and Welfare has deplored our woeful lack of knowledge in this area: "The field of pesticide toxicology exemplifies the absurdity of a situation in which 200 million Americans are undergoing lifelong exposure, yet our knowledge of what is happening to them is at best fragmentary and for the most part indirect and inferential. While there is little ground for forebodings of disaster, there is even less for complacency . . . " (33).

Even today, more than a decade since that report was written, we still do not know what low levels of DDT and other pesticides, over the long run, are doing to our bodies.

Alternative Methods of Pest Control

Although chemical control may indeed substantially reduce a pest population, that success is frequently only temporary and is followed by a resurgence of the pest to higher densities than before control was initiated. Moreover, the cost of that short-term success (in addition to the price of the chemicals) frequently is ecosytem contamination, widespread wildlife mortality, and the development of resistance in the target pest. Cultural and biological control, alternative methods of pest management, are much less expensive than chemical methods and they do not disrupt the normal structure and functioning of ecosystems. Biological control also embraces the use of cultural methods (crop rotation) and the use of pest-resistant crops.

Cultural Control

In *cultural control* the agricultural environment is modified in such a way that crop yields are increased as a result of reduced pest populations (34).

sickness and death among many forms of wildlife. However, for many people who are not hunters, anglers, bird watchers, or nature lovers, this fact, regrettably, does not really cause very much concern. The important question is how the load of DDT in *your* body fat, liver, kidneys, gonads, adrenal glands, and blood affects *your* health. Will you have cancer some day? Researchers have been trying to find definite answers to such questions for almost twenty years.

Autopsies have revealed fairly high levels of DDT and other chlorinated hydrocarbons in the fatty tissues of people who died from cancer, softening of the brain, high blood pressure, stroke, and cirrhosis of the liver (21). In a book entitled *Chemical Carcinogenesis*, D. B. Clayson suggested that the low

427

Among the important methods of cultural control are crop rotation, intercropping, and the planting of trap crops.

CROP ROTATION.   We learned that crop rotation is an important method for curbing soil erosion and increasing soil fertility. It is important in pest control as well. Many species of insects are highly specialized to feed on only one or a few species of crop plants. Thus, the alfalfa weevil feeds mainly on alfalfa, the corn rootworm feeds primarily on corn, and so on. It is apparent, therefore, that if the same crop, say corn, were grown on the same plot year after year, the corn rootworm would have little trouble satisfying its food needs. In such a hospitable environment, growth and reproduction would proceed at a high level of efficiency and the population of the corn rootworm would build up to peak levels. On the other hand, let us assume the corn is alternated with oats. During the oat years it is obvious that the corn rootworm's food supply would be greatly diminished, if not nonexistent, on that particular farm. As a result, its population would greatly decline. Similarly it has been found that the alternation of potato with alfalfa tends to reduce wireworm populations (34).

STRIP HARVESTING.   Under traditional alfalfa harvesting practices, the entire crop is cut at one time. As a result, nothing is left but stubble. How-

ever, in the strip harvest method, shown in Figure 14–33, half of the crop remains standing in the half-grown stage. This technique permits the continued presence of beneficial insects, associated with the alfalfa, that characteristically feed on potentially destructive insect pests. As a result, damage to the alfalfa crop from these pests is held to a minimum (31).

INTERCROPPING.   Intercropping involves planting two different crops in alternate rows, or strips. It has been determined, in experimental work, that damage to corn from the corn borer is reduced by 80 percent when corn and peanuts are intercropped. Although researchers are not sure of the biological explanation, it has been suggested that predators and parasites of the corn borer use the peanut crop as cover (8).

TRAP CROPS.   A trap crop is a low-value crop used to "lure" destructive pests from a high-value crop planted nearby. For example, alfalfa may be used to trap the lygus bug, which otherwise would be a serious pest of cotton crops. Similarly, in the Hawaiian Islands fields of melons and squash are bordered by rows of melon-fly-trapping corn. Once a high population of the pests has been attracted to the trap crop, they can be destroyed with an insecticide or the trap crop with its catch of pests can be plowed under or burned (34).

STRIP HARVESTING

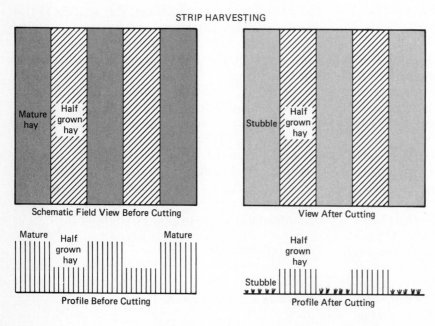

Schematic Field View Before Cutting

Profile Before Cutting

View After Cutting

Profile After Cutting

14–33 *Strip-harvesting of alfalfa as a cultural method of insect-pest control.*

428

Biological Control of Insect Pests

David Pimentel
Department of Entomology
CORNELL UNIVERSITY

Humans have always fought insect pests to prevent them from destroying their crops. Ever since humans first cultivated crops, they probably practiced some form of nonchemical biological control.

The deliberate use of predators and parasites, including micro-organisms, for control of insect pests has proven highly successful against several pests. The first major success occurred late in the 19th century when the Vadalia beetle was brought from Australia to control the cottony-cushion scale that was destroying citrus in California. Since then, several other parasites and predators have been introduced that are providing successful biological control of specific insect pests on several crops such as citrus, olives, alfalfa, apples, and corn.

One of the most successful biological control techniques is host plant resistance. In early times farmers unknowingly applied the technique of using resistant crops when they planted seeds from plants that most successfully survived pest attacks. However, as knowledge of genetics has grown, the scientific selection and breeding of crops resistant to major pest insects has developed. At present, resistant crop cultivars are being planted that effectively resist more than 25 different insect pests, including the Hessian fly pest of wheat, the spotted alfalfa aphid, and the European corn borer.

Several biological control technologies that continue to have widespread use in agriculture include changing crop rotations and planting times, planting diverse crops in combination, employing mechanical tillage, managing water use by controlled irrigation, increasing the use of certain fertilizer elements, and disposing of crop residues that harbor pests.

Few appreciate the fact that biological control in the United States is equally as important as insecticide use for preventing crop losses in agriculture to insect pests.

Biological Control of Insects

In the view of many ecologists, *biological control* is a preferred alternative to the chemical control of pests. Biological control is defined as the deliberate intensification of natural control mechanisms (parasitism and predation) that operate in natural ecosystems — the *density-dependent* mechanisms discussed in Chapter 12. There are several hundred native species of insects, as well as viruses and bacteria, that can be used in controlling crop pests. (See David Pimental's guest article in this chapter and Figure 14–34.)

14–34 *Classic biological control resulting in total elimination of an insect pest as an economic problem. Biological control agents include viruses, predators, and parasites.*

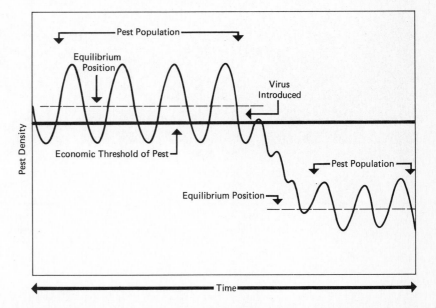

Viruses: Rabbit Control in Australia

The native Australian fauna is unique, being well represented by marsupials such as the kangaroo but being almost completely lacking in placental mammals such as the wolf, fox, coyote, cougar, squirrel, and rabbit. Sheep were introduced to Australia in the nineteenth century. Today they form the basis of a multimillion-dollar wool and mutton industry. Many of the flocks graze on semiarid ranges in the continental interior. Early in the twentieth century the European rabbit was introduced into Australia, apparently at the instigation of European immigrants who longed to indulge once again in their favorite sport of hunting the elusive brushland "bounders." Unfortunately, once they were introduced, their numbers sharply increased. (See Figure 14–35.) Apparently there were no natural predators to serve as limiting factors in controlling their population surge.

As their numbers increased, the rabbits began to invade sheep range. In the semiarid grasslands of interior Australia, forage never had been lush. Now under the combined grazing pressure of both sheep and rabbits, the rangelands rapidly deteriorated. Grasses were clipped to ground level. The denuded earth became vulnerable. (See Figure 14–36.) Dust clouds and sand dunes were the inevitable result. Faced with impending economic ruin, Australian ranchers banded together in an all-out effort to eradicate the rabbits. They tried all the conventional control methods. They poisoned. They trapped. They staged mammoth roundups. They launched huge rabbit-hunting parties, the likes of which Europe had never seen. They even

14–35   *The rabbit explosion in Australia. Rabbits gathering at a water hole during a period of drought. Their population was estimated at one billion in 1950 about the time this picture was taken. Although the Myxomatosis virus, introduced in 1950, has reduced their numbers by 75 percent, they still pose a problem for ranchers.*

14–36 *The effect of a rabbit invasion. The range to the left was consumed by rabbits. The pasture to the right was protected from the rabbit hordes by the intervening fence.*

erected a fence several hundred miles long, from Queenland to North Wales, in an attempt to contain the dispersing rabbit hordes. Their efforts were to no avail. Finally, in 1950 government biologists introduced the *myxoma* virus, lethal to rabbits exclusively, into the target area. It is transmitted to healthy rabbits by virus-carrying mosquitos, which bite only live rabbits. The immediate results were spectacularly successful — only one year later 99.5 percent of Australia's rabbits had succumbed to the virus. Unfortunately, the rabbits gradually developed resistance to the virus and by 1958 the mortality rate from the virus dropped to only 54 percent (15). Whether the rabbits will ultimately develop complete immunity to the myxoma virus and again disrupt Australia's rangeland economy remains to be seen.

STERILIZATION: THE SCREWWORM FLY. Any process that would make it impossible for a female insect to produce eggs or the male to produce sperm is known as *sterilization*. Scientists have developed various methods of sterilization for the purpose of controlling insect pests. The most celebrated example of pest control by this method involves a metallic blue insect known as the screwworm fly — an insect about three times the size of the house fly.

The screwworm fly is widely distributed in South America, Central America, and Mexico and ranges northward into Georgia, Florida, Alabama, Texas, Arizona, New Mexico, and California. During the winter the fly is restricted to the southern portions of those states. Shortly after mating, the adult female will deposit about 100 eggs in the open wound of warm-blooded animals, such as cattle or deer. Occasionally the females will even lay their eggs in the navels of newly born young animals. The eggs soon hatch into parasitic maggots that feed ravenously on the flesh of the host. (See Figure 14 – 37.) As the feeding process continues, the wound dis-

431

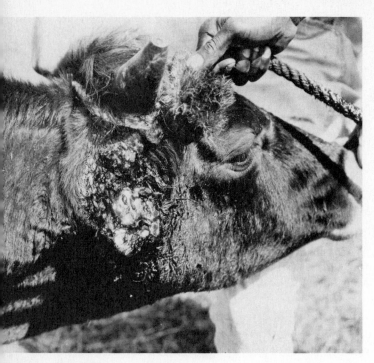

14–37 *Screwworm infestation in the ear of a steer. An untreated, fully grown animal weighing about 1,000 pounds may be killed by several thousand maggots feeding in a single wound.*

charges a fluid that attracts more adult flies. Eventually, in cases of severe infestation, more than 1,000 maggots may feed in a single wound. An infestation such as this can kill a full-grown, 1,000-pound steer within ten days. The scarcity of deer in some parts of Texas has been attributed to the screwworm fly (7). After five days of intensive feeding, the larvae drop to the ground and pupate. Soon after, they emerge as adults. After mating with a male fly, the female will deposit eggs, thus completing the life cycle. The fly may have up to ten generations a year. When breeding conditions and other environmental factors are optimal, the screwworm fly will increase greatly in numbers and cause livestock losses in the United States that may amount to $40 million annually.

Back in the 1930s, Edward Knipling, chief of the USDA's Entomology Research Branch, conceived of controlling this highly destructive pest by sterilizing and releasing male flies. After highly successful preliminary tests on the Caribbean island of Curacao, Dr. Knipling decided to employ this method on the screwworm-fly population of the southeastern

United States. The program was launched in January 1958. It was a most opportune time, for the abnormally cold winter of 1957–1958 had confined the screwworm fly to a small area in southern Florida.

The first step was to set up a sterilization "factory" in a converted airplane hangar, in which 50 million male flies were sterilized each week by exposure to radioactive cobalt. (See Figure 14–38.) Over two billion of those flies were packed in cardboard boxes and flown by airplane over target areas of high infestation and then released (17). Once the boxes fell to the ground, they would pop open, and the sterilized males would disperse. (See Figure 14–39.) The sterilized males would then begin to compete with the normal, wild, fertile males for virgin females. Dr. Knipling and his colleagues determined that a ratio of nine sterilized males to one fertile male would cause 83 percent of the matings

14–38 *Sterilization of male screwworm flies. During the sterilization process, canisters containing 30,000 flies are exposed to a cobalt-60 radiation source at the "sterilization factory."*

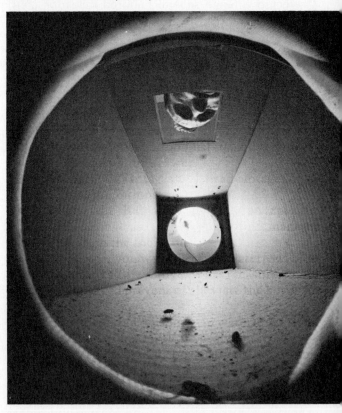

14–39 *Release of sterilized male screwworm flies. Dr. James E. Novy breaks open a box of 2,000 sterile flies near Mission, Texas. Flies disperse in this way when the boxes strike the ground after leaving the aircraft.*

this was "a triumphant demonstration of the worth of scientific creativity, aided by thorough basic research, persistence, and determination" (7). Sterilized male flies continued to be mass produced and released as a preventive measure against the pest's reinvasion.

Regrettably, despite those preventive measures, the fly reappeared. In 1972 over 100,000 cattle became infested with the maggots. Serious cattle losses occurred over the next three years (32). The question arises: How is this resurgence of the fly explained? Several scientists associated with the control project are of the opinion that the flies that were being released for preventive purposes probably had evolved into an inferior domestic strain that was highly susceptible to diseases, predators, and other limiting factors present in the natural, wild environment. It is also possible that this "domestic" strain was incapable of effectively competing for virgin females with the fertile, wild males (32).

SEX ATTRACTANTS: THE CASE OF THE GYPSY MOTH. In 1869 the pupae of the gypsy moth, a native of Europe, were shipped through the mails from France to Medford, Massachusetts. They had been requested by a French astronomer, Leopold Trouvelot, employed by Harvard University, who was interested in developing a disease-resistant silkworm moth (35). Unfortunately, a few of the insects escaped from his laboratory into the surrounding woodlands. Apparently that was the end of the gypsy moth as an invader of the United States. Twenty years later, however, the town of Medford was crawling with an enormous infestation of the brown, bristly, red-and-blue-spotted caterpillars of this moth. Released from such density-dependent control agents as predators and parasites, which had kept this species in check in its native Europe, the gypsy moth population around Medford "exploded." According to one observer "the street was black with them [caterpillars] . . . they were so thick on the trees that they were stuck together like

to be sterile (35). This ratio was attained. In a sense the scientists were employing the insect's reproductive instinct to breed itself into oblivion. (See Figure 14–40.) As a consequence, the screwworm-fly population gradually declined. Only 18 months after the project began, the complete eradication of the screwworm maggot in the Southeast had been achieved. As Rachel Carson has so aptly written,

14–40 *Population reduction of a pest population when a constant number of sterilized males are released in a pest population of one million males and one million females.*

Generation	Number of Virgin Females	Number of Sterile Males Released	Ratio of Sterile to Fertile Males	Number of Fertile Females in the Next Generation
1	1,000,000	2,000,000	2:1	333,333
2	333,333	2,000,000	6:1	47,619
3	47,619	2,000,000	42:1	1107
4	1107	2,000,000	1807:1	less than 1

14–41 *Leaf-eating caterpillars of the gypsy moth damage hundreds of thousands of dollars worth of forest and shade trees in the northeastern states annually. They hatch in April from eggs laid the previous year.*

cold macaroni . . . the foliage was completely stripped from all the trees . . . presenting an awful picture of devastation. . . ." During the quiet of a summer's night one could actually hear the curious sound created by thousands of tiny mandibles shredding foliage in the canopies overhead. Pellets of waste excreted by the multitudinous larvae "rained" down from the trees in a steady drizzle (35).

A single caterpillar can devour one square foot of foliage in one or two hours. Although the larvae prefer oak leaves, they will also consume birch and ash foliage and when full grown will even eat pine needles. Even though defoliation might not kill a tree directly, it might render the tree mortally vulnerable to fungus infections, windstorm, and drought.

Since its momentous escape from Trouvelot's laboratory, the gypsy moth has spread throughout the northeastern states and westward to Michigan, Wisconsin, and California. (See Figure 14–42.) This spread of the pest has been facilitated by the increased use of recreational vehicles because the female moth frequently deposits her egg masses on them (35). In 1980 there were severe gypsy outbreaks both in California and in the northeastern United States. Trees were defoliated throughout a five-million acre region from Maine to Maryland. New York experienced 15 times as much damage as the year before. Fruit farmers in Santa Barbara County in California were very concerned that the caterpillars might cause an estimated $40 million damage to their avocado and citrus crops. Strenuous efforts have been made to control the range extension of the insect. Techniques employed include (a) quarantine of the bark, branches, and soil on which moths may have laid their eggs; (b) the introduction of parasitic flies; (c) the spraying of DDT (prior to its ban) on one million forested acres; and (d) the sterilization-release method of control.

Currently, intensive research is being conducted to determine the effectiveness of *sex attractants* in controlling this pest.

Chemical signals given off by an animal's body are known as *pheromones. Sex attractants* are pheromones that are secreted by an animal to attract a prospective mate for the purpose of reproduction. These scents are species specific. Although the male gypsy moth has strong, functional wings, the female is too heavy-bodied for effective flight. After emerging from her pupa case, the virgin female flutters about near the ground or creeps up tree trunks. She secretes minute quantities (0.00000001-gram) of a sex attractant, known as *gyptol*, from her abdominal glands (20). With the aid of his sensitive antennal receptors, the male moth is able to detect this scent within one-half mile of the female. The male flies upwind along this scent trail until he locates the female. Mating then takes place.

Scientists with the USDA have been able to synthesize a chemically related compound, known as *gyplure*, that has proven just as effective as the natural gyptol as a sex attractant. Researchers have used gyplure in various ways. A minute amount of gyplure may be placed in a trap together with a sticky substance. (See Figure 14–43.) Male gypsy moths are deluded into "thinking" that a virgin female is in the trap, so they enter the traps and cannot extricate themselves. (See Figure 14–44.) (A similar method, employed on the pine sawfly, attracted over 7,000 male sawflies to a single trap within five hours (20).) Thousands of such traps were erected by Californian fruit growers in Los Angeles, Santa Barbara, Carmel, and Monterey, when those areas were invaded by gypsy moths in 1980.

14–42 *Spread of the gypsy moth, 1969–1977, shown by heavy black lines, from the general area of infestation in the Northeast. Male moths were trapped as far west as Wisconsin and as far south as Alabama. The oak forests shown on the map are potentially vulnerable to gypsy moth invasions.*

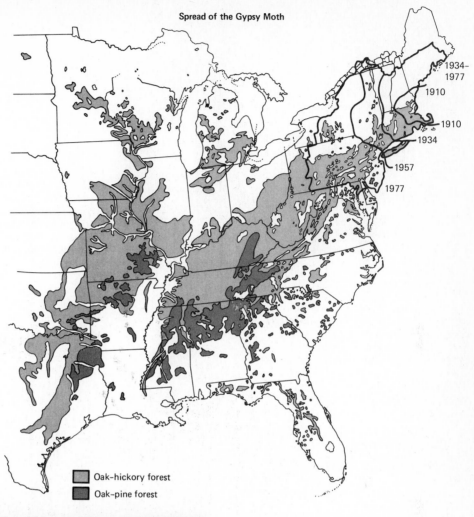

Spread of the Gypsy Moth

1934–1977
1910
1910
1934
1957
1977

Oak-hickory forest
Oak-pine forest

14–43 *Cape Cod, Massachusetts. A scientist at the Gypsy Moth Methods Improvement Laboratory places a small tuft of cotton moistened with gyplure inside a gypsy moth trap. This synthetic attractant is being used to lure male moths to traps and to chemosterilants. It is also being used in a study of a unique method called the confusion technique. An area is saturated with the synthetic attractant in the hope of confusing the male moths to the extent that they will not be able to find and mate with the females.*

14-44 *Cape Cod, Massachusetts. This is a typical gypsy-moth trap picked up in the field. It contains captured gypsy moths lured into the trap by gyplure, a synthetic attractant that confuses male moths into "thinking" a female is inside the trap. Once inside, the moth becomes entangled in a sticky substance and is unable to extricate itself.*

14-45 *Male gypsy moth attracted to a female by the sex attractant gyptol, which she emits (top). Male gypsy moth lured into a trap baited with synthetic gyplure (center). Male gypsy moth, confused by multiple sources of gyplure, is unable to find a female gypsy moth which which to mate.*

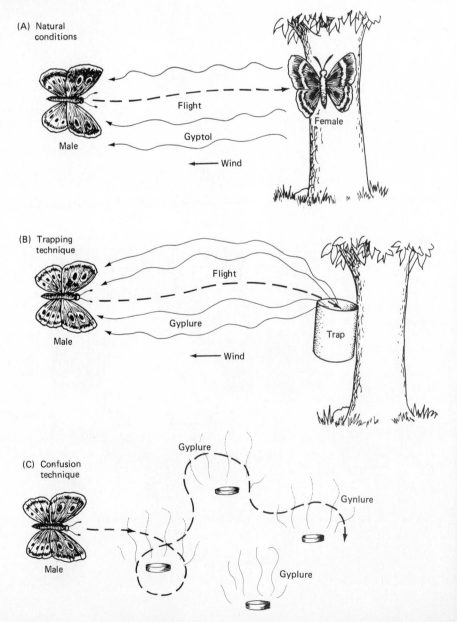

(A) Natural conditions

Flight

Gyptol

Male

Female

Wind

(B) Trapping technique

Flight

Gyplure

Male

Wind

Trap

(C) Confusion technique

Gyplure

Gynlure

Male

Gyplure

436

Predators: Insect Consumption by Humans

We have described the use of *predators*, such as ladybugs, to control crop-destroying insect pests. A type of fish known as *Gambusa* has been used successfully in mosquito control. (See Figure 14–46.) These techniques seem effective. But why not use the greatest predator of all: *humans*? Not only would we in this way save on pesticide costs, but we would be able to utilize an enormous source of otherwise scarce animal protein as well. All we have to do is overcome our fastidiousness. And that should not be too difficult. After all, many people in some parts of the world eat insects. The Japanese dry and salt cockroaches, grind them to a powder, and sprinkle them on rice. Mexicans use the eggs of water beetles to add flavor to cookies and cakes. In South Africa termites are roasted and eaten by the handful, as we eat popcorn (37). Even in the United States fried caterpillars and chocolate-covered locusts are considered, by some, to be culinary delights. Laurent Hodges of Iowa State University has suggested that, for a little gastronomic excitement, we try the following recipe for the common large grasshoppers seen in late summer.

1. Remove head, legs and wings.
2. Add a dash of pepper and salt.
3. Sprinkle with chopped parsley.
4. Fry in butter till crisp (17).

14–46 *Mosquito eater! This minnow, known as* Gambusia affinis, *feeds voraciously on mosquito larvae, as shown in this picture. It is being used in some southern states to control mosquito infestations. In particular, it is hoped that it can reduce population levels of the mosquito* Culex tarsalis, *which transmits encephalitis, and* Anopheles freeborni, *a spreader of malaria.*

All this may sound whimsical, but global food expert Georg Borgstrom of Michigan State University is dead serious about the important and necessary role protein-rich insects may someday play as cheap substitutes for steaks and chops. And, of course, if we focus most of our dietary attention on crop-ravaging insects, pesticide contamination of the human environment should be considerably reduced.

437

A second use of gyplure involves impregnating thousands of tiny wood chips or cardboard squares with the attractant and then releasing them from an airplane over the infested site. If the number of chips outnumbers the virgin females, more males will "mate" with wood chips or cardboard squares than with female gypsy moths. Such squandering of sperm, of course, would cause a population decline of this pest.

A third approach, known as the *confusion technique*, simply involves spraying gyplure broadly over the infested site. The males become confused by the welter of scent trails and spend much time and energy tracking down a nonexistent female. Again, the number of fertile matings is greatly reduced. Under experimental conditions at the USDA's research facility at Beltsville, Maryland, mating activity was reduced by 94 percent when gyplure was applied at concentrations of only 12 grams per acre.

The use of sex attractants in pest control has many advantages over conventional insecticides. Sex attractants are nontoxic, species specific, and nonpersistent. Moreover, it is impossible for an insect to develop resistance to the attractant without at the same time developing resistance to the very act of reproduction. Since its first use on the gypsy moth, the sex-attractant technique has been employed on many other insect pests, such as the cabbage borer, European corn borer, cotton boll weevil, Japanese beetle, tomato hornworm, and the tobacco budworm (25).

Biological Control of Aquatic Weeds

Eutrophication has resulted in "explosions" of aquatic weeds in many lakes and streams throughout the United States. Such weeds hamper navigation and the development of hydropower, clog irrigation channels, detract from scenic beauty, and interfere with such recreational activities as canoeing, swimming, and fishing. Some waters have been virtually blanketed with growths of water chestnut (New York), alligator weed (Florida and Georgia), water hyacinth (Texas, Florida, and Louisiana), and water lotus (Texas and Tennessee). Instead of employing herbicides, whose effect on the aquatic ecosystem may be exceedingly adverse, state and federal agencies are exploring the possibilities of weed control by biological means. Research is being conducted concerning the use of viruses, snails, insects, fish, and even herbivorous mammals, such as

14–47 *Before biological control of water weeds. This tank, which measures 7 × 2½ feet, contains a dense growth of a common water weed called* Florida Elodea.

muskrats. (See Figures 14–47 and 14–48.) Leaf-eating beetles have been employed with considerable success in controlling extensive growths of alligator weed in the lakes and rivers of Georgia and Florida. The *tilapia*, introduced from Africa, has proved effective in the eradication of submerged weeds when the fish is stocked at densities of 1,000 per acre.

Integrated Pest Management (IPM)

Although the biological control of pests holds much promise, many experts believe that the most effective long-term method of control will be *integrated pest management (IPM)*. It employs not only biological control, but cultural and chemical methods as well. The tactics employed in IPM are multiple and diverse: planting pest-resistant strains of crops; timing crop planting so as to avoid pest outbreaks; altering the distance between crop rows; modifications in the use of water and fertilizers;

14-48 *After biological control of water weeds. Six Marisa snails, imported from South America, were placed into the weed-choked tank for a period of 24 weeks, after which this photo was taken. The snail is one of the biological weapons with which the USDA is experimenting. The snails feed on such weeds as Elodea, Southern Naiad, coontail, and pondweed, as well as certain types of algae.*

rotation of crops; strip-cropping; the use of trap crops; using a minimal amount of highly selective insecticides — those that destroy only the target pest; the importation of predators; dispersal of sex attractants to disrupt reproductive activity of the pest; mass introduction of sterile males; and the release of pest viruses. The various strategies may be used singly or in combination, simultaneously or in sequence, depending upon the particular pest problem. Chemicals would not be dispensed in a massive assault on the agricultural ecosystem as was so commonly done in the 1940s and 1950s with disastrous results for wildlife. Instead, the chemicals would be fitted into them. A given pesticide would be employed in a highly selective manner, only after an intensive study had been conducted of its immedi-

ate effects on target pests and of its long-term influences on other organisms (both harmful and beneficial) of the ecosystem. In most cases, the pesticides would be employed only temporarily, to reduce the target population sufficiently to swing the balance in favor of the pest's predators and parasites. Both native and exotic biological control agents would play significant roles. As researchers at the University of California – Berkeley write:

We must realize that man has developed huge monocultures, he has eliminated forests and grasslands, selected special strains of plants and animals, moved them about, and in other ways altered the natural control that had developed over thousands of years. We could not return to those original conditions if it were desirable. We may, however, utilize some of the mechanisms that existed before man's modifications to establish new balances in our favor. (30)

There is mounting evidence, from agricultural regions in South Africa to the apple orchards of Nova Scotia and to the citrus plots of California, that IPM can be extremely effective. IPM has numerous advantages: (1) because it requires minimal amounts of chemicals, it is relatively inexpensive; (2) hazards stemming from food-chain contamination are reduced; (3) the chance for a buildup of resistant insect strains is restricted; (4) it permits the gradual restoration of biotic components of the original ecosystem; and (5) it permits the introduction of exotic agents of control that prior study reveals to be effective against specific target pests (30).

Much of the impetus for IPM was provided by a massive interdisciplinary research project directed by Carl B. Huffaker, entomologist at the University of California – Berkeley. This ambitious project involved the participation of scientists from 18 different universities. Focus was placed on six major crop plants and their pests. In his book *Environmental Awakening*, Rice Odell describes the results of one of the studies concerned with the control of the cotton boll weevil, a quarter-inch pest which invaded Texas from Mexico in 1982:

Consider a Huffaker project experimental program in Texas, where past heavy use of pesticides has proved disastrous. Field tests had revealed that an early-fruiting genetic variety of cotton rapidly became unattractive to boll weevils. In effect, the weevils came too late for their best feeding. It also was found that this effect is enhanced by greatly narrowing the 40-inch spacing between rows.

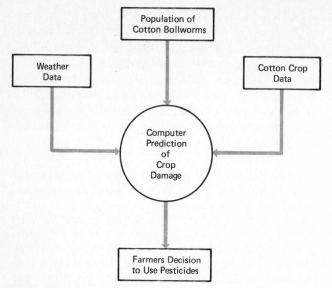

14–49 *Computerized data on weather, cotton crop, and cotton boll weevils serve as the basis on which the cotton farmer makes his decision whether to use chemical pesticides.*

In the experiment, directed by Perry L. Adkisson, head of Texas A&M University's Department of Entomology, irrigation water was cut from the usual 72–80 inches to 30 inches. Nitrogen fertilizer was reduced from 200 pounds to 50 pounds. No late-season pest control was necessary because of early maturation, and *applications of pesticide were cut from twelve to virtually none.* The results, in an area where banks balk at lending money to cotton farmers: a per-acre net *profit* of $364 compared to a *loss* of $1.88 per acre under the old system. *[Italics mine.]*

Under the IPM program boll weevil populations are carefully checked each week by field workers who sweep the cotton fields with insect nets. The "catch" information is then fed into BUGNET, a computer system, which then alerts cotton farmers when weevils are getting too numerous. (See Figure 14–49.) Only then do they spray. As a result of such IPM techniques cotton farmers in Texas have reduced their use of expensive insecticides by 90 percent since the 1960s (3).

Legal Restrictions on Insecticide Use

Because of the potentially harmful effects of the intensive use of some pesticides on humans and wildlife, Congress passed the Federal Insecticide,

Fungicide, and Rodenticide Act (FIFRA) in 1972. Amendments were made in 1975 and 1978. Under this act all pesticides on the market must be officially registered with the EPA. They are then classified for either general or restricted use. EPA's Office of Pesticide Programs evaluates pesticide data submitted by the manufacturers. On the basis of the evaluation, the EPA may refuse to register a given pesticide or may cancel or suspend the use of a pesticide already on the market. About half of the pesticides manufactured in the United States are exported—mainly to underdeveloped nations in Asia, Africa, and South America. Unfortunately, about 20 percent of the exports are either banned for use in the United States (DDT), or have not even been tested by the industry or the EPA concerning their potential threat to humans and wildlife.

On December 31, 1972, a notable triumph was achieved by the proponents of environmental quality. The EPA officially banned DDT for virtually all except emergency situations. (In early 1974 the EPA did permit the U.S. Forest Service to use DDT to control a highly destructive outbreak of the tussock moth in the valuable coniferous timber stands of the Northwest.) In the years since the ban the concentrations of DDT in soil, water, and wildlife have substantially decreased. (See Figure 14–50.)

It must be emphasized, however, that there is currently no ban of DDT in South America, Asia, and Africa, where millions of pounds of DDT are used annually. And where will that DDT eventually cir-

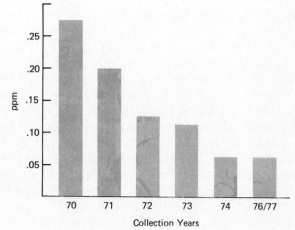

14–50 *Decrease in average concentrations of DDT in freshwater fish collected during the 1970s.*

The insecticide DDT was banned in the United States in 1972 after two decades of battle over its alleged benefits and costs. The DDT story is one of the few pollution sagas in which the final chapters are being written, and it is instructive to examine the impact of this pollution abatement decision.

A major reason (among many others) for the ban was that DDT was causing reproductive failure among certain carnivorous birds. Fifteen years of scientific research showed that DDE, a partial breakdown product of DDT that contaminates the birds by concentrating within their food chains, causes birds to lay thin-shelled eggs that break prematurely, producing no chicks. This effect produced large population declines among many avian species.

Peregrine falcon populations, for example, collapsed during the 1950s and 1960s. Peregrines declined by sixty to ninety-five percent in Western Europe and Western North America, and became extinct as a breeding species in the Eastern United States. By 1970 the outlook for this regal bird was bleak; yet now, a decade after the banning of DDT, Peregrines are staging a dramatic comeback everywhere. They are being bred and raised in captivity, successfully released into the wild, and are reappearing in their former haunts in the Eastern U.S.

The DDT Ban Pays Off

Charles F. Wurster
MARINE SCIENCES RESEARCH CENTER
STATE UNIVERSITY OF NEW YORK AT STONY BROOK

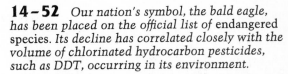

14–52 *Our nation's symbol, the bald eagle, has been placed on the official list of endangered species. Its decline has correlated closely with the volume of chlorinated hydrocarbon pesticides, such as DDT, occurring in its environment.*

14–51 *Down and out? Pesticides are responsible for the drastic decline of the peregrine falcon in the United States. This bird is being studied at the Patuxent Wildlife Research Center, Laurel, Maryland.*

14–53 *Newly hatched bald eagle in nest. One egg has not hatched. DDT-contamination of the eagle's food chain has caused an eggshell-thinning phenomenon. Sometimes the embryos inside the abnormal eggs are crushed under the weight of the incubating female.*

By 1969, the brown pelican, which eats fish, was virtually laying omelets on its breeding grounds on islands off Southern California, and almost no young birds were being produced. Yet by the mid-1970s, after DDT was banned and industrial effluent containing DDT ceased to flow from Los Angeles, pelican reproductive success had soared by 200-fold. Although still subnormal, the population had stabilized.

The bald eagle and osprey, also fish-eaters, followed similar patterns. By the late 1960s, thin-shelled eggs and low reproductive success had caused severe population declines over large regions, but by 1980 dramatic improvements had occurred.

DDT has come full circle. Years of research described the problem, showed DDT as its cause, and even defined the physiological mechanism. A political decision was made: DDT was banned. Now, a decade later, we are reaping great benefits from that decision. Pollution abatement pays. It would be nice to have made as much progress with other pollution problems.

culate? No one knows for certain. But we can be sure that a substantial amount of this DDT will be either airborne or waterborne (rainborne) back to the United States, where it was produced—back to American streams, farms, and backyards—or it will be transported in the form of foods (fish, rice, bananas, and coffee) imported to the American dinner table.

In August 1974, after two years of hearings, the EPA finally banned the general use of two additional chlorinated hydrocarbons, aldrin and dieldrin, considered by some authorities to be even more toxic than DDT. When administered to mice on an experimental basis, both aldrin and dieldrin have caused cancer and birth defects. The ban provoked the usual stereotyped response from the pesticide manufacturers: "Because there is no real proof of the harmful effects of aldrin and dieldrin on wildlife and man, this action by the EPA is blatantly unfair."

The EPA has also suspended the use of heptachlor, endrin, lindane, Kepone, and toxaphene, all chemical "cousins" of DDT. Another note of concern should be sounded, however. The sharp reduction in the use of these pesticides probably means that they will be replaced with organic phosphorus compounds, which, although less persistent in the environment, are *much more acutely toxic to wildlife and humans.* Paradoxically, the chlorinated hydrocarbon bans and suspensions might actually result in an increasing number of pesticide-related human deaths. In order to prevent this, EPA is insisting that all pesticide applicators have proper training and certification.

Rapid Review

1. Insects may attain pest status because humans have (a) simplified ecosystems, (b) introduced them from abroad to areas where they have no natural predators to keep them in check, and (c) changed cultural patterns that now demand "perfection" in the appearance of fruits, vegetables, and grains.

2. Two major groups of insecticides now being manufactured in the United States are the chlorinated hydrocarbon compounds, such as DDT (banned for use in the United States but still being exported) and methoxychlor, and the organic phosphorus compounds, represented by malathion.

3. The chlorinated hydrocarbons generally have the following characteristics: (a) long persistence in the environment, (b) storage in body fat, (c) harmful effects on the nervous system, (d) ease of dispersion through the environment, and (e) the ability to kill a broad spectrum of species, not just the target insect.

4. Since DDT-resistance was first reported in houseflies in California in 1947, more than two-hundred species of insects have developed resistance to one or more insecticides.

5. The concentrations of persistent pesticides, such as some of the chlorinated hydrocarbons, tends to become progressively greater as they "move" from one trophic level to the next in a given ecosystem. This phenomenon is known as biological magnification.

6. Dutch elm disease is caused by a fungus that interferes with the movement of water from the roots to the leaves. The fungus is transported from diseased to healthy trees by means of tiny elm-bark beetles.

7. In 1975 a large amount of Kepone, an insecticide used mainly abroad, was accidentally released into the James River at Hopewell, Virginia. The Kepone eventually contaminated commercially valuable fish, clams, and oysters in the James River-Chesapeake Bay waters.

8. Estrogen is necessary for the production of normal-shelled eggs. DDT stimulates the liver of contaminated birds, such as eagles and pelicans, to produce certain enzymes that cause a reduction in the level of estrogen in the blood stream. As a result, the birds lay eggs with extremely thin shells.

9. Three major methods for the cultural control of pests include (a) crop rotation, (b) intercropping, and (c) trap crops.

10. Australia's rabbit explosion was brought under control by the introduction of the myxoma virus.

11. Livestock losses caused by the screwworm fly have amounted to $40 million annually.

12. The screwworm-fly infestation in Florida was eradicated in 1958 by a sterilization-and-release program launched by the USDA.

13. The gypsy moth was accidentally introduced to the United States from Europe in 1869, when some of the insects escaped from a laboratory at Medford, Massachusetts. The insect has spread westward to Wisconsin and south to Alabama. Infestations have been partly controlled with the use of gyplure, a synthetic sex attractant.

14. Many authorities believe that the most effective long-term control of insects will be integrated pest management (IPM), which employs biological and cultural, as well as chemical, methods of control.

15. During the Vietnam War the United States conducted a defoliation program in order to reduce the hazards of ambush. To this end the vegetation was sprayed with Agent Orange, a mixture of 2,4-D and 2,4,5-T. Since then it has been discovered that 2,4,5-T invariably contains an extremely poisonous contaminant known as TCDD. Hundreds of Viet Nam veterans who had been exposed to Agent Orange are now suing the Veterans Administration for illnesses they claim were caused by the TCDD contaminant.

16. Under the Federal Insecticide, Fungicide, and Rodenticide Act, all pesticides manufactured for use in the United States must first be registered and evaluated by the EPA. Then they are classified for general or restricted use. Some may be banned or suspended by the EPA.

17. A number of strategies have been developed to control the Dutch elm disease and save the American elm. Among them are the following: (a) using insecticides, (b) interplanting elms with other species of trees, (c) developing resistant hybrid elms, (d) using wasps that parasitize the bark-beetle larvae, and (e) inoculating the elms with bacteria that inhibit the growth of fungi.

18. A relatively high rate of spontaneous abortions occurred in the Alsea, Oregon, region where forests had been sprayed annually with 2,4,5-T for the purpose of brush control.

19. An infestation of the Mediterranean fruit fly in 1981 threatened California's $14 billion fruit and vegetable industry. Eventually, with the aid of a combination of quarantines, ground spraying, sterilization-and-release programs, and finally aerial spraying, the pest was brought under control.

Malaria
Malathion
Medfly
Methoxychlor
Mutation
Myxoma virus
Nonpersistent pesticides
Organic pesticide
Organic phosphate compounds
Parasitic wasps
Persistent pesticides
Pest
Pest-resistant crops
Pesticide
Pesticide mobility
Pheromones
Predator
Pyrethrum
Resistance to pesticides
Root grafts
Rotenone
Screwworm fly
Sex attractants
Simplified ecosystem
Spontaneous abortions
Sterilization
2,4-D
2,4,5-T
TCDD
Tilapia
Trap crops
Vedalia beetle
Vietnam defoliation program

Key Words and Phrases

Acetylcholine
Agent Orange
Aldrin
Allied Chemical Company
Aquatic weeds
Australian rabbits
Bald eagle
Biological control
Biological magnification
Bugnet
Chlorinated hydrocarbon
Codistillation
Confusion technique
Cotton boll weevil
Cottony cushion scale
Crop rotation
Cultural control
DDT
Dieldrin
Diversified ecosystem
Dow Chemical Company
Dutch elm disease

Eggshell thinning
Elm bark beetle
EPA
Estrogen
Fat depots
Federal Insecticide, Fungicide, and Rodenticide Act (FIFRA) (1972)
Fungicide
Genetic variability
Governor Jerry Brown
Gyplure
Gypsy moth
Gyptol
Herbicide
Heterotype
Hopewell (Virginia)
Huffaker project
Inorganic pesticide
Insecticide
Integrated Pest Management (IPM)
Intercropping
James River
Kepone
Knipling (Edward)

Questions and Topics for Discussion

1. Explain how the use of insecticides can actually favor insects, the very targets they are supposed to "hit," and threaten carnivores and other higher animals, including humans.
2. How does genetic resistance to pesticides occur? Can humans also develop genetic resistance to them? What is the major advantage insects have over humans in this respect?
3. What is *biological magnification*? Give two examples. What are the characteristics of compounds that can be biologically magnified? Explain how the second law of energy is one of the major factors that accounts for biological magnification.
4. How could the widespread use of DDT in the underdeveloped countries cause even greater outbreaks of malaria than before its use?
5. DDT has been banned in the United States except for a few emergency uses. However, we still ship large quantities to other parts of the world. Debate the pros and cons of allowing this practice to continue.
6. When insect predators are used to control pests, it is undesirable to annihilate the pest populations completely in a given area. Explain.
7. Describe three factors that might cause an initially harmless insect to become a serious pest.

8. Briefly describe the major types of pesticides manufactured in the United States before World War II. After World War II.

9. What effect do the organic phosphorus compounds have on the nervous system?

10. Where are DDT molecules stored in the human body?

11. Describe the benefits derived from the use of insecticides.

12. Give several examples of economic damage caused by insect pests.

13. Name five human diseases that are transmitted by insects.

14. Describe the mechanisms by which the molecules of a chlorinated hydrocarbon pesticide sprayed on a cotton crop in Texas may eventually wind up in the body of a Pacific salmon, an Antarctic penguin, or a college classmate of yours.

15. How was California's cottony-cushion-scale problem brought under control in 1888? Why did the problem reoccur in 1947?

16. In which of the following organisms would you expect pesticide buildup in body tissues to be the greatest: (a) fox, (b) cow, (c) shark? The least? Explain your answer.

17. Discuss the classic case of biological magnification that occurred in the Long Island estuary.

18. Discuss the unexpected effects of the Dutch elm disease control programs.

19. Describe the effects of Kepone poisoning on humans.

20. Low levels of Kepone have been found in fish off the Atlantic coast of New Jersey. Trace the pathway of the kepone molecules from the time of their release into the environment until they enter the body of the fish.

21. The shells of bald eagle eggs laid prior to World War II were considerably thicker than those laid in the 1950s. Explain.

22. Why is crop rotation an effective method of insect pest control?

23. How has the expertise of the geneticist been used to advantage in pest control?

24. Why did the European rabbit population explode in Australia? What strategies were unsuccessfully employed to control the rabbits? Which control method succeeded?

25. Discuss the advantages and disadvantages of sterilization as a method of biological control.

Endnotes

1. "Aftermath of Two Environmental Shocks." *U.S. News and World Report* (Feb. 13, 1978), 43–44.

2. "Around the States: Alabama." *Ecology USA* (July 28, 1980), 119.

3. Boraiko, Allen A. "The Pesticide Dilemma." *National Geographic*, **157** (Feb. 1980), 145–183.

4. "California Uses Sex Trap to Combat Gypsy Moths." *Ecology USA* (July 28, 1980), 116.

5. Carson, Rachel. *Silent Spring.* Boston: Houghton, 1962.

6. Chrispeels, Maarten J., and David Sadava. *Plants, Food and People.* San Francisco: Freeman, 1977.

7. Chrysler, K. M. "Medfly Bites Farmers and Jerry Brown." *U.S. News and World Report* (Aug. 31, 1981), 24.

8. Clayson, D. B. *Chemical Carcinogenesis.* Boston: Little, Brown, 1962.

9. Council on Environmental Quality. *Environmental Quality.* Ninth Annual Report. Washington, D.C.: Government Printing Office, 1978.

10. Environmental Protection Agency. *Research Summary: Integrated Pest Management.* Washington, D.C.: Government Printing Office, 1980.

11. Giesel, James T. *The Biology and Adaptability of Natural Populations.* Saint Louis: Mosby, 1974.

12. "Gypsy Moth Damage Could be Greater This Year, Scientists Warn." *Ecology USA* (Feb. 2, 1981), 20.

13. Hodges, Laurent. *Environmental Pollution.* 2nd ed. New York: Holt, 1977.

14. Keeton, William T. *Biological Science.* 2nd ed. New York: Norton, 1972.

15. Kormondy, Edward J. *Concepts of Ecology.* Englewood Cliffs, N.J.: Prentice-Hall, 1969.

16. Kriebel, David. "The Dioxins: Toxic and Still Troublesome." *Environment*, **23** (Jan.–Feb. 1981), 6–12.

17. "Malathion and the Medfly." *Science News*, **13** (July 18, 1981), 35.

18. Marshall, Eliot. "Man vs. Medfly: Some Tactical Blunders." *Science*, **213** (July 24, 1981), 417–418.

19. McMillen, Wheeler. *Bugs or People?* New York: Appleton, 1965.

20. "Mediterranean Fly Threatens California Crops." *Ecology USA*, **10** (Feb. 2, 1981), 19.

21. Miller, G. Tyler, Jr. *Living in the Environment: Concepts, Problems and Alternatives.* New York: Wadsworth, 1980.

22. Moran, Joseph M., Michael D. Morgan, and James H. Wiersma. *An Introduction to Environmental Sciences.* Boston: Little, Brown, 1973.

23. Moriber, George. *Environmental Science.* Boston: Allyn, 1974.

24. "Spectrum." *Environment*, **23** (Jan.–Feb. 1981), 22.

445

25. Stall, Bill. "U.S. Begins Presenting Case Against Herbicide 2,4,5-T." *Los Angeles Times*, 15 March, 1980, p. 17.

26. Stern, Vernon M., Ray F. Smith, Robert Van den Bosch, and Kenneth S. Hagen. "The Integrated Control Concept." *Hilgardia*, **29** (1959), 81–101.

27. Strobel, Gary A., and Gerald N. Lanier. "Dutch Elm Disease." *Scientific American* 245 (Aug. 1981), 56–66.

28. Thomasson, W. A. "Deadly Legacy: Dioxin and the Viet Nam Veteran." *The Bulletin*, **35** (May 1979), 15–19.

29. Turk, Amos, Janet T. Wittes, Jonathan Turk, and Robert E. Wittes. *Environmental Science*. 2nd ed. Philadelphia: Saunders, 1978.

30. U.S. Dept. of Health, Education and Welfare. *Report of the Secretary's Commission on Pesticides and their Relationship to Environmental Health*. Washington, D.C.: Government Printing Office, 1969.

31. Van den Bosch, Robert, and P. S. Messenger. *Biological Control*. New York: Intext, 1973.

32. Wagner, Richard H. *Environment and Man*. New York: Norton, 1971.

33. *World Book Encyclopedia*. "Hessian Fly." Chicago: Field Enterprises, 1976.

Suggested Readings for the Interested Student

Allen, G. E., and J. E. Bath. "The Conceptual and Institutional Aspects of Integrated Pest Management." *Bioscience*, **30** (Oct. 1980), 658–664. This article is written for a sophisticated reader. It describes the concepts of IPM and its institutionalization at the state, regional, and national levels. It also explains the role of the USDA and the EPA, and outlines future prospects.

Boraiko, Allen. "The Pesticide Dilemma." *National Geographic*, **157** (Feb. 1980), 145–182. This article is written for the general public. It is effectively illustrated with graphs, maps, and color photos. It considers the pros and cons of chemical control, and the advantages of biological and cultural control and IPM. It is highly readable.

Kriebel, David. "The Dioxins: Toxic and Still Troublesome." *Environment*, **23** (Jan./Feb. 1981), 6–12. The author is a researcher at Queens College, Flushing, New York, who has written for the nonspecialist. The article is an easily understood treatment of the source, dispersal, and effects of dioxin on humans in Vietnam and in the United States.

Marshall, Eliot. "Man Versus Medfly: Some Tactical Blunders." *Science*, **213** (July 24, 1981), 417–418. This is a nontechnical account of the accidental release of *fertile* flies in an attempt to control the Medfly by means of the sterilization-and-release method.

Strobel, Gary A., and Gerald N. Lanier. "Dutch Elm Disease." *Scientific American*, **245** (Aug. 1981), 56–66. This is a highly readable account of the causes and symptoms of Dutch elm disease, its spread across the United States, and novel biological techniques that attack both the fungus and the beetles that spread it.

U.S. Office of Technology Assessment. *Pest Management Strategies in Crop Protection. Vol. 1*. Washington, D.C.: Government Printing Office, 1979. This authoritative report evaluates the tactics presently used to control agricultural pests in the United States. It was written with the assistance of a panel of scientists, farmers, consumers, and representatives of industry and public interest groups.

Wallis, Claudia. "Bad News for the Birds." *Time*, **118** (Oct. 5, 1981), 52. This is a nontechnical, highly readable account of how, in the spring of 1981, endrin, a highly toxic chlorinated hydrocarbon, was used to control wheat-eating cutworms in several western states. The aftermath was widespread contamination of waterfowl and a near closing of the duck-goose hunting season.

15 Managing Wastes in the Human Environment

The Volume of Solid Waste in the United States

"America the Beautiful" is the world's champion producer of solid waste: Although we represent only 5 percent of the global population we generate a whopping 70 percent of its solid waste — grim testimony to our nation's *technological overpopulation*. In the early 1980s Americans either directly or indirectly generated 108 pounds of waste per person per day, or 20 tons per year — 15 times as much as the average person living in India.

In a message before Congress, former Senator Gaylord Nelson (D–Wis.) remarked: "It must be viewed with a bitter irony that the enduring pyramid for our affluent and productive age may prove to be a massive pile of indestructible bottles, cans, and plastic containers paid for by the collective sweat of the public brow." That statement was founded in fact: each year twenty million Californians alone produce enough trash to form a gigantic mound 100 feet wide and 30 feet high, extending from Oregon to Mexico. Roughly 10 billion tons of solid waste will have been produced in the United States in just the 35 years from 1965 to 2000. Were this to be compacted, it would still fill a sanitary landfill the size of the entire state of Delaware and would cost American taxpayers $0.5-trillion simply to bury the stuff (18).

Types of Solid Waste

WASTEPAPER. One important cause of America's "paper explosion" is the desire, fostered by the packaging industry, to have almost every imaginable item purchased at the store — from apples and screws to soda crackers and flashlight bulbs — packaged in paper, waxed paper, or cardboard. For example, to get to a simple soda cracker an expectant snacker first has to open its cardboard container and then has to strip away *three* layers of wax paper. Of course the crackers are very crisp, but who needs to hear the "crack" of a cracker at 30 yards anyway? Obviously the packaging industry has a good thing going. In the early 1980s the per capita consumption of packaging materials was around 700 pounds per year.

Wastepaper today forms over 50 percent of municipal refuse. The average American disposes of 540 pounds of old newspapers annually. The *reuse*, or *recycling*, of wastepaper in the United States was only 20 percent in the early 1980s, compared to 40 percent in 1945. (Compare this with Japan, where 50 percent of used paper is recycled.)

One hundred fifty acres of spruce, pine, and poplar have to be logged to provide the paper for a *single* Sunday edition of the *New York Times* (11). The recycling of old newspapers obviously would sharply reduce our nation's pulpwood needs. Simply by recycling a stack of newspapers only three

15 – 1 *Slow strangulation? This encounter between a Canada goose and the plastic frame for a six-pack of beer is an eloquent testimonial to the ubiquitous occurrence of litter and solid waste in the ecosystems of both wildlife and humans.*

15 – 2 *"No Trespassing. Do Not Dump Rubbish." That's what the sign says. But the debris accumulates anyway. Even this farmer's irrigation ditch (foreground) is beginning to be clogged with litter. Such solid-waste pollution has been common in the Central Valley of California. This photo was taken in 1971. Recently developed restrictions may end this problem for the irrigation farmer.*

15–3 *Papers, cans, and birthday suit!*

feet high we could save one living spruce or pine. More than 200,000 acres of spruce and pine forest are required to provide the throw away paper plates, cups, and wrappers discarded yearly by the McDonald hamburger empire (11). A whopping 350 million pulpwood trees could be saved if the United States would increase its paper recycling rate from the current 20 percent to a more desirable 50 percent. At the same time, enough electrical power would be saved to satisfy the demands of ten million people (11).

It should be emphasized that we save more than trees in recycling paper. We also save other resources. For each ton of paper recycled we would save 275 pounds of sulfur, 350 pounds of limestone, 60,000 gallons of water, 9,000 pounds of steam, and 225 kilowatt hours of electricity (20). Moreover, we

would sharply reduce the amount of air and water pollution generated at paper mills.

Recent research by the USDA at Beltsville, Maryland, holds promise for a novel use of wastepaper. Researcher David Dinius has found that cattle will actually put on weight if provided with a diet of 10 percent ground-up newspapers and 90 percent molasses, meal, and vitamins. (See Figure 15–4.) Were wastepaper used in this way on an extensive basis, not only would cattle ranchers cut their feeding costs by 10 percent, but substantial inroads would

15–4 *Conversion of newspapers to beef steaks? A steer at the Agricultural Research Center, Beltsville, Maryland, is shown feeding on a mixture of one part ground newspaper and nine parts concentrates, such as molasses, soybean meal, and cracked corn. The newsprint serves as roughage in the diet and does not appear to have any adverse effect on the animals. In the context of this research, old newspapers would have to be regarded as "resource" rather than as waste.*

be made on the wastepaper disposal problem. It would appear, as one joker put it, that "beef cattle are able to digest and assimilate a Sunday edition of the *New York Times* much more quickly than some human readers" (1).

CANS. We junk 55 billion cans per year, from the beer cans spotting the white "shoulders" of Mount Ranier to the soup cans bobbing in the canoe waters of Michigan. Even parts of the California desert sparkle in the sun, reflecting light from millions of cans flung by absent-minded tourists and mindless "hoods" on motorcycles.

15-5 *"Beauty and the waste." Human thoughtless-ness has caused the desecration of this lovely woodland glade.*

The term *tin can* is a misnomer; it is really a *steel* can in tin clothing. A tin coating has been applied because it presents an attractive, shiny surface and does not react chemically with food contents. However, because it is an energy-consuming and costly process to make steel out of iron ore, more tin cans should be recycled. Wouldn't the steel industry save money by reclaiming the steel from the tin can, thus bypassing the mining and iron-ore-smelting process? It would, except for one thing—the tin alloy. The tin alloy is a mixed-metal contaminant that is unacceptable to the newer steel furnaces. Because of this steel, scrap from tin cans is worth only $20 per ton. Not very much is reused.

Aluminum cans are much more intensively recycled. In the early 1980s America's two largest manufacturers of aluminum cans (Alcoa and Reynolds) collected and recycled more than four billion cans annually—roughly 18 cans for each U.S. citizen. (See Figure 15-6.) This represents one of every four aluminum cans manufactured per year. Much of the collecting was done by youth organizations such as the 4-H Clubs, Boy Scouts, and Girl Scouts. In the process those youngsters sharply reduced the litter strewn across the face of the American landscape. Moreover, they earned 17 cents for every pound they collected. Alcoa and Reynolds were delighted; after all, it takes 19 times as much energy to make a can from "scratch"—from the aluminum ore, as to make it from recycled metal. In addition to substantial fuel savings, the aluminum ore was conserved, and air and water pollution were reduced at plant sites.

BOTTLES. The United States junks about 28 billion bottles each year. That glass forms a substantial 6 percent of the average city's solid waste. This is bad news indeed, because a broken beer or catsup bottle will not disintegrate into granules of silicon dioxide for at least a million years. Part of the problem has been the tendency for industry to use nonreturnable bottles. A returnable bottle, on the other hand, makes about nineteen round trips between the bottler and consumer before it is finally discarded. It appears, however, that the deposits required on returnable bottles should be raised. For example, several years ago the Pepsi Cola company of New York distributed 14.4 million bottles that required a five-cent deposit. Within only six months they had all disappeared, apparently ending up in

15-6 *Through publicity and advertising, the Reynolds Metals Company urges individuals and organizations to collect all-aluminum beverage cans and bring them to one of more than 1,000 collection points. At the Reynolds Recycling Center in Los Angeles each can collector is assigned a bin for his or her scrap.*

15-7 *The cans are placed in a hopper and carried along a moving belt through a magnetic separator that kicks out the steel cans. Payment for aluminum scrap is made at the rate of 10 cents per pound.*

15-8 *"Scotch-on-the-rocks." Jumble of cans and bottles discarded by ice fishermen on a Michigan lake.*

trash cans. Perhaps a 25-cent deposit would work better.

At the time of this writing, support seems to be gathering for an eventual nationwide "bottle bill" that would make the use of returnable bottles mandatory. Such bills have proven enormously successful in Norway and Sweden. The number of bottles littering the roadsides of Oregon was sharply reduced—by more than 80 percent—only six months after that state's bottle bill was passed (11). Vermont, Maine, Michigan, Connecticut, and Iowa have followed Oregon's lead in passing such a bill. About a dozen cities have passed mandatory deposit ordinances as well. Environmental activists organized a campaign that climaxed with a cascade of 10,000 empty bottles and cans flowing into the mailroom at the White House. A federal bottle bill can come none too soon. According to the EPA, such a bill would save our energy-hungry nation at least 80,000 barrels of oil annually, or enough electricity to supply the needs of 1.5 million homes (11). In addition, it would save money for the consumer, create jobs, reduce litter, cut our nation's waste-disposal costs by $40 million annually, and reduce our glass consumption by 40 percent, our aluminum consumption by 10 percent, and our steel consumption by 2 percent (11).

If a bottle bill is so highly desirable, you may well ask: "Why in the world wasn't such a bill passed years ago?" The answer is that there is a massive, well-financed lobby against such a bill. The lobby effort is funded by supermarkets, metal workers' unions, most major breweries, beverage bottlers, and steel and aluminum manufacturers. It has used "scare tactics" (such as predictions of unemployment) to intimidate voters so that they reject bottle-bill legislation (11).

New Uses for Recycled Glass. In recent years waste glass has been used as a valuable raw material in producing everything from road surfacing to floor tiles. Consider these few examples:

1. The crushed glass in incinerator residue has been used to manufacture the glass beads in the *reflective paints* used on highway signs.
2. Recently, crushed glass was used to replace sand in the manufacture of *glasphalt*, a surfacing material used on highways, runways, and parking lots. (See Figure 15–9.) It is much more durable than ordinary asphalt. Moreover, because of its

15–9 *An ingredient of "glasphalt." Ground-up glass crystals that look like rock candy are the glass part of the new "glasphalt" (glass and asphalt) pavement laid at Owens-Illinois Inc.'s Technical Center in Toledo in an experiment by O-I and the University of Missouri (at Rolla) to find a new use for discarded glass containers.*

heat-retaining properties it may permit road paving when the weather is too cold to use ordinary asphalt (2). (See Figure 15–10.)
3. Up to 50 percent waste glass has been used by a Milwaukee concern to manufacture *mineral wool insulation.* This material has been used in a number of construction projects, including an industrial building in Fullerton, California (6).
4. Scientists at the University of California at Los Angeles have developed a technique for making highly durable *floor tiles* from a half-and-half mixture of glass and sewage sludge—a nifty way to reduce two serious waste disposal problems simultaneously (6).

JUNKED CARS. As an environmental eyesore a rusty tin can is bad enough, but how about a whole car? How about seven million cars—the number that affluent Americans were junking every year back in the 1960s? The value of a junked car in those days went down to about $5, so it was not worth having it towed to the salvage yard. Countless car owners, especially teenagers, simply left their cars in the street or alley where they had "conked out." Roughly 60,000 cars were abandoned yearly in New York City alone and up to 200,000 in the nation as a whole. Rusting car hulks appeared everywhere: in

15–10 *Workmen spreading "glasphalt" along a busy street in Toledo, Ohio.*

back yards, on vacant lots, along rural roads, and even in cemeteries.

In the last decade, however, a few technological advances have made it feasible to recover the steel from junked cars. Thus, in Colorado, the National Metal Processing Company launched a "car-eating" operation that employed a gigantic hammer mill capable of "feeding" on 500 cars daily. This mill can convert a rusty old Chevy into compact baseball-sized pellets within 60 seconds. There are similar car-eating operations in other cities, such as Minneapolis-St. Paul. As a result of this new technology, steelmakers can dispense with .5 ton of limestone, 1 ton of coke, and 1.5 tons of iron ore, simply by using one ton of the scrap pellets (10). Moreover, substantial savings in energy are made.

Perhaps car manufacturers should bear more responsibility for ensuring that the metals from their products can be recycled easily. It has been suggested, for example, that the federal government might even prod industry toward this end with tax incentives (17). It should be emphasized that a junked car is a veritable gold mine of resources. To make their cars the industry uses 7 percent of all the copper used annually in the United States, 10 percent of all the aluminum, 13 percent of all the nickel, 20 percent of all the steel, 35 percent of all the zinc, 50 percent of the lead, and 60 percent of the rubber (11). Certainly to write off a junked car as "waste" verges on the ridiculous.

TIRES. One beautiful summer's day as I was driving through the picturesque hills of northern Wisconsin, I noticed a column of dense smoke, black and hideous against the azure sky. Curious, I traced the smoky plume to its source: a pile of burning tires in a nearby village dump. What possible excuse could there be to justify such an atmospheric pollutant, let alone the violation of the scenic beauty? Yet in the 1970s this was still a commonplace method for disposing of many of the 100 million tires annually discarded by American motorists.

453

15–11 *Smoke from the Redding, California, city dump, December 13, 1965, resulting from the burning of trash.*

One reason for the problem has been the low rate of recapping: only 20 percent of tires in the United States are recapped, compared to 80 percent in Europe. Experts believe that auto tires can be made to last for 100,000 miles. If all the tires in use in the United States were 100,000-mile tires, and if each were recapped just once so that it would last another 27,000 miles, multiple benefits would result. Our nation would save $35 million in tire waste-disposal costs, as well as 1.7 million tons of rubber and 23 million barrels of oil (11).

A recent technological breakthrough, resulting from the joint research efforts of the U.S. Bureau of Mines and the Firestone Rubber Company, promises that junked tires can be a valuable source of both chemicals and energy. The tires are first shredded into fine particles and then heated to 500° C in a closed chamber from which oxygen has been removed. The resulting products are 1500 cubic feet of natural gas and 140 gallons of oils from a single ton of scrap tire rubber (3).

PLASTICS. Americans live in a plastic world. In the mid-1980s we will be using six million tons of plastic for packaging material alone. The big problem with plastic is that it resists breakdown by bacterial action. In fact, it takes about 240 years for the average plastic bag to deteriorate. True, plastics can be incinerated, but the result could be highly negative. Corrosive fumes of hydrochloric acid are emitted that would not only destroy surrounding vegetation but could be injurious if inhaled by humans. Recent research may be solving the decay-resistance problem. Japanese chemists, for example, have produced a foam plastic (such as is used in egg cartons) that will disintegrate after only six months of exposure to ultraviolet light from the sun (14). Perhaps some day all containers for food will be *edible.* Whoever invented the ice cream cone was certainly far ahead of his time. At present, however, the plastic-waste problem is still of considerable environmental concern.

Waste Disposal

Collection Methods

In most American cities garbage and other trash is hauled by *packer trucks* that are capable of compressing the waste and reducing its volume by 60 percent. However, this method has a number of drawbacks:

1. It is *expensive.* One truck costs about $65,000. Just to collect and dispose of the Sunday edition of the *New York Times* costs about $5.5 million per year. In general the collection and hauling of urban wastes represent 85 percent of their total disposal cost (11).
2. Trash collection is *hazardous* and results in an extremely high rate of injuries, more than for any other industrial activity except logging.
3. The packer-truck collecting system is *undesirable from an ecological standpoint.* After all, it would be very difficult to separate metal, glass, and paper, as well as other "resources," from a land fill once they have been mixed and mashed by packer trucks (11).
4. The 100 or more packer trucks required by a major city would add significantly to *traffic congestion* and to *noise and air pollution.* Many an urban dweller has been rudely awakened by the predawn crescendos generated by the packer-truck and garbage can "combo."

Things are different in Sundbyberg, Sweden, however. There there are no garbage cans and no packer trucks. The town uses a *vacuum* collection method — the most important advance in collection technology since the invention of the wheel. The housewife simply drops her garbage bags, old news-papers, and so on, into chutes that are recessed into the walls of her apartment. The waste is then whisked at 60 miles per hour to a central collection point. Burning the refuse generates sufficient steam heat to provide hot water for all the apartments using the vacuum system. In addition, it may be used to develop steam at electrical power plants or even to thaw out ice or snow on city streets and sidewalks. The wind velocities created are so high that it takes only 20 minutes to collect the waste from 1,000 apartments. Because only one person, with the aid of electronic panels, removes the waste from 2,200 apartments, labor costs are low (9). France, West Germany, and England are also em-ploying vacuum-collection methods. Several hospi-tals use the method in the United States. A similar system has been employed at Disney World outside of Orlando, Florida. Each day 50 tons of waste — hot dog wrappers, popsicle sticks, paper cups, and so on — are whisked at high speed through an un-derground suction-tube network to a collection center. After the accumulated trash has been baled, it is hauled to an incinerator.

Disposal Methods

DUMP. In the days of the ancient Greeks and Romans, in about 500 B.C., the most widely used method of waste disposal was to haul the stuff out-side the city walls and dump it downwind, so as not to offend the sensibilities of the residents. Today, more than 2,000 years later, there are a substantial number of towns in the United States, the most technologically advanced nation on earth, that still make use of the dump. When trash is burned, a medley of gases and odors assaults the nostrils of downwind inhabitants. Until a relatively few years ago, the Kenilworth Dump in Washington, D.C., operated in this manner. As a result, dense clouds of black smoke issuing from the dump drifted past the windows of the Capitol itself. Not only are such dumps eyesores, but they are fine breeding habitats for disease-transmitting flies, cockroaches, mos-quitoes, rats, and mice. Then too, if the soil under-

15–12 *Moab, Utah. Burning dump creates haze and smoke visible through-out town. Such a dump attracts disease-spreading rats and flies. Note auto "carcass."*

lying the dump is highly permeable, the town's water supplies may easily become contaminated with infectious viruses and bacteria. According to federal law, all such open dumps were supposed to be phased out by 1983.

SANITARY LANDFILL. The most extensively employed disposal method today is the sanitary landfill, in which waste is deposited in a trough that has been excavated at the edge of a town. (See Fig. 15–13.) Sometimes a borrow pit or abandoned gravel pit is selected. At the end of each day's dumping, the accumulated trash is compacted and then covered with a layer of soil. The sanitary landfill method is obviously superior to the dump-and-burn system, because it minimizes air and water pollution, restricts fly and rodent breeding, and reduces the possibility for disease dispersal. There also are fringe benefits that may accrue once the landfill's use for solid waste disposal has ended. Some examples follow:

1. Some sites have been converted into *recreational facilities*. A prime example is Mile-High Stadium in Denver, Colorado, where the Denver Broncos professional football team cavorts. Mount Trashmore, a "hill" in Evanston, Illinois, was built up from solid wastes to a height of 60 feet. It was then converted into a recreational area replete with baseball fields, tennis courts, and toboggan runs. Because it is becoming progressively more difficult and expensive for municipalities to acquire suitable landfill sites, per-

haps more trash hills, or even whole "mountain ranges," may be built in the future.
2. Landfills have also had *landscaping value*. In England, for example, the "hills" formed by the soil-and-vegetation-mantled waste have added interest to an otherwise flat, monotonous terrain.
3. Former landfill sites have been converted to *educational parks* where urban youngsters are provided the opportunity to study wildlife and ecology.
4. Landfill was useful in the *reclamation of strip-mined areas* in Maryland. Waste was transported from 87 roadside dumps to an abandoned strip-mine site characterized by gullies more than fifty feet deep. After the gullies were filled with the waste, the site was covered with a layer of soil. Not only was the original beauty of the area restored to some degree, but acid mine drainage was curbed because of soil compaction, proper grading, and the strategic placement of drainage canals.

THE DISADVANTAGES OF LANDFILLS. One big drawback to landfills is that *they require large acreages of land*. For example, a town of 10,000 people generates so much trash that a single year's accumulation would cover a whole acre to a depth of 10 feet. Gravel pits, abandoned stone quarries, marshes, and "waste" areas are rapidly being filled up in major urban regions such as New York City, Philadelphia, Chicago, and San Francisco. Former landfill operations on the edge of San Francisco Bay

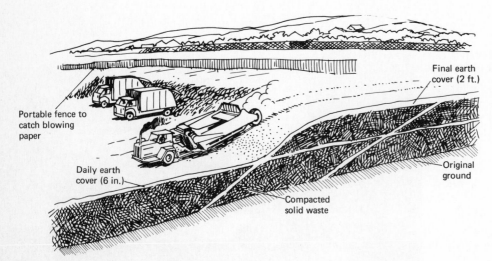

Portable fence to catch blowing paper

Daily earth cover (6 in.)

Compacted solid waste

Final earth cover (2 ft.)

Original ground

15–13 *Sanitary landfill operation. The bulldozer spreads and compacts solid wastes. The scraper (foreground) is used to haul the cover material at the end of the day's operations. Note the portable fence that catches any blowing debris.*

15–14 *Role of the subsurface in determining the movement of leached materials from a landfill. (A) Subsurface is permeable; leached material moves freely. (B) Subsurface is impermeable; leached materials remain in place. (C) Fractured rock underlies subsurface; leached materials move quickly once they reach the fractured-rock zone. (D) Slanting rock aquifer underlies subsurface; leached materials move quickly into aquifer and contaminate drinking water system for nearby community.*

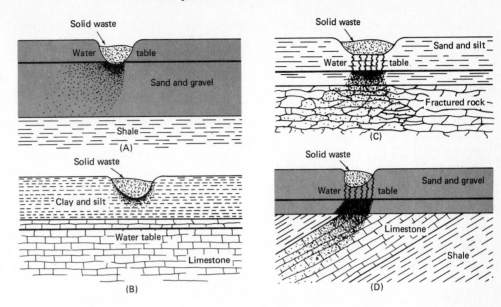

have caused a reduction of the Bay itself, as well as adverse effects on shipping, marine life, and aesthetics.

Despite its name, a "sanitary" landfill may be the *cause of disease outbreaks* within a community. For example, if the soil or rock below the compacted refuse is highly permeable (sand or limestone), it is possible for disease-causing organisms (viruses and bacteria) to be transported downward by percolating water. Eventually those organisms may contaminate an aquifer from which the nearby community had been obtaining its drinking water. (See Figure 15–14.) Another problem is the *production of methane—a potentially explosive gas.* It is generated when organic refuse (garbage) is decomposed by bacterial activity. Ordinarily, the amount of methane produced, which is greatest during the first two years of operation, is no cause for concern. However, if large concentrations accumulate, the possibility exists for an explosion that could be highly destructive to homes built on or adjacent to the site.

COMPOSTING. Composting is a disposal process by which aerobic (oxygen using) bacteria and fungi decompose organic waste to produce a stable humuslike material. The day's garbage (apple cores, bread crusts, corn cobs, grass clippings, and so on) is dumped into a backyard pit. This material can be then spread out, moistened slightly, and covered with a thin layer of soil. The heat of decomposition rises to about 150° F within a few days, sufficient to

destroy any disease-causing bacteria that might be present. After about four months, the end product is a humuslike material that is a valuable soil conditioner; it reduces erosion and promotes aeration and drainage. Organic wastes for composting on a large scale can be derived from sewage sludge, slaughterhouse waste, and residues from fruit and vegetable canneries.

In view of the progressive deterioration of American soils and the increasing food requirements of a growing population, it seems that waste composting should be a highly popular disposal method in this country. However, because the final product is relatively low in nutrients, most farmers have preferred to use commercial fertilizers. Another drawback is the necessity of removing noncompostable materials such as plastics, glass, and metals from the waste—a rather costly and intricate process. A number of commercial composting ventures have failed simply because there has not been sufficient agricultural demand for the finished product. However, as the price of fertilizer zooms ever upward, farmers may show more interest. Composting has had much greater acceptance in Europe. In Holland, for example, a single company produces 200,000 tons of compost annually from the waste generated by one million people (7).

INCINERATION. In contrast to the simple, uncontrolled burning of refuse in an open dump, modern incineration techniques involve highly sophisticated technology, as well as effective control of the overall process. There are several basic phases: (1) the burning of waste in a specially designed furnace at temperatures around 1,900° F, (2) the control and removal of atmospheric pollutants from the stack emissions, (3) the recovery and use of waste heat, and (4) the removal of ash residue to a sanitary landfill. Some of the gaseous pollutants may be removed by burning them in a secondary combustion chamber. Up to 95 percent of the fly ash and other particulates can be removed by means of an electrostatic precipitator.

THE ADVANTAGES OF INCINERATION.
1. The incinerator *requires much less land space* than a landfill.
2. Waste *collection is much less costly* than for a landfill because the incinerator can be located much closer to the point of waste generation— in other words, within the town proper.
3. Incineration can dispose of both domestic garbage and rubbish (furniture, tires, metals, mattresses, wastepaper, and plastic toys) without a costly separation process.
4. One ton of organic waste, when properly incin-

erated, will release about 5,500 BTUs of heat— about 35 percent of that released from coal. If the incinerator is provided with water-containing chambers in its walls, steam can be generated from the waste heat and sold for residential or industrial heating purposes. The huge municipal incinerator in Chicago, which consumes 1,600 tons of refuse daily, generates 44,000 pounds of steam per hour. It is estimated that in the 1980s the number of American communities using incinerator-generated steam to produce electricity will increase rapidly (22).

THE DISADVANTAGES OF INCINERATION.
1. Cost. The consumption of a ton of waste by incineration costs roughly *twice* that of landfill disposal.
2. *The emission of corrosive gases.* A variety of highly corrosive gases may be released during incineration, depending on the waste consumed. Hydrogen chloride (HCl) gas is released during the burning of plastic wastes, which contain the chemical *polyvinyl chloride*, or *PVC*. Over a million tons of this material are produced in the United States annually. It is used in such items as

The Resource Conservation and Recovery Act

The major features of the landmark Resource Conservation and Recovery Act include the following:

1. The act gives the EPA authority to control land (solid waste) pollution that is similar to its authority to control air and water pollution.
2. The EPA is given the responsibility to make a national inventory of all open dumps.
3. The open dumping of solid wastes had to terminate in 1983.
4. The EPA has authority to provide financial assistance to the states to develop their waste-management programs.
5. The EPA is charged to establish criteria for hazardous wastes and establish management standards for each type of hazardous waste, from the moment it is released by industry until its final disposal; in other words, the EPA will monitor and control those chemicals from "the cradle to the grave."
6. Sewage sludge was identified for the first time as a form of solid waste. As Sheldon Meyers, former director of EPA's solid-waste-management program stated: "Sludge is prominent among those wastes which we believe can be put to work to convert a problem into an *environmental asset.* . . . Identifying safe, economic, and acceptable means of sludge disposal and *utilization* [use as soil conditioner, for example] is a matter of high priority for EPA" (4).

plastic toys, garden hoses, shoe soles, and rain-coats. HCl gas is released whenever these objects are burned. If the gas reacts with water, it forms highly corrosive *hydrochloric acid*, which can be very damaging to the internal structures of the furnace (22).

However, despite these disadvantages, it seems that more and more communities, especially those with a population of 200,000 or more, will be turning to incineration to solve at least some of their waste-disposal problems. Certainly the increasing cost of suitable landfill sites, as well as their decreasing availability, will make incineration more and more attractive in the future.

PYROLYSIS. Remember how charcoal used to be made? By excluding air from wood or coal and then applying external heat. The modern name for such a process is *pyrolysis*, which means literally "to break down with fire." During this process, in which the waste is heated to 1,650° C (3,000° F), a number of valuable by-products can be recovered. For example, one ton of ordinary municipal refuse could yield up to 2 gallons of light oil, 5 gallons of pitch and tar, 25 pounds of ammonium sulfate, 230 pounds of char, and 17,000 cubic feet of gas (18). The oil, char, and gas, of course, would be usable as fuel. Acetic acid and methyl alcohol may also be recovered. The first major pyrolysis plant in the United States was constructed in Delaware at a cost of $10 million. After the garbage component in the trash coming to the plant is composted, and the valuable metals and glass have been recycled, the remaining waste is pyrolized. The pyrolysis plant in Baltimore consumes about 900 tons of trash daily. The process of pyrolysis releases several valuable byproducts. The methane gas released is burned to produce steam. The steam, in turn, is piped by the Baltimore Gas and Electric Company to downtown buildings for heating purposes. Residues that are mixed with asphalt are used to increase the durability of road surfaces on the streets of Baltimore (7).

Managing Hazardous Wastes

Remember the Tylenol-and-cyanide scare in the fall of 1982? Millions of American suddenly became concerned that a deadly poison might be lurking

15–15 *Whether a given substance is considered a waste or a valuable resource depends on an industry's point of view. Some industries are now selling their "wastes" to other industries for use as valuable raw materials in their manufacturing processes.*

somewhere in their medicine cabinet — a silent but potent killer. That menace was short-lived and is now behind us. On the other hand, a more real and pervasive problem — low levels of poisonous substances in our very food and drinking water — may plague the American public for decades. How about a "shot" of *chloroform* or *benzene* in your breakfast coffee to start off the day? Or how about a little *mercury* to spice up that salmon you caught? Or how about some *PCBs* (polychlorinated biphenyls) to put some zest in your cereal tomorrow morning? Doesn't sound very appetizing, or nutritious, does it?

The source of the problem is the improper disposal of hundreds of millions of tons of potentially harmful wastes over the last few decades. According to the EPA there are roughly 40,000 sites in the United States where hazardous wastes have either been dumped or injudiciously "stored." And about 1,500 of them have the potential for endangering human health. (See Figure 15–16.) Even worse, an estimated 350 sites almost certainly are chemical "time bombs" that may go off and cause a public health disaster, like the one that occurred at Love Canal in Niagara Falls, New York, in the late 1970s. (See Box p. 464.)

By any measure, the chemical industry is "big business." More than 11,500 firms, employing over 1.1 million workers, manufacture more than

Item	Number of Sites	Status of Sites Operating	Status of Sites Inactive	Description
1	32,000 to 50,000	●	●	Estimates of the number of hazardous waste disposal sites in a 1979 EPA sponsored study.
2	1,200 to 2,000 / 22,000 to 34,000	●	●	Two estimates of the number of sites in item 1 which may pose significant health and/or environmental problems.
3	1,400	●		EPA's estimate of the total number of disposal facilities that have applied for and require permits under current rules implementing RCRA.
4	5,000 to 6,000	●		Number of industrial impoundment sites that may contain potentially hazardous wastes identified in a study conducted by EPA in association with state authorities.
5	127	●		Number of commercial disposal sites identified in a 1980 EPA sponsored study.
6	9,000 to 11,000		●	Number of inactive sites that EPA had identified as of April 1982.
7	400		●	Number of sites that can be given a top priority designation for cleanup under Superfund between 1981 and 1985.
8	115		●	Number of sites EPA has designated as being of highest priority for cleanup under Superfund as of March 1982.

15 – 16 *Estimates of hazardous waste sites in the United States.*

55,000 different chemicals that make possible the "high" standard of living we enjoy. The total annual sales of those chemicals is currently about $180 billion — more than 5 percent of our nation's total GNP. Unfortunately, however, about 2 percent of those chemicals are considered *hazardous*. Just what is a hazardous waste? According to the EPA it is any one of the ninety chemicals that it has placed on its "black list." Each one is either flammable, explosive, corrosive, or (like PCBs, chloroform, mercury, and lead) has the potential for causing severe illness or death, damage to chromosomes (resulting in harmful mutations), unwanted abortions, and deformed babies.

How common are these wastes? Disturbingly so. They form roughly 10 percent of all our industrial waste. For example, about 43 million of the 400 million tons of waste generated by industry in 1981 was considered hazardous. The major industrial sources, in addition to chemical plants, are the metals and electroplating industries. (See Figure 15–17.)

Several federal laws deal with the control of toxic substances. Among them are the Federal Food Drug and Cosmetic Act, the Occupational Safety and Health Act (OSHA), the Clean Air Act, the Clean Water Act, and the Resource Conservation and Recovery Act (RCRA). (See Box p. 458.) However, the most basic, comprehensive, and important of them all is the *Toxic Substances Control Act* of 1976, popularly known as TOSCA. Its major provisions follow:

1. The EPA must keep a record of the identity and volume of all hazardous chemicals produced, as well as the name and location of their American manufacturer.
2. The manufacturer must *pretest* all new chemicals to determine their possible effects on humans and wildlife.
3. The EPA may require the manufacturer to test any chemical already in use if the EPA believes that the chemical may pose a hazard to human health and environment. Toxic chemicals that have already been released into the environment and have accumulated in such sites as dumps, landfill, "storage" lagoons, and so on, must be properly controlled and/or destroyed.
4. The manufacture and distribution of PCBs was banned.

It is expected that under TOSCA's mandate the EPA will be reviewing about 800 new chemical

15 – 17 *Hazardous Waste Generation by Industry, 1980.*

Industry	Quantity (Wet Weight in Thousand Metric Tons)	Percent[1]
Chemicals and allied products	25,509	61.9
Primary metal industries	4,061	9.8
Petroleum and coal products	2,119	5.1
Fabricated metal products	1,997	4.8
Non-manufacturing industries	1,971	4.8
Paper and allied products	1,295	3.1
Transportation equipment	1,240	3.0
Electrical and electronic equipment	1,093	2.7
Leather and leather tanning	474	1.1
Machinery, except electrical	322	0.8
Miscellaneous manufacturing industries	318	0.8
Rubber and miscellaneous plastic products	249	0.6
Textile mill products	203	0.5
Printing and publishing	154	0.4
Instruments and related products	90	0.2
Lumber and food products	87	0.2
Furniture and fixtures	36	0.09
Stone, clay and glass products	17	0.04
Total	41,235	100.0

[1]Figures do not add to total because of rounding.

compounds annually. The cost of the premarket screening of a single chemical is considerable, ranging from the EPA's low estimate of about $100 million to a high estimate of around $800 million made by the Manufacturing Chemists Association.

Something like 100 new federally approved chemical dumps will be needed by the mid-1980s simply to accommodate the chemicals designated as hazardous by the EPA (11). The new EPA regulations require that all operators of such dump sites will be responsible for the chemical wastes at their dumps for *three decades after the closing of the site.* This provision should do much to prevent the occurrence of future Love Canals.

Under the Water Pollution Control Act the chemical industry is required to treat hazardous wastes before they are discharged into lakes, streams, and sewage-disposal systems. Predictably, the industry has complained about the enormous costs involved. However, even with such pretreatment the EPA has estimated that the pollution of our nation's waters

with toxic chemicals will increase substantially in the near future. For example, between 1975 and 1990, as a result of chemical manufacture alone, chromium pollution is expected to increase by 170 percent, zinc by 140 percent, and copper by 4 percent (15).

Another important act dealing with hazardous-waste control is the Comprehensive Environmental Response Compensation and Liability Act, known as CERCLA, passed in 1980. Popularly called the Superfund Act, it created a trust fund of $1.6 billion, largely from taxes on manufacturers of petrochemicals and toxic organic chemicals and importers of crude oil. This fund could be used by the EPA to finance emergency cleanups of potentially dangerous chemical dumps and hazardous releases resulting from tank-truck accidents and deliberate illegal spills.

Funds under the Superfund Act were used to clean up areas in Missouri contaminated with *dioxin.* This chemical is accidentally produced during the

15–18 *Groundwater and surface water pollution at ten Superfund sites, 1981.*

Site	Ground-water Problem	Surface Water Problem	Chemical Nature of Problem
1. Commencement Bay, Takoma, Washington	●	●	Heavy metals, synthetic organics, chlorinated hydrocarbons
2. Keefe Environmental Services, Epping, New Hampshire	●	●	Solvents, acids, caustics, metals, pesticides
3. Lipari Landfill, Pitman, New Jersey	●	●	Methanol, benzene, toluene, sylene, isopropanol, butanol, bis (2-chloroethyl) ether, beryllium, mercury
4. McAdoo Associates, McAdoo, Pennsylvania	●	●	Toluene, benzene, xylene, naphthalene, nitrobenzene, trichloroethylene, cyanide
5. Nyanza Chemical Waste Dump, Ashland, Massachusetts	●	●	Mercury dyes, other chemicals
6. Pollution Abatement Services, Oswego, New York	●	●	Polymer gels, plating wastes, metal sludges, paint wastes, laboratory chemicals, picric acid crystals and boron hydride
7. Price Landfill, Pleasantville, New Jersey	●		Benzene, chloroform, trichloroethylene
8. Tar Creek Ottawa County, Oklahoma	●	●	Acid mine drainage, lead, zinc
9. Tybouts Corner, New Castle, Delaware	●	●	Trichloroethylene, vinyl chloride, 1,2-dichloroethane, benzene
10. Northwest 58th Street Landfill, Hialeah, Florida	●		Arsenic, cadmium, chromium, lead, selenium, phenols, halogenated volatile organic compounds

461

manufacture of herbicides and other products. It is one of the most toxic substances known. In laboratory animals it has caused cancer as well as disorders of the liver and spleen. In the early 1970s dioxin-contaminated oil was sprayed on roads at 20 sites about 30 miles southwest of St. Louis, Missouri. The objective was to settle the dust. Soil samples from one site, analyzed in 1983, revealed dioxin concentrations of 300 parts per billion — 100 times the level considered safe by the EPA. Tests conducted by the Center for Disease Control in Atlanta, Georgia, revealed blood abnormalities in 112 of 130 residents of the contaminated area. Eventually the EPA decided the health risk was so great that it tapped millions of dollars from the Superfund to move many of the residents to new housing elsewhere and to clean up the waste.

PCBs in the Human Environment

In 1968 more than 2,000 Japanese became mysteriously ill. Their skin became strangely discolored with brownish blotches. Many complained of deafness and blindness. Sixteen people died. Some intensive sleuthing by puzzled Japanese health officials revealed one common denominator in the illnesses: all the victims had eaten a particular brand of rice oil. The malady therefore became known as the "Yusho," or "rice oil," disease. Chemical analysis of the rice oil revealed that it had been contaminated with PCBs (polychlorinated biphenyls), which were widely used in industry. Babies born to women who came down with the Yusho disease were not only subnormal in weight, but contained low levels of PCBs in their tissues, indicating that the chemicals had been transferred from mother to infant across the placenta.

The Chemical Nature of PCBs

Just what are PCBs? What do they look like? What is their chemical nature? PCBs are colorless, odorless fluids that have a molasseslike consistency. The term *PCB* is an abbreviation for polychlorinated biphenyls, of which there are at least 105 different kinds already contaminating the world's ecosystems. (See Figure 15–19.) The Monsanto Chemical Company of St. Louis, Missouri, was the sole manufacturer of PCBs in the United States. Between 1930 and 1978 Monsanto produced about 750 million pounds of PCBs. Toxicity to humans and wildlife

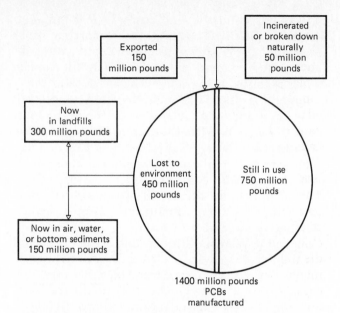

15–19 *Fate of the 1,400 million pounds of PCBs that have been manufactured.*

varies with the type of PCB and appears to be proportionate to the amount of chlorine present in the molecule.

PCBs are the "chemical cousins" of DDT because they have many properties in common. In fact, in the late 1960s, before the techniques of chemical analysis were sufficiently refined, PCBs were apparently mistaken for DDT in soil, water, and body tissue samples. They share the following characteristics: (1) long persistence in the environment because they are not easily decomposed by bacteria, (2) low solubility in water and therefore not easily excreted, (3) high solubility in fat (causing them to concentrate in fatty tissue), (4) biological magnification in the food chains of animals, and (5) ease of dispersal because they adhere to dust particles and evaporate along with water molecules. PCBs have been found in widely diverse ecosystems in such widely separated places as the Arctic, Antarctic, and the Amazon River valley.

Industrial Uses of PCBs

PCBs have been used in the manufacture of a large number and variety of commercial products, including plastics, rubber, and carbonless carbon paper, and as solvents in ink and paint. They are fire-resistant, have high boiling points, and are poor conductors of heat and electricity. Because sparks in electrical devices such as capacitors and transformers could easily start a fire, PCBs are used in them as insulative material. As a result of the environmental problems caused by PCBs and the pressure placed on the manufacturer by environmental action groups and legislators, Monsanto finally decided to restrict their uses to "closed systems," such as transformers and capacitors, where the danger of their escaping into the environment is minimal.

Episodes of PCB Contamination.

1. The initial discovery of the serious problem posed by PCBs was made in New York in December, 1970. High PCB levels were found in chickens that were to become the main ingredient in some Campbell soups. The poultry shipments were stopped, and the USDA ordered the destruction and burial of 146,000 chickens.
2. Some time later federal authorities discovered that a variety of cereal foods, such as shredded wheat, cornmeal, baby food, pancake mixes, and noodle dinners, were contaminated with relatively high PCB levels. Some shredded wheat had 48 times the five parts per million level considered safe by the FDA. Some resourceful detective work on the part of health authorities revealed that the cardboard boxes in which the food was contained was the source of the PCB contamination. The cardboard apparently had been made in part from recycled carbonless carbon paper that had been manufactured with a PCB component.
3. In August 1975 bass and salmon taken from the Hudson River were found to contain more than five parts per million of PCBs — the highest level permissible for commercial fish. As a result, the New York State Commissioner of Environmental Conservation warned the public against eating them. The ensuing investigation revealed

15–20 *The concentration of PCBs in lake trout as a function of age taken from Lake Cayuga in New York State in the early 1970's.*

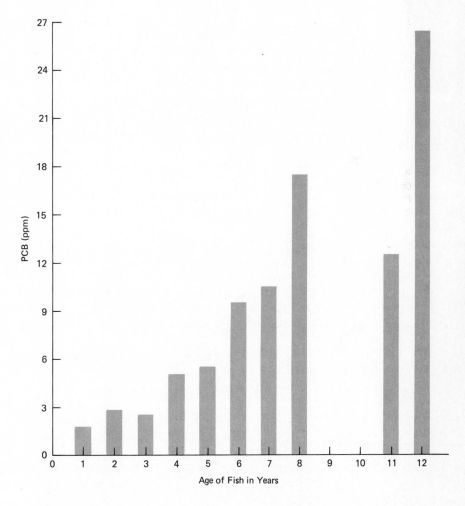

463

The Chemical Time Bomb at Love Canal

The *Love* Canal? That's a misnomer. Maybe it should be renamed the *Hate* Canal, considering the type of emotion generated at the site in the late 1970s. Construction of the Love Canal began more than 100 years ago. The purpose was to provide the rapidly growing community of Niagara Falls, New York, with hydroelectric power and water. Work was abandoned, however, because of economic considerations.

Between 1947 and 1953 the Hooker Chemical Company used the canal site as a dumping ground for 21,000 tons of highly toxic chemicals contained in thousands of steel barrels and drums. After burial the waste was supposedly "sealed off" from the human environment by capping the site with a few meters of clay. In 1953 the city of Niagara Falls threatened to condemn the area, so Hooker sold the land to the city for $1, with the understanding the company would have no further responsibility for it.

Some time later a school was built directly on the site and 239 homes were constructed nearby. More than 700 additional buildings were built in the immediate vicinity. For a few years nobody seemed aware of the chemical time bomb ticking away a few feet below the ground. Then in 1977 unusually heavy rain and snow storms converted the former dump site into a sea of mud. Much of the cap of clay that had sealed off the chemicals was washed away by runoff waters. Through the years corrosion had turned the steel drums containing the chemical wastes into leaking "sieves." The chemical soup began to bubble up to the surface. (See Figure 15–21.) It contaminated vegetable gardens and trickled into basement rooms (11). Residents in the area complained of strange odors. Pets began to die mysteriously. A number of residents were plagued with severe headaches and rectal bleeding. The New York State Health Department became concerned. A study of the health history of Love Canal residents revealed a high incidence of liver, kidney, and respiratory disorders, as well as epilepsy and cancers. In addition the rates of miscarriages and birth defects among Love Canal residents was three times the national average. In July 1978 the New York State Health Department strongly recommended that pregnant women and children under two years of age move out of the contaminated area. In the ensuing investigation *more than eighty toxic chemicals were identified at the site.* They included dioxin, one of the most toxic chemicals made, and 11 others suspected or known to be cancer causing. On May 21, 1980, President Jimmy Carter declared Love Canal an official disaster area. The federal government evacuated 710 families and provided housing for them at a cost of $30 million (11).

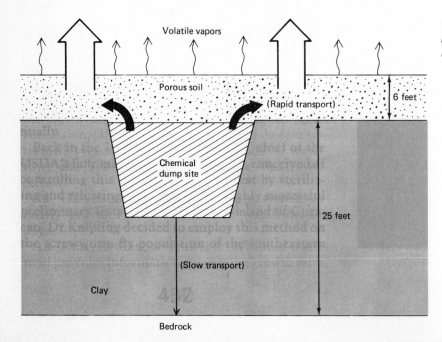

15–21 *Transport of toxic organic chemicals from Love Canal dump site to surrounding homes.*

A massive cleanup of the old dumping site began during the fall of 1978. The vacated homes were boarded up. A tall chain-link fence was erected around the area to prevent looting and trespassing. As might be expected, Hooker Chemical became involved in a number of legal battles. Its position was severely weakened when documents on file with the Securities and Exchange Commission revealed that *the company knew as early as 1958 that their chemical wastes were a serious health hazard to residents of Niagara Falls.* In its defense Hooker Chemical's lawyers have argued that (1) the dumping was legal at the time, (2) there is no proof that the illnesses experienced by the Love Canal residents were indeed caused by its chemical waste, and (3) once it sold the dump site to the city of Niagara Falls it no longer had any responsibility in the matter (11).

that the source of the PCBs in the Hudson River was a *daily* discharge of nearly 50 pounds of PCBs by General Electric over a period of almost two decades. As of 1980 it was estimated that 500,000 pounds of PCBs were still present in the Hudson River. In 1984 the permissible concentration of PCBs in commercial fish, nationwide, was lowered to 2 ppm.

4. The Great Lakes fishery also had a serious PCB problem. Let's focus our attention on just one of the lakes, Lake Michigan. Some of the PCBs have entered the lakes from point sources, such as industries. The Outboard Marine Corporation of Waukegan, Illinois, dumped PCB-contaminated industrial waste into the lake for many years. Interestingly enough, however, an estimated 70 percent of the PCBs were carried over the lake by prevailing winds and then settled into the water. The PCBs adhere to particles in the water and gradually sink, to become part of the bottom sediments. Organisms such as worms, insect larvae, and molluscs, which feed in the bottom ooze, take in the PCBs along with their food. The PCBs then undergo biological magnification as they move from link to link of the aquatic food chain. The PCB contamination in some fish, such as fatty species like lake trout and coho and king salmon, may be 100,000 to *one million* times greater than in the water through which they swim. If PCB inputs to Lake Michigan were stopped immediately, it still might be ten to fifty years before the PCBs would be buried so deeply in bottom sediments that they would no longer be available to trout and salmon via food chains. The PCB concentrations in those fish would drop 70 percent in six years. However, further decreases would occur at slower rates.

HUMAN HEALTH EFFECTS. Suppose that we consumed fairly large numbers of Hudson River or Great Lakes fish with PCB levels of about five parts per million. Or suppose that we occasionally fed on chickens, soup, cereals, and eggs that were contaminated with PCBs. Would our health be adversely affected? This is the overriding concern of the EPA, FDA, and other agencies dealing with the PCB problem. James Allen, a research pathologist at the University of Wisconsin – Madison gave monkeys PCBs in their food three times a week at levels as low as five parts per million in order to match fairly closely the PCB intakes of humans. His findings were that the adult monkeys suffered no ill effects. Interestingly enough, however, pregnant females gave birth to infants that were *subnormal in size*, showed characteristic *blotching of the skin*, and *suffered from behavioral* and *learning disabilities*. Dr. Allen is particularly concerned that thousands of people throughout the United States may be suffering from subtle forms of long-term health damage because they have harbored low levels of PCBs in their tissues for a number of years.

REGULATIONS. The production, sale, and use of PCBs in the United States were finally banned by the EPA in July, 1979. The ban was certainly justified, but it came a little late. After all, a similar ban had already been imposed by Japanese authorities a full ten years earlier. It is fair to wonder why it took our government so long to arrive at the same decision. In 1976 Congress gave the EPA authority to control PCBs under the Toxic Substances Control Act (TOSCA). In 1981 there were more than 66 enforcement actions under the act involving PCBs. More than $500,000 in civil penalties was assessed. In the most important case, a defendant was convicted of the "moonlight" (illegal) dumping of thousands of gallons of PCB-contaminated transformer oil along hundreds of miles of rural roads in North Carolina. The defendant was fined $200,000 and sent to prison for two and one-half years (4).

PCB Disposal. In 1981 the EPA approved two commercial incinerators for destroying PCBs at high temperatures. In that year a commercial incinerator ship, the *Vulcanus*, under EPA permit, burned 700,000 gallons of waste highly contaminated with PCBs in the Gulf of Mexico. It is estimated that the burn achieved the destruction of 99.99 percent of the PCBs. In 1981 the EPA also gave its first approval for the commercial destruction of PCBs by chemical means. By this method the PCBs can be removed from the contaminated oil so that the oil can be reused. The potential hazards resulting from the transport of PCB waste is minimized because the system is mobile and can be brought to the site of the waste (4).

Rapid Review

1. Although the United States represents only 5 percent of the global population, it generates about 70 percent of its solid waste.

2. Wastepaper forms more than half of municipal refuse.

3. The harvesting of 150 acres of spruce, pine, or poplar is required to provide the paper for a single Sunday edition of the *New York Times*.

4. The recycling of paper has many advantages; it (a) conserves trees, (b) conserves fuel, (c) conserves water, (d) reduces air pollution, and (e) reduces water pollution.

5. Because aluminum scrap is worth about $200 per ton, much of it is being collected by scrap dealers and sold to the aluminum industry.

6. It takes 19 times as much energy to make an aluminum can from "scratch" (from aluminum ore) than from recycled metal.

7. A returnable bottle makes 19 round trips between bottler and consumer before it is finally discarded.

8. A nationwide mandatory bottle-deposit law would save the United States 80,000 barrels of oil annually, or enough electricity to supply the needs of 6.5 million homes.

9. Waste glass has been used to manufacture several products, including: (a) reflective highway signs, (b) surfacing materials for highways and parking lots, (c) mineral wool insulation, and (d) floor tiles.

10. About seven million cars are junked annually in the United States.

11. Car manufacturers in the United States use 7 percent of all the copper used in this country, 10 percent of all the aluminum, 13 percent of the nickel, 20 percent of the steel, 35 percent of the zinc, 50 percent of the lead, and 60 percent of the rubber.

12. One hundred million tires are discarded annually in the United States.

13. In most American cities trash and garbage are collected by packer trucks, which are capable of reducing trash volume by 60 percent.

14. Vacuum collection is a highly efficient collection system that has been used in Sweden and was recently introduced into the United States.

15. Open dumps have many negative features, including the following: (a) they are ugly, (b) they are a source of odors, (c) they serve as breeding sites for disease-transmitting insects and rodents, and (c) they contaminate water supplies with disease organisms.

16. The most extensively employed disposal method today is the *sanitary landfill*, in which waste is deposited in a ditch or trough, compacted, and then covered with dirt.

17. Sanitary landfill disposal has several advantages; it minimizes air and water pollution and restricts fly and rodent breeding.

18. Abandoned landfill sites can be used for several different purposes: (a) as recreational facilities, (b) as educational parks (nature study centers), and (c) as landscaping functions.

19. Major disadvantages of sanitary landfill are that (a) large acreages of land are required, (b) wildlife habitat is destroyed by the filling in of marshes and bays, and (c) a safety hazard is created by the generation of potentially explosive methane gas.

20. Composting is a disposal process by which aerobic bacteria and fungi decompose organic waste to produce a stable humuslike material.

21. Compost serves as a valuable soil conditioner that resists compaction, reduces erodibility, and promotes aeration and drainage.

22. Incineration has several advantages: (a) it re-

quires less space than a landfill, (b) collection costs are less than for a landfill, and (c) the heat generated can be used to produce steam to heat homes, stores, and factories or produce electricity.

23. Pyrolysis is simply a new name for an old process called destructive distillation.

24. The pyrolysis of a ton or ordinary municipal refuse could yield (a) two gallons of oil, (b) five gallons of pitch and tar, (c) 25 pounds of ammonium sulfate, (d) 230 pounds of char, and (e) 17,000 cubic feet of gas.

25. The most basic, comprehensive, and significant of all the federal laws designed to control hazardous chemical waste is the Toxic Substances Control Act (TOSCA) of 1976.

26. Full implementation of TOSCA's provisions will be required from industry by 1990.

27. Roughly 100 new federally approved dumps will be needed in the mid-1980s simply to accommodate the 46 different chemicals that have been designated as hazardous by the EPA.

28. New EPA regulations provide that all operators of hazardous chemical dump sites will be responsible for their chemical wastes for three decades after the site is closed.

Key Words and Phrases

Bottle bill	Pyrolysis
Collection	Reclamation of strip-
Composting	mined areas
Disposal	Recycling
Glassphalt	Resource Conservation
Hazardous waste	and Recovery Act
Incineration	(RCRA)
Love Canal	Sanitary landfill
Mineral wool	Superfund Act
Packer trucks	(CERCLA)
Polychlorinated	Toxic Substances
biphenyls (PCBs)	Control Act (TOSCA)
Polyvinyl chlorides	Water Pollution
(PVCs)	Control Act

Questions and Topics for Discussion

1. Discuss what the effect of increasing our nation's recycling rate to 50 percent would have on resource conservation.

2. Discuss the aluminum can recycling program.

3. Discuss the beneficial environmental and economic effects that would result from a nationwide "bottle bill."

4. Describe some of the new uses for recycled glass.

5. Discuss the statement: "A junked car is a veritable gold mine of resources." Is it appropriate? Why or why not?

6. Suppose that all tires in use in the United States were good for 100,000 miles. Suppose further that all those tires were recapped just once. What resource and economic benefits would result?

7. Discuss the disadvantages of the system of collecting waste by packer trucks.

8. Discuss four environmental problems associated with the burning of trash at an open dump.

9. Describe a sanitary landfill operation.

10. Discuss the pros and cons of the sanitary landfill method of waste disposal.

11. Discuss the pros and cons of composting as a method for disposing of waste.

12. Suppose that you were an official of a large town and had to decide between a sanitary landfill and incineration as a method for disposing of municipal waste. What considerations would you have to make before arriving at an informed decision?

13. Identify five valuable by-products that can be recovered from the pyrolysis of municipal waste.

14. List five major features of the Resource Conservation and Recovery Act.

15. What are the characteristics of wastes that have been classified as hazardous by the EPA?

16. What are the major provisions of the Toxic Substances Control Act of 1976?

17. What is the main function of the Superfund Act?

18. What characteristics do PCBs and DDT share?

19. Discuss PCB contamination of the Great Lakes.

20. Briefly describe two approved methods for PCB disposal.

21. What were the circumstances that resulted in the chemical "time bomb" at Love Canal?

22. Do you feel that the Hooker Chemical Company should shoulder 100 percent of the blame for the Love Canal disaster? Why or why not?

Endnotes

1. Benarde, Melvin A. *Our Precarious Habitat.* New York: Norton, 1970.

2. Cailliet, Greg, Paulette Setzer, and Milton Love. *Everyman's Guide to Ecological Living.* New York: Macmillan, 1971.

3. Council on Environmental Quality. *Eighth Annual Report.* Washington, DC: Government Printing Office, 1977.

4. Council on Environmental Quality. *Twelfth Annual Report.* Washington, DC: Government Printing Office, 1982.

5. Environmental Protection Agency. *Environmental News,* **3** (Dec. 8, 1976).

6. "Glass Recycling Makes Strides." *Environmental Science and Technology,* **6** (Nov. 1972), 988–990.

7. Grinstead, Robert R. "The New Resource." *Environment,* **12** (Dec. 1970), 3–17.

8. Hodges, Laurent. *Environmental Pollution.* 2nd ed. New York: Holt, 1977.

9. Johansson, Bertram B. "Whisking the Garbage." *Saturday Review* (July 3, 1971), 40–43.

10. Marx, Wesley. *Man and His Environment: Waste.* New York: Harper, 1971.

11. Miller, G. Tyler., Jr. *Living in the Environment: Concepts, Problems and Alternatives.* New York: Wadsworth, 1975.

12. Moran, Joseph M., Michael D. Morgan, and James H. Wiersma. *An Introduction to Environmental Sciences.* San Francisco: Freeman, 1980.

13. Moriber, George. *Environmental Science.* Boston: Allyn, 1974.

14. Price, F., R. Davidson, and S. Ross, eds., *McGraw-Hill's 1972 Report on Business and the Environment.* New York: McGraw-Hill, 1972.

15. Revelle, Penelope, and Charles Revelle. *The Environment: Issues and Choices for Society.* New York: Van Nostrand, 1981.

16. Rienow, Robert, and Leona Train Rienow. *Moment in the Sun.* New York: Dial, 1967.

17. Segerberg, Osborn, Jr. *Where Have All the Flowers, Fishes, Birds, Trees, Water, and Air Gone?* New York: McKay, 1971.

18. Stanford, Neal. "Atomic Energy Commission Scientists Push Project to Eliminate All Wastes." *Christian Science Monitor* (1969).

19. "Support Piling Up for Requiring Bottle Deposits." *Wisconsin State Journal* (Jan. 20, 1978).

20. Swatek, Paul. *The User's Guide to the Protection of the Environment.* New York: Ballantine, 1970.

21. Turk, Amos, Jonathan Turk, and Janet T. Wittes. *Ecology, Pollution, Environment.* Philadelphia: Saunders, 1972.

22. Turk, Amos, Janet T. Wittes, Jonathan Turk, and Robert E. Wittes. *Environmental Science.* 2nd ed. Philadelphia: Saunders, 1978.

23. Wagner, Richard H. *Environment and Man.* New York: Norton, 1971

Suggested Readings for the Interested Student

Brown, Michel. *Laying Waste: The Poisoning of America by Toxic Wastes.* New York: Pantheon, 1979. This is an outstanding book. The author considers the serious health effects resulting from the contamination of soil, air, and water with hazardous wastes. The Love Canal episode is reviewed.

Brunner, D. R., and D. J. Keller. *Sanitary Landfill Design and Operation.* Washington, DC: US Environmental Protection Agency, 1972. This is a concise and authoritative explanation of the sanitary landfill waste disposal method.

Goldstein, Jerome. *Sensible Sludge: A New Look at a Wasted Natural Resource.* Emmaus, PA: Rodale Press, 1977. This is a superb essay on the beneficial environmental and economic effects of sludge utilization.

Purcell, Arthur H. *The Waste Watchers: A Citizens Handbook for Conserving Energy and Resources.* New York: Anchor Doubleday, 1980. This is an excellent nontechnical blueprint for reducing resource waste.

U.S. Environmental Protection Agency. *Decision Makers Guide in Solid Waste Management.* 2nd ed. Washington, DC: US Environmental Protection Agency, 1977. This is an outstanding treatment of all aspects of solid waste management.

16 Air Pollution

The Breath of Life

Human beings breathe in and out about once every 4 seconds, 16 times a minute, 960 times an hour, 23,040 times per day, 8,409,600 times each year. If a person lives to be seventy years old, he or she will inhale about 75 million gallons of oxygen-containing air into the delicate recesses of the lungs.

In addition to being a vital source of oxygen, the earth's atmosphere is of value to us in many other ways. Without the insulation and heat distribution provided by the atmosphere, we would be subjected to drastic day-night temperature changes completely incompatible with survival. Without an atmosphere, sound vibrations could not be transmitted; the earth would be silent. There would be no weather, no spring rains for crops and lawn, no snow, hail, or fog. Without its atmospheric shield, our planet would not only be more heavily bombarded with meteorites, but would be exposed to potentially lethal radiations from the sun. In summary, without an atmosphere, the Earth would be as lifeless as the moon.

Gases in the Unpolluted Atmosphere

Today, the dry, unpolluted atmosphere has roughly the following composition.

1. Nitrogen (79 percent). Despite our inhalation of 11,000 quarts of nitrogen daily, this chemically inactive gas is not directly usable by us.
2. Oxygen (20 percent). Oxygen is a chemically active gas essential for the respiratory processes of most organisms, including humans, by means of which energy is released to power such biological functions as growth, reproduction, hormone synthesis, nerve-impulse transmission, muscular contraction, perception of stimuli, and even (in humans) thought itself. Fortunately, the world's green plants annually release 400 billion tons of oxygen to the atmosphere in a continuous process of renewal. It has been estimated that were it not for this replenishment, the oxygen supply of the world's atmosphere might become exhausted within 2,000 years.
3. Carbon dioxide (0.03 percent). Although not directly utilized by humans, carbon dioxide (CO_2), a colorless, odorless, tasteless gas, is a raw material for photosynthesis and, therefore, is essential for human survival. It has been estimated that an acre of deciduous forest removes 2,000 pounds of carbon dioxide from the atmosphere annually. The world's green vegetation utilizes an impressive 550 billion tons yearly (14).
4. Inert gases (1 percent). The air also contains negligible quantities of argon, neon, helium, krypton, and xenon, all of which are inert chemically and of relatively little biological importance.

Pollution of the Atmosphere

Natural Pollution

Long before the first white man set foot on American soil, the atmosphere was to some degree polluted, not from man-made sources but from natural causes. Smoke from lightning-triggered forest fires billowed darkly across the land, presumably causing visual and respiratory problems for both Indians and wildlife. Dust clouds occasionally obscured the sun then as now. In May 1980 the massive eruption of Mount St. Helens in Washington released many tons of dust and ash into the air and caused breathing problems for both humans and wildlife for a brief period downwind from the blast. (See Figure 16–2.) A given sample of today's atmosphere may contain a host of natural contaminants, from ragweed pollen to fungal spores and from disease-causing bacteria to minute particles of volcanic ash and salt.

Pollution Caused by Humans

Homo sapiens has been fouling the atmosphere ever since Stone Age people first roasted a deer over an open fire. The smoke smudged some of the otherwise magnificent cave-wall paintings in southern

16–1 *Naturally caused air pollution. A volcanic eruption on Mount Wrangell, Alaska, in 1915, injected many tons of dust and gases into the atmosphere. The particulate matter from such an eruption intercepts sunlight and may have a cooling effect on the global climate.*

France—perhaps the first serious property damage caused by air pollution. In 1306 Parliament passed a law making it illegal to burn coal in a furnace in London; at least one violator was actually tortured for his offense. However, it was not until the industrial revolution that air pollution reached such massive proportions that it seriously affected the health of large segments of society. In 1909 at least 1,063 deaths in Glasgow, Scotland, were directly attributed to polluted air. It was in conjunction with this incident that the word *smog* was coined as a contraction of "smoke and fog" (14). Let us examine the major pollutants that concern us today.

Major Atmospheric Pollutants

Carbon Monoxide. When this writer was in college, carbon monoxide poisoning was usually associated with suicides—the attendant conditions usually being a running car engine and a closed garage. Since then, however, because of the rapidly mounting levels of carbon monoxide (CO) above our city streets and freeway systems, many hundreds of thousands of Americans are suffering from a subtle, unwanted type of carbon monoxide poisoning, not severe enough to cause death, but causing marked effects on human health.

Rather surprisingly, roughly 93 percent of the carbon monoxide in the global atmosphere is derived from natural sources, such as the oxidation of methane (marsh gas), which in turn is formed by the decay of marshland organisms. However, this carbon monoxide does not build up to harmful concentrations because it is soon converted into harmless carbon dioxide. It might reasonably be asked, then, why are we so concerned with carbon monoxide as an atmospheric pollutant? The answer is that the seemingly insignificant 7 percent of the carbon monoxide generated by human activities, largely as the result of the incomplete combustion of fossil fuels, is concentrated in a relatively small volume of air in the world's major cities. In fact, the carbon monoxide concentrations of urban areas must be fifty to one-hundred times greater than the worldwide average (18).

Carbon monoxide forms more than half of all our atmospheric pollution. Over 60 percent of the carbon monoxide generated by human activities has its source in motorcar, truck, and airplane exhaust; 10 percent in the combustion of solid waste; and 10 percent in the gases of industrial smokestacks. (See Figure 16–5.) However, unless stricter control

Day 1   Day 2   Day 3

Mt. St. Helens

Montana

Oregon   Idaho   Wyoming   South Dakota

Nebraska

Colorado

ASH PATH

Kansas

Missouri

Oklahoma

Arkansas

Mich.

Ill.   Ind.   Ohio

Ky.

Tenn.

Miss.   Ala.   Ga.

New York   Penn.

W Va.   Va.

N. Car.

S. Car.

Maine

Vt.   NH

Mass.

Conn.

NJ

Del.

Md.

Daily Progression

16-2 *Shaded area shows approximate path of ashes injected into the air by the eruption of Mount St. Helens, an example of air pollution from natural sources.*

16-3 *Air-sampling operation. A scientist uses this apparatus to analyze samples of the air near Fort Benning, Georgia, to determine types and concentrations of pollutants.*

16-4 *Major pollutants in the air over the United States.*

Major Air Pollutants

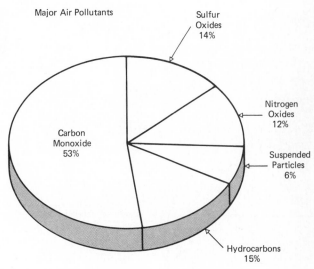

Sulfur Oxides 14%

Nitrogen Oxides 12%

Suspended Particles 6%

Carbon Monoxide 53%

Hydrocarbons 15%

471

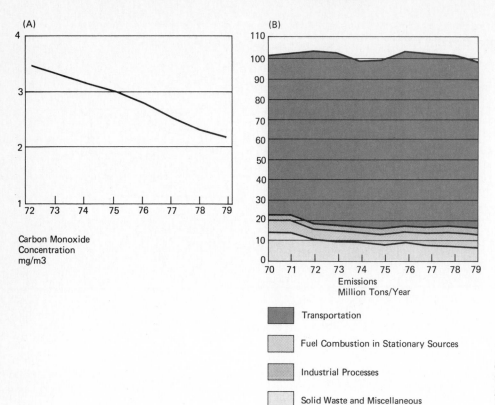

(A)

(B)

Carbon Monoxide
Concentration
mg/m3

Emissions
Million Tons/Year

Transportation

Fuel Combustion in Stationary Sources

Industrial Processes

Solid Waste and Miscellaneous

16–5 *(A) Decline in carbon monoxide concentration in milligrams per cubic meter, 1972–1979. (B) Sources of carbon monoxide emissions, 1970–1979.*

16–6 *(A) Decrease in sulfur dioxide concentrations, 1955–1980. (B) Sources of sulfur dioxide emissions, 1970–1979.*

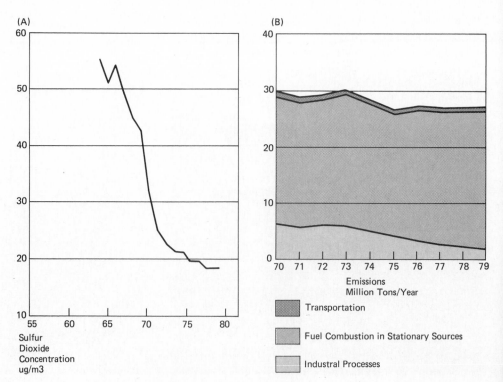

(A)

(B)

Sulfur
Dioxide
Concentration
ug/m3

Emissions
Million Tons/Year

Transportation

Fuel Combustion in Stationary Sources

Industral Processes

472

measures are initiated, carbon monoxide pollution may increase fourfold by the year 2000 (18).

OXIDES OF SULFUR. These gases form whenever sulfur-containing fuels, such as coal, oil, and gas are burned. Coal burning yields 48,000 tons of sulfur dioxide (SO_2) in the United States daily and 1.5 million tons annually in New York City alone. (See Figure 16–6.) As every chemistry student knows, colorless sulfur dioxide stings the eyes and burns the throat. About 1 percent of the population will develop chronic weariness, tortured breathing, sore throat, tonsilitis, coughing, and wheezing when exposed for lengthy periods to the concentrations of sulfur dioxide normally occurring in smog. Because sulfur dioxide may slow down or even halt the cleansing mechanism for the lungs, it contributes importantly to such chronic diseases as bronchitis and emphysema.

HYDROCARBONS. A *hydrocarbon*, as the name suggests, is simply an organic compound that is composed of *hydrogen* and *carbon*. Good examples are methane, benzene, and ethylene. In urban areas humans may generate more than two-hundred kinds of hydrocarbons. Their indirect effects, however, may be more serious: Hydrocarbons will react with nitrogen oxides, in the presence of sunlight, to form *photochemical smog*. Much hydrocarbon pollution results from the evaporation of gasoline from carburetors, crankcases, and gas tanks of cars and trucks. *Methane* is the most abundant of all the hydrocarbon pollutants in the atmosphere. It is produced *naturally* during the decomposition of aquatic vegetation (hence the alternative name *marsh gas*). Some methane, which is the principal component of the natural gas burned in homes and in factories, escapes during its extraction or piping. Methane, a potentially explosive gas, may also be released from landfills, as a result of the decay of garbage and other organic waste that has been buried. Ordinarily the amount of methane released is no cause for concern. However, if large concentrations accumulate, the possibility of an explosion exists that could destroy homes built on the site.

Benzopyrene and at least eight other hydrocarbons have been implicated as possible causes of cancer (12). Some of them occur in cigarette smoke as well as urban smoke. In fact, in terms of these suspected carcinogens, the air breathed in one day by a person living in a badly polluted city would be equivalent to smoking an entire pack of cigarettes.

Benzene is another serious hydrocarbon health hazard. Benzene exposure increases a person's chance of developing leukemia—a form of blood cancer characterized by a dramatic increase in the white-blood-cell count. Benzene, a highly flammable, colorless liquid, forms less than 2 percent of gasoline. However, when gasoline is incompletely burned, considerable amounts of benzene are emitted from the exhaust pipe.

PARTICULATE MATTER. The soot, or fly ash, that issues from industrial smokestacks and blackens backyard laundry or sullies bright yellow sports cars is an example of particulate matter. It can be defined as *small solid particles and liquid droplets suspended in the air*. (See Figure 16–7.) Depending on their size and weight, the particles may remain suspended in the air from a few seconds to several months. Most of the particulate matter is emitted by establishments that use coal as fuel, such as

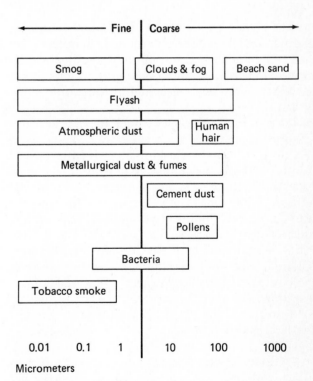

16–7 *Sizes of some airborne particulates. Note that some particles in smog, fly ash, dust, and tobacco smoke are only 0.01-micron in diameter, much too small even to be seen under an ordinary microscope. Perhaps this is one reason why many types of particulates have not yet been identified.*

473

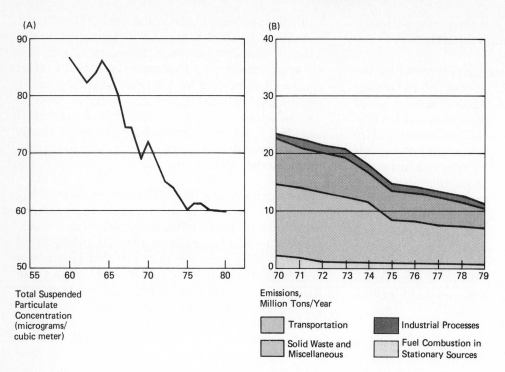

Total Suspended Particulate Concentration (micrograms/ cubic meter)

Emissions, Million Tons/Year

Transportation
Solid Waste and Miscellaneous
Industrial Processes
Fuel Combustion in Stationary Sources

16–8 *(A) Sharply decreasing concentrations of total suspended particulates, 1955–1980. (B) Sources of particulates, 1970–1979.*

power plants, iron and steel mills, and foundries. (See Figure 16–8.) The air around iron mines is frequently reddish because of the large quantity of iron-oxide dust. Twenty-seven million tons of particulate matter are injected into our atmosphere yearly.

Lead, in the form of antiknock fuels, is added to gasoline to enhance its octane rating. We take this lead into our system when inhaling air polluted with motor exhaust. A cumulative poison, it also is ingested with food or water. It can have an injurious effect on the kidneys, blood, and liver. Moreover, it can damage the brains of youngsters, with an ultimately lethal effect. On the basis of lead concentrations in snows at high elevations in the Rockies, Claire C. Patterson, a California Institute of Technology geochemist, has suggested that lead concentrations in humans are one hundred times the level of yesteryear. In 1984 the EPA proposed to reduce lead in gasoline 91 percent by 1986 and eliminate it by 1995.

A variety of other particulates can cause serious illness. Many thousands of coal miners have had their lives shortened because of *black lung disease* —the result of breathing in fine coal dust. In a similar fashion, inhaled cotton fibers cause *brown lung disease* in many textile workers. Minute particles of asbestos fibers derived from the wearing away of

roofing, shingles, insulations, and brake linings have been associated with lung cancer.

OXIDES OF NITROGEN. Nitric oxide (NO) is relatively harmless at ordinary concentrations. It is

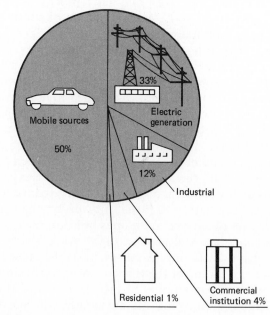

16–9 *Sources of oxides of nitrogen.*

474

formed when atmospheric nitrogen combines with oxygen at the high temperatures generated in the internal-combustion engine. At unusually high concentrations, nitric oxide may have lethal effects, causing death by asphyxiation, because it combines 300,000 times more readily with hemoglobin than does oxygen.

Nitric oxide readily combines with atmospheric oxygen to form nitrogen dioxide (NO_2), a reddish-brown gas with a pungent, choking odor, that may cause a variety of human ailments from gum inflammation and internal bleeding to emphysema and increased susceptibility to pneumonia and lung cancer. Nitrogen dioxide is considered four times as toxic as nitric oxide. Major sources of the oxides of nitrogen are shown in Figure 16–9. Unlike most of our other major pollutants, the levels of nitrogen dioxide have gradually been increasing. (See Figure 16–10A.)

Nitrogen dioxide plays a crucial role in the formation of photochemical smog, the yellow-brown haze characteristic of Los Angeles and other major urban areas. This role of nitrogen dioxide is dependent on its ability to absorb ultraviolet light. At concentrations of nitrogen dioxide normally found in urban air, its direct effect on human health is of little consequence.

PHOTOCHEMICAL SMOG AND OZONE. The yellow-gray haze known as *photochemical smog*,

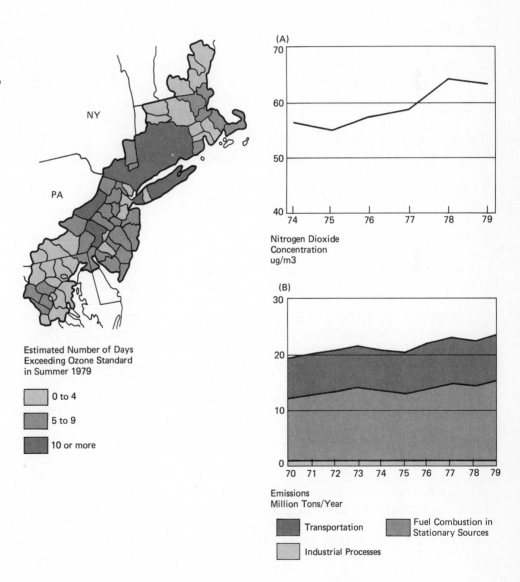

16–10 *(Left) Estimated number of days that ozone standard was exceeded during the summer of 1979 in the Northeast. (A) Nitrogen dioxide concentration trends, 1974–1979. (B) Sources of nitrogen dioxides, 1970–1979.*

Estimated Number of Days Exceeding Ozone Standard in Summer 1979

- 0 to 4
- 5 to 9
- 10 or more

Nitrogen Dioxide Concentration ug/m3

Emissions Million Tons/Year

- Transportation
- Fuel Combustion in Stationary Sources
- Industrial Processes

475

16-11 *Aerial view of smog above New York City.*

which was first recognized in the Los Angeles area, is caused by reactions among hydrocarbons, nitrogen oxides, and atmospheric oxygen in the presence of sunlight. On cloudy days the formation of photochemical smog is somewhat restricted, and at nightfall the process is halted. Various products are formed, one of the most important being *ozone* (O_3). This artificially generated nose-level ozone should not be confused with the layer of ozone that naturally occurs at a height of seven to ten miles. Ozone is severely irritating to human eyes and mucous membranes, as any frequenter of downtown Los Angeles well knows. The EPA keeps careful records of the number of days when ozone levels exceed standards considered safe (Figure 16-10). Temperature can effect the rate at which ozone is produced. Because some fatal traffic accidents may have been caused by ozone-induced tire deterioration, manufacturers now impregnate tires with chemicals that inhibit the effects of ozone on rubber.

At concentrations frequently found in urban areas, ozone will cause nose and throat discomfort after an exposure of only ten minutes. People having prolonged occupational exposure to relatively high levels of ozone have experienced blurred vision, fatigue, recurrent headaches, breathing difficulty, and chest pains. (See Figure 16-12.) It is believed that ozone will cause death by pneumonia in persons in poor health.

Sources of Pollution

Transportation

At present about 150 million motor vehicles in the United States travel an aggregate of one trillion miles yearly. They consume something like 75 billion gallons of fuel a year. From each 1,000 gallons consumed, 1.5 tons of carbon monoxide, 300 pounds of hydrocarbons, and 100 pounds of nitrogen oxides are released into the atmosphere (3). If a

476

16 – 12 *A volunteer is undergoing tests to determine the effects on the human eye of auto exhaust irradiated by sunlight. Pollution-free air is released through one set of tubes and irradiated exhaust-mixed air through the other. The volunteer has no way of knowing which tube carries which type of air. Experiments like this are conducted at the Public Health Service Laboratory to test health effects of automotive air pollution.*

16 – 13 *Jet plane pollutes the air over Washington, D.C.*

16 – 14 *The multibillion-dollar federal interstate highway system has admirably facilitated relatively safe long-distance travel. Unfortunately, however, it also has directly contributed to increased automobile sales, increased motor-vehicle mileage, increased gasoline consumption, and increased atmospheric pollution. The pollutants severely diminish the vitality of vegetables, grain, and trees growing at the highway's edge.*

16 – 15 *Traffic congestion on the Southwest Freeway, Houston, Texas.*

combustion engine were 100 percent efficient, the major exhaust components would be carbon dioxide and water vapor. However, because combustion is sometimes grossly inefficient (especially in some of the "rambling wrecks" chugging down our highways trailing plumes of smoke behind them), roughly two hundred different compounds may be belched from motor exhaust pipes. When we consider all the chemicals added to gasoline, such as rust inhibitors, detergents, deicers, antiknocks, and engine-deposit inhibitors, the chemical mix emerging from an auto's exhaust would have to be complex indeed.

Industry

Foremost among the industries that pour out aerial garbage into the skies over the United States are the coal-burning electrical power plants, which alone emit 15.7 million tons of pollutants yearly, largely from the use of coal. A single ton of coal releases 200 pounds of solids and 48 pounds of sulfur dioxide and nitrogen oxides during its consumption. The refinery industry is also a prime source. With each passing day 12 million barrels of crude oil are processed by our nation's petroleum refineries, with a concomitant injection of particulates, sulfur oxides, hydrocarbons, ammonia, oxides of nitrogen, organic acids, and aldehydes into the air around us. Large ore smelters and metal industries release sulfur dioxide, carbon monoxide, and metallic oxides, as well as lead and arsenic fumes. Chemical industries pollute the air with sulfur dioxide, fluorides, ammonia, hydrogen sulfide, solvents, hydrocarbons, and carbon monoxide. Almost 500,000 tons of sulfur dioxide are released from sulfuric acid plants annually. Massive quantities of dust are produced by the glass, asbestos, and cement industries, as well as in the manufacture of stone products, concrete, and abrasives.

Several air-pollution experts have suggested that the progressive deterioration of air quality that America has experienced might render major cities such as New York, Chicago, Philadelphia, and Los Angeles unlivable by 1990. Such statements have been criticized as being "alarmist." However, air pollution, primarily from an industrial source, actually did cause the death of a European town, Knapsack, Germany, which was officially declared uninhabitable in early 1973. Once the mass exodus of the residents had been completed, the homes of the townsfolk were systematically demolished.

The Influence of Air-Circulation Patterns on Pollution

Thermal Inversion

The buildup of atmospheric contaminants to high levels is facilitated by a meteorological condition known as a *thermal inversion.* Under normal daytime conditions, the air temperature *gradually decreases with altitude,* from ground level to a height of several miles above the earth's surface. With such a thermal pattern it is possible for fly ash, sulfur dioxide, and other contaminants from industrial smokestacks and other sources to disperse either vertically or horizontally, depending on wind currents. However, in the case of a thermal inversion, such dispersion is impossible. Two basic types of inversions are recognized: *radiation* and *subsidence.*

RADIATION INVERSION. At night, heat radiates from the earth's surface into the atmosphere. As a result, both the ground and the air layer next to it cool off rapidly. A condition therefore develops in which a warmer layer of air, perhaps 1,000 feet above the ground, forms a "lid" over the cooler

16–16 *Nature of a temperature inversion.*

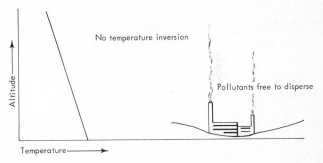

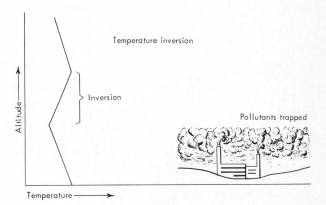

layer beneath it. This effectively prevents any *vertical* mixing of air and airborne contaminants. Pollution buildups, however, need not necessarily occur unless there is little wind present to disperse the pollutants horizontally. Such *radiation inversions* are common but are usually confined to a small area. The inversion usually dissipates by late morning when the earth's surface is warmed by the sun.

SUBSIDENCE INVERSION.   Although it is not as common as the radiation type, subsidence inversion may be of greater duration and may be much more extensive, sometimes forming a canopy over several states. It is formed when a high-pressure air mass (one that is sinking and, hence, warming up) stalls over an area and sinks toward the ground, possibly down to the 2,000-foot level. This type of inversion has caused many of the air-pollution problems in California. (See Figures 16 – 17 and 16 – 18.) During the summer months a warm high-pressure air mass is constantly present above the Pacific Ocean off the California coast. This air mass occasionally moves inland over Los Angeles, Oakland, and other coastal cities and puts a lid on the pollutant-bearing air near the ground that has been cooled by oceanic currents moving along the coast. Coastal California experiences this type of inversion on nine of every ten days in summer (19).

Dust Domes and Heat Islands

Any motorist speeding toward the outskirts of Los Angeles, Chicago, St. Louis, or any other large city has observed the haze of smoke and dust that frequently forms an "umbrella" over the town. This shroud of pollutants, which is known as a *dust dome,* is caused by a unique atmospheric circulation pattern, dependent on the marked temperature dif-

16 – 17   *Aerial view of Los Angeles on a clear day.*

16 – 18   *Aerial view of Los Angeles under smog. The smog is trapped by a temperature inversion at about 300 feet above the ground. The upper portion of the Los Angeles City Hall is visible above the base of the temperature inversion. An inversion is present over the Los Angeles Basin approximately 320 days of the year.*

ferences between the city proper and outlying regions. Although the average annual temperature of a city might be only 1.7° F higher than the surrounding rural areas on a given day, occasionally a city may actually be 27° F warmer and thereby represents a *heat island* (Figure 16 – 19).

As described by Moran, Morgan, and Wiersma (19), several factors contribute to this "heat island" phenomenon:

1. There are many more heat-generating sources in the city than in the rural environment; they include people (with an average body temperature of 98.6° F), motorcars, space heaters, industrial furnaces, and so on.
2. Many of the materials of which streets, parking lots, office buildings, and homes are constructed (brick, concrete, asphalt, and steel) radiate heat much more readily than does, say a field of alfalfa, an oak woods, or a mountain lake.
3. Because water bodies (streams, lakes, farm ponds, potholes, and swamps) are much less numerous per unit area inside the city than in the surrounding countryside, less heat will be lost because of evaporation of water and more will be available for warming up the urban atmosphere.

In any event the urban-rural temperature differential is conducive to an atmospheric circulation pattern in which cool air from the countryside moves into the city to replace warm air rising from the urban center. As a result, smoke dust, nitrogen dioxide, and other aerial "garbage" tend to concen-

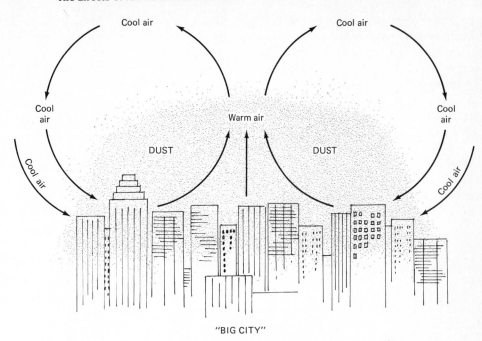

16–19 *Heat-island effect of a city. The air, which is heated up in the city because of large numbers of industrial furnaces, car motors, human bodies, and so on, moves upward and eventually cools off. It may then sink, because of its greater density, move back into the city along with other cool air from the countryside, and be warmed up again. As a result, a circular flow of air occurs. Any dust that is in the air will tend to remain suspended above the city in a mushroom-like formation known as a dust dome.*

trate in a dust dome above the city (see Figure 16–12). *One thousand times as much dust* may be present immediately over an urban industrial area as in the air of the nearby countryside (19).

When the air is calm the dust dome persists; however, when wind speeds get up to eight miles per hour or more the dome is pushed downward and horizontally into an elongated *dust plume.* Such plumes originating in Chicago are occasionally seen from a distance of 150 miles (19).

The Effects of Air Pollution on Climate

One harmful aspect of air pollution is that it may directly modify the intensity of sunlight, temperature, cloud formation, and the distribution, vol-

ume, and acidity of rainfall. Moreover, relatively slight rainfall or temperature changes may disrupt the balance of ecosystems by eliminating key plant and animal species.

ATMOSPHERIC POLLUTION AND SUNLIGHT. Atmospheric pollution can reduce the amount of sunlight that reaches the earth because particulate matter scatters solar radition. For example, Washington, D.C. is receiving 10 percent less sunlight than it did during the beginning of this century when the air was relatively unpolluted. A few years ago smog in downtown Los Angeles reduced the sunlight reaching that city by 10 percent. (See Figure 16–20.) True, these are only two instances, but it is probable that air pollutants cause similar effects in almost every metropolitan area in the United States

16–20 *How bright is the sunshine over Chicago? A solar-radiation-detection instrument is being adjusted atop the John Hancock Center in Chicago. This instrument can aid in the control of air pollution by determining the degree of atmospheric haze present in a given area.*

— and the effects are not limited to urban areas because wind currents disperse particulates widely. The smoke pall of a city, for example, may eventually shroud an area fifty times the size of the urban source (3). Such a reduction of solar energy — the power base of all ecological systems — could conceivably have profound and adverse effects, such as impaired growth in crop plants. With an estimated 13,000 people starving to death somewhere in the world every day, any diminution in foodstuffs would be tragic indeed. Because of darkened skies urban residents are compelled to turn on lights in homes and shops somewhat earlier in the day —

16–21 *"Where did the sun go?" St. Louis, Missouri. The celebrated "Gateway to the West" arch is almost engulfed in smog: November 14, 1966.*

thus resulting in a $16 million increase in our nation's yearly light bills (18).

AIR POLLUTION AND PRECIPITATION. We have previously looked at the conditions that transform cities into heat islands. Warmed urban air combines with the moisture (a by-product of fuel combustion) emitted from industrial smokestacks and motorcars to form clouds above the city. Reinforcing this process are the particulates (soot and dust) — omnipresent in the urban air — that serve as *condensation nuclei* in absorbing tiny moisture droplets. Now, if human-generated air pollution does indeed induce rainfall, we would expect more rainy days from Monday to Friday when factories are operating, and pollutants are generated, than on weekends when plants are closed. This is precisely the case. For example, in Paris, France, the average daily rainfall during weekdays was 31 percent higher than on weekends. Industrial contaminants, such as particulates, generated in Chicago are blown to the general region of La Porte, Indiana, 30 miles to the east, where they trigger considerable amounts of rainfall (3). (See Figure 16–22.)

AIR POLLUTION AND DECREASED AVERAGE TEMPERATURE. Although an increase of carbon dioxide may have a warming influence, an increase in particulate matter may have a cooling effect. Not only may particulates backscatter the incoming rays of the sun, but they may also absorb heat (infrared) rays radiating from the earth's surface into the atmosphere. The cooling effect of particulate matter was impressively demonstrated in 1883 when the island of Krakatoa in the Dutch East Indies partially disintegrated because of a gigantic volcanic eruption that injected countless tons of fine dust particles high into the atmosphere. Over a period of years these particles eventually circled the globe several times. A short time after the eruption, the United States experienced a definite cooling trend; Bostonians, for example, had the rare privilege of throwing snowballs in June. (See Figure 16–23.)

The total annual load of particulates generated directly or indirectly by human activities the world over amounts to 800 million tons. Sources contributing to this particulate load include the combustion of fossil fuels; the razing of old buildings; agricultural activities such as plowing, cultivating, and harvesting; slash-and-burn farming in Asia, Africa,

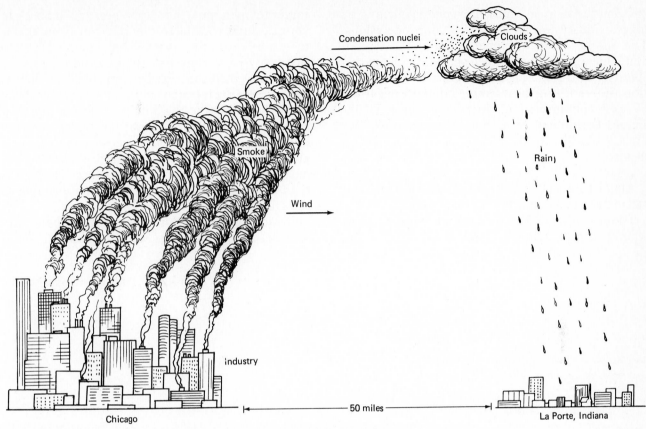

Condensation nuclei — Clouds

Smoke

Wind

Rain

Industry

50 miles

Chicago

La Porte, Indiana

16–22 *Condensation nuclei generated in Chicago are blown eastward and cause increased levels of precipitation in La Porte, Indiana, 50 miles away.*

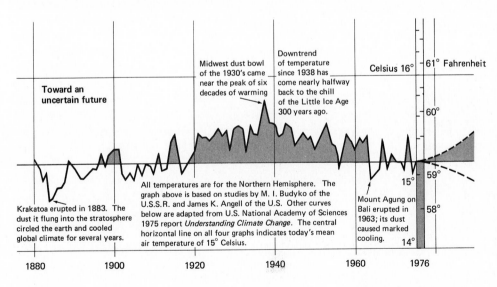

Toward an uncertain future

Midwest dust bowl of the 1930's came near the peak of six decades of warming

Downtrend of temperature since 1938 has come nearly halfway back to the chill of the Little Ice Age 300 years ago.

Celsius 16° — 61° Fahrenheit

60°

15° — 59°

Krakatoa erupted in 1883. The dust it flung into the stratosphere circled the earth and cooled global climate for several years.

All temperatures are for the Northern Hemisphere. The graph above is based on studies by M. I. Budyko of the U.S.S.R. and James K. Angell of the U.S. Other curves below are adapted from U.S. National Academy of Sciences 1975 report *Understanding Climate Change.* The central horizontal line on all four graphs indicates today's mean air temperature of 15° Celsius.

Mount Agung on Bali erupted in 1963; its dust caused marked cooling.

58°

14°

1880   1900   1920   1940   1960   1976

16–23 *Global temperature fluctuations and trends, 1880–1976. The average global temperature is 59° F. The warming trend between 1883 and 1938 can be explained in part as the result of the increasing concentration of heat-trapping carbon dioxide caused by the accelerated consumption of fossil fuels. The sudden temperature drops in 1883 and 1963 were caused by the volcanic eruptions of Krakatoa and Mount Agung, respectively.*

483

and South America; forest fires; debris burning by loggers; dust storms; and strip-mine operations. The annual average temperatures in the United States have gradually declined since 1940. Does this signify that the cooling effects of particulate pollution are overriding the warming influence of carbon dioxide contamination? Just how these trends should be interpreted is not only uncertain, but highly controversial. Much more research is needed.

AIR POLLUTION AND INCREASED AVERAGE TEMPERATURE: THE CARBON DIOXIDE PROBLEM

The Greenhouse Effect. You know what happens when you park your car on a hot summer day and forget to open the windows! When you get back in your car some time later it feels like an oven; that is the *greenhouse effect.* Visible light energy from the sun easily passed through the glass windows. The energy was then converted to infrared heat energy, and because the infrared energy could not pass back through the glass to the outside, it was trapped inside the car. Carbon dioxide molecules act very much like the glass in your car windows or in a greenhouse. They act like an atmospheric trap for heat radiating from the earth's surface. The heat is then radiated back to earth—another example of the greenhouse effect. (See Figure 16–24.)

Carbon Dioxide Buildup in the Atmosphere. Remember the carbon cycle? Since the accelerated use

16–24 *The "greenhouse" effect.*

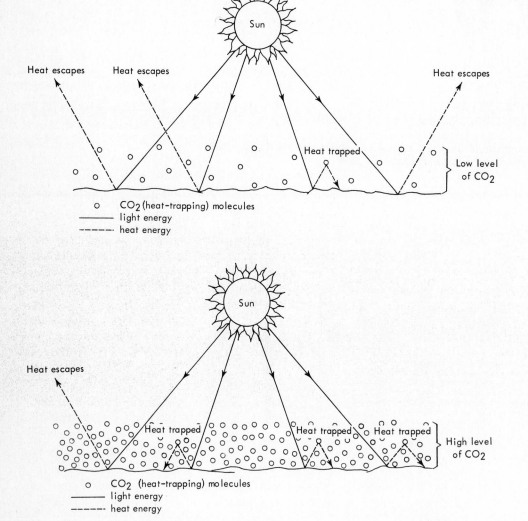

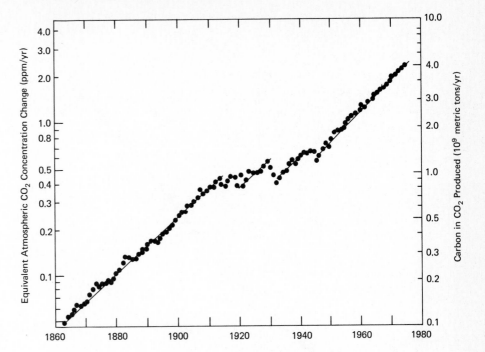

16–25 *The annual world production of carbon dioxide from fossil fuels is plotted since the beginning of the industrial revolution. Except for brief interruptions during the two world wars and the great depression, the release of fossil-fuel carbon has increased at a rate of 4.3 percent per year.*

of fossil fuels, beginning with the industrial revolution in about 1800, the level of carbon dioxide released into the atmosphere has increased by about 20 percent. (See Figure 16–25.) By 2035 the level of carbon dioxide is expected to be twice what it was at the preindustrial level, in around the year 1800. This latter estimate assumes that the rate of fossil-fuel use continues to rise 4 percent annually. It further assumes that the world's vegetation and its oceans continue to remove half of the carbon dioxide released into the atmosphere (18). According to the National Atmospheric and Space Administration (NASA), there should be a statistically significant warming trend worldwide by sometime in the 1980s. Vegetation normally acts as a sink for atmospheric carbon dioxide because it withdraws it during the process of photosynthesis. However, we are now destroying large patches of vegetation all over the world—especially in the tropical forests. This destruction is contributing to the global buildup of atmospheric carbon dioxide. The carbon dioxide buildup has been carefully measured by scientists at Mauna Loa, Hawaii. They have noted an increase in carbon dioxide levels from 316 parts per million in 1959 to 339 parts per million in 1981. Because of this increased level of carbon dioxide the average global temperature is expected to rise three degrees

Centigrade (five degrees Farenheit) by the year 2035. (See Figure 16–26.) However, in the polar regions the warming trend will be even greater—a rise of 7° to 10° C (13° to 18° F).

THE EFFECTS OF CARBON DIOXIDE BUILDUP. The predicted effects of the carbon dioxide buildup and resultant global temperature increase are multiple; a few of them are beneficial, but most of them are harmful to human welfare.

Beneficial Effects. The warming trend should cut fuel bills for heating buildings during the winter season. Moreover, it should increase crop production in some areas because of the extension of the growing season. With more carbon dioxide available for photosynthesis, at least some crops, such as rice, wheat, alfalfa, and soybeans should grow faster and larger.

Harmful Effects. The western two thirds of the United States, including the nation's breadbasket (Kansas and Iowa) will become hotter and drier. The corn belts of Iowa and Indiana will shift northward into Canada where soils are less fertile. Moreover, there will be decreased precipitation and stream flow in many regions which are now agriculturally productive, such as the drainage basins of the Rio Grande, Yang-tze (China), Amu Darya (USSR),

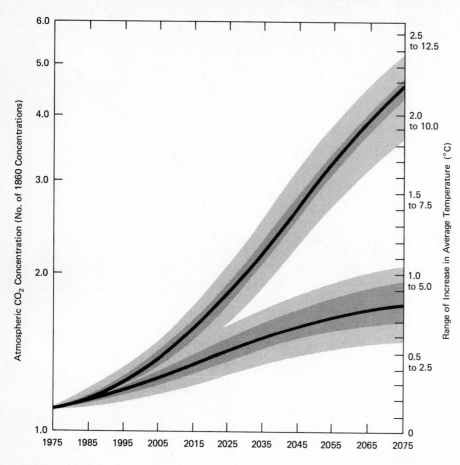

16–26 *The projected growth in atmospheric carbon dioxide and the possible increase in the average surface temperature of the earth are shown for the next 100 years. The range of the increase in average temperature corresponds to 1° to 5° K per doubling of the carbon dioxide concentration.*

Tigris-Euphrates (Middle East), Rhine (Germany), and the Po (Italy). At the same time increased precipitation and serious flooding will occur in the drainage basins of the Mekong (Vietnam) and Brahmaputra (India).

The shift of agriculture northward (in the northern hemisphere) would be disastrous for the malnourished one third of the human race because it would result in a substantial decrease in food production worldwide — at least temporarily. The reason is that the new food-growing regions would not immediately have the necessary multibillion-dollar grain-storage, drainage, irrigation, and transportation systems required for a major agricultural effort (18).

There would probably be a major shift also in the temperature patterns of the oceans — and hence the movements of an oceanic current, such as the Gulf Stream and Aleutian Current. This in turn would cause a change in the migration patterns of valuable food fishes such as tuna and salmon. The effect on

the economy of the American fishing fleet is unpredictable, but it could be highly adverse.

Several species of birds and mammals native to the United States, such as the cardinal, opossum and armadillo, have extended their ranges northward since the beginning of this century, apparently because of the warming trend. Mockingbirds, once considered a symbol of the South, have been found as far north as Ontario, Canada. However, many suitable wildlife habitats have been fragmented by recent human activity, and future range extensions to avoid unsuitable climates may be somewhat restricted.

The increasing temperature in the polar (13° to 18° F or 7° to 10° C) regions may cause the melting of ice caps. The western part of the Antarctic ice sheet could break up within 200 years, according to Terrence Hughes of the University of Maine. As a result, the sea level would rise about 20 feet and gradually flood coastal areas on all continents. In the United States it would cause the exodus and

The Effect of the Carbon Dioxide Buildup in the Atmosphere

Reid Bryson
Director, Institute of
Environmental Studies
UNIVERSITY OF WISCONSIN –
MADISON

The idea that mankind's activities can affect the climate has been with us a very long time. A century ago there was a common saying that the rains followed the plow. In other areas it was said that drought followed the plow or deforestation. While there has been no solid scientific proof of these generalizations, the evidence has grown, over the past quarter-century, that there are ways that vastly expanded populations can affect both regional and global climate.

Two widely discussed cases have been regional climatic modification by cities, and global modification by man-caused increase in the carbon dioxide content of the atmosphere. The former is well established, but debate continues on the latter.

It has been observed that the carbon dioxide content of the atmosphere rose from 260 to 290 parts per million to 330 to 350 parts per million over the past century. This increase has been attributed to the combustion of fossil fuels at ever-increasing rates and/or to the oxidation of stored organic material due to the drain of wetlands, reduction of forests for firewood, and expansion of agriculture.

It is known that carbon dioxide is quite transparent to short-wave radiation (sunlight) but fairly opaque to long-wave or infrared radiation from the earth. This gives rise to the greenhouse concept. The temperature of the earth's surface depends on how much sunlight reaches the surface and the route by and rate at which the absorbed sunlight is transferred to the atmosphere and eventually to space. More carbon dioxide in the atmosphere would be expected to reduce the direct radiative loss of heat from the surface. The temperature of the surface would then be expected to rise to increase the transfer of heat by convection and evaporation and because more heat would be radiated back to the surface by the atmosphere itself. This increased back-radiation by the atmosphere is a consequence of the increased absorption of terrestrial heat by the carbon dioxide in the air.

Up to this point there is little disagreement among atmospheric scientists. When one asks how much global temperatures will rise due to the expected (calculated) doubling of carbon dioxide by the middle of the next century, one gets as many different answers as there are sets of *assumptions* about how the atmospheric machine will respond to these previously unobserved conditions. These assumptions are crucial, since they produce calculated effects that range from slight cooling to a global warming of several degrees Celsius.

The largest number of scientists choose to use a set of assumptions that give a calculated warming of 2° to 3° C, a number which is clearly significant to mankind. However, estimation of the global temperature in A.D. 2050 constitutes a seventy-year forecast. Atmospheric science has no tested capability for making seventy-year forecasts (or ten-year forecasts, for that matter). Nor do we yet have a generally accepted way to identify the onset of such a warming.

Clearly the "carbon dioxide problem" is important. It is just as clear that much more research needs to be done.

abandonment of such cities as Boston, New York, New Orleans, and Los Angeles. The resulting social and economic hardship would be severe.

CONTROLLING ATMOSPHERIC CARBON DIOXIDE. What can be done to slow down or even stop the buildup of atmospheric carbon dioxide? Control strategies are available. All of them, however, require a concerned, dedicated effort by many segments of the global society. First, the destruction of tropical forests, which serve as a sink for atmospheric carbon dioxide, must be stopped. Second, industrial societies must sharply reduce their consumption of fossil fuels, such as oil and coal and switch to geothermal, wind, and solar power. Third, laws must be passed making it mandatory for industrial plants that burn coal or oil to install scrubbers in their stacks to remove carbon dioxide before it is released into the air (18). Fourth, a strenuous, well-organized international approach to the problem is an absolute necessity. Some progress is being made in this direction. For example, at the 1981 meeting of the General Council of the United Nations Environmental Program, a number of nations, including the United States, agreed that the carbon dioxide problem should receive top priority in the UN's efforts to deal with environmental problems of global scope. (See Reid Bryson's guest article for further discussion of this problem.)

The Effects of Air Pollution on Vegetation

Airborne contaminants inflict roughly $1 billion in damage to our nation's agricultural crops, trees, flowers, and shrubs (26). (See Figure 16–27.) The exhaust emissions from the flood of vehicles rushing along our new interstate highway network seriously hamper crop production on nearby farms. It has been estimated that in southern California automotive pollution causes at least $10 million worth of crop damage yearly. Damage has become equally serious along the Atlantic seaboard from Boston to Washington (28).

Among the chemicals causing serious plant injury are ozone, sulfur dioxide, fluorides, hydrocarbons, and herbicides. At least 57 species are susceptible to ozone. Because plants are much more sensitive to this gas than humans are, it frequently causes widespread destruction before we are even aware of the

16–27 Effect of air pollution on potato growth. Plant pathologist Dr. E. H. Heggestad of the USDA's Agricultural Research Service compares two Norland potato plants of the same age during research on air-pollution injury to vegetation at Beltsville, Maryland. The sickly plant on the right was grown in polluted air; the healthy plant on the left was grown in filtered air.

problem. Ozone diffuses through the stomata of plants and kills the palisade cells that carry on photosynthesis. The result is a reddish-brown spotting of the leaf. Ozone has severely damaged the once prosperous flower-growing industry in the Los Angeles area. As little as one part per billion will cause serious injury to tobacco plants after a brief exposure (21). (See Figure 16–28.) Even trees are not immune to ozone.

In the San Bernardino and San Jacinto mountains of southern California, thousands of ponderosa pines have been killed by windborne ozone originating in Los Angeles 60 miles away. Since the 1950s, up to 60 percent of the San Bernardino National Forest's 160,000 pine acres has incurred moderate to severe damage. In the 1970s the smog was destroying about 3 percent of the ponderosa pines annually. According to U.S. Forest Service pathologist Paul Miller, smog concentrations of 0.25-part per million will reduce photosynthesis 66 percent. This in turn reduces the flow of resins under the bark. Because the resins protect the tree to some degree against the ravages of plant diseases and insect pests, smog-triggered forest destruction may be extensive.

During the early years of this century, a mammoth copper smelter at Ducktown, Tennessee, daily belched 40 tons of sulfur dioxide into the air. As a result, over 7,000 acres were completely denuded of vegetation. Thousands of tons of valuable soil were washed from the exposed land, essentially converting the region to a man-made desert. However, in 1913 the smelter initiated a process that converted the waste sulfur dioxide into a valuable by-product, sulfuric acid. Ironically, this by-product became more valuable than the original product, smelted copper. Despite the fact that no additional sulfur dioxide has been emitted since 1913, however, the immediate area around the plant is still desolate and barren fully six decades later (29). At-

16–28 *The leaf of an ozone-sensitive tobacco variety (Beltsville W-3) shows white spots characteristic of air-pollutant damage called "weather fleck." The leaf is shown at the USDA's Research Center, Beltsville, Maryland.*

tempts at artificial restoration have failed. As ecologist Eugene P. Odum has stated, "No one can say how long it will take for natural processes to rebuild the soil and restore the forest, but it will not be within your lifetime, or that of your children" (23).

The Acid Rain Problem

"April showers bring May flowers"—or do they? Many scientists believe that some April showers may cause the death not only of plants, but also of fish, birds, and mammals and even cause serious illness to humans. The problem is *acid rain.*

Where does *acid rain* come from? Surprisingly, a drop of acid rain may originate several hundred miles from where it actually falls to earth. The acid rain problem can be traced directly to atmospheric pollutants such as oxides of sulfur and nitrogen. For example, about 27 million tons of sulfur oxides and 23 million tons of nitrogen oxides are released into our nation's air each year. Oxides of sulfur are released primarily from the smokestacks of coal-fired power plants, smelters, and other industries. In Ohio and nearby states, high-sulfur coal is "king." As a result, Ohio smokestacks alone belch more sulfur dioxide into the air than New York, New Jersey, and the six New England states combined. Nitrogen oxides, on the other hand, are generated primarily by cars, trucks, and buses. Once in the air, the oxides of sulfur and nitrogen may react with moisture to form sulfuric acid (H_2SO_4) and nitric acid (HNO_3), respectively.

Actually, acid rain is only one phase of the more general phenomenon of *acid deposition,* which, in fact, can be either wet or dry. Acid rain, snow, dew, fog, frost, and mist represent the *wet* form of deposition. *Dry* deposition occurs when dust particles containing sulfate or nitrate settle to the earth. Later those chemicals will react with water to form sulfuric and nitric acids. Dry deposition also may occur when gases like sulfur dioxide and nitric oxide come in contact with soil, trees, lakes, and streams and then react with water to form acids.

The pH scale, which ranges from 0 to 14, indicates a substance's degree of acidity or alkalinity. (See Figure 16–29.) A pH of 7 indicates neutrality. Numerical values above 7 indicate alkalinity. For example, lye, with a pH of 13, is extremely alkaline. Values below 7 indicate acidity. Thus, battery acid, with a pH of 1, is extremely acid. Because the scale is logarithmic, rain that has a pH of 4 is ten times as

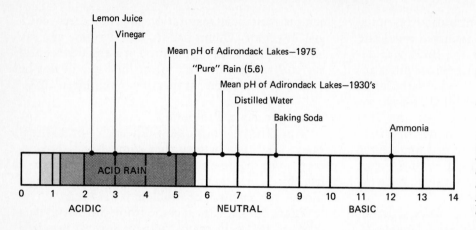

16 – 29 *The pH of acid rain compared with that of "pure" rain and common household substances. Note the sharp decrease in the pH of Adirondack lakes between 1930 and 1975.*

acid as rain with a pH of 5, and one-hundred times as acid as rain with a pH of 6. Rather surprisingly, normal unpolluted rain is weakly acid and has a pH of 5.6. The reason is that carbon dioxide from the air reacts with the water to form carbonic acid.

As seen in Figure 16 – 30 the rain in the eastern United States has become much more acid since 1955. We must remember, of course, that the pH values on the map are average values for an entire year. This trend toward increasing acidity in the northeastern United States appears to be correlated with the increasing volume of sulfur and nitrogen

16 – 30 *Acidity (pH) of North American precipitation. Note the high acidity in northeastern United States and southeastern Canada.*

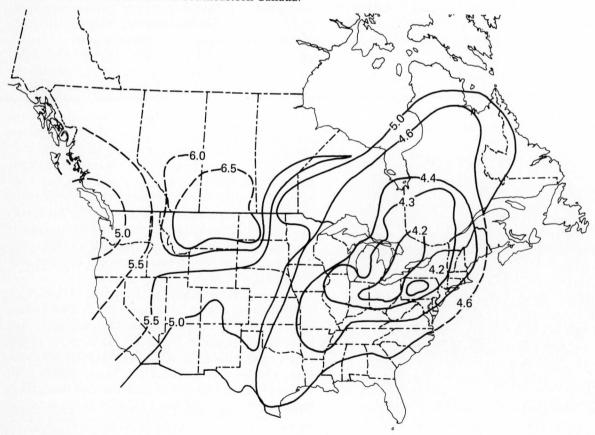

490

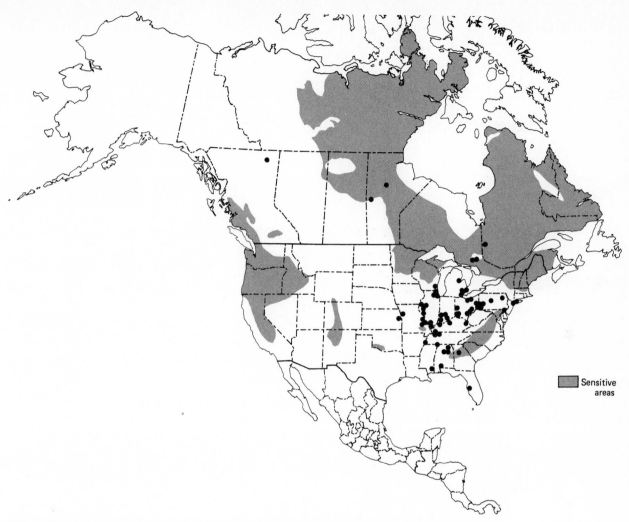

16–31 *The shaded areas are low in natural buffers (e.g., limestone) and are particularly susceptible to acidification. The dots indicate the areas having the heaviest concentration of sulfur dioxide emissions — more than 100,000 tons per year.*

oxides released into the air over the Middle West. In 1979 the average pH for rain in western New York, northern Pennsylvania, and lower Ontario, Canada, was 4.2, many times more acid than normal rain. In Los Angeles a pH of 3 was recorded for a dense fog. The most acid rain ever recorded in the United States fell at Wheeling, West Virginia. It had a pH of 1.4, making it considerably more acid than lemon juice (pH 2.2) and almost as acid as battery acid (pH 1).

Figure 16–31 indicates that some areas of the United States are much more vulnerable to acid rain than others. The most sensitive regions are the eastern United States, northern Minnesota, Wisconsin, and Michigan; certain areas in the Rockies, the Northwest, and the Pacific Coast. The vulnerability of a given region to acid deposition depends on the ability of the rocks and soils in the watershed (or the rocks on a lake bottom) to neutralize, or buffer, the acid. Soils derived from granite, which are therefore low in calcium, are highly vulnerable. Soils derived from limestone, which are therefore rich in calcium, are much more capable of buffering the acid.

Researchers at Colorado State University have found that a given molecule of sulfur dioxide may remain in the atmosphere up to forty hours, whereas a sulfate particle may remain aloft for three weeks. Because of their relatively long air time,

491

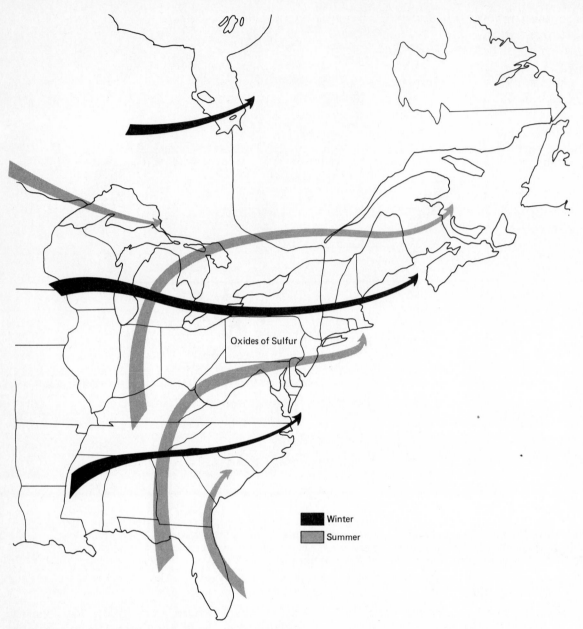

Oxides of Sulfur

■ Winter
▨ Summer

16-32 *Wind patterns relative to acid precipitation.*

these molecules may be wind freighted several hundred miles from their release point. For example, a molecule of sulfur dioxide that originated in Ohio may be transported to New York or New Jersey. (See Figure 16–32.) Those molecules might also be wind blown from the United States into Canada or vice versa. It is estimated that 87 percent of the sulfate in New York and New Jersey, and 92 percent of it in New England, has been brought in by long-

distance transport from outlying areas — most likely the Middle West (30).

The superstack at the mammoth smelter at Sudbury, Ontario, releases 2,500 tons of sulfur dioxide into the air daily (16). It is the largest stack in the world and serves as a symbol of the acid rain problem in North America. Incredibly, this one stack gives off 1 percent of all the sulfur dioxide released *worldwide!* Many superstacks were constructed in

492

recent years so that emissions such as soot, sulfur dioxide, and nitrogen oxide would be diluted before they came down to the nose-and-eye levels of nearby residents. Ironically, by building those extra-tall stacks, the utility people unwittingly facilitated the *long-range* transport of gases and particulates, thus contributing to the widespread acid deposition problem facing the United States and Canada today.

In 1982 a group of environmental activists belonging to the Greenpeace organization (based in Washington, D.C.) zealously protested industry's release of acid-forming chemicals. One of their more spectacular strategies to publicize their cause

was to send six climbers up the vertical face of towering smokestacks in Conesville, Ohio; Madison, Indiana; and San Manuel, Arizona. The daring young men then decorated the stacks with brightly colored banners which read: "For our children, for our land, for our future — Stop Acid Rain. Greenpeace" (9).

EFFECTS ON AQUATIC ECOSYSTEMS.   Acid deposition has seriously disturbed ecosystem functioning in hundreds of lakes in New York and Ontario. (See Figure 16–33.) An estimated 237 lakes in the Adirondacks have a pH of less than 5 — an acidity level considered lethal for many species of fish. In 1982

16–33   *The acidity of the rain that falls on Adirondack lakes in New York and destroys fish and other life has its origin sulfur dioxide emitted from industrial smokestacks in the Midwest.*

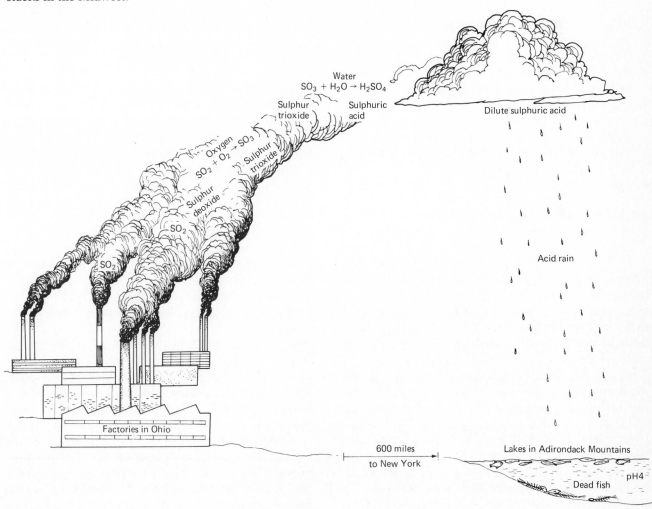

the Office of Technology Assessment made a survey of the acid deposition problem in 27 eastern states. Their conclusions follow:

1. Eighty percent of the lakes and streams in the Northeast and upper Midwest are vulnerable to acidification.
2. Seventeen percent of the lakes and 20 percent of the streams in the 27 states have been damaged by acid rain.
3. Of the 17,059 lakes studied, 2,993 have already been acidified.
4. Of the 117,423 miles of stream investigated, 24,688 have already been damaged. (24)

Scientists further estimate that at least 48,000 lakes in Ontario will be unable to support life in another twenty years at present rates of acid deposition. Among the harmful effects of acid deposition on aquatic ecosystems are the following:

1. Reproduction of many organisms is reduced.
2. Increased numbers of embryos and young are deformed.
3. Important food organisms for fish like crustaceans and insect larvae are destroyed.
4. Heavy metals (aluminum, mercury, and copper) are leached from soils and washed into lakes and streams. Aluminum is toxic to fish at concentrations of less than one part per million. It kills fish by interfering with gill function.
5. The activity of the bacteria of decay is inhibited. As a result, essential nutrients like nitrogen and phosphorus stay locked up in plant and animal remains. Biomass production is therefore reduced, and, of course, fish populations decline.

EFFECTS ON TERRESTRIAL ECOSYSTEMS. Early studies on the effects of acid deposition on terrestrial vegetation indicate reduced rates of photosynthesis and growth as well as increased sensitivity to drought and disease. Growth in a variety of crops such as beans, broccoli, radish, spinach, and beans is retarded. Root systems are damaged by the uptake of aluminum released from the soil. The activity of nitrogen-fixing bacteria is inhibited, thus reducing soil fertility. Nutrients like nitrates may be leached from the soil by acid runoff waters. Trees like spruce, pine, ashes, and birch appear to be especially vulnerable to acid deposition. The adverse effects on valuable timber species like spruce and pine, of course, are very disturbing to the logging industries

of the United States and Canada. In eastern Canada alone, an area highly vulnerable to acid deposition, thousands of people are employed in a forest industry worth $4 billion annually (7). In West Germany, downwind from the smokestacks of the steel industry, beech and spruce forests are suffering serious degradation.

Control Measures

Short-term stop-gap control of the acid deposition problem may be achieved by the use of lime. New York has been liming lakes since 1959. At the present time the state limes seven Adirondack lakes in order to prevent the eradication of brook trout — a highly prized sport fish. Ecologist Voker Hohnen, of the State University of New York, Albany, has suggested applying lime to *entire watersheds*, including forests, rather than just to individual lakes. According to Hohnen, 100,000 acres in Adirondack Park could be limed with converted water-bomber planes at a cost of less than $4 million. By this method acid-susceptible lakes could be placed in a holding pattern until more permanent control measures can be devised (7).

Ann Gorsuch Burford, former EPA administrator, felt that there were so many gaps in our knowledge concerning the acid deposition problem that it would be highly premature to demand that industry sharply reduce its release volume of acid-forming pollutants. In the view of the EPA and the Reagan administration generally, much more research is required before we are in a position where controls, based on a firm foundation of scientific data, can be effectively imposed. As Allan A. Hill, chairman of the Council on Environmental Quality recently stated: "The Administration is well aware of the problem and is committed to conducting an expanded and accelerated acid rain research effort to determine its causes, effects, and possible solutions."

It is true that $30 million was appropriated for research on the acid deposition problem in fiscal years 1981 and 1982 (6). On the other hand, a number of scientists, like acid rain authority Gene Likens of Cornell University, as well as many environmentalist groups like Friends of the Earth, the Audubon Society, and the Sierra Club, argue in this vein: "Research, of course, is needed. But it is not enough. *We also need tough legislation now* which will reduce the volume of acid-forming pollutants being spewed into the atmosphere. When a patient (environment) is dying from cancer (acid rain) the doctor doesn't decide to research the causes of the illness. By the time he learns what causes the cancer, his patient will long since have died and been buried." At the time of this writing, Senator George Mitchell (D–Me.) introduced a bill that would do much to diminish the acid deposition problem. It would require a ten-million-ton reduction in sulfur dioxide emissions in 31 eastern states over the next decade (24).

The Effects of Air Pollution on Humans

It is estimated that the deaths of more than 40,000 Americans each year may be at least partly due to air pollutants. That is about ten times the number of American soldiers who were killed during each year of the Vietnam War.

When most of the air-pollution disasters are studied, a common pattern is revealed: (1) they occur in densely populated areas; (2) they occur in heavily industrialized centers where pollution sources are abundant; (3) they occur in valleys, which might serve as topographical "receptacles" for receiving and retaining pollutants; (4) they are accompanied by fog; it appears that the minute droplets of moisture are absorbed on the surfaces of the pollutants; and (5) they are accompanied by a thermal inversion that effectively puts a meterological lid on the air mass in the valley and contributes to its stagnation (14).

The Donora Disaster

Thirty miles south of Pittsburgh, within a horseshoe-shaped bend of the Monongahela River, nestles the industrial community of Donora, Pennsyl-vania, with a population of 12,000. (See Figure 16–34.) This grimy steel town is almost encircled by hills rising to a height of 350 feet. Factories manufacturing steel, wire, and sulfuric acid, in addition to zinc-smelting plants, are crowded along the river margin for a distance of three miles. On October 26, 1948, a thermal inversion occurred. Soon afterward a fog closed in on the valley. There was hardly a breath of air stirring. The black, red, and yellow smoke fumes that belched from the Donora smokestacks merged to form a multicolored blanket over the valley town. In a short time the pungent odor of sulfur dioxide permeated the air. It was estimated that sulfur dioxide levels ranged from 0.5- to 2 parts per million (14). In addition to sulfur dioxide, the air over Donora contained high levels of nitrogen dioxide and hydrocarbons, which resulted from burning coal to provide heat and electricity for shops and homes. A sluggishly played football game between Donora and Monongahela high schools was cancelled in midplay when several of the gridders complained of chest pains and tortured breathing. Streets, sidewalks, and porches were covered with a film of soot so thick it recorded the footprints of pedestrians. Motorists had to pull off to the side of the road because they could not drive safely. People who had lived in Donora for over half a century got lost in their own hometown. The smog was so dense that it was extremely difficult to see from one side of the street to the other (13). The Donora fire department hauled oxygen tanks around the clock in an effort to provide emergency relief to people experiencing breathing difficulties. Of the total population, roughly 43 percent—5,910 people—became ill, the most prevalent symptoms being nausea, vomiting, and severe headaches; nose, eye, and throat irritation; and labored breathing and

Table 16–1 Major Air-Pollution Disasters

Date	Location	Daily average SO$_2$ levels	Fatalities
Oct. 1948	Donora, Pa.	More than 0.4-ppm (estimated)	20
Dec. 1952	London	1.34-ppm	4,000 (excess)
Dec. 1956	London	0.4-ppm	400 "
Nov. 1953	New York City	0.86-ppm	200 "
Nov. 1966	New York City	0.51-ppm	168 "

Source: National Air Pollution Control Administration, *Air Quality Criteria for Sulfur Oxides.* Washington, DC: U.S. Department of Health, Education and Welfare, January 1969.

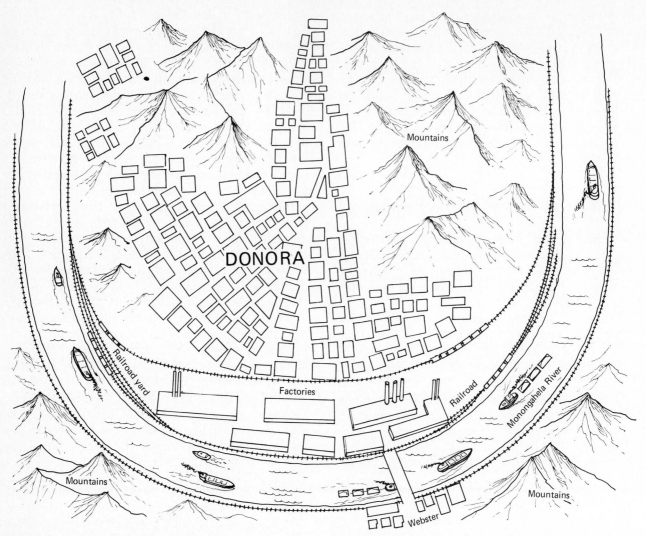

16–34 *Donora, Pennsylvania, the site of America's first well-defined air-pollution disaster, is located in a topographic receptacle rimmed by mountains.*

constriction of the chest. Even pets and wildlife suffered. A veterinarian reported that the dense smoke had caused the death of seven chickens, three canaries, two rats, two rabbits, and two dogs (29).

Evidence of the human loss of life resulting from the air pollution episode is etched on Donora's gravestones. As environmentalist Croswell Bowen writes:

High on the windblown rim of the hill overlooking the bowl-shaped river valley are the town's cemeteries. In St. Dominic's Catholic Cemetery, near the winding road inside the gates, the visitor can see a headstone marking the grave of Iven Ceh: (Born) May 6, 1879, (Died) October 30,

1948. Only the date of his death hints that he figured in the Donora smog tragedy. (2)

But Ceh's death was only the first. One hour after his passing the smog claimed another life, and by 10 A.M. nine corpses were laid out at one mortuary, and one body each at two others (26). The complete death toll for Donora's "Black Saturday" was 17. Two more deaths occurred on Sunday. Then on Sunday night climatic conditions changed. A heavy rain washed some of the pollutants from the air. A breeze drove much of the smoke away. Visibility improved. Breathing became easier. The worst air-pollution disaster in American history was over. Although the smog had persisted only five days, it left twenty deaths in its wake.

Human Illness Caused by Air Pollution

There is substantial evidence that air pollution can kill people. It is most unfortunate, however, that the official cause of death recorded on death certificates does not indicate this fact. For example, instead of stating that the deceased breathed in too much carbon monoxide, sulfur dioxide, nitrogen oxides, or particulates, the death certificate simply states that death was caused by lung cancer, emphysema, or heart attack.

Carbon Monoxide Poisoning

Carbon monoxide combines 210 times more readily with hemoglobin than does oxygen. It therefore tends to *replace* oxygen in the bloodstream. Exposure to 80 parts per million of carbon monoxide for eight hours causes cellular oxygen starvation equivalent to *losing one pint of blood.*

Informed citizens are well aware that smoking is injurious to the health of the smoker. For example, at least one health authority has suggested that we call cigarettes "cancer sticks." But even more discouraging is that smoking may also be injurious to the *nonsmoker.* It has been estimated, for example, that cigarette smoke may contain 300 parts per million of carbon monoxide — sufficient to deactivate roughly *10 percent* of the victimized nonsmoker's hemoglobin [17]. The next time a person gives you the automatic "Mind if I smoke?" as he or she whisks out a cigarette, you can frustrate the attempt by politely responding: "Yes, I do."

The presence of carbon monoxide in the bloodstream of a pregnant woman has been suggested as a possible cause of stillbirths and deformed offspring.

Certain conditions may render some people especially susceptible to carbon monoxide poisoning. They include heart disease, asthma, diseased lungs, high altitudes, and high humidity.

Carbon monoxide may be the indirect cause of many fatal traffic accidents in the United States yearly; the effects of low-level carbon monoxide poisoning can parallel those of alcohol or fatigue in impairing the motorist's ability to control his or her vehicle. (See Figure 16–35.) Because carbon monoxide is colorless and odorless, harmful levels may build up within the car before the driver is aware of them.

Lung Cancer

Several atmospheric contaminants have been strongly implicated as carcinogens — cancer-producing materials. Among them are benzopyrene, asbestos, nickel, and beryllium. For example, cancers have been induced in laboratory animals either by injecting benzopyrene or by implanting it under the skin. The hydrocarbon benzopyrene can get into the lungs from several sources: from the coal smoke issuing from industrial smokestacks or from the smoke issuing from cancer sticks (cigarettes). The smoke generated when fat drippings from a charcoal-broiled steak sputter on the hot coals is a little-suspected source of benzopyrene. Just one smoked steak may contain as much benzopyrene as 600 cigarettes [29].

It has frequently been shown in laboratory experiments on rats and mice that, although two air pollutants (A and B) may not induce cancer independently, cancer *is* induced when an animal is exposed to both pollutants *simultaneously.* Such an effect is called *synergistic.* For example, lung cancers resembling those in humans have been induced in laboratory animals by first exposing the animals to influenza virus and then to *artificial smog.* Tumors have

16–35 *At EPA's Research Triangle Park Laboratory in North Carolina, tests designed specifically to determine the effects of carbon monoxide fumes from automobiles on humans are held, as shown here. The results of this and other tests will be the criteria on which EPA will set national air standards.*

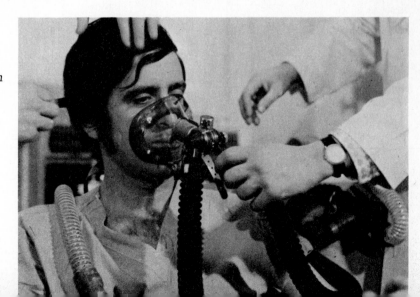

16–36 *Lung taken from patient suffering from "black lung" disease. The lung is shriveled and hardened.*

also been generated in laboratory animals by forcing them to inhale a combination of benzopyrene and sulfur dioxide.

To show a cause-and-effect relationship between benzopyrene and cancer in laboratory animals, of course, does not mean that such a relationship also exists between benzopyrene and cancer in humans. After all, mice are not human. However, both are mammals, and their physiological and cell growth patterns are very similar. Certainly an experiment involving humans would be much more convincing. Fortunately, the results of such an "experiment" are available. For example, researchers have found that the lung cancer rate of men over forty-five living on Staten Island, New York, is 155 per 100,000 in the smoggiest area, as compared to only 40 per 100,000 in the less smoggy region. To research biologists such data strongly indicate a cause-and-effect relationship between atmospheric pollution and lung cancer in humans. The relationship between particulate levels and respiratory cancer rates in humans is shown in Figure 16–37.

Emphysema

When air enters the air sacs, oxygen passes through the membrane of the sac into the blood

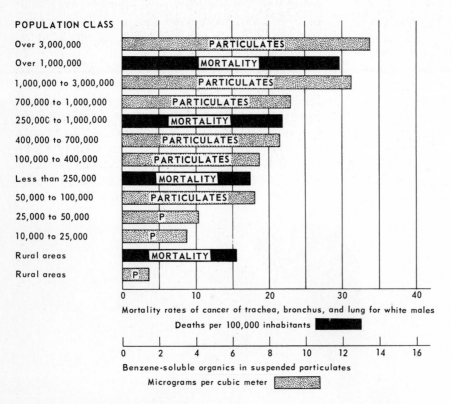

16–37 *Relationship between severity of air pollution and human-mortality rates from cancer in respiratory organs of white males.*

capillaries, while carbon dioxide passes from the capillaries to the air sacs. The total respiratory membrane surface presented by the lung's 300 million air sacs is about the size of a tennis court. In exhalation, the elastic connective tissue in the walls of the alveoli plays an important role. It provides resiliency to the sacs so they can recoil and force air out of the sacs into the air passageway and eventually out of the body. In a person suffering from emphysema, *the elastic tissue is progressively destroyed.* In some cases almost 50 percent of this tissue may be destroyed before the victim is aware

of the problem. As a result, the emphysemic can breathe in easily, thus inflating the lungs. However, it is difficult for such a person to *exhale*. Therefore, the sacs retain more carbon dioxide than they should after exhalation. This carbon dioxide poisons the body. With the next incoming breath the air sac becomes overinflated. This process is repeated many times until the sac "pops" like a burst balloon, resulting in the destruction of both the respiratory membrane and blood capillaries. Eventually, therefore, the area available for the exchange of respiratory gases is greatly reduced. (See Figure 16-38.) In

16-38 *Healthy lung compared with a lung diseased by air pollution.*

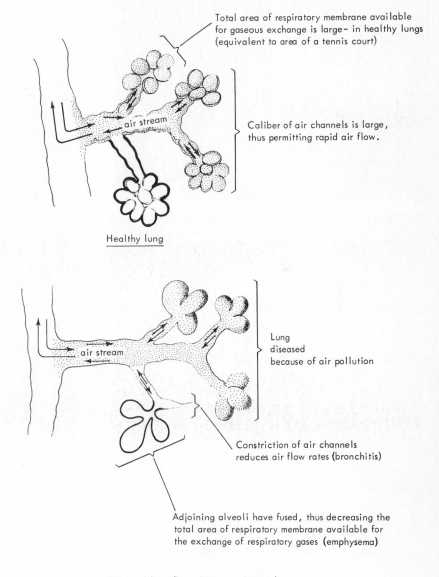

Total area of respiratory membrane available for gaseous exchange is large- in healthy lungs (equivalent to area of a tennis court)

Caliber of air channels is large, thus permitting rapid air flow.

Healthy lung

Lung diseased because of air pollution

Constriction of air channels reduces air flow rates (bronchitis)

Adjoining alveoli have fused, thus decreasing the total area of respiratory membrane available for the exchange of respiratory gases (emphysema)

Diseased lung (bronchitis, emphysema)

16–39 *One of 300 monkeys being exposed to normal, low levels of of pollution of up to seven years' duration in order to determine what harmful effects the pollutants will have on the animals' health.*

a severe case of emphysema, the cells throughout the body tend to suffer from oxygen starvation. To counteract this, the victim's breathing accelerates in a vain attempt to properly aerate the blood. The heart speeds up to dispel the blood more rapidly. The skin of some sufferers turns slightly bluish (cyanosis) as a result of the relatively high level of carbon dioxide. Although the cause of emphysema is unknown, many medical authorities consider air pollution and smoking to be responsible. The emphysema rate is 13 times greater among smokers than among nonsmokers. Evidence suggests that air pollution is an important contributing factor. Indeed, the death toll from emphysema in the United States rose dramatically from a mere 1,500 in 1950 to more than 30,000 in 1970—a twenty-fold increase (31). This mortality increase coincided with increased levels of atmospheric pollution in the areas where the fatalities occurred.

The Pollution Standards Index

In 1976, as a result of the coordinated efforts of a number of federal agencies, a Pollution Standards Index, or PSI, was developed. This index makes it possible to compare the air quality of different urban areas and its potential threat to human health, on a uniform basis. (See Table 16–2.) If the pollutant is at the National Ambient Air Quality Standards (NAAQS) level, it is given an index rating of 100. Any index value below 100 suggests relatively clean air with minimal health effects. However, as the index value rises to about 100, the air is progressively more polluted and the health effects correspondingly severe. An index value of 400 and above suggests that air pollution is "very hazardous." It may cause the premature death of the sick and elderly. Under those conditions, all persons are advised to remain indoors. Such PSI values for various atmospheric contaminants are frequently reported on a daily basis by local newspapers in major urban areas. On the basis of PSI ratings Los Angeles has the most badly polluted air of any city in America. During the three-year period 1978–1980, for example, Los Angeles experienced an annual average of 113 days (or 31.9 percent of the year) in which PSI values indicated that the city's air was either "very un-

16–40 *Air quality in 23 metropolitan areas, 1974–1980, as measured by the Pollutant Standards Index (PSI).*

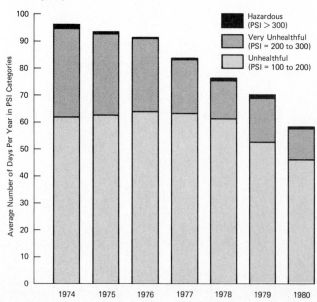

Table 16–2 Pollutant Standards Index (PSI)

Pollutant Levels (in micrograms per liter)		General Health Effects	Cautionary Statements
Index Value	Air-Quality Level		
500	Significant harm	Premature death of ill and elderly. Healthy people will experience adverse symptoms that affect their normal activity.	All persons should remain indoors, keeping windows and doors closed. All persons should minimize physical exertion and avoid traffic.
400	Emergency	Premature onset of certain diseases in addition to significant aggravation of symptoms and decreased exercise tolerance in healthy persons.	Elderly and persons with existing diseases should stay indoors and avoid physical exertion. General population should avoid outdoor activity.
300	Warning	Significant aggravation of symptoms and decreased exercise tolerance in persons with heart or lung disease, with widespread symptoms in the healthy population.	Elderly and persons with existing heart or lung disease should stay indoors and reduce physical activity.
200	Alert	Mild aggravation of symptoms in susceptible persons, with irritation symptoms in the healthy population.	Persons with existing heart or respiratory ailments should reduce physical exertion and outdoor activity.
100	National Ambient Air Quality Standard		
50	50 percent of National Ambient Air Quality Standard		

Source: Environmental Protection Agency, *Guideline for Public Reporting of Daily Air Quality—Pollutant Standards Index (PSI).* EPA-450/2—76-023, OAQPS 1.2-044 (Research Triangle Park, NC: Environmental Protection Agency, 1976), Table 3, p. 10.

healthful, or hazardous" (6). After Los Angeles the cities with the most badly polluted air in the United States are San Bernardino, New York, Denver, Pittsburgh, and Houston. PSI values for the air in 23 American cities are given in Figure 16–40. On the basis of these data one must conclude that the quality of our nation's air is gradually improving.

The Cost of Air Pollution

According to federal estimates, air pollution may be costing each man, woman, and child in the United States a minimum of $75 annually. The average yearly loss sustained by farmers and ranchers alone may approach $0.5-billion. Air pollution costs the nation as a whole at least $16 billion (18). In a recent year the Civil Aeronautics Board cited air pollution as the direct cause of fifteen to twenty air crashes, involving multimillion-dollar plane damage and loss of life. Airborne contaminants tarnish, soil, abrade, corrode, weaken, discolor, and erode a variety of materials. Ozone causes textiles to fade. Sulfuric acid mist can reduce an expensive pair of nylon stockings to shreds in the time it takes a woman to walk to lunch and back.

16–41 *New York City's Central Park provides proof of the corrosive effect of air pollution. Here is evidence of wear on Cleopatra's Needle. What effect does the air pollution have on the delicate lungs of the two boys beneath the statue?*

Store buildings, archways, and monuments are covered with grime and rendered unsightly. Grim testimony to the rapid rate at which we are degrading our atmospheric resource is demonstrated by the fate of Cleopatra's Needle in New York City. Although the famed obelisk was not brought to this country until 1881, it has deteriorated more since its arrival here than during its entire 3,000-year history in Egypt. (See Figure 16–41.) Even the Parthenon, famed symbol of ancient Greece, is undergoing accelerated deterioration because of exposure to twentieth-century air. The "life expectancy" of priceless paintings by masters such as Rembrandt, Picasso, and Van Gogh is threatened by atmospheric contaminants that have penetrated the art galleries of Florence and Paris.

Electric-light bills for many urban families are substantially higher simply because the available sunlight is reduced 15 to 20 percent by smoke and dust. The corrosion of industrial equipment, raw materials, and facilities perhaps is the gravest economic blow dealt by air pollutants. Steel surfaces corrode two to four times faster in urban than in nearby agricultural areas because of sulfur pollution. Add to this the bills for the medical treatment and hospitalization incurred by thousands victimized annually by pollution-caused illness, and the total air-pollution cost to America becomes substantial indeed.

Pollution Control Devices

Although many of the pollution-control devices currently available are not 100 percent efficient in removing industrial contaminants, they often do significantly reduce emission levels. (See Figure 16–42.) Certainly industry cannot wait another few years for the "perfect" control device to be developed; that day may never come.

Controlling Particulates

Four standard types of equipment for controlling particulates are available. The *fabric filter bag house* operates like a giant vacuum cleaner, collecting particles in hugh cloth bags. (See Figure 16–43.) A large filter bag house may consist of more than 1,000 elongated filter bags, each of which is several meters long (10). Up to 99.9 percent of the dust particles may be removed from the gas stream.

The *electrostatic precipitator* removes solid particles (dust, fly ash, asbestos fibers, and lead salts) of less than one micron in diameter from the gases in a smokestack. (See Figure 16–44.) The pollutants pass between pairs of positively and negatively charged electrodes. The particles become negatively charged and are then attracted to a positively charged collector electrode. Although the initial cost of a large precipitator can be more than $1 million, the power and maintenance costs are small. One unfortunate feature, however, is that the precipitators are more effective when high-sulfur rather than low-sulfur coal is burned.

16–42 *Note how the installation of pollution-control equipment at this industrial plant has reduced the emission of soot particles (smoke).*

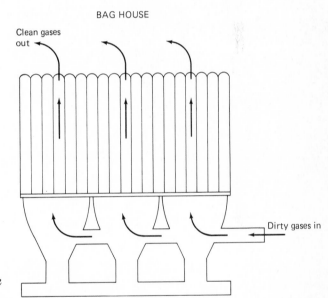

BAG HOUSE

Clean gases out

Dirty gases in

16–43 *Filter bag house. Solid particles are removed from exhaust gases by long "vacuum-cleaner" type bags.*

The *cyclone filter* removes heavy dust particles with the aid of gravity and a downward spiraling air stream. (See Figure 16–45.) Sales of these four standard pollution-control devices are expected to mushroom in the 1980s.

Sulfur Oxides

As we have just seen, the release of sulfur oxides into the atmosphere, whether from transportation, industrial, or residential sources (either directly or indirectly in the form of acid rain) has a highly adverse effect on human health, wildlife, forests, and farm crops, as well as on irreplaceable paintings, monuments, stonework, and statuary. Now, how can the emission of sulfur oxide be controlled? There are several possible approaches. Although no method will be satisfactory by itself, if the following approaches are used in combination, the sulfur oxide problem will at least be greatly reduced.

503

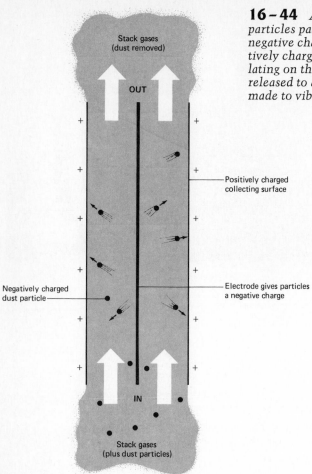

16–44 *An electrostatic precipitator. As the dust particles pass through the precipitator, they are given a negative charge. They are then attracted to the positively charged wall of the precipitator. After accumulating on this collecting surface they are periodically released to a collecting chamber when the surface is made to vibrate.*

Stack gases
(dust removed)

OUT

Positively charged
collecting surface

Electrode gives particles
a negative charge

Negatively charged
dust particle

IN

Stack gases
(plus dust particles)

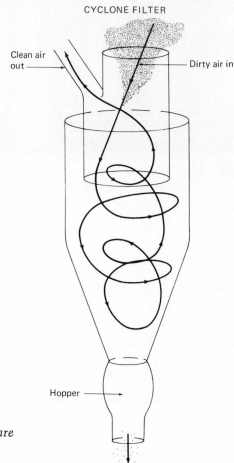

CYCLONE FILTER

Clean air
out

Dirty air in

Hopper

16–45 *Cyclone filter. Solid particles are removed by centrifugal force and are collected in a hopper.*

1. *Shifting from high- to low-sulfur coal.* Much of the industrial coal that had been consumed prior to 1970 had a relatively high sulfur content of up to 3 percent or even more. This coal was taken from mines in Pennsylvania, West Virginia, and Illinois. Once health authorities became aware of the problems posed by oxides of sulfur, however, municipal, state, and federal regulations were eventually passed that made it illegal to burn high-sulfur coal. For example, in 1971 New York City passed an ordinance that made it illegal for industry to burn coal with a sulfur content higher than 0.55 percent. By 1973 the maximum sulfur level for coal permitted in Cleveland was 1 percent; for Chicago, 1.5 percent. Fortunately, there exist vast supplies of low-sulfur coal in such western states as Montana and Wyoming, which can be obtained by strip-mining. (However, because strip-mining can be very destructive to the environment, every precaution must be taken to restore the sites to their original condition.)

2. *Removing sulfur from high-sulfur coal before burning it.* Of course transporting low-sulfur coal a distance of more than 1,000 miles to eastern industrial plants would add greatly to the cost of the coal. An alternative is to mine the high-sulfur coal available in the Middle West and East, where it is close to the industry that will use it, *and then remove much of*

504

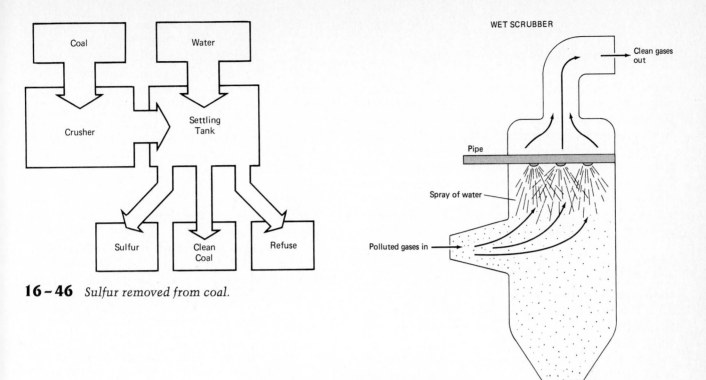

16–46 *Sulfur removed from coal.*

16–47 *Wet scrubber. Downward-streaming water "scrubs out" polluting gases such as sulfur dioxide.*

the sulfur prior to burning the coal. Much of the weight of high-sulfur coal is actually caused by a worthless impurity known as iron pyrite (FeS_2). It can be removed from the coal without sacrificing its fuel value. One commonly employed method depends on the pyrite being considerably *heavier* than the coal itself. Therefore, if the coal is pulverized and then placed in a tank of water, the heavier pyrite particles will settle to the bottom of the tank, while the lighter coal particles remain near the top. (See Figure 16–46.)

3. *Desulfurizing oil.* Crude oil also bears sulfur-containing impurities. One widely used method for their removal is represented by a $120-million desulfurization facility operated by Exxon at Amuay, Venezuela (8). The high-sulfur crude oil, which is composed of a mixture of several different long-chain hydrocarbon compounds, is first heated to a high temperature and is then passed over a catalyst in the presence of hydrogen gas. At this time the complex long-chain hydrocarbon compounds, some of which contain sulfur, are broken down, or cracked, into simpler short-chain compounds. Sulfur is removed and combined with the hydrogen, a process that results in the formation of hydrogen disulfide gas, or HS_2. Later, the sulfur can be rather simply removed from the hydrogen disulfide. At their Venezuelan plant, Exxon daily removes 335 metric tons of sulfur from about 100,000 barrels of crude oil by this method (10). Some authorities feel that industry and government should spend $25 million to $50 million annually on research to develop better methods for desulfurizing coal and fuel oil (28).

4. *Using wet scrubbers.* The wet scrubbers shown in Figure 16–47, will remove 80 to 95 percent of the sulfur dioxide from gases going up industrial stacks.

The cost of control methods and equipment may add substantially to the overall cost of production, varying from 5 percent for a steel mill to 20 percent for a foundry.

505

Air Pollution Abatement and Control

Several years ago, when our nation was just beginning to recognize the grave consequences of mounting atmospheric contamination, John W. Gardner, former Secretary of Health, Education and Welfare, summed up America's options: "Our choices are narrow. We can remain indoors and live like moles for an unspecified number of days each year. We can issue gas masks to a large segment of the population. We can live in domed cities. *Or we can take action to stop fouling the air we breathe.*" [Italics mine.]

Industry

Well over 50 percent of all air pollution has its source in the operations of the 300,000 industrial organizations of our nation. Because our current air-pollution problem represents the cumulative end product of many years of environmental abuse, only a massive and sustained control effort by the industrial establishment will be of much significance.

Converting Pollutants into Valuable By-Products

Although industry as a whole must be prodded repeatedly, an increasing number of concerned, responsible, farsighted industrial leaders are showing not only that aerial contaminants can be markedly curtailed, but that recovery of some commercially valuable wastes may help to absorb the cost of pollution-control equipment. A few examples follow:

1. Detroit Edison's massive St. Clair power plant has been experimentally employing a catalytic process that would reduce offensive sulfur dioxide fumes to easily disposable calcium sulfate (plaster of paris), a procedure that would increase utility costs a negligible 3 percent.
2. Tennessee Corporation once devastated large stretches of the Tennessee hillsides with its sulfur gases; today their wastes are being converted into the company's major product, sulfuric acid.
3. Several large utility companies sell the fly ash recovered from their stack gases for use in the manufacture of cinder blocks, paving materials, abrasives, and portland cement.

Controlling Automotive Emissions

There are three general approaches to the control of automotive pollutants: (1) reducing auto traffic volume in chronically congested urban areas, (2) modifying the conventional internal combustion engine, and (3) developing alternative engine types such as the electric and steam engines.

REDUCING TRAFFIC VOLUME.   Several specific proposals by the EPA to reduce traffic flow include the following:

1. In Washington, D.C., the termination of free parking facilities by employers for their employees.
2. A $5 daily tax added to parking fees in downtown Boston.
3. For one working day per week prohibit commuters from driving to their place of work in

16 – 48   *Before installation of special pollution-control equipment, over 150 tons of smoke used to pour daily from these chimneys at U.S. Steel's Duquesne plant. Now the new equipment wets down the smoke, washes it, and compresses the soot and flyash into disposable briquets.*

16–49 *In Manhattan and some other major urban centers, certain lanes on busy thoroughfares have been reserved for the exclusive use of express buses. This stratagem has proven effective in reducing the commuter traffic volume and hence the level of air pollution.*

downtown Philadelphia and Pittsburgh, thus reducing commuter traffic by 20 percent.

The overall pollution-reduction strategy developed by New York City includes the following features:

1. All street parking in the main business section of Manhattan has been banned.
2. Cruising by Manhattan taxis has been restricted.
3. Several Manhattan bridges have been placed in the toll system.
4. One lane on busy streets has been set aside for the exclusive use of buses. (See Figure 16–49.)

The EPA has assumed that similar measures, instituted in all 31 of the "pollution problem" cities, would be required at least until the mid-1980s. It is hoped that at that time sufficient emission reductions in car engines will have been made, so that the restrictions can be relaxed.

REDUCING POLLUTANT EMISSIONS. The automobile industry once shrugged off its responsibilities for restricting exhaust emissions. For example, a standard Detroit joke in the early 1960s was, "What California needs is filter-tipped people."

16–50 *Traffic congestion in New York City. The exhaust fumes from these cars are contributing to the haze that shrouds the Empire State Building.*

507

Recommendations of the National Commission on Air Quality

In 1977 an amendment to the Clean Air Act established the National Commission on Air Quality. The commission's major function was to determine the most effective methods for upgrading our nation's air quality. Its major recommendations were reported by the Council on Environmental Quality:

1. The current . . . requirements for setting air quality standards at levels necessary to protect public health without consideration of economic factors should remain unchanged. . . .
2. As required by the Clean Air Act, EPA should consider the synergistic and antagonistic characteristics of pollutants.
3. New [pollution] sources should not be required to install additional new [control] equipment during the first ten years of operation unless required for newly regulated or hazardous pollutants.
4. The existing system . . . to protect air quality in national parks and wilderness areas should be retained without change and so should current visibility protection programs. . . .
5. Gasoline and diesel automobile emission standards for hydrocarbon should be retained at 0.41-gram per mile. . . .
6. The statutory standards for emissions of nitrogen oxides by automobiles should be retained at 1.0 gram per mile. . . .
7. The statutory carbon monoxide standard for automobiles should be changed as quickly as practicable to a standard of 7.0 grams per mile through the 1986 model year. After 1986, the EPA should set the standard in the 3.4 to 7.0 range, at a level that would protect the public health expeditiously and effectively. . . .
8. The act should be amended requiring manufacturers to demonstrate that automobiles in the 1984 model year and later, and light trucks in the 1986 model year and later that are sold in areas at least 4,000 feet above sea level will comply with appropriate national emission standards. . . .
9. Vehicle inspection and maintenance programs should be required only in areas with populations greater than 500,000 people where peak 1981 pollution levels for ozone or carbon monoxide are 50 percent greater than air quality standards. . . .
10. Funding should be increased for support of federal, state, and local control efforts, particularly enforcement, and for support of research on air pollution effects, causes, and means of control. . . .
11. Noncompliance penalties should be required against sources not on schedule. Penalties should range up to $5,000 per day for violation.
12. The act should be modified to strengthen provisions requiring a state to reduce emissions which affect other states. . . .
13. Congress should appropriate adequate funds for acid precipitation research. . . .
14. Congress should provide funding for and direct appropriate agencies to develop a long-term nationwide atmospheric [acid] deposition program to assess amounts and effects of deposition. . . .
15. Congress should require a significant reduction by 1990 of sulfur dioxide emissions in the eastern United States. . . . (6)

That early mood of flippancy has long since changed to serious concern. The industry realizes that it has to make radical changes in motor design; mounting pressure from both consumers and pollution-control agencies will demand nothing less. Car manufacturers now regard the pollution issue to be even more of a threat to car sales than the safety issue of the mid-1960s. Henry Ford II branded it "by far the most important problem" the industry will encounter in the immediate future.

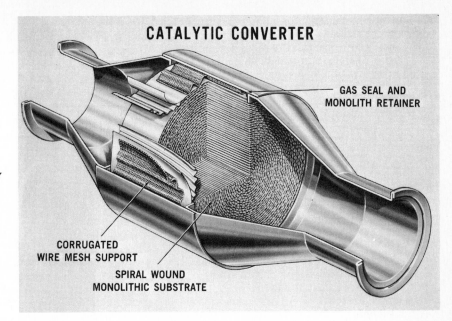

CATALYTIC CONVERTER

GAS SEAL AND MONOLITH RETAINER

CORRUGATED WIRE MESH SUPPORT

SPIRAL WOUND MONOLITHIC SUBSTRATE

16–51 *Cutaway illustration of a catalytic converter of the type used by the Ford Motor Company. Resembling a small muffler, the emission-control device changes vehicle exhaust pollutants into harmless gases and vapors via contact with noble-metal catalysts. The noble metal (platinum, palladium, or a combination of the two) is deposited on the surface of the honeycomblike substrate.*

USING CATALYTIC CONVERTERS. In order to reduce the pollutant emissions from automobiles, as required by the 1977 amendment to the Clean Air Act of 1970, auto manufacturers have relied heavily on a device known as a catalytic converter. (See Figure 16–51.) The converter is a muffler-shaped device that weighs from ten to thirty pounds and is incorporated into the exhaust system of the car. The interior of one type of converter, used by the Ford Motor Company, has a honeycomb-like interior. The cells of the honeycomb are lined with platinum or palladium. As the products of incompletely burned gasoline, such as carbon monoxide and hydrocarbons, pass through the cells of the catalytic converter, the catalyst increases the rate at which they are combined with oxygen. The oxidation of the harmful carbon monoxide and hydrocarbons results in the formation of harmless carbon dioxide and water. (A second type of catalyst is required for the breakdown of nitrogen oxides into harmless nitrogen and oxygen.) (See Figures 16–52 and 16–53.) When the auto industry came out with the catalytic converters they were thought to be too costly (up to $300 each), unreliable, ineffective, and to have a too-short life span of only 12,000 miles, after which they would have to be replaced. Some of these criticisms were valid. Another serious problem associated with their use was that the lead in leaded gasoline, which was used for antiknock purposes,

actually "knocked out" the catalyst. Apparently, the lead eventually formed a thin coating over the catalyst and thus reduced its effective surface area. Because the auto manufacturers would have had an extremely difficult time meeting the federal emission standards without the converter, they put pressure on the oil industry to produce *unleaded gasoline.* Unleaded gasoline became available to the

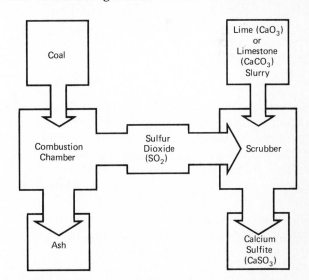

Coal

Lime (CaO₃) or Limestone (CaCO₃) Slurry

Combustion Chamber

Sulfur Dioxide (SO₂)

Scrubber

Ash

Calcium Sulfite (CaSO₃)

16–52 *Method of removing sulfur dioxide from exhaust gases after the combustion of coal. The lime reacts with the sulfur dioxide to form calcium sulfite, a solid that is easily removed.*

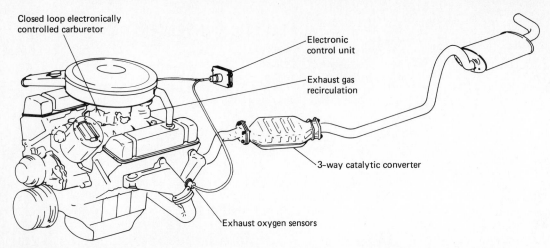

Closed loop electronically
controlled carburetor

Electronic
control unit

Exhaust gas
recirculation

3-way catalytic converter

Exhaust oxygen sensors

16–53 *General Motors' name for its emission control system is C-4, which stands for Computer Controlled Catalytic Converter System. This advanced system provides the technology to meet the stricter emission standards of the 1980s while giving good fuel economy and driveability. The C-4 system uses a three-way converter that, aided by electronic engine controls directed by an onboard computer, reduces oxides of nitrogen, as well as "burning" hydrocarbons and carbon monoxide. It uses rhodium in addition to the platinum-palladium catalyst on current cars.*

motorist in about 1975 and, indeed, had to be used on cars with a catalytic converter. This shift toward nonleaded gasoline was acclaimed by environmentalists and health authorities generally because of the health threat posed by high lead levels in the air of our major cities. Recent studies have shown that roughly 4 percent of our preschool children are suffering from lead poisoning—a problem that could result in anemia, kidney damage, and impaired brain function.

INSPECTION AND MAINTENANCE PROGRAMS. Under the terms of the 1977 amendments to the Clean Air Act, inspection-and-maintenance (IM) programs are mandatory for vehicles in those parts of the country where air-quality standards were not met by 1982 for carbon monoxide and ozone. Under the program, emissions are checked by state or federal inspectors. (See Figures 16–54A and 16–54B.) When levels of pollutants in the exhaust, such as sulfur dioxide and carbon monoxide, for example, are too high, the owner must have his or her vehicle modified so that it will meet EPA's standards. In 1981 about 22 percent of inspected vehicles failed the test. The average cost of repairs required to meet air standards was about $22. In Portland, Oregon, such an IM program resulted in a 40 percent reduction in emissions the very first year.

Alternatives to the Internal Combustion Engine

ELECTRIC CARS. Production of electric cars in Europe, Japan, and the United States amounts to 6,000 vehicles yearly. Several American cities, including San Francisco and New York are making limited use of electric buses and delivery vans. Some experimental cars recently developed have a top speed of 80 miles per hour. Although the electric car itself is relatively pollution-free, the battery eventually has to be recharged—a process that utilizes electricity generated by centrally located power plants. Thus, in one sense, instead of having *numerous, widely dispersed, mobile sources of pollution* (automobiles), the pollution problem is merely transferred to a *few large stationary sources* (the power plants). It is true, however, that effective emission control in this case would be much easier. Another big disadvantage of the electric car is that the batteries required to power the car would be rather bulky. (See Figure 16–55.)

The suitable alternative might be an electric car powered by a *fuel cell*, a special type of battery that is refuelable like a gas engine and that *converts the fuel directly to electricity*, with air-contaminating emissions reduced to zero. John F. Cooper, a research chemist at the Lawrence Livermore National Laboratory, recently announced the development of

16–54A *Auto exhaust monitor. The Energy Research and Development Administration is developing a low-cost, portable device to monitor auto exhausts for three major pollutants: carbon monoxide, unburnt hydrocarbons, and nitrogen oxides. Pollution-control officers and auto-inspection attendants could quickly measure the concentration of the three pollutants with this instrument.*

a fuel cell for electric cars that operates on aluminum, air and tap water! Aluminum serves as the negative electrical terminal as well as the fuel. The water and air which is pumped through the cell undergoes a reaction with aluminum which generates electricity. Cooper estimates that a battery of sixty fuel cells weighing 1,000 pounds (453 kilograms) could power a five-passenger car at a speed of 55 miles per hour for a distance of 300 miles before requiring refueling. Refueling would merely require the removal of hydragillite, (a contaminant), and the addition of tap water. Traditional lead-acid batteries now in use provide only one-fifteenth as much energy as an aluminum fuel cell of equal weight. Cooper predicts the manufacture of a prototype car powered by an aluminum battery by 1989 (32).

HYBRID CARS. One strategy that would eliminate some of the disadvantages of the electric cars now on the road would be to develop *hybrid* cars equipped with both an electric and an internal combustion engine. The hybrid would rely on its electric batteries to power it on short trips through urban areas — for example, on a shopping trip or a Friday night visit to the theater. The motor power for a

16–54B *Examination time. An EPA emission-testing facility at Ann Arbor, Michigan, analyzes and measures the exhaust emitted from newly made automobiles.*

16–55 *Prototype of electric automobile that can be mass produced with existing or near-term technology. Developed by Garrett Corporation, Torrance, California.*

highway trip of several hundred miles would be provided by an alternate source: the conventional internal combustion engine.

STEAM CARS. Another possible alternative to the internal combustion engine. The propulsive steam is generated by burning kerosene. The spent steam is then converted to liquid water and used over again. Because kerosene is virtually totally combusted, the pollutants emitted from the engine would be minimal. The car can be highly durable; it is not too expensive; it runs quietly; there is no need

16–56 *City official in Florissant, Missouri, checks electrolyte level in electric van. The Electra Van is part of Florissant's municipal electric fleet. The city monitors closely the performance, fuel consumption, and operating costs of these vehicles as part of a market demonstration program to promote widespread use of electric vehicles.*

for a transmission system; and its performance, in terms of speed, safety, and reliability is quite acceptable. Why, then, hasn't the motor industry generated any enthusiasm about mass producing the vehicle? The reasons are economic. As environmentalist Virginia Brodine states:

The established automobile industry has too much invested in the internal combustion engine to be interested in developing an alternative, and the costs for an independent manufacturer to enter the market are almost prohibitive. In addition to the enormous initial investment, there would be the difficulties of establishing dealerships and servicing facilities. The petroleum industry also presents an obstacle, since its refineries would have to be revamped to produce low-grade kerosene instead of the present high-octane fuels. (3)

Indoor Air Pollution

When you think of air pollution, what sources come to mind? Industrial smokestacks and city traffic, right? But how about your family living room? Recently scientists have been finding that even the air we breathe in our own homes on a day-to-day basis may be of questionable quality, at best.

Concern about indoor quality is justifiable first of all because most people live indoors much of the time. Not only that, in our recent attempts to reduce our home heating bills, many home owners have heavily insulated their homes, thus effectively "locking" pollutants *inside.* Before the energy crisis the average residence time for a given molecule of gas inside the home was about one hour. However, since our efforts to insulate our homes better, the residence time has increased to about 400 percent (6).

The Lawrence Berkeley Laboratory at Walnut Creek, California, has measured concentrations of pollutants inside a well-insulated house, in which a gas stove and oven were used in ordinary meal preparation. Concentrations of carbon monoxide and nitrogen dioxide exceeded outdoor levels in the kitchen, bedroom, and living room.

You probably remember formaldehyde as the fluid used to preserve frogs and cats in biology class. You may be surprised to learn that it is commonly found in foam insulation, furniture, carpets, particle board, and plywood. A variety of human health problems caused by breathing formaldehyde include eye irritation, nausea, respiratory problems, and cancer (6).

The Occupational Safety and Health Administration (OSHA) has set three parts per million as the minimum formaldehyde concentration permitted inside industrial plants. It is of some concern that studies conducted in Europe and the United States have shown that the formaldehyde levels inside homes have occasionally been even higher. In Mission Viejo, California, formaldehyde concentrations in a research house having no furniture were relatively low. However, when furniture was added, formaldehyde levels increased almost threefold (6).

Radon gas is released when the radium atom decays. Radium is present in trace quantities in brick, concrete, and other building materials. It may even be present in the soil on which a house is built. As a result, an extremely small amount of radon gas probably is inhaled by the residents of almost every home in the United States. The EPA has estimated that 10 percent of all lung cancer deaths in the United States may be caused by radon gas. According to the Council on Environmental Quality, much more research on the concentration, sources, and effects of air pollution inside homes must be conducted as soon as possible (6).

The Clean Air Act

The Clean Air Act of 1970 certainly has been one of the most effective legislative bulwarks for environmental quality ever passed by Congress. Under its terms the EPA was given the responsibility and authority to bring about an extensive cleanup of the nation's "dirty" air. Levels of major types of atmospheric pollutants, such as sulfur dioxide, ozone, lead, particulates, nitrogen oxides, carbon monoxide, and hydrocarbons were closely monitored, and minimum standards for their concentration in the atmosphere were set. A steady reduction in emissions from smokestacks and exhaust pipes was mandated by the act. Under prodding by the EPA, the individual states, some grudgingly, finally came to grips with the serious air-pollution problems within their borders.

The improvement of our nation's air quality since 1970 has been gratifying. For example, the amount of fly ash and soot has been reduced by 16 percent; the volume of carbon monoxide has been lessened by 30 percent; and the volume of sulfur dioxide has decreased by a whopping 44 percent. The gray-brown haze that used to shroud heavily industrialized areas like Gary, Indiana, Cleveland, Baltimore, and Pittsburgh is beginning to dissipate, and the

Controversy: The Political Battle over the Clean Air Act

At the time of this writing the Clean Air Act is the focus of one of the most lively and heated congressional and industrial-environmental debates of the decade. The issue is the retention or relaxation of the tough requirements of the Clean Air Act of 1977. Locked in conflict are environmentalist groups (such as the Audubon Society, Friends of the Earth, and the Sierra Club), public health scientists, and many Democrats who fought ardently for retaining the strict regulations of the act, and their powerful antagonists, represented by the power plant, oil refinery, and automotive industries and other sectors of big business, as well as the Reagan Administration, the EPA, and most Republicans. The latter coalition was fervently committed to relaxing the controls of the Act for purposes of "realism" and the "economic health of the nation."

The fact that the EPA, supposedly our nation's top enforcement agency for pollution control, should side with big business on this issue should not be too surprising. After all, seven of eight appointments to key EPA staff positions were lawyers who had formerly represented clients like Dow Chemical, General Motors, and Exxon — all industrial giants with a vested interest in the "gutting" of the Act.

In order to provide the student with some sense of the intensity and emotion permeating the controversy, as well as an appreciation of the extreme polarization of viewpoints, we can do no better than to list some of the arguments of both sides.

Economics and Budget Cutting

Reagan Administration: "Statutes and regulations should be reasonable and related to the economic and physical realities of the particular areas involved."

General Motors Corporation: "After 10 years' experience with the Clean Air Act, this country ought to be able to make its air-pollution control efforts simpler, less costly, more efficient, and in better balance with other high-priority national concerns. These include reducing inflation, restoring economic growth, creating jobs, producing and conserving energy, and increasing productivity so that the United States industry can compete against its global competition. . . ."

Sierra Club: "Under the guise of budget cutting and eliminating over-regulation this administration is turning its back on the American people."

Controlling Air Pollution

Reagan Administration: "Deadlines for achieving primary air-quality standards should be adjusted to reflect the realities in a particular area. Automobile standards should be adjusted to more reasonable levels."

General Motors Corporation: "GM's approach to automotive emission control is designed to avoid the unnecessary expense, paper work, and redundancy that now characterizes the EPA's enforcement program. . . ." To certify its 1981 models, GM published over 10,000 different pieces of documentation creating a stack over 15 stories high — higher than the GM building in Detroit.

Congressman Henry Waxman (D–Calif.), chairman of the House Subcommittee on Health and the Environment: "The Broyhill-Dingell bill [proposed by pro-Administration forces] is an open invitation for a virtual halt to air pollution control."

Michael McCloskey, executive director, Sierra Club: "Today there is intense pressure in Washington to ignore the interests of the public where . . . environmental protection is concerned."

William A. Butler, vice-president, Audubon Society: In a response to the proposed removal of the Office of Enforcement from the EPA by Administrator Ann Gorsuch: "That move makes [the] federal environment enforcement capability pretty much the toothless tiger it was prior to EPA's creation."

National Clean Air Coalition: "The auto industry executives have also met with the President, with the same appeal for relaxed pollution controls. They came away stating they were accused of his help in working for relaxation of the Clean Air Act."

Public Health

Audubon Society: "More than 2,000 people in the western United States will die prematurely each year by the year 2000 if Congress deletes the reduction of sulfur-in-coal requirements for new coal-fired power plants. Under a worst-possible scenario, premature deaths in the West could rise to 16,000 annually by the year 2000" (1).

Congressman Henry Waxman: "The Administration's philosophical approach in pollution control appears to be no longer based on what happens to the health of the American people, but what the cost might be to industry."

Sierra Club official: "I, for one, am not going to let my health and the health of my loved ones be sacrificed on the altar of budgeting expediency."

National Clean Air Coalition: The amendments to the Clean Air Act proposed by the Reagan Administration forces "would block needed action to protect the ozone layer which guards us from cancer-causing UV radiation for at least two years. . . ."

Acid Rain

Reagan Administration: "Research on acid deposition should be accelerated." (In other words, *action* would be indefinitely postponed until the research is finished.)

Audubon Society: Response to the Reagan Administration's efforts to relax control of sulfur emissions from power plants: "They will cause increased destruction of freshwater ecosystems from acid rain and reduced visibility in the West."

Time Magazine reporter: "Perhaps most startling, the [Administration-backed] legislation makes no mention of acid rain. Environmentalists feel that is a bit like talking about disarmament without any reference to nuclear weapons."

National Clean Air Coalition: "The amendments [proposed by Reagan forces] would do nothing to control acid rain."

reduction in pollution-induced respiratory and heart illness caused by atmospheric pollutants has been considerable (9).

Our nation has about 6,000 stationary pollution sources (power plants and factories) that have the potential for releasing more than 100 tons of criteria pollutants, such as carbon monoxide, particulates, sulfur dioxide, and carbon monoxide, if they are not equipped with proper emission-reduction equipment. It is most encouraging, therefore, from the standpoint of human health, that the controls on more than 90 percent of those sources are adequate to the air standards mandated by the Clean Air Act (6).

Rapid Review

1. Dry, unpolluted air has the following composition: nitrogen (79 percent), oxygen (20 percent),

carbon dioxide (.03 percent), and inert gases (1 percent).

2. Naturally occurring contaminants of the atmosphere include (a) volcanic dust and ash, (b) ragweed and goldenrod pollen, (c) disease-causing bacteria, (d) molds, (e) wind-blown soil particles, (f) salt spray, and (g) methane, carbon monoxide and sulfur dioxide resulting from the decay of organic material.

3. The term *smog* is a contraction of the words smoke and fog.

4. The concentration of carbon monoxide in urban areas may be fifty to one-hundred times the global average.

5. A major source of the sulfur dioxide generated by humans results from the burning of sulfur-containing fossil fuels in power plants and other industries.

6. A *hydrocarbon* is an organic compound composed of hydrogen and carbon. Good examples of hydrocarbon pollutants of the atmosphere are methane and benzene. The most significant effect of the hydrocarbons, generally speaking, is their essential role in the formation of photochemical smog.

7. The solid and liquid particles suspended in the air are known as *particulates.* Major sources are coal-burning industries such as power plants, steel mills, fertilizer plants, and foundries.

8. *Photochemical smog* is caused by the reaction between hydrocarbons, nitrogen oxides, and atmospheric oxygen in the presence of sunlight. Ozone is the principal component of photochemical smog.

9. At present about 150 million motor vehicles in the United States travel an aggregate of one trillion miles yearly and consume 75 billion gallons of fuel per year.

10. The buildup of atmospheric pollution is facilitated by thermal inversions.

11. Because of the *heat-island* effect some cities, such as Cleveland and St. Louis, may be 27° F warmer than the surrounding rural areas.

12. The heat-island effect causes pollutants to concentrate in a *dust dome* above a city.

13. Air pollution may have a number of effects on climate, such as (a) increasing the earth's average temperature, (b) decreasing the earth's average temperature, (c) reducing the amount of sunlight reaching the earth, and (d) inducing precipitation.

14. Atmospheric pollutants are known to damage at least 36 commercially valuable crops.

15. Air pollutants generated in Los Angeles are wind blown sixty miles to the San Bernardino National Forest where they cause extensive damage to ponderosa pine forests.

16. In the early 1900s the release of sulfur dioxide from a copper smelter at Ducktown, Tennessee, caused the destruction of plant cover over 7,000 acres.

17. The pH of normal, nonpolluted rain is about 5.6. This slight acidity is the result of the small amount of carbon dioxide dissolved in the water to form carbonic acid.

18. Rainfall in much of the northeastern states has a pH of 4.5 or lower because of the accelerated release of oxides of sulfur and nitrogen in the Midwest during the last few decades.

19. Because emissions generated in the United States may be transported by winds to Canada and vice versa, the control of the acid rain problem requires international cooperation.

20. The first major air-pollution disaster in the United States occurred in Donora, Pennsylvania, in October 1948; it caused the death of twenty people.

21. Factors that contribute to air pollution disasters include (a) a dense population, (b) dense concentration of industries, (c) location of cities in a topographical receptacle, (d) presence of a thermal inversion, and (e) presence of fog.

22. The release of fluorocarbon gases (Freons) from spray cans in the last few decades has caused chemical reactions in the stratosphere that have resulted in a thinning of the ozone layer. The result has been increased ultraviolet radiation on the earth and increased rates of skin cancer.

23. On the basis of the Pollution Standards Index (PSI), the most badly polluted air in the United States occurs in Los Angeles, the San Bernardino (California) region, New York City, Denver, Pittsburgh, and Houston.

24. Among the major illnesses caused by air pollution are lung cancer, emphysema, chronic bronchitis, "black lung" disease, and skin cancer.

25. Air pollution costs the nation $16 billion yearly.

26. Pollution-control devices employed by industry include electrostatic precipitators, wet scrubbers, cyclone filters, and fabric filter baghouses.

27. Emissions of sulfur dioxide from industrial smokestacks can be reduced by (a) replacing high-sulfur coal with low-sulfur coal, (b) removing sulfur from high-sulfur coal before it is used, (c) removing sulfur from oil, and (d) using wet scrubbers.

28. An increasing number of industries are controlling air pollution by converting the original contaminants into useful products. For example, sulfur dioxide can be converted into sulfuric acid and high-carbon fly ash can be used directly as fuel or can be converted into cinder blocks, paving materials, abrasives, and cement.

29. Four general strategies for controlling auto emissions are (a) reducing traffic volume, (b) modifying the internal combustion engine, (c) replacing the internal combustion engine with electric and steam engines, and (d) developing a hybrid car (combining internal combustion and electric engines).

30. Catalytic converters increase the rate at which carbon monoxide and hydrocarbons are oxidized to carbon dioxide and water, respectively.

31. The wet deposition of acid may be in the form of rain, snow, fog, dew, or frost. The dry deposition of acid-forming materials takes place when dust particles containing nitrates and sulfates settle on the earth, water, or vegetation. Later those materials may react with water to form sulfuric or nitric acid.

32. The pH scale ranges from 0 to 14. A pH of 7 indicates neutrality. Values above 7 indicate increasing alkalinity. Numbers below 7 indicate increasing acidity.

33. The superstack at the nickel smelter at Sudbury, Ontario, releases 1 percent of all the atmospheric sulfur dioxide released worldwide.

34. An estimated 237 lakes in the Adirondacks have a pH of less than 5 — an acidity level considered lethal for many species of fish.

35. Eighty percent of the lakes and streams in the Northeast and upper Midwest are vulnerable to acidification.

36. Acid rain causes reduced photosynthesis and reduced growth in farm crops and forest trees. It also causes increased vulnerability to drought and disease.

37. A short-term solution to the acid-rain problem in lakes is to scatter lime from helicopters; a long-term solution is the reduction of nitrogen and sulfur oxides from the smokestacks of industrial plants in 31 eastern states.

38. Under terms of the Clean Air Act as amended in 1977, inspection and maintenance programs were not met by 1982 for carbon monoxide and ozone.

39. The National Commission on Air Quality made a number of recommendations in 1980 by means of which our nation's air quality could be improved.

40. Recent attempts to insulate homes have caused indoor air-pollution problems from carbon monoxide, formaldehyde, and radon gas.

41. The world's average temperature is projected to increase 3° C (5° F) by the year 2035 if carbon dioxide continues to build up in the atmosphere at current rates. The result would be a gradual northward shift in crop-growing patterns. Moreover, a melting of the polar ice fields would create a 22-foot increase in the level of the ocean. The result would be an inundation of many urban areas along the coastal United States and in other parts of the world.

42. Largely as the result of pollution controls mandated by the Clean Air Act of 1970 and 1977, our nation's air quality has gradually improved. The amount of fly ash and soot has been reduced by 16 percent, carbon monoxide by 30 percent, and sulfur dioxide by 44 percent.

Key Words and Phrases

Acid deposition
Acid rain
Alveoli
Benzene
Benzopyrene
Buffer action
Carbon dioxide
Carbon monoxide
   poisoning
Carcinogens
Catalytic converter
Chronic bronchitis
Clean Air Act (1970, 1977)
Cleopatra's Needle
Cyanosis
Cyclone filter
Donora (Pennsylvania)
Dry deposition

Ducktown, Tennessee
Dust domes
Dust plumes
Electric car
Electrostatic
   precipitator
Emphysema
Fabric filter baghouse
Fluorocarbons
Formaldehyde
Freons
Fuel cell
Greenhouse effect
Heat islands
Hybrid cars
Hydrocarbons
Indoor air pollution
Inspection-and-
   maintenance programs

517

Lead poisoning
Leaded gasoline
Liming lakes
Lung cancer
Marsh gas
Methane
National Commission on Air Quality
Natural pollution
Nitric acid
Nitric oxide
Nitrogen dioxide
Ozone
pH scale
Particulates
Photochemical smog
Pollution disaster

Pollution Standards Index
Radiation inversion
Reagan Administration
San Bernardino National Forest
Skin cancer
Smog
Steam car
Subsidence inversion
Sulfur dioxide
Synergistic
Thermal inversion
Wet deposition
Wet scrubber

Questions and Topics for Discussion

1. Briefly describe the biological significance of the major components of nonpolluted air.
2. Suppose that the percentages for carbon dioxide and oxygen in nonpolluted air were reversed. Would this reversal have any effect on the structure and functioning of ecosystems? How would your life be affected?
3. Briefly list three sources of "natural" pollution.
4. Discuss the health effects of each of the following air pollutants: (a) carbon monoxide, (b) oxides of sulfur, (c) oxides of nitrogen, (d) hydrocarbons, (e) ozone, and (f) lead.
5. List the major human-generated sources of carbon monoxide, oxides of sulfur, oxides of nitrogen, hydrocarbons, ozone, and lead.
6. Describe the formation of photochemical smog.
7. Can you cite an example of how severe air pollution actually caused the "death" of a town?
8. List five conditions that usually are associated with an air-pollution disaster.
9. Describe three conditions that contribute to the "heat island" phenomenon.
10. Discuss the environmental advantages and disadvantages of "superstacks."
11. Which climatic conditions would be most conducive to the rapid dispersal of atmospheric pollutants? To their concentration in a localized area?

12. Is there a possible cause-and-effect relationship between air pollution and the northward extension of the ranges of the armadillo, opossum, cardinal, and mockingbird in the United States during this century?
13. In what way are human beings disrupting the normal flow of carbon dioxide through its cycle?
14. Discuss the advantages and disadvantages of the buildup of carbon dioxide in the atmosphere.
15. Discuss the harmful effects of acid deposition on aquatic ecosystems. On terrestrial ecosystems.
16. Lakes A and B are located only fifty miles apart and receive the same amount of rainfall, the annual average pH of which is 4.5. Yet, Lake A is devoid of fish, whereas Lake B abounds with them. Explain the reason.
17. Many representatives of the electric power and automotive industries feel that much more research on acid rain is needed before stricter controls on the release of acid-forming chemicals are mandated by federal law. Do you support their position? Why or why not?
18. Discuss the advantages and disadvantages of the electric car.
19. Discuss the importance of international cooperation with respect to the control of acid deposition.
20. Discuss the controversy that swirled around proposed relaxation of the regulations of the Clean Air Act in 1982.
21. Discuss the pros and cons of the gradual elimination of leaded gasoline.
22. Debate the relative advantages and disadvantages (environmental, social, and economic) of banning the internal combustion engine by 1990.
23. Now that you have studied this material on air pollution, what changes, if any, do you plan to make with respect to your "love affair" with your automobile?

Endnotes

1. "Audubon Predicts Increased Mortality if Congress Deletes Sulfur Reduction." *Ecology USA*, **11** (June 7, 1982), 85.

2. Bregman, J. I., and Sergei Lenirmand. *The Pollution Paradox*. New York: Spartan, 1966.

3. Brodine, Virginia. *Air Pollution*. New York: Harcourt, 1973.

4. Council on Environmental Quality. *Environmental Quality*. Eighth Annual Report. Washington, DC: Government Printing Office, 1977.

5. ———. *Environmental Quality*. Eleventh Annual Report. Washington, DC: Government Printing Office, 1980.

6. ———. *Environmental Quality*. Twelfth Annual Report. Washington, DC: Government Printing Office, 1981.

7. Ember, Lois R. "Acid Pollutants: Hitchhikers Ride the Wind." *Chemical and Engineering News*, **59** (Sept. 14, 1981), 20.

8. Environmental Protection Agency. *Air Pollution and Your Health*. Washington, DC: Government Printing Office, 1979.

9. Golden, Frederic. "Murky Debate on Clean Air." *Time* (Mar. 1, 1982), 63.

10. Hodges, Laurent. *Environmental Pollution*. New York: Holt, 1977.

11. Kelly, Tom. "How Many More Lakes Have to Die?" *Canada Today*, **12** (Feb. 1981), 1–11.

12. Lessing, Lawrence. "The Revolt Against the Internal Combustion Engine." *Fortune* (July 1967), 79–83, 180–184.

13. "Let's Clear the Air." *The American City* (Aug. 1967), 1324.

14. Lewis, Howard R. *With Every Breath You Take*. New York: Crown, 1965.

15. Lund, Herbert F. "Industrial Air Pollution." *Factory* (Oct. 1965), 11.

16. Luoma, John B. "Troubled Sky, Troubled Waters." *Audubon* (Nov. 1980), 88–111.

17. Maxwell, Kenneth E. *Environment of Life*. Encino, CA: Dickenson, 1973.

18. Miller, G. Tyler. *Living in the Environment: Concepts, Problems, Alternatives*. New York: Wadsworth, 1980.

19. Moran, Joseph M., Michael D. Morgan, and James H. Wiersma. *An Introduction to Environmental Sciences*. Boston: Little, Brown, 1973.

20. Moriber, George. *Environmental Science*. Boston: Allyn, 1974.

21. National Academy of Sciences. *Waste Management and Control*. Publication No. 1400. Washington, DC: National Research Council, 1966.

22. Norris, Ruth. "Fighting for Air." *Audubon*, **83** (Sept. 1981).

23. Odum, Eugene P. *Fundamentals of Ecology*. 3rd ed. Philadelphia: Saunders, 1971.

24. "OTA Acid Rain Study Shows Damage to Lakes and Rivers." *Ecology USA*, **11** (May 24, 1982), 76.

25. "Ozone Depletion: Early Evidence Comes In." *Science News*, **130** (Aug. 22, 1981), 116.

26. Public Health Service. *The Federal Air Pollution Program*. Publication No. 1560. Washington, DC: Division of Air Pollution, Public Health Service, 1966.

27. ———. *The Effects of Air Pollution*. Publication No. 1556. Washington, DC: 1967.

28. Turk, Amos, Janet T. Wittes, Jonathan Turk, and Robert E. Wittes. *Environmental Science*. 2nd ed. Philadelphia: Saunders, 1978.

29. Wagner, Richard H. *Environment and Man*. New York: Norton, 1971.

30. Wolff, George T. "Acid Precipitation." *Science*, **216** (June 11, 1982), 1172.

31. *World Book Encyclopedia*. "Emphysema." Chicago: Field Enterprises, 1976.

32. ———. "Energy." Chicago: Field Enterprises, 1976.

Suggested Readings for the Interested Student

Cowling, Ellis B., and Rick A. Linthurst. "The Acid Precipitation Phenomenon and Its Ecological Consequences." *Bioscience*, **24** (Oct. 1981), 649–652. Researchers from North Carolina State University summarize the effects of acid rain on terrestrial ecosystems. Some beneficial effects of acid rain are described in this highly readable article.

Environmental Protection Agency. *Research Summary: Controlling Nitrogen Oxides*. Washington, DC: Government Printing Office, 1980. This is written in easily understood, nontechnical language. It is an overview of current strategies for controlling nitrogen oxides with excellent graphs, diagrams, and photographs.

———. *Research Summary: Controlling Sulfur Oxides*. Washington, DC: Government Printing Office, 1980. This is a highly readable, well-organized account of strategies for controlling sulfur oxides. It explores sources and effects as well as methods of control and has excellent figures.

———. *Trends in the Quality of the Nation's Air: A Report to the People*. Washington, DC: Government Printing Office, 1980. Written for the nonspecialist, this is an excellent overview of trends in the levels of particulates, sulfur dioxide, carbon monoxide, ozone, and nitrogen dioxide. It has high-quality photographs and colored graphs.

Kelly, Tom. "How Many More Lakes Have to Die?" *Canada Today*, **12** (Feb. 1981). This is a highly readable account of the acid-rain problem from the Canadian point of view. It has excellent maps and colored graphs. The author stresses the need for a coordinated international effort to control acid rain.

Kukla, G., and J. Gavin. "Summer Ice and Carbon Dioxide." *Science,* **214** (Oct. 1981), 497–502. This is an authoritative account by Columbia University researchers concerning the melting of the Antarctic icecap and the possible roles played by increased levels of carbon dioxide in recent years. Its graphs and tables are informative.

Likens, Gene E., Richard F. Wright, James N. Galloway, and Thomas J. Butler. "Acid Rain." *Scientific American,* **241** (Oct. 1979), 43–51. This is "must" reading for students researching the acid-rain literature. It offers highly informative maps, graphs, and photographs. The authors trace the history of the problem from the dawn of the industrial revolution to the present.

17 Minerals, Mining, and Society's Needs

It is fun zooming down the highway, isn't it? It gives you a sense of power and privacy — your own little kingdom on wheels. But have you ever wondered where all the materials that made your metallic kingdom possible came from? Or how many different kinds of metals were involved? To make your car and all the others produced each year, the auto industry uses roughly 7 percent of all the copper consumed in the United States, 10 percent of the aluminum, 13 percent of the nickel, 20 percent of the steel, 35 percent of the zinc, and 50 percent of the lead. The copper may have come from Arizona or Chile; the aluminum from Surinam or Jamaica; the nickel from Ontario or New Caledonia; the iron from Brazil, Russia, or Minnesota; the zinc from Mexico or Peru; and the lead from Missouri and possibly the Yukon Territory. It's hard to believe, but that glistening bit of motorized sophistication you call your car can be traced directly back to small portions of the earth's crust located in widely scattered parts of the world.

The Occurrence and Distribution of Minerals

Unlike forests, wildlife, fisheries, and even soil, mineral resources are *exhaustible* — they cannot be renewed once they are consumed. (They can be recycled, however.) The great majority of minerals now used by society have been extracted from the earth's crust. This crust extends downward from the earth's surface to a depth of about fifteen miles. All

88 of the naturally occurring elements occur in this crust. Some valuable minerals may occur in *elemental* form. Good examples are gold, silver, and diamonds (carbon). Most minerals used by human beings exist as *compounds* of two or more elements however. Copper, for example, exists commonly in the form of copper sulfide (Cu S), aluminum as aluminum oxide (Al_2O_3), and lead as lead carbonate (P_bCO_3). There are actually thousands of different mineral compounds present in the earth's crust, but only about thirty are relatively common, and some of those are valuable. Those mineral compounds are not distributed uniformly. Some are absent or extremely rare in most parts of the world but highly concentrated in a very few isolated areas. An *ore* is any naturally occurring deposit of a desirable mineral in a sufficiently high concentration so that it can be profitably mined. Ores are classified as *high* or *low grade*. For example, a copper ore that is 3 percent copper is considered very high-grade ore; on the other hand, one that is only 0.3 percent copper would be considered low grade (6).

Mineral Production

The value of minerals produced annually in the United States is about $40 billion — about 50 percent of the value of the global production. The leading mining states, based on value of minerals produced annually are Texas, Louisiana, California, and West Virginia. Worldwide, foremost mineral producing nations are the United States, Canada,

West Germany, and Libya. A major goal of the Secretary of the Interior under President Reagan was to stimulate mineral production in the United States. To this end he proposed to open up millions of acres of public lands and wilderness areas to exploration and development by mining interests. His policy has been hotly attacked by environmentalists.

Mineral Consumption in the United States: A Moral Issue?

Although the United States represents only five percent of the world's population, it consumes about twenty percent of the nonfuel minerals removed from the earth's crust each year (5). All the world's people in the entire two-million-year history of human existence have not consumed the quantity of minerals that the United States has used in only the past 35 years. Until very recently our nation was using 45 times as much zinc, 52 times as much aluminum, 64 times as much iron, 102 times as much copper, and 176 times as much lead as *all other people on earth* (5). (Per capita consumption of minerals in the United States as shown in Table 17 – 1.)

Of course without this enormous consumption of minerals the high standard of living we enjoy would not be possible. Very recently, for example, the

Table 17 – 1 Estimated Per Capita Consumption of Metals in the United States

Metal	Pounds per Person per Year
Steel	1550
Aluminum	47
Copper	26
Lead	20
Chromium	20
Zinc	17
Manganese	11
Magnesium	1 to 10
Nickel	2.1
Tin	1.2
Molybdenum	0.4
Cobalt	0.2
Antimony	0.1
Cadmium	0.1
Tungsten	0.1
Beryllium	0.1

Source: Raymond F. Dasmann, *Environmental Conservation,* 4th ed. (New York: Wiley, 1976.)

United States was producing about fifty times as much steel as India. This explains in part why the per capita income of Americans is roughly 33 times that of the residents of India (2). The question naturally arises: "Is it ethical for the United States to consume much more than her fair share of the world's limited mineral wealth? Are we, as a nation, in fact forever preventing the poor countries of the world from ever attaining the life-style we now enjoy? Is it not possible that, because of our insatiable appetite for minerals, the world might run out of the very ones on which the future upgrading of the economy of India, Bangladesh, or Ethiopia might depend?" Enormous amounts of steel, copper, lead, aluminum, zinc, gold, silver, cobalt, and titanium have already been mined, processed, and incorporated into the dishwashers, television sets, electronic games, home computers, speedboats, bridges, and skyscrapers that Americans have learned to expect of their everyday way of life. It has been estimated that to raise the rest of the world up to our level of material wealth would necessitate the extraction of staggering amounts of the world's fixed supply of minerals: more than 30 billion tons of iron, 300 million tons of zinc, and 50 million tons of tin, in addition to mammoth amounts of other minerals (2). Now even if such quantities of minerals were still available, and even if all the mines and smelters on the face of spaceship Earth operated full blast to extract and process those minerals, this production goal could not be accomplished in less than a century!

Strategic Minerals and American Foreign Policy

Minerals that are absolutely essential to the economic health and/or military security of our nation are *strategic minerals.* Among them are aluminum, cadmium, cobalt, copper, lead, mercury, nickel, platinum, silver, tin, uranium, and zinc. Unfortunately, domestic supplies of some of them are very scarce or nonexistent. In fact, it has been estimated that, by the year 2000, the United States *will import all of its chromium* (from the USSR and South Africa), *all of its tin* (Malaysia and Bolivia), *all of its manganese* (USSR and South Africa), *98 percent of its aluminum* (Jamaica and Australia), and *93 percent of its tungsten* (Cuba, Canada, and Peru) (5). (See Figure 17 – 1.) It has been estimated that, by the

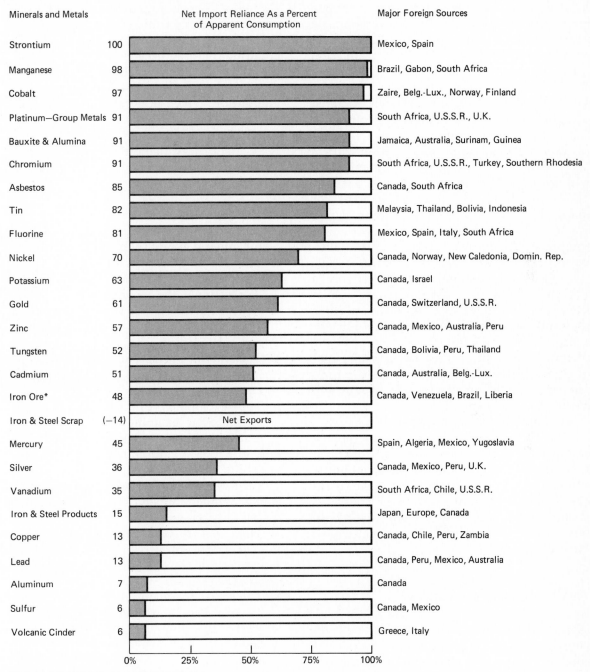

U.S. DEPENDENCE ON IMPORTS OF SELECTED MINERALS AND
METALS AS A PERCENT OF CONSUMPTION

Minerals and Metals		Net Import Reliance As a Percent of Apparent Consumption	Major Foreign Sources
Strontium	100		Mexico, Spain
Manganese	98		Brazil, Gabon, South Africa
Cobalt	97		Zaire, Belg.-Lux., Norway, Finland
Platinum—Group Metals	91		South Africa, U.S.S.R., U.K.
Bauxite & Alumina	91		Jamaica, Australia, Surinam, Guinea
Chromium	91		South Africa, U.S.S.R., Turkey, Southern Rhodesia
Asbestos	85		Canada, South Africa
Tin	82		Malaysia, Thailand, Bolivia, Indonesia
Fluorine	81		Mexico, Spain, Italy, South Africa
Nickel	70		Canada, Norway, New Caledonia, Domin. Rep.
Potassium	63		Canada, Israel
Gold	61		Canada, Switzerland, U.S.S.R.
Zinc	57		Canada, Mexico, Australia, Peru
Tungsten	52		Canada, Bolivia, Peru, Thailand
Cadmium	51		Canada, Australia, Belg.-Lux.
Iron Ore*	48		Canada, Venezuela, Brazil, Liberia
Iron & Steel Scrap	(—14)	Net Exports	
Mercury	45		Spain, Algeria, Mexico, Yugoslavia
Silver	36		Canada, Mexico, Peru, U.K.
Vanadium	35		South Africa, Chile, U.S.S.R.
Iron & Steel Products	15		Japan, Europe, Canada
Copper	13		Canada, Chile, Peru, Zambia
Lead	13		Canada, Peru, Mexico, Australia
Aluminum	7		Canada
Sulfur	6		Canada, Mexico
Volcanic Cinder	6		Greece, Italy

0%   25%   50%   75%   100%

*Substantially higher than normal due to strikes.

17–1 *U.S. net import reliance of selected minerals and metals as a percentage of consumption in 1977.*

year 2000, the United States will be spending at least $60 billion annually on mineral imports. Extreme dependence on a foreign source for a strategic mineral is, of course, foolhardy. For example, much of our cobalt is now obtained from the tiny African nation of Zaire. Our cobalt supply was temporarily threatened when Cuban troops invaded Zaire from nearby Angola in 1978. Zaire's cobalt production was halted for a short period and its price increased sixfold (5). The U.S. government has sharply increased its funding of critical minerals research with the goal of making our nation less vulnerable to a strategic mineral cut-off.

It is always possible that some nation with a "corner" on the world's supply of a strategic mineral will not only demand higher prices, but may hold the United States in economic blackmail. For example, it might decide to sell us the mineral only on the condition that we supply it in turn with military equipment, technical expertise, food, or political favors. China, which holds most of the world's tungsten; Spain, which holds most of the world's mercury; and Russia, with most of the world's palladium, are in a very strong bargaining position. Some experts think that the intense competition for scarce minerals will disrupt global peace. On the other hand, some political theorists consider that the interdependency of nations for necessary minerals should be a stabilizing factor that actually will reduce the prospects of war (5).

To reduce its vulnerable position, in the event that it no longer has access to a continuing supply of strategic minerals, the United States has stockpiled 93 key minerals. The total value of the stockpile is $13 billion. However, in the early 1980s the stockpile was 50 percent short of government goals — to have a sufficient supply of stockpiled minerals so that our nation could wage a conventional war of three years' duration.

The Available Mineral Supply

Have you ever seen, either in person, or possibly on television, a gigantic machine in the process of scooping out several tons of copper ore at a single bite? If so, did you notice the yawning pit left behind after the mining operation was finished? Did you wonder how long such an intensive process of mineral extraction could continue before the supply of copper ore was exhausted?

Geologists carefully distinguish between *total resources* and *mineral reserves.* Total resources is the total amount of minerals that occurs in a given region, nation, or the world. However, just because the minerals *exist*, does not mean that they can actually be *used*. For example, a copper deposit theoretically located ten miles below the surface of the earth could not be used because its extraction would be prohibitively expensive. The term mineral reserves, on the other hand, is used to designate the total amount of a given mineral that can be *mined at a profit*. (See Figure 17-2.) The amount of a mineral reserve is not permanently fixed. The amount in reserve status available to a nation depends on a whole complex of inter-related factors including the following:

1. The discovery of new mineral deposits.
2. The degree to which tax laws provide incentives for mineral exploration and extraction.
3. The degree to which mining activities are restricted as a result of environmental regulations. (For example, the cost of installing a scrubber to remove sulfur dioxide from the smokestack of a smelter or to reclaim a strip-mined area might compel a mining company to shut down.)
4. The amount of relatively cheap energy (electricity, steam power, and diesel fuel) available for extraction and processing.
5. The development of more efficient mining techniques. (For example, the ability to mine at greater depths or to utilize lower-grade deposits.)
6. The degree of durability or obsolescence of a product. (For example, cars built to last twenty years would result in the consumption of only half as much copper, iron, and lead as cars built to last only ten years.)
7. The extent to which a given metal can be recycled. (For example, the reuse of lead from discarded car batteries or the reuse of aluminum from pop and beer cans.)
8. The degree to which substitutes can be found for a scarce metal. (For example, the replacement of steel with aluminum in the manufacture of cars and planes.)

The Great Controversy: Are We Running Out of Minerals?

An intensive debate is raging among geologists, economists, mining experts, and environmentalists concerning the world's future mineral supplies. Ac-

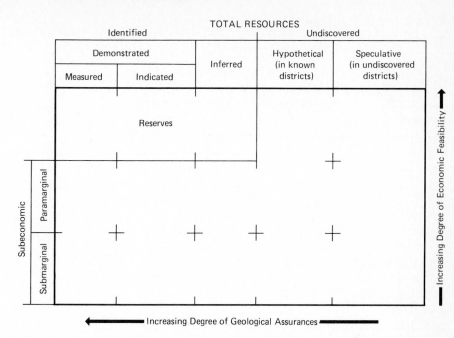

17-2 *Graphic classification of resources and reserves of non-renewable resources.*

cording to the optimists our global mineral reserves will be adequate far into the future. According to the pessimists, the world's mineral supply is diminishing rapidly. For example, usable supplies of gold, silver, and mercury will be depleted within a few decades. The views of both optimists and pessimists are summarized here concerning possible methods for extending our mineral reserves.

THE POSSIBILITY OF IMPORTANT NEW DISCOVERIES

Optimists. A large portion of the earth's surface has not as yet been intensively explored for mineral deposits. With the use of current technologies major finds are possible in Asia, Africa, South America, and Australia. Substantial finds have been made, for example, just recently: (1) billions of tons of iron in Australia, (2) vast deposits of bauxite (aluminum) ore in Brazil, and (3) large quantities of copper in Canada, Papua, New Guinea, and elsewhere.

Pessimists. It is almost certain that extremely rich deposits such as the Comstock silver lode in Nevada or the Mesabi Range iron deposits in Minnesota will not be discovered again. In any event, the search for new deposits is a "hit-or-miss" proposition. Many mining companies simply can't afford to gamble on the high capital investments involved.

Another negative feature is that more than 65 percent of the public lands in the United States, such

as national forests, national parks, and wilderness areas, have been ruled "off-limits" for mining exploration because of the possibility of land abuse, defilement of aesthetics, and pollution.

EXTRACTING MINERALS FROM SEAWATER

Optimists. William Page, a researcher from Great Britain summarizes the viewpoint of the optimists: "Seawater is estimated to contain 1,000 million years' supply of sodium chloride; more than one million years of molybdenum, uranium, tin, and cobalt; more than 1,000 years of nickel and copper. A cubic mile of seawater contains around 47 tons each of aluminum, iron, and zinc. Given around 330 million cubic miles of such water, we are talking of around 16,000 million tons each. Such estimates tend to exclude special concentrations such as the Red Sea brines and sediments; these alone contain perhaps $2,000 million worth of zinc, copper, silver, and gold . . . "(1).

Pessimists. True, there are indeed vast quantities of minerals in seawater. The problem, however, is that except for bromine, magnesium, and ordinary table salt, the concentrations are so very low that the energy costs necessary to extract them are prohibitive. As G. Tyler Miller, a well-known ecologist, has stated, the ocean "miners" would have to process a water volume equal to the combined annual flows of the Hudson and Delaware rivers just to extract

.003 percent of our nation's annual production of zinc (5).

NEW TECHNOLOGIES FOR EXTRACTING MINERALS FROM LOW-GRADE ORES

Optimists. As new extracting techniques are developed, the mining industry will be able to obtain more and more minerals from low-grade ores. The history of copper mining in the United States is a good example. At the start of this century only the very high-grade ore, containing 60 pounds of copper per ton (3 percent copper) was mined. However, as new advances were made in mining techniques, progressively leaner ores, with 50, 40, 30, and 20 pounds of copper per ton could be used. And today, a very low grade of ore that is only 0.3 percent copper, and contains only 6 pounds of copper per ton can be mined at a profit (6).

Pessimists. It is true that new technology has permitted the use of lower-grade ores. However, the gains have been made at the cost of enormous amounts of energy and water — critical resources that our nation is in urgent need of conserving. In fact, during the period 1950 to 1980, mineral production in the United States increased 50 percent, but energy consumption, due in part to the mining of low-grade ores, increased a whopping 600 percent (5). (Figure 17–3). The degree of environmental abuse also increases substantially as lower- and lower-quality ores are used.

THE RELATIVE ABUNDANCE OF LOW-GRADE ORES

Optimists. In many mineral deposits in which there is a gradual decrease in the richness of the ore with depth, the *tonnage of the ore increases at an exponental rate.* This principle was first presented by geologist S. G. Lasky of the U. S. Geological Survey in 1950. The principle holds for such minerals as copper, manganese, aluminum, titanium, nickel, and lead, where the decrease in quality is *gradual.* Therefore, it is logical to assume that, as the technologies for deeper mining and for mineral extraction from poor-grade ores are developed, a literal bonanza of mineral wealth will await the mining industry and society as a whole.

Pessimists. The optimism generated as a result of Lasky's principle is grossly unjustified. The principle certainly does not apply where the quality of ore *drops off sharply* rather than gradually. In any event, the deposits of gold, silver, zinc, lead, tungsten, antimony, and other metals do not conform to

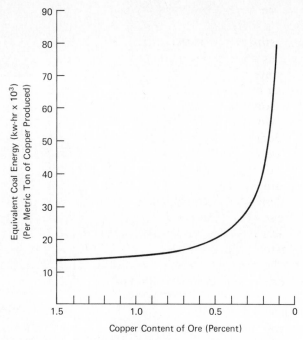

17–3 *Increasing amounts of energy are needed to extract copper from gradually decreasing grades of ore.*

Lasky's principle. The tremendous amount of energy required to mine these abundant, but very low grade, ores would, in many cases, be grossly prohibitive. This concept certainly should not be used in estimating unproved mineral supplies in the United States. As geologist T. S. Lovering states, such a policy would be "not only unwarranted, unscientific, and illogical, it is also downright dangerous in its psychological effects. . . ." In any event, the use of these deep-lying, very low-grade deposits would impose severe environmental impacts on society, even if they were extremely abundant (9).

SUBSTITUTING ONE MINERAL FOR ANOTHER

Optimists. The substitution concept got its impetus during World War II, when considerable amounts of copper were saved for our war effort by making pennies out of steel. Within the last two decades, plastics have replaced at least some steel in everything from fishing rods and speedboats to bathtubs and motor cars. Aluminum has replaced steel in airplanes and many vehicles where light weight is desirable. Magnesium is being substituted for zinc in an increasing number of products such as chemicals and pigments. Indeed, either naturally occurring or synthetic substitutes can now be found for virtually every metal used in today's society.

Pessimists. It is true that aluminum, iron, magnesium, and titanium are among the most abundant elements in the earth's crust and could replace many scarcer metals for a variety of uses. There are, however, some difficulties. For one thing, some substitutes would simply be *inferior* to the original material. For example, there is no other metal that has the unique chemical and physical properties of mercury, or the high melting point of tungsten, or the usefulness of gold in electrical contacts. A second problem is that the proposed substitutes are actually quite scarce in their own right. This is certainly true of the molybdenum that has been substituted for tungsten. Moreover, the cadmium and lead that have been used to replace mercury in some types of batteries are also in very short supply.

DURABILITY AND SIZE OF PRODUCTS. How long did you drive the family car until it "conked out"? Seven, eight — possibly ten — years? In one sense that car was an extremely rich "mine," containing a whole complex of mineral wealth, including about 20 pounds of lead, 35 pounds of zinc, 37 pounds of copper, 66 pounds of aluminum, as well as lots of steel (iron). Of course, the reason your car lasted only seven to ten years is because the manufacturer, General Motors, Ford, or Chrysler, *purposely built obsolescence* into you machine. After all, the quicker the car dies, the quicker you are going to buy a new one — which will keep the stockholders happy. Just suppose, however, that your car lasted twenty years instead of ten. No, that's not asking too much. The technology is available. After all, many European cars already show that kind of durability. By doubling car longevity, the consumption of metals by the automobile industry would be cut in half.

In addition to increasing product durability, minerals could also be conserved by making products *smaller.* There is an increasing tendency for industry to miniaturize its products. This is true of everything from bathtubs to computers. The classic example is the motor car. The enormous gas guzzlers of the 1960s have been replaced with streamlined compacts that are fully 300 pounds lighter. In addition to cars, however, a whole spectrum of household appliances from toasters to electric stoves, from refrigerators to clocks and telephones is available to our mineral-scarce society in smaller and smaller sizes. Calculating machines are another example. Not too many years ago they were bulky and cumbersome — something you wouldn't carry around the campus from one class to another. They were certainly a far cry from today's tiny, compact, pocket-sized calculators, which, again, save considerable mineral resources.

RECYCLING MINERALS. Both optimists and pessimists also agree that extensive mineral recycling will extend the mineral reserves of our nation. Today's sanitary landfill, which is really just an *upgraded dump*, should be regarded as a man-made ore deposit. A major function of the Resource Conservation and Recovery Act of 1976 was to stimulate industry to regard waste as a potential source of valuable metals. Some waste, such as aluminum cans, is already being cycled at a high rate. More than seven billion cans are being recycled yearly — about one in every four produced. Aluminum and other metals that resist corrosion and deterioration, such as copper, lead, zinc, and tin, can be used again and again. Certainly this would be true of the lead in discarded pipes, empty toothpaste tubes, and dead lead-acid car batteries. The recycling industry should indeed be encouraged to "get the lead out."

As a nation we can do a much better recycling job. It depends, in large part, on need and motivation. As Ruben L. Parson, a geography professor at St. Cloud State College, Minnesota, has written: "Under the stress of World War II we reclaimed anything metallic, from abandoned streetcar tracks and worn-out machinery to horseshoes and tin cans. Reclaimed metal gave us the machines that crushed Hitler's armored legions. We became scrap-conscious as never before. But we have too readily reverted to the reckless, wasteful discard of material that is typically American" (8).

Unfortunately, the federal government provides incentives to the mining industry in the form of billions of dollars of tax breaks and depletion allowances to extract the virgin metals from the earth's crust rapidly. Paradoxically, those industries that operate in a more sound manner, both ecologically and economically, and recover scrap metals from urban wastes, do not enjoy such subsidies (5).

When Will the Global Supply of Minerals Become Exhausted?

It is of utmost importance to our economic and national security that we have at least a rough idea

527

as to when the global supplies of our key minerals will be exhausted. Such estimates are made on the basis of (1) the available supply of a given mineral known to be present in the earth's crust, and (2) the known rates of consumption. The depletion time of a given resource is defined by geologists as "the time required until 80 percent of the available mineral supply is consumed."

At least 16 key metals are essential to our nation's industrial economy and national security. Among them are gold, silver, mercury, zinc, lead, copper, tin, and tungsten. Even if new discoveries and or technologies make it possible to mine five times the currently known supply of the global reserves, they will be 80 percent depleted by the year 2040 or before (5). To prevent weakening of our national security, we must carefully conserve these minerals.

Environmental Problems Caused by Mining

LAND ABUSE. Surface mining operations may quickly transform a scenic area of breathtaking beauty into an ugly wasteland. This hideous scarring of the face of our landscape has been brought under at least partial control by the passage of the Surface Mining and Rehabilitation Act. Under the terms of this act, once the minerals have been extracted, the original horizons of soil and rock must be replaced, the original land contours must be restored, and the original vegetative cover must be re-established to the extent that it is technically possible. For example, at the mining communities of Climax and Grand Valley, Colorado, plant ecologists and soil scientists have teamed up in an attempt to establish specially selected hybrid grasses as a pioneer stage of a future plant succession at abandoned surface-mine sites (3). Even with the best techniques available, however, some ecologists feel that in areas of less than ten inches of annual rainfall, the revegetation of abandoned mine sites will be almost impossible.

LAND-USE CONFLICTS. Mining activities have disturbed almost 250,000 acres of land in the Rocky Mountain region alone. The resulting ugliness and desolation make such areas unsuitable for human habitation or for tourists in search of wilderness beauty. Moreover, the potential of the disturbed areas for grain or cattle production has, of course, been seriously impaired.

CONSUMPTIVE USE OF WATER. During the processing of some ores, tremendous quantities of water are needed. The lower the grade of ore, the greater the volume of water required. For example, in the *hydraulic* mining process used to extract gold and silver, powerful blasts of water may be directed against the side of a mountain in which the precious minerals are deposited. Therefore, in some areas the mining industry competes directly with ranchers, irrigationists, industries, and municipalities for a water supply that is already diminishing at record rates.

WATER POLLUTION. Abandoned mine sites can be a source of *acid mine drainage*. As water drains off from displaced soil and rock, chemical reactions occur that result in the formation of sulfuric acid (H_2SO_4). This runoff water then lowers the pH (acidifies) of streams and severely disrupts the normal functioning of the aquatic ecosystem. Massive fish kills are a common result. Drainage from abandoned strip-mined sites also may cause severe water erosion. The resultant increase in stream sedimentation will cause reduced levels of photosynthesis, increased stream temperatures, lowered concentrations of dissolved oxygen, disruption of fish food chains, destruction of fish-spawning sites, serious population declines of many aquatic plants and animals, and the defilement of scenic beauty.

AIR POLLUTION. A variety of toxic materials may be released into the atmosphere as a result of the smelting of ores. Thus, sulfur dioxide and arsenic may be released during the smelting of copper and cadmium when zinc ores are smelted. The devastating effects of sulfur dioxide (and sulfuric acid mist) on the woodland ecosystem adjoining the giant copper smelter at Ducktown, Tennessee, has already been described. During the heating of phosphate rock, toxic fluoride gases are released into the air. Eventually the fluorides may contaminate cattle foods. The intake of the fluoride-contaminated food by cattle results in *fluorosis*, a disease characterized by painful joints, softened bones and teeth, and the inability to stand or walk normally. The result is annual multimillion dollar losses to the livestock industry.

RADIOACTIVE CONTAMINATION OF THE ENVIRONMENT. Uranium is an important fuel for the nuclear power industry. It is extracted as uranium

Problems Facing the Nonfuel Mining Industry

T. B. Thompson
Department of Earth Resources
COLORADO STATE
UNIVERSITY – FORT COLLINS

The nonfuel minerals industry in the United States is the backbone, along with agricultural resources, of the national economy. The minerals industry, however, faces numerous problems: (1) As a supplier of raw materials for the construction and manufacturing industries, activities of the minerals industry fluctuate with the economy. (2) The minerals exploration industry is capital-intensive, with very low discovery rates, attempting to find minerals within land areas that continually shrink as a result of withdrawals; competition with foreign suppliers of minerals is difficult due to foreign government subsidies of their minerals industries, lower labor costs and lower taxation. (3) The United States lacks a policy on strategic minerals; we are dependent on foreign sources for many strategic minerals, making us subject to cartel whims with regard to price and supply. (4) The populace of the United States does not uniformly appreciate their dependence on and the distribution, effects, and importance of the minerals industry in their daily lives; trade deficits due to dependency on foreign sources will continue to increase unless the federal government provides a favorable environment for minerals exploration within the United States.

These problems can be solved by establishment of a national policy with regard to strategic minerals and minerals exploration on federal lands, encouragement of a national base of minerals production, reduced foreign dependence, public education on mineral resources, and development of more precise exploration models.

oxide (U_3O_8) from sandstone deposits in several Western states including Colorado. About one pound of uranium oxide is recovered from every 500 pounds of sandstone. During the early years of the industry the spent sandstone wastes, known as *tailings,* were simply piled up in gigantic mounds near the mine site — an eloquent testimony to the irresponsibility and/or ignorance of both the industry and federal regulatory agencies.

Some of those radioactive tailings were actually used by the construction industry in Grand Junction, Colorado, as fill material for the concrete foundations of about 5,000 homes, schools, and commercial buildings in the 1950s and 1960s. Finally, in 1966 the occupants of those buildings were warned that the radiation to which they were being exposed could increase their chances of getting lung cancer. Nevertheless, in the late 1970s a number of those people had still refused to evacuate the site (2).

Mining the Sea

In recent years the United States has been forced to import at least 23 of the 36 (63.8 percent) basic materials needed to support her industrial economy. Our dependence contrasts sharply with the relative self-sufficiency of Russia, which has needed to import only 8 of the 36 (22.2 percent) basic substances. Now where could the United States possibly obtain additional supplies of these vitally important materials? Certainly not from our land-based mines. After all, many of them are already approaching the stage of exhaustion. Surprisingly, according to some optimists, the answer to our national predicament may be found in the oceans. Minerals occurring in the oceans are found in (1) the seawater itself, (2) the continental shelves, and (3) on the bottom of the deep sea. As of 1982 the federal government made it possible for mining industries to lease certain mineral-rich areas of the ocean bottom within our 200-mile Extended Economic Zone nation's for the purpose of exploration and development.

Minerals of the Continental Shelf

Because a continental shelf is simply an extension of a continent that happens to be "awash," it is not surprising that such a shelf would yield the same types of minerals that can be extracted from land-based mines. In fact, the economic value of the mineral deposits in the continental shelf is estimated (by the optimists) to be about 15 percent of our global terrestrial mineral wealth (4). The United States is extremely interested in the rich deposits of copper and zinc located off the coasts of Washington and Oregon.

Minerals of the Deep Sea Bottom

In the year 1900 an American marine expedition discovered many curious potato-shaped lumps, or nodules, on the bottom of the Pacific Ocean. The aggregate weight of those soft, crumbly two-inch *nodules* in the Pacific alone was estimated at more than 1,700 billion tons. Although rich in manganese, those tiny lumps also contain nickel, iron, copper, cobalt, molybdenum, and aluminum. In aggregate they represent an enormous storehouse of minerals. For example, it is estimated that the supply of industrially valuable copper, at expected usage rates, will become exhausted in only forty years. However, if we are able to extract the 7.9 billion tons of copper available in these ocean-bottom nodules, we would not run out of copper for at least 6,000 years (10).

Problems with Mining the Sea

There are several vexing problems associated with mining the sea. First, there are the technological problems of bringing solid materials, such as the nodules, up from the ocean floor. It has been suggested that this might be done by means of a device that works like a gigantic vacuum cleaner. (It is much easier to extract oil and gas from the ocean floor than to remove and recover solids.) Second, there are *environmental problems.* Certainly any dredging or scooping up of materials from the continental shelves or deep-sea bottom would increase the *turbidity* of the water. It would seem that *thermal pollution* would also be a problem. The mining of the ocean would involve huge machines that would consume large amounts of energy. The massive equipment would most likely be cooled with seawater. Eventually the warmed-up seawater would be discharged back into the ocean. Certainly the increased turbidity and thermal pollution would have a harmful effect on the marine ecosystem in terms of fish and shellfish growth and reproduction.

Third, there are *political problems.* For example, the question of who really owns the floor of the ocean arises. The continental shelves are presumably under the jurisdiction of the adjoining coastal nation. But what about the bottom of the deep sea, say 1,000 miles east of New York City or west of Los Angeles? The deep sea belongs to *no one nation;* therefore, theoretically it is the property of *all nations.* But which nation, among the 350 in the world, should eventually mine the deep ocean floor? As in many situations of this type, the "might makes right" philosophy probably would prevail. Therefore, we might expect that the world's most heavily industrialized and technologically advanced nations (United States, USSR, Great Britain, and Japan) would probably reap most of the mineral wealth. Fourth, this in turn brings up some *ethical* problems. Suppose, for example, that an extremely rich formation of aluminum-containing nodules were discovered on the floor of the Indian Ocean 400 miles off the coast of some small African nation whose people were living in abject poverty. Unfortunately that nation would not have either the financial wealth nor the technological ability to harvest the nodules. However, what if the United States, already the wealthiest nation on earth, were to send her "ocean-mining fleets" halfway around the world to collect them instead? Finally, the mining of the ocean floor poses the problem of a possible *nuclear war.* Suppose, for example, that an extremely rich deposit of copper were found on the ocean floor 300 miles from Cuba. Such an event could eventually lead to a head-to-head confrontation between the United States and the USSR.

The Law of the Sea Treaty

In order to control some of the problems discussed above, 160 nations struggled for several years to develop a Law of the Sea Treaty, under the sponsorship of the United Nations. The draft (unsigned) treaty includes the following provisions:

1. Each nation bordering the sea would have complete control over the harvesting of marine minerals within 200 miles of its coast.
2. An International Seabed Authority would be established to regulate mineral production by private firms outside the 200-mile zone.
3. The Seabed Authority would be funded by a $1-billion-dollar grant from the wealthy coastal nations, such as the United States, England, and Japan.
4. The United Nations would form its own seabed mining company and distribute the profits

among the undeveloped coastal nations like Mexico, Colombia, and India.

5. Private companies, such as those from the United States, the USSR, or France, would be required to sell their latest ocean-mining technology to the United Nations' firm.

Hopes that the treaty would be ratified were rudely shattered when the Reagan Administration refused to sign it in 1981. It felt that the treaty would jeopardize the ocean-mining interests of private American firms (5). The chairman of the House Foreign Affairs Committee, Representative Clement Zablocki (D–Wis.) emphasized that President Reagan's decision "will have serious consequences for the United States" and that the president "unfortunately offered no constructive alternative."

Rapid Review

1. The American automobile industry uses roughly 7 percent of all the copper consumed in the United States, 10 percent of the aluminum, 13 percent of the nickel, 20 percent of the steel, 35 percent of the zinc, and 60 percent of the lead.

2. Mineral resources are classified as *nonrenewable* or *exhaustible*.

3. The nine most abundant elements in the earth's crust are oxygen, silicon, aluminum, iron, calcium, magnesium, sodium, potassium, and titanium.

4. An *ore* is a naturally occurring deposit that has a concentration of a desirable substance.

5. Among the environmental problems caused by mining are (1) land abuse, (2) land-use conflicts, (3) extensive use of water, (4) water pollution, (5) air pollution, and (6) radioactive contamination.

6. Although the United States represents only 5 percent of the world's population, it consumes about 20 percent of the nonfuel minerals mined each year throughout the world. In the minds of some authorities this disproportionate consumption of minerals is unethical.

7. Minerals that are absolutely essential to the economic health or security of our nation, such as copper, cobalt, lead, are classified as *strategic*.

8. By the year 2000 the United States will be spending at least $60 billion on mineral imports.

9. The total amount of a given mineral that is available is known as the *total resources* of that mineral.

10. The term *reserves* refers to the total amount of a given mineral that can be mined at a profit.

11. The extent of reserves available to a nation depends on a number of factors: (a) the discovery of new mineral deposits, (b) the degree to which tax laws provide an incentive for mineral extraction, (c) the degree to which mining activities are hampered by environmental regulations, (d) the amount of cheap energy available for extraction and processing, (e) the level of mining technology, (f) the degree of product durability, (g) the extent to which a given metal can be recycled, and (h) the degree to which substitutes can be found for a scarce metal.

12. The *depletion time* of a mineral is the time required for 80 percent of the mineral to be depleted.

13. The *static reserve index* is the estimate of the time required for 80 percent of the known reserves of the mineral to be depleted at current rates of consumption.

14. The *exponential reserve index* is the estimate of the time required until 80 percent of the reserves of the mineral is depleted, with the assumption that consumption will increase at the rate of 2.5 percent per year.

15. In recent years the United States has been forced to import 23 of the 36 basic minerals needed to support her industrial economy.

16. Sea-mining activities would probably result in increased turbidity as well as thermal pollution.

17. In order to eliminate, or at least control, some of the technological, environmental, political, and ethical problems associated with mining the oceans, 160 nations struggled for several years to develop a Law of the Sea Treaty under the sponsorship of the United Nations.

18. The Reagan Administration refused to sign the Law of the Sea Treaty in 1981 because it felt the treaty would jeopardize the ocean-mining interests of private American firms.

Key Words and Phrases

Acid mine drainage	Fluorosis
Aluminum	High-grade ore
Chromium	Hydraulic mining
Cobalt	International Seabed
Compounds	Authority
Continental shelf	Lasky's principle
Depletion time	Law of the Sea Treaty
Elements	Low-grade ore

Manganese nodules
Mineral
Ocean mining
Ore
Radioactive contamination
Reagan Administration
Recycling
Reserves
Resource Conservation and Recovery Act

Static Reserve Index
Strategic minerals
Substitution
Surface Mining and Rehabilitation Act
Tailings
Thermal pollution
Tin
Titanium
Total mineral resources
Turbidity

Questions and Topics for Discussion

1. Explain the paradoxical statement: "An *American* car, in a sense, is a *foreign* car."
2. How would you *classify* our mineral resources?
3. Distinguish between high- and low-grade ore. Give a specific example.
4. Most minerals used by humans exist in the earth's crust as *compounds.* Name a compound in which copper frequently occurs. Name one in which aluminum occurs.
5. Discuss the statement: "The rate at which the United States is consuming the global supply of minerals is immoral." Do you agree with this statement? Why or why not?
6. Discuss the relationship between the availability of strategic minerals and the national security of the United States.
7. Distinguish between *total mineral resources* and *mineral reserves.*
8. The reserves of a given mineral (such as copper) available to the United States may vary considerably, depending on a number of different interrelated factors. List seven of them.
9. Suppose that you are asked by your instructor to debate the issue of whether our nation is running out of the necessary minerals to keep its economy going strong. What arguments would you advance as an optimist? As a pessimist?
10. Distinguish between the *static reserve index* and the *exponential reserve index.* In your opinion, which index of mineral depletion time is the most realistic?
11. Name the three major sources (or areas) from which ocean minerals might be extracted.
12. Briefly discuss the potential significance of *manganese nodules* as an important mineral source.

13. List two ways in which intensive ocean mining might disrupt marine ecosystems.
14. Discuss some of the political and ethical problems associated with the mining of the sea.
15. List five major provisions of the proposed Law of the Sea Treaty.
16. President Reagan refused to sign the Law of the Sea Treaty in 1981 because he felt it would jeopardize the interests of private American mining firms. In your opinion was President Reagan justified in his actions or do you think his refusal was ill-considered? Discuss your answer.

Endnotes

1. Cole, H. S. D., ed. *Models of Doom.* New York: Universe, 1975.
2. Ehrlich, Paul, Anne H. Ehrlich, and John P. Holdren. *Human Ecology.* San Francisco: Freeman, 1973.
3. Havlick, Spenser W. *The Urban Organism.* New York: Macmillan, 1974.
4. Hunt, Cynthia A., and Robert M. Garrels. *Water: The Web of Life.* New York: Norton, 1972.
5. Miller, G. Tyler. *Living in the Environment.* 3rd ed. New York: Wadsworth, 1982.
6. Moriber, George. *Environmental Science.* Boston: Allyn, 1974.
7. National Academy of Science. *Science and Technology.* San Francisco: Freeman, 1979.
8. Parson, Ruben L. *Conserving American Resources.* 3rd ed. Englewood Cliffs, N.J.: Prentice-Hall, 1972.
9. Treshow, Michael. *The Human Environment.* New York: McGraw-Hill, 1976.
10. Wagner, Richard H. *Environment and Man.* New York: Norton, 1971.

Suggested Readings for the Interested Student

Tilton, J. E. *The Future of Non-Fuel Minerals.* Washington, DC: The Brookings Institution, 1977.
Uyeda, S. *The New View of the Earth.* Translation by O. Masako. San Francisco: Freeman, 1978.
Mineral Resource Perspectives. U.S. Geological Survey Professional Paper 940. Washington, DC: Government Printing Office, 1975.
Government and the Nation's Resources. National Commission on Supplies and Shortages. Washington, DC: Government Printing Office, 1975.
Special Report: Critical Imported Materials. Council on International Economic Policy. Washington, DC: Government Printing Office, 1974.
Cameron, E. N., ed. *Mineral Position of the United States, 1975–2000.* Madison: University of Wisconsin, 1973.

18 Energy

It was symbolic. In early June 1973, America's long-anticipated Skylab mission was in deep trouble. The spaceship had incurred a 6 percent electrical-power deficit because of the failure of 2 of its 18 solar batteries. The implications were grave. In order to conserve energy, lights aboard the spaceship were dimmed, fans were turned off, and a much-heralded long-distance mapping of the earth's mineral resources was canceled. Ironically, the crisis aboard the tiny spaceship, involving three astronauts, was a symbolic vignette of the *global* energy crisis on Spaceship Earth (a luminous sphere 300 miles below), involving four billion people.

The Great Gasoline Shortage

It was the autumn of 1973 when the averge citizen finally realized that the United States was in deep energy trouble. Although college professors, industrial experts, and federal officials had been predicting shortages for months and even years, their pronouncements had always seemed a bit alarmist and unreal. Suddenly, however, the energy crisis was indeed very real. Consider the following developments:

1. Gasoline supplies became so scarce that thousands of independent dealers throughout the nation were forced to stop pumping gas. The personal distress they experienced was expressed in a crudely scrawled sign placed between two pumps at an abandoned Detroit service station:

"Out of gas. Out of patience. Out of business. Bitter? H--- yes!"

2. The price of gasoline suddenly zoomed from 40 cents to 55 cents and more per gallon. A few unscrupulous operators in New York City briefly gouged their customers at the rate of $1.00 per gallon.

3. Motorists lined up in predawn darkness for gas in New York and other major eastern cities, sometimes for two hours, finally receiving only a half-tank of gas.

4. A federal regulation reduced maximum highway speed from 70 to a "crawling" 55 miles per hour — a stratagem that insured more efficient gas consumption (and probably will save 10,000 lives a year as well).

5. The "Big Three" of the auto industry — Ford, Chrysler, and GMC — feverishly converted from the gas-profligate big cars to the gas-conserving compacts.

6. Economic setbacks were severe. Overall, the nation edged closer to a major recession — the GNP growth rate was the lowest since 1971. By early 1974 at least 100,000 workers had lost their jobs in the steel, automobile, auto sales, auto parts, tire, highway-restaurant, camper-trailer, resort, and snowmobile industries, all largely dependent on a bounteous supply of inexpensive gasoline for their vitality.

When the OPEC nations finally lifted their embargo early in 1974, the gasoline pinch finally eased and for several years motorists filled up their tanks

533

almost as casually as before. Then it happened: a revolt in Iran in the winter of 1978–1979, and just like that the world was cut off of 5.5 million barrels of oil per day. In a short time events associated with the first energy crisis were repeated: First in California and then elsewhere, motorists were placed on an alternate-day odd-even number (license plate-calendar day) gas-rationing plan. The extreme shortage of diesel fuel for tractors severely hampered Iowa farmers during the height of the corn-planting season. Gasoline prices zoomed upward rapidly — to more than 90 cents per gallon in 19 states by early June 1979. And even as this writer wrote these words he heard John O'Leary, the assistant secretary of energy intone the somber news on an NBC television program that Nigeria was threatening to cut off the United States from any more of her oil production. The result, according to O'Leary, would be that gasoline prices in America would "hit the roof."

Frustrated American motorists, farmers, and truck drivers searched for scapegoats on which to vent their frustration. The average American blamed a conspiracy of the big oil companies for the nation's gasoline crisis. The oil companies accused the federal government. Congress blamed the Department of Energy and the President. And the President chided the general public. But the branding of a million scapegoats will not put one more drop of oil in America's gas tanks. President Carter bluntly told the "energy facts of life" to a gathering of American businessmen in May 1979: "The American people still refuse to face the inevitable prospect of energy shortages. Even the most well-meaning and patriotic Americans still look for a scapegoat. Many believe there is no energy shortage. Those hopeful and pleasant dreams are not going to come true. . . ."

The very thought of this resource-blessed nation suffering from an energy shortage seems bizarre, indeed. But it is very real and may persist for decades. The gravity of the situation was underscored by John A. Carver, a member of the Federal Power Commission (FPC), who recently stated, "I think our energy shortage is incurable. We're going to have to live with it the rest of our lives" (26).

What Has Caused America's Energy Crisis?

Although the Arab oil embargo was the immediate cause of the 1973–1974 crisis, and the Iranian revolution precipitated the 1979 crisis, a whole complex of long-term factors that have been operating for

18–1 *"Lit up like a Christmas tree." Seattle, Washington, at night — one reason for the nation's energy crisis. (Rollin R. Geppert)*

years was just as significant, even though less obvious, to the general public. Let us examine some of them.

INACCURATE ESTIMATES OF ENERGY NEEDS. Some sources have suggested that the energy demand was grossly underestimated, not only by regulatory agencies such as the FPC, but also by the fuel industry itself.

LACK OF ECONOMIC INCENTIVES FOR GAS AND OIL EXPLORATION. For many years the federal government clamped a lid on gas and oil prices. This policy inevitably caused oil and gas exploration to stagnate. The cost of drilling new wells has risen appreciably because many of the remaining deposits occur at considerable depths. For example, back in 1931, "wildcatter" N. P. Powell made an oil strike in a fabulous East Texas field at a depth of only 3,600 feet, involving a total cost of a mere $15,000. By 1973, however, costs were running as high as $4 *million* per well in western Oklahoma, with deposits being tapped at depths of over 22,000 feet. Between 1956 and 1971 drilling costs rose 85 percent, despite the fact that average prices for gas and oil increased a mere 37 percent and 17 percent, respectively (26).

INADEQUATE REFINING CAPACITY. During the 1970s the EPA directed car manufacturers to produce cars that were adapted to consume unleaded gas. At the same time the EPA required the oil producers to refine increasing amounts of unleaded gasoline. By mid-1979 more than 42 percent of American cars were adapted for unleaded gas. Unfortunately, unleaded gasoline was in short supply. Why? The culprit, according to the oil companies, was federal control of fuel prices. They simply could not expand the capacity of their refineries because gas prices were so low they would not be able to recover the cost of the expensive refining equipment.

ENVIRONMENTAL CONCERNS. In the decade of the 1970s environmentalists were greatly concerned over both the proposed and the actual sitings of numerous nuclear power plants. They were especially disturbed with plant construction in highly populous areas, such as Manhattan, because of the threat to human life and health from radioactive emissions. They also strenuously objected to plant

18–2 *High-voltage transmission lines march across the land. The transmission lines required by the average-sized nuclear power plant will pre-empt 40 acres of land per mile of line and present a visual blight as well.*

siting along lake shores because of resultant thermal pollution, destruction to aquatic life, and accelerated eutrophication. A good case in point was the attempt by environmentalists to delay the operation of the Consumers Power Company on the shores of Lake Michigan. Although the $125-million plant was almost completed, the environmentalists filed a suit to prevent the Atomic Energy Commission from granting the company an operating license. Various groups entered the controversy that ensued—the Michigan Water Resources Commission, the Federal Water Quality Administration, the environmentalists, and the Consumers Power Company. Scientists representing each of the groups could not come to a final agreement. The dilemma was finally resolved when the power company decided to construct a mammoth cooling tower at an initial expense of $15 million and an annual operating expense of $3 million. The environmentalists may have had very sound ecological grounds for intervening, but it is nevertheless true, from the simple-minded standpoint of energy production alone, that such intervention, repeated in conjunction with the sitings of numerous nuclear and fossil-fuel power plants scattered across the nation, undoubtedly has contributed to regional energy shortages. Speaking at an emergency meeting of the Wisconsin Petroleum Institute during the critical oil shortage, which he attended at the time of a subzero cold spell, George Thaler, the institute's president, accused environmentalists of blocking offshore drilling, fighting the development of the trans-Alaskan pipeline, and exerting pressure to decrease oil-depletion allowances. In his words, "Hell, they're the ones who caused the problem, let them solve it . . . " (4). On the other hand, John Steinhart, of the Institute of Environmental Studies at the University of Wisconsin, believes that even if all environmental activism suddenly stopped, the long-range power crisis would still be with us (14).

RESTRICTIONS ON THE USE OF HIGH-SULFUR FUELS. At the present time the great bulk of electrical power is generated in plants fired by fossil fuels (coal, oil, and gas). For almost a century, from 1882 until about 1970, those plants were able to burn any quality of fuel they desired. However, in the past few years, in such major cities as New York, Boston, Chicago, and Los Angeles, the electric utilities, along with other fuel-consuming industries have been required to use only low-sulfur fuels in order to keep sulfur dioxide emissions down to a minimum. Because such low-sulfur fuel is not nearly as abundant as high-sulfur fuel, power production may be hampered as a result.

ENERGY CONSUMPTION FOR POLLUTION CONTROL. It is ironic that the energy crisis confronting America today is in part the result of our attempt to end another problem—pollution. Twenty years ago "pollution abatement" was little more than an academic phrase. Today, however, our nation is committed to clean up the atmospheric, aquatic, and terrestrial garbage that inevitably accumulates as a by-product of our life-style and affluence—and pollution cleanup requires huge amounts of energy. For example, the federal government is currently subsidizing the construction of thousands of modern sewage-treatment plants across the nation; but

to pump sewage water through these plants requires energy—0.5-million kilowatt hours annually for a secondary treatment plant accommodating a city of 90,000 people. We are beginning to control the noxious emissions generated by foundry operations, but it requires the employment of a new type of energy-demanding electric-conduction furnace. We are beginning to reduce the solid-waste problem posed by rusting old Fords and Chevies. This is being done with the aid of a car-crushing machine that mashes the cars into compact blocks of scrap steel; regrettably, however, the machine is activated by an *energy-demanding* 5,000-horsepower electric motor.

AMERICA'S HIGH STANDARD OF LIVING. Through the years the average American has exerted a progressively greater demand for *energy-consuming* creature comforts: high-powered automobiles, color television sets, air-conditioning units, motorbikes, snowmobiles, self-cleaning ovens, power saws, and even motorized golf carts and a whole series of electrical gadgets for slicing meat, opening cans, brushing teeth, polishing shoes, and drying hair. Wisconsin's Senator Gaylord Nelson has observed that *the amount of energy required merely to run America's air conditioners is greater than the total energy used by 800 million Chinese.*

Somehow it seems incongruous (or should we say immoral?) for the United States, with only 6 percent of the world's population, to be consuming 30 percent of the world's energy resources. In other words, you and I are using five times as much energy as the average human inhabitant and fully thirty times as much as a native of India or Africa. (See Figure 18–3.) The American housewife can cook the family meal by using copious quantities of either electricity or natural gas simply by flicking a switch or turning a valve. Contrast this situation with the one in rural India, where the commonest fuel is dried *manure*, of which 300 million tons are used yearly (7). According to energy specialist James P. Lodge, Jr., in terms of energy consumption, the average American has 500 energy slaves at his or her beck and call—the equivalent of 500 human slaves. In this respect the average American is far better off than was the most powerful Roman emperor. The "true" population in America, therefore, is not merely 230 million, but 230 million *plus* 115 billion energy slaves. In contrast, how many energy slaves are available to the rice-paddy farmer in South Viet-

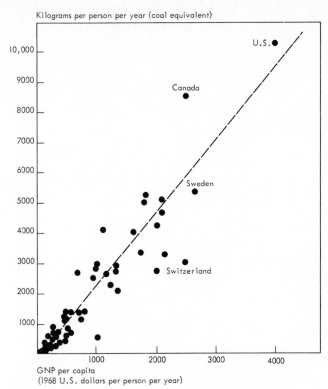

Kilograms per person per year (coal equivalent)

GNP per capita
(1968 U.S. dollars per person per year)

18-3 *Relationship between energy consumption and GNP. Although the nations of the world consume greatly varying amounts of energy per capita, energy consumption correlates fairly well with output per capita (GNP per capita). The relationship is generally linear. The scattering of points is largely the result of climatic differences, local fuel prices, and emphasis on heavy industry. India, Pakistan, and other undeveloped countries would be represented by the clustering of dots in the extreme lower left corner of the graph.*

nam or the berry- and egg-gathering tribesman in South Africa?

These, then, are a few of the factors contributing to our energy crisis. However, even in the act of listing them, the cause of the crisis has probably been grossly oversimplified. According to the nonprofit research corporation Resources for the Future, America's energy dilemma

arises from an extraordinary coincidence of events involving each particular form of commercial energy — factors as diverse as problems with nuclear technology, Middle Eastern politics, the quest for a cleaner environment, the health and safety of mine workers, and the federal government's policies toward natural gas prices and oil imports. All of these strands are so interwoven that it is

difficult to tag this or that factor as contributing this or that much to the overall problem.

The Status of America's Traditional Energy Resources

Coal

It has been estimated that the geologic formation of coal required several hundred million years. Coal was formed as the result of the incomplete oxidation of plant and animal bodies that had been buried under sedimentary deposits of sand and mud. Your ability to read this very page under the electric lamp in your study room may well be possible only because of the sunlight that streamed to earth during the Carboniferous ("coal bearing") period millions of years ago. Some of that solar energy was trapped by green plants during the process of photosynthesis. The tremendous impact the use of coal has had on human culture is described by M. King Hubbert of the U.S. Geological Survey:

Emancipation from this dependence on contemporary solar energy was not possible until some other and hitherto unknown source of energy should become available. This had its beginning about the twelfth or thirteenth century when the inhabitants of the northeastern coast of England discovered that certain black rocks found along the shore, and thereafter known as "sea coales," would burn. From this discovery, there followed in most inevitable succession, the mining of coal and its use for domestic heating and for the smelting of metals, the development

18-4 *The average American uses fully thirty times as much energy as these wretched houseboat-living Pakistani.*

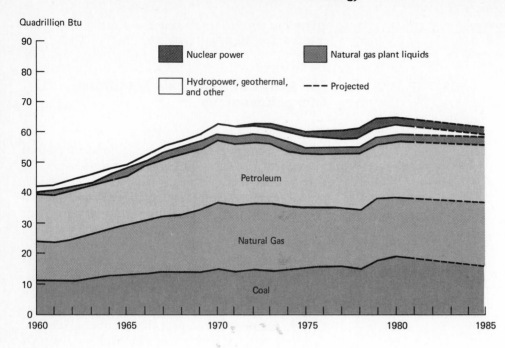

Quadrillion Btu

Nuclear power

Natural gas plant liquids

Hydropower, geothermal, and other

––– Projected

Petroleum

Natural Gas

Coal

18–5 *Production of energy by type, 1960–1981.*

of the steam engine, the locomotive, steamship, and steam-electric power. (14)

The mining of coal started in the United States in the mid-1700s. Nevertheless, it did not replace wood as our nation's major fuel source until the 1880s. Shortly after World War II, oil and gas replaced coal as "energy king" because they could be easily transported by pipeline and were cheaper as well. The importance of coal as an energy source in the United States is shown in Figure 18–5.

Because coal deposits usually occur in continuous seams that frequently lie just below the surface, it has been possible to make fairly accurate estimates of coal abundance by drilling a number of deep, widely spaced borings into the coal-bearing seams. By such techniques the coalfields of the North American continent have been quite thoroughly mapped. (See Figure 18–6.) Geologists estimate, for example, that two trillion tons of minable coal lay buried in North America (8). The United States has so much it has been called the "Saudi Arabia" of coal. It is also known that it is most unlikely that another coal "bonanza" like the Pittsburgh coalfield will be discovered. Although coal has been mined for at least eight centuries, use of this "black gold" has been accelerating at a phenomenal rate — more than half of all the coal ever mined, for example, has been taken in just the last 40 years (2).

THE GRADES OF COAL. Not all coal is of the same quality. The various grades are classified on the basis of carbon content and heat value. They range from *peat*, which is the poorest grade, through *lignite* ("brown coal"), *sub-bituminous* and *bituminous* (soft coal) to *anthracite* ("hard" coal), which is of the highest quality. The change in grades is caused by increasing amounts of heat and pressure generated in the earth's crust. Lignite forms 8 percent of our nation's coal reserves, and is found primarily in the Western states. Since lignite lies near the surface it is easily obtained by strip-mining. Sub-bituminous and bituminous coal form about 83 percent of our nation's coal reserve. It has its main use in coal-fired electric power plants and to some degree in the steel industry. Although anthracite is our top-quality coal, it forms only about 2 percent of our nation's coal reserves.

Environmental Abuse Caused by Strip-Mining

Although the United States has abundant supplies of minable coal, there are two very important environmental concerns attending its use. First, about 50 percent of the coal America burns is strip-mined — scooped from the earth by mighty earth-moving machines. (See Figure 18–8.) This process converts a once-attractive, aesthetically satisfying site (such as the lovely, rolling, wooded mountains of Kentucky and West Virginia) into a sterile, ugly waste-

538

COAL DEPOSITS IN THE UNITED STATES

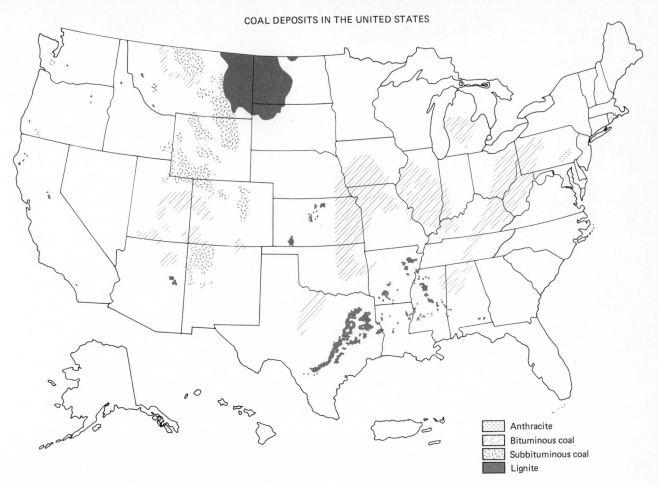

Anthracite
Bituminous coal
Subbituminous coal
Lignite

18-6 *Distribution of U.S. coal resources.*

18-7 *Transporting coal by shuttle car deep below the earth's surface.*

18-8 *Mechanized monster. Mine supervisors (in foreground) observe the operation of the big stripping wheel on a strip mine south of Stanton, North Dakota. This tremendous machine was invented in Germany and was assembled in North Dakota by German technicians.*

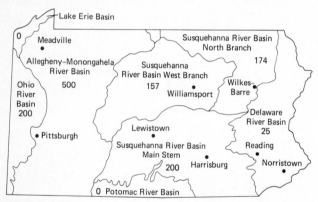

18-9 *Mine acid discharge per day (in tons) into the major rivers of Pennsylvania. Discharges range from zero in the Potomac River Basin to 500 tons per day in the Allegheny-Monongahela River Basin.*

18-10 *Strip-mining for coal in West Virginia.*

land (8). Almost half a million acres of land in the United States are devastated because of strip-mining. Acid mine drainage (see Chapter 8), with its accompanying aquatic-plant and fish kills, is a common strip-mining sequel that has contaminated 6,700 miles of streams. (See Figure 18–9.) In the Four Corners area (near the junction of New Mexico, Arizona, Utah, and Colorado) massive machines have been scooping up 25,000 tons of coal daily to power the gigantic electrical plants that supply the city of Los Angeles 1,000 miles to the west (8). (Perhaps the good citizens of Los Angeles subconsciously are practicing an "out of sight, out of mind" philosophy toward ecosystem abuse.)

Environmental abuses caused by strip-mining were strongly curbed by the Surface Mining Control and Reclamation Act. (See Figure 18–11.) Under the terms of this act, which became effective in 1979, mining companies must restore the original contours of the strip-mined area; replant the de-nuded land with shrubs, trees, and grasses; and control sedimentation and acid contamination of nearby lakes and streams. (See Figure 18–12.) The act placed a federal tax on coal to finance the reclamation of land destroyed by previous strip-mine operations. (Also see E. Willard Miller's guest article concerning strip-mine reclamation.)

The Release of Atmospheric Pollutants by Coal-Burning Plants

A second environmental concern attending the use of coal is the release of carbon dioxide and sulfur into the atmosphere when sulfur-containing coal is burned. The rapid buildup of carbon dioxide may cause dramatic and highly adverse climatic and agricultural effects. It is estimated, for example, that 60 percent of the 14 million tons of sulfur dioxide belched from the American smokestacks annually in the early 1970s had its source in coal. This sulfur dioxide has been largely responsible for the acid rain

Strip-Mining Reclamation

E. Willard Miller
Department of Geography
PENNSYLVANIA STATE
UNIVERSITY

The reclamation of strip-mined land has long been recognized as a serious environmental problem. The first legislation to implement strip-mine reclamation in Pennsylvania was enacted in 1945. This initial Pennsylvania Bituminous Coal Open Pit Mining Conservation Law required each strip-mine operator to cover the exposed face of the unmined coal within one year after completion of mining, and to level and round off the spoil banks sufficiently to permit the planting of trees, shrubs, and grasses. Because of low penalties, the law was largely ineffective. In order to strengthen the law it was revised in 1963, 1968, 1971, 1972, and 1974. The present act is recognized as a model law and was used to formulate many state laws and the national strip-mining law of 1977.

The present Pennsylvania law requires the mining company to secure an operator's license and mining permit, post a bond, and provide a reclamation plan before strip-mining can begin. The reclamation plan must include a statement of the best use of the land before mining, proposed use after mining, the means of conserving the topsoil, a complete planting program, a timetable for accomplishment of each reclamation step, the written consent of the landowner, and the means of controlling surface water and acid mine drainage.

The value of the state and national strip-mining reclamation laws lies primarily in the type of enforcement. Two viewpoints of implementation are still expressed. Conservationists believe that, if the laws are enforced, strip-mining will leave no scars on the landscape. But the conservationists believe that too frequently the laws are disregarded. The other viewpoint by the mining companies is that the state and national agencies have been unfair and inconsistent in applying the reclamation laws. Although much of the strip-mined land is reclaimed, there is little doubt that reclamation laws are being poorly implemented in many areas.

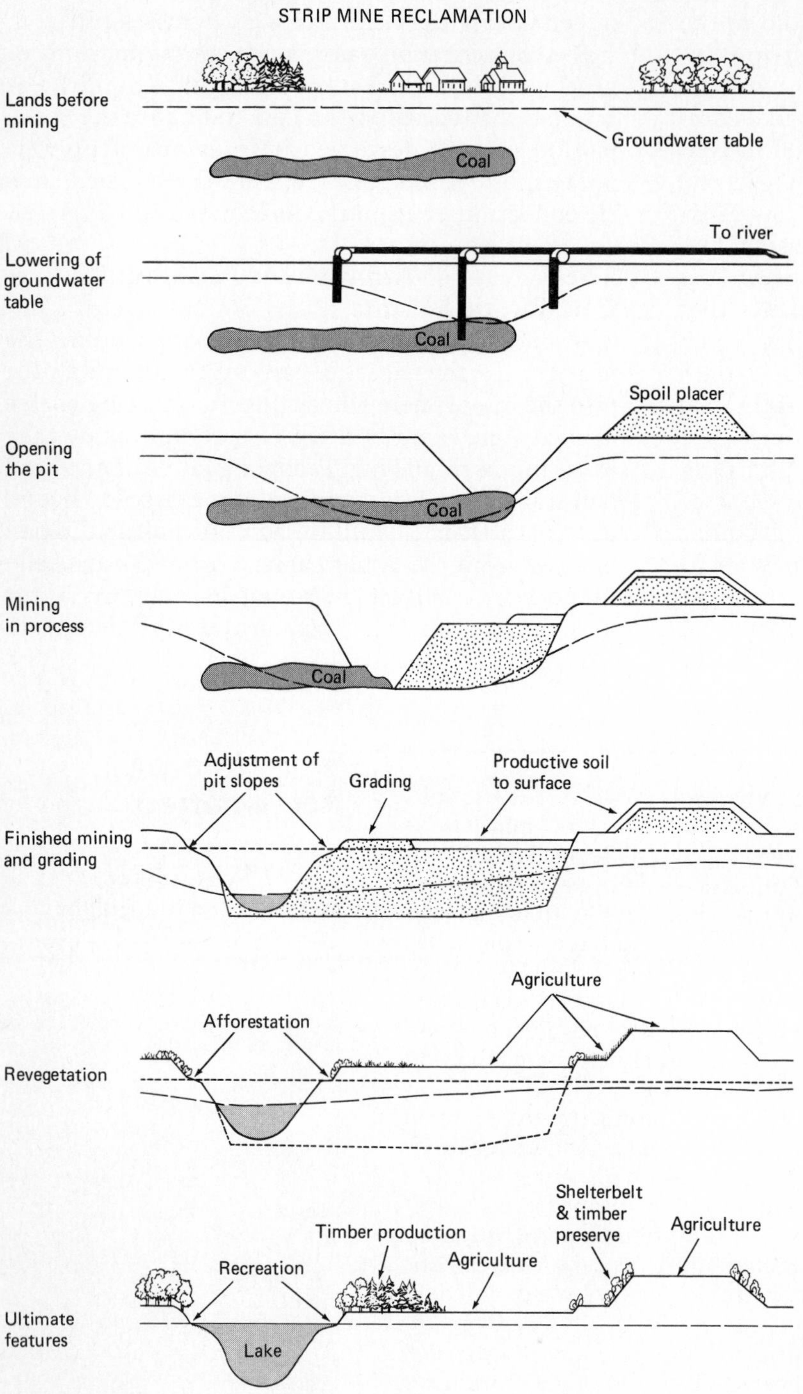

STRIP MINE RECLAMATION

Lands before mining

Groundwater table

Coal

Lowering of groundwater table

To river

Coal

Opening the pit

Spoil placer

Coal

Mining in process

Coal

Finished mining and grading

Adjustment of pit slopes

Grading

Productive soil to surface

Revegetation

Afforestation

Agriculture

Ultimate features

Recreation

Timber production

Agriculture

Shelterbelt & timber preserve

Agriculture

Lake

18-11 *The idealized coal-mine cycle as it occurs in coal beds in Germany, from the start of mining to the completion of reclamation.*

problem in eastern United States and parts of Canada. In order to curb the emissions of sulfur dioxide, many municipalities, such as New York City, Boston, Chicago, and Los Angeles forbid utilities and other industries to burn coal with a sulfur content higher than 1 percent. It is rather ironic, in this era of environmental enlightenment and concern, that a federal agency, the TVA, strip-mined some of the dirtiest coal (in terms of sulfur content) in the nation to power uranium-processing plants operated

18–12 *Use of lime permits lush growth of weeping love grass on strip-mine spoil, White Oak Mountain, West Virginia. The highly acid soil had an original pH of 2.8. The bare spots were seeded but not limed.*

by the former Atomic Energy Commission in Paducah, Kentucky, Oak Ridge, Tennessee, and Portsmouth, Ohio (11).

COAL GASIFICATION. There is hope that high-sulfur coal may yet be used as fuel by *gasification*, a process by which the coal is converted into methane gas by steam heating it under high pressure. (See Figure 18–13.) The largest above-ground coal-gasification plant was opened in 1978 at Windsor, Connecticut. It generates 890,000 cubic feet of gas per hour from the hourly consumption of 4.5 tons of pulverized coal (23). The Bureau of Mines has recently been conducting tests near Hanna, Wyoming, to determine the economic feasibility of gasifying coal subterraneously. (See Figure 18–15.) This would involve pumping air into a coalbed lying 600 feet below the ground surface. After ignition of the bed the resultant gases, including methane (the principal component of natural gas), would be pumped out as the fire smolders. Environmentalists would welcome the substitution of gasification for land-desecrating strip mining. However, Arnold Silverman, chairman of the Western Montana Committee for Environmental Information, has noted the possibility of surface collapse above the caverns formed by extensive gasification (1). Another undesirable feature is the potentially adverse effect on the quality of groundwater.

In the event that gasification proves to be economically feasible, a marked upsurge in the mining of high-sulfur coal is expected in the western states. To date only 4 percent of the nation's coal mining occurs in the West even though the region holds 64 percent of America's coal deposits (11).

18–13 *Coal-gasification research. Coal is placed in the container, then heated under steam pressure to a high temperature. The gases released during the process (principally methane) are carefully identified and measured.*

18–14 *This coal gasifier requires 40 atmospheres pressure.*

18–15 *Coal-gasification research. Researchers at the Department of Energy's Oak Ridge National Laboratory are conducting a study of the pyrolysis (destructive heating) of coal. The large chunks of coal are carefully instrumented with thermocouples, then heated in an oxygen-free environment to temperatures as high as 1,050°C. Gaseous products are collected and analyzed.*

A National Coal Policy to the Year 2010

1. Both domestic and imported supplies of oil will certainly begin to decline, probably around 1990. To compensate for this decrease, the federal government should provide private industry with strong incentives for establishing a synthetic fuel industry, in other words the production of gas and oil from coal and the extraction of oil from shale.

2. Intensive research should be conducted so that new and better methods of using coal can be developed that will be less damaging to the environment and to human health.

3. Develop methods for sharply reducing the incidence of respiratory diseases, such as *black lung,* as well as the incidence of bodily injuries and fatalities among coal miners.

4. Develop intensive long-term studies so that the effects of the atmospheric pollutants resulting from the combustion of coal, such as sulfur dioxide, carbon monoxide, mercury, asbestos, lead, and so on, may be more perfectly understood. This information would place air pollution control legislation on a much firmer scientific basis. As a consequence, much more reliable and efficient standards can be established on which utilities and other coal-using industries can depend in planning for the long term.

5. Because the combustion of coal inevitably causes serious environmental problems, such as the "greenhouse effect" and climate modification, we must develop some other energy source that can be sustained for the long term — many decades into the future.

6. Domestic demand for coal in the United States in the mid-1980s should be about 1 billion tons (20 – 25 quads).

7. By the late 1980s, synthetic fuel technologies should be on the verge of commercialization. By this time knowledge of the health and environmental effects of coal use should be strongly improved so that firm, effective pollution control regulations may rest on a firm foundation.

COAL LIQUEFACTION. Another process that would reduce some of the pollution, transportation, and inconvenience problems associated with the burning of coal is *liquefaction*—a technique by which coal is converted to high-octane gasoline and oil. These products could be transported through pipelines already in existence or stored in existing tanks. A new liquefaction plant, involving the joint participation of Conoco, Shell, and the Department of Energy, began operation in 1979. The plant employed a zinc-chloride catalyst, high pressures, and temperatures up to 825° F. The gasoline produced in this way is equal in quality to petroleum-derived gasoline. Unfortunately, the extensive high-volume production of gasoline by this method awaits the solution of certain technical problems, such as corrosion of the liquefaction plant's reaction chamber (22, 23). In addition phenol-containing wastes which require careful disposal are generated. Some energy experts have suggested that the nation's electrical power plants gradually shift from such fuels as gas and oil, which are short in supply, and convert to the use of relatively abundant coal. Certainly the nation has plenty of coal available — 265 billion tons of proven reserves. But if coal were to be consumed by the United States at the rate suggested by some energy specialists, even this seemingly bounteous energy source will be exhausted by the year 2050 (27).

Oil

The year was 1859 and the place was Titusville, Pennsylvania. "Colonel" Edwin Drake's steel drills penetrated to a depth of seventy feet and — whoosh — the black, foul-smelling fluid that exploded up the well shaft signaled the dawn of a new energy era. (See Figure 18 – 17.) Less than a century later oil had become our nation's most important source of power.

Both oil and natural gas are highly desired fuels

545

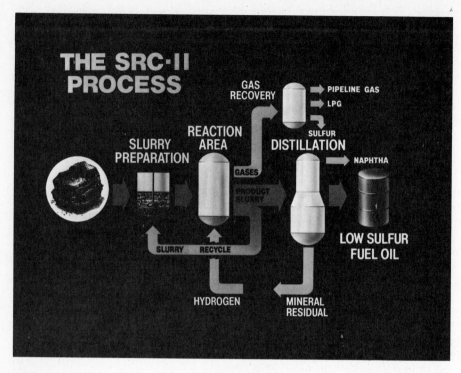

THE SRC-II PROCESS

SLURRY PREPARATION

REACTION AREA

GAS RECOVERY → PIPELINE GAS, LPG

DISTILLATION

SULFUR

GASES

PRODUCT SLURRY

NAPHTHA

LOW SULFUR FUEL OIL

SLURRY RECYCLE

HYDROGEN

MINERAL RESIDUAL

18-16 *Flow diagram illustrating the SRC-II process that is designed to produce primarily a clean, nonpolluting liquid fuel from high-sulfur coal.*

because they emit relatively few atmospheric pollutants when burned. However, both of them are becoming more scarce because America's *consumption is exceeding her production* (19). Although the United States is producing one of every four oil gallons in the world, it is consuming 900 gallons yearly for every man, woman, and child in this nation—about eight times the average consumption rate for the nations of the "free" world (7). In 1980 the United States consumed more than 25 percent of

18-17 *America's first oil well at Titusville, Pennsylvania. Photo taken in 1864.*

PRODUCTS DERIVED FROM ONE BARREL OF CRUDE OIL

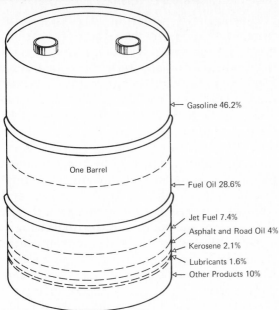

One Barrel

Gasoline 46.2%

Fuel Oil 28.6%

Jet Fuel 7.4%
Asphalt and Road Oil 4%
Kerosene 2.1%
Lubricants 1.6%
Other Products 10%

18-18 *Products derived from one barrel of crude oil.*

the global oil production of 60 million barrels a day. Nearly nine million barrels a day came from American wells—the remainder, more than six million barrels per day, had to be imported. According to S. David Freeman, who once counseled both President Johnson and President Nixon on energy matters, "It doesn't matter that we may have found 30

18-19 *Symbol of the energy crisis. Summer, 1973. "Service is Our Business," but "Sorry No Gas." Will this type of "service" plague American motorists repeatedly in the future?*

billion barrels of oil and more than 20 trillion cubic feet of gas in Alaska. . . . Our rates of consumption are now so large that we can see the *bottom of the barrel* . . . " (19) *[italics mine].* (See Figure 18–19.) Our nation has only nine years of oil reserves left if present rates of oil extraction continue. Already in 1972 the United States was importing 27 percent of its oil, largely from Canada and Venezuela. At the time of this writing about 40 percent is being imported. The price of imported oil has zoomed upward in the past decade. (See Figure 18–21.) Foreign relations and international diplomacy are important factors in determining the adequacy of our imports, for much of this fuel is being secured from OPEC, which includes Algeria, Libya, Nigeria, Kuwait, and Saudi Arabia. Oil analysts are concerned that the oil-producing Arab nations may decide to curb production of the oil upon which Western industry and life-style are so largely based. Prices would thus be artificially inflated, the oil eventually going to the highest bidder, and the acceptable bids being in terms of a combination of money and financial, technical, political, and/or military assistance to the Arab nations in their chronic struggle with Israel (15).

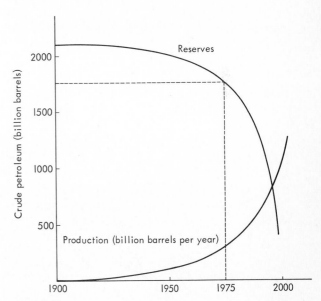

18-20 *World reserves of crude petroleum will not last long at current consumption rates. Note that in 1975, with no more than 15 years left before demand would exceed supply, the total global reserve was depleted by only 12½ percent.*

547

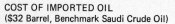

COST OF IMPORTED OIL
($32 Barrel, Benchmark Saudi Crude Oil)

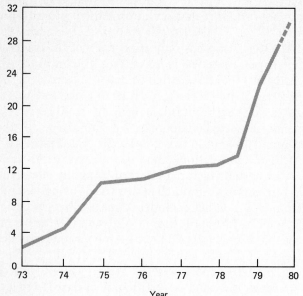

Year

18–21 *The cost of imported oil has zoomed upward from about $3 per barrel in 1973 to $32 per barrel in 1980.*

The Controversial Alaskan Pipeline

Exciting news came out of Alaska during the summer of 1968, for the richest oil deposit in the Western Hemisphere was discovered by the Atlantic Richfield Company, its value being estimated at $50 billion. In order to convey this oil to market in the United States, the Trans-Alaskan Pipeline System (TAPS) built a 789-mile pipeline extending from northern Alaska's Prudhoe Bay to the ice-free port of Valdez on the Gulf of Alaska. (See Figure 18–22.) Pipeline critics pointed up a number of potential environmental problems that might be caused by its construction. Among the problems cited were (1) sagging and breakage of the pipeline as a result of the melting of the underlying permafrost, (2) rupture of the pipeline from earthquake activity, (3) adverse impact on the $150-million Alaskan salmon fishery because of disruption of salmon-spawning sites, (4) contamination of the Gulf of Alaska and the Pacific coast of the United States with oil as a result of tanker accidents caused by heavy tanker traffic and stormy seas, (5) interference with caribou migrations, and (6) the vulnera-

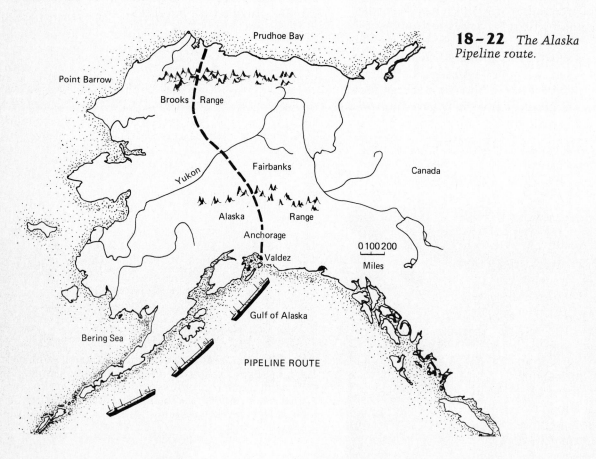

18–22 *The Alaska Pipeline route.*

18–23 *According to the National Petroleum Council, supertankers, such as the one in the picture, will be used to convey Alaskan oil from Valdez to Pacific Coast ports such as Seattle and Portland.*

bility of the pipeline to Russian bombing attacks in the event of war. (See Figure 18–23.)

Despite these many objections to the construction of the pipeline, the federal courts, in late 1973, finally gave TAPS permission to go ahead. The severity of the energy crisis apparently swayed public opinion and, eventually, congressional and court opinion in this direction—environmental objections to the contrary.

Oil Production and the Future

In 1980 American oil companies spent more than $30 billion on oil-exploration projects, in which they drilled more than 60,000 wells. Land probes for oil were made in Pennsylvania, West Virginia, Oklahoma, Texas, and Oregon, as well as in the Rocky Mountains from Colorado to the Canadian border.

In Beverly Hills, California, one company triggered a controversy by planning to drill for oil on the highschool playground. Drilling bits have also been piercing the ocean bottom off the southern California coast, in the Gulf of Alaska, and in the coastal waters of the Atlantic and the Gulf of Mexico. (See Figure 18–24.) Drilling is being done in much deeper water than ever before. In 1978, for example, Texaco constructed a platform in waters off the Newfoundland coast that were over 1 mile deep (23).

18–24 *Offshore oil-drilling platform. Standing on rigid steel legs high above the water off Louisiana's Gulf Coast, this barge-mounted rig drills for oil beneath the bottom of the sea.*

18-25 *A work crew manipulates drilling equipment on an offshore drilling and production platform.*

However, despite all this intensive activity to find more oil, a cloud hangs over the oil horizon. For in 1975, after an exhaustive survey, the U.S. Geological Survey estimated that the undiscovered recoverable oil reserves in the United States would last only about 45 years. Thus deregulation of oil may increase *exploration* for these undiscovered resources but will not result in long term energy-independence for the United States, with oil as the primary energy source. (See Figure 18–26.) The Alaskan North Slope find in 1968 was the richest oil strike ever made by our oilmen. Eventually, it is expected to yield 9.7 billion barrels of oil. Nevertheless, at our current rates of consumption of about 7 billion barrels per year, we could burn up all that Alaskan oil in about 16 months (23)! Because of the potential oil shortage the United States has been building up an oil reserve that could be tapped in emergencies

such as war or another OPEC oil embargo. (See Figure 18–27.)

Natural Gas

Natural gas, which is primarily methane (CH_4), is a fossil fuel like coal and oil, having been formed through long periods of time by the incomplete decomposition of plant and animal remains that had been covered for millennia by sedimentary deposits. Natural gas supplies 26 percent of our nation's energy needs. Much of this gas flows from our nation's 165,000 oil wells. America accounts for roughly 50 percent of the world's consumption of natural gas — 22.1 trillion cubic feet. At this rate of use our nation's proven domestic reserve of 247 trillion cubic feet will be exhausted in the near future (7). The number of producing natural-gas wells drilled in the United States *diminished* by more

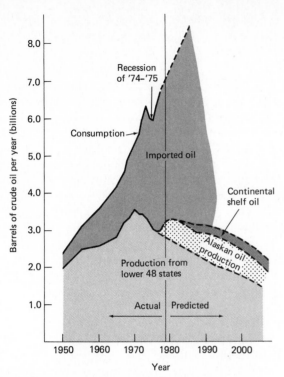

18-26 *Actual and predicted consumption of oil in the United States and the amounts produced in our country or that must be imported.*

than 50 percent during the years from 1955 to 1968. Nevertheless, it is estimated that within the period from 1970 to 1990, America's gas demand will be

one and a half times the total gas volume ever discovered in America since the first American oil gushed from the well at Titusville in 1859. U.S. gas companies state that although there are probably substantial gas reserves, either inland or offshore, current exploration costs are almost prohibitive, with new supplies of gas being reached only after drillers have gone to depths of two to three miles (8). Because of the increased costs incurred by industry, consumer prices are expected to double or even triple within the next few years. A mere doubling of prices would increase the industry's revenues by $4.4 billion annually.

Consumption of natural gas in 1979 exceeded gas *discoveries* by 39 percent. This disturbing trend, however, was apparently reversed by significant discoveries in the early 1980s. What can be done to increase natural gas production? A considerable amount of gas could be obtained by processing such wastes as garbage, sewage, sludge, and livestock manure — procedures that would not only alleviate the solid-waste problem, but also ease the gas shortage. True, such precedures are commendable and should be attempted whenever feasible. Natural-gas production could also be increased by expanding offshore drilling. It must be clear, however, that the production gains will have a proportionate ecological cost measured in oil-spill defilement of the neritic zone, which is already highly productive of shrimp, tuna, and red snapper, if not of natural gas and oil. In the final analysis, however, as in the case

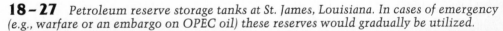

18-27 *Petroleum reserve storage tanks at St. James, Louisiana. In cases of emergency (e.g., warfare or an embargo on OPEC oil) these reserves would gradually be utilized.*

with oil, the only way the United States can meet the demand for gas in the immediate future is by importing large quantities from abroad, especially from Canada and Mexico.

It is estimated that about two trillion cubic feet will be imported annually as liquid natural gas (LNG) by tanker from South America, Africa, Alaska, and the North Sea (10). Currently, America is conveying LNG with a fleet of 130 tankers with an average capacity of 125,000 cubic meters. (Each tanker carries the equivalent of 2.7 billion cubic feet of gas.) The FPC has already approved the plan of El Paso Algeria Corporation to import one billion cubic feet of gas daily from Algeria to supply customers along our densely populated east coast.

James A. Fay of the Massachusetts Institute of Technology and James J. Mackenzie of the National Audubon Society have investigated the possible aftermath of the accidental release of LNG near a densely populated region, caused by either a tanker collision or a faulty transfer operation. They estimate that:

A 100,000-cubic-meter spill . . . would form a vapor cloud more than a mile wide and twenty feet deep in less than fifteen minutes. The cloud could then blow ashore and be ignited in population areas. Given the many possible sources of ignition on land, such as automobiles and home heating units, it is very likely that such a cloud would eventually ignite. A conflagration of that size . . . (equivalent to the burning of 100 Hindenburg zeppelins) . . . in a major city would be a disaster. (10)

The General Accounting Office (GAO) has reported to Congress that the transport of LNG by trains and trucks should not be permitted near major cities. According to the GAO, the contents of a single truck could fill 15 miles of subway tunnel or 110 miles of sewer pipe six feet in diameter with highly explosive gas. The GAO recommendation had considerable significance for the people of Massachusetts, in particular, because two of every three trucks transporting LNG in the United States pass through urban areas in that state (25).

At the time of this writing a fierce debate is being waged between optimists and "realists" concerning a substantial increase in gas production from American wells. The optimists, represented by the American Gas Association, claim that natural gas production could be increased 28 trillion cubic feet. Much of this gas would come from nonconventional

sources as deeply buried salty aquifers of the Texas-Louisiana Gulf Coast, our nation's coal beds, and the Devonian black shales of Appalachia. According to the National Petroleum Council, about 400 trillion cubic feet could be derived from the "hard as cement" geologic formations called *tight sands* that occur in many areas of the country. To enable gas to flow to the well bore, the tight sands must be broken up by the injection of fluids under high pressure. Development of these nonconventional sources would require massive new investments. A more cautious estimate of future nonconventional gas production in the United States is provided by Hans H. Landsberg, a highly respected energy policy researcher. He cautions: "We can't base our hopes on unconventional gas until we've invested the money to find out what can be produced. It could be a huge resource, but we must plan conservatively."

Oil Shale

Oil shale is a grayish-brown sedimentary rock. It was formed millions of years ago from lake-bottom mud. The oil in this shale occurs within a solid organic substance known as *kerogen.* High-grade oil-shale deposits may yield three fourths of a barrel (about 30 gallons) from each ton of rock (18). The most valuable deposits in the United States are held in the Green River Formation, which covers 16,500 square miles in Colorado, Wyoming, and Utah — 80 percent of which is owned by the federal government. (See Figure 18 – 28.) It is estimated that, using currently available technology, at least 80 billion barrels of oil could be extracted from these deposits, sufficient to satisfy our oil needs at current consumption rates for about seven and one-half years. The shale may be removed either by deep or open-pit mining, depending on the depth of the deposits. Some deposits form outcrops along cliffs. (See Figure 18 – 29.) The shale is crushed and then heated to 1,000° F to break down the kerogen and release the oil (17). (See Figures 18 – 30 and 18 – 31.)

You well might ask: "If oil shale represents such a massive energy source, why is the industry so slow to develop it?" The reasons are twofold. First, the production costs are very high — up to $28 for just one barrel of oil (20). Second, production may cause the following severe environmental problems.

1. Fifty million tons of waste shale per year would litter the landscape yearly from the operation of a

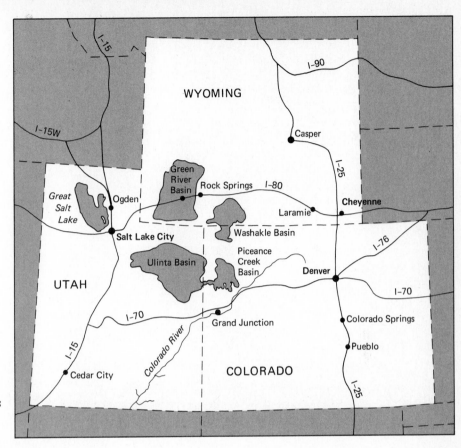

18–28 *Location of our nation's main oil-shale deposits in Colorado, Utah, and Wyoming.*

single 100,000-barrel-per-day plant. The resulting visual blight would be enormous. A precedent has already been set. "People point to the miles of naked rock piles thrown up on the banks of the Blue River near Breckenridge, Colorado, by gold dredges in the 1890s that remain as an eyesore today . . . " (17).

2. The production of each barrel of oil will result in the generation of two and one-half pounds of toxic gases, such as sulfur dioxide and carbon monoxide. In addition, cadmium, mercury and lead, all toxic to humans, may be released into the atmosphere.

3. Enormous quantities of water will be required, up to 19,000 acre-feet per year, for an oil-shale industry that is producing 100,000 barrels of oil per day. This is the equivalent of two and one-half barrels of water for each barrel of oil produced. Some day this water might be sorely needed for irrigation farming or for watering livestock. Sharply depleted water supplies can

18–29 *Oil-shale hills. Oil deposits in Colorado shale and in Alberta tar sands could extend American industrial use of oil considerably.*

553

18–30 *Drilling and loading operations in an oil-shale demonstration project at Rifle, Colorado.*

18–31 *Block of oil shale and a beaker of the oil that can be extracted from the shale. This project is located in Laramie, Wyoming.*

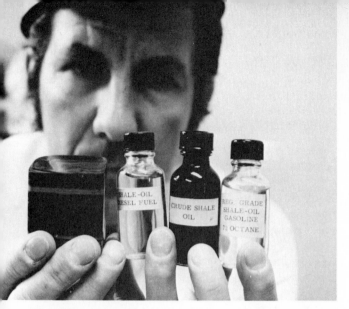

18–32 *Oil from shale. Ed Piper, project manager for Paraho Development Company, holds samples of shale-oil derivatives produced at Anvil Points, Colorado. In his hands are a bottle each of diesel fuel (left), crude shale oil (center), and 72-octane gasoline (right). Almost 300 years ago, medicinal oils were produced from bituminous shales in England. A patent was issued as early as 1684 to produce "oyle from a kind of stone."*

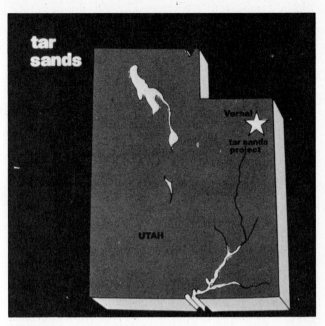

18–33 *Location of tar sands project at Vernal, Utah. An estimated 28 billion barrels of oil are available from the tar sands of Utah.*

only have a detrimental effect on the large populations of elk, antelope, and mule deer that occur in that region (17).

4. The discharge of the wastewater into the Colorado River would substantially increase the salinity of this agriculturally vital stream. This might cause the United States some international embarassment: by treaty with Mexico we are committed to keep the salinity of the Colorado as low as possible; once this water flows over the border, it is intensively used by Mexican farmers for irrigation purposes (17).

Tar Sands

In some parts of the world oil has migrated upward to the earth's surface. Such is the case in northern Alberta, where tarlike oil deposits have stained sandstone black. It is estimated that these deposits could yield 300 billion barrels of oil—fully ten times the proven oil reserves in the United States (20). It is estimated that the tar sands in Utah could yield about 28 billion barrels of oil. (Figures 18–33 and 18–34.) A Canadian company, Great Canadian

18–34 *Transporting tar sands mined near Vernal, Utah.*

Oil Sands Limited, has begun large-scale development of the tar fields in northern Alberta. Their plant is designed to produce 45,000 barrels of oil per day; two barrels of crude oil are extracted from every three tons of rock.

The Future Use of Fossil Fuels as Energy Sources

We have seen that although there do exist relatively large amounts of fossil fuels (coal, oil, and natural gas) either on the North American continent or elsewhere in the world, their availability and actual use by the American people are fraught with problems — economic, political, technological, environmental, and moral. Even if the fossil fuels were readily available, however, there has been considerable criticism directed at their continued intensive use as energy sources. Recently the National Academy of Sciences established a Committee on Resources and Man to evaluate the adequacy of America's resources. Composed of some of this nation's leading authorities, the committee strongly recommended "that the fossil fuels be conserved for uses which cannot be met by other sources. . . . " According to the committee,

The fossil fuels are needed for petrochemicals, synthetic polymers, and essential liquid fuels, *for which suitable substitutes are as yet unknown.* They might also play a part in synthetic or bacterial food production. They should not be spent in the generation of electricity, for heating, and for industrial purposes where substitutes can qualify. The Department of the Interior should be autho-

rized and directed to develop and institute a practicable and effective hydrocarbon conservation program. (18) *[Italics mine.]*

Alternative Energy Sources

Some authorities think that we should gradually derive more and more of our energy from sources other than fossil fuels. Among such alternative forms of energy are solar power, wind, biomass, tides, water power, geothermal energy, and ocean thermal energy. (See Figure 18–35.)

Solar Energy

Perhaps our nation should hitch her "energy wagon" to a star — the sun. Sunlight is the ultimate source of the energy locked up in fossil fuels, the ultimate source of the energy powering the world's ecosystems, and the ultimate source of the energy that permits you to read these words and for thoughts concerning the energy crisis to flash through your mind. (See Figure 18–36.) However, as we learned in the earlier discussion of the second law of thermodynamics, fully 99 percent of the radiant energy from the sun is "lost"; in other words, it is converted into heat energy that in turn dissipates from the earth's surface and becomes irretrievable by humans. The possibility of harnessing this wasted solar energy has piqued the human mind for ages. Solar power has in fact been harnessed at least since the 1860s, when a still was set up in Chile to provide 5,000 gallons of fresh water to thirsty

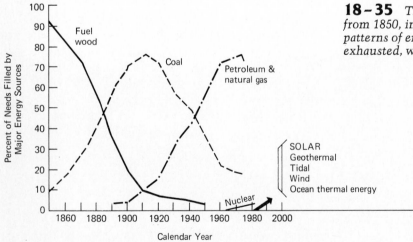

18–35 *The pattern of U.S. energy consumption from 1850, including a question about our future patterns of energy use. As supplies of petroleum become exhausted, what alternative sources will be exploited?*

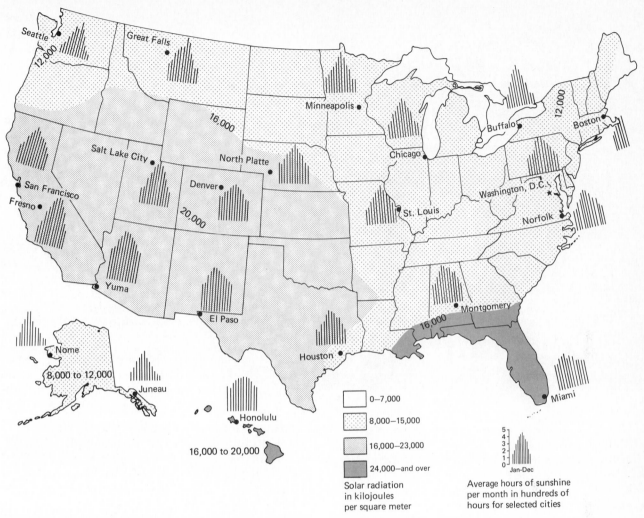

18–36 *The potential for solar energy use in different regions of the United States.*

miners. Solar-powered engines were also constructed in the nineteenth century by John Ericsson, better remembered as the builder of the *Monitor,* the famed combat ship of the Civil War.

The amount of solar energy flooding the earth's surface on a cloudless day is roughly *100,000 times greater than the world's presently installed total electric-power capacity.* Unlike the hydrocarbon (fossil fuel) energy sources, solar energy will continue to be available at a uniform rate for millions of years, long after the human species has become extinct. The world's largest solar furnace, near Odeillo in the French Pyrenees, provides us with an example of sunlight's awesome power. This furnace is pro-

vided with a 148-foot mirror. (See Figure 18–37.) The mirror focuses the sunlight on a furnace where temperatures reach 6,300° F. This is sufficiently hot to melt a one-foot-wide hole in a steel plate that is three eighth of an inch thick in only 60 seconds (29). The solar potential for heating purposes is enormous. In fact, without the warming influence of the sun, our planet Earth would be cold indeed — about −450° F.

Solar Heating

Solar heating systems installed in the average home could provide 50 to 75 percent of the occupant's hot-water needs. The initial cost of a hot-

557

18 – 37 *French solar furnace. This solar furnace, located near Odeillo in the Pyrenees Mountains of southern France, was built to test materials under extremely high temperatures. In the foreground, an array of 63 mirrors (heliostats), each measuring 6 meters by 7½ meters, reflects sunlight onto the curved mirror surface of the office building in the background. This in turn focuses the sunlight on an aperture in the tower at the center, where temperatures of 7,000°F can be produced — enough heat to melt any known material.*

water system, $1,500 for the average home, can be written off in only ten years (5).

Of the many solar homes currently operating in the United States, one of the most successful is the four-bedroom experimental home constructed by researchers at the University of Delaware. It derives 80 percent of its heat and power from the sunshine beaming down on heat-collecting panels on its roof and front walls. The heat-collecting panels are relatively simple in basic design and include the following components:

1. A black metal plate that absorbs the sun's rays and gets hot.
2. Styrofoam insulation beneath the plate.
3. A glass cover to prevent the radiation of heat to the atmosphere (the greenhouse effect).
4. A system of channels (air ducts or water pipes) for transporting heated air to other parts of the house.

The heat is stored in a six-foot cube of special salts from which it may be withdrawn as needed by the home's residents. Two basic types of solar space-heating systems are shown in Figure 18 – 38.

The number of solar-heated homes in the United States is rapidly increasing. For example, although California had only 25 such dwellings in 1975, by the early 1980s the number of solar-heated homes in California had risen to well over 200,000. In order to meet the expected demand for solar heating systems, Grumman Corporation recently opened a $1-million plant in the San Joaquin Valley that is capable of manufacturing 12,000 systems annually (25).

It must be emphasized that the use of solar power plants and solar heating systems for homes must be augmented with conventional energy sources (oil, gas, wood, etc.). This would certainly be true of a home located in the cloudy Pacific Northwest. It is also true, however, for *any* region in the United States. For example, although the average household of four requires 55,000 kilojoules of energy daily, not even the sunny Southwest receives that much solar energy.

Sunshine may be converted *directly* into electricity by *solar (photovoltaic) cells.* These cells were developed by American scientists to power the rockets that put man on the moon. In 1980 solar cells powered the first flight of the "Gossamer Penguin"— the world's first piloted solar airplane.

HEATING SYSTEM USING WATER

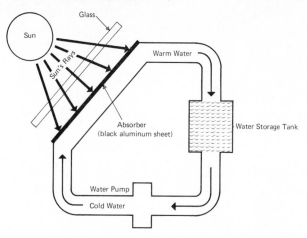

HEATING SYSTEM USING AIR

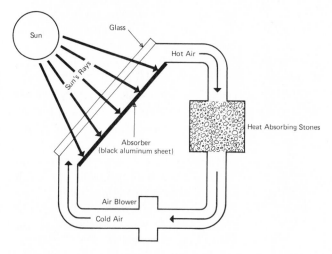

18–38 *Two types of solar space-heating systems.*

The generation of electricity from solar cells is highly attractive. The fuel — solar energy — is inexhaustible. There is no land scarring from strip mining, no acid mine drainage, no release of atmospheric pollutants such as sulfur dioxide; no pollution-caused deaths from emphysema and lung cancer; no fission of nuclear fuel, and no problems of nuclear waste disposal. There are no moving parts to wear out. So why can't the solar age dawn in America? Because of the cost. The silicon from which solar cells are made is one of the most abundant elements on earth, it is derived from sand — *silicon dioxide* (SiO_2). Each 3-inch solar cell provides about .5 watt of power. Many extremely technical and sophisticated processes are involved between sand and the completed solar cell, however. As a result, the solar cells are very expensive, costing roughly $15,000 to deliver one kilowatt of electrical power, compared to the $1,000 cost per kilowatt from conventional power plants (20).

All the electrical power required by the United States could theoretically be produced by twelve thousand square kilometers of solar cells. This is roughly equivalent to the area occupied by buildings in the contiguous 48 states. A small solar-cell power plant could be installed on the rooftop of an average building and would be able to satisfy all of that building's energy needs. However, it is possible that the building's owner would not care to have the responsibility of installing and maintaining the mini power plant. In that case, perhaps utility companies could rent rooftop space from the building owner. Brown University professor Joseph Loferski has estimated that if such mini power plants were

18–39 *Mt. Rushmore goes solar. Mt. Rushmore, South Dakota, site of the famed sculpted faces of former presidents, has a new solar-energy system. Solar collectors on the roof of the Visitor's Center transform the rays of the sun into energy for heating and air conditioning. The solar panels were developed by Honeywell. The system provides energy for 53 percent of the heating and 41 percent of the cooling for the 9,250-square-foot building.*

placed on only 20 percent of Rhode Island's rooftops, the power needs of the entire state could be met. One big advantage of rooftop solar-cell plants is that they would effectively decentralize electrical power production in this country. The electrical power would be generated only a few feet from where it would be used by the occupants of the building, thus removing the need for costly, inefficient, and ugly transmission-tower networks and power lines (23). One minor environmental problem would be the necessity of removing considerable numbers of shade trees to permit maximum exposure of the solar cells to the sunlight.

Now what about the possibility of constructing a central heating plant, in the 1,000-megawatt range, comparable to major electrical plants now powered by coal, oil, or gas? Such a plant is indeed technologically possible.

There are drawbacks, however.

Firstly, such a plant would require a considerable amount of space. A plant capable of supplying the electrical needs of a city of 1.5 million people, such as Cleveland, would require the collection of solar energy from a 16-square-mile area, and that much space is in notoriously short supply, especially near urban centers (7).

Secondly, the electricity produced would be extremely expensive. For example, the solar power plant in Barstow, California is capable of generating 10 megawatts of electricity. However the electricity costs 10 times as much per kilowatt as that generated by a nuclear plant, and 20 times as much as that produced by a coal-fired plant.

SOLAR POWER TOWERS. The solar *power tower* approach to generating electricity on a commercial basis from a central location is being evaluated at Sandia, New Mexico and Barstow, California. These prototype power towers, which were completed in 1977, are one megawatt plants,—each theoretically capable of satisfying the electrical needs of a city of 3,000 people. The power tower, standing about 15 stories high, is located in the center of a large field which is occupied by hundreds of movable mirrors known as *heliostats.* Under computerized control, the heliostats track the course of the sun in the sky, and, in unison, focus the solar rays on a boiler located at the top of the tower. The intense heat thus produced then converts water in the boiler to steam. The steam in turn then drives turbines to produce electricity. (See Fig-

ures 18–40, 18–41, 18–42.) If the evaluations currently being conducted by the Department of Energy are encouraging, power towers of considerably larger scope will be constructed in the near future (17, 21).

The Satellite Solar Power Station (SSPS)

In recent years considerable controversy has been raging among energy experts concerning the possibility of generating electrical power by means of a satellite solar power station (SSPS). An SSPS generating 5,000 megawatts of power would be eight miles long and three miles wide. Its components, weighing 20,000 tons, would be assembled by workers aboard a space station. The incident sunshine would be converted to electrical energy by the satellite. This energy in turn would be converted into microwaves (high-frequency electromagnetic waves), which would be directed earthward in a beam about 5 miles in diameter. After being picked up by a receiving antenna on earth, the microwave beam would be reconverted into electrical power (6, 23).

One big advantage of tapping solar energy outside the earth's atmosphere is that it is about eight times greater than on the earth's surface. A second advantage is that the "on again-off again" problem of power generation from solar stations on earth caused by the day-night cycle would be averted. The successful completion of the project would require roughly the same expenditure of time, effort, money, and dedication that characterized the Apollo Program that sent human beings to the moon. Moreover, if we started the program in 1990 it would probably not be completed until the year 2010 (6, 23).

Although a number of university professors, space scientists, and utility people enthusiastically support the SSPS program, certain of its negative aspects should be considered:

1. Its construction would require enormous amounts of energy. The satellite would require seven to ten years of operation just to pay it back.
2. The satellite would be extremely expensive — each would cost about $100 million.
3. The microwave beams would probably disrupt military and commercial radar systems.
4. The microwaves would destroy large numbers of migrating birds — roasting them almost as if they were in a microwave oven (16).

18-40 *The solar-power tower. The concentrated rays of the sun convert water to steam, which in turn propels the turbine.*

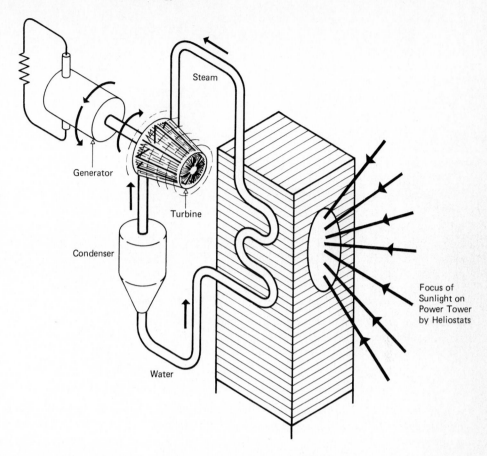

18-41 *View of solar-power tower located at the Department of Energy's test facility at Sandia Laboratories in Albuquerque, New Mexico.*

18-42 *The concentrated rays of the sun focused on this half-inch steel plate melted this hole within a few seconds at the Sandia Laboratories' solar "power tower" test facility at Albuquerque, New Mexico.*

561

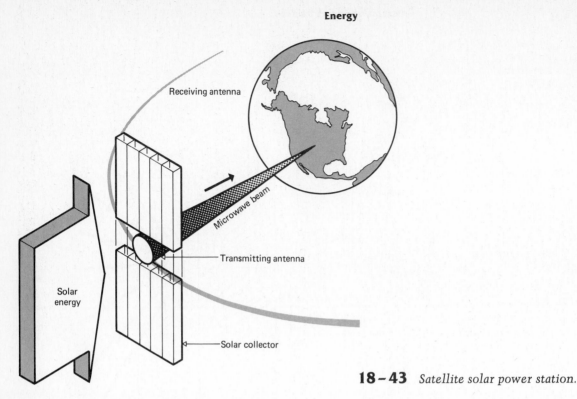

18–43 *Satellite solar power station.*

5. The microwaves could damage the human nervous system, cause eye cataracts, and inflict genetic damage.
6. The distribution of solar power would be centralized in a few large utilities.
7. A considerable volume of hydrochloric acid would be released into the atmosphere by the space shuttle needed to assemble and maintain the SSPS.

Our Solar Future

We are pouring billions of dollars into nuclear-power research. On the other hand, we are spending ridiculously small amounts on the development of solar power. Solar energy is abundant, inexhaustible, and pollution-free, but the operation of nuclear power plants, and particularly the transport and storage of nuclear wastes, poses formidable environmental problems, indeed.

Of the $3.23-billion federal energy budget for fiscal year 1979, only 4 percent ($373 million) was allotted for the research and development of solar power. This is shocking, for it is $17 million less than was appropriated for the fiscal year 1978. Both the development of nuclear power and that of fossil fuels were funded with a whopping $1 billion each. The Council on Environmental Quality has forecasted that solar enery will satisfy 25 percent of our nation's energy needs by the year 2000, and more than 50 percent by the year 2020. Certainly if solar energy is ever to play the significant role predicted for it, Congress will have to provide much more substantial funding for its development (3, 5).

It would be gross folly for the nation to emphasize a more and more intensive extraction of fossil fuels while we turn a relatively cold shoulder to the development of solar power. Eventually our "energy wagon" indeed will be hitched to the sun. But this "hitching" should be done with much more commitment on the federal, state, and local levels than has been demonstrated to date. Professor Kurt H. Hohenemser of Washington University, Saint Louis, recently discussed this problem:

The transition to the solar future of the world is a gigantic technological enterprise probably requiring a *century*. It would be made much easier if we began it *soon*, while we still have cheap fossil energy available. The question should not be how to extend our growth-based industrial and economic system a little longer by still faster extraction of our finite resources, but rather how to spend some of our remaining resources *wisely* so as to accomplish a smooth transition to the solar-based equilibrium system in which all nations will share equitably in the sun-produced wealth. (15) *[Italics mine.]*

Tidal Power

Former President Franklin Roosevelt often observed the rise and fall of the tides near his summer home on Campobello Island on the Bay of Fundy. He was impressed with the power potential of the surging waters, for the tides of Fundy are the largest on earth — up to a height of 52 feet (21). Those tides could be used to spin the blades of turbines to produce electrical power.

Tidal power has many advantages: It is inexpensive, produces no noxious wastes, and would be available long after the human species has become extinct. The big drawbacks are that there is not enough of it and that massive machinery is involved, including dams, dikes, and levees.

There are several disadvantages to tidal power development. First, there is not much available. The total world potential is only 2.9 million megawatts, less than 1 percent of the world's water power potential. Second, the structural components involved, such as dams, levees, and dikes, are expen-sive. Third, the operation of a tidal power station might have an adverse effect on the spawning activities of commercially valuable marine organisms such as crabs and oysters (20).

Small tidal mills have been used for grinding grain since the twelfth century. However, the world's first major tidal-electric installation at the La Rance estuary in France was not built until 1966. At present it is operating successfully, producing 240,000 kilowatts of power. Other plants have since been constructed in Russia. The U.S. and Canadian governments have been investigating the economic feasibility of a tidal-electric plant in the Passamaquoddy Bay off the Bay of Fundy on the United States-Canadian border, where the average tidal range is 5.5 meters (16).

Geothermal Energy

The word *geothermal* means "earth heat." (See Figure 18–44.) This heat is released when rocks undergo radioactive decay. As a result, with each kilo-

18–44 *Map of geothermal areas in the world. Most are located in regions of volcanic activity, past or present.*

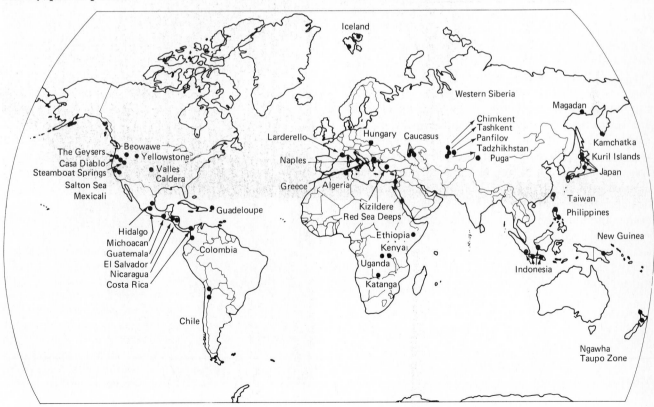

meter of depth the earth's temperature increases about 25° C. In a few special geological situations, underground water that is trapped in layers of porous rock will become very hot. Vulcanism and mountain-building are associated with the development of geothermal deposits. For example, of the known geothermal areas in the United States, three are located in the Black Hills of South Dakota, six in the Ouachita Mountains (Oklahoma), 46 in the Appalachians, and about 1,000 in the Rockies.

USE IN HEATING BUILDINGS. If wells are drilled into such steam reservoirs, the steam that issues up the well shaft can be utilized to heat buildings. For example, almost all the houses in the town of Reykjavik, Iceland, a city of 81,000 people, are heated by geothermal steam (6). And in the United States, Klamath Falls, Oregon, and Boise, Idaho are partially heated by nearby geothermal wells (6). At least 300 communities in the United States, including Reno, Nevada, could use geothermal energy to advantage. The water doesn't have to be geyser-hot. Plain hot water, often less than boiling, can be used in numerous industrial processes, ranging from dehydrating potatoes to washing beer bottles. It is difficult to realize that the warm comfort of the sprawling ranch house at Hilltop Ring Ranch, 40 miles north of Midland, South Dakota, is made possible because of some "hot rocks" lying 4,000 feet below the surface of the ground. As reported by the Associated Press this ranch home comfort is just one of the benefits resulting from a three-year federally funded geothermal-energy research project conducted jointly by the Department of Energy and the South Dakota School of Mines. The rocks heat water in an adjacent aquifer to a fairly constant temperature of 153° F. After being tapped by a deep natural well the water is transported by subterranean pipes to the ranch, where it heats the ranch house and a number of other buildings and dries several thousand bushels of grain yearly. George Armstrong, the owner of the ranch, is very pleased. Every year those "hot rocks" save him about $5,500 in fuel bills.

USE IN GENERATING ELECTRICITY. The first use of geothermal energy to generate electricity was initiated at Larderello, Italy, in 1904. Other geothermal plants have been set up in New Zealand, Japan, Mexico, Iceland, and the Soviet Union. The world's third largest geothermal project, operated by the Pacific Gas and Electric Company, is located at The Geysers on the steep slope of Cobb Mountain, an extinct volcano, in northern California, where production began in 1960. (See Figure 18–45.) The plant, which has a capacity of 900 megawatts, supplies half of the electrical needs of San Francisco. The San Diego Gas and Electric Company constructed a plant in this region in 1973. (See Figure 18–46.) Do not get the impression, however, that significant amounts of electrical power are currently being derived from geothermal power. For example, the total capacity of all the geothermal plants the world over is only about 1,200 megawatts — equivalent to the power generated by just one large coal-fueled plant (6).

Geothermal power is cheap and relatively clean compared to power derived from burning coal. Capital investment is minimal, costing only $150 per kilowatt, compared to $250 for a coal-fired plant

18 – 45 *Geothermal wells at The Geysers, California. More than 100 wells have been drilled at The Geysers, in an area 2 × 8 miles in extent. The deepest of these is more than 8,000 feet. Temperatures of the underground reservoirs from which the heat is drawn are about 255°C (480°F). The basic source appears to be a mass of heated rocks at a depth of three to five miles and covering an area of about 100 to 500 square miles.*

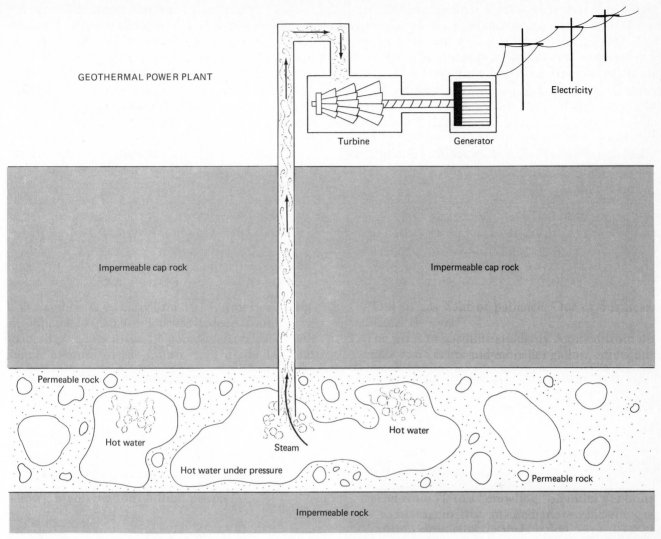

GEOTHERMAL POWER PLANT

Turbine

Generator

Electricity

Impermeable cap rock

Impermeable cap rock

Permeable rock

Hot water

Hot water

Steam

Hot water under pressure

Permeable rock

Impermeable rock

18 – 46 *Schematic view of a geothermal-power-plant operation.*

and $500 for a nuclear-power station. However, there are also drawbacks. For one thing, minerals dissolved in the steam may corrode pipes and turbine blades. Another problem is that gaseous contaminants may be present in the steam. For example, at The Geysers the steam contains small amounts of "rotten-egg" gas (hydrogen sulfide), as well as carbon dioxide, ammonia, and methane (6). Then, too, only negligible amounts of geothermal energy are available in the populous eastern United States where the demand would be greatest. Furthermore, land "sinking" may occur following the sinking of a geothermal well.

THE FUTURE OF GEOTHERMAL ENERGY. Nevertheless, despite the disadvantages, Joseph Barnes, United Nations director of resources, is quite optimistic and considers that geothermal energy is making a breakthrough. Another United Nations expert, Tsvi Meidav, has speculated that geothermal sources *could yield double the energy represented by the world's total deposits of oil, gas, and coal.* Some experts believe that all the power needs of twenty million people could be satisfied with the steam that underlies the Imperial Valley in southern California (11). Leases have been granted for the development of geothermal energy in 13 states embracing an area of 58 million acres. A panel of Interior Department experts, perhaps rather optimistically, have estimated that, by the end of this century, 395 million kilowatts could be supplied by geothermal sources — more electrical power than is produced by all the generating capacity in the United States today. A more realistic estimate, perhaps, is that, by the year 2020, our nation will derive 18.5 quads of energy annually from geothermal sources, which is roughly 10 percent of our nation's energy needs.

Hydropower

Waterpower has been employed to serve human needs since the time of the Romans. In the United States hydropower was extensively used in the nineteenth century for grinding wheat and corn, sawing logs (whether white pine from Minnesota and Wisconsin or redwoods from California), and powering textile mills along the New England coast.

18-47 *Hydroelectric power. Aerial view of Hoover Dam and Lake Mead on the Arizona-Nevada border. This world-famous dam spans the Colorado River. Built in 1935, the dam provides multiple benefits, such as flood protection, water storage for irrigation purposes, and hydroelectric power.*

Hydropower has several advantages: (1) it is relatively inexpensive, (2) it is pollution-free, (3) it certainly will never be exhausted during human survival on the planet Earth, and (4) it has been estimated that the global potential of hydropower is equivalent to all the energy derived from fossil fuels today. As a matter of fact, the installed hydropower capacity of the world is only about 8 percent of its potential capacity.

It might be supposed, therefore, that when the supply of fossil fuels is eventually exhausted, the world could simply shift over to full development of the hitherto unrealized hydropower potential. However, the situation is not quite that simple. Several complexities cloud the picture:

1. The greatest hydropower potential exists in such underdeveloped continents as Africa and South America. For example, the potential in the United States is only 161,000 megawatts, compared to 577,000 megawatts for South America and 780,000 for Africa (14). Because, however, the countries involved are poorly endowed with many other essential resources, and in any event are not highly industrialized, the prospects for actually developing this hydropower potential are not bright.

2. The massive, multimillion-dollar dams necessary in hydropower development would have an abbreviated life expectancy (as previously discussed in connection with water sources) because of as yet unsolved reservoir-sedimentation problems. For example, even Egypt's Aswan Dam, the world's largest, probably will have a functional life of less than two centuries. In the United States, several California dams, such as the Mono Dam at Santa Barbara, have been killed by silt in fewer than twenty years.

3. There are aesthetic objections to converting some of the world's most lovely wilderness spectacles — wild, rushing white streams cutting their way through craggy mountain gorges — into chains of drab, unexciting man-made reservoirs. In the event that we were eventually put in an increasingly tight energy squeeze, would we really be willing to trade off environmental grandeur for kilowatts? Or would we look elsewhere? The Colorado River is already closed to future dam projects by Congressional mandate. Mounting public opposition has also blocked the devel-

opment of dam sites on the Columbia and Snake rivers of the Northwest, as well as on the Eel and Mad rivers of California.

4. The reservoir (artificial lake) that forms behind the dam inundates and destroys valuable forests, wildlife habitat and agricultural land.

5. The development of hydropower may damage the ecological balance of estuaries due to a drastic change in water flow patterns.

6. Dams interfere with the spawning migrations of salmon and other anadromous species. Elimination of endangered species of fishes below the dams may occur due to changes in flow rates and water volume.

7. In hot arid areas the extremely high rates of water evaporation from the reservoir would result in increased levels of salinity. This would lower the use of this water for irrigation purposes.

8. Dam collapse may cause human death and injury. For example, during the 40-year period from 1918 to 1958 thirty-three dams collapsed. The failure of just five of these dams resulted in 1,680 deaths.

9. More ecological damage is caused for each unit of energy produced by hydropower than by any other energy source, according to the National Research Council.

Windpower

For many decades Great Plains farmers harnessed the winds sweeping across their rolling grasslands and wheatfields with the aid of picturesque windmills, once a characteristic barnyard feature. They used windpower to pump water, grind grain, and generate enough electricity to light up their barns. Once rural electrification programs came into existence in the 1930s, the sight of windmill silhouettes etched darkly agains the blue prairie skies gradually became a rarity. In recent years, however, with the cost of fuels ever spiralling, interest in windpower has sharply revived. And there is plenty of power waiting to be tapped. The potential windpower available in this country at an elevation of 500 feet is estimated to be 400 quadrillion BTUs. (One quadrillion is 1 followed by 15 zeros.) However, World Meteorological Organization estimates that realis-

18 – 48 *The windmill of the past. Many-bladed windmills like these were once characteristic landmarks on American farms. They were used to pump water. Farmers stopped using them following the successful rural electrification program of the 1930s. Now farmers need alternative power sources to pump irrigation water because of high prices for gas and other fuels.*

18–49 *The windmill of the future! This large wind-turbine generator is supplying part of the electric power used by the people of Clayton, New Mexico. The 200-kilowatt wind machine is part of a Department of Energy project to test the economics and performance of large wind systems interconnected with conventional power plants and used to supply electric power through existing utility lines. The blades on this wind machine are 40 feet long.*

tically 7–19 percent of electricity used in the U.S. will be generated by wind power by the year 2000.

Many modern versions of the old Great Plains windmill are currently being studied by the Department of Energy. For proponents of wind-energy systems the date July 1979, had special significance. For at that time the world's largest wind-turbine generator began operation at Boone, North Carolina. The blades on Boone's giant "windmill" measure 200 feet in diameter and rotate 35 times per minute. They are mounted atop a 140-foot tower. Two megawatts of power can be generated at wind speeds of 30 miles per hour—sufficient to supply the electrical needs of 500 homes (28).

DISADVANTAGES OF WINDPOWER

1. Suitable areas for the generation of windpower are limited. It would take 300,000 to one million giant wind turbines in the Plains states to generate just half of current U.S. electrical needs. The only other feasible area is the Mid-Atlantic seaboard. (See Figure 18–50.)
2. A considerable amount of farm and rangeland would be converted to access roads required for the maintenance of the wind turbines.
3. Once-attractive landscapes would be dominated by a "forest" of wind turbines and extensive systems of transmission lines.
4. Materials tend to fatigue in the rotors of large wind turbines.
5. The microclimate downwind from the turbines would be altered.
6. The giant array of turbines would disrupt television communication systems and interfere with bird migration.

Biomass Fuels

It is possible to derive energy from the organic compounds in the bodies or organisms as well as from their waste products, such as manure. Such materials are known as *biomass fuels*. Experts have esti-

18–50 *Offshore windmills. Some day there may be groups of large wind-energy conversion systems in offshore areas near the coastlines of the United States. Scientists are studying the concept because offshore areas have strong prevailing winds. The idea may not be economical, however, because of the high cost of the support platforms for the wind machines and for the lengthy underwater cables required to carry the electricity to shore.*

18–51 *An "energy plantation." Note the size of these rapidly growing hybrid poplars. They are only six years old but are more than 15 feet tall. This is part of an energy farm experimental program conducted by the U.S. Forest Service at Rhinelander, Wisconsin.*

mated that up to 10 percent of our nation's energy requirements could be satisfied with biomass fuels. Of course, such energy is really an indirect form of solar energy because all the chemical energy occurring in the bodies of plants and animals originally was derived from the process of photosynthesis. The chemical energy in the vegetation covering the planet Earth is fully 20 times the energy consumed by mankind for all purposes. Even when we consider the United States alone, where energy consumption is greater than in any other country of the world, the chemical energy produced by terrestrial plants is equivalent to our nation's total energy demands. Of course, it would not be wise to use up all the vegetation in this way. After all, grasses are needed to control erosion; Douglas fir and white pine are needed as timber, and so on.

Researchers are excited over the prospects of "energy plantations"—intensely managed forests of trees especially selected because of their rapid growth—as a potential source of fuel. (See Figure 18–51.) For example, in Pennsylvania hybrid poplar plantations are yielding twenty metric tons of wood per hectare per year. Of course, large-scale energy plantations are associated with certain limiting factors, such as availability of land, water, and costly fertilizer. Then, too, if the plantations are developed as monotypes, outbreaks of diseases and insect pests could be highly destructive. The energy-equivalent of twenty million tons of coal could be obtained merely by utilizing the wood now rotting on the forest floor of the Tennessee Valley. The TVA is considering using some of this wood as fuel to heat public schools in Tennessee (25).

569

18–52 *This biomass-to-fuel oil plant in Albany, Oregon, converts feedstock, such as Douglas fir wood chips in the foreground, into fuel oil. The wood chips are combined with carbon monoxide and hydrogen at high temperatures and pressures.*

Biomass energy can be secured from such diverse sources as seaweed, scrub trees, waterweeds (resulting from eutrophication), cannery waste, pulp and paper mill residues, livestock manure that has accu-

mulated in feedlots, and household garbage. Biomass such as sewage sludge can be converted into methane gas by the activity of anaerobic bacteria, and alcohol can be derived from biomass materials by fermentation.

The production of char (a solid fuel), oil, and such gaseous fuels as methane, carbon monoxide, and hydrogen by the pyrolysis of garbage and other organic wastes has already been discussed in Chapter 15 in connection with solid-waste-disposal strategies. Much interest is currently being shown using *gasohol* to power motor cars. Gasohol is a mixture of 10 percent alcohol and 90 percent gasoline. It has already been sold at some service stations. Until now much of the alcohol has been derived from the bacterial fermentation of corn, and that poses the problem of choosing between food and fuel. After all, most of the best corn-producing farmland is already in production. However, researchers at Colorado State University have demonstrated that alcohol can be efficiently produced from agricultural residues. For example, they have been able to produce one quart of ethanol from just ten pounds of wheat straw. It is estimated that the residues from just nine major agricultural crops amounts to 71 million tons annually. The Colorado State scientists estimate that roughly three billion gallons of alcohol could be derived from residues annually. Of course, one big advantage is that our nation's food supply would not be threatened. It should be mentioned, however, that agricultural residues such as corn and wheat stubble do increase the organic content of the soil as they decay. Moreover, they serve in controlling the loss of valuable topsoil to erosion. These functions must be taken into consideration in any intensive program to use farm residues for alcohol production.

The Gasoline Plant

It may sound bizarre, but in the year 2000 farmers in the Southwest may be growing cash crops that yield oil and gasoline rather than food. A University of California biochemist, Nobel Prize winner Melvin Calvin, has found that the hydrocarbons occurring abundantly in the milky sap of a desert shrub, *Euphorbia lathyris*, commonly called the *gopher plant*, are the same ones occurring in gasoline. (See Figures 18–53 and 18–54.) Calvin discovered that an acre of these "gas plants" could produce ten barrels of oil after a seven-month growing season. The plants are cut off and crushed to remove the oil, which can then be converted into gasoline in already existing refineries. (See Figure 18–55.) Calvin estimates that sufficient gasoline can be derived from a gopher-plant farm the size of Arizona to satisfy all of our

18–53 *Biomass power.* Euphorbia lathyris, *the "gasoline plant," is shown growing wild in the hills of Berkeley, California.*

18–54 *Biomass power. Dr. Melvin Calvin of the University of California-Berkeley examines the gasoline weed (Euphorbia lathyris). According to Dr. Calvin, this weed, which now grows in the wild, could be cultivated on semiarid land to produce petroleum.*

18–55 *Biomass power. A laboratory assistant at the University of California's laboratory of Chemical Biodynamics prepares test samples of the gasoline weed. She is searching for the most effective method of extracting petroleum from this plant.*

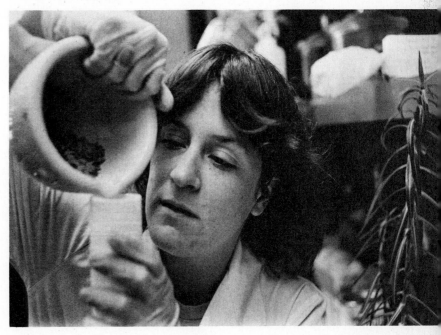

nation's gasoline requirements. The cost of producing the oil is about $20 per barrel — twice the cost of current Middle East oil. However, it is estimated that by 1988 the cost of fossil-fuel oil will be so high that gopher-plant oil will be commercially attractive (27).

Ocean Thermal Energy Conversion (OTEC)

The ocean is a vast storehouse of indirect solar energy, and the technology is available for converting it into electricity by exploiting the temperature differential between warm surface waters and cold bottom waters in tropical seas. Each OTEC plant includes a floating platform with enormous pipes extending downward to a depth of 3,000 feet (905 meters). (See Figure 18–56.) The operational design of the plant is simple. A fluid, such as ammonia, that boils at a relatively low temperature is continuously circulated through a closed system of tubes. The warm temperature at the surface converts the ammonia to a gas that in turn drives the blades of an electric turbine. (See Figure 18–57.) The spent ammonia gas is then condensed by cold water pumped up from the ocean depths. This liquid ammonia is then converted to gaseous form by the warm surface water and the cycle starts once again. The electrical energy produced may then be conducted to shore; or it could be used directly in the desalination of sea water. One enthusiast believes that OTEC power plants could be generating up to 5 percent of our nation's energy needs by 2000.

ECONOMIC PROBLEMS. Unfortunately, the energy-conversion efficiency is only about 3 percent. Moreover, there is considerable uncertainty concerning the financial costs of a large-scale OTEC system. Costs are at least $1,500 per kilowatt, compared to a cost of $1,000 per kilowatt generated at a nuclear plant. Another drawback is that suitable locations for OTEC plants would be limited to a relatively few locations such as the Gulf Coast and the waters off Hawaii, Guam, and Puerto Rico. The high cost is partly the result of the vast amount of water that must be pumped through the system. In a moderate-sized plant generating 100 megawatts, the volume of water pumped would be greater than the average flow of the Potomac River (17).

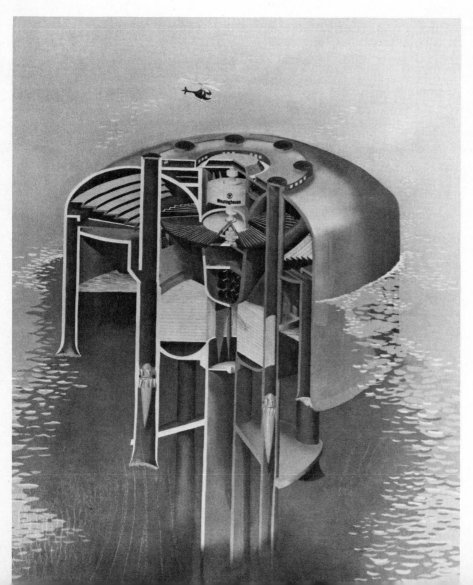

18–56 *Artist's conception of a 100-MWE ocean thermal energy conversion plant. Seawater is vaporized. The steam drives a turbine with a 125-foot diameter. The steam is then condensed, using 40 F water pumped from an ocean depth of 3,000 feet. This plant would make significant amounts of fresh water as a byproduct.*

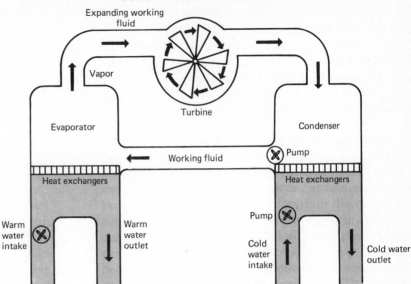

OCEAN THERMAL POWER PLANT

18–57 *Schematic diagram of a closed-cycle ocean thermal power plant.*

ENVIRONMENTAL PROBLEMS WITH OTEC. A number of environmental problems cloud the OTEC energy horizon:

1. The release of carbon dioxide into the atmosphere by the OTEC plant resulting from the upwelling of cold water would be roughly one third that of an equivalent coal-fired plant (NRC).
2. The cooling of surface waters may adversely affect commercial fisheries.
3. Rainfall patterns may be changed if many plants are constructed (NRC).

Hydrogen

As every grade school student knows, the supply of hydrogen is super-abundant, as part of the water molecule H_2O. Hydrogen gas burns readily in air, as it combines rapidly with oxygen. It has the potential for being a very useful and versatile fuel. Hydrogen gas may also be obtained by processing natural gas (CH_4) or petroleum gas. An electric power plant based on hydrogen fuel is being installed in New York City. This plant would produce electricity directly from hydrogen fuel cells.

Hydrogen may also be used to replace gasoline in trucks, buses, and motor cars. It also has been considered as a fuel for the turbine engines of jet planes. Its advantages are considerable. Air, thermal, and noise pollution would be reduced to a minimum,

hence it would be more readily accepted by a city than would a dirty coal-burning plant or a potentially hazardous nuclear plant. Moreover, when hydrogen burns, no environmentally damaging pollutants like soot, sulfur dioxide, carbon monoxide, lead, mercury, or radioactive materials are released into the air. In fact, the only product resulting from the combustion of hydrogen is water — plain H_2O! Nevertheless, there are some drawbacks associated with its use. Firstly, it is not a *primary* fuel source. For example, first some other fuel like coal must be burned to produce the electricity to break down water by electrolysis to release the hydrogen. Secondly, when using hydrogen as a fuel, there is always the potential for a flammable reaction. Thirdly, the metals that come in contact with hydrogen tend to become brittle after a prolonged period of time.

Conserving Energy

In America's attempt to satisfy its prospective energy needs, most of the attention has been focused on methods of producing more hydrocarbon (fossil) fuels or on developing alternative, less conventional energy sources. Not enough attention has been directed toward devising methods of *reducing energy consumption*. Nevertheless, the opportunities are

573

great. In a Harvard Business School report entitled *Energy Future*, conservation was described as "no less an energy alternative than oil, gas, coal or nuclear. Indeed in the near term, conservation could do more than any of the conventional sources to help the country deal with the energy problem." For example, Wisconsin's Senator Gaylord Nelson has observed that the United States wastes more energy than is consumed by all of Japan—the world's third-largest industrial nation. Allen L. Hammond, writing in *Science*, has emphasized that "five sixths of the energy used in transportation, two thirds of the fuel consumed to generate electricity, and nearly one third of the remaining energy—amounting in all to more than 50 percent of the energy consumed in the United States—is discarded as waste heat . . . " (12). Some experts believe that it is possible for the United States to save from 10 to 40 percent of the energy it now consumes. Even if we saved only 1 percent of the 63×10^{15} BTUs our nation consumes each year, our annual energy gain would be equivalent to 100 million barrels of petroleum (12).

Fuel-savings potential has been further underscored by the U.S. Office of Emergency Preparedness, which is of the opinion that we could cut energy consumption by 15 percent through such strategems as energy taxes, increased recycling and reuse, improved freight-handling systems, and expanded mass transit. The office feels that such devices could save our nation 7.3 million barrels of oil daily by 1985.

Energy savings can be made in many sectors of American life: home construction, the design of factories and commercial buildings, transportation, industry, and others. Let us examine just a few of those areas.

Home Construction

Americans have been notoriously mindless in building residences with minimal regard for the soundness of their architectural design in relation to climate. Today's homes consume twice as much energy as those built just a few decades ago. The philosophy of the architect and homebuilder has been that, if a home gets uncomfortably warm, it can be cooled off with energy-demanding air conditioning; if a house gets too chilly, it can always be warmed up with an energy-demanding heat plant. Architects can play an important role in energy conservation.

S. David Freeman, director of a Ford Foundation study of national energy problems, has had some revealing discussions with American architects. Freeman writes:

One architect told me that he looked over the plans for a building he's just finished. He found that with a few small changes in the design—that would not have added a *penny* to the cost of the building—he could have cut down the energy consumption by 35 percent *simply by replacing half the glass with walls*. . . . Glass is an excellent conductor and a poor insulator. Heat flows right through it. By cutting down on the area of glass you cut down the heat loss tremendously. *[Italics mine.]*

Ironically, the glass-walled United Nations building in New York City is a classic example of profligate energy waste caused by faulty architectural design. (See Figure 18–58.)

A study of model homes in Atlanta, Minneapolis, and New York has indicated that the use of more insulation, weather stripping, and storm windows would reduce energy consumption for space-heating purposes by 42 percent. Substantial energy savings can be made simply by flicking the thermostat in the proper direction. For example, in Minneapolis, Minnesota, where winters are frequently severely cold, keeping the thermostat at 68° F during the day and turning it down to 55° F at night will reduce the fuel costs of the average homeowner by 23 percent. The newly constructed Federal Office Building in Manchester, New Hampshire, is an excellent example of how proper design can reduce energy consumption. The building incorporates such energy-saving features as a low window-to-wall ratio; several windows in the south-facing wall to provide solar warmth during the winter; extra thick insulation in the roof, walls, and floors; and improved lighting systems. True, the building cost 10 percent more than the conventional variety, but energy consumption is being reduced by 50 percent (6).

In many buildings solar hot-water heaters could replace about half of the gas or electric heaters now employed, thus gaining an additional 1 percent of energy. Deciduous tree plantings next to a house will shade it in the summer, thus reducing the need for energy-extravagant air conditioning and permitting the sun's rays to warm it during the winter. Architectural designs in modern commercial buildings often involve excessive use of mortar and steel, material whose manufacture is highly energy-con-

18-58 *View of the United Nations from the East River. The glass-walled Secretariat Building in the left foreground, ironically, is a classic example of heat- (and energy-) wasting architectural design.*

suming. A substantial saving in electricity might be made in many department stores, clothing stores, and drugstores, whose managers apparently feel their places of business have to be lit up like a Christmas tree in order to attract customers. It has been estimated that the World Trade Center, the celebrated high-rise building in New York City, consumes more energy than the entire city of Cambridge, Massachusetts, a community of over 100,000 inhabitants. (See Figure 18-61.)

18-59 *Energy conservation. Many families throughout the United States are concerned with energy conservation. They turn lights off, don't waste hot water, and set thermostats back. However, many families are losing energy and dollars unknowingly through poorly insulated roofs. To maintain a comfortable temperature in their home, they are forced to make their furnace work harder and consume more fuel than necessary.*

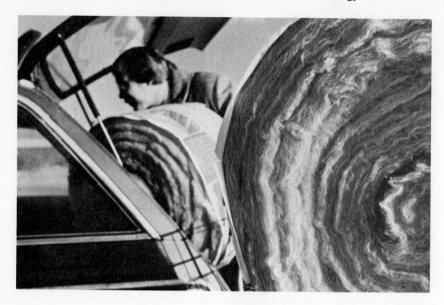

18–60 *Getting ready for winter. Adding insulation yourself will result in both energy and money savings. Many families in the northern states — New York, Pennsylvania, and Michigan — are investing in insulation, caulking, weather stripping, and storm windows. Their homes will be snug despite the icy blasts of winter.*

18–61 *Twin energy consumers: the towers of the World Trade Center in New York, each 110 stories, or one-quarter mile, high. Each day these twin towers use more energy than the entire city of Cambridge, Massachusetts.*

The federal government has instituted several programs that have energy-conserving objectives for homeowners. For example, federal funds are available to provide home insulation for low-income families. Then too, low interest loans and tax credits may be obtained by homeowners for the purpose of adopting energy-saving systems such as solar water heaters. It is rather discouraging, however, that the amount of federal money being spent to stimulate *conservation* is "peanuts" compared to the large amounts being used to boost energy *production.* For example, a four-year sum of only $2.5 billion was authorized for energy conservation loans. Compare this with the $88 billion federal expenditure earmarked for the development of synthetic fuels.

Transportation

The usual expansion pattern of the average American city is in the form of an irregular "doughnut," with many millions of people, the nation over, moving into the suburbs, the outer "rim" of the doughnut, even though their employment may be in the doughnut's "hole." Obviously much valuable fuel is consumed simply because these people must commute between home and work, with some unfortunates easily driving a round trip of 60 miles per working day, or about 15,000 miles yearly. Because about 25 percent of all energy consumed by Americans is used in transportation (either of humans or materials), billions of dollars worth of energy could be saved annually if urban expansion patterns were changed.

Because four times as much fuel is used to transport one pound of freight by truck as by rail, the shifting of long-distance transport from trucks to trains would seem to make much better energy sense. Substantial fuel savings could also be made if the commuter were to use a *public transportation system* instead of a personal automobile (a car consumes twice as much fuel as a bus per person transported). Apparently Americans are learning this

18–62 *"Much valuable fuel is consumed simply because these people must commute between home and work, some unfortunate ones easily driving a round trip of 60 miles per working day, or about 15,000 miles yearly. . . ."*

National Energy Policy

Earl Cook
Distinguished Professor of
Geology
TEXAS A&M UNIVERSITY

National energy policy tends to shift dramatically with the short-term perception of energy scarcity. When energy is high priced and the nation appears increasingly dependent on imports, national policy is directed toward conservation and substitution. When conservation and economic recession relieve the pressure on energy supplies and bring about a decline in energy prices, the national mood returns to complacency and support evaporates for development of synthetic fuels, solar energy, and gasohol. It is conveniently forgotten that adequate supplies now result from a decrease in consumption rather than an increase in supply.

National energy policy should have three aims: (1) to provide access for all citizens to the minimum supply of energy needed to maintain life and dignity in a mechanized society; (2) to guard against political or military interdiction of necessary energy imports; and (3) to move toward substitution, both adequate in quantity and reasonable in cost, of other energy systems for the systems now based on domestic supplies of crude oil and natural gas, supplies that are diminishing and that probably will diminish faster in the closing years of this century.

Consequently, energy policy should provide financial assistance for the poor to purchase the energy they need; a workable standby fuel-rationing system; maintenance of the strategic petroleum reserve at a level equivalent to at least ninety days of imports; continued government assistance for the development of alternative domestic sources of energy, based on coal, uranium, sunshine, and biomass; and renewed encouragement of conservation and severe discouragement of energy waste.

mass-transit lesson in fuel economy, for the number of passenger trips by bus, train, and subway increased from 6.5 billion in 1972 to more than 9 billion in the early 1980s — an encouraging increase of 39 percent. Moreover, if the commuter were willing to sacrifice a little privacy, comfort, and independence, substantial energy savings could be made by the formation of *car pools*, thus easing both the *energy and air-pollution problems simultaneously.*

A considerable degree of gasoline savings could be made if automobile manufacturers used the best technology for obtaining maximal fuel efficiency. Much progress already has been made. For example, by the mid-1980s the average American car is expected to get at least 27.5 miles per gallon — roughly twice the average mileage of the mid-1970s. But this is only the beginning. According to some manufacturers the technology should soon be available to enable some cars to attain 50 miles per gallon by 1990, and even 80 miles per gallon by 1995! Such dramatic fuel efficiencies may be obtained only in small cars specifically designed for in-town use.

Industry

Industry consumes about 40 percent of all energy used in the United States. What is more, over 50 percent of the energy used by industry is wasted as heat. It is apparent, therefore, that any large-scale saving in the industrial area would be very desirable. It is encouraging that with fuel costs zooming, some American industrial corporations are beginning to make concerted efforts to reduce fuel wastage.

More important, these energy savings have been made at the same time that the GNP has not only been maintained but actually has risen. The *energy/ GNP ratio* shows how many thousands of BTUs are consumed per dollar of GNP (in 1972 dollars). It is both significant and highly encouraging that this index has steadily decreased. For example, in 1970 it was at a relatively high 62.4. However, by 1980 it had dropped to 53.0. Although our nation's GNP increased at an annual rate of 2.65 from 1973–1979, the rate of energy consumption rose much more slowly — only .88 percent per year. These figures are highly significant since they show that gross energy consumption can be separated from real economic growth. They do not necessarily have to increase at the same rate.

Consider some items:

1. U.S. Steel is now capturing large amounts of natural gas emitted from its coke ovens and using this formerly wasted fuel in other plant operations (21).
2. The utility bill at one large General Motors plant was reduced by almost $1 million simply by cut-ting down on superfluous electric lighting during daytime hours (21).
3. United Air Lines is considering reducing jet-flight speeds in an effort to conserve fuel. For example, it could save at least 350 gallons on the New York–San Francisco 747 flight simply by reducing the cruising speed from 588 to 574 miles per hour. Moreover, the flight time would be extended by a negligible seven minutes (21).
4. It is most gratifying that the car industry has reduced the size of their giant gasoline-guzzling

Energy Policy Issues for the United States

Supply and Demand of Energy

1. Should the United States adopt a policy of self-sufficiency in energy resource development and production? Or should the United States pursue a policy of maximum importation of energy sources in order to conserve domestic supplies?
2. How dependent can the United States become on imported petroleum? Should the nation pursue a policy designed to increase the development of its urban, onshore and offshore oil reserves?
3. Should the United States seek ways to negotiate contracts that guarantee delivery of imported natural gas?
4. Should tax policies be designed to provide increased incentives for the development of potential energy reserves? To increase oil refining capacities?
5. Can synthetic fuels close the energy gap? What are the prospects for solar power, geothermal, nuclear fusion or other alternative sources?
6. What are the air quality implications of increased use of high sulfur oil and coal?
7. Should the nation adopt policies to alter existing building codes that would reduce energy demand? How effective would they be?
8. How can the energy demand from tranportation be lowered?

Implementation of Policy

1. Are national security, clean energy and a low-cost national energy base compatible?
2. Should the price of energy be allowed to be set by a free-market system or an alternative system?
3. Should there be established a "one-step" approval procedure for energy-related projects, such as the siting of power plants, urban and off-shore oil drilling, geothermal development, and so on?
4. Should a coordinated federal-state energy research and development effort be developed?

Modified from Richard C. Dorf, *Energy, Resources and Policy* (Reading, Mass.: Addison-Wesley Publishing Company, 1978).

models. Thus, Charles M. Heinen, Chrysler's chief engineer, announced at a California energy conference, "I've instructed my entire staff to concentrate on energy-waste reduction right now. We're aiming for cuts of 500 to 700 pounds and that alone would save the consumer all the extra gas consumption required as a result of new pollution control and safety measures . . ." (23). Who needs the "roar" of a Cougar, Jaguar, or any of the other "metallic monsters" to bolster one's faded ego, anyway? Why were cars built with 450 "horses under the hood" when 95 percent of the time the driver needs only one tenth as much power?

5. Rather admirably, even the gasoline companies, which are in the business to sell gasoline, have stressed its conservation. The time when a motorist could blithely say "Fill 'er up!" may soon be past. Noteworthy is the following newspaper "advertisement" by Mobil, which appeared in the Minneapolis *Star*: "So we're trying to sell you *conservation* right now, instead of gasoline. We think it's the thing to do while shortages persist.

We know, for instance, that if every driver in the United States used just a gallon less gasoline a week, the nation probably could get along without gasoline imports. This would save about $800 million yearly in foreign exchange payments. . . ." *[Italics mine.]*

Energy savings could also be effected were industry to produce more durable products. Planned obsolescence for many manufacturing corporations appears to be a way of business life. Last Christmas's plastic toys and mechanical gadgets for youngsters all wind up in the trash can before New Year's. But that's small potatoes compared with the car business. If a Ford or Chevy were built to last 12 years instead of 6, the amount of energy consumed in the car-manufacturing process would be reduced by 50 percent.

A large array of energy-saving methods are available to industry. Among them are: (1) cogeneration systems, which produce both heat and electricity, (2) methods for recovering waste heat, (3) more efficient boilers and furnaces, (4) electric motors whose

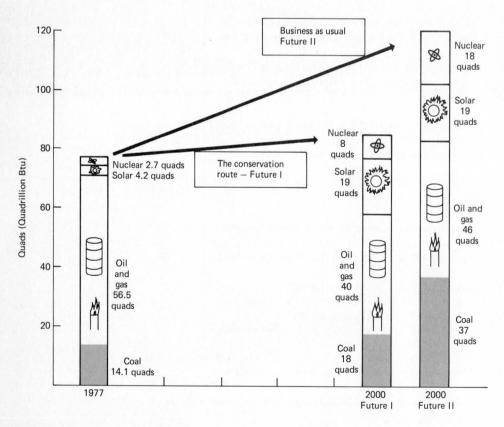

18–63 *Two possible energy-consumption patterns for the United States. We can follow the conservation route—a procedure that is highly desirable—or we can continue our foolhardy waste of energy. Environmental degradation will be proportional to the amount of energy we consume.*

Technology	Status	Environmental concerns
Gasification	Low-energy process in use in Europe. High-energy process to be available in the 1990s.	On-site subsidence. Air and water contamination.
Liquefaction	Solvent refined coal process near commercialization. Availability of other processes expected about 1990.	Air and water contamination.
Fluidized-bed combustion	Pilot plants being tested. Availability expected in the 1990s.	Thermal pollution. Disposal of spent sorbent. Air and water contamination.
Oil shale	Pilot plant in operation. Availability of surface and in situ processes expected in 1985.	Disposal of overburden and spent shale. Air and water contamination.
Nuclear fission	In use. Plutonium reprocessing, waste solidification, and potentials for armament proliferation under study.	Radioactive waste disposal. Water contamination. Thermal pollution.
Fusion	In early testing stage. A 21st century technology.	Decommissioned reactors. Radioactive wastes.
Geothermal	In use. Increased application expected in the 1990s.	Subsidence. Noise. Air and water contamination. Thermal pollution.
Solar	Heating of buildings commercialized. Cooling of buildings and biomass fuels expected in the 1980s. Availability of thermal electric technology project for the 21st century. Demonstration of Ocean Thermal Energy Conversion expected by 1985. Production of clean fuels from biomass, post-1990.	Toxicity of working fluids. Land and water use. Climatic change. Marine pollution.

18-64 *Status of the various energy technologies and a brief listing of the environmental concerns associated with each.*

speed can be controlled, (5) devices for controlling air-to-fuel ratios. *Cogeneration* can reduce fuel consumption by 30 percent, compared to the fuel needed to generate the same amount of steam and electricity separately. A presidential energy commission has estimated that cogeneration systems could save 3.5 quads annually by the year 2000 — equivalent to a savings of 1.75 million barrels of oil per day.

It is encouraging that America's energy demands in the near future will be somewhat less than was originally predicted. This is due in part to the employment of a combination of the energy saving methods and practices described above for the residential, transportational, and industrial sectors. For example, Shell Oil predicts that annual growth increases in energy demand that averaged 1.8 percent in the 1970s will drop to 1.2 percent in the 1980s. A recent estimate predicts an annual national demand of about 100 quads by the year 2000 — fully 33 percent below the 150 quads widely forecasted in the late 1970s.

The energy crisis is for real. It may be with us for the remaining years of this century. It can be solved. But at a cost, measured in fuel price increases to the consumer, by possible fuel rationing, by a new energy-conserving rather than energy-spending lifestyle on the part of the American people. (See Figure 18-63.) Regrettably, part of the cost would be some seemingly unavoidable environmental damage—

such as the air pollution resulting from intensified use of coal. For the short term, the nation's accelerating energy demands can be met by a combination of such programs as energy conservation, coal gasification, the construction of the Alaskan gas pipeline, the increased tempo of gas and oil exploration, the development of oil-shale resources, and increasing imports of foreign oil. In addition, intensive development must be made of solar-, hydro-, wind-, biomass-, geothermal- and tidal-energy sources. However, for the long term, beyond the 1980s and into the twenty-first century, most authorities agree that America will be compelled to derive more and more of its energy from nuclear power. The production of nuclear power, which is highly controversial and poses grave implications for environmental damage, will be discussed in the next chapter. (See Earl Cook's guest article concerning a national energy policy.)

Rapid Review

1. The great gasoline shortages of 1973 and 1978–1979 were characterized by sharply increased gas prices, mandatory reductions in highway speeds, a shift from gas-guzzling big cars to gas-conserving compacts, a stagnant economy, and increased levels of unemployment.

2. America's energy crisis was caused by a number of factors: (a) inaccurate estimates of energy needs, (b) lack of economic incentives for gas and oil exploration, (c) inadequate refining capacity, (d) restrictions on the use of high-sulfur fuels, (e) energy consumption for pollution control, (f) our nation's high standard of living, and (g) excessive energy waste.

3. The North American continent holds two trillion tons of minable coal, sufficient to last several centuries.

4. The use of coal, however, has several disadvantages: (a) the desecration of the land by strip-mining, (b) acid mine drainage, and (c) the release of atmospheric pollutants such as sulfur dioxide, carbon dioxide, mercury, and fly ash.

5. Gasification and liquefaction are two processes that permit the use of high-sulfur coal without releasing large amounts of sulfur dioxide into the atmosphere.

6. Our nation consumes about eight times the average consumption rate for the nations of the free world.

7. Foreign relations and international diplomacy are important factors in determining the adequacy of America's oil imports. Much of this imported oil is purchased from the Organization of Petroleum Exporting Countries (OPEC), which includes Algeria, Libya, Nigeria, Saudi Arabia, and Kuwait.

8. In 1969 the richest ($50 billion) oil deposit in the Western Hemisphere was discovered on the North Slope of Alaska. This oil is being transported to the Port of Valdez via a 789 mile Trans-Alaskan Pipeline.

9. The U.S. Geological Survey has estimated that undiscovered recoverable oil reserves in the United States would last only about 45 years.

10. The United States accounts for approximately 50 percent of the world's consumption of natural gas.

11. Because of the increased costs associated with exploration hand drilling, the cost of natural gas and oil in the United States is expected to rise sharply in the near future.

12. The most valuable oil-shale deposits in the United States are located in Colorado, Wyoming, and Utah.

13. The United States will import about two trillion cubic feet of natural gas annually in liquid form (LNG) from Africa, South America, and the North Sea.

14. High-grade oil-shale deposits may yield three-fourths of a barrel (about thirty gallons) of oil per ton of crushed rock.

15. The large-scale processing of shale oil may result in a number of environmental problems, including (a) littering the landscape with millions of tons of wasted shale, (b) the release of atmospheric pollutants such as sulfur dioxide, carbon monoxide, lead, mercury, and cadmium, and (c) the discharge of salty water into the Colorado River.

16. In the future the United States will be deriving more and more of its energy from nonfossil-fuel sources such as (a) direct solar power, (b) indirect solar power (wind, biomass, tides, water-power, and ocean thermal energy), and (c) geothermal energy.

17. The amount of solar energy flooding the earth's surface on a cloudless day is roughly 100,000

times greater than the world's presently installed electric power capacity.

18. Solar heating systems installed in the average home could provide up to 75 percent of the occupants' hot water.

19. Solar energy can be converted directly into electricity by means of solar (photovoltaic) cells. The large-scale production of electricity solar cells awaits a reduction in cost that will make it competitive with electricity from fossil-fuel-powered electric plants.

20. Satellite solar power systems (SSPS) theoretically could tap solar energy outside the earth's atmosphere and convert it into electricity. However, there are disadvantages: (1) a cost of $100 billion per satellite and (2) several adverse effects from the microwaves beamed to earth, such as (a) the destruction of migratory birds, (b) the disruption of radar systems, and (c) genetic and nervous system damage to humans.

21. The huge tides in the Bay of Fundy may someday be used to develop electricity under a joint U.S.-Canadian program.

22. Geothermal energy is currently being used to heat homes in Klamath Falls, Oregon; Boise, Idaho; and Midland, South Dakota.

23. The Pacific Gas and Electric Company operates the world's third largest geothermal program at The Geysers, California, and supplies half of San Francisco's electrical needs with it.

24. The drawbacks of geothermal power are that (a) most potential sites are located too far from population centers, (b) some atmospheric pollutants, such as hydrogen sulfide (rotten-egg gas), ammonia, methane, and carbon dioxide are released, (c) minerals dissolved in the water may corrode pipes and turbine blades, and (d) some land mining may occur.

25. Hydropower has several advantages: (a) it is relatively inexpensive, (b) it inflicts minimal environmental damage, (c) it is inexhaustible, and (d) its global potential is equivalent to all the energy derived from fossil fuels today.

26. There are disadvantages to hydropower development: (a) the sites with greatest potential are frequently far removed from population centers, (b) reservoirs associated with hydropower development would have a silt-abbreviated life span, and (c) wild, rushing streams of considerable beauty would be converted into a chain of drab, man-made reservoirs.

27. In 1979 the world's largest wind turbine generator began operations at Boone, North Carolina.

28. Up to 10 percent of our nation's energy requirements may be satisfied with biomass fuels such as seaweeds, scrub trees, paper mill and cannery residues, agricultural waste, household garbage, and sewage sludge.

29. Ocean thermal energy conversion systems (OTEC) could be generating up to 5 percent of our nation's energy requirements by 2000. Major drawbacks are (a) local shifts in climate and rainfall patterns, (b) destruction of marine life as a result of accidental release of working fluids, and (c) the accelerated release of carbon dioxide into the atmosphere.

30. The United States wastes more energy than is consumed by all of Japan.

31. More than 50 percent of the energy consumed in the United States is discarded as waste heat.

32. Experts estimate that the United States could save 10 to 40 percent of the energy it now consumes. Substantial savings could be made in many sectors of American life, including: (a) home construction, (b) the design of commercial and industrial buildings, (c) transportation, and (d) manufacturing processes.

Key Words and Phrases

Acid mine drainage
Alaskan North Slope
Alaskan Pipeline
Ammonia
Bay of Fundy
Biomass
Boone (North Carolina)
British Thermal Unit (BTU)
Coal
Department of Energy
Drake (Col. Edwin)
Energy conservation
Energy slaves
Federal Power Commission
Four Corners Power Plant
Gasification

Gasohol
Geothermal energy
Geysers (The)
High-sulfur fuel
Hybrid poplar
Hydropower
Kerogen
Kilowatt
Liquefaction
Liquid natural gas
Megawatt
Methane
Microwave
Natural gas
Ocean thermal energy conversion (OTEC)
Offshore oil drilling
Oil
Oil embargo

Oil exploration
Oil shale
Oil wells
Organization of
   Petroleum Exporting
   Countries (OPEC)
Photovoltaic cells
Prudhoe Bay
Refining capacity
Satellite solar power
   station (SSPS)
Shale oil
Silicon
Solar cells

Solar energy
Solar furnace
Solar heating
Solar panels
Solar satellites
Surface Mining Control
   and Reclamation Act
Tar sands
Tidal power
Titusville
   (Pennsylvania)
Wind power
World Trade Center

Questions and Topics for Discussion

1. Describe some of the adverse social and economic effects caused by the oil shortages of 1973 and 1978–1979.
2. Briefly discuss seven factors that have contributed to our nation's energy crisis.
3. Do you feel that our nation should make an intensive effort to derive a much larger percentage of our electrical power from coal-fired power plants? What would be the advantages? The disadvantages?
4. Briefly describe the process of coal liquefaction and of coal gasification.
5. Discuss the statement: "Now that deregulated oil and gas prices have provided the incentive for intensive exploration and drilling, our nation's energy-shortage problems are a thing of the past."
6. Discuss the statement: "Considering the seriousness of our nation's energy problems, our abundant high-sulfur coal resource should be intensively utilized, regardless of environmental concerns such as land desecration from strip-mining or the release of atmospheric pollutants such as sulfur dioxide, carbon dioxide, and fly ash from power plants."
7. Some experts have stated: "In terms of energy consumption the average American has 500 *energy slaves* at his or her beck and call." How many energy slaves do you think might be available to tribesmen in South Africa? To rice-paddy farmers in Laos? Discuss the ethical and

moral problems involved. Can these problems be solved? If so, how?
8. Discuss the statement: "Now that the United States is exploiting the oil reserves on the North Slope of Alaska, the richest deposit ($30 billion) on the North American continent, America's energy problems are over."
9. Intensive exploration and drilling are now occurring along our Pacific, Gulf, and Atlantic coasts. Discuss the economic and environmental problems that this activity may create.
10. Do you feel that the intensive development of oil-shale deposits in Colorado, Wyoming, and Utah is worth the probable environmental cost? Discuss your answer.
11. Some authorities feel that the United States should hitch her "energy wagon" to a star — the sun. What do you think? What are the advantages? What economic and environmental problems might be involved?
12. Briefly list and describe the basic structural components of a simple solar-heating plant for a home.
13. Would the geographic location of the solar-heated home be an important consideration? Explain your answer.
14. In simple terms, describe how a satellite solar-power station works. Discuss the economic and environmental problems involved.
15. In simple terms, describe the operation of a geothermal power plant. Discuss some of the problems associated with the intensive and wide-scale development of geothermal power sources in the United States.
16. Hydropower, wind power, biomass power, tidal power, and ocean thermal energy are all considered indirect forms of solar energy. Explain.
17. Briefly list six sources of biomass fuels.
18. Discuss the possible environmental consequences of using much of our forests as a source of biomass fuels.
19. Discuss the potential of the gopher plant as a source of gasoline in the United States.
20. Why would OTEC systems be limited to the tropical oceans?
21. Discuss three effective methods for energy conservation in each of the following sectors: (a) transportation, (b) residential, and (c) industrial.

22. What effect, if any, will your study of our nation's energy problems have on *your* future lifestyle?

Endnotes

1. Aaronson, Terri, and George Kohl. "Spectrum." *Environment*, **14** (1972), 24–26.
2. Bengelsdorf, Irvin. "Are We Running Out of Fuel?" *National Wildlife*, **20** (Feb.-Mar. 1971).
3. Bregman, Sandra E. "Solar Energy Comes of Age." *Environment* (June 1978), 25–31.
4. Carlson, Dave. "Oil Shortage Gets Worse." *Eau Claire Leader-Telegram*, 11 Jan. 1973.
5. Council on Environmental Quality. *Environmental Quality. Eighth Annual Report.* Washington, DC: Government Printing Office, 1977.
6. Dorf, Richard C. *Energy, Resources and Policy.* Reading, MA: Addison, 1978.
7. Ehrlich, Paul R., and Anne H. Ehrlich. *Population, Resources, Environment.* San Francisco: Freeman, 1970.
8. "Energy Crisis: Are We Running Out?" *Time* (June 12, 1972).
9. Epping, Norm. "Converting Manure to Methane Gas." *Wisconsin Agriculturist* (Jan. 10, 1976).
10. Fay, James A., and James J. MacKenzie. "Cold Cargo." *Environment*, **14** (1972), 21–22, 27–29.
11. Gannon, Robert. "Special Report: Atomic Power — What Are Our Alternatives?" *Science Digest* (Dec. 1971), 19–22.
12. Gore, Rick. *National Geographic* (Feb. 1981), 34–57.
13. Hammond, Allen L. "Conservation of Energy: The Potential for More Efficient Use." *Science*, **178** (Dec. 8, 1972), 1079–1081.
14. Hohenemser, Kurt H. "Sun Day Thoughts." *Environment* (May 1978), 2–4.
15. Hubbert, M. King. "Energy Resources." In National Academy of Sciences, *Resources and Man.* San Francisco: Freeman, 1969.
16. Longworth, Richard C. "Scramble Looms Unless Nations Cooperate on Oil." *Minneapolis Tribune*, 27 May 1973.
17. Miller, G. Tyler, Jr. *Living in the Environment: Concepts, Problems, Alternatives.* New York: Wadsworth, 1980.
18. Myers, Dave, Phyllis Dorset, and Tom Parker. *Oil Shale and the Environment.* Washington, DC: Environmental Protection Agency, 1977.
19. National Academy of Sciences. *Resources and Man.* San Francisco: Freeman, 1969.
20. O'Toole, Thomas. "United States Energy Crisis Called Incurable." Washington Post Service, 30 April 1972.
21. Revelle, Penelope, and Charles Revelle. *The Environment: Issues and Choices for Society.* New York: Van Nostrand, 1981.
22. "Save a Watt." *Newsweek* (May 28, 1973), 90–91.
23. *Science Year 1978.* Chicago: Worldbook, Childcraft International, 1977.
24. *Science Year 1979.* Chicago: Worldbook, Childcraft International, 1978.
25. Sheets, Kenneth R. "Five Years After Embargo: No End to Energy Woes." *U.S. News and World Report* (Oct. 23, 1978), 30.
26. "Spectrum." *Environment*, **20** (Sept. 1978), 21–23.
27. "There'll Be Enough Gas and Oil if People Pay the Price." *U.S. News and World Report* (June 4, 1973), 27–28.
28. University of Wisconsin Sea Grant Program. *Earthwatching II.* Public Information Report No. 129. Madison: University of Wisconsin, 1978.
29. Visich, Marian, Jr. "Energy." *Science Year 1981: World Book Encyclopedia.* Chicago: Field Enterprises Educational Corporation, 1980.
30. Weaver, Kenneth F., and Emory Kristof. "The Search for Tomorrow's Power." *National Geographic*, **142** (Nov. 1972), 650–681.

Suggested Readings for the Interested Student

Glass, David. "Senate Studies Alcohol Fuels from Biomass." *Bioscience*, **31** (June 1981), 425–428. Witnesses at Senate hearings wax enthusiastic about the future role of alcohol fuels in the United States.

Kerr, Richard. "How Much Oil? It Depends Upon Whom You Ask." *Science*, **212** (Apr. 24, 1981), 427–429. The author discusses the varied estimates of our nation's oil reserves in this well-written article.

Norman, Colin. "Reagan's Energy Policy and Other Myths." *Science*, **213** (Sept. 25, 1981), 1481. This is a critical examination of President Reagan's energy policy.

———. "Energy Conservation: The Debate Begins." *Science*, **212** (Apr. 24, 1981), 424–426. This is a highly readable examination of the effectiveness of the Reagan Administration's approach to energy conservation.

Sheets, Kenneth R., and Joseph Benham. "Oil Fever Rages and So Does an Old Debate." *U.S. News and World Report* (May 4, 1981), 49–51. Witnesses at Senate hearings wax enthusiastic about the future role of alcohol fuels in the United States.

585

Tracy, Eleanor Johnson. "Exxon Gets Serious About Shale." *Fortune* (May 18, 1981), 62–64. The author describes a $3 billion oil-shale development in Colorado that is scheduled to produce 47,000 barrels per day.

Walton, Susan. "Fast-Growing Fuelwoods Could Ease Pressure on Forests." *Bioscience*, **31** (Apr. 1981), 291–292. This is a highly readable discussion of a Natural Academy of Science report concerning the selection of rapidly growing species of trees for deliberate use as firewood.

19 Nuclear Energy, Radiation, and Human Life

The world's first atom bomb hurtled earthward. Far below was Hiroshima. The blinding flash of light, awesome explosion, and mushroom-shaped cloud that followed not only brought World War II to an abrupt end, but ushered in the Nuclear Age. The development of nuclear power has become a two-edged technological "sword," bearing vast potential for destruction on the one hand and holding bright promise for promoting human welfare on the other.

What Is Nuclear Energy?

Atomic Structure

All matter, whether a solid, liquid, or gas, is composed of submicroscopic particles called *atoms*. An element, such as sodium or chlorine, is composed of one basic type of atom. Each atom is composed of a dense, centrally located *nucleus* composed of positively charged *protons* and electrically neutral *neutrons*. The nucleus contains virtually all the mass (and hence weight) of the atom. Surrounding the nucleus are one or more rings of negatively charged *electrons*. Atoms combine with other atoms to form *molecules*. Thus, an atom of sodium combines with an atom of chlorine to form one molecule of sodium chloride, or common table salt.

The Nature of Radiation

In 1896 the famed scientist Henri Becquerel accidentally discovered that even though a photo-graphic plate was carefully covered, it would nevertheless be exposed, even in total darkness, if radium were placed on top of the film. Later the French scientists Pierre and Marie Curie found that radium was also *radioactive*, or had the capacity of emitting radiation. It is now known that radium spontaneously disintegrates to give off three radiation types: *alpha particles* (rays), which are *positively* charged protons; *beta particles* (rays), which are *negatively* charged electrons; and *gamma rays*, which are electrically *neutral* and are similar to X rays. An alpha particle is capable of traveling a distance of up to three inches through the air. (See Figure 19–2.) It can easily be stopped by a sheet of paper or the human skin and is dangerous only if breathed into the lungs or ingested with contaminated food or water. Beta particles are capable of penetrating the skin a short distance; however, they can be blocked by a wooden shield. Gamma rays are potentially the most dangerous to the human body, for they can pass completely through the skin and penetrate the soft internal organs such as the stomach, intestines, and liver. A thick concrete or lead shield is necessary to block gamma rays (8).

If an atom of uranium is hit by a neutron, its nucleus will break up into fragments; at the same time, a certain amount of energy is released in the form of heat and radioactivity. The term *fission* is given to such a nuclear-splitting process. Most nuclear reactors generate energy as the result of the fission of radioactive fuel, such as uranium.

587

19 – 1 *Nuclear bomb detonation in the Pacific test area on February 28, 1954. Note the characteristic mushroom-shaped cloud of highly radioactive dust.*

Isotopes are forms of an element that have identical atomic structures except for a difference in the number of neutrons in the nucleus. Good examples are the different isotopes of uranium, all of which have 92 protons in their nucleus. One uranium isotope has 146 neutrons in its nucleus. Its mass number is 238, obtained by adding 92 plus 146, the number of protons and neutrons in the nucleus. Isotopes may either be *stable* or *unstable*. A good example of a stable isotope is heavy hydrogen, or *deuterium*. Unstable isotopes are said to be radioactive. They undergo spontaneous disintegration, releasing nuclear particles and large quantities of energy. The time required for 50 percent of the radioactive element to disintegrate is known as its *half-life*. For example, if a given radioactive element has a half-life of ten years and one pound of it is placed in a

container in the year 1985, by the year 1995 only one-half pound would be left. The half-lives of isotopes vary from a fraction of a second to millions of years. For example, iodine-131 has a half-life of eight days; cesium-137, 27 years; strontium-90, 28 years; carbon-14, 5,600 years; and plutonium-239, 24,000 years. With the aid of sensitive instruments, such as Geiger counters, which detect the emitted radiations, radioisotopes can be traced as they move through soil, air, water, and the bodies of living organisms.

Chain Reactions

The nucleus of uranium-238 bears 146 neutrons. When bombarded by neutrons the uranium atom absorbs one neutron so that its nucleus has a total of 147 neutrons. The atom then disintegrates to form

ABILITY OF RAYS TO PENETRATE THE BODY

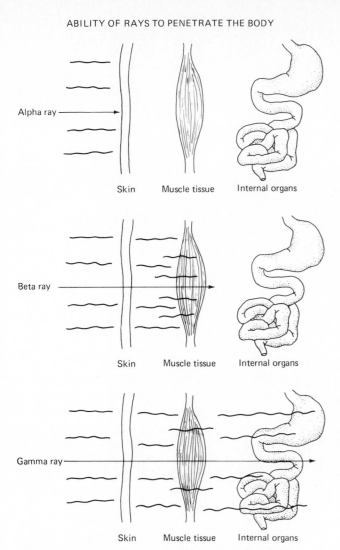

Alpha ray

Skin   Muscle tissue   Internal organs

Beta ray

Skin   Muscle tissue   Internal organs

Gamma ray

Skin   Muscle tissue   Internal organs

19–2 *Relative ability of alpha, beta, gamma rays to penetrate the body.*

one fragment with 47 neutrons and another fragment with 82. Forty-seven and 82 equal 129, meaning that 18 free *neutrons are left over*; in other words, they are released into the environment (14). In the event that each of these free neutrons in turn bombarded other uranium atoms, large quantities of additional neutrons could be released. This process could be repeated again and again as long as the uranium fuel supply remained, resulting in a *chain reaction*. (See Figure 19–3.) The tremendous implications of nuclear chain reactions as a power source can be appreciated when it is realized that the explosive force resulting from the fissioning of only one

pound of uranium is equivalent to that of 10,000 tons of TNT. (Remember, of course, that a nuclear reactor is designed not to explode like a bomb.) The fissioning of one pound of uranium can release as much heat as can be gotten from burning 1,500 short tons of coal. (See Figure 19–4.)

Background Radiation

In this discussion we are primarily concerned with the possible human health hazards resulting from induced radiation exposures — that is, exposures resulting from technological developments, such as the atomic bomb and nuclear power plants. In considering this problem, however, we should be aware that we are also exposed to *natural*, or *background*, radiation over which we have absolutely no control. (See Figure 19–5.) We eat, drink, and breathe materials that, although radioactive, are part of the natural world around us. We are exposed, for example, to cosmic rays from outer space. Cosmic rays are high-energy charged particles of extraterrestrial origin, most of which are protons. The greater the elevation of a town above sea level, the greater the cosmic radiation to which its population is exposed. Thus, people living in Leadville, Colorado, at an elevation of three kilometers receive four times the cosmic radiation received by inhabitants of a coastal city like Boston. The crew of a supersonic transport plane, which averages about 480 hours flying time per year, receives a radiation dose just under the maximum dose permitted by the International Commission on Radiologic Protection (18). Radioactive gases are naturally emitted from soil and rocks. The amount of radiation from the soil varies greatly. For example, in some parts of Brazil, uranium deposits are so rich that the terrestrial radiation to which a person is exposed may be forty times what is received by the average inhabitant of the United States (5). Even coal contains radioactive material, which is emitted from the smokestacks of coal-fired power plants and other coal-using industries.

Natural radiation sources can be internal as well as external. Thus, physicist Walter C. Patterson estimates that because the human body harbors about one-ten-thousand-millionth gram of radium, about four radium atoms are disintegrating inside the body every second, releasing destructive alpha particles to surrounding tissues (10). In essence, therefore, every man, woman, and child on earth is natu-

589

NUCLEAR FISSION CHAIN REACTION

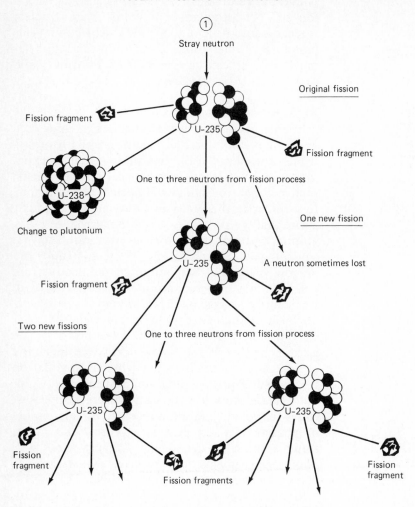

19-3 *Nuclear fission chain reaction.*

rally radioactive. Background radiation is an inescapable part of the ecological system to which we belong. You can compute the amount of radiation to which you are exposed after referring to Figure 19–6.

Radioactive Fallout from Nuclear Bomb Blasts

When an atomic bomb is detonated, only 50 percent of the energy released goes into the blast. Of the remainder, 35 percent is dissipated as heat, whereas only 15 percent is released as radioactivity (17). The radioactive dust resulting from the explosion eventually becomes suspended at a height of six to nine miles above the earth's surface and may ultimately be transported by air currents several times around the globe. Eventually, after several years, the bulk of the radioactive material either settles to the earth or

is partially scrubbed from the air by the cleansing action of rain or snow.

One major isotope entering biological systems from such radioactive fallout is strontium-90. Although extremely scarce, strontium-90 mimics the

19-4 *One pound of uranium-235 is the energy equivalent of 1,500 tons of coal.*

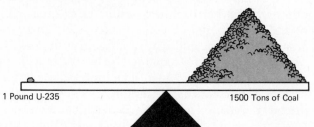

1 Pound U-235   1500 Tons of Coal

What are some typical radiation exposure levels?

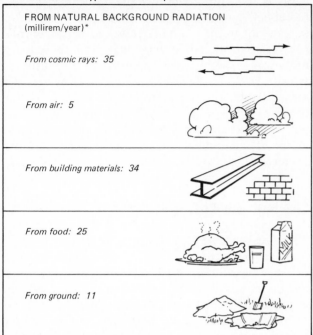

FROM NATURAL BACKGROUND RADIATION
(millirem/year)*

From cosmic rays: 35

From air: 5

From building materials: 34

From food: 25

From ground: 11

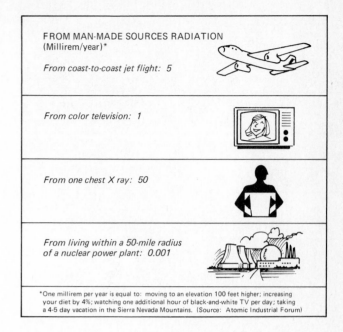

FROM MAN-MADE SOURCES RADIATION
(Millirem/year)*

From coast-to-coast jet flight: 5

From color television: 1

From one chest X ray: 50

*From living within a 50-mile radius
of a nuclear power plant: 0.001*

*One millirem per year is equal to: moving to an elevation 100 feet higher; increasing
your diet by 4%; watching one additional hour of black-and-white TV per day; taking
a 4-5 day vacation in the Sierra Nevada Mountains. (Source: Atomic Industrial Forum)

19–5 *Typical radiation exposure levels.*

19–6 *Compute your own radiation dosage.*

COMPUTE YOUR OWN RADIATION DOSAGE

We live in a radioactive world. Radiation is all about us and is part of our natural environment.
By filling out this form, you will get an idea of the amount you are exposed to every year.

	Common Source of Radiation	Your Annual Inventory
WHERE YOU LIVE	Location: Cosmic radiation at sea level Add 1 for every 100 feet of elevation Typical elevations: Pittsburgh 1200; Minneapolis 815; Atlanta 1050; Las Vegas 2000; Denver 5280; St. Louis 455; Salt Lake City 4400; Dallas 435; Bangor 20; Spokane 1890; Chicago 595 (Coastal cities are assumed to be zero, or sea level)	<u>40</u>
	House construction (¾ time factor): Wood 35; Concrete 45; Brick 45; Stone 50	___
	Ground: (¼ time factor): U.S. Average	<u>15</u>
WHAT YOU EAT, DRINK, & BREATHE	Water, Food, and Air: U.S. Average	<u>25</u>
HOW YOU LIVE	Jet Airplanes: Number of 6000-mile flights _____ x 4	___
	Television viewing: Black and white Number of hours per day _____ x 1 Color Number of hours per day _____ x 2	___
	X-ray diagnosis and treatment: Chest x-ray _____ x 100-200 Gastrointestinal tract x-ray _____ x 2000 Dental x-ray _____ x 20	___ ___ ___
	Compare your annual dose to the U.S. Annual Average of 225	Sub Total ___ mrem
HOW CLOSE YOU LIVE TO A NUCLEAR PLANT	At site boundary: Annual average number of hours per day _____ x 0.2 One mile away: Annual average number of hours per day _____ x 0.02 Five miles away: Annual average number of hours per day _____ x 0.002 Over 5 miles away: None	
		Total ___ mrem

19–7 *Biologists collect samples of vegetation growing in the Los Alamos (New Mexico) National Environmental Research Park, where nuclear bomb testing had been made several years ago. The plants will be brought to a laboratory and their tissues will be analyzed to determine their radioactivity.*

physiological characteristics of the much more abundant calcium in biological systems. As a result, therefore, the radioactive strontium is transmitted eventually to animal tissues (including human tissues) via food chains. Plants require calcium as a component of *calcium pectate*, the cementive substance found between cell walls that holds adjoining plant cells together. The radioactive strontium is rapidly absorbed by plant root systems, especially in *calcium-deficient* soils. The radioactive strontium tends to concentrate in herbivores such as rodents, deer, and cattle. Humans get radioactive strontium in their system by consuming contaminated cereals and milk. The radioactive strontium becomes concentrated in the milk of a lactating mother and is then ingested by the suckling baby. (See Figure 19–8.) In either case, most of the radioactive stron-

tium is deposited in the bones. Because all red-blood-cell and much white-blood-cell production takes place in the bone marrow, the effects of marrow irradiation can be very serious. Although any radiation is potentially harmful, the quantity of strontium-90 in the environment at present is still rather small. The total amount of strontium-90 in the five million acres of the Netherlands, for example, is less than one gram, compared to the 1,000 grams of calcium carried around in a single human skeleton (17).

The Nuclear Power Plant

The Design and Operation of the Nuclear Reactor

It has been estimated that America's energy requirements will continue to increase through the year 2000. Because coal-fired power plants are prime sources of atmospheric contamination, and because our supplies of oil are rapidly diminishing, a substantial amount of additional electrical power probably will be generated by nuclear plants during the remaining years of this century. Although America had only 23 nuclear plants operating in 1972, the number increased to 72 by 1985. Whereas in 1975 only 6 percent of our electrical power was derived from nuclear sources, by the year 2000 almost 15 percent may be so derived. Unfortunately, nuclear power plants also pose a contaminant threat — not with sulfur dioxide, carbon dioxide, benzopyrene, or fly ash (the principal pollutants from coal-fired plants), but with thermal and radioactive pollution. To understand this problem it will be necessary first to examine the design and operation of a nuclear-fueled plant and the nature of the fuel.

The uranium fuel used in all large nuclear power plants is uranium-235. It is obtained from an ore, such as pitchblende, that contains a mixture of uranium-235, which is fissionable but scarce, and uranium-238, which is nonfissionable but relatively abundant. Unfortunately, uranium-235 forms less than 1 percent of most uranium ores; over 99 percent is uranium-238. However, at a fuel *enrichment plant* the percentage of uranium-235 is increased to about 3 percent. This mixture of 3 percent uranium-235 and 97 percent uranium-238 is the fuel used by most conventional nuclear plants (16). This

592

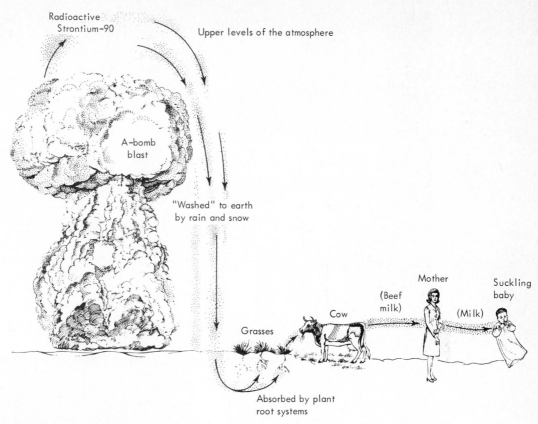

Radioactive
Strontium-90

Upper levels of the atmosphere

A-bomb
blast

"Washed" to earth
by rain and snow

Mother

Suckling
baby

(Beef
milk)

(Milk)

Cow

Grasses

Absorbed by plant
root systems

19-8 *Movement of radioactive strontium through the human ecosystem.*

19-9 *The largest operating nuclear power plant in New England. This is the Millstone Nuclear Power Station, Waterford, Connecticut, located on the north shore of Long Island Sound.*

593

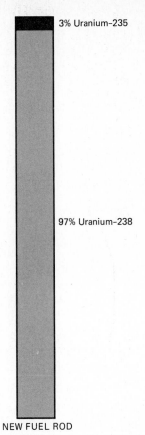

3% Uranium–235

97% Uranium–238

NEW FUEL ROD

19 – 10 *Fuel content of a fresh fuel rod.*

The chain reactions generate a large quantity of heat that produces the steam required to drive the turbines to produce electrical power. (See Figure 19 – 15, page 596.) The core becomes very hot but is maintained at about 1,000° F by a water-cooling system.

Thermal Pollution

Although nuclear plants are preferable to fossil-fuel plants from the standpoint of atmospheric quality, they do pose a much more formidable threat with respect to *thermal pollution*, the nuclear plant generating 40 percent more waste heat per kilowatt of power produced. (This problem was discussed in Chapter 8.) The thermal pollution is controlled by means of cooling towers of the type shown in Figure 19 – 16.

19 – 11 *A nuclear-fuel-assembly storage rack at the Yankee Nuclear Power Station.*

fuel, in the form of bright orange pellets of uranium oxide, is placed in thin, stainless-steel tubes, known as *fuel rods*, that are about 12 feet long and one-half inch in diameter (17). (See Figure 19 – 10.) Thirty to 300 of these *fuel rods* are then bundled together to form a *bundle*, or *fuel assembly*, that weighs about 1,000 pounds. (See Figure 19 – 11.) The part of the reactor containing the fuel assemblies, and hence the part where nuclear fission and the chain reactions actually occur, is known as the *core*. The core, in turn, is located at the bottom of a *pressure vessel* equipped with six-inch-thick steel walls. (See Figure 19 – 12.)

About 100 tons of uranium oxide fuel may be contained in this core. The intensity of the chain reaction is controlled by neutron-absorbing *control rods* made of cadmium or boron steel that can be gradually inserted into, or withdrawn from, the reactor core. Therefore, insertion of the control rods slows down the chain reaction, whereas withdrawal of the rods causes it to accelerate.

19–12 *An 800-ton nuclear vessel dwarfs on-lookers as it leaves the site at Mount Vernon, Indiana, where it was fabricated. It is 72 feet long and 22 feet in diameter. Heat from the nuclear reactions contained in the vessel will produce steam sufficient to generate 809 megawatts of electrical power.*

19–13 *Loading nuclear fuel. The first fuel bundle at the Duane Arnold Energy Center near Palo, Iowa, is being lowered into its slot in the nuclear reactor. The reactor contains a grid guide structure (visible in the reactor vessel), control rods, and water. The 600-pound fuel bundle is supported by a cable in the center. The cartridge-like posts ringing the reactor are the bolts for fastening the reactor vessel head in place. This reactor has a capacity of 550 megawatts. It would require burning 25,000 acres of redwoods or 3½ million tons of garbage each year to furnish the energy equivalent to that from the 19 tons of nuclear fuel that will be consumed each year in this reactor.*

595

19–14 *Reactor vessel. This is the "heart" of the 500,000-kilowatt nuclear-fueled electric generating plant near Monticello, Minnesota. The tubular structures seen in the picture contain the uranium oxide fuel. A reactor vessel such as this may receive over 100,000 pounds of uranium oxide. Cooling water keeps the heat generated by the vessel at about 1,000°F.*

Radiation Emissions from the Properly Functioning Nuclear Plant

Despite the alarms generated by the scare tactics of some environmental activists, the radiation emission from a properly designed and operated modern nuclear power plant is negligible. (See Figure 19–17.) The cumulative radiation dose after six years of operation would be roughly equivalent to the radiation received from a single dental X ray (16). Radioactivity released from the most recently constructed nuclear power plants is probably less than 1 percent of the permissible levels (3). F. L. Parker of Vanderbilt University has estimated that, even in the year 2000, when America will probably have many more nuclear plants in operation, the total radiation emitted would be only 1 percent of

19–15 *Comparison of cooling systems for fossil-fuel power plant and nuclear power plant (boiling water reactor).*

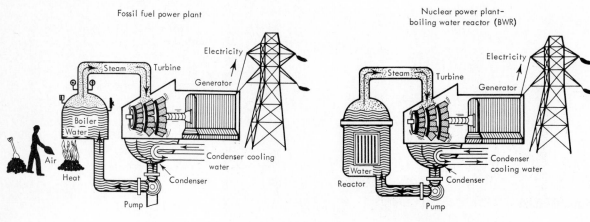

596

19-16 *This is the Portland General Electric Nuclear Plant on the shores of the Columbia River at Rainier, Oregon. The dome that shields the reactor is a characteristic feature of nuclear plants. Note the mammoth cooling tower to the left.*

the natural background radiation (2). In fact, the *smokestacks of a coal-fired power plant may emit more radioactive material than a properly operating nuclear plant.*

19-17 *Major features of the containment building that houses the nuclear reactor.*

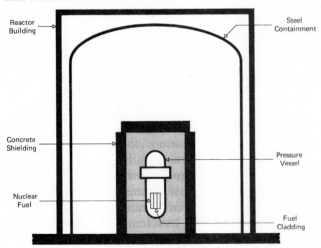

Reactor Building

Steel Containment

Concrete Shielding

Pressure Vessel

Nuclear Fuel

Fuel Cladding

Detailed studies have been conducted by various agencies of the amount of radiation (in addition to background radiation) to which residents were exposed who had been living in the vicinity of nuclear power plants that had been in operation for 10 to 12 years. On the basis of its study of the Dresden Nuclear Power Station in Illinois, the EPA concluded that "exposure to the surrounding population through consumption of food and water from radio-nuclides released at Dresden was not measurable . . . " (3).

Three Mile Island: A Case Study of a Nuclear Accident

The present writer had the opportunity to discuss with several utility officials the environmental damage that might be caused by the operation of a mammoth nuclear power plant that the utility was planning to construct in western Wisconsin. To allay the concern of various biology, physics, chemistry, and public health professors at the meeting, one official stated that the chance of their power plant undergoing a major malfunction that might

597

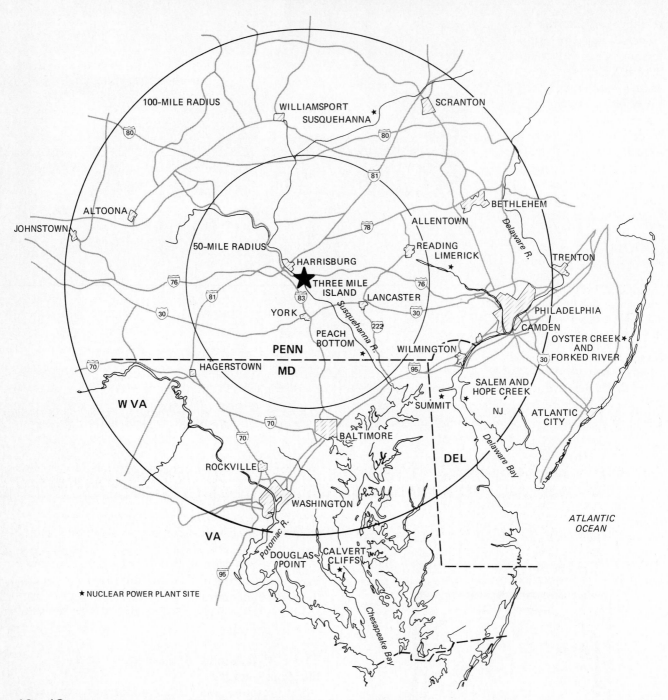

19–18 *Map of area within 100 miles of Three Mile Island nuclear plant.*

expose the public to dangerously high levels of radiation was infinitely small. He likened it to the probability that a person might get struck by lightning — one in many million.

But lightning did strike on March 28, 1979. It struck at Three Mile Island (TMI), a nuclear power plant located on an island in the Susquehanna River, only ten miles from Harrisburg, Pennsylvania. (See Figure 19–18.) I have visited the TMI nuclear complex several times since the accident and each time the startling contrast between the massive cooling towers, shaped by human technology, and the lovely Susquehanna Valley, shaped by aeons of geological activity, have sent shock waves through me. Those enormous towers have now become symbols of the most serious accident that the American nuclear industry has ever experienced. The scene that unfolded inside TMI's Unit Two just moments before a series of sirens, buzzers, whistles, and flashing lights shattered its peace and quiet, has been vividly described by a special inquiry group established by the Nuclear Regulatory Commission shortly after the accident. Excerpts from their report follow:

It is approaching 4 A.M., the downhill side of the graveyard shift, and four operators are moving through the routines of Unit 1 plant on Three Mile Island. This is a billion-dollar facility, and just now it is under the complete control of this youthful quartet, all high school graduates, all veterans of the nuclear Navy. Control room operators Craig Faust and Edward Frederick are quietly

monitoring and making adjustments at the more critical of hundreds of instruments in the brightly lighted control room. (See Figure 19–19.)

In a glass-enclosed office at the rear of the control room, partially obscured from the operators, William Zewe, shift supervisor . . . is trying to overtake his paperwork. Zewe is a licensed senior operator, qualified to run either unit.

Here at TMI-2, the control room itself, despite the array of instrumentation, has an improvised (and disorganized) look; it would not be mistaken for the Starship *Enterprise.* The control panels nearer at hand are arranged in an arc, effectively fencing off the operators from [emergency alarm] panels that stand at the far side of the room. An operator needing quick access to these more distant [alarm] panels [would have to] make a choice between an end run and a vault. Repair tags . . . obscure the faces of other instruments.

Almost on the nose at 4 A.M. Bill Zewe's concentration is broken by the warble of an [emergency] alarm out in the control room — a sound as . . . persistent as a continued tugging at a sleeve. Zewe looks out into the control room;

19–19 *The "brain center" of a nuclear power plant. Note the many control panels. In the event of a plant malfunction, the panels light up and alarm sirens alert the control-room technicians.*

The TMI Story No One Ever Told

Thomas M. Gerusky
Director
PENNSYLVANIA BUREAU OF
RADIATION PROTECTION

The Three Mile Island accident on March 28, 1979 was an event no one was adequately prepared to cope with. In particular the communications between the reactor facility, the Nuclear Regulatory Commission (NRC) on-site team and NRC headquarters were extremely bad during the first few days of the accident.

The poor communications resulted in two specific actions taken by the Nuclear Regulatory Commission headquarters that caused the voluntary evacuation and considerable fear among the thousands of residents in the general vicinity of the plant.

The first occurred on Friday morning, March 30, the second about one day later. The NRC staff, having obtained information from the plant, misinterpreted the problem and believed that a massive release of radioactive gases would occur. Without consulting their field staff at the plant or the State Bureau of Radiation Protection, they ordered the Pennsylvania Emergency Management Agency to evacuate everyone within ten miles of the facility. In fact, the releases from the plant were planned, monitored by aircraft and on the ground, and were lower than what had been released a day earlier. By the time the problem was resolved, near panic had occurred among the residents.

The second action occurred as a result of the lack of proper information concerning the condition of the reactor core. NRC believed that oxygen was being generated and released into the reactor vessel, mixing with accident-generated hydrogen and giving rise to serious risk of an explosion. In their calculations, NRC did not give any weight to the fact that the reactor was pressurized and that hydrogen is normally injected into pressurized water reactors to prevent the release of oxygen by quenching the normal radiation-induced water molecule disassociation (radiolysis). No explosion was possible under the conditions then existing at the plant.

Unfortunately, the public was never told of the NRC errors and many still believe their lives were in jeopardy.

In the future, decisions should be made at an accident site and not by long-distance telephone.

Today, several years after the accident at TMI, and even after numerous emergency exercises and drills, it appears that the NRC still has not learned the most important lesson: be *sure* before you act, consult with others also knowledgeable, and try to resolve conflicts between or among agencies before reacting. A few minutes of time will not jeopardize any protective action recommendation or the health and safety of the general public.

---

several [alarm] lights are blinking to life on the control system panel. He hurries out to . . . figure out what's going wrong. . . .

Down in the turbine building, the quiet has just been destroyed by loud thunderous noises, like a couple of freight trains. [A moment later] Zewe's voice crackles over the paging system "Turbine shutdown—reactor shutdown." Upon hearing this, Fred Scheimann, the fourth operator on duty, drops everything and bolts for the control room . . . (13).

In essence it was the malfunction of two small pumps and a sticking automatic valve in the cooling system that caused the problems at TMI. With better training, the four operators in the plant might have been able to respond properly. *But they had not received the best training. Moreover, their judgment under conditions of stress was questionable.*

Shortly after the malfunction occurred a cloud of radioactive steam escaped into the atmosphere and drifted through the valley. On the floor of one building 250,000 gallons of radioactive water accumulated to ankle depth. Harold Denton, director of operations for the Nuclear Regulatory Commission (NRC) branded the episode the "most serious accident in the licensed reactor program." There was extensive damage to the fuel rods. Denton stated that "a *fuel meltdown* was the worst possible thing that could happen. A meltdown would not result in any (immediate) fatalities. It would result in latent cancer, land contamination, and heavy economic loss." *[Italics mine.]*

Eight workers inside the plant were exposed to abnormally high levels of radiation. (See Figure 19–20.) Increased radiation levels were detected in Harrisburg, ten miles to the northeast. There was considerable concern for 13,000 people living in the dairy farm belt surrounding the plant. Pennsylva-

nia's then Lieutenant Governor William Scranton, III, stated: "The full impact on public health is being evaluated as environmental samples [vegetation, milk, and so on] are being analyzed. We are concerned most with radioactive iodine, which can accumulate in the thyroid either through breathing or through drinking milk." The four counties in the immediate vicinity of the plant, Lancaster, York, Dauphin, and Cumberland, have nearly one million residents. About 130,000 people living within a ten-mile radius of Three Mile Island were advised by Governor Dick Thornburgh to remain indoors to escape excessive radiation. Furthermore, the Gover-

19–20 *Three Mile Island nuclear accident, March 28, 1979.*

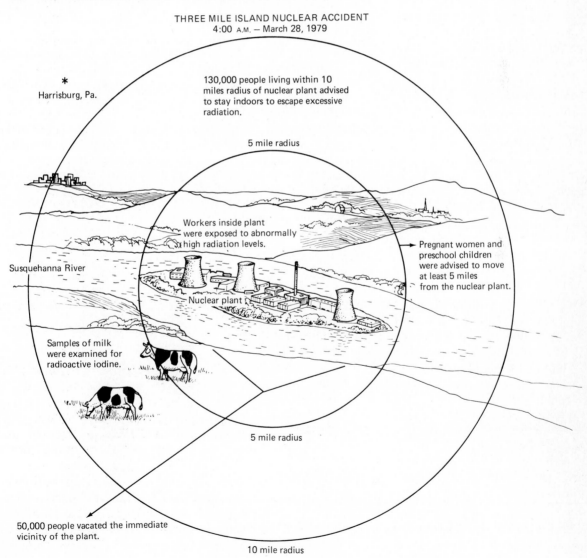

THREE MILE ISLAND NUCLEAR ACCIDENT
4:00 A.M. — March 28, 1979

* Harrisburg, Pa.

130,000 people living within 10 miles radius of nuclear plant advised to stay indoors to escape excessive radiation.

5 mile radius

Workers inside plant were exposed to abnormally high radiation levels.

Pregnant women and preschool children were advised to move at least 5 miles from the nuclear plant.

Susquehanna River

Nuclear plant

Samples of milk were examined for radioactive iodine.

5 mile radius

50,000 people vacated the immediate vicinity of the plant.

10 mile radius

601

nor advised pregnant women and preschool children (who are especially sensitive to nuclear radiation) to move to at least a five-mile distance from the reactor. Eventually an estimated 50,000 residents vacated the vicinity of the plant. On Sunday, April 2, the bishop of the Roman Catholic Diocese of Harrisburg granted general absolution (forgiveness of sins) at several Sunday masses, an action usually performed by priests in cases of dire emergency where human life is threatened.

In a whirlwind inspection tour of the plant, President Jimmy Carter wore a radiation-measuring device and protective clothing to protect him against contaminated dust. Carter announced that he would "be personally responsible for informing the American public about this particular incident and the status of nuclear safety in the future."

After several days of feverish efforts nuclear engineers from the NRC and Metropolitan Edison (owners of the plant) were able to bring about a "cold shutdown" of the reactor, thus terminating any further radiation release. Nevertheless, the accident necessitated a mammoth cleanup and decontamination operation, at a cost of more than a billion dollars, which was still not completed at the time of this writing.

In the aftermath of the near disaster, an intensive investigation was conducted to reveal the precise cause of the accident. *It was concluded that human error, as well as both mechanical and design problems, were responsible.* NRC engineer Darrell Eisenhut listed the following operational errors:

1. The main emergency core cooling system was turned off at the wrong time.
2. Valves on an emergency pumping system were closed when they should have been open.
3. Four auxiliary water pumps were disengaged *in violation of NRC regulations, when they should have been ready for use.*

Apparently the episode did not cause any severe immediate illness. There were no fatalities. In Washington, Joseph Califano, secretary of the Department of Health, Education and Welfare, stated that the increased radiation released from the Three Mile Island reactor could result in *one to ten additional cancers during the lifetime of the exposed population.*

So nuclear plant "lightning" struck, with appar-

ently little adverse effect on human beings. But if it strikes again, the effects on human health and survival might be much worse.

Reprocessing Spent Fuel

The biggest concern of environmentalists, as well as of the NRC (which assumed the regulatory functions of the old Atomic Energy Commission), is not the routine radiation emissions from the nuclear plant itself, but the *disposal of high-level radioactive fission products in the spent fuel.* After a reactor has been operating for one to two years, there is a tendency for those waste products to slow down the chain reaction. Because a large number of free neutrons is absorbed by the wastes, the quantity of neutrons available for continued nuclear bombardment is progressively reduced. Once this critical stage has been reached, the spent fuel rods are replaced with

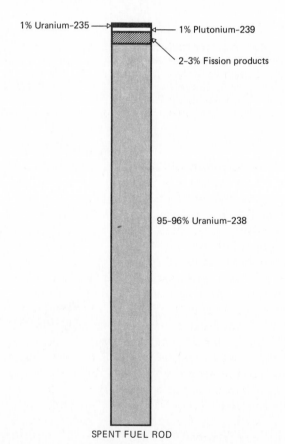

1% Uranium-235

1% Plutonium-239

2-3% Fission products

95-96% Uranium-238

SPENT FUEL ROD

19-21 *Fuel content of a spent fuel rod. When neutrons are captured by the nucleus of uranium-238, a new element, plutonium-239, is formed.*

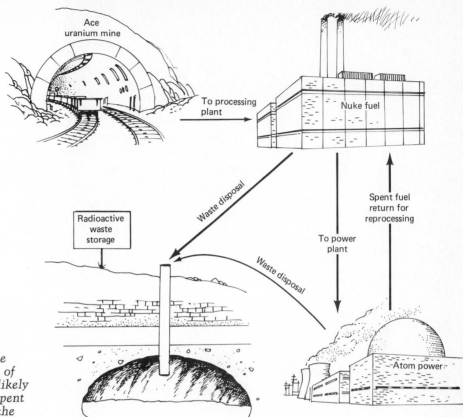

19–22 *Nuclear fuel-and-waste cycle. Radioactive contamination of the human environment is most likely to occur during the transport of spent fuel for reprocessing and during the transport and disposal of nuclear waste.*

fresh rods. About one third of the fuel rods in a reactor are replaced each year. (See Figure 19–21.) The spent rods are then transported to a *reprocessing plant.* (See Figure 19–22.) At this time the wastes are most highly concentrated, most intensely radioactive, and of greatest potential threat to human safety (9). To reduce the radiation hazard the spent fuel rods are transported from the reactor by way of underwater canals to swimming pool-like water storage chambers, where they remain under twenty feet of water for several months. (See Figure 19–23.) During this time much of the radioactivity, such as that of iodine-131, is dissipated. Several years ago the Atomic Energy Commission proposed to transport such radioactive waste by truck from the Shoreham, Long Island, nuclear plant through New York City for reprocessing in upstate New York. (See Figures 19–24 and 19–25.) The EPA became quite concerned. After all, the route would pass through areas where population density reaches 8,000 per square mile. The EPA recommended that the wastes be shipped instead by barge to reprocessing facilities in Illinois or South Carolina (1).

The function of the fuel-reprocessing plant is to salvage any usable fuel left in the spent fuel rods. The usable fuel is of two types: uranium-235 that has not fissioned and a small amount of fissionable plutonium that was formed from some of the uranium-238 during the fission process.

At the processing plant the fuel rods are "chopped up" into small pieces and the contents dissolved in acid. The usable uranium-235 fuel, as well as the plutonium that was generated from the uranium-238, is recovered and separated from the radioactive waste. The recovery of uranium and plutonium is dictated by raw economics because the fuels are very expensive. Roughly 100 gallons of highly radioactive liquid waste must be disposed of for every ton of spent fuel. A reprocessing plant emits roughly 100 times as much radiation as a properly operating nuclear power plant (7).

19–23 *Spent nuclear fuel "cooling off" under water. The spent fuel assemblies from the Savannah River Plant in Georgia illuminate a cooling basin. In the photo, spent fuel of three different "ages" is shown under 20 feet of water. The brightest assemblies (top center) were just discharged from the reactor. In front of them are assemblies that were discharged a month earlier. Barely visible on the lower extreme left are assemblies that have "cooled" by radioactive decay for 3½ months.*

19–24 *Method of transporting highly radioactive spent-fuel assemblies.*

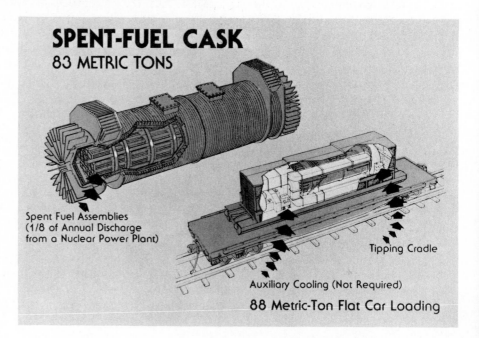

SPENT-FUEL CASK
83 METRIC TONS

Spent Fuel Assemblies
(1/8 of Annual Discharge
from a Nuclear Power Plant)

Tipping Cradle

Auxiliary Cooling (Not Required)

88 Metric-Ton Flat Car Loading

604

19–25 *In an experiment conducted by the Department of Energy, a train and a trailer carrying a spent-fuel shipping cask collide head-on at a speed of 81 miles per hour. The cask was undamaged.*

Unfortunately, for one reason or another, during most of the 1970s no reprocessing plants were available to the nuclear power industry for the reprocessing of fuel. A plant at West Valley, New York, just south of Buffalo, experienced serious waste-disposal problems. (See Figure 19–26.) It closed down in the early 1970s. Failure to meet federal licensing standards prevented the opening of a plant at Barnwell, South Carolina. At Morris Plains, Illinois, a plant owned by General Electric was scheduled to start operating about 1973, but it was never started up because of faulty design (12).

As a result of the lack of active fuel-reprocessing plants, large numbers of spent fuel rods have been accumulating in the underwater storage systems at nuclear plant sites. In the early 1980s many plants were greatly increasing their spent fuel-rod storage capacities — sufficient in some cases to handle a *15-year accumulation of rods*. Of course, the lack of

reprocessing facilities, as well as the pileup of highly radioactive fuel rods at nuclear plants is a problem of considerable concern that the Department of Energy and the NRC will have to solve in the near future.

The Disposal of Liquid Waste from Reprocessing Plants

One method of storing liquid waste is to place it in containers with thick steel walls and bury it underground. *Ninety million gallons* of high-level radioactive liquid waste are now being stored by the NRC in subterranean tanks in Idaho, Washington, and South Carolina. Although this disposal method has been extensively employed in the past, there are three vexing problems associated with it. First, the precise location for such sites must be selected with extreme care and intensive planning. (Apparently this was not the case during World War II, when a

19–26 *Reprocessing spent fuels. The Nuclear Fuels Services Reprocessing Plant in West Valley, New York. Currently, not one such plant is operational. All have been shut down because of technological and economic problems. Separation of the highly radioactive fission products from the unconsumed uranium and plutonium is the job of reprocessing plants. These heavily shielded facilities purify the uranium and plutonium for reuse in other reactors and concentrate the radioactive wastes into small volumes for storage on-site, pending transfer to the U.S. Department of Energy for final disposition.*

subterranean dumping site was selected at Hanford, Washington. The burial site is located *above a major geological fault*, which makes the area susceptible to an earthquake. Possibly the poor choice of site was the result of the urgency associated with the Manhattan Project — the development of the atomic bomb. However, were the tanks to be ruptured by an earthquake, the released radioactivity would have a severely detrimental effect on human health and life in the immediate area.)

Nuclear Industry Still Can't Solve Its Waste Problem

Dean Abrahamson
Director
HUBERT H. HUMPHREY
INSTITUTE OF PUBLIC AFFAIRS
UNIVERSITY OF MINNESOTA

During the springtime of optimism regarding civilian nuclear power — the days of promises that electricity would be too cheap to meter and projections of 1,000 reactors operating in the United States by the year 2000 — there was little discussion of nuclear wastes.

Radioactive waste management was regarded as a minor technical issue that would be taken care of in due time with little diversion of financial resources from productive ends.

There now are about 80 civilian atomic power plants in the United States, and we have neither the technical means to sequester the radioactive wastes safely nor the political means to locate waste repositories. The situation is both a major embarrassment for the industry and a potential public health disaster.

One year of operation of a typical 1,000-megawatt reactor produced tens of thousands of cubic meters of radioactive uranium mill tailings, hundreds of cubic meters of low-level waste, and tens of cubic meters of extremely high-level radioactive waste. And the reactors themselves become radioactive waste at the time of their decommissioning.

It is sobering to realize that the 60 pounds of cesium-137 produced by operating a nuclear power plant for a year has the potential, should it escape, of excluding humans from hundreds of square miles for decades. Cesium-137 is but one of several long-lasting radioisotopes found in reactor wastes.

The half-lives of some radioactive material are so long that the waste remains toxic for hundreds of thousands of years. The wastes must be protected from contact with living things virtually in perpetuity. The overriding imperative is the protection of future generations from the release of such material into the biosphere.

In January 1983, President Reagan signed a nuclear-waste bill that requires, among other things, that the first site for the perpetual storage of radioactive wastes be identified by 1987.

Also in January 1983, a review of "the radwaste paradox" in *Science*, the most prestigious American science journal, documented serious unresolved scientific and technical problems with every one of the several waste-storage schemes now being investigated.

The nuclear-waste bill was the latest in a series of political responses to a scientific and technical problem. The bill may help by focusing attention on the issues and by providing resources for an adequate program of research and development.

If there is reliable evidence that an adequate waste storage program is finally under way, we should continue operation of those reactors for which emergency evacuation has been shown to be possible. If not, we should simply stop producing these highly toxic radioactive wastes. Considering that there is a nearly 40 percent excess in electrical generating capacity in the United States, we do *not* need the existing nuclear capacity to meet our country's electricity needs.

There is another problem attending this disposal method. Even if a geologically appropriate site were selected, the wastes would continue to boil because of the intensely generated internal heat, for many decades or even centuries, depending on the half-life of the isotopes involved. The tanks holding the wastes, however, might have a longevity of only a hundred years at best, thus making it mandatory to maintain, repair, and ultimately replace them with new containers. It is apparent that such vigilance will have to be perpetuated by generations of mankind as yet unborn. To date the monitoring of this nuclear waste has been less than commendable. At least 16 cases of leakage have occurred that have resulted in the escape of 350,000 gallons of radioactive liquids (7).

The Disposal of Solid Nuclear Wastes

Because of the limitations of liquid-waste burial, federal regulations have made it mandatory for reprocessing waste to be stored in *solid* form, encased in solid ceramic bricks or in a glasslike material. (See Figure 19-27.) In the solid state the waste is not as capable of escaping into the environment as a result of accident, sabotage, or some natural catastrophe. Almost 400,000 tons of radioactive solid wastes have accumulated as a result of nuclear-power generation in the United States. Those wastes will have to be safely stored for centuries.

It is surprising, however, that even though these solid wastes pose a potentially serious health and life threat to humans, their volume is amazingly small. For example, if all the energy that you, the reader, used during your life span of about seventy years were derived from nuclear power, the total amount of solid radioactive waste that would have accumulated as a result could be stuffed into just one 16-ounce beer can. In fact, all the solid radioactive waste generated in the United States for peaceful purposes by the year 2000 could be stored in a 12.5-foot-high building the size of a football field (7).

The AEC proposed to store such solid waste in abandoned salt mines, of which there are a considerable number in Kansas, New York, and the Gulf Coast region. (See Figure 19-28.) Salt mines are attractive for such purposes for several reasons: (1) salt is a good conductor of the heat generated by the waste; (2) salt mines have been separated from groundwater supplies for thousands of years, and (3) the walls of salt mines are "plastic" and hence

19-27 *Glassification of nuclear waste. The Department of Energy is developing methods for converting high-level liquid waste into a dry, stable form such as these borosilicate glass pellets (shown next to a 25-cent coin). It is hoped that when nuclear waste is immobilized in this form required safety, health, and environmental standards may be met and maintained.*

would incur minimal damage in the event of an earthquake. However, in 1972, after spending $25 million to develop a salt-mine disposal site at Lyons, Kansas, the NRC finally decided to abandon the site because of the possibility of groundwater contamination. At the time of this writing the Department of Energy is investigating the possibility of radioactive waste disposal in New York and Wisconsin, much to the concern of local residents.

Recently a team of Australian scientists described a technique for radioactive-waste disposal that might be the safest yet devised. It involves "locking" radioactive waste in the crystalline structure of a special type of rock that the scientists have synthesized. This rock is relatively insoluble in water, is stable, and is capable of imprisoning the wastes for millions of years. According to Professor Ted Ringwood, a geochemist at Australian National University, the waste-holding rocks should then be enclosed in containers made of a nickel-iron alloy and inserted into holes that have been drilled in solid granite to a depth of almost two miles. (See Figure

METHODS FOR STORAGE OF NUCLEAR WASTE

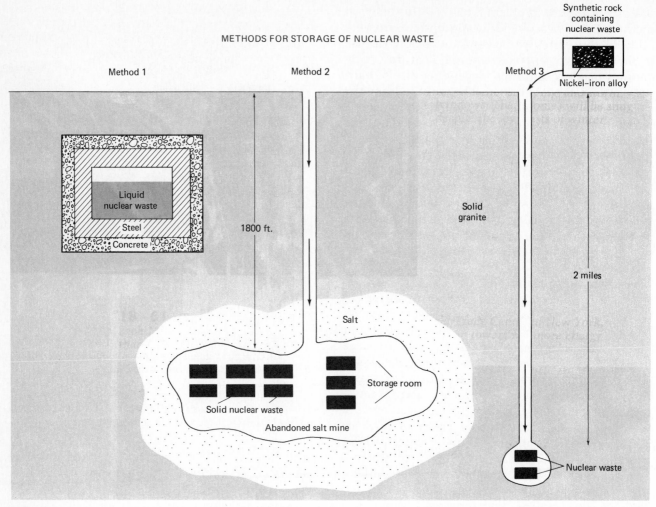

19–28 *Methods for storing nuclear waste.*

19–28.) All the radioactive waste generated by an 8,000-megawatt power plant over a period of forty years could be held by only twenty drill holes. The cost of such burial would be only 1 percent of the cost of power production by the plant (15). (See Dean Abrahamson's guest article concerning our nation's waste disposal problems.)

The Effects of Radiation on Human Health

The extensive use of nuclear energy for electrical-power production, at least for the next few decades, as well as its increasing employment in agriculture,

medical and biological research and therapy, and in spaceship and submarine propulsion, means that human beings will be subjected to ever-increasing levels of radiation. It would be instructive, therefore, to consider the possible effects that ionizing radiation might have on the human body. We will consider two types of effects: *nongenetic* and *genetic*.

Nongenetic Effects

First of all, it should be emphasized that the radiation sensitivity of human beings varies with age. Thus, fetuses and newborns are much more sensitive than adults. Sensitivity also varies with the type of tissue or organ radiated. The bone marrow (where red blood cells are produced) and the white blood cells (which fight bacterial infections) are highly sensitive to radiation. Cartilage, muscle, and nervous tissue are much more resistant.

The effects of radiation on the human body vary with the intensity of the radiation to which a person is exposed. Radiation dosages are frequently measured in rads.* As shown in Figure 19–29, if the radiation dose is about 300 rads or less, all individuals will survive at least three weeks after exposure. However, as the dosage increases to a little under 500 rads, only 50 percent of the people exposed will survive for three weeks. Finally, at a dosage of 900 rads (or greater) all people will die within three weeks (16).

What are some of the symptoms shown by people exposed to radiation dosages of gradually increasing intensity? A person receiving less than 25 rads would be aware of no changes in his or her health. However, when the dose rises to 100 rads, the char-

---

* A rad is equal to the absorption of 100 *ergs* per gram of living tissue. An erg is an extremely small amount of energy, about the amount that is transferred by a mosquito when it alights on your arm.

19–29 *Effect of varying levels of radiation dosage on human survival.*

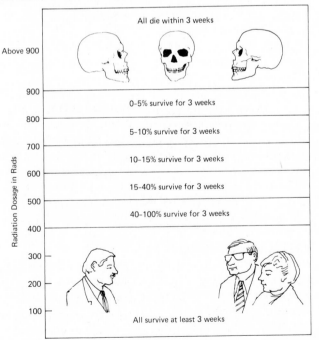

acteristic effects are feelings of weakness and fatigue, together with repeated bouts of vomiting and diarrhea. Hair may begin to fall out a few days after exposure (16). Eventually, however, these people will recover and be able to operate normally again. At a radiation exposure of 400 to 500 rads a person will again become nauseated, vomit, show fatigue, and lose hair, but, more importantly and more ominously for survival abilities, will incur radiation-induced destruction of the red-blood-cell-manufacturing tissues inside the bones. Because red blood cells die at the rate of about five million every second even in a healthy person, and red-bone-marrow destruction quickly results in a severe anemia. White-blood-cell-forming centers in the red bone marrow are also destroyed. These cells actually "feed" on disease-causing bacteria, so that the marked reduction of their numbers in the human bloodstream would make the body highly vulnerable to widespread infections. A radiation dosage of 400 to 500 rads will also cause a reduction in the number of platelets—microscopic cell fragments that are essential to the blood-clotting process. The eventual result is massive hemorrhaging and excessive blood loss. At a dosage of 400 to 500 rads, therefore, roughly 50 percent of the people will die, usually as a result of anemia, hemorrhaging, or severe bacterial infections. (See Table 19–1.) Animal experiments have shown that at extremely high dosages of 10,000 rads, death results within a few hours from heart and brain damage (16).

Radiation Effects from the Bombing of Hiroshima

It is of interest to examine the radiation effects (other than immediate fatalities) caused by the detonation of the nuclear bombs near Hiroshima and Nagasaki during World War II. Thousands of people were exposed to radiation dosages ranging from 100 to 150 rads. The *immediate effects* included burns, fever, loss of hair, and intestinal bleeding. In cases of radiation damage to the bone marrow, *delayed effects* occurred such as anemia, blood cancer (leukemia), and infections.

The children of mothers who while pregnant had been within 1,200 meters of the center of the explosion suffered mongoloid mental retardation, deformity of the skull, hip dislocation, heart disease, clubfoot, glaucoma (resulting in blindness), partial albinism, and misshapen chest and ears (18).

Table 19–1 The Effects of Radiation on Humans

Radiation Dosage in Rads	Percent that Will Die	Other Symptoms
above 10,000	100%	Death in two days due to brain and heart damage.
3,000	100%	Permanent damage of brain, spinal cord, bone marrow and intestines; bleeding, infections.
2,000	100%	Permanent destruction of bone marrow and intestines; severe dehydration, bleeding and infections.
1,000	100%	Permanent destruction of bone marrow and permanent damage to intestines.
600	60%	Permanent destruction of bone marrow.
400–500	50%	Fatigue, nausea, vomiting, loss of hair; reduced number of blood platelets and white blood cells; bleeding and infections.
100–250*	0%	Fatigue, nausea, vomiting, loss of hair, diarrhea, ulcers of gut; some may suffer permanent loss of fertility.
25–100	0%	No visible effects; lower number of white blood cells.
0–25	0%	No measurable effects.

Note: All individuals exposed to 100 rads or more will experience fatigue, nausea, vomiting, diarrhea, and hair loss.

Radiation and Cancer

Experiments on laboratory animals such as mice, rats, and rabbits have indicated that radiation can induce cancer in a variety of organs such as lymph glands, mammary glands, lungs, ovaries, and skin (14). Considerable evidence now indicates that ionizing radiation can cause cancer in humans as well, even though the cancer may not actually materialize for decades after the radiation exposure. Consider the following items:

1. A high incidence of *skin cancer* was found among radiologists during the early days of their profession when adequate safeguards had not as yet been instituted (14).
2. A number of women who painted radium on watch dials during World War II developed *bone cancer* some years later. Apparently they accidentally ingested the radioactive material when placing the brushes to their lips to draw them to a "point" (14).
3. Over a period of several years at least 5,000 miners who had been employed in a uranium mine in Joachimsthal, Czechoslovakia, eventually died from *lung cancer* (14).
4. Children irradiated within the mother's uterus during pelvic X ray examinations (of the mother) have also shown a high cancer rate.
5. The rate of *blood cancer* (leukemia) was substantially higher among Japanese who had been exposed to the bombs dropped on Hiroshima and Nagasaki than among Japanese not so exposed. Blood cancers appeared in these people in increasing numbers more than three decades after the bombings.

Nevertheless, despite these disturbing facts, it must be emphasized that the cumulative radiation dosages to which those unfortunate people were exposed were considerably higher than the dosage to which the average human being would be exposed to even were he or she to live in the immediate vicinity of a properly functioning nuclear power plant in full operation. A study by the National Academy of Sciences has suggested that if a population of one million people were subjected to a dose of one rad (a much higher dosage than they would get from normal nuclear-power-plant operations) a maximum of twenty leukemia cases and 145 other types of cancer would be produced during that population's lifetime (14). Environmental disease expert Merrill Eisenbud of New York University states that human exposure to radioactivity from the nuclear-power industry could produce a maximum of 12 cases of cancer per year in the United States population. "Since the annual incidence of cancer in the United States is about 1,600 cases per million persons, the 12 cases would occur against a background of nearly 500,000 cancers from other causes . . . " (3).

The Genetic Effects of Radiation

When radiation causes chromosome damage in the sperm cells produced in the male's testes or in the eggs produced in the female's ovary, the effects are said to be *genetic*. Such genetic damage will adversely affect the children born to the radiation-exposed parent(s). The genes contained in the sperm (produced by the male testis) and in the egg (produced by the female ovary) may undergo *mutations* — spontaneous changes that can be inherited by fu-

610

ture offspring. During the long two-million-year history of human evolution, many of the harmful mutations have been weeded out by natural selection, whereas the beneficial mutations have been incorporated into the human gene pool. This means that if a gene in a modern human being undergoes a mutation, it probably will be a harmful one, resulting in such possible defects as mental impairment or malformed limbs. Such mutations, caused possibly by natural or background radiation, occur spontaneously at the rate of about one per million sperm or eggs produced. However, as a result of Herman Muller's Nobel Prize-winning research on fruit flies, we now know that mutation rates can be artificially increased with the use of X rays, a form of radiation similar to the gamma rays emitted from a nuclear reactor. James F. Crow, an eminent University of Wisconsin geneticist and former president of the Genetics Society of America, suggests that *any amount of radiation exposure, no matter how slight, is potentially damaging to genetic material.* If so, it certainly behooves us to keep the radiation emissions generated by our technology down to an absolute minimum. Failure to exercise every precaution may eventually result in some genetic damage to the sex cells of people now living, at a cost that will be paid by generations of Americans yet unborn. (See Table 19 – 1.)

The Breeder Reactor

Only 0.7 percent of the uranium found in nature is *fissionable* uranium-235. At present rates of consumption our nation's supply will be exhausted in about forty years. The solution to this potential scarcity of uranium fuel would be the ultimate replacement of the conventional uranium-235 "spending" reactor with a uranium-235 "conserving" *breeder* reactor. The *breeder reactor* utilizes a relatively small amount of scarce but fissionable uranium-235. This material releases neutrons that bombard the "blanket" of nonfissionable uranium-238 around it and converts it into fissionable plutonium-239, from which the heat energy required to generate electrical power is ultimately derived.

The supply of fissionable uranium-235 is considered so limited that the development of a suitable commercial breeder reactor is considered of great importance to the nuclear industry. It is anticipated that the breeder reactors will replace the conventional nonbreeder type by the year 2000. When this occurs it will be possible for breeder enthusiasts to tap extensive uranium deposits that previously could not be used.

For example, uranium-bearing Chattanooga shale underlies a considerable portion of Ohio, Kentucky, Tennessee, Illinois, and Indiana. One part of the formation, which is 15 feet thick, embraces hundreds of square miles and bears many hundreds of thousands of tons of shale. Every 100,000 pounds of shale yields about six pounds of uranium (5). We might well ask the question: If we were using the breeder reactor, how much energy could be derived from this single shale formation? It is estimated that an area of shale of *fewer than three square miles* would yield as much energy as our nation's total supply of producible crude oil, amounting to *200 billion barrels* (5).

Nuclear proponents consider it of utmost importance that we shift from the uranium-235 *spending* nonbreeder reactor to the uranium-235 *conserving* breeder reactor before we exhaust our restricted supplies of this essential "trigger" for the release of the nuclear energy bounty.

The Plutonium Controversy

Nevertheless, despite the obvious benefits derived from the breeder in the form of additional high-quality nuclear fuel, strenuous criticism has been leveled against the breeder program. Criticism has focused on the highly radioactive plutonium fuel "bred" by the reactor. Consumer advocate Ralph Nader's group has branded plutonium-239 *the most toxic substance known to science.* According to these critics just *one pound* of plutonium-239 could eventually cause lung cancer in *eight billion people,* in other words, destroy all of humankind, with 3.5 billion deaths left over. Although such a statement is probably a bit extreme, plutonium-239 certainly has the potential for massive human illness and death, if not properly used and monitored. If the plutonium could be used directly at the site where it is bred, the environmental and health threat would be somewhat diminished. Unfortunately, the plutonium must first be removed from the reactor that bred it and then transported for considerable distances by truck or rail to a processing plant that will change it into a form in which it can be effectively used by a conventional nonbreeder nuclear reactor. During transport the plutonium is contained in extremely thick steel-walled casks. In the event of an accident, however, such as a head-on collision with another truck or a train derailment (perhaps as the result of sabotage), it is theoretically possible that the casks might break open and release the highly radioactive plutonium. If the accident were to occur in a densely populated area, the health and/or lives of thousands of people might be in jeopardy. It is more probable, however, that the plutonium might be hijacked by a terrorist group or by agents working for a foreign power, such as Russia, because the very costly plutonium could be used to fuel atomic bombs or other nuclear weapons. Certainly if the breeder program expands as rapidly as its proponents hope, by the end of this century literally thousands of specially trained federal militia will be required as permanent "watchdogs" at breeder-reactor sites, at plutonium-reprocessing plants, and along the routes taken by plutonium-transporting trucks and trains. Current federal regulations require that each 15-pound drum of plutonium be invested with at least three layers of steel. Each truck would haul about 40 drums, or 600 pounds of plutonium. It is estimated that by 1990 about 360 plutonium shipments, totaling 108 tons, would be made annually. The trucks would travel a total distance of 108,000 miles each year (12).

Nuclear Fusion

That brilliant sunshine that helps to "brighten" your day had its origin in countless trillions of nuclear fusion reactions occurring on the surface of the sun. In a sense nuclear fusion is exactly the opposite of nuclear fission. Fission is a "splitting apart" of nuclei, whereas fusion involves a "coming together" of nuclei. In nuclear fission heavy nuclei like those of uranium are used because they tend to be unstable. If nuclear fusion is to take place, the tendency for nuclei to repel each other because they are all positively charged must be overcome. In the case of fusion reactions, therefore, it is desirable to use extremely light atoms, such as those of hydrogen, because the repulsive forces (positive charges of the nuclei) are less in light atoms than in heavy atoms. When two hydrogen nuclei fuse, energy is

released that eventually can be used by humans in the form of electricity. Hydrogen is usually used in experimental fusion reactions because it is the lightest element known to science and has only one proton in its nucleus. Its repulsive force, therefore, is extremely small, and theoretically it should be relatively easy for two hydrogen atoms to come together and fuse. Another advantage of using hydrogen as a fuel is that it is extremely abundant — every molecule of water is composed of two atoms of hydrogen and one atom of oxygen. The isotopes of hydrogen, *deuterium* and *tritium*, are identical to ordinary hydrogen except that deuterium has two neutrons in its nucleus and tritium has three. Two potentially valuable types of fusion reactions involve deuterium-deuterium (D-D) or deuterium-tritium (D-T) (7). (See Figure 19–30.)

Because the positively charged nuclei in these reactions tend to repel each other, a powerful force is required to "push" the nuclei toward each other and cause them to fuse. This can be done only by heating the deuterium and tritium atoms to at least 40 million° C. At these extremely high temperatures the nuclei of the atoms are separated from their electrons. The result is an extremely hot mixture of nuclei and electrons known as *plasma*. Under these conditions nuclei can speed toward each other, collide, and fuse; when this occurs, energy is released. For a sustained reaction to occur, however, some sort of "container" must keep the nuclei together for a minimum of one second. At a temperature of 40 million° C, however, there is no known substance that can remain intact to serve as an effective container; therefore, fusion scientists have developed a doughnut-shaped electromagnetic bottle to hold the plasma together. (See Figure 19–31.) The heat generated by the fusion reaction is transferred to liquid lithium, then to liquid potassium, and finally to water to form steam. The steam is then employed to drive a turbine to produce electricity.

Nuclear fusion has several advantages over nuclear fission as a method of generating electricity:

1. The fuel for the fusion reaction is both abundant and inexpensive. For example, the deuterium in only one square kilometer of seawater could provide us with as much energy as 1,500 billion barrels of crude oil or 300 billion tons of coal (8). Each pound of deuterium could provide as much energy as 300 gallons of gasoline.

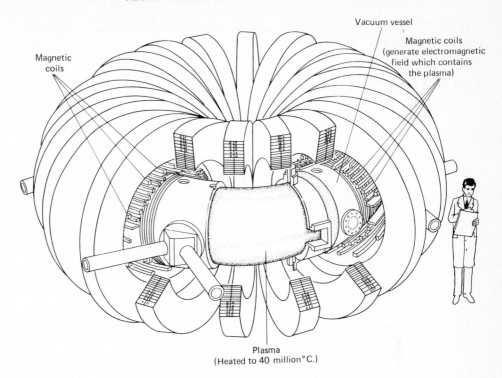

Vacuum vessel

Magnetic coils
(generate electromagnetic
field which contains
the plasma)

Magnetic
coils

Plasma
(Heated to 40 million°C.)

19–30 *Fusion Research Device. This diagram shows one research device that could bring the United States closer to controlling fusion, the force that powers the sun and the stars. Because it is easier to work with, this device will use hydrogen as its fusion fuel. Later-generation devices will employ deuterium and tritium as fuels. This device is known as the Princeton Large Torus (PLT).*

19–31 *Nuclear-fusion research. Magnetic coils used to confine and compress fusion plasma are visible in this fusion device. Microwave power levels are increased for the early-stage testing of a technique to heat plasma to the very high temperatures needed for fusion reactions. This device, known as the Elmo Bumpy Torus, is located at the Department of Energy's Holifield National Laboratory.*

Nuclear Development: Politics, Economics and the Safety Issue

During the mid-1950s the Atomic Energy Commission (AEC) was absorbed with promoting and developing new reactors. The perspective of the industry and AEC was that accidents with those small reactors would be limited and could be dealt with if they happened. Safety design concentrated on protection systems to prevent accidents from happening and was accompanied by a philosophy of placing small Light Water Reactors in remote sites and surrounding some of them with a containment so that, in the event of an accident, any fission products would be isolated from the environment.

This view of postaccident mitigation was reflected in the Price-Anderson Act in 1957, which provided insurance for utilities operating nuclear units. The industry had argued, and continues to argue, that this type of government sharing of risks was necessary to encourage development of the new, dangerous technology. Still, safety as such was not adequately emphasized. In the 1960s utilities were pressing the AEC to allow siting closer to major load centers (such as cities and factories) to minimize transmission costs and power losses. In the promotional atmosphere of the AEC, such arguments had appeal. The AEC accepted proposals to site close to cities, such as at Indian Point, above New York City, but gagged at a proposal for a large plant in the middle of that city's borough of Queens.

A 1967 report on the proposed 1,000 megawatt units concluded convincingly that a containment system alone would not prevent the emission of radioactive material in the event of a core meltdown — the most serious accident postulated in a reactor. The result was a drastic shift in AEC regulation away from only preventing accidents toward complex ways to mitigate the consequences of accidents as well. The AEC began requiring that the new, larger units include quality-assurance programs, redundancy of critical equipment, the addition of an Emergency Core Cooling System (ECCS), and other measures — as well as retaining the existing containment approach. There was a trade-off in the new requirements: closer siting would be allowed, on the demonstration that engineering fixes had been installed to ensure the safety of the larger population.

Nonetheless, with thirty units ordered, 1967 was a boom year for the industry. Nor did the new safety requirements deter orders. As the 1963 units came on line and utilities studied the low-cost power available from a nuclear unit, the demand for them jumped. Ninety-one units were ordered in 1969 and 160 by the end of 1972.

But the easy, nonabrasive days of government-industry relationships began to draw to a close as the activism generated by the Vietnam War began to seep into the nuclear energy issue. Aided by the 1971 Calvert Cliffs decision, which imposed environmental responsibilities on the AEC, and by the government's liberal intervention policies, intervenors began challenging the ability of utilities to build safe, environmentally sound nuclear plants. This challenge perhaps reached its peak in the heavily publicized debate over the Midland, Michigan, nuclear power plant, which applied for its construction permit in 1968 and was still in the early stages of construction in 1979.

The old issue of a conflict of interest between the AEC's promotional and regulatory roles finally impressed both the Nixon Administration and Congress. In 1974 the Energy Reorganization Act split the AEC into the Energy Research and Development Administration (ERDA) (the promotional side) and the Nuclear Regulatory Commission (NRC).

The 1970s did not hold up to the promise for the industry that prevailed in the 1960s and, to an extent, the 1950s. Although the industry believes the

614

technology is sound, legal and economic constraints are once again limiting its development. The increasing regulatory demands of the NRC and the various state governments are forcing utilities and vendors to add costly new equipment and procedures. Further, it is alleged that intervenors have lengthened the time necessary to obtain a license by raising costly court challenges. Economically, tight capital markets and construction cost over-runs have made the larger, more expensive nuclear plant less competitive with other types of generation. Scores of orders have been canceled.

It was this environment of deep uncertainty throughout the industry in which the accident at Three Mile Island occurred . . . (13).

Source: Nuclear Regulatory Commission Special Inquiry Group. *Three Mile Island, Volume I: A Report to the Commissioners and to the Public.* Washington, DC: Government Printing Office, 1980.

2. Nuclear fusion is much safer than nuclear fission. For example, were a fusion reactor to malfunction, the reaction would simply come to a stop, with no harm to humans or the environment. Nuclear experts agree that there is no possible chance for an explosion. There would be no massive release of radiation. (However, the wall of the reactor vessel would be bombarded by high-speed neutrons and become radioactive.)
3. Because a fusion reaction is much more *efficient* than a fission reaction, less waste heat is released. As a result, the fusion reactor's potential for thermal pollution is considerably less. Moreover, less coolant water will be needed, thus releasing water for other purposes, such as irrigation, sewage treatment, and community water supplies (7).

As ecologist G. Tyler Miller has stated, the most important hazard associated with fusion reactors could be the release of radioactive tritium gas into the environment. At high temperatures it is extremely difficult to control and is capable of passing through metal shields (7).

So what are the prospects of shifting to fusion in this century? They are not very good. Fusion research is being intensively conducted at such universities as Princeton and the University of California, as well as in federal laboratories at Oak Ridge, Tennessee. Unfortunately, federal funding for fusion research has, until recently, lagged behind funding for conventional fission reactors and the controversial breeder. All this changed, however, in 1980, when Congress passed the Magnetic Fusion Energy Emergency Act. This act authorizes the De-partment of Energy to spend roughly $1 billion per year from 1980 to the year 2000. The goal is a workable fusion energy reactor by the end of this century (7). This financial support is encouraging. Certainly from the standpoint of human safety, economics, and effective energy production, the fusion reaction is superior to fission. Of course, there exists a number of technical difficulties with the development of fusion power that may never be solved. It may not be until 2010 or later that your stereo or TV will be powered with energy derived from seawater.

America's Energy Future

What will our nation's energy future be? Is it just possible that we should relegate nuclear power to the (radioactive) ash heap of history? Certainly, at the present time, because of the almost prohibitive construction costs, as well as mounting public opposition, it seems likely that fission will fizzle as a viable energy source by the end of this decade. What about coal? America has enough proven reserves to last for centuries. But serious environmental problems are associated with its use, such as acid rain, carbon dioxide buildup (the greenhouse effect), and strip-mined devastation.

How about oil? Certainly we will continue to rely on oil substantially until our domestic supplies run out — perhaps in fifty years. But more and more, oil should be conserved as a raw material in the manufacture of medicines, fertilizers, and pesticides. Should the federal government launch a crash program, complete with substantial subsidies of money and technical expertise, to develop energy technologies such as solar, wind, small hydroplants, biomass, and geothermal? Such small-scale, decentralized sources of electrical power lend themselves to cooperative development and management by the very people who directly use the power. These "soft" energy technologies would not be nearly as environmentally destructive as are the "hard," centralized energy systems represented by today's coal-fired and nuclear-fired plants.

Suppose that the $50 billion (more or less) of tax payers' money that was poured into what is now a dying nuclear-fission power industry had been channeled into the development of solar, wind, small hydro-, biomass and geothermal technologies instead. The tantalizing question is, if that had happened, would we now, as a nation (with some temporary assistance from coal-fired power plants equipped with sophisticated air-pollution controls) be very close to being independent of foreign oil imports? In other words, would America have achieved her long-cherished goal of *energy independence?* There are many well-informed energy specialists who firmly believe that the shift to softer, decentralized (in other words, not controlled by a few big utilities) sources of energy is the most appropriate method for satisfying our energy needs.

The shift would include multiple social, economic, political, and environmental fringe benefits as well.

In their recent book "The Menace of Atomic Energy," consumer advocate Ralph Nader and John Abbotts described what they think are the two major energy options for America:

The obstacles to an enlightened energy policy are great. Citizens must overcome giant corporations with multi-billion-dollar investments, as well as governments determined to prop up an expiring technology. But the stakes are also great. There are two choices for future energy systems. One is a future increasingly dependent on energy-supply options that are expensive, in need of massive subsidies, complicated, dangerous, destructive to workers and the environment, and which, by requiring large amounts of capital investment, lend themselves to control by large corporate entities. The second future would turn to energy options that are simpler, safer, economical, job-creating, decentralized, local, socially and environmentally beneficial, and inherently more democratic and susceptible to citizen control. Because different interest groups will benefit from the two futures, they are probably mutually exclusive. The world's citizens and future generations, who will benefit from the second path, cannot afford to lose this struggle . . . " (9).

Controversy: The Pros and Cons of Nuclear Power

Few environmental-technological issues have been as hotly contested as that concerning the development of nuclear power. This debate has been waged with intensity and conviction by proponents and opponents of nuclear power alike in college classrooms, on city street corners, on commuter trains, in the laboratories of nuclear physicists, during coffee breaks in the offices of big business, at ladies' bridge clubs, and, of course, in the cloakrooms and marbled halls of Congress itself. The arguments pro and con have been presented by press, radio, and television. Referendums on the nuclear issue have appeared on the ballots of at least seven states.

Among the organizations that have taken a strong antinuclear stand are Critical Mass (sponsored by consumer advocate Ralph Nader), Friends of the Earth, the Sierra Club, and the Union of Concerned Scientists. Grass roots resistance to nuclear-power development was in dramatic expression at California's Diablo Canyon Nuclear Station. The twin-domed plant is located near San Luis Obispo, between a range of lovely mountains and the sea. Construction of the plant was launched by the Pacific Gas and Electric Company in 1969. It was scheduled to be operational by 1973. Yet, as late as 1981, not a single atom of uranium had been split. The reason? In 1972 a major earthquake fault line had been discovered less than three miles away, much to the embarrassment and frustration of utility officials. Follow-up studies by engineers concerning the ability of the Diablo plant to withstand a possible earthquake revealed it to be highly vulnerable. Nevertheless, despite the potential hazards involved, the Nuclear Regulatory Commission refused to cancel Diablo's license *because of the large financial loss involved and the severe impact such action would have on the nuclear industry.*

Because the antinuclear activists in the area could get no appropriate legal satisfaction, they decided to resort to direct action, such as camping on the nuclear site, passively interfering with plant activities, and picketing. In 1976 a total of eight protesters were arrested. The number of arrests grew to 47 by 1977 and to 487 by 1978. Finally, in the summer of 1979, more than 20,000 demonstrators converged on Diablo in a massive expression of antinuclear sentiment. Similar demonstrations occurred at a beleaguered nuclear plant at Seabrook, New Hampshire, in 1979.

In controversies such as this it is useful to list the major arguments of opposing groups side by side.

Arguments for Nuclear Power

1. *Adequacy of fuel supply.* Once the breeder reactor has been perfected, the nuclear industry will be able to tap a virtually unlimited supply of uranium-238 in the Chattanooga shale deposits of Kentucky, Tennessee, Indiana, and Illinois.
2. *Oil conservation.* The development of nuclear power will free considerable amounts of otherwise limited supplies of oil for other purposes, such as the manufacture of medicines, pesticides, and fertilizers. Nuclear power is the only source of energy that can reduce our dependency on oil imports from the OPEC nations.
3. *Cost of electrical power.* Cost per kilowatt is considerably lower than that generated by coal- or oil-fired power plants.
4. *Possibility of terrorists making atomic bombs from nuclear fuel.* "Reactor"-grade plutonium is not suitable for use in the manufacture of nuclear bombs.
5. *Radiation releases from routine plant operations.* The operation of nuclear plants in the United States exposes the average American to just .003-millirem of radioactivity above the 250 millirems received from all other sources. The added risk of cancer a person would experience by living immediately adjacent to a nuclear plant would be equal to that of smoking just one cigarette per year.
6. *Probability of a nuclear-power-plant accident.* The probability of an accident in the United States that would release large amounts of radioactivity is less than one in a thousand years. Other sources of electric power also have the potential for many fatalities. A University of California study has shown that the failure of some large hydropower dams might result in up to 260,000 deaths (6). For each large coal-fired power plant operating in the United States, an estimated 31 to 111 people lose their lives each year as a result of mine accidents, mishaps during coal transport, and the effects of the air pollution resulting from the burning of coal.
7. *Environmental pollution.* A properly functioning nuclear plant is a much "cleaner" source of energy than a coal-fired plant. In one year a coal-fired plant of 1,000 megawatts generates 300,000 tons of coal ash waste, compared to a ton of fission waste from a nuclear plant. The coal-fired plant releases sulfur dioxide, nitrogen oxides, carbon dioxide, particulates, and mercury through the stacks. Solid wastes from coal-fired plants contain nonradioactive materials such as selenium, mercury, and benzopyrene, as well as radioactive uranium and thorium. The level of radioactivity from a coal-fired plant is actually *greater* than from a nuclear power plant.
8. *Plutonium transport.* With the proper shielding (lead, concrete, or steel) of suitable containers, as well as the restriction of transport to areas of low population density, the chance of an accident causing radiation damage to large numbers of people is minimal.
9. *Danger of plutonium radiation.* If the world switched to an all-breeder-reactor power system, the total amount of plutonium produced, if dispersed throughout the earth's crust, would be no more dangerous than the radium occurring *naturally* in the upper four millimeters of the earth's surface.

Arguments Against Nuclear Power

1. *Adequacy of the nuclear fuel supply.* The breeder reactor program has been fraught with many technical problems that remain to be solved, despite the spending of many billions of dollars of public tax moneys. If the breeder reactor program never gets off the ground, the nuclear industry will be forced to rely on relatively scarce uranium-235 — the supply of which will probably be exhausted within 50 years.

2. *Oil conservation.* Not much oil will actually be freed up for other use. After all, most of the power plants today consume coal rather than oil. A number of alternative energy sources, such as wind, biomass, and solar (which are more efficient, economical, and safe, as well as less damaging to the environment), can be more intensively developed so that oil can be conserved for other functions.

3. *Cost of electrical power.* The cost of producing a kilowatt of electricity is rising higher and higher because of the need for the industry to comply with steadily upgraded safety and environmental standards imposed by the federal government. Then, too, we must remember that the life span of a given reactor is only about thirty to forty years. When it finally dies it must be decommissioned, or dismantled, and its highly radioactive core must be properly disposed of. This will cost about $100 million, or 10 percent of the original cost of the power station.

4. *Possibility of terrorists making atomic bombs from nuclear fuel.* Crude nuclear bombs could easily be made from only ten pounds of plutonium-239 metal or 22 pounds of plutonium oxide. Such bombs could be used to destroy industrial plants and paralyze communication systems.

5. *Radiation releases from routine nuclear plant operations.* Although the radiation released from a "properly functioning" nuclear plant is very small, the exposure to such radiation year after year will increase the probability, even though admittedly small, for some genetic damage or the eventual development of cancer.

6. *Probability of a nuclear plant accident.* Several nuclear reactor accidents (the Enrico Fermi plant in Michigan and the Three Mile Island plant in Pennsylvania) have already occurred. A near meltdown of the reactor fuel was caused in 1975 by a fire at the Browns Ferry plant in Alabama. As the number of nuclear plants increases, the possibility of nuclear plant accidents increases accordingly. No private insurance company will insure against nuclear accidents because the risk and potential damage to health and property are so great.

7. *Environmental pollution.* In addition to being a potential source of massive environmental contamination with radiation, the nuclear power industry generates 40 percent more thermal pollution per kilowatt than a coal-fired plant. The huge demonstrations by 15,000 protesters at the Seabrook, New Hampshire, plant were in part because of the harmful effects that thermal pollution would have on the commercially valuable marine life near the reactor site.

8. *Plutonium transport.* According to one conservative estimate, the total annual mileage of plutonium shipments could reach 108,000 miles per year by 1990. The possibility of a serious accident in which high levels of radioactivity would be released is omnipresent. Even though shipments are heavily guarded, fanatic terrorists might hijack the plutonium for the purpose of making nuclear weapons.

9. *Danger of plutonium radiation.* A mass of plutonium the size of a grapefruit, if dispersed into extremely fine particles, and inhaled, has the potential of destroying the total world population of 4.8 billion people, with more than three billion deaths left over.

Rapid Review

1. An atom is composed of a dense, centrally located nucleus composed of positively charged protons and electrically neutral neutrons. Surrounding the nucleus are one or more rings of electrically negative electrons.

2. Radioactive elements spontaneously disintegrate to give off three different types of radiation: alpha rays, beta rays, and gamma rays. Of these types the gamma rays are potentially the most harmful to the human body.

3. Man eats, breathes, and drinks materials that are naturally radioactive. Soil and rocks are also radioactive. All of this natural radiation is collectively known as *background radiation.*

4. Radioactive strontium undergoes *biological magnification* as it moves through food chains. It mimics the physiological characteristics of calcium in the human body. As a result, it tends to concentrate in the human skeleton.

5. The number of nuclear power plants operating in the United States increased from 23 in 1972 to 72 in 1983.

6. Uranium ore contains a mixture of fissionable uranium-235, which forms only 1 percent of the ore, and nonfissionable uranium-238, which forms the remaining 99 percent.

7. About 100 tons of uranium oxide fuel may be contained in the core of a nuclear reactor.

8. Nuclear power plants generate 40 percent more waste heat per kilowatt than is produced by a power plant fuelled with coal or oil.

9. Even in the year 2000, when the U.S. will have many more nuclear plants than at present, the total radiation emitted should be only about 1 percent of the background radiation, if the plants are operating properly.

10. The most serious nuclear plant malfunction in United States history occurred on March 28, 1979 at Three Mile Island, ten miles from Harrisburg, Pennsylvania.

11. To reduce the radiation hazard the spent fuel rods, which must be removed from the reactor core after one to two years of operation, are stored under 20 feet of water in swimming pool-like chambers. After several months much of the radioactivity is dissipated.

12. The function of a fuel-reprocessing plant is to salvage any usable fuel left in the spent fuel rods.

13. Federal regulations have made it mandatory for high-level radioactive waste to be stored in solid form, encased either in ceramic bricks or in a glass-like material.

14. The Department of Energy is searching for an adequate site for the burial of highly radioactive waste. Sites in Wisconsin and New York are being considered.

15. The effects of radiation on the human body vary with the intensity of the radiation to which the person is exposed. Radiation dosage is usually measured in rads. As the dosage increases to a little under 500 rads, only 50 percent of the people exposed will survive for three weeks.

16. The Japanese population exposed to radiation released from atomic bombs suffered from both immediate effects — burns, fever, loss of hair, and intestinal bleeding — and delayed effects — anemia, blood cancer, and infections.

17. Any amount of radiation, no matter how slight, is potentially damaging to genetic material and increases the risk of cancer.

18. The breeder reactor uses a relatively small amount of fissionable uranium-235. This material releases neutrons that bombard a "blanket" of nonfissionable uranium-238 and convert it into fissionable plutonium-239, from which the heat energy required to generate electrical power is ultimately derived.

19. In a sense nuclear fusion is exactly the opposite of nuclear fission. Fission is a "splitting apart" of nuclei, whereas fusion involves a "coming together" of nuclei. When two hydrogen nuclei fuse in a nuclear fusion reactor, energy is released that eventually can be used by man in the form of electricity.

20. The Magnetic Fusion Energy Emergency Act authorizes the Department of Energy to spend roughly $1 billion annually from 1980 to the year 2000 to develop a workable fusion energy reactor.

21. Among the arguments for the development of nuclear power are the following: (a) once the breeder reactor is operational the nuclear fuel supply will be adequate; (b) it will reduce our dependency on oil; (c) nuclear power is cheap; (d) release of radiation from routine plant operations is minimal; (e) the probability of a massive nuclear plant accident releasing large amounts of radiation is extremely small; other sources of electric power also have the potential for many fatalities; and (f) nuclear power generation is very "clean" compared to power generation by a fossil fuel plant.

22. Among the arguments against the development of nuclear power are the following: (a) the supply of uranium-235 will be exhausted in about 50 years if the breeder reactor is not successfully developed; reduced dependency on oil could better be achieved by shifting to alternative energy sources such as solar, wind, and so on; (b) the cost of nuclear power is rising rapidly; (c) terrorists could easily make nuclear bombs from only 10 pounds of plutonium-239; (d) even a small amount of radiation can cause some genetic damage; (e) no private insurance agency will insure against nuclear accidents because the risk of damage to human health and property is so high; and (f) a nuclear power plant generates 40 percent more waste heat per kilowatt than a fossil-fuel-fired plant.

Key Words and Phrases

Alpha ray	Isotope
Atom	Leukemia
Atom bomb	Lyons, Kansas
Atomic Energy	Magnetic Fusion Energy
Commission (AEC)	Emergency Act
Beta ray	Mutation
Bone cancer	Nader, Ralph
Cancer	Neutron
Cesium-137	Nongenetic effects of
Chain reaction	radiation
Chattanooga shale	Nuclear bomb
Control rod	Nuclear Regulatory
Decommissioned	Commission
reactor	Pitchblende
Deuterium	Plasma
Electromagnetic bottle	Plutonium-239
Electron	Pressure vessel
Enrichment plant	Proton
Environmental	Rad
Protection Agency	Radioactive fallout
Fuel assembly	Radioactive waste
Fuel rod	disposal
Fusion reactor	Radioactivity
Gamma ray	Reprocessing plant
Half life	Sabotage
Hanford, Washington	Salt mine
Hiroshima bomb	Skin cancer
Hydrogen	Solid waste
Iodine-131	Spent fuel

Strontium-90	Tritium
Terrorists	Uranium oxide pellets
Thermal pollution	Uranium-235
Three Mile Island	Uranium-238

Questions and Topics for Discussion

1. Define or identify each of the key words and phrases listed on the previous page.
2. Describe the structure of an atom.
3. What are the relative health hazards of alpha, beta, and gamma rays?
4. Which phase of the nuclear fuel cycle poses the greatest radiation threat to man?
5. Why does nuclear fuel have to be reprocessed?
6. Discuss the basic differences between nuclear fission and nuclear fusion.
7. What are the advantages and disadvantages of power generation by nuclear fusion?
8. Make a tour of a nuclear power plant. Have the tour guide explain the design and operation of the plant as well as the various devices for minimizing the release of radiation to the environment. Report back to your class on your nuclear plant visit.
9. Discuss the statement: "There is a strong possibility that incidents like the one at Three Mile Island will occur with increasing frequency in the United States."
10. Form a panel with several of your other classmates and be prepared to discuss the topic, "Possible methods for the disposal of high-level radioactive waste." Consult literature available in the college library for aspects of the problem not covered in the text.
11. Be prepared to become involved in a debate on the pros and cons of nuclear power development. Consult literature available in your college library for pertinent material above and beyond that presented in this text.
12. Suppose that a utility proposed to construct a mammoth nuclear plant one mile from your college campus. Suppose also that the construction, maintenance, and operation of this plant would revitalize the stagnant economy of the area. What would be your response to the proposed project? Discuss with other members of your class.

Endnotes

1. Aaronson, Terri and George Kohl. "Spectrum." *Environment*, **14** (1972), 24–26.
2. Benarde, Melvin A. *Our Precarious Habitat.* New York: Norton, 1970.
3. Eisenbud, Merril. "Health Hazards from Radioactive Emissions." Paper presented at AMA Cong. Environ. Health, Chicago, April 29–30, 1973.
4. Hodges, Laurent. *Environmental Pollution.* New York: Holt, 1977.
5. Hubbert, M. King. "Energy Resources," in National Academy of Sciences, *Resources and Man.* San Francisco: Freeman, 1969.
6. McCracken, Samuel. "The War Against the Atom." *Commentary* (Sept. 1977), pp. 1–16.
7. Miller, G. Tyler. *Living in the Environment: Concepts, Problems and Alternatives.* Belmont, CA: Wadsworth, 1981.
8. Moriber, George. *Environmental Science.* Boston: Allyn and Bacon, 1974.
9. Nader, Ralph and John Abbotts. *The Menace of Atomic Energy.* New York: Norton, 1979.
10. Odum, Eugene P. *Fundamentals of Ecology.* 3rd ed. Philadelphia: Saunders, 1971.
11. Patterson, Walter C. "Hazards of Radioactive Waste," in Robert M. Chute, *Environmental Insight.* New York: Harper, 1971.
12. Revelle, Penelope and Charles Revelle. *The Environment: Issues and Choices for Society.* New York: Van Nostrand, 1981.
13. Rogovin, Mitchell and George T. Frampton, Jr. *Three Mile Island*, Vol. 1 Nuclear Regulatory Commission. Special Inquiry Group. Washington, DC: U.S.G.P.O., 1980.
14. Sartwell, Phillip E. in K. F. Maxcy and M. J. Rosenau, eds., *Preventive Medicine and Public Health.* 9th ed. Chapter 25. New York: Appleton.
15. "Spectrum." *Environment*, **20** (1978), p. 21.
16. Turk, Amos, Jonathon Turk, and Janet T. Wittes. *Ecology, Pollution, Environment.* 2nd ed. Philadelphia: Saunders, 1978.
17. Wagner, Richard H. *Environment and Man.* New York: Norton, 1971.
18. Waldbott, George L. *Health Effects of Environmental Pollutants.* Saint Louis: Mosby, 1973.
19. *World Book Encyclopedia.* Chicago: Field Enterprises Educational Corporation, 1976.

Suggested Readings for the Interested Student

Dingel, David A. "Fusion Power." *Chemical and Engineering News* (Apr. 2, 1979), 32–47. This is an outstanding summary of the nature and prospects of fusion power.

Gofman, John W., and Arthur R. Tamplin. *Poisoned Power: The Case Against Nuclear Power.* 2nd ed. Emmaus, PA: Rodale, 1979. This is a scathing indictment of nuclear power development.

Kemeny, John G. "Saving American Democracy: The Lessons of Three Mile Island." *Technology Review* (June–July 1980), 65–75. This is a superb discussion of the Three Mile Island incident.

Kendall, H. W., ed. *The Risks of Nuclear Power Reactors.* Washington, DC: Union of Concerned Scientists, 1977. This is an outstanding analysis of the possible health and environmental damage resulting from nuclear power plant mishaps.

"Nuclear Dilemma: The Atoms Fizzle in an Energy Short World." *Business Week* (Dec. 25, 1978), 54. This article discusses the diminishing status of nuclear power as a viable energy source for America.

Weaver, Kenneth F., and Emory Kristof. "The Promise and Peril of Nuclear Energy." *National Geographic,* **155** (Apr. 1979), 458–493.

Appendix: Information Sources for Environmental Research

Sources

1. *University library.* Your school library will be a major source of information for preparing your report.

    a. *Newspapers.* Such newspapers as the *Christian Science Monitor, Milwaukee Journal, New York Times, San Francisco Chronicle*, and *St.Louis Post-Dispatch* frequently devote an entire page to resource and other environmental problems. Editorials often deal with environmental issues. Moreover the editorial page frequently will include "Letters to the Editor," written by scientists, legislators, and industrialists, on topics pertinent to your report.

    b. *Periodicals.* Consult important journals and magazines dealing with resource-environment matters.

    c. *Books.* An excellent way to get started in your library research is to examine the "Suggested Readings for the Interested Student" at the end of the chapters in this book. After gleaning information from a given publication, examine its bibliography. Select three or four of the most interesting titles you find there, take notes on what is pertinent, and then examine *their* bibliography. This technique is known as chainbibbing. If a computer terminal is available in the library, ask the librarian to show you how to use it to quickly compile a list of relevant sources.

2. *University faculty.* A number of different departments in your school have staff members with expertise in resource conservation and other environmental issues. If you make an advance appointment they probably would be happy to assist you by suggesting an interesting report topic and by guiding you in your literary search. Among the depart-that might be of assistance to you are the following:

    Agronomy: Soil chemistry, soil erosion, buckshot urbanization.

    Biology: Ecological concepts, wildlife extinction, predator control.

    Chemistry: Environmental pollution, pesticide problems.

    Entomology: Crop and forest pest outbreaks, pesticide problems.

    Fisheries: Introduction of exotics, artificial propagation, fish farming, extended economic zone (EEZ).

    Forestry: Multiple-use management, clear-cutting problems, fire suppression, pest control, energy plantations.

    Geography: Soil erosion, flooding, drought, watershed management.

    Meteorology: Acid rain, air pollution, carbon dioxide problem, weather modification, drought, flooding.

    Physics: Nuclear reactors, effects of radiation on man, laws of thermodynamics (energy laws).

    Wildlife Ecology: Game management, wildlife extinction, introduction of exotics, effects of pesticides on wildlife.

3. *Local agencies.* City Health Department, Parks and Recreation Department, Public Works Department (waterworks, sewage disposal).

4. *Local industries.* Automobile manufacturing,

steel, pulp and paper, oil refining, chemical, pesticides.

5. *County agencies.* Parks and Forests, Soil and Water Conservation District, Public Works (sanitary landfill operations).

6. *State agencies.* Consult the list of agencies appearing on the following pages. (Many of these agencies will provide free literature on a specific area of environmental concern.)

7. *Congressional committees and federal agencies.* Consult the list appearing on the following pages. (Many of these agencies and committees will provide you with free information.)

U.S. Congressional Committees

U.S. Senate
Committee on Agriculture, Nutrition and Forestry, Room 322, Russell Bldg., Washington, DC 20510 (202) 224-2035

Committee on Appropriations, Room 132, Russell Bldg., Washington, DC 20501 (202) 224-3471

Committee on Energy and Natural Resources, Rm. 3106, Dirksen Building, Washington, DC 20510 (202) 224-4971

Committee on Environment and Public Works, Room 4204, Dirksen Building, Washington, DC 20510 (202) 224-6176

House of Representatives
Committee on Agriculture, Room 1301, Longworth House Office Building, Washington, DC 20515 (202) 225-2171

Committee on Appropriations, Room H-218, Capitol Building, Washington, DC 20515 (202) 225-2771

Committee on Merchant Marine and Fisheries, Rm. 1334, Longworth House Office Building, Washington, DC 20515 (202) 225-4047

Committee on Public Works and Transportation, Room 2165, Rayburn House Office Building, Washington, DC 20515 (202) 225-4472

U.S. Government — Executive Branch

Council on Environmental Quality, 722 Jackson Place, N.W., Washington, DC 20006 (202)395-5700

Agricultural Stabilization and Conservation Service, Washington, DC 20013 (202) 44 plus extension; information: Ext. 75237

Forest Service, P.O. Box 2417, Washington, DC 20013 (202) 447-3957 for information

National Marine Fisheries Service, U.S. Department of Commerce, NOAA, Washington, DC 20235 (202) 634 plus extension

National Oceanic and Atmospheric Administration, Rockville, MD 20852 (301) 443-8910

Army Corps of Engineers, Office of the Chief of Engineers, Forrestal Building, Washington, DC 20314

Federal Energy Regulatory Commission, 825 N. Capitol St., N.E., Washington, DC 20426 (202) 27 plus extension

Food and Drug Administration, 5600 Fishers Lane, Rockville, MD 20857 (301) 443 plus extension; information: Ext. 1544

Bureau of Land Management, Washington, DC 20240 (202) 343 plus extension; information; Ext. 1100

Bureau of Mines, Washington, DC 20241 (202) 634 plus extension; information: Ext. 1004

Bureau of Reclamation, Washington, DC 20240 (202) 343 plus extension; information: Ext. 4662

Geological Survey, National Center, Reston, VA 22092 (703) 860-7000

Office of Surface Mining, U.S. Department of the Interior, 1951 Constitution Avenue, N.W., Washington, DC 20240

Office of Water Research and Technology, Washington, DC 20240 (202) 343-4608

U.S. Fish and Wildlife Service, Washington, DC 20240 (202) 343 plus extension

Urban Mass Transportation Administration, 400 Seventh Street, S.W., Washington, DC 20590 (202) 426-4043

U.S. Government — Independent Agencies

Endangered Species Scientific Authority, 18th and C Streets, N.W., Washington, DC 20240 (202) 653-5948

Environmental Protection Agency, 401 M Street, S.W., Washington, DC 20460 (202) 755-2673

Nuclear Regulatory Commission, Washington, DC 20555 (301) 492-7000

Tennessee Valley Authority, 400 Commerce Avenue, Knoxville, TN 37902 (615) 632-2101

State Agencies

Alabama:
Department of Agriculture and Industries, The Richard Beard Building, 1445 Federal Drive, Montgomery 36109 (205) 832-6693

Department of Conservation and Natural Resources, 64 N. Union Street, Montgomery 36130 (205) 832-6361

Alaska:
Department of Environmental Conservation, Pouch O, Juneau 99811 (907) 465-2600

Arizona:
Game and Fish Department, 2222 W. Greenway Road, Phoenix 85023 (602) 942-3000

Arkansas:
Department of Pollution Control and Ecology, 80001 National Drive, P.O. Box 9583, Little Rock 72219 (501) 371-1701

Forestry Commission, P.O. Box 4523, Asher Station, 3821 West Roosevelt Road, Little Rock 72214 (501) 371-1732

California:
California Cooperative Fishery Research Unit, U.S. Department of the Interior, Fisheries Department, Humboldt State University, Arcata 95521 (707) 826-3268

Department of Food and Agriculture, 1220 N Street, Sacramento 95814 (916) 445-9280

Department of Forestry, 1416 Ninth Street, Sacramento 95814 (916) 445-3976

Department of Water Resources, 1416 Ninth Street, Sacramento 95814 (916) 445-6582

Department of Fish and Game, 1416 Ninth Street, Sacramento 95814 (916) 445-3535

Air Resources Board, P.O. Box 2815, Sacramento 95812 (916) 322-2990

Solid Waste Management Board, 1416 Ninth Street, Room 605-2, Sacramento 95814 (916) 445-3993

Colorado:
Colorado Cooperative Fishery Research Unit, U.S. Department of the Interior, Room 102, Cooperative Units Building, Colorado State University, Ft. Collins 80523 (303) 892-2471

Department of Agriculture, 1525 Sherman Street, Denver 80203 (303) 839-2811

Department of Natural Resources, 1313 Sherman, Room 718, Denver 80203 (303) 892-3311

Connecticut:
Council on Environmental Quality, Room 141, 165 Capitol Avenue, Hartford 06115 (203) 566-3510

Department of Environmental Protection, State Office Building, 165 Capitol Avenue, Hartford 06115 (203) 566-5599

Delaware:
Department of Natural Resources and Environmental Control, The Elward Tatnall Building, P.O. Box 1401, Dover 19901

Florida:
Department of Natural Resource, Commonwealth Building, Tallahassee 32303 (904) 488-1555

Georgia:
Department of Natural Resources, 270 Washington Street, S.W., Atlanta 30334 (404) 656-3530

Idaho:
Bureau of Mines and Geology, Moscow 83843

Fish and Game Department, 600 S. Walnut , P.O. Box 25, Boise 83707

Illinois:
Department of Agriculture, State Fairgrounds, Springfield 62706 (217) 782-2172

Department of Conservation, 605 Stratton Office Building, Springfield 62706 (217) 782-6302

Environmental Protection Agency, 2200 Churchill Road, Springfield 62706 (217) 782-3397

Indiana:
Department of Natural Resources, 608 State Office Building, Indianapolis 46204

Iowa:
Department of Agriculture, Wallace State Office Building, Des Moines 50319 (515) 281-5322

Department of Environmental Quality, Henry A. Wallace Building, 900 East Grand, Des Moines 50319, (515) 281-8690

Kansas:
State Department of Health and Environment, Forbes Field, Building 740, Topeka 66620

Kentucky:
Department of Natural Resources and Environmental Protection, 5th Floor, Capital Plaza Tower, Frankfort 40601 (502) 564-3350

625

Louisiana:
Department of Natural Resources, Office of Forestry, P.O. Box 1628, Baton Rouge 70821 (504) 925-4510

Department of Wildlife and Fisheries, 400 Royal Street, New Orleans 70130 (504) 568-5665

Maine:
Department of Conservation, State Office Building, Augusta 04333 (207) 289-2212

Maryland:
Agricultural Commission, Department of Agriculture, Parole Plaza Office Building, Annapolis 21401 (301) 269-2332, 2333

Department of Natural Resources, Tawes State Office Building, Annapolis 21401 (301) 269 plus extension

University of Maryland Center for Environmental and Estuaries Studies, Cambridge 21613 (301) 228-9250

Massachusetts:
Department of Fisheries, Wildlife and Recreational Vehicles, 100 Cambridge Street, Boston 02202

Michigan:
Department of Agriculture, 5th Floor, Lewis Cass Building, P.O. Box 30017, Lansing 48909 (517) 373-1050

Department of Natural Resources, Box 30028, Lansing 48909 (517) 373-1220

Minnesota:
Department of Agriculture, 90 W. Plato Blvd., St. Paul 55107 (612) 296-3391

Department of Natural Resources, 300 Centennial Building, 658 Cedar Street, St. Paul 55155 (612) 296 plus extension

Pollution Control Agency, 1935 W. County Road B2, Roseville 55113 (612) 296-7373

Mississippi:
Department of Natural Resources, Bureau of Pollution Control, P.O. Box 827, Jackson 39205 (601) 354-2550

Missouri:
Department of Conservation, P.O. Box 180, Jefferson City 65102 (314) 751-4115

Montana:
Bureau of Mines and Geology, c/o Montana College of Mineral Science and Technology, Butte 59701 (406) 792-8321

Department of Natural Resources and Conservation, 32 South Ewing, Helena 59601 (406) 449-3712

Nebraska:
Department of Agriculture, 301 Centennial Mall South, P.O. Box 94947 Lincoln 68509 (402) 471-2341

Department of Environmental Control, State House Station, P.O. Box 94877, Lincoln 68509

Nevada:
Bureau of Mines and Geology, University of Nevada, Reno 89557 (702) 784-6691

Department of Conservation and Natural Resources, Capitol Complex, Nye Building, 201 S. Fall Street, Carson City 89710 (702) 885-4360

New Hampshire:
Fish and Game Department, 34 Bridge Street, Concord 03301, (603) 271-3421

New Jersey:
Department of Environmental Protection, Labor and Industry Building, P.O. Box 1390, Trenton 08625

Division of Fish, Game and Shellfisheries, P.O. Box 1809, Trenton 08625 (609) 292-2965

New Mexico:
Natural Resources Department, Villagra Building, Santa Fe 87503 (505) 827-3167

New York:
Department of Environmental Conservation, 50 Wolf Road, Albany 12233

Marine Sciences Research Center, State University of New York, Stony Brook 11794 (516) 246-7710

North Carolina:
Department of Agriculture, P.O. Box 27647, Raleigh, 27611

Department of Natural Resources, P.O. Box 27687, Raleigh 27611

North Dakota:
Department of Agriculture, State Capitol, Bismarck 58505

Institute for Ecological Studies, University of North Dakota, Grand Forks 58202 (701) 777-2851

Ohio:
Department of Agriculture, 65 South Front Street, Columbus 43215 (614) 466-2732

Department of Natural Resources, Fountain Square, Columbus, 43224 (614) 466-3066

Oklahoma:
Department of Wildlife Conservation, 1801 North Lincoln, P.O. Box 53465, Oklahoma City 73152 (405) 521-3851

Oregon:
Department of Environmental Quality, 522 S.W. Fifth Avenue, P.O. Box 1760, Portland 97207

Department of Fish and Wildlife, P.O. Box 3503, Portland 97208 (503) 229-5551

Pennsylvania:
Department of Agriculture, 2301 N. Cameron Street, Harrisburg 17120 (717) 787-4737

Department of Environmental Resources, Public Information, Ninth Floor, Fulton Building, P.O. Box 2063, Harrisburg, 17120

Pennsylvania Cooperative Wildlife Research Unit, 113 Ferguson Building, Pennsylvania State University, University Park 16802 (814) 865-4511

Rhode Island:
Department of Environmental Management, 83 Park Street, Providence 02903 (401) 227 plus extension

South Carolina:
Department of Agriculture, Wade Hampton Office Building, P.O. Box 11280, Columbia 29211 (803) 758-2426

Department of Health and Environmental Control, J. Marion Sims Building, 2600 Bull Street, Columbia 29201

South Dakota:
Board of Environmental Protection, Joe Foss Building, Pierre, 57501

Department of Agriculture, Sigurd Anderson Building, Pierre 57501 (605) 773-3375

Tennessee:
Department of Conservation, 2611 West End Avenue, Nashville, 37203 (615) 741-2301

Texas:
Bureau of Economic Geology, The University of Texas at Austin, University Station, Box X, Austin 78712 (512) 471-1534

Utah:
State Department of Natural Resources, 400 Empire Building, 231 East Fourth South, Salt Lake City 84111

Vermont:
Agency of Environmental Conservation, Montpelier 05602 (802) 828-3357

Virginia:
Commission of Game and Inland Fisheries, 4010 West Broad Street, P.O. Box 11104, Richmond 23230 (804) 257-1000

Council on the Environment, 903 Ninth Street Office Building, Richmond 23219 (804) 786-4500

Institute of Marine Science, Gloucester Point 23062 (804) 642-2111

Washington:
Department of Agriculture, 406 General Administration Building, Olympia 98504 (206) 753-6780

Department of Ecology, Olympia 98504 (206) 753-2800

Department of Fisheries, 115 General Administration Building, Olympia, 98504 (206) 753-6600

West Virginia:
Department of Natural Resources, 1800 Washington Street, East, Charleston, 25305 (304) 348-2754

Wisconsin:
Department of Agriculture, P.O. Box 8911, 801 W. Badger Road, Madison 53708 (608) 266-1721

Department of Natural Resources, P.O. Box 7921, Madison, 53707 (608) 266-2621

Wisconsin Cooperative Wildlife Research Unit, U.S. Department of the Interior, Department of Wildlife Ecology, 226 Russell Laboratories, University of Wisconsin-Madison 53706 (608) 262-2671

Wyoming:
Environmental Quality Department, Hathaway Building, Cheyenne 82002 (307) 777-7631

Game and Fish Department, Cheyenne 82002 (307) 777-7631

GLOSSARY

Abortion. The premature expulsion of the fetus from the uterus.

Abyssal Zone. The bottom zone of the ocean; characterized by darkness, close to freezing temperatures, and high water pressures.

Accelerated Erosion. A rapid type of soil erosion that is induced by human activities, in contrast to the relatively slow processes of geological erosion.

Acid Rain. Rain that has a lower pH than "normal" rain — in other words, lower than pH 5.8. It is caused by the release of oxides of sulfur and nitrogen into the atmosphere.

Activated Sludge. The solid organic waste that has been intensively aerated and "seeded" with bacteria (in a secondary or tertiary sewage-treatment process) to promote rapid bacterial decomposition.

Adsorption. The process by which nutrient particles form a loose chemical bond with the surface of a clay particle.

Aggregate. A grouping of soil particles. Soil aeration, moisture content, fertility, and erosion resistance are in part dependent on the aggregate patterns of soil particles.

Alfisols. An order of soils that develops under deciduous forest (elms, maples, beech, and oak) forest cover; aluminum and iron are characteristic components of the B horizon.

Alluvial Soil. A type of soil that develops from waterborne sediment; frequently very fertile.

Alpha Particle. A positively charged particle (proton) that is emitted from the nucleus of a radioactive atom.

Altitudinal Migration. Seasonal movement of birds (grosbeaks and finches) and mammals (elk and bighorn sheep) up and down mountain slopes.

Ammocoetes Larva. The immature stages of the sea lamprey.

Ammonification. The process by which the bacteria of decay convert complex nitrogenous compounds occurring in animal carcasses and the excretions of animals, as well as the dead bodies of plants, into relatively simple ammonia (NH_3) compounds.

Anadromous Fish. A fish, such as the Pacific salmon, that spawns and spends its early life in fresh water but moves into the ocean where it attains sexual maturity and spends most of its life span.

Annular Ring. A concentric ring, visible in the cross-section of a tree trunk, that is useful in determining the age of the tree.

Antimycin. A toxic substance that has been rather extensively used by fisheries biologists to eradicate carp.

Aquifer. A subterranean layer of porous water-bearing rock, gravel, or sand.

Aridisol. An order of soils that develops under desert vegetation. The thin band of topsoil contains a relatively small amount of organic matter.

Artificial Insemination. The technique employed by cattle breeders in which sperm from a bull of one breed, such as Hereford, might be refrigerated and used, over a period of time, to fertilize the eggs of the same breed or other breeds of cattle, possibly from widely separated localities.

Artificial Reef. A reef constructed of housing debris, rubble, junked automobile bodies, tires, and so on, frequently placed in relatively shallow water near the coast. A method for increasing the number of breeding sites and providing more cover for marine fish.

Biomonitor. A biological monitor, such as a lichen or soybean plant, that detects very small levels of pollutants (such as sulfur dioxide) in the environment.

Biotic Potential (BP). The theoretical reproductive capacity of a species.

Black Lung Disease. An occupational disease frequently contracted by coal miners.

Blister Rust. A fungus-caused disease of the white pine; characterized by the appearance of orange "blisters" on the bark.

Botulism. A waterfowl disease caused by a bacterium and characterized by eventual respiratory paralysis and death.

Breeder Reactor. A nuclear reactor that uses a relatively small amount of uranium-235 as a "primer" to release energy from the much more abundant uranium-238.

Broadcasting. A method of reseeding range or forest; seeds are dispersed broadly by hand, machine, or plane.

Brown Lung Disease. An occupational disease frequently contracted by textile workers.

Browse Line. A line delimiting the browsed and unbrowsed portions of shrubs and trees in an area where the deer population exceeds the carrying capacity of the range.

Buckshot Urbanization. The random hit-and-miss pattern of urban development that has effectively reduced the acreage of prime agricultural land and suitable wildlife habitat in the United States within the past few decades.

Buffer Action. The action of limestone-derived soils in neutralizing the acidity of acid rain.

Cambium. The layer of rapidly dividing cells located between the xylem and phloem in the trunk of a tree; it permits growth of the diameter of the trunk.

Carbon Absorption. A process employed by a tertiary sewage-treatment plant by which dissolved organic compounds are removed from the effluent as they pass through a tower packed with small particles of carbon.

Carbon Dioxide Fixation. The incorporation of carbon dioxide into glucose molecules during the process of photosynthesis.

Carcinogen. A cancer-causing chemical.

Carrying Capacity. The capacity of a given habitat to sustain a population of animals for an indefinite period of time.

Catadromous Fish. A type of fish, such as the American eel, that grows to sexual maturity in fresh water but migrates to the ocean for spawning purposes.

Central Arizona Project. A multimillion-dollar project that has been proposed to alleviate water-shortage problems in Arizona by transporting water from the Colorado River.

Chain Reaction. The sequence of events that occurs when neutrons that have been emitted from a radioactive atom bombard another atom and cause it to emit neutrons that in turn bombard yet another atom, and so on.

Channelization. The process by which a natural stream is converted into a ditch for the ostensible purpose of flood control. Attendant environmental abuse is severe.

Chlorinated Hydrocarbon. A "family" of nondegradable pesticides such as DDT, dieldrin, and toxaphene. They may have a harmful effect on nontarget organisms such as fish and birds. They have long persistence in the environment and undergo biological magnification as they move through food chains.

Chlororganics. Potentially toxic organic compounds that form in water treated with chlorine. A good example is chloroform and carbon tetrachloride.

Chlorosis. An abnormal condition in plants characterized by a chlorophyll deficiency.

Clear Cutting. A method of harvesting timber in which *all* trees are removed from a given patch or block of forest. This is the method of choice when harvesting a stand composed of a single species in which all trees are of the same age.

Climax Community. The stable terminal stage of an ecological succession.

Closed-Cycle Cooling System. A method of cooling power plants in which the cooling water is continuously recirculated instead of being discharged into a stream and causing thermal pollution.

Coliform Bacteria. A type of bacterium occurring in the human gut. It is used as an index of the degree to which stream or lake water has been contaminated with human sewage.

Community. The total number of organisms of all species living in a given area. For example, the community of an oak woods, an abandoned field, or a cattail marsh.

Compensation Depth. The depth in a lake at which photosynthesis balances respiration. This level delimits the upper limnetic zone from the lower profundal zone.

Compost. Partially decomposed organic matter (garbage) that can be used as a soil conditioner and fertilizer.

Conservation Tillage. Sometimes called minimal tillage, this is a method of cultivating farmland with a minimal amount of disturbance to the soil. Soil erosion is minimized.

Consumer. A term used for any animal "link" in a food chain.

Contour Farming. Plowing, cultivating, and harvesting crops along the contour of the land rather than up and down the slope. An effective technique for controlling soil erosion.

Crown Fire. The most destructive type of forest fire. A fire that consumes the entire tree, including the crown.

Cyanosis. A disease characterized by a bluish discoloration of the skin. This is caused by the impaired effectiveness of hemoglobin in carrying oxygen. An infant that drinks water carrying too high a level of nitrates may undergo chemical changes of its hemoglobin that in turn will result in cyanosis of the skin.

Cyclic Population. A population that peaks and troughs at regular intervals. Good examples are the four-year cycle of the lemming and the ten-year cycle of the ruffed grouse.

Cyclone Filter. A type of air-pollution control device that removes particulate matter (dust) with the aid of gravity and a downward spiraling air stream.

Death Rate. The number of deaths per 1,000 individuals in a given year.

Demographic Transition. A change in a population that is characterized by decreasing birth and death rates. It usually occurs when a nation becomes industrialized.

Denitrification. The decomposition of ammonia compounds, nitrites and nitrates by bacteria that results in the eventual release of nitrogen into the atmosphere.

Density-Dependent Factor. A population-regulating factor, such as predation or infectious disease, whose effect on a population is dependent upon the population density.

Density-Independent Factor. A population-regulating factor such as storm, drought, flood, or volcanic eruption, whose effect is independent of population density.

Depletion Time. The time required until 80 percent of the available mineral supply is consumed.

Desalinization. The removal of salt from seawater in order to make it usable to humans, crops, and wildlife.

Desert Pavement. The stony surface of some deserts caused by excessive erosion of the thin topsoil resulting from occasionally heavy rainfall.

Deuterium. An isotope of hydrogen that may serve as fuel in nuclear fusion reactions.

Dioxin. An extremely toxic impurity occurring in the herbicide 2,4,5-T. In some areas it is suspected of causing birth defects and miscarriages.

Dust Dome. A shroud of dust particles characteristically found over urban areas. It is caused by the unique atmospheric circulation pattern that results from the marked temperature differences between the urban area and outlying farmlands.

Ecology. The study of the interrelationships that occur between organisms and their environment.

Ecosphere. The total area in which living organisms occur.

Ecosystem. A contraction for ecological system.

Edge. The interspersion of various habitat types; densities of game animals tend to be greater in areas that have a substantial amount of edge.

Electron. A negatively charged particle occurring in the orbit of an atom.

Electrostatic Precipitator. A pollution-control device that removes solid particles from smokestacks by providing them with a negative charge and then attracting them to a positively charged plate.

Elemental Cycle. The "circular" movement of an element (nitrogen, carbon) from the nonliving environment (air, water, soil) into the bodies of living organisms and then back into the nonliving environment.

Emphysema. A potentially lethal disease characterized by a reduction in the number of alveoli in the lungs as well as a reduction in total respiratory membrane area.

Environmental Resistance (ER). Any factor in the environment of an organism that tends to limit its numbers.

Epilimnion. The upper stratum of a lake that is characterized by a temperature gradient of less than 1° C per meter of depth.

Estrogen. The female sex hormone, produced by the egg follicle in the ovary, which is responsible for many female characteristics, such as development of the vagina, uterus, and oviducts, the growth of pubic and armpit hair, the widening of the hips, and the sexual urge.

Eugenicists. A dedicated group of people who would like to "improve" the quality of the human species by making sterilization mandatory for "inferior" individuals such as cripples, criminals, and the mentally retarded.

Euphotic Zone. The open-water zone of the ocean, characterized by sufficient sunlight penetration to support photosynthesis; located just above the bathyal zone.

Euryphagous. An organism having a highly varied diet, such as a pheasant or opossum, in contrast to an animal having a narrow or stenophagous diet, such as an ivory-billed woodpecker.

Eutrophication. The enrichment of an aquatic ecosystem with nutrients (nitrates, phosphates) that promote biological productivity (growth of algae and weeds).

Extended Economic Zone (EEZ). The 200-mile zone extending from the coastline, over which a nation has control over such commercial activities as fishing and mineral extraction.

Fabric Filter Baghouse. An air-pollution-control device that operates somewhat like a giant vacuum cleaner in removing solid particles from industrial smokestacks.

Fall Overturn. The thorough mixing of lake waters during autumn that occurs because water temperature and density are uniform from top to bottom.

Fenuron. A herbicide that has been used extensively to control rangeland pests such as the mesquite bush. Use of fenuron should be held to a minimum.

Fibrous Root System. A complex root system, such as that of grass plants, in which there are several major roots and a great number of primary, sec-ondary, and tertiary branches; useful in "binding" soil in place and preventing erosion.

Field Capacity. The amount of water that remains in the soil after the excess has drained away from soil that had been water saturated.

Fluorocarbons. A group of chemical compounds containing the elements carbon, chlorine, and fluorine. One group of these compounds manufactured by Dupont under the trade name Freons has been used in refrigerators, air conditioners, and aerosol spray bombs.

Fluorosis. A disease in animals caused by fluoride poisoning; symptoms in livestock include thickened bones and stiff joints.

Flyway. One of the major migration pathways used by waterfowl, for example, Atlantic Flyway and Pacific Flyway.

Food Chain. The flow of nutrients and energy from one organism to another by means of a series of eating processes.

Food Web. An interconnected series of food chains.

Freons. A group of fluorocarbon compounds manufactured by Dupont for use in refrigerators, air conditioners, and aerosol spray bombs. Unfortunately, Freons have contributed to the breakdown of the shield of ozone in the upper stratosphere that protects humans from ultraviolet radiation.

Furunculosis. A serious bacterial disease occurring in fish.

Gamma Radiation. An intense type of radiation, similar to X rays, that is easily capable of penetrating the human body.

Genetic Diversity. A term used to indicate a great variety of organisms (many different species) occupying a given area.

Genetic Shift Mechanism. A deterioration of the genes of a species of animal at very high population levels that results in higher mortality rates and ensures a reduction of the population.

Glassification. A method of disposing of radioactive waste, by concentrating it and enclosing it in solid ceramic bricks.

Glasphalt. A type of road surfacing material that employs crushed glass in its manufacture rather than sand; more durable than ordinary asphalt.

Greenhouse Effect. The warming influence caused by the increased concentration of carbon dioxide in the earth's atmosphere.

Green Manure. The bodies of green plants (alfalfa,

vetch, for example) that have been plowed under to increase soil fertility.

Green Revolution. The increased food-production capability made possible in recent years because of selective breeding, increased use of fertilizer, development of seed banks, and more intensive use of herbicides and insecticides.

Gross National Product (GNP). The sum total of expenditures by governments and individuals for goods, services, and investments.

Groundwater. Water that has infiltrated the ground, in contrast to runoff water, which flows over the ground surface.

Gully Reclamation. The mending of a gully by either physical methods (check dams of boulders or cement) or vegetational means (planting of rapidly growing shrubs on the slopes).

Gyptol. The sex attractant produced by the female gypsy moth, which serves to attract the male moth from considerable distances.

Habitat. The immediate environment in which an organism lives; it includes such components as cover, food, shelter, water, and breeding sites.

Hair Cells. Sensory cells in the inner ear (cochlea) that are concerned with the sensation of hearing.

Half-life. The time required for one half of the radioactivity of a given radioactive isotope (uranium, strontium) to be dissipated.

Hardwood. A species of tree, such as oak, hickory, and maple, that has relatively hard wood in contrast to the soft woods of the conifers such as spruce and pine; synonymous with deciduous.

Heartwood. The dark central portion of a tree trunk characterized by the presence of dead xylem cells that have become filled with gums and resins.

Heat Island. The tendency for the atmosphere of a city to be warmer than the air in the surrounding farmlands. This is partly the result of the greater number of heat-generating sources (autos, factories, human bodies) in the city.

Home Range. The total area occupied by an animal during its life cycle — that is, the area required for feeding, breeding, loafing, and securing refuge from the weather and from predators.

Horizon. One of the horizontal layers (A, B, C, and D) visible in a cross section of soil.

Hybrid. The offspring that results from a cross of two different species or strains of animals or plants; for example, the Santa Gertrudis cattle re-

sulted from a series of crosses involving two parental types, the Brahmin cattle and the shorthorn.

Hybrid Car. A car that can be powered either by gasoline or by electricity.

Hydraulic Mining. A mining technique used to extract gold and silver in which a powerful stream of water is directed against the face of the rock containing the minerals.

Hydrocoele. A type of radiation-induced birth defect characterized by the accumulation of fluid around the testes.

Hydrologic Cycle. The circular movement of water from the ocean reservoir to the air (clouds), to the earth in the form of rain and snow, and finally back to the ocean reservoir via streams and estuaries.

Hydrolysis. A type of chemical reaction in which a compound is broken down into simpler components by the action of water.

Hydroponics. The technique of growing crops in an aqueous nutrient solution without soil.

Hydroseeder. A machine employed to disperse grass seed, water, and fertilizer on steep banks.

Hypolimnion. The bottom layer of water in a lake characterized by a temperature gradient of less than 1° C per meter of depth.

Incendiary. A person who maliciously starts a forest fire.

Industrial Fixation. The "fixing" of nitrogen (in other words, combining it with hydrogen to form ammonia) by industrial means rather than by natural methods such as bacterial action.

Integrated Pest Control. A method of pest control that judiciously employs chemical, biological, and other methods (cultural), depending on the specific problem; the use of chemicals is minimized to avoid environmental damage.

Intercropping. A cultural method of pest control in which the farmer intermixes a number of different crops in a small area instead of devoting the entire area to a single crop.

Introduction. The bringing in of an exotic plant or animal to a new region — for example, the introduction of the European carp into the United States and of the coho salmon from the Pacific Coast to Lake Michigan.

Invader. A term employed in rangeland management that refers to establishing a pioneer species of plant, usually a noxious weed, in an overgrazed pasture.

Irruption. A sudden increase in the population of an organism that is followed by a precipitous decline (crash); frequently the carrying capacity of the habitat is reduced for many years thereafter — for example, the Kaibab deer irruption.

Isotope. A form of an element identical to the regular element except for a difference in atomic weight. Thus, deuterium is an isotope of hydrogen.

Juvenile Dispersal. The dispersal of young animals (bald eagles, ruffed grouse, muskrats) from the general region of their hatching or birth site; the presumed function is to prevent overpopulation in the parental area.

Kepone. A highly toxic insecticide manufactured by a company in Hopewell, Virginia. As a result of carelessness the chemical was allowed to contaminate the James River and destroy much aquatic life.

Kerogen. The solid organic material that contains shale oil.

Krill. The crustaceans and other small marine organisms that are used as food by the baleen whales.

Landfill. A method of solid waste disposal in which the waste is dumped, compacted, and then covered with a layer of soil.

Lasky's Principle. The principle that, in many mineral deposits in which there is a gradual decrease in the richness of the ore with depth, the tonnage of the ore increases at an exponential rate.

Latitudinal Migration. The north-south migration characteristic of caribou, gray whale, and waterfowl.

Levee. A dike composed of earth, stone, or concrete that is erected along the margin of a river for purposes of flood control.

Limiting Factors. Any factor in the environment of an organism, such as radiation, excessive heat, floods, drought, disease, or lack of micronutrients, that tends to reduce the population of that organism.

Limnetic Zone. The region of open water in a lake, beyond the littoral zone, down to the maximal depth at which there is sufficient sunlight for photosynthesis.

Littoral Zone. The shallow, marginal region of a lake characterized by rooted vegetation.

Loam. The most desirable type of soil from an agricultural viewpoint; composed of a mixture of sand, silt, and clay.

Macronutrient. Mineral nutrient used by organisms in relatively large quantities (calcium, nitrogen, potassium, phosphorus).

Macropores. A large space that occurs between the individual soil particles.

Malthusian Overpopulation. The type of overpopulation described by Robert Malthus; it results in an overtaxing of available food supplies and eventual massive starvation.

Mass Emigration. The mass movement of a given species from an area. For example, the mass movement of the snowy owl from the tundra to the United States during periods of lemming scarcity.

Mass Number. The mass number of an element is based on the total number of protons and neutrons present in the nucleus of the atom.

Maximization. The most efficient use of a resource that is possible with current technology. Waste is minimized.

Metabolic Reserve. The lower 50 percent of a grass shoot that is required by a grazed plant for survival; contains the minimum amount of photosynthetic equipment needed for food-production purposes.

Microcephaly. A birth defect characterized by an abnormally small brain; associated with mental retardation; may be induced by radiation.

Microhabitat. The immediate, localized environment of an organism.

Micronutrient. A mineral nutrient required by organisms in only minute quantities (iodine, zinc, copper, iron).

Millirem. One thousandth of a *rem*, which is a unit for measuring the effect of radiation on the body of a living organism.

Mollisols. The order of soils developing under a prairie type of vegetation, characterized by a fertile, thick, blackish-brown topsoil.

Monotype. An agricultural or forest planting composed of only one species.

Mulch. Dead plant material that accumulates on the ground surface; a reliable indicator of range condition.

Mycelia. The branching "root system" of a fungus.

Mycorrhiza. An intimate relationship between the root systems of trees and soil fungi.

Myxomatosis Virus. The virus that was used to

control the rabbit outbreak in Australia; animals become infected when they consume contaminated forage.

Natural Resource. Any component of the natural environment, such as soil, water, rangeland, forest, wildlife, minerals, that humans can use to promote their welfare.

Nematode. An extremely abundant and ubiquitous type of worm (roundworm) that occurs in soil, water, and the bodies of plants and animals; some are free-living, others are parasitic.

Neomalthusian Overpopulation. The type of overpopulation that results in massive pollution and resource exhaustion because of the high technological level maintained by the population. People die because of toxic contamination of the environment rather than because of food shortages.

Neritic Zone. The relatively warm, nutrient-rich, shallow water zone of the ocean that overlies the continental shelf; valuable in terms of fish production.

Net Production. The total energy incorporated into the body of a plant as a result of photosynthesis minus the energy required for respiration.

Neutron. The electrically neutral particle in the nucleus of an atom.

Nitrate Bacteria. Bacteria that have the ability to convert nitrites into nitrates; essential bacteria in the cycling of nitrogen.

Nitrogen Stripping. A technique employed in tertiary sewage treatment plants in which air is forced through wastewater and strips ammonia gas (NH_3) from the water.

Nonbiodegradable Material. Material not susceptible to decomposition by bacteria. For example, DDT and other chlorinated hydrocarbon pesticides would be relatively nonbiodegradable.

North American Water and Power Alliance (NAWAPA). Scheme for transferring water from the water-rich, lowly populous areas of northwestern Canada to the water-deficient areas of the United States and Mexico.

Nuclear Fusion. The generation of energy by causing the fusion of the nuclei of two atoms of a very light element such as hydrogen under temperatures of around 40 million°C.

Oak Wilt. A fungus-caused disease that has threatened extensive oak forests in the southern Appalachians and the upper Mississippi valley.

Ocean Thermal Energy Conversion. A method of using the temperature differential between different levels of the ocean to alternately gasify and condense a working fluid such as ammonia and in this way propel a turbine for the purpose of electrical power production.

Oligotrophic Lake. A nutrient-poor lake occurring in the northern states and in high mountain areas, characterized by great depth, sandy or gravelly bottom, sparse amount of rooted vegetation, low production of plankton and fish; for example, Lake Superior, Finger Lakes of New York.

Organic Phosphorus Pesticides. A group of pesticides (malathion and parathion, for example) that are lethal to insects because they reduce the supply of cholinesterase at the junction (synapse) between two nerve cells in a nerve cell chain.

Oxidation. The chemical union of oxygen with metals (iron, aluminum) or organic compounds (sugars); the former process is an important factor in soil formation; the latter process permits the release of energy from cellular fuels (sugars, fats).

Oyster Watch. A well-coordinated program employed along our coast that involves the use of oysters as biological monitors of marine pollutants.

Ozone. A gaseous component of the atmosphere; normally occurs at elevations of about 20 miles; important to humans because it shields us from the ultraviolet radiation of the sun; also represents one of the products resulting from the action of sunlight on the hydrocarbons emitted from the internal combustion engine.

Particulate Matter. Minute solid and liquid particles in the atmosphere (soot).

Phloem. The elongate food-conducting cells of the trunk and branches of a tree; these cells convey food from the leaves downward to the root system.

Photochemical Smog. The type of smog that has plagued Los Angeles and other California towns, as well as other areas in the United States; formed as a result of the action of sunlight on the hydrocarbon emissions from motor cars and other sources; at nightfall the production of this type of smog ceases.

Photolysis. A phase of photosynthesis in which solar energy splits water molecules into hydrogen and oxygen.

Photosynthesis. The process occurring in green

plants by which solar energy is utilized in the conversion of carbon dioxide and water into sugar.

Phreatophyte. A type of plant, such as cattail, willow, and saltcedar, that uses unusually large quantities of water to the disadvantage of more desirable species of plants such as range grasses.

Phytoactin. A type of antibiotic that has been used successfully to control the blister rust disease in western white pine.

Phytoplankton. Minute plants, such as algae, living in lakes, streams, and oceans, that are passively transported by water currents or wave action.

Pioneer Community. The initial community in an ecological succession; such a community (weeds, lichens) is frequently capable of surviving under severe conditions such as drought, extreme heat, or cold.

Plankton. Tiny plants (algae) and animals (protozoa, small crustaceans, fish embryos, insect larvae) that live in aquatic ecosystems and are moved about by water currents and wave action.

Point Pollution. Pollution that is discharged from an extremely restricted area or "point," such as the discharge of sulfur dioxide from a smokestack or the discharge of carbon monoxide from the exhaust pipe of a motor car. This contrasts with nonpoint pollution, such as the runoff from a farm or urban area.

Population. The total number of individuals of a species occurring in a given area; for example, the population of deer in a cedar swamp, the population of black bass in a lake.

Prescribed Burning. A type of surface burning (used by foresters, wildlife biologists, and ranchers) in which the utmost precaution is taken in terms of dryness of fuel, wind velocity, and relative humidity; prescribed burning attempts to improve the quality of forest, range, or wildlife habitat.

Primary Production. The total chemical energy produced by photosynthesis; on a global basis it amounts to about 270 billion tons annually.

Primary Succession. An ecological succession that develops in an area not previously occupied by a community; for example, a succession that develops on a granite outcrop or on lava.

Primary Sewage Treatment. A rudimentary sewage treatment that removes a substantial amount of the settleable solids and about 90 percent of the biological oxygen demand (BOD).

Producer. A plant that can carry on photosynthesis and thus produce food for itself and indirectly for other organisms in the food chain of which it is a part.

Profundal Zone. The bottom zone of a lake, which extends from the lake bottom upward to the limnetic zone; characterized by insufficient sunlight for photosynthesis.

Progesterone. A hormone produced by the corpus luteum of the ovary, which is responsible for preparing the uterus to receive the fertilized egg.

Proton. A positively charged particle in the nucleus of an atom.

Purse Seine. A seine used by commercial fishermen that closes to entrap fish somewhat as a drawstring purse closes to "trap" money.

Pyramid of Energy. The graphic expression of the second law of thermodynamics as applied to the energy transfer in food chains — a certain amount of energy is lost in the form of heat as it moves through the links of a food chain, the greatest amount being present in the basal link (producer) and the least amount being present in the terminal link (carnivore).

Pyramid of Biomass. The graphic expression of the fact that there is a progressive reduction in total biomass (protoplasm) with each successive level in a food chain.

Pyramid of Numbers. The graphic expression of the fact that the number of individuals in a given food chain is greatest at the producer level, less at the herbivore level, and least at the carnivore level.

Pyrolysis. The destructive distillation of solid waste.

Quadrillion. The number 1 followed by 15 zeros.

Quercitin. A substance derived from tree bark that is useful in checking bleeding.

Rad. A unit devised to measure the amount of radiation absorbed by living tissue; a rad is 100 ergs (unit of energy) absorbed by one gram of tissue; about 1 roentgen, which is about the amount of radioactivity received from a single dental X ray.

Range of Tolerance. The tolerance range of a species for certain factors in its environment such as moisture, temperature, radiation, micronutrients, and oxygen.

Resource Conservation and Recovery Act (RCRA). Under terms of this act the EPA was given full authority to control pollution by solid waste just as it had authority for controlling air and water pollution.

Rem. A unit of absorbed radiation dose taking into account the relative biological effect of various types of radiation; about 1 roentgen, which is roughly the amount of radiation received from a single dental X ray.

Respiration. The process by means of which cellular fuels are burned with the aid of oxygen to permit the release of the energy required to sustain life; during respiration oxygen is used up and carbon dioxide is given off.

Rhizobium. One of a genus of nitrogen-fixing bacteria that lives in the root nodules of legumes (alfalfa, clover).

Rhizome. An underground stem; occurs in grasses; permits vegetative reproduction because the tip of the rhizome may develop a bud that can develop into a new plant.

Rhizosphere. The soil in the immediate vicinity of a plant root system.

Rotenone. A poisonous substance derived from the roots of an Asiatic legume; has been extensively used to control rough fish populations.

Rough Fish. Undesirable trash fish such as garpike and carp.

Runoff Water. The water that flows over the land surface after rainfall or snowmelt and eventually forms streams, lakes, and marshes.

Salinization. An adverse aftereffect of irrigating land that has poor drainage properties; as a result, especially in the arid western states, evaporation of the salty water leaves a salt accumulation on the land, which renders the soil unsuitable for crop production.

Saltwater Intrusion. The contamination of freshwater aquifers with salt water as the result of excessive exploitation of those aquifers in coastal regions near the ocean.

Sapwood. The lighter, moist, more porous layer of xylem tissue immediately ensheathing the heartwood; composed of water and nutrient-transporting xylem cells.

Secondary Sewage Treatment. An advanced type of sewage treatment that involves both mechanical and biological (bacterial action) phases; although superior to primary treatment, much of the phosphates and nitrates remain in the effluent.

Secondary Succession. An ecological succession that occurs in an area that had at one time already supported living organisms; for example, a succession developing in a burned-over forest or in an abandoned field.

Septic Tank. A part of a rudimentary type of sewage treatment system used commonly by families who are located in rural areas; the sewage flows into the subterranean septic tank and is gradually decomposed by bacterial action.

Shade-Tolerant Plants. A species of plant, such as the sugar maple, that reproduces well under conditions of reduced light intensity.

Sheet Irrigation. A type of irrigation in which water flows slowly over the land in the form of a "sheet."

Shelter Belt. Rows of trees and shrubs arranged at right angles to the prevalent wind for the purpose of diminishing the desiccating and eroding effects of the wind on crop and range land; commonly employed in the Great Plains.

Sigmoid Growth Curve. The S-shaped curve commonly followed by the population of an animal (deer, grouse, rabbit) when it has been newly introduced into a habitat with good carrying capacity.

Siltation. The filling up of a stream or reservoir with water-borne sediment.

Slash-and-Burn Agriculture. A type of agriculture maintained by natives of tropical rain-forest regions in which a patch of forest is cut and burned, crops are grown in the clearing for a few years until the fertility of the soil is exhausted, and then the area is deserted because the farmers move to another part of the forest to repeat the process.

Softwood. A species of tree such as spruce, pine, and fir, that has softer wood than hardwoods such as oak and hickory; usually synonymous with conifer.

Soil Fire. A slowly burning fire that consumes the organic material in the earth; characterized by little flame but considerable smoke.

Soil Profile. A cross-sectional view of a particular soil type in which the characteristic layers or horizons are well represented.

Soil Structure. The arrangement or grouping of the soil's primary particles into granules or aggregates; a soil with good structure has a spongy or crumbly quality with an abundance of pores through which water and oxygen can move.

Soil Texture. The size of the individual soil particles; the four textural categories ranging from the smallest to the largest sized particles are clay, silt, sand, and gravel.

Solar Cell. A platelike device composed of two layers of silicon that converts solar energy directly into electricity.

Solar Energy. The radiant energy generated by the sun that "powers" all energy-consuming processes on earth, whether biological or nonbiological.

Spodosols. An order of soils that develops under coniferous forest cover. This soil is relatively acid and infertile.

Spoil Bank. The mounds of overburden that accumulate during a strip-mining operation; unless properly limed and then vegetated, these spoil banks may be an important source of acid mine drainage and erosion.

Spring Overturn. The complete top-to-bottom mixing of water in a lake during the spring of the year when all the water is of about the same temperature and density.

Stamen. The club-shaped, pollen-producing part of a flower.

Stenophagous. Having a very specialized diet; for example, the ivory-billed woodpecker, which consumes beetle larvae secured only from recently dead trees, or the Everglade kite, which feeds almost exclusively on the snail *Pomacea caliginosa*.

Sterilization. A method of human population control involving the cutting and tying of the sperm ducts in the male and the oviducts (egg tubes) in the female.

Strategic Minerals. Minerals that are essential to the economic well-being and/or security of a nation.

Strip-Cropping. An agricultural practice in which an open row crop (potatoes, corn, cotton) is alternated with a cover crop (alfalfa, clover) to minimize soil erosion.

Strip-Mining. The type of mining in which coal or iron, for example, is scooped from the earth by giant earth-moving machines; the results are frequently a badly scarred landscape, soil erosion, and acid mine drainage.

Subsidence. Land collapse resulting from mining underground water reservoirs (aquifers).

Superfund Act (CERCLA). The act that provided a fund to the EPA for the purpose of cleaning up extremely hazardous waste sites.

Surface Fire. A type of forest fire that moves along the surface of the forest floor; it consumes litter, herbs, shrubs, and seedlings.

Surface Mining Control and Reclamation Act. Under terms of this act, which became effective in 1979, mining companies must restore a strip-mined area to its original condition, within the limits of available technology.

Succession. The replacement of one community by another in an orderly and predictable manner. The succession begins with a pioneer community and terminates with a climax community.

Sustained Yield. The concept that a forest or wildlife resource can be managed in such a way that a modest crop can be harvested year after year without depletion of the resource as long as annual decrements are counterbalanced by annual growth increments.

Synergistic Effect. A condition in which the toxic effect of two or more pollutants (copper, zinc, heat) is much greater than the sum of the effects of the pollutants when operating individually.

Taiga. The northern coniferous forest biome, which is typically composed of spruce, fir, and pine.

Tannin. A substance derived from tree bark that is employed in tanning leather.

Taproot. The type of root system characterized by one large main root; for example, that of a beet or carrot.

Telemetry. The electronic technique involving a transmitter-receiver system in which the movements and behavior of animals (deer, elk, grizzly bear, salmon) are monitored from a distance.

Terracing. A soil-conservation technique in which steep slopes are converted into a series of broad-based "steps"; the velocity of runoff water is thus retarded and soil erosion is arrested.

Territory. An area that is defended by a member of one species against other members of that same species.

Tertiary Sewage Treatment. The most advanced type of sewage treatment, which not only removes the BOD and the solids, but also the phosphates and nitrates; the installation of such a plant at Lake Tahoe has arrested eutrophication of the lake.

Thermal Inversion. An abnormal temperature stratification of the lower atmosphere in which a layer of warm air overlies a layer of cooler air.

Such an inversion frequently occurs at heights from 100 to 3,000 feet, resulting in stagnation of the air mass below the inversion; it contributes to air-pollution problems, especially in industrial areas.

Thermocline. The middle layer of water in a lake in summer characterized by a temperature gradient of more than 1° C per meter of depth.

Throughput. An economics term that relates to the amount of materials being produced and consumed in a given society.

Toxic Substances Control Act (TOSCA). This act makes it mandatory for a company to notify the EPA 90 days in advance of its intention to manufacture a new chemical. If the EPA concluded that the chemical may be harmful to human health or may be environmentally destructive, the EPA would not give the company permission to produce the chemical.

Transpiration. The evaporation of water from the breathing pores of a plant leaf.

Tritium. An isotope of hydrogen. A potential fuel for a nuclear fusion reactor.

Tundra. The type of biome occurring in northern Canada and Eurasia north of the timberline. It is characterized by fewer than 10 inches of annual rainfall, subzero weather in winter, a low-lying vegetation composed of grasses, dwarf willows, and lichens, and a fauna consisting of lemmings, Arctic foxes, Arctic wolves, caribou, and snowy owls, among other species. The growing season lasts only six to seven weeks.

2,4-D. A herbicide that kills a weed because it mimics the plant's growth hormones, causing more rapid growth than can be sustained by its supply of oxygen and food materials.

2,4,5-T. A herbicide that operates on the same principle as 2,4-D. It kills a weed because it mimics the plant's growth hormones, causing more rapid growth than can be sustained by its supply of food, moisture, and oxygen.

Upwelling. The movement of nutrient-rich cold water from the ocean bottom to higher levels by means of vertically moving currents.

Vessel Element. The elongate xylem cell in a tree trunk or branch that has water transportation as a major function.

Watershed. The total area drained by a particular stream; may range from a few square miles in the case of a small stream to thousands of square miles in the case of the Mississippi River.

Water Table. The upper level of water-saturated ground.

Wet Scrubber. An air-pollution control device that washes contaminants from the outgoing air stream by means of a water spray.

Xerophytes. Specialized plants that are well adapted to survive in arid regions because of such water-conserving features as reduced leaves, recessed stomata, thick cuticles, accelerated life cycles, periodic dormancy and the presence of water-storing (succulent) tissues.

Xylem. A type of tissue occurring in the trunks and branches of trees (and other plants) that serves to transport water and nutrients from the roots to the leaves and also provides support.

Zone of Deposition. Refers to the B horizon, or subsoil, which receives and accumulates the soluble salts and organic matter carried downward from the A horizon by percolating water.

Zone of Leaching. Refers to the A horizon, or topsoil, because many soluble salts are carried downward or leached from this horizon to the B horizon below it.

Zooplankton. Minute animals (protozoans, crustaceans, fish embryos, insect larvae) that live in a lake, stream, or ocean and are moved aimlessly by water currents and wave action.

639

ILLUSTRATION ACKNOWLEDGMENTS

1-1. National Aeronautics and Space Administration photo by Astronaut Eugene A. Cernan

1-2. U.S. National Park Service

1-4. New York State Department of Health photo by M. Dixon

1-5. Environmental Protection Administration —Documerica photo by Marc St. Gill

1-6 and 1-7. After David Van Vleck, *The Crucial Generation* (Charlotte, Vt.: Optimum Population Inc., 1971). Original source: Donella E. Meadows et al., *The Limits to Growth* (New York: Universe Books, 1974, graphics by Potomac Associates.)

1-8. Modified after. Van Vleck, *op. cit.*

1-9. U.S. Department of Agriculture

1-10. Tennessee Valley Authority

2-3. After Amos Turk, Jonathan Turk, and Janet T. Wittes, *Ecology, Pollution, and Environment* (Philadelphia: Saunders, 1972)

2-6. U.S. Department of Agriculture, Soil Conservation Service photo by Morrison W. Liston

2-24. Eugene P. Odum, *Fundamentals of Ecology* (Philadelphia: W. B. Saunders, 1959)

2-26. U.S. Fish and Wildlife Service photo by V. B. Scheffer

2-27. U.S. Fish and Wildlife Service photo by Paul Adams

2-28. U.S. Fish and Wildlife Service photo by J. Malcolm Greany

2-29. U.S. Department of Agriculture, Soil Conservation Service

2-30. U.S. Fish and Wildlife Service photo by E. P. Haddon

2-32. U.S. Department of Agriculture

2-33. U.S. Fish and Wildlife Service photo by W. P. Taylor.

3-4. U.S. Bureau of the Census

3-8. After P. Walton Purdom and Stanley H. Anderson, *Environmental Science*, 2nd ed. (Columbus, Ohio: Merrill, 1983)

3-10. U.S. Bureau of the Census

3-12. World Food Programme

3-13. U.N. Food and Agriculture Organization

4-2. From Paul R. Ehrlich, Anne H. Ehrlich, and John P. Holdren, *Ecoscience, Population, Resources, Environment* (San Francisco: Freeman, 1977)

4-3. U.S. Forest Service

4-4. U.S. Department of Agriculture, Soil Conservation Service

4-5. Nyle C. Brady, *The Nature and Properties of Soils*, 8th ed. (New York: Macmillan, 1974)

4-9. W. B. Clapham, Jr., *Human Ecosystems* (New York: Macmillan, 1981).

4-10. After David Greenland, *Guidelines for Modern Resource Management* (Columbus, Ohio: Merrill, 1983)

4-11. From Clapham, *op. cit.*

4–12 and 4–13. U.S. Department of Agriculture

4–14. Adapted from Raymond F. Dasmann, *Environmental Conservation* (New York: Wiley, 1968)

4–17. U.S. Department of Agriculture, Soil Conservation Service

5–1. U.S. Department of Agriculture

5–3. U.S. Department of Agriculture, Soil Conservation Service

5–4. From Rice Odell, *Environmental Awakening* (Cambridge, Mass.: Ballenger, 1980)

5–5. U.S. Department of Agriculture, Soil Conservation Service

5–6. From Dasmann, *op. cit.*

5–7. U.S. Department of Agriculture, Soil Conservation Service photo by B. C. McLean)

5–8. From U.S. Department of Agriculture, *America's Soil Water: Conditions and Trends* (Washington, D.C.: U.S. Government Printing Office, 1981)

5–9 and 5–10. U.S. Department of Agriculture, Soil Conservation Service

5–12. U.S. Department of Agriculture: *Soil and Water Resources Conservation Act: 1980 —Appraisal, Part One* (Washington, D.C.: U.S. Government Printing Office)

5–13. U.S. Department of Agriculture

5–15. From Allen and Leonard, *Conserving Natural Resources* (New York: McGraw-Hill, 1966. Copyright © 1966 by McGraw-Hill, Inc. Used by permission of McGraw-Hill Book Company)

5–16, 5–17, and 5–18. U.S. Department of Agriculture, Soil Conservation Service

5–19. From U.S. Department of Agriculture, *America's Soil and Water*

5–20, 5–21, and 5–22. U.S. Department of Agriculture, Soil Conservation Service

5–24. U.S. Department of Agriculture, Soil Conservation Service

5–25. U.S. Department of Agriculture

5–26. U.S. Department of Agriculture, Soil Conservation Service photo by Erwin W. Cole

5–27. U.S. Department of Agriculture, Soil Conservation Service photo by Fred Fortney

5–28. U.S. Department of Agriculture, *Soil and Water Resources Conservation Act: 1980 —Reappraisal, Part One*

6–1. Paul R. Ehrlich and Anne H. Ehrlich, *Population, Resources, and the Environment* (San Francisco: Freeman, 1970)

6–3. U.S. Department of Agriculture

6–4 and 6–5. U.N. Food and Agriculture Organization photos by P. Pitter

6–7 and 6–8. U.N. Food and Agriculture Organization

6–9. Adapted from Guy-Harold Smith, *Conservation of Natural Resources* (New York: Wiley, 1965)

6–10. Courtesy Carolina Biological Supply Company

6–11. U.S. Department of Agriculture

6–12. U.N. Food and Agriculture Organization photo by G. Tortoli

6–13. U.S. Department of Agriculture Photo by Murray Lemmon

6–14 and 6–15. U.S. Department of Agriculture

6–16. World Food Programme photo by Peyton Johnson

6–17. U.N. Food and Agriculture Organization photo by D. Mason

6–18. U.N. Food and Agriculture Organization photo by H. Null

6–19. U.N. Food and Agriculture Organization

6–20. National Aeronautics and Space Administration

7–1. From Ben Osborn and Phoebe Harrison, *Water . . . and the Land* (Washington, D.C.: U.S. Department of Agriculture, Soil Conservation Service, SCS-TP-147, July, 1965)

7–2. U.S. Forest Service

7–3. After Purdom and Anderson, *op. cit.*

7–4. From U.S. Department of Agriculture, *Soil and Water Resources Conservation Act: 1980—Appraisal, Part One* (Washington, D.C.: U.S. Government Printing Office, 1981)

7–5. U.S. Department of Agriculture

7–7. California Department of Water Resources

7–10. Edwin G. Gutentag and John B. Weeks, "Water Table in the High Plains Aquifer in 1978 in Parts of Colorado, Kansas, Nebraska, New Mexico, Oklahoma, South Dakota, Texas and Wyoming," *Hydrologic Investigations Atlas* HA-642 (Reston, VA.: U.S. Geological Survey, 1980)

7–11. From U.S. Department of Agriculture, *Soil and Water Resources Conservation Act: 1980—Appraisal, Part One* (Washington, D.C.: U.S. Government Printing Office, 1981)

7–12. National Aeronautics and Space Administration

7–13. U.S. Department of Agriculture photo by *Harrison Daily Times*

7–14. U.S. Department of Agriculture, *America's Soil and Water*

7–15. U.S. Department of Agriculture photo by Frank M. Roadman

7–17. Bureau of Reclamation photo by E. E. Hertzog

7–18. From U.S. Department of Agriculture, *Soil and Water Resources Conservation Act 1980—Appraisal, Part One.* (Washington, D.C.: U.S. Government Printing Office, 1981)

7–19. U.S. Department of Agriculture, Soil Conservation Service photo by John McConnell

7–20. U.S. Department of the Interior, Bureau of Reclamation photo by Glade Walker

7–21. Photo by A. G. D'Alessandro

7–22. Bureau of Reclamation photo by E. E. Hertzog

7–23. From *Soil and Water Resources Conservation Act: 1980—Appraisal, Part One* (Washington, D.C.: U.S. Government Printing Office)

7–24. Arthur F. Pillsbury, "The Salinity of Rivers," *Scientific American,* July 1981

7–25. Bureau of Reclamation

7–26 and 7–27. California Department of Water Resources

7–28 and 7–29. Bureau of Reclamation photos by E. E. Hertzog

7–30. From *Soil and Water Resources Conservation Act: 1980—Appraisal, Part One.* Washington, D.C.: U.S. Government Printing Office, 1981.

7–31. From *The New York Times,* May 12, 1981.

7–32. Harold Dregne, "Desertification of Arid Lands," *Economic Geography,* **53** (1977) 325

7–34 and 7–35. California Department of Water Resources

8–1. Hammond, Indiana, *Times*

8–2. J. Edwin Becht and L. D. Belzung, *World Resource Management* (Englewood Cliffs, N.J.: Prentice-Hall, 1975; adapted from American Geographical Society)

8–3. Environmental Protection Administration —Documerica photo by Belinda Rain

8–5. U.S. Department of Agriculture, *America's Soil and Water: Condition and Trends* (Washington, D.C.: U.S. Government Printing Office, 1981)

8–7. U.S. Department of Agriculture

8–8. Environmental Protection Administration —Documerica photo by Gene Daniels

8–9. U.S. Department of Agriculture, Soil Conservation Service photo by Erwin W. Cole

8–10. U.S. Department of Agriculture

8–11. Wisconsin Natural Resources Department, Madison

8–12. After James M. Moran, Michael D. Morgan, and James H. Wiersma, *An Introduction to Environmental Sciences* (Boston: Little, Brown, 1973. Copyright © 1973 by Little, Brown and Company)

8–13 and 8–14. Penelope Revelle and Charles Revelle, *The Environment: Issues and Choices for Society* (New York: Van Nostrand, 1981)

8–16. Top, center, and bottom photos courtesy Carolina Biological Supply Company

8–17 and 8–18. Pennsylvania Power and Light

8–19. After Revelle and Revelle, *op. cit.*

8–20. Council on Environmental Quality, *Environmental Quality,* 1977

8–21. U.S. Environmental Protection Agency, Office of Water Supply and Solid Waste Management Programs, *Waste Disposal Practices and Their Effects on Ground Water: Executive Summary* (Washington, D.C.: U.S. Government Printing Office, 1977, p. 8)

8–22. U.S. Department of Agriculture, Soil Conservation Service

8–25. After Revelle and Revelle, *op. cit.*

8–26. New York State Department of Health

8–28. From Environmental Protection Agency, *A Primer on Wastewater Treatment* (Washington, D.C.: U.S. Government Printing Office, 1976)

8–29. Bureau of Reclamation

8–30 and 8–31. After Revelle and Revelle, *op. cit.*

643

8–32. Environmental Protection Administration photo by Belinda Rain

8–33. After Revelle and Revelle, *op. cit.*

8–34. Soil Conservation Service, *Soils and Septic Tanks*, Agriculture Information Bulletin No. 349 (Washington, D.C.: U.S. Government Printing Office, 1978)

9–1. Wisconsin Natural Resources Department, Madison

9–2. Adapted from Robert L. Smith, *Ecology and Field Biology* (New York: Harper & Row, 1966; used by permission of the publishers)

9–3. From G. E. Hutchinson, *A Treatise on Limnology* (New York: Wiley, 1967)

9–4, 9–5, and 9–6. Adapted from Robert L. Smith, *op. cit.*

9–7. New York State Conservation Department photo by Nick Drahos

9–8. Data from G. W. Burton and E. P. Odum, "The Distribution of Stream Fish in the Vicinity of Mountain Lake, Virginia," *Ecology*, 26:182–193)

9–10, 9–11, and 9–12. From Environmental Protection Administration, *Fish Kills Caused by Pollution in 1975* (Washington, D.C.: U.S. Government Printing Office, 1976)

9–13. Michigan Department of Natural Resources

9–14. U.S. Department of Agriculture

9–15. U.S. Atomic Energy Commission (now Nuclear Regulatory Commission)

9–16. From Environmental Protection Agency, *Environmental Midwest* (Washington, D.C.: U.S. Government Printing Office, 1978)

9–17. Wisconsin Natural Resources Department, Madison

9–18. From Environmental Protection Administration, *Clean Lakes and Us* (Washington, D.C.: U.S. Government Printing Office, 1979)

9–20. California Department of Water Resources

9–21. U.S. Department of the Interior

9–22. Bureau of Reclamation photo by F. K. Noonan

9–23. From Howard E. Snow, "The Constant Northern," *Wisconsin Conservation Bulletin*, May–June 1973, Wisconsin Department of Natural Resources

9–24. From George W. Bennett, *Management of Lakes and Ponds* (New York: Van Nostrand, 1971)

9–25. Michigan Department of Natural Resources

9–26. U.S. Fish and Wildlife Service

9–27. California Department of Water Resources

9–28. U.S. Department of the Interior

9–29. Wisconsin Natural Resources Department, Madison

9–30. U.S. Department of Agriculture, Soil Conservation Service

9–31. J. Michael Migel, *The Stream Conservation Handbook* (New York: Crown Publishers, 1974)

9–32 and 9–33. Wisconsin Natural Resources Department, Madison

9–34. U.S. Fish and Wildlife Service

9–35. From "Grass Carp Threatens Wisconsin," *Wisconsin Conservation Bulletin*, May–June 1975, p. 23, Wisconsin Natural Resources Department

9–37. New York State Conservation Department photo by Nick Drahos

9–38. Adapted from Karl F. Lagler, *Freshwater Fishery Biology* (Dubuque, Iowa: William C. Brown Company, Publishers, 1956)

9–39. From Agricultural Extension Service, *Proceedings of the Upper Midwest Trout Symposium*, I and II, University of Minnesota, St. Paul, Minn., 1978)

9–40. From K. D. Karlander, *Journal of the Fisheries Research Board of Canada*, Vol. 12, No. 4, 1955

9–41. Courtesy Carolina Biological Supply Company

9–42. Michigan Department of Natural Resources

9–43. U.S. Fish and Wildlife Service

9–44. New York State Conservation Department photo by Chuck McNulty

9–45. New York State Conservation Department

9–46. U.S. Environmental Protection Agency

9–47. U.S. Department of Agriculture, Soil Conservation Service

10–2. From Environmental Protection Agency, *Research Summary: Chesapeake Bay* (Washington, D.C.: U.S. Government Printing Office, May 1980)

10-3. From George L. Clarke, *Elements of Ecology* (New York: Wiley, 1954)

10-4A. Adapted from Eugene P. Odum, *Fundamentals of Ecology* (Philadelphia: Saunders, 1959)

10-4B. From Revelle and Revelle, *op. cit.* Adapted from John D. Isaacs, "The Nature of Oceanic Life," *Scientific American*, September 1969

10-5. University of California, Scripps Institute of Oceanography

10-6. California Department of Water Resources

10-7. National Aeronautics and Space Administration

10-8, 10-9, and 10-10. From Environmental Protection Agency, *Research Summary: Chesapeake Bay* (Washington, D.C.: U.S. Government Printing Office, May 1980)

10-11. From U.S. Department of Commerce, *U.S. Ocean Policy in the 1970s: Statutes and Issues* (Washington, D.C.: U.S. Government Printing Office, 1978)

10-12. From Environmental Protection Agency, *Research Outlook 1978* (Washington, D.C.: U.S. Government Printing Office, 1978)

10-13. From Environmental Protection Agency, *Research Summary: Oil Spills* (Washington, D.C.: U.S. Government Printing Office, February 1979)

10-14. National Oceanic and Atmospheric Administration

10-15. From Environmental Protection Agency, *Research Summary: Oil Spills* (Washington, D.C.: U.S. Government Printing Office, February 1979)

10-16. Environmental Protection Agency

10-17. Phillips Petroleum Company

10-18. Environmental Protection Agency photo by Dick Smith

10-19. Official U.S. Coast Guard photo

10-20 and 10-21. California Department of Water Resources

10-22. From Clapham, *op. cit.* Data from G. I. Murphy, "Population Biology of the Pacific Sardine (*Sardinops caerulea*)," *Proc. Calif. Acad. Science* (4th Ser.) **34** (1):1-84

10-23. From S. J. Holt, "The Food Resources of the Ocean," *Scientific American*, 1969

10-24 and 10-25. After Bernard J. Nebel, *Environmental Science* (Englewood Cliffs, N.J.: Prentice-Hall, 1981)

10-26. *Commercial Fisheries Review*, Bureau of Commercial Fisheries, U.S.G.P.O., Washington, D.C.

10-27. Adapted from Guy-Harold Smith, *op. cit.*

10-28. Courtesy Carolina Biological Supply Company

10-29. U.S. Department of the Interior

10-30. Cooper and Stevens, "An Experiment in Marine Fish Cultivation," *Nature*, **161** (1948), pp. 631-633

10-31. U.S. Department of the Interior, Bureau of Commercial Fisheries

10-32. Environmental Protection Agency Regional Profiles

10-33. Clapham, W.B., *op. cit.* After *Atlas of Living Resources of the Sea*, U.N. Food and Agricultural Organization

10-34. U.N. Food and Agriculture Organization photo

10-35. Courtesy Raymond Gilmore of the San Diego Natural History Museum

10-36. U.S. Fish and Wildlife Service

11-1. U.S. Department of Agriculture

11-2. U.S. Department of Agriculture, Forest Service

11-3. New York State Conservation Department

11-4. Adapted from Richard M. Highsmith, J. Granville Jensen, and Robert D. Rudd, *Conservation in the United States* (Chicago: Rand McNally, 1962)

11-5. U.S. Department of Agriculture

11-6. Adapted from Highsmith, Jensen, and Rudd, *op. cit.*; Weyerhaeuser Company map

11-7. U.S. Forest Service photo by P. F. Heim

11-8. U.S. Department of Agriculture

11-9. Courtesy Crown-Zellerbach Corporation

11-9. U.S. Department of Agriculture

11-10. U.S. Department of Agriculture

11-11. U.S. Forest Service photo by Daniel O. Todd

11-12. U.S. Forest Service

11-13. Adapted from Guy-Harold Smith, *op. cit.* Data from *Timber Resources Review*, U.S. Forest Service

11-14. From Charles J. Krebs, *Ecology: The Experimental Analysis of Distribution and Abundance*, 2nd ed. (New York: Harper & Row, 1978). After W. C. Grimm, *Familiar Trees* of America (New York: Harper & Row, 1967)

11–15 and 11–16. U.S. Department of Agriculture

11–18. U.S. Department of Agriculture photo by Miller Cowlin

11–19. National Aeronautics and Space Administration

11–20. U.S. Department of Agriculture

11–21. U.S. Forest Service

11–22. U.S. Department of Agriculture

11–23. U.S. Department of Agriculture photo by Bluford W. Muir

11–24. U.S. Department of Agriculture photo by Paul S. Bieler

11–25. U.S. Forest Service

11–26. U.S. Department of Agriculture

11–27. Bureau of Land Management

11–28 and 11–29. U.S. Forest Service

11–30. U.S. Department of Agriculture photo by Robert W. Neelands

11–31. U.S. Department of Agriculture, Soil Conservation Service photo by Al Crouch

11–32. Courtesy Morbark Industries

11–33. From *Environmental Quality*, Seventh Annual Report of the Council of Environmental Quality (Washington, D.C.: U.S. Government Printing Office, 1976)

12–2. Adapted from Edward J. Kormondy, *Concepts of Ecology* (Englewood Cliffs, N.J.: Prentice-Hall, 1969). After A. S. Leopold, *Wisconsin Conservation Bulletin* No. 321, 1943

12–6. Michigan Department of Natural Resources

12–7. U.S. Fish and Wildlife Service

12–9A and 12–9B. From Chandler S. Robbins, "Effect of Forest Fragmentation on Bird Populations," in *Management of North Central and Northeastern Forests for Nongame Birds* (U.S. Forest Service General Technical Report NC-51, St. Paul, Minn., 1979)

12–10 and 12–11. State Historical Society of Wisconsin

12–12, 12–13, 12–14, and 12–15. U.S. Fish and Wildlife Service

13–1. U.S. Fish and Wildlife Service

13–2. From James O. Evrard, "The Energy Crisis for Wildlife," *Wisconsin Conservation Bulletin*, Jan. – Feb. 1975

13–3. U.S. Fish and Wildlife Service

13–4. U.S. National Park Service photo by Richard Frear

13–5. California Department of Fish and Game

13–6. Los Alamos Scientific Laboratory

13–7. U.S. Fish and Wildlife Service

13–9. Wisconsin Natural Resources Department, Madison

13–10. U.S. Department of Agriculture

13–11. Wisconsin Conservation Department, Madison

13–12. From F. C. Lincoln and B. Hines, *Migration of Birds*, Circular 16 (Washington, D.C.: U.S. Government Printing Office, 1950)

13–13. National Park Service photo by M. Woodbridge Williams

13–14. From Joseph Linduska, ed., U.S. Fish and Wildlife Service, *Waterfowl Tomorrow* (Washington, D.C.: U.S. Government Printing Office, 1964)

13–15. U.S. Department of the Interior, Bureau of Sport Fisheries and Wildlife

13–16. Environmental Protection Agency

13–17 and 13–18. U.S. Department of the Interior, Bureau of Sport Fisheries and Wildlife

13–19. Michigan Department of Highway Resources

13–20. Wisconsin Natural Resources Department, Madison

13–21. Wisconsin Conservation Department, Madison

13–22. Minnesota Department of Natural Resources photo by Walter H. Wettschreck

13–23. After Dasmann, *op. cit.*

13–24. U.S. Department of Agriculture, Soil Conservation Service

13–25. U.S. Department of Agriculture photo by Tom Beemers

13–26 and 13–27. From *Making Land Produce Useful Wildlife*, Farmer's Bulletin No. 2035 (Washington, D.C.: Department of Agriculture, May 1969)

13–28. Minnesota Department of Natural Resources photo by Walter H. Wettschreck

13–29. U.S. Department of Agriculture

13–30, 13–31, and 13–32. U.S. Department of the Interior, Bureau of Reclamation photos by Lyle C. Axthelm

13-33. Adapted from R. Kahler Martinson, "Wood Duck Nest Box Utilization, 1961," in Kenneth W. Laub, ed., *Game Research in Ohio*, Vol. 2, August, 1963 (Columbus, Ohio: Ohio Conservation Department)

13-34. U.S. Fish and Wildlife Service

13-35. U.S. Fish and Wildlife Service photo by Peter J. Van Huizen

13-36. From Richard A. Hunt and Harold C. Hanson, "The Spring Canada Goose Migration in Wisconsin," *Wisconsin Conservation Bulletin*, March–April 1975, pp. 7–9)

13-37. U.S. Fish and Wildlife Service

13-38. New York State Conservation Department photo by David G. Allen

13-39. U.S. Fish and Wildlife Service photo by Rex Gary Schmidt

13-40. U.S. Department of the Interior, Bureau of Sport Fisheries and Wildlife

13-41. Adapted from Robert T. Orr, *Vertebrate Biology*, 2nd ed. (Philadelphia: Saunders, 1961)

13-42. U.S. Department of the Interior, Bureau of Sport Fisheries and Wildlife

14-1. U.S. Department of the Interior, Bureau of Reclamation photo by E. E. Hertzog

14-2. From C. A. I. Goring, "The Costs of Commercializing Pesticides," in D. L. Watson and A. W. A. Brown, eds., *Pesticide Management and Insecticide Resistance* (New York: Academic Press, 1977)

14-3. Michigan Department of Natural Resources

14-4. U.S. Department of Agriculture photo by Fred S. Witte

14-5 and 14-6. U.S. Department of Agriculture

14-7. Environmental Protection Agency — Documerica

14-8. U.S. Department of Agriculture photo by Robert Bjork

14-9. Courtesy Carolina Biological Supply Company

14-10. Courtesy General Biological Supply House, Inc., Chicago, Ill.; from W. K. Beaver and G. B. Noland, *General Biology*, 8th ed. (St. Louis: Mosby, 1970)

14-12. U.S. Department of Agriculture

14-13. From Amos Turk, Janet T. Wittes, Jonathan Turk, and Robert E. Wittes, *Environ-mental Science* (Philadelphia: Saunders, 1978)

14-14. Environmental Protection Administration — Documerica photo by Charles O'Rear

14-15. Michigan Department of Natural Resources

14-16 and 14-17. U.S. Department of Agriculture

14-19. From Arthur S. Boughey, *Man and the Environment* (New York: Macmillan, 1975)

14-20. From Clapham, *op. cit.*

14-21. From James W. Berry, David W. Osgood, and Philip A. St. John, *Chemical Villains: A Biology of Pollution* (St. Louis: Mosby, 1974)

14-23. From Gary A. Strobel and Gerald N. Lanier, "The Dutch Elm Disease," in *Scientific American* **245**, August 1981, pp. 56–66

14-24 and 14-25. U.S. Department of Agriculture

14-26. From G. L. Worf, C. F. Koval, and E. B. Smalley, "Dutch Elm Disease in Wisconsin" (Madison, Wis.: University of Wisconsin Extention, September 1977)

14-27 and 14-28. U.S. Department of Agriculture

14-30 and 14-31. U.S. Department of Agriculture

14-32. U.S. Dept. of Health, Education and Welfare (Washington, D.C.: U.S.G.P.O.)

14-33 and 14-34. From Robert Van Den Bosch and P. S. Messenger, *Biological Control* (New York: Intext, 1973)

14-35 and 14-36. Australian News and Information Bureau

14-37 and 14-38. U.S. Department of Agriculture

14-39. U.S. Department of Agriculture photo by Murray Lemmon

14-40. Amos Turk, Janet T. Wittes, Jonathan Turk, and Robert E. Wittes, *Environmental Science* (Philadelphia: Saunders, 1978)

14-41. U.S. Department of Agriculture

14-42. From "The Gypsy Moth" (Washington, D.C.: U.S. Department of Agriculture, 1972)

14-43 and 14-44. U.S. Department of Agriculture

14-46, 14-47, and 14-48. U.S. Department of Agriculture

14-50. U.S. Department of Agriculture

14-51. U.S. Department of the Interior, Bureau of Sport Fisheries and Wildlife

14-52 and 14-53. Michigan Department of Natural Resources

15–1. Michigan Department of Natural Resources

15–2. U.S. Department of the Interior, Bureau of Reclamation

15–3. Environmental Protection Agency— Documerica photo by Ken Hwyman

15–4. U.S. Department of Agriculture photo by Murray Lemmon

15–5. Michigan Department of Natural Resources

15–6 and 15–7. Courtesy Reynolds Metals Company

15–8. Michigan Department of Natural Resources

15–9 and 15–10. Courtesy Owens-Illinois

15–11. National Air Pollution Control Administration

15–12. Environmental Protection Agency— Documerica photo by David Hiser

15–13. From Bureau of Solid Waste Management, *Sanitary Landfill Facts* (Washington, D.C.: U.S. Government Printing Office, 1970)

15–14. W. J. Schneider, "Hydrologic Implications of Solid Waste Disposal," U.S. Geological Survey Circular 601F (Washington, D.C.: U.S.G.P.O., 1970)

15–15. From Environmental Protection Agency, *Environment Midwest* (Washington: D.C.: U.S. Government Printing Office, 1981)

15–16, 15–17, and 15–18. From Environmental Protection Agency, *State of the Environment, 1982* (Washington, D.C.: The Conservation Foundation, 1982)

15–19. Revelle and Revelle, *op. cit.*

15–20. After C. A. Bache et al., "Polychlorinated Biphenyl Residues: Accumulation in Cayuga Lake Trout with Age," *Science* **177** (Sept. 29, 1972), pp. 1191–1192. Copyright 1972 by the American Association for the Advancement of Science

15–21. From Thomas G. Spiro and William M. Stigliani, *Environmental Science in Perspective* (Albany: State University of New York Press, 1980)

16–1. U.S. Department of Agriculture

16–2. Associated Press map from *Salt Lake City Tribune*, May 1980

16–3. Columbus, Georgia, *Ledger-Enquirer* and the Environmental Protection Agency

16–4. From Environmental Protection Agency, *National Air Quality, Monitoring, and Emissions Trends Report, 1977* (Washington, D.C.: U.S. Government Printing Office, 1978)

16–5 and 16–6. Environmental Protection Agency

16–7. From Environmental Protection Agency, *Research Outlook 1978* (Washington, D.C.: U.S. Government Printing Office, 1978)

16–8, 16–9, and 16–10. Environmental Protection Agency

16–11. Fairchild Aerial Surveys

16–12. National Air Pollution Control Administration

16–13. U.S. Public Health Service

16–14. U.S. Department of Housing and Urban Development

16–15. Environmental Protection Agency — Documerica photo by Blair Pittman

16–17 and 16–18. Los Angeles County Air Pollution Control District

16–20. Argonne National Laboratory

16–21. World Wide Photo — Environmental Protection Administration

16–23. From *Environmental Quality*, Eighth Annual Report of the Council on Environmental Quality (Washington, D.C.: U.S. Government Printing Office, 1978)

16–25 and 16–26. Charles F. Baes, "Carbon Dioxide and Climate: The Uncontrolled Experiment," *American Scientist* **65**: 310–320 (1977)

16–27. U.S. Department of Agriculture

16–28. U.S. Department of Agriculture photo by Murray Lemmon

16–29 and 16–30. Environmental Protection Agency

16–31. From *Canada Today*, Vol. 12, No. 2, Feb. 1981

16–32. Environmental Protection Agency

16–35. Environmental Protection Agency

16–36. Environmental Protection Agency — Documerica photo by LeRoy Woodson

16–37. Adapted from Harold Wolozin, ed., *The Economics of Air Pollution* (New York: Norton, 1966); used by permission of W. W. Norton & Company, Inc.; copyright © 1966 by W. W. Norton & Company, Inc.

16–39. Washington, D.C., *Evening Star*

16–40. Council on Environmental Quality, *State of*

the Environment, 1982 (Washington, D.C.: The Conservation Foundation, 1982)

16-41. National Air Pollution Control Administration

16-42. U.S. Public Health Service

16-48. U.S. Public Health Service

16-50. U.S. Public Health Service

16-51. Courtesy Ford Motor Company

16-52. Environmental Protection Agency, *Trends in the Quality of Our Nation's Air, October 1980* (Washington, D.C.: U.S. Government Printing Office, 1980)

16-53. Courtesy General Motors Corporation

16-54A. ERDA/Panametrics photo

16-54B. Environmental Protection Agency — Documerica photo by Joe Clark

16-55 and 16-56. U.S. Department of Energy

17-1. U.S. Department of the Interior, Bureau of Mines, in Nebel, *op. cit.*

17-2. Clapham, *op. cit.* After J. J. Schanz, Jr., "Problems and Opportunities in Adapting U.S. Geological Survey Terminology to Energy Resources," in M. Grenon, ed., *Energy Resources,* Int. Inst. Appl. Syst. Anal. Conf. Proceedings, CP-76-4: 85-120, 1976

17-3. From Nebel, *op. cit.* Adapted from Earl Cook, "Limits to Exploitation of Nonrenewable Resources," in P. H. Abelson and A. L. Hammond, eds., *Materials: Renewable and Nonrenewable Resources* (Washington, D.C.: American Association for the Advancement of Science, 1976)

18-1. Rollin R. Geppert

18-2. Courtesy Northern States Power

18-3. From Meadows *et al., op. cit.*

18-4. World Food Programme/U.N. Food and Agriculture Organization photo by E. Ragazzini

18-5. From U.S. Department of Energy, *State of the Environment, 1982* (Washington, D.C.: The Conservation Foundation, 1982)

18-6. Revelle and Revelle, *op cit.* Source: Bureau of Land Management, 1974

18-7. Courtesy Joy Manufacturing Company and U.S. Department of the Interior, Bureau of Mines

18-10. U.S. Department of Agriculture, Soil Conservation Service

18-11. Knabe, "Idealized Coal Mine Cycle as It Occurs in Coal Beds in Germany from the Start of Mining to the Completion of Reclamation," *Ohio Journal of Science,* 1964

18-12. U.S. Department of Agriculture

18-13. U.S. Department of Energy

18-14. U.S. Department of the Interior, Bureau of Mines

18-15 and 18-16. U.S. Department of Energy

18-17. U.S. Department of the Interior

18-18. U.S. Bureau of Mines, *Minerals Yearbook,* U.S.G.P.O., 1971

18-19. Rollin R. Geppert

18-23. Courtesy Skyfotos — Texaco

18-24. Courtesy Humble Oil and Refining Company

18-25. Courtesy Clark Oil and Refining Corporation

18-26. Nebel, *op. cit.* Data from the U.S. Department of Energy.

18-27 and 18-28. U.S. Department of Energy

18-29 and 18-30. U.S. Department of the Interior, Bureau of Mines

18-31, 18-32, 18-33, and 18-34. U.S. Department of Energy

18-35. From Revelle and Revelle, *op. cit.,* as adapted from "A National Plan for Energy Research, Development, and Demonstration," issued by the Energy Research and Development Administration, now part of the U.S. Department of Energy

18-36. "Special Energy Report," *National Geographic,* February 1981, page 68, National Geographic Society, Washington, D.C.

18-37. U.S. Department of Energy

18-39. U.S. Department of Energy

18-40. From Revelle and Revelle, *op. cit.,* as adapted from D. Kash et al., *Energy Alternatives,* Report to the President's Council on Environmental Quality (Washington, D.C.: U.S. Government Printing Office, 1975)

18-41 and 18-42. U.S. Department of Energy

18-43. Adapted from Revelle and Revelle, *op. cit.;* Revelle version adapted from "Space Shuttle Payloads," Hearings of the Committee on Aeronautical and Space Sciences of the U.S. Senate, October 31, 1973

18-44. A. J. Ellis, "Geothermal Systems and Power Development," *American Scientist,* **63:** 510-521 (1975)

18-45. U.S. Department of Energy

18–47. U.S. Department of the Interior, Bureau of Reclamation

18–48. U.S. Department of Agriculture

18–49. U.S. Department of Energy

18–50. Artist's conception by Westinghouse

18–51 and 18–52. U.S. Department of Energy

18–53, 18–54, and 18–55. U.S. Department of Energy photos by Schneider

18–56. U.S. Department of Energy

18–57. Adapted from John R. Justus, "Renewable Sources of Energy from the Ocean," in *Project Interdependence,* Committee Print 95-3, U.S. Congress, November 1977

18–58. New York Convention and Visitors Bureau

18–59 and 18–60. U.S. Department of Energy

18–61. New York Convention and Visitors Bureau

18–62. Michigan Department of Natural Resources

18–63. Adapted from Revelle and Revelle, *op. cit.*

18–64. Environmental Protection Agency, *Research Outlook 1978* (Washington, D.C.: U.S. Government Printing Office, 1978)

19–3, 19–4, and 19–5. From *Nuclear Power,* Edison Electric Institute Publication No. 78-24

19–6. *Nuclear Power and the Environment* (Hinsdale, Ill.: American Nuclear Society, 1973)

19–7. ERDA's Los Alamos Scientific Laboratory

19–9. Courtesy C-E Power Systems

19–11. Courtesy Westinghouse Atomic Power Division

19–12. Babcock and Wilcox

19–13. Courtesy Iowa Light and Power Company

19–14. Earl Chambers — Northern States Power Company

19–15. From *Nuclear Power and the Environment* (Hinsdale, Ill.: American Nuclear Society, 1973)

19–16. Rollin R. Geppert

19–17. *Nuclear Power,* Edison Electric Institute Publication No. 78-24

19–18. U.S. Nuclear Regulatory Commission

19–19. U.S. Department of Energy

19–22. Berry, Osgood, and St. John, *op. cit.*

19–23. Courtesy E. I. Du Pont de Nemours & Company

19–24 and 19–25. U.S. Department of Energy

19–26. Raymond Reczek

19–28. U.S. Department of Energy

19–31. Courtesy Union Carbide

Additional Acknowledgments

page 137. Box: A Master Plan for Feeding a Hungry World. G. Tyler Miller, Jr. *Living in the Environment* (Belmont, Calif.: Wadsworth Publishing Company, 1982).

page 213. Table 8-4: Water Pollution: Sources, Effects, and Control. Adapted from G. Tyler Miller, *op. cit.*

page 305. Section entitled "Constraints." Derived in part from Theodore W. Daniel, John A. Helms, Frederick S. Baker, *Principles of Silviculture,* 2nd ed. (New York: McGraw-Hill Book Company, 1979).

page 310. Section entitled "Fertilization." Derived in part from Theodore W. Daniel, John A. Helms and Frederick S. Baker, *op. cit.*

page 312. Section entitled "Development of Genetically Superior Trees." Derived in part from Theodore W. Daniel, John A. Helms and Frederick S. Baker, *op. cit.*

page 623. Appendix: Information Sources for Environmental Research. Derived in part from *Conservation Directory,* 1980. The National Wildlife Federation, Washington, D.C., 1980.

INDEX